**INSTRUCTORS...**

Would you like your **students** to show up for class **more prepared**? *(Let's face it, class is much more fun if everyone is engaged and prepared...)*

Want an **easy way to assign** homework online and track student **progress**? *(Less time grading means more time teaching...)*

Want an **instant view** of student or class performance relative to learning objectives? *(No more wondering if students understand...)*

Need to **collect data and generate reports** required for administration or accreditation? *(Say goodbye to manually tracking student learning outcomes...)*

Want to **record and post your lectures** for students to view online?

 With **McGraw-Hill's Connect™ Plus Accounting,**

## INSTRUCTORS GET:

- Simple **assignment management**, allowing you to spend more time teaching.
- **Auto-graded** assignments, quizzes, and tests.
- **Detailed Visual Reporting** where student and section results can be viewed and analyzed.
- Sophisticated **online testing** capability.
- A **filtering and reporting** function that allows you to easily assign and report on materials that are correlated to accreditation standards, learning outcomes, and Bloom's taxonomy.
- An easy-to-use **lecture capture** tool.
- The option to **upload course documents** for student access.

Want an online, **searchable version** of your textbook?

Wish your textbook could be **available online** while you're doing your assignments?

 *Connect™ Plus Accounting* eBook

If you choose to use *Connect™ Plus Accounting*, you have an affordable and searchable online version of your book integrated with your other online tools.

*Connect™ Plus Accounting* eBook offers features like:

- Topic search
- Direct links from assignments
- Adjustable text size
- Jump to page number
- Print by section

 Want to get more **value** from your textbook purchase?

Think learning accounting should be a bit more **interesting**?

 **Check out the STUDENT RESOURCES section under the *Connect™* Library tab.**

Here you'll find a wealth of resources designed to help you achieve your goals in the course. You'll find things like **quizzes, PowerPoints, and Internet activities** to help you study. Every student has different needs, so explore the STUDENT RESOURCES to find the materials best suited to you.

# Principles of Financial Accounting

**20**th edition

**John J. Wild**

*University of Wisconsin at Madison*

**Ken W. Shaw**

*University of Missouri at Columbia*

**Barbara Chiappetta**

*Nassau Community College*

**McGraw-Hill Irwin**

To my students and family, especially **Kimberly, Jonathan, Stephanie,** and **Trevor.**
To my wife **Linda** and children, **Erin, Emily,** and **Jacob.**
To my mother, husband **Bob,** and sons **Michael** and **David.**

FUNDAMENTAL ACCOUNTING PRINCIPLES
Published by McGraw-Hill/Irwin, a business unit of The McGraw-Hill Companies, Inc., 1221 Avenue of the Americas, New York, NY, 10020. Copyright © 2011, 2009, 2007, 2005, 2002, 1999, 1996, 1993, 1990, 1987, 1984, 1981, 1978, 1975, 1972, 1969, 1966, 1963, 1959, 1955 by The McGraw-Hill Companies, Inc. All rights reserved. No part of this publication may be reproduced or distributed in any form or by any means, or stored in a database or retrieval system, without the prior written consent of The McGraw-Hill Companies, Inc., including, but not limited to, in any network or other electronic storage or transmission, or broadcast for distance learning.

Some ancillaries, including electronic and print components, may not be available to customers outside the United States.

This book is printed on acid-free paper.

4 5 6 7 8 9 0 DOW/DOW 1 0 9 8 7 6 5 4 3 2

ISBN-13: 978-0-07-811087-0 (combined edition)
ISBN-10: 0-07-811087-4 (combined edition)
ISBN-13: 978-0-07-733825-1 (volume 1, chapters 1-12)
ISBN-10: 0-07-733825-1 (volume 1, chapters 1-12)
ISBN-13: 978-0-07-733824-4 (volume 2, chapters 12-25)
ISBN-10: 0-07-733824-3 (volume 2, chapters 12-25)
ISBN-13: 978-0-07-733826-8 (with working papers volume 1, chapters 1-12)
ISBN-10: 0-07-733826-X (with working papers volume 1, chapters 1-12)
ISBN-13: 978-0-07-733827-5 (with working papers volume 2, chapters 12-25)
ISBN-10: 0-07-733827-8 (with working papers volume 2, chapters 12-25)
ISBN-13: 978-0-07-733823-7 (principles, chapters 1-17)
ISBN-10: 0-07-733823-5 (principles, chapters 1-17)

Vice president and editor-in-chief: *Brent Gordon*
Editorial director: *Stewart Mattson*
Publisher: *Tim Vertovec*
Executive editor: *Steve Schuetz*
Director of development: *Ann Torbert*
Senior development editor: *Christina A. Sanders*
Vice president and director of marketing: *Robin J. Zwettler*
Marketing director: *Brad Parkins*
Marketing manager: *Michelle Heaster*
Vice president of editing, design, and production: *Sesha Bolisetty*
Managing editor: *Lori Koetters*

Senior buyer: *Carol A. Bielski*
Lead designer: *Matthew Baldwin*
Senior photo research coordinator: *Jeremy Cheshareck*
Photo researcher: *Sarah Evertson*
Lead media project manager: *Brian Nacik*
Media project manager: *Ron Nelms*
Interior and cover design: *Laurie Entringer*
Cover image: © *Getty Images*
Typeface: *10.5/12 Times Roman*
Compositor: *Aptara®, Inc.*
Printer: *R. R. Donnelley*

**The Library of Congress has cataloged the single volume edition of this work as follows**

Wild, John J.
    Fundamental accounting principles / John J. Wild, Ken W. Shaw, Barbara Chiappetta.—20th ed.
        p. cm.
    Includes index.
    ISBN-13: 978-0-07-811087-0 (combined edition : alk. paper)
    ISBN-10: 0-07-811087-4 (combined edition : alk. paper)
    ISBN-13: 978-0-07-733825-1 (volume 1 ch. 1-12 : alk. paper)
    ISBN-10: 0-07-733825-1 (volume 1 ch. 1-12 : alk. paper)
    [etc.]
    1. Accounting. I. Shaw, Ken W. II. Chiappetta, Barbara. III. Title.
HF5636.W675 2011
657—dc22
                                                            2010026205

www.mhhe.com

Dear Colleagues/Friends,

As we roll out the new edition of *Fundamental Accounting Principles*, we thank each of you who provided suggestions to improve our textbook. As teachers, we know how important it is to select the right book for our course. This new edition reflects the advice and wisdom of many dedicated reviewers, symposium and workshop participants, students, and instructors. Our book consistently rates number one in customer loyalty because of you. Together, we have created the most readable, concise, current, accurate, and innovative accounting book available today.

Throughout the writing process, we steered this book in the manner you directed. Reviewers, instructors, and students say this book's enhanced presentation, graphics, and technology cater to different learning styles and helps students better understand accounting. *Connect Accounting Plus* offers new features to improve student learning and to assist instructor teaching and grading. Our iPod content lets students study on the go, while our Algorithmic Test Bank provides an infinite variety of exam problems. You and your students will find all these tools easy to apply.

We owe the success of this book to our colleagues who graciously took time to help us focus on the changing needs of today's instructors and students. We feel fortunate to have witnessed our profession's extraordinary devotion to teaching. Your feedback and suggestions are reflected in everything we write. Please accept our heartfelt thanks for your dedication in helping today's students learn, understand, and appreciate accounting.

With kindest regards,

John J. Wild        Ken W. Shaw        Barbara Chiappetta

# About the Authors

**JOHN J. WILD** is a distinguished professor of accounting at the University of Wisconsin at Madison. He previously held appointments at Michigan State University and the University of Manchester in England. He received his BBA, MS, and PhD from the University of Wisconsin.

Professor Wild teaches accounting courses at both the undergraduate and graduate levels. He has received numerous teaching honors, including the Mabel W. Chipman Excellence-in-Teaching Award, the departmental Excellence-in-Teaching Award, and the Teaching Excellence Award from the 2003 and 2005 business graduates at the University of Wisconsin. He also received the Beta Alpha Psi and Roland F. Salmonson Excellence-in-Teaching Award from Michigan State University. Professor Wild has received several research honors and is a past KPMG Peat Marwick National Fellow and is a recipient of fellowships from the American Accounting Association and the Ernst and Young Foundation.

Professor Wild is an active member of the American Accounting Association and its sections. He has served on several committees of these organizations, including the Outstanding Accounting Educator Award, Wildman Award, National Program Advisory, Publications, and Research Committees. Professor Wild is author of Financial Accounting, Managerial Accounting, and College Accounting, each published by McGraw-Hill/Irwin. His research articles on accounting and analysis appear in The Accounting Review, Journal of Accounting Research, Journal of Accounting and Economics, Contemporary Accounting Research, Journal of Accounting, Auditing and Finance, Journal of Accounting and Public Policy, and other journals. He is past associate editor of Contemporary Accounting Research and has served on several editorial boards including The Accounting Review.

In his leisure time, Professor Wild enjoys hiking, sports, travel, people, and spending time with family and friends.

**KEN W. SHAW** is an associate professor of accounting and the Deloitte Professor at the University of Missouri. He previously was on the faculty at the University of Maryland at College Park. He received an accounting degree from Bradley University and an MBA and PhD from the University of Wisconsin. He is a Certified Public Accountant with work experience in public accounting.

Professor Shaw teaches financial accounting at the undergraduate and graduate levels. He received the Williams-Keepers LLC Teaching Excellence award in 2007, was voted the "Most Influential Professor" by the 2005, 2006, and 2010 School of Accountancy graduating classes, and is a two-time recipient of the O'Brien Excellence in Teaching Award. He is the advisor to his School's chapter of the Association of Certified Fraud Examiners.

Professor Shaw is an active member of the American Accounting Association and its sections. He has served on many committees of these organizations and presented his research papers at national and regional meetings. Professor Shaw's research appears in The Accounting Review; Journal of Accounting Research; Contemporary Accounting Research; Journal of Financial and Quantitative Analysis; Journal of the American Taxation Association; Journal of Accounting, Auditing, and Finance; Journal of Financial Research; Research in Accounting Regulation; and other journals. He has served on the editorial boards of Issues in Accounting Education, the Journal of Business Research, and Research in Accounting Regulation. Professor Shaw is co-author of Financial and Managerial Accounting and College Accounting, both published by McGraw-Hill.

In his leisure time, Professor Shaw enjoys tennis, cycling, music, and coaching his children's sports teams.

**BARBARA CHIAPPETTA** received her BBA in Accountancy and MS in Education from Hofstra University and is a tenured full professor at Nassau Community College. For the past two decades, she has been an active executive board member of the Teachers of Accounting at Two-Year Colleges (TACTYC), serving 10 years as vice president and as president from 1993 through 1999. As an active member of the American Accounting Association, she has served on the Northeast Regional Steering Committee, chaired the Curriculum Revision Committee of the Two-Year Section, and participated in numerous national committees. Professor Chiappetta has been inducted into the American Accounting Association Hall of Fame for the Northeast Region. She had also received the Nassau Community College dean of instruction's Faculty Distinguished Achievement Award. Professor Chiappetta was honored with the State University of New York Chancellor's Award for Teaching Excellence in 1997. As a confirmed believer in the benefits of the active learning pedagogy, Professor Chiappetta has authored Student Learning Tools, an active learning workbook for a first-year accounting course, published by McGraw-Hill/Irwin.

In her leisure time, Professor Chiappetta enjoys tennis and participates on a U.S.T.A. team. She also enjoys the challenge of bridge. Her husband, Robert, is an entrepreneur in the leisure sport industry. She has two sons—Michael, a lawyer, specializing in intellectual property law in New York, and David, a composer, pursuing a career in music for film in Los Angeles.

# Helping Students Achieve Peak Performance

## *Fundamental Accounting Principles 20e*

Great performances result from pushing the limits through quality practices and reinforcing feedback to strengthen abilities and motivation. Assist your students in achieving their peak performance by giving them what they need to succeed in today's accounting principles course.

Whether the goal is to become an accountant or a businessperson, or simply to be an informed consumer of accounting information, *Fundamental Accounting Principles (FAP)* has helped generations of students succeed by giving them support in the form of leading-edge accounting content that engages students, paired with state-of-the-art technology that elevates their understanding of key accounting principles.

With *FAP* on your side, you'll be provided with **engaging content** in a **motivating style** to help students see the relevance of accounting. Students are motivated when reading materials that are clear and pertinent. *FAP* excels at engaging students. Its chapter-opening vignettes showcase dynamic, successful entrepreneurial individuals and companies guaranteed to **interest and excite students**. This edition's featured companies—**Research In Motion** (maker of BlackBerry), **Apple**, **Nokia**, and **Palm**—captivate students with their products and annual reports, which are a pathway for learning financial statements. Further, this book's coverage of the accounting cycle fundamentals is widely praised for its clarity and effectiveness.

*FAP* also delivers innovative technology to help student performance. **Connect Accounting** provides students with instant grading and feedback for assignments that are completed online. **Connect Accounting Plus** integrates an online version of the textbook with *Connect Accounting*. Our algorithmic test bank offers infinite variations of numerical test bank questions. The Self-Quiz and Study, Interactive Presentations, and LearnSmart all provide additional support to help reinforce concepts and keep students motivated.

We're confident you'll agree that **FAP will help your students achieve peak performance**.

# Your Students' Connection to

McGraw-Hill *Connect Accounting* is an online assignment and assessment solution that connects your students with the tools and resources needed to achieve success through faster learning, more efficient studying, and higher retention of knowledge.

**Online Assignments:** *Connect Accounting* helps students learn more efficiently by providing feedback and practice material when they need it, where they need it. *Connect* grades homework automatically and gives immediate feedback on any questions students may have missed.

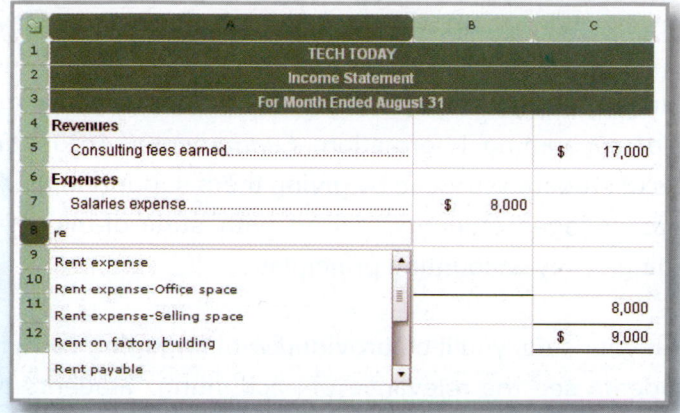

**Interactive Presentations:** The interactive presentations provide engaging narratives of all chapter learning objectives in an interactive online format. The presentations are tied specifically to *Fundamental Accounting Principles*, 20e. They follow the structure of the text and are organized to match the learning objectives within each chapter. While the interactive presentations are not meant to replace the textbook in this course, they provide additional explanation and enhancement of material from the text chapter, allowing students to learn, study, and practice with instant feedback at their own pace.

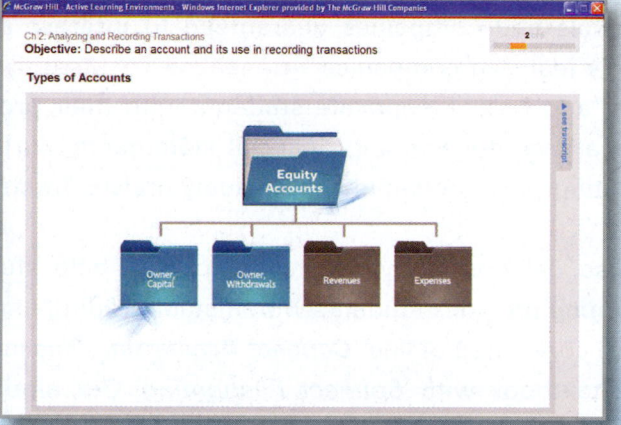

**Student Resource Library:** The *Connect Accounting* Student Study Center gives access to additional resources such as recorded lectures, online practice materials, an eBook, and more.

# Reach Peak Performance!

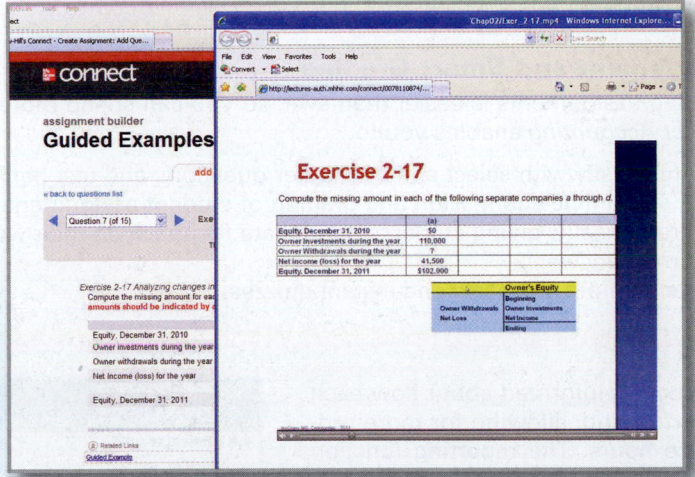

**Guided Examples:** The Guided Examples in *Connect Accounting* provide a narrated, animated, step-by-step walk-through of select exercises similar to those assigned. These short presentations provide reinforcement when students need it most.

**LearnSmart:** LearnSmart adaptive self-study technology within *Connect Accounting* helps students make the best use of their study time. LearnSmart provides a seamless combination of practice, assessment, and remediation for every concept in the textbook. LearnSmart's intelligent software adapts to students by supplying questions on a new concept when they are ready to learn it. With LearnSmart, students will spend less time on topics they understand and practice more on those they have yet to master.

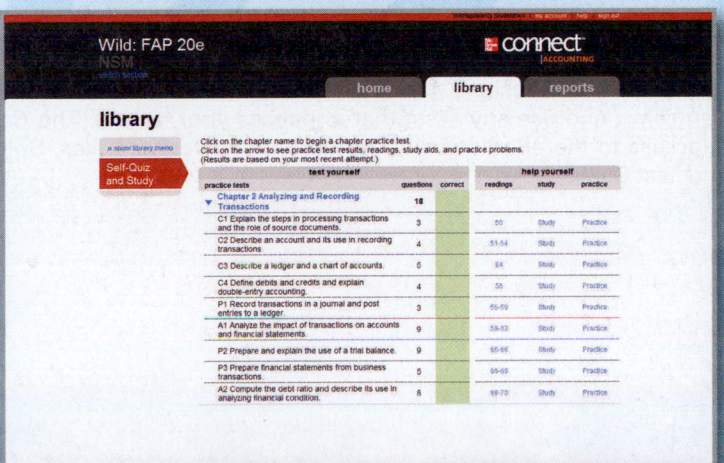

**Self-Quiz and Study:** The Self-Quiz and Study (SQS) connects students to the learning resources students need to succeed in the course. For each chapter, students can take a practice quiz and immediately see how well they performed. A study plan then recommends specific readings from the text, supplemental study material, and practice exercises that will improve students' understanding and mastery of each learning objective.

# Connect Accounting

*Connect Accounting* offers a number of powerful tools and features to make managing assignments easier, so faculty can spend more time teaching. With *Connect Accounting*, students can engage with their coursework anytime and anywhere, making the learning process more accessible and efficient. (Please see previous page for a description of the student tools available within *Connect Accounting*.)

## Simple Assignment Management and Smart Grading

With *Connect Accounting*, creating assignments is easier than ever, so you can spend more time teaching and less time managing. *Connect Accounting* enables you to:

- Create and deliver assignments easily with select end-of-chapter questions and test bank items.
- Go paperless with the eBook and online submission and grading of student assignments.
- Have assignments scored automatically, giving students immediate feedback on their work and side-by-side comparisons with correct answers.
- Reinforce classroom concepts with practice tests and instant quizzes.

## Student Reporting

*Connect Accounting* keeps instructors informed about how each student, section, and class is performing, allowing for more productive use of lecture and office hours. The reporting function enables you to:

- View scored work immediately and track individual or group performance with assignment and grade reports.
- Access an instant view of student or class performance relative to learning objectives.
- Collect data and generate reports required by many accreditation organizations, such as AACSB and AICPA.

© Svetlana Gryankina; iStockphoto

## Instructor Library

The *Connect Accounting* Instructor Library is your repository for additional resources to improve student engagement in and out of class. You can select and use any asset that enhances your lecture. The *Connect Accounting* Instructor Library includes: access to the eBook version of the text, PowerPoint files, Solutions Manual, Instructor Resource Manual, and Test Bank.

© David Pedre; iStockphoto

# Tools for Instructors

## McGraw-Hill *Connect Plus Accounting*

McGraw-Hill reinvents the textbook learning experience for the modern student with *Connect Plus Accounting*. A seamless integration of an eBook and *Connect Accounting, Connect Plus Accounting* provides all of the *Connect Accounting* features plus:

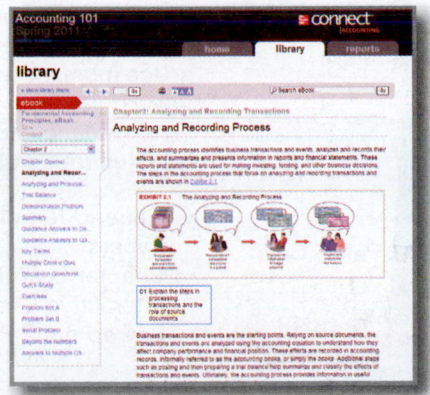

- An integrated eBook, allowing for anytime, anywhere access to the textbook.
- Dynamic links between the problems or questions you assign to your students and the location in the eBook where that problem or question is covered.
- A powerful search function to pinpoint and connect key concepts in a snap.

For more information about *Connect*, go to **www.mcgrawhillconnect.com**, or contact your local McGraw-Hill sales representative.

## Tegrity Campus: Lectures 24/7

Tegrity Campus is a service that makes class time available 24/7 by automatically capturing every lecture. With a simple one-click start-and-stop process, you capture all computer screens and corresponding audio in a format that is easily searchable, frame by frame. Students can replay any part of any class with easy-to-use browser-based viewing on a PC or Mac, an iPod, or other mobile device.

Educators know that the more students can see, hear, and experience class resources, the better they learn. In fact, studies prove it. Tegrity Campus's unique search feature helps students efficiently find what they need, when they need it, across an entire semester of class recordings. Help turn your students' study time into learning moments immediately supported by your lecture. With Tegrity Campus, you also increase intent listening and class participation by easing students' concerns about note-taking. Lecture Capture will make it more likely you will see students' faces, not the tops of their heads.

To learn more about Tegrity watch a two-minute Flash demo at **http://tegritycampus.mhhe.com**.

## McGraw-Hill Customer Care Contact Information

At McGraw-Hill, we understand that getting the most from new technology can be challenging. That's why our services don't stop after you purchase our products. You can e-mail our Product Specialists 24 hours a day to get product training online. Or you can search our knowledge bank of Frequently Asked Questions on our support Website. For Customer Support, call 800-331-5094 or visit **www.mhhe.com/support**. One of our Technical Support Analysts will be able to assist you in a timely fashion.

# How Can Text-Related Web Resources Enrich My Course?

## Online Learning Center (OLC)

© Okea; iStockphoto

We offer an Online Learning Center (OLC) that follows *Fundamental Accounting Principles* chapter by chapter. It doesn't require any building or maintenance on your part. It's ready to go the moment you and your students type in the URL: *www.mhhe.com/wildFAP20e*

As students study and learn from *Fundamental Accounting Principles*, they can visit the Student Edition of the OLC Website to work with a multitude of helpful tools:

- Generic Template Working Papers
- Chapter Learning Objectives
- Interactive Chapter Quizzes
- PowerPoint® Presentations
- Narrated PowerPoint® Presentations*
- Video Library
- Excel Template Assignments
- iPod Content*

\* indicates Premium Content

A secured Instructor Edition stores essential course materials to save you prep time before class. Everything you need to run a lively classroom and an efficient course is included. All resources available to students, plus . . .

- Instructor's Resource Manual
- Solutions Manual
- Solutions to Excel Template Assignments
- Test Bank
- Solutions to CYGL, Peachtree, and QuickBooks templates

The OLC Website also serves as a doorway to other technology solutions, like course management systems.

> "There are numerous materials and resources available for the instructor. I love how everything is on one Website and there is no need for a CD or different supplements/materials that need to be carried around."
>
> —**Jeanine Metzler, Northampton Community College, on the OLC**

### Online Course Management

No matter what online course management system you use (WebCT, BlackBoard, or eCollege), we have a course content ePack available for *FAP* 20e. Our new ePacks are specifically designed to make it easy for students to navigate and access content online. They are easier than ever to install on the latest version of the course management system available today.

Don't forget that you can count on the highest level of service from McGraw-Hill. Our online course management specialists are ready to assist you with your online course needs. They provide training and will answer any questions you have throughout the life of your adoption. So try our new ePack for *FAP* 20e and make online course content delivery easy and fun.

## CourseSmart

CourseSmart is a new way to find and buy eTextbooks. CourseSmart has the largest selection of eTextbooks available anywhere, offering thousands of the most commonly adopted textbooks from a wide variety of higher education publishers. CourseSmart eTextbooks are available in one standard online reader with full text search, notes, and highlighting, and email tools for sharing between classmates. Visit **www.CourseSmart.com** for more information on ordering.

## How Students Can Study On the Go Using Their iPods

### iPod Content

Harness the power of one of the most popular technology tools students use today—the Apple iPod. Our innovative approach allows students to download audio and video presentations right into their iPod and take learning materials with them wherever they go. Students just need to visit the Online Learning Center at **www.mhhe.com/wildFAP20e** to download our iPod content. For each chapter of the book they will be able to download audio narrated lecture presentations for use on various versions of iPods. iPod Touch users can even access self-quizzes.

It makes review and study time as easy as putting on headphones.

## How Can McGraw-Hill Help Teach My Course Online?

### Improve Student Learning Outcomes and Save Instructor Time with ALEKS®

ALEKS is an assessment and learning program that provides individualized instruction in accounting. Available online in partnership with McGraw-Hill/Irwin, ALEKS interacts with students much like a skilled human tutor, with the ability to assess precisely a student's knowledge and provide instruction on the exact topics the student is most ready to learn. By providing topics to meet individual students' needs, allowing students to move between explanation and practice, correcting and analyzing errors, and defining terms, ALEKS helps students to master course content quickly and easily.

ALEKS also includes an Instructor Module with powerful, assignment-driven features and extensive content flexibility. The complimentary Instructor Module provides a course calendar, a customizable gradebook with automatically graded homework, textbook integration, and dynamic reports to monitor student and class progress. ALEKS simplifies course management and allows instructors to spend less time with administrative tasks and more time directing student learning.

To learn more about ALEKS, visit **www.aleks.com/highered/business**.

ALEKS is a registered trademark of ALEKS Corporation.

# Innovative Textbook Features

## Using Accounting for Decisions

Whether we prepare, analyze, or apply accounting information, one skill remains essential: decision-making. To help develop good decision-making habits and to illustrate the relevance of accounting, our book uses a unique pedagogical framework we call the Decision Center. This framework is comprised of a variety of approaches and subject areas, giving students insight into every aspect of business decision-making; see three examples to the right and one below. Answers to Decision Maker and Ethics boxes are at the end of each chapter.

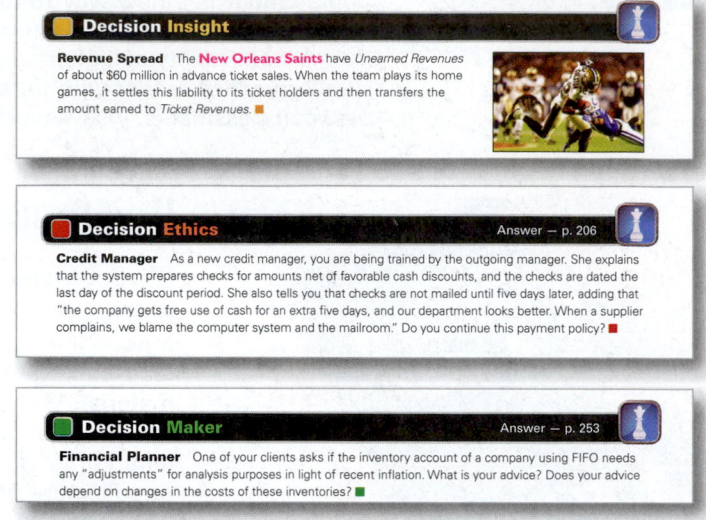

**Decision Insight**

**Revenue Spread** The **New Orleans Saints** have *Unearned Revenues* of about $60 million in advance ticket sales. When the team plays its home games, it settles this liability to its ticket holders and then transfers the amount earned to *Ticket Revenues.* ■

**Decision Ethics** — Answer — p. 206

**Credit Manager** As a new credit manager, you are being trained by the outgoing manager. She explains that the system prepares checks for amounts net of favorable cash discounts, and the checks are dated the last day of the discount period. She also tells you that checks are not mailed until five days later, adding that "the company gets free use of cash for an extra five days, and our department looks better. When a supplier complains, we blame the computer system and the mailroom." Do you continue this payment policy? ■

**Decision Maker** — Answer — p. 253

**Financial Planner** One of your clients asks if the inventory account of a company using FIFO needs any "adjustments" for analysis purposes in light of recent inflation. What is your advice? Does your advice depend on changes in the costs of these inventories? ■

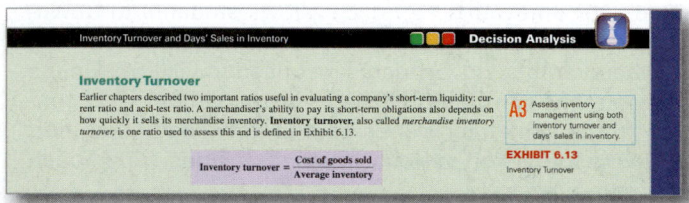

## CAP Model

The Conceptual/Analytical/Procedural (CAP) Model allows courses to be specially designed to meet your teaching needs or those of a diverse faculty. This model identifies learning objectives, textual materials, assignments, and test items by C, A, or P, allowing different instructors to teach from the same materials, yet easily customize their courses toward a conceptual, analytical, or procedural approach (or a combination thereof) based on personal preferences.

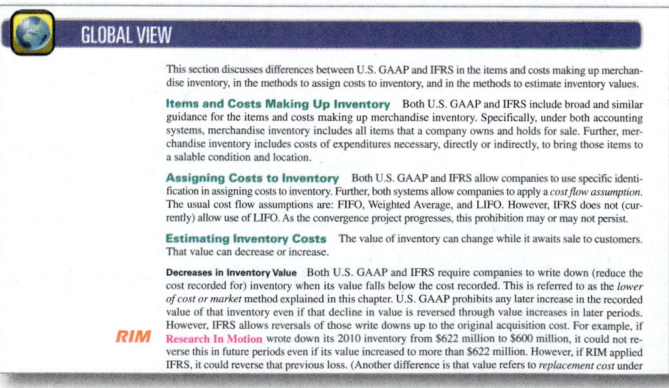

## New Global View

This section explains international accounting practices relating to the material covered in that chapter. This section is purposefully located at the end of each chapter so that each instructor can decide what emphasis, if at all, is to be assigned to it. The aim of this Global View section is to describe accounting practices and to identify the similarities and differences in international accounting practices versus that in the U.S. As we move toward global convergence in accounting practices, and as we witness the likely conversion of U.S. GAAP to IFRS, the importance of student familiarity with international accounting grows. This innovative section helps us begin down that path of learning and teaching global accounting practices.

"...the chapter openers are absolutely excellent and include entrepreneurs that the students can easily relate to. This helps the students understand the need/importance of accounting in a small business."

—Michelle Grant, Bossier Parish Community College

# Bring Accounting To Life

## Chapter Preview With Flowchart

This feature provides a handy textual/visual guide at the start of every chapter. Students can now begin their reading with a clear understanding of what they will learn and when, allowing them to stay more focused and organized along the way.

## Quick Check

These short question/answer features reinforce the material immediately preceding them. They allow the reader to pause and reflect on the topics described, then receive immediate feedback before going on to new topics. Answers are provided at the end of each chapter.

"The author(s) are doing an excellent job of using learning and study aids. The examples are real-world and easy to understand. I cannot think of anything else that I would add."

—Shirly Kleiner, Johnson County Community College

g transactions is to post journal entries to
ledger is up-to-date, entries are posted as
en time permits. All entries must be posted
l to ensure that account balances are up-to-
bits in journal entries are transferred into

**Point:** Computerized systems often provide a code beside a balance such as *dr.* or *cr.* to identify its balance. Posting is automatic and immediate with accounting software.

## Marginal Student Annotations

These annotations provide students with additional hints, tips, and examples to help them more fully understand the concepts and retain what they have learned. The annotations also include notes on global implications of accounting and further examples.

# Outstanding Assignment Material

*Once a student has finished reading the chapter, how well he or she retains the material can depend greatly on the questions, exercises, and problems that reinforce it. This book leads the way in comprehensive, accurate assignments.*

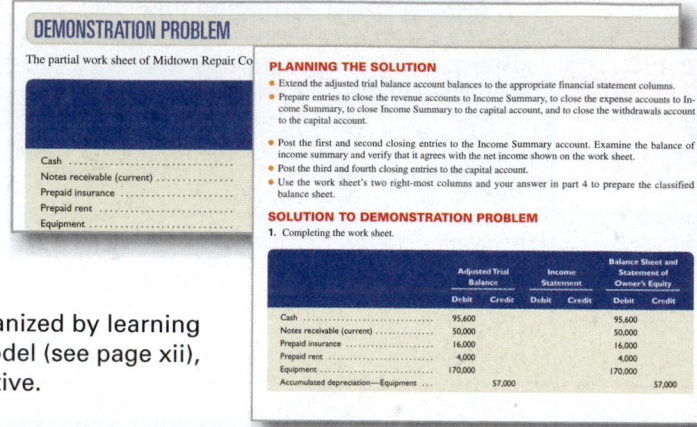

**Demonstration Problems** present both a problem and a complete solution, allowing students to review the entire problem-solving process and achieve success.

**Chapter Summaries** provide students with a review organized by learning objectives. Chapter Summaries are a component of the CAP model (see page xii), which recaps each conceptual, analytical, and procedural objective.

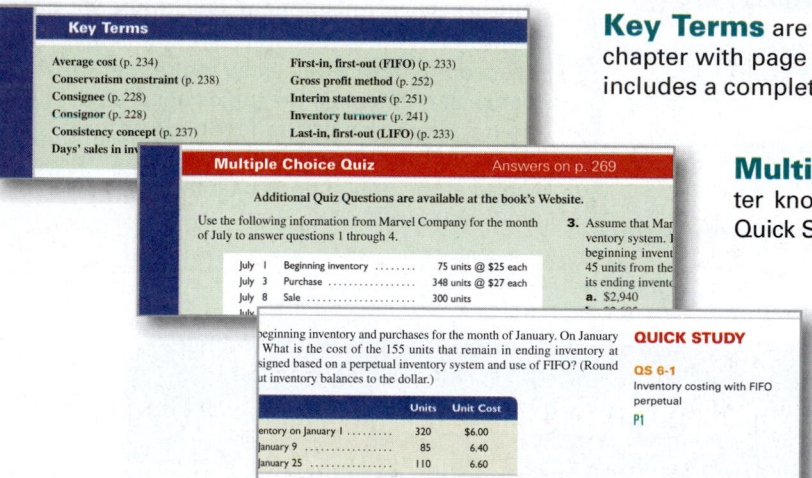

**Key Terms** are bolded in the text and repeated at the end of the chapter with page numbers indicating their location. The book also includes a complete Glossary of Key Terms.

**Multiple Choice Quiz** Questions quickly test chapter knowledge before a student moves on to complete Quick Studies, Exercises, and Problems.

**Quick Study** assignments are short exercises that often focus on one learning objective. Most are included in *Connect Accounting*. There are usually 8-10 Quick Study assignments per chapter.

**Exercises** are one of this book's many strengths and a competitive advantage. There are about 10-15 per chapter and most are included in *Connect Accounting*.

**Problem Sets A & B** are proven problems that can be assigned as homework or for in-class projects. All problems are coded according to the CAP model (see page xii), and Set A is included in *Connect Accounting*.

## PUT AWAY YOUR RED PEN!

We pride ourselves on the accuracy of this book's assignment materials. Independent research reports that instructors and reviewers point to the accuracy of this book's assignment materials as one of its key competitive advantages.

# Helps Students Master Key Concepts

**Beyond the Numbers** exercises ask students to use accounting figures and understand their meaning. Students also learn how accounting applies to a variety of business situations. These creative and fun exercises are all new or updated, and are divided into sections:

- Reporting in Action
- Comparative Analysis
- Ethics Challenge
- Communicating in Practice
- Taking It To The Net
- Teamwork in Action
- Hitting the Road
- Entrepreneurial Decision
- Global Decision

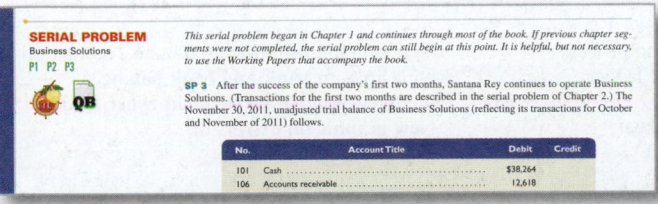

**Serial Problem** uses a continuous running case study to illustrate chapter concepts in a familiar context. The Serial Problem can be followed continuously from the first chapter or picked up at any later point in the book; enough information is provided to ensure students can get right to work.

> "Well planned, and very organized. A very thorough coverage of all topics. Easy to read and comprehend."
>
> — Linda Bolduc, Mount Wachusett Community College

**The End of the Chapter Is Only the Beginning** Our valuable and proven assignments aren't just confined to the book. From problems that require technological solutions to materials found exclusively online, this book's end-of-chapter material is fully integrated with its technology package.

- Quick Studies, Exercises, and Problems available in *Connect* are marked with an icon.

- Problems supported by the General Ledger Application Software, Peachtree, or Quickbooks are marked with an icon.

- Online Learning Center (OLC) includes Interactive Quizzes, Excel template assignments, and more.

- Problems supported with Microsoft Excel template assignments are marked with an icon.

- Material that receives additional coverage (slide shows, videos, audio, etc.) available in iPod ready format are marked with an icon.

- Assignments that focus on global accounting practices and companies are often identified with an icon.

The authors extend a special thanks to accuracy checkers Barbara Schnathorst, The Write Solution, Inc.; Helen Roybark, Radford University; Beth Woods, CPA, Accuracy Counts; and David Krug, Johnson County Community College.

# Enhancements in This Edition

This edition's revisions are driven by instructors and students. General revisions to the entire book follow (including chapter-by-chapter revisions):

- Revised and updated assignments throughout
- Updated ratio (tool) analyses for each chapter
- New material on International Financial Reporting Standards (IFRS) in most chapters, including global examples
- New and revised entrepreneurial examples and elements
- Revised serial problem through nearly all chapters
- New art program, visual info-graphics and text layout

- New Research In Motion (maker of BlackBerry) annual report with comparisons to Apple, Palm, and Nokia (IFRS) with new assignments
- Updated graphics added to each chapter's analysis section
- New technology content integrated and referenced in the book
- New Global View section in each chapter referencing international accounting including examples using global companies
- New assignments covering international accounting

## Chapter 1

Facebook NEW opener with new entrepreneurial assignment
Streamlined and consolidated learning objectives
New section on International Standards and convergence
Revised section on accounting principles, assumptions, and constraints
New visual layouts for conceptual framework and the building blocks of GAAP
New discussion of conceptual framework linked to IFRSs
New graphic discussing fraud control in accounting
Updated compensation data in exhibit

## Chapter 2

CitySlips NEW opener with new entrepreneurial assignment
Reorganized and streamlined learning objectives
Revised introduction of double-entry accounting
New 4-step process for analyzing, recording, and posting transactions
Revised layout for transaction analysis
New discussion on accounting quality

## Chapter 3

Cheezburger Network NEW opener with new entrepreneurial assignment
Updated 3-step process for adjusting accounts
Enhanced and streamlined presentation of accounting adjustments
Revised info-graphics for adjusting entries
Enhanced exhibit on steps in preparing financial statements
Expanded discussion of global accounting

## Chapter 4

Gamer Grub NEW opener with new entrepreneurial assignment
Slightly revised steps 1 and 2 of work sheet

Enhanced graphics for closing process
Enhanced details for general ledger after the closing process
Updated color-coded work sheet

## Chapter 5

Heritage Link Brands NEW opener with new entrepreneurial assignment
Streamlined learning objectives
New 2-step presentation for recording merchandise sales and its costs
Revised presentation on purchase returns
New discussion on fraud and invoices
Revised discussion of gross margin

## Chapter 6

Fitness Anywhere NEW opener with new entrepreneurial assignment
Streamlined presentation for lower of cost or market (LCM)
Color-coded graphic for introducing cost flow assumptions
Enhanced graphics for learning inventory errors
Expanded discussion on inventory controls
Expanded explanation of inventory accounting under IFRS

## Chapter 7

New Belgium Brewing Company NEW opener with new entrepreneurial assignment
Streamlined learning objectives
Enhanced graphics for special journals
Detailed four benefits from subsidiary ledgers
Updated ERP presentation
Revised discussion of segment returns

## Chapter 8

Dylan's Candy Bar REVISED opener with new entrepreneurial assignment
Enhanced SOX discussion of controls, including the role of COSO
Streamlined learning objectives
New material on drivers of human fraud

New graphic introducing a bank reconciliation with links to bank and book balances
Updated graphic on frequent cyber frauds
New graphic on drivers of financial misconduct

## Chapter 9

LaserMonks NEW opener with new entrepreneurial assignment
Streamlined learning objectives
Reorganized recording of credit sales
Further clarification of interest formula
Enhanced graphics for bad debts estimation

## Chapter 10

Games2U NEW opener with new entrepreneurial assignment
Reorganized learning objectives
Added entry to record impairment
Enhanced discussion of asset sales
Expanded explanation of asset valuation under IFRS
Updated all real world examples and graphics

## Chapter 11

SnorgTees NEW opener with new entrepreneurial assignment
Updated tax illustrations and assignments using most recent government rates
New data on frauds involving employee payroll
New entry to reclassify long- to short-term debt
Updated all real world examples and graphics

## Chapter 12

Kids Konserve NEW opener with new entrepreneurial assignment
New 3-step process for partnership liquidation
New *statement of liquidation* introduced
Enhanced discussion of partnership liquidation

# For Better Learning

## Chapter 13
Clean Air Lawn Care NEW opener with new entrepreneurial assignment
Streamlined learning objectives
Inserted numerous key margin computations for entries involving equity
Updated statement of stockholders' equity
Updated all real world examples and graphics
Explained accounting for equity under IFRS

## Chapter 14
CakeLove NEW opener with new entrepreneurial assignment
Enhanced graphics for bonds and notes
Revised discussion of debt-to-equity
Enhanced explanation of how U.S. GAAP and IFRS determine fair value
New arrow lines linking effective interest amortization tables to journal entries

## Chapter 15
Blackboard NEW opener with new entrepreneurial assignment
Streamlined learning objectives
Phrase "fair value" used in lieu of "market value"
Enhanced exhibit summarizing accounting for securities
Revised explanation of investments in securities with significant influence
New, enhanced section on comprehensive income

## Chapter 16
Animoto NEW opener with new entrepreneurial assignment
Streamlined learning objectives
Enhanced graphics on cash inflows and outflows involving operating, investing, and financing
Highlighted 5-step process to prepare the statement of cash flows
New discussion of different classifications for certain cash flows under IFRS
Increased number and range of assignments

## Chapter 17
Motley Fool REVISED opener with new entrepreneurial assignment
Streamlined learning objectives
New companies—Research In Motion, Apple, Palm and Nokia—data throughout the chapter, exhibits, and illustrations

Enhanced horizontal and vertical analysis using new company and industry data
Enhanced discussion of common-size graphics
Enhanced ratio analysis using new company and industry data

## Chapter 18
Hot Box Cookies NEW opener with new entrepreneurial assignment
Revised learning objectives
Enhanced discussion of trends in managerial accounting, including e-commerce and role of services
New exhibit and discussion of the value chain
Discussion of fraud and ethics in managerial accounting moved to earlier in chapter
New discussion of global trends in managerial accounting

## Chapter 19
Liberty Tax Service NEW opener with new entrepreneurial assignment
Enhanced explanation of events in job order costing, including new 3-step process
Added new arrow lines to exhibits as learning aids
Enhanced discussion of adjusting factory overhead
New factory overhead T-account exhibit
New exhibit on entries to adjust factory overhead account
Added several new assignments

## Chapter 20
IdeaPaint NEW opener with new entrepreneurial assignment
Streamlined learning objectives
Updated list of companies applying process operations
Enhanced several exhibits for better learning
New section on trends in process operations, including discussion of just-in-time, automation, role of services, and customer focus
Increased number and range of assignments

## Chapter 21
Skullcandy NEW opener with new entrepreneurial assignment
Streamlined learning objectives
Enhanced activity-based costing exhibits
Revised discussion and exhibits for comparisons between activity-based costing and two-stage cost allocation
Added summary of cost allocation methods with exhibit

Deleted section on departmental reporting and analysis
Added Serial Problem to end of chapter assignments

## Chapter 22
Johnny Cupcakes NEW opener with new entrepreneurial assignment
Streamlined learning objectives
Revised cost exhibits for added clarity and learning
New discussion on global use of contribution margin

## Chapter 23
Smathers and Branson NEW opener with new entrepreneurial assignment
Reorganized learning objectives
New discussion on potential outcomes of participatory budgeting
Enhanced discussion and exhibits for cash budgets
New exhibit on general formula for preparing the cash budget
Added Decision Insight box on Apple's cash cushion
Enhanced discussion of computing cash disbursements for purchases, including new exhibit
Increased number and range of assignments

## Chapter 24
SewWhat? NEW opener with new entrepreneurial assignment
Streamlined learning objectives
Simplified presentation of overhead variances to focus on controllable and volume variances
Moved detailed overhead variances and standard cost system journal entries to (new) Appendix 24A
Increased number and range of assignments

## Chapter 25
Dogswell NEW opener with new entrepreneurial assignment
Streamlined learning objectives
Updated graphic on industry cost of capital estimates
Added section and assignments on decision to keep or replace equipment
Increased number and range of assignments

# Instructor Supplements

## Instructor's Resource CD-ROM
*Chapters 1-25*
*ISBN13: 978007338107*
*ISBN10: 0077338103*

This is your all-in-one resource. It allows you to create custom presentations from your own materials or from the following text-specific materials provided in the CD's asset library:

- **Instructor's Resource Manual**
  *Written by Barbara Chiappetta, Nassau Community College, and Patricia Walczak, Lansing Community College.*

  This manual contains (for each chapter) a Lecture Outline, a chart linking all assignment materials to Learning Objectives, a list of relevant active learning activities, and additional visuals with transparency masters.

- **Solutions Manual**
- **Test Bank, Computerized Test Bank**
- **PowerPoint® Presentations**
  *Prepared by Jon Booker, Charles Caldwell, Cindy Rooney, and Susan Galbreth.*

  Presentations allow for revision of lecture slides, and includes a viewer, allowing screens to be shown with or without the software.

- **Link to PageOut**

## Test Bank
*Vol. 1, Chapters 1-12*
*ISBN13: 9780077338183*
*ISBN10: 0077338189*

*Vol. 2, Chapters 13-25*
*ISBN13: 9780077338190*
*ISBN10: 0077338197*

*Revised by Barbara Gershowitz, Nashville State Technical Community College.*

## Solutions Manual
*Vol. 1, Chapters 1-12*
*ISBN13: 9780077338152*
*ISBN10: 0077338154*

*Vol. 2, Chapters 13-25*
*ISBN13: 9780077338145*
*ISBN10: 0077338146*

*Written by John J. Wild, Ken W. Shaw, and Anita Kroll, University of Wisconsin–Madison.*

# Student Supplements

## Excel Working Papers CD
*ISBN13: 9780077338084*
*ISBN10: 0077338081*

*Written by John J. Wild.*

Working Papers (for Chapters 1-25) delivered in Excel spreadsheets. These Excel Working Papers are available on CD-ROM and can be bundled with the printed Working Papers; see your representative for information.

## Working Papers
*Vol. 1, Chapters 1-12*
*ISBN13: 9780077338220*
*ISBN10: 0077338227*

*Vol. 2, Chapters 12-25*
*ISBN13: 9780077338206*
*ISBN10: 0077338200*

*Principles of Financial Accounting Chapters 1-17*
*ISBN13: 9780077338213*
*ISBN10: 0077338219*

*Written by John J. Wild.*

## Study Guide
*Vol. 1, Chapters 1-12*
*ISBN13: 9780077338169*
*ISBN10: 0077338162*

*Vol. 2, Chapters 12-25*
*ISBN13: 9780077338176*
*ISBN10: 0077338170*

*Written by Barbara Chiapetta, Nassau Community College, and Patricia Walczak, Lansing Community College.*

Covers each chapter and appendix with reviews of the learning objectives, outlines of the chapters, summaries of chapter materials, and additional problems with solutions.

## Carol Yacht's General Ledger CD-ROM
*ISBN13: 9780077338039*
*ISBN10: 0077338030*

The CD-ROM includes fully functioning versions of McGraw-Hill's own General Ledger Application software. Problem templates prepared by Carol Yacht and student user guides are included that allow you to assign text problems for working in Yacht's General Ledger or Peachtree.

## QuickBooks Pro 2011 Student Guide and Templates
*ISBN13: 9780077455309*
*ISBN10: 0077455304*

*Prepared by Carol Yacht.*

To better prepare students for accounting in the real world, select end-of-chapter material in the text is tied to QuickBooks software. The accompanying student guide provides a step-by-step walkthrough for students on how to complete the problem in the software.

### Assurance of Learning Ready

Many educational institutions today are focused on the notion of assurance of learning, an important element of some accreditation standards. *Fundamental Accounting Principles* is designed specifically to support your assurance of learning initiatives with a simple, yet powerful solution. Each test bank question for *Fundamental Accounting Principles* maps to a specific chapter learning objective listed in the text. You can use our test bank software, EZ Test and EZ Test Online, or *Connect Accounting* to easily query for learning objectives that directly relate to the learning objectives for your course. You can then use the reporting features of EZ Test to aggregate student results in similar fashion, making the collection and presentation of assurance of learning data simple and easy.

> "Best on the market! Great examples, complete coverage of principle's topics, and great resources!"
>
> — David Alldredge, Salt Lake Community College

### AACSB Statement

The McGraw-Hill Companies is a proud corporate member of AACSB International. Understanding the importance and value of AACSB accreditation, *Fundamental Accounting Principles* recognizes the curricula guidelines detailed in the AACSB standards for business accreditation by connecting selected questions in the test bank to the six general knowledge and skill guidelines in the AACSB standards. The statements contained in *Fundamental Accounting Principles* are provided only as a guide for the users of this textbook. The AACSB leaves content coverage and assessment within the purview of individual schools, the mission of the school, and the faculty. While *Fundamental Accounting Principles* and the teaching package make no claim of any specific AACSB qualification or evaluation, we have within *Fundamental Accounting Principles* labeled select questions according to the six general knowledge and skills areas.

*The authors extend a special thanks to our contributing and technology supplement authors:*

**Contributing Author:** Anita Kroll, University of Wisconsin–Madison
**LearnSmart Authors:** Anna Boulware, St. Charles Community College; Brenda Mattison, Tri County Technical College; and Dominique Svarc, William Rainey Harper College
**Online Quizzes:** Gina Jones, Aims County Community College
**Connect Self-Quiz and Study:** Jeannine Metzler, Northampton Community College
**Interactive Presentations:** Kathleen O'Donnell, Onongada Community College, and Jeannie Folk, College of DuPage

# Acknowledgments

John J. Wild, Ken W. Shaw, Barbara Chiappetta, and McGraw-Hill/Irwin would like to recognize the following instructors for their valuable feedback and involvement in the development of *Fundamental Accounting Principles* 20e. We are thankful for their suggestions, counsel, and encouragement.

**Nelson Alino,** Quinnipiac University

**David Alldredge,** Salt Lake Community College

**Sheila Ammons,** Austin Community College

**Victoria Badura,** Chadron State College

**Susan Baker,** University of Michigan-Dearborn

**Charles Scott Barhight**, Northampton Community College

**Robert Beebe,** Morrisville State University

**Teri Bernstein,** Santa Monica College

**Swati Bhandarkar,** University of Georgia

**Jaswinder Bhangal,** Chabot College

**Linda Bolduc,** Mount Wachusett Community College

**Anna Boulware,** St. Charles Community College

**Philip Brown,** Harding University

**Jay Buchanon,** Burlington County College-Pemberton

**Mary Burnell,** Fairmont State University

**Nathaniel Calloway,** University of Maryland

**Sal Cardiel,** Chaffey College

**Lloyd Carroll,** Borough of Manhattan Community College

**Hong Chen,** Northeastern Illinois University

**Stanley Chu,** Borough of Manhattan Community College

**Kwang-Hyun Chung,** Pace University

**Shiefei Chung,** Rowan University

**Robert Churchman,** Harding University

**Marilyn Ciolino,** Delgado Community College

**Lisa Cole,** Johnson County Community College

**Howard A. Collins**, SUNY at Stony Brook

**William Cooper,** North Carolina A &T University

**Suzie Cordes,** Johnson County Community College

**James Cosby,** John Tyler Community College

**Richard Culp,** Ball State University

**Alan Czyzewski,** Indiana State University-Terre Haute

**Judy Daulton,** Piedmont Technical College

**Walter DeAguero,** Saddleback College

**Mike Deschamps,** Mira Costa College

**Rosemond Desir,** Colorado State University

**Vincent Dicalogero,** Suffolk County Community College

**Roger Dorsey,** University of Arkansas-Little Rock

**Jap Efendi,** University of Texas-Arlington

**Terry Elliott** Morehead State University

**James M. Emig**, Villanova University

**Steven Englert,** Ivy Tech Community College

**Caroline Falconetti,** Nassau Community College

**Stephanie Farewell,** University of Arkansas-Little Rock

**Laura Farrell,** Wagner College

**Charles Fazzi,** Saint Vincent College

**Ronald A. Feinberg**, Suffolk Community College

**Kathleen Fitzpatrick,** University of Toledo-Scott Park

**Jeannie Folk,** College of DuPage

**Mary Foster,** Illinois Central College

**Mitchell Franklin,** Syracuse University

**Paul Franklin,** Kaplan University Online

**Kim Gatzke,** Delgado Community College

**Rich Geglien,** Ivy Tech Community College

**Barbara Gershowitz,** Nashville State Technical Community College

**Richard Gordon,** Columbia Southern

**Michelle Grant,** Bossier Parish Community College

**Richard P. Green II**, Texas A& M University

**Tony Greig,** Purdue University

**Joyce Griffin,** Kansas City Kansas Community College

**Lillian Grose,** Delgado Community College

**Denise Guest,** Germanna Community College

**Amy Haas,** Kingsborough Community College

**Betty Habiger,** New Mexico State University

**Francis Haggerty,** Lee College

**Betty Harper,** Middle Tennessee State University

**Jeannie Harrington,** Middle Tennessee State University

**John L. Haverty**, St. Joseph's University

**Laurie Hays,** Western Michigan University

**Shelley Henke,** Fox Valley Technical College

**Geoffrey Heriot,** Greenville Technical College

**Lyle Hicks,** Danville Area Community College

**Cecil Hill,** Jackson State University

**Patricia Holmes,** Des Moines Area Community College

**Margaret Houston,** Wright State University

**Constance Hylton,** George Mason University

**Gary Allen Hypes,** Mount Aloysius College

**Catherine Jeppson,** Caifornia State University–Northridge

**Gina M. Jones,** Aims Community College

**Rita Jones,** Columbus State University

**Christine Jonick,** Gainesville State College

**Thomas Kam,** Hawaii Pacific University

**Jack Karbens,** Hawaii Pacific University

**Connie Kelt,** San Juan College

**Karen Kettelson,** Western Technical College

**Randy Kidd,** Longview Community College

**Irene Kim,** George Washington University

**James Kinard,** Ohio State University-Columbus

**Rita Kingery-Cook,** University of Delaware

**Frank Klaus,** Cleveland State University

**Shirly A. Kleiner,** Johnson County Community College

**Robert F. Koch,** Saint Peter's College

**Phillip Korb,** University of Baltimore

**David Krug,** Johnson County Community College

**Jill Kolody,** Anne Arundel Community College

**Charles Lacey,** Henry Ford Community College

**Tara Laken,** Joliet Junior College

Beth Lasky, Delgado Community College

Phillip Lee, Nashville State Technical Community College

Jerry Lehman, Madison Area Technical College

Frederic Lerner, New York University

Roger Lewis, West Virginia University-Parkersburg

Eric Lindquist, Lansing Community College

Jeannie Liu, Chaffey College

Rebecca Lohmann, Southeast Missouri State University

Debra Luna, El Paso Community College

Sylvester A. Maorino, SUNY Westchester Community College

Thomas S. Marsh, Northern Virginia Community College-Annadale

Stacie Mayes, Rose State College

Brenda Mattison, Tri-County Technical College

Jeanine Metzler, Northampton Community College

Kathleen Michele, Prairieville University

Tim Miller, El Camino College

Roger L. Moore, Arkansas State University-Beebe

Robbie Morse, Ivy Tech Community College

Linda Muren, Cuyahoga Community College—West Campus

Andrea Murowski, Brookdale Community College

Ramesh Narasimhan, Montclair State University

Mary Beth Nelson, North Shore Community College

Deborah Niemer, Oakland Community College

Kathleen O'Donnell, Onongada Community College

Ahmed Omar, Burlington County College

Deborah Pauly, Loras College

Joel Peralto, Hawaii Community College

Yvonne Phang, Borough of Manhattan Community College

Gary Pieroni, Diablo Valley College

Susan Pope, University of Akron

Jean Price, Marshall University

Debbie Rankin, Lincoln University

Susan Reeves, University of South Carolina

Jenny Resnick, Santa Monica College

Ruthie Reynolds, Howard University

Carla Rich, Pensacola Junior College

Paul Rivers, Bunker Hill Community College

Jill Roberts, Campbellsville University

Karen Robinson, Morgan State University

Richard Roding, Red Rocks Community College

Joel Rosenfeld, New York University

Pamela Rouse, Butler University

Helen Roybark, Radford University

Alphonse Ruggiero, Suffolk County Community College

Martin Sabo, Community College of Denver

Judith Sage, Texas A&M International University

Nathaniel Samba, Ivy Tech Community College

Linda Schain, Hoefstra University

Christine Schalow, University of Wisconsin-Stevens Point

Bunney Schmidt, Keiser University

Geeta Shankhar, University of Dayton

Regina Shea, Community College of Baltimore County—Essex

Jay Siegel, Union County College

Lois Slutsky, Broward College-South

Gerald Smith, University of Northern Iowa

Kathleen Sobieralski, University of Maryland

Charles Spector, State University of New York College

Jane Stam, Onondaga Community College

Douglas P. Stives, Monmouth University

Jacqueline Stoute, Baruch University

Beverly Strachan, Troy University

John Suckow, Lansing Community College

Dominique Svarc, William Rainey Harper College

Anthony Teng, Saddleback College

Sue Terizan, Wright State University

Leslie Thysell, John Tyler Community College

Michael Ulinski, Pace University-Pleasantville

Bob Urell, Irvine Valley College

Alonda Vaughn, Strayer University-Tampa East

Ari Vega, Fashion Institute of Technology

Adam Vitalis, University of Wisconsin

Patricia Walczak, Lansing Community College

Li Wang, University of Akron

Doris Warmflash, SUNY Westchester Community College

David Welch, Franklin University

Jean Wells, Howard University

Robert A. Widman, Brooklyn College CUNY

Christopher Widmer, Tidewater Community College

Jane Wiese, Valencia Community College

Kenneth L. Wild, University of London

Scott Williams, County College of Morris

Wanda Wong, Chabot College

Darryl Woolley, University of Idaho

Gloria Worthy, Southwest Tennessee Community College-Macon

Lorenzo Ybarra, West Los Angeles College

Laura Young, University of Central Arkansas

Judy Zander, Grossmont College

In addition to the helpful and generous colleagues listed above, we thank the entire McGraw-Hill/Irwin *Fundamental Accounting Principles* 20e team, including Stewart Mattson, Tim Vertovec, Steve Schuetz, Christina Sanders, Aaron Downey of Matrix Productions, Lori Koetters, Matthew Baldwin, Carol Bielski, Patricia Plumb, and Brian Nacik. We also thank the great marketing and sales support staff, including Michelle Heaster, Kathleen Klehr, and Simi Dutt. Many talented educators and professionals worked hard to create the supplements for this book, and for their efforts we're grateful. Finally, many more people we either did not meet or whose efforts we did not personally witness nevertheless helped to make this book everything that it is, and we thank them all.

John J. Wild        Ken W. Shaw        Barbara Chiappetta

# Brief Contents

# Contents

# 13 Accounting for Corporations 506

# 14 Long-Term Liabilities 550

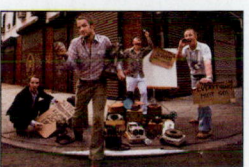

# Principles of
# Financial Accounting

# 1

# Accounting in Business

## A Look at This Chapter

Accounting is crucial in our information age. In this chapter, we discuss the importance of accounting to different types of organizations and describe its many users and uses. We explain that ethics are essential to accounting. We also explain business transactions and how they are reflected in financial statements.

## A Look Ahead

Chapter 2 describes and analyzes business transactions. We explain the analysis and recording of transactions, the ledger and trial balance, and the double-entry system. More generally, Chapters 2 through 4 show (via the accounting cycle) how financial statements reflect business activities.

## Learning Objectives

*Learning Objectives* are classified as conceptual, analytical, or procedural.

### CONCEPTUAL

**C1** Explain the purpose and importance of accounting. (p. 4)

**C2** Identify users and uses of, and opportunities in, accounting. (p. 5)

**C3** Explain why ethics are crucial to accounting. (p. 8)

**C4** Explain generally accepted accounting principles and define and apply several accounting principles. (p. 9)

**C5** *Appendix 1B*—Identify and describe the three major activities of organizations. (p. 26)

### ANALYTICAL

**A1** Define and interpret the accounting equation and each of its components. (p. 14)

**A2** Compute and interpret return on assets. (p. 22)

**A3** *Appendix 1A*—Explain the relation between return and risk. (p. 26)

LP1

### PROCEDURAL

**P1** Analyze business transactions using the accounting equation. (p. 15)

**P2** Identify and prepare basic financial statements and explain how they interrelate. (p. 19)

## Decision Insight

### Accounting for Facebook

*"We are focused on . . . helping people share information"*
—MARK ZUCKERBERG

PALO ALTO, CA—"Open Society" conjures up philosophical thoughts and political ideologies. However, for Mark Zuckerberg, his vision of an open society "is to give people the power to share and make the world more open and connected." That vision led Mark to create **Facebook** (**Facebook.com**) from his college dorm. Today, Facebook is the highest-profile social networking site. Along the way, Mark had to learn accounting and the details of preparing and interpreting financial statements.

"It's all been very interesting," says Mark. Important questions involving business formation, transaction analysis, and financial reporting arose. Mark answered them and in the process has set his company apart. "I'm here to build something for the long term," declares Mark. "Anything else is a distraction."

Information is the focus—both within Facebook and within its accounting records. Mark recalls that when he launched his business, there were "all these reasons why they could not aggregate this [personal] information." He took a similar tactic in addressing accounting information. "There's an intense focus on . . . information, as both an ideal and a practical strategy to get things done," insists Mark. This includes using accounting information to make key business decisions.

While Facebook is the language of social networking, accounting is the language of business networking. "As a company we are very focused on what we are building," says Mark. "We are adding a certain amount of value to people's lives if we build a very good product." That value is reflected in its financial statements, which are based on transaction analysis and accounting concepts.

Facebook's success is reflected in its revenues, which continue to grow and exhibit what people call the monetizing of social networking. "Social Ads are doing pretty well," asserts Mark. "We are happy with how we are doing in terms of numbers of advertisers and revenue." Facebook also tracks its expenses and asset purchases. "We expect to achieve . . . profitability next year," states Mark. "It means we will be able to fund all of our operations and server purchases from the cash we generate." This is saying a lot as Facebook's operating expenditures must support nearly 1 billion photo uploads and 8 million video uploads per day.

Mark emphasizes that his financial house must be in order for Facebook to realize its full potential—and that potential is in his sights. "We believe really deeply that if people are sharing more, then the world will be a more open place where people can understand what is going on with the people around them."

[Sources: *Facebook Website*, January 2011; *CNN*, October 2008; *Mercury News*, April 2009; *VentureBeat*, March 2008; *FastCompany.com*, May 2007; *Wired*, June 2009]

Today's world is one of information—its preparation, communication, analysis, and use. Accounting is at the core of this information age. Knowledge of accounting gives us career opportunities and the insight to take advantage of them. This book introduces concepts, procedures, and analyses that help us make better decisions, including career choices. In this chapter we describe accounting, the users and uses of accounting information, the forms and activities of organizations, and several accounting principles. We also introduce transaction analysis and financial statements.

## Accounting in Business

| Importance of Accounting | Fundamentals of Accounting | Transaction Analysis | Financial Statements |
|---|---|---|---|
| • Accounting information users<br>• Opportunities in accounting | • Ethics—key concept<br>• Generally accepted accounting principles<br>• International standards | • Accounting equation<br>• Transaction analysis—illustrated | • Income statement<br>• Statement of owner's equity<br>• Balance sheet<br>• Statement of cash flows |

# IMPORTANCE OF ACCOUNTING

**C1** Explain the purpose and importance of accounting.

Why is accounting so popular on campuses? Why are there so many accounting jobs for graduates? Why is accounting so important to companies? Why do politicians and business leaders focus on accounting regulations? The answer is that we live in an information age, where that information, and its reliability, impacts the financial well-being of us all.

**Accounting** is an information and measurement system that identifies, records, and communicates relevant, reliable, and comparable information about an organization's business activities. *Identifying* business activities requires selecting transactions and events relevant to an organization. Examples are the sale of iPhones by **Apple** and the receipt of ticket money by **TicketMaster**. *Recording* business activities requires keeping a chronological log of transactions and events measured in dollars and classified and summarized in a useful format. *Communicating* business activities requires preparing accounting reports such as financial statements. It also requires analyzing and interpreting such reports. (The financial statements and notes of **Research In Motion**, the maker of *BlackBerry*, are shown in Appendix A near the end of this book. This appendix also shows the financial statements of **Apple**, **Palm**, and **Nokia**.) Exhibit 1.1 summarizes accounting activities.

*Real company names are printed in bold magenta.*

We must guard against a narrow view of accounting. Our most common contact with accounting is through credit approvals, checking accounts, tax forms, and payroll. These experiences are limited and tend to focus on the recordkeeping parts of accounting. **Recordkeeping,** or **bookkeeping,** is the recording of transactions and events, either manually or electronically. This is just one part of accounting. Accounting also identifies and communicates information on transactions and events, and it includes the crucial processes of analysis and interpretation.

**EXHIBIT 1.1**

Accounting Activities

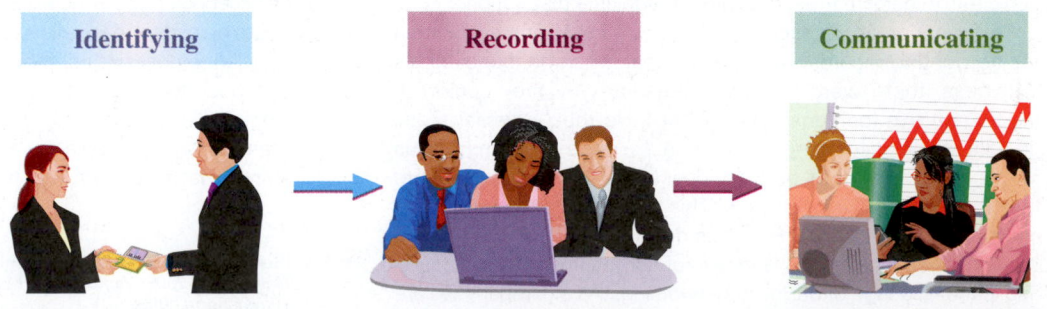

| Identifying | Recording | Communicating |
|---|---|---|
| Select transactions and events | Input, measure, and classify | Prepare, analyze, and interpret |

Technology is a key part of modern business and plays a major role in accounting. Technology reduces the time, effort, and cost of recordkeeping while improving clerical accuracy. Some small organizations continue to perform various accounting tasks manually, but even they are impacted by technology. As technology has changed the way we store, process, and summarize masses of data, accounting has been freed to expand. Consulting, planning, and other financial services are now closely linked to accounting. These services require sorting through data, interpreting their meaning, identifying key factors, and analyzing their implications.

## Users of Accounting Information

Accounting is often called the *language of business* because all organizations set up an accounting information system to communicate data to help people make better decisions. Exhibit 1.2 shows that the accounting information system serves many kinds of users (this is a partial listing) who can be divided into two groups: external users and internal users.

**External users**

- Lenders        • Consumer groups
- Shareholders   • External auditors
- Governments    • Customers

**Internal users**

- Officers           • Sales staff
- Managers           • Budget officers
- Internal auditors  • Controllers

**EXHIBIT 1.2**

Users of Accounting Information

*Infographics reinforce key concepts through visual learning.*

**C2** Identify users and uses of, and opportunities in, accounting.

**External Information Users**    **External users** of accounting information are *not* directly involved in running the organization. They include shareholders (investors), lenders, directors, customers, suppliers, regulators, lawyers, brokers, and the press. External users have limited access to an organization's information. Yet their business decisions depend on information that is reliable, relevant, and comparable.

**Financial accounting** is the area of accounting aimed at serving external users by providing them with *general-purpose financial statements*. The term *general-purpose* refers to the broad range of purposes for which external users rely on these statements.

Each external user has special information needs depending on the types of decisions to be made. *Lenders* (creditors) loan money or other resources to an organization. Banks, savings and loans, co-ops, and mortgage and finance companies are lenders. Lenders look for information to help them assess whether an organization is likely to repay its loans with interest. *Shareholders* (investors) are the owners of a corporation. They use accounting reports in deciding whether to buy, hold, or sell stock. Shareholders typically elect a *board of directors* to oversee their interests in an organization. Since directors are responsible to shareholders, their information needs are similar. *External* (independent) *auditors* examine financial statements to verify that they are prepared according to generally accepted accounting principles. *Nonexecutive employees* and *labor unions* use financial statements to judge the fairness of wages, assess job prospects, and bargain for better wages. *Regulators* often have legal authority over certain activities of organizations. For example, the Internal Revenue Service (IRS) and other tax authorities require organizations to file accounting reports in computing taxes. Other regulators include utility boards that use accounting information to set utility rates and securities regulators that require reports for companies that sell their stock to the public.

Accounting serves the needs of many other external users. *Voters, legislators,* and *government officials* use accounting information to monitor and evaluate government receipts and expenses. *Contributors* to nonprofit organizations use accounting information to evaluate the use and impact of their donations. *Suppliers* use accounting information to judge the soundness of a customer before making sales on credit, and *customers* use financial reports to assess the staying power of potential suppliers.

**Internal Information Users** **Internal users** of accounting information are those directly involved in managing and operating an organization. They use the information to help improve the efficiency and effectiveness of an organization. **Managerial accounting** is the area of accounting that serves the decision-making needs of internal users. Internal reports are not subject to the same rules as external reports and instead are designed with the special needs of internal users in mind.

There are several types of internal users, and many are managers of key operating activities. *Research and development managers* need information about projected costs and revenues of any proposed changes in products and services. *Purchasing managers* need to know what, when, and how much to purchase. *Human resource managers* need information about employees' payroll, benefits, performance, and compensation. *Production managers* depend on information to monitor costs and ensure quality. *Distribution managers* need reports for timely, accurate, and efficient delivery of products and services. *Marketing managers* use reports about sales and costs to target consumers, set prices, and monitor consumer needs, tastes, and price concerns. *Service managers* require information on the costs and benefits of looking after products and services. Decisions of these and other internal users depend on accounting reports.

Both internal and external users rely on internal controls to monitor and control company activities. *Internal controls* are procedures set up to protect company property and equipment, ensure reliable accounting reports, promote efficiency, and encourage adherence to company policies. Examples are good records, physical controls (locks, passwords, guards), and independent reviews.

### Decision **Insight**

**Virtuous Returns** Virtue is not always its own reward. Compare the S&P 500 with the Domini Social Index (DSI), which covers 400 companies that have especially good records of social responsibility. We see that returns for companies with socially responsible behavior are at least as high as those of the S&P 500. ■

Copyright © 2009 by KLD Research & Analytics, Inc. The "Domini 400 Social Index" is a service mark of KLD Research & Analytics.

## Opportunities in Accounting

Accounting information affects many aspects of our lives. When we earn money, pay taxes, invest savings, budget earnings, and plan for the future, we are influenced by accounting. Accounting has four broad areas of opportunities: financial, managerial, taxation, and accounting-related. Exhibit 1.3 lists selected opportunities in each area.

**EXHIBIT 1.3**

Accounting Opportunities

| Financial | Managerial | Taxation | Accounting-related | |
|---|---|---|---|---|
| • Preparation | • General accounting | • Preparation | • Lenders | • FBI investigators |
| • Analysis | • Cost accounting | • Planning | • Consultants | • Market researchers |
| • Auditing | • Budgeting | • Regulatory | • Analysts | • Systems designers |
| • Regulatory | • Internal auditing | • Investigations | • Traders | • Merger services |
| • Consulting | • Consulting | • Consulting | • Directors | • Business valuation |
| • Planning | • Controller | • Enforcement | • Underwriters | • Forensic accounting |
| • Criminal investigation | • Treasurer | • Legal services | • Planners | • Litigation support |
| | • Strategy | • Estate plans | • Appraisers | • Entrepreneurs |

The majority of accounting opportunities are in *private accounting,* which are employees working for businesses, as shown in Exhibit 1.4. *Public accounting* offers the next largest number of opportunities, which involve services such as auditing and tax advice to a vast range of businesses. Still other opportunities exist in government and not-for-profit agencies, including business regulation and investigation of law violations.

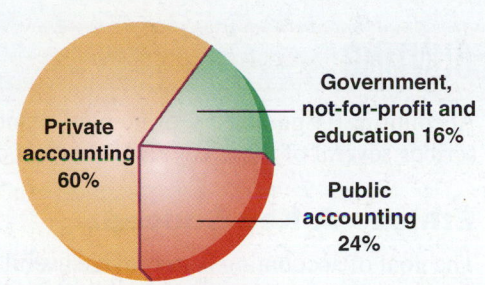

**EXHIBIT 1.4**

Accounting Jobs by Area

Accounting specialists are highly regarded. Their professional standing often is denoted by a certificate. Certified public accountants (CPAs) must meet education and experience requirements, pass an examination, and exhibit ethical character. Many accounting specialists hold certificates in addition to or instead of the CPA. Two of the most common are the certificate in management accounting (CMA) and the certified internal auditor (CIA). Employers also look for specialists with designations such as certified bookkeeper (CB), certified payroll professional (CPP), personal financial specialist (PFS), certified fraud examiner (CFE), and certified forensic accountant (CrFA).

**Point:** The largest accounting firms are Deloitte, Ernst & Young, KPMG, and PricewaterhouseCoopers.

Individuals with accounting knowledge are always in demand as they can help with financial analysis, strategic planning, e-commerce, product feasibility analysis, information technology, and financial management. Benefit packages can include flexible work schedules, telecommuting options, career path alternatives, casual work environments, extended vacation time, and child and elder care.

Demand for accounting specialists is strong. Exhibit 1.5 reports average annual salaries for several accounting positions. Salary variation depends on location, company size, professional designation, experience, and other factors. For example, salaries for chief financial officers (CFO) range from under $75,000 to more than $1 million per year. Likewise, salaries for bookkeepers range from under $30,000 to more than $80,000.

**Point:** Census Bureau (2009) reports that for workers 18 and over, higher education yields higher average pay:
Advanced degree . . . . . . . . . .   $80,977
Bachelor's degree . . . . . . . . . .     57,181
High school degree . . . . . . . .     31,286
No high school degree . . . . . .     21,484

**EXHIBIT 1.5**

Accounting Salaries for Selected Fields

| Field | Title (experience) | 2009 Salary | 2014 Estimate* |
|---|---|---|---|
| **Public Accounting** | Partner . . . . . . . . . . . . . . . . . . . . . . . . . . | $191,000 | $211,000 |
| | Manager (6–8 years) . . . . . . . . . . . . . . . | 94,500 | 104,000 |
| | Senior (3–5 years) . . . . . . . . . . . . . . . . . | 72,000 | 79,500 |
| | Junior (0–2 years) . . . . . . . . . . . . . . . . . | 51,500 | 57,000 |
| **Private Accounting** | CFO . . . . . . . . . . . . . . . . . . . . . . . . . . | 232,000 | 256,000 |
| | Controller/Treasurer . . . . . . . . . . . . . . | 147,500 | 163,000 |
| | Manager (6–8 years) . . . . . . . . . . . . . . . | 87,500 | 96,500 |
| | Senior (3–5 years) . . . . . . . . . . . . . . . . . | 72,500 | 80,000 |
| | Junior (0–2 years) . . . . . . . . . . . . . . . . . | 49,000 | 54,000 |
| **Recordkeeping** | Full-charge bookkeeper . . . . . . . . . . . . | 57,500 | 63,500 |
| | Accounts manager . . . . . . . . . . . . . . . . . | 51,000 | 56,500 |
| | Payroll manager . . . . . . . . . . . . . . . . . . . | 54,500 | 60,000 |
| | Accounting clerk (0–2 years) . . . . . . . . . | 37,500 | 41,500 |

\* Estimates assume a 2% compounded annual increase over current levels (rounded to nearest $500).

**Point:** For updated salary information:
Abbott-Langer.com
www.AICPA.org
Kforce.com

## Quick Check

Answers — p. 28

**Quick Check** *is a chance to stop and reflect on key points.*

1. What is the purpose of accounting?
2. What is the relation between accounting and recordkeeping?
3. Identify some advantages of technology for accounting.
4. Who are the internal and external users of accounting information?
5. Identify at least five types of managers who are internal users of accounting information.
6. What are internal controls and why are they important?

## FUNDAMENTALS OF ACCOUNTING

Accounting is guided by principles, standards, concepts, and assumptions. This section describes several of these key fundamentals of accounting.

### Ethics—A Key Concept

 **C3** Explain why ethics are crucial to accounting.

The goal of accounting is to provide useful information for decisions. For information to be useful, it must be trusted. This demands ethics in accounting. **Ethics** are beliefs that distinguish right from wrong. They are accepted standards of good and bad behavior.

Identifying the ethical path is sometimes difficult. The preferred path is a course of action that avoids casting doubt on one's decisions. For example, accounting users are less likely to trust an auditor's report if the auditor's pay depends on the success of the client's business. To avoid such concerns, ethics rules are often set. For example, auditors are banned from direct investment in their client and cannot accept pay that depends on figures in the client's reports. Exhibit 1.6 gives guidelines for making ethical decisions.

**Point: Sarbanes-Oxley Act** requires each issuer of securities to disclose whether it has adopted a code of ethics for its senior financial officers and the contents of that code.

**EXHIBIT 1.6**

Guidelines for Ethical Decision Making

| Identify ethical concerns | Analyze options | Make ethical decision |
|---|---|---|
| Use personal ethics to recognize an ethical concern. | Consider all good and bad consequences. | Choose best option after weighing all consequences. |

Providers of accounting information often face ethical choices as they prepare financial reports. These choices can affect the price a buyer pays and the wages paid to workers. They can even affect the success of products and services. Misleading information can lead to a wrongful closing of a division that harms workers, customers, and suppliers. There is an old saying: *Good ethics are good business.*

Some people extend ethics to *social responsibility,* which refers to a concern for the impact of actions on society. An organization's social responsibility can include donations to hospitals, colleges, community programs, and law enforcement. It also can include programs to reduce pollution, increase product safety, improve worker conditions, and support continuing education. These programs are not limited to large companies. For example, many small businesses offer discounts to students and senior citizens. Still others help sponsor events such as the Special Olympics and summer reading programs.

**Point:** The American Institute of Certified Public Accountants' *Code of Professional Conduct* is available at **www.AICPA.org.**

### Decision Insight

**They Fought the Law**   Our economic and social welfare depends on reliable accounting. Some individuals forgot that and are now paying their dues. They include Bernard Madoff (in photo) of **Madoff Investment Securities**, convicted of falsifying securities records; Bernard Ebbers of **WorldCom**, convicted of an $11 billion accounting scandal; Andrew Fastow of **Enron**, guilty of hiding debt and inflating income; and Ramalinga Raju of **Satyam Computers**, accused of overstating assets by $1.5 billion. ■

### Generally Accepted Accounting Principles

Financial accounting practice is governed by concepts and rules known as **generally accepted accounting principles (GAAP).** To use and interpret financial statements effectively, we need to understand these principles, which can change over time in response to the demands of users.

GAAP aims to make information in financial statements *relevant, reliable,* and *comparable.* Relevant information affects the decisions of its users. Reliable information is trusted by users. Comparable information is helpful in contrasting organizations.

In the United States, the **Securities and Exchange Commission (SEC),** a government agency, has the legal authority to set GAAP. The SEC also oversees proper use of GAAP by companies that raise money from the public through issuances of their stock and debt. Those companies that issue their stock on U.S. exchanges include both *U.S. SEC registrants* (companies incorporated in the United States) and *non-U.S. SEC registrants* (companies incorporated under non-U.S. laws). The SEC has largely delegated the task of setting U.S. GAAP to the **Financial Accounting Standards Board (FASB),** which is a private-sector group that sets both broad and specific principles.

C4  Explain generally accepted accounting principles and define and apply several accounting principles.

**Point:** State ethics codes require CPAs who audit financial statements to disclose areas where those statements fail to comply with GAAP. If CPAs fail to report noncompliance, they can lose their licenses and be subject to criminal and civil actions and fines.

## International Standards

In today's global economy, there is increased demand by external users for comparability in accounting reports. This demand often arises when companies wish to raise money from lenders and investors in different countries. To that end, the **International Accounting Standards Board (IASB),** an independent group (consisting of individuals from many countries), issues **International Financial Reporting Standards (IFRS)** that identify preferred accounting practices.

If standards are harmonized, one company can potentially use a single set of financial statements in all financial markets. Differences between U.S. GAAP and IFRS are slowly fading as the FASB and IASB pursue a *convergence* process aimed to achieve a single set of accounting standards for global use. More than 115 countries now require or permit companies to prepare financial reports following IFRS. Further, non-U.S. SEC registrants can use IFRS in financial reports filed with the SEC (with no reconciliation to U.S. GAAP). This means there are *two* sets of accepted accounting principles in the United States: (1) U.S. GAAP for U.S. SEC registrants and (2) either IFRS or U.S. GAAP for non-U.S. SEC registrants.

The convergence process continues and, in late 2008, the SEC set a roadmap for use of IFRS by publicly traded U.S. companies. This roadmap proposes that large U.S. companies adopt IFRS by 2014, with midsize and small companies following in 2015 and 2016, respectively. Early adoption is permitted for large multinationals that meet certain criteria. For updates on this roadmap, we can check with the AICPA (**IFRS.com**), FASB (**FASB.org**), and IASB (**IASB.org.uk**).

 **IFRS** _____

Like the FASB, the IASB uses a conceptual framework to aid in revising or drafting new standards. However, unlike the FASB, the IASB's conceptual framework is used as a reference when specific guidance is lacking. The IASB also requires that transactions be accounted for according to their substance (not only their legal form), and that financial statements give a fair presentation, whereas the FASB narrows that scope to fair presentation *in accordance with U.S. GAAP.* ∎

## Conceptual Framework and Convergence

The FASB and IASB are attempting to converge and enhance the **conceptual framework** that guides standard setting. The framework consists broadly of the following:

- **Objectives**—to provide information useful to investors, creditors, and others.
- **Qualitative Characteristics**—to require information that is relevant, reliable, and comparable.
- **Elements**—to define items that financial statements can contain.
- **Recognition and Measurement**—to set criteria that an item must meet for it to be recognized as an element; and how to measure that element.

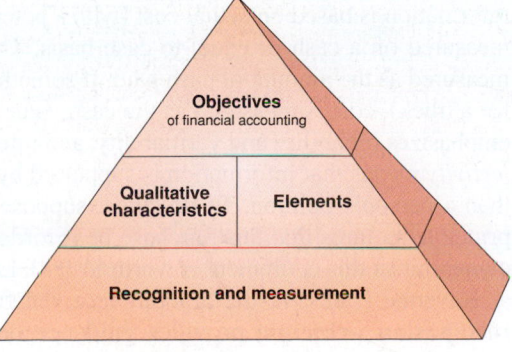

For updates on this joint FASB and IASB conceptual framework convergence we can check with **FASB.org** or **IASB.org.uk** Websites. We must remember that U.S. GAAP and IFRS are two similar, but not identical, systems. However, their similarities greatly outweigh any differences. The remainder of this section describes key principles and assumptions of accounting.

### Decision Insight

**Principles and Scruples**   Auditors, directors, and lawyers are using principles to improve accounting reports. Examples include accounting restatements at **Navistar**, financial restatements at **Nortel**, accounting reviews at **Echostar**, and expense adjustments at **Electronic Data Systems**. Principles-based accounting has led accounting firms to drop clients deemed too risky. Examples include **Grant Thornton**'s resignation as auditor of **Fremont General** due to alleged failures in providing information when promised, and **Ernst and Young**'s resignation as auditor of **Catalina Marketing** due to alleged accounting errors. ■

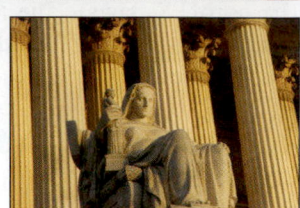

**Principles and Assumptions of Accounting**   Accounting principles (and assumptions) are of two types. *General principles* are the basic assumptions, concepts, and guidelines for preparing financial statements. *Specific principles* are detailed rules used in reporting business transactions and events. General principles stem from long-used accounting practices. Specific principles arise more often from the rulings of authoritative groups.

We need to understand both general and specific principles to effectively use accounting information. Several general principles are described in this section that are relied on in later chapters. General principles (in purple font with white shading) and assumptions (in red font with yellow shading) are portrayed as building blocks of GAAP in Exhibit 1.7. The specific principles are described as we encounter them in the book.

**EXHIBIT 1.7**

Building Blocks for GAAP

**Accounting Principles**   General principles consist of at least four basic principles, four assumptions, and two constraints.

**Point:** The cost principle is also called the *historical cost principle.*

The **measurement principle,** also called the **cost principle,** usually means that accounting information is based on actual cost (with a potential for subsequent adjustments to market). Cost is measured on a cash or equal-to-cash basis. This means if cash is given for a service, its cost is measured as the amount of cash paid. If something besides cash is exchanged (such as a car traded for a truck), cost is measured as the cash value of what is given up or received. The cost principle emphasizes reliability and verifiability, and information based on cost is considered objective. *Objectivity* means that information is supported by independent, unbiased evidence; it demands more than a person's opinion. To illustrate, suppose a company pays $5,000 for equipment. The cost principle requires that this purchase be recorded at a cost of $5,000. It makes no difference if the owner thinks this equipment is worth $7,000. Later in the book we introduce *fair value* measures.

Revenue (sales) is the amount received from selling products and services. The **revenue recognition principle** provides guidance on when a company must recognize revenue. To *recognize* means to record it. If revenue is recognized too early, a company would look more profitable than it is. If revenue is recognized too late, a company would look less profitable than it is.

Three concepts are important to revenue recognition. (1) *Revenue is recognized when earned.* The earnings process is normally complete when services are performed or a seller transfers ownership of products to the buyer. (2) *Proceeds from selling products and services need not be in cash.* A common noncash proceed received by a seller is a customer's promise to pay at a future date, called *credit sales.* (3) *Revenue is measured by the cash received plus the cash value of any other items received.*

The **expense recognition principle,** also called the **matching principle,** prescribes that a company record the expenses it incurred to generate the revenue reported. The principles of matching and revenue recognition are key to modern accounting.

The **full disclosure principle** prescribes that a company report the details behind financial statements that would impact users' decisions. Those disclosures are often in footnotes to the statements.

**Example:** When a bookstore sells a textbook on credit is its earnings process complete? *Answer:* A bookstore can record sales for these books minus an amount expected for returns.

## Decision Insight

Revenues for the **Green Bay Packers** and **Dallas Cowboys** football teams include ticket sales, television and cable broadcasts, radio rights, concessions, and advertising. Revenues from ticket sales are earned when the NFL team plays each game. Advance ticket sales are not revenues; instead, they represent a liability until the NFL team plays the game for which the ticket was sold. At that point, the liability is removed and revenues are reported. ■

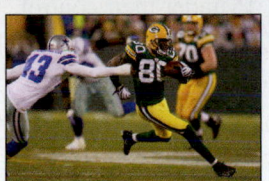

**Accounting Assumptions**    There are four accounting assumptions: the going concern assumption, the monetary unit assumption, the time period assumption, and the business entity assumption.

The **going-concern assumption** means that accounting information reflects a presumption that the business will continue operating instead of being closed or sold. This implies, for example, that property is reported at cost instead of, say, liquidation values that assume closure.

The **monetary unit assumption** means that we can express transactions and events in monetary, or money, units. Money is the common denominator in business. Examples of monetary units are the dollar in the United States, Canada, Australia, and Singapore; and the peso in Mexico, the Philippines, and Chile. The monetary unit a company uses in its accounting reports usually depends on the country where it operates, but many companies today are expressing reports in more than one monetary unit.

**Point:** For currency conversion: xe.com

The **time period assumption** presumes that the life of a company can be divided into time periods, such as months and years, and that useful reports can be prepared for those periods.

The **business entity assumption** means that a business is accounted for separately from other business entities, including its owner. The reason for this assumption is that separate information about each business is necessary for good decisions. A business entity can take one of three legal forms: *proprietorship, partnership,* or *corporation.*

**Point:** Abuse of the entity assumption was a main culprit in **Enron's** collapse.

1. A **sole proprietorship,** or simply **proprietorship,** is a business owned by one person. No special legal requirements must be met to start a proprietorship. It is a separate entity for accounting purposes, but it is *not* a separate legal entity from its owner. This means, for example, that a court can order an owner to sell personal belongings to pay a proprietorship's debt. This *unlimited liability* of a proprietorship is a disadvantage. However, an advantage is that a proprietorship's income is not subject to a business income tax but is instead reported and taxed on the owner's personal income tax return. Proprietorship attributes are summarized in Exhibit 1.8, including those for partnerships and corporations.

2. A **partnership** is a business owned by two or more people, called *partners.* Like a proprietorship, no special legal requirements must be met in starting a partnership. The only

**EXHIBIT 1.8**

Attributes of Businesses

| Attribute Present | Proprietorship | Partnership | Corporation |
|---|---|---|---|
| One owner allowed . . . . . . . . . . . | yes | no | yes |
| Business taxed . . . . . . . . . . . . . . | no | no | yes |
| Limited liability . . . . . . . . . . . . . . | no* | no* | yes |
| Business entity . . . . . . . . . . . . . . | yes | yes | yes |
| Legal entity . . . . . . . . . . . . . . . . | no | no | yes |
| Unlimited life . . . . . . . . . . . . . . | no | no | yes |

\* Proprietorships and partnerships that are set up as LLCs provide limited liability.

requirement is an agreement between partners to run a business together. The agreement can be either oral or written and usually indicates how income and losses are to be shared. A partnership, like a proprietorship, is *not* legally separate from its owners. This means that each partner's share of profits is reported and taxed on that partner's tax return. It also means *unlimited liability* for its partners. However, at least three types of partnerships limit liability. A *limited partnership* (*LP*) includes a general partner(s) with unlimited liability and a limited partner(s) with liability restricted to the amount invested. A *limited liability partnership* (*LLP*) restricts partners' liabilities to their own acts and the acts of individuals under their control. This protects an innocent partner from the negligence of another partner, yet all partners remain responsible for partnership debts. A *limited liability company* (*LLC*) offers the limited liability of a corporation and the tax treatment of a partnership (and proprietorship). Most proprietorships and partnerships are now organized as LLCs.

3. A **corporation** is a business legally separate from its owners, meaning it is responsible for its own acts and its own debts. Separate legal status means that a corporation can conduct business with the rights, duties, and responsibilities of a person. A corporation acts through its managers, who are its legal agents. Separate legal status also means that its owners, who are called **shareholders** (or **stockholders**), are not personally liable for corporate acts and debts. This limited liability is its main advantage. A main disadvantage is what's called *double taxation*—meaning that (1) the corporation income is taxed and (2) any distribution of income to its owners through dividends is taxed as part of the owners' personal income, usually at the 15% rate. (For lower income taxpayers, the dividend tax is less than 15%, and in some cases zero.) An *S corporation,* a corporation with special attributes, does not owe corporate income tax. Owners of S corporations report their share of corporate income with their personal income. Ownership of all corporations is divided into units called **shares** or **stock.** When a corporation issues only one class of stock, we call it **common stock** (or *capital stock*).

**Point:** Proprietorships and partnerships are usually managed by their owners. In a corporation, the owners (shareholders) elect a board of directors who appoint managers to run the business.

*Decision Ethics boxes are role-playing exercises that stress ethics in accounting and business.*

### ■ Decision Ethics                                                      Answer — p. 27

**Entrepreneur**  You and a friend develop a new design for in-line skates that improves speed by 25% to 30%. You plan to form a business to manufacture and market those skates. You and your friend want to minimize taxes, but your prime concern is potential lawsuits from individuals who might be injured on these skates. What form of organization do you set up? ■

**Accounting Constraints**   There are two basic constraints on financial reporting. The **materiality constraint** prescribes that only information that would influence the decisions of a reasonable person need be disclosed. This constraint looks at both the importance and relative size of an amount. The **cost-benefit constraint** prescribes that only information with benefits of disclosure greater than the costs of providing it need be disclosed.

## Sarbanes–Oxley (SOX)

**Point:** An audit examines whether financial statements are prepared using GAAP. It does *not* attest to absolute accuracy of the statements.

Congress passed the **Sarbanes–Oxley Act,** also called *SOX,* to help curb financial abuses at companies that issue their stock to the public. SOX requires that these public companies apply both accounting oversight and stringent internal controls. The desired results include more transparency, accountability, and truthfulness in reporting transactions.

Compliance with SOX requires documentation and verification of internal controls and increased emphasis on internal control effectiveness. Failure to comply can yield financial penalties, stock market delisting, and criminal prosecution of executives. Management must issue a report stating that internal controls are effective. CEOs and CFOs who knowingly sign off on bogus accounting reports risk millions of dollars in fines and years in prison. **Auditors** also must verify the effectiveness of internal controls.

A listing of some of the more publicized accounting scandals in recent years follows.

| Company | Alleged Accounting Abuses |
| --- | --- |
| Enron ....................... | Inflated income, hid debt, and bribed officials |
| WorldCom .................... | Understated expenses to inflate income and hid debt |
| Fannie Mae ................... | Inflated income |
| Adelphia Communications ........ | Understated expenses to inflate income and hid debt |
| AOL Time Warner................ | Inflated revenues and income |
| Xerox......................... | Inflated income |
| Bristol-Myers Squibb............. | Inflated revenues and income |
| Nortel Networks ............... | Understated expenses to inflate income |
| Global Crossing................. | Inflated revenues and income |
| Tyco ........................ | Hid debt, and CEO evaded taxes |
| Halliburton .................... | Inflated revenues and income |
| Qwest Communications........... | Inflated revenues and income |

**Point:** *BusinessWeek* reports that external audit costs run about $35,000 for start-ups, up from $15,000 pre-SOX.

To reduce the risk of accounting fraud, companies set up *governance systems*. A company's governance system includes its owners, managers, employees, board of directors, and other important stakeholders, who work together to reduce the risk of accounting fraud and increase confidence in accounting reports.

The impact of SOX regulations for accounting and business is discussed throughout this book. Ethics and investor confidence are key to company success. Lack of confidence in accounting numbers impacts company value as evidenced by huge stock price declines for **Enron**, **WorldCom**, **Tyco**, and **ImClone** after accounting misconduct was uncovered.

## Decision Insight

**Economic Downturn, Fraud Upturn?** Executives polled show that 80% believe that the economic downturn has or will have a significant impact on fraud control in their companies (Deloitte 2009). The top three responses to the question "What activity would best counter this increased fraud risk?" are tallied in the graphic to the right. ■

Increased fraud awareness training — 38.7%
Greater fraud assessment — 21.5%
Expanded internal auditing — 20.3%

(0% 10% 20% 30% 40%)

## Quick Check

Answers — p. 28

7. What three-step guidelines can help people make ethical decisions?
8. Why are ethics and social responsibility valuable to organizations?
9. Why are ethics crucial in accounting?
10. Who sets U.S. accounting rules?
11. How are U.S. companies affected by international accounting standards?
12. How are the objectivity concept and cost principle related?
13. Why is the business entity assumption important?
14. Why is the revenue recognition principle important?
15. What are the three basic forms of business organization?
16. Identify the owners of corporations and the terminology for ownership units.

## TRANSACTION ANALYSIS AND THE ACCOUNTING EQUATION

To understand accounting information, we need to know how an accounting system captures relevant data about transactions, and then classifies, records, and reports data.

### Accounting Equation

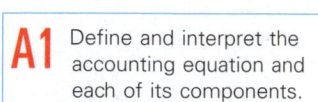

**A1** Define and interpret the accounting equation and each of its components.

Assets  =  Liabilities + Equity

The accounting system reflects two basic aspects of a company: what it owns and what it owes. *Assets* are resources a company owns or controls. Examples are cash, supplies, equipment, and land, where each carries expected benefits. The claims on a company's assets—what it owes—are separated into owner and nonowner claims. *Liabilities* are what a company owes its nonowners (creditors) in future payments, products, or services. *Equity* (also called owner's equity or capital) refers to the claims of its owner(s). Together, liabilities and equity are the source of funds to acquire assets. The relation of assets, liabilities, and equity is reflected in the following **accounting equation:**

$$\text{Assets} = \text{Liabilities} + \text{Equity}$$

Liabilities are usually shown before equity in this equation because creditors' claims must be paid before the claims of owners. (The terms in this equation can be rearranged; for example, Assets − Liabilities = Equity.) The accounting equation applies to all transactions and events, to all companies and forms of organization, and to all points in time. For example, **Research In Motion**'s assets equal $10,204,409, its liabilities equal $2,601,746, and its equity equals $7,602,663 ($ in thousands). Let's now look at the accounting equation in more detail.

**Assets**  Assets are resources a company owns or controls. These resources are expected to yield future benefits. Examples are Web servers for an online services company, musical instruments for a rock band, and land for a vegetable grower. The term *receivable* is used to refer to an asset that promises a future inflow of resources. A company that provides a service or product on credit is said to have an account receivable from that customer.

**Point:** The phrases "on credit" and "on account" imply that cash payment will occur at a future date.

**Liabilities**  Liabilities are creditors' claims on assets. These claims reflect company obligations to provide assets, products or services to others. The term *payable* refers to a liability that promises a future outflow of resources. Examples are wages payable to workers, accounts payable to suppliers, notes payable to banks, and taxes payable to the government.

**Equity**  Equity is the owner's claim on assets. Equity is equal to assets minus liabilities. This is the reason equity is also called *net assets* or *residual equity*.

Equity for a noncorporate entity—commonly called owner's equity—increases and decreases as follows: owner investments and revenues *increase* equity, whereas owner withdrawals and expenses *decrease* equity. **Owner investments** are assets an owner puts into the company and are included under the generic account **Owner, Capital**. **Revenues** are sales of products or services to customers. Revenues increase equity (via net income) and result from a company's earnings activities. Examples are consulting services provided, sales of products, facilities rented to others, and commissions from services. **Owner withdrawals** are assets an owner takes from the company for personal use. **Expenses** are the costs necessary to earn revenues. Expenses decrease equity. Examples are costs of employee time, use of supplies, and advertising, utilities, and insurance services from others. In sum, equity is the accumulated revenues and owner investments less the accumulated expenses and withdrawals since the company began. This breakdown of equity yields the following **expanded accounting equation.**

Key **terms** are printed in bold and defined again in the end-of-book **glossary.**

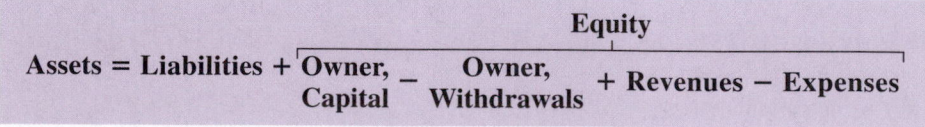

$$\text{Assets} = \text{Liabilities} + \overbrace{\underset{\text{Capital}}{\text{Owner,}} - \underset{\text{Withdrawals}}{\text{Owner,}} + \text{Revenues} - \text{Expenses}}^{\text{Equity}}$$

**Net income** occurs when revenues exceed expenses. Net income increases equity. A **net loss** occurs when expenses exceed revenues, which decreases equity.

**Web Info**   Most organizations maintain Websites that include accounting data—see **Research in Motion** (**RIM.com**) as an example. The SEC keeps an online database called **EDGAR** (**www.sec.gov/edgar.shtml**), which has accounting information for thousands of companies that issue stock to the public (EDGAR is being upgraded and renamed **IDEA**). Information services such as **Finance.Google.com** and **Finance. Yahoo.com** offer additional online data and analysis. ■

## Transaction Analysis

Business activities can be described in terms of transactions and events. **External transactions** are exchanges of value between two entities, which yield changes in the accounting equation. An example is the sale of ad space by **Facebook**. **Internal transactions** are exchanges within an entity, which may or may not affect the accounting equation. An example is Facebook's use of its supplies, which are reported as expenses when used. **Events** refer to happenings that affect the accounting equation *and* are reliably measured. They include business events such as changes in the market value of certain assets and liabilities and natural events such as floods and fires that destroy assets and create losses. They do not include, for example, the signing of service or product contracts, which by themselves do not impact the accounting equation.

This section uses the accounting equation to analyze 11 selected transactions and events of FastForward, a start-up consulting (service) business, in its first month of operations. Remember that each transaction and event leaves the equation in balance and that assets *always* equal the sum of liabilities and equity.

| P1 | Analyze business transactions using the accounting equation. |

### Transaction 1: Investment by Owner

On December 1, Chas Taylor forms a consulting business, named FastForward and set up as a proprietorship, that focuses on assessing the performance of footwear and accessories. Taylor owns and manages the business. The marketing plan for the business is to focus primarily on publishing online reviews and consulting with clubs, athletes, and others who place orders for footwear and accessories with manufacturers. Taylor personally invests $30,000 cash in the new company and deposits the cash in a bank account opened under the name of FastForward. After this transaction, the cash (an asset) and the owner's equity each equal $30,000. The source of increase in equity is the owner's investment, which is included in the column titled C. Taylor, Capital. (Owner investments are always included under the title *'Owner name,' Capital.*) The effect of this transaction on FastForward is reflected in the accounting equation as follows:

**Point:** There are 3 basic types of company operations: (1) **Services**—providing customer services for profit, (2) **Merchandisers**—buying products and re-selling them for profit, and (3) **Manufacturers**—creating products and selling them for profit.

|  | Assets | = | Liabilities | + | Equity |
|---|---|---|---|---|---|
|  | Cash | = |  |  | C. Taylor, Capital |
| (1) | +$30,000 | = |  |  | +$30,000 |

### Transaction 2: Purchase Supplies for Cash

FastForward uses $2,500 of its cash to buy supplies of brand name footwear for performance testing over the next few months. This transaction is an exchange of cash, an asset, for another kind of asset, supplies. It merely changes the form of assets from cash to supplies. The decrease in cash is exactly equal to the increase in supplies. The supplies of footwear are assets because of the expected future benefits from the test results of their performance. This transaction is reflected in the accounting equation as follows:

|  | Assets | | | = | Liabilities | + | Equity |
|---|---|---|---|---|---|---|---|
|  | Cash | + | Supplies | = |  |  | C. Taylor, Capital |
| Old Bal. | $30,000 |  |  | = |  |  | $30,000 |
| (2) | −2,500 | + | $2,500 |  |  |  |  |
| New Bal. | $27,500 | + | $ 2,500 | = |  |  | $30,000 |
|  |  | $30,000 | | | | $30,000 | |

**Transaction 3: Purchase Equipment for Cash**   FastForward spends $26,000 to acquire equipment for testing footwear. Like transaction 2, transaction 3 is an exchange of one asset, cash, for another asset, equipment. The equipment is an asset because of its expected future benefits from testing footwear. This purchase changes the makeup of assets but does not change the asset total. The accounting equation remains in balance.

| | Assets | | | | | = | Liabilities | + | Equity |
|---|---|---|---|---|---|---|---|---|---|
| | Cash | + | Supplies | + | Equipment | = | | | C. Taylor, Capital |
| Old Bal. | $27,500 | + | $2,500 | | | = | | | $30,000 |
| (3) | −26,000 | | | + | $26,000 | = | | | |
| New Bal. | $ 1,500 | + | $2,500 | + | $ 26,000 | = | | | $30,000 |
| | | | $30,000 | | | | | $30,000 | |

**Example:** If FastForward pays $500 cash in transaction 4, how does this partial payment affect the liability to CalTech? What would be FastForward's cash balance? *Answers:* The liability to CalTech would be reduced to $6,600 and the cash balance would be reduced to $1,000.

**Transaction 4: Purchase Supplies on Credit**   Taylor decides more supplies of footwear and accessories are needed. These additional supplies total $7,100, but as we see from the accounting equation in transaction 3, FastForward has only $1,500 in cash. Taylor arranges to purchase them on credit from CalTech Supply Company. Thus, FastForward acquires supplies in exchange for a promise to pay for them later. This purchase increases assets by $7,100 in supplies, and liabilities (called *accounts payable* to CalTech Supply) increase by the same amount. The effects of this purchase follow:

| | Assets | | | | | = | Liabilities | + | Equity |
|---|---|---|---|---|---|---|---|---|---|
| | Cash | + | Supplies | + | Equipment | = | Accounts Payable | + | C. Taylor, Capital |
| Old Bal. | $1,500 | + | $2,500 | + | $26,000 | = | | | $30,000 |
| (4) | | + | 7,100 | | | = | +$7,100 | | |
| New Bal. | $1,500 | + | $9,600 | + | $26,000 | = | $ 7,100 | + | $30,000 |
| | | | $37,100 | | | | | $37,100 | |

**Transaction 5: Provide Services for Cash**   FastForward earns revenues by selling online ad space to manufacturers and by consulting with clients about test results on footwear and accessories. It earns net income only if its revenues are greater than its expenses incurred in earning them. In one of its first jobs, FastForward provides consulting services to a power-walking club and immediately collects $4,200 cash. The accounting equation reflects this increase in cash of $4,200 and in equity of $4,200. This increase in equity is identified in the far right column under Revenues because the cash received is earned by providing consulting services.

| | Assets | | | | | = | Liabilities | + | Equity | | |
|---|---|---|---|---|---|---|---|---|---|---|---|
| | Cash | + | Supplies | + | Equipment | = | Accounts Payable | + | C. Taylor, Capital | + | Revenues |
| Old Bal. | $1,500 | + | $9,600 | + | $26,000 | = | $7,100 | + | $30,000 | | |
| (5) | +4,200 | | | | | = | | | | + | $4,200 |
| New Bal. | $5,700 | + | $9,600 | + | $26,000 | = | $7,100 | + | $30,000 | + | $ 4,200 |
| | | | $41,300 | | | | | | $41,300 | | |

**Transactions 6 and 7: Payment of Expenses in Cash**   FastForward pays $1,000 rent to the landlord of the building where its facilities are located. Paying this amount allows FastForward to occupy the space for the month of December. The rental payment is reflected in the following accounting equation as transaction 6. FastForward also pays the biweekly $700 salary of the company's only employee. This is reflected in the accounting equation as transaction 7. Both transactions 6 and 7 are December expenses for FastForward. The costs of both rent and salary are expenses, as opposed to assets, because their benefits are used in December (they have no future benefits after December). These transactions also use up an asset (cash) in carrying out FastForward's operations. The accounting equation shows that both transactions reduce cash and equity. The far right column identifies these decreases as Expenses.

*By definition, increases in expenses yield decreases in equity.*

| | Assets | | | | = | Liabilities | + | | | Equity | | |
|---|---|---|---|---|---|---|---|---|---|---|---|---|
| | Cash | + | Supplies | + | Equipment | = | Accounts Payable | + | C. Taylor, Capital | + | Revenues | − | Expenses |
| Old Bal. | $5,700 | + | $9,600 | + | $26,000 | = | $7,100 | + | $30,000 | + | $4,200 | | |
| (6) | −1,000 | | | | | | | | | | | − | $1,000 |
| Bal. | 4,700 | + | 9,600 | + | 26,000 | = | 7,100 | + | 30,000 | + | 4,200 | − | 1,000 |
| (7) | − 700 | | | | | | | | | | | − | 700 |
| New Bal. | $4,000 | + | $9,600 | + | $26,000 | = | $7,100 | + | $30,000 | + | $4,200 | − | $ 1,700 |

$39,600 = $39,600

### Transaction 8: Provide Services and Facilities for Credit
FastForward provides consulting services of $1,600 and rents its test facilities for $300 to a podiatric services center. The rental involves allowing members to try recommended footwear and accessories at FastForward's testing area. The center is billed for the $1,900 total. This transaction results in a new asset, called *accounts receivable,* from this client. It also yields an increase in equity from the two revenue components reflected in the Revenues column of the accounting equation:

| | Assets | | | | | | | = | Liabilities | + | | | Equity | | |
|---|---|---|---|---|---|---|---|---|---|---|---|---|---|---|---|
| | Cash | + | Accounts Receivable | + | Supplies | + | Equipment | = | Accounts Payable | + | C. Taylor, Capital | + | Revenues | − | Expenses |
| Old Bal. | $4,000 | + | | + | $9,600 | + | $26,000 | = | $7,100 | + | $30,000 | + | $4,200 | − | $1,700 |
| (8) | | + | $1,900 | | | | | | | | | + | 1,600 | | |
| | | | | | | | | | | | | + | 300 | | |
| New Bal. | $4,000 | + | $ 1,900 | + | $9,600 | + | $26,000 | = | $7,100 | + | $30,000 | + | $6,100 | − | $1,700 |

$41,500 = $41,500

### Transaction 9: Receipt of Cash from Accounts Receivable
The client in transaction 8 (the podiatric center) pays $1,900 to FastForward 10 days after it is billed for consulting services. This transaction 9 does not change the total amount of assets and does not affect liabilities or equity. It converts the receivable (an asset) to cash (another asset). It does not create new revenue. Revenue was recognized when FastForward rendered the services in transaction 8, not when the cash is now collected. This emphasis on the earnings process instead of cash flows is a goal of the revenue recognition principle and yields useful information to users. The new balances follow:

**Point:** Receipt of cash is not always a revenue.

| | Assets | | | | | | | = | Liabilities | + | | | Equity | | |
|---|---|---|---|---|---|---|---|---|---|---|---|---|---|---|---|
| | Cash | + | Accounts Receivable | + | Supplies | + | Equipment | = | Accounts Payable | + | C. Taylor, Capital | + | Revenues | − | Expenses |
| Old Bal. | $4,000 | + | $1,900 | + | $9,600 | + | $26,000 | = | $7,100 | + | $30,000 | + | $6,100 | − | $1,700 |
| (9) | +1,900 | − | 1,900 | | | | | | | | | | | | |
| New Bal. | $5,900 | + | $ 0 | + | $9,600 | + | $26,000 | = | $7,100 | + | $30,000 | + | $6,100 | − | $1,700 |

$41,500 = $41,500

### Transaction 10: Payment of Accounts Payable
FastForward pays CalTech Supply $900 cash as partial payment for its earlier $7,100 purchase of supplies (transaction 4), leaving $6,200 unpaid. The accounting equation shows that this transaction decreases FastForward's cash by $900 and decreases its liability to CalTech Supply by $900. Equity does not change. This event does not create an expense even though cash flows out of FastForward (instead the expense is recorded when FastForward derives the benefits from these supplies).

| | Cash | + | Accounts Receivable | + | Supplies | + | Equipment | = | Accounts Payable | + | C. Taylor, Capital | + | Revenues | − | Expenses |
|---|---|---|---|---|---|---|---|---|---|---|---|---|---|---|---|
| Old Bal. | $5,900 | + | $ 0 | + | $9,600 | + | $26,000 | = | $7,100 | + | $30,000 | + | $6,100 | − | $1,700 |
| (10) | − 900 | | | | | | | | − 900 | | | | | | |
| New Bal. | $5,000 | + | $ 0 | + | $9,600 | + | $26,000 | = | $6,200 | + | $30,000 | + | $6,100 | − | $1,700 |

$40,600          $40,600

**Transaction 11: Withdrawal of Cash by Owner**   The owner of FastForward withdraws $200 cash for personal use. Withdrawals (decreases in equity) are not reported as expenses because they are not part of the company's earnings process. Since withdrawals are not company expenses, they are not used in computing net income.

*By definition, increases in withdrawals yield decreases in equity.*

| | Cash | + | Accounts Receivable | + | Supplies | + | Equipment | = | Accounts Payable | + | C. Taylor, Capital | − | C. Taylor, Withdrawals | + | Revenues | − | Expenses |
|---|---|---|---|---|---|---|---|---|---|---|---|---|---|---|---|---|---|
| Old Bal. | $5,000 | + | $ 0 | + | $9,600 | + | $26,000 | = | $6,200 | + | $30,000 | | | + | $6,100 | − | $1,700 |
| (11) | − 200 | | | | | | | | | | | − | $200 | | | | |
| New Bal. | $4,800 | + | $ 0 | + | $9,600 | + | $26,000 | = | $6,200 | + | $30,000 | − | $200 | + | $6,100 | − | $1,700 |

$40,400          $40,400

## Summary of Transactions

We summarize in Exhibit 1.9 the effects of these 11 transactions of FastForward using the accounting equation. First, we see that the accounting equation remains in balance after each transaction. Second, transactions can be analyzed by their effects on components of the

**EXHIBIT 1.9**

Summary of Transactions Using the Accounting Equation

| | Cash | + | Accounts Receivable | + | Supplies | + | Equipment | = | Accounts Payable | + | C. Taylor, Capital | − | C. Taylor, Withdrawals | + | Revenues | − | Expenses |
|---|---|---|---|---|---|---|---|---|---|---|---|---|---|---|---|---|---|
| (1) | $30,000 | | | | | | | = | | | $30,000 | | | | | | |
| (2) | − 2,500 | | | + | $2,500 | | | | | | | | | | | | |
| Bal. | 27,500 | | | + | 2,500 | | | = | | | 30,000 | | | | | | |
| (3) | −26,000 | | | | | + | $26,000 | | | | | | | | | | |
| Bal. | 1,500 | | | + | 2,500 | + | 26,000 | = | | | 30,000 | | | | | | |
| (4) | | | | + | 7,100 | | | | +$7,100 | | | | | | | | |
| Bal. | 1,500 | | | + | 9,600 | + | 26,000 | = | 7,100 | + | 30,000 | | | | | | |
| (5) | + 4,200 | | | | | | | | | | | | | + | $4,200 | | |
| Bal. | 5,700 | | | + | 9,600 | + | 26,000 | = | 7,100 | + | 30,000 | | | + | 4,200 | | |
| (6) | − 1,000 | | | | | | | | | | | | | | | − | $1,000 |
| Bal. | 4,700 | | | + | 9,600 | + | 26,000 | = | 7,100 | + | 30,000 | | | + | 4,200 | − | 1,000 |
| (7) | − 700 | | | | | | | | | | | | | | | − | 700 |
| Bal. | 4,000 | | | + | 9,600 | + | 26,000 | = | 7,100 | + | 30,000 | | | + | 4,200 | − | 1,700 |
| (8) | | | + $1,900 | | | | | | | | | | | + | 1,600 | | |
| | | | | | | | | | | | | | | + | 300 | | |
| Bal. | 4,000 | + | 1,900 | + | 9,600 | + | 26,000 | = | 7,100 | + | 30,000 | | | + | 6,100 | − | 1,700 |
| (9) | + 1,900 | − | 1,900 | | | | | | | | | | | | | | |
| Bal. | 5,900 | + | 0 | + | 9,600 | + | 26,000 | = | 7,100 | + | 30,000 | | | + | 6,100 | − | 1,700 |
| (10) | − 900 | | | | | | | | − 900 | | | | | | | | |
| Bal. | 5,000 | + | 0 | + | 9,600 | + | 26,000 | = | 6,200 | + | 30,000 | | | + | 6,100 | − | 1,700 |
| (11) | − 200 | | | | | | | | | | | − | $200 | | | | |
| Bal. | $ 4,800 | + | $ 0 | + | $ 9,600 | + | $ 26,000 | = | $ 6,200 | + | $ 30,000 | − | $ 200 | + | $6,100 | − | $1,700 |

accounting equation. For example, in transactions 2, 3, and 9, one asset increased while another asset decreased by equal amounts.

**Point:** Knowing how financial statements are prepared improves our analysis of them. We develop the skills for analysis of financial statements throughout the book. Chapter 17 focuses on financial statement analysis.

## Quick Check
Answers — p. 28

**17.** When is the accounting equation in balance, and what does that mean?
**18.** How can a transaction not affect any liability and equity accounts?
**19.** Describe a transaction increasing equity and one decreasing it.
**20.** Identify a transaction that decreases both assets and liabilities.

# FINANCIAL STATEMENTS

This section introduces us to how financial statements are prepared from the analysis of business transactions. The four financial statements and their purposes are:

**P2** Identify and prepare basic financial statements and explain how they interrelate.

1. **Income statement**—describes a company's revenues and expenses along with the resulting net income or loss over a period of time due to earnings activities.
2. **Statement of owner's equity**—explains changes in equity from net income (or loss) and from any owner investments and withdrawals over a period of time.
3. **Balance sheet**—describes a company's financial position (types and amounts of assets, liabilities, and equity) at a point in time.
4. **Statement of cash flows**—identifies cash inflows (receipts) and cash outflows (payments) over a period of time.

We prepare these financial statements, in this order, using the 11 selected transactions of FastForward. (These statements are technically called *unadjusted*—we explain this in Chapters 2 and 3.)

## Income Statement

FastForward's income statement for December is shown at the top of Exhibit 1.10. Information about revenues and expenses is conveniently taken from the Equity columns of Exhibit 1.9. Revenues are reported first on the income statement. They include consulting revenues of $5,800 from transactions 5 and 8 and rental revenue of $300 from transaction 8. Expenses are reported after revenues. (For convenience in this chapter, we list larger amounts first, but we can sort expenses in different ways.) Rent and salary expenses are from transactions 6 and 7. Expenses reflect the costs to generate the revenues reported. Net income (or loss) is reported at the bottom of the statement and is the amount earned in December. Owner's investments and withdrawals are *not* part of income.

**Point:** Net income is sometimes called *earnings* or *profit.*

## Statement of Owner's Equity

The statement of owner's equity reports information about how equity changes over the reporting period. This statement shows beginning capital, events that increase it (owner investments and net income), and events that decrease it (withdrawals and net loss). Ending capital is computed in this statement and is carried over and reported on the balance sheet. FastForward's statement of owner's equity is the second report in Exhibit 1.10. The beginning capital balance is measured as of the start of business on December 1. It is zero because FastForward did not exist before then. An existing business reports a beginning balance equal to that as of the end of the prior reporting period (such as from November 30). FastForward's statement of owner's equity shows that Taylor's initial investment created $30,000 of equity. It also shows the $4,400 of net income earned during the period. This links the income statement to the statement of owner's equity (see line ①). The statement also reports Taylor's $200 cash withdrawal and Fast-Forward's end-of-period capital balance.

**Point:** The statement of owner's equity is also called the *statement of changes in owner's equity.* Note: Beg. Capital + Net Income − Withdrawals = Ending Capital

**EXHIBIT 1.10**

Financial Statements and
Their Links

**Point:** A statement's heading identifies the company, the statement title, and the date or time period.

**Point:** Arrow lines show how the statements are linked. ① Net income is used to compute equity. ② Owner capital is used to prepare the balance sheet. ③ Cash from the balance sheet is used to reconcile the statement of cash flows.

**Point:** The income statement, the statement of owner's equity, and the statement of cash flows are prepared for a *period* of time. The balance sheet is prepared as of a *point* in time.

**FASTFORWARD**
**Income Statement**
**For Month Ended December 31, 2011**

| | | |
|---|---|---|
| Revenues | | |
| Consulting revenue ($4,200 + $1,600)................ | $ 5,800 | |
| Rental revenue ....................................... | 300 | |
| Total revenues ..................................... | | $ 6,100 |
| Expenses | | |
| Rent expense ...................................... | 1,000 | |
| Salaries expense .................................. | 700 | |
| Total expenses ................................... | | 1,700 |
| Net income ........................................ | | **$ 4,400** ← |

**FASTFORWARD**
**Statement of Owner's Equity**
**For Month Ended December 31, 2011**

| | | |
|---|---|---|
| C. Taylor, Capital, December 1, 2011 ..................... | | $ 0 |
| Plus: Investments by owner ......................... | $30,000 | |
| Net income ................................ | 4,400 | 34,400 |
| | | 34,400 |
| Less: Withdrawals by owner ......................... | | 200 |
| C. Taylor, Capital, December 31, 2011 ................... | | **$34,200** ← |

**FASTFORWARD**
**Balance Sheet**
**December 31, 2011**

| **Assets** | | **Liabilities** | |
|---|---|---|---|
| Cash ............ | **$ 4,800** | Accounts payable............. | $ 6,200 |
| Supplies ........ | 9,600 | Total liabilities ............... | 6,200 |
| Equipment ........ | 26,000 | | |
| | | **Equity** | |
| | | C. Taylor, Capital.............. | 34,200 ← |
| Total assets ....... | $ 40,400 | Total liabilities and equity ...... | $ 40,400 |

**Point:** A single ruled line denotes an addition or subtraction. Final totals are double underlined. Negative amounts are often in parentheses.

**FASTFORWARD**
**Statement of Cash Flows**
**For Month Ended December 31, 2011**

| | | |
|---|---|---|
| Cash flows from operating activities | | |
| Cash received from clients ($4,200 + $1,900).......... | $ 6,100 | |
| Cash paid for supplies ($2,500 + $900)............... | (3,400) | |
| Cash paid for rent ................................. | (1,000) | |
| Cash paid to employee ............................ | (700) | |
| Net cash provided by operating activities ............. | | $ 1,000 |
| Cash flows from investing activities | | |
| Purchase of equipment ............................ | (26,000) | |
| Net cash used by investing activities ................. | | (26,000) |
| Cash flows from financing activities | | |
| Investments by owner ............................. | 30,000 | |
| Withdrawals by owner.............................. | (200) | |
| Net cash provided by financing activities ............. | | 29,800 |
| Net increase in cash ................................ | | $ 4,800 |
| Cash balance, December 1, 2011 ...................... | | 0 |
| Cash balance, December 31, 2011 ..................... | | **$ 4,800** |

## Balance Sheet

FastForward's balance sheet is the third report in Exhibit 1.10. This statement refers to Fast-Forward's financial condition at the close of business on December 31. The left side of the balance sheet lists FastForward's assets: cash, supplies, and equipment. The upper right side of the balance sheet shows that FastForward owes $6,200 to creditors. Any other liabilities (such as a bank loan) would be listed here. The equity (capital) balance is $34,200. Line ② shows the link between the ending balance of the statement of owner's equity and the equity balance on the balance sheet. (This presentation of the balance sheet is called the *account form:* assets on the left and liabilities and equity on the right. Another presentation is the *report form:* assets on top, followed by liabilities and then equity at the bottom. Either presentation is acceptable.) As always, we see the accounting equation applies: Assets of $40,400 = Liabilities of $6,200 + Equity of $34,200.

*Decision Maker boxes are role-playing exercises that stress the relevance of accounting.*

**▢ Decision Maker**  Answer — p. 28

**Retailer**  You open a wholesale business selling entertainment equipment to retail outlets. You find that most of your customers demand to buy on credit. How can you use the balance sheets of these customers to help you decide which ones to extend credit to? ■

## Statement of Cash Flows

FastForward's statement of cash flows is the final report in Exhibit 1.10. The first section reports cash flows from *operating activities.* It shows the $6,100 cash received from clients and the $5,100 cash paid for supplies, rent, and employee salaries. Outflows are in parentheses to denote subtraction. Net cash provided by operating activities for December is $1,000. If cash paid exceeded the $5,100 cash received, we would call it "cash used by operating activities." The second section reports *investing activities,* which involve buying and selling assets such as land and equipment that are held for *long-term use* (typically more than one year). The only investing activity is the $26,000 purchase of equipment. The third section shows cash flows from *financing activities,* which include the *long-term* borrowing and repaying of cash from lenders and the cash investments from, and withdrawals by, the owner. FastForward reports $30,000 from the owner's initial investment and the $200 cash withdrawal. The net cash effect of all financing transactions is a $29,800 cash inflow. The final part of the statement shows FastForward increased its cash balance by $4,800 in December. Since it started with no cash, the ending balance is also $4,800—see line ③. We see that cash flow numbers are different from income statement (*accrual*) numbers, which is common.

**Point:** Statement of cash flows has three main sections: operating, investing, and financing.

**Point:** Payment for supplies is an operating activity because supplies are expected to be used up in short-term operations (typically less than one year).

**Point:** Investing activities refer to long-term asset investments by the company, *not* to owner investments.

**Quick Check**  Answers — p. 28

21. Explain the link between the income statement and the statement of owner's equity.
22. Describe the link between the balance sheet and the statement of owner's equity.
23. Discuss the three major sections of the statement of cash flows.

## GLOBAL VIEW

Accounting according to U.S. GAAP is similar, but not identical, to IFRS. Throughout the book we use this last section to identify major similarities and differences between IFRS and U.S. GAAP for the materials in each chapter.

**Basic Principles**  Both U.S. GAAP and IFRS include broad and similar guidance for accounting. However, neither system specifies particular account names nor the detail required. (A typical *chart of accounts* is shown near the end of this book.) IFRS does require certain minimum line items be reported in the balance sheet along with other minimum disclosures that U.S. GAAP does not. On the other hand, U.S. GAAP requires disclosures for the current and prior two years for the income statement, statement of cash flows, and statement of retained earnings (equity), while IFRS requires disclosures for the current and prior year. Still, the basic principles behind these two systems are similar.

**Transaction Analysis**   Both U.S. GAAP and IFRS apply transaction analysis identically as shown in this chapter. Although some variations exist in revenue and expense recognition and other principles, all of the transactions in this chapter are accounted for identically under these two systems. It is often said that U.S. GAAP is more *rules-based* whereas IFRS is more *principles-based*. The main difference on the rules versus principles focus is with the approach in deciding how to account for certain transactions. Under U.S. GAAP, the approach is more focused on strictly following the accounting rules; under IFRS, the approach is more focused on a review of the situation and how accounting can best reflect it. This difference typically impacts advanced topics beyond the introductory course.

**Financial Statements**   Both U.S. GAAP and IFRS prepare the same four basic financial statements. To illustrate, a condensed version of **Nokia**'s income statement follows (numbers are in Euros millions). Nokia is a leader in mobile technology, from smartphones to mobile computers. Similar condensed versions can be prepared for the other three statements.

| NOKIA | |
| --- | --- |
| Income Statement (in € millions) | |
| For Year Ended December 31, 2009 | |
| Net sales | 40,984 |
| Cost of sales | 27,720 |
| Research, selling, administrative, and other expenses | 12,302 |
| Taxes | 702 |
| Net income (profit) | 260 |

*Decision Analysis (a section at the end of each chapter) introduces and explains ratios helpful in decision making using real company data. Instructors can skip this section and cover all ratios in Chapter 17.*

 **Decision Analysis** 🟩🟨🟥                                                    Return on Assets

**A2** Compute and interpret return on assets.

A *Decision Analysis* section at the end of each chapter is devoted to financial statement analysis. We organize financial statement analysis into four areas: (1) liquidity and efficiency, (2) solvency, (3) profitability, and (4) market prospects—Chapter 17 has a ratio listing with definitions and groupings by area. When analyzing ratios, we need benchmarks to identify good, bad, or average levels. Common benchmarks include the company's prior levels and those of its competitors.

This chapter presents a profitability measure: return on assets. Return on assets is useful in evaluating management, analyzing and forecasting profits, and planning activities. **Dell** has its marketing department compute return on assets for *every* order. **Return on assets (ROA),** also called *return on investment* (*ROI*), is defined in Exhibit 1.11.

**EXHIBIT 1.11**

Return on Assets

$$\text{Return on assets} = \frac{\text{Net income}}{\text{Average total assets}}$$

Net income is from the annual income statement, and average total assets is computed by adding the beginning and ending amounts for that same period and dividing by 2. To illustrate, **Best Buy** reports net income of $1,317 million for fiscal year 2010. At the beginning of fiscal 2010, its total assets are $15,826 million and at the end of fiscal 2010, they total $18,302 million. Best Buy's return on assets for fiscal 2010 is:

$$\text{Return on assets} = \frac{\$1,317 \text{ million}}{(\$15,826 \text{ million} + \$18,302 \text{ million})/2} = 7.7\%$$

Is a 7.7% return on assets good or bad for Best Buy? To help answer this question, we compare (benchmark) Best Buy's return with its prior performance, the returns of competitors (such as **RadioShack**, **Conn's**, and **Rex Stores**), and the returns from alternative investments. Best Buy's return for each of the prior five years is in the second column of Exhibit 1.12, which ranges from 7.0% to 10.8%.

| | Return on Assets | |
| --- | --- | --- |
| **Fiscal Year** | **Best Buy** | **Industry** |
| 2010 . . . . . . . . . . . . . . | 7.7% | 2.9% |
| 2009 . . . . . . . . . . . . . . | 7.0 | 2.5 |
| 2008 . . . . . . . . . . . . . . | 10.7 | 3.4 |
| 2007 . . . . . . . . . . . . . . | 10.8 | 3.5 |
| 2006 . . . . . . . . . . . . . . | 10.3 | 3.3 |

**EXHIBIT 1.12**

Best Buy and Industry Returns

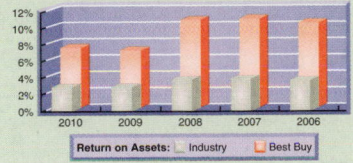

Best Buy shows a fairly stable pattern of good returns that reflect its productive use of assets. There is a decline in its 2009 return reflecting the recessionary period. We compare Best Buy's return to the normal return for similar merchandisers of electronic products (third column). Industry averages are available from services such as **Dun & Bradstreet**'s *Industry Norms and Key Ratios* and **The Risk Management Association**'s *Annual Statement Studies*. When compared to the industry, Best Buy performs well.

*Each **Decision Analysis** section ends with a role-playing scenario to show the usefulness of ratios.*

### ▢ Decision Maker

Answer — p. 28

**Business Owner** You own a small winter ski resort that earns a 21% return on its assets. An opportunity to purchase a winter ski equipment manufacturer is offered to you. This manufacturer earns a 19% return on its assets. The industry return for this manufacturer is 14%. Do you purchase this manufacturer? ■

*The **Demonstration Problem** is a review of key chapter content. The Planning the Solution offers strategies in solving the problem.*

## DEMONSTRATION PROBLEM

After several months of planning, Jasmine Worthy started a haircutting business called Expressions. The following events occurred during its first month of business.

**a.** On August 1, Worthy invested $3,000 cash and $15,000 of equipment in Expressions.

**b.** On August 2, Expressions paid $600 cash for furniture for the shop.

**c.** On August 3, Expressions paid $500 cash to rent space in a strip mall for August.

**d.** On August 4, it purchased $1,200 of equipment on credit for the shop (using a long-term note payable).

**e.** On August 5, Expressions opened for business. Cash received from haircutting services in the first week and a half of business (ended August 15) was $825.

**f.** On August 15, it provided $100 of haircutting services on account.

**g.** On August 17, it received a $100 check for services previously rendered on account.

**h.** On August 17, it paid $125 cash to an assistant for hours worked during the grand opening.

**i.** Cash received from services provided during the second half of August was $930.

**j.** On August 31, it paid a $400 installment toward principal on the note payable entered into on August 4.

**k.** On August 31, Worthy made a $900 cash withdrawal from the company for personal use.

### Required

1. Arrange the following asset, liability, and equity titles in a table similar to the one in Exhibit 1.9: Cash; Accounts Receivable; Furniture; Store Equipment; Note Payable; J. Worthy, Capital; J. Worthy, Withdrawals; Revenues; and Expenses. Show the effects of each transaction using the accounting equation.

2. Prepare an income statement for August.

3. Prepare a statement of owner's equity for August.

4. Prepare a balance sheet as of August 31.

5. Prepare a statement of cash flows for August.

6. Determine the return on assets ratio for August.

## PLANNING THE SOLUTION

- Set up a table like Exhibit 1.9 with the appropriate columns for accounts.
- Analyze each transaction and show its effects as increases or decreases in the appropriate columns. Be sure the accounting equation remains in balance after each transaction.
- Prepare the income statement, and identify revenues and expenses. List those items on the statement, compute the difference, and label the result as *net income* or *net loss*.
- Use information in the Equity columns to prepare the statement of owner's equity.
- Use information in the last row of the transactions table to prepare the balance sheet.
- Prepare the statement of cash flows; include all events listed in the Cash column of the transactions table. Classify each cash flow as operating, investing, or financing.
- Calculate return on assets by dividing net income by average assets.

## SOLUTION TO DEMONSTRATION PROBLEM

**1.**

| | Assets | | | | | | | | = | Liabilities | + | | | | | Equity | | | | |
|---|---|---|---|---|---|---|---|---|---|---|---|---|---|---|---|---|---|---|---|---|
| | Cash | + | Accounts Receivable | + | Furniture | + | Store Equipment | = | Note Payable | + | J. Worthy, Capital | − | J. Worthy, Withdrawals | + | Revenues | − | Expenses |
| a. | $3,000 | | | | | | $15,000 | | | | $18,000 | | | | | | |
| b. | − 600 | | | + | $600 | | | | | | | | | | | | |
| Bal. | 2,400 | + | | + | 600 | + | 15,000 | = | | | 18,000 | | | | | | |
| c. | − 500 | | | | | | | | | | | | | | | | − | $500 |
| Bal. | 1,900 | + | | + | 600 | + | 15,000 | = | | | 18,000 | | | | | | − | 500 |
| d. | | | | | | + | 1,200 | | +$1,200 | | | | | | | | |
| Bal. | 1,900 | + | | + | 600 | + | 16,200 | = | 1,200 | + | 18,000 | | | | | | − | 500 |
| e. | + 825 | | | | | | | | | | | | | + | $ 825 | | |
| Bal. | 2,725 | + | | + | 600 | + | 16,200 | = | 1,200 | + | 18,000 | | | + | 825 | − | 500 |
| f. | | + | $100 | | | | | | | | | | | + | 100 | | |
| Bal. | 2,725 | + | 100 | + | 600 | + | 16,200 | = | 1,200 | + | 18,000 | | | + | 925 | − | 500 |
| g. | + 100 | − | 100 | | | | | | | | | | | | | | |
| Bal. | 2,825 | + | 0 | + | 600 | + | 16,200 | = | 1,200 | + | 18,000 | | | + | 925 | − | 500 |
| h. | − 125 | | | | | | | | | | | | | | | − | 125 |
| Bal. | 2,700 | + | 0 | + | 600 | + | 16,200 | = | 1,200 | + | 18,000 | | | + | 925 | − | 625 |
| i. | + 930 | | | | | | | | | | | | | + | 930 | | |
| Bal. | 3,630 | + | 0 | + | 600 | + | 16,200 | = | 1,200 | + | 18,000 | | | + | 1,855 | − | 625 |
| j. | − 400 | | | | | | | | − 400 | | | | | | | |
| Bal. | 3,230 | + | 0 | + | 600 | + | 16,200 | = | 800 | + | 18,000 | | | + | 1,855 | − | 625 |
| k. | − 900 | | | | | | | | | | | − | $900 | | | |
| Bal. | $ 2,330 | + | 0 | + | $600 | + | $ 16,200 | = | $ 800 | + | $ 18,000 | − | $900 | + | $1,855 | − | $625 |

**2.**

| | EXPRESSIONS |
|---|---|
| | **Income Statement** |
| | **For Month Ended August 31** |

| Revenues | | |
|---|---|---|
| Haircutting services revenue . . . . . . . . . | | $1,855 |
| Expenses | | |
| Rent expense . . . . . . . . . . . . . . . . . . . . | $500 | |
| Wages expense . . . . . . . . . . . . . . . . . . . | 125 | |
| Total expenses . . . . . . . . . . . . . . . . . . | | 625 |
| Net Income . . . . . . . . . . . . . . . . . . . . . | | $1,230 |

**3.**

| EXPRESSIONS | | |
|---|---|---|
| Statement of Owner's Equity | | |
| For Month Ended August 31 | | |
| J. Worthy, Capital, August 1*.......... | | $   0 |
| Plus:  Investments by owner ......... | $18,000 | |
| Net income.................. | 1,230 | 19,230 |
| | | 19,230 |
| Less:  Withdrawals by owner.......... | | 900 |
| J. Worthy, Capital, August 31.......... | | $18,330 |

* If Expressions had been an existing business from a prior period, the beginning capital balance would equal the Capital account balance from the end of the prior period.

**4.**

| EXPRESSIONS | | | |
|---|---|---|---|
| Balance Sheet | | | |
| August 31 | | | |
| **Assets** | | **Liabilities** | |
| Cash ................. | $  2,330 | Note payable ................... | $   800 |
| Furniture ............. | 600 | **Equity** | |
| Store equipment ....... | 16,200 | J. Worthy, Capital .............. | 18,330 |
| Total assets ........... | $19,130 | Total liabilities and equity ........ | $19,130 |

**5.**

| EXPRESSIONS | | |
|---|---|---|
| Statement of Cash Flows | | |
| For Month Ended August 31 | | |
| Cash flows from operating activities | | |
| Cash received from customers ..................... | $1,855 | |
| Cash paid for rent .............................. | (500) | |
| Cash paid for wages ........................... | (125) | |
| Net cash provided by operating activities ........... | | $1,230 |
| Cash flows from investing activities | | |
| Cash paid for furniture ........................ | | (600) |
| Cash flows from financing activities | | |
| Cash investments by owner...................... | 3,000 | |
| Cash withdrawals by owner ..................... | (900) | |
| Partial repayment of (long-term) note payable ........ | (400) | |
| Net cash provided by financing activities ............ | | 1,700 |
| Net increase in cash........................... | | $2,330 |
| Cash balance, August 1 ........................ | | 0 |
| Cash balance, August 31........................ | | $2,330 |

**6.** Return on assets $= \dfrac{\text{Net income}}{\text{Average assets}} = \dfrac{\$1,230}{(\$18,000^* + \$19,130)/2} = \dfrac{\$1,230}{\$18,565} = \underline{\underline{\mathbf{6.63\%}}}$

* Uses the initial $18,000 investment as the beginning balance for the *start-up period only*.

# 1A

# Return and Risk Analysis

**A3** Explain the relation between return and risk.

This appendix explains return and risk analysis and its role in business and accounting.

Net income is often linked to **return.** Return on assets (ROA) is stated in ratio form as income divided by assets invested. For example, banks report return from a savings account in the form of an interest return such as 4%. If we invest in a savings account or in U.S. Treasury bills, we expect a return of around 2% to 7%. We could also invest in a company's stock, or even start our own business. How do we decide among these investment options? The answer depends on our trade-off between return and risk.

**Risk** is the uncertainty about the return we will earn. All business investments involve risk, but some investments involve more risk than others. The lower the risk of an investment, the lower is our expected return. The reason that savings accounts pay such a low return is the low risk of not being repaid with interest (the government guarantees most savings accounts from default). If we buy a share of eBay or any other company, we might obtain a large return. However, we have no guarantee of any return; there is even the risk of loss.

**EXHIBIT 1A.1**

Average Returns for Bonds with Different Risks

The bar graph in Exhibit 1A.1 shows recent returns for 10-year bonds with different risks. *Bonds* are written promises by organizations to repay amounts loaned with interest. U.S. Treasury bonds provide a low expected return, but they also offer low risk since they are backed by the U.S. government. High-risk corporate bonds offer a much larger potential return but with much higher risk.

The trade-off between return and risk is a normal part of business. Higher risk implies higher, but riskier, expected returns. To help us make better decisions, we use accounting information to assess both return and risk.

# 1B

# Business Activities and the Accounting Equation

**C5** Identify and describe the three major activities of organizations.

This appendix explains how the accounting equation is derived from business activities.

There are three major types of business activities: financing, investing, and operating. Each of these requires planning. *Planning* involves defining an organization's ideas, goals, and actions. Most public corporations use the *Management Discussion and Analysis* section in their annual reports to communicate plans. However, planning is not cast in stone. This adds *risk* to both setting plans and analyzing them.

**Point:** Management must understand accounting data to set financial goals, make financing and investing decisions, and evaluate operating performance.

**Financing**   *Financing activities* provide the means organizations use to pay for resources such as land, buildings, and equipment to carry out plans. Organizations are careful in acquiring and managing financing activities because they can determine success or failure. The two sources of financing are owner and nonowner. *Owner financing* refers to resources contributed by the owner along with any income the owner leaves in the organization. *Nonowner* (or *creditor*) *financing* refers to resources contributed by creditors (lenders). *Financial management* is the task of planning how to obtain these resources and to set the right mix between owner and creditor financing.

**Point:** Investing (assets) and financing (liabilities plus equity) totals are *always* equal.

**Investing**   *Investing activities* are the acquiring and disposing of resources (assets) that an organization uses to acquire and sell its products or services. Assets are funded by an organization's financing. Organizations differ on the amount and makeup of assets. Some require land and factories to operate. Others need only an office. Determining the amount and type of assets for operations is called *asset management.* Invested amounts are referred to as *assets.* Financing is made up of creditor and owner financing, which hold claims on assets. Creditors' claims are called *liabilities,* and the owner's claim is called *equity.* This basic equality is called the *accounting equation* and can be written as: Assets = Liabilities + Equity.

**Operating**  *Operating activities* involve using resources to research, develop, purchase, produce, distribute, and market products and services. Sales and revenues are the inflow of assets from selling products and services. Costs and expenses are the outflow of assets to support operating activities. *Strategic management* is the process of determining the right mix of operating activities for the type of organization, its plans, and its market.

Exhibit 1B.1 summarizes business activities. Planning is part of each activity and gives them meaning and focus. Investing (assets) and financing (liabilities and equity) are set opposite each other to stress their balance. Operating activities are below investing and financing activities to show that operating activities are the result of investing and financing.

**EXHIBIT 1B.1**

Activities of Organizations

# Summary

← *A **Summary** organized by learning objectives concludes each chapter.*

**C1**  **Explain the purpose and importance of accounting.** Accounting is an information and measurement system that aims to identify, record, and communicate relevant, reliable, and comparable information about business activities. It helps assess opportunities, products, investments, and social and community responsibilities.

**C2**  **Identify users and uses of, and opportunities in, accounting.** Users of accounting are both internal and external. Some users and uses of accounting include (a) managers in controlling, monitoring, and planning; (b) lenders for measuring the risk and return of loans; (c) shareholders for assessing the return and risk of stock; (d) directors for overseeing management; and (e) employees for judging employment opportunities. Opportunities in accounting include financial, managerial, and tax accounting. They also include accounting-related fields such as lending, consulting, managing, and planning.

**C3**  **Explain why ethics are crucial to accounting.** The goal of accounting is to provide useful information for decision making. For information to be useful, it must be trusted. This demands ethical behavior in accounting.

**C4**  **Explain generally accepted accounting principles and define and apply several accounting principles.** Generally accepted accounting principles are a common set of standards applied by accountants. Accounting principles aid in producing relevant, reliable, and comparable information. Four principles underlying financial statements were introduced: cost, revenue recognition, matching, and full disclosure. Financial statements also reflect four assumptions: going-concern, monetary unit, time period, and business entity.

**C5ᴮ**  **Identify and describe the three major activities of organizations.** Organizations carry out three major activities: financing, investing, and operating. Financing is the means used to pay for resources such as land, buildings, and machines. Investing refers to the buying and selling of resources used in acquiring and selling products and services. Operating activities are those necessary for carrying out the organization's plans.

**A1**  **Define and interpret the accounting equation and each of its components.** The accounting equation is: Assets = Liabilities + Equity. Assets are resources owned by a company. Liabilities are creditors' claims on assets. Equity is the owner's claim on assets (*the residual*). The expanded accounting equation is: Assets = Liabilities + [Owner Capital − Owner Withdrawals + Revenues − Expenses].

**A2**  **Compute and interpret return on assets.** Return on assets is computed as net income divided by average assets. For example, if we have an average balance of $100 in a savings account and it earns $5 interest for the year, the return on assets is $5/$100, or 5%.

**A3ᴬ**  **Explain the relation between return and risk.** *Return* refers to income, and *risk* is the uncertainty about the return we hope to make. All investments involve risk. The lower the risk of an investment, the lower is its expected return. Higher risk implies higher, but riskier, expected return.

**P1**  **Analyze business transactions using the accounting equation.** A *transaction* is an exchange of economic consideration between two parties. Examples include exchanges of products, services, money, and rights to collect money. Transactions always have at least two effects on one or more components of the accounting equation. This equation is always in balance.

**P2**  **Identify and prepare basic financial statements and explain how they interrelate.** Four financial statements report on an organization's activities: balance sheet, income statement, statement of owner's equity, and statement of cash flows.

## Guidance Answers to Decision Maker and Decision Ethics

**Entrepreneur** (p. 12) You should probably form the business as a corporation if potential lawsuits are of prime concern. The corporate form of organization protects your personal property from lawsuits directed at the business and places only the corporation's resources at risk. A downside of the corporate form is double taxation: The corporation must pay taxes on its income, and you normally must pay taxes on any money distributed to you from the business (even though the corporation already paid taxes on this money). You should also examine the ethical and socially responsible aspects of starting a business in which you anticipate injuries to others. Formation as an LLC or S corp. should also be explored.

**Retailer**   (p. 21) You can use the accounting equation (Assets = Liabilities + Equity) to help identify risky customers to whom you would likely not want to extend credit. A balance sheet provides amounts for each of these key components. The lower a customer's equity is relative to liabilities, the less likely you would be to extend credit. A low equity means the business has little value that does not already have creditor claims to it.

**Business Owner**   (p. 23) The 19% return on assets for the manufacturer exceeds the 14% industry return (and many others). This is a positive factor for a potential purchase. Also, the purchase of this manufacturer is an opportunity to spread your risk over two businesses as opposed to one. Still, you should hesitate to purchase a business whose return of 19% is lower than your current resort's return of 21%. You are probably better off directing efforts to increase investment in your resort, assuming you can continue to earn a 21% return.

## Guidance Answers to Quick Checks

1. Accounting is an information and measurement system that identifies, records, and communicates relevant information to help people make better decisions.

2. Recordkeeping, also called *bookkeeping,* is the recording of financial transactions and events, either manually or electronically. Recordkeeping is essential to data reliability; but accounting is this and much more. Accounting includes identifying, measuring, recording, reporting, and analyzing business events and transactions.

3. Technology offers increased accuracy, speed, efficiency, and convenience in accounting.

4. External users of accounting include lenders, shareholders, directors, customers, suppliers, regulators, lawyers, brokers, and the press. Internal users of accounting include managers, officers, and other internal decision makers involved with strategic and operating decisions.

5. Internal users (managers) include those from research and development, purchasing, human resources, production, distribution, marketing, and servicing.

6. Internal controls are procedures set up to protect assets, ensure reliable accounting reports, promote efficiency, and encourage adherence to company policies. Internal controls are crucial for relevant and reliable information.

7. Ethical guidelines are threefold: (1) identify ethical concerns using personal ethics, (2) analyze options considering all good and bad consequences, and (3) make ethical decisions after weighing all consequences.

8. Ethics and social responsibility yield good behavior, and they often result in higher income and a better working environment.

9. For accounting to provide useful information for decisions, it must be trusted. Trust requires ethics in accounting.

10. Two major participants in setting rules include the SEC and the FASB. (*Note:* Accounting rules reflect society's needs, not those of accountants or any other single constituency.)

11. Most U.S. companies are not directly affected by international accounting standards. International standards are put forth as preferred accounting practices. However, stock exchanges and other parties are increasing the pressure to narrow differences in worldwide accounting practices. International accounting standards are playing an important role in that process.

12. The objectivity concept and cost principle are related in that most users consider information based on cost as objective. Information prepared using both is considered highly reliable and often relevant.

13. Users desire information about the performance of a specific entity. If information is mixed between two or more entities, its usefulness decreases.

14. The revenue recognition principle gives preparers guidelines on when to recognize (record) revenue. This is important; for example, if revenue is recognized too early, the statements report revenue sooner than it should and the business looks more profitable than it is. The reverse is also true.

15. The three basic forms of business organization are sole proprietorships, partnerships, and corporations.

16. Owners of corporations are called *shareholders* (or *stockholders*). Corporate ownership is divided into units called *shares* (or *stock*). The most basic of corporate shares is common stock (or capital stock).

17. The accounting equation is: Assets = Liabilities + Equity. This equation is always in balance, both before and after each transaction.

18. A transaction that changes the makeup of assets would not affect liability and equity accounts. FastForward's transactions 2 and 3 are examples. Each exchanges one asset for another.

19. Earning revenue by performing services, as in FastForward's transaction 5, increases equity (and assets). Incurring expenses while servicing clients, such as in transactions 6 and 7, decreases equity (and assets). Other examples include owner investments that increase equity and withdrawals that decrease equity.

20. Paying a liability with an asset reduces both asset and liability totals. One example is FastForward's transaction 10 that reduces a payable by paying cash.

21. An income statement reports a company's revenues and expenses along with the resulting net income or loss. A statement of owner's equity shows changes in equity, including that from net income or loss. Both statements report transactions occurring over a period of time.

22. The balance sheet describes a company's financial position (assets, liabilities, and equity) at a point in time. The equity amount in the balance sheet is obtained from the statement of owner's equity.

23. Cash flows from operating activities report cash receipts and payments from the primary business the company engages in. Cash flows from investing activities involve cash transactions from buying and selling long-term assets. Cash flows from financing activities include long-term cash borrowings and repayments to lenders and the cash investments from and withdrawals by the owner.

*A list of key terms with page references concludes each chapter (a complete glossary is at the end of the book and also on the book's Website).*

## Key Terms                                      mhhe.com/wildFAP20e

Accounting (p. 4)
Accounting equation (p. 14)
Assets (p. 14)
Audit (p. 12)
Auditors (p. 13)
Balance sheet (p. 19)
Bookkeeping (p. 4)
Business entity assumption (p. 11)
Common stock (p. 12)
Conceptual framework (p. 9)
Corporation (p. 12)
Cost-benefit constraint (p. 12)
Cost principle (p. 10)
Equity (p. 14)
Ethics (p. 8)
Events (p. 15)
Expanded accounting equation (p. 14)
Expense recognition principle (p. 11)
Expenses (p. 14)
External transactions (p. 15)
External users (p. 5)
Financial accounting (p. 5)

Financial Accounting Standards Board (FASB) (p. 9)
Full disclosure principle (p. 11)
Generally accepted accounting principles (GAAP) (p. 8)
Going-concern assumption (p. 11)
Income statement (p. 19)
Internal transactions (p. 15)
Internal users (p. 6)
International Accounting Standards Board (IASB) (p. 9)
International Financial Reporting Standards (IFRS) (p. 9)
Liabilities (p. 14)
Managerial accounting (p. 6)
Matching principle (p. 11)
Materiality constraint (p. 12)
Measurement principle (p. 10)
Monetary unit assumption (p. 11)
Net income (p. 14)
Net loss (p. 14)
Owner, Capital (p. 14)
Owner investment (p. 14)

Owner withdrawals (p. 14)
Partnership (p. 11)
Proprietorship (p. 11)
Recordkeeping (p. 4)
Return (p. 26)
Return on assets (p. 22)
Revenue recognition principle (p. 10)
Revenues (p. 14)
Risk (p. 26)
Sarbanes–Oxley Act (p. 12)
Securities and Exchange Commission (SEC) (p. 9)
Shareholders (p. 12)
Shares (p. 12)
Sole proprietorship (p. 11)
Statement of cash flows (p. 19)
Statement of owner's equity (p. 19)
Stock (p. 12)
Stockholders (p. 12)
Time period assumption (p. 11)
Withdrawals (p. 14)

## Multiple Choice Quiz          Answers on p. 47          mhhe.com/wildFAP20e

**Additional Quiz Questions are available at the book's Website.**

1. A building is offered for sale at $500,000 but is currently assessed at $400,000. The purchaser of the building believes the building is worth $475,000, but ultimately purchases the building for $450,000. The purchaser records the building at:
   a. $50,000
   b. $400,000
   c. $450,000
   d. $475,000
   e. $500,000

2. On December 30, 2010, **KPMG** signs a $150,000 contract to provide accounting services to one of its clients in 2011. KPMG has a December 31 year-end. Which accounting principle or assumption requires KPMG to record the accounting services revenue from this client in 2011 and not 2010?
   a. Business entity assumption
   b. Revenue recognition principle
   c. Monetary unit assumption
   d. Cost principle
   e. Going-concern assumption

3. If the assets of a company increase by $100,000 during the year and its liabilities increase by $35,000 during the same

year, then the change in equity of the company during the year must have been:
   a. An increase of $135,000.
   b. A decrease of $135,000.
   c. A decrease of $65,000.
   d. An increase of $65,000.
   e. An increase of $100,000.

4. **Brunswick** borrows $50,000 cash from Third National Bank. How does this transaction affect the accounting equation for Brunswick?
   a. Assets increase by $50,000; liabilities increase by $50,000; no effect on equity.
   b. Assets increase by $50,000; no effect on liabilities; equity increases by $50,000.
   c. Assets increase by $50,000; liabilities decrease by $50,000; no effect on equity.
   d. No effect on assets; liabilities increase by $50,000; equity increases by $50,000.
   e. No effect on assets; liabilities increase by $50,000; equity decreases by $50,000.

**5.** **Geek Squad** performs services for a customer and bills the customer for $500. How would Geek Squad record this transaction?
 **a.** Accounts receivable increase by $500; revenues increase by $500.
 **b.** Cash increases by $500; revenues increase by $500.
 **c.** Accounts receivable increase by $500; revenues decrease by $500.
 **d.** Accounts receivable increase by $500; accounts payable increase by $500.
 **e.** Accounts payable increase by $500; revenues increase by $500.

A(B)  *Superscript letter A (B) denotes assignments based on Appendix 1A (1B).*

[i] Icon denotes assignments that involve decision making.

## Discussion Questions

**1.** What is the purpose of accounting in society?

**2.** Technology is increasingly used to process accounting data. Why then must we study and understand accounting?

**3.** [i] Identify four kinds of external users and describe how they use accounting information.

**4.** [i] What are at least three questions business owners and managers might be able to answer by looking at accounting information?

**5.** Identify three actual businesses that offer services and three actual businesses that offer products.

**6.** [i] Describe the internal role of accounting for organizations.

**7.** Identify three types of services typically offered by accounting professionals.

**8.** [i] What type of accounting information might be useful to the marketing managers of a business?

**9.** Why is accounting described as a service activity?

**10.** What are some accounting-related professions?

**11.** How do ethics rules affect auditors' choice of clients?

**12.** What work do tax accounting professionals perform in addition to preparing tax returns?

**13.** What does the concept of *objectivity* imply for information reported in financial statements? Why?

**14.** A business reports its own office stationery on the balance sheet at its $400 cost, although it cannot be sold for more than $10 as scrap paper. Which accounting principle and/or assumption justifies this treatment?

**15.** Why is the revenue recognition principle needed? What does it demand?

**16.** Describe the three basic forms of business organization and their key attributes.

**17.** Define (*a*) *assets,* (*b*) *liabilities,* (*c*) *equity,* and (*d*) *net assets.*

**18.** What events or transactions change equity?

**19.** Identify the two main categories of accounting principles.

**20.** What do accountants mean by the term *revenue?*

**21.** Define *net income* and explain its computation.

**22.** Identify the four basic financial statements of a business.

**23.** [i] What information is reported in an income statement?

**24.** Give two examples of expenses a business might incur.

**25.** What is the purpose of the statement of owner's equity?

**26.** [i] What information is reported in a balance sheet?

**27.** The statement of cash flows reports on what major activities?

**28.** [i] Define and explain return on assets.

**29.**A [i] Define return and risk. Discuss the trade-off between them.

**30.**B Describe the three major business activities in organizations.

**31.**B Explain why investing (assets) and financing (liabilities and equity) totals are always equal.

**32.** Refer to the financial statements of **Research In Motion** in Appendix A near the end of the book. To what level of significance are dollar amounts rounded? What time period does its income statement cover? **RIM**

**33.** Identify the dollar amounts of **Apple**'s 2009 assets, liabilities, and equity as reported in its statements in Appendix A near the end of the book. **Apple**

**34.** Refer to **Nokia**'s balance sheet in Appendix A near the end of the book. Confirm that its total assets equal its total liabilities plus total equity. **NOKIA**

**35.** [i] Access the SEC EDGAR database (**www.SEC. gov**) and retrieve **Palm**'s 2009 10-K (filed July 24, 2009). Identify its auditor. What responsibility does its independent auditor claim regarding Palm's financial statements? **Palm**

*Connect* reproduces assignments online, in static or algorithmic mode, which allows instructors to monitor, promote, and assess student learning. It can be used for practice, homework, or exams.

*Quick Study* exercises give readers a brief test of key elements.

## QUICK STUDY

**QS 1-1**

Identifying accounting terms   **C1**

Reading and interpreting accounting reports requires some knowledge of accounting terminology. (*a*) Identify the meaning of these accounting-related acronyms: GAAP, SEC, FASB, IASB and IFRS. (*b*) Briefly explain the importance of the knowledge base or organization that is referred to for each of the accounting-related acronyms.

An important responsibility of many accounting professionals is to design and implement internal control procedures for organizations. Explain the purpose of internal control procedures. Provide two examples of internal controls applied by companies.

**QS 1-2**
Explaining internal control
**C1**

---

Identify the following users as either external users (E) or internal users (I).

**a.** Lenders      **d.** Sales staff      **g.** Brokers      **j.** Managers

**b.** Controllers      **e.** FBI and IRS      **h.** Suppliers      **k.** Business press

**c.** Shareholders      **f.** Consumer group      **i.** Customers      **l.** District attorney

**QS 1-3**
Identifying accounting users
**C2**

---

There are many job opportunities for those with accounting knowledge. Identify at least three main areas of opportunities for accounting professionals. For each area, identify at least three job possibilities linked to accounting.

**QS 1-4**
Accounting opportunities   **C2**

---

Accounting professionals must sometimes choose between two or more acceptable methods of accounting for business transactions and events. Explain why these situations can involve difficult matters of ethical concern.

**QS 1-5**
Identifying ethical concerns   **C3**

*This icon highlights assignments that enhance decision-making skills.*

---

Identify which accounting principle or assumption best describes each of the following practices:

**a.** If $51,000 cash is paid to buy land, the land is reported on the buyer's balance sheet at $51,000.

**b.** Alissa Kees owns both Sailing Passions and Dockside Supplies. In preparing financial statements for Dockside Supplies, Kees makes sure that the expense transactions of Sailing Passions are kept separate from Dockside's transactions and financial statements.

**c.** In December 2010, Ace Landscaping received a customer's order and cash prepayment to install sod at a new house that would not be ready for installation until March 2011. Ace should record the revenue from the customer order in March 2011, not in December 2010.

**QS 1-6**
Identifying accounting principles
**C4**

---

**a.** Total assets of Caldwell Company equal $40,000 and its equity is $10,000. What is the amount of its liabilities?

**b.** Total assets of Waterworld equal $55,000 and its liabilities and equity amounts are equal to each other. What is the amount of its liabilities? What is the amount of its equity?

**QS 1-7**
Applying the accounting equation
**A1**

---

Use the accounting equation to compute the missing financial statement amounts (*a*), (*b*), and (*c*).

| Company | Assets | = | Liabilities | + | Equity |
|---------|--------|---|-------------|---|--------|
| 1 | $ 30,000 | | $ *(a)* | | $ 20,000 |
| 2 | *(b)* | | 50,000 | | 30,000 |
| 3 | 90,000 | | 10,000 | | *(c)* |

**QS 1-8**
Applying the accounting equation
**A1**

---

Accounting provides information about an organization's business transactions and events that both affect the accounting equation and can be reliably measured. Identify at least two examples of both (*a*) business transactions and (*b*) business events that meet these requirements.

**QS 1-9**
Identifying transactions and events   **P1**

---

Use **Apple**'s September 26, 2009, financial statements, in Appendix A near the end of the book, to answer the following:

**a.** Identify the dollar amounts of Apple's 2009 (1) assets, (2) liabilities, and (3) equity.

**b.** Using Apple's amounts from part *a*, verify that Assets = Liabilities + Equity.

**QS 1-10**
Identifying and computing assets, liabilities, and equity
**P1**

**QS 1-11**
Computing and interpreting return on assets

**A2**

In a recent year's financial statements, **Home Depot** reported the following results. Compute and interpret Home Depot's return on assets (assume competitors average a 5% return on assets).

| | |
|---|---|
| Sales . . . . . . . . . . . . . . . . . . . . . . | $71,288 million |
| Net income . . . . . . . . . . . . . . . | 2,260 million |
| Average total assets . . . . . . . . . | 42,744 million |

**QS 1-12**
Identifying items with financial statements

**P2**

Indicate in which financial statement each item would most likely appear: income statement (I), balance sheet (B), statement of owner's equity (OE), or statement of cash flows (CF).

**a.** Assets      **d.** Equipment      **g.** Total liabilities and equity

**b.** Revenues      **e.** Withdrawals      **h.** Cash from operating activities

**c.** Liabilities      **f.** Expenses      **i.** Net decrease (or increase) in cash

**QS 1-13**
International accounting standards  **C4**

*This icon highlights assignments that focus on IFRS-related content.*

Answer each of the following questions related to international accounting standards.

**a.** The International Accounting Standards Board (IASB) issues preferred accounting practices that are referred to as what?

**b.** The FASB and IASB are working on a convergence process for what purpose?

**c.** The SEC has proposed a roadmap for use of IFRS by U.S. companies. What is the proposed adoption date for large U.S. companies to adopt IFRS?

**connect**

## EXERCISES

**Exercise 1-1**
Classifying activities reflected in the accounting system

**C1**

Accounting is an information and measurement system that identifies, records, and communicates relevant, reliable, and comparable information about an organization's business activities. Classify the following activities as part of the identifying (I), recording (R), or communicating (C) aspects of accounting.

_____ **1.** Determining employee tasks behind a service.

_____ **2.** Establishing revenues generated from a product.

_____ **3.** Maintaining a log of service costs.

_____ **4.** Measuring the costs of a product.

_____ **5.** Preparing financial statements.

_____ **6.** Analyzing and interpreting reports.

_____ **7.** Presenting financial information.

**Exercise 1-2**
Identifying accounting users and uses

**C2**

Part A. Identify the following users of accounting information as either an internal (I) or an external (E) user.

_____ **1.** Shareholders

_____ **2.** Creditors

_____ **3.** Nonexecutive employee

_____ **4.** Research and development director

_____ **5.** Purchasing manager

_____ **6.** Human resources director

_____ **7.** Production supervisors

_____ **8.** Distribution managers

Part B. Identify the following questions as most likely to be asked by an internal (I) or an external (E) user of accounting information.

_____ **1.** What are the costs of our service to customers?

_____ **2.** Should we make a five-year loan to that business?

_____ **3.** Should we spend further research on our product?

_____ **4.** Do income levels justify the current stock price?

_____ **5.** What are reasonable payroll benefits and wages?

_____ **6.** Which firm reports the highest sales and income?

_____ **7.** What are the costs of our product's ingredients?

**Exercise 1-3**
Describing accounting responsibilities

**C2**

Many accounting professionals work in one of the following three areas:

**A.** Managerial accounting     **B.** Financial accounting     **C.** Tax accounting

Identify the area of accounting that is most involved in each of the following responsibilities:

_____ **1.** Reviewing reports for SEC compliance.

_____ **2.** Planning transactions to minimize taxes.

_____ **3.** Investigating violations of tax laws.

_____ **4.** Preparing external financial statements.

_____ **5.** Budgeting.

_____ **6.** Cost accounting.

_____ **7.** External auditing.

_____ **8.** Internal auditing.

Assume the following role and describe a situation in which ethical considerations play an important part in guiding your decisions and actions:

a. You are a student in an introductory accounting course.

b. You are an accounting professional with audit clients that are competitors in business.

c. You are an accounting professional preparing tax returns for clients.

d. You are a manager with responsibility for several employees.

**Exercise 1-4**
Identifying ethical concerns
C3

Match each of the numbered descriptions with the term or phrase it best reflects. Indicate your answer by writing the letter for the term or phrase in the blank provided.

A. Audit        C. Ethics        E. SEC        G. Net income

B. GAAP        D. Tax accounting        F. Public accountants        H. IASB

_____ **1.** Amount a business earns after paying all expenses and costs associated with its sales and revenues.

_____ **2.** An examination of an organization's accounting system and records that adds credibility to financial statements.

_____ **3.** Principles that determine whether an action is right or wrong.

_____ **4.** Accounting professionals who provide services to many clients.

_____ **5.** An accounting area that includes planning future transactions to minimize taxes paid.

**Exercise 1-5**
Learning the language of business
C1–C3

Match each of the numbered descriptions with the principle or assumption it best reflects. Enter the letter for the appropriate principle or assumption in the blank space next to each description.

A. Cost principle        E. General accounting principle

B. Matching principle        F. Business entity assumption

C. Specific accounting principle        G. Revenue recognition principle

D. Full disclosure principle        H. Going-concern assumption

_____ **1.** Revenue is recorded only when the earnings process is complete.

_____ **2.** Information is based on actual costs incurred in transactions.

_____ **3.** Usually created by a pronouncement from an authoritative body.

_____ **4.** Financial statements reflect the assumption that the business continues operating.

_____ **5.** A company reports details behind financial statements that would impact users' decisions.

_____ **6.** A company records the expenses incurred to generate the revenues reported.

_____ **7.** Derived from long-used and generally accepted accounting practices.

_____ **8.** Every business is accounted for separately from its owner or owners.

**Exercise 1-6**
Identifying accounting principles and assumptions
C4

The following describe several different business organizations. Determine whether the description refers to a sole proprietorship, partnership, or corporation.

a. A-1 pays its own income taxes and has two owners.

b. Ownership of Zeller Company is divided into 1,000 shares of stock.

c. Waldron is owned by Mary Malone, who is personally liable for the company's debts.

d. Micah Douglas and Nathan Logan own Financial Services, a financial services provider. Neither Douglas nor Logan has personal responsibility for the debts of Financial Services.

e. Bailey and Kay own Squeaky Clean, a cleaning service. Both are personally liable for the debts of the business.

f. Plasto Products does not pay income taxes and has one owner.

g. Ian LLC does not have separate legal existence apart from the one person who owns it.

**Exercise 1-7**
Distinguishing business organizations
C4

Answer the following questions. (*Hint:* Use the accounting equation.)

a. Office Mart has assets equal to $123,000 and liabilities equal to $53,000 at year-end. What is the total equity for Office Mart at year-end?

b. At the beginning of the year, Logan Company's assets are $200,000 and its equity is $150,000. During the year, assets increase $70,000 and liabilities increase $30,000. What is the equity at the end of the year?

c. At the beginning of the year, Keller Company's liabilities equal $60,000. During the year, assets increase by $80,000, and at year-end assets equal $180,000. Liabilities decrease $10,000 during the year. What are the beginning and ending amounts of equity?

**Exercise 1-8**
Using the accounting equation
A1  P1

**Check**  (c) Beg. equity, $40,000

**Exercise 1-9**
Using the accounting equation
A1

Determine the missing amount from each of the separate situations *a*, *b*, and *c* below.

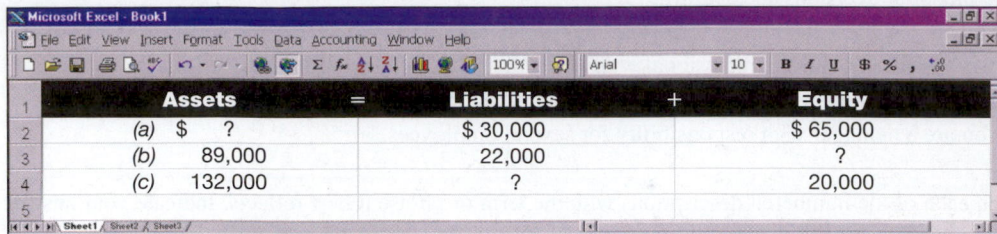

| | Assets | = | Liabilities | + | Equity |
|---|---|---|---|---|---|
| (a) | $     ? | | $ 30,000 | | $ 65,000 |
| (b) | 89,000 | | 22,000 | | ? |
| (c) | 132,000 | | ? | | 20,000 |

**Exercise 1-10**
Identifying effects of transactions on the accounting equation
P1

Provide an example of a transaction that creates the described effects for the separate cases *a* through *g*.

a. Increases an asset and decreases an asset.
b. Decreases an asset and decreases a liability.
c. Decreases a liability and increases a liability.
d. Increases an asset and increases a liability.
e. Decreases an asset and decreases equity.
f. Increases a liability and decreases equity.
g. Increases an asset and increases equity.

**Exercise 1-11**
Identifying effects of transactions using the accounting equation
P1

Lena Gold began a professional practice on June 1 and plans to prepare financial statements at the end of each month. During June, Gold (the owner) completed these transactions:

a. Owner invested $50,000 cash in the company along with equipment that had a $10,000 market value.
b. The company paid $1,600 cash for rent of office space for the month.
c. The company purchased $12,000 of additional equipment on credit (payment due within 30 days).
d. The company completed work for a client and immediately collected the $2,000 cash earned.
e. The company completed work for a client and sent a bill for $7,000 to be received within 30 days.
f. The company purchased additional equipment for $8,000 cash.
g. The company paid an assistant $2,400 cash as wages for the month.
h. The company collected $5,000 cash as a partial payment for the amount owed by the client in transaction *e*.
i. The company paid $12,000 cash to settle the liability created in transaction *c*.
j. Owner withdrew $500 cash from the company for personal use.

**Required**

**Check**   Net income, $5,000

Create a table like the one in Exhibit 1.9, using the following headings for columns: Cash; Accounts Receivable; Equipment; Accounts Payable; L. Gold, Capital; L. Gold, Withdrawals; Revenues; and Expenses. Then use additions and subtractions to show the effects of the transactions on individual items of the accounting equation. Show new balances after each transaction.

**Exercise 1-12**
Analysis using the accounting equation
P1

Zelda began a new consulting firm on January 5. The accounting equation showed the following balances after each of the company's first five transactions. Analyze the accounting equation for each transaction and describe each of the five transactions with their amounts.

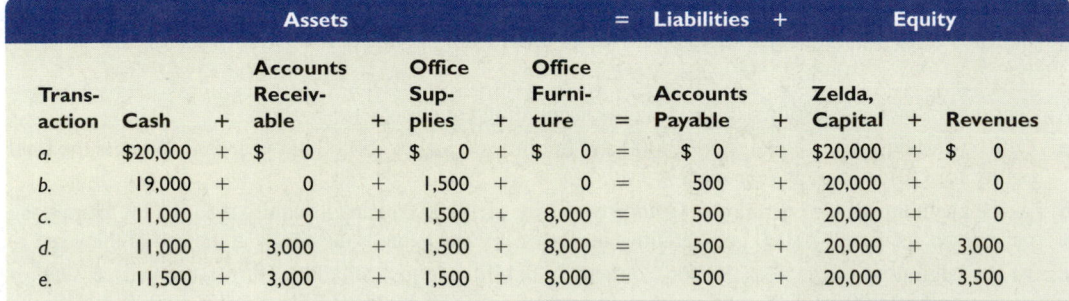

| | | | Assets | | | | | = | Liabilities | + | | Equity | |
| Trans-action | Cash | + | Accounts Receivable | + | Office Supplies | + | Office Furniture | = | Accounts Payable | + | Zelda, Capital | + | Revenues |
|---|---|---|---|---|---|---|---|---|---|---|---|---|---|
| a. | $20,000 | + | $   0 | + | $   0 | + | $   0 | = | $   0 | + | $20,000 | + | $   0 |
| b. | 19,000 | + | 0 | + | 1,500 | + | 0 | = | 500 | + | 20,000 | + | 0 |
| c. | 11,000 | + | 0 | + | 1,500 | + | 8,000 | = | 500 | + | 20,000 | + | 0 |
| d. | 11,000 | + | 3,000 | + | 1,500 | + | 8,000 | = | 500 | + | 20,000 | + | 3,000 |
| e. | 11,500 | + | 3,000 | + | 1,500 | + | 8,000 | = | 500 | + | 20,000 | + | 3,500 |

The following table shows the effects of five transactions (*a* through *e*) on the assets, liabilities, and equity of Vera's Boutique. Write short descriptions of the probable nature of each transaction.

| | Assets | | | | | = | Liabilities | + | | Equity | | |
|---|---|---|---|---|---|---|---|---|---|---|---|---|
| | Cash | + | Accounts Receivable | + | Office Supplies | + | Land | = | Accounts Payable | + | Vera, Capital | + | Revenues |
| | $ 10,500 | + | $ 0 | + | $1,500 | + | $ 9,500 | = | $ 0 | + | $21,500 | + | $ 0 |
| a. | − 2,000 | | | | | + | 2,000 | | | | | | |
| b. | | | | + | 500 | | | | +500 | | | | |
| c. | | + | 950 | | | | | | | | | + | 950 |
| d. | − 500 | | | | | | | | −500 | | | | |
| e. | + 950 | − | 950 | | | | | | | | | | |
| | $ 8,950 | + | $ 0 | + | $2,000 | + | $11,500 | = | $ 0 | + | $21,500 | + | $950 |

On October 1, Natalie King organized Real Solutions, a new consulting firm. On October 31, the company's records show the following items and amounts. Use this information to prepare an October income statement for the business.

| | | | | |
|---|---|---|---|---|
| Cash..................... | $ 2,000 | Cash withdrawals by owner ......... | $ 3,360 |
| Accounts receivable ........ | 13,000 | Consulting fees earned ............. | 15,000 |
| Office supplies ............. | 4,250 | Rent expense ................... | 2,550 |
| Land ..................... | 36,000 | Salaries expense ................. | 6,000 |
| Office equipment .......... | 28,000 | Telephone expense ............... | 660 |
| Accounts payable........... | 7,500 | Miscellaneous expenses ........... | 680 |
| Owner investments ......... | 74,000 | | |

Use the information in Exercise 1-14 to prepare an October statement of owner's equity for Real Solutions.

Use the information in Exercise 1-14 (if completed, you can also use your solution to Exercise 1-15) to prepare an October 31 balance sheet for Real Solutions.

Use the information in Exercise 1-14 to prepare an October 31 statement of cash flows for Real Solutions. Also assume the following:

**a.** The owner's initial investment consists of $38,000 cash and $36,000 in land.

**b.** The company's $28,000 equipment purchase is paid in cash.

**c.** The accounts payable balance of $7,500 consists of the $4,250 office supplies purchase and $3,250 in employee salaries yet to be paid.

**d.** The company's rent, telephone, and miscellaneous expenses are paid in cash.

**e.** $2,000 has been collected on the $15,000 consulting fees earned.

Geneva Group reports net income of $20,000 for 2011. At the beginning of 2011, Geneva Group had $100,000 in assets. By the end of 2011, assets had grown to $150,000. What is Geneva Group's 2011 return on assets? How would you assess its performance if competitors average a 10% return on assets?

Indicate the section where each of the following would appear on the statement of cash flows.

**A.** Cash flows from operating activity

**B.** Cash flows from investing activity

**C.** Cash flows from financing activity

_____ **1.** Cash paid for wages            _____ **5.** Cash paid on an account payable

_____ **2.** Cash withdrawal by owner        _____ **6.** Cash investment by owner

_____ **3.** Cash purchase of equipment      _____ **7.** Cash received from clients

_____ **4.** Cash paid for advertising       _____ **8.** Cash paid for rent

**Exercise 1-20ᴮ**
Identifying business activities
C5

Match each transaction or event to one of the following activities of an organization: financing activities (F), investing activities (I), or operating activities (O).

**1.** _____ An owner contributes resources to the business.
**2.** _____ An organization purchases equipment.
**3.** _____ An organization advertises a new product.
**4.** _____ The organization borrows money from a bank.
**5.** _____ An organization sells some of its land.

**Exercise 1-21**
Preparing an income statement for a global company

P2

**Nintendo Company** reports the following income statement accounts for the year ended March 31, 2009. (Japanese yen in millions.)

| | |
|---|---:|
| Net sales . . . . . . . . . . . . . . . . . . . . . . . . . . . . . . . . . . . . . . . | ¥1,838,622 |
| Cost of sales . . . . . . . . . . . . . . . . . . . . . . . . . . . . . . . . . . . . | 1,044,981 |
| Selling, general and administrative expenses . . . . . . . . . | 238,378 |
| Other expenses . . . . . . . . . . . . . . . . . . . . . . . . . . . . . . . | 276,174 |

Use this information to prepare Nintendo's income statement for the year ended March 31, 2009.

*Problem Set B located at the end of Problem Set A is provided for each problem to reinforce the learning process.*

## PROBLEM SET A

**Problem 1-1A**
Identifying effects of transactions on financial statements

A1  P1

Identify how each of the following separate transactions affects financial statements. For the balance sheet, identify how each transaction affects total assets, total liabilities, and total equity. For the income statement, identify how each transaction affects net income. For the statement of cash flows, identify how each transaction affects cash flows from operating activities, cash flows from financing activities, and cash flows from investing activities. For increases, place a "+" in the column or columns. For decreases, place a "−" in the column or columns. If both an increase and a decrease occur, place a "+/−" in the column or columns. The first transaction is completed as an example.

| | Transaction | Balance Sheet Total Assets | Balance Sheet Total Liab. | Balance Sheet Total Equity | Income Statement Net Income | Statement of Cash Flows Operating Activities | Statement of Cash Flows Financing Activities | Statement of Cash Flows Investing Activities |
|---|---|---|---|---|---|---|---|---|
| 1 | Owner invests cash in business | + | | + | | | + | |
| 2 | Incurs legal costs on credit | | | | | | | |
| 3 | Pays cash for employee wages | | | | | | | |
| 4 | Borrows cash by signing long-term note payable | | | | | | | |
| 5 | Receives cash for services provided | | | | | | | |
| 6 | Buys land by signing note payable | | | | | | | |
| 7 | Buys office equipment for cash | | | | | | | |
| 8 | Provides services on credit | | | | | | | |
| 9 | Collects cash on receivable from (8) | | | | | | | |
| 10 | Owner withdraws cash | | | | | | | |

The following financial statement information is from five separate companies:

| | Company A | Company B | Company C | Company D | Company E |
|---|---|---|---|---|---|
| **December 31, 2010** | | | | | |
| Assets.......................... | $45,000 | $35,000 | $29,000 | $80,000 | $123,000 |
| Liabilities ...................... | 23,500 | 22,500 | 14,000 | 38,000 | ? |
| **December 31, 2011** | | | | | |
| Assets.......................... | 48,000 | 41,000 | ? | 125,000 | 112,500 |
| Liabilities ...................... | ? | 27,500 | 19,000 | 64,000 | 75,000 |
| **During year 2011** | | | | | |
| Owner investments.............. | 5,000 | 1,500 | 7,750 | ? | 4,500 |
| Net income (loss) ............... | 7,500 | ? | 9,000 | 12,000 | 18,000 |
| Owner cash withdrawals ......... | 2,500 | 3,000 | 3,875 | 0 | 9,000 |

**Required**

1. Answer the following questions about Company A:
   a. What is the amount of equity on December 31, 2010?
   b. What is the amount of equity on December 31, 2011?
   c. What is the amount of liabilities on December 31, 2011?
2. Answer the following questions about Company B:
   a. What is the amount of equity on December 31, 2010?
   b. What is the amount of equity on December 31, 2011?
   c. What is net income for year 2011?
3. Calculate the amount of assets for Company C on December 31, 2011.
4. Calculate the amount of owner investments for Company D during year 2011.
5. Calculate the amount of liabilities for Company E on December 31, 2010.

**Problem 1-2A**
Computing missing information using accounting knowledge
A1  P1

**Check**    (1*b*) $31,500

(2*c*) $2,500

(3) $46,875

---

The following is selected financial information for Affiliated Company as of December 31, 2011: liabilities, $34,000; equity, $56,000; assets, $90,000.

**Required**

Prepare the balance sheet for Affiliated Company as of December 31, 2011.

**Problem 1-3A**
Preparing a balance sheet
P2

---

The following is selected financial information for Sun Energy Company for the year ended December 31, 2011: revenues, $65,000; expenses, $50,000; net income, $15,000.

**Required**

Prepare the 2011 calendar-year income statement for Sun Energy Company.

**Problem 1-4A**
Preparing an income statement
P2

---

Following is selected financial information for Boardwalk for the year ended December 31, 2011.

| | | | |
|---|---|---|---|
| B. Walk, Capital, Dec. 31, 2011.......... | $15,000 | B. Walk, Withdrawals ................ | $2,000 |
| Net income ...................... | 9,000 | B. Walk, Capital, Dec. 31, 2010 .......... | 8,000 |

**Required**

Prepare the 2011 statement of owner's equity for Boardwalk.

**Problem 1-5A**
Preparing a statement of owner's equity
P2

**Problem 1-6A**
Preparing a statement of
cash flows

**P2**

Following is selected financial information of Trimark for the year ended December 31, 2011.

| | |
|---|---:|
| Cash used by investing activities . . . . . . . . . | $(3,000) |
| Net increase in cash . . . . . . . . . . . . . . . . . | 200 |
| Cash used by financing activities . . . . . . . . . | (3,800) |
| Cash from operating activities . . . . . . . . . . | 7,000 |
| Cash, December 31, 2010 . . . . . . . . . . . . . | 3,300 |

**Check** Cash balance, Dec. 31,
2011, $3,500

**Required**

Prepare the 2011 statement of cash flows for Trimark Company.

---

**Problem 1-7A**
Analyzing effects of transactions

**C4  P1  P2  A1**

Miranda Right started Right Consulting, a new business, and completed the following transactions during its first year of operations.

**a.** M. Right invests $60,000 cash and office equipment valued at $30,000 in the company.

**b.** The company purchased a $300,000 building to use as an office. Right paid $50,000 in cash and signed a note payable promising to pay the $250,000 balance over the next ten years.

**c.** The company purchased office equipment for $6,000 cash.

**d.** The company purchased $4,000 of office supplies and $1,000 of office equipment on credit.

**e.** The company paid a local newspaper $1,000 cash for printing an announcement of the office's opening.

**f.** The company completed a financial plan for a client and billed that client $4,000 for the service.

**g.** The company designed a financial plan for another client and immediately collected an $8,000 cash fee.

**h.** M. Right withdrew $1,800 cash from the company for personal use.

**i.** The company received $3,000 cash as partial payment from the client described in transaction *f.*

**j.** The company made a partial payment of $500 cash on the equipment purchased in transaction *d.*

**k.** The company paid $2,500 cash for the office secretary's wages for this period.

**Required**

**1.** Create a table like the one in Exhibit 1.9, using the following headings for the columns: Cash; Accounts Receivable; Office Supplies; Office Equipment; Building; Accounts Payable; Notes Payable; M. Right, Capital; M. Right, Withdrawals; Revenues; and Expenses.

**Check** (2) Ending balances: Cash,
$9,200; Expenses, $3,500; Notes
Payable, $250,000

(3) Net income, $8,500

**2.** Use additions and subtractions within the table created in part *1* to show the dollar effects of each transaction on individual items of the accounting equation. Show new balances after each transaction.

**3.** Once you have completed the table, determine the company's net income.

---

**Problem 1-8A**
Analyzing transactions and
preparing financial statements

**C4  P1  P2**

mhhe.com/wildFAP20e

J. D. Simpson started The Simpson Co., a new business that began operations on May 1. The Simpson Co. completed the following transactions during its first month of operations.

May  1   J. D. Simpson invested $60,000 cash in the company.
      1   The company rented a furnished office and paid $3,200 cash for May's rent.
      3   The company purchased $1,680 of office equipment on credit.
      5   The company paid $800 cash for this month's cleaning services.
      8   The company provided consulting services for a client and immediately collected $4,600 cash.
     12   The company provided $3,000 of consulting services for a client on credit.
     15   The company paid $850 cash for an assistant's salary for the first half of this month.
     20   The company received $3,000 cash payment for the services provided on May 12.
     22   The company provided $2,800 of consulting services on credit.
     25   The company received $2,800 cash payment for the services provided on May 22.
     26   The company paid $1,680 cash for the office equipment purchased on May 3.
     27   The company purchased $60 of advertising in this month's (May) local paper on credit; cash payment is due June 1.
     28   The company paid $850 cash for an assistant's salary for the second half of this month.
     30   The company paid $200 cash for this month's telephone bill.
     30   The company paid $480 cash for this month's utilities.
     31   J. D. Simpson withdrew $1,200 cash from the company for personal use.

**Required**

**1.** Arrange the following asset, liability, and equity titles in a table like Exhibit 1.9: Cash; Accounts Receivable; Office Equipment; Accounts Payable; J. D. Simpson, Capital; J. D. Simpson, Withdrawals; Revenues; and Expenses.

**2.** Show effects of the transactions on the accounts of the accounting equation by recording increases and decreases in the appropriate columns. Do not determine new account balances after each transaction. Determine the final total for each account and verify that the equation is in balance.

**3.** Prepare an income statement for May, a statement of owner's equity for May, a May 31 balance sheet, and a statement of cash flows for May.

**Check**  (2) Ending balances: Cash, $61,140; Expenses, $6,440

(3) Net income, $3,960; Total assets, $62,820

Curtis Hamilton started a new business and completed these transactions during December.

Dec.  1  Curtis Hamilton transferred $56,000 cash from a personal savings account to a checking account in the name of Hamilton Electric.
     2  The company rented office space and paid $800 cash for the December rent.
     3  The company purchased $14,000 of electrical equipment by paying $3,200 cash and agreeing to pay the $10,800 balance in 30 days.
     5  The company purchased office supplies by paying $900 cash.
     6  The company completed electrical work and immediately collected $1,000 cash for these services.
     8  The company purchased $3,800 of office equipment on credit.
    15  The company completed electrical work on credit in the amount of $4,000.
    18  The company purchased $500 of office supplies on credit.
    20  The company paid $3,800 cash for the office equipment purchased on December 8.
    24  The company billed a client $600 for electrical work completed; the balance is due in 30 days.
    28  The company received $4,000 cash for the work completed on December 15.
    29  The company paid the assistant's salary of $1,200 cash for this month.
    30  The company paid $440 cash for this month's utility bill.
    31  C. Hamilton withdrew $700 cash from the company for personal use.

**Problem 1-9A**

Analyzing transactions and preparing financial statements

**C4  P1  P2**

**eXcel**

mhhe.com/wildFAP20e

*Required*

**1.** Arrange the following asset, liability, and equity titles in a table like Exhibit 1.9: Cash; Accounts Receivable; Office Supplies; Office Equipment; Electrical Equipment; Accounts Payable; C. Hamilton, Capital; C. Hamilton, Withdrawals; Revenues; and Expenses.

**2.** Use additions and subtractions to show the effects of each transaction on the accounts in the accounting equation. Show new balances after each transaction.

**3.** Use the increases and decreases in the columns of the table from part 2 to prepare an income statement, a statement of owner's equity, and a statement of cash flows—each of these for the current month. Also prepare a balance sheet as of the end of the month.

**Check**  (2) Ending balances: Cash, $49,960, Accounts Payable, $11,300

(3) Net income, $3,160; Total assets, $69,760

*Analysis Component*

**4.** Assume that the owner investment transaction on December 1 was $40,000 cash instead of $56,000 and that Hamilton Electric obtained another $16,000 in cash by borrowing it from a bank. Explain the effect of this change on total assets, total liabilities, and total equity.

Nolan manufactures, markets, and sells cellular telephones. The average total assets for Nolan is $250,000. In its most recent year, Nolan reported net income of $55,000 on revenues of $455,000.

**Problem 1-10A**

Determining expenses, liabilities, equity, and return on assets

**A1  A2**

*Required*

**1.** What is Nolan's return on assets?

**2.** Does return on assets seem satisfactory for Nolan given that its competitors average a 12% return on assets?

**3.** What are total expenses for Nolan in its most recent year?

**4.** What is the average total amount of liabilities plus equity for Nolan?

**Check**  (3) $400,000
(4) $250,000

**Coca-Cola** and **PepsiCo** both produce and market beverages that are direct competitors. Key financial figures (in $ millions) for these businesses over the past year follow.

**Problem 1-11A**

Computing and interpreting return on assets

**A2**

| Key Figures ($ millions) | Coca-Cola | PepsiCo |
|---|---|---|
| Sales | $30,990 | $43,232 |
| Net income | 6,906 | 5,979 |
| Average assets | 44,595 | 37,921 |

*Required*

**1.** Compute return on assets for (*a*) Coca-Cola and (*b*) PepsiCo.

**2.** Which company is more successful in its total amount of sales to consumers?

**3.** Which company is more successful in returning net income from its assets invested?

*Analysis Component*

**4.** Write a one-paragraph memorandum explaining which company you would invest your money in and why. (Limit your explanation to the information provided.)

---

**Problem 1-12A**<sup>A</sup>

Identifying risk and return

A3

All business decisions involve aspects of risk and return.

*Required*

Identify both the risk and the return in each of the following activities:

**1.** Investing $1,000 in a 4% savings account.

**2.** Placing a $1,000 bet on your favorite sports team.

**3.** Investing $10,000 in Yahoo! stock.

**4.** Taking out a $10,000 college loan to earn an accounting degree.

---

**Problem 1-13A**<sup>B</sup>

Describing organizational activities   C5

An organization undertakes various activities in pursuit of business success. Identify an organization's three major business activities, and describe each activity.

---

**Problem 1-14A**<sup>B</sup>

Describing organizational activities

C5

A start-up company often engages in the following transactions in its first year of operations. Classify those transactions in one of the three major categories of an organization's business activities.

**F.** Financing     **I.** Investing     **O.** Operating

_____ **1.** Owner investing land in business.     _____ **5.** Purchasing equipment.

_____ **2.** Purchasing a building.     _____ **6.** Selling and distributing products.

_____ **3.** Purchasing land.     _____ **7.** Paying for advertising.

_____ **4.** Borrowing cash from a bank.     _____ **8.** Paying employee wages.

---

## PROBLEM SET B

**Problem 1-1B**

Identifying effects of transactions on financial statements   A1   P1

Identify how each of the following separate transactions affects financial statements. For the balance sheet, identify how each transaction affects total assets, total liabilities, and total equity. For the income statement, identify how each transaction affects net income. For the statement of cash flows, identify how each transaction affects cash flows from operating activities, cash flows from financing activities, and cash flows from investing activities. For increases, place a "+" in the column or columns. For decreases, place a "−" in the column or columns. If both an increase and a decrease occur, place "+/−" in the column or columns. The first transaction is completed as an example.

| | Transaction | Balance Sheet | | | Income Statement | Statement of Cash Flows | | |
| --- | --- | --- | --- | --- | --- | --- | --- | --- |
| | | Total Assets | Total Liab. | Total Equity | Net Income | Operating Activities | Financing Activities | Investing Activities |
| 1 | Owner invests cash in business | + | | + | | | + | |
| 2 | Buys building by signing note payable | | | | | | | |
| 3 | Pays cash for salaries incurred | | | | | | | |
| 4 | Provides services for cash | | | | | | | |
| 5 | Pays cash for rent incurred | | | | | | | |
| 6 | Incurs utilities costs on credit | | | | | | | |
| 7 | Buys store equipment for cash | | | | | | | |
| 8 | Owner withdraws cash | | | | | | | |
| 9 | Provides services on credit | | | | | | | |
| 10 | Collects cash on receivable from (9) | | | | | | | |

The following financial statement information is from five separate companies.

|  | Company V | Company W | Company X | Company Y | Company Z |
|---|---|---|---|---|---|
| **December 31, 2010** | | | | | |
| Assets........................ | $45,000 | $70,000 | $121,500 | $82,500 | $124,000 |
| Liabilities ..................... | 30,000 | 50,000 | 58,500 | 61,500 | ? |
| **December 31, 2011** | | | | | |
| Assets........................ | 49,000 | 90,000 | 136,500 | ? | 160,000 |
| Liabilities ..................... | 26,000 | ? | 55,500 | 72,000 | 52,000 |
| **During year 2011** | | | | | |
| Owner investments.............. | 6,000 | 10,000 | ? | 38,100 | 40,000 |
| Net income or (loss)............. | ? | 30,000 | 16,500 | 24,000 | 32,000 |
| Owner cash withdrawals......... | 4,500 | 2,000 | 0 | 18,000 | 6,000 |

**Problem 1-2B**
Computing missing information using accounting knowledge
A1  P1

**Required**

1. Answer the following questions about Company V:
   a. What is the amount of equity on December 31, 2010?
   b. What is the amount of equity on December 31, 2011?
   c. What is the net income or loss for the year 2011?
2. Answer the following questions about Company W:
   a. What is the amount of equity on December 31, 2010?
   b. What is the amount of equity on December 31, 2011?
   c. What is the amount of liabilities on December 31, 2011?
3. Calculate the amount of owner investments for Company X during 2011.
4. Calculate the amount of assets for Company Y on December 31, 2011.
5. Calculate the amount of liabilities for Company Z on December 31, 2010.

**Check** (1*b*) $23,000

(2*c*) $32,000

(4) $137,100

---

The following is selected financial information for RWB Company as of December 31, 2011.

| Liabilities ........ | $74,000 | Equity ........ | $40,000 | Assets ........ | $114,000 |
|---|---|---|---|---|---|

**Problem 1-3B**
Preparing a balance sheet
P2

**Required**

Prepare the balance sheet for RWB Company as of December 31, 2011.

---

Selected financial information for Online Co. for the year ended December 31, 2011, follows.

| Revenues ....... | $58,000 | Expenses ........ | $30,000 | Net income ....... | $28,000 |
|---|---|---|---|---|---|

**Problem 1-4B**
Preparing an income statement
P2

**Required**

Prepare the 2011 income statement for Online Company.

---

Following is selected financial information of ComEx for the year ended December 31, 2011.

| C. Tex, Capital, Dec. 31, 2011 ........... | $47,000 | C. Tex, Withdrawals .................. | $ 8,000 |
|---|---|---|---|
| Net income ........................ | 6,000 | C. Tex, Capital, Dec. 31, 2010 ........... | 49,000 |

**Problem 1-5B**
Preparing a statement of owner's equity
P2

**Required**

Prepare the 2011 statement of owner's equity for ComEx.

**Problem 1-6B**
Preparing a statement of
cash flows

**P2**

Selected financial information of BuyRight Co. for the year ended December 31, 2011, follows.

| | |
|---|---|
| Cash from investing activities . . . . . . . . . . . | $2,600 |
| Net increase in cash . . . . . . . . . . . . . . . . . . | 1,400 |
| Cash from financing activities . . . . . . . . . . . . | 2,800 |
| Cash used by operating activities . . . . . . . . | (4,000) |
| Cash, December 31, 2010 . . . . . . . . . . . . . . | 1,300 |

**Required**

Prepare the 2011 statement of cash flows for BuyRight Company.

**Problem 1-7B**
Analyzing effects of transactions

**C4 P1 P2 A1**

Tiana Moore started a new business, Tiana's Solutions, and completed the following transactions during its first year of operations.

**a.** T. Moore invests $95,000 cash and office equipment valued at $20,000 in the company.

**b.** The company purchased a $120,000 building to use as an office. It paid $20,000 in cash and signed a note payable promising to pay the $100,000 balance over the next ten years.

**c.** The company purchased office equipment for $20,000 cash.

**d.** The company purchased $1,400 of office supplies and $3,000 of office equipment on credit.

**e.** The company paid a local newspaper $400 cash for printing an announcement of the office's opening.

**f.** The company completed a financial plan for a client and billed that client $1,800 for the service.

**g.** The company designed a financial plan for another client and immediately collected a $2,000 cash fee.

**h.** T. Moore withdrew $5,000 cash from the company for personal use.

**i.** The company received $1,800 cash from the client described in transaction *f*.

**j.** The company made a payment of $2,000 cash on the equipment purchased in transaction *d*.

**k.** The company paid $2,000 cash for the office secretary's wages.

**Required**

**Check** (2) Ending balances: Cash,
$49,400; Expenses, $2,400; Notes
Payable, $100,000

(3) Net income, $1,400

**1.** Create a table like the one in Exhibit 1.9, using the following headings for the columns: Cash; Accounts Receivable; Office Supplies; Office Equipment; Building; Accounts Payable; Notes Payable; T. Moore, Capital; T. Moore, Withdrawals; Revenues; and Expenses.

**2.** Use additions and subtractions within the table created in part *1* to show the dollar effects of each transaction on individual items of the accounting equation. Show new balances after each transaction.

**3.** Once you have completed the table, determine the company's net income.

**Problem 1-8B**
Analyzing transactions and
preparing financial statements

**C4 P1 P2**

Ken Stone launched a new business, Ken's Maintenance Co., that began operations on June 1. The following transactions were completed by the company during that first month.

| June | 1 | K. Stone invested $120,000 cash in the company. |
|---|---|---|
| | 2 | The company rented a furnished office and paid $4,500 cash for June's rent. |
| | 4 | The company purchased $2,400 of equipment on credit. |
| | 6 | The company paid $1,125 cash for this month's advertising of the opening of the business. |
| | 8 | The company completed maintenance services for a customer and immediately collected $750 cash. |
| | 14 | The company completed $6,300 of maintenance services for City Center on credit. |
| | 16 | The company paid $900 cash for an assistant's salary for the first half of the month. |
| | 20 | The company received $6,300 cash payment for services completed for City Center on June 14. |
| | 21 | The company completed $3,500 of maintenance services for Skyway Co. on credit. |
| | 24 | The company completed $825 of maintenance services for Comfort Motel on credit. |
| | 25 | The company received $3,500 cash payment from Skyway Co. for the work completed on June 21. |
| | 26 | The company made payment of $2,400 cash for equipment purchased on June 4. |
| | 28 | The company paid $900 cash for an assistant's salary for the second half of this month. |
| | 29 | K. Stone withdrew $2,000 cash from the company for personal use. |
| | 30 | The company paid $120 cash for this month's telephone bill. |
| | 30 | The company paid $525 cash for this month's utilities. |

**Required**

**1.** Arrange the following asset, liability, and equity titles in a table like Exhibit 1.9: Cash; Accounts Receivable; Equipment; Accounts Payable; K. Stone, Capital; K. Stone, Withdrawals; Revenues; and Expenses.

**2.** Show the effects of the transactions on the accounts of the accounting equation by recording increases and decreases in the appropriate columns. Do not determine new account balances after each transaction. Determine the final total for each account and verify that the equation is in balance.

**3.** Prepare a June income statement, a June statement of owner's equity, a June 30 balance sheet, and a June statement of cash flows.

**Check**   (2) Ending balances: Cash, $118,080; Expenses, $8,070

(3) Net income, $3,306; Total assets, $121,305

---

Swender Excavating Co., owned by Patrick Swender, began operations in July and completed these transactions during that first month of operations.

**Problem 1-9B**
Analyzing transactions and preparing financial statements

C4 P1 P2

| July | 1 | P. Swender invested $60,000 cash in the company. |
|---|---|---|
| | 2 | The company rented office space and paid $500 cash for the July rent. |
| | 3 | The company purchased excavating equipment for $4,000 by paying $800 cash and agreeing to pay the $3,200 balance in 30 days. |
| | 6 | The company purchased office supplies for $500 cash. |
| | 8 | The company completed work for a customer and immediately collected $2,200 cash for the work. |
| | 10 | The company purchased $3,800 of office equipment on credit. |
| | 15 | The company completed work for a customer on credit in the amount of $2,400. |
| | 17 | The company purchased $1,920 of office supplies on credit. |
| | 23 | The company paid $3,800 cash for the office equipment purchased on July 10. |
| | 25 | The company billed a customer $5,000 for work completed; the balance is due in 30 days. |
| | 28 | The company received $2,400 cash for the work completed on July 15. |
| | 30 | The company paid an assistant's salary of $1,260 cash for this month. |
| | 31 | The company paid $260 cash for this month's utility bill. |
| | 31 | P. Swender withdrew $1,200 cash from the company for personal use. |

**Required**

**1.** Arrange the following asset, liability, and equity titles in a table like Exhibit 1.9: Cash; Accounts Receivable; Office Supplies; Office Equipment; Excavating Equipment; Accounts Payable; P. Swender, Capital; P. Swender, Withdrawals; Revenues; and Expenses.

**2.** Use additions and subtractions to show the effects of each transaction on the accounts in the accounting equation. Show new balances after each transaction.

**3.** Use the increases and decreases in the columns of the table from part 2 to prepare an income statement, a statement of owner's equity, and a statement of cash flows—each of these for the current month. Also prepare a balance sheet as of the end of the month.

**Check**   (2) Ending balances: Cash, $56,280;  Accounts Payable, $5,120

(3) Net income, $7,580; Total assets, $71,500

**Analysis Component**

**4.** Assume that the $4,000 purchase of excavating equipment on July 3 was financed from an owner investment of another $4,000 cash in the business (instead of the purchase conditions described in the transaction). Explain the effect of this change on total assets, total liabilities, and total equity.

---

Aspen Company manufactures, markets, and sells ATV and snowmobile equipment and accessories. The average total assets for Aspen is $2,000,000. In its most recent year, Aspen reported net income of $100,000 on revenues of $1,200,000.

**Problem 1-10B**
Determining expenses, liabilities, equity, and return on assets

A1   A2

**Required**

**1.** What is Aspen Company's return on assets?

**2.** Does return on assets seem satisfactory for Aspen given that its competitors average a 9.5% return on assets?

**3.** What are the total expenses for Aspen Company in its most recent year?

**4.** What is the average total amount of liabilities plus equity for Aspen Company?

**Check**   (3) $1,100,000

(4) $2,000,000

---

**AT&T** and **Verizon** produce and market telecommunications products and are competitors. Key financial figures (in $ millions) for these businesses over the past year follow.

**Problem 1-11B**
Computing and interpreting return on assets

A2

| Key Figures ($ millions) | AT&T | Verizon |
|---|---|---|
| Sales . . . . . . . . . . . . . . . . . . . . . . . | $123,018 | $107,808 |
| Net income . . . . . . . . . . . . . . . . . | 12,535 | 10,358 |
| Average assets . . . . . . . . . . . . . . . | 266,999 | 214,937 |

*Required*

**1.** Compute return on assets for (*a*) AT&T and (*b*) Verizon.

**2.** Which company is more successful in the total amount of sales to consumers?

**3.** Which company is more successful in returning net income from its assets invested?

*Analysis Component*

**4.** Write a one-paragraph memorandum explaining which company you would invest your money in and why. (Limit your explanation to the information provided.)

**Problem 1-12B**[A]

Identifying risk and return

A3

All business decisions involve aspects of risk and return.

*Required*

Identify both the risk and the return in each of the following activities:

**1.** Stashing $1,000 cash under your mattress.

**2.** Placing a $500 bet on a horse running in the Kentucky Derby.

**3.** Investing $10,000 in Nike stock.

**4.** Investing $10,000 in U.S. Savings Bonds.

**Problem 1-13B**[B]

Describing organizational activities C5

Identify in outline format the three major business activities of an organization. For each of these activities, identify at least two specific transactions or events normally undertaken by the business's owners or its managers.

**Problem 1-14B**[B]

Describing organizational activities

C5

A start-up company often engages in the following activities during its first year of operations. Classify each of the following activities into one of the three major activities of an organization.

**A.** Financing     **B.** Investing     **C.** Operating

_____ **1.** Providing client services.     _____ **5.** Supervising workers.

_____ **2.** Obtaining a bank loan.     _____ **6.** Owner investing money in business.

_____ **3.** Purchasing machinery.     _____ **7.** Renting office space.

_____ **4.** Research for its products.     _____ **8.** Paying utilities expenses.

*This serial problem starts in this chapter and continues throughout most chapters of the book. It is most readily solved if you use the Working Papers that accompany this book (but working papers are not required).*

**SERIAL PROBLEM**

Business Solutions

C4   P1

**SP 1**    On October 1, 2011, Santana Rey launched a computer services company, **Business Solutions,** that is organized as a proprietorship and provides consulting services, computer system installations, and custom program development. Rey adopts the calendar year for reporting purposes and expects to prepare the company's first set of financial statements on December 31, 2011.

*Required*

Create a table like the one in Exhibit 1.9 using the following headings for columns: Cash; Accounts Receivable; Computer Supplies; Computer System; Office Equipment; Accounts Payable; S. Rey, Capital; S. Rey, Withdrawals; Revenues; and Expenses. Then use additions and subtractions within the table created to show the dollar effects for each of the following October transactions for Business Solutions on the individual items of the accounting equation. Show new balances after each transaction.

Oct.   1    S. Rey invested $45,000 cash, a $20,000 computer system, and $8,000 of office equipment in the company.

     3    The company purchased $1,420 of computer supplies on credit from Harris Office Products.

     6    The company billed Easy Leasing $4,800 for services performed in installing a new Web server.

     8    The company paid $1,420 cash for the computer supplies purchased from Harris Office Products on October 3.

   10    The company hired Lyn Addie as a part-time assistant for $125 per day, as needed.

   12    The company billed Easy Leasing another $1,400 for services performed.

   15    The company received $4,800 cash from Easy Leasing as partial payment toward its account.

   17    The company paid $805 cash to repair computer equipment damaged when moving it.

   20    The company paid $1,728 cash for advertisements published in the local newspaper.

   22    The company received $1,400 cash from Easy Leasing toward its account.

   28    The company billed IFM Company $5,208 for services performed.

   31    The company paid $875 cash for Lyn Addie's wages for seven days of work this month.

   31    S. Rey withdrew $3,600 cash from the company for personal use.

*Beyond the Numbers (BTN) is a special problem section aimed to refine communication, conceptual, analysis, and research skills. It includes many activities helpful in developing an active learning environment.*

## Beyond the Numbers

**BTN 1-1** Key financial figures for **Research In Motion**'s fiscal year ended February 27, 2010, follow.

| Key Figure | In Millions |
|---|---|
| Liabilities + Equity........ | $10,204 |
| Net income ............. | 2,457 |
| Revenues ............... | 14,953 |

**REPORTING IN ACTION**

A1 A2 A3

*RIM*

### Required

1. What is the total amount of assets invested in Research In Motion?
2. What is Research In Motion's return on assets? Its assets at February 28, 2009, equal $8,101 (in millions).
3. How much are total expenses for Research In Motion for the year ended February 27, 2010?
4. Does Research In Motion's return on assets seem satisfactory if competitors average an 18% return?

**Check** (2) 26.8%

### Fast Forward

5. Access Research In Motion's financial statements (Form 10-K) for fiscal years ending after February 27, 2010, from its Website (**RIM.com**) or from the SEC Website (**www.sec.gov**) and compute its return on assets for those fiscal years. Compare the February 27, 2010, fiscal year-end return on assets to any subsequent years' returns you are able to compute, and interpret the results.

---

**BTN 1-2** Key comparative figures ($ millions) for both **Research In Motion** and **Apple** follow.

| Key Figure | Research In Motion | Apple |
|---|---|---|
| Liabilities + Equity......... | $10,204 | $47,501 |
| Net income ............. | 2,457 | 8,235 |
| Revenues and sales ........ | 14,953 | 42,905 |

**COMPARATIVE ANALYSIS**

A1 A2 A3

*RIM*

Apple

### Required

1. What is the total amount of assets invested in (a) Research In Motion and (b) Apple?
2. What is the return on assets for (a) Research In Motion and (b) Apple? Research In Motion's beginning-year assets equal $8,101 (in millions) and Apple's beginning-year assets equal $36,171 (in millions).
3. How much are expenses for (a) Research In Motion and (b) Apple?
4. Is return on assets satisfactory for (a) Research In Motion and (b) Apple? (Assume competitors average an 18% return.)
5. What can you conclude about Research In Motion and Apple from these computations?

**Check** (2b) 19.7%

---

**BTN 1-3** Madison Thorne works in a public accounting firm and hopes to eventually be a partner. The management of Allnet Company invites Thorne to prepare a bid to audit Allnet's financial statements. In discussing the audit fee, Allnet's management suggests a fee range in which the amount depends on the reported profit of Allnet. The higher its profit, the higher will be the audit fee paid to Thorne's firm.

**ETHICS CHALLENGE**

C3 C4

### Required

1. Identify the parties potentially affected by this audit and the fee plan proposed.
2. What are the ethical factors in this situation? Explain.
3. Would you recommend that Thorne accept this audit fee arrangement? Why or why not?
4. Describe some ethical considerations guiding your recommendation.

## COMMUNICATING IN PRACTICE

A1  C2

**BTN 1-4**   Refer to this chapter's opening feature about **Facebook**.® Assume that Mark Zuckerberg desires to expand his online services to meet people's demands. He decides to meet with his banker to discuss a loan to allow Facebook to expand.

**Required**

1. Prepare a half-page report outlining the information you would request from Mark Zuckerberg if you were the loan officer.
2. Indicate whether the information you request and your loan decision are affected by the form of business organization for Facebook.

## TAKING IT TO THE NET

A2

**BTN 1-5**   Visit the EDGAR database at (**www.SEC.gov**). Access the Form 10-K report of **Rocky Mountain Chocolate Factory** (ticker RMCF) filed on May 26, 2009, covering its 2009 fiscal year.

**Required**

1. Item 6 of the 10-K report provides comparative financial highlights of RMCF for the years 2005–2009. How would you describe the revenue trend for RMCF over this five-year period?
2. Has RMCF been profitable (see net income) over this five-year period? Support your answer.

## TEAMWORK IN ACTION

C1

**BTN 1-6**   Teamwork is important in today's business world. Successful teams schedule convenient meetings, maintain regular communications, and cooperate with and support their members. This assignment aims to establish support/learning teams, initiate discussions, and set meeting times.

**Required**

1. Form teams and open a team discussion to determine a regular time and place for your team to meet between each scheduled class meeting. Notify your instructor via a memorandum or e-mail message as to when and where your team will hold regularly scheduled meetings.
2. Develop a list of telephone numbers and/or e-mail addresses of your teammates.

## ENTREPRENEURIAL DECISION

A1  P1

**BTN 1-7**   Refer to this chapter's opening feature about **Facebook**. Assume that Mark Zuckerberg decides to open a new Website devoted to social networking for accountants and those studying accounting. This new company will be called AccountBook.

**Required**

1. AccountBook obtains a $500,000 loan and Mark Zuckerberg contributes $250,000 of his own assets in exchange for common stock in the new company.
   a. What is the new company's total amount of liabilities plus equity?
   b. What is the new company's total amount of assets?

**Check**   (2) 10.7%

2. If the new company earns $80,000 in net income in the first year of operation, compute its return on asset (assume average assets equal $750,000). Assess its performance if competitors average a 10% return.

## HITTING THE ROAD

C2

**BTN 1-8**   You are to interview a local business owner. (This can be a friend or relative.) Opening lines of communication with members of the business community can provide personal benefits of business networking. If you do not know the owner, you should call ahead to introduce yourself and explain your position as a student and your assignment requirements. You should request a thirty minute appointment for a face-to-face or phone interview to discuss the form of organization and operations of the business. Be prepared to make a good impression.

**Required**

1. Identify and describe the main operating activities and the form of organization for this business.
2. Determine and explain why the owner(s) chose this particular form of organization.
3. Identify any special advantages and/or disadvantages the owner(s) experiences in operating with this form of business organization.

**BTN 1-9**   Nokia (www.Nokia.com) is a leading manufacturer of mobile devices and services, and it competes to some extent with both **Research In Motion** and **Apple**. Key financial figures for Nokia follow.

**GLOBAL DECISION**

A1  A2  A3

**NOKIA**

*RIM*

Apple

| Key Figure* | Euro (EUR) in Millions |
|---|---|
| Average assets . . . . . . . . . . . . . . . . . | 37,660 |
| Net income . . . . . . . . . . . . . . . . . . . | 260 |
| Revenue . . . . . . . . . . . . . . . . . . . . . | 40,984 |
| Return on assets . . . . . . . . . . . . . . | 0.7% |

\* Figures prepared in accordance with International Financial Reporting Standards.

**Required**

1. Identify any concerns you have in comparing Nokia's income and revenue figures to those of Research In Motion and Apple (in BTN 1-2) for purposes of making business decisions.

2. Identify any concerns you have in comparing Nokia's return on assets ratio to those of Research In Motion and Apple (computed for BTN 1-2) for purposes of making business decisions.

## ANSWERS TO MULTIPLE CHOICE QUIZ

1. c; $450,000 is the actual cost incurred.
2. b; revenue is recorded when earned.
3. d;

| Assets | = | Liabilities | + | Equity |
|---|---|---|---|---|
| +$100,000 | = | +35,000 | + | ? |

Change in equity = $100,000 − $35,000 = $65,000

4. a
5. a

# 2

# Analyzing and Recording Transactions

## A Look Back

Chapter 1 defined accounting and introduced financial statements. We described forms of organizations and identified users and uses of accounting. We defined the accounting equation and applied it to transaction analysis.

## A Look at This Chapter

This chapter focuses on the accounting process. We describe transactions and source documents, and we explain the analysis and recording of transactions. The accounting equation, T-account, general ledger, trial balance, and debits and credits are key tools in the accounting process.

## A Look Ahead

Chapter 3 extends our focus on processing information. We explain the importance of adjusting accounts and the procedures in preparing financial statements.

## Learning Objectives

**CAP**

### CONCEPTUAL

**C1** Explain the steps in processing transactions and the role of source documents. (p. 50)

**C2** Describe an account and its use in recording transactions. (p. 51)

**C3** Describe a ledger and a chart of accounts. (p. 54)

**C4** Define *debits* and *credits* and explain double-entry accounting. (p. 55)

### ANALYTICAL

**A1** Analyze the impact of transactions on accounts and financial statements. (p. 59)

**A2** Compute the debt ratio and describe its use in analyzing financial condition. (p. 69)

LP2

### PROCEDURAL

**P1** Record transactions in a journal and post entries to a ledger. (p. 56)

**P2** Prepare and explain the use of a trial balance. (p. 65)

**P3** Prepare financial statements from business transactions. (p. 66)

# Sole Sisters

*"Every way we can cut costs, we do!"*

—**SUSIE LEVITT** (on right)

NEW YORK—"High heels were killing our feet, but we didn't want to give them up because we aren't the tallest people out there," insists Susie Levitt, who stands no taller than 5'2". "So we came up with the idea of emergency footwear." Susie, along with Katie Shea, designed a stylish, foldable slip-on ballet flat with a pouch that is readily tucked into a handbag and pulled out when their feet cry for mercy. The empty pouch then expands into a tote bag to hold their "killer" heels for carrying home. Launched from their college apartment, Susie and Katie invested "less than $10,000" for the cost of their first order of 1,000 pairs, including Website design, to launch **CitySlips** (**www.cityslips.com**).

To pursue their business ambitions, Susie and Katie took business courses, including accounting. They learned and applied recordkeeping processes, transaction analysis, inventory accounting, and financial statement reporting. We were careful to get a handle on our financial situation, says Katie. Today, the two are running a profitable business and have a reliable accounting system to help them make good business decisions.

We had to account for product costs, design expenses, supplier payments, patent fees, and other expenses, says Susie. At the same time, the two have grown sales and expanded their product line. "It was all done online," says Susie. "We became nocturnal!"

The two insist that it is crucial to track and account for all revenues and expenses, and what is invested in the business. They maintain that success requires proper accounting for and analysis of the financial side. Susie also suggests that young entrepreneurs "network with your professors and other staff members. They have years of experience and can often help you, or introduce you to people who can help you, with your business."

The bigger message of our company, says Susie, is promoting comfort and confidence for women. Adds Katie, "Regardless of what your business is, the story of starting while in college, differentiates you from the beginning!"

[Sources: *CitySlips Website,* January 2011; *Entrepreneur,* December 2009; *Examiner.com,* December 2009; *CNN.com,* August 2009; *Daily News,* May 2009.]

Financial statements report on the financial performance and condition of an organization. Knowledge of their preparation, organization, and analysis is important. A main goal of this chapter is to illustrate how transactions are recorded, how they are reflected in financial statements, and how they impact analysis of financial statements. Debits and credits are introduced and identified as a tool in helping analyze and process transactions.

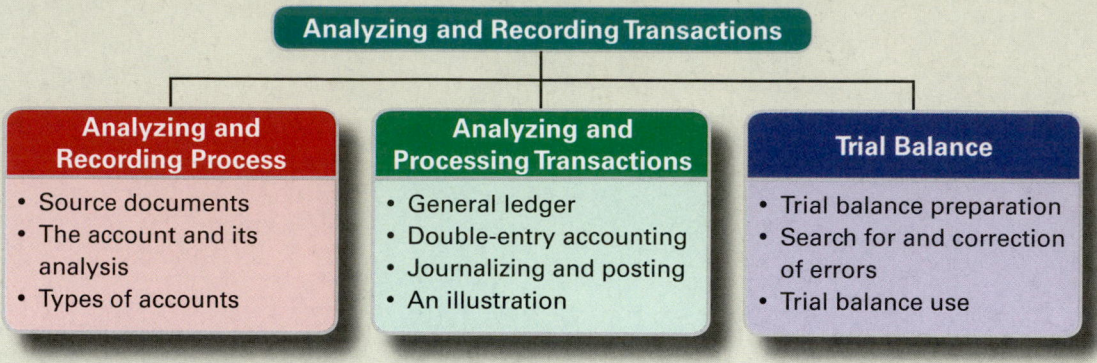

**Analyzing and Recording Transactions**

| **Analyzing and Recording Process** | **Analyzing and Processing Transactions** | **Trial Balance** |
|---|---|---|
| • Source documents<br>• The account and its analysis<br>• Types of accounts | • General ledger<br>• Double-entry accounting<br>• Journalizing and posting<br>• An illustration | • Trial balance preparation<br>• Search for and correction of errors<br>• Trial balance use |

# ANALYZING AND RECORDING PROCESS

The accounting process identifies business transactions and events, analyzes and records their effects, and summarizes and presents information in reports and financial statements. These reports and statements are used for making investing, lending, and other business decisions. The steps in the accounting process that focus on *analyzing and recording* transactions and events are shown in Exhibit 2.1.

**EXHIBIT 2.1**

The Analyzing and Recording Process

Analyze each transaction and event from source documents

Record relevant transactions and events in a journal

Post journal information to ledger accounts

Prepare and analyze the trial balance

**C1** Explain the steps in processing transactions and the role of source documents.

Business transactions and events are the starting points. Relying on source documents, the transactions and events are analyzed using the accounting equation to understand how they affect company performance and financial position. These effects are recorded in accounting records, informally referred to as the *accounting books,* or simply the *books.* Additional steps such as posting and then preparing a trial balance help summarize and classify the effects of transactions and events. Ultimately, the accounting process provides information in useful reports or financial statements to decision makers.

## Source Documents

**Source documents** identify and describe transactions and events entering the accounting process. They are the sources of accounting information and can be in either hard copy or electronic form. Examples are sales tickets, checks, purchase orders, bills from suppliers, employee earnings records, and bank statements. To illustrate, when an item is purchased on credit, the seller usually prepares at least two copies of a sales invoice. One copy is given to the buyer. Another copy, often sent electronically, results in an entry in the seller's information system to record the sale. Sellers use invoices for recording sales and for control; buyers use them for recording purchases and for monitoring purchasing activity. Many cash registers record information for each sale on a tape or electronic file locked inside the register. This record can be used as a source document for recording sales in the accounting records. Source documents, especially if obtained from outside the organization, provide objective and reliable evidence about transactions and events and their amounts.

**Point:** To ensure that all sales are rung up on the register, most sellers require customers to have their receipts to exchange or return purchased items.

**Decision Ethics**                                      Answer — p. 74

**Cashier**   Your manager requires that you, as cashier, immediately enter each sale. Recently, lunch hour traffic has increased and the assistant manager asks you to avoid delays by taking customers' cash and making change without entering sales. The assistant manager says she will add up cash and enter sales after lunch. She says that, in this way, the register will always match the cash amount when the manager arrives at three o'clock. What do you do? ∎

## The Account and Its Analysis

An **account** is a record of increases and decreases in a specific asset, liability, equity, revenue, or expense item. Information from an account is analyzed, summarized, and presented in reports and financial statements. The **general ledger,** or simply **ledger,** is a record containing all accounts used by a company. The ledger is often in electronic form. While most companies' ledgers contain similar accounts, a company often uses one or more unique accounts because of its type of operations. As shown in Exhibit 2.2, accounts are classified into three general categories based on the accounting equation: asset, liability, or equity.

**C2** Describe an account and its use in recording transactions.

 =  +

**Asset Accounts**     **Liability Accounts**     **Equity Accounts**

**EXHIBIT 2.2**

Accounts Organized by the Accounting Equation

**Asset Accounts**   Assets are resources owned or controlled by a company and that have expected future benefits. Most accounting systems include (at a minimum) separate accounts for the assets described here.

A *Cash* account reflects a company's cash balance. All increases and decreases in cash are recorded in the Cash account. It includes money and any medium of exchange that a bank accepts for deposit (coins, checks, money orders, and checking account balances).

*Accounts receivable* are held by a seller and refer to promises of payment from customers to sellers. These transactions are often called *credit sales* or *sales on account* (or *on credit*). Accounts receivable are increased by credit sales and are decreased by customer payments. A company needs a separate record for each customer, but for now, we use the simpler practice of recording all increases and decreases in receivables in a single account called Accounts Receivable.

**Point:** Customers and others who owe a company are called its **debtors.**

A *note receivable,* or promissory note, is a written promise of another entity to pay a definite sum of money on a specified future date to the holder of the note. A company holding a promissory note signed by another entity has an asset that is recorded in a Note (or Notes) Receivable account.

*Prepaid accounts* (also called *prepaid expenses*) are assets that represent prepayments of future expenses (*not* current expenses). When the expenses are later incurred, the amounts in prepaid accounts are transferred to expense accounts. Common examples of prepaid accounts include prepaid insurance, prepaid rent, and prepaid services (such as club memberships). Prepaid accounts expire with the passage of time (such as with rent) or through use (such as with prepaid meal tickets). When financial statements are prepared, prepaid accounts are adjusted so that (1) all expired and used prepaid accounts are recorded as regular expenses and (2) all unexpired and unused prepaid accounts are recorded as assets (reflecting future use in

**Point:** A college parking fee is a prepaid account from the student's standpoint. At the beginning of the term, it represents an asset that entitles a student to park on or near campus. The benefits of the parking fee expire as the term progresses. At term-end, prepaid parking (asset) equals zero as it has been entirely recorded as parking expense.

**Point:** Prepaid accounts that apply to current and future periods are assets. These assets are adjusted at the end of each period to reflect only those amounts that have not yet expired, and to record as expenses those amounts that have expired.

future periods). To illustrate, when an insurance fee, called a *premium,* is paid in advance, the cost is typically recorded in the asset account Prepaid Insurance. Over time, the expiring portion of the insurance cost is removed from this asset account and reported in expenses on the income statement. Any unexpired portion remains in Prepaid Insurance and is reported on the balance sheet as an asset. (An exception exists for prepaid accounts that will expire or be used before the end of the current accounting period when financial statements are prepared. In this case, the prepayments *can* be recorded immediately as expenses.)

*Supplies* are assets until they are used. When they are used up, their costs are reported as expenses. The costs of unused supplies are recorded in a Supplies asset account. Supplies are often grouped by purpose—for example, office supplies and store supplies. *Office supplies* include stationery, paper, toner, and pens. *Store supplies* include packaging materials, plastic and paper bags, gift boxes and cartons, and cleaning materials. The costs of these unused supplies can be recorded in an Office Supplies or a Store Supplies asset account. When supplies are used, their costs are transferred from the asset accounts to expense accounts.

**Point:** Some assets are described as *intangible* because they do not have physical existence or their benefits are highly uncertain. A recent balance sheet for **Coca-Cola Company** shows nearly $1 billion in intangible assets.

*Equipment* is an asset. When equipment is used and gets worn down, its cost is gradually reported as an expense (called depreciation). Equipment is often grouped by its purpose—for example, office equipment and store equipment. *Office equipment* includes computers, printers, desks, chairs, and shelves. Costs incurred for these items are recorded in an Office Equipment asset account. The Store Equipment account includes the costs of assets used in a store, such as counters, showcases, ladders, hoists, and cash registers.

*Buildings* such as stores, offices, warehouses, and factories are assets because they provide expected future benefits to those who control or own them. Their costs are recorded in a Buildings asset account. When several buildings are owned, separate accounts are sometimes kept for each of them.

The cost of *land* owned by a business is recorded in a Land account. The cost of buildings located on the land is separately recorded in one or more building accounts.

## Decision Insight

**Women Entrepreneurs**   The Center for Women's Business Research reports that women-owned businesses, such as **CitySlips**, are growing and that they:

- Total approximately 11 million and employ nearly 20 million workers.
- Generate $2.5 trillion in annual sales and tend to embrace technology.
- Are philanthropic—70% of owners volunteer at least once per month.
- Are more likely funded by individual investors (73%) than venture firms (15%). ∎

**Liability Accounts**   Liabilities are claims (by creditors) against assets, which means they are obligations to transfer assets or provide products or services to others. **Creditors** are individuals and organizations that have rights to receive payments from a company. If a company fails to pay its obligations, the law gives creditors a right to force the sale of that company's assets to obtain the money to meet creditors' claims. When assets are sold under these conditions, creditors are paid first, but only up to the amount of their claims. Any remaining money, the residual, goes to the owners of the company. Creditors often use a balance sheet to help decide whether to loan money to a company. A loan is less risky if the borrower's liabilities are small in comparison to assets because this means there are more resources than claims on resources. Common liability accounts are described here.

**Point:** Accounts payable are also called *trade payables.*

*Accounts payable* refer to oral or implied promises to pay later, which usually arise from purchases of merchandise. Payables can also arise from purchases of supplies, equipment, and services. Accounting systems keep separate records about each creditor. We describe these individual records in Chapter 5.

A *note payable* refers to a formal promise, usually denoted by the signing of a promissory note, to pay a future amount. It is recorded in either a short-term Note Payable account or a long-term Note Payable account, depending on when it must be repaid. We explain details of short- and long-term classification in Chapter 3.

**Unearned revenue** refers to a liability that is settled in the future when a company delivers its products or services. When customers pay in advance for products or services (before revenue is earned), the revenue recognition principle requires that the seller consider this payment as unearned revenue. Examples of unearned revenue include magazine subscriptions collected in advance by a publisher, sales of gift certificates by stores, and season ticket sales by sports teams. The seller would record these in liability accounts such as Unearned Subscriptions, Unearned Store Sales, and Unearned Ticket Revenue. When products and services are later delivered, the earned portion of the unearned revenue is transferred to revenue accounts such as Subscription Fees, Store Sales, and Ticket Sales.[1]

*Accrued liabilities* are amounts owed that are not yet paid. Examples are wages payable, taxes payable, and interest payable. These are often recorded in separate liability accounts by the same title. If they are not large in amount, one or more ledger accounts can be added and reported as a single amount on the balance sheet. (Financial statements often have amounts reported that are a summation of several ledger accounts.)

**Point:** If a subscription is canceled, the publisher is expected to refund the unused portion to the subscriber.

### Decision Insight

**Revenue Spread** The **New Orleans Saints** have *Unearned Revenues* of about $60 million in advance ticket sales. When the team plays its home games, it settles this liability to its ticket holders and then transfers the amount earned to *Ticket Revenues*. ■

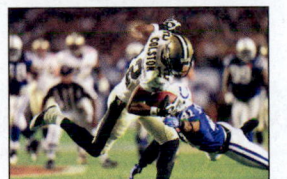

**Equity Accounts** The owner's claim on a company's assets is called *equity* or *owner's equity*. Equity is the owner's *residual interest* in the assets of a business after deducting liabilities. Equity is impacted by four types of accounts: owner's capital, owner's withdrawals, revenues, and expenses. We show this visually in Exhibit 2.3 by expanding the accounting equation.

**Point:** Equity is also called *net assets*.

**EXHIBIT 2.3**

Expanded Accounting Equation

When an owner invests in a company, the invested amount is recorded in an account titled Owner, Capital (where the owner's name is inserted in place of "owner"). The account titled *C. Taylor, Capital* is used for FastForward. Any further owner investments are recorded in this account. When an owner withdraws assets for personal use it decreases both company assets and total equity. Withdrawals are not expenses of the business; they are simply the opposite of owner investments. The Owner, Withdrawals account is used to record asset distributions to the owner. The account titled *C. Taylor, Withdrawals* is used for FastForward. (Owners of proprietorships cannot receive company salaries because they are not legally separate from their companies; and they cannot enter into company contracts with themselves.)

Revenues and expenses also impact equity. Examples of revenue accounts are Sales, Commissions Earned, Professional Fees Earned, Rent Revenue, and Interest Revenue. *Revenues increase equity* and result from products and services provided to customers. Examples of expense accounts are Advertising Expense, Store Supplies Expense, Office Salaries Expense, Office Supplies Expense, Rent Expense, Utilities Expense, and Insurance Expense. *Expenses decrease equity* and result from assets and services used in a company's operations. The variety of revenues and expenses can be seen by looking at the *chart of accounts* that follows the index at the

**Point:** The Owner's Withdrawals account is a *contra equity* account because it reduces the normal balance of equity.

**Point:** The withdrawal of assets by the owners of a corporation is called a *dividend*.

---

[1] In practice, account titles vary. As one example, Subscription Fees is sometimes called Subscription Fees Revenue, Subscription Fees Earned, or Earned Subscription Fees. As another example, Rent Earned is sometimes called Rent Revenue, Rental Revenue, or Earned Rent Revenue. We must use good judgment when reading financial statements because titles can differ even within the same industry. For example, product sales are called *revenue* at **Research In Motion**, but *net sales* at **Apple**. Generally, the term *revenues* or *fees* is more commonly used with service businesses, and *net sales* or *sales* with product businesses.

back of this book. (Different companies sometimes use different account titles than those in this book's chart of accounts. For example, some might use Interest Revenue instead of Interest Earned, or Rental Expense instead of Rent Expense. It is important only that an account title describe the item it represents.)

### Decision Insight

**Sporting Accounts**  The **Los Angeles Lakers** and the other NBA teams have the following major revenue and expense accounts:

| Revenues | Expenses |
|---|---|
| Basketball ticket sales | Team salaries |
| TV & radio broadcast fees | Game costs |
| Advertising revenues | NBA franchise costs |
| Basketball playoff receipts | Promotional costs ■ |

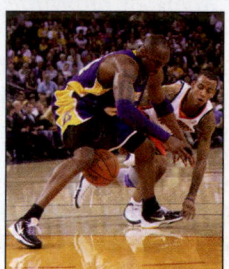

# ANALYZING AND PROCESSING TRANSACTIONS

This section explains several tools and processes that comprise an accounting system. These include a ledger, T-account, debits and credits, double-entry accounting, journalizing, and posting.

## Ledger and Chart of Accounts

**C3**  Describe a ledger and a chart of accounts.

The collection of all accounts and their balances for an information system is called a *ledger* (or *general ledger*). If accounts are in files on a hard drive, the sum of those files is the ledger. If the accounts are pages in a file, that file is the ledger. A company's size and diversity of operations affect the number of accounts needed. A small company can get by with as few as 20 or 30 accounts; a large company can require several thousand. The **chart of accounts** is a list of all ledger accounts and includes an identification number assigned to each account. A small business might use the following numbering system for its accounts:

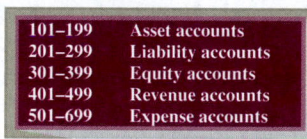

| | |
|---|---|
| 101–199 | Asset accounts |
| 201–299 | Liability accounts |
| 301–399 | Equity accounts |
| 401–499 | Revenue accounts |
| 501–699 | Expense accounts |

These numbers provide a three-digit code that is useful in recordkeeping. In this case, the first digit assigned to asset accounts is a 1, the first digit assigned to liability accounts is a 2, and so on. The second and third digits relate to the accounts' subcategories. Exhibit 2.4 shows a partial chart of accounts for FastForward, the focus company of Chapter 1. (Please review the more complete chart of accounts that follows the index at the back of this book.)

**EXHIBIT 2.4**

Partial Chart of Accounts for FastForward

| Acct. No. | Account Name | Acct. No. | Account Name | Acct. No. | Account Name |
|---|---|---|---|---|---|
| 101 | Cash | 236 | Unearned consulting revenue | 622 | Salaries expense |
| 106 | Accounts receivable | | | 637 | Insurance expense |
| 126 | Supplies | 301 | C. Taylor, Capital | 640 | Rent expense |
| 128 | Prepaid insurance | 302 | C. Taylor, Withdrawals | 652 | Supplies expense |
| 167 | Equipment | 403 | Consulting revenue | 690 | Utilities expense |
| 201 | Accounts payable | 406 | Rental revenue | | |

## Debits and Credits

A **T-account** represents a ledger account and is a tool used to understand the effects of one or more transactions. Its name comes from its shape like the letter **T**. The layout of a T-account, shown in Exhibit 2.5, is (1) the account title on top, (2) a left, or debit side, and (3) a right, or credit, side.

The left side of an account is called the **debit** side, often abbreviated *Dr*. The right side is called the **credit** side, abbreviated *Cr*.[2] To enter amounts on the left side of an account is to *debit* the account. To enter amounts on the right side is to *credit* the account. Do not make the error of thinking that the terms *debit* and *credit* mean increase or decrease. Whether a debit or a credit is an increase or decrease depends on the account. For an account where a debit is an increase, the credit is a decrease; for an account where a debit is a decrease, the credit is an increase. The difference between total debits and total credits for an account, including any beginning balance, is the **account balance.** When the sum of debits exceeds the sum of credits, the account has a *debit balance.* It has a *credit balance* when the sum of credits exceeds the sum of debits. When the sum of debits equals the sum of credits, the account has a *zero balance.*

| Account Title | |
|---|---|
| (Left side) | (Right side) |
| **Debit** | **Credit** |

**EXHIBIT 2.5**

The T-Account

**Point:** Think of *debit* and *credit* as accounting directions for left and right.

## Double-Entry Accounting

**Double-entry accounting** requires that for each transaction:

- At least two accounts are involved, with at least one debit and one credit.
- The total amount debited must equal the total amount credited.
- The accounting equation must not be violated.

This means the sum of the debits for all entries must equal the sum of the credits for all entries, and the sum of debit account balances in the ledger must equal the sum of credit account balances.

The system for recording debits and credits follows from the usual accounting equation—see Exhibit 2.6. Two points are important here. First, like any simple mathematical relation, net increases or decreases on one side have equal net effects on the other side. For example, a net increase in assets must be accompanied by an identical net increase on the liabilities and equity

"Total debits equal total credits for each entry."

**EXHIBIT 2.6**

Debits and Credits in the Accounting Equation

side. Recall that some transactions affect only one side of the equation, meaning that two or more accounts on one side are affected, but their net effect on this one side is zero. Second, the left side is the *normal balance* side for assets, and the right side is the *normal balance* side for liabilities and equity. This matches their layout in the accounting equation where assets are on the left side of this equation, and liabilities and equity are on the right.

Recall that equity increases from revenues and owner investments and it decreases from expenses and owner withdrawals. These important equity relations are conveyed by expanding the accounting equation to include debits and credits in double-entry form as shown in Exhibit 2.7.

Increases (credits) to owner's capital and revenues *increase* equity; increases (debits) to withdrawals and expenses *decrease* equity. The normal balance of each account (asset, liability, capital, withdrawals, revenue, or expense) refers to the left or right (debit or credit) side where

**Point:** Debits and credits do not mean favorable or unfavorable. A debit to an asset increases it, as does a debit to an expense. A credit to a liability increases it, as does a credit to a revenue.

---

[2] These abbreviations are remnants of 18th-century English recordkeeping practices where the terms *debitor* and *creditor* were used instead of *debit* and *credit*. The abbreviations use the first and last letters of these terms, just as we still do for Saint (St.) and Doctor (Dr.).

**C4** Define *debits* and *credits* and explain double-entry accounting.

**EXHIBIT 2.7**

Debit and Credit Effects for Component Accounts

*increases* are recorded. Understanding these diagrams and rules is required to prepare, analyze, and interpret financial statements.

The T-account for FastForward's Cash account, reflecting its first 11 transactions (from Exhibit 1.9), is shown in Exhibit 2.8. The total increases in its Cash account are $36,100, the total decreases are $31,300, and the account's debit balance is $4,800. (We illustrate use of T-accounts later in this chapter.)

**EXHIBIT 2.8**

Computing the Balance for a T-Account

| Cash | | | |
|---|---|---|---|
| Receive investment by owner | 30,000 | Purchase of supplies | 2,500 |
| Consulting services revenue earned | 4,200 | Purchase of equipment | 26,000 |
| Collection of account receivable | 1,900 | Payment of rent | 1,000 |
| | | Payment of salary | 700 |
| | | Payment of account payable | 900 |
| | | Withdrawal by owner | 200 |
| Balance | 4,800 | | |

**Point:** The ending balance is on the side with the larger dollar amount. Also, a plus (+) and minus (−) are not used in a T-account.

**Quick Check**                    Answers — p. 75

1. Identify examples of accounting source documents.
2. Explain the importance of source documents.
3. Identify each of the following as either an asset, a liability, or equity: (*a*) Prepaid Rent, (*b*) Unearned Fees, (*c*) Building, (*d*) Wages Payable, and (*e*) Office Supplies.
4. What is an account? What is a ledger?
5. What determines the number and types of accounts a company uses?
6. Does *debit* always mean increase and *credit* always mean decrease?
7. Describe a chart of accounts.

## Journalizing and Posting Transactions

**P1** Record transactions in a journal and post entries to a ledger.

Processing transactions is a crucial part of accounting. The four usual steps of this process are depicted in Exhibit 2.9. Steps 1 and 2—involving transaction analysis and the accounting equation—were introduced in prior sections. This section extends that discussion and focuses on steps 3 and 4 of the accounting process. Step 3 is to record each transaction chronologically in a journal. A **journal** gives a complete record of each transaction in one place. It also shows debits and credits for each transaction. The process of recording transactions in a journal is called **journalizing.** Step 4 is to transfer (or *post*) entries from the journal to the ledger. The process of transferring journal entry information to the ledger is called **posting.**

**Journalizing Transactions**    The process of journalizing transactions requires an understanding of a journal. While companies can use various journals, every company uses a **general journal.** It can be used to record any transaction and includes the following information about each transaction: ⓐ date of transaction, ⓑ titles of affected accounts, ⓒ dollar amount of each

**Step 1:** Identify transactions and source documents.

**Step 2:** Analyze transactions using the accounting equation.

**Step 3:** Record journal entry.

**Step 4:** Post entry to ledger.

**EXHIBIT 2.9**

Steps in Processing Transactions

debit and credit, and ⓓ explanation of the transaction. Exhibit 2.10 shows how the first two transactions of FastForward are recorded in a general journal. This process is similar for manual and computerized systems. Computerized journals are often designed to look like a manual journal page, and also include error-checking routines that ensure debits equal credits for each entry. Shortcuts allow recordkeepers to select account names and numbers from pull-down menus.

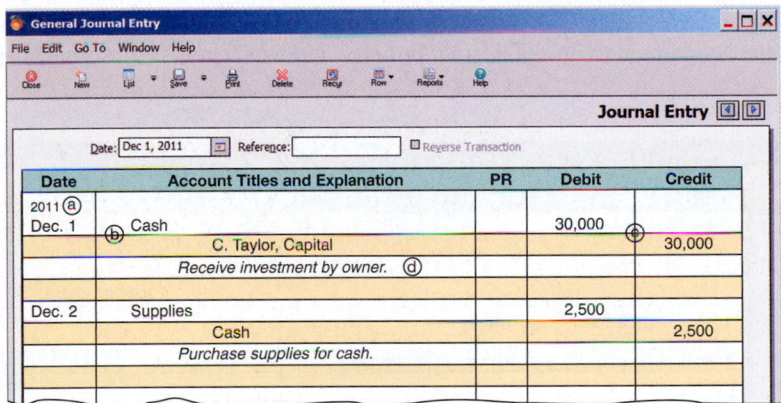

**EXHIBIT 2.10**

Partial General Journal for FastForward

To record entries in a general journal, apply these steps; refer to the entries in Exhibit 2.10 when reviewing these steps. (1) Date the transaction: Enter the year at the top of the first column and the month and day on the first line of each journal entry. (2) Enter titles of accounts debited and then enter amounts in the Debit column on the same line. Account titles are taken from the chart of accounts and are aligned with the left margin of the Account Titles and Explanation column. (3) Enter titles of accounts credited and then enter amounts in the Credit column on the same line. Account titles are from the chart of accounts and are indented from the left margin of the Account Titles and Explanation column to distinguish them from debited accounts. (4) Enter a brief explanation of the transaction on the line below the entry (it often references a source document). This explanation is indented about half as far as the credited account titles to avoid confusing it with accounts, and it is italicized.

**Point:** There are no exact rules for writing journal entry explanations. An explanation should be short yet describe why an entry is made.

 **IFRS**

IFRS requires that companies report the following four basic financial statements with explanatory notes:

- Balance sheet
- Income statement
- Statement of changes in equity (or statement of recognized revenue and expense)
- Statement of cash flows

IFRS does not prescribe specific formats; and comparative information is required for the preceding period only. ■

A blank line is left between each journal entry for clarity. When a transaction is first recorded, the **posting reference (PR) column** is left blank (in a manual system). Later, when posting entries to the ledger, the identification numbers of the individual ledger accounts are entered in the PR column.

**Balance Column Account**   T-accounts are simple and direct means to show how the accounting process works. However, actual accounting systems need more structure and therefore use **balance column accounts,** such as that in Exhibit 2.11.

**EXHIBIT 2.11**

Cash Account in Balance Column Format

| Cash | | | | | | Account No. 101 |
|------|------|------|------|------|------|------|
| Date | Explanation | PR | Debit | Credit | | Balance |
| 2011 | | | | | | |
| Dec.  1 | | G1 | 30,000 | | | 30,000 |
| Dec.  2 | | G1 | | 2,500 | | 27,500 |
| Dec.  3 | | G1 | | 26,000 | | 1,500 |
| Dec. 10 | | G1 | 4,200 | | | 5,700 |

The balance column account format is similar to a T-account in having columns for debits and credits. It is different in including transaction date and explanation columns. It also has a column with the balance of the account after each entry is recorded. To illustrate, FastForward's Cash account in Exhibit 2.11 is debited on December 1 for the $30,000 owner investment, yielding a $30,000 debit balance. The account is credited on December 2 for $2,500, yielding a $27,500 debit balance. On December 3, it is credited again, this time for $26,000, and its debit balance is reduced to $1,500. The Cash account is debited for $4,200 on December 10, and its debit balance increases to $5,700; and so on.

**Point:** Explanations are typically included in ledger accounts only for unusual transactions or events.

The heading of the Balance column does not show whether it is a debit or credit balance. Instead, an account is assumed to have a *normal balance*. Unusual events can sometimes temporarily

**EXHIBIT 2.12**

Posting an Entry to the Ledger

**Point:** The fundamental concepts of a manual (pencil-and-paper) system are identical to those of a computerized information system.

Key:   ① Identify debit account in Ledger: enter date, journal page, amount, and balance.
② Enter the debit account number from the Ledger in the PR column of the journal.
③ Identify credit account in Ledger: enter date, journal page, amount, and balance.
④ Enter the credit account number from the Ledger in the PR column of the journal.

give an account an abnormal balance. An *abnormal balance* refers to a balance on the side where decreases are recorded. For example, a customer might mistakenly overpay a bill. This gives that customer's account receivable an abnormal (credit) balance. An abnormal balance is often identified by circling it or by entering it in red or some other unusual color. A zero balance for an account is usually shown by writing zeros or a dash in the Balance column to avoid confusion between a zero balance and one omitted in error.

**Posting Journal Entries**  Step 4 of processing transactions is to post journal entries to ledger accounts (see Exhibit 2.9). To ensure that the ledger is up-to-date, entries are posted as soon as possible. This might be daily, weekly, or when time permits. All entries must be posted to the ledger before financial statements are prepared to ensure that account balances are up-to-date. When entries are posted to the ledger, the debits in journal entries are transferred into ledger accounts as debits, and credits are transferred into ledger accounts as credits. Exhibit 2.12 shows the *four steps to post a journal entry.* First, identify the ledger account that is debited in the entry; then, in the ledger, enter the entry date, the journal and page in its PR column, the debit amount, and the new balance of the ledger account. (The letter *G* shows it came from the General Journal.) Second, enter the ledger account number in the PR column of the journal. Steps 3 and 4 repeat the first two steps for credit entries and amounts. The posting process creates a link between the ledger and the journal entry. This link is a useful cross-reference for tracing an amount from one record to another.

> **Point:** Computerized systems often provide a code beside a balance such as *dr.* or *cr.* to identify its balance. Posting is automatic and immediate with accounting software.

> **Point:** A journal is often referred to as the *book of original entry.* The ledger is referred to as the *book of final entry* because financial statements are prepared from it.

## Analyzing Transactions—An Illustration

We return to the activities of FastForward to show how double-entry accounting is useful in analyzing and processing transactions. Analysis of each transaction follows the four steps of Exhibit 2.9.

**Step 1** Identify the transaction and any source documents.
**Step 2** Analyze the transaction using the accounting equation.
**Step 3** Record the transaction in journal entry form applying double-entry accounting.
**Step 4** Post the entry (for simplicity, we use T-accounts to represent ledger accounts).

Study each transaction thoroughly before proceeding to the next. The first 11 transactions are from Chapter 1, and we analyze five additional December transactions of FastForward (numbered 12 through 16) that were omitted earlier.

> **A1** Analyze the impact of transactions on accounts and financial statements.

### 1. Receive investment by Owner

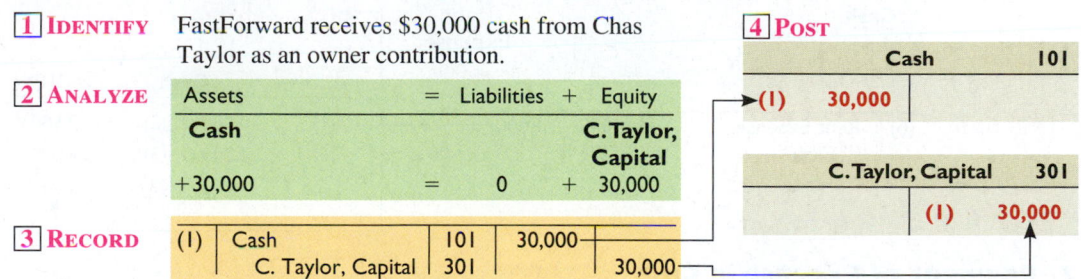

**1 IDENTIFY**  FastForward receives $30,000 cash from Chas Taylor as an owner contribution.

**2 ANALYZE**

| Assets | = | Liabilities | + | Equity |
|---|---|---|---|---|
| **Cash** | | | | **C. Taylor, Capital** |
| +30,000 | = | 0 | + | 30,000 |

**3 RECORD**

| (1) | Cash | 101 | 30,000 | |
| | C. Taylor, Capital | 301 | | 30,000 |

**4 POST**

| Cash | | 101 |
|---|---|---|
| (1)  30,000 | | |

| C. Taylor, Capital | | 301 |
|---|---|---|
| | (1) | 30,000 |

### 2. Purchase Supplies for Cash

**1 IDENTIFY**  FastForward pays $2,500 cash for supplies.

**2 ANALYZE**

| Assets | | = | Liabilities | + | Equity |
|---|---|---|---|---|---|
| **Cash** | **Supplies** | | | | |
| −2,500 | +2,500 | = | 0 | + | 0 |

Changes the composition of assets but not the total.

**3 RECORD**

| (2) | Supplies | 126 | 2,500 | |
| | Cash | 101 | | 2,500 |

**4 POST**

| Supplies | | 126 |
|---|---|---|
| (2)  2,500 | | |

| Cash | | 101 |
|---|---|---|
| (1)  30,000 | (2) | 2,500 |

*FASTForward*

### 3. Purchase Equipment for Cash

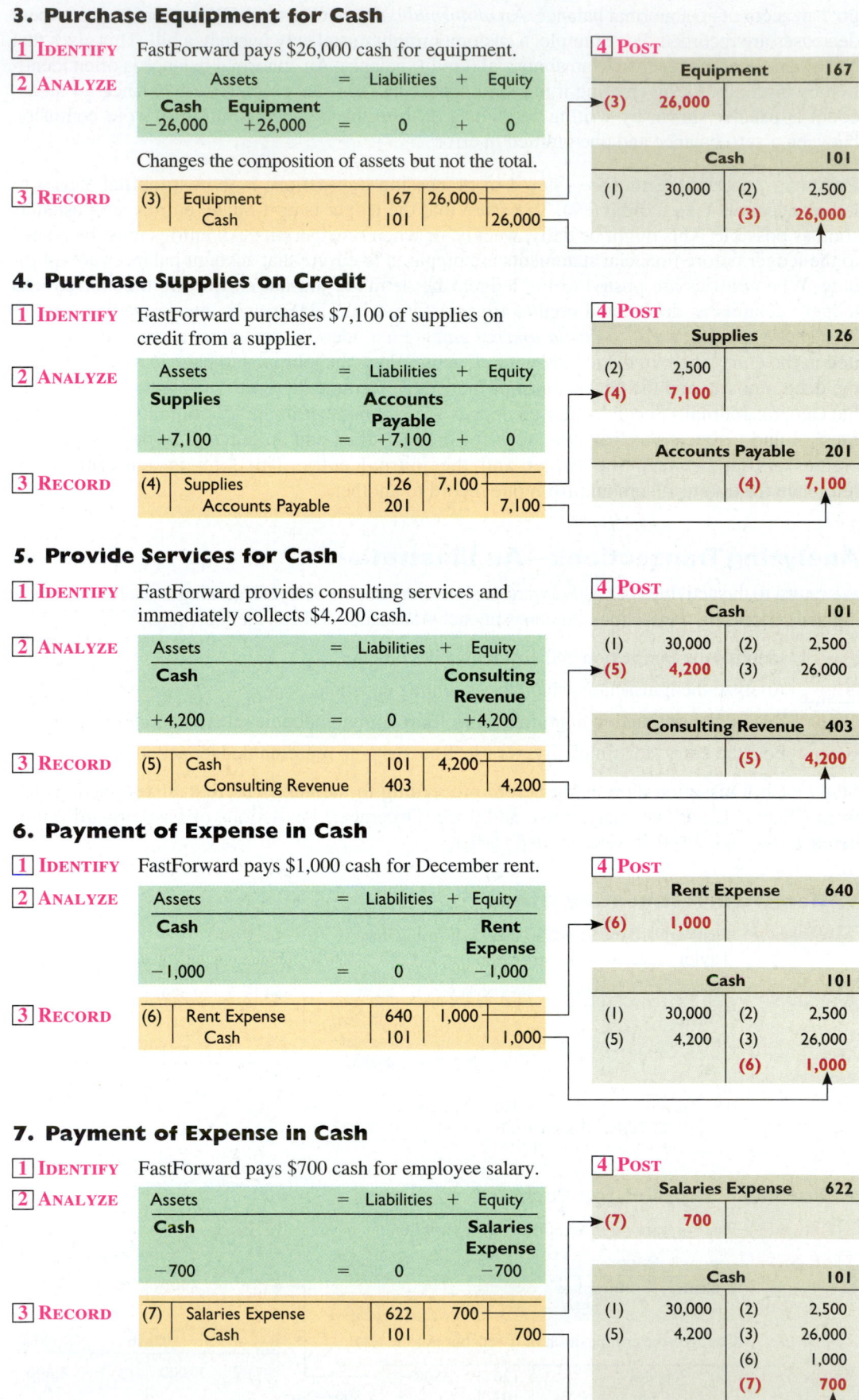

**1 IDENTIFY**   FastForward pays $26,000 cash for equipment.

**2 ANALYZE**

| Assets | | = | Liabilities | + | Equity |
|---|---|---|---|---|---|
| **Cash** | **Equipment** | | | | |
| −26,000 | +26,000 | = | 0 | + | 0 |

Changes the composition of assets but not the total.

**3 RECORD**

| (3) | Equipment | 167 | 26,000 | |
|---|---|---|---|---|
| | Cash | 101 | | 26,000 |

**4 POST**

| Equipment | | 167 |
|---|---|---|
| (3) | 26,000 | |

| Cash | | | 101 |
|---|---|---|---|
| (1) | 30,000 | (2) | 2,500 |
| | | (3) | 26,000 |

### 4. Purchase Supplies on Credit

**1 IDENTIFY**   FastForward purchases $7,100 of supplies on credit from a supplier.

**2 ANALYZE**

| Assets | = | Liabilities | + | Equity |
|---|---|---|---|---|
| **Supplies** | | **Accounts Payable** | | |
| +7,100 | = | +7,100 | + | 0 |

**3 RECORD**

| (4) | Supplies | 126 | 7,100 | |
|---|---|---|---|---|
| | Accounts Payable | 201 | | 7,100 |

**4 POST**

| Supplies | | 126 |
|---|---|---|
| (2) | 2,500 | |
| (4) | 7,100 | |

| Accounts Payable | | 201 |
|---|---|---|
| | (4) | 7,100 |

### 5. Provide Services for Cash

**1 IDENTIFY**   FastForward provides consulting services and immediately collects $4,200 cash.

**2 ANALYZE**

| Assets | = | Liabilities | + | Equity |
|---|---|---|---|---|
| **Cash** | | | | **Consulting Revenue** |
| +4,200 | = | 0 | | +4,200 |

**3 RECORD**

| (5) | Cash | 101 | 4,200 | |
|---|---|---|---|---|
| | Consulting Revenue | 403 | | 4,200 |

**4 POST**

| Cash | | | 101 |
|---|---|---|---|
| (1) | 30,000 | (2) | 2,500 |
| (5) | 4,200 | (3) | 26,000 |

| Consulting Revenue | | 403 |
|---|---|---|
| | (5) | 4,200 |

### 6. Payment of Expense in Cash

**1 IDENTIFY**   FastForward pays $1,000 cash for December rent.

**2 ANALYZE**

| Assets | = | Liabilities | + | Equity |
|---|---|---|---|---|
| **Cash** | | | | **Rent Expense** |
| −1,000 | = | 0 | | −1,000 |

**3 RECORD**

| (6) | Rent Expense | 640 | 1,000 | |
|---|---|---|---|---|
| | Cash | 101 | | 1,000 |

**4 POST**

| Rent Expense | | 640 |
|---|---|---|
| (6) | 1,000 | |

| Cash | | | 101 |
|---|---|---|---|
| (1) | 30,000 | (2) | 2,500 |
| (5) | 4,200 | (3) | 26,000 |
| | | (6) | 1,000 |

### 7. Payment of Expense in Cash

**Point:** *Salary* usually refers to compensation for an employee who receives a fixed amount for a given time period, whereas *wages* usually refers to compensation based on time worked.

**1 IDENTIFY**   FastForward pays $700 cash for employee salary.

**2 ANALYZE**

| Assets | = | Liabilities | + | Equity |
|---|---|---|---|---|
| **Cash** | | | | **Salaries Expense** |
| −700 | = | 0 | | −700 |

**3 RECORD**

| (7) | Salaries Expense | 622 | 700 | |
|---|---|---|---|---|
| | Cash | 101 | | 700 |

**4 POST**

| Salaries Expense | | 622 |
|---|---|---|
| (7) | 700 | |

| Cash | | | 101 |
|---|---|---|---|
| (1) | 30,000 | (2) | 2,500 |
| (5) | 4,200 | (3) | 26,000 |
| | | (6) | 1,000 |
| | | (7) | 700 |

## 8. Provide Consulting and Rental Services on Credit

**1 IDENTIFY**  FastForward provides consulting services of $1,600 and rents its test facilities for $300. The customer is billed $1,900 for these services.

**2 ANALYZE**

| Assets | = | Liabilities | + | Equity | |
|---|---|---|---|---|---|
| **Accounts Receivable** | | | | **Consulting Revenue** | **Rental Revenue** |
| +1,900 | = | 0 | | +1,600 | +300 |

**3 RECORD**

| (8) | Accounts Receivable | 106 | 1,900 | |
|---|---|---|---|---|
| | Consulting Revenue | 403 | | 1,600 |
| | Rental Revenue | 406 | | 300 |

**4 POST**

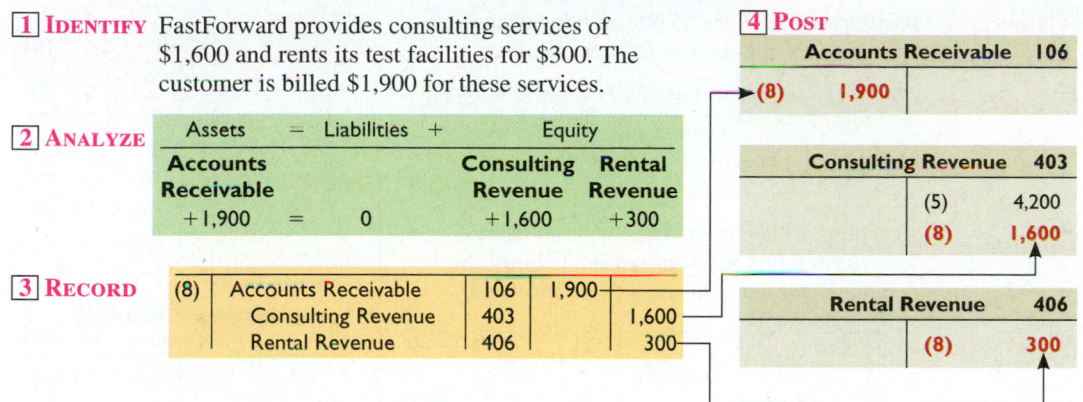

| Accounts Receivable | | 106 |
|---|---|---|
| (8) | 1,900 | |

| Consulting Revenue | | 403 |
|---|---|---|
| | (5) | 4,200 |
| | (8) | 1,600 |

| Rental Revenue | | 406 |
|---|---|---|
| | (8) | 300 |

**Point:** Transaction 8 is a **compound journal entry,** which affects three or more accounts.

## 9. Receipt of Cash on Account

**1 IDENTIFY**  FastForward receives $1,900 cash from the client billed in transaction 8.

**2 ANALYZE**

| Assets | | = | Liabilities | + | Equity |
|---|---|---|---|---|---|
| **Cash** | **Accounts Receivable** | | | | |
| +1,900 | −1,900 | = | 0 | + | 0 |

**3 RECORD**

| (9) | Cash | 101 | 1,900 | |
|---|---|---|---|---|
| | Accounts Receivable | 106 | | 1,900 |

**4 POST**

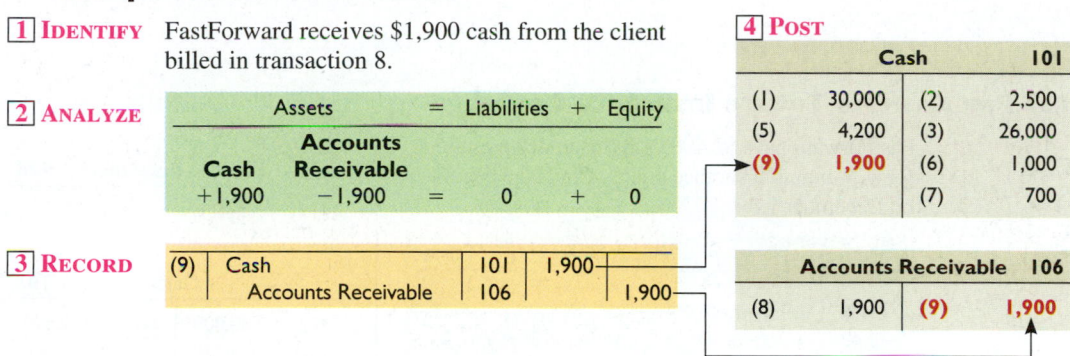

| | | Cash | | 101 |
|---|---|---|---|---|
| (1) | 30,000 | (2) | | 2,500 |
| (5) | 4,200 | (3) | | 26,000 |
| (9) | 1,900 | (6) | | 1,000 |
| | | (7) | | 700 |

| Accounts Receivable | | 106 |
|---|---|---|
| (8) | 1,900 | (9) | 1,900 |

**Point:** The *revenue recognition principle* requires revenue to be recognized when earned, which is when the company provides products and services to a customer. This is not necessarily the same time that the customer pays. A customer can pay before or after products or services are provided.

## 10. Partial Payment of Accounts Payable

**1 IDENTIFY**  FastForward pays CalTech Supply $900 cash toward the payable of transaction 4.

**2 ANALYZE**

| Assets | = | Liabilities | + | Equity |
|---|---|---|---|---|
| **Cash** | | **Accounts Payable** | | |
| −900 | = | −900 | + | 0 |

**3 RECORD**

| (10) | Accounts Payable | 201 | 900 | |
|---|---|---|---|---|
| | Cash | 101 | | 900 |

**4 POST**

| Accounts Payable | | 201 |
|---|---|---|
| (10) | 900 | (4) | 7,100 |

| | | Cash | | 101 |
|---|---|---|---|---|
| (1) | 30,000 | (2) | | 2,500 |
| (5) | 4,200 | (3) | | 26,000 |
| (9) | 1,900 | (6) | | 1,000 |
| | | (7) | | 700 |
| | | (10) | | 900 |

## 11. Withdrawal of Cash by Owner

**1 IDENTIFY**  Chas Taylor withdraws $200 cash from FastForward for personal use.

**2 ANALYZE**

| Assets | = | Liabilities | + | Equity |
|---|---|---|---|---|
| **Cash** | | | | **C. Taylor, Withdrawals** |
| −200 | = | 0 | | −200 |

**3 RECORD**

| (11) | C. Taylor, Withdrawals | 302 | 200 | |
|---|---|---|---|---|
| | Cash | 101 | | 200 |

**4 POST**

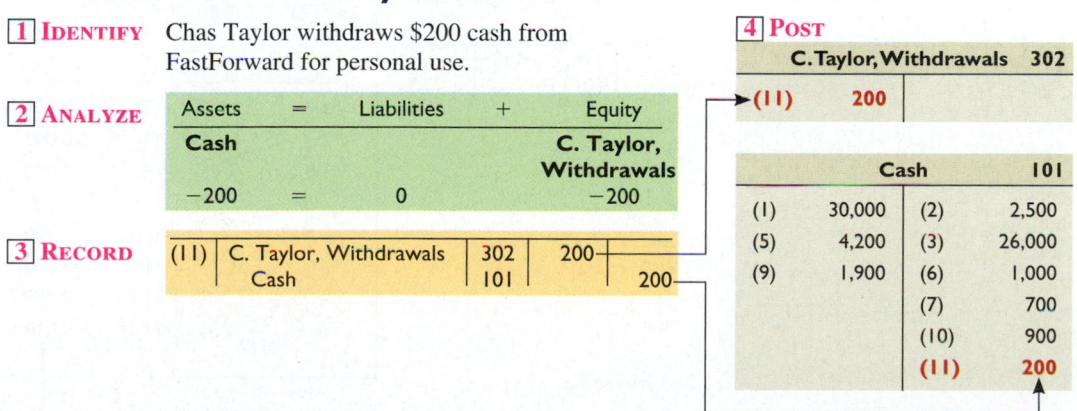

| C. Taylor, Withdrawals | | 302 |
|---|---|---|
| (11) | 200 | |

| | | Cash | | 101 |
|---|---|---|---|---|
| (1) | 30,000 | (2) | | 2,500 |
| (5) | 4,200 | (3) | | 26,000 |
| (9) | 1,900 | (6) | | 1,000 |
| | | (7) | | 700 |
| | | (10) | | 900 |
| | | (11) | | 200 |

## 12. Receipt of Cash for Future Services

**1 IDENTIFY**  FastForward receives $3,000 cash in advance of providing consulting services to a customer.

**2 ANALYZE**

Accepting $3,000 cash obligates FastForward to perform future services and is a liability. No revenue is earned until services are provided.

**3 RECORD**

| (12) | Cash | 101 | 3,000 | |
| | Unearned Consulting Revenue | 236 | | 3,000 |

**4 POST**

| Cash | | | 101 |
|---|---|---|---|
| (1) | 30,000 | (2) | 2,500 |
| (5) | 4,200 | (3) | 26,000 |
| (9) | 1,900 | (6) | 1,000 |
| (12) | 3,000 | (7) | 700 |
| | | (10) | 900 |
| | | (11) | 200 |

| Unearned Consulting Revenue | | 236 |
|---|---|---|
| | (12) | 3,000 |

**Point:** Luca Pacioli, a 15th-century monk, is considered a pioneer in accounting and the first to devise double-entry accounting.

## 13. Pay Cash for Future Insurance Coverage

**1 IDENTIFY**  FastForward pays $2,400 cash (insurance premium) for a 24-month insurance policy. Coverage begins on December 1.

**2 ANALYZE**

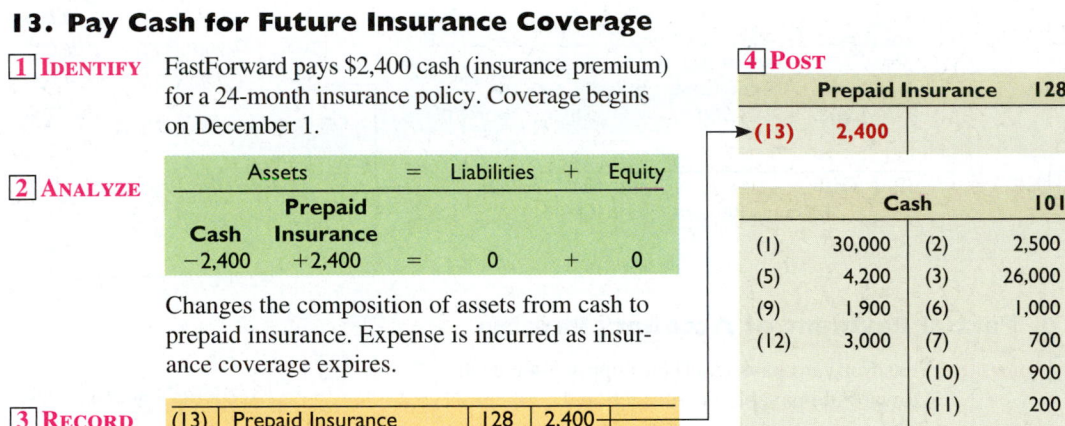

Changes the composition of assets from cash to prepaid insurance. Expense is incurred as insurance coverage expires.

**3 RECORD**

| (13) | Prepaid Insurance | 128 | 2,400 | |
| | Cash | 101 | | 2,400 |

**4 POST**

| Prepaid Insurance | | 128 |
|---|---|---|
| (13) | 2,400 | |

| Cash | | | 101 |
|---|---|---|---|
| (1) | 30,000 | (2) | 2,500 |
| (5) | 4,200 | (3) | 26,000 |
| (9) | 1,900 | (6) | 1,000 |
| (12) | 3,000 | (7) | 700 |
| | | (10) | 900 |
| | | (11) | 200 |
| | | (13) | 2,400 |

## 14. Purchase Supplies for Cash

**1 IDENTIFY**  FastForward pays $120 cash for supplies.

**2 ANALYZE**

**3 RECORD**

| (14) | Supplies | 126 | 120 | |
| | Cash | 101 | | 120 |

**4 POST**

| Supplies | | 126 |
|---|---|---|
| (2) | 2,500 | |
| (4) | 7,100 | |
| (14) | 120 | |

| Cash | | | 101 |
|---|---|---|---|
| (1) | 30,000 | (2) | 2,500 |
| (5) | 4,200 | (3) | 26,000 |
| (9) | 1,900 | (6) | 1,000 |
| (12) | 3,000 | (7) | 700 |
| | | (10) | 900 |
| | | (11) | 200 |
| | | (13) | 2,400 |
| | | (14) | 120 |

### 15. Payment of Expense in Cash

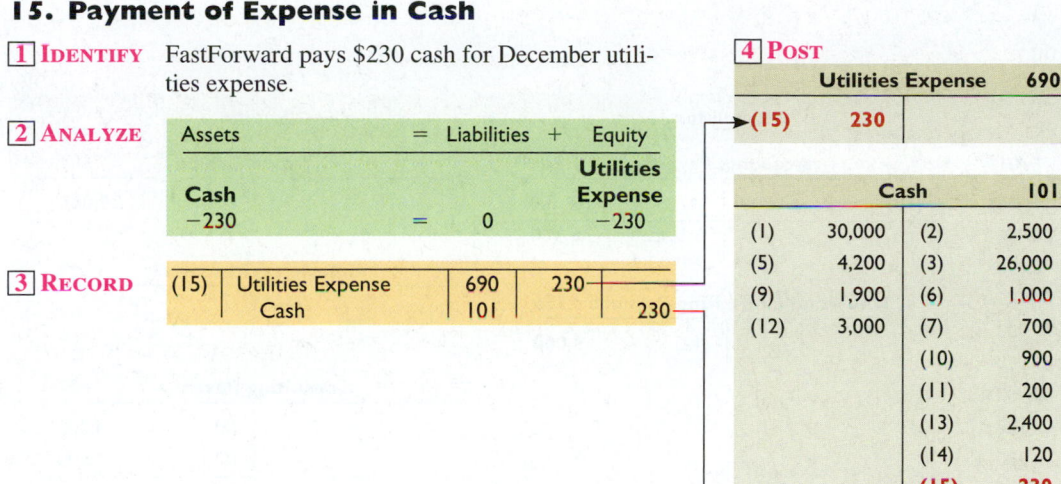

**1 IDENTIFY**  FastForward pays $230 cash for December utilities expense.

**2 ANALYZE**

| Assets | = Liabilities + | Equity |
|---|---|---|
| **Cash** | | **Utilities Expense** |
| −230 | = 0 | −230 |

**3 RECORD**

| (15) | Utilities Expense | 690 | 230 | |
|---|---|---|---|---|
| | Cash | 101 | | 230 |

**4 POST**

| Utilities Expense | | 690 |
|---|---|---|
| (15) | 230 | |

| | Cash | | 101 |
|---|---|---|---|
| (1) | 30,000 | (2) | 2,500 |
| (5) | 4,200 | (3) | 26,000 |
| (9) | 1,900 | (6) | 1,000 |
| (12) | 3,000 | (7) | 700 |
| | | (10) | 900 |
| | | (11) | 200 |
| | | (13) | 2,400 |
| | | (14) | 120 |
| | | **(15)** | **230** |

### 16. Payment of Expense in Cash

**1 IDENTIFY**  FastForward pays $700 cash in employee salary for work performed in the latter part of December.

**2 ANALYZE**

| Assets | = Liabilities + | Equity |
|---|---|---|
| **Cash** | | **Salaries Expense** |
| −700 | = 0 | −700 |

**3 RECORD**

| (16) | Salaries Expense | 622 | 700 | |
|---|---|---|---|---|
| | Cash | 101 | | 700 |

**4 POST**

| Salaries Expense | | 622 |
|---|---|---|
| (7) | 700 | |
| (16) | 700 | |

| | Cash | | 101 |
|---|---|---|---|
| (1) | 30,000 | (2) | 2,500 |
| (5) | 4,200 | (3) | 26,000 |
| (9) | 1,900 | (6) | 1,000 |
| (12) | 3,000 | (7) | 700 |
| | | (10) | 900 |
| | | (11) | 200 |
| | | (13) | 2,400 |
| | | (14) | 120 |
| | | (15) | 230 |
| | | **(16)** | **700** |

**Point:** We could merge transactions 15 and 16 into one *compound entry.*

## Accounting Equation Analysis

Exhibit 2.13 shows the ledger accounts (in T-account form) of FastForward after all 16 transactions are recorded and posted and the balances computed. The accounts are grouped into three major columns corresponding to the accounting equation: assets, liabilities, and equity. Note several important points. First, as with each transaction, the totals for the three columns must obey the accounting equation. Specifically, assets equal $42,470 ($4,350 + $0 + $9,720 + $2,400 + $26,000); liabilities equal $9,200 ($6,200 + $3,000); and equity equals $33,270 ($30,000 − $200 + $5,800 + $300 − $1,400 − $1,000 − $230). These numbers prove the accounting equation: Assets of $42,470 = Liabilities of $9,200 + Equity of $33,270. Second, the capital, withdrawals, revenue, and expense accounts reflect the transactions that change equity. These account categories underlie the statement of owner's equity. Third, the revenue and expense account balances will be summarized and reported in the income statement. Fourth, increases and decreases in the cash account make up the elements reported in the statement of cash flows.

| | **Debit and Credit Rules** | |
|---|---|---|
| | **Increase** | |
| **Accounts** | **(normal bal.)** | **Decrease** |
| Asset . . . . . . . . . . . . | Debit | Credit |
| Liability . . . . . . . . . . | Credit | Debit |
| Capital . . . . . . . . . . . | Credit | Debit |
| Withdrawals . . . . . . . | Debit | Credit |
| Revenue . . . . . . . . . . | Credit | Debit |
| Expense . . . . . . . . . . | Debit | Credit |

**Point:** Technology does not provide the judgment required to analyze most business transactions. Analysis requires the expertise of skilled and ethical professionals.

**EXHIBIT 2.13**

Ledger for FastForward (in T-Account Form)

| Assets | | | | = | Liabilities | | | + | Equity | | |
|---|---|---|---|---|---|---|---|---|---|---|---|

**Assets**

**Cash** 101

| | | | |
|---|---|---|---|
| (1) | 30,000 | (2) | 2,500 |
| (5) | 4,200 | (3) | 26,000 |
| (9) | 1,900 | (6) | 1,000 |
| (12) | 3,000 | (7) | 700 |
| | | (10) | 900 |
| | | (11) | 200 |
| | | (13) | 2,400 |
| | | (14) | 120 |
| | | (15) | 230 |
| | | (16) | 700 |
| Balance | 4,350 | | |

**Accounts Receivable** 106

| | | | |
|---|---|---|---|
| (8) | 1,900 | (9) | 1,900 |
| Balance | 0 | | |

**Supplies** 126

| | | |
|---|---|---|
| (2) | 2,500 | |
| (4) | 7,100 | |
| (14) | 120 | |
| Balance | 9,720 | |

**Prepaid Insurance** 128

| | | |
|---|---|---|
| (13) | 2,400 | |

**Equipment** 167

| | | |
|---|---|---|
| (3) | 26,000 | |

**$42,470**   =

**Liabilities**

**Accounts Payable** 201

| | | | |
|---|---|---|---|
| (10) | 900 | (4) | 7,100 |
| | | Balance | 6,200 |

**Unearned Consulting Revenue** 236

| | | | |
|---|---|---|---|
| | | (12) | 3,000 |

**$9,200**   +

**Equity**

**C. Taylor, Capital** 301

| | | | |
|---|---|---|---|
| | | (1) | 30,000 |

**C. Taylor, Withdrawals** 302

| | | |
|---|---|---|
| (11) | 200 | |

**Consulting Revenue** 403

| | | | |
|---|---|---|---|
| | | (5) | 4,200 |
| | | (8) | 1,600 |
| | | Balance | 5,800 |

**Rental Revenue** 406

| | | | |
|---|---|---|---|
| | | (8) | 300 |

**Salaries Expense** 622

| | | |
|---|---|---|
| (7) | 700 | |
| (16) | 700 | |
| Balance | 1,400 | |

**Rent Expense** 640

| | | |
|---|---|---|
| (6) | 1,000 | |

**Utilities Expense** 690

| | | |
|---|---|---|
| (15) | 230 | |

Accounts in this white area reflect those reported on the income statement.

**$33,270**

---

## Quick Check

Answers — p. 75

8. What types of transactions increase equity? What types decrease equity?

9. Why are accounting systems called *double-entry?*

10. For each transaction, double-entry accounting requires which of the following? (*a*) Debits to asset accounts must create credits to liability or equity accounts, (*b*) a debit to a liability account must create a credit to an asset account, or (*c*) total debits must equal total credits.

11. An owner invests $15,000 cash along with equipment having a market value of $23,000 in a company. Prepare the necessary journal entry.

12. Explain what a compound journal entry is.

13. Why are posting reference numbers entered in the journal when entries are posted to ledger accounts?

## TRIAL BALANCE

Double-entry accounting requires the sum of debit account balances to equal the sum of credit account balances. A trial balance is used to confirm this. A **trial balance** is a list of accounts and their balances at a point in time. Account balances are reported in their appropriate debit or credit columns of a trial balance. A trial balance can be used to confirm this and to follow up on any abnormal or unusual balances. Exhibit 2.14 shows the trial balance for FastForward after its 16 entries have been posted to the ledger. (This is an *unadjusted* trial balance—Chapter 3 explains the necessary adjustments.)

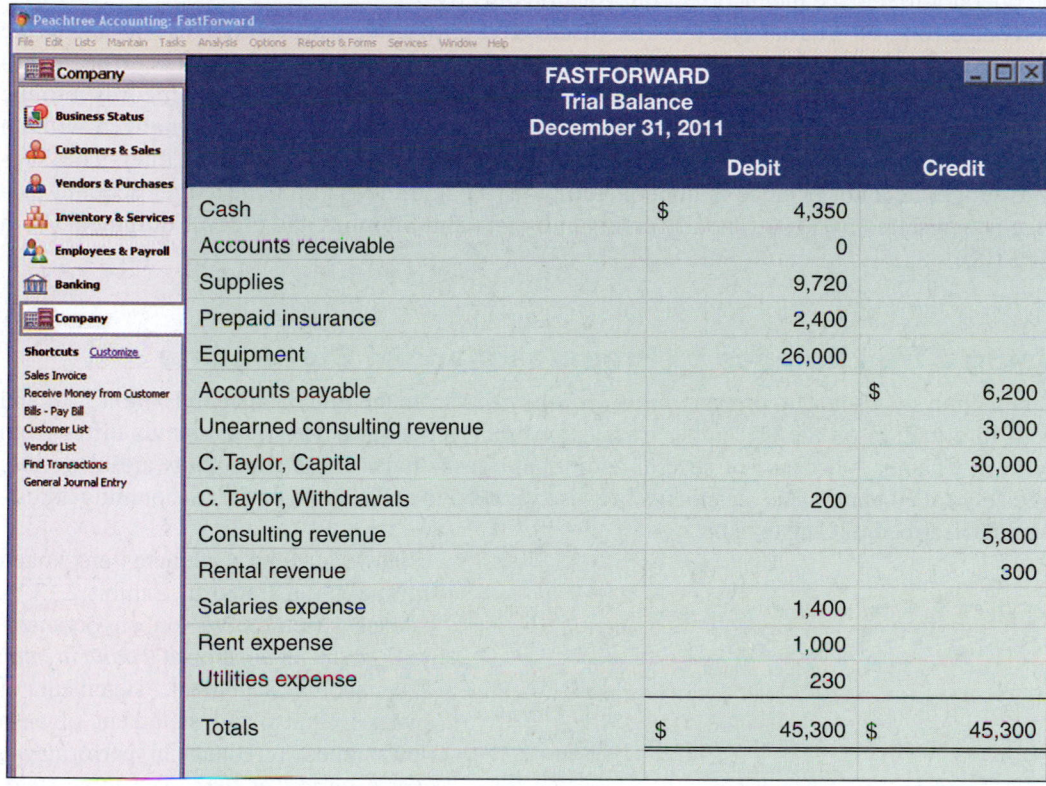

**EXHIBIT 2.14**

Trial Balance (Unadjusted)

**FASTFORWARD**
**Trial Balance**
**December 31, 2011**

| | Debit | Credit |
|---|---|---|
| Cash | $ 4,350 | |
| Accounts receivable | 0 | |
| Supplies | 9,720 | |
| Prepaid insurance | 2,400 | |
| Equipment | 26,000 | |
| Accounts payable | | $ 6,200 |
| Unearned consulting revenue | | 3,000 |
| C. Taylor, Capital | | 30,000 |
| C. Taylor, Withdrawals | 200 | |
| Consulting revenue | | 5,800 |
| Rental revenue | | 300 |
| Salaries expense | 1,400 | |
| Rent expense | 1,000 | |
| Utilities expense | 230 | |
| Totals | $ 45,300 | $ 45,300 |

**Point:** The ordering of accounts in a trial balance typically follows their identification number from the chart of accounts.

## Preparing a Trial Balance

Preparing a trial balance involves three steps:

**P2**  Prepare and explain the use of a trial balance.

1.  List each account title and its amount (from ledger) in the trial balance. If an account has a zero balance, list it with a zero in its normal balance column (or omit it entirely).
2.  Compute the total of debit balances and the total of credit balances.
3.  Verify (*prove*) total debit balances equal total credit balances.

The total of debit balances equals the total of credit balances for the trial balance in Exhibit 2.14. Equality of these two totals does not guarantee that no errors were made. For example, the column totals still will be equal when a debit or credit of a correct amount is made to a wrong account. Another error that does not cause unequal column totals occurs when equal debits and credits of an incorrect amount are entered.

**Point:** A trial balance is *not* a financial statement but a mechanism for checking equality of debits and credits in the ledger. Financial statements do not have debit and credit columns.

**Searching for and Correcting Errors**  If the trial balance does not balance (when its columns are not equal), the error (or errors) must be found and corrected. An efficient

**Example:** If a credit to Unearned Revenue was incorrectly posted from the journal as a credit to the Revenue ledger account, would the ledger still balance? Would the financial statements be correct? *Answers:* The ledger would balance, but liabilities would be understated, equity would be overstated, and income would be overstated (all because of overstated revenues).

way to search for an error is to check the journalizing, posting, and trial balance preparation in *reverse order.* Step 1 is to verify that the trial balance columns are correctly added. If step 1 fails to find the error, step 2 is to verify that account balances are accurately entered from the ledger. Step 3 is to see whether a debit (or credit) balance is mistakenly listed in the trial balance as a credit (or debit). A clue to this error is when the difference between total debits and total credits equals twice the amount of the incorrect account balance. If the error is still undiscovered, Step 4 is to recompute each account balance in the ledger. Step 5 is to verify that each journal entry is properly posted. Step 6 is to verify that the original journal entry has equal debits and credits. At this point, the errors should be uncovered.[3]

**Point:** The IRS requires companies to keep records that can be audited.

If an error in a journal entry is discovered before the error is posted, it can be corrected in a manual system by drawing a line through the incorrect information. The correct information is written above it to create a record of change for the auditor. Many computerized systems allow the operator to replace the incorrect information directly.

If an error in a journal entry is not discovered until after it is posted, we do not strike through both erroneous entries in the journal and ledger. Instead, we correct this error by creating a *correcting entry* that removes the amount from the wrong account and records it to the correct account. As an example, suppose a $100 purchase of supplies is journalized with an incorrect debit to Equipment, and then this incorrect entry is posted to the ledger. The Supplies ledger account balance is understated by $100, and the Equipment ledger account balance is overstated by $100. The correcting entry is: debit Supplies and credit Equipment (both for $100).

## Using a Trial Balance to Prepare Financial Statements

**P3** Prepare financial statements from business transactions.

This section shows how to prepare *financial statements* from the trial balance in Exhibit 2.14 and from information on the December transactions of FastForward. These statements differ from those in Chapter 1 because of several additional transactions. These statements are also more precisely called *unadjusted statements* because we need to make some further accounting adjustments (described in Chapter 3).

**EXHIBIT 2.15**

Links between Financial Statements across Time

How financial statements are linked in time is illustrated in Exhibit 2.15. A balance sheet reports on an organization's financial position at a *point in time.* The income statement, statement of owner's equity, and statement of cash flows report on financial performance over a *period of time.* The three statements in the middle column of Exhibit 2.15 link balance sheets from the beginning to the end of a reporting period. They explain how financial position changes from one point to another.

Preparers and users (including regulatory agencies) determine the length of the reporting period. A one-year, or

---

[3] *Transposition* occurs when two digits are switched, or transposed, within a number. If transposition is the only error, it yields a difference between the two trial balance totals that is evenly divisible by 9. For example, assume that a $691 debit in an entry is incorrectly posted to the ledger as $619. Total credits in the trial balance are then larger than total debits by $72 ($691 − $619). The $72 error is *evenly* divisible by 9 (72/9 = 8). The first digit of the quotient (in our example it is 8) equals the difference between the digits of the two transposed numbers (the 9 and the 1). The number of digits in the quotient also tells the location of the transposition, starting from the right. The quotient in our example had only one digit (8), so it tells us the transposition is in the first digit. Consider another example where a transposition error involves posting $961 instead of the correct $691. The difference in these numbers is $270, and its quotient is 30 (270/9). The quotient has two digits, so it tells us to check the second digit from the right for a transposition of two numbers that have a difference of 3.

annual, reporting period is common, as are semiannual, quarterly, and monthly periods. The one-year reporting period is known as the *accounting,* or *fiscal, year.* Businesses whose accounting year begins on January 1 and ends on December 31 are known as *calendar-year* companies. Many companies choose a fiscal year ending on a date other than December 31. **Research In Motion** is a *noncalendar-year* company as reflected in the headings of its February 27 year-end financial statements in Appendix A near the end of the book.

**Income Statement**   An income statement reports the revenues earned less the expenses incurred by a business over a period of time. FastForward's income statement for December is shown at the top of Exhibit 2.16. Information about revenues and expenses is conveniently taken from the trial balance in Exhibit 2.14. Net income of $3,470 is reported at the bottom of the statement. Owner investments and withdrawals are *not* part of income.

**Statement of Owner's Equity**   The statement of owner's equity reports information about how equity changes over the reporting period. FastForward's statement of owner's equity is the second report in Exhibit 2.16. It shows the $30,000 owner investment, the $3,470 of net income, the $200 withdrawal, and the $33,270 end-of-period (capital) balance. (The beginning

**EXHIBIT 2.16**

Financial Statements and Their Links

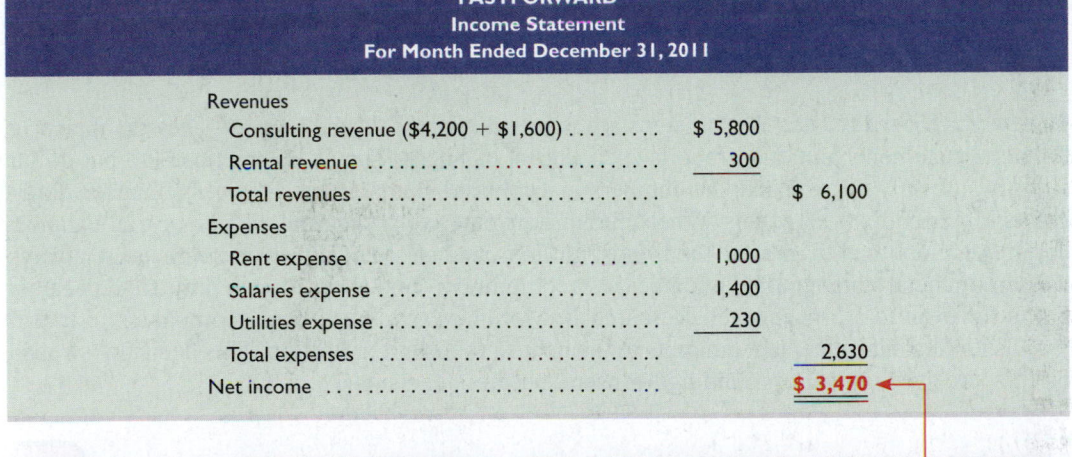

balance in the statement of owner's equity is rarely zero; an exception is for the first period of operations. The beginning capital balance in January 2012 is $33,270, which is December's ending balance.)

**Point:** An income statement is also called an *earnings statement, a statement of operations,* or a *P&L (profit and loss) statement.* A balance sheet is also called a *statement of financial position.*

**Balance Sheet**    The balance sheet reports the financial position of a company at a point in time, usually at the end of a month, quarter, or year. FastForward's balance sheet is the third report in Exhibit 2.16. This statement refers to financial condition at the close of business on December 31. The left side of the balance sheet lists its assets: cash, supplies, prepaid insurance, and equipment. The upper right side of the balance sheet shows that it owes $6,200 to creditors and $3,000 in services to customers who paid in advance. The equity section shows an ending balance of $33,270. Note the link between the ending balance of the statement of owner's equity and the capital balance. (Recall that this presentation of the balance sheet is called the *account form:* assets on the left and liabilities and equity on the right. Another presentation is the *report form:* assets on top, followed by liabilities and then equity. Either presentation is acceptable.)

**Point:** While revenues increase equity, and expenses decrease equity, the amounts are not reported in detail in the statement of owner's equity. Instead, their effects are reflected through net income.

### Decision Maker

Answer — p. 74

**Entrepreneur**    You open a wholesale business selling entertainment equipment to retail outlets. You find that most of your customers demand to buy on credit. How can you use the balance sheets of these customers to decide which ones to extend credit to? ■

**Point:** Knowing how financial statements are prepared improves our analysis of them.

**Presentation Issues**    Dollar signs are not used in journals and ledgers. They do appear in financial statements and other reports such as trial balances. The usual practice is to put dollar signs beside only the first and last numbers in a column. **Research In Motion**'s financial statements in Appendix A show this. When amounts are entered in a journal, ledger, or trial balance, commas are optional to indicate thousands, millions, and so forth. However, commas are always used in financial statements. Companies also commonly round amounts in reports to the nearest dollar, or even to a higher level. Research In Motion is typical of many companies in that it rounds its financial statement amounts to the nearest thousand or million. This decision is based on the perceived impact of rounding for users' business decisions.

### Quick Check

Answers — p. 75

14. Where are dollar signs typically entered in financial statements?
15. If a $4,000 debit to Equipment in a journal entry is incorrectly posted to the ledger as a $4,000 credit, and the ledger account has a resulting debit balance of $20,000, what is the effect of this error on the Trial Balance column totals?
16. Describe the link between the income statement and the statement of owner's equity.
17. Explain the link between the balance sheet and the statement of owner's equity.
18. Define and describe revenues and expenses.
19. Define and describe assets, liabilities, and equity.

## GLOBAL VIEW

Financial accounting according to U.S. GAAP is similar, but not identical, to IFRS. This section discusses differences in analyzing and recording transactions, and with the preparation of financial statements.

**Analyzing and Recording Transactions**    Both U.S. GAAP and IFRS include broad and similar guidance for financial accounting. As the FASB and IASB work toward a common conceptual framework over the next few years, even those differences will fade. Further, both U.S. GAAP and IFRS apply transaction analysis and recording as shown in this chapter—using the same debit and credit system and accrual account-ing. Although some variations exist in revenue and expense recognition and other accounting principles, all of the transactions in this chapter are accounted for identically under these two systems.

**Financial Statements**   Both U.S. GAAP and IFRS prepare the same four basic financial state-ments. A few differences within each statement do exist and we will discuss those throughout the book. For example, both U.S. GAAP and IFRS require balance sheets to separate current items from noncurrent items. However, while U.S. GAAP balance sheets report current items first, IFRS balance sheets normally (but are not required to) present noncurrent items first, and equity before liabilities. To illustrate, a con-densed version of **Nokia**'s balance sheet follows (numbers using Euros in millions).

**NOKIA**

| NOKIA Balance Sheet (in EUR millions) December 31, 2009 | | | |
|---|---|---|---|
| **Assets** | | **Equity and Liabilities** | |
| Noncurrent assets . . . . . . . . | 12,125 | Total equity . . . . . . . . . . . . . . | 14,749 |
| Current assets . . . . . . . . . . | 23,613 | Noncurrent liabilities . . . . . . . | 5,801 |
| | | Current liabilities . . . . . . . . . . | 15,188 |
| Total assets . . . . . . . . . . . . . | 35,738 | Total equity and liabilities . . . . | 35,738 |

**Accounting Controls and Assurance**   Accounting systems depend on control procedures that assure the proper principles were applied in processing accounting information. The passage of SOX leg-islation strengthened U.S. control procedures in recent years. However, global standards for control are diverse and so are enforcement activities. Consequently, while global accounting standards are converg-ing, their application in different countries can yield different outcomes depending on the quality of their auditing standards and enforcement.

---

## Decision Insight

**Accounting Control**   Recording valid transactions, and not recording fraudulent transactions, enhances the quality of financial statements. The graph here shows the percentage of employees in information technology that report observing specific types of misconduct within the past year. ■

[Source: KPMG 2009]

| | Percent |
|---|---|
| Breaching database controls | 23% |
| Mishandling private information | 22% |
| Breaching customer privacy | 16% |
| Falsifying accounting data | 9% |

**Percent Citing Misconduct**

---

## Decision Analysis

Debt Ratio

An important business objective is gathering information to help assess a company's risk of failing to pay its debts. Companies finance their assets with either liabilities or equity. A company that finances a rela-tively large portion of its assets with liabilities is said to have a high degree of *financial leverage*. Higher financial leverage involves greater risk because liabilities must be repaid and often require regular interest payments (equity financing does not). The risk that a company might not be able to meet such required payments is higher if it has more liabilities (is more highly leveraged). One way to assess the risk associ-ated with a company's use of liabilities is to compute the **debt ratio** as in Exhibit 2.17.

A2   Compute the debt ratio and describe its use in analyzing financial condition.

$$\text{Debt ratio} = \frac{\text{Total liabilities}}{\text{Total assets}}$$

**EXHIBIT 2.17**

Debt Ratio

To see how to apply the debt ratio, let's look at **Skechers**'s liabilities and assets. The company designs, markets, and sells footwear for men, women, and children under the Skechers brand. Exhibit 2.18 computes and reports its debt ratio at the end of each year from 2005 to 2009.

**EXHIBIT 2.18**

Computation and Analysis of Debt Ratio

| $ in millions | 2009 | 2008 | 2007 | 2006 | 2005 |
|---|---|---|---|---|---|
| Total liabilities ............. | $246 | $204 | $201 | $288 | $238 |
| Total assets .............. | $996 | $876 | $828 | $737 | $582 |
| Debt ratio ............. | 0.25 | 0.23 | 0.24 | 0.39 | 0.41 |
| Industry debt ratio ........ | 0.51 | 0.50 | 0.46 | 0.48 | 0.47 |

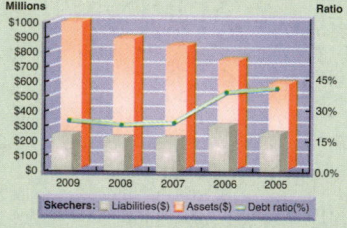

Skechers's debt ratio ranges from a low of 0.23 to a high of 0.41—also, see graph in margin. Its ratio is lower, and has been generally declining, compared with the industry ratio. This analysis implies a low risk from its financial leverage. Is financial leverage good or bad for Skechers? To answer that question we need to compare the company's return on the borrowed money to the rate it is paying creditors. If the company's return is higher, it is successfully borrowing money to make more money. A company's success with making money from borrowed money can quickly turn unprofitable if its own return drops below the rate it is paying creditors.

**Decision Maker**                                                Answer — p. 74

**Investor**   You consider buying stock in **Converse**. As part of your analysis, you compute its debt ratio for 2009, 2010, and 2011 as: 0.35, 0.74, and 0.94, respectively. Based on the debt ratio, is Converse a low-risk investment? Has the risk of buying Converse stock changed over this period? (The industry debt ratio averages 0.40.) ■

# DEMONSTRATION PROBLEM

(This problem extends the demonstration problem of Chapter 1.) After several months of planning, Jasmine Worthy started a haircutting business called Expressions. The following events occurred during its first month.

**a.** On August 1, Worthy invested $3,000 cash and $15,000 of equipment in Expressions.

**b.** On August 2, Expressions paid $600 cash for furniture for the shop.

**c.** On August 3, Expressions paid $500 cash to rent space in a strip mall for August.

**d.** On August 4, it purchased $1,200 of equipment on credit for the shop (using a long-term note payable).

**e.** On August 5, Expressions opened for business. Cash received from haircutting services in the first week and a half of business (ended August 15) was $825.

**f.** On August 15, it provided $100 of haircutting services on account.

**g.** On August 17, it received a $100 check for services previously rendered on account.

**h.** On August 17, it paid $125 to an assistant for hours worked during the grand opening.

**i.** Cash received from services provided during the second half of August was $930.

**j.** On August 31, it paid a $400 installment toward principal on the note payable entered into on August 4.

**k.** On August 31, Worthy withdrew $900 cash for personal use.

### Required

**1.** Open the following ledger accounts in balance column format (account numbers are in parentheses): Cash (101); Accounts Receivable (102); Furniture (161); Store Equipment (165); Note Payable (240); J. Worthy, Capital (301); J. Worthy, Withdrawals (302); Haircutting Services Revenue (403); Wages Expense (623); and Rent Expense (640). Prepare general journal entries for the transactions.

**2.** Post the journal entries from (1) to the ledger accounts.

3. Prepare a trial balance as of August 31.
4. Prepare an income statement for August.
5. Prepare a statement of owner's equity for August.
6. Prepare a balance sheet as of August 31.
7. Determine the debt ratio as of August 31.

**Extended Analysis**

8. In the coming months, Expressions will experience a greater variety of business transactions. Identify which accounts are debited and which are credited for the following transactions. (*Hint:* We must use some accounts not opened in part 1.)
   a. Purchase supplies with cash.
   b. Pay cash for future insurance coverage.
   c. Receive cash for services to be provided in the future.
   d. Purchase supplies on account.

## PLANNING THE SOLUTION

- Analyze each transaction and use the debit and credit rules to prepare a journal entry for each.
- Post each debit and each credit from journal entries to their ledger accounts and cross-reference each amount in the posting reference (PR) columns of the journal and ledger.
- Calculate each account balance and list the accounts with their balances on a trial balance.
- Verify that total debits in the trial balance equal total credits.
- To prepare the income statement, identify revenues and expenses. List those items on the statement, compute the difference, and label the result as *net income* or *net loss*.
- Use information in the ledger to prepare the statement of owner's equity.
- Use information in the ledger to prepare the balance sheet.
- Calculate the debt ratio by dividing total liabilities by total assets.
- Analyze the future transactions to identify the accounts affected and apply debit and credit rules.

## SOLUTION TO DEMONSTRATION PROBLEM

1. General journal entries:

**General Journal Entry**                                            Page 1

| Date | Account Titles and Explanation | PR | Debit | Credit |
|---|---|---|---|---|
| Aug. 1 | Cash ........................................ | 101 | 3,000 | |
| | Store Equipment .................................. | 165 | 15,000 | |
| | J. Worthy, Capital ............................. | 301 | | 18,000 |
| | *Owner's investment.* | | | |
| 2 | Furniture ....................................... | 161 | 600 | |
| | Cash ....................................... | 101 | | 600 |
| | *Purchased furniture for cash.* | | | |
| 3 | Rent Expense ..................................... | 640 | 500 | |
| | Cash ....................................... | 101 | | 500 |
| | *Paid rent for August.* | | | |
| 4 | Store Equipment ..................................... | 165 | 1,200 | |
| | Note Payable ............................. | 240 | | 1,200 |
| | *Purchased additional equipment on credit.* | | | |
| 15 | Cash ........................................ | 101 | 825 | |
| | Haircutting Services Revenue .................... | 403 | | 825 |
| | *Cash receipts from first half of August.* | | | |

[continued on next page]

[continued from previous page]

| | | | | | |
|---|---|---|---|---|---|
| 15 | Accounts Receivable ............................... | 102 | 100 | |
| | Haircutting Services Revenue ..................... | 403 | | 100 |
| | *To record revenue for services provided on account.* | | | |
| 17 | Cash .......................................... | 101 | 100 | |
| | Accounts Receivable .......................... | 102 | | 100 |
| | *To record cash received as payment on account.* | | | |
| 17 | Wages Expense ................................... | 623 | 125 | |
| | Cash ......................................... | 101 | | 125 |
| | *Paid wages to assistant.* | | | |
| 31 | Cash .......................................... | 101 | 930 | |
| | Haircutting Services Revenue ..................... | 403 | | 930 |
| | *Cash receipts from second half of August.* | | | |
| 31 | Note Payable .................................. | 240 | 400 | |
| | Cash ......................................... | 101 | | 400 |
| | *Paid an installment on the note payable.* | | | |
| 31 | J. Worthy, Withdrawals ............................ | 302 | 900 | |
| | Cash ......................................... | 101 | | 900 |
| | *Cash withdrawal by owner.* | | | |

**2.** Post journal entries from part 1 to the ledger accounts:

## General Ledger

**Cash**      Account No. 101

| Date | PR | Debit | Credit | Balance |
|---|---|---|---|---|
| Aug. 1 | G1 | 3,000 | | 3,000 |
| 2 | G1 | | 600 | 2,400 |
| 3 | G1 | | 500 | 1,900 |
| 15 | G1 | 825 | | 2,725 |
| 17 | G1 | 100 | | 2,825 |
| 17 | G1 | | 125 | 2,700 |
| 31 | G1 | 930 | | 3,630 |
| 31 | G1 | | 400 | 3,230 |
| 31 | G1 | | 900 | 2,330 |

**Accounts Receivable**      Account No. 102

| Date | PR | Debit | Credit | Balance |
|---|---|---|---|---|
| Aug. 15 | G1 | 100 | | 100 |
| 17 | G1 | | 100 | 0 |

**Furniture**      Account No. 161

| Date | PR | Debit | Credit | Balance |
|---|---|---|---|---|
| Aug. 2 | G1 | 600 | | 600 |

**Store Equipment**      Account No. 165

| Date | PR | Debit | Credit | Balance |
|---|---|---|---|---|
| Aug. 1 | G1 | 15,000 | | 15,000 |
| 4 | G1 | 1,200 | | 16,200 |

**Note Payable**      Account No. 240

| Date | PR | Debit | Credit | Balance |
|---|---|---|---|---|
| Aug. 4 | G1 | | 1,200 | 1,200 |
| 31 | G1 | 400 | | 800 |

**J. Worthy, Capital**      Account No. 301

| Date | PR | Debit | Credit | Balance |
|---|---|---|---|---|
| Aug. 1 | G1 | | 18,000 | 18,000 |

**J. Worthy, Withdrawals**      Account No. 302

| Date | PR | Debit | Credit | Balance |
|---|---|---|---|---|
| Aug. 31 | G1 | 900 | | 900 |

**Haircutting Services Revenue**      Account No. 403

| Date | PR | Debit | Credit | Balance |
|---|---|---|---|---|
| Aug. 15 | G1 | | 825 | 825 |
| 15 | G1 | | 100 | 925 |
| 31 | G1 | | 930 | 1,855 |

**Wages Expense**      Account No. 623

| Date | PR | Debit | Credit | Balance |
|---|---|---|---|---|
| Aug. 17 | G1 | 125 | | 125 |

**Rent Expense**      Account No. 640

| Date | PR | Debit | Credit | Balance |
|---|---|---|---|---|
| Aug. 3 | G1 | 500 | | 500 |

**3.** Prepare a trial balance from the ledger:

| EXPRESSIONS<br>Trial Balance<br>August 31 | | |
|---|---|---|
| | **Debit** | **Credit** |
| Cash | $ 2,330 | |
| Accounts receivable | 0 | |
| Furniture | 600 | |
| Store equipment | 16,200 | |
| Note payable | | $   800 |
| J. Worthy, Capital | | 18,000 |
| J. Worthy, Withdrawals | 900 | |
| Haircutting services revenue | | 1,855 |
| Wages expense | 125 | |
| Rent expense | 500 | |
| Totals | $20,655 | $20,655 |

**4.**

| EXPRESSIONS<br>Income Statement<br>For Month Ended August 31 | | |
|---|---|---|
| Revenues | | |
| Haircutting services revenue | | $1,855 |
| Operating expenses | | |
| Rent expense | $500 | |
| Wages expense | 125 | |
| Total operating expenses | | 625 |
| Net income | | $1,230 |

**5.**

| EXPRESSIONS<br>Statement of Owner's Equity<br>For Month Ended August 31 | | |
|---|---|---|
| J. Worthy, Capital, August 1 | | $    0 |
| Plus:   Investments by owner | $18,000 | |
| Net income | 1,230 | 19,230 |
| | | 19,230 |
| Less:   Withdrawals by owner | | 900 |
| J. Worthy, Capital, August 31 | | $18,330 |

**6.**

| EXPRESSIONS<br>Balance Sheet<br>August 31 | | | |
|---|---|---|---|
| **Assets** | | **Liabilities** | |
| Cash | $ 2,330 | Note payable | $   800 |
| Furniture | 600 | **Equity** | |
| Store equipment | 16,200 | J. Worthy, Capital | 18,330 |
| Total assets | $19,130 | Total liabilities and equity | $19,130 |

**7.** Debt ratio $= \dfrac{\text{Total liabilities}}{\text{Total assets}} = \dfrac{\$800}{\$19{,}130} = \underline{\underline{\mathbf{4.18\%}}}$

**8a.** Supplies *debited*
       Cash *credited*

**8b.** Prepaid Insurance *debited*
       Cash *credited*

**8c.** Cash *debited*
       Unearned Services Revenue *credited*

**8d.** Supplies *debited*
       Accounts Payable *credited*

# Summary

**C1** **Explain the steps in processing transactions and the role of source documents.** The accounting process identifies business transactions and events, analyzes and records their effects, and summarizes and prepares information useful in making decisions. Transactions and events are the starting points in the accounting process. Source documents identify and describe transactions and events. Examples are sales tickets, checks, purchase orders, bills, and bank statements. Source documents provide objective and reliable evidence, making information more useful. The effects of transactions and events are recorded in journals. Posting along with a trial balance helps summarize and classify these effects.

**C2** **Describe an account and its use in recording transactions.** An account is a detailed record of increases and decreases in a specific asset, liability, equity, revenue, or expense. Information from accounts is analyzed, summarized, and presented in reports and financial statements for decision makers.

**C3** **Describe a ledger and a chart of accounts.** The ledger (or general ledger) is a record containing all accounts used by a company and their balances. It is referred to as the *books*. The chart of accounts is a list of all accounts and usually includes an identification number assigned to each account.

**C4** **Define *debits* and *credits* and explain double-entry accounting.** *Debit* refers to left, and *credit* refers to right. Debits increase assets, expenses, and withdrawals while credits decrease them. Credits increase liabilities, owner capital, and revenues; debits decrease them. Double-entry accounting means each transaction affects at least two accounts and has at least one debit and one credit. The system for recording debits and credits follows from the accounting equation. The left side of an account is the normal balance for assets, withdrawals, and expenses, and the right side is the normal balance for liabilities, capital, and revenues.

**A1** **Analyze the impact of transactions on accounts and financial statements.** We analyze transactions using concepts of double-entry accounting. This analysis is performed by determining a transaction's effects on accounts. These effects are recorded in journals and posted to ledgers.

**A2** **Compute the debt ratio and describe its use in analyzing financial condition.** A company's debt ratio is computed as total liabilities divided by total assets. It reveals how much of the assets are financed by creditor (nonowner) financing. The higher this ratio, the more risk a company faces because liabilities must be repaid at specific dates.

**P1** **Record transactions in a journal and post entries to a ledger.** Transactions are recorded in a journal. Each entry in a journal is posted to the accounts in the ledger. This provides information that is used to produce financial statements. Balance column accounts are widely used and include columns for debits, credits, and the account balance.

**P2** **Prepare and explain the use of a trial balance.** A trial balance is a list of accounts from the ledger showing their debit or credit balances in separate columns. The trial balance is a summary of the ledger's contents and is useful in preparing financial statements and in revealing recordkeeping errors.

**P3** **Prepare financial statements from business transactions.** The balance sheet, the statement of owner's equity, the income statement, and the statement of cash flows use data from the trial balance (and other financial statements) for their preparation.

---

## Guidance Answers to Decision Maker and Decision Ethics

**Cashier** The advantages to the process proposed by the assistant manager include improved customer service, fewer delays, and less work for you. However, you should have serious concerns about internal control and the potential for fraud. In particular, the assistant manager could steal cash and simply enter fewer sales to match the remaining cash. You should reject her suggestion without the manager's approval. Moreover, you should have an ethical concern about the assistant manager's suggestion to ignore store policy.

**Entrepreneur** We can use the accounting equation (Assets = Liabilities + Equity) to help us identify risky customers to whom we would likely not want to extend credit. A balance sheet provides amounts for each of these key components. The lower a customer's equity is relative to liabilities, the less likely you would extend credit. A low equity means the business has little value that does not already have creditor claims to it.

**Investor** The debt ratio suggests the stock of Converse is of higher risk than normal and that this risk is rising. The average industry ratio of 0.40 further supports this conclusion. The 2011 debt ratio for Converse is twice the industry norm. Also, a debt ratio approaching 1.0 indicates little to no equity.

## Guidance Answers to Quick Checks

1. Examples of source documents are sales tickets, checks, purchase orders, charges to customers, bills from suppliers, employee earnings records, and bank statements.

2. Source documents serve many purposes, including record-keeping and internal control. Source documents, especially if obtained from outside the organization, provide objective and reliable evidence about transactions and their amounts.

3.

| Assets | Liabilities | Equity |
|--------|-------------|--------|
| a,c,e  | b,d         | —      |

4. An account is a record in an accounting system that records and stores the increases and decreases in a specific asset, liability, equity, revenue, or expense. The ledger is a collection of all the accounts of a company.

5. A company's size and diversity affect the number of accounts in its accounting system. The types of accounts depend on information the company needs to both effectively operate and report its activities in financial statements.

6. No. Debit and credit both can mean increase or decrease. The particular meaning in a circumstance depends on the *type of account*. For example, a debit increases the balance of asset, withdrawals, and expense accounts, but it decreases the balance of liability, capital, and revenue accounts.

7. A chart of accounts is a list of all of a company's accounts and their identification numbers.

8. Equity is increased by revenues and by owner investments. Equity is decreased by expenses and owner withdrawals.

9. The name *double-entry* is used because all transactions affect at least two accounts. There must be at least one debit in one account and at least one credit in another account.

10. The answer is (c).

11.

| | | |
|---|---|---|
| Cash .............................. | 15,000 | |
| Equipment ........................... | 23,000 | |
|     Owner, Capital .................... | | 38,000 |
| *Investment by owner of cash and equipment.* | | |

12. A compound journal entry affects three or more accounts.

13. Posting reference numbers are entered in the journal when posting to the ledger as a cross-reference that allows the record-keeper or auditor to trace debits and credits from one record to another.

14. At a minimum, dollar signs are placed beside the first and last numbers in a column. It is also common to place dollar signs beside any amount that appears after a ruled line to indicate that an addition or subtraction has occurred.

15. The Equipment account balance is incorrectly reported at $20,000—it should be $28,000. The effect of this error understates the trial balance's Debit column total by $8,000. This results in an $8,000 difference between the column totals.

16. An income statement reports a company's revenues and expenses along with the resulting net income or loss. A statement of owner's equity reports changes in equity, including that from net income or loss. Both statements report transactions occurring over a period of time.

17. The balance sheet describes a company's financial position (assets, liabilities, and equity) at a point in time. The capital amount in the balance sheet is obtained from the statement of owner's equity.

18. Revenues are inflows of assets in exchange for products or services provided to customers as part of the main operations of a business. Expenses are outflows or the using up of assets that result from providing products or services to customers.

19. Assets are the resources a business owns or controls that carry expected future benefits. Liabilities are the obligations of a business, representing the claims of others against the assets of a business. Equity reflects the owner's claims on the assets of the business after deducting liabilities.

## Key Terms                                        mhhe.com/wildFAP20e

Account (p. 51)
Account balance (p. 55)
Balance column account (p. 58)
Chart of accounts (p. 54)
Compound journal entry (p. 61)
Credit (p. 55)
Creditors (p. 52)
Debit (p. 55)

Debtors (p. 51)
Debt ratio (p. 69)
Double-entry accounting (p. 55)
General journal (p. 56)
General ledger (p. 51)
Journal (p. 56)
Journalizing (p. 56)
Ledger (p. 51)

Posting (p. 56)
Posting reference (PR) column (p. 58)
Source documents (p. 50)
T-account (p. 55)
Trial balance (p. 65)
Unearned revenue (p. 52)

## Multiple Choice Quiz    Answers on p. 91    mhhe.com/wildFAP20e

Additional Quiz Questions are available at the book's Website.

1. Amalia Company received its utility bill for the current period of $700 and immediately paid it. Its journal entry to record this transaction includes a
   a. Credit to Utility Expense for $700.
   b. Debit to Utility Expense for $700.
   c. Debit to Accounts Payable for $700.
   d. Debit to Cash for $700.
   e. Credit to capital for $700.

2. On May 1, Mattingly Lawn Service collected $2,500 cash from a customer in advance of five months of lawn service. Mattingly's journal entry to record this transaction includes a
   a. Credit to Unearned Lawn Service Fees for $2,500.
   b. Debit to Lawn Service Fees Earned for $2,500.
   c. Credit to Cash for $2,500.
   d. Debit to Unearned Lawn Service Fees for $2,500.
   e. Credit to capital for $2,500.

3. Liang Shue contributed $250,000 cash and land worth $500,000 to open his new business, Shue Consulting. Which of the following journal entries does Shue Consulting make to record this transaction?
   a. Cash Assets . . . . . . . . . . .    750,000
       L. Shue, Capital . . . . . .          750,000
   b. L. Shue, Capital . . . . . . . .    750,000
       Assets . . . . . . . . . . . . . .          750,000
   c. Cash . . . . . . . . . . . . . . . .    250,000
      Land . . . . . . . . . . . . . . . .    500,000
       L. Shue, Capital . . . . . .          750,000

   d. L. Shue, Capital . . . . . . . .    750,000
      Cash . . . . . . . . . . . . . . .          250,000
      Land . . . . . . . . . . . . . . .          500,000

4. A trial balance prepared at year-end shows total credits exceed total debits by $765. This discrepancy could have been caused by
   a. An error in the general journal where a $765 increase in Accounts Payable was recorded as a $765 decrease in Accounts Payable.
   b. The ledger balance for Accounts Payable of $7,650 being entered in the trial balance as $765.
   c. A general journal error where a $765 increase in Accounts Receivable was recorded as a $765 increase in Cash.
   d. The ledger balance of $850 in Accounts Receivable was entered in the trial balance as $85.
   e. An error in recording a $765 increase in Cash as a credit.

5. Bonaventure Company has total assets of $1,000,000, liabilities of $400,000, and equity of $600,000. What is its debt ratio (rounded to a whole percent)?
   a. 250%
   b. 167%
   c. 67%
   d. 150%
   e. 40%

[i] Icon denotes assignments that involve decision making.

## Discussion Questions

1. Provide the names of two (a) asset accounts, (b) liability accounts, and (c) equity accounts.

2. What is the difference between a note payable and an account payable?

3. [i] Discuss the steps in processing business transactions.

4. What kinds of transactions can be recorded in a general journal?

5. Are debits or credits typically listed first in general journal entries? Are the debits or the credits indented?

6. If assets are valuable resources and asset accounts have debit balances, why do expense accounts also have debit balances?

7. Should a transaction be recorded first in a journal or the ledger? Why?

8. [i] Why does the recordkeeper prepare a trial balance?

9. If an incorrect amount is journalized and posted to the accounts, how should the error be corrected?

10. Identify the four financial statements of a business.

11. [i] What information is reported in an income statement?

12. [i] Why does the user of an income statement need to know the time period that it covers?

13. [i] What information is reported in a balance sheet?

14. Define (a) assets, (b) liabilities, (c) equity, and (d) net assets.

15. Which financial statement is sometimes called the statement of financial position?

16. [i] Review the **Research in Motion** balance sheet in Appendix A. Identify three accounts on its balance **RIM** sheet that carry debit balances and three accounts on its balance sheet that carry credit balances.

17. Review the **Apple** balance sheet in Appendix A. Identify an asset with the word receivable in its account **Apple** title and a liability with the word payable in its account title.

18. Locate **Palm**'s income statement in Appendix A. **Palm** What is the title of its revenue account?

19. Refer to **Nokia**'s balance sheet in Appendix A. **NOKIA** What does Nokia title its current asset referring to merchandise available for sale?

Identify the financial statement(s) where each of the following items appears. Use I for income statement, E for statement of owner's equity, and B for balance sheet.

**a.** Accounts payable
**b.** Cash
**c.** Rent expense
**d.** Office supplies
**e.** Prepaid insurance
**f.** Revenue
**g.** Office equipment
**h.** Cash withdrawal by owner
**i.** Unearned rent revenue

**QUICK STUDY**

**QS 2-1**
Identifying financial statement items
C2  P3

Identify the items from the following list that are likely to serve as source documents.

**a.** Bank statement
**b.** Sales ticket
**c.** Income statement
**d.** Trial balance
**e.** Telephone bill
**f.** Invoice from supplier
**g.** Company revenue account
**h.** Balance sheet
**i.** Prepaid rent

**QS 2-2**
Identifying source documents
C1

Identify whether a debit or credit yields the indicated change for each of the following accounts.

**a.** To increase Store Equipment
**b.** To increase Land
**c.** To decrease Cash
**d.** To increase Utilities Expense
**e.** To increase Fees Earned
**f.** To decrease Unearned Revenue
**g.** To decrease Prepaid Insurance
**h.** To increase Notes Payable
**i.** To decrease Accounts Receivable
**j.** To increase Owner Capital

**QS 2-3**
Analyzing debit or credit by account
A1

Identify the normal balance (debit or credit) for each of the following accounts.

**a.** Equipment
**b.** Wages Expense
**c.** Repair Services Revenue
**d.** Office Supplies
**e.** Owner Withdrawals
**f.** Accounts Receivable
**g.** Prepaid Insurance
**h.** Wages Payable
**i.** Owner Capital

**QS 2-4**
Identifying normal balance
C4

Indicate whether a debit or credit *decreases* the normal balance of each of the following accounts.

**a.** Land
**b.** Service Revenue
**c.** Interest Payable
**d.** Accounts Receivable
**e.** Salaries Expense
**f.** Owner Capital
**g.** Prepaid Insurance
**h.** Buildings
**i.** Interest Revenue
**j.** Owner Withdrawals
**k.** Unearned Revenue
**l.** Accounts Payable

**QS 2-5**
Linking debit or credit with normal balance
C4

Prepare journal entries for each of the following selected transactions.

**a.** On January 15, Kolby Anderson opens a remodeling company called Fancy Kitchens by investing $75,000 cash along with equipment having a $30,000 value.
**b.** On January 21, Fancy Kitchens purchases office supplies on credit for $650.
**c.** On January 25, Fancy Kitchens receives $8,700 cash for performing remodeling services.
**d.** On January 30, Fancy Kitchens receives $4,000 cash in advance of providing remodeling services to a customer.

**QS 2-6**
Preparing journal entries
P1

A trial balance has total debits of $20,000 and total credits of $24,500. Which one of the following errors would create this imbalance? Explain.

**a.** A $2,250 debit posting to Accounts Receivable was posted mistakenly to Cash.
**b.** A $4,500 debit posting to Equipment was posted mistakenly to Supplies.
**c.** An entry debiting Cash and crediting Accounts Payable for $4,500 was mistakenly not posted.
**d.** A $2,250 credit to Revenue in a journal entry is incorrectly posted to the ledger as a $2,250 debit, leaving the Revenue account with a $6,300 credit balance.
**e.** A $4,500 debit to Rent Expense in a journal entry is incorrectly posted to the ledger as a $4,500 credit, leaving the Rent Expense account with a $750 debit balance.
**f.** A $2,250 debit to Utilities Expense in a journal entry is incorrectly posted to the ledger as a $2,250 credit, leaving the Utilities Expense account with a $3,000 debit balance.

**QS 2-7**
Identifying a posting error
P2

**QS 2-8**
Classifying accounts in
financial statements

**P3**

Indicate the financial statement on which each of the following items appears. Use I for income statement, E for statement of owner's equity, and B for balance sheet.

| | | |
|---|---|---|
| **a.** Buildings | **e.** Rental Revenue | **i.** Accounts Receivable |
| **b.** Interest Expense | **f.** Insurance Expense | **j.** Salaries Expense |
| **c.** Owner Withdrawals | **g.** Services Revenue | **k.** Equipment |
| **d.** Office Supplies | **h.** Interest Payable | **l.** Prepaid Insurance |

**QS 2-9**
International accounting
standards

**C4**

Answer each of the following questions related to international accounting standards.

**a.** What type of entry system is applied when accounting follows IFRS?

**b.** Identify the number and usual titles of the financial statements prepared under IFRS.

**c.** How do differences in accounting controls and enforcement impact accounting reports prepared across different countries?

# EXERCISES

**Exercise 2-1**
Steps in analyzing and recording
transactions   **C1**

Order the following steps in the accounting process that focus on analyzing and recording transactions.

_____ **a.** Record relevant transactions in a journal.

_____ **b.** Prepare and analyze the trial balance.

_____ **c.** Analyze each transaction from source documents.

_____ **d.** Post journal information to ledger accounts.

**Exercise 2-2**
Identifying and classifying
accounts

**C2**

Enter the number for the item that best completes each of the descriptions below.

**1.** Account     **3.** Asset     **5.** Equity

**2.** Three     **4.** Liability

**a.** Owner, capital and owner, withdrawals are examples of _____ accounts.

**b.** Accounts payable, unearned revenue, and note payable are examples of _____ accounts.

**c.** Accounts receivable, prepaid accounts, supplies, and land are examples of _____ accounts.

**d.** Accounts are arranged into _____ general categories

**e.** An _____ is a record of increases and decreases in a specific asset, liability, equity, revenue, or expense item.

**Exercise 2-3**
Identifying a ledger and chart
of accounts

**C3**

Enter the number for the item that best completes each of the descriptions below.

**1.** General ledger     **2.** Chart

**a.** The _____ is a record containing all accounts used by a company.

**b.** A _____ of accounts is a list of all accounts a company uses.

**Exercise 2-4**
Identifying type and normal
balances of accounts

**C4**

For each of the following (1) identify the type of account as an asset, liability, equity, revenue, or expense, (2) identify the normal balance of the account, and (3) enter *debit* (*Dr.*) or *credit* (*Cr.*) to identify the kind of entry that would increase the account balance.

| | | |
|---|---|---|
| **a.** Fees Earned | **e.** Cash | **i.** Accounts Receivable |
| **b.** Equipment | **f.** Legal Expense | **j.** Owner Withdrawals |
| **c.** Notes Payable | **g.** Prepaid Insurance | **k.** License Fee Revenue |
| **d.** Owner Capital | **h.** Land | **l.** Unearned Revenue |

**Exercise 2-5**
Analyzing effects of
transactions on accounts

**A1**

Taylor Co. bills a client $48,000 for services provided and agrees to accept the following three items in full payment: (1) $7,500 cash, (2) computer equipment worth $75,000, and (3) to assume responsibility for a $34,500 note payable related to the computer equipment. The entry Taylor makes to record this transaction includes which one or more of the following?

| | |
|---|---|
| **a.** $34,500 increase in a liability account | **d.** $48,000 increase in an asset account |
| **b.** $7,500 increase in the Cash account | **e.** $48,000 increase in a revenue account |
| **c.** $7,500 increase in a revenue account | **f.** $34,500 increase in an equity account |

Use the information in each of the following separate cases to calculate the unknown amount.

**a.** During October, Shandra Company had $97,500 of cash receipts and $101,250 of cash disbursements. The October 31 Cash balance was $16,800. Determine how much cash the company had at the close of business on September 30.

**b.** On September 30, Mordish Co. had a $97,500 balance in Accounts Receivable. During October, the company collected $88,950 from its credit customers. The October 31 balance in Accounts Receivable was $100,500. Determine the amount of sales on account that occurred in October.

**c.** Nasser Co. had $147,000 of accounts payable on September 30 and $136,500 on October 31. Total purchases on account during October were $270,000. Determine how much cash was paid on accounts payable during October.

**Exercise 2-6**
Analyzing account entries and balances

A1

---

Prepare general journal entries for the following transactions of a new company called Pose for Pics.

Aug.  1   Kasey Madison, the owner, invested $7,500 cash and $32,500 of photography equipment in the company.
      2   The company paid $3,000 cash for an insurance policy covering the next 24 months.
      5   The company purchased office supplies for $1,400 cash.
     20   The company received $2,650 cash in photography fees earned.
     31   The company paid $875 cash for August utilities.

**Exercise 2-7**
Preparing general journal entries

P1

---

Use the information in Exercise 2-7 to prepare an August 31 trial balance for Pose for Pics. Begin by opening these T-accounts: Cash; Office Supplies; Prepaid Insurance; Photography Equipment; K. Madison, Capital; Photography Fees Earned; and Utilities Expense. Then, post the general journal entries to these T-accounts (which will serve as the ledger), and prepare the trial balance.

**Exercise 2-8**
Preparing T-accounts (ledger) and a trial balance  P2

---

Prepare general journal entries to record the transactions below for Dexter Company by using the following accounts: Cash; Accounts Receivable; Office Supplies; Office Equipment; Accounts Payable; M. Dexter, Capital; M. Dexter, Withdrawals; Fees Earned; and Rent Expense. Use the letters beside each transaction to identify entries. After recording the transactions, post them to T-accounts, which serves as the general ledger for this assignment. Determine the ending balance of each T-account.

**a.** Macy Dexter, owner, invested $12,750 cash in the company.
**b.** The company purchased office supplies for $375 cash.
**c.** The company purchased $7,050 of office equipment on credit.
**d.** The company received $1,500 cash as fees for services provided to a customer.
**e.** The company paid $7,050 cash to settle the payable for the office equipment purchased in transaction *c*.
**f.** The company billed a customer $2,700 as fees for services provided.
**g.** The company paid $525 cash for the monthly rent.
**h.** The company collected $1,125 cash as partial payment for the account receivable created in transaction *f*.
**i.** Macy Dexter withdrew $1,000 cash from the company for personal use.

**Exercise 2-9**
Recording effects of transactions in T-accounts

A1

**Check**  Cash ending balance, $6,425

---

After recording the transactions of Exercise 2-9 in T-accounts and calculating the balance of each account, prepare a trial balance. Use May 31, 2011, as its report date.

**Exercise 2-10**
Preparing a trial balance  P2

---

Examine the following transactions and identify those that create revenues for Jade Services, a company owned by Mia Jade. Prepare general journal entries to record those revenue transactions and explain why the other transactions did not create revenues.

**a.** Mia Jade invests $38,250 cash in the company.
**b.** The company provided $1,350 of services on credit.
**c.** The company provided services to a client and immediately received $1,575 cash.
**d.** The company received $9,150 cash from a client in payment for services to be provided next year.
**e.** The company received $4,500 cash from a client in partial payment of an account receivable.
**f.** The company borrowed $150,000 cash from the bank by signing a promissory note.

**Exercise 2-11**
Analyzing and journalizing revenue transactions

A1  P1

**Exercise 2-12**

Analyzing and journalizing expense transactions

A1　P1　

Examine the following transactions and identify those that create expenses for Jade Services. Prepare general journal entries to record those expense transactions and explain why the other transactions did not create expenses.

**a.** The company paid $14,100 cash for payment on a 14-month old liability for office supplies.

**b.** The company paid $1,125 cash for the just completed two-week salary of the receptionist.

**c.** The company paid $45,000 cash for equipment purchased.

**d.** The company paid $930 cash for this month's utilities.

**e.** Owner (Jade) withdrew $5,000 cash from the company for personal use.

---

**Exercise 2-13**

Preparing an income statement

C3　P3

Dominick Lopez operates a consulting firm called Tech Today. On August 31, the company's records show the following accounts and amounts for the month of August. Use this information to prepare an August income statement for the business.

| | | | | |
|---|---|---|---|---|
| Cash............................ | $ 8,360 | | D. Lopez, Withdrawals......... | $ 3,000 |
| Accounts receivable ............ | 17,000 | | Consulting fees earned......... | 17,000 |
| Office supplies ................. | 3,250 | | Rent expense ................. | 4,550 |
| Land .......................... | 46,000 | | Salaries expense .............. | 8,000 |
| Office equipment .............. | 18,000 | | Telephone expense............ | 560 |
| Accounts payable .............. | 8,000 | | Miscellaneous expenses ........ | 280 |
| D. Lopez, Capital, July 31......... | 4,000 | | Owner investments ........... | 80,000 |

**Check**　Net income, $3,610

---

**Exercise 2-14**

Preparing a statement of owner's equity　P3

**Check**　End. Capital, $84,610

Use the information in Exercise 2-13 to prepare an August statement of owner's equity for Tech Today. (The owner invested $84,000 cash in the company during the first week of August.)

---

**Exercise 2-15**

Preparing a balance sheet　P3

Use the information in Exercise 2-13 (if completed, you can also use your solution to Exercise 2-14) to prepare an August 31 balance sheet for Tech Today.

---

**Exercise 2-16**

Computing net income

A1　

A sole proprietorship had the following assets and liabilities at the beginning and end of this year.

| | Assets | Liabilities |
|---|---|---|
| Beginning of the year ......... | $ 70,000 | $30,000 |
| End of the year ............. | 115,000 | 46,000 |

Determine the net income earned or net loss incurred by the business during the year for each of the following *separate* cases:

**a.** Owner made no investments in the business and no withdrawals were made during the year.

**b.** Owner made no investments in the business but withdrew $1,250 cash per month for personal use.

**c.** Owner made no withdrawals during the year but did invest an additional $45,000 cash.

**d.** Owner withdrew $1,250 cash per month for personal use and invested an additional $25,000 cash.

---

**Exercise 2-17**

Analyzing changes in a company's equity

P3　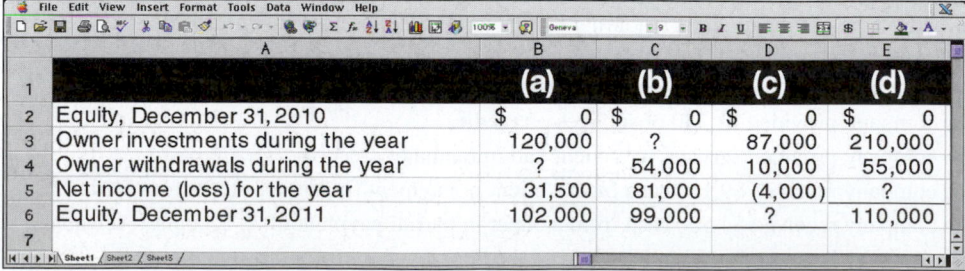

Compute the missing amount for each of the following separate companies a through d.

Assume the following T-accounts reflect Joy Co.'s general ledger and that seven transactions *a* through *g* are posted to them. Provide a short description of each transaction. Include the amounts in your descriptions.

**Exercise 2-18**
Interpreting and describing transactions from T-accounts

A1

| Cash | | | |
|---|---|---|---|
| (a) | 7,000 | (b) | 3,600 |
| (e) | 2,500 | (c) | 600 |
| | | (f) | 2,400 |
| | | (g) | 700 |

| Automobiles | |
|---|---|
| (a) | 11,000 |

| Accounts Payable | | | |
|---|---|---|---|
| (f) | 2,400 | (d) | 9,600 |

| Office Supplies | |
|---|---|
| (c) | 600 |
| (d) | 200 |

| D. Joy, Capital | | | |
|---|---|---|---|
| | | (a) | 23,600 |

| Prepaid Insurance | |
|---|---|
| (b) | 3,600 |

| Delivery Services Revenue | | | |
|---|---|---|---|
| | | (e) | 2,500 |

| Equipment | |
|---|---|
| (a) | 5,600 |
| (d) | 9,400 |

| Gas and Oil Expense | |
|---|---|
| (g) | 700 |

Use information from the T-accounts in Exercise 2-18 to prepare general journal entries for each of the seven transactions *a* through *g*.

**Exercise 2-19**
Preparing general journal entries

P1

Posting errors are identified in the following table. In column (1), enter the amount of the difference between the two trial balance columns (debit and credit) due to the error. In column (2), identify the trial balance column (debit or credit) with the larger amount if they are not equal. In column (3), identify the account(s) affected by the error. In column (4), indicate the amount by which the account(s) in column (3) is under- or overstated. Item (a) is completed as an example.

**Exercise 2-20**
Identifying effects of posting errors on the trial balance

A1 P2

| | Description of Posting Error | (1) Difference between Debit and Credit Columns | (2) Column with the Larger Total | (3) Identify Account(s) Incorrectly Stated | (4) Amount that Account(s) Is Over- or Understated |
|---|---|---|---|---|---|
| a. | $2,400 debit to Rent Expense is posted as a $1,590 debit. | $810 | Credit | Rent Expense | Rent Expense understated $810 |
| b. | $4,050 credit to Cash is posted twice as two credits to Cash. | | | | |
| c. | $9,900 debit to the Withdrawals account is debited to Owner's Capital. | | | | |
| d. | $2,250 debit to Prepaid Insurance is posted as a debit to Insurance Expense. | | | | |
| e. | $42,000 debit to Machinery is posted as a debit to Accounts Payable. | | | | |
| f. | $4,950 credit to Services Revenue is posted as a $495 credit. | | | | |
| g. | $1,440 debit to Store Supplies is not posted. | | | | |

You are told the column totals in a trial balance are not equal. After careful analysis, you discover only one error. Specifically, a correctly journalized credit purchase of a computer for $16,950 is posted from the journal to the ledger with a $16,950 debit to Office Equipment and another $16,950 debit to Accounts Payable. The Office Equipment account has a debit balance of $40,100 on the trial balance. Answer each of the following questions and compute the dollar amount of any misstatement.

**Exercise 2-21**
Analyzing a trial balance error

A1 P2

**a.** Is the debit column total of the trial balance overstated, understated, or correctly stated?

**b.** Is the credit column total of the trial balance overstated, understated, or correctly stated?

**c.** Is the Office Equipment account balance overstated, understated, or correctly stated in the trial balance?

**d.** Is the Accounts Payable account balance overstated, understated, or correctly stated in the trial balance?

**e.** If the debit column total of the trial balance is $360,000 before correcting the error, what is the total of the credit column before correction?

---

**Exercise 2-22**

Interpreting the debt ratio and return on assets

A2

**a.** Calculate the debt ratio and the return on assets using the year-end information for each of the following six separate companies ($ thousands).

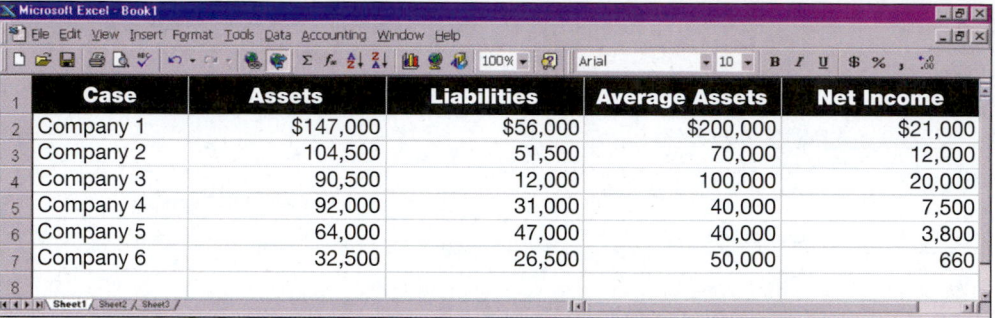

| Case | Assets | Liabilities | Average Assets | Net Income |
|------|--------|-------------|----------------|------------|
| Company 1 | $147,000 | $56,000 | $200,000 | $21,000 |
| Company 2 | 104,500 | 51,500 | 70,000 | 12,000 |
| Company 3 | 90,500 | 12,000 | 100,000 | 20,000 |
| Company 4 | 92,000 | 31,000 | 40,000 | 7,500 |
| Company 5 | 64,000 | 47,000 | 40,000 | 3,800 |
| Company 6 | 32,500 | 26,500 | 50,000 | 660 |

**b.** Of the six companies, which business relies most heavily on creditor financing?

**c.** Of the six companies, which business relies most heavily on equity financing?

**d.** Which two companies indicate the greatest risk?

**e.** Which two companies earn the highest return on assets?

**f.** Which one company would investors likely prefer based on the risk–return relation?

---

**Exercise 2-23**

Preparing a balance sheet following IFRS

P3

**BMW** reports the following balance sheet accounts for the year ended December 31, 2009 (euro in millions). Prepare the balance sheet for this company as of December 31, 2009, following the usual IFRS formats.

| | | | | |
|---|---|---|---|---|
| Current liabilities | € 8,350 | | Noncurrent liabilities | €10,943 |
| Current assets | 17,663 | | Noncurrent assets | 6,984 |
| Total equity | 5,354 | | | |

---

**PROBLEM SET A**

**Problem 2-1A**

Preparing and posting journal entries; preparing a trial balance

C3  C4  A1  P1  P2

mhhe.com/wildFAP20e

Gary Bauer opens a computer consulting business called Technology Consultants and completes the following transactions in April.

April   1   Bauer invested $100,000 cash along with $24,000 in office equipment in the company.
       2   The company prepaid $7,200 cash for twelve months' rent for an office. (*Hint:* Debit Prepaid Rent for $7,200.)
       3   The company made credit purchases of office equipment for $12,000 and office supplies for $2,400. Payment is due within 10 days.
       6   The company completed services for a client and immediately received $2,000 cash.
       9   The company completed an $8,000 project for a client, who must pay within 30 days.
      13   The company paid $14,400 cash to settle the account payable created on April 3.
      19   The company paid $6,000 cash for the premium on a 12-month insurance policy. (*Hint:* Debit Prepaid Insurance for $6,000.)
      22   The company received $6,400 cash as partial payment for the work completed on April 9.
      25   The company completed work for another client for $2,640 on credit.
      28   Bauer withdrew $6,200 cash from the company for personal use.
      29   The company purchased $800 of additional office supplies on credit.
      30   The company paid $700 cash for this month's utility bill.

*Required*

**1.** Prepare general journal entries to record these transactions (use the account titles listed in part 2).

**2.** Open the following ledger accounts—their account numbers are in parentheses (use the balance column format): Cash (101); Accounts Receivable (106); Office Supplies (124); Prepaid Insurance (128);

Prepaid Rent (131); Office Equipment (163); Accounts Payable (201); G. Bauer, Capital (301); G. Bauer, Withdrawals (302); Services Revenue (403); and Utilities Expense (690). Post the journal entries from part 1 to the ledger accounts and enter the balance after each posting.

**3.** Prepare a trial balance as of the end of April.

**Check** (2) Ending balances: Cash, $73,900; Accounts Receivable, $4,240; Accounts Payable, $800

(3) Total debits, $137,440

Shelton Engineering completed the following transactions in the month of June.

**a.** Shana Shelton, the owner, invested $105,000 cash, office equipment with a value of $6,000, and $45,000 of drafting equipment to launch the company.

**b.** The company purchased land worth $54,000 for an office by paying $5,400 cash and signing a long-term note payable for $48,600.

**c.** The company purchased a portable building with $75,000 cash and moved it onto the land acquired in b.

**d.** The company paid $6,000 cash for the premium on an 18-month insurance policy.

**e.** The company completed and delivered a set of plans for a client and collected $5,700 cash.

**f.** The company purchased $22,500 of additional drafting equipment by paying $10,500 cash and signing a long-term note payable for $12,000.

**g.** The company completed $12,000 of engineering services for a client. This amount is to be received in 30 days.

**h.** The company purchased $2,250 of additional office equipment on credit.

**i.** The company completed engineering services for $18,000 on credit.

**j.** The company received a bill for rent of equipment that was used on a recently completed job. The $1,200 rent cost must be paid within 30 days.

**k.** The company collected $7,200 cash in partial payment from the client described in transaction g.

**l.** The company paid $1,500 cash for wages to a drafting assistant.

**m.** The company paid $2,250 cash to settle the account payable created in transaction h.

**n.** The company paid $675 cash for minor maintenance of its drafting equipment.

**o.** S. Shelton withdrew $9,360 cash from the company for personal use.

**p.** The company paid $1,500 cash for wages to a drafting assistant.

**q.** The company paid $3,000 cash for advertisements in the local newspaper during June.

*Required*

**1.** Prepare general journal entries to record these transactions (use the account titles listed in part 2).

**2.** Open the following ledger accounts—their account numbers are in parentheses (use the balance column format): Cash (101); Accounts Receivable (106); Prepaid Insurance (108); Office Equipment (163); Drafting Equipment (164); Building (170); Land (172); Accounts Payable (201); Notes Payable (250); S. Shelton, Capital (301); S. Shelton, Withdrawals (302); Engineering Fees Earned (402); Wages Expense (601); Equipment Rental Expense (602); Advertising Expense (603); and Repairs Expense (604). Post the journal entries from part 1 to the accounts and enter the balance after each posting.

**3.** Prepare a trial balance as of the end of June.

**Problem 2-2A**
Preparing and posting journal entries; preparing a trial balance
**C3 C4 A1 P1 P2**

**Check** (2) Ending balances: Cash, $2,715; Accounts Receivable, $22,800; Accounts Payable, $1,200

(3) Trial balance totals, $253,500

The accounting records of Fabiano Distribution show the following assets and liabilities as of December 31, 2010 and 2011.

| December 31 | 2010 | 2011 |
|---|---|---|
| Cash | $ 52,500 | $ 18,750 |
| Accounts receivable | 28,500 | 22,350 |
| Office supplies | 4,500 | 3,300 |
| Office equipment | 138,000 | 147,000 |
| Trucks | 54,000 | 54,000 |
| Building | 0 | 180,000 |
| Land | 0 | 45,000 |
| Accounts payable | 7,500 | 37,500 |
| Note payable | 0 | 105,000 |

**Problem 2-3A**
Computing net income from equity analysis, preparing a balance sheet, and computing the debt ratio
**C2 A1 A2 P3**

mhhe.com/wildFAP20e

Late in December 2011, the business purchased a small office building and land for $225,000. It paid $120,000 cash toward the purchase and a $105,000 note payable was signed for the balance. Mr. Fabiano had to invest $35,000 cash in the business to enable it to pay the $120,000 cash. Mr. Fabiano withdraws $3,000 cash per month for personal use.

**Required**

1. Prepare balance sheets for the business as of December 31, 2010 and 2011. (*Hint:* Report only total equity on the balance sheet and remember that total equity equals the difference between assets and liabilities.)

2. By comparing equity amounts from the balance sheets and using the additional information presented in this problem, prepare a calculation to show how much net income was earned by the business during 2011.

3. Compute the 2011 year-end debt ratio for the business.

---

**Problem 2-4A**
Preparing and posting journal entries; preparing a trial balance

**C3  C4  A1  P1  P2**

Santo Birch opens a Web consulting business called Show-Me-the-Money and completes the following transactions in its first month of operations.

| | | |
|---|---|---|
| March | 1 | Birch invests $150,000 cash along with office equipment valued at $22,000 in the company. |
| | 2 | The company prepaid $6,000 cash for twelve months' rent for office space. (*Hint:* Debit Prepaid Rent for $6,000.) |
| | 3 | The company made credit purchases for $3,000 in office equipment and $1,200 in office supplies. Payment is due within 10 days. |
| | 6 | The company completed services for a client and immediately received $4,000 cash. |
| | 9 | The company completed a $7,500 project for a client, who must pay within 30 days. |
| | 13 | The company paid $4,200 cash to settle the account payable created on March 3. |
| | 19 | The company paid $5,000 cash for the premium on a 12-month insurance policy. (*Hint:* Debit Prepaid Insurance for $5,000.) |
| | 22 | The company received $3,500 cash as partial payment for the work completed on March 9. |
| | 25 | The company completed work for another client for $3,820 on credit. |
| | 29 | Birch withdrew $5,100 cash from the company for personal use. |
| | 30 | The company purchased $600 of additional office supplies on credit. |
| | 31 | The company paid $200 cash for this month's utility bill. |

**Required**

1. Prepare general journal entries to record these transactions (use account titles listed in part 2).

2. Open the following ledger accounts—their account numbers are in parentheses (use the balance column format): Cash (101); Accounts Receivable (106); Office Supplies (124); Prepaid Insurance (128); Prepaid Rent (131); Office Equipment (163); Accounts Payable (201); S. Birch, Capital (301); S. Birch, Withdrawals (302); Services Revenue (403); and Utilities Expense (690). Post journal entries from part 1 to the ledger accounts and enter the balance after each posting.

3. Prepare a trial balance as of April 30.

---

**Problem 2-5A**
Recording transactions; posting to ledger; preparing a trial balance

**C3  A1  P1  P2**

Business transactions completed by Eric Pense during the month of September are as follows.

a. Pense invested $23,000 cash along with office equipment valued at $12,000 in a new sole proprietorship named EP Consulting.

b. The company purchased land valued at $8,000 and a building valued at $33,000. The purchase is paid with $15,000 cash and a long-term note payable for $26,000.

c. The company purchased $600 of office supplies on credit.

d. Pense invested his personal automobile in the company. The automobile has a value of $7,000 and is to be used exclusively in the business.

e. The company purchased $1,100 of additional office equipment on credit.

f. The company paid $800 cash salary to an assistant.

g. The company provided services to a client and collected $2,700 cash.

h. The company paid $430 cash for this month's utilities.

i. The company paid $600 cash to settle the account payable created in transaction c.

j. The company purchased $4,000 of new office equipment by paying $4,000 cash.

k. The company completed $2,400 of services for a client, who must pay within 30 days.

l. The company paid $800 cash salary to an assistant.

m. The company received $1,000 cash in partial payment on the receivable created in transaction k.

n. Pense withdrew $1,050 cash from the company for personal use.

**Required**

**1.** Prepare general journal entries to record these transactions (use account titles listed in part 2).

**2.** Open the following ledger accounts—their account numbers are in parentheses (use the balance column format): Cash (101); Accounts Receivable (106); Office Supplies (108); Office Equipment (163); Automobiles (164); Building (170); Land (172); Accounts Payable (201); Notes Payable (250); E. Pense, Capital (301); E. Pense, Withdrawals (302); Fees Earned (402); Salaries Expense (601); and Utilities Expense (602). Post the journal entries from part 1 to the ledger accounts and enter the balance after each posting.

**3.** Prepare a trial balance as of the end of September.

**Check**  (2) Ending balances: Cash, $4,020; Office Equipment, $17,100

(3) Trial balance totals, $74,200

---

Carlos Beltran started an engineering firm called Beltran Engineering. He began operations and completed seven transactions in May, which included his initial investment of $17,000 cash. After those seven transactions, the ledger included the following accounts with normal balances.

**Problem 2-6A**
Analyzing account balances and reconstructing transactions

C1  C3  A1  P2

| | |
|---|---:|
| Cash ....................... | $26,660 |
| Office supplies ................ | 660 |
| Prepaid insurance ............ | 3,200 |
| Office equipment ............ | 16,500 |
| Accounts payable ............ | 16,500 |
| C. Beltran, Capital ............ | 17,000 |
| C. Beltran, Withdrawals ........ | 3,740 |
| Engineering fees earned ........ | 24,000 |
| Rent expense ............... | 6,740 |

**Required**

**1.** Prepare a trial balance for this business as of the end of May.

**Check**  (1) Trial balance totals, $57,500

**Analysis Components**

**2.** Analyze the accounts and their balances and prepare a list that describes each of the seven most likely transactions and their amounts.

**3.** Prepare a report of cash received and cash paid showing how the seven transactions in part 2 yield the $26,660 ending Cash balance.

(3) Cash paid, $14,340

---

Shaw Management Services opens for business and completes these transactions in November.

Nov.  1   Kita Shaw, the owner, invested $30,000 cash along with $15,000 of office equipment in the company.

2   The company prepaid $4,500 cash for six months' rent for an office. (*Hint:* Debit Prepaid Rent for $4,500.)

4   The company made credit purchases of office equipment for $2,500 and of office supplies for $600. Payment is due within 10 days.

8   The company completed work for a client and immediately received $3,400 cash.

12   The company completed a $10,200 project for a client, who must pay within 30 days.

13   The company paid $3,100 cash to settle the payable created on November 4.

19   The company paid $1,800 cash for the premium on a 24-month insurance policy.

22   The company received $5,200 cash as partial payment for the work completed on November 12.

24   The company completed work for another client for $1,750 on credit.

28   K. Shaw withdrew $5,300 cash from the company for personal use.

29   The company purchased $249 of additional office supplies on credit.

30   The company paid $531 cash for this month's utility bill.

**PROBLEM SET B**

**Problem 2-1B**
Preparing and posting journal entries; preparing a trial balance

C3  C4  A1  P1  P2

**Required**

**1.** Prepare general journal entries to record these transactions (use account titles listed in part 2).

**2.** Open the following ledger accounts—their account numbers are in parentheses (use the balance column format): Cash (101); Accounts Receivable (106); Office Supplies (124); Prepaid Insurance (128); Prepaid Rent (131); Office Equipment (163); Accounts Payable (201); K. Shaw, Capital (301); K. Shaw, Withdrawals (302); Services Revenue (403); and Utilities Expense (690). Post the journal entries from part 1 to the ledger accounts and enter the balance after each posting.

**3.** Prepare a trial balance as of the end of November.

**Check**  (2) Ending balances: Cash, $23,369; Accounts Receivable, $6,750; Accounts Payable, $249

(3) Total debits, $60,599

**Problem 2-2B**

Preparing and posting journal entries; preparing a trial balance

C3  C4  A1  P1  P2

At the beginning of April, Brooke Gable launched a custom computer solutions company called Softways. The company had the following transactions during April.

**a.** Brooke Gable invested $45,000 cash, office equipment with a value of $4,500, and $28,000 of computer equipment in the company.

**b.** The company purchased land worth $24,000 for an office by paying $4,800 cash and signing a long-term note payable for $19,200.

**c.** The company purchased a portable building with $21,000 cash and moved it onto the land acquired in *b*.

**d.** The company paid $6,600 cash for the premium on a two-year insurance policy.

**e.** The company provided services to a client and immediately collected $3,200 cash.

**f.** The company purchased $3,500 of additional computer equipment by paying $700 cash and signing a long-term note payable for $2,800.

**g.** The company completed $3,750 of services for a client. This amount is to be received within 30 days.

**h.** The company purchased $750 of additional office equipment on credit.

**i.** The company completed client services for $9,200 on credit.

**j.** The company received a bill for rent of a computer testing device that was used on a recently completed job. The $320 rent cost must be paid within 30 days.

**k.** The company collected $4,600 cash in partial payment from the client described in transaction *i*.

**l.** The company paid $1,600 cash for wages to an assistant.

**m.** The company paid $750 cash to settle the payable created in transaction *h*.

**n.** The company paid $425 cash for minor maintenance of the company's computer equipment.

**o.** B. Gable withdrew $3,875 cash from the company for personal use.

**p.** The company paid $1,600 cash for wages to an assistant.

**q.** The company paid $800 cash for advertisements in the local newspaper during April.

*Required*

**1.** Prepare general journal entries to record these transactions (use account titles listed in part 2).

**Check**  (2) Ending balances: Cash, $10,650; Accounts Receivable, $8,350; Accounts Payable, $320

**2.** Open the following ledger accounts—their account numbers are in parentheses (use the balance column format): Cash (101); Accounts Receivable (106); Prepaid Insurance (108); Office Equipment (163); Computer Equipment (164); Building (170); Land (172); Accounts Payable (201); Notes Payable (250); B. Gable, Capital (301); B. Gable, Withdrawals (302); Fees Earned (402); Wages Expense (601); Computer Rental Expense (602); Advertising Expense (603); and Repairs Expense (604). Post the journal entries from part 1 to the accounts and enter the balance after each posting.

(3) Trial balance totals, $115,970

**3.** Prepare a trial balance as of the end of April.

**Problem 2-3B**

Computing net income from equity analysis, preparing a balance sheet, and computing the debt ratio

C2  A1  A2  P3

The accounting records of Schmit Co. show the following assets and liabilities as of December 31, 2010 and 2011.

| December 31 | 2010 | 2011 |
|---|---|---|
| Cash | $14,000 | $ 10,000 |
| Accounts receivable | 25,000 | 30,000 |
| Office supplies | 10,000 | 12,500 |
| Office equipment | 60,000 | 60,000 |
| Machinery | 30,500 | 30,500 |
| Building | 0 | 260,000 |
| Land | 0 | 65,000 |
| Accounts payable | 5,000 | 15,000 |
| Note payable | 0 | 260,000 |

Late in December 2011, the business purchased a small office building and land for $325,000. It paid $65,000 cash toward the purchase and a $260,000 note payable was signed for the balance. Janet Schmit, the owner, had to invest an additional $25,000 cash to enable it to pay the $65,000 cash toward the purchase. The owner withdraws $1,000 cash per month for personal use.

*Required*

**1.** Prepare balance sheets for the business as of December 31, 2010 and 2011. (*Hint:* Report only total equity on the balance sheet and remember that total equity equals the difference between assets and liabilities.)

**2.** By comparing equity amounts from the balance sheets and using the additional information presented in the problem, prepare a calculation to show how much net income was earned by the business during 2011.

**3.** Calculate the December 31, 2011, debt ratio for the business.

**Check**  (2) Net income, $45,500

(3) Debt ratio, 58.76%

---

Lummus Management Services opens for business and completes these transactions in September.

| | | |
|---|---|---|
| Sept. | 1 | Rhonda Lummus, the owner, invests $28,000 cash along with office equipment valued at $25,000 in the company. |
| | 2 | The company prepaid $10,500 cash for 12 months' rent for office space. (*Hint:* Debit Prepaid Rent for $10,500.) |
| | 4 | The company made credit purchases for $9,000 in office equipment and $1,200 in office supplies. Payment is due within 10 days. |
| | 8 | The company completed work for a client and immediately received $2,600 cash. |
| | 12 | The company completed a $13,400 project for a client, who must pay within 30 days. |
| | 13 | The company paid $10,200 cash to settle the payable created on September 4. |
| | 19 | The company paid $5,200 cash for the premium on an 18-month insurance policy. (*Hint:* Debit Prepaid Insurance for $5,200.) |
| | 22 | The company received $7,800 cash as partial payment for the work completed on September 12. |
| | 24 | The company completed work for another client for $1,900 on credit. |
| | 28 | Lummus withdrew $5,300 cash from the company for personal use. |
| | 29 | The company purchased $1,700 of additional office supplies on credit. |
| | 30 | The company paid $460 cash for this month's utility bill. |

**Problem 2-4B**
Preparing and posting journal entries; preparing a trial balance
C3  C4  A1  P1  P2

**Required**

**1.** Prepare general journal entries to record these transactions (use account titles listed in part 2).

**2.** Open the following ledger accounts—their account numbers are in parentheses (use the balance column format): Cash (101); Accounts Receivable (106); Office Supplies (124); Prepaid Insurance (128); Prepaid Rent (131); Office Equipment (163); Accounts Payable (201); R. Lummus, Capital (301); R. Lummus, Withdrawals (302); Service Fees Earned (401); and Utilities Expense (690). Post journal entries from part 1 to the ledger accounts and enter the balance after each posting.

**3.** Prepare a trial balance as of the end of September.

**Check**  (2) Ending balances: Cash, $6,740; Accounts Receivable, $7,500; Accounts Payable, $1,700

(3) Total debits, $72,600

---

Cooke Consulting completed the following transactions during June.

**a.** Chris Cooke, the owner, invested $80,000 cash along with office equipment valued at $30,000 in the new company.

**b.** The company purchased land valued at $30,000 and a building valued at $170,000. The purchase is paid with $40,000 cash and a long-term note payable for $160,000.

**c.** The company purchased $2,400 of office supplies on credit.

**d.** C. Cooke invested his personal automobile in the company. The automobile has a value of $18,000 and is to be used exclusively in the business.

**e.** The company purchased $6,000 of additional office equipment on credit.

**f.** The company paid $1,500 cash salary to an assistant.

**g.** The company provided services to a client and collected $6,000 cash.

**h.** The company paid $800 cash for this month's utilities.

**i.** The company paid $2,400 cash to settle the payable created in transaction *c*.

**j.** The company purchased $20,000 of new office equipment by paying $20,000 cash.

**k.** The company completed $5,200 of services for a client, who must pay within 30 days.

**l.** The company paid $1,500 cash salary to an assistant.

**m.** The company received $3,800 cash in partial payment on the receivable created in transaction *k*.

**n.** C. Cooke withdrew $6,400 cash from the company for personal use.

**Problem 2-5B**
Recording transactions; posting to ledger; preparing a trial balance
C3  A1  P1  P2

**Required**

**1.** Prepare general journal entries to record these transactions (use account titles listed in part 2).

**2.** Open the following ledger accounts—their account numbers are in parentheses (use the balance column format): Cash (101); Accounts Receivable (106); Office Supplies (108); Office Equipment (163); Automobiles (164); Building (170); Land (172); Accounts Payable (201); Notes Payable (250); C. Cooke, Capital (301); C. Cooke, Withdrawals (302); Fees Earned (402); Salaries Expense (601); and Utilities Expense (602). Post the journal entries from part 1 to the ledger accounts and enter the balance after each posting.

**3.** Prepare a trial balance as of the end of June.

**Check**  (2) Ending balances: Cash, $17,200; Office Equipment, $56,000

(3) Trial balance totals, $305,200

**Problem 2-6B**
Analyzing account balances
and reconstructing
transactions

C1 C3 A1 P2

Michael Gould started a Web consulting firm called Gould Solutions. He began operations and completed seven transactions in April that resulted in the following accounts, which all have normal balances.

| | |
|---|---:|
| Cash ........................ | $12,485 |
| Office supplies ................ | 560 |
| Prepaid rent ................. | 1,500 |
| Office equipment ............. | 11,450 |
| Accounts payable ............. | 11,450 |
| M. Gould, Capital ............. | 10,000 |
| M. Gould, Withdrawals ......... | 6,200 |
| Consulting fees earned ......... | 16,400 |
| Operating expenses ........... | 5,655 |

**Required**

**Check**   (1) Trial balance total, $37,850

**1.** Prepare a trial balance for this business as of the end of April.

**Analysis Component**

**2.** Analyze the accounts and their balances and prepare a list that describes each of the seven most likely transactions and their amounts.

(3) Cash paid, $13,915

**3.** Prepare a report of cash received and cash paid showing how the seven transactions in part 2 yield the $12,485 ending Cash balance.

## SERIAL PROBLEM
Business Solutions

A1 P1 P2

*(This serial problem started in Chapter 1 and continues through most of the chapters. If the Chapter 1 segment was not completed, the problem can begin at this point. It is helpful, but not necessary, to use the Working Papers that accompany this book.)*

**SP 2** On October 1, 2011, Santana Rey launched a computer services company called **Business Solutions,** which provides consulting services, computer system installations, and custom program development. Rey adopts the calendar year for reporting purposes and expects to prepare the company's first set of financial statements on December 31, 2011. The company's initial chart of accounts follows.

| Account | No. | Account | No. |
|---|---|---|---|
| Cash ..................... | 101 | S. Rey, Capital ................... | 301 |
| Accounts Receivable ......... | 106 | S. Rey, Withdrawals ............... | 302 |
| Computer Supplies .......... | 126 | Computer Services Revenue ......... | 403 |
| Prepaid Insurance .......... | 128 | Wages Expense ................... | 623 |
| Prepaid Rent .............. | 131 | Advertising Expense ............... | 655 |
| Office Equipment .......... | 163 | Mileage Expense ................... | 676 |
| Computer Equipment ........ | 167 | Miscellaneous Expenses ............ | 677 |
| Accounts Payable .......... | 201 | Repairs Expense—Computer......... | 684 |

**Required**

**1.** Prepare journal entries to record each of the following transactions for Business Solutions.

Oct.  1   S. Rey invested $45,000 cash, a $20,000 computer system, and $8,000 of office equipment in the company.
     2   The company paid $3,300 cash for four months' rent. (*Hint:* Debit Prepaid Rent for $3,300.)
     3   The company purchased $1,420 of computer supplies on credit from Harris Office Products.
     5   The company paid $2,220 cash for one year's premium on a property and liability insurance policy. (*Hint:* Debit Prepaid Insurance for $2,220.)
     6   The company billed Easy Leasing $4,800 for services performed in installing a new Web server.
     8   The company paid $1,420 cash for the computer supplies purchased from Harris Office Products on October 3.
    10   The company hired Lyn Addie as a part-time assistant for $125 per day, as needed.
    12   The company billed Easy Leasing another $1,400 for services performed.

| | | |
|---|---|---|
| 15 | The company received $4,800 cash from Easy Leasing as partial payment on its account. | |
| 17 | The company paid $805 cash to repair computer equipment that was damaged when moving it. | |
| 20 | The company paid $1,728 cash for advertisements published in the local newspaper. | |
| 22 | The company received $1,400 cash from Easy Leasing on its account. | |
| 28 | The company billed IFM Company $5,208 for services performed. | |
| 31 | The company paid $875 cash for Lyn Addie's wages for seven days' work. | |
| 31 | S. Rey withdrew $3,600 cash from the company for personal use. | |

Nov. 1  The company reimbursed S. Rey in cash for business automobile mileage allowance (Rey logged 1,000 miles at $0.32 per mile).

2  The company received $4,633 cash from Liu Corporation for computer services performed.

5  The company purchased computer supplies for $1,125 cash from Harris Office Products.

8  The company billed Gomez Co. $5,668 for services performed.

13  The company received notification from Alex's Engineering Co. that Business Solutions' bid of $3,950 for an upcoming project is accepted.

18  The company received $2,208 cash from IFM Company as partial payment of the October 28 bill.

22  The company donated $250 cash to the United Way in the company's name.

24  The company completed work for Alex's Engineering Co. and sent it a bill for $3,950.

25  The company sent another bill to IFM Company for the past-due amount of $3,000.

28  The company reimbursed S. Rey in cash for business automobile mileage (1,200 miles at $0.32 per mile).

30  The company paid $1,750 cash for Lyn Addie's wages for 14 days' work.

30  S. Rey withdrew $2,000 cash from the company for personal use.

**2.** Open ledger accounts (in balance column format) and post the journal entries from part 1 to them.

**3.** Prepare a trial balance as of the end of November.

**Check**  (2) Cash, Nov. 30 bal., $38,264
(3) Trial bal. totals, $98,659

## Beyond the Numbers

**BTN 2-1**  Refer to **Research In Motion**'s financial statements in Appendix A for the following questions.

*Required*

**1.** What amount of total liabilities does it report for each of the fiscal years ended February 28, 2009, and February 27, 2010?

**2.** What amount of total assets does it report for each of the fiscal years ended February 28, 2009, and February 27, 2010?

**3.** Compute its debt ratio for each of the fiscal years ended February 28, 2009, and February 27, 2010.

**4.** In which fiscal year did it employ more financial leverage (February 28, 2009, or February 27, 2010)? Explain.

**REPORTING IN ACTION**

A1  A2

*RIM*

*Fast Forward*

**5.** Access its financial statements (10-K report) for a fiscal year ending after February 27, 2010, from its Website (**RIM.com**) or the SEC's EDGAR database (**www.SEC.gov**). Recompute its debt ratio for any subsequent year's data and compare it with the debt ratio for 2009 and 2010.

**BTN 2-2**  Key comparative figures for **Research In Motion** and **Apple** follow.

| ($ millions) | Research In Motion | | Apple | |
|---|---|---|---|---|
| | Current Year | Prior Year | Current Year | Prior Year |
| Total liabilities ......... | $ 2,602 | $ 2,227 | $15,861 | $13,874 |
| Total assets ........... | 10,204 | 8,101 | 47,501 | 36,171 |

**COMPARATIVE ANALYSIS**

A1  A2

*RIM*
Apple

**1.** What is the debt ratio for Research In Motion in the current year and for the prior year?

**2.** What is the debt ratio for Apple in the current year and for the prior year?

**3.** Which of the two companies has the higher degree of financial leverage? What does this imply?

**ETHICS CHALLENGE**

C1

**BTN 2-3**   Review the *Decision Ethics* case from the first part of this chapter involving the cashier. The guidance answer suggests that you should not comply with the assistant manager's request.

**Required**

Propose and evaluate two other courses of action you might consider, and explain why.

**COMMUNICATING IN PRACTICE**

C1  C2  A1  P3

**BTN 2-4**   Mora Stanley is an aspiring entrepreneur and your friend. She is having difficulty understanding the purposes of financial statements and how they fit together across time.

**Required**

Write a one-page memorandum to Stanley explaining the purposes of the four financial statements and how they are linked across time.

**TAKING IT TO THE NET**

A1

**BTN 2-5**   Access EDGAR online (www.SEC.gov) and locate the 2009 year 10-K report of **Amazon.com** (ticker AMZN) filed on January 29, 2010. Review its financial statements reported for years ended 2009, 2008, and 2007 to answer the following questions.

**Required**

1. What are the amounts of its net income or net loss reported for each of these three years?
2. Does Amazon's operating activities provide cash or use cash for each of these three years?
3. If Amazon has a 2009 net income of more than $900 million and 2009 operating cash flows of more than $3,000 million, how is it possible that its cash balance at December 31, 2009, increases by less than $700 million relative to its balance at December 31, 2008?

**TEAMWORK IN ACTION**

C1  C2  C4  A1

**BTN 2-6**   The expanded accounting equation consists of assets, liabilities, capital, withdrawals, revenues, and expenses. It can be used to reveal insights into changes in a company's financial position.

**Required**

1. Form *learning teams* of six (or more) members. Each team member must select one of the six components and each team must have at least one expert on each component: (*a*) assets, (*b*) liabilities, (*c*) capital, (*d*) withdrawals, (*e*) revenues, and (*f*) expenses.
2. Form *expert teams* of individuals who selected the same component in part 1. Expert teams are to draft a report that each expert will present to his or her learning team addressing the following:
   **a.** Identify for its component the (i) increase and decrease side of the account and (ii) normal balance side of the account.
   **b.** Describe a transaction, with amounts, that increases its component.
   **c.** Using the transaction and amounts in (*b*), verify the equality of the accounting equation and then explain any effects on the income statement and statement of cash flows.
   **d.** Describe a transaction, with amounts, that decreases its component.
   **e.** Using the transaction and amounts in (*d*), verify the equality of the accounting equation and then explain any effects on the income statement and statement of cash flows.
3. Each expert should return to his/her learning team. In rotation, each member presents his/her expert team's report to the learning team. Team discussion is encouraged.

**ENTREPRENEURIAL DECISION**

A1  A2  P3

**BTN 2-7**   Assume Susie Levitt and Katie Shea of **CitySlips** plan on expanding their business to accommodate more product lines. They are considering financing their expansion in one of two ways: (1) contributing more of their own funds to the business or (2) borrowing the funds from a bank.

**Required**

Identify at least two issues that Susie and Katie should consider when trying to decide on the method for financing their expansion.

**BTN 2-8** Lisa Langely is a young entrepreneur who operates Langely Music Services, offering singing lessons and instruction on musical instruments. Langely wishes to expand but needs a $15,000 loan. The bank requests Langely to prepare a balance sheet and key financial ratios. Langely has not kept formal records but is able to provide the following accounts and their amounts as of December 31, 2011.

**ENTREPRENEURIAL DECISION**

A1 A2 P3

| | | | | | |
|---|---|---|---|---|---|
| Cash .............. | $ 1,800 | Accounts Receivable .... | $4,800 | Prepaid Insurance ..... | $ 750 |
| Prepaid Rent ........ | 4,700 | Store Supplies ......... | 3,300 | Equipment ........... | 25,000 |
| Accounts Payable .... | 1,100 | Unearned Lesson Fees ... | 7,800 | Total Equity* ......... | 31,450 |
| Annual net income ... | 20,000 | | | | |

\* The total equity amount reflects all owner investments, withdrawals, revenues, and expenses as of December 31, 2011.

**Required**

1. Prepare a balance sheet as of December 31, 2011, for Langely Music Services. (Report only the total equity amount on the balance sheet.)
2. Compute Langely's debt ratio and its return on assets (the latter ratio is defined in Chapter 1). Assume average assets equal its ending balance.
3. Do you believe the prospects of a $15,000 bank loan are good? Why or why not?

**BTN 2-9** Obtain a recent copy of the most prominent newspaper distributed in your area. Research the classified section and prepare a report answering the following questions (attach relevant classified clippings to your report). Alternatively, you may want to search the Web for the required information. One suitable Website is **CareerOneStop** (**www.CareerOneStop.org**). For documentation, you should print copies of Websites accessed.

**HITTING THE ROAD**

C1

1. Identify the number of listings for accounting positions and the various accounting job titles.
2. Identify the number of listings for other job titles, with examples, that require or prefer accounting knowledge/experience but are not specifically accounting positions.
3. Specify the salary range for the accounting and accounting-related positions if provided.
4. Indicate the job that appeals to you, the reason for its appeal, and its requirements.

**BTN 2-10** **Nokia** (**www.Nokia.com**) is a leading global manufacturer of mobile devices and services, and it competes to some extent with both **Research In Motion** and **Apple**. Key financial ratios for the current fiscal year follow.

**GLOBAL DECISION**

A2

**NOKIA**

*RIM*

Apple

| Key Figure | Nokia | Research In Motion | Apple |
|---|---|---|---|
| Return on assets ......... | 0.7% | 26.8% | 19.7% |
| Debt ratio .............. | 58.7% | 25.5% | 33.4% |

**Required**

1. Which company is most profitable according to its return on assets?
2. Which company is most risky according to the debt ratio?
3. Which company deserves increased investment based on a joint analysis of return on assets and the debt ratio? Explain.

## ANSWERS TO MULTIPLE CHOICE QUIZ

1. b; debit Utility Expense for $700, and credit Cash for $700.
2. a; debit Cash for $2,500, and credit Unearned Lawn Service Fees for $2,500.
3. c; debit Cash for $250,000, debit Land for $500,000, and credit L. Shue, Capital for $750,000.
4. d
5. e; Debt ratio = $400,000/$1,000,000 = 40%

# 3

# Adjusting Accounts and Preparing Financial Statements

## A Look Back

Chapter 2 explained the analysis and recording of transactions. We showed how to apply and interpret company accounts, T-accounts, double-entry accounting, ledgers, postings, and trial balances.

## A Look at This Chapter

This chapter explains the timing of reports and the need to adjust accounts. Adjusting accounts is important for recognizing revenues and expenses in the proper period. We describe the adjusted trial balance and how it is used to prepare financial statements.

## A Look Ahead

Chapter 4 highlights the completion of the accounting cycle. We explain the important final steps in the accounting process. These include closing procedures, the post-closing trial balance, and reversing entries.

## Learning Objectives

### CONCEPTUAL

**C1** Explain the importance of periodic reporting and the time period assumption. (p. 94)

**C2** Explain accrual accounting and how it improves financial statements. (p. 95)

**C3** Identify the types of adjustments and their purpose. (p. 96)

### ANALYTICAL

**A1** Explain how accounting adjustments link to financial statements. (p. 105)

**A2** Compute profit margin and describe its use in analyzing company performance. (p. 109)

LP3

### PROCEDURAL

**P1** Prepare and explain adjusting entries. (p. 97)

**P2** Explain and prepare an adjusted trial balance. (p. 106)

**P3** Prepare financial statements from an adjusted trial balance. (p. 106)

**P4** *Appendix 3A*—Explain the alternatives in accounting for prepaids. (p. 113)

## Huh? Yes!

*"Make sure that whatever commitment you make . . . you keep"*
—BEN HUH

SEATTLE—"When we were starting this thing, people asked who was going to run it, and I said, 'I will, and my wife.' And they said, 'You're crazy.' And I said, 'Yes!' " Meet Ben Huh. His thing? **Cheezburger Network (Cheezburger.com/sites),** which controls over 30 Websites devoted to Internet memes. (Memes are running gags, usually in JPEG or video format, which spawn and spread on the Web.) His sites include ICanHasCheezburger?, FailBlog, IHasAHotdog!, ROFLrazzi, and TotallyLooksLike. Since launching his company just a few years ago, his network has nearly 200 million page views per month and annual revenue in the millions. Revenue comes from display ads, along with some merchandise sales.

Ben explains that he set up an accounting system early on to account for all business activities, including cash, revenues, receivables, and payables. He also had to learn about the deferral and accrual of revenues and expenses. Setting up a good accounting system is an important part of success, explains Ben. "I learned how to keep costs low."

In spite of his quirky business, Ben insists "it is very serious business." He also seriously monitors the adjusting of accounts so that revenues and expenses are properly reported so that good decisions are made. Adds Ben, "No matter how strange or ridiculous a business looks, those fundamentals still need to be there."

Financial statement preparation and analysis is a process that Ben emphasizes. Although he insists on timely and accurate accounting reports, Ben says "we're just having fun . . . we've always been very much counterculture." To achieve the fun part, Ben first took time to understand accounting adjustments and their effects. It is part of the larger picture. We "make people happy for five minutes every day." But, for Ben to do that, he insists that a reliable accounting system is necessary . . . otherwise his business would fail.

"We'd like to continue to do what we do . . . build bigger communities and just kind of evangelize the idea that the user is great at creating excellent content," says Ben. "The market is far more efficient than any one company . . . but we haven't applied that theory to [Web] content."

[Sources: *Cheezburger Website* and *BenHuh Website,* January 2011; *Entrepreneur,* August 2009; *Wired,* February 2010; *The New York Times,* April 2009; *Time,* August 2009]

Financial statements reflect revenues when earned and expenses when incurred. This is known as *accrual accounting,* which was the focus of Chapter 2. We showed how companies use accounting systems to collect information about *external* transactions and events. We also explained how journals, ledgers, and other tools are useful in preparing financial statements. This chapter describes the accounting process for producing useful information involving *internal* transactions and events. An important part of this process is adjusting the account balances so that financial statements at the end of a reporting period reflect the effects of all transactions. We then explain the important steps in preparing financial statements.

### Adjusting Accounts and Preparing Financial Statements

| Timing and Reporting | Adjusting Accounts | Preparing Financial Statements |
|---|---|---|
| • Accounting period<br>• Accrual versus cash<br>• Recognition of revenues and expenses | • Prepaid expenses<br>• Unearned revenues<br>• Accrued expenses<br>• Accrued revenues<br>• Adjusted trial balance | • Income statement<br>• Statement of owner's equity<br>• Balance sheet |

## TIMING AND REPORTING

This section describes the importance of reporting accounting information at regular intervals and its impact for recording revenues and expenses.

### The Accounting Period

**C1** Explain the importance of periodic reporting and the time period assumption.

The value of information is often linked to its timeliness. Useful information must reach decision makers frequently and promptly. To provide timely information, accounting systems prepare reports at regular intervals. This results in an accounting process impacted by the time period (or periodicity) assumption. The **time period assumption** presumes that an organization's activities can be divided into specific time periods such as a month, a three-month quarter, a six-month interval, or a year. Exhibit 3.1 shows various **accounting,** or *reporting,* **periods.** Most organizations use a year as their primary accounting period. Reports covering a one-year period are known as **annual financial statements.** Many organizations also prepare **interim financial statements** covering one, three, or six months of activity.

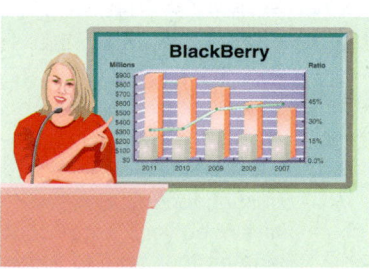

"RIM announces annual income of . . ."

**EXHIBIT 3.1**

Accounting Periods

The annual reporting period is not always a calendar year ending on December 31. An organization can adopt a **fiscal year** consisting of any 12 consecutive months. It is also acceptable to adopt an annual reporting period of 52 weeks. For example, **Gap**'s fiscal year consistently ends the final week of January or the first week of February each year.

Companies with little seasonal variation in sales often choose the calendar year as their fiscal year. The financial statements of **The Kellogg Company** (the company that controls characters such as Tony the Tiger, Snap! Crackle! Pop!, and Keebler Elf) reflect a fiscal year that ends on the Saturday nearest December 31. Companies experiencing seasonal variations in sales often choose a **natural business year** end, which is when sales activities are at their lowest level for the year. The natural business year for retailers such as **Walmart**, **Target**, and **Macy's** usually ends around January 31, after the holiday season.

## Accrual Basis versus Cash Basis

After external transactions and events are recorded, several accounts still need adjustments before their balances appear in financial statements. This need arises because internal transactions and events remain unrecorded. **Accrual basis accounting** uses the adjusting process to recognize revenues when earned and expenses when incurred (matched with revenues).

**C2** Explain accrual accounting and how it improves financial statements.

**Cash basis accounting** recognizes revenues when cash is received and records expenses when cash is paid. This means that cash basis net income for a period is the difference between cash receipts and cash payments. Cash basis accounting is not consistent with generally accepted accounting principles (neither U.S. GAAP nor IFRS).

It is commonly held that accrual accounting better reflects business performance than information about cash receipts and payments. Accrual accounting also increases the *comparability* of financial statements from one period to another. Yet cash basis accounting is useful for several business decisions—which is the reason companies must report a statement of cash flows.

To see the difference between these two accounting systems, let's consider FastForward's Prepaid Insurance account. FastForward paid $2,400 for 24 months of insurance coverage that began on December 1, 2011. Accrual accounting requires that $100 of insurance expense be reported on December 2011's income statement. Another $1,200 of expense is reported in year 2012, and the remaining $1,100 is reported as expense in the first 11 months of 2013. Exhibit 3.2 illustrates this allocation of insurance cost across these three years. Any unexpired premium is reported as a Prepaid Insurance asset on the accrual basis balance sheet.

**EXHIBIT 3.2**

Accrual Accounting for Allocating Prepaid Insurance to Expense

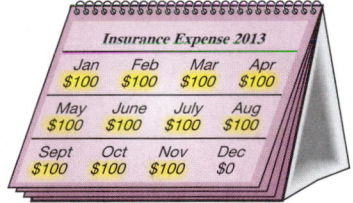

Alternatively, a cash basis income statement for December 2011 reports insurance expense of $2,400, as shown in Exhibit 3.3. The cash basis income statements for years 2012 and 2013 report no insurance expense. The cash basis balance sheet never reports an insurance asset because it is immediately expensed. This shows that cash basis income for 2011–2013 fails to match the cost of insurance with the insurance benefits received for those years and months.

**EXHIBIT 3.3**

Cash Accounting for Allocating Prepaid Insurance to Expense

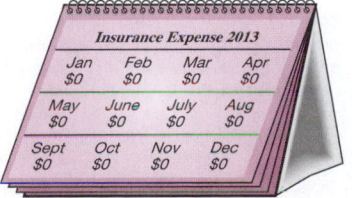

## Recognizing Revenues and Expenses

**Point:** Recording revenue early over-states current-period revenue and income; recording it late understates current-period revenue and income.

**Point:** Recording expense early over-states current-period expense and understates current-period income; recording it late understates current-period expense and overstates current-period income.

We use the time period assumption to divide a company's activities into specific time periods, but not all activities are complete when financial statements are prepared. Thus, adjustments often are required to get correct account balances.

We rely on two principles in the adjusting process: revenue recognition and expense recognition (the latter is often referred to as matching). Chapter 1 explained that the *revenue recognition principle* requires that revenue be recorded when earned, not before and not after. Most companies earn revenue when they provide services and products to customers. A major goal of the adjusting process is to have revenue recognized (reported) in the time period when it is earned. The **expense recognition** (or **matching**) **principle** aims to record expenses in the same accounting period as the revenues that are earned as a result of those expenses. This matching of expenses with the revenue benefits is a major part of the adjusting process.

Matching expenses with revenues often requires us to predict certain events. When we use financial statements, we must understand that they require estimates and therefore include measures that are not precise. **Walt Disney**'s annual report explains that its production costs from movies, such as *Alice in Wonderland,* are matched to revenues based on a ratio of current revenues from the movie divided by its predicted total revenues.

### Quick Check                                          Answers — p. 116

1. Describe a company's annual reporting period.
2. Why do companies prepare interim financial statements?
3. What two accounting principles most directly drive the adjusting process?
4. Is cash basis accounting consistent with the matching principle? Why or why not?
5. If your company pays a $4,800 premium on April 1, 2011, for two years' insurance coverage, how much insurance expense is reported in 2012 using cash basis accounting?

# ADJUSTING ACCOUNTS

Adjusting accounts is a 3-step process:

**Step 1:** **Determine what the current account balance** *equals.*

**Step 2:** **Determine what the current account balance** *should equal.*

**Step 3:** **Record an adjusting entry to get from step** *1* **to step** *2.*

## Framework for Adjustments

**C3**   Identify the types of adjustments and their purpose.

Adjustments are necessary for transactions and events that extend over more than one period. It is helpful to group adjustments by the timing of cash receipt or cash payment in relation to the recognition of the related revenues or expenses. Exhibit 3.4 identifies four types of adjustments.

The upper half of this exhibit shows prepaid expenses (including depreciation) and unearned revenues, which reflect transactions when cash is paid or received *before* a related expense or revenue is recognized. They are also called *deferrals* because the recognition of an expense (or revenue) is *deferred* until after the related cash is paid (or received). The lower half of this exhibit shows accrued expenses and accrued revenues, which reflect transactions when cash is paid or received *after* a related expense or revenue is recognized. Adjusting entries are necessary for each of these so that revenues, expenses, assets, and liabilities are correctly reported. Specifically, an **adjusting entry** is made at the end of an accounting period to reflect a transaction or event that is not yet recorded. Each adjusting entry affects one or more income statement accounts *and* one or more balance sheet accounts (but never the Cash account).

**Point:** Source documents provide information for most daily transactions, and in many businesses the recordkeepers record them. Adjustments require more knowledge and are usually handled by senior accounting professionals.

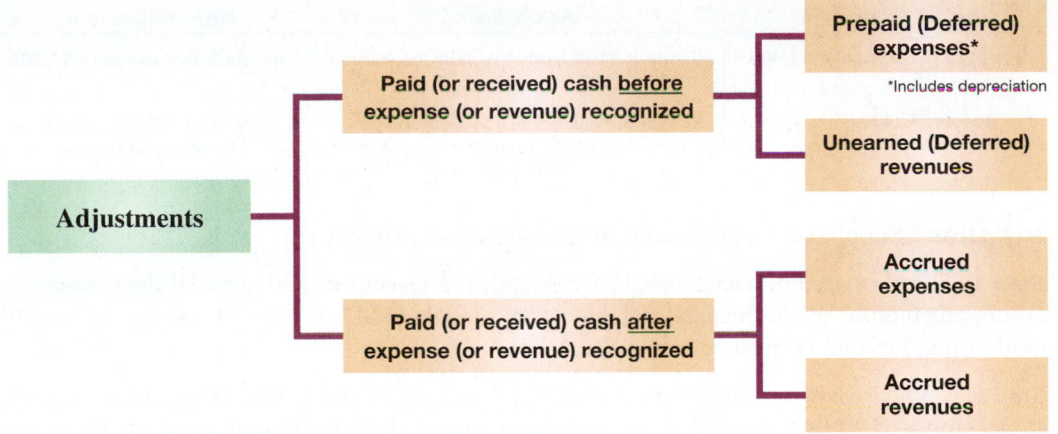

**EXHIBIT 3.4**

Types of Adjustments

## Prepaid (Deferred) Expenses

**Prepaid expenses** refer to items *paid for* in advance of receiving their benefits. Prepaid expenses are assets. When these assets are used, their costs become expenses. Adjusting entries for prepaids increase expenses and decrease assets as shown in the T-accounts of Exhibit 3.5. Such adjustments reflect transactions and events that use up prepaid expenses (including passage of time). To illustrate the accounting for prepaid expenses, we look at prepaid insurance, supplies, and depreciation.

**P1** Prepare and explain adjusting entries.

**EXHIBIT 3.5**

Adjusting for Prepaid Expenses

**Prepaid Insurance**   We use our 3-step process for this and all accounting adjustments.

**Step 1:**   We determine that the current balance of FastForward's prepaid insurance is equal to its $2,400 payment for 24 months of insurance benefits that began on December 1, 2011.

**Step 2:**   With the passage of time, the benefits of the insurance gradually expire and a portion of the Prepaid Insurance asset becomes expense. For instance, one month's insurance coverage expires by December 31, 2011. This expense is $100, or 1/24 of $2,400, which leaves $2,300.

**Step 3:**   The adjusting entry to record this expense and reduce the asset, along with T-account postings, follows:

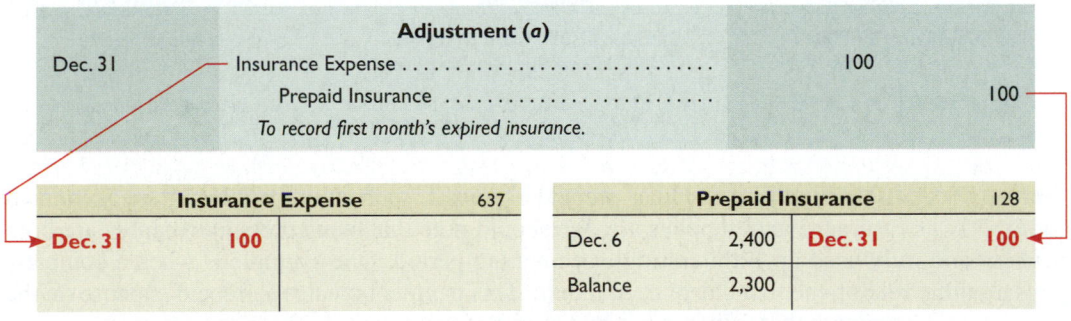

Assets = Liabilities + Equity
−100                      −100

**Explanation**   After adjusting and posting, the $100 balance in Insurance Expense and the $2,300 balance in Prepaid Insurance are ready for reporting in financial statements. *Not* making the adjustment on or before December 31 would (1) understate expenses by $100 and overstate net income by $100 for the December income statement and (2) overstate both prepaid insurance (assets) and equity (because of net income) by $100 in the December 31 balance sheet. (Exhibit 3.2 showed that 2012's adjustments must transfer a total of $1,200 from Prepaid Insurance to Insurance Expense, and 2013's adjustments must transfer the remaining $1,100 to Insurance Expense.) The following table highlights the December 31, 2011, adjustment for prepaid insurance.

**Point:** Many companies record adjusting entries only at the end of each year because of the time and cost necessary.

| Before Adjustment | Adjustment | After Adjustment |
|---|---|---|
| **Prepaid Insurance = $2,400** | **Deduct $100 from Prepaid Insurance Add $100 to Insurance Expense** | **Prepaid Insurance = $2,300** |
| Reports $2,400 policy for 24-months' coverage. | Record current month's $100 insurance expense and $100 reduction in prepaid amount. | Reports $2,300 in coverage for remaining 23 months. |

**Supplies**   Supplies are a prepaid expense requiring adjustment.

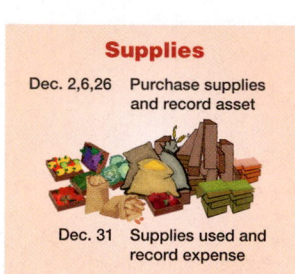

**Supplies**

Dec. 2,6,26  Purchase supplies and record asset

Dec. 31  Supplies used and record expense

**Step 1:**   FastForward purchased $9,720 of supplies in December and some of them were used during this month. When financial statements are prepared at December 31, the cost of supplies used during December must be recognized.

**Step 2:**   When FastForward computes (takes physical count of) its remaining unused supplies at December 31, it finds $8,670 of supplies remaining of the $9,720 total supplies. The $1,050 difference between these two amounts is December's supplies expense.

**Step 3:**   The adjusting entry to record this expense and reduce the Supplies asset account, along with T-account postings, follows:

Assets = Liabilities + Equity
−1,050              −1,050

**Adjustment (b)**

| Dec. 31 | Supplies Expense | .............................. | 1,050 | |
| | Supplies | .............................. | | 1,050 |
| | *To record supplies used.* | | | |

| **Supplies Expense** | | 652 |
|---|---|---|
| **Dec. 31** | **1,050** | |

| **Supplies** | | | 126 |
|---|---|---|---|
| Dec.  2 | 2,500 | **Dec. 31** | **1,050** |
| 6 | 7,100 | | |
| 26 | 120 | | |
| Balance | 8,670 | | |

**Explanation**   The balance of the Supplies account is $8,670 after posting—equaling the cost of the remaining supplies. *Not* making the adjustment on or before December 31 would (1) understate expenses by $1,050 and overstate net income by $1,050 for the December income statement and (2) overstate both supplies and equity (because of net income) by $1,050 in the December 31 balance sheet. The following table highlights the adjustment for supplies.

| Before Adjustment | Adjustment | After Adjustment |
|---|---|---|
| **Supplies = $9,720** | **Deduct $1,050 from Supplies Add $1,050 to Supplies Expense** | **Supplies = $8,670** |
| Reports $9,720 in supplies. | Record $1,050 in supplies used and $1,050 as supplies expense. | Reports $8,670 in supplies. |

**Other Prepaid Expenses**   Other prepaid expenses, such as Prepaid Rent, are accounted for exactly as Insurance and Supplies are. We should note that some prepaid expenses are both paid for and fully used up within a single accounting period. One example is when a company pays monthly rent on the first day of each month. This payment creates a prepaid expense on the first day of each month that fully expires by the end of the month. In these special cases, we can record the cash paid with a debit to an expense account instead of an asset account. This practice is described more completely later in the chapter.

**Point:** We assume that prepaid and unearned items are recorded in balance sheet accounts. An alternative is to record them in income statement accounts; Appendix 3A discusses this alternative. The adjusted financial statements are identical.

 **Decision Maker**                                        Answer — p. 115

**Investor**   A small publishing company signs a well-known athlete to write a book. The company pays the athlete $500,000 to sign plus future book royalties. A note to the company's financial statements says that "prepaid expenses include $500,000 in author signing fees to be matched against future expected sales." Is this accounting for the signing bonus acceptable? How does it affect your analysis? ■

**Depreciation**  A special category of prepaid expenses is **plant assets,** which refers to long-term tangible assets used to produce and sell products and services. Plant assets are expected to provide benefits for more than one period. Examples of plant assets are buildings, machines, vehicles, and fixtures. All plant assets, with a general exception for land, eventually wear out or decline in usefulness. The costs of these assets are deferred but are gradually reported as expenses in the income statement over the assets' useful lives (benefit periods). **Depreciation** is the process of allocating the costs of these assets over their expected useful lives. Depreciation expense is recorded with an adjusting entry similar to that for other prepaid expenses.

**Point:** Plant assets are also called *Plant & Equipment,* or *Property, Plant & Equipment.*

**Point:** Depreciation does not necessarily measure decline in market value.

**Point:** An asset's expected value at the end of its useful life is called *salvage value.*

*Step 1:*  Recall that FastForward purchased equipment for $26,000 in early December to use in earning revenue. This equipment's cost must be depreciated.

*Step 2:*  The equipment is expected to have a useful life (benefit period) of four years and to be worth about $8,000 at the end of four years. This means the *net* cost of this equipment over its useful life is $18,000 ($26,000 − $8,000). We can use any of several methods to allocate this $18,000 net cost to expense. FastForward uses a method called **straight-line depreciation,** which allocates equal amounts of the asset's net cost to depreciation during its useful life. Dividing the $18,000 net cost by the 48 months in the asset's useful life gives a monthly cost of $375 ($18,000/48).

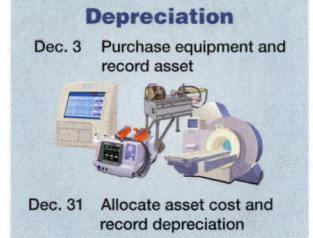

**Depreciation**

Dec. 3  Purchase equipment and record asset

Dec. 31  Allocate asset cost and record depreciation

*Step 3:*  The adjusting entry to record monthly depreciation expense, along with T-account postings, follows:

| Adjustment (c) | | | |
|---|---|---|---|
| Dec. 31 | Depreciation Expense ........................... | 375 | |
| | Accumulated Depreciation—Equipment ........ | | 375 |
| | *To record monthly equipment depreciation.* | | |

Assets = Liabilities + Equity
−375                         −375

| Depreciation Expense—Equipment | 612 | | Equipment | 167 | | Accumulated Depreciation—Equipment | 168 |
|---|---|---|---|---|---|---|---|
| Dec. 31 | 375 | | Dec. 3 | 26,000 | | | Dec. 31 | 375 |

**Explanation**  After posting the adjustment, the Equipment account ($26,000) less its Accumulated Depreciation ($375) account equals the $25,625 net cost (made up of $17,625 for the 47 remaining months in the benefit period plus the $8,000 value at the end of that time). The $375 balance in the Depreciation Expense account is reported in the December income statement. *Not* making the adjustment at December 31 would (1) understate expenses by $375 and overstate net income by $375 for the December income statement and (2) overstate both assets and equity (because of income) by $375 in the December 31 balance sheet. The following table highlights the adjustment for depreciation.

| Before Adjustment | Adjustment | After Adjustment |
|---|---|---|
| Equipment, net = $26,000 | Deduct $375 from Equipment, net Add $375 to Depreciation Expense | Equipment, net = $25,625 |
| Reports $26,000 in equipment. | Record $375 in depreciation and $375 as accumulated depreciation, which is deducted from equipment. | Reports $25,625 in equipment, net of accumulated depreciation. |

Accumulated depreciation is kept in a separate contra account. A **contra account** is an account linked with another account, it has an opposite normal balance, and it is reported as a subtraction from that other account's balance. For instance, FastForward's contra account of Accumulated Depreciation—Equipment is subtracted from the Equipment account in the balance sheet (see Exhibit 3.7). This contra account allows balance sheet readers to know both the full costs of assets and the total depreciation.

The title of the contra account, *Accumulated Depreciation,* reveals that this account includes total depreciation expense for all prior periods for which the asset was used. To illustrate, the Equipment and the Accumulated Depreciation accounts appear as in Exhibit 3.6 on February 28, 2012, after three months of adjusting entries. The $1,125 balance in the accumulated depreciation account can be subtracted from its related $26,000 asset cost. The difference ($24,875) between these two balances is the cost of the asset that has not yet been depreciated. This difference is

**Point:** The cost principle requires an asset to be initially recorded at acquisition cost. Depreciation causes the asset's book value (cost less accumulated depreciation) to decline over time.

**EXHIBIT 3.6**

Accounts after Three Months of
Depreciation Adjustments

| Equipment | | 167 |
|---|---|---|
| Dec. 3 | 26,000 | |

| Accumulated<br>Depreciation—Equipment | | 168 |
|---|---|---|
| | Dec. 31 | 375 |
| | Jan. 31 | 375 |
| | Feb. 28 | 375 |
| | Balance | **1,125** |

**Point:** The net cost of equipment is
also called the *depreciable basis.*

called the **book value,** or the *net amount,* which equals the asset's costs less its accumulated
depreciation.

These account balances are reported in the assets section of the February 28 balance sheet in
Exhibit 3.7.

**EXHIBIT 3.7**

Equipment and Accumulated
Depreciation on February 28
Balance Sheet

| Assets (at February 28, 2012) | | |
|---|---|---|
| Cash | | $ |
| Equipment | $26,000 | |
| Less accumulated depreciation | 1,125 | 24,875 |
| Total Assets | | $ |

Commonly titled
*Equipment, net*

**Decision Maker**     Answer — p. 116

**Entrepreneur**   You are preparing an offer to purchase a family-run restaurant. The depreciation schedule
for the restaurant's building and equipment shows costs of $175,000 and accumulated depreciation of
$155,000. This leaves a net for building and equipment of $20,000. Is this information useful in helping you
decide on a purchase offer? ■

## Unearned (Deferred) Revenues

The term **unearned revenues** refers to cash received in advance of providing products and
services. Unearned revenues, also called *deferred revenues,* are liabilities. When cash is accepted, an obligation to provide products
or services is accepted. As products or services are provided, the unearned revenues
become *earned* revenues. Adjusting entries
for unearned revenues involve increasing
revenues and decreasing unearned revenues, as shown in Exhibit 3.8.

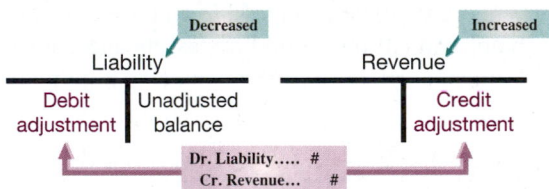

**EXHIBIT 3.8**

Adjusting for Unearned Revenues

**Point:** To *defer* is to postpone. We
postpone reporting amounts received
as revenues until they are earned.

An example of unearned revenues is from **The New York Times Company**, which reports
unexpired (unearned) subscriptions of $81 million: "Proceeds from … subscriptions are de-
ferred at the time of sale and are recognized in earnings on a pro rata basis over the terms of
the subscriptions." Unearned revenues are nearly 10% of the current liabilities for the Times.
Another example comes from the **Boston Celtics**. When the Celtics receive cash from advance
ticket sales and broadcast fees, they record it in an unearned revenue account called *Deferred
Game Revenues.* The Celtics recognize this unearned revenue with adjusting entries on a game-
by-game basis. Since the NBA regular season begins in October and ends in April, revenue
recognition is mainly limited to this period. For a recent season, the Celtics' quarterly revenues were $0 million for July–September; $34 million for October–December; $48 million
for January–March; and $17 million for April–June.

Returning to FastForward, it also has unearned revenues. It agreed on December 26 to provide consulting services to a client for a fixed fee of $3,000 for 60 days.

***Step 1:***   On December 26, the client paid the 60-day fee in advance, covering the period
December 27 to February 24. The entry to record the cash received in advance is

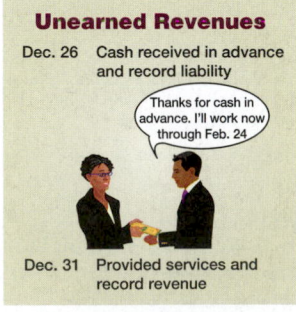

**Unearned Revenues**

Dec. 26   Cash received in advance
and record liability

Thanks for cash in
advance. I'll work now
through Feb. 24

Dec. 31   Provided services and
record revenue

| Dec. 26 | Cash . . . . . . . . . . . . . . . . . . . . . . . . . . . . . . . . . . . . . . . . . | 3,000 | |
| | Unearned Consulting Revenue . . . . . . . . . . . . . . . | | 3,000 |
| | *Received advance payment for services over the next 60 days.* | | |

Assets = Liabilities + Equity
+3,000      +3,000

This advance payment increases cash and creates an obligation to do consulting work over the next 60 days.

**Step 2:**   As time passes, FastForward earns this payment through consulting. By December 31, it has provided five days' service and earned 5/60 of the $3,000 unearned revenue. This amounts to $250 ($3,000 × 5/60). The *revenue recognition principle* implies that $250 of unearned revenue must be reported as revenue on the December income statement.

**Step 3:**   The adjusting entry to reduce the liability account and recognize earned revenue, along with T-account postings, follows:

| | **Adjustment (d)** | | |
| Dec. 31 | Unearned Consulting Revenue . . . . . . . . . . . . . . . . . . . . | 250 | |
| | Consulting Revenue . . . . . . . . . . . . . . . . . . . . . . . | | 250 |
| | *To record earned revenue that was received in advance ($3,000 × 5/60).* | | |

Assets = Liabilities + Equity
          −250       +250

| **Unearned Consulting Revenue** | 236 | | |
| **Dec. 31** | **250** | Dec. 26 | 3,000 |
| | | Balance | 2,750 |

| **Consulting Revenue** | 403 |
| | Dec.  5 | 4,200 |
| | 12 | 1,600 |
| | **31** | **250** |
| | Balance | 6,050 |

**Explanation**   The adjusting entry transfers $250 from unearned revenue (a liability account) to a revenue account. *Not* making the adjustment (1) understates revenue and net income by $250 in the December income statement and (2) overstates unearned revenue and understates equity by $250 on the December 31 balance sheet. The following highlights the adjustment for unearned revenue.

| **Before Adjustment** | **Adjustment** | **After Adjustment** |
| --- | --- | --- |
| **Unearned Consulting Revenue = $3,000** | **Deduct $250 from Unearned Consulting Revenue** **Add $250 to Consulting Revenue** | **Unearned Consulting Revenue = $2,750** |
| Reports $3,000 in unearned revenue for consulting services promised for 60 days. | Record 5 days of earned consulting revenue, which is 5/60 of unearned amount. | Reports $2,750 in unearned revenue for consulting services owed over next 55 days. |

Accounting for unearned revenues is crucial to many companies. For example, the **National Retail Federation** reports that gift card sales, which are unearned revenues for sellers, exceed $20 billion annually. Gift cards are now the top selling holiday gift.

## Accrued Expenses

**Accrued expenses** refer to costs that are incurred in a period but are both unpaid and unrecorded. Accrued expenses must be reported on the income statement of the period when incurred. Adjusting entries for recording accrued expenses involve increasing expenses and increasing liabilities as shown in Exhibit 3.9. This adjustment recognizes expenses incurred in a period but not yet paid. Common examples of accrued expenses are salaries, interest, rent, and taxes. We use salaries and interest to show how to adjust accounts for accrued expenses.

**Point:** Accrued expenses are also called accrued liabilities.

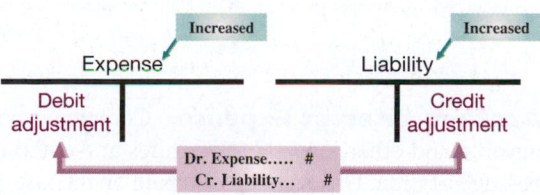

**EXHIBIT 3.9**

Adjusting for Accrued Expenses

**Accrued Salaries Expense**    FastForward's employee earns $70 per day, or $350 for a five-day workweek beginning on Monday and ending on Friday.

**Step 1:**    Its employee is paid every two weeks on Friday. On December 12 and 26, the wages are paid, recorded in the journal, and posted to the ledger.

**Step 2:**    The calendar in Exhibit 3.10 shows three working days after the December 26 payday (29, 30, and 31). This means the employee has earned three days' salary by the close of business

**EXHIBIT 3.10**

Salary Accrual and Paydays

Pay period begins

Salary expense incurred        Payday                              Payday

**Point:** An employer records salaries expense and a vacation pay liability when employees earn vacation pay.

on Wednesday, December 31, yet this salary cost has not been paid or recorded. The financial statements would be incomplete if FastForward fails to report the added expense and liability to the employee for unpaid salary from December 29, 30, and 31.

**Step 3:**    The adjusting entry to account for accrued salaries, along with T-account postings, follows:

Assets = Liabilities + Equity
       +210       −210

**Explanation**    Salaries expense of $1,610 is reported on the December income statement and $210 of salaries payable (liability) is reported in the balance sheet. *Not* making the adjustment (1) understates salaries expense and overstates net income by $210 in the December income statement and (2) understates salaries payable (liabilities) and overstates equity by $210 on the December 31 balance sheet. The following highlights the adjustment for salaries incurred.

| Before Adjustment | Adjustment | After Adjustment |
|---|---|---|
| Salaries Payable = $0 | Add $210 to Salaries Payable<br>Add $210 to Salaries Expense | Salaries Payable = $210 |
| Reports $0 from employee salaries incurred but not yet paid in cash. | Record 3 days' salaries owed to employee, but not yet paid, at $70 per day. | Reports $210 salaries payable to employee but not yet paid. |

**Accrued Interest Expense**    Companies commonly have accrued interest expense on notes payable and other long-term liabilities at the end of a period. Interest expense is incurred with the passage of time. Unless interest is paid on the last day of an accounting period, we need to adjust for interest expense incurred but not yet paid. This means we must accrue interest cost from the most recent payment date up to the end of the period. The formula for computing accrued interest is:

**Principal amount owed × Annual interest rate × Fraction of year since last payment date.**

To illustrate, if a company has a $6,000 loan from a bank at 6% annual interest, then 30 days' accrued interest expense is $30—computed as $6,000 × 0.06 × 30/360. The adjusting entry would be to debit Interest Expense for $30 and credit Interest Payable for $30.

**Point:** Interest computations assume a 360-day year; known as the *bankers' rule.*

**Future Payment of Accrued Expenses**  Adjusting entries for accrued expenses foretell cash transactions in future periods. Specifically, accrued expenses at the end of one accounting period result in *cash payment* in a *future period*(s). To illustrate, recall that FastForward recorded accrued salaries of $210. On January 9, the first payday of the next period, the following entry settles the accrued liability (salaries payable) and records salaries expense for seven days of work in January:

| Jan. 9 | Salaries Payable (3 days at $70 per day) . . . . . . . . . . . . . | 210 | |
|--------|--------------------------------------------------------------|-----|-----|
| | Salaries Expense (7 days at $70 per day) . . . . . . . . . . . | 490 | |
| | Cash . . . . . . . . . . . . . . . . . . . . . . . . . . . . . . . . . . . . | | 700 |
| | *Paid two weeks' salary including three days accrued in December.* | | |

Assets = Liabilities + Equity
−700     −210     −490

The $210 debit reflects the payment of the liability for the three days' salary accrued on December 31. The $490 debit records the salary for January's first seven working days (including the New Year's Day holiday) as an expense of the new accounting period. The $700 credit records the total amount of cash paid to the employee.

## Accrued Revenues

The term **accrued revenues** refers to revenues earned in a period that are both unrecorded and not yet received in cash (or other assets). An example is a technician who bills customers only when the job is done. If one-third of a job is complete by the end of a period, then the technician must record one-third of the expected billing as revenue in that period—even though there is no billing or collection. The adjusting entries for accrued revenues increase assets and increase revenues as shown in Exhibit 3.11. Accrued revenues commonly arise from services, products, interest, and rent. We use service fees and interest to show how to adjust for accrued revenues.

**Point:** Accrued revenues are also called *accrued assets.*

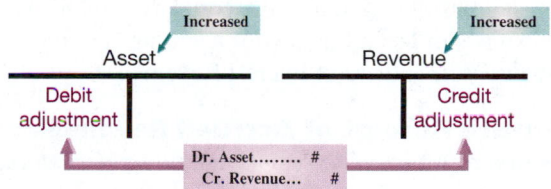

**EXHIBIT 3.11**

Adjusting for Accrued Revenues

**Accrued Services Revenue**  Accrued revenues are not recorded until adjusting entries are made at the end of the accounting period. These accrued revenues are earned but unrecorded because either the buyer has not yet paid for them or the seller has not yet billed the buyer. FastForward provides an example.

*Step 1:*  In the second week of December, it agreed to provide 30 days of consulting services to a local fitness club for a fixed fee of $2,700. The terms of the initial agreement call for FastForward to provide services from December 12, 2011, through January 10, 2012, or 30 days of service. The club agrees to pay FastForward $2,700 on January 10, 2012, when the service period is complete.

*Step 2:*  At December 31, 2011, 20 days of services have already been provided. Since the contracted services have not yet been entirely provided, FastForward has neither billed the club nor recorded the services already provided. Still, FastForward has earned two-thirds of the 30-day fee, or $1,800 ($2,700 × 20/30). The *revenue recognition principle* implies that it must report the $1,800 on the December income statement. The balance sheet also must report that the club owes FastForward $1,800.

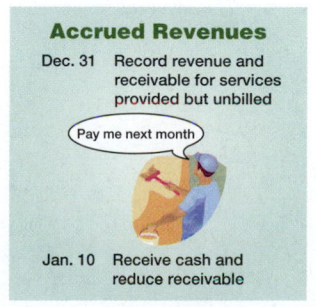

**Accrued Revenues**

Dec. 31  Record revenue and receivable for services provided but unbilled

Pay me next month

Jan. 10  Receive cash and reduce receivable

**Step 3:**   The year-end adjusting entry to account for accrued services revenue is

Assets  =  Liabilities  +  Equity
+1,800                        +1,800

| Adjustment (f) | | |
|---|---|---|
| Dec. 31    Accounts Receivable ........................... | 1,800 | |
| Consulting Revenue ....................... | | 1,800 |
| *To record 20 days' accrued revenue.* | | |

| Accounts Receivable | | | 106 |
|---|---|---|---|
| Dec. 12 | 1,900 | Dec. 22 | 1,900 |
| **31** | **1,800** | | |
| Balance | 1,800 | | |

| Consulting Revenue | | 403 |
|---|---|---|
| | Dec.  5 | 4,200 |
| | 12 | 1,600 |
| | 31 | 250 |
| | **31** | **1,800** |
| | Balance | 7,850 |

Example: What is the adjusting entry
if the 30-day consulting period began on
December 22? Answer: One-third of the
fee is earned:
Accounts Receivable .......   900
   Consulting Revenue....         900

**Explanation**   Accounts receivable are reported on the balance sheet at $1,800, and the $7,850 total of consulting revenue is reported on the income statement. *Not* making the adjustment would understate (1) both consulting revenue and net income by $1,800 in the December income statement and (2) both accounts receivable (assets) and equity by $1,800 on the December 31 balance sheet. The following table highlights the adjustment for accrued revenue.

| Before Adjustment | Adjustment | After Adjustment |
|---|---|---|
| **Accounts Receivable = $0** | **Add $1,800 to Accounts Receivable**<br>**Add $1,800 to Consulting Revenue** | **Accounts Receivable = $1,800** |
| Reports $0 from revenue earned but not yet received in cash. | Record 20 days of earned consulting revenue, which is 20/30 of total contract amount. | Reports $1,800 in accounts receivable from consulting services provided. |

**Accrued Interest Revenue**   In addition to the accrued interest expense we described earlier, interest can yield an accrued revenue when a debtor owes money (or other assets) to a company. If a company is holding notes or accounts receivable that produce interest revenue, we must adjust the accounts to record any earned and yet uncollected interest revenue. The adjusting entry is similar to the one for accruing services revenue. Specifically, we debit Interest Receivable (asset) and credit Interest Revenue.

**Future Receipt of Accrued Revenues**   Accrued revenues at the end of one accounting period result in *cash receipts* in a *future period*(s). To illustrate, recall that FastForward made an adjusting entry for $1,800 to record 20 days' accrued revenue earned from its consulting contract. When FastForward receives $2,700 cash on January 10 for the entire contract amount, it makes the following entry to remove the accrued asset (accounts receivable) and recognize the revenue earned in January. The $2,700 debit reflects the cash received. The $1,800 credit reflects the removal of the receivable, and the $900 credit records the revenue earned in January.

Assets  =  Liabilities  +  Equity
+2,700                         +900
−1,800

| Jan. 10    Cash ......................................... | 2,700 | |
|---|---|---|
| Accounts Receivable (20 days at $90 per day) ...... | | 1,800 |
| Consulting Revenue (10 days at $90 per day) ..... | | 900 |
| *Received cash for the accrued asset and recorded*<br>*earned consulting revenue for January.* | | |

**Decision Maker**                                                    Answer – p. 116

**Loan Officer**   The owner of an electronics store applies for a business loan. The store's financial statements reveal large increases in current-year revenues and income. Analysis shows that these increases are due to a promotion that let consumers buy now and pay nothing until January 1 of next year. The store recorded these sales as accrued revenue. Does your analysis raise any concerns? ■

## Links to Financial Statements

The process of adjusting accounts is intended to bring an asset or liability account balance to its correct amount. It also updates a related expense or revenue account. These adjustments are necessary for transactions and events that extend over more than one period. (Adjusting entries are posted like any other entry.)

**A1** Explain how accounting adjustments link to financial statements.

Exhibit 3.12 summarizes the four types of transactions requiring adjustment. Understanding this exhibit is important to understanding the adjusting process and its importance to financial statements. Remember that each adjusting entry affects one or more income statement accounts *and* one or more balance sheet accounts (but never cash).

| Category | BEFORE Adjusting | | Adjusting Entry |
| | Balance Sheet | Income Statement | |
|---|---|---|---|
| **Prepaid expenses†** | Asset overstated | Expense understated | **Dr. Expense** |
| | Equity overstated | | **Cr. Asset*** |
| **Unearned revenues†** | Liability overstated | Revenue understated | **Dr. Liability** |
| | Equity understated | | **Cr. Revenue** |
| **Accrued expenses** | Liability understated | Expense understated | **Dr. Expense** |
| | Equity overstated | | **Cr. Liability** |
| **Accrued revenues** | Asset understated | Revenue understated | **Dr. Asset** |
| | Equity understated | | **Cr. Revenue** |

**EXHIBIT 3.12**

Summary of Adjustments and Financial Statement Links

\* For depreciation, the credit is to Accumulated Depreciation (contra asset).

† Exhibit assumes that prepaid expenses are initially recorded as assets and that unearned revenues are initially recorded as liabilities.

Information about some adjustments is not always available until several days or even weeks after the period-end. This means that some adjusting and closing entries are recorded later than, but dated as of, the last day of the period. One example is a company that receives a utility bill on January 10 for costs incurred for the month of December. When it receives the bill, the company records the expense and the payable as of December 31. Other examples include long-distance phone usage and costs of many Web billings. The December income statement reflects these additional expenses incurred, and the December 31 balance sheet includes these payables, although the amounts were not actually known on December 31.

**Decision Ethics**  Answer — p. 116

**Financial Officer**   At year-end, the president instructs you, the financial officer, not to record accrued expenses until next year because they will not be paid until then. The president also directs you to record in current-year sales a recent purchase order from a customer that requires merchandise to be delivered two weeks after the year-end. Your company would report a net income instead of a net loss if you carry out these instructions. What do you do? ■

**Quick Check**  Answers — p. 116

6. If an adjusting entry for accrued revenues of $200 at year-end is omitted, what is this error's effect on the year-end income statement and balance sheet?
7. What is a contra account? Explain its purpose.
8. What is an accrued expense? Give an example.
9. Describe how an unearned revenue arises. Give an example.

## Adjusted Trial Balance

**P2**   Explain and prepare an adjusted trial balance.

An **unadjusted trial balance** is a list of accounts and balances prepared *before* adjustments are recorded. An **adjusted trial balance** is a list of accounts and balances prepared *after* adjusting entries have been recorded and posted to the ledger.

Exhibit 3.13 shows both the unadjusted and the adjusted trial balances for FastForward at December 31, 2011. The order of accounts in the trial balance is usually set up to match the order in the chart of accounts. Several new accounts arise from the adjusting entries.

**EXHIBIT 3.13**

Unadjusted and Adjusted
Trial Balances

### FASTFORWARD
### Trial Balances
### December 31, 2011

| Acct. No. | Account Title | Unadjusted Trial Balance Dr. | Unadjusted Trial Balance Cr. | Adjustments Dr. | Adjustments Cr. | Adjusted Trial Balance Dr. | Adjusted Trial Balance Cr. |
|---|---|---|---|---|---|---|---|
| 101 | Cash | $ 4,350 | | | | $ 4,350 | |
| 106 | Accounts receivable | 0 | | (f) $1,800 | | 1,800 | |
| 126 | Supplies | 9,720 | | | (b) $1,050 | 8,670 | |
| 128 | Prepaid insurance | 2,400 | | | (a) 100 | 2,300 | |
| 167 | Equipment | 26,000 | | | | 26,000 | |
| 168 | Accumulated depreciation—Equip. | | $ 0 | | (c) 375 | | $ 375 |
| 201 | Accounts payable | | 6,200 | | | | 6,200 |
| 209 | Salaries payable | | 0 | | (e) 210 | | 210 |
| 236 | Unearned consulting revenue | | 3,000 | (d) 250 | | | 2,750 |
| 301 | C. Taylor, Capital | | 30,000 | | | | 30,000 |
| 302 | C. Taylor, Withdrawals | 200 | | | | 200 | |
| 403 | Consulting revenue | | 5,800 | | (d) 250 | | 7,850 |
| | | | | | (f) 1,800 | | |
| 406 | Rental revenue | | 300 | | | | 300 |
| 612 | Depreciation expense—Equip. | 0 | | (c) 375 | | 375 | |
| 622 | Salaries expense | 1,400 | | (e) 210 | | 1,610 | |
| 637 | Insurance expense | 0 | | (a) 100 | | 100 | |
| 640 | Rent expense | 1,000 | | | | 1,000 | |
| 652 | Supplies expense | 0 | | (b) 1,050 | | 1,050 | |
| 690 | Utilities expense | 230 | | | | 230 | |
| | Totals | $45,300 | $45,300 | $3,785 | $3,785 | $47,685 | $47,685 |

Each adjustment (see middle columns) is identified by a letter in parentheses that links it to an adjusting entry explained earlier. Each amount in the Adjusted Trial Balance columns is computed by taking that account's amount from the Unadjusted Trial Balance columns and adding or subtracting any adjustment(s). To illustrate, Supplies has a $9,720 Dr. balance in the unadjusted columns. Subtracting the $1,050 Cr. amount shown in the adjustments columns yields an adjusted $8,670 Dr. balance for Supplies. An account can have more than one adjustment, such as for Consulting Revenue. Also, some accounts might not require adjustment for this period, such as Accounts Payable.

## PREPARING FINANCIAL STATEMENTS

**P3**   Prepare financial statements from an adjusted trial balance.

**Point: Sarbanes-Oxley Act** requires that financial statements filed with the SEC be certified by the CEO and CFO, including a declaration that the statements fairly present the issuer's operations and financial condition. Violators can receive fines and/or prison terms.

We can prepare financial statements directly from information in the *adjusted* trial balance. An adjusted trial balance (see the right-most columns in Exhibit 3.13) includes all accounts and balances appearing in financial statements, and is easier to work from than the entire ledger when preparing financial statements.

Exhibit 3.14 shows how revenue and expense balances are transferred from the adjusted trial balance to the income statement (red lines). The net income and the withdrawals amount are then used to prepare the statement of owner's equity (black lines). Asset and liability balances on the adjusted trial balance are then transferred to the balance sheet (blue lines). The ending capital is determined on the statement of owner's equity and transferred to the balance sheet (green lines).

**EXHIBIT 3.14**

Preparing Financial Statements (Adjusted Trial Balance from Exhibit 3.13)

**Step 3** Prepare balance sheet

### FASTFORWARD — Adjusted Trial Balance — December 31, 2011

| Acct. No. | Account Title | Debit | Credit |
|---|---|---|---|
| 101 | Cash ................................................ | $ 4,350 | |
| 106 | Accounts receivable ......................... | 1,800 | |
| 126 | Supplies .......................................... | 8,670 | |
| 128 | Prepaid insurance ............................ | 2,300 | |
| 167 | Equipment ....................................... | 26,000 | |
| 168 | Accumulated depreciation—Equip. ... | | $ 375 |
| 201 | Accounts payable ............................. | | 6,200 |
| 209 | Salaries payable ............................... | | 210 |
| 236 | Unearned consulting revenue ............ | | 2,750 |
| 301 | C. Taylor, Capital ............................. | | 30,000 |
| 302 | C. Taylor, Withdrawals ..................... | 200 | |
| 403 | Consulting revenue ........................... | | 7,850 |
| 406 | Rental revenue ................................. | | 300 |
| 612 | Depreciation expense—Equip. .......... | 375 | |
| 622 | Salaries expense .............................. | 1,610 | |
| 637 | Insurance expense ............................ | 100 | |
| 640 | Rent expense ................................... | 1,000 | |
| 652 | Supplies expense .............................. | 1,050 | |
| 690 | Utilities expense ............................... | 230 | |
| | Totals ............................................. | $47,685 | $47,685 |

### FASTFORWARD — Balance Sheet — December 31, 2011

**Assets**

| | | |
|---|---|---|
| Cash ............................................. | | $ 4,350 |
| Accounts receivable ...................... | | 1,800 |
| Supplies ....................................... | | 8,670 |
| Prepaid insurance ......................... | | 2,300 |
| Equipment ................................... | $26,000 | |
| Less accumulated depreciation .... | 375 | 25,625 |
| Total assets ................................. | | $ 42,745 |

**Liabilities**

| | |
|---|---|
| Accounts payable ......................... | $ 6,200 |
| Salaries payable ........................... | 210 |
| Unearned consulting revenue ....... | 2,750 |
| Total liabilities ............................. | 9,160 |

**Equity**

| | |
|---|---|
| C. Taylor, Capital .......................... | 33,585 |
| Total liabilities and equity ............. | $ 42,745 |

**Step 2** Prepare statement of owner's equity

### FASTFORWARD — Statement of Owner's Equity — For Month Ended December 31, 2011

| | | |
|---|---|---|
| C. Taylor, Capital, December 1..... | | $ 0 |
| Plus: Investments by owner .......... | $30,000 | |
| Net income ........................... | 3,785 | |
| | | 33,785 |
| Less: Withdrawals by owner .......... | | 200 |
| C. Taylor, Capital, December 31 ..... | | $33,585 |

**Step 1** Prepare income statement

### FASTFORWARD — Income Statement — For Month Ended December 31, 2011

| | | |
|---|---|---|
| Revenues | | |
| Consulting revenue ....................... | $7,850 | |
| Rental revenue ............................. | 300 | |
| Total revenues ............................. | | $8,150 |
| Expenses | | |
| Depreciation expense—Equip....... | 375 | |
| Salaries expense........................... | 1,610 | |
| Insurance expense......................... | 100 | |
| Rent expense................................ | 1,000 | |
| Supplies expense........................... | 1,050 | |
| Utilities expense............................ | 230 | |
| Total expenses.............................. | | 4,365 |
| Net income................................... | | $3,785 |

### Steps to Prepare Financial Statements

**Step 1** Prepare income statement using revenue and expense accounts from trial balance.

**Step 2** Prepare statement of owner's equity using withdrawals account from trial balance; and pull net income from step 1.

**Step 3** Prepare balance sheet using asset and liability account from trial balance; and pull updated capital balance from step 2.

**Step 4** Prepare statement of cash flows from changes in cash flows for the period (not illustrated here).

We prepare financial statements in the following order: income statement, statement of owner's equity, and balance sheet. This order makes sense because the balance sheet uses information from the statement of owner's equity, which in turn uses information from the income statement. The statement of cash flows is usually the final statement prepared.

**Point:** Each trial balance amount is used in only *one* financial statement and, when financial statements are completed, each account will have been used once.

## Quick Check

Answers — p. 116

**10.** Music-Mart records $1,000 of accrued salaries on December 31. Five days later, on January 5 (the next payday), salaries of $7,000 are paid. What is the January 5 entry?

**11.** Jordan Air has the following information in its unadjusted and adjusted trial balances. What are the adjusting entries that Jordan Air likely recorded?

|  | Unadjusted | | Adjusted | |
|---|---|---|---|---|
|  | Debit | Credit | Debit | Credit |
| Prepaid insurance .......... | $6,200 |  | $5,900 |  |
| Salaries payable .......... |  | $ 0 |  | $1,400 |

**12.** What accounts are taken from the adjusted trial balance to prepare an income statement?

**13.** In preparing financial statements from an adjusted trial balance, what statement is usually prepared second?

# GLOBAL VIEW

We explained that accounting under U.S. GAAP is similar, but not identical, to that under IFRS. This section discusses differences in adjusting accounts, preparing financial statements, and reporting assets and liabilities on a balance sheet.

**Adjusting Accounts**    Both U.S. GAAP and IFRS include broad and similar guidance for adjusting accounts. Although some variations exist in revenue and expense recognition and other principles, all of the adjustments in this chapter are accounted for identically under the two systems. In later chapters we describe how certain assets and liabilities can result in different adjusted amounts using fair value measurements.

**Preparing Financial Statements**    Both U.S. GAAP and IFRS prepare the same four basic financial statements following the same process discussed in this chapter. Chapter 2 explained how both U.S. GAAP and IFRS require current items to be separated from noncurrent items on the balance sheet (yielding a classified balance sheet). U.S. GAAP balance sheets report current items first. Assets are listed from most liquid to least liquid, where liquid refers to the ease of converting an asset to cash. Liabilities are listed from nearest to maturity to furthest from maturity, maturity refers to the nearness of paying off the liability. IFRS balance sheets normally present noncurrent items first (and equity before liabilities), but this is not a requirement. Other differences with financial statements exist, which we identify in later chapters. Nokia provides the following example of IFRS reporting for its assets, liabilities, and equity within the balance sheet:

**NOKIA**

| NOKIA Balance Sheet (in EUR millions) December 31, 2009 | | | | |
|---|---|---|---|---|
| **Assets** | | **Equity and Liabilities** | | |
| Noncurrent assets | | Total equity ........................... | | 14,749 |
| Goodwill and other intangibles ............ | 8,076 | Noncurrent liabilities | | |
| Property, plant and equipment ............. | 1,867 | Long-term interest-bearing liabilities ....... | | 4,432 |
| Other noncurrent assets ................. | 2,182 | Other long-term liabilities ............... | | 1,369 |
| Total noncurrent assets ................ | 12,125 | Total noncurrent liabilities ............. | | 5,801 |
| Current assets | | Current liabilities | | |
| Inventories............................. | 1,865 | Current portion of long-term loans........ | | 44 |
| Accounts receivable, net ................. | 7,981 | Short-term borrowings and other liabilities ... | | 972 |
| Prepaid expenses and accrued income ...... | 4,551 | Accounts payable ...................... | | 4,950 |
| Other current assets .................... | 8,074 | Accrued expenses ..................... | | 6,504 |
| Cash ................................. | 1,142 | Provisions ............................ | | 2,718 |
| Total current assets .................... | 23,613 | Total current liabilities ................ | | 15,188 |
| Total assets .......................... | 35,738 | Total equity and liabilities ............... | | 35,738 |

## IFRS

Revenue and expense recognition are key to recording accounting adjustments. IFRS tends to be more *principles-based* relative to U.S. GAAP, which is viewed as more *rules-based*. A principles-based system depends heavily on control procedures to reduce the potential for fraud or misconduct. Failure in judgment led to improper accounting adjustments at **Fannie Mae**, **Xerox**, **WorldCom**, and others. A KPMG 2009 survey of accounting and finance employees found that 13% of them had witnessed falsification or manipulation of accounting data within the past year. Internal controls and governance processes are directed at curtailing such behavior. ■

---

| Profit Margin |  **Decision Analysis** |  |

A useful measure of a company's operating results is the ratio of its net income to net sales. This ratio is called **profit margin,** or *return on sales,* and is computed as in Exhibit 3.15.

> **A2** Compute profit margin and describe its use in analyzing company performance.

**EXHIBIT 3.15**

Profit Margin

$$\text{Profit margin} = \frac{\text{Net income}}{\text{Net sales}}$$

This ratio is interpreted as reflecting the percent of profit in each dollar of sales. To illustrate how we compute and use profit margin, let's look at the results of **Limited Brands, Inc.**, in Exhibit 3.16 for its fiscal years 2006 through 2010.

**EXHIBIT 3.16**

Limited Brands' Profit Margin

| $ in millions | 2010 | 2009 | 2008 | 2007 | 2006 |
|---|---|---|---|---|---|
| Net income ................. | $ 448 | $ 220 | $ 718 | $ 676 | $ 683 |
| Net sales .................... | $8,632 | $9,043 | $10,134 | $10,671 | $9,699 |
| Profit margin .............. | 5.2% | 2.4% | 7.1% | 6.3% | 7.0% |
| Industry profit margin ......... | 0.9% | 0.3% | 1.1% | 1.6% | 1.5% |

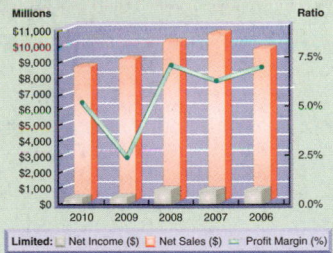

The Limited's average profit margin is 5.6% during this 5-year period. This favorably compares to the average industry profit margin of 1.1%. However, Limited's profit margin has declined in the most recent two years—from 7.1% in 2008 to 2.4% and 5.2% for the recent recessionary periods (see margin graph). Future success depends on Limited maintaining its market share and increasing its profit margin.

## DEMONSTRATION PROBLEM 1

The following information relates to Fanning's Electronics on December 31, 2011. The company, which uses the calendar year as its annual reporting period, initially records prepaid and unearned items in balance sheet accounts (assets and liabilities, respectively).

**a.** The company's weekly payroll is $8,750, paid each Friday for a five-day workweek. Assume December 31, 2011, falls on a Monday, but the employees will not be paid their wages until Friday, January 4, 2012.

**b.** Eighteen months earlier, on July 1, 2010, the company purchased equipment that cost $20,000. Its useful life is predicted to be five years, at which time the equipment is expected to be worthless (zero salvage value).

**c.** On October 1, 2011, the company agreed to work on a new housing development. The company is paid $120,000 on October 1 in advance of future installation of similar alarm systems in 24 new homes. That amount was credited to the Unearned Services Revenue account. Between October 1 and December 31, work on 20 homes was completed.

**d.** On September 1, 2011, the company purchased a 12-month insurance policy for $1,800. The transaction was recorded with an $1,800 debit to Prepaid Insurance.

**e.** On December 29, 2011, the company completed a $7,000 service that has not been billed and not recorded as of December 31, 2011.

**Required**

**1.** Prepare any necessary adjusting entries on December 31, 2011, in relation to transactions and events *a* through *e*.

**2.** Prepare T-accounts for the accounts affected by adjusting entries, and post the adjusting entries. Determine the adjusted balances for the Unearned Revenue and the Prepaid Insurance accounts.

**3.** Complete the following table and determine the amounts and effects of your adjusting entries on the year 2011 income statement and the December 31, 2011, balance sheet. Use up (down) arrows to indicate an increase (decrease) in the Effect columns.

| Entry | Amount in the Entry | Effect on Net Income | Effect on Total Assets | Effect on Total Liabilities | Effect on Total Equity |
|-------|--------------------|--------------------|----------------------|-------------------------|----------------------|
|       |                    |                    |                      |                         |                      |

## PLANNING THE SOLUTION

- Analyze each situation to determine which accounts need to be updated with an adjustment.
- Calculate the amount of each adjustment and prepare the necessary journal entries.
- Show the amount of each adjustment in the designated accounts, determine the adjusted balance, and identify the balance sheet classification of the account.
- Determine each entry's effect on net income for the year and on total assets, total liabilities, and total equity at the end of the year.

## SOLUTION TO DEMONSTRATION PROBLEM 1

**1.** Adjusting journal entries.

| | | | |
|---|---|---|---|
| (a) Dec. 31 | Wages Expense ................................. | 1,750 | |
| | Wages Payable ............................. | | 1,750 |
| | *To accrue wages for the last day of the year ($8,750 × 1/5).* | | |
| (b) Dec. 31 | Depreciation Expense—Equipment ................ | 4,000 | |
| | Accumulated Depreciation—Equipment ........ | | 4,000 |
| | *To record depreciation expense for the year ($20,000/5 years = $4,000 per year).* | | |
| (c) Dec. 31 | Unearned Services Revenue ...................... | 100,000 | |
| | Services Revenue ........................... | | 100,000 |
| | *To recognize services revenue earned ($120,000 × 20/24).* | | |
| (d) Dec. 31 | Insurance Expense ............................. | 600 | |
| | Prepaid Insurance .......................... | | 600 |
| | *To adjust for expired portion of insurance ($1,800 × 4/12).* | | |
| (e) Dec. 31 | Accounts Receivable .......................... | 7,000 | |
| | Services Revenue ........................... | | 7,000 |
| | *To record services revenue earned.* | | |

**2.** T-accounts for adjusting journal entries *a* through *e*.

| Wages Expense | | Wages Payable | |
|---|---|---|---|
| (a) | 1,750 | | (a) 1,750 |

| Depreciation Expense—Equipment | | Accumulated Depreciation—Equipment | |
|---|---|---|---|
| (b) | 4,000 | | (b) 4,000 |

| Unearned Revenue | | Services Revenue | |
|---|---|---|---|
| (c) 100,000 | Unadj. Bal. 120,000 | | (c) 100,000 |
| | Adj. Bal. 20,000 | | (e) 7,000 |
| | | | Adj. Bal. 107,000 |

| Insurance Expense | | Prepaid Insurance | |
|---|---|---|---|
| (d) | 600 | Unadj. Bal. 1,800 | (d) 600 |
| | | Adj. Bal. 1,200 | |

| Accounts Receivable | |
|---|---|
| (e) | 7,000 |

**3.** Financial statement effects of adjusting journal entries.

| Entry | Amount in the Entry | Effect on Net Income | Effect on Total Assets | Effect on Total Liabilities | Effect on Total Equity |
|---|---|---|---|---|---|
| a | $ 1,750 | $ 1,750 ↓ | No effect | $ 1,750 ↑ | $ 1,750 ↓ |
| b | 4,000 | 4,000 ↓ | $4,000 ↓ | No effect | 4,000 ↓ |
| c | 100,000 | 100,000 ↑ | No effect | $100,000 ↓ | 100,000 ↑ |
| d | 600 | 600 ↓ | $ 600 ↓ | No effect | 600 ↓ |
| e | 7,000 | 7,000 ↑ | $7,000 ↑ | No effect | 7,000 ↑ |

# DEMONSTRATION PROBLEM 2

Use the following adjusted trial balance to answer questions 1–3.

**CHOI COMPANY**
**Adjusted Trial Balance**
**December 31**

| | Debit | Credit |
|---|---|---|
| Cash | $ 3,050 | |
| Accounts receivable | 400 | |
| Prepaid insurance | 830 | |
| Supplies | 80 | |
| Equipment | 217,200 | |
| Accumulated depreciation—Equipment | | $ 29,100 |
| Wages payable | | 880 |

[continued on next page]

[continued from previous page]

| | | |
|---|---:|---:|
| Interest payable | | 3,600 |
| Unearned rent | | 460 |
| Long-term notes payable | | 150,000 |
| M. Choi, Capital | | 40,340 |
| M. Choi, Withdrawals | 21,000 | |
| Rent earned | | 57,500 |
| Wages expense | 25,000 | |
| Utilities expense | 1,900 | |
| Insurance expense | 3,200 | |
| Supplies expense | 250 | |
| Depreciation expense—Equipment | 5,970 | |
| Interest expense | 3,000 | |
| Totals | $281,880 | $281,880 |

**1.** Prepare the annual income statement from the adjusted trial balance of Choi Company.

*Answer:*

**CHOI COMPANY**
**Income Statement**
**For Year Ended December 31**

| | | |
|---|---:|---:|
| Revenues | | |
| Rent earned | | $57,500 |
| Expenses | | |
| Wages expense | $25,000 | |
| Utilities expense | 1,900 | |
| Insurance expense | 3,200 | |
| Supplies expense | 250 | |
| Depreciation expense—Equipment | 5,970 | |
| Interest expense | 3,000 | |
| Total expenses | | 39,320 |
| Net income | | $18,180 |

**2.** Prepare a statement of owner's equity from the adjusted trial balance of Choi Company. Choi's capital account balance of $40,340 consists of a $30,340 balance from the prior year-end, plus a $10,000 owner investment during the current year.

*Answer:*

**CHOI COMPANY**
**Statement of Owner's Equity**
**For Year Ended December 31**

| | | |
|---|---:|---:|
| M. Choi, Capital, December 31 prior year-end | | $30,340 |
| Plus: Owner investments | $10,000 | |
| Net income | 18,180 | 28,180 |
| | | 58,520 |
| Less: Withdrawals by owner | | 21,000 |
| M. Choi, Capital, December 31 current year-end | | $37,520 |

**3.** Prepare a balance sheet from the adjusted trial balance of Choi Company.

*Answer:*

| CHOI COMPANY<br>Balance Sheet<br>December 31 | | |
|---|---:|---:|
| **Assets** | | |
| Cash . . . . . . . . . . . . . . . . . . . . . . . . . . . . . . | | $  3,050 |
| Accounts receivable  . . . . . . . . . . . . . . . . | | 400 |
| Prepaid insurance  . . . . . . . . . . . . . . . . . | | 830 |
| Supplies  . . . . . . . . . . . . . . . . . . . . . . . . | | 80 |
| Equipment . . . . . . . . . . . . . . . . . . . . . . . | $217,200 | |
| Less accumulated depreciation  . . . . . . . . | 29,100 | 188,100 |
| Total assets  . . . . . . . . . . . . . . . . . . . . . . | | $192,460 |
| **Liabilities** | | |
| Wages payable . . . . . . . . . . . . . . . . . . . . . | | $    880 |
| Interest payable . . . . . . . . . . . . . . . . . . . . | | 3,600 |
| Unearned rent . . . . . . . . . . . . . . . . . . . . . . | | 460 |
| Long-term notes payable  . . . . . . . . . . . . . | | 150,000 |
| Total liabilities  . . . . . . . . . . . . . . . . . . . . . | | 154,940 |
| **Equity** | | |
| M. Choi, Capital . . . . . . . . . . . . . . . . . . . . . | | 37,520 |
| Total liabilities and equity  . . . . . . . . . . . . . | | $192,460 |

# Alternative Accounting for Prepayments

This appendix explains an alternative in accounting for prepaid expenses and unearned revenues.

**Recording Prepayment of Expenses in Expense Accounts**   An alternative method is to record *all* prepaid expenses with debits to expense accounts. If any prepaids remain unused or unexpired at the end of an accounting period, then adjusting entries must transfer the cost of the unused portions from expense accounts to prepaid expense (asset) accounts. This alternative method is acceptable. The financial statements are identical under either method, but the adjusting entries are different. To illustrate the differences between these two methods, let's look at FastForward's cash payment of December 6 for 24 months of insurance coverage beginning on December 1. FastForward recorded that payment with a debit to an asset account, but it could have recorded a debit to an expense account. These alternatives are shown in Exhibit 3A.1.

**P4**   Explain the alternatives in accounting for prepaids.

**EXHIBIT 3A.1**

Alternative Initial Entries for Prepaid Expenses

| | | Payment Recorded<br>as Asset | Payment Recorded<br>as Expense |
|---|---|---:|---:|
| Dec. 6 | Prepaid Insurance  . . . . . . . . . | 2,400 | |
| | Cash  . . . . . . . . . . . . . . . | | 2,400 |
| Dec. 6 | Insurance Expense  . . . . . . . . | | 2,400 |
| | Cash  . . . . . . . . . . . . . . . | | 2,400 |

At the end of its accounting period on December 31, insurance protection for one month has expired. This means $100 ($2,400/24) of insurance coverage expired and is an expense for December. The adjusting entry depends on how the original payment was recorded. This is shown in Exhibit 3A.2.

**EXHIBIT 3A.2**

Adjusting Entry for Prepaid Expenses for the Two Alternatives

| | | | Payment Recorded as Asset | Payment Recorded as Expense |
|---|---|---|---|---|
| Dec. 31 | Insurance Expense ............. | | 100 | |
| | Prepaid Insurance ......... | | 100 | |
| Dec. 31 | Prepaid Insurance ............. | | | 2,300 |
| | Insurance Expense ........ | | | 2,300 |

When these entries are posted to the accounts in the ledger, we can see that these two methods give identical results. The December 31 adjusted account balances in Exhibit 3A.3 show Prepaid Insurance of $2,300 and Insurance Expense of $100 for both methods.

**EXHIBIT 3A.3**

Account Balances under Two Alternatives for Recording Prepaid Expenses

| Payment Recorded as Asset | | | |
|---|---|---|---|
| **Prepaid Insurance** | | | 128 |
| Dec. 6 | 2,400 | Dec. 31 | 100 |
| Balance | **2,300** | | |

| **Insurance Expense** | | | 637 |
|---|---|---|---|
| Dec. 31 | **100** | | |

| Payment Recorded as Expense | | | |
|---|---|---|---|
| **Prepaid Insurance** | | | 128 |
| Dec. 31 | **2,300** | | |

| **Insurance Expense** | | | 637 |
|---|---|---|---|
| Dec. 6 | 2,400 | Dec. 31 | 2,300 |
| Balance | **100** | | |

**Recording Prepayment of Revenues <u>in Revenue Accounts</u>**   As with prepaid expenses, an alternative method is to record *all* unearned revenues with credits to revenue accounts. If any revenues are unearned at the end of an accounting period, then adjusting entries must transfer the unearned portions from revenue accounts to unearned revenue (liability) accounts. This alternative method is acceptable. The adjusting entries are different for these two alternatives, but the financial statements are identical. To illustrate the accounting differences between these two methods, let's look at FastForward's December 26 receipt of $3,000 for consulting services covering the period December 27 to February 24. FastForward recorded this transaction with a credit to a liability account. The alternative is to record it with a credit to a revenue account, as shown in Exhibit 3A.4.

**EXHIBIT 3A.4**

Alternative Initial Entries for Unearned Revenues

| | | | Receipt Recorded as Liability | Receipt Recorded as Revenue |
|---|---|---|---|---|
| Dec. 26 | Cash ................................. | | 3,000 | |
| | Unearned Consulting Revenue ......... | | 3,000 | |
| Dec. 26 | Cash ................................. | | | 3,000 |
| | Consulting Revenue ................ | | | 3,000 |

By the end of its accounting period on December 31, FastForward has earned $250 of this revenue. This means $250 of the liability has been satisfied. Depending on how the initial receipt is recorded, the adjusting entry is as shown in Exhibit 3A.5.

**EXHIBIT 3A.5**

Adjusting Entry for Unearned Revenues for the Two Alternatives

| | | | Receipt Recorded as Liability | Receipt Recorded as Revenue |
|---|---|---|---|---|
| Dec. 31 | Unearned Consulting Revenue ............. | | 250 | |
| | Consulting Revenue ................ | | 250 | |
| Dec. 31 | Consulting Revenue ..................... | | | 2,750 |
| | Unearned Consulting Revenue ......... | | | 2,750 |

After adjusting entries are posted, the two alternatives give identical results. The December 31 adjusted account balances in Exhibit 3A.6 show unearned consulting revenue of $2,750 and consulting revenue of $250 for both methods.

**EXHIBIT 3A.6**

Account Balances under Two Alternatives for Recording Unearned Revenues

| Receipt Recorded as Liability | | | |
|---|---|---|---|
| **Unearned Consulting Revenue** | | | 236 |
| Dec. 31 | 250 | Dec. 26 | 3,000 |
| | | Balance | **2,750** |

| | | | |
|---|---|---|---|
| **Consulting Revenue** | | | 403 |
| | | Dec. 31 | **250** |

| Receipt Recorded as Revenue | | | |
|---|---|---|---|
| **Unearned Consulting Revenue** | | | 236 |
| | | Dec. 31 | **2,750** |

| | | | |
|---|---|---|---|
| **Consulting Revenue** | | | 403 |
| Dec. 31 | 2,750 | Dec. 26 | 3,000 |
| | | Balance | **250** |

# Summary

**C1** **Explain the importance of periodic reporting and the time period assumption.** The value of information is often linked to its timeliness. To provide timely information, accounting systems prepare periodic reports at regular intervals. The time period assumption presumes that an organization's activities can be divided into specific time periods for periodic reporting.

**C2** **Explain accrual accounting and how it improves financial statements.** Accrual accounting recognizes revenue when earned and expenses when incurred—not necessarily when cash inflows and outflows occur. This information is valuable in assessing a company's financial position and performance.

**C3** **Identify the types of adjustments and their purpose.** Adjustments can be grouped according to the timing of cash receipts and cash payments relative to when they are recognized as revenues or expenses as follows: prepaid expenses, unearned revenues, accrued expenses, and accrued revenues. Adjusting entries are necessary so that revenues, expenses, assets, and liabilities are correctly reported.

**A1** **Explain how accounting adjustments link to financial statements.** Accounting adjustments bring an asset or liability account balance to its correct amount. They also update related expense or revenue accounts. Every adjusting entry affects one or more income statement accounts *and* one or more balance sheet accounts. An adjusting entry never affects cash.

**A2** **Compute profit margin and describe its use in analyzing company performance.** *Profit margin* is defined as the reporting period's net income divided by its net sales. Profit margin reflects on a company's earnings activities by showing how much income is in each dollar of sales.

**P1** **Prepare and explain adjusting entries.** *Prepaid expenses* refer to items paid for in advance of receiving their benefits.

Prepaid expenses are assets. Adjusting entries for prepaids involve increasing (debiting) expenses and decreasing (crediting) assets. *Unearned* (or *prepaid*) *revenues* refer to cash received in advance of providing products and services. Unearned revenues are liabilities. Adjusting entries for unearned revenues involve increasing (crediting) revenues and decreasing (debiting) unearned revenues. *Accrued expenses* refer to costs incurred in a period that are both unpaid and unrecorded. Adjusting entries for recording accrued expenses involve increasing (debiting) expenses and increasing (crediting) liabilities. *Accrued revenues* refer to revenues earned in a period that are both unrecorded and not yet received in cash. Adjusting entries for recording accrued revenues involve increasing (debiting) assets and increasing (crediting) revenues.

**P2** **Explain and prepare an adjusted trial balance.** An adjusted trial balance is a list of accounts and balances prepared after recording and posting adjusting entries. Financial statements are often prepared from the adjusted trial balance.

**P3** **Prepare financial statements from an adjusted trial balance.** Revenue and expense balances are reported on the income statement. Asset, liability, and equity balances are reported on the balance sheet. We usually prepare statements in the following order: income statement, statement of owner's equity, balance sheet, and statement of cash flows.

**P4A** **Explain the alternatives in accounting for prepaids.** Charging all prepaid expenses to expense accounts when they are purchased is acceptable. When this is done, adjusting entries must transfer any unexpired amounts from expense accounts to asset accounts. Crediting all unearned revenues to revenue accounts when cash is received is also acceptable. In this case, the adjusting entries must transfer any unearned amounts from revenue accounts to unearned revenue accounts.

## Guidance Answers to Decision Maker and Decision Ethics

**Investor**   Prepaid expenses are items paid for in advance of receiving their benefits. They are assets and are expensed as they are used up. The publishing company's treatment of the signing bonus is

acceptable provided future book sales can at least match the $500,000 expense. As an investor, you are concerned about the risk of future book sales. The riskier the likelihood of future book sales is, the more likely your analysis is to treat the $500,000, or a portion of it, as an expense, not a prepaid expense (asset).

**Entrepreneur**   Depreciation is a process of cost allocation, not asset valuation. Knowing the depreciation schedule is not especially useful in your estimation of what the building and equipment are currently worth. Your own assessment of the age, quality, and usefulness of the building and equipment is more important.

**Loan Officer**   Your concern in lending to this store arises from analysis of current-year sales. While increased revenues and income are fine, your concern is with collectibility of these promotional sales. If the owner sold products to customers with poor records of paying bills, then collectibility of these sales is low. Your analysis must assess this possibility and recognize any expected losses.

**Financial Officer**   Omitting accrued expenses and recognizing revenue early can mislead financial statement users. One action is to request a second meeting with the president so you can explain that accruing expenses when incurred and recognizing revenue when earned are required practices. If the president persists, you might discuss the situation with legal counsel and any auditors involved. Your ethical action might cost you this job, but the potential pitfalls for falsification of statements, reputation and personal integrity loss, and other costs are too great.

## Guidance Answers to Quick Checks

1. An annual reporting (or accounting) period covers one year and refers to the preparation of annual financial statements. The annual reporting period is not always a calendar year that ends on December 31. An organization can adopt a fiscal year consisting of any consecutive 12 months or 52 weeks.

2. Interim financial statements (covering less than one year) are prepared to provide timely information to decision makers.

3. The revenue recognition principle and the matching principle lead most directly to the adjusting process.

4. No. Cash basis accounting is not consistent with the matching principle because it reports revenue when received, not necessarily when earned, and expenses when paid, not necessarily in the period when the expenses were incurred as a result of the revenues earned.

5. No expense is reported in 2012. Under cash basis accounting, the entire $4,800 is reported as an expense in April 2011 when the premium is paid.

6. If the accrued revenues adjustment of $200 is not made, then both revenues and net income are understated by $200 on the current year's income statement, and both assets and equity are understated by $200 on the balance sheet.

7. A contra account is an account that is subtracted from the balance of a related account. Use of a contra account provides more information than simply reporting a net amount.

8. An accrued expense is a cost incurred in a period that is both unpaid and unrecorded prior to adjusting entries. One example is salaries earned but not yet paid at period-end.

9. An unearned revenue arises when a firm receives cash (or other assets) from a customer before providing the services or products to the customer. A magazine subscription paid in advance is one example; season ticket sales is another.

10.
| | | |
|---|---|---|
| Salaries Payable | 1,000 | |
| Salaries Expense | 6,000 | |
| Cash | | 7,000 |

*Paid salary including accrual from December.*

11. The probable adjusting entries of Jordan Air are:

| | | |
|---|---|---|
| Insurance Expense | 300 | |
| Prepaid Insurance | | 300 |

*To record insurance expired.*

| | | |
|---|---|---|
| Salaries Expense | 1,400 | |
| Salaries Payable | | 1,400 |

*To record accrued salaries.*

12. Revenue accounts and expense accounts.

13. Statement of owner's equity.

## Key Terms

mhhe.com/wildFAP20e

**Accounting period** (p. 94)
**Accrual basis accounting** (p. 95)
**Accrued expenses** (p. 101)
**Accrued revenues** (p. 103)
**Adjusted trial balance** (p. 106)
**Adjusting entry** (p. 96)
**Annual financial statements** (p. 94)
**Book value** (p. 100)

**Cash basis accounting** (p. 95)
**Contra account** (p. 99)
**Depreciation** (p. 99)
**Expense recognition** (or **matching**) **principle** (p. 96)
**Fiscal year** (p. 95)
**Interim financial statements** (p. 94)
**Natural business year** (p. 95)

**Plant assets** (p. 99)
**Prepaid expenses** (p. 97)
**Profit margin** (p. 109)
**Straight-line depreciation method** (p. 99)
**Time period assumption** (p. 94)
**Unadjusted trial balance** (p. 106)
**Unearned revenues** (p. 100)

**Multiple Choice Quiz**          Answers on p. 135          mhhe.com/wildFAP20e

Additional Quiz Questions are available at the book's Website.

**1.** A company forgot to record accrued and unpaid employee wages of $350,000 at period-end. This oversight would
  **a.** Understate net income by $350,000.
  **b.** Overstate net income by $350,000.
  **c.** Have no effect on net income.
  **d.** Overstate assets by $350,000.
  **e.** Understate assets by $350,000.

**2.** Prior to recording adjusting entries, the Supplies account has a $450 debit balance. A physical count of supplies shows $125 of unused supplies still available. The required adjusting entry is:
  **a.** Debit Supplies $125; Credit Supplies Expense $125.
  **b.** Debit Supplies $325; Credit Supplies Expense $325.
  **c.** Debit Supplies Expense $325; Credit Supplies $325.
  **d.** Debit Supplies Expense $325; Credit Supplies $125.
  **e.** Debit Supplies Expense $125; Credit Supplies $125.

**3.** On May 1, 2011, a two-year insurance policy was purchased for $24,000 with coverage to begin immediately. What is the amount of insurance expense that appears on the company's income statement for the year ended December 31, 2011?
  **a.** $4,000
  **b.** $8,000

  **c.** $12,000
  **d.** $20,000
  **e.** $24,000

**4.** On November 1, 2011, Stockton Co. receives $3,600 cash from Hans Co. for consulting services to be provided evenly over the period November 1, 2011, to April 30, 2012—at which time Stockton credited $3,600 to Unearned Consulting Fees. The adjusting entry on December 31, 2011 (Stockton's year-end) would include a
  **a.** Debit to Unearned Consulting Fees for $1,200.
  **b.** Debit to Unearned Consulting Fees for $2,400.
  **c.** Credit to Consulting Fees Earned for $2,400.
  **d.** Debit to Consulting Fees Earned for $1,200.
  **e.** Credit to Cash for $3,600.

**5.** If a company had $15,000 in net income for the year, and its sales were $300,000 for the same year, what is its profit margin?
  **a.** 20%
  **b.** 2,000%
  **c.** $285,000
  **d.** $315,000
  **e.** 5%

[A] *Superscript letter A denotes assignments based on Appendix 3A.*
[i] Icon denotes assignments that involve decision making.

## Discussion Questions

**1.** What is the difference between the cash basis and the accrual basis of accounting?

**2.** [i] Why is the accrual basis of accounting generally preferred over the cash basis?

**3.** What type of business is most likely to select a fiscal year that corresponds to its natural business year instead of the calendar year?

**4.** What is a prepaid expense and where is it reported in the financial statements?

**5.** [i] What type of assets require adjusting entries to record depreciation?

**6.** [i] What contra account is used when recording and reporting the effects of depreciation? Why is it used?

**7.** **Apple** has unearned revenue. What is unearned revenue and where is it reported in financial statements?  *Apple*

**8.** What is an accrued revenue? Give an example.

**9.**[A] If a company initially records prepaid expenses with debits to expense accounts, what type of account is debited in the adjusting entries for those prepaid expenses?

**10.** [i] Review the balance sheet of **Research In Motion** in Appendix A. Identify one asset account that requires adjustment before annual financial statements can be prepared. What would be the effect on the income statement if this asset account were not adjusted?  *RIM*

**11.** [i] Review the balance sheet of **Nokia** in Appendix A. Identify the amount for property, plant, and equipment. What adjusting entry is necessary (no numbers required) for this account when preparing financial statements?  *NOKIA*

**12.** [i] Refer to **Palm**'s balance sheet in Appendix A. If it made an adjustment for unpaid wages at year-end, where would the accrued wages be reported on its balance sheet?  *Palm*

## connect

Classify the following adjusting entries as involving prepaid expenses (PE), unearned revenues (UR), accrued expenses (AE), or accrued revenues (AR).

**a.** _____ To record revenue earned that was previously received as cash in advance.

**b.** _____ To record annual depreciation expense.

**c.** _____ To record wages expense incurred but not yet paid (nor recorded).

**d.** _____ To record revenue earned but not yet billed (nor recorded).

**e.** _____ To record expiration of prepaid insurance.

**QUICK STUDY**

**QS 3-1**
Identifying accounting adjustments
P1

**QS 3-2**

Adjusting prepaid expenses

P1

a. On July 1, 2011, Baxter Company paid $1,800 for six months of insurance coverage. No adjustments have been made to the Prepaid Insurance account, and it is now December 31, 2011. Prepare the journal entry to reflect expiration of the insurance as of December 31, 2011.

b. Tyrell Company has a Supplies account balance of $1,000 on January 1, 2011. During 2011, it purchased $3,000 of supplies. As of December 31, 2011, a supplies inventory shows $1,300 of supplies available. Prepare the adjusting journal entry to correctly report the balance of the Supplies account and the Supplies Expense account as of December 31, 2011.

**QS 3-3**

Adjusting for depreciation

P1

a. Carlos Company purchases $30,000 of equipment on January 1, 2011. The equipment is expected to last five years and be worth $5,000 at the end of that time. Prepare the entry to record one year's depreciation expense of $5,000 for the equipment as of December 31, 2011.

b. Chaves Company purchases $40,000 of land on January 1, 2011. The land is expected to last indefinitely. What depreciation adjustment, if any, should be made with respect to the Land account as of December 31, 2011?

**QS 3-4**

Adjusting for unearned revenues

A1  P1

a. Eager Co. receives $20,000 cash in advance for 4 months of legal services on October 1, 2011, and records it by debiting Cash and crediting Unearned Revenue both for $20,000. It is now December 31, 2011, and Eager has provided legal services as planned. What adjusting entry should Eager make to account for the work performed from October 1 through December 31, 2011?

b. Rutherford Co. started a new publication called *Contest News*. Its subscribers pay $48 to receive 12 issues. With every new subscriber, Rutherford debits Cash and credits Unearned Subscription Revenue for the amounts received. The company has 100 new subscribers as of July 1, 2011. It sends *Contest News* to each of these subscribers every month from July through December. Assuming no changes in subscribers, prepare the journal entry that Rutherford must make as of December 31, 2011, to adjust the Subscription Revenue account and the Unearned Subscription Revenue account.

**QS 3-5**

Accruing salaries

A1  P1

Marsha Moder employs one college student every summer in her coffee shop. The student works the five weekdays and is paid on the following Monday. (For example, a student who works Monday through Friday, June 1 through June 5, is paid for that work on Monday, June 8.) Moder adjusts her books monthly, if needed, to show salaries earned but unpaid at month-end. The student works the last week of July—Friday is August 1. If the student earns $100 per day, what adjusting entry must Moder make on July 31 to correctly record accrued salaries expense for July?

**QS 3-6**

Recording and analyzing adjusting entries

A1

Adjusting entries affect at least one balance sheet account and at least one income statement account. For the following entries, identify the account to be debited and the account to be credited. Indicate which of the accounts is the income statement account and which is the balance sheet account.

a. Entry to record revenue earned that was previously received as cash in advance.

b. Entry to record annual depreciation expense.

c. Entry to record wage expenses incurred but not yet paid (nor recorded).

d. Entry to record revenue earned but not yet billed (nor recorded).

e. Entry to record expiration of prepaid insurance.

**QS 3-7**

Computing accrual and cash income

P1  C2

In its first year of operations, Harden Co. earned $39,000 in revenues and received $33,000 cash from these customers. The company incurred expenses of $22,500 but had not paid $2,250 of them at year-end. The company also prepaid $3,750 cash for expenses that would be incurred the next year. Calculate the first year's net income under both the cash basis and the accrual basis of accounting.

The following information is taken from Cruz Company's unadjusted and adjusted trial balances.

|  | Unadjusted | | Adjusted | |
|  | Debit | Credit | Debit | Credit |
| --- | --- | --- | --- | --- |
| Prepaid insurance......... | $4,100 | | $3,700 | |
| Interest payable .......... | | $ 0 | | $800 |

Given this information, which of the following is likely included among its adjusting entries?

**a.** A $400 credit to Prepaid Insurance and an $800 debit to Interest Payable.

**b.** A $400 debit to Insurance Expense and an $800 debit to Interest Payable.

**c.** A $400 debit to Insurance Expense and an $800 debit to Interest Expense.

**QS 3-8**
Interpreting adjusting entries

C2 P2

In making adjusting entries at the end of its accounting period, Gomez Consulting failed to record $1,600 of insurance coverage that had expired. This $1,600 cost had been initially debited to the Prepaid Insurance account. The company also failed to record accrued salaries expense of $1,000. As a result of these two oversights, the financial statements for the reporting period will [choose one] (1) understate assets by $1,600; (2) understate expenses by $2,600; (3) understate net income by $1,000; or (4) overstate liabilities by $1,000.

**QS 3-9**
Determining effects of adjusting entries

C3 A1

During the year, Lyle Co. recorded prepayments of expenses in asset accounts, and cash receipts of unearned revenues in liability accounts. At the end of its annual accounting period, the company must make three adjusting entries: (1) accrue salaries expense, (2) adjust the Unearned Services Revenue account to recognize earned revenue, and (3) record services revenue earned for which cash will be received the following period. For each of these adjusting entries (1), (2), and (3), indicate the account from *a* through *i* to be debited and the account to be credited.

**a.** Prepaid Salaries    **d.** Salaries Payable    **g.** Unearned Services Revenue

**b.** Salaries Expense    **e.** Equipment    **h.** Accounts Receivable

**c.** Services Revenue    **f.** Cash    **i.** Accounts Payable

**QS 3-10**
Preparing adjusting entries

C3 P1

Yang Company reported net income of $37,925 and net sales of $390,000 for the current year. Calculate the company's profit margin and interpret the result. Assume that its competitors earn an average profit margin of 15%.

**QS 3-11**
Analyzing profit margin

A2

Diego Consulting initially records prepaid and unearned items in income statement accounts. Given this company's accounting practices, which of the following applies to the preparation of adjusting entries at the end of its first accounting period?

**a.** Earned but unbilled (and unrecorded) consulting fees are recorded with a debit to Unearned Consulting Fees and a credit to Consulting Fees Earned.

**b.** Unpaid salaries are recorded with a debit to Prepaid Salaries and a credit to Salaries Expense.

**c.** The cost of unused office supplies is recorded with a debit to Supplies Expense and a credit to Office Supplies.

**d.** Unearned fees (on which cash was received in advance earlier in the period) are recorded with a debit to Consulting Fees Earned and a credit to Unearned Consulting Fees.

**QS 3-12**<sup>A</sup>
Preparing adjusting entries

C3 P4

Answer each of the following questions related to international accounting standards.

**a.** Do financial statements prepared under IFRS normally present assets from least liquid to most liquid or vice-versa?

**b.** Do financial statements prepared under IFRS normally present liabilities from furthest from maturity to nearest to maturity or vice-versa?

**QS 3-13**
International accounting standards

P3

## EXERCISES

**Exercise 3-1**

Classifying adjusting entries

**C3**

In the blank space beside each adjusting entry, enter the letter of the explanation A through F that most closely describes the entry.

**A.** To record this period's depreciation expense.

**B.** To record accrued salaries expense.

**C.** To record this period's use of a prepaid expense.

**D.** To record accrued interest revenue.

**E.** To record accrued interest expense.

**F.** To record the earning of previously unearned income.

| | | | |
|---|---|---|---|
| _____ 1. | Salaries Expense ............................... | 13,280 | |
| | Salaries Payable ............................... | | 13,280 |
| _____ 2. | Interest Expense ............................... | 2,208 | |
| | Interest Payable ............................... | | 2,208 |
| _____ 3. | Insurance Expense ............................ | 3,180 | |
| | Prepaid Insurance ............................ | | 3,180 |
| _____ 4. | Unearned Professional Fees .................... | 19,250 | |
| | Professional Fees Earned ..................... | | 19,250 |
| _____ 5. | Interest Receivable ............................ | 3,300 | |
| | Interest Revenue ............................. | | 3,300 |
| _____ 6. | Depreciation Expense ......................... | 38,217 | |
| | Accumulated Depreciation ...................... | | 38,217 |

**Exercise 3-2**

Preparing adjusting entries

**P1**

For each of the following separate cases, prepare adjusting entries required of financial statements for the year ended (date of) December 31, 2011. (Assume that prepaid expenses are initially recorded in asset accounts and that fees collected in advance of work are initially recorded as liabilities.)

**a.** One-third of the work related to $30,000 cash received in advance is performed this period.

**b.** Wages of $9,000 are earned by workers but not paid as of December 31, 2011.

**c.** Depreciation on the company's equipment for 2011 is $19,127.

**d.** The Office Supplies account had a $480 debit balance on December 31, 2010. During 2011, $5,349 of office supplies are purchased. A physical count of supplies at December 31, 2011, shows $587 of supplies available.

**Check**  (e) Dr. Insurance Expense, $2,800; (f) Cr. Interest Revenue, $750

**e.** The Prepaid Insurance account had a $5,000 balance on December 31, 2010. An analysis of insurance policies shows that $2,200 of unexpired insurance benefits remain at December 31, 2011.

**f.** The company has earned (but not recorded) $750 of interest from investments in CDs for the year ended December 31, 2011. The interest revenue will be received on January 10, 2012.

**g.** The company has a bank loan and has incurred (but not recorded) interest expense of $3,500 for the year ended December 31, 2011. The company must pay the interest on January 2, 2012.

**Exercise 3-3**

Preparing adjusting entries

**P1**

Prepare adjusting journal entries for the year ended (date of) December 31, 2011, for each of these separate situations. Assume that prepaid expenses are initially recorded in asset accounts. Also assume that fees collected in advance of work are initially recorded as liabilities.

**a.** Depreciation on the company's equipment for 2011 is computed to be $16,000.

**b.** The Prepaid Insurance account had a $7,000 debit balance at December 31, 2011, before adjusting for the costs of any expired coverage. An analysis of the company's insurance policies showed that $1,040 of unexpired insurance coverage remains.

**Check**  (c) Dr. Office Supplies Expense, $2,626; (e) Dr. Insurance Expense, $4,600

**c.** The Office Supplies account had a $300 debit balance on December 31, 2010; and $2,680 of office supplies were purchased during the year. The December 31, 2011, physical count showed $354 of supplies available.

**d.** One-half of the work related to $10,000 of cash received in advance was performed this period.

**e.** The Prepaid Insurance account had a $5,600 debit balance at December 31, 2011, before adjusting for the costs of any expired coverage. An analysis of insurance policies showed that $4,600 of coverage had expired.

**f.** Wage expenses of $4,000 have been incurred but are not paid as of December 31, 2011.

The following three separate situations require adjusting journal entries to prepare financial statements as of April 30. For each situation, present both the April 30 adjusting entry and the subsequent entry during May to record the payment of the accrued expenses.

**a.** On April 1, the company retained an attorney for a flat monthly fee of $2,500. This amount is paid to the attorney on the 12th day of the following month in which it was earned.

**b.** A $780,000 note payable requires 9.6% annual interest, or $6,240 to be paid at the 20th day of each month. The interest was last paid on April 20 and the next payment is due on May 20. As of April 30, $2,080 of interest expense has accrued.

**c.** Total weekly salaries expense for all employees is $9,000. This amount is paid at the end of the day on Friday of each five-day workweek. April 30 falls on Tuesday of this year, which means that the employees had worked two days since the last payday. The next payday is May 3.

**Exercise 3-4**
Adjusting and paying accrued expenses

A1  P1

**Check**  (b) May 20 Dr. Interest Expense, $4,160

---

Determine the missing amounts in each of these four separate situations *a* through *d*.

| | a | b | c | d |
|---|---|---|---|---|
| Supplies available—prior year-end ............... | $ 300 | $1,600 | $1,360 | ? |
| Supplies purchased during the current year ......... | 2,100 | 5,400 | ? | $6,000 |
| Supplies available—current year-end ............. | 750 | ? | 1,840 | 800 |
| Supplies expense for the current year ............ | ? | 1,300 | 9,600 | 6,575 |

**Exercise 3-5**
Determining cost flows through accounts

C1  A1  P1

---

Pablo Management has five part-time employees, each of whom earns $100 per day. They are normally paid on Fridays for work completed Monday through Friday of the same week. They were paid in full on Friday, December 28, 2011. The next week, the five employees worked only four days because New Year's Day was an unpaid holiday. Show (*a*) the adjusting entry that would be recorded on Monday, December 31, 2011, and (*b*) the journal entry that would be made to record payment of the employees' wages on Friday, January 4, 2012.

**Exercise 3-6**
Adjusting and paying accrued wages

C1  P1

---

Following are two income statements for Kendall Co. for the year ended December 31. The left column is prepared before any adjusting entries are recorded, and the right column includes the effects of adjusting entries. The company records cash receipts and payments related to unearned and prepaid items in balance sheet accounts. Analyze the statements and prepare the eight adjusting entries that likely were recorded. (*Note:* 30% of the $6,000 adjustment for Fees Earned has been earned but not billed, and the other 70% has been earned by performing services that were paid for in advance.)

**Exercise 3-7**
Analyzing and preparing adjusting entries

A1  P1  P3

**KENDALL CO.**
**Income Statements**
**For Year Ended December 31**

| | Unadjusted | Adjusted |
|---|---|---|
| **Revenues** | | |
| Fees earned ................................. | $24,000 | $30,000 |
| Commissions earned ....................... | 42,500 | 42,500 |
| Total revenues .............................. | 66,500 | 72,500 |
| **Expenses** | | |
| Depreciation expense—Computers ............ | 0 | 1,500 |
| Depreciation expense—Office furniture ......... | 0 | 1,750 |
| Salaries expense ............................ | 12,500 | 14,950 |
| Insurance expense ........................... | 0 | 1,300 |
| Rent expense ............................... | 4,500 | 4,500 |
| Office supplies expense ...................... | 0 | 480 |
| Advertising expense ......................... | 3,000 | 3,000 |
| Utilities expense ............................ | 1,250 | 1,320 |
| Total expenses .............................. | 21,250 | 28,800 |
| Net income ................................. | $45,250 | $43,700 |

**Exercise 3-8**
Determining assets and
expenses for accrual and
cash accounting

C2

On March 1, 2009, a company paid a $16,200 premium on a 36-month insurance policy for coverage begin-
ning on that date. Refer to that policy and fill in the blanks in the following table.

| | Balance Sheet Prepaid Insurance Asset Using | | | Insurance Expense Using | | |
|---|---|---|---|---|---|---|
| | Accrual Basis | Cash Basis | | | Accrual Basis | Cash Basis |
| Dec. 31, 2009 | $_____ | $_____ | 2009 | | $_____ | $_____ |
| Dec. 31, 2010 | _____ | _____ | 2010 | | _____ | _____ |
| Dec. 31, 2011 | _____ | _____ | 2011 | | _____ | _____ |
| Dec. 31, 2012 | _____ | _____ | 2012 | | _____ | _____ |
| | | | Total | | $_____ | $_____ |

**Check**  2011 insurance expense:
Accrual, $5,400; Cash, $0.
Dec. 31, 2011, asset: Accrual, $900;
Cash, $0.

---

**Exercise 3-9**
Computing and interpreting
profit margin

A2

Use the following information to compute profit margin for each separate company *a* through *e*.

| | Net Income | Net Sales | | | Net Income | Net Sales |
|---|---|---|---|---|---|---|
| **a.** | $ 5,390 | $ 44,830 | | **d.** | $55,234 | $1,458,999 |
| **b.** | 87,644 | 398,954 | | **e.** | 70,158 | 435,925 |
| **c.** | 93,385 | 257,082 | | | | |

Which of the five companies is the most profitable according to the profit margin ratio? Interpret that company's profit margin ratio.

---

**Exercise 3-10ᴬ**
Recording and reporting
revenues received in advance

P4

Corbel Company experienced the following events and transactions during July.

July  1  Received $2,000 cash in advance of performing work for Beth Oker.
     6  Received $8,400 cash in advance of performing work for Lisa Poe.
    12  Completed the job for Oker.
    18  Received $7,500 cash in advance of performing work for Henry Coe.
    27  Completed the job for Poe.
    31  None of the work for Coe has been performed.

**a.** Prepare journal entries (including any adjusting entries as of the end of the month) to record these
events using the procedure of initially crediting the Unearned Fees account when payment is received
from a customer in advance of performing services.

**b.** Prepare journal entries (including any adjusting entries as of the end of the month) to record these
events using the procedure of initially crediting the Fees Earned account when payment is received
from a customer in advance of performing services.

**Check**  (*c*) Fees Earned—using
entries from part *b*, $10,400

**c.** Under each method, determine the amount of earned fees reported on the income statement for July
and the amount of unearned fees reported on the balance sheet as of July 31.

---

**Exercise 3-11ᴬ**
Adjusting for prepaids recorded
as expenses and unearned
revenues recorded as revenues

P4

On-The-Mark Construction began operations on December 1. In setting up its accounting procedures, the
company decided to debit expense accounts when it prepays its expenses and to credit revenue accounts
when customers pay for services in advance. Prepare journal entries for items *a* through *d* and the adjusting
entries as of its December 31 period-end for items *e* through *g*.

**a.** Supplies are purchased on December 1 for $3,000 cash.

**b.** The company prepaid its insurance premiums for $1,440 cash on December 2.

**c.** On December 15, the company receives an advance payment of $12,000 cash from a customer for
remodeling work.

**d.** On December 28, the company receives $3,600 cash from another customer for remodeling work to be
performed in January.

**e.** A physical count on December 31 indicates that On-The-Mark has $1,920 of supplies available.

**f.** An analysis of the insurance policies in effect on December 31 shows that $240 of insurance coverage had expired.

**g.** As of December 31, only one remodeling project has been worked on and completed. The $6,300 fee for this project had been received in advance.

**Check**   (*f*) Cr. Insurance Expense, $1,200; (*g*) Dr. Remodeling Fees Earned, $9,300

---

**adidas AG** reports the following balance sheet accounts for the year ended December 31, 2009 (euros in millions). Prepare the balance sheet for this company as of December 31, 2009, following usual IFRS practices.

**Exercise 3-12**
Preparing a balance sheet following IFRS

P3

| | | | |
|---|---|---|---|
| Tangible and other assets | €1,410 | Intangible assets | €2,980 |
| Total equity | 3,776 | Total current liabilities | 2,836 |
| Receivables and financial assets | 1,753 | Inventories | 1,471 |
| Total noncurrent liabilities | 2,263 | Total liabilities | 5,099 |
| Cash and cash equivalents | 775 | Other current assets | 486 |
| Total current assets | 4,485 | Total noncurrent assets | 4,390 |

---

**connect**

Meyer Co. follows the practice of recording prepaid expenses and unearned revenues in balance sheet accounts. The company's annual accounting period ends on December 31, 2011. The following information concerns the adjusting entries to be recorded as of that date.

**a.** The Office Supplies account started the year with a $3,000 balance. During 2011, the company purchased supplies for $12,400, which was added to the Office Supplies account. The inventory of supplies available at December 31, 2011, totaled $2,640.

**b.** An analysis of the company's insurance policies provided the following facts.

**PROBLEM SET A**

**Problem 3-1A**
Preparing adjusting and subsequent journal entries

C1  A1  P1

| Policy | Date of Purchase | Months of Coverage | Cost |
|---|---|---|---|
| A | April 1, 2010 | 24 | $15,840 |
| B | April 1, 2011 | 36 | 13,068 |
| C | August 1, 2011 | 12 | 2,700 |

The total premium for each policy was paid in full (for all months) at the purchase date, and the Prepaid Insurance account was debited for the full cost. (Year-end adjusting entries for Prepaid Insurance were properly recorded in all prior years.)

**c.** The company has 15 employees, who earn a total of $2,100 in salaries each working day. They are paid each Monday for their work in the five-day workweek ending on the previous Friday. Assume that December 31, 2011, is a Tuesday, and all 15 employees worked the first two days of that week. Because New Year's Day is a paid holiday, they will be paid salaries for five full days on Monday, January 6, 2012.

**d.** The company purchased a building on January 1, 2011. It cost $855,000 and is expected to have a $45,000 salvage value at the end of its predicted 30-year life. Annual depreciation is $27,000.

**e.** Since the company is not large enough to occupy the entire building it owns, it rented space to a tenant at $2,400 per month, starting on November 1, 2011. The rent was paid on time on November 1, and the amount received was credited to the Rent Earned account. However, the tenant has not paid the December rent. The company has worked out an agreement with the tenant, who has promised to pay both December and January rent in full on January 15. The tenant has agreed not to fall behind again.

**f.** On November 1, the company rented space to another tenant for $2,175 per month. The tenant paid five months' rent in advance on that date. The payment was recorded with a credit to the Unearned Rent account.

**Check** (1*b*) Dr. Insurance Expense, $12,312 (1*d*) Dr. Depreciation Expense, $27,000

*Required*

**1.** Use the information to prepare adjusting entries as of December 31, 2011.

**2.** Prepare journal entries to record the first subsequent cash transaction in 2012 for parts *c* and *e*.

---

**Problem 3-2A**

Identifying adjusting entries with explanations

C3   P1

For each of the following entries, enter the letter of the explanation that most closely describes it in the space beside each entry. (You can use letters more than once.)

**A.** To record receipt of unearned revenue.

**B.** To record this period's earning of prior unearned revenue.

**C.** To record payment of an accrued expense.

**D.** To record receipt of an accrued revenue.

**E.** To record an accrued expense.

**F.** To record an accrued revenue.

**G.** To record this period's use of a prepaid expense.

**H.** To record payment of a prepaid expense.

**I.** To record this period's depreciation expense.

| | | | |
|---|---|---|---|
| _____ | 1. | Rent Expense .................................... | 2,000 |
| | | Prepaid Rent .................................. | | 2,000 |
| _____ | 2. | Interest Expense ................................ | 1,000 |
| | | Interest Payable ............................... | | 1,000 |
| _____ | 3. | Depreciation Expense ............................ | 4,000 |
| | | Accumulated Depreciation ..................... | | 4,000 |
| _____ | 4. | Unearned Professional Fees ....................... | 3,000 |
| | | Professional Fees Earned ...................... | | 3,000 |
| _____ | 5. | Insurance Expense ............................... | 4,200 |
| | | Prepaid Insurance ............................. | | 4,200 |
| _____ | 6. | Salaries Payable ................................ | 1,400 |
| | | Cash ........................................ | | 1,400 |
| _____ | 7. | Prepaid Rent ................................... | 4,500 |
| | | Cash ........................................ | | 4,500 |
| _____ | 8. | Salaries Expense ................................ | 6,000 |
| | | Salaries Payable .............................. | | 6,000 |
| _____ | 9. | Interest Receivable .............................. | 5,000 |
| | | Interest Revenue .............................. | | 5,000 |
| _____ | 10. | Cash .......................................... | 9,000 |
| | | Accounts Receivable (from consulting) ........... | | 9,000 |
| _____ | 11. | Cash .......................................... | 7,500 |
| | | Unearned Professional Fees .................... | | 7,500 |
| _____ | 12. | Cash .......................................... | 2,000 |
| | | Interest Receivable ........................... | | 2,000 |

---

**Problem 3-3A**

Preparing adjusting entries, adjusted trial balance, and financial statements

A1   P1   P2   P3

mhhe.com/wildFAP20e

Watson Technical Institute (WTI), a school owned by Tom Watson, provides training to individuals who pay tuition directly to the school. WTI also offers training to groups in off-site locations. Its unadjusted trial balance as of December 31, 2011, follows. WTI initially records prepaid expenses and unearned revenues in balance sheet accounts. Descriptions of items *a* through *h* that require adjusting entries on December 31, 2011, follow.

*Additional Information Items*

**a.** An analysis of WTI's insurance policies shows that $3,000 of coverage has expired.

**b.** An inventory count shows that teaching supplies costing $2,600 are available at year-end 2011.

**c.** Annual depreciation on the equipment is $12,000.

**d.** Annual depreciation on the professional library is $6,000.

**e.** On November 1, WTI agreed to do a special six-month course (starting immediately) for a client. The contract calls for a monthly fee of $2,200, and the client paid the first five months' fees in advance. When the cash was received, the Unearned Training Fees account was credited. The fee for the sixth month will be recorded when it is collected in 2012.

**f.** On October 15, WTI agreed to teach a four-month class (beginning immediately) for an individual for $3,000 tuition per month payable at the end of the class. The class started on October 15, but no payment has yet been received. (WTI's accruals are applied to the nearest half-month; for example, October recognizes one-half month accrual.)

**g.** WTI's two employees are paid weekly. As of the end of the year, two days' salaries have accrued at the rate of $100 per day for each employee.

**h.** The balance in the Prepaid Rent account represents rent for December.

| WATSON TECHNICAL INSTITUTE Unadjusted Trial Balance December 31, 2011 | Debit | Credit |
|---|---|---|
| Cash | $ 26,000 | |
| Accounts receivable | 0 | |
| Teaching supplies | 10,000 | |
| Prepaid insurance | 15,000 | |
| Prepaid rent | 2,000 | |
| Professional library | 30,000 | |
| Accumulated depreciation—Professional library | | $ 9,000 |
| Equipment | 70,000 | |
| Accumulated depreciation—Equipment | | 16,000 |
| Accounts payable | | 36,000 |
| Salaries payable | | 0 |
| Unearned training fees | | 11,000 |
| T. Watson, Capital | | 63,600 |
| T. Watson, Withdrawals | 40,000 | |
| Tuition fees earned | | 102,000 |
| Training fees earned | | 38,000 |
| Depreciation expense—Professional library | 0 | |
| Depreciation expense—Equipment | 0 | |
| Salaries expense | 48,000 | |
| Insurance expense | 0 | |
| Rent expense | 22,000 | |
| Teaching supplies expense | 0 | |
| Advertising expense | 7,000 | |
| Utilities expense | 5,600 | |
| Totals | $ 275,600 | $ 275,600 |

### Required

1. Prepare T-accounts (representing the ledger) with balances from the unadjusted trial balance.

2. Prepare the necessary adjusting journal entries for items *a* through *h* and post them to the T-accounts. Assume that adjusting entries are made only at year-end.

3. Update balances in the T-accounts for the adjusting entries and prepare an adjusted trial balance.

4. Prepare Watson Technical Institute's income statement and statement of owner's equity for the year 2011 and prepare its balance sheet as of December 31, 2011.

**Check**  (2*e*) Cr. Training Fees Earned, $4,400; (2*f*) Cr. Tuition Fees Earned, $7,500; (3) Adj. Trial balance totals, $301,500; (4) Net income, $38,500; Ending T. Watson, Capital $62,100

---

A six-column table for JJW Company follows. The first two columns contain the unadjusted trial balance for the company as of July 31, 2011. The last two columns contain the adjusted trial balance as of the same date.

### Required

#### Analysis Component

1. Analyze the differences between the unadjusted and adjusted trial balances to determine the eight adjustments that likely were made. Show the results of your analysis by inserting these adjustment amounts in the table's two middle columns. Label each adjustment with a letter *a* through *h* and provide a short description of it at the bottom of the table.

**Problem 3-4A**
Interpreting unadjusted and adjusted trial balances, and preparing financial statements

C3  A1  P1  P2  P3

mhhe.com/wildFAP20e

**Preparation Component**

**2.** Use the information in the adjusted trial balance to prepare the company's (*a*) income statement and its statement of owner's equity for the year ended July 31, 2011 (*note:* J. Winner, Capital at July 31, 2010, was $28,420, and the current-year withdrawals were $10,000), and (*b*) the balance sheet as of July 31, 2011.

| | Unadjusted Trial Balance | | Adjustments | | Adjusted Trial Balance | |
|---|---|---|---|---|---|---|
| Cash ........................ | $ 27,000 | | | | $ 27,000 | |
| Accounts receivable ........... | 12,000 | | | | 22,460 | |
| Office supplies ............... | 18,000 | | | | 3,000 | |
| Prepaid insurance ............. | 7,320 | | | | 4,880 | |
| Office equipment ............. | 92,000 | | | | 92,000 | |
| Accum. depreciation— Office equip. ............... | | $ 12,000 | | | | $ 18,000 |
| Accounts payable ............. | | 9,300 | | | | 10,200 |
| Interest payable ............... | | 0 | | | | 800 |
| Salaries payable ............... | | 0 | | | | 6,600 |
| Unearned consulting fees ....... | | 16,000 | | | | 14,300 |
| Long-term notes payable ....... | | 44,000 | | | | 44,000 |
| J. Winner, Capital ............. | | 28,420 | | | | 28,420 |
| J. Winner, Withdrawals ......... | 10,000 | | | | 10,000 | |
| Consulting fees earned ......... | | 156,000 | | | | 168,160 |
| Depreciation expense— Office equip. ............... | 0 | | | | 6,000 | |
| Salaries expense .............. | 71,000 | | | | 77,600 | |
| Interest expense .............. | 1,400 | | | | 2,200 | |
| Insurance expense ............ | 0 | | | | 2,440 | |
| Rent expense ................ | 13,200 | | | | 13,200 | |
| Office supplies expense ........ | 0 | | | | 15,000 | |
| Advertising expense ........... | 13,800 | | | | 14,700 | |
| Totals ...................... | $265,720 | $265,720 | | | $290,480 | $290,480 |

---

**Problem 3-5A**

Preparing financial statements
from the adjusted trial balance
and calculating profit margin

**P3  A1  A2**

The adjusted trial balance for Callahay Company as of December 31, 2011, follows.

| | Debit | Credit |
|---|---|---|
| Cash ...................................... | $ 22,000 | |
| Accounts receivable ......................... | 44,000 | |
| Interest receivable ......................... | 10,000 | |
| Notes receivable (due in 90 days) .............. | 160,000 | |
| Office supplies ............................. | 8,000 | |
| Automobiles ............................... | 160,000 | |
| Accumulated depreciation—Automobiles ......... | | $ 42,000 |
| Equipment ................................. | 130,000 | |
| Accumulated depreciation—Equipment .......... | | 10,000 |
| Land ...................................... | 70,000 | |
| Accounts payable ........................... | | 88,000 |
| Interest payable ............................ | | 12,000 |
| Salaries payable ............................ | | 11,000 |
| Unearned fees .............................. | | 22,000 |
| Long-term notes payable ..................... | | 130,000 |
| J. Callahay, Capital ......................... | | 247,800 |
| J. Callahay, Withdrawals ...................... | 38,000 | |

[continued on next page]

[continued from previous page]

| | | |
|---|---:|---:|
| Fees earned | | 420,000 |
| Interest earned | | 16,000 |
| Depreciation expense—Automobiles | 18,000 | |
| Depreciation expense—Equipment | 10,000 | |
| Salaries expense | 180,000 | |
| Wages expense | 32,000 | |
| Interest expense | 24,000 | |
| Office supplies expense | 26,000 | |
| Advertising expense | 50,000 | |
| Repairs expense—Automobiles | 16,800 | |
| Totals | $998,800 | $998,800 |

**Required**

1. Use the information in the adjusted trial balance to prepare (a) the income statement for the year ended December 31, 2011; (b) the statement of owner's equity for the year ended December 31, 2011; and (c) the balance sheet as of December 31, 2011.

2. Calculate the profit margin for year 2011.

**Check** (1) Total assets, $552,000

Quisp Co. had the following transactions in the last two months of its year ended December 31.

Nov. 1 Paid $1,500 cash for future newspaper advertising.
1 Paid $2,160 cash for 12 months of insurance through October 31 of the next year.
30 Received $3,300 cash for future services to be provided to a customer.
Dec. 1 Paid $2,700 cash for a consultant's services to be received over the next three months.
15 Received $7,650 cash for future services to be provided to a customer.
31 Of the advertising paid for on November 1, $900 worth is not yet used.
31 A portion of the insurance paid for on November 1 has expired. No adjustment was made in November to Prepaid Insurance.
31 Services worth $1,200 are not yet provided to the customer who paid on November 30.
31 One-third of the consulting services paid for on December 1 have been received.
31 The company has performed $3,000 of services that the customer paid for on December 15.

**Problem 3-6A[A]**
Recording prepaid expenses and unearned revenues

P1 P4

**Required**

1. Prepare entries for these transactions under the method that records prepaid expenses as assets and records unearned revenues as liabilities. Also prepare adjusting entries at the end of the year.

2. Prepare entries for these transactions under the method that records prepaid expenses as expenses and records unearned revenues as revenues. Also prepare adjusting entries at the end of the year.

**Analysis Component**

3. Explain why the alternative sets of entries in requirements 1 and 2 do not result in different financial statement amounts.

Nomo Co. follows the practice of recording prepaid expenses and unearned revenues in balance sheet accounts. The company's annual accounting period ends on October 31, 2011. The following information concerns the adjusting entries that need to be recorded as of that date.

**PROBLEM SET B**

**Problem 3-1B**
Preparing adjusting and subsequent journal entries

C1 A1 P1

a. The Office Supplies account started the fiscal year with a $500 balance. During the fiscal year, the company purchased supplies for $3,650, which was added to the Office Supplies account. The supplies available at October 31, 2011, totaled $700.

b. An analysis of the company's insurance policies provided the following facts.

| Policy | Date of Purchase | Months of Coverage | Cost |
|:---:|:---:|:---:|:---:|
| A | April 1, 2010 | 24 | $3,000 |
| B | April 1, 2011 | 36 | 3,600 |
| C | August 1, 2011 | 12 | 660 |

The total premium for each policy was paid in full (for all months) at the purchase date, and the Prepaid Insurance account was debited for the full cost. (Year-end adjusting entries for Prepaid Insurance were properly recorded in all prior fiscal years.)

**c.** The company has four employees, who earn a total of $800 for each workday. They are paid each Monday for their work in the five-day workweek ending on the previous Friday. Assume that October 31, 2011, is a Monday, and all four employees worked the first day of that week. They will be paid salaries for five full days on Monday, November 7, 2011.

**d.** The company purchased a building on November 1, 2010, that cost $155,000 and is expected to have a $20,000 salvage value at the end of its predicted 25-year life. Annual depreciation is $5,400.

**e.** Since the company does not occupy the entire building it owns, it rented space to a tenant at $600 per month, starting on September 1, 2011. The rent was paid on time on September 1, and the amount received was credited to the Rent Earned account. However, the October rent has not been paid. The company has worked out an agreement with the tenant, who has promised to pay both October and November rent in full on November 15. The tenant has agreed not to fall behind again.

**f.** On September 1, the company rented space to another tenant for $525 per month. The tenant paid five months' rent in advance on that date. The payment was recorded with a credit to the Unearned Rent account.

### Required

**1.** Use the information to prepare adjusting entries as of October 31, 2011.

**2.** Prepare journal entries to record the first subsequent cash transaction in November 2011 for parts c and e.

---

**Problem 3-2B**
Identifying adjusting entries with explanations

C3  P1

For each of the following entries, enter the letter of the explanation that most closely describes it in the space beside each entry. (You can use letters more than once.)

**A.** To record payment of a prepaid expense.

**B.** To record this period's use of a prepaid expense.

**C.** To record this period's depreciation expense.

**D.** To record receipt of unearned revenue.

**E.** To record this period's earning of prior unearned revenue.

**F.** To record an accrued expense.

**G.** To record payment of an accrued expense.

**H.** To record an accrued revenue.

**I.** To record receipt of accrued revenue.

| | | | |
|---|---|---|---|
| _____ | 1. | Unearned Professional Fees ....................... | 6,000 |
| | | Professional Fees Earned ...................... | | 6,000 |
| _____ | 2. | Interest Receivable ............................. | 3,500 |
| | | Interest Revenue ............................. | | 3,500 |
| _____ | 3. | Salaries Payable ............................... | 9,000 |
| | | Cash ....................................... | | 9,000 |
| _____ | 4. | Depreciation Expense ........................... | 8,000 |
| | | Accumulated Depreciation ..................... | | 8,000 |
| _____ | 5. | Cash ........................................ | 9,000 |
| | | Unearned Professional Fees ................... | | 9,000 |
| _____ | 6. | Insurance Expense ............................. | 4,000 |
| | | Prepaid Insurance ........................... | | 4,000 |
| _____ | 7. | Interest Expense .............................. | 5,000 |
| | | Interest Payable ............................. | | 5,000 |
| _____ | 8. | Cash ........................................ | 1,500 |
| | | Accounts Receivable (from services) ............. | | 1,500 |
| _____ | 9. | Salaries Expense .............................. | 7,000 |
| | | Salaries Payable ............................. | | 7,000 |
| _____ | 10. | Cash ........................................ | 1,000 |
| | | Interest Receivable .......................... | | 1,000 |
| _____ | 11. | Prepaid Rent ................................. | 3,000 |
| | | Cash ....................................... | | 3,000 |
| _____ | 12. | Rent Expense ................................ | 7,500 |
| | | Prepaid Rent ................................ | | 7,500 |

Following is the unadjusted trial balance for Alcorn Institute as of December 31, 2011, which initially records prepaid expenses and unearned revenues in balance sheet accounts. The Institute provides one-on-one training to individuals who pay tuition directly to the business and offers extension training to groups in off-site locations. Shown after the trial balance are items *a* through *h* that require adjusting entries as of December 31, 2011.

**Problem 3-3B**
Preparing adjusting entries, adjusted trial balance, and financial statements
A1  P1  P2  P3

**ALCORN INSTITUTE**
**Unadjusted Trial Balance**
**December 31, 2011**

| | Debit | Credit |
|---|---|---|
| Cash | $ 50,000 | |
| Accounts receivable | 0 | |
| Teaching supplies | 60,000 | |
| Prepaid insurance | 18,000 | |
| Prepaid rent | 2,600 | |
| Professional library | 10,000 | |
| Accumulated depreciation—Professional library | | $ 1,500 |
| Equipment | 30,000 | |
| Accumulated depreciation—Equipment | | 16,000 |
| Accounts payable | | 12,200 |
| Salaries payable | | 0 |
| Unearned training fees | | 27,600 |
| M. Alcorn, Capital | | 68,500 |
| M. Alcorn, Withdrawals | 20,000 | |
| Tuition fees earned | | 105,000 |
| Training fees earned | | 62,000 |
| Depreciation expense—Professional library | 0 | |
| Depreciation expense—Equipment | 0 | |
| Salaries expense | 43,200 | |
| Insurance expense | 0 | |
| Rent expense | 28,600 | |
| Teaching supplies expense | 0 | |
| Advertising expense | 18,000 | |
| Utilities expense | 12,400 | |
| Totals | $ 292,800 | $292,800 |

***Additional Information Items***

**a.** An analysis of the Institute's insurance policies shows that $6,400 of coverage has expired.

**b.** An inventory count shows that teaching supplies costing $2,500 are available at year-end 2011.

**c.** Annual depreciation on the equipment is $4,000.

**d.** Annual depreciation on the professional library is $2,000.

**e.** On November 1, the Institute agreed to do a special four-month course (starting immediately) for a client. The contract calls for a $4,600 monthly fee, and the client paid the first two months' fees in advance. When the cash was received, the Unearned Training Fees account was credited. The last two month's fees will be recorded when collected in 2012.

**f.** On October 15, the Institute agreed to teach a four-month class (beginning immediately) to an individual for $2,200 tuition per month payable at the end of the class. The class started on October 15, but no payment has yet been received. (Alcorn's accruals are applied to the nearest half-month; for example, October recognizes one-half month accrual.)

**g.** The Institute's only employee is paid weekly. As of the end of the year, three days' salaries have accrued at the rate of $180 per day.

**h.** The balance in the Prepaid Rent account represents rent for December.

## Required

**1.** Prepare T-accounts (representing the ledger) with balances from the unadjusted trial balance.

**2.** Prepare the necessary adjusting journal entries for items *a* through *h*, and post them to the T-accounts. Assume that adjusting entries are made only at year-end.

**3.** Update balances in the T-accounts for the adjusting entries and prepare an adjusted trial balance.

**4.** Prepare the company's income statement and statement of owner's equity for the year 2011, and prepare its balance sheet as of December 31, 2011.

---

**Problem 3-4B**

Interpreting unadjusted and
adjusted trial balances, and
preparing financial statements

C3   A1   P1   P2   P3  

A six-column table for Daxu Consulting Company follows. The first two columns contain the unadjusted trial balance for the company as of December 31, 2011, and the last two columns contain the adjusted trial balance as of the same date.

| | Unadjusted Trial Balance | | Adjustments | | Adjusted Trial Balance | |
|---|---:|---:|---|---|---:|---:|
| Cash ......................... | $ 48,000 | | | | $ 48,000 | |
| Accounts receivable ........... | 70,000 | | | | 76,660 | |
| Office supplies .............. | 30,000 | | | | 7,000 | |
| Prepaid insurance ............. | 13,200 | | | | 8,600 | |
| Office equipment ............. | 150,000 | | | | 150,000 | |
| Accumulated depreciation— Office equip. ............... | | $ 30,000 | | | | $ 40,000 |
| Accounts payable ............ | | 36,000 | | | | 42,000 |
| Interest payable .............. | | 0 | | | | 1,600 |
| Salaries payable .............. | | 0 | | | | 11,200 |
| Unearned consulting fees ....... | | 30,000 | | | | 17,800 |
| Long-term notes payable ....... | | 80,000 | | | | 80,000 |
| D. Chen, Capital .............. | | 70,200 | | | | 70,200 |
| D. Chen, Withdrawals .......... | 10,000 | | | | 10,000 | |
| Consulting fees earned ......... | | 264,000 | | | | 282,860 |
| Depreciation expense— Office equip. ............... | 0 | | | | 10,000 | |
| Salaries expense ............. | 115,600 | | | | 126,800 | |
| Interest expense ............. | 6,400 | | | | 8,000 | |
| Insurance expense ............ | 0 | | | | 4,600 | |
| Rent expense ................ | 24,000 | | | | 24,000 | |
| Office supplies expense ........ | 0 | | | | 23,000 | |
| Advertising expense ........... | 43,000 | | | | 49,000 | |
| Totals ..................... | $510,200 | $510,200 | | | $545,660 | $545,660 |

## Required

### Analysis Component

**1.** Analyze the differences between the unadjusted and adjusted trial balances to determine the eight adjustments that likely were made. Show the results of your analysis by inserting these adjustment amounts in the table's two middle columns. Label each adjustment with a letter *a* through *h* and provide a short description of it at the bottom of the table.

### Preparation Component

**2.** Use the information in the adjusted trial balance to prepare this company's (*a*) income statement and its statement of owner's equity for the year ended December 31, 2011 (*note:* D. Chen, Capital at December 31, 2010, was $70,200, and the current-year withdrawals were $10,000), and (*b*) the balance sheet as of December 31, 2011.

The adjusted trial balance for Lightning Courier as of December 31, 2011, follows.

**Problem 3-5B**
Preparing financial statements
from the adjusted trial balance
and calculating profit margin

P3  A1  A2

| | Debit | Credit |
|---|---|---|
| Cash .................................... | $ 48,000 | |
| Accounts receivable ...................... | 110,000 | |
| Interest receivable ...................... | 6,000 | |
| Notes receivable (due in 90 days) ............. | 200,000 | |
| Office supplies ........................... | 12,000 | |
| Trucks .................................... | 124,000 | |
| Accumulated depreciation—Trucks ............. | | $ 48,000 |
| Equipment ................................. | 260,000 | |
| Accumulated depreciation—Equipment ........ | | 190,000 |
| Land ...................................... | 90,000 | |
| Accounts payable ......................... | | 124,000 |
| Interest payable .......................... | | 22,000 |
| Salaries payable .......................... | | 30,000 |
| Unearned delivery fees ..................... | | 110,000 |
| Long-term notes payable ................... | | 190,000 |
| J. Hallam, Capital ......................... | | 115,000 |
| J. Hallam, Withdrawals ..................... | 40,000 | |
| Delivery fees earned ....................... | | 580,000 |
| Interest earned ........................... | | 24,000 |
| Depreciation expense—Trucks ............... | 24,000 | |
| Depreciation expense—Equipment ........... | 46,000 | |
| Salaries expense .......................... | 64,000 | |
| Wages expense ........................... | 290,000 | |
| Interest expense .......................... | 25,000 | |
| Office supplies expense ................... | 33,000 | |
| Advertising expense ...................... | 26,400 | |
| Repairs expense—Trucks ................... | 34,600 | |
| Totals .................................... | $1,433,000 | $1,433,000 |

**Required**

1. Use the information in the adjusted trial balance to prepare (*a*) the income statement for the year ended December 31, 2011, (*b*) the statement of owner's equity for the year ended December 31, 2011, and (*c*) the balance sheet as of December 31, 2011.

2. Calculate the profit margin for year 2011.

**Check**  (1) Total assets, $612,000

Quake Co. had the following transactions in the last two months of its fiscal year ended May 31.

**Problem 3-6B**<sup>A</sup>
Recording prepaid expenses and
unearned revenues

P1  P4

Apr.  1  Paid $3,450 cash to an accounting firm for future consulting services.
  1  Paid $2,700 cash for 12 months of insurance through March 31 of the next year.
  30  Received $7,500 cash for future services to be provided to a customer.
May  1  Paid $3,450 cash for future newspaper advertising.
  23  Received $9,450 cash for future services to be provided to a customer.
  31  Of the consulting services paid for on April 1, $1,500 worth has been received.
  31  A portion of the insurance paid for on April 1 has expired. No adjustment was made in April to Prepaid Insurance.
  31  Services worth $3,600 are not yet provided to the customer who paid on April 30.
  31  Of the advertising paid for on May 1, $1,050 worth is not yet used.
  31  The company has performed $4,500 of services that the customer paid for on May 23.

**Required**

1. Prepare entries for these transactions under the method that records prepaid expenses and unearned revenues in balance sheet accounts. Also prepare adjusting entries at the end of the year.

**2.** Prepare entries for these transactions under the method that records prepaid expenses and unearned revenues in income statement accounts. Also prepare adjusting entries at the end of the year.

*Analysis Component*

**3.** Explain why the alternative sets of entries in parts 1 and 2 do not result in different financial statement amounts.

---

**SERIAL PROBLEM**
Business Solutions
P1  P2  P3

*This serial problem began in Chapter 1 and continues through most of the book. If previous chapter segments were not completed, the serial problem can still begin at this point. It is helpful, but not necessary, to use the Working Papers that accompany the book.*

**SP 3**   After the success of the company's first two months, Santana Rey continues to operate Business Solutions. (Transactions for the first two months are described in the serial problem of Chapter 2.) The November 30, 2011, unadjusted trial balance of Business Solutions (reflecting its transactions for October and November of 2011) follows.

| No. | Account Title | Debit | Credit |
|-----|---------------|-------|--------|
| 101 | Cash ............................................. | $38,264 | |
| 106 | Accounts receivable ............................. | 12,618 | |
| 126 | Computer supplies ............................... | 2,545 | |
| 128 | Prepaid insurance ............................... | 2,220 | |
| 131 | Prepaid rent .................................... | 3,300 | |
| 163 | Office equipment ................................ | 8,000 | |
| 164 | Accumulated depreciation—Office equipment ....... | | $    0 |
| 167 | Computer equipment .............................. | 20,000 | |
| 168 | Accumulated depreciation—Computer equipment ..... | | 0 |
| 201 | Accounts payable ................................ | | 0 |
| 210 | Wages payable ................................... | | 0 |
| 236 | Unearned computer services revenue .............. | | 0 |
| 301 | S. Rey, Capital ................................. | | 73,000 |
| 302 | S. Rey, Withdrawals ............................. | 5,600 | |
| 403 | Computer services revenue ....................... | | 25,659 |
| 612 | Depreciation expense—Office equipment ........... | 0 | |
| 613 | Depreciation expense—Computer equipment ......... | 0 | |
| 623 | Wages expense ................................... | 2,625 | |
| 637 | Insurance expense ............................... | 0 | |
| 640 | Rent expense .................................... | 0 | |
| 652 | Computer supplies expense ....................... | 0 | |
| 655 | Advertising expense ............................. | 1,728 | |
| 676 | Mileage expense ................................. | 704 | |
| 677 | Miscellaneous expenses .......................... | 250 | |
| 684 | Repairs expense—Computer ........................ | 805 | |
| | Totals ......................................... | $98,659 | $98,659 |

Business Solutions had the following transactions and events in December 2011.

Dec.  2  Paid $1,025 cash to Hillside Mall for Business Solutions' share of mall advertising costs.
      3  Paid $500 cash for minor repairs to the company's computer.
      4  Received $3,950 cash from Alex's Engineering Co. for the receivable from November.
    10  Paid cash to Lyn Addie for six days of work at the rate of $125 per day.
    14  Notified by Alex's Engineering Co. that Business Solutions' bid of $7,000 on a proposed project has been accepted. Alex's paid a $1,500 cash advance to Business Solutions.
    15  Purchased $1,100 of computer supplies on credit from Harris Office Products.
    16  Sent a reminder to Gomez Co. to pay the fee for services recorded on November 8.
    20  Completed a project for Liu Corporation and received $5,625 cash.
22–26  Took the week off for the holidays.
    28  Received $3,000 cash from Gomez Co. on its receivable.

29 Reimbursed S. Rey for business automobile mileage (600 miles at $0.32 per mile).
31 S. Rey withdrew $1,500 cash from the company for personal use.

The following additional facts are collected for use in making adjusting entries prior to preparing financial statements for the company's first three months:

**a.** The December 31 inventory count of computer supplies shows $580 still available.

**b.** Three months have expired since the 12-month insurance premium was paid in advance.

**c.** As of December 31, Lyn Addie has not been paid for four days of work at $125 per day.

**d.** The company's computer is expected to have a four-year life with no salvage value.

**e.** The office equipment is expected to have a five-year life with no salvage value.

**f.** Three of the four months' prepaid rent has expired.

### Required

**1.** Prepare journal entries to record each of the December transactions and events for Business Solutions. Post those entries to the accounts in the ledger.

**2.** Prepare adjusting entries to reflect *a* through *f*. Post those entries to the accounts in the ledger.

**3.** Prepare an adjusted trial balance as of December 31, 2011.

**4.** Prepare an income statement for the three months ended December 31, 2011.

**5.** Prepare a statement of owner's equity for the three months ended December 31, 2011.

**6.** Prepare a balance sheet as of December 31, 2011.

**Check** (3) Adjusted trial balance totals, $109,034

(6) Total assets, $83,460

## Beyond the Numbers

**BTN 3-1** Refer to **Research In Motion**'s financial statements in Appendix A to answer the following.

**1.** Identify and write down the revenue recognition principle as explained in the chapter.

**2.** Review Research In Motion's footnotes to discover how it applies the revenue recognition principle and when it recognizes revenue. Report what you discover.

**3.** What is Research In Motion's profit margin for fiscal years ended February 28, 2009, and February 27, 2010.

**REPORTING IN ACTION**

C1 C2 A1 A2

**RIM**

### Fast Forward

**4.** Access RIM's annual report (10-K) for fiscal years ending after February 27, 2010, at its Website (**RIM.com**) or the SEC's EDGAR database (**www.sec.gov**). Assess and compare the February 27, 2010, fiscal year profit margin to any subsequent year's profit margin that you compute.

**BTN 3-2** Key figures for the recent two years of both **Research In Motion** and **Apple** follow.

| ($ millions) | Research In Motion | | Apple | |
| --- | --- | --- | --- | --- |
| | Current Year | Prior Year | Current Year | Prior Year |
| Net income . . . . . . . . . . . . . | $ 2,457 | $ 1,893 | $ 8,235 | $ 6,119 |
| Net sales . . . . . . . . . . . . . . . | 14,953 | 11,065 | 42,905 | 37,491 |
| Current assets . . . . . . . . . . . | 5,813 | 4,842 | 31,555 | 30,006 |
| Current liabilities . . . . . . . . | 2,432 | 2,115 | 11,506 | 11,361 |

**COMPARATIVE ANALYSIS**

A2

**RIM**

Apple

### Required

**1.** Compute profit margins for (*a*) Research In Motion and (*b*) Apple for the two years of data shown.

**2.** Which company is more successful on the basis of profit margin? Explain.

**BTN 3-3** Jackie Bergez works for Sea Biscuit Co. She and Bob Welch, her manager, are preparing adjusting entries for annual financial statements. Bergez computes depreciation and records it as

**ETHICS CHALLENGE**

C1 C2 A1

| Depreciation Expense—Equipment . . . . . . . . . . . . . . . | 123,000 | |
| --- | --- | --- |
| Accumulated Depreciation—Equipment . . . . . . . . | | 123,000 |

Welch agrees with her computation but says the credit entry should be directly to the Equipment account. Welch argues that while accumulated depreciation is technically correct, "it is less hassle not to use a contra account and just credit the Equipment account directly. And besides, the balance sheet shows the same amount for total assets under either method."

**Required**

**1.** How should depreciation be recorded? Do you support Bergez or Welch?

**2.** Evaluate the strengths and weaknesses of Welch's reasons for preferring his method.

**3.** Indicate whether the situation Bergez faces is an ethical problem. Explain.

---

**COMMUNICATING IN PRACTICE**

C1   A2

**BTN 3-4**   The class should be divided into teams. Teams are to select an industry (such as automobile manufacturing, airlines, defense contractors), and each team member is to select a different company in that industry. Each team member is to acquire the annual report of the company selected. Annual reports can be downloaded from company Websites or from the SEC's EDGAR database at (**www.SEC.gov**).

**Required**

**1.** Use the annual report to compute the return on assets, debt ratio, and profit margin.

**2.** Communicate with team members via a meeting, e-mail, or telephone to discuss the meaning of the ratios, how different companies compare to each other, and the industry norm. The team must prepare a single memo reporting the ratios for each company and identifying the conclusions or consensus of opinion reached during the team's discussion. The memo is to be copied and distributed to the instructor and all classmates.

---

**TAKING IT TO THE NET**

C1   A2

**BTN 3-5**   Access EDGAR online (**www.SEC.gov**) and locate the 10-K report of **The Gap, Inc.,** (ticker GPS) filed on March 26, 2010. Review its financial statements reported for the year ended January 30, 2010, to answer the following questions.

**Required**

**1.** What are Gap's main brands?

**2.** What is Gap's fiscal year-end?

**3.** What is Gap's net sales for the period ended January 30, 2010?

**4.** What is Gap's net income for the period ended January 30, 2010?

**5.** Compute Gap's profit margin for the year ended January 30, 2010.

**6.** Do you believe Gap's decision to use a year-end of late January or early February relates to its natural business year? Explain.

---

**TEAMWORK IN ACTION**

C3   A1   P1

**BTN 3-6**   Four types of adjustments are described in the chapter: (1) prepaid expenses, (2) unearned revenues, (3) accrued expenses, and (4) accrued revenues.

**Required**

**1.** Form *learning teams* of four (or more) members. Each team member must select one of the four adjustments as an area of expertise (each team must have at least one expert in each area).

**2.** Form *expert teams* from the individuals who have selected the same area of expertise. Expert teams are to discuss and write a report that each expert will present to his or her learning team addressing the following:

   **a.** Description of the adjustment and why it's necessary.

   **b.** Example of a transaction or event, with dates and amounts, that requires adjustment.

   **c.** Adjusting entry(ies) for the example in requirement *b*.

   **d.** Status of the affected account(s) before and after the adjustment in requirement *c*.

   **e.** Effects on financial statements of not making the adjustment.

**3.** Each expert should return to his or her learning team. In rotation, each member should present his or her expert team's report to the learning team. Team discussion is encouraged.

**BTN 3-7**   Review the opening feature of this chapter dealing with **Cheezburger Network**.

**ENTREPRENEURIAL DECISION**

A2

*Required*

1. Assume that Cheezburger Network sells a $300 gift certificate to a customer, collecting the $300 cash in advance. Prepare the journal entry for the (*a*) collection of the cash for delivery of the gift certificate to the customer and (*b*) revenue from the subsequent delivery of merchandise when the gift certificate is used.

2. How can keeping less inventory help to improve Cheezburger Network's profit margin?

3. Ben Huh understands that many companies carry considerable inventory, and Ben is thinking of carrying additional inventory of merchandise for sale. Ben desires your advice on the pros and cons of carrying such inventory. Provide at least one reason for and one reason against carrying additional inventory.

**BTN 3-8**   Visit the Website of a major company that interests you. Use the Investor Relations link at the Website to obtain the toll-free telephone number of the Investor Relations Department. Call the company, ask to speak to Investor Relations, and request a copy of the company's most recent annual report. You should receive the requested report within one to two weeks. Once you have received your report, use it throughout the term to see that the principles you are learning in class are being applied in practice.

**HITTING THE ROAD**

C1

**BTN 3-9**   **Nokia** (**www.Nokia.com**) is a leading global manufacturer of mobile devices and services.

**GLOBAL DECISION**

A2   C1   C2

**NOKIA**

*Required*

1. Locate the notes to its December 31, 2009, financial statements at the company's Website, and read note *1 Accounting Principles—Revenue Recognition,* first paragraph only. When is revenue recognized by Nokia?

2. Refer to Nokia's financials in Appendix A. What is Nokia's profit margin for the year ended December 31, 2009?

## ANSWERS TO MULTIPLE CHOICE QUIZ

1. b; the forgotten adjusting entry is: *dr.* Wages Expense, *cr.* Wages Payable.
2. c; Supplies used = $450 − $125 = $325
3. b; Insurance expense = $24,000 × (8/24) = $8,000; adjusting entry is: *dr.* Insurance Expense for $8,000, *cr.* Prepaid Insurance for $8,000.

4. a; Consulting fees earned = $3,600 × (2/6) = $1,200; adjusting entry is: *dr.* Unearned Consulting Fee for $1,200, *cr.* Consulting Fees Earned for $1,200.
5. e; Profit margin = $15,000/$300,000 = 5%

# 4

# Completing the Accounting Cycle

### A Look Back

Chapter 3 explained the timing of reports. We described why adjusting accounts is key for recognizing revenues and expenses in the proper period. We prepared an adjusted trial balance and used it to prepare financial statements.

### A Look at This Chapter

This chapter emphasizes the final steps in the accounting process and reviews the entire accounting cycle. We explain the closing process, including accounting procedures and the use of a post-closing trial balance. We show how a work sheet aids in preparing financial statements.

### A Look Ahead

Chapter 5 looks at accounting for merchandising activities. We describe the sale and purchase of merchandise and their implications for preparing and analyzing financial statements.

## Learning Objectives

**CAP**

### CONCEPTUAL

**C1** Explain why temporary accounts are closed each period. (p. 142)

**C2** Identify steps in the accounting cycle. (p. 146)

**C3** Explain and prepare a classified balance sheet. (p. 147)

### ANALYTICAL

**A1** Compute the current ratio and describe what it reveals about a company's financial condition. (p. 150)

LP4

### PROCEDURAL

**P1** Prepare a work sheet and explain its usefulness. (p. 138)

**P2** Describe and prepare closing entries. (p. 143)

**P3** Explain and prepare a post-closing trial balance. (p. 144)

**P4** *Appendix 4A*—Prepare reversing entries and explain their purpose. (p. 154)

# Gamer Grub!

*"Be in front of your customer . . . [and] have a little bit of an edge"*
—**KEITH MULLIN** (far left)

SAN DIEGO—"I have been battling greasy fingers and keyboard crumbs," complained gamer Keith Mullin. "I thought '*there has to be a better way*!'" So, Keith-the-gamer morphed into Keith-the-entrepreneur. In 2008, Keith set up what he calls his "garage startup" and introduced **Gamer Grub**® (**GamerGrub.com**), which is performance snack food for gamers. "I got tired of wiping my hands on my jeans," laughs Keith. "And, I like to multi-task."

Success, however, requires Keith to monitor and minimize costs. "I made the first Gamer Grub prototypes in my mom's kitchen," explains Keith. He eventually set up an accounting system to track costs and match them with revenues. But, Keith says, it is a constant struggle as his business has been tripling in revenues each month. He explains that properly applying the accounting cycle, preparing classified financial statements, and acting on that information has helped in his success. However, admits Keith, "it is more of a collaborative effort."

To date, Keith has successfully controlled his costs while monitoring both revenues and customer needs. "You need to be in front of your customer, watch them taste it, watch them understand what you're doing," says Keith. "You have to be out there . . . we have given out at least 16,000 samples!" Keith adds that he applies the accounting cycle, including closing entries, to help identify and match costs with revenues for specific time periods. He also relies on classified balance sheets to plan payment schedules. But, what keeps him going, admits Keith, is knowing that he offers "different ways to snack while you're computer gaming or multi-tasking."

Keith is on a mission. What motivates him, explains Keith, is the "Wow! If you get that 'Wow' reaction, that's a really good thing." To make that happen, he tracks the accounting numbers to be sure his "Wow food" is a money-making venture. "Gamer Grub allows gamers to consume healthy, game-enhancing snacks," insists Keith. "Without greasy fingers or keyboard crumbs!"

[Sources: *GamerGrub* Website, January 2011; *Entrepreneur,* October 2009; *Business Wire,* September 2008; *MGC* Website, January 2010]

Many of the important steps leading to financial statements were explained in earlier chapters. We described how transactions and events are analyzed, journalized, and posted. This chapter explains the closing process that readies revenue, expense, and withdrawal accounts for the next reporting period and updates the capital account. A work sheet is shown to be a useful tool for these final steps and in preparing financial statements. It also explains how accounts are classified on a balance sheet to increase their usefulness to decision makers.

### Completing the Accounting Cycle

| Work Sheet | Closing Process | Accounting Cycle | Classified Balance Sheet |
|---|---|---|---|
| • Benefits of a work sheet<br>• Use of a work sheet | • Temporary and permanent accounts<br>• Closing entries<br>• Post-closing trial balance | • Definition of accounting cycle<br>• Review of accounting cycle | • Classification structure<br>• Classification categories |

# WORK SHEET AS A TOOL

Information preparers use various analyses and internal documents when organizing information for internal and external decision makers. Internal documents are often called **working papers.** One widely used working paper is the **work sheet,** which is a useful tool for preparers in working with accounting information. It is usually not available to external decision makers.

## Benefits of a Work Sheet (Spreadsheet)

**P1** Prepare a work sheet and explain its usefulness.

A work sheet is *not* a required report, yet using a manual or electronic work sheet has several potential benefits. Specifically, a work sheet

- Aids the preparation of financial statements.
- Reduces the possibility of errors when working with many accounts and adjustments.
- Links accounts and adjustments to their impacts in financial statements.
- Assists in planning and organizing an audit of financial statements—as it can be used to reflect any adjustments necessary.
- Helps in preparing interim (monthly and quarterly) financial statements when the journalizing and posting of adjusting entries are postponed until year-end.
- Shows the effects of proposed or "what-if" transactions.

### Decision Insight

**High-Tech Work Sheet**  An electronic work sheet using spreadsheet software such as Excel allows us to easily change numbers, assess the impact of alternative strategies, and quickly prepare financial statements at less cost. It can also increase the available time for analysis and interpretation. ■

## Use of a Work Sheet

**Point:** Since a work sheet is *not* a required report or an accounting record, its format is flexible and can be modified by its user to fit his/her preferences.

When a work sheet is used to prepare financial statements, it is constructed at the end of a period before the adjusting process. The complete work sheet includes a list of the accounts, their balances and adjustments, and their sorting into financial statement columns. It provides two columns each for the unadjusted trial balance, the adjustments, the adjusted trial balance, the income statement, and the balance sheet (including the statement of owner's equity). To describe and interpret the work sheet, we use the information from FastForward. Preparing the work sheet has five important steps. Each step, 1 through 5, is color-coded and explained with reference to Exhibits 4.1 and 4.2.

### ① Step 1. Enter Unadjusted Trial Balance

*Refer to Exhibit 4.1.* The first step in preparing a work sheet is to list the title of every account and its account number that is expected to appear on its financial statements. This includes all accounts in the ledger plus any new ones from adjusting entries. Most adjusting entries—including expenses from salaries, supplies, depreciation, and insurance—are predictable and recurring. The unadjusted balance for each account is then entered in the appropriate Debit or Credit column of the unadjusted trial balance columns. The totals of these two columns must be equal. Exhibit 4.1 shows FastForward's work sheet after completing this first step. Sometimes blank lines are left on the work sheet based on past experience to indicate where lines will be needed for adjustments to certain accounts. Exhibit 4.1 shows Consulting Revenue as one example. An alternative is to squeeze adjustments on one line or to combine the effects of two or more adjustments in one amount. In the unusual case when an account is not predicted, we can add a new line for such an account following the *Totals* line.

### ② Step 2. Enter Adjustments

*Refer to Exhibit 4.1a (turn over first transparency).* The second step in preparing a work sheet is to enter adjustments in the Adjustments columns. The adjustments shown are the same ones shown in Exhibit 3.13. An identifying letter links the debit and credit of each adjusting entry. This is called *keying* the adjustments. After preparing a work sheet, adjusting entries must still be entered in the journal and posted to the ledger. The Adjustments columns provide the information for those entries.

**Point:** A recordkeeper often can complete the procedural task of journalizing and posting adjusting entries by using a work sheet and the guidance that *keying* provides.

### ③ Step 3. Prepare Adjusted Trial Balance

*Refer to Exhibit 4.1b (turn over second transparency).* The adjusted trial balance is prepared by combining the adjustments with the unadjusted balances for each account. As an example, the Prepaid Insurance account has a $2,400 debit balance in the Unadjusted Trial Balance columns. This $2,400 debit is combined with the $100 credit in the Adjustments columns to give Prepaid Insurance a $2,300 debit in the Adjusted Trial Balance columns. The totals of the Adjusted Trial Balance columns confirm the equality of debits and credits.

**Point:** To avoid omitting the transfer of an account balance, start with the first line (cash) and continue in account order.

### ④ Step 4. Sort Adjusted Trial Balance Amounts to Financial Statements

*Refer to Exhibit 4.1c (turn over third transparency).* This step involves sorting account balances from the adjusted trial balance to their proper financial statement columns. Expenses go to the Income Statement Debit column and revenues to the Income Statement Credit column. Assets and withdrawals go to the Balance Sheet & Statement of Owner's Equity Debit column. Liabilities and owner's capital go to the Balance Sheet & Statement of Owner's Equity Credit column.

### ⑤ Step 5. Total Statement Columns, Compute Income or Loss, and Balance Columns

*Refer to Exhibit 4.1d (turn over fourth transparency).* Each financial statement column (from Step 4) is totaled. The difference between the totals of the Income Statement columns is net income or net loss. This occurs because revenues are entered in the Credit column and expenses in the Debit column. If the Credit total exceeds the Debit total, there is net income. If the Debit total exceeds the Credit total, there is a net loss. For FastForward, the Credit total exceeds the Debit total, giving a $3,785 net income.

The net income from the Income Statement columns is then entered in the Balance Sheet & Statement of Owner's Equity Credit column. Adding net income to the last Credit column implies that it is to be added to owner's capital. If a loss occurs, it is added to the Debit column. This implies that it is to be subtracted from owner's capital. The ending balance of owner's capital does not appear in the last two columns as a single amount, but it is computed in the statement of owner's equity using these account balances. When net income or net loss is added

[continued on p. 142]

## EXHIBIT 4.1

Work Sheet with Unadjusted Trial Balance

**FastForward**
**Work Sheet**
**For Month Ended December 31, 2011**

| No. | Account | Unadjusted Trial Balance Dr. | Unadjusted Trial Balance Cr. | Adjustments Dr. | Adjustments Cr. | Adjusted Trial Balance Dr. | Adjusted Trial Balance Cr. | Income Statement Dr. | Income Statement Cr. | Balance Sheet & Statement of Owner's Equity Dr. | Balance Sheet & Statement of Owner's Equity Cr. |
|---|---|---|---|---|---|---|---|---|---|---|---|
| 101 | Cash | 4,350 | | | | | | | | | |
| 126 | Supplies | 9,720 | | | | | | | | | |
| 128 | Prepaid insurance | 2,400 | | | | | | | | | |
| 167 | Equipment | 26,000 | | | | | | | | | |
| 201 | Accounts payable | | 6,200 | | | | | | | | |
| 236 | Unearned consulting revenue | | 3,000 | | | | | | | | |
| 301 | C. Taylor, Capital | | 30,000 | | | | | | | | |
| 302 | C. Taylor, Withdrawals | 200 | | | | | | | | | |
| 403 | Consulting revenue | | 5,800 | | | | | | | | |
| 406 | Rental revenue | | 300 | | | | | | | | |
| 622 | Salaries expense | 1,400 | | | | | | | | | |
| 640 | Rent expense | 1,000 | | | | | | | | | |
| 690 | Utilities expense | 230 | | | | | | | | | |
| | Totals | 45,300 | 45,300 | | | | | | | | |

List all accounts from the ledger (can include those expected to arise from adjusting entries).

Enter all amounts available from ledger accounts. Column totals must be equal.

A work sheet collects and summarizes information used to prepare adjusting entries, financial statements, and closing entries.

**EXHIBIT 4.2**

Financial Statements Prepared
from the Work Sheet

**FASTFORWARD**
**Income Statement**
**For Month Ended December 31, 2011**

| | | |
|---|---:|---:|
| Revenues | | |
| Consulting revenue . . . . . . . . . . . . . . . . . . . . | $ 7,850 | |
| Rental revenue . . . . . . . . . . . . . . . . . . . . . . . | 300 | |
| Total revenues . . . . . . . . . . . . . . . . . . . . . . . | | $ 8,150 |
| Expenses | | |
| Depreciation expense—Equipment . . . . . . . | 375 | |
| Salaries expense . . . . . . . . . . . . . . . . . . . . . . | 1,610 | |
| Insurance expense . . . . . . . . . . . . . . . . . . . | 100 | |
| Rent expense . . . . . . . . . . . . . . . . . . . . . . . | 1,000 | |
| Supplies expense . . . . . . . . . . . . . . . . . . . . . | 1,050 | |
| Utilities expense . . . . . . . . . . . . . . . . . . . . . | 230 | |
| Total expenses . . . . . . . . . . . . . . . . . . . . . . | | 4,365 |
| Net income . . . . . . . . . . . . . . . . . . . . . . . . . | | $ 3,785 |

**FASTFORWARD**
**Statement of Owner's Equity**
**For Month Ended December 31, 2011**

| | | |
|---|---:|---:|
| C. Taylor, Capital, December 1 . . . . . . . . . . . . . | | $ 0 |
| Add: Investment by owner. . . . . . . . . . . . . . . . | $30,000 | |
| Net income . . . . . . . . . . . . . . . . . . . | 3,785 | 33,785 |
| | | 33,785 |
| Less: Withdrawals by owner . . . . . . . . . . . . . . | | 200 |
| C. Taylor, Capital, December 31 . . . . . . . . . . . . | | $33,585 |

**FASTFORWARD**
**Balance Sheet**
**December 31, 2011**

| | | |
|---|---:|---:|
| **Assets** | | |
| Cash . . . . . . . . . . . . . . . . . . . . . . . . . . . . . . | | $ 4,350 |
| Accounts receivable . . . . . . . . . . . . . . . . . . . . | | 1,800 |
| Supplies . . . . . . . . . . . . . . . . . . . . . . . . . . . . | | 8,670 |
| Prepaid insurance . . . . . . . . . . . . . . . . . . . . . | | 2,300 |
| Equipment . . . . . . . . . . . . . . . . . . . . . . . . . . | $26,000 | |
| Accumulated depreciation—Equipment . . . . | (375) | 25,625 |
| Total assets . . . . . . . . . . . . . . . . . . . . . . . | | $42,745 |
| **Liabilities** | | |
| Accounts payable . . . . . . . . . . . . . . . . . . . . . | | $ 6,200 |
| Salaries payable . . . . . . . . . . . . . . . . . . . . . . . | | 210 |
| Unearned consulting revenue . . . . . . . . . . . . . | | 2,750 |
| Total liabilities . . . . . . . . . . . . . . . . . . . . . . | | 9,160 |
| **Equity** | | |
| C. Taylor, Capital . . . . . . . . . . . . . . . . . . . . . | | 33,585 |
| Total liabilities and equity . . . . . . . . . . . . . . | | $42,745 |

to the proper Balance Sheet & Statement of Owner's Equity column, the totals of the last two columns must balance. If they do not, one or more errors have been made. The error can either be mathematical or involve sorting one or more amounts to incorrect columns.

 **Decision** Maker                                    Answer — p. 156

**Entrepreneur**   You make a printout of the electronic work sheet used to prepare financial statements. There is no depreciation adjustment, yet you own a large amount of equipment. Does the absence of depreciation adjustment concern you? ■

## Work Sheet Applications and Analysis

A work sheet does not substitute for financial statements. It is a tool we can use at the end of an accounting period to help organize data and prepare financial statements. FastForward's financial statements are shown in Exhibit 4.2. Its income statement amounts are taken from the Income Statement columns of the work sheet. Similarly, amounts for its balance sheet and its statement of owner's equity are taken from the Balance Sheet & Statement of Owner's Equity columns of the work sheet.

Information from the Adjustments columns of a work sheet can be used to journalize adjusting entries. It is important to remember that a work sheet is not a journal. This means that even when a work sheet is prepared, it is necessary to both journalize adjustments and post them to the ledger.

Work sheets are also useful in analyzing the effects of proposed, or what-if, transactions. This is done by entering financial statement amounts in the Unadjusted (what-if) columns. Proposed transactions are then entered in the Adjustments columns. We then compute "adjusted" amounts from these proposed transactions. The extended amounts in the financial statement columns show the effects of these proposed transactions. These financial statement columns yield **pro forma financial statements** because they show the statements *as if* the proposed transactions occurred.

**Quick Check**                                              Answers — p. 156

1. Where do we get the amounts to enter in the Unadjusted Trial Balance columns of a work sheet?
2. What are the advantages of using a work sheet to help prepare adjusting entries?
3. What are the overall benefits of a work sheet?

# CLOSING PROCESS

**C1**  Explain why temporary accounts are closed each period.

The **closing process** is an important step at the end of an accounting period *after* financial statements have been completed. It prepares accounts for recording the transactions and the events of the *next* period. In the closing process we must (1) identify accounts for closing, (2) record and post the closing entries, and (3) prepare a post-closing trial balance. The purpose of the closing process is twofold. First, it resets revenue, expense, and withdrawals account balances to zero at the end of each period. This is done so that these accounts can properly measure income and withdrawals for the next period. Second, it helps in summarizing a period's revenues and expenses. This section explains the closing process.

**Temporary Accounts**
(closed at period-end)
Revenues
Expenses
Owner Withdrawals
Income Summary

## Temporary and Permanent Accounts

**Temporary** (or *nominal*) **accounts** accumulate data related to one accounting period. They include all income statement accounts, the withdrawals account, and the Income Summary account. They are temporary because the accounts are opened at the beginning of a period, used to record transactions and events for that period, and then closed at the end of the period. *The closing process applies only to temporary accounts.* **Permanent** (or *real*) **accounts** report on activities related to one or more future accounting periods. They carry their ending balances into the next period and generally consist of all balance sheet accounts. These asset, liability, and equity accounts are not closed.

**Permanent Accounts**
(not closed at period-end)
Assets
Liabilities
Owner Capital

# Recording Closing Entries

To record and post **closing entries** is to transfer the end-of-period balances in revenue, expense, and withdrawals accounts to the permanent capital account. Closing entries are necessary at the end of each period after financial statements are prepared because

- Revenue, expense, and withdrawals accounts must begin each period with zero balances.
- Owner's capital must reflect prior periods' revenues, expenses, and withdrawals.

An income statement aims to report revenues and expenses for a *specific accounting period*. The statement of owner's equity reports similar information, including withdrawals. Since revenue, expense, and withdrawals accounts must accumulate information separately for each period, they must start each period with zero balances. To close these accounts, we transfer their balances first to an account called *Income Summary*. **Income Summary** is a temporary account (only used for the closing process) that contains a credit for the sum of all revenues (and gains) and a debit for the sum of all expenses (and losses). Its balance equals net income or net loss and it is transferred to the capital account. Next the withdrawals account balance is transferred to the capital account. After these closing entries are posted, the revenue, expense, withdrawals, and Income Summary accounts have zero balances. These accounts are then said to be *closed* or *cleared*.

Exhibit 4.3 uses the adjusted account balances of FastForward (from the Adjusted Trial Balance columns of Exhibit 4.1 or from the left side of Exhibit 4.4) to show the four steps necessary to close its temporary accounts. We explain each step.

**Point:** To understand the closing process, focus on its *outcomes — updating* the capital account balance to its proper ending balance, and getting *temporary accounts* to show *zero balances* for purposes of accumulating data for the next period.

**EXHIBIT 4.3**

Four-Step Closing Process

**Point:** C. Taylor, Capital is the only *permanent account* in Exhibit 4.3.

## Step 1: Close Credit Balances in Revenue Accounts to Income Summary

The first closing entry transfers credit balances in revenue (and gain) accounts to the Income Summary account. We bring accounts with credit balances to zero by debiting them. For FastForward, this journal entry is step 1 in Exhibit 4.4. This entry closes revenue accounts and leaves them with zero balances. The accounts are now ready to record revenues when they occur in the next period. The $8,150 credit entry to Income Summary equals total revenues for the period.

**P2** Describe and prepare closing entries.

## Step 2: Close Debit Balances in Expense Accounts to Income Summary

The second closing entry transfers debit balances in expense (and loss) accounts to the Income Summary account. We bring expense accounts' debit balances to zero by crediting them. With a balance of zero, these accounts are ready to accumulate a record of expenses for the next

**Point:** It is possible to close revenue and expense accounts directly to owner's capital. Computerized accounting systems do this.

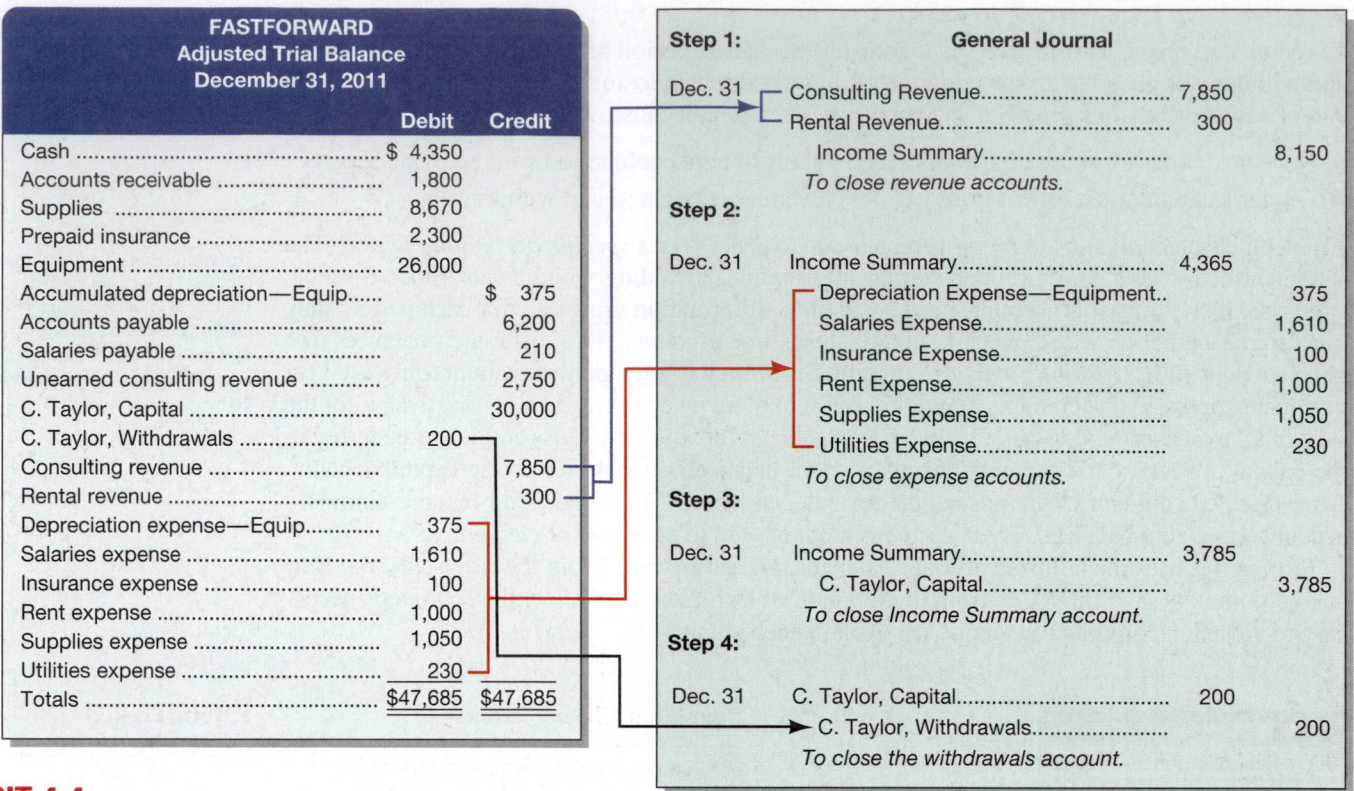

**EXHIBIT 4.4**

Preparing Closing Entries

period. This second closing entry for FastForward is step 2 in Exhibit 4.4. Exhibit 4.3 shows that posting this entry gives each expense account a zero balance.

**Step 3: Close Income Summary to Owner's Capital** After steps 1 and 2, the balance of Income Summary is equal to December's net income of $3,785 ($8,150 credit less $4,365 debit). The third closing entry transfers the balance of the Income Summary account to the capital account. This entry closes the Income Summary account–see step 3 in Exhibit 4.4. The Income Summary account has a zero balance after posting this entry. It continues to have a zero balance until the closing process again occurs at the end of the next period. (If a net loss occurred because expenses exceeded revenues, the third entry is reversed: debit Owner Capital and credit Income Summary.)

**Step 4: Close Withdrawals Account to Owner's Capital** The fourth closing entry transfers any debit balance in the withdrawals account to the owner's capital account—see step 4 in Exhibit 4.4. This entry gives the withdrawals account a zero balance, and the account is now ready to accumulate next period's withdrawals. This entry also reduces the capital account balance to the $33,585 amount reported on the balance sheet.

We could also have selected the accounts and amounts needing to be closed by identifying individual revenue, expense, and withdrawals accounts in the ledger. This is illustrated in Exhibit 4.4 where we prepare closing entries using the adjusted trial balance.[1] (Information for closing entries is also in the financial statement columns of a work sheet.)

## Post-Closing Trial Balance

**P3** Explain and prepare a post-closing trial balance.

Exhibit 4.5 shows the entire ledger of FastForward as of December 31 after adjusting and closing entries are posted. (The transaction and adjusting entries are in Chapters 2 and 3.) The temporary accounts (revenues, expenses, and withdrawals) have ending balances equal to zero.

---

[1] The closing process has focused on proprietorships. It is identical for partnerships with the exception that each owner has separate capital and withdrawals accounts (for steps 3 and 4). The closing process for a corporation is similar with the exception that it uses a Retained Earnings account instead of a Capital account, and a Dividend account instead of a Withdrawals account.

## EXHIBIT 4.5

General Ledger after the Closing Process for FastForward

### Asset Accounts

**Cash**     Acct. No. 101

| Date | Explan. | PR | Debit | Credit | Balance |
|---|---|---|---|---|---|
| 2011 | | | | | |
| Dec. 1 | (1) | G1 | 30,000 | | 30,000 |
| 2 | (2) | G1 | | 2,500 | 27,500 |
| 3 | (3) | G1 | | 26,000 | 1,500 |
| 5 | (5) | G1 | 4,200 | | 5,700 |
| 6 | (13) | G1 | | 2,400 | 3,300 |
| 12 | (6) | G1 | | 1,000 | 2,300 |
| 12 | (7) | G1 | | 700 | 1,600 |
| 22 | (9) | G1 | 1,900 | | 3,500 |
| 24 | (10) | G1 | | 900 | 2,600 |
| 24 | (11) | G1 | | 200 | 2,400 |
| 26 | (12) | G1 | 3,000 | | 5,400 |
| 26 | (14) | G1 | | 120 | 5,280 |
| 26 | (15) | G1 | | 230 | 5,050 |
| 26 | (16) | G1 | | 700 | 4,350 |

**Accounts Receivable**     Acct. No. 106

| Date | Explan. | PR | Debit | Credit | Balance |
|---|---|---|---|---|---|
| 2011 | | | | | |
| Dec. 12 | (8) | G1 | 1,900 | | 1,900 |
| 22 | (9) | G1 | | 1,900 | 0 |
| 31 | Adj.(f) | G1 | 1,800 | | 1,800 |

**Supplies**     Acct. No. 126

| Date | Explan. | PR | Debit | Credit | Balance |
|---|---|---|---|---|---|
| 2011 | | | | | |
| Dec. 2 | (2) | G1 | 2,500 | | 2,500 |
| 6 | (4) | G1 | 7,100 | | 9,600 |
| 26 | (14) | G1 | 120 | | 9,720 |
| 31 | Adj.(b) | G1 | | 1,050 | 8,670 |

**Prepaid Insurance**     Acct. No. 128

| Date | Explan. | PR | Debit | Credit | Balance |
|---|---|---|---|---|---|
| 2011 | | | | | |
| Dec. 6 | (13) | G1 | 2,400 | | 2,400 |
| 31 | Adj.(a) | G1 | | 100 | 2,300 |

**Equipment**     Acct. No. 167

| Date | Explan. | PR | Debit | Credit | Balance |
|---|---|---|---|---|---|
| 2011 | | | | | |
| Dec. 3 | (3) | G1 | 26,000 | | 26,000 |

**Accumulated Depreciation— Equipment**     Acct. No. 168

| Date | Explan. | PR | Debit | Credit | Balance |
|---|---|---|---|---|---|
| 2011 | | | | | |
| Dec. 31 | Adj.(c) | G1 | | 375 | 375 |

### Liability and Equity Accounts

**Accounts Payable**     Acct. No. 201

| Date | Explan. | PR | Debit | Credit | Balance |
|---|---|---|---|---|---|
| 2011 | | | | | |
| Dec. 6 | (4) | G1 | | 7,100 | 7,100 |
| 24 | (10) | G1 | 900 | | 6,200 |

**Salaries Payable**     Acct. No. 209

| Date | Explan. | PR | Debit | Credit | Balance |
|---|---|---|---|---|---|
| 2011 | | | | | |
| Dec. 31 | Adj.(e) | G1 | | 210 | 210 |

**Unearned Consulting Revenue**     Acct. No. 236

| Date | Explan. | PR | Debit | Credit | Balance |
|---|---|---|---|---|---|
| 2011 | | | | | |
| Dec. 26 | (12) | G1 | | 3,000 | 3,000 |
| 31 | Adj.(d) | G1 | 250 | | 2,750 |

**C. Taylor, Capital**     Acct. No. 301

| Date | Explan. | PR | Debit | Credit | Balance |
|---|---|---|---|---|---|
| 2011 | | | | | |
| Dec. 1 | (1) | G1 | | 30,000 | 30,000 |
| 31 | Clos.(3) | G1 | | 3,785 | 33,785 |
| 31 | Clos.(4) | G1 | 200 | | 33,585 |

**C. Taylor, Withdrawals**     Acct. No. 302

| Date | Explan. | PR | Debit | Credit | Balance |
|---|---|---|---|---|---|
| 2011 | | | | | |
| Dec. 24 | (11) | G1 | 200 | | 200 |
| 31 | Clos.(4) | G1 | | 200 | 0 |

### Revenue and Expense Accounts (Including Income Summary)

**Consulting Revenue**     Acct. No. 403

| Date | Explan. | PR | Debit | Credit | Balance |
|---|---|---|---|---|---|
| 2011 | | | | | |
| Dec. 5 | (5) | G1 | | 4,200 | 4,200 |
| 12 | (8) | G1 | | 1,600 | 5,800 |
| 31 | Adj.(d) | G1 | | 250 | 6,050 |
| 31 | Adj.(f) | G1 | | 1,800 | 7,850 |
| 31 | Clos.(1) | G1 | 7,850 | | 0 |

**Rental Revenue**     Acct. No. 406

| Date | Explan. | PR | Debit | Credit | Balance |
|---|---|---|---|---|---|
| 2011 | | | | | |
| Dec. 12 | (8) | G1 | | 300 | 300 |
| 31 | Clos.(1) | G1 | 300 | | 0 |

**Depreciation Expense— Equipment**     Acct. No. 612

| Date | Explan. | PR | Debit | Credit | Balance |
|---|---|---|---|---|---|
| 2011 | | | | | |
| Dec. 31 | Adj.(c) | G1 | 375 | | 375 |
| 31 | Clos.(2) | G1 | | 375 | 0 |

**Salaries Expense**     Acct. No. 622

| Date | Explan. | PR | Debit | Credit | Balance |
|---|---|---|---|---|---|
| 2011 | | | | | |
| Dec. 12 | (7) | G1 | 700 | | 700 |
| 26 | (16) | G1 | 700 | | 1,400 |
| 31 | Adj.(e) | G1 | 210 | | 1,610 |
| 31 | Clos.(2) | G1 | | 1,610 | 0 |

**Insurance Expense**     Acct. No. 637

| Date | Explan. | PR | Debit | Credit | Balance |
|---|---|---|---|---|---|
| 2011 | | | | | |
| Dec. 31 | Adj.(a) | G1 | 100 | | 100 |
| 31 | Clos.(2) | G1 | | 100 | 0 |

**Rent Expense**     Acct. No. 640

| Date | Explan. | PR | Debit | Credit | Balance |
|---|---|---|---|---|---|
| 2011 | | | | | |
| Dec. 12 | (6) | G1 | 1,000 | | 1,000 |
| 31 | Clos.(2) | G1 | | 1,000 | 0 |

**Supplies Expense**     Acct. No. 652

| Date | Explan. | PR | Debit | Credit | Balance |
|---|---|---|---|---|---|
| 2011 | | | | | |
| Dec. 31 | Adj.(b) | G1 | 1,050 | | 1,050 |
| 31 | Clos.(2) | G1 | | 1,050 | 0 |

**Utilities Expense**     Acct. No. 690

| Date | Explan. | PR | Debit | Credit | Balance |
|---|---|---|---|---|---|
| 2011 | | | | | |
| Dec. 26 | (15) | G1 | 230 | | 230 |
| 31 | Clos.(2) | G1 | | 230 | 0 |

**Income Summary**     Acct. No. 901

| Date | Explan. | PR | Debit | Credit | Balance |
|---|---|---|---|---|---|
| 2011 | | | | | |
| Dec. 31 | Clos.(1) | G1 | | 8,150 | 8,150 |
| 31 | Clos.(2) | G1 | 4,365 | | 3,785 |
| 31 | Clos.(3) | G1 | 3,785 | | 0 |

A **post-closing trial balance** is a list of permanent accounts and their balances from the ledger after all closing entries have been journalized and posted. It lists the balances for all accounts not closed. These accounts comprise a company's assets, liabilities, and equity, which are identical to those in the balance sheet. The aim of a post-closing trial balance is to verify that (1) total debits equal total credits for permanent accounts and (2) all temporary accounts have zero balances. FastForward's post-closing trial balance is shown in Exhibit 4.6. The post-closing trial balance usually is the last step in the accounting process.

**EXHIBIT 4.6**

Post-Closing Trial Balance

| FASTFORWARD Post-Closing Trial Balance December 31, 2011 | | |
|---|---|---|
| | **Debit** | **Credit** |
| Cash . . . . . . . . . . . . . . . . . . . . . . . . . . . . . . . . . . . | $ 4,350 | |
| Accounts receivable . . . . . . . . . . . . . . . . . . . . . . | 1,800 | |
| Supplies . . . . . . . . . . . . . . . . . . . . . . . . . . . . . . . . | 8,670 | |
| Prepaid insurance . . . . . . . . . . . . . . . . . . . . . . . | 2,300 | |
| Equipment . . . . . . . . . . . . . . . . . . . . . . . . . . . . . | 26,000 | |
| Accumulated depreciation—Equipment . . . . . . . . | | $    375 |
| Accounts payable . . . . . . . . . . . . . . . . . . . . . . . . | | 6,200 |
| Salaries payable . . . . . . . . . . . . . . . . . . . . . . . . . | | 210 |
| Unearned consulting revenue . . . . . . . . . . . . . . . | | 2,750 |
| C. Taylor, Capital . . . . . . . . . . . . . . . . . . . . . . . . | | 33,585 |
| Totals . . . . . . . . . . . . . . . . . . . . . . . . . . . . . . . . | $43,120 | $43,120 |

## ACCOUNTING CYCLE

 **C2** Identify steps in the accounting cycle.

The term **accounting cycle** refers to the steps in preparing financial statements. It is called a *cycle* because the steps are repeated each reporting period. Exhibit 4.7 shows the 10 steps in the cycle, beginning with analyzing transactions and ending with a post-closing trial balance or

**EXHIBIT 4.7**

Steps in the Accounting Cycle*

Explanations

| | |
|---|---|
| 1. Analyze transactions | Analyze transactions to prepare for journalizing. |
| 2. Journalize | Record accounts, including debits and credits, in a journal. |
| 3. Post | Transfer debits and credits from the journal to the ledger. |
| 4. Prepare unadjusted trial balance | Summarize unadjusted ledger accounts and amounts. |
| 5. Adjust | Record adjustments to bring account balances up to date; journalize and post adjustments. |
| 6. Prepare adjusted trial balance | Summarize adjusted ledger accounts and amounts. |
| 7. Prepare statements | Use adjusted trial balance to prepare financial statements. |
| 8. Close | Journalize and post entries to close temporary accounts. |
| 9. Prepare post-closing trial balance | Test clerical accuracy of the closing procedures. |
| 10. Reverse (optional) | Reverse certain adjustments in the next period—optional step; see Appendix 4A. |

* Steps 4, 6, and 9 can be done on a work sheet. A work sheet is useful in planning adjustments, but adjustments (step 5) must always be journalized and posted. Steps 3, 4, 6, and 9 are automatic with a computerized system.

reversing entries. Steps 1 through 3 usually occur regularly as a company enters into transactions. Steps 4 through 9 are done at the end of a period. *Reversing entries* in step 10 are optional and are explained in Appendix 4A.

## Quick Check

Answers — p. 156

4. What are the major steps in preparing closing entries?
5. Why are revenue and expense accounts called *temporary?* Identify and list the types of temporary accounts.
6. What accounts are listed on the post-closing trial balance?

# CLASSIFIED BALANCE SHEET

Our discussion to this point has been limited to unclassified financial statements. This section describes a classified balance sheet. The next chapter describes a classified income statement. An **unclassified balance sheet** is one whose items are broadly grouped into assets, liabilities, and equity. One example is FastForward's balance sheet in Exhibit 4.2. A **classified balance sheet** organizes assets and liabilities into important subgroups that provide more information to decision makers.

**C3** Explain and prepare a classified balance sheet.

## Classification Structure

A classified balance sheet has no required layout, but it usually contains the categories in Exhibit 4.8. One of the more important classifications is the separation between current and noncurrent items for both assets and liabilities. Current items are those expected to come due (either collected or owed) within one year or the company's operating cycle, whichever is longer. The **operating cycle** is the time span from when *cash is used* to acquire goods and services until *cash is received* from the sale of goods and services. "Operating" refers to company operations and "cycle" refers to the circular flow of cash used for company inputs and then cash received from its outputs. The length of a company's operating cycle depends on its activities. For a service company, the operating cycle is the time span between (1) paying employees who perform the services and (2) receiving cash from customers. For a merchandiser selling products, the operating cycle is the time span between (1) paying suppliers for merchandise and (2) receiving cash from customers.

| Assets | Liabilities and Equity |
|---|---|
| Current assets | Current liabilities |
| Noncurrent assets | Noncurrent liabilities |
|    Long-term investments | Equity |
|    Plant assets | |
|    Intangible assets | |

**EXHIBIT 4.8**

Typical Categories in a Classified Balance Sheet

Most operating cycles are less than one year. This means most companies use a one-year period in deciding which assets and liabilities are current. A few companies have an operating cycle longer than one year. For instance, producers of certain beverages (wine) and products (ginseng) that require aging for several years have operating cycles longer than one year. A balance sheet lists current assets before noncurrent assets and current liabilities before noncurrent liabilities. This consistency in presentation allows users to quickly identify current assets that are most easily converted to cash and current liabilities that are shortly coming due. Items in current assets and current liabilities are listed in the order of how quickly they will be converted to, or paid in, cash.

**EXHIBIT 4.9**

Example of a Classified
Balance Sheet

| SNOWBOARDING COMPONENTS Balance Sheet January 31, 2011 | | |
|---|---|---|
| **Assets** | | |
| **Current assets** | | |
| Cash ................................................. | $ 6,500 | |
| Short-term investments ......................... | 2,100 | |
| Accounts receivable, net ....................... | 4,400 | |
| Merchandise inventory .......................... | 27,500 | |
| Prepaid expenses ................................ | 2,400 | |
| Total current assets ............................. | | $ 42,900 |
| **Long-term investments** | | |
| Notes receivable ................................. | 1,500 | |
| Investments in stocks and bonds ............... | 18,000 | |
| Land held for future expansion ................. | 48,000 | |
| Total long-term investments .................... | | 67,500 |
| **Plant assets** | | |
| Equipment and buildings ........................ | 203,200 | |
| Less accumulated depreciation .................. | 53,000 | |
| Equipment and buildings, net ................... | | 150,200 |
| Land ............................................... | | 73,200 |
| Total plant assets ............................... | | 223,400 |
| **Intangible assets** ............................... | | 10,000 |
| Total assets ...................................... | | $343,800 |
| | | |
| **Liabilities** | | |
| **Current liabilities** | | |
| Accounts payable ............................... | $ 15,300 | |
| Wages payable .................................. | 3,200 | |
| Notes payable ................................... | 3,000 | |
| Current portion of long-term liabilities .......... | 7,500 | |
| Total current liabilities ......................... | | $ 29,000 |
| **Long-term liabilities** (net of current portion) ......... | | 150,000 |
| Total liabilities .................................. | | 179,000 |
| | | |
| **Equity** | | |
| T. Hawk, Capital ................................ | | 164,800 |
| Total liabilities and equity ...................... | | $343,800 |

## Classification Categories

This section describes the most common categories in a classified balance sheet. The balance sheet for Snowboarding Components in Exhibit 4.9 shows the typical categories. Its assets are classified as either current or noncurrent. Its noncurrent assets include three main categories: long-term investments, plant assets, and intangible assets. Its liabilities are classified as either current or long-term. Not all companies use the same categories of assets and liabilities for their balance sheets. **K2 Inc.**, a manufacturer of snowboards, reported a balance sheet with only three asset classes: current assets; property, plant and equipment; and other assets.

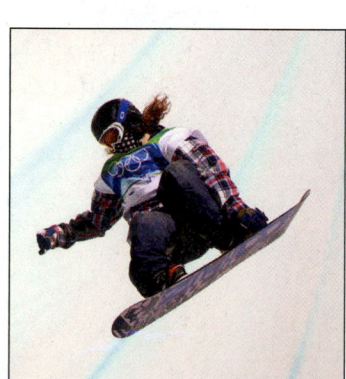

**Current Assets**   **Current assets** are cash and other resources that are expected to be sold, collected, or used within one year or the company's operating cycle, whichever is longer. Examples are cash, short-term investments, accounts receivable, short-term notes receivable, goods for sale (called *merchandise* or *inventory*), and prepaid expenses. The individual prepaid expenses of a company are usually small in amount compared to many other assets and are often combined and shown as a single item. The prepaid expenses in Exhibit 4.9 likely include items such as prepaid insurance, prepaid rent, office supplies, and store supplies. Prepaid expenses are usually listed last because they will not be converted to cash (instead, they are used).

**Long-Term Investments**    A second major balance sheet classification is **long-term** (or *noncurrent*) **investments.** Notes receivable and investments in stocks and bonds are long-term assets when they are expected to be held for more than the longer of one year or the operating cycle. Land held for future expansion is a long-term investment because it is *not* used in operations.

**Point:** Current is also called *short-term,* and noncurrent is also called *long-term.*

**Plant Assets**    Plant assets are tangible assets that are both *long-lived* and *used to produce* or *sell products and services.* Examples are equipment, machinery, buildings, and land that are used to produce or sell products and services. The order listing for plant assets is usually from most liquid to least liquid such as equipment and machinery to buildings and land.

**Point:** Plant assets are also called *fixed assets; property, plant and equipment;* or *long-lived assets.*

**Intangible Assets**    **Intangible assets** are long-term resources that benefit business operations, usually lack physical form, and have uncertain benefits. Examples are patents, trademarks, copyrights, franchises, and goodwill. Their value comes from the privileges or rights granted to or held by the owner. **K2, Inc.,** reported intangible assets of $228 million, which is nearly 20 percent of its total assets. Its intangibles included trademarks, patents, and licensing agreements.

**Current Liabilities**    **Current liabilities** are obligations due to be paid or settled within one year or the operating cycle, whichever is longer. They are usually settled by paying out current assets such as cash. Current liabilities often include accounts payable, notes payable, wages payable, taxes payable, interest payable, and unearned revenues. Also, any portion of a long-term liability due to be paid within one year or the operating cycle, whichever is longer, is a current liability. Unearned revenues are current liabilities when they will be settled by delivering products or services within one year or the operating cycle, whichever is longer. Current liabilities are reported in the order of those to be settled first.

**Point:** Many financial ratios are distorted if accounts are not classified correctly.

**Long-Term Liabilities**    **Long-term liabilities** are obligations *not* due within one year or the operating cycle, whichever is longer. Notes payable, mortgages payable, bonds payable, and lease obligations are common long-term liabilities. If a company has both short- and long-term items in each of these categories, they are commonly separated into two accounts in the ledger.

**Point:** Only assets and liabilities are classified as current or noncurrent.

**Equity**    Equity is the owner's claim on assets. For a proprietorship, this claim is reported in the equity section with an owner's capital account. (For a partnership, the equity section reports a capital account for each partner. For a corporation, the equity section is divided into two main subsections, common stock and retained earnings.)

---

## Quick Check    Answers — p. 156

7. Classify the following assets as (1) current assets, (2) plant assets, or (3) intangible assets: (*a*) land used in operations, (*b*) office supplies, (*c*) receivables from customers due in 10 months, (*d*) insurance protection for the next 9 months, (*e*) trucks used to provide services to customers, (*f*) trademarks.
8. Cite at least two examples of assets classified as investments on the balance sheet.
9. Explain the operating cycle for a service company.

# GLOBAL VIEW

We explained that accounting under U.S. GAAP is similar, but not identical, to that under IFRS. This section discusses differences in the closing process and in reporting assets and liabilities on a balance sheet.

**Closing Process**   The closing process is identical under U.S. GAAP and IFRS. Although unique accounts can arise under either system, the closing process remains the same.

**Reporting Assets and Liabilities**   The definition of an asset is similar under U.S. GAAP and IFRS and involves three basic criteria: (1) the company owns or controls the right to use the item, (2) the right arises from a past transaction or event, and (3) the item can be reliably measured. Both systems define the initial asset value as historical cost for nearly all assets. After acquisition, one of two asset measurement systems is applied: historical cost or fair value. Generally, U.S. GAAP defines fair value as the amount to be received in an orderly sale. IFRS defines fair value as *exchange value*—either replacement cost or selling price. We describe these differences, and the assets to which they apply, in later chapters.

The definition of a liability is similar under U.S. GAAP and IFRS and involves three basic criteria: (1) the item is a *present* obligation requiring a probable future resource outlay, (2) the obligation arises from a past transaction or event, and (3) the obligation can be reliably measured. As with assets, both systems apply one of two measurement systems to liabilities: historical cost or fair value. Later chapters discuss specific differences.

**Decision Analysis**                                                                     Current Ratio

**A1**  Compute the current ratio and describe what it reveals about a company's financial condition.

An important use of financial statements is to help assess a company's ability to pay its debts in the near future. Such analysis affects decisions by suppliers when allowing a company to buy on credit. It also affects decisions by creditors when lending money to a company, including loan terms such as interest rate, due date, and collateral requirements. It can also affect a manager's decisions about using cash to pay debts when they come due. The **current ratio** is one measure of a company's ability to pay its short-term obligations. It is defined in Exhibit 4.10 as current assets divided by current liabilities.

**EXHIBIT 4.10**

Current Ratio

$$\text{Current ratio} = \frac{\text{Current assets}}{\text{Current liabilities}}$$

Using financial information from **Limited Brands, Inc.**, we compute its current ratio for the recent four-year period. The results are in Exhibit 4.11.

**EXHIBIT 4.11**

Limited Brands' Current Ratio

| $ in millions | 2010 | 2009 | 2008 | 2007 | 2006 |
|---|---|---|---|---|---|
| Current assets . . . . . . . . . . . . . . . . | $3,250 | $2,867 | $2,919 | $2,771 | $2,784 |
| Current liabilities . . . . . . . . . . . . . | $1,322 | $1,255 | $1,374 | $1,709 | $1,575 |
| **Current ratio** . . . . . . . . . . . . . . | **2.5** | **2.3** | **2.1** | **1.6** | **1.8** |
| Industry current ratio . . . . . . . . . | 1.9 | 2.0 | 2.1 | 2.3 | 2.4 |

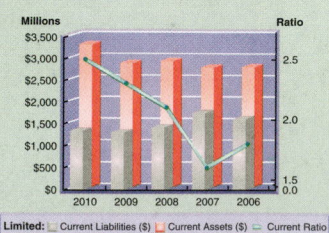

Limited Brands' current ratio averaged 2.1 for its fiscal years 2006 through 2010. The current ratio for each of these years suggests that the company's short-term obligations can be covered with its short-term assets. However, if its ratio would approach 1.0, Limited would expect to face challenges in covering liabilities. If the ratio were *less* than 1.0, current liabilities would exceed current assets, and the company's ability to pay short-term obligations could be in doubt.

**Decision** Maker          Answer — p. 156

**Analyst**   You are analyzing the financial condition of a company to assess its ability to meet upcoming loan payments. You compute its current ratio as 1.2. You also find that a major portion of accounts receivable is due from one client who has not made any payments in the past 12 months. Removing this receivable from current assets lowers the current ratio to 0.7. What do you conclude? ■

# DEMONSTRATION PROBLEM

The partial work sheet of Midtown Repair Company at December 31, 2011, follows.

| | Adjusted Trial Balance | | Income Statement | | Balance Sheet and Statement of Owner's Equity | |
|---|---|---|---|---|---|---|
| | Debit | Credit | Debit | Credit | Debit | Credit |
| Cash ............................... | 95,600 | | | | | |
| Notes receivable (current) .............. | 50,000 | | | | | |
| Prepaid insurance ..................... | 16,000 | | | | | |
| Prepaid rent ......................... | 4,000 | | | | | |
| Equipment ........................... | 170,000 | | | | | |
| Accumulated depreciation—Equipment .... | | 57,000 | | | | |
| Accounts payable ..................... | | 52,000 | | | | |
| Long-term notes payable ............... | | 63,000 | | | | |
| C. Trout, Capital ...................... | | 178,500 | | | | |
| C. Trout, Withdrawals .................. | 30,000 | | | | | |
| Repair services revenue ................ | | 180,800 | | | | |
| Interest revenue ...................... | | 7,500 | | | | |
| Depreciation expense—Equipment ........ | 28,500 | | | | | |
| Wages expense ....................... | 85,000 | | | | | |
| Rent expense ........................ | 48,000 | | | | | |
| Insurance expense .................... | 6,000 | | | | | |
| Interest expense ..................... | 5,700 | | | | | |
| Totals .............................. | 538,800 | 538,800 | | | | |

## Required

1. Complete the work sheet by extending the adjusted trial balance totals to the appropriate financial statement columns.
2. Prepare closing entries for Midtown Repair Company.
3. Set up the Income Summary and the C. Trout, Capital account in the general ledger (in balance column format) and post the closing entries to these accounts.
4. Determine the balance of the C. Trout, Capital account to be reported on the December 31, 2011, balance sheet.
5. Prepare an income statement, statement of owner's equity, and classified balance sheet (in report form) as of December 31, 2011.

## PLANNING THE SOLUTION

- Extend the adjusted trial balance account balances to the appropriate financial statement columns.
- Prepare entries to close the revenue accounts to Income Summary, to close the expense accounts to Income Summary, to close Income Summary to the capital account, and to close the withdrawals account to the capital account.

- Post the first and second closing entries to the Income Summary account. Examine the balance of income summary and verify that it agrees with the net income shown on the work sheet.
- Post the third and fourth closing entries to the capital account.
- Use the work sheet's two right-most columns and your answer in part 4 to prepare the classified balance sheet.

## SOLUTION TO DEMONSTRATION PROBLEM

**1.** Completing the work sheet.

| | Adjusted Trial Balance | | Income Statement | | Balance Sheet and Statement of Owner's Equity | |
|---|---|---|---|---|---|---|
| | Debit | Credit | Debit | Credit | Debit | Credit |
| Cash .............................. | 95,600 | | | | 95,600 | |
| Notes receivable (current) .............. | 50,000 | | | | 50,000 | |
| Prepaid insurance .................... | 16,000 | | | | 16,000 | |
| Prepaid rent ........................ | 4,000 | | | | 4,000 | |
| Equipment .......................... | 170,000 | | | | 170,000 | |
| Accumulated depreciation—Equipment ... | | 57,000 | | | | 57,000 |
| Accounts payable .................... | | 52,000 | | | | 52,000 |
| Long-term notes payable .............. | | 63,000 | | | | 63,000 |
| C. Trout, Capital ..................... | | 178,500 | | | | 178,500 |
| C. Trout, Withdrawals ................ | 30,000 | | | | 30,000 | |
| Repair services revenue .............. | | 180,800 | | 180,800 | | |
| Interest revenue .................... | | 7,500 | | 7,500 | | |
| Depreciation expense—Equipment ....... | 28,500 | | 28,500 | | | |
| Wages expense ...................... | 85,000 | | 85,000 | | | |
| Rent expense ....................... | 48,000 | | 48,000 | | | |
| Insurance expense ................... | 6,000 | | 6,000 | | | |
| Interest expense .................... | 5,700 | | 5,700 | | | |
| Totals ............................ | 538,800 | 538,800 | 173,200 | 188,300 | 365,600 | 350,500 |
| Net income ......................... | | | 15,100 | | | 15,100 |
| Totals ............................ | | | 188,300 | 188,300 | 365,600 | 365,600 |

**2.** Closing entries.

| Dec. 31 | Repair Services Revenue ......................... | 180,800 | |
| | Interest Revenue ............................... | 7,500 | |
| | Income Summary ............................ | | 188,300 |
| | *To close revenue accounts.* | | |
| Dec. 31 | Income Summary ............................... | 173,200 | |
| | Depreciation Expense—Equipment ............ | | 28,500 |
| | Wages Expense ............................. | | 85,000 |
| | Rent Expense ............................... | | 48,000 |
| | Insurance Expense ........................... | | 6,000 |
| | Interest Expense ............................ | | 5,700 |
| | *To close expense accounts.* | | |
| Dec. 31 | Income Summary ............................... | 15,100 | |
| | C. Trout, Capital ............................. | | 15,100 |
| | *To close the Income Summary account.* | | |
| Dec. 31 | C. Trout, Capital ............................... | 30,000 | |
| | C. Trout, Withdrawals ........................ | | 30,000 |
| | *To close the withdrawals account.* | | |

**3.** Set up the Income Summary and the capital ledger accounts and post the closing entries.

| Income Summary | | | | | Account No. 901 |
| --- | --- | --- | --- | --- | --- |
| Date | Explanation | PR | Debit | Credit | Balance |
| 2011 | | | | | |
| Jan.  1 | Beginning balance ................. | | | | 0 |
| Dec. 31 | Close revenue accounts ............ | | | 188,300 | 188,300 |
| 31 | Close expense accounts ............ | | 173,200 | | 15,100 |
| 31 | Close income summary ............ | | 15,100 | | 0 |

| C. Trout, Capital | | | | | Account No. 301 |
| --- | --- | --- | --- | --- | --- |
| Date | Explanation | PR | Debit | Credit | Balance |
| 2011 | | | | | |
| Jan.  1 | Beginning balance ................. | | | | 178,500 |
| Dec. 31 | Close Income Summary ............ | | | 15,100 | 193,600 |
| 31 | Close C. Trout, Withdrawals ........ | | 30,000 | | 163,600 |

**4.** The final capital balance of $163,600 (from part 3) will be reported on the December 31, 2011, balance sheet. The final capital balance reflects the increase due to the net income earned during the year and the decrease for the owner's withdrawals during the year.

**5.**

| MIDTOWN REPAIR COMPANY |
| --- |
| Income Statement |
| For Year Ended December 31, 2011 |

| | | |
| --- | --- | --- |
| Revenues | | |
| Repair services revenue ................. | $180,800 | |
| Interest revenue ....................... | 7,500 | |
| Total revenues ........................ | | $188,300 |
| Expenses | | |
| Depreciation expense—Equipment ......... | 28,500 | |
| Wages expense ....................... | 85,000 | |
| Rent expense ........................ | 48,000 | |
| Insurance expense .................... | 6,000 | |
| Interest expense ..................... | 5,700 | |
| Total expenses ....................... | | 173,200 |
| Net income ........................... | | $ 15,100 |

| MIDTOWN REPAIR COMPANY |
| --- |
| Statement of Owner's Equity |
| For Year Ended December 31, 2011 |

| | | | |
| --- | --- | --- | --- |
| C. Trout, Capital, December 31, 2010 ............ | | | $178,500 |
| Add:  Investment by owner .................... | $ | 0 | |
| Net income ......................... | | 15,100 | 15,100 |
| | | | 193,600 |
| Less:  Withdrawals by owner ................... | | | 30,000 |
| C. Trout, Capital, December 31, 2011 ............ | | | $163,600 |

**MIDTOWN REPAIR COMPANY**
**Balance Sheet**
**December 31, 2011**

**Assets**

| | | |
|---|---|---|
| Current assets | | |
| Cash | | $ 95,600 |
| Notes receivable | | 50,000 |
| Prepaid insurance | | 16,000 |
| Prepaid rent | | 4,000 |
| Total current assets | | 165,600 |
| Plant assets | | |
| Equipment | $170,000 | |
| Less: Accumulated depreciation—Equipment | (57,000) | |
| Total plant assets | | 113,000 |
| Total assets | | $278,600 |

**Liabilities**

| | | |
|---|---|---|
| Current liabilities | | |
| Accounts payable | | $ 52,000 |
| Long-term liabilities | | |
| Long-term notes payable | | 63,000 |
| Total liabilities | | 115,000 |

**Equity**

| | | |
|---|---|---|
| C. Trout, Capital | | 163,600 |
| Total liabilities and equity | | $278,600 |

**APPENDIX**

# 4A

# Reversing Entries

**Reversing entries** are optional. They are recorded in response to accrued assets and accrued liabilities that were created by adjusting entries at the end of a reporting period. The purpose of reversing entries is to simplify a company's recordkeeping. Exhibit 4A.1 shows an example of FastForward's reversing entries. The top of the exhibit shows the adjusting entry FastForward recorded on December 31 for its employee's earned but unpaid salary. The entry recorded three days' salary of $210, which increased December's total salary expense to $1,610. The entry also recognized a liability of $210. The expense is reported on December's income statement. The expense account is then closed. The ledger on January 1, 2012, shows a $210 liability and a zero balance in the Salaries Expense account. At this point, the choice is made between using or not using reversing entries.

**Point:** As a general rule, adjusting entries that create new asset or liability accounts are likely candidates for reversing.

**Accounting *without* Reversing Entries**    The path down the left side of Exhibit 4A.1 is described in the chapter. To summarize here, when the next payday occurs on January 9, we record payment with a compound entry that debits both the expense and liability accounts and credits Cash. Posting that entry creates a $490 balance in the expense account and reduces the liability account balance to zero because the debt has been settled. The disadvantage of this approach is the slightly more complex entry required on January 9. Paying the accrued liability means that this entry differs from the routine entries made on all other paydays. To construct the proper entry on January 9, we must recall the effect of the December 31 adjusting entry. Reversing entries overcome this disadvantage.

**Accounting *with* Reversing Entries**    The right side of Exhibit 4A.1 shows how a reversing entry on January 1 overcomes the disadvantage of the January 9 entry when not using reversing entries. A reversing entry is the exact opposite of an adjusting entry. For FastForward, the Salaries Payable liability account is debited for $210, meaning that this account now has a zero balance after the entry is posted. The Salaries Payable account temporarily understates the liability, but this is not a problem since

**P4**    Prepare reversing entries and explain their purpose.

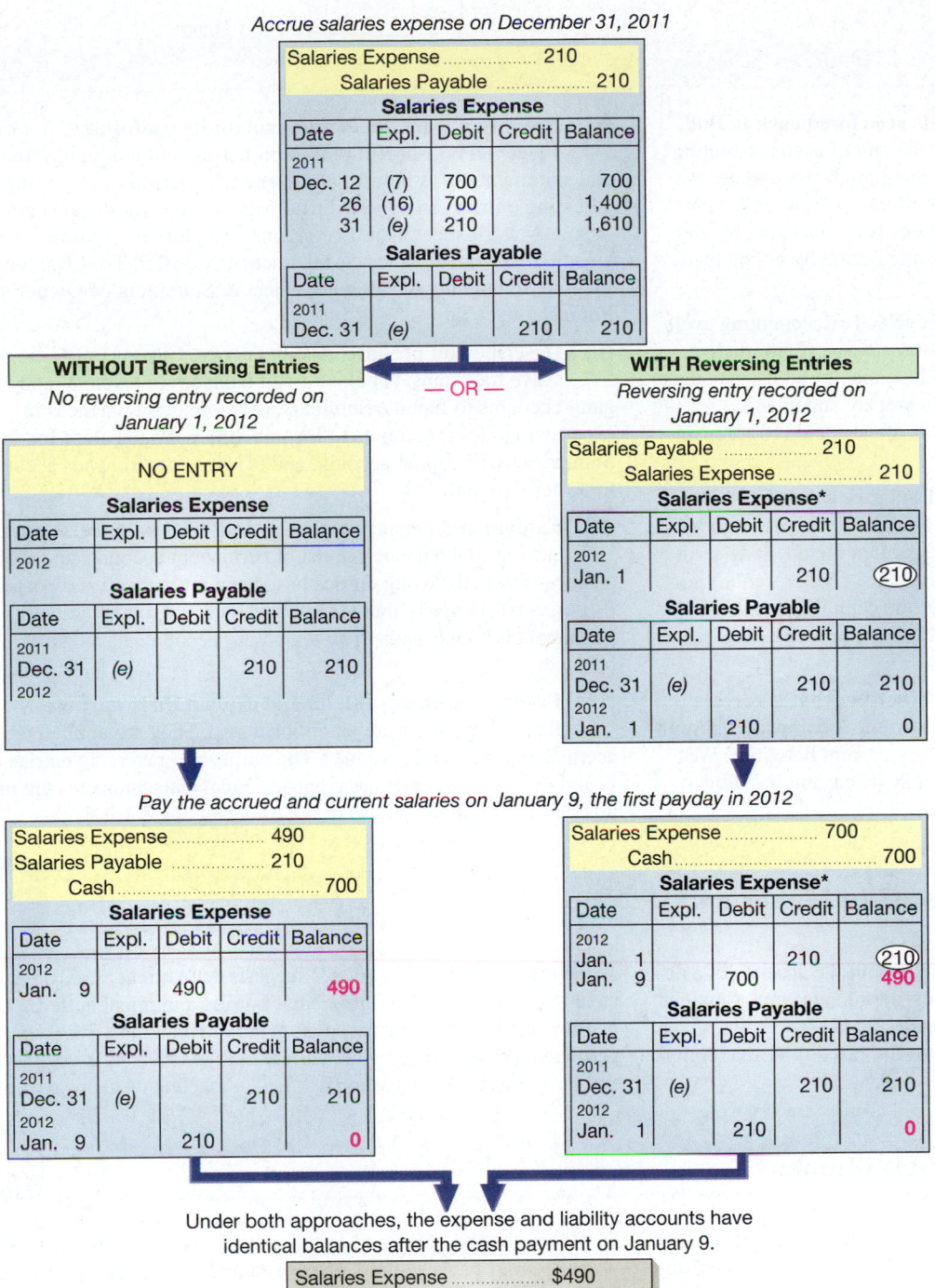

**EXHIBIT 4A.1**

Reversing Entries for an Accrued Expense

*Accrue salaries expense on December 31, 2011*

Salaries Expense .............. 210
    Salaries Payable .............. 210

**Salaries Expense**

| Date | Expl. | Debit | Credit | Balance |
|------|-------|-------|--------|---------|
| 2011 | | | | |
| Dec. 12 | (7) | 700 | | 700 |
| 26 | (16) | 700 | | 1,400 |
| 31 | (e) | 210 | | 1,610 |

**Salaries Payable**

| Date | Expl. | Debit | Credit | Balance |
|------|-------|-------|--------|---------|
| 2011 | | | | |
| Dec. 31 | (e) | | 210 | 210 |

**WITHOUT Reversing Entries**

— OR —

*No reversing entry recorded on January 1, 2012*

NO ENTRY

**Salaries Expense**

| Date | Expl. | Debit | Credit | Balance |
|------|-------|-------|--------|---------|
| 2012 | | | | |

**Salaries Payable**

| Date | Expl. | Debit | Credit | Balance |
|------|-------|-------|--------|---------|
| 2011 | | | | |
| Dec. 31 | (e) | | 210 | 210 |
| 2012 | | | | |

**WITH Reversing Entries**

*Reversing entry recorded on January 1, 2012*

Salaries Payable .............. 210
    Salaries Expense .............. 210

**Salaries Expense***

| Date | Expl. | Debit | Credit | Balance |
|------|-------|-------|--------|---------|
| 2012 | | | | |
| Jan. 1 | | | 210 | (210) |

**Salaries Payable**

| Date | Expl. | Debit | Credit | Balance |
|------|-------|-------|--------|---------|
| 2011 | | | | |
| Dec. 31 | (e) | | 210 | 210 |
| 2012 | | | | |
| Jan. 1 | | 210 | | 0 |

*Pay the accrued and current salaries on January 9, the first payday in 2012*

Salaries Expense .............. 490
Salaries Payable .............. 210
    Cash .............. 700

**Salaries Expense**

| Date | Expl. | Debit | Credit | Balance |
|------|-------|-------|--------|---------|
| 2012 | | | | |
| Jan. 9 | | 490 | | **490** |

**Salaries Payable**

| Date | Expl. | Debit | Credit | Balance |
|------|-------|-------|--------|---------|
| 2011 | | | | |
| Dec. 31 | (e) | | 210 | 210 |
| 2012 | | | | |
| Jan. 9 | | 210 | | **0** |

Salaries Expense .............. 700
    Cash .............. 700

**Salaries Expense***

| Date | Expl. | Debit | Credit | Balance |
|------|-------|-------|--------|---------|
| 2012 | | | | |
| Jan. 1 | | | 210 | (210) |
| Jan. 9 | | 700 | | **490** |

**Salaries Payable**

| Date | Expl. | Debit | Credit | Balance |
|------|-------|-------|--------|---------|
| 2011 | | | | |
| Dec. 31 | (e) | | 210 | 210 |
| 2012 | | | | |
| Jan. 1 | | 210 | | **0** |

Under both approaches, the expense and liability accounts have
identical balances after the cash payment on January 9.

Salaries Expense .............. $490
Salaries Payable .............. $  0

*Circled numbers in the *Balance* column indicate abnormal balances.

financial statements are not prepared before the liability is settled on January 9. The credit to the Salaries Expense account is unusual because it gives the account an *abnormal credit balance*. We highlight an abnormal balance by circling it. Because of the reversing entry, the January 9 entry to record payment is straightforward. This entry debits the Salaries Expense account and credits Cash for the full $700 paid. It is the same as all other entries made to record 10 days' salary for the employee. Notice that after the payment entry is posted, the Salaries Expense account has a $490 balance that reflects seven days' salary of $70 per day (see the lower right side of Exhibit 4A.1). The zero balance in the Salaries Payable account is now correct. The lower section of Exhibit 4A.1 shows that the expense and liability accounts have exactly the same balances whether reversing entries are used or not. This means that both approaches yield identical results.

# Summary

**C1**  **Explain why temporary accounts are closed each period.** Temporary accounts are closed at the end of each accounting period for two main reasons. First, the closing process updates the capital account to include the effects of all transactions and events recorded for the period. Second, it prepares revenue, expense, and withdrawals accounts for the next reporting period by giving them zero balances.

**C2**  **Identify steps in the accounting cycle.** The accounting cycle consists of 10 steps: (1) analyze transactions, (2) journalize, (3) post, (4) prepare an unadjusted trial balance, (5) adjust accounts, (6) prepare an adjusted trial balance, (7) prepare statements, (8) close, (9) prepare a post-closing trial balance, and (10) prepare (optional) reversing entries.

**C3**  **Explain and prepare a classified balance sheet.** Classified balance sheets report assets and liabilities in two categories: current and noncurrent. Noncurrent assets often include long-term investments, plant assets, and intangible assets. Owner's equity for proprietorships (and partnerships) report the capital account balance. A corporation separates equity into common stock and retained earnings.

**A1**  **Compute the current ratio and describe what it reveals about a company's financial condition.** A company's current ratio is defined as current assets divided by current liabilities. We use it to evaluate a company's ability to pay its current liabilities out of current assets.

**P1**  **Prepare a work sheet and explain its usefulness.** A work sheet can be a useful tool in preparing and analyzing financial statements. It is helpful at the end of a period in preparing adjusting entries, an adjusted trial balance, and financial statements. A work sheet usually contains five pairs of columns: Unadjusted Trial Balance, Adjustments, Adjusted Trial Balance, Income Statement, and Balance Sheet & Statement of Owner's Equity.

**P2**  **Describe and prepare closing entries.** Closing entries involve four steps: (1) close credit balances in revenue (and gain) accounts to Income Summary, (2) close debit balances in expense (and loss) accounts to Income Summary, (3) close Income Summary to the capital account, and (4) close withdrawals account to owner's capital.

**P3**  **Explain and prepare a post-closing trial balance.** A post-closing trial balance is a list of permanent accounts and their balances after all closing entries have been journalized and posted. Its purpose is to verify that (1) total debits equal total credits for permanent accounts and (2) all temporary accounts have zero balances.

**P4**A  **Prepare reversing entries and explain their purpose.** Reversing entries are an optional step. They are applied to accrued expenses and revenues. The purpose of reversing entries is to simplify subsequent journal entries. Financial statements are unaffected by the choice to use or not use reversing entries.

## Guidance Answers to Decision Maker and Decision Ethics

**Entrepreneur**  Yes, you are concerned about the absence of a depreciation adjustment. Equipment does depreciate, and financial statements must recognize this occurrence. Its absence suggests an error or a misrepresentation (there is also the possibility that equipment is fully depreciated).

**Analyst**  A current ratio of 1.2 suggests that current assets are sufficient to cover current liabilities, but it implies a minimal buffer in case of errors in measuring current assets or current liabilities. Removing the past due receivable reduces the current ratio to 0.7. Your assessment is that the company will have some difficulty meeting its loan payments.

## Guidance Answers to Quick Checks

1. Amounts in the Unadjusted Trial Balance columns are taken from current account balances in the ledger. The balances for new accounts expected to arise from adjusted entries can be left blank or set at zero.

2. A work sheet offers the advantage of listing on one page all necessary information to make adjusting entries.

3. A work sheet can help in (a) accounting efficiency and avoiding errors, (b) linking transactions and events to their effects in financial statements, (c) showing adjustments for audit purposes, (d) preparing interim financial statements, and (e) showing effects from proposed, or what-if, transactions.

4. The major steps in preparing closing entries are to close (1) credit balances in revenue accounts to Income Summary, (2) debit balances in expense accounts to Income Summary, (3) Income Summary to owner's capital, and (4) any withdrawals account to owner's capital.

5. Revenue (and gain) and expense (and loss) accounts are called *temporary* because they are opened and closed each period. The Income Summary and owner's withdrawals accounts are also temporary.

6. Permanent accounts make up the post-closing trial balance, which consist of asset, liability, and equity accounts.

7. Current assets: (*b*), (*c*), (*d*). Plant assets: (*a*), (*e*). Item (*f*) is an intangible asset.

8. Investment in common stock, investment in bonds, and land held for future expansion.

9. For a service company, the operating cycle is the usual time between (1) paying employees who do the services and (2) receiving cash from customers for services provided.

## Key Terms                                                    mhhe.com/wildFAP20e

Accounting cycle (p. 146)

Classified balance sheet (p. 147)

Closing entries (p. 143)

Closing process (p. 142)

Current assets (p. 148)

Current liabilities (p. 149)

Current ratio (p. 150)

Income summary (p. 143)

Intangible assets (p. 149)

Long-term investments (p. 149)

Long-term liabilities (p. 149)

Operating cycle (p. 147)

Permanent accounts (p. 142)

Post-closing trial balance (p. 146)

Pro forma financial statements (p. 142)

Reversing entries (p. 154)

Temporary accounts (p. 142)

Unclassified balance sheet (p. 147)

Working papers (p. 138)

Work sheet (p. 138)

## Multiple Choice Quiz          Answers on p. 177          mhhe.com/wildFAP20e

Additional Quiz Questions are available at the book's Website.

**1.** G. Venda, owner of Venda Services, withdrew $25,000 from the business during the current year. The entry to close the withdrawals account at the end of the year is:

| | | | |
|---|---|---|---|
| **a.** | G. Venda, Withdrawals . . . . . . . . . . . . . . | 25,000 | |
| | G. Venda, Capital . . . . . . . . . . . . . | | 25,000 |
| **b.** | Income Summary . . . . . . . . . . . . . . . . . | 25,000 | |
| | G. Venda, Capital . . . . . . . . . . . . . | | 25,000 |
| **c.** | G. Venda, Withdrawals . . . . . . . . . . . . . | 25,000 | |
| | Cash . . . . . . . . . . . . . . . . . . . . . | | 25,000 |
| **d.** | G. Venda, Capital . . . . . . . . . . . . . . . . | 25,000 | |
| | Salary Expense . . . . . . . . . . . . . . . | | 25,000 |
| **e.** | G. Venda, Capital . . . . . . . . . . . . . . . . | 25,000 | |
| | G. Venda, Withdrawals . . . . . . . . . . | | 25,000 |

**2.** The following information is available for the R. Kandamil Company before closing the accounts. After all of the closing entries are made, what will be the balance in the R. Kandamil, Capital account?

| | |
|---|---|
| Total revenues . . . . . . . . . . . . . . . . . | $300,000 |
| Total expenses . . . . . . . . . . . . . . . | 195,000 |
| R. Kandamil, Capital . . . . . . . . . . . | 100,000 |
| R. Kandamil, Withdrawals . . . . . . . | 45,000 |

**a.** $360,000    **d.** $150,000

**b.** $250,000    **e.**  $60,000

**c.** $160,000

**3.** Which of the following errors would cause the balance sheet and statement of owner's equity columns of a work sheet to be out of balance?

**a.** Entering a revenue amount in the balance sheet and statement of owner's equity debit column.

**b.** Entering a liability amount in the balance sheet and statement of owner's equity credit column.

**c.** Entering an expense account in the balance sheet and statement of owner's equity debit column.

**d.** Entering an asset account in the income statement debit column.

**e.** Entering a liability amount in the income statement credit column.

**4.** The temporary account used only in the closing process to hold the amounts of revenues and expenses before the net difference is added or subtracted from the owner's capital account is called the

**a.** Closing account.

**b.** Nominal account.

**c.** Income Summary account.

**d.** Balance Column account.

**e.** Contra account.

**5.** Based on the following information from Repicor Company's balance sheet, what is Repicor Company's current ratio?

| | |
|---|---|
| Current assets . . . . . . . . . . . . | $ 75,000 |
| Investments . . . . . . . . . . . . . . | 30,000 |
| Plant assets . . . . . . . . . . . . . . | 300,000 |
| Current liabilities . . . . . . . . . . | 50,000 |
| Long-term liabilities . . . . . . . . | 60,000 |
| D. Repicor, Capital . . . . . . . . . | 295,000 |

**a.** 2.10    **d.** 0.95

**b.** 1.50    **e.** 0.67

**c.** 1.00

<sup>A</sup> *Superscript letter A denotes assignments based on Appendix 4A.*

Icon denotes assignments that involve decision making.

## Discussion Questions

1. What accounts are affected by closing entries? What accounts are not affected?
2. What two purposes are accomplished by recording closing entries?
3. What are the steps in recording closing entries?
4. What is the purpose of the Income Summary account?
5. Explain whether an error has occurred if a post-closing trial balance includes a Depreciation Expense account.
6. What tasks are aided by a work sheet?
7. Why are the debit and credit entries in the Adjustments columns of the work sheet identified with letters?
8. What is a company's operating cycle?
9. What classes of assets and liabilities are shown on a typical classified balance sheet?
10. How is unearned revenue classified on the balance sheet?

11. What are the characteristics of plant assets?
12.<sup>A</sup> How do reversing entries simplify recordkeeping?
13.<sup>A</sup> If a company recorded accrued salaries expense of $500 at the end of its fiscal year, what reversing entry could be made? When would it be made?
14. Refer to the balance sheet for **Research In Motion** in Appendix A. What five main noncurrent asset categories are used on its classified balance sheet?    **RIM**
15. Refer to **Nokia**'s balance sheet in Appendix A. Identify and list its 9 current assets.    **NOKIA**
16. Refer to **Apple**'s balance sheet in Appendix A. Identify the three accounts listed as current liabilities.    Apple
17. Refer to **Palm**'s financial statements in Appendix A. What journal entry was likely recorded as of May 31, 2009, to close its Income Summary account?    **Palm**

---

**Mc Graw Hill** connect™

## QUICK STUDY

**QS 4-1**

Identifying the accounting cycle

C2

List the following steps of the accounting cycle in their proper order.
a. Preparing the post-closing trial balance.
b. Posting the journal entries.
c. Journalizing and posting adjusting entries.
d. Preparing the adjusted trial balance.
e. Journalizing and posting closing entries.
f. Analyzing transactions and events.
g. Preparing the financial statements.
h. Preparing the unadjusted trial balance.
i. Journalizing transactions and events.

---

**QS 4-2**

Explaining temporary and permanent accounts

C1

Complete the following descriptions related to temporary and permanent accounts.
1. Temporary accounts accumulate data related to _____ accounting period.
2. Permanent accounts report on activities related to _____ future accounting periods, and they carry their ending balances into the next period.
3. _____ accounts include all income statement accounts, the withdrawals account, and the Income Summary account.
4. _____ accounts generally consist of all balance sheet accounts, and these accounts are not closed.

---

**QS 4-3**

Identifying current accounts and computing the current ratio

A1

Compute Jamar Company's current ratio using the following information.

| | | | | |
|---|---|---|---|---|
| Accounts receivable ........ | $15,000 | | Long-term notes payable .......... | $20,000 |
| Accounts payable .......... | 10,000 | | Office supplies ................... | 1,800 |
| Buildings ................. | 42,000 | | Prepaid insurance ............... | 2,500 |
| Cash ................... | 6,000 | | Unearned services revenue ........ | 4,000 |

---

**QS 4-4**

Classifying balance sheet items

C3

The following are common categories on a classified balance sheet.
A. Current assets
B. Long-term investments
C. Plant assets
D. Intangible assets
E. Current liabilities
F. Long-term liabilities

For each of the following items, select the letter that identifies the balance sheet category where the item typically would appear.

| | |
|---|---|
| _____ **1.** Trademarks | _____ **5.** Cash |
| _____ **2.** Accounts receivable | _____ **6.** Wages payable |
| _____ **3.** Land not currently used in operations | _____ **7.** Store equipment |
| _____ **4.** Notes payable (due in three years) | _____ **8.** Accounts payable |

---

In preparing a work sheet, indicate the financial statement Debit column to which a normal balance in the following accounts should be extended. Use IS for the Income Statement Debit column and BS for the Balance Sheet and Statement of Owner's Equity Debit column.

**QS 4-5**
Applying a work sheet
**P1**

| | |
|---|---|
| _____ **a.** Insurance expense | _____ **d.** Depreciation expense—Equipment |
| _____ **b.** Equipment | _____ **e.** Prepaid rent |
| _____ **c.** Owner, Withdrawals | _____ **f.** Accounts receivable |

---

List the following steps in preparing a work sheet in their proper order by writing numbers 1–5 in the blank spaces provided.

**QS 4-6**
Ordering work sheet steps
**P1**

**a.** _____ Prepare an adjusted trial balance on the work sheet.

**b.** _____ Prepare an unadjusted trial balance on the work sheet.

**c.** _____ Enter adjustments data on the work sheet.

**d.** _____ Extend adjusted balances to appropriate financial statement columns.

**e.** _____ Total the statement columns, compute net income (loss), and complete work sheet.

---

The following selected information is taken from the work sheet for Wayman Company as of December 31, 2011. Using this information, determine the amount for K. Wayman, Capital, that should be reported on its December 31, 2011, balance sheet.

**QS 4-7**
Interpreting a work sheet
**P1**

| | Income Statement | | Balance Sheet and Statement of Owner's Equity | |
|---|---|---|---|---|
| | **Dr.** | **Cr.** | **Dr.** | **Cr.** |
| ⋮ | | | | |
| K. Wayman, Capital . . . . . . . . . . . . | | | | 65,000 |
| K. Wayman, Withdrawals . . . . . . . | | | 32,000 | |
| ⋮ | | | | |
| Totals . . . . . . . . . . . . . . . . . . . . . . | 115,000 | 174,000 | | |

---

The ledger of Terrel Company includes the following unadjusted normal balances: Prepaid Rent $800, Services Revenue $11,600, and Wages Expense $5,000. Adjusting entries are required for **(a)** accrued rent expense $240; **(b)** accrued services revenue $180; and **(c)** accrued wages expense $160. Enter these unadjusted balances and the necessary adjustments on a work sheet and complete the work sheet for these accounts. *Note:* Also include the following accounts: Accounts Receivable, Wages Payable, and Rent Expense.

**QS 4-8**
Preparing a partial work sheet
**P1**

---

The ledger of Avril Company includes the following accounts with normal balances: L. Avril, Capital $6,000; L. Avril, Withdrawals $400; Services Revenue $10,000; Wages Expense $5,200; and Rent Expense $800. Prepare the necessary closing entries from the available information at December 31.

**QS 4-9**
Prepare closing entries from the ledger **P2**

---

Identify the accounts listed in QS 4-9 that would be included in a post-closing trial balance.

**QS 4-10**
Identify post-closing accounts **P3**

---

On December 31, 2010, Lester Co. prepared an adjusting entry for $6,700 of earned but unrecorded management fees. On January 16, 2011, Lester received $15,500 cash in management fees, which included the accrued fees earned in 2010. Assuming the company uses reversing entries, prepare the January 1, 2011, reversing entry and the January 16, 2011, cash receipt entry.

**QS 4-11^A**
Reversing entries
**P4**

**QS 4-12**

International accounting standards **P2**

Answer each of the following questions related to international accounting standards.

**a.** Explain how the closing process is different between accounting under IFRS versus U.S. GAAP.

**b.** What basic principle do U.S. GAAP and IFRS rely upon in recording the initial acquisition value for nearly all assets?

# EXERCISES

**Exercise 4-1**

Preparing and posting closing entries

**P2**

Use the March 31 fiscal year-end information from the following ledger accounts (assume that all accounts have normal balances) to prepare closing journal entries and then post those entries to the appropriate ledger accounts.

**Check** M. Mallon, Capital (ending balance), $38,900

| General Ledger | | | | | | | | | | |
|---|---|---|---|---|---|---|---|---|---|---|

**M. Mallon, Capital**   Acct. No. 301

| Date | PR | Debit | Credit | Balance |
|---|---|---|---|---|
| Mar. 31 | G2 | | | 42,000 |

**M. Mallon, Withdrawals**   Acct. No. 302

| Date | PR | Debit | Credit | Balance |
|---|---|---|---|---|
| Mar. 31 | G2 | | | 25,000 |

**Services Revenue**   Acct. No. 401

| Date | PR | Debit | Credit | Balance |
|---|---|---|---|---|
| Mar. 31 | G2 | | | 74,000 |

**Depreciation Expense**   Acct. No. 603

| Date | PR | Debit | Credit | Balance |
|---|---|---|---|---|
| Mar. 31 | G2 | | | 17,000 |

**Salaries Expense**   Acct. No. 622

| Date | PR | Debit | Credit | Balance |
|---|---|---|---|---|
| Mar. 31 | G2 | | | 21,000 |

**Insurance Expense**   Acct. No. 637

| Date | PR | Debit | Credit | Balance |
|---|---|---|---|---|
| Mar. 31 | G2 | | | 4,500 |

**Rent Expense**   Acct. No. 640

| Date | PR | Debit | Credit | Balance |
|---|---|---|---|---|
| Mar. 31 | G2 | | | 9,600 |

**Income Summary**   Acct. No. 901

| Date | PR | Debit | Credit | Balance |
|---|---|---|---|---|
| | | | | |

**Exercise 4-2**

Preparing closing entries and a post-closing trial balance

**P2 P3**

The adjusted trial balance for Sundance Marketing Co. follows. Complete the four right-most columns of the table by first entering information for the four closing entries (keyed *1* through *4*) and second by completing the post-closing trial balance.

| No. | Account Title | Adjusted Trial Balance | | Closing Entry Information | | Post-Closing Trial Balance | |
|---|---|---|---|---|---|---|---|
| | | Dr. | Cr. | Dr. | Cr. | Dr. | Cr. |
| 101 | Cash | $ 8,200 | | | | | |
| 106 | Accounts receivable | 24,000 | | | | | |
| 153 | Equipment | 41,000 | | | | | |
| 154 | Accumulated depreciation—Equipment | | $ 16,500 | | | | |
| 193 | Franchise | 30,000 | | | | | |
| 201 | Accounts payable | | 14,000 | | | | |
| 209 | Salaries payable | | 3,200 | | | | |
| 233 | Unearned fees | | 2,600 | | | | |
| 301 | H. Sundance, Capital | | 64,500 | | | | |
| 302 | H. Sundance, Withdrawals | 14,400 | | | | | |
| 401 | Marketing fees earned | | 79,000 | | | | |
| 611 | Depreciation expense—Equipment | 11,000 | | | | | |
| 622 | Salaries expense | 31,500 | | | | | |
| 640 | Rent expense | 12,000 | | | | | |
| 677 | Miscellaneous expenses | 7,700 | | | | | |
| 901 | Income summary | | | | | | |
| | Totals | $179,800 | $179,800 | | | | |

The following adjusted trial balance contains the accounts and balances of Showers Company as of December 31, 2011, the end of its fiscal year. (1) Prepare the December 31, 2011, closing entries for Showers Company. (2) Prepare the December 31, 2011, post-closing trial balance for Showers Company.

**Exercise 4-3**
Preparing closing entries and a post-closing trial balance
**P2  P3**

| No. | Account Title | Debit | Credit |
|-----|---------------|-------|--------|
| 101 | Cash | $18,000 | |
| 126 | Supplies | 12,000 | |
| 128 | Prepaid insurance | 2,000 | |
| 167 | Equipment | 23,000 | |
| 168 | Accumulated depreciation—Equipment | | $ 6,500 |
| 301 | R. Showers, Capital | | 46,600 |
| 302 | R. Showers, Withdrawals | 6,000 | |
| 404 | Services revenue | | 36,000 |
| 612 | Depreciation expense—Equipment | 2,000 | |
| 622 | Salaries expense | 21,000 | |
| 637 | Insurance expense | 1,500 | |
| 640 | Rent expense | 2,400 | |
| 652 | Supplies expense | 1,200 | |
| | Totals | $89,100 | $89,100 |

**Check**  (2) R. Showers, Capital (ending), $48,500; Total debits, $55,000

Use the following adjusted trial balance of Webb Trucking Company to prepare the (1) income statement and (2) statement of owner's equity, for the year ended December 31, 2011. The K. Webb, Capital, account balance is $161,000 at December 31, 2010.

**Exercise 4-4**
Preparing the financial statements
**C2**

| Account Title | Debit | Credit |
|---------------|-------|--------|
| Cash | $ 7,000 | |
| Accounts receivable | 16,500 | |
| Office supplies | 2,000 | |
| Trucks | 170,000 | |
| Accumulated depreciation—Trucks | | $ 35,000 |
| Land | 75,000 | |
| Accounts payable | | 11,000 |
| Interest payable | | 3,000 |
| Long-term notes payable | | 52,000 |
| K. Webb, Capital | | 161,000 |
| K. Webb, Withdrawals | 19,000 | |
| Trucking fees earned | | 128,000 |
| Depreciation expense—Trucks | 22,500 | |
| Salaries expense | 60,000 | |
| Office supplies expense | 7,000 | |
| Repairs expense—Trucks | 11,000 | |
| Totals | $390,000 | $390,000 |

Use the information in the adjusted trial balance reported in Exercise 4-4 to prepare Webb Trucking Company's classified balance sheet as of December 31, 2011.

**Exercise 4-5**
Preparing a classified balance sheet **C3**

**Check**  Total assets, $235,500; K. Webb, Capital, $169,500

**Exercise 4-6**

Computing the current ratio

A1

Use the information in the adjusted trial balance reported in Exercise 4-4 to compute the current ratio as of the balance sheet date (round the ratio to two decimals). Interpret the current ratio for the Webb Trucking Company. (Assume that the industry average for the current ratio is 1.5.)

**Exercise 4-7**

Computing and analyzing the current ratio

A1

Calculate the current ratio in each of the following separate cases (round the ratio to two decimals). Identify the company case with the strongest liquidity position. (These cases represent competing companies in the same industry.)

| | Current Assets | Current Liabilities |
|---|---|---|
| Case 1 ........ | $ 78,000 | $31,000 |
| Case 2 ........ | 104,000 | 75,000 |
| Case 3 ........ | 44,000 | 48,000 |
| Case 4 ........ | 84,500 | 80,600 |
| Case 5 ........ | 60,000 | 99,000 |

**Exercise 4-8**

Extending adjusted account balances on a work sheet

P1

These 16 accounts are from the Adjusted Trial Balance columns of a company's 10-column work sheet. In the blank space beside each account, write the letter of the appropriate financial statement column (A, B, C, or D) to which a normal account balance is extended.

**A.** Debit column for the Income Statement columns.

**B.** Credit column for the Income Statement columns.

**C.** Debit column for the Balance Sheet and Statement of Owner's Equity columns.

**D.** Credit column for the Balance Sheet and Statement of Owner's Equity columns.

_____ **1.** Office Supplies       _____ **9.** Service Fees Revenue

_____ **2.** Accounts Payable       _____ **10.** Insurance Expense

_____ **3.** Owner, Capital       _____ **11.** Accumulated Depreciation

_____ **4.** Wages Payable       _____ **12.** Interest Revenue

_____ **5.** Machinery       _____ **13.** Accounts Receivable

_____ **6.** Interest Receivable       _____ **14.** Rent Expense

_____ **7.** Interest Expense       _____ **15.** Depreciation Expense

_____ **8.** Owner, Withdrawals       _____ **16.** Cash

**Exercise 4-9**

Preparing adjusting entries from a work sheet  P1

Use the following information from the Adjustments columns of a 10-column work sheet to prepare the necessary adjusting journal entries (a) through (e).

| | A | B | C | D | E | F | G | H | I | J | K | L |
|---|---|---|---|---|---|---|---|---|---|---|---|---|
| 1 | | | | | | | | | | | Balance Sheet and Statement of Owner's Equity | |
| 2 | | | Unadjusted Trial Balance | | Adjustments | | Adjusted Trial Balance | | Income Statement | | | |
| 3 | | | | | | | | | | | | |
| 4 | **No.** | **Account Title** | **Dr.** | **Cr.** | **Dr.** | **Cr.** | **Dr.** | **Cr.** | **Dr.** | **Cr.** | **Dr.** | **Cr.** |
| 5 | 109 | Interest receivable | | | | | (d) $ 580 | | | | | |
| 6 | 124 | Office supplies | | | | | | (b) $1,650 | | | | |
| 7 | 128 | Prepaid insurance | | | | | | (a) 900 | | | | |
| 8 | 164 | Accumulated depreciation—Office equipment | | | | | | (c) 3,300 | | | | |
| 9 | 209 | Salaries payable | | | | | | (e) 660 | | | | |
| 10 | 409 | Interest revenue | | | | | | (d) 580 | | | | |
| 11 | 612 | Depreciation expense—Office equipment | | | | | (c) 3,300 | | | | | |
| 12 | 620 | Office salaries expense | | | | | (e) 660 | | | | | |
| 13 | 636 | Insurance expense—Office equipment | | | | | (a) 432 | | | | | |
| 14 | 637 | Insurance expense—Store equipment | | | | | (a) 468 | | | | | |
| 15 | 650 | Office supplies expense | | | | | (b) 1,650 | | | | | |
| 16 | | Totals | | | | | $7,090 | $7,090 | | | | |
| 17 | | | | | | | | | | | | |

The Adjusted Trial Balance columns of a 10-column work sheet for Propel Company follow. Complete the work sheet by extending the account balances into the appropriate financial statement columns and by entering the amount of net income for the reporting period.

**Exercise 4-10**
Extending accounts in a work sheet **P1**

| A | B | C | D | E | F | G | H | I | J | K | L |
|---|---|---|---|---|---|---|---|---|---|---|---|
| | | Unadjusted Trial Balance | | Adjustments | | Adjusted Trial Balance | | Income Statement | | Balance Sheet and Statement of Owner's Equity | |
| No. | Account Title | Dr. | Cr. | Dr. | Cr. | Dr. | Cr. | Dr. | Cr. | Dr. | Cr. |
| 101 | Cash | | | | | $ 6,000 | | | | | |
| 106 | Accounts receivable | | | | | 26,200 | | | | | |
| 153 | Trucks | | | | | 41,000 | | | | | |
| 154 | Accumulated depreciation—Trucks | | | | | | $ 16,500 | | | | |
| 183 | Land | | | | | 30,000 | | | | | |
| 201 | Accounts payable | | | | | | 14,000 | | | | |
| 209 | Salaries payable | | | | | | 3,200 | | | | |
| 233 | Unearned fees | | | | | | 2,600 | | | | |
| 301 | J. Propel, Capital | | | | | | 64,500 | | | | |
| 302 | J. Propel, Withdrawals | | | | | 14,400 | | | | | |
| 401 | Plumbing fees earned | | | | | | 79,000 | | | | |
| 611 | Depreciation expense—Trucks | | | | | 5,500 | | | | | |
| 622 | Salaries expense | | | | | 37,000 | | | | | |
| 640 | Rent expense | | | | | 12,000 | | | | | |
| 677 | Miscellaneous expenses | | | | | 7,700 | | | | | |
| | Totals | | | | | $179,800 | $179,800 | | | | |

**Check** Net income, $16,800

These partially completed Income Statement columns from a 10-column work sheet are for Welch's Red Sail Rental Company. (1) Use the information to determine the amount that should be entered on the net income line of the work sheet. (2) Prepare the company's closing entries. The owner, L. Welch, did not make any withdrawals this period.

**Exercise 4-11**
Completing the income statement columns and preparing closing entries
**P1 P2**

| Account Title | Debit | Credit |
|---|---|---|
| Rent earned | | 102,000 |
| Salaries expense | 45,300 | |
| Insurance expense | 6,400 | |
| Dock rental expense | 15,000 | |
| Boat supplies expense | 3,200 | |
| Depreciation expense—Boats | 19,500 | |
| Totals | | |
| Net income | | |
| Totals | | |

**Check** Net income, $12,600

The following unadjusted trial balance contains the accounts and balances of Dalton Delivery Company as of December 31, 2011, its first year of operations.

(1) Use the following information about the company's adjustments to complete a 10-column work sheet.

**a.** Unrecorded depreciation on the trucks at the end of the year is $35,000.

**b.** The total amount of accrued interest expense at year-end is $8,000.

**c.** The cost of unused office supplies still available at the year-end is $1,000.

(2) Prepare the year-end closing entries for this company, and determine the capital amount to be reported on its year-end balance sheet.

**Exercise 4-12**
Preparing a work sheet and recording closing entries
**P1 P2**

| | A | B | C |
|---|---|---|---|
| 1 | | Unadjusted Trial Balance | |
| 2 | **Account Title** | Debit | Credit |
| 3 | Cash | $ 14,000 | |
| 4 | Accounts receivable | 33,000 | |
| 5 | Office supplies | 4,000 | |
| 6 | Trucks | 340,000 | |
| 7 | Accumulated depreciation—Trucks | | $70,000 |
| 8 | Land | 150,000 | |
| 9 | Accounts payable | | 22,000 |
| 10 | Interest payable | | 6,000 |
| 11 | Long-term notes payable | | 104,000 |
| 12 | V. Dalton, Capital | | 322,000 |
| 13 | V. Dalton, Withdrawals | 38,000 | |
| 14 | Delivery fees earned | | 256,000 |
| 15 | Depreciation expense—Truck | 45,000 | |
| 16 | Salaries expense | 120,000 | |
| 17 | Office supplies expense | 14,000 | |
| 18 | Interest expense | 6,000 | |
| 19 | Repairs expense—Trucks | 16,000 | |
| 20 | Totals | $780,000 | $780,000 |
| 21 | | | |

**Check**   Adj. trial balance totals, $817,000; Net income, $15,000

---

**Exercise 4-13ᴬ**

Preparing reversing entries

P4

The following two events occurred for Tanger Co. on October 31, 2011, the end of its fiscal year.

**a.** Tanger rents a building from its owner for $3,200 per month. By a prearrangement, the company delayed paying October's rent until November 5. On this date, the company paid the rent for both October and November.

**b.** Tanger rents space in a building it owns to a tenant for $750 per month. By prearrangement, the tenant delayed paying the October rent until November 8. On this date, the tenant paid the rent for both October and November.

**Required**

**1.** Prepare adjusting entries that the company must record for these events as of October 31.

**2.** Assuming Tanger does *not* use reversing entries, prepare journal entries to record Tanger's payment of rent on November 5 and the collection of rent on November 8 from Tanger's tenant.

**3.** Assuming that the company uses reversing entries, prepare reversing entries on November 1 and the journal entries to record Tanger's payment of rent on November 5 and the collection of rent on November 8 from Tanger's tenant.

---

**Exercise 4-14ᴬ**

Preparing reversing entries

P4

Hinson Company records prepaid assets and unearned revenues in balance sheet accounts. The following information was used to prepare adjusting entries for the company as of August 31, the end of the company's fiscal year.

**a.** The company has earned $5,000 in service fees that were not yet recorded at period-end.

**b.** The expired portion of prepaid insurance is $2,700.

**c.** The company has earned $1,900 of its Unearned Service Fees account balance.

**d.** Depreciation expense for office equipment is $2,300.

**e.** Employees have earned but have not been paid salaries of $2,400.

Prepare any necessary reversing entries for the accounting adjustments *a* through *e* assuming that the company uses reversing entries in its accounting system.

---

**Exercise 4-15**

Determining effects of closing entries

C1

Argosy Company began the current period with a $14,000 credit balance in the D. Argosy, Capital account. At the end of the period, the company's adjusted account balances include the following temporary accounts with normal balances.

| | | | | |
|---|---|---|---|---|
| Service fees earned | $35,000 | Interest revenue | $3,500 |
| Salaries expense | 19,000 | D. Argosy, Withdrawals | 6,000 |
| Depreciation expense | 4,000 | Utilities expense | 2,300 |

After closing the revenue and expense accounts, what will be the balance of the Income Summary account? After all closing entries are journalized and posted, what will be the balance of the D. Argosy, Capital account?

Following are **Nintendo**'s revenue and expense accounts for a recent calendar year (yen in millions). Prepare the company's closing entries for its revenues and its expenses.

| | |
|---|---|
| Net sales . . . . . . . . . . . . . . . | ¥1,838,622 |
| Cost of sales . . . . . . . . . . . . . | 1,044,981 |
| Advertising expense . . . . . . . . | 117,308 |
| Other expense, net . . . . . . . . . | 397,244 |

**Exercise 4-16**
Preparing closing entries

P2

The following data are taken from the unadjusted trial balance of the Madison Company at December 31, 2011. Each account carries a normal balance and the accounts are shown here in alphabetical order.

**Exercise 4-17**
Completing a worksheet

P1

| | | | | | |
|---|---|---|---|---|---|
| Accounts Payable . . . . . . . . . . . . . . . | $ 2 | Prepaid Insurance . . | $ 6 | T. Madison, Withdrawals . . . | $2 |
| Accounts Receivable . . . . . . . . . . . . . | 4 | Revenue . . . . . . . . . | 25 | Unearned Revenue . . . . . . . | 4 |
| Accumulated Depreciation—Equip. . . | 5 | Salaries Expense . . . . | 6 | Utilities Expense . . . . . . . . | 4 |
| Cash . . . . . . . . . . . . . . . . . . . . . . . . | 7 | Supplies . . . . . . . . . | 8 | | |
| Equipment . . . . . . . . . . . . . . . . . . . | 13 | T. Madison, Capital . . | 14 | | |

1. Use the data above to prepare a worksheet. Enter the accounts in proper order and enter their balances in the correct debit or credit column.

2. Use the following adjustment information to complete the worksheet.
   a. Depreciation on equipment, $1
   b. Accrued salaries, $2
   c. The $4 of unearned revenue has been earned
   d. Supplies available at December 31, 2011, $5
   e. Expired insurance, $5

**connect**

In the blank space beside each numbered balance sheet item, enter the letter of its balance sheet classification. If the item should not appear on the balance sheet, enter a *Z* in the blank.

**A.** Current assets    **D.** Intangible assets    **F.** Long-term liabilities
**B.** Long-term investments    **E.** Current liabilities    **G.** Equity
**C.** Plant assets

**PROBLEM SET A**

**Problem 4-1A**
Determining balance sheet classifications

C3

| | |
|---|---|
| _____ **1.** Office equipment | _____ **11.** Depreciation expense—Building |
| _____ **2.** Office supplies | _____ **12.** Prepaid rent |
| _____ **3.** Buildings | _____ **13.** Interest receivable |
| _____ **4.** Store supplies | _____ **14.** Taxes payable |
| _____ **5.** Accumulated depreciation—Trucks | _____ **15.** Automobiles |
| _____ **6.** Land (used in operations) | _____ **16.** Notes payable (due in 3 years) |
| _____ **7.** Repairs expense | _____ **17.** Accounts payable |
| _____ **8.** Cash | _____ **18.** Prepaid insurance |
| _____ **9.** Current portion of long-term note payable | _____ **19.** Owner, Capital |
| _____ **10.** Long-term investment in stock | _____ **20.** Unearned services revenue |

On April 1, 2011, Jennifer Stafford created a new travel agency, See-It-Now Travel. The following transactions occurred during the company's first month.

**Problem 4-2A**
Applying the accounting cycle

C1 C2 P2 P3

mhhe.com/wildFAP20e

| | | |
|---|---|---|
| April | 1 | Stafford invested $20,000 cash and computer equipment worth $40,000 in the company. |
| | 2 | The company rented furnished office space by paying $1,700 cash for the first month's (April) rent. |
| | 3 | The company purchased $1,100 of office supplies for cash. |
| | 10 | The company paid $3,600 cash for the premium on a 12-month insurance policy. Coverage begins on April 11. |
| | 14 | The company paid $1,800 cash for two weeks' salaries earned by employees. |
| | 24 | The company collected $7,900 cash on commissions from airlines on tickets obtained for customers. |
| | 28 | The company paid $1,800 cash for two weeks' salaries earned by employees. |
| | 29 | The company paid $250 cash for minor repairs to the company's computer. |
| | 30 | The company paid $650 cash for this month's telephone bill. |
| | 30 | Stafford withdrew $1,500 cash from the company for personal use. |

The company's chart of accounts follows:

| No. | Account | No. | Account |
|---|---|---|---|
| 101 | Cash | 405 | Commissions Earned |
| 106 | Accounts Receivable | 612 | Depreciation Expense—Computer Equip. |
| 124 | Office Supplies | 622 | Salaries Expense |
| 128 | Prepaid Insurance | 637 | Insurance Expense |
| 167 | Computer Equipment | 640 | Rent Expense |
| 168 | Accumulated Depreciation—Computer Equip. | 650 | Office Supplies Expense |
| 209 | Salaries Payable | 684 | Repairs Expense |
| 301 | J. Stafford, Capital | 688 | Telephone Expense |
| 302 | J. Stafford, Withdrawals | 901 | Income Summary |

### Required

**Check**    (3) Unadj. trial balance totals, $67,900

1. Use the balance column format to set up each ledger account listed in its chart of accounts.
2. Prepare journal entries to record the transactions for April and post them to the ledger accounts. The company records prepaid and unearned items in balance sheet accounts.
3. Prepare an unadjusted trial balance as of April 30.

(4a) Dr. Insurance Expense, $200

4. Use the following information to journalize and post adjusting entries for the month:
   a. Two-thirds of one month's insurance coverage has expired.
   b. At the end of the month, $700 of office supplies are still available.
   c. This month's depreciation on the computer equipment is $600.
   d. Employees earned $320 of unpaid and unrecorded salaries as of month-end.
   e. The company earned $1,650 of commissions that are not yet billed at month-end.

(5) Net income, $1,830;
J. Stafford, Capital (4/30/2011),
$60,330; Total assets, $60,650

5. Prepare the income statement and the statement of owner's equity for the month of April and the balance sheet at April 30, 2011.
6. Prepare journal entries to close the temporary accounts and post these entries to the ledger.

(7) P-C trial balance totals, $61,250

7. Prepare a post-closing trial balance.

---

**Problem 4-3A**
Preparing trial balances, closing entries, and financial statements

C3 P2 P3

mhhe.com/wildFAP20e

The adjusted trial balance of Kobe Repairs on December 31, 2011, follows.

| | **KOBE REPAIRS** Adjusted Trial Balance December 31, 2011 | | |
|---|---|---|---|
| **No.** | **Account Title** | **Debit** | **Credit** |
| 101 | Cash | $ 13,000 | |
| 124 | Office supplies | 1,200 | |
| 128 | Prepaid insurance | 1,950 | |
| 167 | Equipment | 48,000 | |
| 168 | Accumulated depreciation—Equipment | | $ 4,000 |
| 201 | Accounts payable | | 12,000 |
| 210 | Wages payable | | 500 |
| 301 | S. Kobe, Capital | | 40,000 |
| 302 | S. Kobe, Withdrawals | 15,000 | |
| 401 | Repair fees earned | | 77,750 |
| 612 | Depreciation expense—Equipment | 4,000 | |
| 623 | Wages expense | 36,500 | |
| 637 | Insurance expense | 700 | |
| 640 | Rent expense | 9,600 | |
| 650 | Office supplies expense | 2,600 | |
| 690 | Utilities expense | 1,700 | |
| | Totals | $134,250 | $134,250 |

### Required

**Check**    (1) Ending capital balance, $47,650; net income, $22,650

1. Prepare an income statement and a statement of owner's equity for the year 2011, and a classified balance sheet at December 31, 2011. There are no owner investments in 2011.

2. Enter the adjusted trial balance in the first two columns of a six-column table. Use columns three and four for closing entry information and the last two columns for a post-closing trial balance. Insert an Income Summary account as the last item in the trial balance.

(2) P-C trial balance totals, $64,150

3. Enter closing entry information in the six-column table and prepare journal entries for it.

**Analysis Component**

4. Assume for this part only that

   **a.** None of the $700 insurance expense had expired during the year. Instead, assume it is a prepayment of the next period's insurance protection.

   **b.** There are no earned and unpaid wages at the end of the year. (*Hint:* Reverse the $500 wages payable accrual.)

Describe the financial statement changes that would result from these two assumptions.

---

The adjusted trial balance for Sharp Construction as of December 31, 2011, follows.

**Problem 4-4A**
Preparing closing entries, financial statements, and ratios

**C3 A1 P2**

| | SHARP CONSTRUCTION<br>Adjusted Trial Balance<br>December 31, 2011 | | |
|---|---|---|---|
| **No.** | **Account Title** | **Debit** | **Credit** |
| 101 | Cash | $ 4,000 | |
| 104 | Short-term investments | 22,000 | |
| 126 | Supplies | 7,100 | |
| 128 | Prepaid insurance | 6,000 | |
| 167 | Equipment | 39,000 | |
| 168 | Accumulated depreciation—Equipment | | $ 20,000 |
| 173 | Building | 130,000 | |
| 174 | Accumulated depreciation—Building | | 55,000 |
| 183 | Land | 45,000 | |
| 201 | Accounts payable | | 15,500 |
| 203 | Interest payable | | 1,500 |
| 208 | Rent payable | | 2,500 |
| 210 | Wages payable | | 1,500 |
| 213 | Property taxes payable | | 800 |
| 233 | Unearned professional fees | | 6,500 |
| 251 | Long-term notes payable | | 66,000 |
| 301 | J. Sharp, Capital | | 82,700 |
| 302 | J. Sharp, Withdrawals | 12,000 | |
| 401 | Professional fees earned | | 96,000 |
| 406 | Rent earned | | 13,000 |
| 407 | Dividends earned | | 1,900 |
| 409 | Interest earned | | 1,000 |
| 606 | Depreciation expense—Building | 10,000 | |
| 612 | Depreciation expense—Equipment | 5,000 | |
| 623 | Wages expense | 31,000 | |
| 633 | Interest expense | 4,100 | |
| 637 | Insurance expense | 9,000 | |
| 640 | Rent expense | 12,400 | |
| 652 | Supplies expense | 6,400 | |
| 682 | Postage expense | 3,200 | |
| 683 | Property taxes expense | 4,000 | |
| 684 | Repairs expense | 7,900 | |
| 688 | Telephone expense | 2,200 | |
| 690 | Utilities expense | 3,600 | |
| | Totals | $363,900 | $363,900 |

J. Sharp invested $50,000 cash in the business during year 2011 (the December 31, 2010, credit balance of the J. Sharp, Capital account was $32,700). Sharp Construction is required to make a $6,600 payment on its long-term notes payable during 2012.

**Required**

**Check** (1) Total assets (12/31/2011), $178,100; Net income, $13,100

**1.** Prepare the income statement and the statement of owner's equity for the calendar year 2011 and the classified balance sheet at December 31, 2011.

**2.** Prepare the necessary closing entries at December 31, 2011.

**3.** Use the information in the financial statements to compute these ratios: (*a*) return on assets (total assets at December 31, 2010, was $200,000), (*b*) debt ratio, (*c*) profit margin ratio (use total revenues as the denominator), and (*d*) current ratio.

---

**Problem 4-5A**

Preparing a work sheet, adjusting and closing entries, and financial statements

C3 P1 P2

The following unadjusted trial balance is for Adams Construction Co. as of the end of its 2011 fiscal year. The June 30, 2010, credit balance of the owner's capital account was $52,660, and the owner invested $25,000 cash in the company during the 2011 fiscal year.

| | A | B | C | D |
|---|---|---|---|---|
| 1 | | **ADAMS CONSTRUCTION CO.** | | |
| 2 | | **Unadjusted Trial Balance** | | |
| 3 | | **June 30, 2011** | | |
| 4 | **No.** | **Account Title** | **Debit** | **Credit** |
| 5 | 101 | Cash | $ 17,500 | |
| 6 | 126 | Supplies | 8,900 | |
| 7 | 128 | Prepaid insurance | 6,200 | |
| 8 | 167 | Equipment | 131,000 | |
| 9 | 168 | Accumulated depreciation—Equipment | | $ 25,250 |
| 10 | 201 | Accounts payable | | 5,800 |
| 11 | 203 | Interest payable | | 0 |
| 12 | 208 | Rent payable | | 0 |
| 13 | 210 | Wages payable | | 0 |
| 14 | 213 | Property taxes payable | | 0 |
| 15 | 251 | Long-term notes payable | | 24,000 |
| 16 | 301 | S. Adams, Capital | | 77,660 |
| 17 | 302 | S. Adams, Withdrawals | 30,000 | |
| 18 | 401 | Construction fees earned | | 134,000 |
| 19 | 612 | Depreciation expense—Equipment | 0 | |
| 20 | 623 | Wages expense | 45,860 | |
| 21 | 633 | Interest expense | 2,640 | |
| 22 | 637 | Insurance expense | 0 | |
| 23 | 640 | Rent expense | 13,200 | |
| 24 | 652 | Supplies expense | 0 | |
| 25 | 683 | Property taxes expense | 4,600 | |
| 26 | 684 | Repairs expense | 2,810 | |
| 27 | 690 | Utilities expense | 4,000 | |
| 28 | | Totals | $266,710 | $266,710 |
| 29 | | | | |

**Required**

**1.** Prepare a 10-column work sheet for fiscal year 2011, starting with the unadjusted trial balance and including adjustments based on these additional facts.

**a.** The supplies available at the end of fiscal year 2011 had a cost of $3,200.

**b.** The cost of expired insurance for the fiscal year is $3,900.

**c.** Annual depreciation on equipment is $8,500.

**d.** The June utilities expense of $550 is not included in the unadjusted trial balance because the bill arrived after the trial balance was prepared. The $550 amount owed needs to be recorded.

**e.** The company's employees have earned $1,600 of accrued wages at fiscal year-end.

**f.** The rent expense incurred and not yet paid or recorded at fiscal year-end is $200.

**g.** Additional property taxes of $900 have been assessed for this fiscal year but have not been paid or recorded in the accounts.

**h.** The long-term note payable bears interest at 12% per year. The unadjusted Interest Expense account equals the amount paid for the first 11 months of the 2011 fiscal year. The $240 accrued interest for June has not yet been paid or recorded. (The company is required to make a $5,000 payment toward the note payable during the 2012 fiscal year.)

**2.** Enter adjusting and closing information in the work sheet; then journalize the adjusting and closing entries.

**3.** Prepare the income statement and the statement of owner's equity for the year ended June 30 and the classified balance sheet at June 30, 2011.

**Check**  (3) Total assets, $120,250; Current liabilities, $14,290; Net income, $39,300

### Analysis Component

**4.** Analyze the following separate errors and describe how each would affect the 10-column work sheet. Explain whether the error is likely to be discovered in completing the work sheet and, if not, the effect of the error on the financial statements.

   **a.** Assume that the adjustment for supplies used consisted of a credit to Supplies and a debit to Supplies Expense for $3,200, when the correct amount was $5,700.

   **b.** When the adjusted trial balance in the work sheet is completed, assume that the $17,500 Cash balance is incorrectly entered in the Credit column.

---

The following six-column table for Bullseye Ranges includes the unadjusted trial balance as of December 31, 2011.

**Problem 4-6A**[A]

Preparing adjusting, reversing, and next period entries

**P4**

|  | A | B | C | D | E | F | G |
|---|---|---|---|---|---|---|---|
| 1 |  | **BULLSEYE RANGES** | | | | | |
| 2 |  | **December 31, 2011** | | | | | |
| 3 |  | **Unadjusted** | | | | **Adjusted** | |
| 4 |  | **Trial Balance** | | **Adjustments** | | **Trial Balance** | |
| 5 | **Account Title** | **Dr.** | **Cr.** | **Dr.** | **Cr.** | **Dr.** | **Cr.** |
| 6 | Cash | $ 13,000 | | | | | |
| 7 | Accounts receivable | 0 | | | | | |
| 8 | Supplies | 5,500 | | | | | |
| 9 | Equipment | 130,000 | | | | | |
| 10 | Accumulated depreciation—Equipment | | $ 25,000 | | | | |
| 11 | Interest payable | | 0 | | | | |
| 12 | Salaries payable | | 0 | | | | |
| 13 | Unearned member fees | | 14,000 | | | | |
| 14 | Notes payable | | 50,000 | | | | |
| 15 | T. Allen, Capital | | 58,250 | | | | |
| 16 | T. Allen, Withdrawals | 20,000 | | | | | |
| 17 | Member fees earned | | 53,000 | | | | |
| 18 | Depreciation expense—Equipment | 0 | | | | | |
| 19 | Salaries expense | 28,000 | | | | | |
| 20 | Interest expense | 3,750 | | | | | |
| 21 | Supplies expense | 0 | | | | | |
| 22 | Totals | $200,250 | $200,250 | | | | |
| 23 | | | | | | | |

### Required

**1.** Complete the six-column table by entering adjustments that reflect the following information.

   **a.** As of December 31, 2011, employees had earned $900 of unpaid and unrecorded salaries. The next payday is January 4, at which time $1,600 of salaries will be paid.

   **b.** The cost of supplies still available at December 31, 2011, is $2,700.

   **c.** The notes payable requires an interest payment to be made every three months. The amount of unrecorded accrued interest at December 31, 2011, is $1,250. The next interest payment, at an amount of $1,500, is due on January 15, 2012.

   **d.** Analysis of the unearned member fees account shows $5,600 remaining unearned at December 31, 2011.

   **e.** In addition to the member fees included in the revenue account balance, the company has earned another $9,100 in unrecorded fees that will be collected on January 31, 2012. The company is also expected to collect $8,000 on that same day for new fees earned in January 2012.

   **f.** Depreciation expense for the year is $12,500.

**Check**  (1) Adjusted trial balance totals, $224,000

**2.** Prepare journal entries for the adjustments entered in the six-column table for part 1.

**3.** Prepare journal entries to reverse the effects of the adjusting entries that involve accruals.

**4.** Prepare journal entries to record the cash payments and cash collections described for January.

## PROBLEM SET B

**Problem 4-1B**
Determining balance sheet classifications

C3

In the blank space beside each numbered balance sheet item, enter the letter of its balance sheet classification. If the item should not appear on the balance sheet, enter a *Z* in the blank.

**A.** Current assets　　　　　**E.** Current liabilities

**B.** Long-term investments　　**F.** Long-term liabilities

**C.** Plant assets　　　　　　**G.** Equity

**D.** Intangible assets

_____　**1.** Machinery

_____　**2.** Prepaid insurance

_____　**3.** Current portion of long-term note payable

_____　**4.** Interest receivable

_____　**5.** Rent receivable

_____　**6.** Land (used in operations)

_____　**7.** Copyrights

_____　**8.** Rent revenue

_____　**9.** Depreciation expense—Trucks

_____　**10.** Long-term investment in stock

_____　**11.** Office supplies

_____　**12.** Interest payable

_____　**13.** Owner, Capital

_____　**14.** Notes receivable (due in 120 days)

_____　**15.** Accumulated depreciation—Trucks

_____　**16.** Salaries payable

_____　**17.** Commissions earned

_____　**18.** Income taxes payable

_____　**19.** Office equipment

_____　**20.** Notes payable (due in 15 years)

---

**Problem 4-2B**
Applying the accounting cycle

C1　C2　P2　P3　

On July 1, 2011, Lucinda Fogle created a new self-storage business, KeepSafe Co. The following transactions occurred during the company's first month.

July　1　Fogle invested $20,000 cash and buildings worth $120,000 in the company.
　　　2　The company rented equipment by paying $1,800 cash for the first month's (July) rent.
　　　5　The company purchased $2,300 of office supplies for cash.
　　　10　The company paid $5,400 cash for the premium on a 12-month insurance policy. Coverage begins on July 11.
　　　14　The company paid an employee $900 cash for two weeks' salary earned.
　　　24　The company collected $8,800 cash for storage fees from customers.
　　　28　The company paid $900 cash for two weeks' salary earned by an employee.
　　　29　The company paid $850 cash for minor repairs to a leaking roof.
　　　30　The company paid $300 cash for this month's telephone bill.
　　　31　Fogle withdrew $1,600 cash from the company for personal use.

The company's chart of accounts follows:

| | | | | |
|---|---|---|---|---|
| 101 | Cash | | 401 | Storage Fees Earned |
| 106 | Accounts Receivable | | 606 | Depreciation Expense—Buildings |
| 124 | Office Supplies | | 622 | Salaries Expense |
| 128 | Prepaid Insurance | | 637 | Insurance Expense |
| 173 | Buildings | | 640 | Rent Expense |
| 174 | Accumulated Depreciation—Buildings | | 650 | Office Supplies Expense |
| 209 | Salaries Payable | | 684 | Repairs Expense |
| 301 | L. Fogle, Capital | | 688 | Telephone Expense |
| 302 | L. Fogle, Withdrawals | | 901 | Income Summary |

**Required**

**1.** Use the balance column format to set up each ledger account listed in its chart of accounts.

**2.** Prepare journal entries to record the transactions for July and post them to the ledger accounts. Record prepaid and unearned items in balance sheet accounts.

**3.** Prepare an unadjusted trial balance as of July 31.

**Check** (3) Unadj. trial balance totals, $148,800

**4.** Use the following information to journalize and post adjusting entries for the month:

   **a.** Two-thirds of one month's insurance coverage has expired.

   **b.** At the end of the month, $1,550 of office supplies are still available.

   **c.** This month's depreciation on the buildings is $1,200.

   **d.** An employee earned $180 of unpaid and unrecorded salary as of month-end.

   **e.** The company earned $950 of storage fees that are not yet billed at month-end.

**5.** Prepare the income statement and the statement of owner's equity for the month of July and the balance sheet at July 31, 2011.

**6.** Prepare journal entries to close the temporary accounts and post these entries to the ledger.

**7.** Prepare a post-closing trial balance.

(4a) Dr. Insurance Expense, $300

(5) Net income, $2,570; L. Fogle, Capital (7/31/2011), $140,970; Total assets, $141,150

(7) P-C trial balance totals, $142,350

---

Heel-To-Toe Shoes' adjusted trial balance on December 31, 2011, follows.

**Problem 4-3B**

Preparing trial balances, closing entries, and financial statements

**C3  P2  P3**

| No. | Account Title | Debit | Credit |
|-----|--------------|-------|--------|
| | **HEEL-TO-TOE SHOES**<br>**Adjusted Trial Balance**<br>**December 31, 2011** | | |
| 101 | Cash | $ 13,450 | |
| 125 | Store supplies | 4,140 | |
| 128 | Prepaid insurance | 2,200 | |
| 167 | Equipment | 33,000 | |
| 168 | Accumulated depreciation—Equipment | | $ 9,000 |
| 201 | Accounts payable | | 1,000 |
| 210 | Wages payable | | 3,200 |
| 301 | P. Holt, Capital | | 31,650 |
| 302 | P. Holt, Withdrawals | 16,000 | |
| 401 | Repair fees earned | | 62,000 |
| 612 | Depreciation expense—Equipment | 3,000 | |
| 623 | Wages expense | 28,400 | |
| 637 | Insurance expense | 1,100 | |
| 640 | Rent expense | 2,400 | |
| 651 | Store supplies expense | 1,300 | |
| 690 | Utilities expense | 1,860 | |
| | Totals | $106,850 | $106,850 |

**Required**

**1.** Prepare an income statement and a statement of owner's equity for the year 2011, and a classified balance sheet at December 31, 2011. There are no owner investments in 2011.

**2.** Enter the adjusted trial balance in the first two columns of a six-column table. Use the middle two columns for closing entry information and the last two columns for a post-closing trial balance. Insert an Income Summary account (No. 901) as the last item in the trial balance.

**3.** Enter closing entry information in the six-column table and prepare journal entries for it.

**Check** (1) Ending capital balance, $39,590

(2) P-C trial balance totals, $52,790

*Analysis Component*

**4.** Assume for this part only that

   **a.** None of the $1,100 insurance expense had expired during the year. Instead, assume it is a prepayment of the next period's insurance protection.

   **b.** There are no earned and unpaid wages at the end of the year. (*Hint:* Reverse the $3,200 wages payable accrual.)

Describe the financial statement changes that would result from these two assumptions.

**Problem 4-4B**
Preparing closing entries,
financial statements, and ratios

C3  A1  P2

The adjusted trial balance for Giovanni Co. as of December 31, 2011, follows.

| | GIOVANNI COMPANY<br>Adjusted Trial Balance<br>December 31, 2011 | | |
|---|---|---|---|
| **No.** | **Account Title** | **Debit** | **Credit** |
| 101 | Cash ...................................... | $  6,400 | |
| 104 | Short-term investments ..................... | 10,200 | |
| 126 | Supplies .................................. | 3,600 | |
| 128 | Prepaid insurance ......................... | 800 | |
| 167 | Equipment .............................. | 18,000 | |
| 168 | Accumulated depreciation—Equipment ........ | | $  3,000 |
| 173 | Building ................................. | 90,000 | |
| 174 | Accumulated depreciation—Building .......... | | 9,000 |
| 183 | Land ..................................... | 28,500 | |
| 201 | Accounts payable ......................... | | 2,500 |
| 203 | Interest payable .......................... | | 1,400 |
| 208 | Rent payable ............................. | | 200 |
| 210 | Wages payable ........................... | | 1,180 |
| 213 | Property taxes payable ..................... | | 2,330 |
| 233 | Unearned professional fees .................. | | 650 |
| 251 | Long-term notes payable .................... | | 32,000 |
| 301 | J. Giovanni, Capital ......................... | | 91,800 |
| 302 | J. Giovanni, Withdrawals ................... | 6,000 | |
| 401 | Professional fees earned .................... | | 47,000 |
| 406 | Rent earned .............................. | | 3,600 |
| 407 | Dividends earned .......................... | | 500 |
| 409 | Interest earned ........................... | | 1,120 |
| 606 | Depreciation expense—Building .............. | 2,000 | |
| 612 | Depreciation expense—Equipment ............ | 1,000 | |
| 623 | Wages expense ........................... | 17,500 | |
| 633 | Interest expense .......................... | 1,200 | |
| 637 | Insurance expense ........................ | 1,425 | |
| 640 | Rent expense ............................. | 1,800 | |
| 652 | Supplies expense ......................... | 900 | |
| 682 | Postage expense .......................... | 310 | |
| 683 | Property taxes expense ..................... | 3,825 | |
| 684 | Repairs expense .......................... | 579 | |
| 688 | Telephone expense ........................ | 421 | |
| 690 | Utilities expense .......................... | 1,820 | |
| | Totals .................................. | $196,280 | $196,280 |

J. Giovanni invested $30,000 cash in the business during year 2011 (the December 31, 2010, credit balance of the J. Giovanni, Capital account was $61,800). Giovanni Company is required to make a $6,400 payment on its long-term notes payable during 2012.

**Required**

**Check**  (1) Total assets (12/31/2011), $145,500; Net income, $19,440

1. Prepare the income statement and the statement of owner's equity for the calendar year 2011 and the classified balance sheet at December 31, 2011.

2. Prepare the necessary closing entries at December 31, 2011.

3. Use the information in the financial statements to calculate these ratios: (*a*) return on assets (total assets at December 31, 2010, were $150,000), (*b*) debt ratio, (*c*) profit margin ratio (use total revenues as the denominator), and (*d*) current ratio.

The following unadjusted trial balance is for Crush Demolition Company as of the end of its April 30, 2011, fiscal year. The April 30, 2010, credit balance of the owner's capital account was $36,900, and the owner invested $30,000 cash in the company during the 2011 fiscal year.

**Problem 4-5B**
Preparing a work sheet, adjusting and closing entries, and financial statements

**C3  P1  P2**

|     | No. | Account Title | Debit | Credit |
|-----|-----|---------------|-------|--------|
| 1 | | CRUSH DEMOLITION COMPANY | | |
| 2 | | Unadjusted Trial Balance | | |
| 3 | | April 30, 2011 | | |
| 4 | No. | Account Title | Debit | Credit |
| 5 | 101 | Cash | $ 9,000 | |
| 6 | 126 | Supplies | 18,000 | |
| 7 | 128 | Prepaid insurance | 14,600 | |
| 8 | 167 | Equipment | 140,000 | |
| 9 | 168 | Accumulated depreciation—Equipment | | $ 10,000 |
| 10 | 201 | Accounts payable | | 16,000 |
| 11 | 203 | Interest payable | | 0 |
| 12 | 208 | Rent payable | | 0 |
| 13 | 210 | Wages payable | | 0 |
| 14 | 213 | Property taxes payable | | 0 |
| 15 | 251 | Long-term notes payable | | 20,000 |
| 16 | 301 | J. Bonair, Capital | | 66,900 |
| 17 | 302 | J. Bonair, Withdrawals | 24,000 | |
| 18 | 401 | Demolition fees earned | | 177,000 |
| 19 | 612 | Depreciation expense—Equipment | 0 | |
| 20 | 623 | Wages expense | 51,400 | |
| 21 | 633 | Interest expense | 2,200 | |
| 22 | 637 | Insurance expense | 0 | |
| 23 | 640 | Rent expense | 8,800 | |
| 24 | 652 | Supplies expense | 0 | |
| 25 | 683 | Property taxes expense | 8,400 | |
| 26 | 684 | Repairs expense | 6,700 | |
| 27 | 690 | Utilities expense | 6,800 | |
| 28 | | Totals | $289,900 | $289,900 |
| 29 | | | | |

**Required**

1. Prepare a 10-column work sheet for fiscal year 2011, starting with the unadjusted trial balance and including adjustments based on these additional facts.

   a. The supplies available at the end of fiscal year 2011 had a cost of $8,100.

   b. The cost of expired insurance for the fiscal year is $11,500.

   c. Annual depreciation on equipment is $18,000.

   d. The April utilities expense of $700 is not included in the unadjusted trial balance because the bill arrived after the trial balance was prepared. The $700 amount owed needs to be recorded.

   e. The company's employees have earned $2,200 of accrued wages at fiscal year-end.

   f. The rent expense incurred and not yet paid or recorded at fiscal year-end is $5,360.

   g. Additional property taxes of $450 have been assessed for this fiscal year but have not been paid or recorded in the accounts.

   h. The long-term note payable bears interest at 12% per year. The unadjusted Interest Expense account equals the amount paid for the first 11 months of the 2011 fiscal year. The $200 accrued interest for April has not yet been paid or recorded. (Note that the company is required to make a $4,000 payment toward the note payable during the 2012 fiscal year.)

2. Enter adjusting and closing information in the work sheet; then journalize the adjusting and closing entries.

3. Prepare the income statement and the statement of owner's equity for the year ended April 30 and the classified balance sheet at April 30, 2011.

**Check**  (3) Total assets, $132,200; current liabilities, $28,910; Net income, $44,390

**Analysis Component**

4. Analyze the following separate errors and describe how each would affect the 10-column work sheet. Explain whether the error is likely to be discovered in completing the work sheet and, if not, the effect of the error on the financial statements.

   a. Assume the adjustment for expiration of the insurance coverage consisted of a credit to Prepaid Insurance and a debit to Insurance Expense for $3,100, when the correct amount was $11,500.

   b. When the adjusted trial balance in the work sheet is completed, assume that the $6,700 Repairs Expense account balance is extended to the Debit column of the balance sheet columns.

**Problem 4-6B**[A]

Preparing adjusting, reversing, and next period entries

P4

The following six-column table for Solutions Co. includes the unadjusted trial balance as of December 31, 2011.

|  | A | B | C | D | E | F | G |
|---|---|---|---|---|---|---|---|
| 1 |  | SOLUTIONS COMPANY | | | | | |
| 2 |  | December 31, 2011 | | | | | |
| 3 |  | Unadjusted | | Adjustments | | Adjusted | |
| 4 |  | Trial Balance | | | | Trial Balance | |
| 5 | Account Title | Dr. | Cr. | Dr. | Cr. | Dr. | Cr. |
| 6 | Cash | $ 9,000 | | | | | |
| 7 | Accounts receivable | 0 | | | | | |
| 8 | Supplies | 6,600 | | | | | |
| 9 | Machinery | 40,100 | | | | | |
| 10 | Accumulated depreciation—Machinery | | $15,800 | | | | |
| 11 | Interest payable | | 0 | | | | |
| 12 | Salaries payable | | 0 | | | | |
| 13 | Unearned rental fees | | 5,200 | | | | |
| 14 | Notes payable | | 20,000 | | | | |
| 15 | G. Clay, Capital | | 13,200 | | | | |
| 16 | G. Clay, Withdrawals | 10,500 | | | | | |
| 17 | Rental fees earned | | 37,000 | | | | |
| 18 | Depreciation expense—Machinery | 0 | | | | | |
| 19 | Salaries expense | 23,500 | | | | | |
| 20 | Interest expense | 1,500 | | | | | |
| 21 | Supplies expense | 0 | | | | | |
| 22 | Totals | $91,200 | $91,200 | | | | |
| 23 |  | | | | | | |

**Required**

1. Complete the six-column table by entering adjustments that reflect the following information:

   a. As of December 31, 2011, employees had earned $420 of unpaid and unrecorded wages. The next payday is January 4, at which time $1,250 in wages will be paid.

   b. The cost of supplies still available at December 31, 2011, is $2,450.

   c. The notes payable requires an interest payment to be made every three months. The amount of unrecorded accrued interest at December 31, 2011, is $500. The next interest payment, at an amount of $600, is due on January 15, 2012.

   d. Analysis of the unearned rental fees shows that $3,100 remains unearned at December 31, 2011.

   e. In addition to the machinery rental fees included in the revenue account balance, the company has earned another $2,350 in unrecorded fees that will be collected on January 31, 2012. The company is also expected to collect $4,400 on that same day for new fees earned in January 2012.

   f. Depreciation expense for the year is $3,800.

**Check** (1) Adjusted trial balance totals, $98,270

2. Prepare journal entries for the adjustments entered in the six-column table for part 1.

3. Prepare journal entries to reverse the effects of the adjusting entries that involve accruals.

4. Prepare journal entries to record the cash payments and cash collections described for January.

**SERIAL PROBLEM**

Business Solutions

P2  P3

*(This serial problem began in Chapter 1 and continues through most of the book. If previous chapter segments were not completed, the serial problem can begin at this point. It is helpful, but not necessary, to use the Working Papers that accompany the book.)*

**SP 4**   The December 31, 2011, adjusted trial balance of Business Solutions (reflecting its transactions from October through December of 2011) follows.

| No. | Account Title | Debit | Credit |
|---|---|---|---|
| 101 | Cash | $ 48,372 | |
| 106 | Accounts receivable | 5,668 | |
| 126 | Computer supplies | 580 | |
| 128 | Prepaid insurance | 1,665 | |

[continued on next page]

[continued from previous page]

| | | | |
|---|---|---:|---:|
| 131 | Prepaid rent | 825 | |
| 163 | Office equipment | 8,000 | |
| 164 | Accumulated depreciation—Office equipment | | $ 400 |
| 167 | Computer equipment | 20,000 | |
| 168 | Accumulated depreciation—Computer equipment | | 1,250 |
| 201 | Accounts payable | | 1,100 |
| 210 | Wages payable | | 500 |
| 236 | Unearned computer services revenue | | 1,500 |
| 301 | S. Rey, Capital | | 73,000 |
| 302 | S. Rey, Withdrawals | 7,100 | |
| 403 | Computer services revenue | | 31,284 |
| 612 | Depreciation expense—Office equipment | 400 | |
| 613 | Depreciation expense—Computer equipment | 1,250 | |
| 623 | Wages expense | 3,875 | |
| 637 | Insurance expense | 555 | |
| 640 | Rent expense | 2,475 | |
| 652 | Computer supplies expense | 3,065 | |
| 655 | Advertising expense | 2,753 | |
| 676 | Mileage expense | 896 | |
| 677 | Miscellaneous expenses | 250 | |
| 684 | Repairs expense—Computer | 1,305 | |
| 901 | Income summary | | 0 |
| | Totals | $109,034 | $109,034 |

## Required

1. Record and post the necessary closing entries for Business Solutions.
2. Prepare a post-closing trial balance as of December 31, 2011.

**Check**  Post-closing trial balance totals, $85,110

## Beyond the Numbers

**BTN 4-1**  Refer to **Research In Motion**'s financial statements in Appendix A to answer the following.

**REPORTING IN ACTION**

C1  P2

**RIM**

### Required

1. For the fiscal year ended February 27, 2010, what amount is credited to Income Summary to summarize its revenues earned?
2. For the fiscal year ended February 27, 2010, what amount is debited to Income Summary to summarize its expenses incurred?
3. For the fiscal year ended February 27, 2010, what is the balance of its Income Summary account before it is closed?
4. In its statement of cash flows for the year ended February 27, 2010, what amount of cash is paid in dividends to common stockholders?

### Fast Forward

5. Access RIM's annual report for fiscal years ending after February 27, 2010, at its Website (**RIM.com**) or the SEC's EDGAR database (**www.sec.gov**). How has the amount of net income closed to Income Summary changed in the fiscal years ending after February 27, 2010? How has the amount of cash paid as dividends changed in the fiscal years ending after February 27, 2010?

**BTN 4-2**  Key figures for the recent two years of **Research In Motion** and **Apple** follow.

**COMPARATIVE ANALYSIS**

A1

**RIM**

Apple

| Key Figures ($ millions) | Research In Motion | | Apple | |
|---|---|---|---|---|
| | Current Year | Prior Year | Current Year | Prior Year |
| Current assets | $5,813 | $4,842 | $31,555 | $30,006 |
| Current liabilities | 2,432 | 2,115 | 11,506 | 11,361 |

***Required***

1. Compute the current ratio for both years for both companies.
2. Which company has the better ability to pay short-term obligations according to the current ratio?
3. Analyze and comment on each company's current ratios for the past two years.
4. How do RIM's and Apple's current ratios compare to their industry (assumed) average ratio of 2.4?

**ETHICS CHALLENGE**

C2

**BTN 4-3**   On January 20, 2011, Tamira Nelson, the accountant for Picton Enterprises, is feeling pressure to complete the annual financial statements. The company president has said he needs up-to-date financial statements to share with the bank on January 21 at a dinner meeting that has been called to discuss Picton's obtaining loan financing for a special building project. Tamira knows that she will not be able to gather all the needed information in the next 24 hours to prepare the entire set of adjusting entries. Those entries must be posted before the financial statements accurately portray the company's performance and financial position for the fiscal period ended December 31, 2010. Tamira ultimately decides to estimate several expense accruals at the last minute. When deciding on estimates for the expenses, she uses low estimates because she does not want to make the financial statements look worse than they are. Tamira finishes the financial statements before the deadline and gives them to the president without mentioning that several account balances are estimates that she provided.

***Required***

1. Identify several courses of action that Tamira could have taken instead of the one she took.
2. If you were in Tamira's situation, what would you have done? Briefly justify your response.

**COMMUNICATING IN PRACTICE**

C1   P2

**BTN 4-4**   Assume that one of your classmates states that a company's books should be ongoing and therefore not closed until that business is terminated. Write a half-page memo to this classmate explaining the concept of the closing process by drawing analogies between (1) a scoreboard for an athletic event and the revenue and expense accounts of a business or (2) a sports team's record book and the capital account. (*Hint:* Think about what would happen if the scoreboard is not cleared before the start of a new game.)

**TAKING IT TO THE NET**

A1

**BTN 4-5**   Access **Motley Fool**'s discussion of the current ratio at **Fool.com/School/Valuation/ CurrentAndQuickRatio.htm**. (If the page changed, search that site for the *current ratio*.)

***Required***

1. What level for the current ratio is generally regarded as sufficient to meet near-term operating needs?
2. Once you have calculated the current ratio for a company, what should you compare it against?
3. What are the implications for a company that has a current ratio that is too high?

**TEAMWORK IN ACTION**

P1   P2   P3

**BTN 4-6**   The unadjusted trial balance and information for the accounting adjustments of Noseworthy Investigators follow. Each team member involved in this project is to assume one of the four responsibilities listed. After completing each of these responsibilities, the team should work together to prove the accounting equation utilizing information from teammates (1 and 4). If your equation does not balance, you are to work as a team to resolve the error. The team's goal is to complete the task as quickly and accurately as possible.

| Unadjusted Trial Balance | | |
|---|---|---|
| **Account Title** | **Debit** | **Credit** |
| Cash | $15,000 | |
| Supplies | 11,000 | |
| Prepaid insurance | 2,000 | |
| Equipment | 24,000 | |
| Accumulated depreciation—Equipment | | $ 6,000 |
| Accounts payable | | 2,000 |
| D. Noseworthy, Capital | | 31,000 |
| D. Noseworthy, Withdrawals | 5,000 | |
| Investigation fees earned | | 32,000 |
| Rent expense | 14,000 | |
| Totals | $71,000 | $71,000 |

### Additional Year-End Information

**a.** Insurance that expired in the current period amounts to $1,200.
**b.** Equipment depreciation for the period is $3,000.
**c.** Unused supplies total $4,000 at period-end.
**d.** Services in the amount of $500 have been provided but have not been billed or collected.

### Responsibilities for Individual Team Members

**1.** Determine the accounts and adjusted balances to be extended to the balance sheet columns of the work sheet for Noseworthy. Also determine total assets and total liabilities.
**2.** Determine the adjusted revenue account balance and prepare the entry to close this account.
**3.** Determine the adjusted account balances for expenses and prepare the entry to close these accounts.
**4.** Prepare T-accounts for both D. Noseworthy, Capital (reflecting the unadjusted trial balance amount) and Income Summary. Prepare the third and fourth closing entries. Ask teammates assigned to parts 2 and 3 for the postings for Income Summary. Obtain amounts to complete the third closing entry and post both the third and fourth closing entries. Provide the team with the ending capital account balance.
**5.** The entire team should prove the accounting equation using post-closing balances.

---

**BTN 4-7** Review this chapter's opening feature involving Keith Mullin and his **Gamer Grub** business.
**1.** Explain how a classified balance sheet can help Keith Mullin know what bills are due when, and whether he has the resources to pay those bills.
**2.** Why is it important for Keith Mullin to match costs and revenues in a specific time period? How do closing entries help him in this regard?
**3.** What objectives are met when Keith Mullin applies closing procedures each fiscal year-end?

**ENTREPRENEURIAL DECISION**

A1 C3 P2

---

**BTN 4-8** Select a company that you can visit in person or interview on the telephone. Call ahead to the company to arrange a time when you can interview an employee (preferably an accountant) who helps prepare the annual financial statements. Inquire about the following aspects of its *accounting cycle:*
**1.** Does the company prepare interim financial statements? What time period(s) is used for interim statements?
**2.** Does the company use the cash or accrual basis of accounting?
**3.** Does the company use a work sheet in preparing financial statements? Why or why not?
**4.** Does the company use a spreadsheet program? If so, which software program is used?
**5.** How long does it take after the end of its reporting period to complete annual statements?

**HITTING THE ROAD**

C2

---

**BTN 4-9** Nokia (www.Nokia.com) is a leading global manufacturer of mobile devices and services. The following selected information is available from Nokia's financial statements.

**GLOBAL DECISION**

A1

**NOKIA**

| (Euro millions) | Current Year | Prior Year |
|---|---|---|
| Current assets . . . . . . . . . . | 23,613 | 24,470 |
| Current liabilities . . . . . . . . | 15,188 | 20,355 |

### Required

**1.** Compute Nokia's current ratio for both the current year and the prior year.
**2.** Comment on any change from the prior year to the current year for the current ratio.

---

## ANSWERS TO MULTIPLE CHOICE QUIZ

**1.** e
**2.** c
**3.** a

**4.** c
**5.** b

# 5

# Accounting for Merchandising Operations

### A Look Back

Chapters 3 and 4 focused on the final steps of the accounting process. We explained the importance of proper revenue and expense recognition and described the adjusting and closing processes. We also prepared financial statements.

### A Look at This Chapter

This chapter emphasizes merchandising activities. We explain how reporting merchandising activities differs from reporting service activities. We also analyze and record merchandise purchases and sales transactions, and explain the adjustments and closing process for merchandisers.

### A Look Ahead

Chapter 6 extends our analysis of merchandising activities and focuses on the valuation of inventory. Topics include the items in inventory, costs assigned, costing methods used, and inventory estimation techniques.

## Learning Objectives

## CAP

### CONCEPTUAL

**C1** Describe merchandising activities and identify income components for a merchandising company. (p. 180)

**C2** Identify and explain the inventory asset and cost flows of a merchandising company. (p. 181)

### ANALYTICAL

**A1** Compute the acid-test ratio and explain its use to assess liquidity. (p. 196)

**A2** Compute the gross margin ratio and explain its use to assess profitability. (p. 196)

LP5

### PROCEDURAL

**P1** Analyze and record transactions for merchandise purchases using a perpetual system. (p. 182)

**P2** Analyze and record transactions for merchandise sales using a perpetual system. (p. 187)

**P3** Prepare adjustments and close accounts for a merchandising company. (p. 190)

**P4** Define and prepare multiple-step and single-step income statements. (p. 192)

**P5** *Appendix 5A*—Record and compare merchandising transactions using both periodic and perpetual inventory systems. (p. 201)

## Decision Insight

## Out of Africa

*"We are changing history and . . . we are all going to make a whole lot of money"*

—SELENA CUFFE

LOS ANGELES—Selena Cuffe was in Johannesburg as part of a student exchange program when she discovered wine at the Soweto Wine Festival. "They have wine here?" asked a puzzled Selena. That festival unleashed Selena's passion to pursue the merchandising of wine. But not just any wine—she would import and distribute wine produced by indigenous African vintners. She and her husband, Khary, launched **Heritage Link Brands (HeritageLinkBrands.com).** Our mission, says Selena, is "to showcase the very best wines from Africa and the African Diaspora."

But the start-up was a struggle. "Our business is a family business so whatever decisions we make have to be made with the best interest of my family and those we work with," explains Selena. She describes how the business required a merchandising accounting system to account for purchases and sales transactions and to effectively track the levels of the various wines. Inventory was especially important to account for and monitor. Khary explains, "It is very easy to underestimate expenses."

To succeed, Selena and Khary needed to make smart business decisions. They set up an accounting system to capture and communicate costs and sales information. Tracking merchandising activities was necessary to set prices and to manage discounts, allowances, and returns of both sales and purchases. A perpetual inventory system enabled them to stock the right kind and amount of merchandise and to avoid the costs of out-of-stock and excess inventory. Khary stressed that they monitored current assets and current liabilities (working capital). "Understand working capital," insists Khary. "If you don't understand working capital, stop right here and open an accounting book."

Mastering accounting for merchandising is a means to an end for Selena and Khary. "My training is really about how to run a successful business," says Selena. "How to get the most profit you can out of something." Still, Selena recognizes that her merchandising business is more than profits and losses. "What we're able to do and how we're able to make an impact with this business only matters in as much as the people here and on the continent are able to be successful and thrive."

[Sources: *Heritage Link Brands Website,* January 2011; *TIME,* September 2007; *Black Enterprise,* May 2009; *Inc,* March 2009]

Buyers of merchandise expect many products, discount prices, inventory on demand, and high quality. This chapter introduces the accounting practices used by companies engaged in merchandising. We show how financial statements reflect merchandising activities and explain the new financial statement items created by merchandising activities. We also analyze and record merchandise purchases and sales, and explain the adjustments and the closing process for these companies.

## Accounting for Merchandising Operations

| **Merchandising Activities** | **Merchandising Purchases** | **Merchandising Sales** | **Accounting Cycle** | **Financial Statement Formats** |
|---|---|---|---|---|
| • Reporting income<br>• Reporting inventory<br>• Operating cycles<br>• Inventory systems | • Purchase discounts<br>• Purchase returns and allowances<br>• Transportation costs | • Sales of merchandise<br>• Sales discounts<br>• Sales returns and allowances | • Adjusting entries<br>• Preparing financial statements<br>• Closing entries | • Multiple-step income statement<br>• Single-step income statement<br>• Classified balance sheet |

# MERCHANDISING ACTIVITIES

**C1** Describe merchandising activities and identify income components for a merchandising company.

Previous chapters emphasized the accounting and reporting activities of service companies. A merchandising company's activities differ from those of a service company. **Merchandise** consists of products, also called *goods,* that a company acquires to resell to customers. A **merchandiser** earns net income by buying and selling merchandise. Merchandisers are often identified as either wholesalers or retailers. A **wholesaler** is an *intermediary* that buys products from manufacturers or other wholesalers and sells them to retailers or other wholesalers. A **retailer** is an intermediary that buys products from manufacturers or wholesalers and sells them to consumers. Many retailers sell both products and services.

## Reporting Income for a Merchandiser

Net income for a merchandiser equals revenues from selling merchandise minus both the cost of merchandise sold to customers and the cost of other expenses for the period, see Exhibit 5.1. The

**EXHIBIT 5.1**

Computing Income for a Merchandising Company versus a Service Company

**Service Company**

Revenues — Minus → Expenses — Equals → Net income

**Merchandiser**

Net sales — Minus → Cost of goods sold — Equals → Gross profit — Minus → Expenses — Equals → Net income

usual accounting term for revenues from selling merchandise is *sales,* and the term used for the expense of buying and preparing the merchandise is **cost of goods sold.** (Some service companies use the term *sales* instead of revenues; and cost of goods sold is also called *cost of sales.*)

The income statement for Z-Mart in Exhibit 5.2 illustrates these key components of a merchandiser's net income. The first two lines show that products are acquired at a cost of $230,400 and sold for $314,700. The third line shows an $84,300 **gross profit,** also called

**Point: Fleming, SuperValu,** and **SYSCO** are wholesalers. **Gap, Oakley, Target,** and **Walmart** are retailers.

**EXHIBIT 5.2**

Merchandiser's Income Statement

| Z-MART | |
|---|---|
| Income Statement | |
| For Year Ended December 31, 2011 | |
| Net sales . . . . . . . . . . . . . . . . . . . | $314,700 |
| **Cost of goods sold** . . . . . . . . . | 230,400 |
| **Gross profit** . . . . . . . . . . . . . . . | 84,300 |
| Expenses . . . . . . . . . . . . . . . . . . | 71,400 |
| Net income . . . . . . . . . . . . . . . | $  12,900 |

**gross margin,** which equals net sales less cost of goods sold. Additional expenses of $71,400 are reported, which leaves $12,900 in net income.

**Point:** Analysis of gross profit is important to effective business decisions, and is described later in the chapter.

## Reporting Inventory for a Merchandiser

A merchandiser's balance sheet includes a current asset called *merchandise inventory,* an item not on a service company's balance sheet. **Merchandise inventory,** or simply *inventory,* refers to products that a company owns and intends to sell. The cost of this asset includes the cost incurred to buy the goods, ship them to the store, and make them ready for sale.

**C2** Identify and explain the inventory asset and cost flows of a merchandising company.

## Operating Cycle for a Merchandiser

A merchandising company's operating cycle begins by purchasing merchandise and ends by collecting cash from selling the merchandise. The length of an operating cycle differs across the types of businesses. Department stores often have operating cycles of two to five months. Operating cycles for grocery merchants usually range from two to eight weeks.

Exhibit 5.3 illustrates an operating cycle for a merchandiser with credit sales. The cycle moves from (*a*) cash purchases of merchandise to (*b*) inventory for sale to (*c*) credit sales to (*d*) accounts receivable to (*e*) cash. Companies try to keep their operating cycles short because assets tied up in inventory and receivables are not productive. Cash sales shorten operating cycles.

**EXHIBIT 5.3**

Merchandiser's Operating Cycle

## Inventory Systems

Cost of goods sold is the cost of merchandise sold to customers during a period. It is often the largest single expense on a merchandiser's income statement. **Inventory** refers to products a company owns and expects to sell in its normal operations. Exhibit 5.4 shows that a company's merchandise available for sale consists of what it begins with (beginning inventory) and what it

**EXHIBIT 5.4**

Merchandiser's Cost Flow for a Single Time Period

**Point:** Mathematically, Exhibit 5.4 says
$$BI + NP = MAS,$$
where BI is beginning inventory, NP is net purchases, and MAS is merchandise available for sale. Exhibit 5.4 also says
$$MAS = EI + COGS,$$
which can be rewritten as MAS − EI = COGS or MAS − COGS = EI, where EI is ending inventory and COGS is cost of goods sold.

purchases (net purchases). The merchandise available is either sold (cost of goods sold) or kept for future sales (ending inventory).

Two alternative inventory accounting systems can be used to collect information about cost of goods sold and cost of inventory: *perpetual system* or *periodic system*. The **perpetual inventory system** continually updates accounting records for merchandising transactions—specifically, for those records of inventory available for sale and inventory sold. The **periodic inventory system** updates the accounting records for merchandise transactions only at the *end of a period*. Technological advances and competitive pressures have dramatically increased the use of the perpetual system. It gives managers immediate access to detailed information on sales and inventory levels, where they can strategically react to sales trends, cost changes, consumer tastes, and so forth, to increase gross profit. (Some companies use a *hybrid* system where the perpetual system is used for tracking units available and the periodic system is used to compute cost of sales.)

## Quick Check    Answers — p. 207

1. Describe a merchandiser's cost of goods sold.
2. What is gross profit for a merchandising company?
3. Explain why use of the perpetual inventory system has dramatically increased.

*The following sections, consisting of the next 10 pages on purchasing, selling, and adjusting merchandise, use the perpetual system. Appendix 5A uses the periodic system (with the perpetual results on the side). An instructor can choose to cover either one or both inventory systems.*

# ACCOUNTING FOR MERCHANDISE PURCHASES

**P1** Analyze and record transactions for merchandise purchases using a perpetual system.

The cost of merchandise purchased for resale is recorded in the Merchandise Inventory asset account. To illustrate, Z-Mart records a $1,200 cash purchase of merchandise on November 2 as follows:

Assets = Liabilities + Equity
+1,200
−1,200

| Nov. 2 | Merchandise Inventory ............................ | 1,200 | |
|--------|---------------------------------------------------|-------|-------|
| | Cash ...................................... | | 1,200 |
| | *Purchased merchandise for cash.* | | |

The invoice for this merchandise is shown in Exhibit 5.5. The buyer usually receives the original invoice, and the seller keeps a copy. This *source document* serves as the purchase invoice of Z-Mart (buyer) and the sales invoice for Trex (seller). The amount recorded for merchandise inventory includes its purchase cost, shipping fees, taxes, and any other costs necessary to make it ready for sale. This section explains how we compute the recorded cost of merchandise purchases.

**Point:** The Merchandise Inventory account reflects the cost of goods available for resale.

## Decision Insight

**Trade Discounts**    When a manufacturer or wholesaler prepares a catalog of items it has for sale, it usually gives each item a **list price,** also called a *catalog price.* However, an item's intended *selling price* equals list price minus a given percent called a **trade discount.** The amount of trade discount usually depends on whether a buyer is a wholesaler, retailer, or final consumer. A wholesaler buying in large quantities is often granted a larger discount than a retailer buying in smaller quantities. A buyer records the net amount of list price minus trade discount. For example, in the November 2 purchase of merchandise by Z-Mart, the merchandise was listed in the seller's catalog at $2,000 and Z-Mart received a 40% trade discount. This meant that Z-Mart's purchase price was $1,200, computed as $2,000 − (40% × $2,000). ■

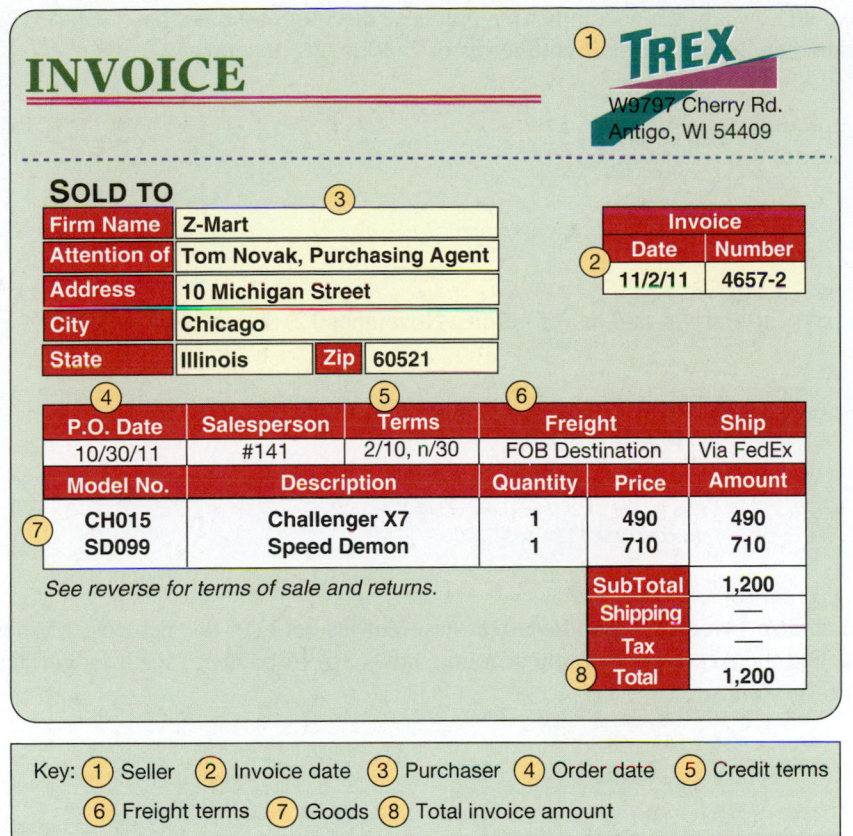

**EXHIBIT 5.5**

Invoice

## Purchase Discounts

The purchase of goods on credit requires a clear statement of expected future payments and dates to avoid misunderstandings. **Credit terms** for a purchase include the amounts and timing of payments from a buyer to a seller. Credit terms usually reflect an industry's practices. To illustrate, when sellers require payment within 10 days after the end of the month of the invoice date, the invoice will show credit terms as "n/10 EOM," which stands for net 10 days after end of month (**EOM**). When sellers require payment within 30 days after the invoice date, the invoice shows credit terms of "n/30," which stands for *net 30 days*.

Exhibit 5.6 portrays credit terms. The amount of time allowed before full payment is due is called the **credit period.** Sellers can grant a **cash discount** to encourage buyers to pay earlier. A buyer views a cash discount as a **purchase discount.** A seller views a cash discount as a **sales discount.** Any cash discounts are described in the credit terms on the invoice. For example, credit terms of "2/10, n/60" mean that full payment is due within a 60-day credit period, but the buyer can deduct 2% of the invoice amount if payment is made within 10 days of the invoice date. This reduced payment applies only for the **discount period.**

**Point:** Since both the buyer and seller know the invoice date, this date is used in setting the discount and credit periods.

**EXHIBIT 5.6**

Credit Terms

**Point:** Appendix 5A repeats journal entries *a* through *f* using a periodic inventory system.

To illustrate how a buyer accounts for a purchase discount, assume that Z-Mart's $1,200 purchase of merchandise is on credit with terms of 2/10, n/30. Its entry is

Assets = Liabilities + Equity
+1,200     +1,200

| *(a)* Nov. 2 | Merchandise Inventory .......................... | 1,200 | |
|---|---|---|---|
| | Accounts Payable ........................... | | 1,200 |
| | *Purchased merchandise on credit, invoice dated Nov. 2, terms 2/10, n/30.* | | |

If Z-Mart pays the amount due on (or before) November 12, the entry is

Assets = Liabilities + Equity
−24     −1,200
−1,176

| *(b)* Nov. 12 | Accounts Payable ................................ | 1,200 | |
|---|---|---|---|
| | Merchandise Inventory ...................... | | 24 |
| | Cash ..................................... | | 1,176 |
| | *Paid for the $1,200 purchase of Nov. 2 less the discount of $24 (2% × $1,200).* | | |

**Point:** These entries illustrate what is called the *gross method* of accounting for purchases with discount terms.

The Merchandise Inventory account after these entries reflects the net cost of merchandise purchased, and the Accounts Payable account shows a zero balance. Both ledger accounts, in T-account form, follow:

| Merchandise Inventory | | | |
|---|---|---|---|
| Nov. 2 | 1,200 | Nov. 12 | 24 |
| Balance | 1,176 | | |

| Accounts Payable | | | |
|---|---|---|---|
| Nov. 12 | 1,200 | Nov. 2 | 1,200 |
| | | Balance | 0 |

A buyer's failure to pay within a discount period can be expensive. To illustrate, if Z-Mart does not pay within the 10-day 2% discount period, it can delay payment by 20 more days. This delay costs Z-Mart $24, computed as 2% × $1,200. Most buyers take advantage of a purchase discount because of the usually high interest rate implied from not taking it.[1] Also, good cash management means that no invoice is paid until the last day of the discount or credit period.

---

 **Decision Maker**      Answer — p. 206

**Entrepreneur**   You purchase a batch of products on terms of 3/10, n/90, but your company has limited cash and you must borrow funds at an 11% annual rate if you are to pay within the discount period. Do you take advantage of the purchase discount? ■

## Purchase Returns and Allowances

*Purchase returns* refer to merchandise a buyer acquires but then returns to the seller. A *purchase allowance* is a reduction in the cost of defective or unacceptable merchandise that a buyer acquires. Buyers often keep defective but still marketable merchandise if the seller grants an acceptable allowance. When a buyer returns or takes an allowance on merchandise, the buyer issues a **debit memorandum** to inform the seller of a debit made to the seller's account in the buyer's records.

**Point:** The sender (maker) of a *debit memorandum* will debit the account of the memo's receiver. The memo's receiver will credit the sender's account.

---

[1] The *implied annual interest rate* formula is:

(365 days ÷ [Credit period − Discount period]) × Cash discount rate.

For terms of 2/10, n/30, missing the 2% discount for an additional 20 days is equal to an annual interest rate of 36.5%, computed as [365 days/(30 days − 10 days)] × 2% discount rate. *Favorable purchase discounts* are those with implied annual interest rates that exceed the purchaser's annual rate for borrowing money.

**Purchase Allowances** To illustrate purchase allowances, assume that on November 15, Z-Mart (buyer) issues a $300 debit memorandum for an allowance from Trex for defective merchandise. Z-Mart's November 15 entry to update its Merchandise Inventory account to reflect the purchase allowance is

| (c) Nov. 15 | Accounts Payable . . . . . . . . . . . . . . . . . . . . . . . . . . . . . . . | 300 | |
| | Merchandise Inventory . . . . . . . . . . . . . . . . . . . . . | | 300 |
| | *Allowance for defective merchandise.* | | |

Assets = Liabilities + Equity
−300      −300

The buyer's allowance for defective merchandise is usually offset against the buyer's current account payable balance to the seller. When cash is refunded, the Cash account is debited instead of Accounts Payable.

**Purchase Returns** Returns are recorded at the net costs charged to buyers. To illustrate the accounting for returns, suppose Z-Mart purchases $1,000 of merchandise on June 1 with terms 2/10, n/60. Two days later, Z-Mart returns $100 of goods before paying the invoice. When Z-Mart later pays on June 11, it takes the 2% discount only on the $900 remaining balance. When goods are returned, a buyer can take a purchase discount on only the remaining balance of the invoice. The resulting discount is $18 (2% × $900) and the cash payment is $882 ($900 − $18). The following entries reflect this illustration.

| June 1 | Merchandise Inventory . . . . . . . . . . . . . . . . . . . . . . . . . | 1,000 | |
| | Accounts Payable . . . . . . . . . . . . . . . . . . . . . . . . . | | 1,000 |
| | *Purchased merchandise, invoice dated June 1,* | | |
| | *terms 2/10, n/60.* | | |
| June 3 | Accounts Payable . . . . . . . . . . . . . . . . . . . . . . . . . . . . . | 100 | |
| | Merchandise Inventory . . . . . . . . . . . . . . . . . . . . . | | 100 |
| | *Returned merchandise to seller.* | | |
| June 11 | Accounts Payable . . . . . . . . . . . . . . . . . . . . . . . . . . . . . | 900 | |
| | Merchandise Inventory . . . . . . . . . . . . . . . . . . . . . | | 18 |
| | Cash . . . . . . . . . . . . . . . . . . . . . . . . . . . . . . . . . . . . . | | 882 |
| | *Paid for $900 merchandise ($1,000 − $100)* | | |
| | *less $18 discount (2% × $900).* | | |

**Example:** Assume Z-Mart pays $980 cash for $1,000 of merchandise purchased within its 2% discount period. Later, it returns $100 of the original $1,000 merchandise. The return entry is
Cash . . . . . . . . . . . . . . . . . . . . . . 98
     Merchandise Inventory . . . .      98

**Decision Ethics**      Answer — p. 206

**Credit Manager** As a new credit manager, you are being trained by the outgoing manager. She explains that the system prepares checks for amounts net of favorable cash discounts, and the checks are dated the last day of the discount period. She also tells you that checks are not mailed until five days later, adding that "the company gets free use of cash for an extra five days, and our department looks better. When a supplier complains, we blame the computer system and the mailroom." Do you continue this payment policy? ■

## Transportation Costs and Ownership Transfer

The buyer and seller must agree on who is responsible for paying any freight costs and who bears the risk of loss during transit for merchandising transactions. This is essentially the same as asking at what point ownership transfers from the seller to the buyer. The point of transfer is called the **FOB** (*free on board*) point, which determines who pays transportation costs (and often other incidental costs of transit such as insurance).

Exhibit 5.7 identifies two alternative points of transfer. (1) *FOB shipping point,* also called *FOB factory,* means the buyer accepts ownership when the goods depart the seller's place of business. The buyer is then responsible for paying shipping costs and bearing the risk of damage or loss when goods are in transit. The goods are part of the buyer's inventory when they are in transit since ownership has transferred to the buyer. **1-800-FLOWERS.COM**, a floral and gift

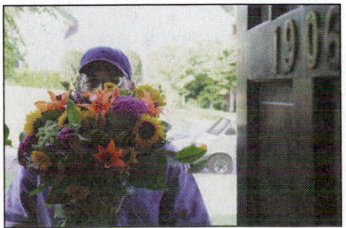

## EXHIBIT 5.7

Ownership Transfer and
Transportation Costs

| | Shipping point | Carrier | Destination |
|---|---|---|---|

| | Ownership Transfers When Goods Passed to | Transportation Costs Paid by |
|---|---|---|
| FOB shipping point | Carrier | Buyer |
| FOB destination | Buyer | Seller |

**Point:** The party not responsible for shipping costs sometimes pays the carrier. In these cases, the party paying these costs either bills the party responsible or, more commonly, adjusts its account payable or account receivable with the other party. For example, a buyer paying a carrier when terms are FOB destination can decrease its account payable to the seller by the amount of shipping cost.

merchandiser, and **Bare Escentuals**, a cosmetic manufacturer, both use FOB shipping point. (2) *FOB destination* means ownership of goods transfers to the buyer when the goods arrive at the buyer's place of business. The seller is responsible for paying shipping charges and bears the risk of damage or loss in transit. The seller does not record revenue from this sale until the goods arrive at the destination because this transaction is not complete before that point. **Kyocera**, a manufacturer, uses FOB destination.

Z-Mart's $1,200 purchase on November 2 is on terms of FOB destination. This means Z-Mart is not responsible for paying transportation costs. When a buyer is responsible for paying transportation costs, the payment is made to a carrier or directly to the seller depending on the agreement. The cost principle requires that any necessary transportation costs of a buyer (often called *transportation-in* or *freight-in*) be included as part of the cost of purchased merchandise. To illustrate, Z-Mart's entry to record a $75 freight charge from an independent carrier for merchandise purchased FOB shipping point is

Assets = Liabilities + Equity
+75
−75

| **(d)** Nov. 24 | Merchandise Inventory . . . . . . . . . . . . . . . . . . . . . . . . . | 75 | |
|---|---|---|---|
| | Cash . . . . . . . . . . . . . . . . . . . . . . . . . . . . . . . . . | | 75 |
| | *Paid freight costs on purchased merchandise.* | | |

A seller records the costs of shipping goods to customers in a Delivery Expense account when the seller is responsible for these costs. Delivery Expense, also called *transportation-out* or *freight-out,* is reported as a selling expense in the seller's income statement.

In summary, purchases are recorded as debits to Merchandise Inventory. Any later purchase discounts, returns, and allowances are credited (decreases) to Merchandise Inventory. Transportation-in is debited (added) to Merchandise Inventory. Z-Mart's itemized costs of merchandise purchases for year 2011 are in Exhibit 5.8.

## EXHIBIT 5.8

Itemized Costs of
Merchandise Purchases

| Z-MART |
|---|
| **Itemized Costs of Merchandise Purchases** |
| **For Year Ended December 31, 2011** |

| | |
|---|---|
| Invoice cost of merchandise purchases . . . . . . . . . . . . | $ 235,800 |
| Less: Purchase discounts received . . . . . . . . . . . . . . . | (4,200) |
| Purchase returns and allowances . . . . . . . . . . . | (1,500) |
| Add: Costs of transportation-in . . . . . . . . . . . . . . . . . | 2,300 |
| **Total cost of merchandise purchases** . . . . . . . . | **$232,400** |

**Point:** Some companies have separate accounts for purchase discounts, returns and allowances, and transportation-in. These accounts are then transferred to Merchandise Inventory at period-end. This is a *hybrid system* of perpetual and periodic. That is, Merchandise Inventory is updated on a perpetual basis but only for purchases and cost of goods sold.

The accounting system described here does not provide separate records (accounts) for total purchases, total purchase discounts, total purchase returns and allowances, and total transportation-in. Yet nearly all companies collect this information in supplementary records because managers need this information to evaluate and control each of these cost elements. **Supplementary records,** also called *supplemental records,* refer to information outside the usual general ledger accounts.

## Quick Check

Answers — p. 207

4. How long are the credit and discount periods when credit terms are 2/10, n/60?
5. Identify which items are subtracted from the *list* amount and not recorded when computing purchase price: (*a*) freight-in; (*b*) trade discount; (*c*) purchase discount; (*d*) purchase return.
6. What does *FOB* mean? What does *FOB destination* mean?

## ACCOUNTING FOR MERCHANDISE SALES

Merchandising companies also must account for sales, sales discounts, sales returns and allowances, and cost of goods sold. A merchandising company such as Z-Mart reflects these items in its gross profit computation, as shown in Exhibit 5.9. This section explains how this information is derived from transactions.

**P2** Analyze and record transactions for merchandise sales using a perpetual system.

**EXHIBIT 5.9**

Gross Profit Computation

| **Z-MART**<br>**Computation of Gross Profit**<br>**For Year Ended December 31, 2011** | | |
|---|---|---|
| Sales. . . . . . . . . . . . . . . . . . . . . . . . . . . . . . . | | $321,000 |
| Less: Sales discounts . . . . . . . . . . . . . . . . . . . | $4,300 | |
| Sales returns and allowances . . . . . . . . | 2,000 | 6,300 |
| Net sales . . . . . . . . . . . . . . . . . . . . . . . | | 314,700 |
| Cost of goods sold . . . . . . . . . . . . . . . . . . . | | 230,400 |
| **Gross profit** . . . . . . . . . . . . . . . . . . . . . . | | **$ 84,300** |

## Sales of Merchandise

Each sales transaction for a seller of merchandise involves two parts.

1. **Revenue received in the form of an asset from the customer.**
2. **Recognition of the cost of merchandise sold to the customer.**

Accounting for a sales transaction under the perpetual system requires recording information about both parts. This means that each sales transaction for merchandisers, whether for cash or on credit, requires *two entries:* one for revenue and one for cost. To illustrate, Z-Mart sold $2,400 of merchandise on credit on November 3. The revenue part of this transaction is recorded as

| (e) Nov. 3 | Accounts Receivable . . . . . . . . . . . . . . . . . . . . . . . . . | 2,400 | |
|---|---|---|---|
| | Sales . . . . . . . . . . . . . . . . . . . . . . . . . . . . . . . | | 2,400 |
| | *Sold merchandise on credit.* | | |

Assets = Liabilities + Equity
+2,400                      +2,400

This entry reflects an increase in Z-Mart's assets in the form of accounts receivable. It also shows the increase in revenue (Sales). If the sale is for cash, the debit is to Cash instead of Accounts Receivable.

The cost part of each sales transaction ensures that the Merchandise Inventory account under a perpetual inventory system reflects the updated cost of the merchandise available for sale. For example, the cost of the merchandise Z-Mart sold on November 3 is $1,600, and the entry to record the cost part of this sales transaction is

| (e) Nov. 3 | Cost of Goods Sold . . . . . . . . . . . . . . . . . . . . . . . . . | 1,600 | |
|---|---|---|---|
| | Merchandise Inventory . . . . . . . . . . . . . . . . . . . . | | 1,600 |
| | *To record the cost of Nov. 3 sale.* | | |

Assets = Liabilities + Equity
−1,600                      −1,600

## Decision Insight

**Suppliers and Demands**   Large merchandising companies often bombard suppliers with demands. These include discounts for bar coding and technology support systems, and fines for shipping errors. Merchandisers' goals are to reduce inventories, shorten lead times, and eliminate errors. ■

## Sales Discounts

*Sales discounts* on credit sales can benefit a seller by decreasing the delay in receiving cash and reducing future collection efforts. At the time of a credit sale, a seller does not know whether a customer will pay within the discount period and take advantage of a discount. This means the seller usually does not record a sales discount until a customer actually pays within the discount period. To illustrate, Z-Mart completes a credit sale for $1,000 on November 12 with terms of 2/10, n/60. The entry to record the revenue part of this sale is

Assets = Liabilities + Equity
+1,000          +1,000

| Nov. 12 | Accounts Receivable ........................... | 1,000 | |
| |      Sales ..................................... | | 1,000 |
| | *Sold merchandise under terms of 2/10, n/60.* | | |

This entry records the receivable and the revenue as if the customer will pay the full amount. The customer has two options, however. One option is to wait 60 days until January 11 and pay the full $1,000. In this case, Z-Mart records that payment as

Assets = Liabilities + Equity
+1,000
−1,000

| Jan. 11 | Cash ......................................... | 1,000 | |
| |      Accounts Receivable ...................... | | 1,000 |
| | *Received payment for Nov. 12 sale.* | | |

The customer's second option is to pay $980 within a 10-day period ending November 22. If the customer pays on (or before) November 22, Z-Mart records the payment as

Assets = Liabilities + Equity
+980          −20
−1,000

| Nov. 22 | Cash ......................................... | 980 | |
| | Sales Discounts .............................. | 20 | |
| |      Accounts Receivable ...................... | | 1,000 |
| | *Received payment for Nov. 12 sale less discount.* | | |

Sales Discounts is a contra revenue account, meaning the Sales Discounts account is deducted from the Sales account when computing a company's net sales (see Exhibit 5.9). Management monitors Sales Discounts to assess the effectiveness and cost of its discount policy.

## Sales Returns and Allowances

**Point:** Published income statements rarely disclose sales discounts, returns and allowances.

*Sales returns* refer to merchandise that customers return to the seller after a sale. Many companies allow customers to return merchandise for a full refund. *Sales allowances* refer to reductions in the selling price of merchandise sold to customers. This can occur with damaged or defective merchandise that a customer is willing to purchase with a decrease in selling price. Sales returns and allowances usually involve dissatisfied customers and the possibility of lost future sales, and managers monitor information about returns and allowances.

**Sales Returns**   To illustrate, recall Z-Mart's sale of merchandise on November 3 for $2,400 that had cost $1,600. Assume that the customer returns part of the merchandise on

November 6, and the returned items sell for $800 and cost $600. The revenue part of this transaction must reflect the decrease in sales from the customer's return of merchandise as follows:

| (f) Nov. 6 | Sales Returns and Allowances ..................... | 800 | |
|---|---|---|---|
| | Accounts Receivable ........................ | | 800 |
| | *Customer returns merchandise of Nov. 3 sale.* | | |

Assets = Liabilities + Equity
−800            −800

If the merchandise returned to Z-Mart is not defective and can be resold to another customer, Z-Mart returns these goods to its inventory. The entry to restore the cost of such goods to the Merchandise Inventory account is

| Nov. 6 | Merchandise Inventory ......................... | 600 | |
|---|---|---|---|
| | Cost of Goods Sold ........................ | | 600 |
| | *Returned goods added to inventory.* | | |

Assets = Liabilities + Equity
+600            +600

*This entry changes if the goods returned are defective.* In this case the returned inventory is recorded at its estimated value, not its cost. To illustrate, if the goods (costing $600) returned to Z-Mart are defective and estimated to be worth $150, the following entry is made: Dr. Merchandise Inventory for $150, Dr. Loss from Defective Merchandise for $450, and Cr. Cost of Goods Sold for $600.

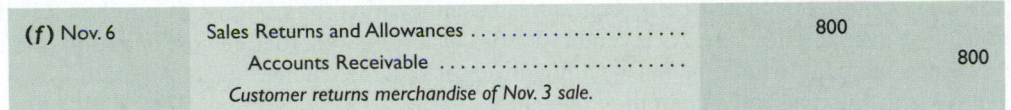

## Decision Insight

**Return to Sender**   Book merchandisers such as **Barnes & Noble**, **Borders Books**, **Books-A-Million**, and **Waldenbooks** can return unsold books to publishers at purchase price. Publishers say returns of new hardcover books run between 35% and 50%. ■

**Sales Allowances**   To illustrate sales allowances, assume that $800 of the merchandise Z-Mart sold on November 3 is defective but the buyer decides to keep it because Z-Mart offers a $100 price reduction. Z-Mart records this allowance as follows:

| Nov. 6 | Sales Returns and Allowances ..................... | 100 | |
|---|---|---|---|
| | Accounts Receivable ........................ | | 100 |
| | *To record sales allowance on Nov. 3 sale.* | | |

Assets = Liabilities + Equity
−100            −100

The seller usually prepares a credit memorandum to confirm a buyer's return or allowance. A seller's **credit memorandum** informs a buyer of the seller's credit to the buyer's Account Receivable (on the seller's books).

**Point:** The sender (maker) of a credit memorandum will *credit* the account of the receiver. The receiver of a credit memorandum will *debit* the sender's account.

## Quick Check       Answers — p. 207

7. Why are sales discounts and sales returns and allowances recorded in contra revenue accounts instead of directly in the Sales account?
8. Under what conditions are two entries necessary to record a sales return?
9. When merchandise is sold on credit and the seller notifies the buyer of a price allowance, does the seller create and send a credit memorandum or a debit memorandum?

## COMPLETING THE ACCOUNTING CYCLE

Exhibit 5.10 shows the flow of merchandising costs during a period and where these costs are reported at period-end. Specifically, beginning inventory plus the net cost of purchases is the merchandise available for sale. As inventory is sold, its cost is recorded in cost of goods sold on the income statement; what remains is ending inventory on the balance sheet. A period's ending inventory is the next period's beginning inventory.

**EXHIBIT 5.10**

Merchandising Cost Flow in the Accounting Cycle

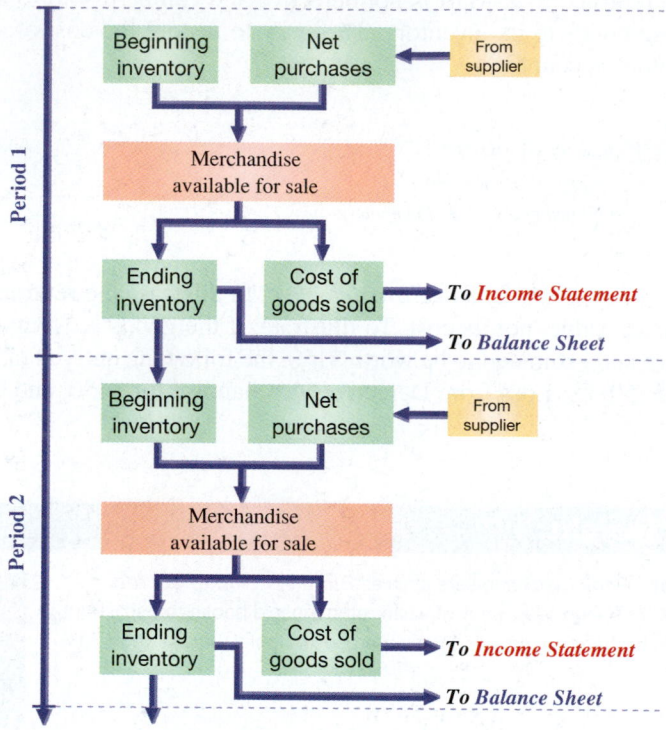

### Adjusting Entries for Merchandisers

P3   Prepare adjustments and close accounts for a merchandising company.

Each of the steps in the accounting cycle described in the prior chapter for a service company applies to a merchandiser. This section and the next two further explain three steps of the accounting cycle for a merchandiser—adjustments, statement preparation, and closing.

Adjusting entries are generally the same for merchandising companies and service companies, including those for prepaid expenses (including depreciation), accrued expenses, unearned revenues, and accrued revenues. However, a merchandiser using a perpetual inventory system is usually required to make another adjustment to update the Merchandise Inventory account to reflect any loss of merchandise, including theft and deterioration. **Shrinkage** is the term used to refer to the loss of inventory and it is computed by comparing a physical count of inventory with recorded amounts. A physical count is usually performed at least once annually.

**Point:** About two-thirds of shoplifting losses are thefts by employees.

To illustrate, Z-Mart's Merchandise Inventory account at the end of year 2011 has a balance of $21,250, but a physical count reveals that only $21,000 of inventory exists. The adjusting entry to record this $250 shrinkage is

Assets = Liabilities + Equity
−250                  −250

| Dec. 31 | Cost of Goods Sold ............................. | 250 | |
| | Merchandise Inventory ...................... | | 250 |
| | *To adjust for $250 shrinkage revealed by a physical count of inventory.* | | |

## Preparing Financial Statements

The financial statements of a merchandiser, and their preparation, are similar to those for a service company described in Chapters 2 through 4. The income statement mainly differs by the inclusion of *cost of goods sold* and *gross profit*. Also, net sales is affected by discounts, returns, and allowances, and some additional expenses are possible such as delivery expense and loss from defective merchandise. The balance sheet mainly differs by the inclusion of *merchandise inventory* as part of current assets. The statement of owner's equity is unchanged. A work sheet can be used to help prepare these statements, and one is illustrated in Appendix 5B for Z-Mart.

**Point:** Staples's costs of shipping merchandise to its stores is included in its costs of inventories as required by the cost principle.

## Closing Entries for Merchandisers

Closing entries are similar for service companies and merchandising companies using a perpetual system. The difference is that we must close some new temporary accounts that arise from merchandising activities. Z-Mart has several temporary accounts unique to merchandisers: Sales (of goods), Sales Discounts, Sales Returns and Allowances, and Cost of Goods Sold. Their existence in the ledger means that the first two closing entries for a merchandiser are slightly different from the ones described in the prior chapter for a service company. These differences are set in **red boldface** in the closing entries of Exhibit 5.11.

**Point:** The Inventory account is not affected by the closing process under a perpetual system.

**EXHIBIT 5.11**

Closing Entries for a Merchandiser

| **Step 1: Close Credit Balances in Temporary Accounts to Income Summary.** | | | |
|---|---|---|---|
| Dec. 31 | **Sales** .......................................... | **321,000** | |
| | Income Summary .......................... | | 321,000 |
| | *To close credit balances in temporary accounts.* | | |

| **Step 2: Close Debit Balances in Temporary Accounts to Income Summary.** | | | |
|---|---|---|---|
| Dec. 31 | Income Summary ............................... | 308,100 | |
| | **Sales Discounts** .......................... | | **4,300** |
| | **Sales Returns and Allowances** ............. | | **2,000** |
| | **Cost of Goods Sold** ...................... | | **230,400** |
| | Depreciation Expense ...................... | | 3,700 |
| | Salaries Expense .......................... | | 43,800 |
| | Insurance Expense ......................... | | 600 |
| | Rent Expense ............................. | | 9,000 |
| | Supplies Expense ......................... | | 3,000 |
| | Advertising Expense ...................... | | 11,300 |
| | *To close debit balances in temporary accounts.* | | |

**Step 3: Close Income Summary to Owner's Capital.**

The third closing entry is identical for a merchandising company and a service company. The $12,900 amount is net income reported on the income statement.

| | | | |
|---|---|---|---|
| Dec. 31 | Income Summary ............................... | 12,900 | |
| | K. Marty, Capital ........................... | | 12,900 |
| | *To close the Income Summary account.* | | |

**Step 4: Close Withdrawals Account to Owner's Capital.**

The fourth closing entry is identical for a merchandising company and a service company. It closes the Withdrawals account and adjusts the Owner's Capital account to the amount shown on the balance sheet.

| | | | |
|---|---|---|---|
| Dec. 31 | K. Marty, Capital ............................. | 4,000 | |
| | K. Marty, Withdrawals ...................... | | 4,000 |
| | *To close the Withdrawals account.* | | |

## Summary of Merchandising Entries

Exhibit 5.12 summarizes the key adjusting and closing entries of a merchandiser (using a perpetual inventory system) that are different from those of a service company described in prior chapters (the Demonstration Problem 2 illustrates these merchandising entries).

**EXHIBIT 5.12**

Summary of Merchandising Entries

| Merchandising Transactions | | Merchandising Entries | Dr. | Cr. |
|---|---|---|---|---|
| **Purchases** | Purchasing merchandise for resale. | Merchandise Inventory . . . . . . . . . . . . . . . . | # | |
| | | Cash or Accounts Payable . . . . . . . . . . | | # |
| | Paying freight costs on purchases; FOB shipping point. | Merchandise Inventory . . . . . . . . . . . . . . | # | |
| | | Cash . . . . . . . . . . . . . . . . . . . . . . . . . . | | # |
| | Paying within discount period. | Accounts Payable . . . . . . . . . . . . . . . . . | # | |
| | | Merchandise Inventory . . . . . . . . . . . . | | # |
| | | Cash . . . . . . . . . . . . . . . . . . . . . . . . . . | | # |
| | Recording purchase returns or allowances. | Cash or Accounts Payable . . . . . . . . . . . . . | # | |
| | | Merchandise Inventory . . . . . . . . . . . . | | # |
| **Sales** | Selling merchandise. | Cash or Accounts Receivable . . . . . . . . . . | # | |
| | | Sales . . . . . . . . . . . . . . . . . . . . . . . . . . | | # |
| | | Cost of Goods Sold . . . . . . . . . . . . . . . . | # | |
| | | Merchandise Inventory . . . . . . . . . . . . | | # |
| | Receiving payment within discount period. | Cash . . . . . . . . . . . . . . . . . . . . . . . . . . . | # | |
| | | Sales Discounts . . . . . . . . . . . . . . . . . . . | # | |
| | | Accounts Receivable . . . . . . . . . . . . . | | # |
| | Granting sales returns or allowances. | Sales Returns and Allowances . . . . . . . . . . | # | |
| | | Cash or Accounts Receivable . . . . . . . | | # |
| | | Merchandise Inventory . . . . . . . . . . . . . . | # | |
| | | Cost of Goods Sold . . . . . . . . . . . . . | | # |
| | Paying freight costs on sales; FOB destination. | Delivery Expense . . . . . . . . . . . . . . . . . . . | # | |
| | | Cash . . . . . . . . . . . . . . . . . . . . . . . . . | | # |

| Merchandising Events | | Adjusting and Closing Entries | | |
|---|---|---|---|---|
| **Adjusting** | Adjusting due to shrinkage (occurs when recorded amount larger than physical inventory). | Cost of Goods Sold . . . . . . . . . . . . . . . . . . | # | |
| | | Merchandise Inventory . . . . . . . . . . . . | | # |
| **Closing** | Closing temporary accounts with credit balances. | Sales . . . . . . . . . . . . . . . . . . . . . . . . . . . . | # | |
| | | Income Summary . . . . . . . . . . . . . . . . | | # |
| | Closing temporary accounts with debit balances. | Income Summary . . . . . . . . . . . . . . . . . . . | # | |
| | | Sales Returns and Allowances . . . . . . . | | # |
| | | Sales Discounts . . . . . . . . . . . . . . . . . . | | # |
| | | Cost of Goods Sold . . . . . . . . . . . . . . | | # |
| | | Delivery Expense . . . . . . . . . . . . . . . . | | # |
| | | "Other Expenses" . . . . . . . . . . . . . . . . | | # |

## Quick Check

Answers — p. 207

10. When a merchandiser uses a perpetual inventory system, why is it sometimes necessary to adjust the Merchandise Inventory balance with an adjusting entry?

11. What temporary accounts do you expect to find in a merchandising business but not in a service business?

12. Describe the closing entries normally made by a merchandising company.

# FINANCIAL STATEMENT FORMATS

**P4** Define and prepare multiple-step and single-step income statements.

Generally accepted accounting principles do not require companies to use any one presentation format for financial statements so we see many different formats in practice. This section describes two common income statement formats: multiple-step and single-step. The classified balance sheet of a merchandiser is also explained.

# Multiple-Step Income Statement

A **multiple-step income statement** format shows detailed computations of net sales and other costs and expenses, and reports subtotals for various classes of items. Exhibit 5.13 shows a multiple-step income statement for Z-Mart. The statement has three main parts: (1) *gross profit,* determined by net sales less cost of goods sold, (2) *income from operations,* determined by gross profit less operating expenses, and (3) *net income,* determined by income from operations adjusted for nonoperating items.

**EXHIBIT 5.13**

Multiple-Step Income Statement

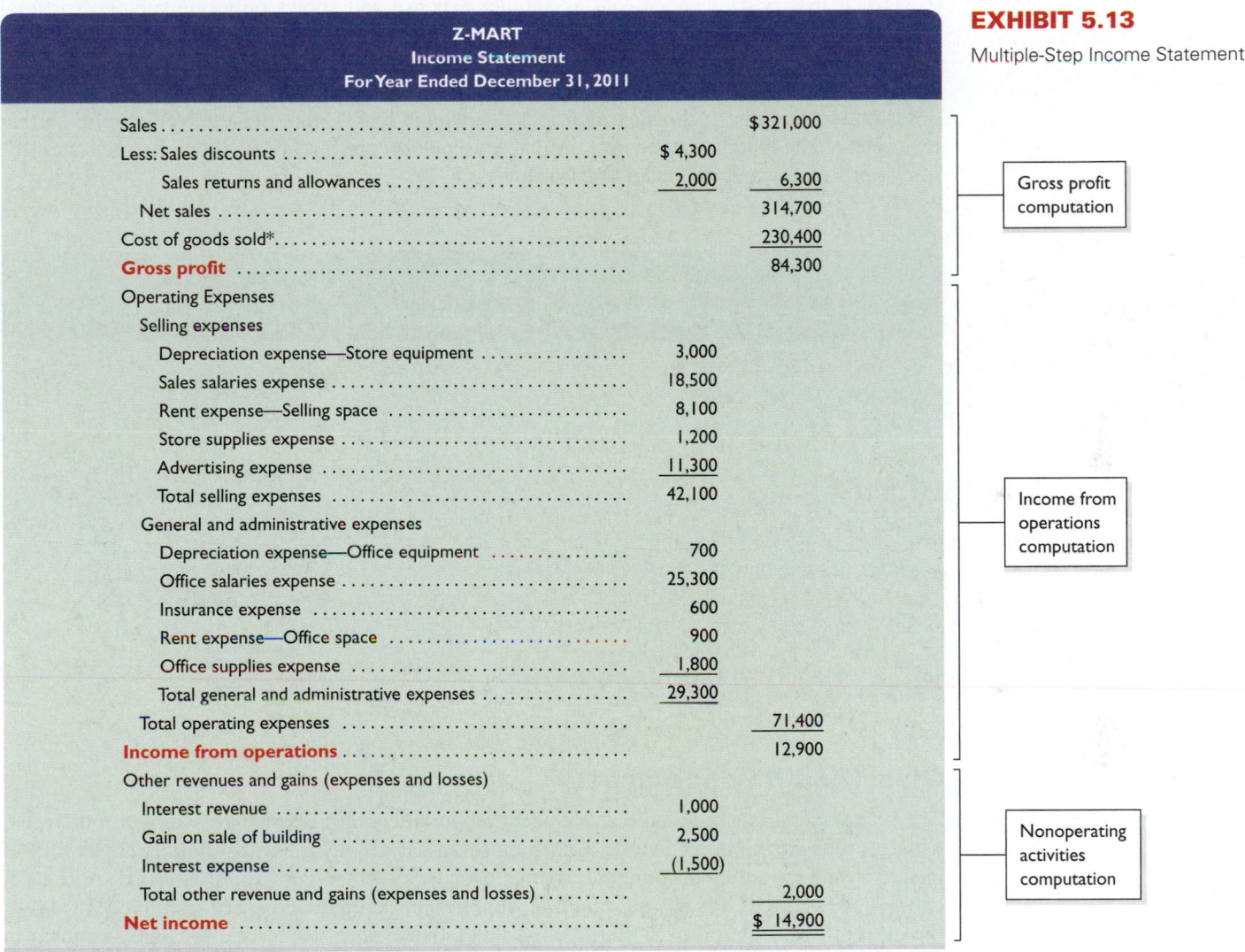

| Z-MART<br>Income Statement<br>For Year Ended December 31, 2011 | | | |
|---|---|---|---|
| Sales..................................................... | | | $321,000 |
| Less: Sales discounts ......................................... | | $4,300 | |
| Sales returns and allowances ........................... | | 2,000 | 6,300 |
| Net sales ..................................................... | | | 314,700 |
| Cost of goods sold*......................................... | | | 230,400 |
| **Gross profit** ............................................. | | | 84,300 |
| Operating Expenses | | | |
| Selling expenses | | | |
| Depreciation expense—Store equipment ................ | 3,000 | | |
| Sales salaries expense ................................... | 18,500 | | |
| Rent expense—Selling space ......................... | 8,100 | | |
| Store supplies expense ............................... | 1,200 | | |
| Advertising expense ................................... | 11,300 | | |
| Total selling expenses ............................... | 42,100 | | |
| General and administrative expenses | | | |
| Depreciation expense—Office equipment ............... | 700 | | |
| Office salaries expense ................................. | 25,300 | | |
| Insurance expense ..................................... | 600 | | |
| Rent expense—Office space ......................... | 900 | | |
| Office supplies expense ............................... | 1,800 | | |
| Total general and administrative expenses ............... | 29,300 | | |
| Total operating expenses ............................... | | 71,400 | |
| **Income from operations** ............................ | | 12,900 | |
| Other revenues and gains (expenses and losses) | | | |
| Interest revenue ....................................... | 1,000 | | |
| Gain on sale of building ............................... | 2,500 | | |
| Interest expense ....................................... | (1,500) | | |
| Total other revenue and gains (expenses and losses).......... | | 2,000 | |
| **Net income** ......................................... | | $14,900 | |

Gross profit computation

Income from operations computation

Nonoperating activities computation

*Cost of goods sold consists of the following:

| | |
|---|---|
| Beginning inventory..................... | $ 19,000 |
| Cost of goods purchased ............... | 232,400 |
| Cost of goods available for sale.......... | 251,400 |
| Less ending inventory ................. | 21,000 |
| Cost of goods sold..................... | $230,400 |

Operating expenses are classified into two sections. **Selling expenses** include the expenses of promoting sales by displaying and advertising merchandise, making sales, and delivering goods to customers. **General and administrative expenses** support a company's overall operations and include expenses related to accounting, human resource management, and financial management. Expenses are allocated between sections when they contribute to more than one. Z-Mart allocates rent expense of $9,000 from its store building between two sections: $8,100 to selling expense and $900 to general and administrative expense.

*Nonoperating activities* consist of other expenses, revenues, losses, and gains that are unrelated to a company's operations. *Other revenues and gains* commonly include interest revenue,

**Point:** Z-Mart did not have any non-operating activities; however, Exhibit 5.13 includes some for illustrative purposes.

dividend revenue, rent revenue, and gains from asset disposals. *Other expenses and losses* commonly include interest expense, losses from asset disposals, and casualty losses. When a company has no reportable nonoperating activities, its income from operations is simply labeled net income.

## Single-Step Income Statement

**Point:** Many companies report interest expense and interest revenue in separate categories after operating income and before subtracting income tax expense. As one example, see **Palm**'s income statement in Appendix A.

A **single-step income statement** is another widely used format and is shown in Exhibit 5.14 for Z-Mart. It lists cost of goods sold as another expense and shows only one subtotal for total expenses. Expenses are grouped into very few, if any, categories. Many companies use formats that combine features of both the single- and multiple-step statements. Provided that income statement items are shown sensibly, management can choose the format. (In later chapters, we describe some items, such as extraordinary gains and losses, that must be reported in certain locations on the income statement.) Similar presentation options are available for the statement of owner's equity and statement of cash flows.

**EXHIBIT 5.14**

Single-Step Income Statement

| Z-MART Income Statement For Year Ended December 31, 2011 | | |
|---|---:|---:|
| **Revenues** | | |
| Net sales | | $314,700 |
| Interest revenue | | 1,000 |
| Gain on sale of building | | 2,500 |
| Total revenues | | 318,200 |
| **Expenses** | | |
| Cost of goods sold | $230,400 | |
| Selling expenses | 42,100 | |
| General and administrative expenses | 29,300 | |
| Interest expense | 1,500 | |
| Total expenses | | 303,300 |
| **Net income** | | $ 14,900 |

## Classified Balance Sheet

The merchandiser's classified balance sheet reports merchandise inventory as a current asset, usually after accounts receivable according to an asset's nearness to liquidity. Inventory is usually less liquid than accounts receivable because inventory must first be sold before cash can be received; but it is more liquid than supplies and prepaid expenses. Exhibit 5.15 shows the current asset section of Z-Mart's classified balance sheet (other sections are as shown in Chapter 4).

**EXHIBIT 5.15**

Classified Balance Sheet (partial) of a Merchandiser

| Z-MART Balance Sheet (partial) December 31, 2011 | |
|---|---:|
| **Current assets** | |
| Cash | $ 8,200 |
| Accounts receivable | 11,200 |
| **Merchandise inventory** | **21,000** |
| Office supplies | 550 |
| Store supplies | 250 |
| Prepaid insurance | 300 |
| Total current assets | $ 41,500 |

## Decision Insight

**Merchandising Shenanigans** Accurate invoices are important to both sellers and buyers. Merchandisers rely on invoices to make certain they receive all monies for products provided—no more, no less. To achieve this, controls are set up. Still, failures arise. A survey reports that 9% of employees in sales and marketing witnessed false or misleading invoices sent to customers. Another 14% observed employees violating contract terms with customers (KPMG 2009). ■

## GLOBAL VIEW

This section discusses similarities and differences between U.S. GAAP and IFRS in accounting and reporting for merchandise purchases and sales, and for the income statement.

**Accounting for Merchandise Purchases and Sales** Both U.S. GAAP and IFRS include broad and similar guidance for the accounting of merchandise purchases and sales. Specifically, all of the transactions presented and illustrated in this chapter are accounted for identically under the two systems. The closing process for merchandisers also is identical for U.S. GAAP and IFRS. In the next chapter we describe how inventory valuation can, in some cases, be different for the two systems.

**Income Statement Presentation** We explained that net income, profit, and earnings refer to the same (*bottom line*) item. However, IFRS tends to use the term *profit* more than any other term, whereas U.S. statements tend to use *net income* more than any other term. Both U.S. GAAP and IFRS income statements begin with the net sales or net revenues (*top line*) item. For merchandisers and manufacturers, this is followed by cost of goods sold. The presentation is similar for the remaining items with the following differences.

- U.S. GAAP offers little guidance about the presentation or order of expenses. IFRS requires separate disclosures for financing costs (interest expense), income tax expense, and some other special items.
- Both systems require separate disclosure of items when their size, nature, or frequency are important for proper interpretation.
- IFRS permits expenses to be presented by their function or their nature. U.S. GAAP provides no direction but the SEC requires presentation by function.
- Neither U.S. GAAP nor IFRS define *operating* income; this means classification of expenses into operating or nonoperating reflects considerable management discretion.
- IFRS permits alternative measures of income on the income statement; U.S. GAAP prohibits disclosure of alternative income measures in financial statements.

**Nokia** provides the following example of income statement reporting.

NOKIA

| NOKIA<br>Income Statement (in Euros million)<br>For Year Ended December 31, 2009 | |
| --- | --- |
| Net sales . . . . . . . . . . . . . . . . . . . . . . . . . . . . . . | 40,984 |
| Cost of sales . . . . . . . . . . . . . . . . . . . . . . . . . . | 27,720 |
| Gross profit . . . . . . . . . . . . . . . . . . . . . . . . . . . | 13,264 |
| Research and development expenses . . . . . . . . . . . . | 5,909 |
| Selling and marketing expenses . . . . . . . . . . . . . . . . | 3,933 |
| Administrative and general expenses . . . . . . . . . . . . | 1,145 |
| Other income and expenses . . . . . . . . . . . . . . . . . . | 1,080 |
| Operating profit . . . . . . . . . . . . . . . . . . . . . . | 1,197 |
| Financial income and expenses (and other) . . . . . . . . | 235 |
| Profit before tax . . . . . . . . . . . . . . . . . . . . . . . | 962 |
| Tax . . . . . . . . . . . . . . . . . . . . . . . . . . . . . . . . . . | 702 |
| Profit . . . . . . . . . . . . . . . . . . . . . . . . . . . . . . . | 260 |

**Balance Sheet Presentation** Chapters 2 and 3 explained how both U.S. GAAP and IFRS require current items to be separated from noncurrent items on the balance sheet (yielding a *classified balance sheet*). As discussed, U.S. GAAP balance sheets report current items first. Assets are listed from most liquid to least liquid, whereas liabilities are listed from nearest to maturity to furthest from maturity. IFRS balance sheets normally present noncurrent items first (and equity before liabilities), but this is *not* a requirement. **Nokia** provides an example of IFRS reporting for the balance sheet in Appendix A.

## Decision Analysis                                     Acid-Test and Gross Margin Ratios

## Acid-Test Ratio

**A1** Compute the acid-test ratio and explain its use to assess liquidity.

For many merchandisers, inventory makes up a large portion of current assets. Inventory must be sold and any resulting accounts receivable must be collected before cash is available. Chapter 4 explained that the current ratio, defined as current assets divided by current liabilities, is useful in assessing a company's ability to pay current liabilities. Because it is sometimes unreasonable to assume that inventories are a source of payment for current liabilities, we look to other measures.

One measure of a merchandiser's ability to pay its current liabilities (referred to as its *liquidity*) is the acid-test ratio. It differs from the current ratio by excluding less liquid current assets such as inventory and prepaid expenses that take longer to be converted to cash. The **acid-test ratio,** also called *quick ratio*, is defined as *quick assets* (cash, short-term investments, and current receivables) divided by current liabilities—see Exhibit 5.16.

**EXHIBIT 5.16**

Acid-Test (Quick) Ratio

$$\text{Acid-test ratio} = \frac{\text{Cash and cash equivalents + Short-term investments + Current receivables}}{\text{Current liabilities}}$$

Exhibit 5.17 shows both the acid-test and current ratios of retailer **JCPenney** for fiscal years 2007 through 2010—also see margin graph. JCPenney's acid-test ratio reveals a general increase from 2007 through 2010 that exceeds the industry average. Further, JCPenney's current ratio (never less than 1.90) suggests that its short-term obligations can be confidently covered with short-term assets.

**EXHIBIT 5.17**

JCPenney's Acid-Test and Current Ratios

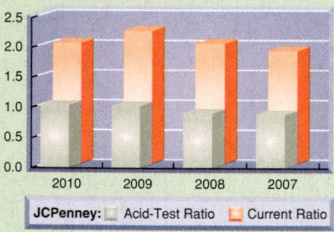

| ($ millions) | 2010 | 2009 | 2008 | 2007 |
|---|---|---|---|---|
| Total quick assets . . . . . . . . . . . . . | $3,406 | $2,704 | $2,845 | $2,901 |
| Total current assets . . . . . . . . . . . | $6,652 | $6,220 | $6,751 | $6,648 |
| Total current liabilities . . . . . . . . | $3,249 | $2,794 | $3,338 | $3,492 |
| **Acid-test ratio** . . . . . . . . . . . . . | **1.05** | **0.97** | **0.85** | **0.83** |
| **Current ratio** . . . . . . . . . . . . . . | **2.05** | **2.23** | **2.02** | **1.90** |
| Industry acid-test ratio . . . . . . . . . | 0.59 | 0.63 | 0.62 | 0.58 |
| Industry current ratio . . . . . . . . . . | 2.15 | 2.31 | 2.39 | 2.43 |

**Point:** Successful use of a just-in-time inventory system can narrow the gap between the acid-test ratio and the current ratio.

An acid-test ratio less than 1.0 means that current liabilities exceed quick assets. A rule of thumb is that the acid-test ratio should have a value near, or higher than, 1.0 to conclude that a company is unlikely to face near-term liquidity problems. A value much less than 1.0 raises liquidity concerns unless a company can generate enough cash from inventory sales or if much of its liabilities are not due until late in the next period. Similarly, a value slightly larger than 1.0 can hide a liquidity problem if payables are due shortly and receivables are not collected until late in the next period. Analysis of JCPenney shows no need for concern regarding its liquidity even though its acid-test ratio is less than one. This is because retailers such as JCPenney pay many current liabilities from inventory sales. Further, in all years, JCPenney's acid-test ratios exceed the industry norm (and its inventory is fairly liquid).

### ◼ Decision Maker                                             Answer — p. 206

**Supplier**   A retailer requests to purchase supplies on credit from your company. You have no prior experience with this retailer. The retailer's current ratio is 2.1, its acid-test ratio is 0.5, and inventory makes up most of its current assets. Do you extend credit? ◼

## Gross Margin Ratio

**A2** Compute the gross margin ratio and explain its use to assess profitability.

The cost of goods sold makes up much of a merchandiser's expenses. Without sufficient gross profit, a merchandiser will likely fail. Users often compute the gross margin ratio to help understand this relation. It differs from the profit margin ratio in that it excludes all costs except cost of goods sold. The **gross margin ratio** (also called *gross profit ratio*) is defined as *gross margin* (net sales minus cost of goods sold) divided by net sales—see Exhibit 5.18.

**EXHIBIT 5.18**

Gross Margin Ratio

$$\text{Gross margin ratio} = \frac{\text{Net sales } - \text{ Cost of goods sold}}{\text{Net sales}}$$

Exhibit 5.19 shows the gross margin ratio of **JCPenney** for fiscal years 2007 through 2010. For JCPenney, each $1 of sales in 2010 yielded about 39.4¢ in gross margin to cover all other expenses and still produce a net income. This 39.4¢ margin is up from 39.3¢ in 2007. This slight increase is a favorable development. Success for merchandisers such as JCPenney depends on adequate gross margin. For example, the 0.1¢ increase in the gross margin ratio, computed as 39.4¢ − 39.3¢, means that JCPenney has $17.6 million more in gross margin! (This is computed as net sales of $17,556 million multiplied by the 0.1% increase in gross margin.) Management's discussion in its annual report attributes this improvement to its "strategy to sell a greater portion of merchandise at regular promotional prices and less at clearance prices."

**Point:** The power of a ratio is often its ability to identify areas for more detailed analysis.

**EXHIBIT 5.19**

JCPenney's Gross Margin Ratio

| ($ millions) | 2010 | 2009 | 2008 | 2007 |
|---|---|---|---|---|
| Gross margin | $ 6,910 | $ 6,915 | $ 7,671 | $ 7,825 |
| Net sales | $17,556 | $18,486 | $19,860 | $19,903 |
| Gross margin ratio | 39.4% | 37.4% | 38.6% | 39.3% |

■ **Decision Maker**                                    Answer − p. 207

**Financial Officer**  Your company has a 36% gross margin ratio and a 17% net profit margin ratio. Industry averages are 44% for gross margin and 16% for net profit margin. Do these comparative results concern you? ■

# DEMONSTRATION PROBLEM 1

Use the following adjusted trial balance and additional information to complete the requirements.

**KC ANTIQUES**
**Adjusted Trial Balance**
**December 31, 2011**

| | Debit | Credit |
|---|---|---|
| Cash | $ 7,000 | |
| Accounts receivable | 13,000 | |
| Merchandise inventory | 60,000 | |
| Store supplies | 1,500 | |
| Equipment | 45,600 | |
| Accumulated depreciation—Equipment | | $ 16,600 |
| Accounts payable | | 9,000 |
| Salaries payable | | 2,000 |
| K. Carter, Capital | | 79,000 |
| K. Carter, Withdrawals | 10,000 | |
| Sales | | 343,250 |
| Sales discounts | 5,000 | |
| Sales returns and allowances | 6,000 | |
| Cost of goods sold | 159,900 | |
| Depreciation expense—Store equipment | 4,100 | |
| Depreciation expense—Office equipment | 1,600 | |
| Sales salaries expense | 30,000 | |
| Office salaries expense | 34,000 | |
| Insurance expense | 11,000 | |
| Rent expense (70% is store, 30% is office) | 24,000 | |
| Store supplies expense | 5,750 | |
| Advertising expense | 31,400 | |
| Totals | $449,850 | $449,850 |

KC Antiques' *supplementary records* for 2011 reveal the following itemized costs for merchandising activities:

| | |
|---|---:|
| Invoice cost of merchandise purchases ........ | $150,000 |
| Purchase discounts received ................. | 2,500 |
| Purchase returns and allowances ............. | 2,700 |
| Cost of transportation-in ................... | 5,000 |

**Required**

1. Use the supplementary records to compute the total cost of merchandise purchases for 2011.
2. Prepare a 2011 multiple-step income statement. (Inventory at December 31, 2010, is $70,100.)
3. Prepare a single-step income statement for 2011.
4. Prepare closing entries for KC Antiques at December 31, 2011.
5. Compute the acid-test ratio and the gross margin ratio. Explain the meaning of each ratio and interpret them for KC Antiques.

## PLANNING THE SOLUTION

- Compute the total cost of merchandise purchases for 2011.
- To prepare the multiple-step statement, first compute net sales. Then, to compute cost of goods sold, add the net cost of merchandise purchases for the year to beginning inventory and subtract the cost of ending inventory. Subtract cost of goods sold from net sales to get gross profit. Then classify expenses as selling expenses or general and administrative expenses.
- To prepare the single-step income statement, begin with net sales. Then list and subtract the expenses.
- The first closing entry debits all temporary accounts with credit balances and opens the Income Summary account. The second closing entry credits all temporary accounts with debit balances. The third entry closes the Income Summary account to the capital account, and the fourth entry closes the withdrawals account to the capital account.
- Identify the quick assets on the adjusted trial balance. Compute the acid-test ratio by dividing quick assets by current liabilities. Compute the gross margin ratio by dividing gross profit by net sales.

## SOLUTION TO DEMONSTRATION PROBLEM 1

**1.**

| | |
|---|---:|
| Invoice cost of merchandise purchases ........ | $150,000 |
| Less: Purchases discounts received ........... | 2,500 |
| Purchase returns and allowances ......... | 2,700 |
| Add: Cost of transportation-in .............. | 5,000 |
| Total cost of merchandise purchases .......... | $149,800 |

**2.** Multiple-step income statement

| KC ANTIQUES | | |
|---|---|---|
| Income Statement | | |
| For Year Ended December 31, 2011 | | |
| Sales ........................................ | | $343,250 |
| Less: Sales discounts ............................... | $ 5,000 | |
|     Sales returns and allowances ................... | 6,000 | 11,000 |
|     Net sales ...................................... | | 332,250 |
| Cost of goods sold* .............................. | | 159,900 |
| Gross profit .................................... | | 172,350 |
| Expenses | | |
|    Selling expenses | | |
|       Depreciation expense—Store equipment ......... | 4,100 | |
|       Sales salaries expense ....................... | 30,000 | |
|       Rent expense—Selling space ................... | 16,800 | |
|       Store supplies expense ...................... | 5,750 | |
|       Advertising expense .......................... | 31,400 | |
|      Total selling expenses ...................... | 88,050 | |

[continued on next page]

[continued from previous page]

| General and administrative expenses | | |
|---|---|---|
| Depreciation expense—Office equipment . . . . . . . . . | 1,600 | |
| Office salaries expense . . . . . . . . . . . . . . . . . . . . . . | 34,000 | |
| Insurance expense . . . . . . . . . . . . . . . . . . . . . . . . | 11,000 | |
| Rent expense—Office space . . . . . . . . . . . . . . . . . | 7,200 | |
| Total general and administrative expenses . . . . . . . . . | 53,800 | |
| Total operating expenses . . . . . . . . . . . . . . . . . . . . | | 141,850 |
| Net income . . . . . . . . . . . . . . . . . . . . . . . . . . . . . . | | $ 30,500 |

\* Cost of goods sold can also be directly computed (applying concepts from Exhibit 5.4):

| | |
|---|---|
| Merchandise inventory, December 31, 2010 . . . . . . . . . . . . . | $ 70,100 |
| Total cost of merchandise purchases (from part 1) . . . . . . . . . | 149,800 |
| Goods available for sale . . . . . . . . . . . . . . . . . . . . . . . . . . | 219,900 |
| Merchandise inventory, December 31, 2011 . . . . . . . . . . . . . | 60,000 |
| Cost of goods sold . . . . . . . . . . . . . . . . . . . . . . . . . . . . . | $159,900 |

**3.** Single-step income statement

| KC ANTIQUES | | |
|---|---|---|
| **Income Statement** | | |
| **For Year Ended December 31, 2011** | | |
| Net sales . . . . . . . . . . . . . . . . . . . . . . . . . . . . . | | $332,250 |
| Expenses | | |
| Cost of goods sold . . . . . . . . . . . . . . . . . . . . | $159,900 | |
| Selling expenses . . . . . . . . . . . . . . . . . . . . . . | 88,050 | |
| General and administrative expenses . . . . . . . . | 53,800 | |
| Total expenses . . . . . . . . . . . . . . . . . . . . . . . | | 301,750 |
| Net income . . . . . . . . . . . . . . . . . . . . . . . . . . | | $ 30,500 |

**4.**

| Dec. 31 | Sales . . . . . . . . . . . . . . . . . . . . . . . . . . . . . . . . . . . . | 343,250 | |
|---|---|---|---|
| | Income Summary . . . . . . . . . . . . . . . . . . . . . . . . . | | 343,250 |
| | *To close credit balances in temporary accounts.* | | |
| Dec. 31 | Income Summary . . . . . . . . . . . . . . . . . . . . . . . . . | 312,750 | |
| | Sales Discounts . . . . . . . . . . . . . . . . . . . . . . . . . . | | 5,000 |
| | Sales Returns and Allowances . . . . . . . . . . . . . . . . | | 6,000 |
| | Cost of Goods Sold . . . . . . . . . . . . . . . . . . . . . . . | | 159,900 |
| | Depreciation Expense—Store Equipment . . . . . . . | | 4,100 |
| | Depreciation Expense—Office Equipment . . . . . . | | 1,600 |
| | Sales Salaries Expense . . . . . . . . . . . . . . . . . . . . . | | 30,000 |
| | Office Salaries Expense . . . . . . . . . . . . . . . . . . . . | | 34,000 |
| | Insurance Expense . . . . . . . . . . . . . . . . . . . . . . . . | | 11,000 |
| | Rent Expense . . . . . . . . . . . . . . . . . . . . . . . . . . . | | 24,000 |
| | Store Supplies Expense . . . . . . . . . . . . . . . . . . . . | | 5,750 |
| | Advertising Expense . . . . . . . . . . . . . . . . . . . . . . | | 31,400 |
| | *To close debit balances in temporary accounts.* | | |
| Dec. 31 | Income Summary . . . . . . . . . . . . . . . . . . . . . . . . . | 30,500 | |
| | K. Carter, Capital . . . . . . . . . . . . . . . . . . . . . . . . | | 30,500 |
| | *To close the Income Summary account.* | | |
| Dec. 31 | K. Carter, Capital . . . . . . . . . . . . . . . . . . . . . . . . . | 10,000 | |
| | K. Carter, Withdrawals . . . . . . . . . . . . . . . . . . . . | | 10,000 |
| | *To close the Withdrawals account.* | | |

**5.** Acid-test ratio = (Cash and equivalents + Short-term investments + Current receivables)/
Current liabilities

= (Cash + Accounts receivable/(Accounts payable + Salaries payable)

= ($7,000 + $13,000)/($9,000 + $2,000) = $20,000/$11,000 = <u>1.82</u>

Gross margin ratio = Gross profit/Net sales = $172,350/$332,250 = <u>0.52</u> (or 52%)

KC Antiques has a healthy acid-test ratio of 1.82. This means it has more than $1.80 in liquid assets to satisfy each $1.00 in current liabilities. The gross margin of 0.52 shows that KC Antiques spends 48¢ ($1.00 − $0.52) of every dollar of net sales on the costs of acquiring the merchandise it sells. This leaves 52¢ of every dollar of net sales to cover other expenses incurred in the business and to provide a net profit.

# DEMONSTRATION PROBLEM 2

Prepare journal entries to record the following merchandising transactions for both the seller (BMX) and buyer (Sanuk).

| | |
|---|---|
| May 4 | BMX sold $1,500 of merchandise on account to Sanuk, terms FOB shipping point, n/45, invoice dated May 4. The cost of the merchandise was $900. |
| May 6 | Sanuk paid transportation charges of $30 on the May 4 purchase from BMX. |
| May 8 | BMX sold $1,000 of merchandise on account to Sanuk, terms FOB destination, n/30, invoice dated May 8. The cost of the merchandise was $700. |
| May 10 | BMX paid transportation costs of $50 for delivery of merchandise sold to Sanuk on May 8. |
| May 16 | BMX issued Sanuk a $200 credit memorandum for merchandise returned. The merchandise was purchased by Sanuk on account on May 8. The cost of the merchandise returned was $140. |
| May 18 | BMX received payment from Sanuk for purchase of May 8. |
| May 21 | BMX sold $2,400 of merchandise on account to Sanuk, terms FOB shipping point, 2/10, n/EOM. BMX prepaid transportation costs of $100, which were added to the invoice. The cost of the merchandise was $1,440. |
| May 31 | BMX received payment from Sanuk for purchase of May 21, less discount (2% × $2,400). |

## SOLUTION TO DEMONSTRATION PROBLEM 2

| | BMX (Seller) | | | Sanuk (Buyer) | | |
|---|---|---|---|---|---|---|
| May 4 | Accounts Receivable—Sanuk | 1,500 | | Merchandise Inventory | 1,500 | |
| | Sales | | 1,500 | Accounts Payable—BMX | | 1,500 |
| | Cost of Goods Sold | 900 | | | | |
| | Merchandise Inventory | | 900 | | | |
| 6 | No entry. | | | Merchandise Inventory | 30 | |
| | | | | Cash | | 30 |
| 8 | Accounts Receivable—Sanuk | 1,000 | | Merchandise Inventory | 1,000 | |
| | Sales | | 1,000 | Accounts Payable—BMX | | 1,000 |
| | Cost of Goods Sold | 700 | | | | |
| | Merchandise Inventory | | 700 | | | |
| 10 | Delivery Expense | 50 | | No entry. | | |
| | Cash | | 50 | | | |
| 16 | Sales Returns & Allowances | 200 | | Accounts Payable—BMX | 200 | |
| | Accounts Receivable—Sanuk | | 200 | Merchandise Inventory | | 200 |
| | Merchandise Inventory | 140 | | | | |
| | Cost of Goods Sold | | 140 | | | |
| 18 | Cash | 800 | | Accounts Payable—BMX | 800 | |
| | Accounts Receivable—Sanuk | | 800 | Cash | | 800 |
| 21 | Accounts Receivable—Sanuk | 2,400 | | Merchandise Inventory | 2,500 | |
| | Sales | | 2,400 | Accounts Payable—BMX | | 2,500 |
| | Accounts Receivable—Sanuk | 100 | | | | |
| | Cash | | 100 | | | |
| | Cost of Goods Sold | 1,440 | | | | |
| | Merchandise Inventory | | 1,440 | | | |
| 31 | Cash | 2,452 | | Accounts Payable—BMX | 2,500 | |
| | Sales Discounts | 48 | | Merchandise Inventory | | 48 |
| | Accounts Receivable—Sanuk | | 2,500 | Cash | | 2,452 |

# Periodic Inventory System

A periodic inventory system requires updating the inventory account only at the *end of a period* to reflect the quantity and cost of both the goods available and the goods sold. Thus, during the period, the Merchandise Inventory balance remains unchanged. It reflects the beginning inventory balance until it is updated at the end of the period. During the period the cost of merchandise is recorded in a temporary *Purchases* account. When a company sells merchandise, it records revenue **but not the cost of the goods sold.** At the end of the period when a company prepares financial statements, it takes a *physical count of inventory* by counting the quantities and costs of merchandise available. The cost of goods sold is then computed by subtracting the ending inventory amount from the cost of merchandise available for sale.

**Recording Merchandise Transactions**    Under a periodic system, purchases, purchase returns and allowances, purchase discounts, and transportation-in transactions are recorded in separate temporary accounts. At period-end, each of these temporary accounts is closed and the Merchandise Inventory account is updated. To illustrate, journal entries under the periodic inventory system are shown for the most common transactions (codes *a* through *f* link these transactions to those in the chapter, and we drop explanations for simplicity). For comparison, perpetual system journal entries are shown to the right of each periodic entry, where differences are in green font.

> **P5** Record and compare merchandising transactions using both periodic and perpetual inventory systems.

**Purchases**    The periodic system uses a temporary *Purchases* account that accumulates the cost of all purchase transactions during each period. Z-Mart's November 2 entry to record the purchase of merchandise for $1,200 on credit with terms of 2/10, n/30 is

(*a*)

| Periodic | | | Perpetual | | |
|---|---|---|---|---|---|
| Purchases ............... | 1,200 | | Merchandise Inventory ......... | 1,200 | |
| Accounts Payable ..... | | 1,200 | Accounts Payable ......... | | 1,200 |

**Purchase Discounts**    The periodic system uses a temporary *Purchase Discounts* account that accumulates discounts taken on purchase transactions during the period. If payment in (*a*) is delayed until after the discount period expires, the entry is to debit Accounts Payable and credit Cash for $1,200 each. However, if Z-Mart pays the supplier for the previous purchase in (*a*) within the discount period, the required payment is $1,176 ($1,200 × 98%) and is recorded as

(*b*)

| Periodic | | | Perpetual | | |
|---|---|---|---|---|---|
| Accounts Payable ......... | 1,200 | | Accounts Payable ............. | 1,200 | |
| Purchase Discounts .... | | 24 | Merchandise Inventory ..... | | 24 |
| Cash ............... | | 1,176 | Cash .................. | | 1,176 |

**Purchase Returns and Allowances**    Z-Mart returned merchandise purchased on November 2 because of defects. In the periodic system, the temporary *Purchase Returns and Allowances* account accumulates the cost of all returns and allowances during a period. The recorded cost (including discounts) of the defective merchandise is $300, and Z-Mart records the November 15 return with this entry:

(*c*)

| Periodic | | | Perpetual | | |
|---|---|---|---|---|---|
| Accounts Payable ......... | 300 | | Accounts Payable ............. | 300 | |
| Purchase Returns and Allowances ....... | | 300 | Merchandise Inventory ..... | | 300 |

**Transportation-In**    Z-Mart paid a $75 freight charge to transport merchandise to its store. In the periodic system, this cost is charged to a temporary *Transportation-In* account.

(d)

| Periodic | | | Perpetual | | |
|---|---|---|---|---|---|
| Transportation-In . . . . . . . . . | 75 | | Merchandise Inventory . . . . . . . . . | 75 | |
| Cash . . . . . . . . . . . . . . | | 75 | Cash . . . . . . . . . . . . . . . . . . | | 75 |

**Sales**   Under the periodic system, the cost of goods sold is *not* recorded at the time of each sale. (We later show how to compute total cost of goods sold at the end of a period.) Z-Mart's November 3 entry to record sales of $2,400 in merchandise on credit (when its cost is $1,600) is:

(e)

| Periodic | | | Perpetual | | |
|---|---|---|---|---|---|
| Accounts Receivable . . . . . . | 2,400 | | Accounts Receivable . . . . . . . . . . | 2,400 | |
| Sales . . . . . . . . . . . . . . | | 2,400 | Sales . . . . . . . . . . . . . . . . . . | | 2,400 |
| | | | Cost of Goods Sold . . . . . . . . . . . | 1,600 | |
| | | | Merchandise Inventory . . . . | | 1,600 |

**Sales Returns**   A customer returned part of the merchandise from the transaction in (*e*), where the returned items sell for $800 and cost $600. (*Recall:* The periodic system records only the revenue effect, not the cost effect, for sales transactions.) Z-Mart restores the merchandise to inventory and records the November 6 return as

(f)

| Periodic | | | Perpetual | | |
|---|---|---|---|---|---|
| Sales Returns and | | | Sales Returns and | | |
| Allowances . . . . . . . . . . . . . | 800 | | Allowances . . . . . . . . . . . . . . . . | 800 | |
| Accounts Receivable. . . | | 800 | Accounts Receivable . . . . . . | | 800 |
| | | | Merchandise Inventory . . . . . . . . . | 600 | |
| | | | Cost of Goods Sold . . . . . . . | | 600 |

**Sales Discounts**   To illustrate sales discounts, assume that the remaining $1,600 of receivables (computed as $2,400 from *e* less $800 for *f* ) has credit terms of 3/10, n/90 and that customers all pay within the discount period. Z-Mart records this payment as

| Periodic | | | Perpetual | | |
|---|---|---|---|---|---|
| Cash . . . . . . . . . . . . . . . . . . | 1,552 | | Cash . . . . . . . . . . . . . . . . . . . . | 1,552 | |
| Sales Discounts ($1,600 × .03) | 48 | | Sales Discounts ($1,600 × .03) . . . | 48 | |
| Accounts Receivable . . . | | 1,600 | Accounts Receivable . . . . . . | | 1,600 |

**Adjusting and Closing Entries**   The periodic and perpetual inventory systems have slight differences in adjusting and closing entries. The period-end Merchandise Inventory balance (unadjusted) is $19,000 under the periodic system and $21,250 under the perpetual system. Since the periodic system does not update the Merchandise Inventory balance during the period, the $19,000 amount is the beginning inventory. However, the $21,250 balance under the perpetual system is the recorded ending inventory before adjusting for any inventory shrinkage.

A physical count of inventory taken at the end of the period reveals $21,000 of merchandise available. The adjusting and closing entries for the two systems are shown in Exhibit 5A.1. The periodic system records the ending inventory of $21,000 in the Merchandise Inventory account (which includes

**EXHIBIT 5A.1**

Comparison of Adjusting and Closing Entries—Periodic and Perpetual

| PERIODIC | | | PERPETUAL | | |
|---|---|---|---|---|---|
| Adjusting Entry—Shrinkage | | | Adjusting Entry—Shrinkage | | |
| None | | | Cost of Goods Sold . . . . . . . . . . . . . . . . . . . | 250 | |
| | | | Merchandise Inventory . . . . . . . . . . . . . | | 250 |

[continued on next page]

[continued from previous page]

| PERIODIC | | |
|---|---|---|
| **Closing Entries** | | |
| (1) Sales ........................................ | 321,000 | |
| **Merchandise Inventory** ................ | **21,000** | |
| **Purchase Discounts** ................... | **4,200** | |
| **Purchase Returns and Allowances** ..... | **1,500** | |
| Income Summary .................. | | 347,700 |
| (2) Income Summary | 334,800 | |
| Sales Discounts .................... | | 4,300 |
| Sales Returns and Allowances ....... | | 2,000 |
| **Merchandise Inventory** .......... | | **19,000** |
| **Purchases** ...................... | | **235,800** |
| **Transportation-In** ............... | | **2,300** |
| Depreciation Expense ............... | | 3,700 |
| Salaries Expense ................... | | 43,800 |
| Insurance Expense ................ | | 600 |
| Rent Expense .................... | | 9,000 |
| Supplies Expense ................... | | 3,000 |
| Advertising Expense ............... | | 11,300 |
| (3) Income Summary .................... | 12,900 | |
| K. Marty, Capital ................... | | 12,900 |
| (4) K. Marty, Capital ...................... | 4,000 | |
| K. Marty, Withdrawals ............. | | 4,000 |

| PERPETUAL | | |
|---|---|---|
| **Closing Entries** | | |
| (1) Sales ..................................... | 321,000 | |
| Income Summary ................... | | 321,000 |
| (2) Income Summary ..................... | 308,100 | |
| Sales Discounts .................... | | 4,300 |
| Sales Returns and Allowances ....... | | 2,000 |
| **Cost of Goods Sold** ............. | | **230,400** |
| Depreciation Expense ............... | | 3,700 |
| Salaries Expense ................... | | 43,800 |
| Insurance Expense ................ | | 600 |
| Rent Expense .................... | | 9,000 |
| Supplies Expense ................... | | 3,000 |
| Advertising Expense ............... | | 11,300 |
| (3) Income Summary .................... | 12,900 | |
| K. Marty, Capital ................... | | 12,900 |
| (4) K. Marty, Capital ...................... | 4,000 | |
| K. Marty, Withdrawals ............. | | 4,000 |

shrinkage) in the first closing entry and removes the $19,000 beginning inventory balance from the account in the second closing entry.[2]

By updating Merchandise Inventory and closing Purchases, Purchase Discounts, Purchase Returns and Allowances, and Transportation-In, the periodic system transfers the cost of goods sold amount to Income Summary. Review the periodic side of Exhibit 5A.1 and notice that the **boldface** items affect Income Summary as follows.

| | |
|---|---:|
| Credit to Income Summary in the first closing entry includes amounts from: | |
| Merchandise inventory (ending) ............................................ | $   21,000 |
| Purchase discounts ....................................................... | 4,200 |
| Purchase returns and allowances ......................................... | 1,500 |
| Debit to Income Summary in the second closing entry includes amounts from: | |
| Merchandise inventory (beginning) ......................................... | (19,000) |
| Purchases ................................................................ | (235,800) |
| Transportation-in ........................................................ | (2,300) |
| **Net effect on Income Summary** ......................................... | **$(230,400)** |

This $230,400 effect on Income Summary is the cost of goods sold amount. The periodic system transfers cost of goods sold to the Income Summary account but without using a Cost of Goods Sold account. Also, the periodic system does not separately measure shrinkage. Instead, it computes cost of goods available

---

[2] This approach is called the *closing entry method*. An alternative approach, referred to as the *adjusting entry method*, would not make any entries to Merchandise Inventory in the closing entries of Exhibit 5A.1, but instead would make two adjusting entries. Using Z-Mart data, the two adjusting entries would be: (1) Dr. Income Summary and Cr. Merchandise Inventory for $19,000 each, and (2) Dr. Merchandise Inventory and Cr. Income Summary for $21,000 each. The first entry removes the beginning balance of Merchandise Inventory, and the second entry records the actual ending balance.

for sale, subtracts the cost of ending inventory, and defines the difference as cost of goods sold, which includes shrinkage.

**Preparing Financial Statements**   The financial statements of a merchandiser using the periodic system are similar to those for a service company described in prior chapters. The income statement mainly differs by the inclusion of *cost of goods sold* and *gross profit*—of course, net sales is affected by discounts, returns, and allowances. The cost of goods sold section under the periodic system follows

| Calculation of Cost of Goods Sold For Year Ended December 31, 2011 | |
|---|---|
| Beginning inventory .................. | $ 19,000 |
| Cost of goods purchased ............. | 232,400 |
| Cost of goods available for sale ........ | 251,400 |
| Less ending inventory ............... | 21,000 |
| Cost of goods sold ................. | $230,400 |

The balance sheet mainly differs by the inclusion of *merchandise inventory* in current assets—see Exhibit 5.15. The statement of owner's equity is unchanged. A work sheet can be used to help prepare these statements. The only differences under the periodic system from the work sheet illustrated in Appendix 5B using the perpetual system are highlighted as follows in blue boldface font.

File  Edit  View  Insert  Format  Tools  Data  Accounting  Window  Help

| | No. | Account | Unadjusted Trial Balance Dr. | Cr. | Adjustments Dr. | Cr. | Adjusted Trial Balance Dr. | Cr. | Income Statement Dr. | Cr. | Balance Sheet Dr. | Cr. |
|---|---|---|---|---|---|---|---|---|---|---|---|---|
| 3 | 101 | Cash | 8,200 | | | | 8,200 | | | | 8,200 | |
| 4 | 106 | Accounts receivable | 11,200 | | | | 11,200 | | | | 11,200 | |
| 5 | 119 | **Merchandise Inventory** | 19,000 | | | | 19,000 | | 19,000 | 21,000 | 21,000 | |
| 6 | 126 | Supplies | 3,800 | | | (b) 3,000 | 800 | | | | 800 | |
| 7 | 128 | Prepaid insurance | 900 | | | (a)  600 | 300 | | | | 300 | |
| 8 | 167 | Equipment | 34,200 | | | | 34,200 | | | | 34,200 | |
| 9 | 168 | Accumulated depr.—Equip. | | 3,700 | | (c) 3,700 | | 7,400 | | | | 7,400 |
| 10 | 201 | Accounts payable | | 16,000 | | | | 16,000 | | | | 16,000 |
| 11 | 209 | Salaries payable | | | | (d)  800 | | 800 | | | | 800 |
| 12 | 301 | K. Marty, Capital | | 42,600 | | | | 42,600 | | | | 42,600 |
| 13 | 302 | K. Marty, Withdrawals | 4,000 | | | | 4,000 | | | | 4,000 | |
| 14 | 413 | Sales | | 321,000 | | | | 321,000 | | 321,000 | | |
| 15 | 414 | Sales returns and allowances | 2,000 | | | | 2,000 | | 2,000 | | | |
| 16a | 415 | Sales discounts | 4,300 | | | | 4,300 | | 4,300 | | | |
| 16b | 505 | **Purchases** | 235,800 | | | | 235,800 | | 235,800 | | | |
| 16c | 506 | **Purchases returns & allowance** | | 1,500 | | | | 1,500 | | 1,500 | | |
| 16d | 507 | **Purchases discounts** | | 4,200 | | | | 4,200 | | 4,200 | | |
| 17 | 508 | **Transportation-in** | 2,300 | | | | 2,300 | | 2,300 | | | |
| 18 | 612 | Depreciation expense—Equip. | | | (c) 3,700 | | 3,700 | | 3,700 | | | |
| 19 | 622 | Salaries expense | 43,000 | | (d)  800 | | 43,800 | | 43,800 | | | |
| 20 | 637 | Insurance expense | | | (a)  600 | | 600 | | 600 | | | |
| 21 | 640 | Rent expense | 9,000 | | | | 9,000 | | 9,000 | | | |
| 22 | 652 | Supplies expense | | | (b) 3,000 | | 3,000 | | 3,000 | | | |
| 23 | 655 | Advertising expense | 11,300 | | | | 11,300 | | 11,300 | | | |
| 24 | | Totals | 389,000 | 389,000 | 8,100 | 8,100 | 393,500 | 393,500 | 334,800 | 347,700 | 79,700 | 66,800 |
| 25 | | Net income | | | | | | | 12,900 | | | 12,900 |
| 26 | | Totals | | | | | | | 347,700 | 347,700 | 79,700 | 79,700 |

Sheet1  Sheet2  Sheet3

## Quick Check

Answers — p. 207

**13.** What account is used in a perpetual inventory system but not in a periodic system?

**14.** Which of the following accounts are temporary accounts under a periodic system?
(*a*) Merchandise Inventory; (*b*) Purchases; (*c*) Transportation-In.

**15.** How is cost of goods sold computed under a periodic inventory system?

**16.** Do reported amounts of ending inventory and net income differ if the adjusting entry method of recording the change in inventory is used instead of the closing entry method?

---

APPENDIX

# Work Sheet—Perpetual System

# 5B

Exhibit 5B.1 shows the work sheet for preparing financial statements of a merchandiser. It differs slightly from the work sheet layout in Chapter 4—the differences are in **red boldface**. Also, the adjustments in the work sheet reflect the following: (*a*) Expiration of $600 of prepaid insurance. (*b*) Use of $3,000 of supplies. (*c*) Depreciation of $3,700 for equipment. (*d*) Accrual of $800 of unpaid salaries. (*e*) Inventory shrinkage of $250. Once the adjusted amounts are extended into the financial statement columns, the information is used to develop financial statements.

**EXHIBIT 5B.1**

Work Sheet for Merchandiser (using a perpetual system)

File Edit View Insert Format Tools Data Accounting Window Help

| No. | Account | Unadjusted Trial Balance Dr. | Cr. | Adjustments Dr. | Cr. | Adjusted Trial Balance Dr. | Cr. | Income Statement Dr. | Cr. | Balance Sheet Dr. | Cr. |
|---|---|---|---|---|---|---|---|---|---|---|---|
| 101 | Cash | 8,200 | | | | 8,200 | | | | 8,200 | |
| 106 | Accounts receivable | 11,200 | | | | 11,200 | | | | 11,200 | |
| 119 | **Merchandise Inventory** | 21,250 | | | (e) 250 | 21,000 | | | | 21,000 | |
| 126 | Supplies | 3,800 | | | (b) 3,000 | 800 | | | | 800 | |
| 128 | Prepaid insurance | 900 | | | (a) 600 | 300 | | | | 300 | |
| 167 | Equipment | 34,200 | | | | 34,200 | | | | 34,200 | |
| 168 | Accumulated depr.—Equip. | | 3,700 | | (c) 3,700 | | 7,400 | | | | 7,400 |
| 201 | Accounts payable | | 16,000 | | | | 16,000 | | | | 16,000 |
| 209 | Salaries payable | | | | (d) 800 | | 800 | | | | 800 |
| 301 | K. Marty, Capital | | 42,600 | | | | 42,600 | | | | 42,600 |
| 302 | K. Marty, Withdrawals | 4,000 | | | | 4,000 | | | | 4,000 | |
| 413 | **Sales** | | 321,000 | | | | 321,000 | | 321,000 | | |
| 414 | **Sales returns and allowances** | 2,000 | | | | 2,000 | | 2,000 | | | |
| 415 | **Sales discounts** | 4,300 | | | | 4,300 | | 4,300 | | | |
| 502 | **Cost of goods sold** | 230,150 | | (e) 250 | | 230,400 | | 230,400 | | | |
| 612 | Depreciation expense—Equip. | | | (c) 3,700 | | 3,700 | | 3,700 | | | |
| 622 | Salaries expense | 43,000 | | (d) 800 | | 43,800 | | 43,800 | | | |
| 637 | Insurance expense | | | (a) 600 | | 600 | | 600 | | | |
| 640 | Rent expense | 9,000 | | | | 9,000 | | 9,000 | | | |
| 652 | Supplies expense | | | (b) 3,000 | | 3,000 | | 3,000 | | | |
| 655 | Advertising expense | 11,300 | | | | 11,300 | | 11,300 | | | |
| | Totals | 383,300 | 383,300 | 8,350 | 8,350 | 387,800 | 387,800 | 308,100 | 321,000 | 79,700 | 66,800 |
| | Net income | | | | | | | 12,900 | | | 12,900 |
| | Totals | | | | | | | 321,000 | 321,000 | 79,700 | 79,700 |

Sheet1 / Sheet2 / Sheet3

# Summary

**C1** **Describe merchandising activities and identify income components for a merchandising company.** Merchandisers buy products and resell them. Examples of merchandisers include Walmart, Home Depot, The Limited, and Barnes & Noble. A merchandiser's costs on the income statement include an amount for cost of goods sold. Gross profit, or gross margin, equals sales minus cost of goods sold.

**C2** **Identify and explain the inventory asset and cost flows of a merchandising company.** The current asset section of a merchandising company's balance sheet includes *merchandise inventory,* which refers to the products a merchandiser sells and are available for sale at the balance sheet date. Cost of merchandise purchases flows into Merchandise Inventory and from there to Cost of Goods Sold on the income statement. Any remaining inventory is reported as a current asset on the balance sheet.

**A1** **Compute the acid-test ratio and explain its use to assess liquidity.** The acid-test ratio is computed as quick assets (cash, short-term investments, and current receivables) divided by current liabilities. It indicates a company's ability to pay its current liabilities with its existing quick assets. An acid-test ratio equal to or greater than 1.0 is often adequate.

**A2** **Compute the gross margin ratio and explain its use to assess profitability.** The gross margin ratio is computed as gross margin (net sales minus cost of goods sold) divided by net sales. It indicates a company's profitability before considering other expenses.

**P1** **Analyze and record transactions for merchandise purchases using a perpetual system.** For a perpetual inventory system, purchases of inventory (net of trade discounts) are added to the Merchandise Inventory account. Purchase discounts and purchase returns and allowances are subtracted from Merchandise Inventory, and transportation-in costs are added to Merchandise Inventory.

**P2** **Analyze and record transactions for merchandise sales using a perpetual system.** A merchandiser records sales at list price less any trade discounts. The cost of items sold is transferred from Merchandise Inventory to Cost of Goods Sold. Refunds or credits given to customers for unsatisfactory merchandise are recorded in Sales Returns and Allowances, a contra account to Sales. If merchandise is returned and restored to inventory, the cost of this merchandise is removed from Cost of Goods Sold and transferred back to Merchandise Inventory. When cash discounts from the sales price are offered and customers pay within the discount period, the seller records Sales Discounts, a contra account to Sales.

**P3** **Prepare adjustments and close accounts for a merchandising company.** With a perpetual system, it is often necessary to make an adjustment for inventory shrinkage. This is computed by comparing a physical count of inventory with the Merchandise Inventory balance. Shrinkage is normally charged to Cost of Goods Sold. Temporary accounts closed to Income Summary for a merchandiser include Sales, Sales Discounts, Sales Returns and Allowances, and Cost of Goods Sold.

**P4** **Define and prepare multiple-step and single-step income statements.** Multiple-step income statements include greater detail for sales and expenses than do single-step income statements. They also show details of net sales and report expenses in categories reflecting different activities.

**P5<sup>A</sup>** **Record and compare merchandising transactions using both periodic and perpetual inventory systems.** A perpetual inventory system continuously tracks the cost of goods available for sale and the cost of goods sold. A periodic system accumulates the cost of goods purchased during the period and does not compute the amount of inventory or the cost of goods sold until the end of a period. Transactions involving the sale and purchase of merchandise are recorded and analyzed under both the periodic and perpetual inventory systems. Adjusting and closing entries for both inventory systems are illustrated and explained.

---

## Guidance Answers to Decision Maker and Decision Ethics

**Entrepreneur** For terms of 3/10, n/90, missing the 3% discount for an additional 80 days equals an implied annual interest rate of 13.69%, computed as (365 days ÷ 80 days) × 3%. Since you can borrow funds at 11% (assuming no other processing costs), it is better to borrow and pay within the discount period. You save 2.69% (13.69% − 11%) in interest costs by paying early.

**Credit Manager** Your decision is whether to comply with prior policy or to create a new policy and not abuse discounts offered by suppliers. Your first step should be to meet with your superior to find out if the late payment policy is the actual policy and, if so, its rationale. If it is the policy to pay late, you must apply your own sense of ethics. One point of view is that the late payment policy is unethical. A deliberate plan to make late payments means the company lies when it pretends to make payment within the discount period. Another view is that the late payment policy is acceptable. In some markets, attempts to take discounts through late payments are accepted as a continued phase of "price negotiation." Also, your company's suppliers can respond by billing your company for the discounts not accepted because of late payments. However, this is a dubious viewpoint, especially since the prior manager proposes that you dishonestly explain late payments as computer or mail problems and since some suppliers have complained.

**Supplier** A current ratio of 2.1 suggests sufficient current assets to cover current liabilities. An acid-test ratio of 0.5 suggests, however, that quick assets can cover only about one-half of current liabilities. This implies that the retailer depends on money from sales of inventory to pay current liabilities. If sales of inventory decline or profit margins decrease, the likelihood that this retailer will default on its payments increases. Your decision is probably not to extend credit. If you do extend credit, you are likely to closely monitor the retailer's financial condition. (It is better to hold unsold inventory than uncollectible receivables.)

**Financial Officer**  Your company's net profit margin is about equal to the industry average and suggests typical industry performance. However, gross margin reveals that your company is paying far more in cost of goods sold or receiving far less in sales price than competitors. Your attention must be directed to finding the problem with cost of goods sold, sales, or both. One positive note is that your company's expenses make up 19% of sales (36% − 17%). This favorably compares with competitors' expenses that make up 28% of sales (44% − 16%).

## Guidance Answers to Quick Checks

1. Cost of goods sold is the cost of merchandise purchased from a supplier that is sold to customers during a specific period.

2. Gross profit (or gross margin) is the difference between net sales and cost of goods sold.

3. Widespread use of computing and related technology has dramatically increased the use of the perpetual inventory system.

4. Under credit terms of 2/10, n/60, the credit period is 60 days and the discount period is 10 days.

5. (b) trade discount.

6. *FOB* means "free on board." It is used in identifying the point when ownership transfers from seller to buyer. *FOB destination* means that the seller transfers ownership of goods to the buyer when they arrive at the buyer's place of business. It also means that the seller is responsible for paying shipping charges and bears the risk of damage or loss during shipment.

7. Recording sales discounts and sales returns and allowances separately from sales gives useful information to managers for internal monitoring and decision making.

8. When a customer returns merchandise *and* the seller restores the merchandise to inventory, two entries are necessary. One entry records the decrease in revenue and credits the customer's account. The second entry debits inventory and reduces cost of goods sold.

9. Credit memorandum—seller credits accounts receivable from buyer.

10. Merchandise Inventory may need adjusting to reflect shrinkage.

11. Sales (of goods), Sales Discounts, Sales Returns and Allowances, and Cost of Goods Sold (and maybe Delivery Expense).

12. Four closing entries: (1) close credit balances in temporary accounts to Income Summary, (2) close debit balances in temporary accounts to Income Summary, (3) close Income Summary to owner's capital, and (4) close withdrawals account to owner's capital.

13. Cost of Goods Sold.

14. (b) Purchases and (c) Transportation-In.

15. Under a periodic inventory system, the cost of goods sold is determined at the end of an accounting period by adding the net cost of goods purchased to the beginning inventory and subtracting the ending inventory.

16. Both methods report the same ending inventory and income.

## Key Terms

mhhe.com/wildFAP20e

Acid-test ratio (p. 196)
Cash discount (p. 183)
Cost of goods sold (p. 180)
Credit memorandum (p. 189)
Credit period (p. 183)
Credit terms (p. 183)
Debit memorandum (p. 184)
Discount period (p. 183)
EOM (p. 183)
FOB (p. 185)
General and administrative expenses (p. 193)

Gross margin (p. 181)
Gross margin ratio (p. 196)
Gross profit (p. 180)
Inventory (p. 181)
List price (p. 182)
Merchandise (p. 180)
Merchandise inventory (p. 181)
Merchandiser (p. 180)
Multiple-step income statement (p. 192)
Periodic inventory system (p. 182)
Perpetual inventory system (p. 182)

Purchase discount (p. 183)
Retailer (p. 180)
Sales discount (p. 183)
Selling expenses (p. 193)
Shrinkage (p. 190)
Single-step income statement (p. 193)
Supplementary records (p. 186)
Trade discount (p. 182)
Wholesaler (p. 180)

## Multiple Choice Quiz

Answers on p. 225

mhhe.com/wildFAP20e

Additional Quiz Questions are available at the book's Website.

1. A company has $550,000 in net sales and $193,000 in gross profit. This means its cost of goods sold equals
    a. $743,000
    b. $550,000
    c. $357,000
    d. $193,000
    e. $(193,000)

**2.** A company purchased $4,500 of merchandise on May 1 with terms of 2/10, n/30. On May 6, it returned $250 of that merchandise. On May 8, it paid the balance owed for merchandise, taking any discount it is entitled to. The cash paid on May 8 is
  **a.** $4,500
  **b.** $4,250
  **c.** $4,160
  **d.** $4,165
  **e.** $4,410

**3.** A company has cash sales of $75,000, credit sales of $320,000, sales returns and allowances of $13,700, and sales discounts of $6,000. Its net sales equal
  **a.** $395,000
  **b.** $375,300
  **c.** $300,300
  **d.** $339,700
  **e.** $414,700

**4.** A company's quick assets are $37,500, its current assets are $80,000, and its current liabilities are $50,000. Its acid-test ratio equals
  **a.** 1.600
  **b.** 0.750
  **c.** 0.625
  **d.** 1.333
  **e.** 0.469

**5.** A company's net sales are $675,000, its costs of goods sold are $459,000, and its net income is $74,250. Its gross margin ratio equals
  **a.** 32%
  **b.** 68%
  **c.** 47%
  **d.** 11%
  **e.** 34%

---

$^{A(B)}$ *Superscript letter A (B) denotes assignments based on Appendix 5A (5B).*

🔧 Icon denotes assignments that involve decision making.

## Discussion Questions

**1.** In comparing the accounts of a merchandising company with those of a service company, what additional accounts would the merchandising company likely use, assuming it employs a perpetual inventory system?

**2.** What items appear in financial statements of merchandising companies but not in the statements of service companies?

**3.** 🔧 Explain how a business can earn a positive gross profit on its sales and still have a net loss.

**4.** 🔧 Why do companies offer a cash discount?

**5.** How does a company that uses a perpetual inventory system determine the amount of inventory shrinkage?

**6.** Distinguish between cash discounts and trade discounts. Is the amount of a trade discount on purchased merchandise recorded in the accounts?

**7.** What is the difference between a sales discount and a purchase discount?

**8.** 🔧 Why would a company's manager be concerned about the quantity of its purchase returns if its suppliers allow unlimited returns?

**9.** Does the sender (maker) of a debit memorandum record a debit or a credit in the recipient's account? What entry (debit or credit) does the recipient record?

**10.** What is the difference between the single-step and multiple-step income statement formats?

**11.** 🔧 Refer to the balance sheet and income statement for **Research In Motion** in Appendix A. What does the company title its inventory account? Does the company present a detailed calculation of its cost of sales? **RIM**

**12.** Refer to **Nokia**'s income statement in Appendix A. What title does it use for cost of goods sold? **NOKIA**

**13.** Refer to the income statement for **Apple** in Appendix A. What does Apple title its cost of goods sold account? **Apple**

**14.** Refer to the income statement of **Palm** in Appendix A. Does its income statement report a gross profit figure? If yes, what is the amount? **Palm**

**15.** 🔧 Buyers negotiate purchase contracts with suppliers. What type of shipping terms should a buyer attempt to negotiate to minimize freight-in costs?

---

connect

## QUICK STUDY

**QS 5-1**

Applying merchandising terms

C1

Enter the letter for each term in the blank space beside the definition that it most closely matches.

  **A.** Cash discount
  **B.** Credit period
  **C.** Discount period
  **D.** FOB destination
  **E.** FOB shipping point
  **F.** Gross profit
  **G.** Merchandise inventory
  **H.** Purchase discount
  **I.** Sales discount
  **J.** Trade discount

——— **1.** Ownership of goods is transferred when delivered to the buyer's place of business.
——— **2.** Time period in which a cash discount is available.
——— **3.** Difference between net sales and the cost of goods sold.
——— **4.** Reduction in a receivable or payable if it is paid within the discount period.
——— **5.** Purchaser's description of a cash discount received from a supplier of goods.
——— **6.** Ownership of goods is transferred when the seller delivers goods to the carrier.
——— **7.** Reduction below list or catalog price that is negotiated in setting the price of goods.
——— **8.** Seller's description of a cash discount granted to buyers in return for early payment.
——— **9.** Time period that can pass before a customer's payment is due.
——— **10.** Goods a company owns and expects to sell to its customers.

---

The cost of merchandise inventory includes which of the following:

**a.** Costs incurred to buy the goods.
**b.** Costs incurred to ship the goods to the store(s).
**c.** Costs incurred to make the goods ready for sale.
**d.** Both a and b.
**e.** a, b, and c.

**QS 5-2**
Identifying inventory costs
C2

---

Prepare journal entries to record each of the following purchases transactions of a merchandising company. Show supporting calculations and assume a perpetual inventory system.

Mar. 5   Purchased 500 units of product at a cost of $5 per unit. Terms of the sale are 2/10, n/60; the invoice is dated March 5.
Mar. 7   Returned 50 defective units from the March 5 purchase and received full credit.
Mar. 15   Paid the amount due from the March 5 purchase, less the return on March 7.

**QS 5-3**
Recording purchases—perpetual system
P1

---

Prepare journal entries to record each of the following sales transactions of a merchandising company. Show supporting calculations and assume a perpetual inventory system.

Apr. 1   Sold merchandise for $2,000, granting the customer terms of 2/10, EOM; invoice dated April 1. The cost of the merchandise is $1,400.
Apr. 4   The customer in the April 1 sale returned merchandise and received credit for $500. The merchandise, which had cost $350, is returned to inventory.
Apr. 11   Received payment for the amount due from the April 1 sale less the return on April 4.

**QS 5-4**
Recording sales—perpetual system
P2

---

Compute net sales, gross profit, and the gross margin ratio for each separate case *a* through *d*. Interpret the gross margin ratio for case *a*.

**QS 5-5**
Computing and analyzing gross margin
A2

| | a | b | c | d |
|---|---|---|---|---|
| Sales | $130,000 | $512,000 | $35,700 | $245,700 |
| Sales discounts | 4,200 | 16,500 | 400 | 3,500 |
| Sales returns and allowances | 17,000 | 5,000 | 5,000 | 700 |
| Cost of goods sold | 76,600 | 326,700 | 21,300 | 125,900 |

---

Nix'It Company's ledger on July 31, its fiscal year-end, includes the following selected accounts that have normal balances (Nix'It uses the perpetual inventory system).

**QS 5-6**
Accounting for shrinkage—perpetual system
P3

| | | | |
|---|---|---|---|
| Merchandise inventory | $ 34,800 | Sales returns and allowances | $ 3,500 |
| T. Nix, Capital | 115,300 | Cost of goods sold | 102,000 |
| T. Nix, Withdrawals | 7,000 | Depreciation expense | 7,300 |
| Sales | 157,200 | Salaries expense | 29,500 |
| Sales discounts | 1,700 | Miscellaneous expenses | 2,000 |

A physical count of its July 31 year-end inventory discloses that the cost of the merchandise inventory still available is $32,900. Prepare the entry to record any inventory shrinkage.

**QS 5-7**
Closing entries **P3**

Refer to QS 5-6 and prepare journal entries to close the balances in temporary revenue and expense accounts. Remember to consider the entry for shrinkage that is made to solve QS 5-6.

**QS 5-8**
Computing and interpreting acid-test ratio

**A1**

Use the following information on current assets and current liabilities to compute and interpret the acid-test ratio. Explain what the acid-test ratio of a company measures.

| | | | | |
|---|---|---|---|---|
| Cash | $1,200 | | Prepaid expenses | $ 600 |
| Accounts receivable | 2,700 | | Accounts payable | 4,750 |
| Inventory | 5,000 | | Other current liabilities | 950 |

**QS 5-9**
Contrasting liquidity ratios **A1**

Identify similarities and differences between the acid-test ratio and the current ratio. Compare and describe how the two ratios reflect a company's ability to meet its current obligations.

**QS 5-10**
Multiple-step income statement

**P4**

The multiple-step income statement normally includes which of the following:
**a.** Detailed computations of net sales.
**b.** Detailed computations of expenses, including subtotals for various expense categories.
**c.** Operating expenses are usually classified into (1) selling expenses and (2) general and administrative expenses.
**d.** Both a and c.
**e.** a, b, and c.

**QS 5-11**<sup>A</sup>
Contrasting periodic and perpetual systems

**P5**

Identify whether each description best applies to a periodic or a perpetual inventory system.
**a.** Provides more timely information to managers.
**b.** Requires an adjusting entry to record inventory shrinkage.
**c.** Markedly increased in frequency and popularity in business within the past decade.
**d.** Records cost of goods sold each time a sales transaction occurs.
**e.** Updates the inventory account only at period-end.

**QS 5-12**<sup>A</sup>
Recording purchases— periodic system **P5**

Refer to QS 5-3 and prepare journal entries to record each of the merchandising transactions assuming that the periodic inventory system is used.

**QS 5-13**<sup>A</sup>
Recording purchases— periodic system **P5**

Refer to QS 5-4 and prepare journal entries to record each of the merchandising transactions assuming that the periodic inventory system is used.

**QS 5-14**
IFRS income statement presentation

**P4**

Income statement information for **adidas Group**, a German footwear, apparel, and accessories manufacturer, for the year ended December 31, 2009, follows. The company applies IFRS, as adopted by the European Union, and reports its results in millions of Euros. Prepare its calendar year 2009 (1) multiple-step income statement and (2) single-step income statement.

| | |
|---|---|
| Net income | € 245 |
| Financial income | 19 |
| Financial expenses | 169 |
| Operating profit | 508 |
| Cost of sales | 5,669 |
| Income taxes | 113 |
| Income before taxes | 358 |
| Gross profit | 4,712 |
| Royalty and commission income | 86 |
| Other operating income | 100 |
| Other operating expenses | 4,390 |
| Net sales | 10,381 |

Answer each of the following questions related to international accounting standards.

**a.** Explain how the accounting for merchandise purchases and sales is different between accounting un- der IFRS versus U.S. GAAP.

**b.** Income statements prepared under IFRS usually report an item titled *finance costs*. What do finance costs refer to?

**c.** U.S. GAAP prohibits alternative measures of income reported on the income statement. Does IFRS permit such alternative measures on the income statement?

**QS 5-15**
International accounting standards
C1

---

![McGraw Hill connect]

---

Prepare journal entries to record the following transactions for a retail store. Assume a perpetual inventory system.

Apr. 2 Purchased merchandise from Blue Company under the following terms: $3,600 price, invoice dated April 2, credit terms of 2/15, n/60, and FOB shipping point.

3 Paid $200 for shipping charges on the April 2 purchase.

4 Returned to Blue Company unacceptable merchandise that had an invoice price of $600.

17 Sent a check to Blue Company for the April 2 purchase, net of the discount and the returned merchandise.

18 Purchased merchandise from Fox Corp. under the following terms: $7,500 price, invoice dated April 18, credit terms of 2/10, n/30, and FOB destination.

21 After negotiations, received from Fox a $2,100 allowance on the April 18 purchase.

28 Sent check to Fox paying for the April 18 purchase, net of the discount and allowance.

**EXERCISES**

**Exercise 5-1**
Recording entries for merchandise purchases

**P1**

**Check**   April 28, Cr. Cash $5,292

---

Taos Company purchased merchandise for resale from Tuscon Company with an invoice price of $22,000 and credit terms of 3/10, n/60. The merchandise had cost Tuscon $15,000. Taos paid within the discount period. Assume that both buyer and seller use a perpetual inventory system.

**1.** Prepare entries that the buyer should record for (*a*) the purchase and (*b*) the cash payment.

**2.** Prepare entries that the seller should record for (*a*) the sale and (*b*) the cash collection.

**3.** Assume that the buyer borrowed enough cash to pay the balance on the last day of the discount period at an annual interest rate of 11% and paid it back on the last day of the credit period. Compute how much the buyer saved by following this strategy. (Assume a 365-day year and round dollar amounts to the nearest cent, including computation of interest per day.)

**Exercise 5-2**
Analyzing and recording merchandise transactions— both buyer and seller

**P1 P2**

**Check**   (3) $338.50 savings (rounded)

---

The operating cycle of a merchandiser with credit sales includes the following five activities. Starting with merchandise acquisition, identify the chronological order of these five activities.

**a.** _____ purchases of merchandise.

**b.** _____ credit sales to customers.

**c.** _____ inventory made available for sale.

**d.** _____ cash collections from customers.

**e.** _____ accounts receivable accounted for.

**Exercise 5-3**
Operating cycle for merchandiser

**C2**

---

Spare Parts was organized on May 1, 2011, and made its first purchase of merchandise on May 3. The pur- chase was for 1,000 units at a price of $10 per unit. On May 5, Spare Parts sold 600 of the units for $14 per unit to DeSoto Co. Terms of the sale were 2/10, n/60. Prepare entries for Spare Parts to record the May 5 sale and each of the following separate transactions *a* through *c* using a perpetual inventory system.

**a.** On May 7, DeSoto returns 200 units because they did not fit the customer's needs. Spare Parts restores the units to its inventory.

**b.** On May 8, DeSoto discovers that 50 units are damaged but are still of some use and, therefore, keeps the units. Spare Parts sends DeSoto a credit memorandum for $300 to compensate for the damage.

**c.** On May 15, DeSoto discovers that 72 units are the wrong color. DeSoto keeps 43 of these units because Spare Parts sends a $92 credit memorandum to compensate. DeSoto returns the remaining 29 units to Spare Parts. Spare Parts restores the 29 returned units to its inventory.

**Exercise 5-4**
Recording sales returns and allowances  **P2**

**Check**   (c) Dr. Merchandise Inventory $290

---

Refer to Exercise 5-4 and prepare the appropriate journal entries for DeSoto Co. to record the May 5 pur- chase and each of the three separate transactions *a* through *c*. DeSoto is a retailer that uses a perpetual inventory system and purchases these units for resale.

**Exercise 5-5**
Recording purchase returns and allowances  **P1**

**Exercise 5-6**

Analyzing and recording
merchandise transactions—
both buyer and seller

P1  P2

**Check** (1) May 20, Cr. Cash $27,936

On May 11, Smythe Co. accepts delivery of $30,000 of merchandise it purchases for resale from Hope Corporation. With the merchandise is an invoice dated May 11, with terms of 3/10, n/90, FOB shipping point. The goods cost Hope $20,000. When the goods are delivered, Smythe pays $335 to Express Shipping for delivery charges on the merchandise. On May 12, Smythe returns $1,200 of goods to Hope, who receives them one day later and restores them to inventory. The returned goods had cost Hope $800. On May 20, Smythe mails a check to Hope Corporation for the amount owed. Hope receives it the following day. (Both Smythe and Hope use a perpetual inventory system.)

1. Prepare journal entries that Smythe Co. records for these transactions.

2. Prepare journal entries that Hope Corporation records for these transactions.

**Exercise 5-7**

Sales returns and allowances

C1

Business decision makers desire information on sales returns and allowances. (1) Explain why a company's manager wants the accounting system to record customers' returns of unsatisfactory goods in the Sales Returns and Allowances account instead of the Sales account. (2) Explain whether this information would be useful for external decision makers.

**Exercise 5-8**

Recording effects of
merchandising activities

P1  P2

The following supplementary records summarize Titus Company's merchandising activities for year 2011. Set up T-accounts for Merchandise Inventory and Cost of Goods Sold. Then record the summarized activities in those T-accounts and compute account balances.

| | |
|---|---:|
| Cost of merchandise sold to customers in sales transactions ................... | $186,000 |
| Merchandise inventory, December 31, 2010 ............................... | 27,000 |
| Invoice cost of merchandise purchases ......................................... | 190,500 |
| Shrinkage determined on December 31, 2011 ............................... | 700 |
| Cost of transportation-in ......................................................... | 1,900 |
| Cost of merchandise returned by customers and restored to inventory .......... | 2,200 |
| Purchase discounts received ....................................................... | 1,600 |
| Purchase returns and allowances ................................................ | 4,100 |

**Check** Year-End Merchandise
Inventory Dec. 31, $29,200

**Exercise 5-9**

Computing revenues, expenses,
and income

C1  C2

Using your accounting knowledge, fill in the blanks in the following separate income statements *a* through *e*. Identify any negative amount by putting it in parentheses.

| | a | b | c | d | e |
|---|---:|---:|---:|---:|---:|
| Sales ....................................... | $60,000 | $42,500 | $36,000 | $ ? | $23,600 |
| Cost of goods sold | | | | | |
|   Merchandise inventory (beginning) ........... | 6,000 | 17,050 | 7,500 | 7,000 | 2,560 |
|     Total cost of merchandise purchases ......... | 36,000 | ? | ? | 32,000 | 5,600 |
|   Merchandise inventory (ending) ............. | ? | (2,700) | (9,000) | (6,600) | ? |
|     Cost of goods sold ...................... | 34,050 | 15,900 | ? | ? | 5,600 |
| Gross profit ................................... | ? | ? | 3,750 | 45,600 | ? |
| Expenses .................................... | 9,000 | 10,650 | 12,150 | 2,600 | 6,000 |
| Net income (loss) .......................... | $ ? | $15,950 | $ (8,400) | $43,000 | $ ? |

**Exercise 5-10**

Preparing adjusting and closing
entries for a merchandiser

P3

The following list includes selected permanent accounts and all of the temporary accounts from the December 31, 2011, unadjusted trial balance of Deacon Co., a business owned by Julie Deacon. Use these account balances along with the additional information to journalize (*a*) adjusting entries and (*b*) closing entries. Deacon Co. uses a perpetual inventory system.

| | Debit | Credit |
|---|---:|---:|
| Merchandise inventory ............. | $ 28,000 | |
| Prepaid selling expenses ............ | 5,000 | |
| J. Deacon, Withdrawals ............. | 2,200 | |
| Sales ........................... | | $429,000 |
| Sales returns and allowances ........ | 16,500 | |
| Sales discounts .................. | 4,000 | |
| Cost of goods sold ............... | 211,000 | |
| Sales salaries expense ............. | 47,000 | |
| Utilities expense ................. | 14,000 | |
| Selling expenses ................. | 35,000 | |
| Administrative expenses ........... | 95,000 | |

**Additional Information**

Accrued sales salaries amount to $1,600. Prepaid selling expenses of $2,000 have expired. A physical count of year-end merchandise inventory shows $27,450 of goods still available.

**Check**   Entry to close Income
Summary: Cr. J. Deacon, Capital
$2,350

---

A retail company recently completed a physical count of ending merchandise inventory to use in preparing adjusting entries. In determining the cost of the counted inventory, company employees failed to consider that $2,000 of incoming goods had been shipped by a supplier on December 31 under an FOB shipping point agreement. These goods had been recorded in Merchandise Inventory as a purchase, but they were not included in the physical count because they were in transit. Explain how this overlooked fact affects the company's financial statements and the following ratios: return on assets, debt ratio, current ratio, and acid-test ratio.

**Exercise 5-11**
Interpreting a physical count error as inventory shrinkage

**A1**

---

Refer to the information in Exercise 5-11 and explain how the error in the physical count affects the company's gross margin ratio and its profit margin ratio.

**Exercise 5-12**
Physical count error and profits

**A2**

---

Compute the current ratio and acid-test ratio for each of the following separate cases. (Round ratios to two decimals.) Which company case is in the best position to meet short-term obligations? Explain.

|  | Case A | Case B | Case C |
|---|---|---|---|
| Cash . . . . . . . . . . . . . . . . . . . . . . . | $ 800 | $ 510 | $3,200 |
| Short-term investments . . . . . . . . | 0 | 0 | 1,100 |
| Current receivables . . . . . . . . . . . . | 0 | 790 | 800 |
| Inventory . . . . . . . . . . . . . . . . . . . . | 2,000 | 1,600 | 1,900 |
| Prepaid expenses . . . . . . . . . . . . . . | 1,200 | 600 | 300 |
| Total current assets . . . . . . . . . . . | $4,000 | $3,500 | $7,300 |
| Current liabilities . . . . . . . . . . . . . . | $2,200 | $1,100 | $3,650 |

**Exercise 5-13**
Computing and analyzing acid-test and current ratios

**A1**

---

Journalize the following merchandising transactions for CSI Systems assuming it uses a perpetual inventory system.

1. On November 1, CSI Systems purchases merchandise for $1,400 on credit with terms of 2/5, n/30, FOB shipping point; invoice dated November 1.
2. On November 5, CSI Systems pays cash for the November 1 purchase.
3. On November 7, CSI Systems discovers and returns $100 of defective merchandise purchased on November 1 for a cash refund.
4. On November 10, CSI Systems pays $80 cash for transportation costs with the November 1 purchase.
5. On November 13, CSI Systems sells merchandise for $1,500 on credit. The cost of the merchandise is $750.
6. On November 16, the customer returns merchandise from the November 13 transaction. The returned items sell for $200 and cost $100.

**Exercise 5-14**
Preparing journal entries— perpetual system

**P1   P2**

---

A company reports the following sales related information: Sales (gross) of $100,000; Sales discounts of $2,000; Sales returns and allowances of $8,000; Sales salaries expense of $5,000. Prepare the net sales portion only of this company's multiple-step income statement.

**Exercise 5-15**
Multiple-step income statement

**P4**

---

Refer to Exercise 5-1 and prepare journal entries to record each of the merchandising transactions assuming that the periodic inventory system is used.

**Exercise 5-16ᴬ**
Recording purchases— periodic system   **P5**

---

Refer to Exercise 5-2 and prepare journal entries to record each of the merchandising transactions assuming that the periodic inventory system is used by both the buyer and the seller. (Skip the part 3 requirement.)

**Exercise 5-17ᴬ**
Recording purchases and sales— periodic system   **P5**

**Exercise 5-18^A**
Buyer and seller transactions—periodic system   P5

Refer to Exercise 5-6 and prepare journal entries to record each of the merchandising transactions assuming that the periodic inventory system is used by both the buyer and the seller.

**Exercise 5-19^A**
Recording purchases—periodic system   P5

Refer to Exercise 5-14 and prepare journal entries to record each of the merchandising transactions assuming that the periodic inventory system is used.

**Exercise 5-20**
Preparing an income statement following IFRS

P4

**L'Oréal** reports the following income statement accounts for the year ended December 31, 2009 (euros in millions). Prepare the income statement for this company for the year ended December 31, 2009, following usual IFRS practices.

| | | | | |
|---|---|---|---|---|
| Net profit | € 1,794.9 | Income tax expense | € 676.1 |
| Finance costs | 76.0 | Profit before tax expense | 2,471.0 |
| Net sales | 17,472.6 | Research and development expense | 609.2 |
| Gross profit | 12,311.0 | Selling, general and administrative expense | 3,735.5 |
| Other expense | 30.6 | Advertising and promotion expense | 5,388.7 |
| Cost of sales | 5,161.6 | | |

**connect**

# PROBLEM SET A

**Problem 5-1A**
Preparing journal entries for merchandising activities—perpetual system

P1  P2

**Check**  Aug. 9, Dr. Delivery Expense, $120

Aug. 18, Cr. Cash $4,695

Aug. 29, Dr. Cash $2,970

Prepare journal entries to record the following merchandising transactions of Stone Company, which applies the perpetual inventory system. (*Hint:* It will help to identify each receivable and payable; for example, record the purchase on August 1 in Accounts Payable—Abilene.)

Aug.  1   Purchased merchandise from Abilene Company for $6,000 under credit terms of 1/10, n/30, FOB destination, invoice dated August 1.

     4   At Abilene's request, Stone paid $100 cash for freight charges on the August 1 purchase, reducing the amount owed to Abilene.

     5   Sold merchandise to Lux Corp. for $4,200 under credit terms of 2/10, n/60, FOB destination, invoice dated August 5. The merchandise had cost $3,000.

     8   Purchased merchandise from Welch Corporation for $5,300 under credit terms of 1/10, n/45, FOB shipping point, invoice dated August 8. The invoice showed that at Stone's request, Welch paid the $240 shipping charges and added that amount to the bill. (*Hint:* Discounts are not applied to freight and shipping charges.)

     9   Paid $120 cash for shipping charges related to the August 5 sale to Lux Corp.

     10  Lux returned merchandise from the August 5 sale that had cost Stone $500 and been sold for $700. The merchandise was restored to inventory.

     12  After negotiations with Welch Corporation concerning problems with the merchandise purchased on August 8, Stone received a credit memorandum from Welch granting a price reduction of $800.

     15  Received balance due from Lux Corp. for the August 5 sale less the return on August 10.

     18  Paid the amount due Welch Corporation for the August 8 purchase less the price reduction granted.

     19  Sold merchandise to Trax Co. for $3,600 under credit terms of 1/10, n/30, FOB shipping point, invoice dated August 19. The merchandise had cost $2,500.

     22  Trax requested a price reduction on the August 19 sale because the merchandise did not meet specifications. Stone sent Trax a $600 credit memorandum to resolve the issue.

     29  Received Trax's cash payment for the amount due from the August 19 sale.

     30  Paid Abilene Company the amount due from the August 1 purchase.

**Problem 5-2A**
Preparing journal entries for merchandising activities—perpetual system

P1  P2

Prepare journal entries to record the following merchandising transactions of Bask Company, which applies the perpetual inventory system. (*Hint:* It will help to identify each receivable and payable; for example, record the purchase on July 1 in Accounts Payable—Black.)

July  1   Purchased merchandise from Black Company for $6,000 under credit terms of 1/15, n/30, FOB shipping point, invoice dated July 1.

     2   Sold merchandise to Coke Co. for $800 under credit terms of 2/10, n/60, FOB shipping point, invoice dated July 2. The merchandise had cost $500.

     3   Paid $100 cash for freight charges on the purchase of July 1.

8 Sold merchandise that had cost $1,200 for $1,600 cash.
9 Purchased merchandise from Lane Co. for $2,300 under credit terms of 2/15, n/60, FOB destination, invoice dated July 9.
11 Received a $200 credit memorandum from Lane Co. for the return of part of the merchandise purchased on July 9.
12 Received the balance due from Coke Co. for the invoice dated July 2, net of the discount.
16 Paid the balance due to Black Company within the discount period.
19 Sold merchandise that cost $900 to AKP Co. for $1,250 under credit terms of 2/15, n/60, FOB shipping point, invoice dated July 19.
21 Issued a $150 credit memorandum to AKP Co. for an allowance on goods sold on July 19.
24 Paid Lane Co. the balance due after deducting the discount.
30 Received the balance due from AKP Co. for the invoice dated July 19, net of discount.
31 Sold merchandise that cost $3,200 to Coke Co. for $5,000 under credit terms of 2/10, n/60, FOB shipping point, invoice dated July 31.

**Check** July 12, Dr. Cash $784
July 16, Cr. Cash $5,940

July 24, Cr. Cash $2,058
July 30, Dr. Cash $1,078

---

The following unadjusted trial balance is prepared at fiscal year-end for Rex Company.

**Problem 5-3A**
Preparing adjusting entries and income statements; and computing gross margin, acid-test, and current ratios

 A1 A2 P3 P4

mhhe.com/wildFAP20e

| REX COMPANY Unadjusted Trial Balance January 31, 2011 | | |
|---|---|---|
| | **Debit** | **Credit** |
| Cash | $ 2,200 | |
| Merchandise inventory | 11,500 | |
| Store supplies | 4,800 | |
| Prepaid insurance | 2,300 | |
| Store equipment | 41,900 | |
| Accumulated depreciation—Store equipment | | $ 15,000 |
| Accounts payable | | 9,000 |
| T. Rex, Capital | | 32,000 |
| T. Rex, Withdrawals | 2,000 | |
| Sales | | 104,000 |
| Sales discounts | 1,000 | |
| Sales returns and allowances | 2,000 | |
| Cost of goods sold | 37,400 | |
| Depreciation expense—Store equipment | 0 | |
| Salaries expense | 31,000 | |
| Insurance expense | 0 | |
| Rent expense | 14,000 | |
| Store supplies expense | 0 | |
| Advertising expense | 9,900 | |
| Totals | $160,000 | $160,000 |

Rent expense and salaries expense are equally divided between selling activities and the general and administrative activities. Rex Company uses a perpetual inventory system.

**Required**

**1.** Prepare adjusting journal entries to reflect each of the following:
   **a.** Store supplies still available at fiscal year-end amount to $1,650.
   **b.** Expired insurance, an administrative expense, for the fiscal year is $1,500.
   **c.** Depreciation expense on store equipment, a selling expense, is $1,400 for the fiscal year.
   **d.** To estimate shrinkage, a physical count of ending merchandise inventory is taken. It shows $11,100 of inventory is still available at fiscal year-end.

**2.** Prepare a multiple-step income statement for fiscal year 2011.

**3.** Prepare a single-step income statement for fiscal year 2011.

**4.** Compute the current ratio, acid-test ratio, and gross margin ratio as of January 31, 2011.

---

**Problem 5-4A**
Computing merchandising
amounts and formatting
income statements

C2   P4

BizKid Company's adjusted trial balance on August 31, 2011, its fiscal year-end, follows.

|  | Debit | Credit |
|---|---|---|
| Merchandise inventory | $ 31,000 | |
| Other (noninventory) assets | 120,400 | |
| Total liabilities | | $ 35,000 |
| N. Kidman, Capital | | 101,650 |
| N. Kidman, Withdrawals | 8,000 | |
| Sales | | 212,000 |
| Sales discounts | 3,250 | |
| Sales returns and allowances | 14,000 | |
| Cost of goods sold | 82,600 | |
| Sales salaries expense | 29,000 | |
| Rent expense—Selling space | 10,000 | |
| Store supplies expense | 2,500 | |
| Advertising expense | 18,000 | |
| Office salaries expense | 26,500 | |
| Rent expense—Office space | 2,600 | |
| Office supplies expense | 800 | |
| Totals | $348,650 | $348,650 |

On August 31, 2010, merchandise inventory was $25,000. Supplementary records of merchandising activities for the year ended August 31, 2011, reveal the following itemized costs.

| | |
|---|---|
| Invoice cost of merchandise purchases | $91,000 |
| Purchase discounts received | 1,900 |
| Purchase returns and allowances | 4,400 |
| Costs of transportation-in | 3,900 |

**Required**

**1.** Compute the company's net sales for the year.

**2.** Compute the company's total cost of merchandise purchased for the year.

**3.** Prepare a multiple-step income statement that includes separate categories for selling expenses and for general and administrative expenses.

**4.** Prepare a single-step income statement that includes these expense categories: cost of goods sold, selling expenses, and general and administrative expenses.

---

**Problem 5-5A**
Preparing closing entries and
interpreting information about
discounts and returns

C2   P3

Use the data for BizKid Company in Problem 5-4A to complete the following requirements.

**Required**

**1.** Prepare closing entries as of August 31, 2011 (the perpetual inventory system is used).

**Analysis Component**

**2.** The company makes all purchases on credit, and its suppliers uniformly offer a 3% sales discount. Does it appear that the company's cash management system is accomplishing the goal of taking all available discounts? Explain.

**3.** In prior years, the company experienced a 5% returns and allowance rate on its sales, which means approximately 5% of its gross sales were eventually returned outright or caused the company to grant allowances to customers. How do this year's results compare to prior years' results?

Refer to the data and information in Problem 5-3A.

*Required*

Prepare and complete the entire 10-column work sheet for Rex Company. Follow the structure of Exhibit 5B.1 in Appendix 5B.

**Problem 5-6A**[B]
Preparing a work sheet for a merchandiser

P3

Prepare journal entries to record the following merchandising transactions of Wave Company, which applies the perpetual inventory system. (*Hint:* It will help to identify each receivable and payable; for example, record the purchase on July 3 in Accounts Payable—CAP.)

**PROBLEM SET B**

**Problem 5-1B**
Preparing journal entries for merchandising activities—perpetual system

P1  P2

| | | |
|---|---|---|
| July | 3 | Purchased merchandise from CAP Corp. for $15,000 under credit terms of 1/10, n/30, FOB destination, invoice dated July 3. |
| | 4 | At CAP's request, Wave paid $250 cash for freight charges on the July 3 purchase, reducing the amount owed to CAP. |
| | 7 | Sold merchandise to Morris Co. for $10,500 under credit terms of 2/10, n/60, FOB destination, invoice dated July 7. The merchandise had cost $7,500. |
| | 10 | Purchased merchandise from Murdock Corporation for $14,200 under credit terms of 1/10, n/45, FOB shipping point, invoice dated July 10. The invoice showed that at Wave's request, Murdock paid the $600 shipping charges and added that amount to the bill. (*Hint:* Discounts are not applied to freight and shipping charges.) |
| | 11 | Paid $300 cash for shipping charges related to the July 7 sale to Morris Co. |
| | 12 | Morris returned merchandise from the July 7 sale that had cost Wave $1,250 and been sold for $1,750. The merchandise was restored to inventory. |
| | 14 | After negotiations with Murdock Corporation concerning problems with the merchandise purchased on July 10, Wave received a credit memorandum from Murdock granting a price reduction of $2,000. |
| | 17 | Received balance due from Morris Co. for the July 7 sale less the return on July 12. |
| | 20 | Paid the amount due Murdock Corporation for the July 10 purchase less the price reduction granted. |
| | 21 | Sold merchandise to Ulsh for $9,000 under credit terms of 1/10, n/30, FOB shipping point, invoice dated July 21. The merchandise had cost $6,250. |
| | 24 | Ulsh requested a price reduction on the July 21 sale because the merchandise did not meet specifications. Wave sent Ulsh a credit memorandum for $1,500 to resolve the issue. |
| | 30 | Received Ulsh's cash payment for the amount due from the July 21 sale. |
| | 31 | Paid CAP Corp. the amount due from the July 3 purchase. |

**Check**   July 17, Dr. Cash $8,575
July 20, Cr. Cash $12,678


July 30, Dr. Cash $7,425

Prepare journal entries to record the following merchandising transactions of Yang Company, which applies the perpetual inventory system. (*Hint:* It will help to identify each receivable and payable; for example, record the purchase on May 2 in Accounts Payable—Bots.)

**Problem 5-2B**
Preparing journal entries for merchandising activities—perpetual system

P1  P2

| | | |
|---|---|---|
| May | 2 | Purchased merchandise from Bots Co. for $9,000 under credit terms of 1/15, n/30, FOB shipping point, invoice dated May 2. |
| | 4 | Sold merchandise to Chase Co. for $1,200 under credit terms of 2/10, n/60, FOB shipping point, invoice dated May 4. The merchandise had cost $750. |
| | 5 | Paid $150 cash for freight charges on the purchase of May 2. |
| | 9 | Sold merchandise that had cost $1,800 for $2,400 cash. |
| | 10 | Purchased merchandise from Snyder Co. for $3,450 under credit terms of 2/15, n/60, FOB destination, invoice dated May 10. |
| | 12 | Received a $300 credit memorandum from Snyder Co. for the return of part of the merchandise purchased on May 10. |
| | 14 | Received the balance due from Chase Co. for the invoice dated May 4, net of the discount. |
| | 17 | Paid the balance due to Bots Co. within the discount period. |
| | 20 | Sold merchandise that cost $1,450 to Tex Co. for $2,800 under credit terms of 2/15, n/60, FOB shipping point, invoice dated May 20. |
| | 22 | Issued a $400 credit memorandum to Tex Co. for an allowance on goods sold from May 20. |
| | 25 | Paid Snyder Co. the balance due after deducting the discount. |
| | 30 | Received the balance due from Tex Co. for the invoice dated May 20, net of discount and allowance. |
| | 31 | Sold merchandise that cost $4,800 to Chase Co. for $7,500 under credit terms of 2/10, n/60, FOB shipping point, invoice dated May 31. |

**Check**   May 14, Dr. Cash $1,176
May 17, Cr. Cash $8,910


May 30, Dr. Cash $2,352

**Problem 5-3B**
Preparing adjusting entries
and income statements; and
computing gross margin,
acid-test, and current ratios

A1   A2   P3   P4

The following unadjusted trial balance is prepared at fiscal year-end for FAB Products Company.

File   Edit   View   Insert   Format   Tools   Data   Accounting   Window   Help

100%   Arial   10   B   I   U   $   %

### FAB PRODUCTS COMPANY
### Unadjusted Trial Balance
### October 31, 2011

|    |                                              | Debit      | Credit     |
|----|----------------------------------------------|------------|------------|
| 1  |                                              |            |            |
| 2  | Cash                                         | $   4,400  |            |
| 3  | Merchandise inventory                        | 23,000     |            |
| 4  | Store supplies                               | 9,600      |            |
| 5  | Prepaid insurance                            | 4,600      |            |
| 6  | Store equipment                              | 83,800     |            |
| 7  | Accumulated depreciation—Store equipment     |            | $  30,000  |
| 8  | Accounts payable                             |            | 16,000     |
| 9  | A. Fab, Capital                              |            | 64,000     |
| 10 | A. Fab, Withdrawals                          | 2,000      |            |
| 11 | Sales                                        |            | 208,000    |
| 12 | Sales discounts                              | 2,000      |            |
| 13 | Sales returns and allowances                 | 4,000      |            |
| 14 | Cost of goods sold                           | 74,800     |            |
| 15 | Depreciation expense—Store equipment         | 0          |            |
| 16 | Salaries expense                             | 62,000     |            |
| 17 | Insurance expense                            | 0          |            |
| 18 | Rent expense                                 | 28,000     |            |
| 19 | Store supplies expense                       | 0          |            |
| 20 | Advertising expense                          | 19,800     |            |
| 21 | Totals                                       | $318,000   | $318,000   |
| 22 |                                              |            |            |

Sheet1   Sheet2   Sheet3

Rent expense and salaries expense are equally divided between selling activities and the general and administrative activities. FAB Products Company uses a perpetual inventory system.

*Required*

**1.** Prepare adjusting journal entries to reflect each of the following.

   **a.** Store supplies still available at fiscal year-end amount to $3,300.

   **b.** Expired insurance, an administrative expense, for the fiscal year is $3,000.

   **c.** Depreciation expense on store equipment, a selling expense, is $2,800 for the fiscal year.

   **d.** To estimate shrinkage, a physical count of ending merchandise inventory is taken. It shows $22,200 of inventory is still available at fiscal year-end.

**Check**  (2) Gross profit, $126,400;
(3) Total expenses, $197,500;
Net income, $4,500

**2.** Prepare a multiple-step income statement for fiscal year 2011.

**3.** Prepare a single-step income statement for fiscal year 2011.

**4.** Compute the current ratio, acid-test ratio, and gross margin ratio as of October 31, 2011.

---

**Problem 5-4B**
Computing merchandising
amounts and formatting
income statements

C1   C2   P4

Albin Company's adjusted trial balance on March 31, 2011, its fiscal year-end, follows.

|                                  | Debit     | Credit     |
|----------------------------------|-----------|------------|
| Merchandise inventory .............. | $ 46,500  |            |
| Other (noninventory) assets ......... | 190,600   |            |
| Total liabilities .................... |           | $ 52,500   |
| R. Albin, Capital ................... |           | 152,475    |
| R. Albin, Withdrawals ............. | 2,000     |            |

[continued on next page]

[continued from previous page]

| | | |
|---|---:|---:|
| Sales .............................. | | 318,000 |
| Sales discounts ................... | 4,875 | |
| Sales returns and allowances ........ | 21,000 | |
| Cost of goods sold ............... | 123,900 | |
| Sales salaries expense ............. | 43,500 | |
| Rent expense—Selling space ........ | 15,000 | |
| Store supplies expense ............. | 3,750 | |
| Advertising expense ............... | 27,000 | |
| Office salaries expense ............. | 39,750 | |
| Rent expense—Office space ........ | 3,900 | |
| Office supplies expense ........... | 1,200 | |
| Totals ......................... | $522,975 | $522,975 |

On March 31, 2010, merchandise inventory was $37,500. Supplementary records of merchandising activities for the year ended March 31, 2011, reveal the following itemized costs.

| | |
|---|---:|
| Invoice cost of merchandise purchases ........ | $136,500 |
| Purchase discounts received ................. | 2,850 |
| Purchase returns and allowances ............. | 6,600 |
| Costs of transportation-in ................. | 5,850 |

**Required**

1. Calculate the company's net sales for the year.
2. Calculate the company's total cost of merchandise purchased for the year.
3. Prepare a multiple-step income statement that includes separate categories for selling expenses and for general and administrative expenses.
4. Prepare a single-step income statement that includes these expense categories: cost of goods sold, selling expenses, and general and administrative expenses.

**Check**   (2) $132,900;

(3) Gross profit, $168,225;
Net income, $34,125;

(4) Total expenses, $258,000

---

Use the data for Albin Company in Problem 5-4B to complete the following requirements.

**Problem 5-5B**
Preparing closing entries and interpreting information about discounts and returns

**C2  P3**

**Required**

1. Prepare closing entries as of March 31, 2011 (the perpetual inventory system is used).

*Analysis Component*

2. The company makes all purchases on credit, and its suppliers uniformly offer a 3% sales discount. Does it appear that the company's cash management system is accomplishing the goal of taking all available discounts? Explain.
3. In prior years, the company experienced a 5% returns and allowance rate on its sales, which means approximately 5% of its gross sales were eventually returned outright or caused the company to grant allowances to customers. How do this year's results compare to prior years' results?

**Check**   (1) $34,125 Dr. to close Income Summary

(3) Current-year rate, 6.6%

---

Refer to the data and information in Problem 5-3B.

**Problem 5-6B**[B]
Preparing a work sheet for a merchandiser

**P3**

**Required**

Prepare and complete the entire 10-column work sheet for FAB Products Company. Follow the structure of Exhibit 5B.1 in Appendix 5B.

**SERIAL PROBLEM**

Business Solutions

P1 P2 P3 P4

*(This serial problem began in Chapter 1 and continues through most of the book. If previous chapter segments were not completed, the serial problem can begin at this point. It is helpful, but not necessary, to use the Working Papers that accompany the book.)*

**SP 5**   Santana Rey created Business Solutions on October 1, 2011. The company has been successful, and its list of customers has grown. To accommodate the growth, the accounting system is modified to set up separate accounts for each customer. The following chart of accounts includes the account number used for each account and any balance as of December 31, 2011. Santana Rey decided to add a fourth digit with a decimal point to the 106 account number that had been used for the single Accounts Receivable account. This change allows the company to continue using the existing chart of accounts.

| No. | Account Title | Dr. | Cr. |
|---|---|---|---|
| 101 | Cash | $48,372 | |
| 106.1 | Alex's Engineering Co. | 0 | |
| 106.2 | Wildcat Services | 0 | |
| 106.3 | Easy Leasing | 0 | |
| 106.4 | IFM Co. | 3,000 | |
| 106.5 | Liu Corp. | 0 | |
| 106.6 | Gomez Co. | 2,668 | |
| 106.7 | Delta Co. | 0 | |
| 106.8 | KC, Inc. | 0 | |
| 106.9 | Dream, Inc. | 0 | |
| 119 | Merchandise inventory | 0 | |
| 126 | Computer supplies | 580 | |
| 128 | Prepaid insurance | 1,665 | |
| 131 | Prepaid rent | 825 | |
| 163 | Office equipment | 8,000 | |
| 164 | Accumulated depreciation—Office equipment | | $ 400 |
| 167 | Computer equipment | 20,000 | |
| 168 | Accumulated depreciation—Computer equipment | | 1,250 |
| 201 | Accounts payable | | 1,100 |

| No. | Account Title | Dr. | Cr. |
|---|---|---|---|
| 210 | Wages payable | | $ 500 |
| 236 | Unearned computer services revenue | | 1,500 |
| 301 | S. Rey, Capital | | 80,360 |
| 302 | S. Rey, Withdrawals | $0 | |
| 403 | Computer services revenue | | 0 |
| 413 | Sales | | 0 |
| 414 | Sales returns and allowances | 0 | |
| 415 | Sales discounts | 0 | |
| 502 | Cost of goods sold | 0 | |
| 612 | Depreciation expense—Office equipment | 0 | |
| 613 | Depreciation expense—Computer equipment | 0 | |
| 623 | Wages expense | 0 | |
| 637 | Insurance expense | 0 | |
| 640 | Rent expense | 0 | |
| 652 | Computer supplies expense | 0 | |
| 655 | Advertising expense | 0 | |
| 676 | Mileage expense | 0 | |
| 677 | Miscellaneous expenses | 0 | |
| 684 | Repairs expense—Computer | 0 | |

In response to requests from customers, S. Rey will begin selling computer software. The company will extend credit terms of 1/10, n/30, FOB shipping point, to all customers who purchase this merchandise. However, no cash discount is available on consulting fees. Additional accounts (Nos. 119, 413, 414, 415, and 502) are added to its general ledger to accommodate the company's new merchandising activities. Also, Business Solutions does not use reversing entries and, therefore, all revenue and expense accounts have zero beginning balances as of January 1, 2012. Its transactions for January through March follow:

Jan. 4   The company paid cash to Lyn Addie for five days' work at the rate of $125 per day. Four of the five days relate to wages payable that were accrued in the prior year.

     5   Santana Rey invested an additional $25,000 cash in the company.

     7   The company purchased $5,800 of merchandise from Kansas Corp. with terms of 1/10, n/30, FOB shipping point, invoice dated January 7.

     9   The company received $2,668 cash from Gomez Co. as full payment on its account.

     11   The company completed a five-day project for Alex's Engineering Co. and billed it $5,500, which is the total price of $7,000 less the advance payment of $1,500.

**Check**   Jan. 11, Dr. Unearned Computer Services Revenue $1,500

13  The company sold merchandise with a retail value of $5,200 and a cost of $3,560 to Liu Corp., invoice dated January 13.

15  The company paid $600 cash for freight charges on the merchandise purchased on January 7.

16  The company received $4,000 cash from Delta Co. for computer services provided.

17  The company paid Kansas Corp. for the invoice dated January 7, net of the discount.

20  Liu Corp. returned $500 of defective merchandise from its invoice dated January 13. The returned merchandise, which had a $320 cost, is discarded. (The policy of Business Solutions is to leave the cost of defective products in cost of goods sold.)

**Check**  Jan. 20, No entry to Cost of Goods Sold

22  The company received the balance due from Liu Corp., net of both the discount and the credit for the returned merchandise.

24  The company returned defective merchandise to Kansas Corp. and accepted a credit against future purchases. The defective merchandise invoice cost, net of the discount, was $496.

26  The company purchased $9,000 of merchandise from Kansas Corp. with terms of 1/10, n/30, FOB destination, invoice dated January 26.

26  The company sold merchandise with a $4,640 cost for $5,800 on credit to KC, Inc., invoice dated January 26.

29  The company received a $496 credit memorandum from Kansas Corp. concerning the merchandise returned on January 24.

31  The company paid cash to Lyn Addie for 10 days' work at $125 per day.

Feb.  1  The company paid $2,475 cash to Hillside Mall for another three months' rent in advance.

3  The company paid Kansas Corp. for the balance due, net of the cash discount, less the $496 amount in the credit memorandum.

5  The company paid $600 cash to the local newspaper for an advertising insert in today's paper.

11  The company received the balance due from Alex's Engineering Co. for fees billed on January 11.

15  Santana Rey withdrew $4,800 cash from the company for personal use.

23  The company sold merchandise with a $2,660 cost for $3,220 on credit to Delta Co., invoice dated February 23.

26  The company paid cash to Lyn Addie for eight days' work at $125 per day.

27  The company reimbursed Santana Rey for business automobile mileage (600 miles at $0.32 per mile).

Mar.  8  The company purchased $2,730 of computer supplies from Harris Office Products on credit, invoice dated March 8.

9  The company received the balance due from Delta Co. for merchandise sold on February 23.

11  The company paid $960 cash for minor repairs to the company's computer.

16  The company received $5,260 cash from Dream, Inc., for computing services provided.

19  The company paid the full amount due to Harris Office Products, consisting of amounts created on December 15 (of $1,100) and March 8.

24  The company billed Easy Leasing for $9,047 of computing services provided.

25  The company sold merchandise with a $2,002 cost for $2,800 on credit to Wildcat Services, invoice dated March 25.

30  The company sold merchandise with a $1,048 cost for $2,220 on credit to IFM Company, invoice dated March 30.

31  The company reimbursed Santana Rey for business automobile mileage (400 miles at $0.32 per mile).

The following additional facts are available for preparing adjustments on March 31 prior to financial statement preparation:

**a.** The March 31 amount of computer supplies still available totals $2,005.

**b.** Three more months have expired since the company purchased its annual insurance policy at a $2,220 cost for 12 months of coverage.

**c.** Lyn Addie has not been paid for seven days of work at the rate of $125 per day.

**d.** Three months have passed since any prepaid rent has been transferred to expense. The monthly rent expense is $825.

**e.** Depreciation on the computer equipment for January 1 through March 31 is $1,250.

**f.** Depreciation on the office equipment for January 1 through March 31 is $400.

**g.** The March 31 amount of merchandise inventory still available totals $704.

**Required**

1. Prepare journal entries to record each of the January through March transactions.
2. Post the journal entries in part 1 to the accounts in the company's general ledger. (*Note:* Begin with the ledger's post-closing adjusted balances as of December 31, 2011.)
3. Prepare a partial work sheet consisting of the first six columns (similar to the one shown in Exhibit 5B.1) that includes the unadjusted trial balance, the March 31 adjustments (*a*) through (*g*), and the adjusted trial balance. Do not prepare closing entries and do not journalize the adjustments or post them to the ledger.
4. Prepare an income statement (from the adjusted trial balance in part 3) for the three months ended March 31, 2012. Use a single-step format. List all expenses without differentiating between selling expenses and general and administrative expenses.
5. Prepare a statement of owner's equity (from the adjusted trial balance in part 3) for the three months ended March 31, 2012.
6. Prepare a classified balance sheet (from the adjusted trial balance) as of March 31, 2012.

## Beyond the Numbers

### REPORTING IN ACTION

A1

**RIM**

**BTN 5-1**   Refer to **Research In Motion**'s financial statements in Appendix A to answer the following.

**Required**

1. Assume that the amounts reported for inventories and cost of sales reflect items purchased in a form ready for resale. Compute the net cost of goods purchased for the fiscal year ended February 27, 2010.
2. Compute the current ratio and acid-test ratio as of February 27, 2010, and February 28, 2009. Interpret and comment on the ratio results. How does Research In Motion compare to the industry average of 2.4 for the current ratio and 1.5 for the acid-test ratio?

*Fast Forward*

3. Access Research In Motion's financial statements (form 10-K) for fiscal years ending after February 27, 2010, from its Website (**RIM.com**) or the SEC's EDGAR database (**www.sec.gov**). Recompute and interpret the current ratio and acid-test ratio for these current fiscal years.

### COMPARATIVE ANALYSIS

A2

**RIM**

Apple

**BTN 5-2**   Key comparative figures for both **Research In Motion** and **Apple** follow.

| ($ millions) | Research In Motion | | Apple | |
| --- | --- | --- | --- | --- |
| | Current Year | Prior Year | Current Year | Prior Year |
| Revenues (net sales) . . . . . . . . . | $14,953 | $11,065 | $42,905 | $37,491 |
| Cost of sales . . . . . . . . . . . . . . | 8,369 | 5,968 | 25,683 | 24,294 |

**Required**

1. Compute the dollar amount of gross margin and the gross margin ratio for the two years shown for each of these companies.
2. Which company earns more in gross margin for each dollar of net sales? How do they compare to the industry average of 40.0%?
3. Did the gross margin ratio improve or decline for these companies?

**BTN 5-3** Ashton Martin is a student who plans to attend approximately four professional events a year at her college. Each event necessitates a financial outlay of $100 to $200 for a new suit and accessories. After incurring a major hit to her savings for the first event, Ashton developed a different approach. She buys the suit on credit the week before the event, wears it to the event, and returns it the next week to the store for a full refund on her charge card.

**Required**

1. Comment on the ethics exhibited by Ashton and possible consequences of her actions.
2. How does the merchandising company account for the suits that Ashton returns?

**BTN 5-4** You are the financial officer for Music Plus, a retailer that sells goods for home entertainment needs. The business owner, Jamie Madsen, recently reviewed the annual financial statements you prepared and sent you an e-mail stating that he thinks you overstated net income. He explains that although he has invested a great deal in security, he is sure shoplifting and other forms of inventory shrinkage have occurred, but he does not see any deduction for shrinkage on the income statement. The store uses a perpetual inventory system.

**Required**

Prepare a brief memorandum that responds to the owner's concerns.

**BTN 5-5** Access the SEC's EDGAR database (www.SEC.gov) and obtain the March 19, 2010, filing of its fiscal 2010 10-K report (for year ended January 30, 2010) for **J. Crew Group, Inc** (ticker: JCG).

**Required**

Prepare a table that reports the gross margin ratios for J. Crew using the revenues and cost of goods sold data from J. Crew's income statement for each of its most recent three years. Analyze and comment on the trend in its gross margin ratio.

**BTN 5-6** Best Brands' general ledger and supplementary records at the end of its current period reveal the following.

| | | | |
|---|---|---|---|
| Sales . . . . . . . . . . . . . . . . . . . . . . | $430,000 | Merchandise inventory (beginning of period) . . . . . . | $ 49,000 |
| Sales returns . . . . . . . . . . . . . . | 18,000 | Invoice cost of merchandise purchases . . . . . . . . . . . | 180,000 |
| Sales discounts . . . . . . . . . . . . | 6,600 | Purchase discounts received . . . . . . . . . . . . . . . . . . . | 4,500 |
| Cost of transportation-in . . . . | 11,000 | Purchase returns and allowances . . . . . . . . . . . . . . . | 5,500 |
| Operating expenses . . . . . . . . | 20,000 | Merchandise inventory (end of period) . . . . . . . . . . . | 42,000 |

**Required**

1. *Each* member of the team is to assume responsibility for computing *one* of the following items. You are not to duplicate your teammates' work. Get any necessary amounts to compute your item from the appropriate teammate. Each member is to explain his or her computation to the team in preparation for reporting to the class.

   **a.** Net sales
   **b.** Total cost of merchandise purchases
   **c.** Cost of goods sold

   **d.** Gross profit
   **e.** Net income

2. Check your net income with the instructor. If correct, proceed to step 3.
3. Assume that a physical inventory count finds that actual ending inventory is $38,000. Discuss how this affects previously computed amounts in step 1.

**ENTREPRENEURIAL DECISION**

C1  C2  P4

**BTN 5-7**   Refer to the opening feature about **Heritage Link Brands**. Assume that Selena and Khary Cuffe report current annual sales at approximately $10 million and disclose the following income statement.

| Heritage Link Brands Income Statement For Year Ended January 31, 2010 | |
| --- | --- |
| Net sales ............................... | $10,000,000 |
| Cost of sales .......................... | 6,100,000 |
| Expenses (other than cost of sales) ........ | 2,000,000 |
| Net income ........................... | $ 1,900,000 |

Selena and Khary Cuffe sell to various individuals and retailers, ranging from small shops to large chains. Assume that they currently offer credit terms of 1/15, n/60, and ship FOB destination. To improve their cash flow, they are considering changing credit terms to 3/10, n/30. In addition, they propose to change shipping terms to FOB shipping point. They expect that the increase in discount rate will increase net sales by 9%, but the gross margin ratio (and ratio of cost of sales divided by net sales) is expected to remain unchanged. They also expect that delivery expenses will be zero under this proposal; thus, expenses other than cost of sales are expected to increase only 6%.

**Required**

**1.** Prepare a forecasted income statement for the year ended January 31, 2011, based on the proposal.

**2.** Based on the forecasted income statement alone (from your part 1 solution), do you recommend that Selena and Khary implement the new sales policies? Explain.

**3.** What else should Selena and Khary consider before deciding whether or not to implement the new policies? Explain.

**HITTING THE ROAD**

C1

**Point:** This activity complements the Ethics Challenge assignment.

**BTN 5-8**   Arrange an interview (in person or by phone) with the manager of a retail shop in a mall or in the downtown area of your community. Explain to the manager that you are a student studying merchandising activities and the accounting for sales returns and sales allowances. Ask the manager what the store policy is regarding returns. Also find out if sales allowances are ever negotiated with customers. Inquire whether management perceives that customers are abusing return policies and what actions management takes to counter potential abuses. Be prepared to discuss your findings in class.

**GLOBAL DECISION**

A2  P4

**NOKIA**

**RIM**

Apple

**BTN 5-9**   **Nokia** (**www.Nokia.com**), **Research In Motion**, and **Apple** are competitors in the global marketplace. Key comparative figures for each company follow.

| | Net Sales | Cost of Sales |
| --- | --- | --- |
| Nokia* .................... | 40,984 | 27,720 |
| Research In Motion[†] ........ | $14,953 | $ 8,369 |
| Apple[†] ................... | $42,905 | $25,683 |

\* EUR millions for Nokia.

[†] $ millions for Research In Motion and Apple.

**Required**

**1.** Rank the three companies (highest to lowest) based on the gross margin ratio.

**2.** Which of the companies uses a multiple-step income statement format? (These companies' income statements are in Appendix A.)

## ANSWERS TO MULTIPLE CHOICE QUIZ

**1.** c; Gross profit = $550,000 − $193,000 = $357,000

**2.** d; ($4,500 − $250) × (100% − 2%) = $4,165

**3.** b; Net sales = $75,000 + $320,000 − $13,700 − $6,000 = $375,300

**4.** b; Acid-test ratio = $37,500/$50,000 = 0.750

**5.** a; Gross margin ratio = ($675,000 − $459,000)/$675,000 = 32%

# 6

# Inventories and Cost of Sales

## A Look Back

Chapter 5 focused on merchandising activities and how they are reported. We analyzed and recorded purchases and sales and explained accounting adjustments and closing for merchandisers.

## A Look at This Chapter

This chapter emphasizes accounting for inventory. We describe methods for assigning costs to inventory and we explain the items and costs making up merchandise inventory. We also discuss methods of estimating and measuring inventory.

## A Look Ahead

Chapter 7 emphasizes accounting information systems. We describe system principles, the system components, use of special journals and subsidiary ledgers, and technology-based systems.

## Learning Objectives

CAP

### CONCEPTUAL

**C1** Identify the items making up merchandise inventory. (p. 228)

**C2** Identify the costs of merchandise inventory. (p. 229)

### ANALYTICAL

**A1** Analyze the effects of inventory methods for both financial and tax reporting. (p. 236)

**A2** Analyze the effects of inventory errors on current and future financial statements. (p. 238)

**A3** Assess inventory management using both inventory turnover and days' sales in inventory. (p. 241)

LP6

### PROCEDURAL

**P1** Compute inventory in a perpetual system using the methods of specific identification, FIFO, LIFO, and weighted average. (p. 230)

**P2** Compute the lower of cost or market amount of inventory. (p. 237)

**P3** *Appendix 6A*—Compute inventory in a periodic system using the methods of specific identification, FIFO, LIFO, and weighted average. (p. 246)

**P4** *Appendix 6B*—Apply both the retail inventory and gross profit methods to estimate inventory. (p. 251)

## Decision Insight

# The Gizmo!

*"I wanted to re-create the SEAL team environment"*
—**RANDY HETRICK**

SAN FRANCISCO—The Navy SEALs call it "the gizmo." This gizmo, created by former Navy SEAL Randy Hetrick, CEO of Fitness Anywhere, Inc and the inventor of Suspension Training®, is a resistance exercise device officially named the TRX Suspension Trainer. It is the hallmark product of Randy's start-up exercise equipment business, **Fitness Anywhere Inc. (FitnessAnywhere.com).**

Randy explains that to keep himself in shape for clandestine missions, he stitched parachute webbing into straps that he could fasten to almost anything and then use as a pulley system where his own body weight served as resistance. After leaving the Navy, Randy headed to business school and devoted himself to producing and marketing his new invention.

However, the entrepreneurial road was rough. Randy struggled with inventory production and sales planning, and had to deal with discounts, returns, and allowances. A major challenge was maintaining appropriate inventories while controlling costs. Randy admits that mistakes are part of entrepreneurial endeavors, but that he just had to throw himself into it and learn.

And, learn he did. Applying inventory management, and old-fashion trial-and-error, Randy learned to fill orders, collect money, and maintain the right inventory. "I wanted to re-create the SEAL team environment," explains Randy. To help, he set up a perpetual inventory system to account for inventory sales and purchases in real time. Randy insists that it is really important to serve customers' needs, which demands sound inventory accounting.

But business success requires more than good products and perpetual inventory management, explains Randy. It requires commitment, patience, energy, faith, and maybe some luck. "I thought this was a commando tool, pure and simple," laughs Randy. "Man, was I wrong!"

While Randy continues to measure, monitor, and manage inventories and costs, his success and growth are pushing him into new products and opportunities. He explains that he now has a line of portable, resistance exercise devices. Still, Randy demands that his business stay true to "the small, flat, high-performance . . . kind of [SEALs] culture." His inventory procedures and office setting contribute to that lean and mean culture. "Working out [in the office] is not only sanctioned," says Randy, "it almost is required."

[Sources: *FitnessAnywhere Website,* January 2011; *Entrepreneur,* February 2010; *Triathlete Magazine,* December 2009; *Wall Street Journal,* September 2009]

Merchandisers' activities include the purchasing and reselling of merchandise. We explained accounting for merchandisers in Chapter 5, including that for purchases and sales. In this chapter, we extend the study and analysis of inventory by explaining the methods used to assign costs to merchandise inventory *and* to cost of goods sold. Retailers, wholesalers, and other merchandising companies that purchase products for resale use the principles and methods described here. Understanding inventory accounting helps in the analysis and interpretation of financial statements and helps people run their businesses.

### Inventories and Cost of Sales

| Inventory Basics | Inventory Costing under a Perpetual System | Inventory Valuation and Errors |
|---|---|---|
| • Determining inventory items<br>• Determining inventory costs<br>• Internal control of inventory<br>• Taking a physical count | • Cost flow assumptions<br>• Specific identification<br>• First-in, first-out<br>• Last-in, first-out<br>• Weighted average<br>• Financial statement effects | • Inventory valuation at lower of cost or market<br>• Financial statement effects of inventory errors |

# INVENTORY BASICS

This section identifies the items and costs making up merchandise inventory. It also describes the importance of internal controls in taking a physical count of inventory.

## Determining Inventory Items

**C1** Identify the items making up merchandise inventory.

Merchandise inventory includes all goods that a company owns and holds for sale. This rule holds regardless of where the goods are located when inventory is counted. Certain inventory items require special attention, including goods in transit, goods on consignment, and goods that are damaged or obsolete.

**Goods in Transit**  Does a purchaser's inventory include goods in transit from a supplier? The answer is that if ownership has passed to the purchaser, the goods are included in the purchaser's inventory. We determine this by reviewing the shipping terms: *FOB destination* or *FOB shipping point.* If the purchaser is responsible for paying freight, ownership passes when goods are loaded on the transport vehicle. If the seller is responsible for paying freight, ownership passes when goods arrive at their destination.

**Goods on Consignment**  Goods on consignment are goods shipped by the owner, called the **consignor,** to another party, the **consignee.** A consignee sells goods for the owner. The consignor continues to own the consigned goods and reports them in its inventory. **Upper Deck**, for instance, pays sports celebrities such as Tony Romo of the Dallas Cowboys to sign memorabilia, which are offered to shopping networks on consignment. Upper Deck, the consignor, must report these items in its inventory until sold.

**Goods Damaged or Obsolete**  Damaged and obsolete (and deteriorated) goods are not counted in inventory if they cannot be sold. If these goods can be sold at a reduced price, they are included in inventory at a conservative estimate of their **net realizable value.** Net realizable value is sales price minus the cost of making the sale. The period when damage or obsolescence (or deterioration) occurs is the period when the loss in value is reported.

## Decision **Insight**

A wireless portable device with a two-way radio allows clerks to quickly record inventory by scanning bar codes and to instantly send and receive inventory data. It gives managers access to up-to-date information on inventory and its location. ■

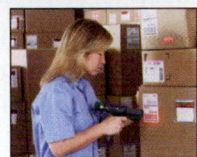

## Determining Inventory Costs

Merchandise inventory includes costs of expenditures necessary, directly or indirectly, to bring an item to a salable condition and location. This means that the cost of an inventory item includes its invoice cost minus any discount, and plus any incidental costs necessary to put it in a place and condition for sale. Incidental costs can include import duties, freight, storage, insurance, and costs incurred in an aging process (for example, aging wine or cheese).

> **C2** Identify the costs of merchandise inventory.

Accounting principles prescribe that incidental costs be added to inventory. Also, the *matching (expense recognition) principle* states that inventory costs should be recorded against revenue in the period when inventory is sold. However, some companies use the *materiality constraint (cost-to-benefit constraint)* to avoid assigning some incidental costs of acquiring merchandise to inventory. Instead, they expense them when incurred. These companies argue either that those incidental costs are immaterial or that the effort in assigning them outweighs the benefit.

## Internal Controls and Taking a Physical Count

The Inventory account under a perpetual system is updated for each purchase and sale, but events can cause the Inventory account balance to differ from the actual inventory available. Such events include theft, loss, damage, and errors. Thus, nearly all companies take a *physical count of inventory* at least once each year—informally called *taking an inventory*. This often occurs at the end of a fiscal year or when inventory amounts are low. This physical count is used to adjust the Inventory account balance to the actual inventory available.

A company applies internal controls when taking a physical count of inventory that usually include the following:

- *Prenumbered inventory tickets* are prepared and distributed to the *counters*—each ticket must be accounted for.
- Counters of inventory are assigned and do not include those responsible for inventory.
- Counters confirm the validity of inventory, including its existence, amount, and quality.
- A second count is taken by a different counter.
- A manager confirms that all inventories are ticketed once, and only once.

> **Point:** The Inventory account is a controlling account for the inventory subsidiary ledger. This *subsidiary ledger* contains a separate record (units and costs) for each separate product, and it can be in electronic or paper form. Subsidiary records assist managers in planning and monitoring inventory.

## Quick Check                                    Answers — p. 253

1. What accounting principle most guides the allocation of cost of goods available for sale between ending inventory and cost of goods sold?
2. If **Skechers** sells goods to **Target** with terms FOB shipping point, which company reports these goods in its inventory while they are in transit?
3. An art gallery purchases a painting for $11,400 on terms FOB shipping point. Additional costs in obtaining and offering the artwork for sale include $130 for transportation-in, $150 for import duties, $100 for insurance during shipment, $180 for advertising, $400 for framing, and $800 for office salaries. For computing inventory, what cost is assigned to the painting?

## INVENTORY COSTING UNDER A PERPETUAL SYSTEM

Accounting for inventory affects both the balance sheet and the income statement. A major goal in accounting for inventory is to properly match costs with sales. We use the *matching principle* to decide how much of the cost of the goods available for sale is deducted from sales and how much is carried forward as inventory and matched against future sales.

Management decisions in accounting for inventory involve the following:

- Items included in inventory and their costs.
- Costing method (specific identification, FIFO, LIFO, or weighted average).
- Inventory system (perpetual or periodic).
- Use of market values or other estimates.

The first point was explained on the prior two pages. The second and third points will be addressed now. The fourth point is the focus at the end of this chapter. Decisions on these points affect the reported amounts for inventory, cost of goods sold, gross profit, income, current assets, and other accounts.

One of the most important issues in accounting for inventory is determining the per unit costs assigned to inventory items. When all units are purchased at the same unit cost, this process is simple. When identical items are purchased at different costs, however, a question arises as to which amounts to record in cost of goods sold and which amounts remain in inventory.

Four methods are commonly used to assign costs to inventory and to cost of goods sold: (1) specific identification; (2) first-in, first-out; (3) last-in, first-out; and (4) weighted average.

**EXHIBIT 6.1**

Frequency in Use of Inventory Methods

Other* 3%

Weighted Average 20%

FIFO 50%

LIFO 27%

*Includes specific identification.

Exhibit 6.1 shows the frequency in the use of these methods.

Each method assumes a particular pattern for how costs flow through inventory. Each of these four methods is acceptable whether or not the actual physical flow of goods follows the cost flow assumption. Physical flow of goods depends on the type of product and the way it is stored. (Perishable goods such as fresh fruit demand that a business attempt to sell them in a first-in, first-out physical flow. Other products such as crude oil and minerals such as coal, gold, and decorative stone can be sold in a last-in, first-out physical flow.) **Physical flow and cost flow need not be the same.**

## Inventory Cost Flow Assumptions

**P1** Compute inventory in a perpetual system using the methods of specific identification, FIFO, LIFO, and weighted average.

This section introduces inventory cost flow assumptions. For this purpose, assume that three identical units are purchased separately at the following three dates and costs: May 1 at $45, May 3 at $65, and May 6 at $70. One unit is then sold on May 7 for $100. Exhibit 6.2 gives a visual layout of the flow of costs to either the gross profit section of the income statement or the inventory reported on the balance sheet for FIFO, LIFO, and weighted average.

(1) *FIFO assumes costs flow in the order incurred.* The unit purchased on May 1 for $45 is the earliest cost incurred—it is sent to cost of goods sold on the income statement first. The remaining two units ($65 and $70) are reported in inventory on the balance sheet.

(2) *LIFO assumes costs flow in the reverse order incurred.* The unit purchased on May 6 for $70 is the most recent cost incurred—it is sent to cost of goods sold on the income statement. The remaining two units ($45 and $65) are reported in inventory on the balance sheet.

(3) *Weighted average assumes costs flow at an average of the costs available.* The units available at the May 7 sale average $60 in cost, computed as ($45 + $65 + $70)/3. One unit's $60 average cost is sent to cost of goods sold on the income statement. The remaining two units' average costs are reported in inventory at $120 on the balance sheet.

Cost flow assumptions can markedly impact gross profit and inventory numbers. Exhibit 6.2 shows that gross profit as a percent of net sales ranges from 30% to 55% due to nothing else but the cost flow assumption.

**Point:** It is helpful to recall the cost flow of inventory from Exhibit 5.4.

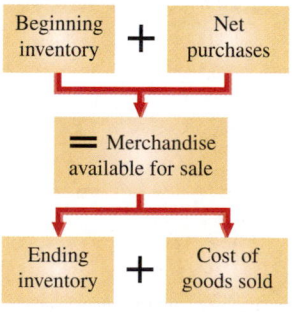

Beginning inventory **+** Net purchases

**=** Merchandise available for sale

Ending inventory **+** Cost of goods sold

*The following sections on inventory costing use the perpetual system. Appendix 6A uses the periodic system. An instructor can choose to cover either one or both systems. If the perpetual system is skipped, then read Appendix 6A and return to the section (seven pages ahead) titled "Valuing Inventory at LCM and . . ."*

**EXHIBIT 6.2**

Cost Flow Assumptions

## Inventory Costing Illustration

This section provides a comprehensive illustration of inventory costing methods. We use information from Trekking, a sporting goods store. Among its many products, Trekking carries one type of mountain bike whose sales are directed at resorts that provide inexpensive mountain bikes for complimentary guest use. Its customers usually purchase in amounts of 10 or more bikes. We use Trekking's data from August. Its mountain bike (unit) inventory at the beginning of August and its purchases and sales during August are shown in Exhibit 6.3. It ends August with 12 bikes remaining in inventory.

| Date | Activity | Units Acquired at Cost | Units Sold at Retail | Unit Inventory |
|------|----------|------------------------|----------------------|----------------|
| Aug.  1 | Beginning inventory .... | 10 units @ $  91 = $   910 |  | 10 units |
| Aug.  3 | Purchases ............. | 15 units @ $106 = $ 1,590 |  | 25 units |
| Aug. 14 | Sales ................ |  | 20 units @ $130 | 5 units |
| Aug. 17 | Purchases ............ | 20 units @ $115 = $ 2,300 |  | 25 units |
| Aug. 28 | Purchases ............ | 10 units @ $119 = $ 1,190 |  | 35 units |
| Aug. 31 | Sales ................ |  | 23 units @ $150 | **12 units** |
|  | Totals ............. | **55 units**       **$5,990** | **43 units** |  |

**EXHIBIT 6.3**

Purchases and Sales of Goods

Trekking uses the perpetual inventory system, which means that its merchandise inventory account is continually updated to reflect purchases and sales. **(Appendix 6A describes the assignment of costs to inventory using a periodic system.)** Regardless of what inventory method or system is used, cost of goods available for sale must be allocated between cost of goods sold and ending inventory.

**Point:** The perpetual inventory system is now the most dominant system for U.S. businesses.

**Point:** Cost of goods sold plus ending inventory equals cost of goods available for sale.

## Specific Identification

When each item in inventory can be identified with a specific purchase and invoice, we can use **specific identification** (also called *specific invoice inventory pricing*) to assign costs. We also need sales records that identify exactly which items were sold and when. Trekking's internal documents reveal the following specific unit sales:

| | |
|---|---|
| August 14 | Sold 8 bikes costing $91 each and 12 bikes costing $106 each |
| August 31 | Sold 2 bikes costing $91 each, 3 bikes costing $106 each, 15 bikes costing $115 each, and 3 bikes costing $119 each |

**Point:** Three key variables determine the dollar value of ending inventory: (1) inventory quantity, (2) costs of inventory, and (3) cost flow assumption.

Applying specific identification, and using the information above and from Exhibit 6.3, we prepare Exhibit 6.4. This exhibit starts with 10 bikes at $91 each in beginning inventory. On August 3, 15 more bikes are purchased at $106 each for $1,590. Inventory available now consists of 10 bikes at $91 each and 15 bikes at $106 each, for a total of $2,500. On August 14 (see sales above), 20 bikes costing $2,000 are sold—leaving 5 bikes costing $500 in inventory. On August 17, 20 bikes costing $2,300 are purchased, and on August 28, another 10 bikes costing $1,190 are purchased, for a total of 35 bikes costing $3,990 in inventory. On August 31 (see sales above), 23 bikes costing $2,582 are sold, which leaves 12 bikes costing $1,408 in ending inventory. Carefully study this exhibit and the boxed explanations to see the flow of costs both in and out of inventory. Each unit, whether sold or remaining in inventory, has its own specific cost attached to it.

**EXHIBIT 6.4**

Specific Identification Computations

For the 20 units sold on Aug. 14, the company specifically identified that 8 of those had cost $91 and 12 had cost $106.

For the 23 units sold on Aug. 31, the company specifically identified each bike sold and its acquisition cost from prior purchases.

\* Identification of items sold (and their costs) is obtained from internal documents that track each unit from its purchase to its sale.

When using specific identification, Trekking's cost of goods sold reported on the income statement totals **$4,582**, the sum of $2,000 and $2,582 from the third column of Exhibit 6.4. Trekking's ending inventory reported on the balance sheet is **$1,408**, which is the final inventory balance from the fourth column of Exhibit 6.4.

**Point:** Specific identification is usually practical only for companies with expensive, custom-made inventory.

The purchases and sales entries for Exhibit 6.4 follow (the colored boldface numbers are those impacted by the cost flow assumption).

| Purchases | | | |
|---|---|---|---|
| Aug. 3 | Merchandise Inventory | 1,590 | |
| | Accounts Payable | | 1,590 |
| 17 | Merchandise Inventory | 2,300 | |
| | Accounts Payable | | 2,300 |
| 28 | Merchandise Inventory | 1,190 | |
| | Accounts Payable | | 1,190 |

| Sales | | | |
|---|---|---|---|
| Aug. 14 | Accounts Receivable | 2,600 | |
| | Sales | | 2,600 |
| 14 | Cost of Goods Sold | **2,000** | |
| | Merchandise Inventory | | **2,000** |
| 31 | Accounts Receivable | 3,450 | |
| | Sales | | 3,450 |
| 31 | Cost of Goods Sold | **2,582** | |
| | Merchandise Inventory | | **2,582** |

# First-In, First-Out

The **first-in, first-out (FIFO)** method of assigning costs to both inventory and cost of goods sold assumes that inventory items are sold in the order acquired. When sales occur, the costs of the earliest units acquired are charged to cost of goods sold. This leaves the costs from the most recent purchases in ending inventory. Use of FIFO for computing the cost of inventory and cost of goods sold is shown in Exhibit 6.5.

This exhibit starts with beginning inventory of 10 bikes at $91 each. On August 3, 15 more bikes costing $106 each are bought for $1,590. Inventory now consists of 10 bikes at $91 each and 15 bikes at $106 each, for a total of $2,500. On August 14, 20 bikes are sold—applying FIFO, the first 10 sold cost $91 each and the next 10 sold cost $106 each, for a total cost of $1,970. This leaves 5 bikes costing $106 each, or $530, in inventory. On August 17, 20 bikes costing $2,300 are purchased, and on August 28, another 10 bikes costing $1,190 are purchased, for a total of 35 bikes costing $4,020 in inventory. On August 31, 23 bikes are sold—applying FIFO, the first 5 bikes sold cost $530 and the next 18 sold cost $2,070, which leaves 12 bikes costing $1,420 in ending inventory.

**Point:** The "Goods Purchased" column is identical for all methods. Data are taken from Exhibit 6.3.

| Date | Goods Purchased | Cost of Goods Sold | | Inventory Balance | |
|---|---|---|---|---|---|
| Aug. 1 | Beginning balance | | | 10 @ $ 91 | = $ 910 |
| Aug. 3 | 15 @ $106 = $1,590 | | | 10 @ $ 91 ⎱ 15 @ $106 ⎰ | = $2,500 |
| Aug. 14 | | 10 @ $ 91 = $ 910 ⎱ 10 @ $106 = $1,060 ⎰ = **$1,970** | | 5 @ $106 | = $ 530 |
| Aug. 17 | 20 @ $115 = $2,300 | | | 5 @ $106 ⎱ 20 @ $115 ⎰ | = $2,830 |
| Aug. 28 | 10 @ $119 = $1,190 | | | 5 @ $106 ⎱ 20 @ $115 ⎬ 10 @ $119 ⎰ | = $4,020 |
| Aug. 31 | | 5 @ $106 = $ 530 ⎱ 18 @ $115 = $2,070 ⎰ = **$2,600** $4,570 | | 2 @ $115 ⎱ 10 @ $119 ⎰ | = **$1,420** |

**EXHIBIT 6.5**

FIFO Computations—Perpetual System

> For the 20 units sold on Aug. 14, the first 10 sold are assigned the earliest cost of $91 (from beg. bal.). The next 10 sold are assigned the next earliest cost of $106.

> For the 23 units sold on Aug. 31, the first 5 sold are assigned the earliest available cost of $106 (from Aug. 3 purchase). The next 18 sold are assigned the next earliest cost of $115 (from Aug. 17 purchase).

Trekking's FIFO cost of goods sold reported on its income statement (reflecting the 43 units sold) is **$4,570** ($1,970 + $2,600), and its ending inventory reported on the balance sheet (reflecting the 12 units unsold) is **$1,420**.

The purchases and sales entries for Exhibit 6.5 follow (the colored boldface numbers are those affected by the cost flow assumption).

**Point:** Under FIFO, a unit sold is assigned the earliest (oldest) cost from inventory. This leaves the most recent costs in ending inventory.

### Purchases

| | | | |
|---|---|---|---|
| Aug. 3 | Merchandise Inventory | 1,590 | |
| | Accounts Payable | | 1,590 |
| 17 | Merchandise Inventory | 2,300 | |
| | Accounts Payable | | 2,300 |
| 28 | Merchandise Inventory | 1,190 | |
| | Accounts Payable | | 1,190 |

### Sales

| | | | |
|---|---|---|---|
| Aug. 14 | Accounts Receivable | 2,600 | |
| | Sales | | 2,600 |
| 14 | Cost of Goods Sold | **1,970** | |
| | Merchandise Inventory | | **1,970** |
| 31 | Accounts Receivable | 3,450 | |
| | Sales | | 3,450 |
| 31 | Cost of Goods Sold | **2,600** | |
| | Merchandise Inventory | | **2,600** |

# Last-In, First-Out

The **last-in, first-out (LIFO)** method of assigning costs assumes that the most recent purchases are sold first. These more recent costs are charged to the goods sold, and the costs of the earliest purchases are assigned to inventory. As with other methods, LIFO is acceptable even when the physical flow of goods does not follow a last-in, first-out pattern. One appeal of LIFO is that by assigning costs from the most recent purchases to cost of goods sold, LIFO comes closest to matching current costs of goods sold with revenues (compared to FIFO or weighted average).

Exhibit 6.6 shows the LIFO computations. It starts with beginning inventory of 10 bikes at $91 each. On August 3, 15 more bikes costing $106 each are bought for $1,590. Inventory now consists of 10 bikes at $91 each and 15 bikes at $106 each, for a total of $2,500. On August 14, 20 bikes are sold—applying LIFO, the first 15 sold are from the most recent purchase costing $106 each, and the next 5 sold are from the next most recent purchase costing $91 each, for a total cost of $2,045. This leaves 5 bikes costing $91 each, or $455, in inventory. On August 17, 20 bikes costing $2,300 are purchased, and on August 28, another 10 bikes costing $1,190 are purchased, for a total of 35 bikes costing $3,945 in inventory. On August 31, 23 bikes are sold—applying LIFO, the first 10 bikes sold are from the most recent purchase costing $1,190, and the next 13 sold are from the next most recent purchase costing $1,495, which leaves 12 bikes costing $1,260 in ending inventory.

**EXHIBIT 6.6**

LIFO Computations—
Perpetual System

For the 20 units sold on Aug. 14, the first 15 sold are assigned the most recent cost of $106. The next 5 sold are assigned the next most recent cost of $91.

For the 23 units sold on Aug. 31, the first 10 sold are assigned the most recent cost of $119. The next 13 sold are assigned the next most recent cost of $115.

| Date | Goods Purchased | Cost of Goods Sold | Inventory Balance |
|---|---|---|---|
| Aug. 1 | Beginning balance | | 10 @ $ 91    = $  910 |
| Aug. 3 | 15 @ $106 = $1,590 | | 10 @ $ 91 ⎱ = $ 2,500<br>15 @ $106 ⎰ |
| Aug. 14 | | 15 @ $106 = $1,590 ⎱ = **$2,045**<br>5 @ $ 91 = $ 455 ⎰ | 5 @ $ 91    = $  455 |
| Aug. 17 | 20 @ $115 = $2,300 | | 5 @ $ 91 ⎱ = $ 2,755<br>20 @ $115 ⎰ |
| Aug. 28 | 10 @ $119 = $1,190 | | 5 @ $ 91 ⎫<br>20 @ $115 ⎬ = $ 3,945<br>10 @ $119 ⎭ |
| Aug. 31 | | 10 @ $119 = $1,190 ⎱ = **$2,685**<br>13 @ $115 = $1,495 ⎰ | 5 @ $ 91 ⎱ = **$1,260**<br>7 @ $115 ⎰ |
| | | **$4,730** | |

Trekking's LIFO cost of goods sold reported on the income statement is **$4,730** ($2,045 + $2,685), and its ending inventory reported on the balance sheet is **$1,260**.

The purchases and sales entries for Exhibit 6.6 follow (the colored boldface numbers are those affected by the cost flow assumption).

**Purchases**

| | | | | |
|---|---|---|---|---|
| Aug. 3 | Merchandise Inventory | | 1,590 | |
| | Accounts Payable | | | 1,590 |
| 17 | Merchandise Inventory | | 2,300 | |
| | Accounts Payable | | | 2,300 |
| 28 | Merchandise Inventory | | 1,190 | |
| | Accounts Payable | | | 1,190 |

**Sales**

| | | | | |
|---|---|---|---|---|
| Aug. 14 | Accounts Receivable | | 2,600 | |
| | Sales | | | 2,600 |
| 14 | Cost of Goods Sold | | **2,045** | |
| | Merchandise Inventory | | | **2,045** |
| 31 | Accounts Receivable | | 3,450 | |
| | Sales | | | 3,450 |
| 31 | Cost of Goods Sold | | **2,685** | |
| | Merchandise Inventory | | | **2,685** |

## Weighted Average

The **weighted average** (also called **average cost**) method of assigning cost requires that we use the weighted average cost per unit of inventory at the time of each sale. Weighted average cost per unit at the time of each sale equals the cost of goods available for sale divided by the units available. The results using weighted average (WA) for Trekking are shown in Exhibit 6.7.

This exhibit starts with beginning inventory of 10 bikes at $91 each. On August 3, 15 more bikes costing $106 each are bought for $1,590. Inventory now consists of 10 bikes at $91 each and 15 bikes at $106 each, for a total of $2,500. The average cost per bike for that inventory is $100, computed as $2,500/(10 bikes + 15 bikes). On August 14, 20 bikes are sold—applying

| Date | Goods Purchased | Cost of Goods Sold | Inventory Balance |
|------|-----------------|--------------------|--------------------|
| Aug. 1 | Beginning balance | | 10 @ \$ 91  = \$ 910 |
| Aug. 3 | 15 @ \$106 = \$1,590 | | 10 @ \$ 91 }<br>15 @ \$106 }  = \$2,500 (or \$100 per unit)[a] |
| Aug. 14 | | 20 @ \$100 = **\$2,000** | 5 @ \$100   = \$ 500 (or \$100 per unit)[b] |
| Aug. 17 | 20 @ \$115 = \$2,300 | | 5 @ \$100 }<br>20 @ \$115 }  = \$2,800 (or \$112 per unit)[c] |
| Aug. 28 | 10 @ \$119 = \$1,190 | | 5 @ \$100 }<br>20 @ \$115 }  = \$3,990 (or \$114 per unit)[d]<br>10 @ \$119 } |
| Aug. 31 | | 23 @ \$114 = **\$2,622** | 12 @ \$114   = **\$1,368** (or \$114 per unit)[e] |
| | | **\$4,622** | |

**EXHIBIT 6.7**

Weighted Average
Computations—Perpetual System

> For the 20 units sold on Aug. 14, the cost assigned is the \$100 *average cost* per unit from the inventory balance column at the time of sale.

> For the 23 units sold on Aug. 31, the cost assigned is the \$114 *average cost* per unit from the inventory balance column at the time of sale.

[a] \$100 per unit = (\$2,500 inventory balance ÷ 25 units in inventory).
[b] \$100 per unit = (\$500 inventory balance ÷ 5 units in inventory).
[c] \$112 per unit = (\$2,800 inventory balance ÷ 25 units in inventory).
[d] \$114 per unit = (\$3,990 inventory balance ÷ 35 units in inventory).
[e] \$114 per unit = (\$1,368 inventory balance ÷ 12 units in inventory).

WA, the 20 sold are assigned the \$100 average cost, for a total cost of \$2,000. This leaves 5 bikes with an average cost of \$100 each, or \$500, in inventory. On August 17, 20 bikes costing \$2,300 are purchased, and on August 28, another 10 bikes costing \$1,190 are purchased, for a total of 35 bikes costing \$3,990 in inventory at August 28. The average cost per bike for the August 28 inventory is \$114, computed as \$3,990/(5 bikes + 20 bikes + 10 bikes). On August 31, 23 bikes are sold—applying WA, the 23 sold are assigned the \$114 average cost, for a total cost of \$2,622. This leaves 12 bikes costing \$1,368 in ending inventory.

Trekking's cost of goods sold reported on the income statement (reflecting the 43 units sold) is **\$4,622** (\$2,000 + \$2,622), and its ending inventory reported on the balance sheet (reflecting the 12 units unsold) is **\$1,368**.

The purchases and sales entries for Exhibit 6.7 follow (the colored boldface numbers are those affected by the cost flow assumption).

**Point:** Under weighted average, a unit sold is assigned the average cost of all items currently available for sale at the date of each sale.

| **Purchases** | | | | **Sales** | | |
|------|-----------------------------|-------|-------|------|-----------------------------|-------|
| Aug. 3 | Merchandise Inventory . . . . . . . . . | 1,590 | | Aug. 14 | Accounts Receivable . . . . . . . . . | 2,600 |
| | Accounts Payable . . . . . . . . | | 1,590 | | Sales . . . . . . . . . . . . . . . . . | | 2,600 |
| 17 | Merchandise Inventory . . . . . . . . . | 2,300 | | 14 | Cost of Goods Sold . . . . . . . . . | **2,000** |
| | Accounts Payable . . . . . . . . | | 2,300 | | Merchandise Inventory . . . . | | **2,000** |
| 28 | Merchandise Inventory . . . . . . . . . | 1,190 | | 31 | Accounts Receivable . . . . . . . . . | 3,450 |
| | Accounts Payable . . . . . . . . | | 1,190 | | Sales . . . . . . . . . . . . . . . . . | | 3,450 |
| | | | | 31 | Cost of Goods Sold . . . . . . . . . | **2,622** |
| | | | | | Merchandise Inventory . . . . | | **2,622** |

This completes computations under the four most common perpetual inventory costing methods. Advances in technology have greatly reduced the cost of a perpetual inventory system. Many companies now ask whether they can afford *not* to have a perpetual inventory system because timely access to inventory information is a competitive advantage and it can help reduce the amount of inventory, which reduces costs.

## Decision Insight

**Inventory Control**   SOX demands that companies safeguard inventory and properly report it. Safeguards include restricted access, use of authorized requisitions, security measures, and controlled environments to prevent damage. Proper accounting includes matching inventory received with purchase order terms and quality requirements, preventing misstatements, and controlling access to inventory records. A study reports that 23% of employees in purchasing and procurement observed inappropriate kickbacks or gifts from suppliers (KPMG 2009). Another 23% of employees in production witnessed fabrication of product quality results. ■

# Financial Statement Effects of Costing Methods

A1  Analyze the effects of inventory methods for both financial and tax reporting.

When purchase prices do not change, each inventory costing method assigns the same cost amounts to inventory and to cost of goods sold. When purchase prices are different, however, the methods nearly always assign different cost amounts. We show these differences in Exhibit 6.8 using Trekking's data.

**EXHIBIT 6.8**

Financial Statement Effects of Inventory Costing Methods

| TREKKING COMPANY<br>For Month Ended August 31 | | | | |
|---|---|---|---|---|
| | Specific Identification | FIFO | LIFO | Weighted Average |
| **Income Statement** | | | | |
| Sales .......................... | $ 6,050 | $ 6,050 | $ 6,050 | $ 6,050 |
| **Cost of goods sold** ............ | **4,582** | **4,570** | **4,730** | **4,622** |
| Gross profit ................. | 1,468 | 1,480 | 1,320 | 1,428 |
| Expenses ...................... | 450 | 450 | 450 | 450 |
| Income before taxes ............. | 1,018 | 1,030 | 870 | 978 |
| Income tax expense (30%) ........ | 305 | 309 | 261 | 293 |
| **Net income** .................. | **$ 713** | **$ 721** | **$ 609** | **$ 685** |
| **Balance Sheet** | | | | |
| **Inventory** .................... | **$1,408** | **$1,420** | **$1,260** | **$1,368** |

This exhibit reveals two important results. First, when purchase costs *regularly rise,* as in Trekking's case, the following occurs:

**Point:** Managers prefer FIFO when costs are rising *and* incentives exist to report higher income for reasons such as bonus plans, job security, and reputation.

- FIFO assigns the lowest amount to cost of goods sold—yielding the highest gross profit and net income.
- LIFO assigns the highest amount to cost of goods sold—yielding the lowest gross profit and net income, which also yields a temporary tax advantage by postponing payment of some income tax.
- Weighted average yields results between FIFO and LIFO.
- Specific identification always yields results that depend on which units are sold.

**Point:** LIFO inventory is often less than the inventory's replacement cost because LIFO inventory is valued using the oldest inventory purchase costs.

Second, when costs *regularly decline,* the reverse occurs for FIFO and LIFO. Namely, FIFO gives the highest cost of goods sold—yielding the lowest gross profit and income. However, LIFO then gives the lowest cost of goods sold—yielding the highest gross profit and income.

All four inventory costing methods are acceptable. However, a company must disclose the inventory method it uses in its financial statements or notes. Each method offers certain advantages as follows:

- FIFO assigns an amount to inventory on the balance sheet that approximates its current cost; it also mimics the actual flow of goods for most businesses.
- LIFO assigns an amount to cost of goods sold on the income statement that approximates its current cost; it also better matches current costs with revenues in computing gross profit.
- Weighted average tends to smooth out erratic changes in costs.
- Specific identification exactly matches the costs of items with the revenues they generate.

 **Decision Maker**        Answer – p. 253

**Financial Planner**    One of your clients asks if the inventory account of a company using FIFO needs any "adjustments" for analysis purposes in light of recent inflation. What is your advice? Does your advice depend on changes in the costs of these inventories? ■

**Tax Effects of Costing Methods**    Trekking's segment income statement in Exhibit 6.8 includes income tax expense (at a rate of 30%) because it was formed as a corporation. Since inventory costs affect net income, they have potential tax effects. Trekking gains a temporary tax advantage by using LIFO. Many companies use LIFO for this reason.

Companies can and often do use different costing methods for financial reporting and tax reporting. *The only exception is when LIFO is used for tax reporting; in this case, the IRS requires that it also be used in financial statements*—called the LIFO conformity rule.

## Consistency in Using Costing Methods

The **consistency concept** prescribes that a company use the same accounting methods period after period so that financial statements are comparable across periods—the only exception is when a change from one method to another will improve its financial reporting. The *full-disclosure principle* prescribes that the notes to the statements report this type of change, its justification, and its effect on income.

The consistency concept does *not* require a company to use one method exclusively. For example, it can use different methods to value different categories of inventory.

**Decision Ethics**                                     Answer — p. 253

**Inventory Manager**   Your compensation as inventory manager includes a bonus plan based on gross profit. Your superior asks your opinion on changing the inventory costing method from FIFO to LIFO. Since costs are expected to continue to rise, your superior predicts that LIFO would match higher current costs against sales, thereby lowering taxable income (and gross profit). What do you recommend? ■

**Quick Check**                                         Answers — p. 253

4. Describe one advantage for each of the inventory costing methods: specific identification, FIFO, LIFO, and weighted average.
5. When costs are rising, which method reports higher net income—LIFO or FIFO?
6. When costs are rising, what effect does LIFO have on a balance sheet compared to FIFO?
7. A company takes a physical count of inventory at the end of 2010 and finds that ending inventory is understated by $10,000. Would this error cause cost of goods sold to be overstated or understated in 2010? In year 2011? If so, by how much?

# VALUING INVENTORY AT LCM AND THE EFFECTS OF INVENTORY ERRORS

This section examines the role of market costs in determining inventory on the balance sheet and also the financial statement effects of inventory errors.

## Lower of Cost or Market

We explained how to assign costs to ending inventory and cost of goods sold using one of four costing methods (FIFO, LIFO, weighted average, or specific identification). However, *accounting principles require that inventory be reported at the market value (cost) of replacing inventory when market value is lower than cost.* Merchandise inventory is then said to be reported on the balance sheet at the **lower of cost or market (LCM).**

**P2** Compute the lower of cost or market amount of inventory.

**Computing the Lower of Cost or Market**   *Market* in the term *LCM* is defined as the current replacement cost of purchasing the same inventory items in the usual manner. A decline in replacement cost reflects a loss of value in inventory. When the recorded cost of inventory is higher than the replacement cost, a loss is recognized. When the recorded cost is lower, no adjustment is made.

LCM is applied in one of three ways: (1) to each individual item separately, (2) to major categories of items, or (3) to the whole of inventory. The less similar the items that make up inventory, the more likely companies are to apply LCM to individual items or categories. With the increasing application of technology and inventory tracking, companies increasingly apply

**EXHIBIT 6.9**

Lower of Cost or Market
Computations

$140,000 is the lower of $160,000
or $140,000

Market amount of $265,000 is lower
than the $295,000 recorded cost

| Inventory Items | Units | Per Unit | | Total Cost | Total Market | LCM Applied to Items |
|---|---|---|---|---|---|---|
| | | Cost | Market | | | |
| **Cycles** | | | | | | |
| Roadster ......... | 20 | $8,000 | $7,000 | $160,000 | $140,000 | $ 140,000 |
| Sprint ........... | 10 | 5,000 | 6,000 | 50,000 | 60,000 | 50,000 |
| **Off-Road** | | | | | | |
| Trax-4 ........... | 8 | 5,000 | 6,500 | 40,000 | 52,000 | 40,000 |
| Blazer ........... | 5 | 9,000 | 7,000 | 45,000 | 35,000 | 35,000 |
| Totals ........... | | | | $295,000 | | **$265,000** |

LCM to each individual item separately. Accordingly, we show that method only; however, advanced courses cover the other two methods. To illustrate LCM, we apply it to the ending inventory of a motorsports retailer in Exhibit 6.9.

**LCM Applied to Individual Items**   When LCM is applied to individual *items* of inventory, the number of comparisons equals the number of items. For Roadster, $140,000 is the lower of the $160,000 cost and the $140,000 market. For Sprint, $50,000 is the lower of the $50,000 cost and the $60,000 market. For Trax-4, $40,000 is the lower of the $40,000 cost and the $52,000 market. For Blazer, $35,000 is the lower of the $45,000 cost and the $35,000 market. This yields a $265,000 reported inventory, computed from $140,000 for Roadster plus $50,000 for Sprint plus $40,000 for Trax-4 plus $35,000 for Blazer.

**Point:** Advances in technology encourage the individual-item approach for LCM.

*RIM*     The manufacturer **Research In Motion** applies LCM and reports that its "inventories are stated at the lower of cost and net realizable value [or replacement cost]."

**Recording the Lower of Cost or Market**   Inventory must be adjusted downward when market is less than cost. To illustrate, if LCM is applied to the individual items of inventory in Exhibit 6.9, the Merchandise Inventory account must be adjusted from the $295,000 recorded cost down to the $265,000 market amount as follows.

| | | |
|---|---|---|
| Cost of Goods Sold ........................... | 30,000 | |
| Merchandise Inventory ...................... | | 30,000 |
| *To adjust inventory cost to market.* | | |

Accounting rules require that inventory be adjusted to market when market is less than cost, but inventory normally cannot be written up to market when market exceeds cost. If recording inventory down to market is acceptable, why are companies not allowed to record inventory up to market? One view is that a gain from a market increase should not be realized until a sales transaction verifies the gain. However, this problem also applies when market is less than cost. A second and primary reason is the **conservatism constraint,** which prescribes the use of the less optimistic amount when more than one estimate of the amount to be received or paid exists and these estimates are about equally likely.

## Financial Statement Effects of Inventory Errors

**A2**  Analyze the effects of inventory errors on current and future financial statements.

Companies must take care in both taking a physical count of inventory and in assigning a cost to it. An inventory error causes misstatements in cost of goods sold, gross profit, net income, current assets, and equity. It also causes misstatements in the next period's statements because ending inventory of one period is the beginning inventory of the next. As we consider the financial statement effects in this section, it is helpful if we recall the following *inventory relation.*

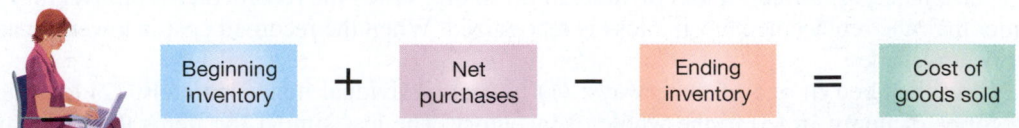

**Income Statement Effects**   Exhibit 6.10 shows the effects of inventory errors on key amounts in the current and next periods' income statements. Let's look at row 1 and year 1. We see that understating ending inventory overstates cost of goods sold. This can be seen from the above inventory relation where we subtract a smaller ending inventory amount in computing cost of goods sold. Then a higher cost of goods sold yields a lower income.

To understand year 2 of row 1, remember that an understated ending inventory for year 1 becomes an understated beginning inventory for year 2. Using the above inventory relation, we see that if beginning inventory is understated, then cost of goods sold is understated (because we are starting with a smaller amount). A lower cost of goods sold yields a higher income.

Turning to overstatements, let's look at row 2 and year 1. If ending inventory is overstated, we use the inventory relation to see that cost of goods sold is understated. A lower cost of goods sold yields a higher income.

For year 2 of row 2, we again recall that an overstated ending inventory for year 1 becomes an overstated beginning inventory for year 2. If beginning inventory is overstated, we use the inventory relation to see that cost of goods sold is overstated. A higher cost of goods sold yields a lower income.

**EXHIBIT 6.10**

Effects of Inventory Errors on the Income Statement

|  | Year 1 | | Year 2 | |
| --- | --- | --- | --- | --- |
| **Ending Inventory** | **Cost of Goods Sold** | **Net Income** | **Cost of Goods Sold** | **Net Income** |
| Understated↓ ......... | Overstated↑ | Understated↓ | Understated↓ | Overstated↑ |
| Overstated*↑ ......... | Understated↓ | Overstated↑ | Overstated↑ | Understated↓ |

\* This error is less likely under a perpetual system because it implies more inventory than is recorded (or less shrinkage than expected). Management will normally follow up and discover and correct this error before it impacts any accounts.

To illustrate, consider an inventory error for a company with $100,000 in sales for each of the years 2010, 2011, and 2012. If this company maintains a steady $20,000 inventory level during this period and makes $60,000 in purchases in each of these years, its cost of goods sold is $60,000 and its gross profit is $40,000 each year.

**Ending Inventory Understated—Year 1**   Assume that this company errs in computing its 2010 ending inventory and reports $16,000 instead of the correct amount of $20,000. The effects of this error are shown in Exhibit 6.11. The $4,000 understatement of 2010 ending inventory causes a $4,000 overstatement in 2010 cost of goods sold and a $4,000 understatement in both gross profit and net income for 2010. We see that these effects match the effects predicted in Exhibit 6.10.

**EXHIBIT 6.11**

Effects of Inventory Errors on Three Periods' Income Statements

| Income Statements | | | | | |
| --- | --- | --- | --- | --- | --- |
| | | **2010** | | **2011** | **2012** |
| Sales ...................... | | $100,000 | | $100,000 | $100,000 |
| Cost of goods sold | | | | | |
| Beginning inventory ........ | $20,000 | | →$16,000* | | →$20,000 |
| Cost of goods purchased ..... | 60,000 | | 60,000 | | 60,000 |
| Goods available for sale ..... | 80,000 | | 76,000 | | 80,000 |
| Ending inventory .......... | 16,000* | | 20,000 | | 20,000 |
| Cost of goods sold ......... | | 64,000† | | 56,000† | 60,000 |
| Gross profit ................ | | 36,000 | | 44,000 | 40,000 |
| Expenses ................... | | 10,000 | | 10,000 | 10,000 |
| Net income ................. | | $ 26,000 | | $ 34,000 | $ 30,000 |

Correct income is $30,000 for each year

\* Correct amount is $20,000.        † Correct amount is $60,000.

**Ending Inventory Understated—Year 2**   The 2010 understated ending inventory becomes the 2011 understated *beginning* inventory. We see in Exhibit 6.11 that this error causes an understatement in 2011 cost of goods sold and a $4,000 overstatement in both gross profit and net income for 2011.

**Ending Inventory Understated—Year 3**   Exhibit 6.11 shows that the 2010 ending inventory error affects only that period and the next. It does not affect 2012 results or any period thereafter. An inventory error is said to be *self-correcting* because it always yields an offsetting error in the next period. This does not reduce the severity of inventory errors. Managers, lenders, owners, and others make important decisions from analysis of income and costs.

**Example:** If 2010 ending inventory in Exhibit 6.11 is overstated by $3,000 (not understated by $4,000), what is the effect on cost of goods sold, gross profit, assets, and equity? *Answer:* Cost of goods sold is understated by $3,000 in 2010 and overstated by $3,000 in 2011. Gross profit and net income are overstated in 2010 and understated in 2011. Assets and equity are overstated in 2010.

**Point:** A former internal auditor at **Coca-Cola** alleges that just before midnight at a prior calendar year-end, fully loaded Coke trucks were ordered to drive about 2 feet away from the loading dock so that Coke could record millions of dollars in extra sales.

We can also do an analysis of beginning inventory errors. The income statement effects are the opposite of those for ending inventory.

**Balance Sheet Effects**    Balance sheet effects of an inventory error can be seen by considering the accounting equation: Assets = Liabilities + Equity. For example, understating ending inventory understates both current and total assets. An understatement in ending inventory also yields an understatement in equity because of the understatement in net income. Exhibit 6.12 shows the effects of inventory errors on the current period's balance sheet amounts. Errors in *beginning* inventory do not yield misstatements in the end-of-period balance sheet, but they do affect that current period's income statement.

**EXHIBIT 6.12**

Effects of Inventory Errors on Current Period's Balance Sheet

| Ending Inventory | Assets | Equity |
| --- | --- | --- |
| Understated↓ . . . . . . . . . . . . . . . | Understated↓ | Understated↓ |
| Overstated↑ . . . . . . . . . . . . . . . | Overstated↑ | Overstated↑ |

### Quick Check

Answers — p. 254

8. Use LCM applied separately to the following individual items to compute ending inventory.

| Product | Units | Unit Recorded Cost | Unit Market Cost |
| --- | --- | --- | --- |
| A . . . . . . . . . . | 20 | $ 6 | $ 5 |
| B . . . . . . . . . . | 40 | 9 | 8 |
| C . . . . . . . . . | 10 | 12 | 15 |

## GLOBAL VIEW

This section discusses differences between U.S. GAAP and IFRS in the items and costs making up merchandise inventory, in the methods to assign costs to inventory, and in the methods to estimate inventory values.

**Items and Costs Making Up Inventory**    Both U.S. GAAP and IFRS include broad and similar guidance for the items and costs making up merchandise inventory. Specifically, under both accounting systems, merchandise inventory includes all items that a company owns and holds for sale. Further, merchandise inventory includes costs of expenditures necessary, directly or indirectly, to bring those items to a salable condition and location.

**Assigning Costs to Inventory**    Both U.S. GAAP and IFRS allow companies to use specific identification in assigning costs to inventory. Further, both systems allow companies to apply a *cost flow assumption*. The usual cost flow assumptions are: FIFO, Weighted Average, and LIFO. However, IFRS does not (currently) allow use of LIFO. As the convergence project progresses, this prohibition may or may not persist.

**Estimating Inventory Costs**    The value of inventory can change while it awaits sale to customers. That value can decrease or increase.

**Decreases in Inventory Value**    Both U.S. GAAP and IFRS require companies to write down (reduce the cost recorded for) inventory when its value falls below the cost recorded. This is referred to as the *lower of cost or market* method explained in this chapter. U.S. GAAP prohibits any later increase in the recorded value of that inventory even if that decline in value is reversed through value increases in later periods. However, IFRS allows reversals of those write downs up to the original acquisition cost. For example, if *RIM* **Research In Motion** wrote down its 2010 inventory from $622 million to $600 million, it could not reverse this in future periods even if its value increased to more than $622 million. However, if RIM applied IFRS, it could reverse that previous loss. (Another difference is that value refers to *replacement cost* under U.S. GAAP, but *net realizable value* under IFRS.)

**Increases in Inventory Value**    Neither U.S. GAAP nor IFRS allow inventory to be adjusted upward beyond the original cost. (One exception is that IFRS requires agricultural assets such as animals, forests, and plants to be measured at fair value less point-of-sale costs.)

Nokia provides the following description of its inventory valuation procedures:

> Inventories are stated at the lower of cost or net realizable value. Cost ... approximates actual cost on a FIFO (First-in First-out) basis. Net realizable value is the amount that can be realized from the sale of the inventory in the normal course of business after allowing for the costs of realization.

---

**Inventory Turnover and Days' Sales in Inventory**      **Decision Analysis**

## Inventory Turnover

Earlier chapters described two important ratios useful in evaluating a company's short-term liquidity: current ratio and acid-test ratio. A merchandiser's ability to pay its short-term obligations also depends on how quickly it sells its merchandise inventory. **Inventory turnover,** also called *merchandise inventory turnover,* is one ratio used to assess this and is defined in Exhibit 6.13.

**A3** Assess inventory management using both inventory turnover and days' sales in inventory.

**EXHIBIT 6.13**

Inventory Turnover

$$\text{Inventory turnover} = \frac{\text{Cost of goods sold}}{\text{Average inventory}}$$

This ratio reveals how many *times* a company turns over (sells) its inventory during a period. If a company's inventory greatly varies within a year, average inventory amounts can be computed from interim periods such as quarters or months.

Users apply inventory turnover to help analyze short-term liquidity and to assess whether management is doing a good job controlling the amount of inventory available. A low ratio compared to that of competitors suggests inefficient use of assets. The company may be holding more inventory than it needs to support its sales volume. Similarly, a very high ratio compared to that of competitors suggests inventory might be too low. This can cause lost sales if customers must back-order merchandise. Inventory turnover has no simple rule except to say *a high ratio is preferable provided inventory is adequate to meet demand.*

**Point:** We must take care when comparing turnover ratios across companies that use different costing methods (such as FIFO and LIFO).

## Days' Sales in Inventory

To better interpret inventory turnover, many users measure the adequacy of inventory to meet sales demand. **Days' sales in inventory,** also called *days' stock on hand,* is a ratio that reveals how much inventory is available in terms of the number of days' sales. It can be interpreted as the number of days one can sell from inventory if no new items are purchased. This ratio is often viewed as a measure of the buffer against out-of-stock inventory and is useful in evaluating liquidity of inventory. It is defined in Exhibit 6.14.

**Point:** Inventory turnover is higher and days' sales in inventory is lower for industries such as foods and other perishable products. The reverse holds for nonperishable product industries.

$$\text{Days' sales in inventory} = \frac{\text{Ending inventory}}{\text{Cost of goods sold}} \times 365$$

**EXHIBIT 6.14**

Days' Sales in Inventory

Days' sales in inventory focuses on ending inventory and it estimates how many days it will take to convert inventory at the end of a period into accounts receivable or cash. Days' sales in inventory focuses on *ending* inventory whereas inventory turnover focuses on *average* inventory.

**Point:** Days' sales in inventory for many Ford models has risen: Freestyle, 122 days; Montego, 109 days; Five Hundred, 118 days. The industry average is 73 days. (*BusinessWeek*)

   **Decision Insight**

**Dell-ocity**   From its roots in a college dorm room, **Dell** now sells over 50 million dollars' worth of computers each day from its Website. The speed of Web technology has allowed Dell to slash inventories. Dell's inventory turnover is 88 and its days' sales in inventory is 5 days. Michael Dell asserts, "Speed is everything in this business." ∎

## Analysis of Inventory Management

Inventory management is a major emphasis for merchandisers. They must both plan and control inventory purchases and sales. **Toys "R" Us** is one of those merchandisers. Its inventory in fiscal year 2009 was $1,781 million. This inventory constituted 59% of its current assets and 21% of its total assets. We apply the analysis tools in this section to Toys "R" Us, as shown in Exhibit 6.15—also see margin graph.

**EXHIBIT 6.15**

Inventory Turnover and Days' Sales in Inventory for Toys "R" Us

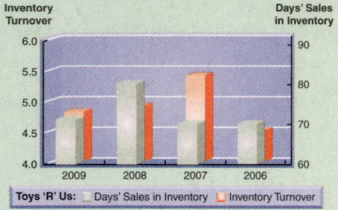

| ($ millions) | 2009 | 2008 | 2007 | 2006 |
|---|---|---|---|---|
| Cost of goods sold | $8,976 | $8,987 | $8,638 | $7,652 |
| Ending inventory | $1,781 | $1,998 | $1,690 | $1,488 |
| **Inventory turnover** | **4.8** times | **4.9** times | **5.4** times | **4.5** times |
| *Industry* inventory turnover | 3.2 times | 3.4 times | 3.0 times | 2.8 times |
| **Days' sales in inventory** | **72** days | **81** days | **71** days | **71** days |
| *Industry* days' sales in inventory | 124 days | 135 days | 129 days | 135 days |

Its 2009 inventory turnover of 4.8 times means that Toys "R" Us turns over its inventory 4.8 times per year, or once every 76 days (365 days ÷ 4.8). We prefer inventory turnover to be high provided inventory is not out of stock and the company is not losing customers. The second metric, the 2009 days' sales in inventory of 72 days, reveals that it is carrying 72 days of sales in inventory. This inventory buffer seems more than adequate. Toys "R" Us would benefit from further management efforts to increase inventory turnover and reduce inventory levels.

**Decision Maker**                                    Answer — p. 253

**Entrepreneur**  Analysis of your retail store yields an inventory turnover of 5.0 and a days' sales in inventory of 73 days. The industry norm for inventory turnover is 4.4 and for days' sales in inventory is 74 days. What is your assessment of inventory management? ■

TAKE THESE FIGURES, FREEBLE, AND SHROUD THEM IN MYSTERY AND LEGEND.

# DEMONSTRATION PROBLEM

Craig Company uses a perpetual inventory system for its one product. Its beginning inventory, purchases, and sales during calendar year 2011 follow.

| Date | Activity | Units Acquired at Cost | Units Sold at Retail | Unit Inventory |
|---|---|---|---|---|
| Jan. 1 | Beg. Inventory .... | 400 units @ $14 = $ 5,600 | | 400 units |
| Jan. 15 | Sale ............ | | 200 units @ $30 | 200 units |
| March 10 | Purchase ........ | 200 units @ $15 = $ 3,000 | | 400 units |
| April 1 | Sale ............ | | 200 units @ $30 | 200 units |
| May 9 | Purchase ........ | 300 units @ $16 = $ 4,800 | | 500 units |
| Sept. 22 | Purchase ........ | 250 units @ $20 = $ 5,000 | | 750 units |
| Nov. 1 | Sale ............ | | 300 units @ $35 | 450 units |
| Nov. 28 | Purchase ........ | 100 units @ $21 = $ 2,100 | | 550 units |
| | Totals ......... | 1,250 units      $20,500 | 700 units | |

**Additional tracking data for specific identification:** (1) January 15 sale—200 units @ $14, (2) April 1 sale—200 units @ $15, and (3) November 1 sale—200 units @ $14 and 100 units @ $20.

**Required**

1. Calculate the cost of goods available for sale.

2. Apply the four different methods of inventory costing (FIFO, LIFO, weighted average, and specific identification) to calculate ending inventory and cost of goods sold under each method.

3. Compute gross profit earned by the company for each of the four costing methods in part 2. Also, report the inventory amount reported on the balance sheet for each of the four methods.

4. In preparing financial statements for year 2011, the financial officer was instructed to use FIFO but failed to do so and instead computed cost of goods sold according to LIFO. Determine the impact on year 2011's income from the error. Also determine the effect of this error on year 2012's income. Assume no income taxes.

5. Management wants a report that shows how changing from FIFO to another method would change net income. Prepare a table showing (1) the cost of goods sold amount under each of the four methods, (2) the amount by which each cost of goods sold total is different from the FIFO cost of goods sold, and (3) the effect on net income if another method is used instead of FIFO.

## PLANNING THE SOLUTION

- Compute cost of goods available for sale by multiplying the units of beginning inventory and each purchase by their unit costs to determine the total cost of goods available for sale.
- Prepare a perpetual FIFO table starting with beginning inventory and showing how inventory changes after each purchase and after each sale (see Exhibit 6.5).
- Prepare a perpetual LIFO table starting with beginning inventory and showing how inventory changes after each purchase and after each sale (see Exhibit 6.6).
- Make a table of purchases and sales recalculating the average cost of inventory prior to each sale to arrive at the weighted average cost of ending inventory. Total the average costs associated with each sale to determine cost of goods sold (see Exhibit 6.7).
- Prepare a table showing the computation of cost of goods sold and ending inventory using the specific identification method (see Exhibit 6.4).
- Compare the year-end 2011 inventory amounts under FIFO and LIFO to determine the misstatement of year 2011 income that results from using LIFO. The errors for year 2011 and 2012 are equal in amount but opposite in effect.
- Create a table showing cost of goods sold under each method and how net income would differ from FIFO net income if an alternate method is adopted.

## SOLUTION TO DEMONSTRATION PROBLEM

1. Cost of goods available for sale (this amount is the same for all methods).

| Date | | | Units | Unit Cost | Cost |
|---|---|---|---|---|---|
| Jan. | 1 | Beg. Inventory . . . . . . . . . . | 400 | $14 | $ 5,600 |
| March 10 | | Purchase . . . . . . . . . . . . . . | 200 | 15 | 3,000 |
| May | 9 | Purchase . . . . . . . . . . . . . . | 300 | 16 | 4,800 |
| Sept. | 22 | Purchase . . . . . . . . . . . . . . | 250 | 20 | 5,000 |
| Nov. | 28 | Purchase . . . . . . . . . . . . . . | 100 | 21 | 2,100 |
| | | Total goods available for sale . . . . . . . . | 1,250 | | $20,500 |

2a. FIFO perpetual method.

| Date | Goods Purchased | Cost of Goods Sold | Inventory Balance |
|---|---|---|---|
| Jan. 1 | Beginning balance | | 400 @ $14 = $ 5,600 |
| Jan. 15 | | 200 @ $14 = $2,800 | 200 @ $14 = $ 2,800 |
| Mar. 10 | 200 @ $15 = $3,000 | | 200 @ $14 ⎱ = $ 5,800<br>200 @ $15 ⎰ |
| April 1 | | 200 @ $14 = $2,800 | 200 @ $15 = $ 3,000 |
| May 9 | 300 @ $16 = $4,800 | | 200 @ $15 ⎱ = $ 7,800<br>300 @ $16 ⎰ |
| Sept. 22 | 250 @ $20 = $5,000 | | 200 @ $15 ⎫<br>300 @ $16 ⎬ = $12,800<br>250 @ $20 ⎭ |
| Nov. 1 | | 200 @ $15 = $3,000<br>100 @ $16 = $1,600 | 200 @ $16 ⎱ = $ 8,200<br>250 @ $20 ⎰ |
| Nov. 28 | 100 @ $21 = $2,100 | | 200 @ $16 ⎫<br>250 @ $20 ⎬ = $10,300<br>100 @ $21 ⎭ |
| **Total cost of goods sold** | | **$10,200** | |

*Note to students:* **In a classroom situation,** once we compute cost of goods available for sale, we can compute the amount for either cost of goods sold or ending inventory—it is a matter of preference. **In practice,** the costs of items sold are identified as sales are made and immediately transferred from the inventory account to the cost of goods sold account. The previous solution showing the line-by-line approach illustrates actual application in practice. The following alternate solutions illustrate that, once the concepts are understood, other solution approaches are available. Although this is only shown for FIFO, it could be shown for all methods.

### Alternate Methods to Compute FIFO Perpetual Numbers

[FIFO Alternate No. 1: Computing cost of goods sold first]

| | | |
|---|---|---|
| Cost of goods available for sale (from part 1) . . . . . . . . . . . . | | $ 20,500 |
| **Cost of goods sold** | | |
| Jan.   15    Sold (200 @ $14) . . . . . . . . . . . . . . . . . . . . . . | $2,800 | |
| April   1    Sold (200 @ $14) . . . . . . . . . . . . . . . . . . . . . . | 2,800 | |
| Nov.   1    Sold (200 @ $15 and 100 @ $16) . . . . . . . . . | 4,600 | 10,200 |
| **Ending inventory** . . . . . . . . . . . . . . . . . . . . . . . . . . . . . | | **$10,300** |

[FIFO Alternate No. 2: Computing ending inventory first]

| | | |
|---|---|---|
| Cost of goods available for sale (from part 1) . . . . . . . . . | | $ 20,500 |
| Ending inventory* | | |
| Nov.  28    Purchase (100 @ $21) . . . . . . . . . . . . . . . . | $2,100 | |
| Sept.  22    Purchase (250 @ $20) . . . . . . . . . . . . . . . . | 5,000 | |
| May    9    Purchase (200 @ $16) . . . . . . . . . . . . . . . . | 3,200 | |
| **Ending inventory** . . . . . . . . . . . . . . . . . . . . . . . . . . . . . | | 10,300 |
| **Cost of goods sold** . . . . . . . . . . . . . . . . . . . . . . . . . . . . | | **$10,200** |

\* Since FIFO assumes that the earlier costs are the first to flow out, we determine ending inventory by assigning the most recent costs to the remaining items.

**2b.**  LIFO perpetual method.

| Date | Goods Purchased | Cost of Goods Sold | Inventory Balance | |
|---|---|---|---|---|
| Jan.   1 | Beginning balance | | 400 @ $14 | = $ 5,600 |
| Jan.  15 | | 200 @ $14 = $2,800 | 200 @ $14 | = $ 2,800 |
| Mar. 10 | 200 @ $15 = $3,000 | | 200 @ $14 <br> 200 @ $15 } | = $ 5,800 |
| April  1 | | 200 @ $15 = $3,000 | 200 @ $14 | = $ 2,800 |
| May   9 | 300 @ $16 = $4,800 | | 200 @ $14 <br> 300 @ $16 } | = $ 7,600 |
| Sept. 22 | 250 @ $20 = $5,000 | | 200 @ $14 <br> 300 @ $16 <br> 250 @ $20 } | = $12,600 |
| Nov.   1 | | 250 @ $20 = $5,000 <br> 50 @ $16 = $  800 | 200 @ $14 <br> 250 @ $16 } | = $ 6,800 |
| Nov. 28 | 100 @ $21 = $2,100 | | 200 @ $14 <br> 250 @ $16 <br> 100 @ $21 } | = **$ 8,900** |
| **Total cost of goods sold** | | **$11,600** | | |

**2c.** Weighted average perpetual method.

| Date | Goods Purchased | Cost of Goods Sold | Inventory Balance | |
|------|-----------------|--------------------|--------------------|---|
| Jan. 1 | Beginning balance | | 400 @ $14 | = $ 5,600 |
| Jan. 15 | | 200 @ $14 = $2,800 | 200 @ $14 | = $ 2,800 |
| Mar. 10 | 200 @ $15 = $3,000 | | 200 @ $14 ⎫<br>200 @ $15 ⎬<br>(avg. cost is $14.5) | = $ 5,800 |
| April 1 | | 200 @ $14.5 = $2,900 | 200 @ $14.5 | = $ 2,900 |
| May 9 | 300 @ $16 = $4,800 | | 200 @ $14.5 ⎫<br>300 @ $16 ⎬<br>(avg. cost is $15.4) | = $ 7,700 |
| Sept. 22 | 250 @ $20 = $5,000 | | 200 @ $14.5 ⎫<br>300 @ $16 ⎬<br>250 @ $20 ⎭<br>(avg. cost is $16.93) | = $ 12,700 |
| Nov. 1 | | 300 @ $16.93 = $5,079 | 450 @ $16.93 | = $ 7,618.5 |
| Nov. 28 | 100 @ $21 = $2,100 | | 450 @ $16.93 ⎫<br>100 @ $21 ⎬ | = **$9,718.5** |
| **Total cost of goods sold*** | | **$10,779** | | |

* The cost of goods sold ($10,779) plus ending inventory ($9,718.5) is $2.5 less than the cost of goods available for sale ($20,500) due to rounding.

**2d.** Specific identification method.

| Date | Goods Purchased | Cost of Goods Sold | Inventory Balance | |
|------|-----------------|--------------------|--------------------|---|
| Jan. 1 | Beginning balance | | 400 @ $14 | = $ 5,600 |
| Jan. 15 | | 200 @ $14 = $2,800 | 200 @ $14 | = $ 2,800 |
| Mar. 10 | 200 @ $15 = $3,000 | | 200 @ $14 ⎫<br>200 @ $15 ⎬ | = $ 5,800 |
| April 1 | | 200 @ $15 = $3,000 | 200 @ $14 | = $ 2,800 |
| May 9 | 300 @ $16 = $4,800 | | 200 @ $14 ⎫<br>300 @ $16 ⎬ | = $ 7,600 |
| Sept. 22 | 250 @ $20 = $5,000 | | 200 @ $14 ⎫<br>300 @ $16 ⎬<br>250 @ $20 ⎭ | = $ 12,600 |
| Nov. 1 | | 200 @ $14 = $2,800<br>100 @ $20 = $2,000 | 300 @ $16 ⎫<br>150 @ $20 ⎬ | = $ 7,800 |
| Nov. 28 | 100 @ $21 = $2,100 | | 300 @ $16 ⎫<br>150 @ $20 ⎬<br>100 @ $21 ⎭ | = **$ 9,900** |
| **Total cost of goods sold** | | **$10,600** | | |

3.

| | FIFO | LIFO | Weighted Average | Specific Identification |
|---|---|---|---|---|
| **Income Statement** | | | | |
| Sales* . . . . . . . . . . . . . . . . . . . . . . . | $ 22,500 | $22,500 | $ 22,500 | $22,500 |
| **Cost of goods sold** . . . . . . . . . . . . | 10,200 | 11,600 | 10,779 | 10,600 |
| Gross profit . . . . . . . . . . . . . . . . | $ 12,300 | $10,900 | $ 11,721 | $11,900 |
| **Balance Sheet** | | | | |
| **Inventory** . . . . . . . . . . . . . . . . . . . | **$10,300** | **$ 8,900** | **$9,718.5** | **$ 9,900** |

\* Sales = (200 units × $30) + (200 units × $30) + (300 units × $35) = $22,500

4. Mistakenly using LIFO when FIFO should have been used overstates cost of goods sold in year 2011 by $1,400, which is the difference between the FIFO and LIFO amounts of ending inventory. It understates income in 2011 by $1,400. In year 2012, income is overstated by $1,400 because of the understatement in beginning inventory.

5. Analysis of the effects of alternative inventory methods.

| | Cost of Goods Sold | Difference from FIFO Cost of Goods Sold | Effect on Net Income If Adopted Instead of FIFO |
|---|---|---|---|
| FIFO . . . . . . . . . . . . . . . . . . . . . . | $10,200 | — | — |
| LIFO . . . . . . . . . . . . . . . . . . . . . . | 11,600 | +$1,400 | $1,400 lower |
| Weighted average . . . . . . . . . . . | 10,779 | + 579 | 579 lower |
| Specific identification . . . . . . . . . | 10,600 | + 400 | 400 lower |

---

# 6A Inventory Costing under a Periodic System

**P3** Compute inventory in a periodic system using the methods of specific identification, FIFO, LIFO, and weighted average.

The basic aim of the periodic system and the perpetual system is the same: to assign costs to inventory and cost of goods sold. The same four methods are used to assign costs under both systems: specific identification; first-in, first-out; last-in, first-out; and weighted average. We use information from Trekking to show how to assign costs using these four methods with a periodic system. Data for sales and purchases are in Exhibit 6A.1. Also, recall that we explained the accounting entries under a periodic system in Appendix 5A.

**EXHIBIT 6A.1**

Purchases and Sales of Goods

| Date | Activity | Units Acquired at Cost | Units Sold at Retail | Unit Inventory |
|---|---|---|---|---|
| Aug. 1 | Beginning inventory . . . . | 10 units @ $ 91 = $ 910 | | 10 units |
| Aug. 3 | Purchases . . . . . . . . . . . . | 15 units @ $106 = $ 1,590 | | 25 units |
| Aug. 14 | Sales . . . . . . . . . . . . . . | | 20 units @ $130 | 5 units |
| Aug. 17 | Purchases . . . . . . . . . . . . | 20 units @ $115 = $ 2,300 | | 25 units |
| Aug. 28 | Purchases. . . . . . . . . . . . . | 10 units @ $119 = $ 1,190 | | 35 units |
| Aug. 31 | Sales. . . . . . . . . . . . . . . | | 23 units @ $150 | **12 units** |
| | Totals . . . . . . . . . . . . . . | **55 units**    **$5,990** | **43 units** | |

**Specific Identification** We use the above sales and purchases information and the specific identification method to assign costs to ending inventory and units sold. Trekking's internal data reveal the following specific unit sales:

**August 14**   Sold 8 bikes costing $91 each and 12 bikes costing $106 each

**August 31**   Sold 2 bikes costing $91 each, 3 bikes costing $106 each, 15 bikes costing $115 each, and 3 bikes costing $119 each

Applying specific identification and using the information above, we prepare Exhibit 6A.2. This exhibit starts with 10 bikes at $91 each in beginning inventory. On August 3, 15 more bikes are purchased at $106 each for $1,590. Inventory available now consists of 10 bikes at $91 each and 15 bikes at $106 each, for a total of $2,500. On August 14 (see specific sales data above), 20 bikes costing $2,000 are sold—leaving 5 bikes costing $500 in inventory. On August 17, 20 bikes costing $2,300 are purchased, and on August 28, another 10 bikes costing $1,190 are purchased, for a total of 35 bikes costing $3,990 in inventory. On August 31 (see specific sales above), 23 bikes costing $2,582 are sold, which leaves 12 bikes costing $1,408 in ending inventory. Carefully study Exhibit 6A.2 to see the flow of costs both in and out of inventory. Each unit, whether sold or remaining in inventory, has its own specific cost attached to it.

**EXHIBIT 6A.2**

Specific Identification Computations

* Identification of items sold (and their costs) is obtained from internal documents that track each unit from its purchase to its sale.

When using specific identification, Trekking's cost of goods sold reported on the income statement totals **$4,582**, the sum of $2,000 and $2,582 from the third column of Exhibit 6A.2. Trekking's ending inventory reported on the balance sheet is **$1,408**, which is the final inventory balance from the fourth column. The purchases and sales entries for Exhibit 6A.2 follow (the colored boldface numbers are those affected by the cost flow assumption).

**Point:** The assignment of costs to the goods sold and to inventory using specific identification is the same for both the perpetual and periodic systems.

| | Purchases | | |
|---|---|---|---|
| Aug. 3 | Purchases .................. | 1,590 | |
| | Accounts Payable ......... | | 1,590 |
| 17 | Purchases .................. | 2,300 | |
| | Accounts Payable ......... | | 2,300 |
| 28 | Purchases .................. | 1,190 | |
| | Accounts Payable ......... | | 1,190 |

| | Sales | | |
|---|---|---|---|
| Aug. 14 | Accounts Receivable ........... | 2,600 | |
| | Sales.................... | | 2,600 |
| 31 | Accounts Receivable .......... | 3,450 | |
| | Sales.................... | | 3,450 |
| | **Adjusting Entry** | | |
| 31 | Merchandise Inventory ......... | **1,408** | |
| | Income Summary......... | | 498 |
| | Merchandise Inventory .... | | **910** |

**First-In, First-Out**  The first-in, first-out (FIFO) method of assigning costs to inventory assumes that inventory items are sold in the order acquired. When sales occur, the costs of the earliest units acquired are charged to cost of goods sold. This leaves the costs from the most recent purchases in ending inventory. Use of FIFO for computing the cost of inventory and cost of goods sold is shown in Exhibit 6A.3.

This exhibit starts with computing $5,990 in total units available for sale—this is given to us at the start of this appendix. Applying FIFO, we know that the 12 units in ending inventory will be reported at the cost of the most recent 12 purchases. Reviewing purchases in reverse order, we assign costs to the 12 bikes in ending inventory as follows: $119 cost to 10 bikes and $115 cost to 2 bikes. This yields 12 bikes costing $1,420 in ending inventory. We then subtract this $1,420 in ending inventory from $5,990 in cost of goods available to get $4,570 in cost of goods sold.

**EXHIBIT 6A.3**

FIFO Computations—
Periodic System

Exhibit 6A.1 shows that the 12 units in ending inventory consist of 10 units from the latest purchase on Aug. 28 and 2 units from the next latest purchase on Aug. 17.

| | | |
|---|---|---|
| Total cost of 55 units available for sale (from Exhibit 6A.1) ......... | | $5,990 |
| Less ending inventory priced using FIFO | | |
| 10 units from August 28 purchase at $119 each ............... | $1,190 | |
| 2 units from August 17 purchase at $115 each ............... | 230 | |
| **Ending inventory** ........................................ | | 1,420 |
| **Cost of goods sold** ..................................... | | $4,570 |

**Point:** The assignment of costs to the goods sold and to inventory using FIFO is the same for both the perpetual and periodic systems.

Trekking's ending inventory reported on the balance sheet is **$1,420**, and its cost of goods sold reported on the income statement is **$4,570**. These amounts are the same as those computed using the perpetual system. This always occurs because the most recent purchases are in ending inventory under both systems. The purchases and sales entries for Exhibit 6A.3 follow (the colored boldface numbers are those affected by the cost flow assumption).

| **Purchases** | | |
|---|---|---|
| Aug. 3 | Purchases..................... 1,590 | |
| | Accounts Payable.......... | 1,590 |
| 17 | Purchases..................... 2,300 | |
| | Accounts Payable.......... | 2,300 |
| 28 | Purchases..................... 1,190 | |
| | Accounts Payable.......... | 1,190 |

| **Sales** | | |
|---|---|---|
| Aug. 14 | Accounts Receivable ........... 2,600 | |
| | Sales .................... | 2,600 |
| 31 | Accounts Receivable ........... 3,450 | |
| | Sales .................... | 3,450 |
| | **Adjusting Entry** | |
| 31 | Merchandise Inventory ..........**1,420** | |
| | Income Summary ......... | 510 |
| | Merchandise Inventory ..... | **910** |

**Last-In, First-Out**    The last-in, first-out (LIFO) method of assigning costs assumes that the most recent purchases are sold first. These more recent costs are charged to the goods sold, and the costs of the earliest purchases are assigned to inventory. LIFO results in costs of the most recent purchases being assigned to cost of goods sold, which means that LIFO comes close to matching current costs of goods sold with revenues. Use of LIFO for computing cost of inventory and cost of goods sold is shown in Exhibit 6A.4.

This exhibit starts with computing $5,990 in total units available for sale—this is given to us at the start of this appendix. Applying LIFO, we know that the 12 units in ending inventory will be reported at the cost of the earliest 12 purchases. Reviewing the earliest purchases in order, we assign costs to the 12 bikes in ending inventory as follows: $91 cost to 10 bikes and $106 cost to 2 bikes. This yields 12 bikes costing $1,122 in ending inventory. We then subtract this $1,122 in ending inventory from $5,990 in cost of goods available to get $4,868 in cost of goods sold.

**EXHIBIT 6A.4**

LIFO Computations—
Periodic System

Exhibit 6A.1 shows that the 12 units in ending inventory consist of 10 units from the earliest purchase (beg. inv.) and 2 units from the next earliest purchase on Aug. 3.

| | | |
|---|---|---|
| Total cost of 55 units available for sale (from Exhibit 6A.1) .......... | | $5,990 |
| Less ending inventory priced using LIFO | | |
| 10 units in beginning inventory at $91 each ................... | $910 | |
| 2 units from August 3 purchase at $106 each.................. | 212 | |
| **Ending inventory** ....................................... | | 1,122 |
| **Cost of goods sold** ..................................... | | $4,868 |

Trekking's ending inventory reported on the balance sheet is $1,122, and its cost of goods sold reported on the income statement is $4,868. When LIFO is used with the periodic system, cost of goods sold is assigned costs from the most recent purchases for the period. With a perpetual system, cost of goods sold is assigned costs from the most recent purchases at the point of *each sale*. The purchases and sales entries for Exhibit 6A.4 follow (the colored boldface numbers are those affected by the cost flow assumption).

| Purchases | | | | Sales | | |
|---|---|---|---|---|---|---|
| Aug. 3 Purchases | 1,590 | | Aug. 14 | Accounts Receivable | 2,600 | |
| Accounts Payable | | 1,590 | | Sales | | 2,600 |
| 17 Purchases | 2,300 | | 31 | Accounts Receivable | 3,450 | |
| Accounts Payable | | 2,300 | | Sales | | 3,450 |
| 28 Purchases | 1,190 | | | **Adjusting Entry** | | |
| Accounts Payable | | 1,190 | 31 | Merchandise Inventory | **1,122** | |
| | | | | Income Summary | | 212 |
| | | | | Merchandise Inventory | | **910** |

**Weighted Average**   The **weighted average** or **WA** (also called **average cost**) method of assigning cost requires that we use the average cost per unit of inventory at the end of the period. Weighted average cost per unit equals the cost of goods available for sale divided by the units available. The weighted average method of assigning cost involves three important steps. The first two steps are shown in Exhibit 6A.5. First, multiply the per unit cost for beginning inventory and each particular purchase by the corresponding number of units (from Exhibit 6A.1). Second, add these amounts and divide by the total number of units available for sale to find the weighted average cost per unit.

**EXHIBIT 6A.5**

Weighted Average Cost per Unit

| Step 1: | 10 units @ $ 91 = $ 910 |
| | 15 units @ $106 = 1,590 |
| | 20 units @ $115 = 2,300 |
| | 10 units @ $119 = 1,190 |
| | 55             $5,990 |
| Step 2: | $5,990/55 units = **$108.91** weighted average cost per unit |

The third step is to use the weighted average cost per unit to assign costs to inventory and to the units sold as shown in Exhibit 6A.6.

| Step 3: | Total cost of 55 units available for sale (from Exhibit 6A.1) | $ 5,990 |
| | Less **ending inventory** priced on a weighted average cost basis: 12 units at $108.91 each (from Exhibit 6A.5) | 1,307 |
| | **Cost of goods sold** | $4,683 |

**Example:** In Exhibit 6A.5, if 5 more units had been purchased at $120 each, what would be the weighted average cost per unit?
*Answer:* $109.83 ($6,590/60)

**EXHIBIT 6A.6**

Weighted Average Computations—Periodic

Trekking's ending inventory reported on the balance sheet is $1,307, and its cost of goods sold reported on the income statement is $4,683 when using the weighted average (periodic) method. The purchases and sales entries for Exhibit 6A.6 follow (the colored boldface numbers are those affected by the cost flow assumption).

**Point:** Weighted average usually yields different results for the perpetual and the periodic systems because under a perpetual system it recomputes the per unit cost prior to each sale, whereas under a periodic system, the per unit cost is computed only at the end of a period.

| Purchases | | | | Sales | | |
|---|---|---|---|---|---|---|
| Aug. 3 Purchases | 1,590 | | Aug. 14 | Accounts Receivable | 2,600 | |
| Accounts Payable | | 1,590 | | Sales | | 2,600 |
| 17 Purchases | 2,300 | | 31 | Accounts Receivable | 3,450 | |
| Accounts Payable | | 2,300 | | Sales | | 3,450 |
| 28 Purchases | 1,190 | | | **Adjusting Entry** | | |
| Accounts Payable | | 1,190 | 31 | Merchandise Inventory | **1,307** | |
| | | | | Income Summary | | 397 |
| | | | | Merchandise Inventory | | **910** |

**Point:** LIFO inventory is often less than the inventory's replacement cost because LIFO inventory is valued using the oldest inventory purchase costs.

**Financial Statement Effects**   When purchase prices do not change, each inventory costing method assigns the same cost amounts to inventory and to cost of goods sold. When purchase prices are different, however, the methods nearly always assign different cost amounts. We show these differences in Exhibit 6A.7 using Trekking's data.

**EXHIBIT 6A.7**

Financial Statement Effects of Inventory Costing Methods

| TREKKING COMPANY<br>For Month Ended August 31 | | | | |
|---|---|---|---|---|
| | Specific<br>Identification | FIFO | LIFO | Weighted<br>Average |
| **Income Statement** | | | | |
| Sales ......................... | $ 6,050 | $ 6,050 | $ 6,050 | $ 6,050 |
| **Cost of goods sold** ............. | 4,582 | 4,570 | 4,868 | 4,683 |
|    Gross profit ................. | 1,468 | 1,480 | 1,182 | 1,367 |
| Expenses...................... | 450 | 450 | 450 | 450 |
| Income before taxes............. | 1,018 | 1,030 | 732 | 917 |
| Income tax expense (30%)......... | 305 | 309 | 220 | 275 |
| **Net income** ................... | $ 713 | $ 721 | $ 512 | $ 642 |
| **Balance Sheet** | | | | |
| **Inventory** ..................... | $1,408 | $1,420 | $1,122 | $1,307 |

This exhibit reveals two important results. First, when purchase costs *regularly rise,* as in Trekking's case, observe the following:

- FIFO assigns the lowest amount to cost of goods sold—yielding the highest gross profit and net income.
- LIFO assigns the highest amount to cost of goods sold—yielding the lowest gross profit and net income, which also yields a temporary tax advantage by postponing payment of some income tax.
- Weighted average yields results between FIFO and LIFO.
- Specific identification always yields results that depend on which units are sold.

Second, when costs *regularly decline,* the reverse occurs for FIFO and LIFO. FIFO gives the highest cost of goods sold—yielding the lowest gross profit and income. And LIFO gives the lowest cost of goods sold—yielding the highest gross profit and income.

    All four inventory costing methods are acceptable in practice. A company must disclose the inventory method it uses. Each method offers certain advantages as follows:

- FIFO assigns an amount to inventory on the balance sheet that approximates its current cost; it also mimics the actual flow of goods for most businesses.
- LIFO assigns an amount to cost of goods sold on the income statement that approximates its current cost; it also better matches current costs with revenues in computing gross profit.
- Weighted average tends to smooth out erratic changes in costs.
- Specific identification exactly matches the costs of items with the revenues they generate.

## Quick Check
Answers — p. 254

9. A company reports the following beginning inventory and purchases, and it ends the period with 30 units in inventory.

| | |
|---|---|
| Beginning inventory .......... | 100 units at $10 cost per unit |
| Purchase 1 ................. | 40 units at $12 cost per unit |
| Purchase 2 ................. | 20 units at $14 cost per unit |

    **a.** Compute ending inventory using the FIFO periodic system.

    **b.** Compute cost of goods sold using the LIFO periodic system.

# Inventory Estimation Methods

# 6B

**P4** Apply both the retail inventory and gross profit methods to estimate inventory.

Inventory sometimes requires estimation for two reasons. First, companies often require **interim statements** (financial statements prepared for periods of less than one year), but they only annually take a physical count of inventory. Second, companies may require an inventory estimate if some casualty such as fire or flood makes taking a physical count impossible. Estimates are usually only required for companies that use the periodic system. Companies using a perpetual system would presumably have updated inventory data.

This appendix describes two methods to estimate inventory.

**Retail Inventory Method**   To avoid the time-consuming and expensive process of taking a physical inventory each month or quarter, some companies use the **retail inventory method** to estimate cost of goods sold and ending inventory. Some companies even use the retail inventory method to prepare the annual statements. **Home Depot**, for instance, says in its annual report: "Inventories are stated at the lower of cost (first-in, first-out) or market, as determined by the retail inventory method." A company may also estimate inventory for audit purposes or when inventory is damaged or destroyed.

The retail inventory method uses a three-step process to estimate ending inventory. We need to know the amount of inventory a company had at the beginning of the period in both *cost* and *retail* amounts. We already explained how to compute the cost of inventory. The *retail amount of inventory* refers to its dollar amount measured using selling prices of inventory items. We also need to know the net amount of goods purchased (minus returns, allowances, and discounts) in the period, both at cost and at retail. The amount of net sales at retail is also needed. The process is shown in Exhibit 6B.1.

The reasoning behind the retail inventory method is that if we can get a good estimate of the cost-to-retail ratio, we can multiply ending inventory at retail by this ratio to estimate ending inventory at cost. We show in Exhibit 6B.2 how these steps are applied to estimate ending inventory for a typical company. First, we find that $100,000 of goods (at retail selling prices) were available for sale. We see that $70,000 of these goods were sold, leaving $30,000 (retail value) of merchandise in ending inventory. Second, the cost of these goods is 60% of the $100,000 retail value. Third, since cost for these goods is 60% of retail, the estimated cost of ending inventory is $18,000.

**Point:** When a retailer takes a physical inventory, it can restate the retail value of inventory to a cost basis by applying the cost-to-retail ratio. It can also estimate the amount of shrinkage by comparing the inventory computed with the amount from a physical inventory.

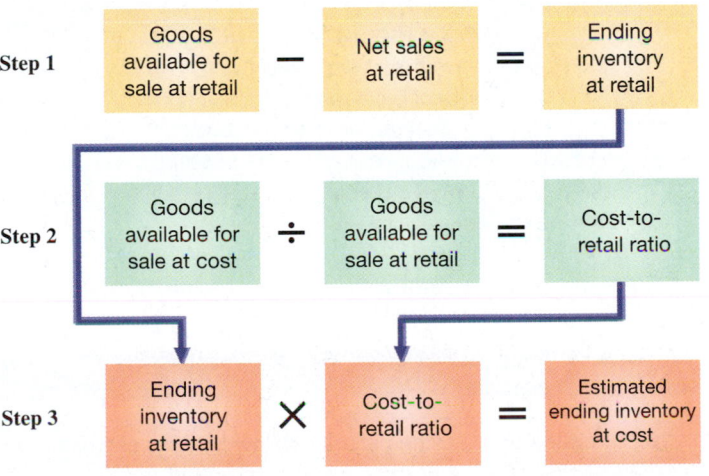

**EXHIBIT 6B.1**

Retail Inventory Method of Inventory Estimation

**Example:** What is the cost of ending inventory in Exhibit 6B.2 if the cost of beginning inventory is $22,500 and its retail value is $34,500? *Answer:* $30,000 × 62% = $18,600

**EXHIBIT 6B.2**

Estimated Inventory Using the Retail Inventory Method

| | At Cost | At Retail |
|---|---|---|
| Goods available for sale | | |
|   Beginning inventory . . . . . . . . . . . . . . . . . . . . . . . . . . . . . . . . . . | $ 20,500 | $ 34,500 |
|   Cost of goods purchased. . . . . . . . . . . . . . . . . . . . . . . . . . . . . . | 39,500 | 65,500 |
|   Goods available for sale . . . . . . . . . . . . . . . . . . . . . . . . . . . . . | 60,000 | 100,000 |
| **Step 1:**   **Deduct net sales at retail** . . . . . . . . . . . . . . . . . . . . . . . . . | | 70,000 |
|   **Ending inventory at retail** . . . . . . . . . . . . . . . . . . . . . . . . . . . | | $ 30,000 |
| **Step 2:**   **Cost-to-retail ratio: ($60,000 ÷ $100,000) = 60%** | | |
| **Step 3:**   **Estimated ending inventory at cost ($30,000 × 60%)** . . . . . . . . . | $18,000 | |

**Gross Profit Method**   The **gross profit method** estimates the cost of ending inventory by applying the gross profit ratio to net sales (at retail). This type of estimate often is needed when inventory is destroyed, lost, or stolen. These cases require an inventory estimate so that a company can file a claim with its insurer. Users also apply this method to see whether inventory amounts from a physical count are reasonable. This method uses the historical relation between cost of goods sold and net sales to estimate the proportion of cost of goods sold making up current sales. This cost of goods sold estimate is then subtracted from cost of goods available for sale to estimate the ending inventory at cost. These two steps are shown in Exhibit 6B.3.

**EXHIBIT 6B.3**

Gross Profit Method of Inventory Estimation

To illustrate, assume that a company's inventory is destroyed by fire in March 2011. When the fire occurs, the company's accounts show the following balances for January through March: sales, $31,500; sales returns, $1,500; inventory (January 1, 2011), $12,000; and cost of goods purchased, $20,500. If this company's gross profit ratio is 30%, then 30% of each net sales dollar is gross profit and 70% is cost of goods sold. We show in Exhibit 6B.4 how this 70% is used to estimate lost inventory of $11,500. To understand this exhibit, think of subtracting the cost of goods sold from the goods available for sale to get the ending inventory.

**Point:** A fire or other catastrophe can result in an insurance claim for lost inventory or income. Backup and off-site storage of data help ensure coverage for such losses.

**Point:** Reliability of the gross profit method depends on a good estimate of the gross profit ratio.

**EXHIBIT 6B.4**

Estimated Inventory Using the Gross Profit Method

| | | |
|---|---|---:|
| Goods available for sale | | |
| Inventory, January 1, 2011 . . . . . . . . . . . . . . . . . . . . . . . . . . . . | | $12,000 |
| Cost of goods purchased . . . . . . . . . . . . . . . . . . . . . . . . . . | | 20,500 |
| Goods available for sale (at cost) . . . . . . . . . . . . . . . . . . . . | | 32,500 |
| Net sales at retail ($31,500 − $1,500) . . . . . . . . . . . . . . . . . | | $30,000⌐ |
| **Step 1:** | **Estimated cost of goods sold ($30,000 × 70%)** . . . . . . . . | **(21,000)** ← ☐ × 0.70 |
| **Step 2:** | **Estimated March inventory at cost** . . . . . . . . . . . . . . . . | **$11,500** |

## Quick Check

Answer — p. 254

**10.** Using the retail method and the following data, estimate the cost of ending inventory.

| | Cost | Retail |
|---|---:|---:|
| Beginning inventory . . . . . . . . . . . . . . . | $324,000 | $530,000 |
| Cost of goods purchased . . . . . . . . . . | 195,000 | 335,000 |
| Net sales . . . . . . . . . . . . . . . . . . . . . . | | 320,000 |

# Summary

**C1** **Identify the items making up merchandise inventory.**
Merchandise inventory refers to goods owned by a company and held for resale. Three special cases merit our attention. Goods in transit are reported in inventory of the company that holds ownership rights. Goods on consignment are reported in the consignor's inventory. Goods damaged or obsolete are reported in inventory at their net realizable value.

**C2** **Identify the costs of merchandise inventory.** Costs of merchandise inventory include expenditures necessary to bring an

item to a salable condition and location. This includes its invoice cost minus any discount plus any added or incidental costs necessary to put it in a place and condition for sale.

**A1** **Analyze the effects of inventory methods for both financial and tax reporting.** When purchase costs are rising or falling, the inventory costing methods are likely to assign different costs to inventory. Specific identification exactly matches costs and revenues. Weighted average smooths out cost changes. FIFO assigns an amount to inventory closely approximating current replacement cost. LIFO assigns the most recent costs incurred to cost of goods sold and likely better matches current costs with revenues.

**A2    Analyze the effects of inventory errors on current and future financial statements.** An error in the amount of ending inventory affects assets (inventory), net income (cost of goods sold), and equity for that period. Since ending inventory is next period's beginning inventory, an error in ending inventory affects next period's cost of goods sold and net income. Inventory errors in one period are offset in the next period.

**A3    Assess inventory management using both inventory turnover and days' sales in inventory.** We prefer a high inventory turnover, provided that goods are not out of stock and customers are not turned away. We use days' sales in inventory to assess the likelihood of goods being out of stock. We prefer a small number of days' sales in inventory if we can serve customer needs and provide a buffer for uncertainties.

**P1    Compute inventory in a perpetual system using the methods of specific identification, FIFO, LIFO, and weighted average.** Costs are assigned to the cost of goods sold account *each time* a sale occurs in a perpetual system. Specific identification assigns a cost to each item sold by referring to its actual cost (for example, its net invoice cost). Weighted average assigns a cost to items sold by dividing the current balance in the inventory account by the total items available for sale to determine cost per unit. We then multiply the number of units sold by this cost per unit to get the cost of each sale. FIFO assigns cost to items sold assuming that the earliest units purchased are the first units sold. LIFO assigns cost to items sold assuming that the most recent units purchased are the first units sold.

**P2    Compute the lower of cost or market amount of inventory.** Inventory is reported at market cost when market is *lower* than recorded cost, called the *lower of cost or market (LCM) inventory.* Market is typically measured as replacement cost. Lower of cost or market can be applied separately to each item, to major categories of items, or to the entire inventory.

**P3ᴬ    Compute inventory in a periodic system using the methods of specific identification, FIFO, LIFO, and weighted average.** Periodic inventory systems allocate the cost of goods available for sale between cost of goods sold and ending inventory *at the end of a period.* Specific identification and FIFO give identical results whether the periodic or perpetual system is used. LIFO assigns costs to cost of goods sold assuming the last units purchased for the period are the first units sold. The weighted average cost per unit is computed by dividing the total cost of beginning inventory and net purchases for the period by the total number of units available. Then, it multiplies cost per unit by the number of units sold to give cost of goods sold.

**P4ᴮ    Apply both the retail inventory and gross profit methods to estimate inventory.** The retail inventory method involves three steps: (1) goods available at retail minus net sales at retail equals ending inventory at retail, (2) goods available at cost divided by goods available at retail equals the cost-to-retail ratio, and (3) ending inventory at retail multiplied by the cost-to-retail ratio equals estimated ending inventory at cost. The gross profit method involves two steps: (1) net sales at retail multiplied by 1 minus the gross profit ratio equals estimated cost of goods sold, and (2) goods available at cost minus estimated cost of goods sold equals estimated ending inventory at cost.

---

## Guidance Answers to Decision Maker and Decision Ethics

**Financial Planner**    The FIFO method implies that the oldest costs are the first ones assigned to cost of goods sold. This leaves the most recent costs in ending inventory. You report this to your client and note that in most cases, the ending inventory of a company using FIFO is reported at or near its replacement cost. This means that your client need not in most cases adjust the reported value of inventory. Your answer changes only if there are major increases in replacement cost compared to the cost of recent purchases reported in inventory. When major increases in costs occur, your client might wish to adjust inventory (for internal reports) for the difference between the reported cost of inventory and its replacement cost. (*Note:* Decreases in costs of purchases are recognized under the lower of cost or market adjustment.)

**Inventory Manager**    It seems your company can save (or at least postpone) taxes by switching to LIFO, but the switch is likely to reduce bonus money that you think you have earned and deserve. Since

the U.S. tax code requires companies that use LIFO for tax reporting also to use it for financial reporting, your options are further constrained. Your best decision is to tell your superior about the tax savings with LIFO. You also should discuss your bonus plan and how this is likely to hurt you unfairly. You might propose to compute inventory under the LIFO method for reporting purposes but use the FIFO method for your bonus calculations. Another solution is to revise the bonus plan to reflect the company's use of the LIFO method.

**Entrepreneur**    Your inventory turnover is markedly higher than the norm, whereas days' sales in inventory approximates the norm. Since your turnover is already 14% better than average, you are probably best served by directing attention to days' sales in inventory. You should see whether you can reduce the level of inventory while maintaining service to customers. Given your higher turnover, you should be able to hold less inventory.

---

## Guidance Answers to Quick Checks

1. The matching principle.
2. Target reports these goods in its inventory.
3. Total cost assigned to the painting is $12,180, computed as $11,400 + $130 + $150 + $100 + $400.
4. Specific identification exactly matches costs and revenues. Weighted average tends to smooth out cost changes. FIFO

assigns an amount to inventory that closely approximates current replacement cost. LIFO assigns the most recent costs incurred to cost of goods sold and likely better matches current costs with revenues.

5. FIFO—it gives a lower cost of goods sold, a higher gross profit, and a higher net income when costs are rising.

**6.** When costs are rising, LIFO gives a lower inventory figure on the balance sheet as compared to FIFO. FIFO's inventory amount approximates current replacement costs.

**7.** Cost of goods sold would be overstated by $10,000 in 2010 and understated by $10,000 in year 2011.

**8.** The reported LCM inventory amount (using items) is $540, computed as $[(20 \times \$5) + (40 \times \$8) + (10 \times \$12)]$.

**9.^A a.** FIFO periodic inventory = $(20 \times \$14) + (10 \times \$12)$
$$= \$400$$

    **b.** LIFO periodic cost of goods sold
$$= (20 \times \$14) + (40 \times \$12) + (70 \times \$10)$$
$$= \$1,460$$

**10.^B** Estimated ending inventory (at cost) is $327,000. It is computed as follows:

Step 1:  $(\$530,000 + \$335,000) - \$320,000 = \$545,000$

Step 2:  $\dfrac{\$324,000 + \$195,000}{\$530,000 + \$335,000} = 60\%$

Step 3:  $\$545,000 \times 60\% = \underline{\$327,000}$

---

## Key Terms

mhhe.com/wildFAP20e

**Average cost** (p. 234)
**Conservatism constraint** (p. 238)
**Consignee** (p. 228)
**Consignor** (p. 228)
**Consistency concept** (p. 237)
**Days' sales in inventory** (p. 241)

**First-in, first-out (FIFO)** (p. 233)
**Gross profit method** (p. 252)
**Interim statements** (p. 251)
**Inventory turnover** (p. 241)
**Last-in, first-out (LIFO)** (p. 233)
**Lower of cost or market (LCM)** (p. 237)

**Net realizable value** (p. 228)
**Retail inventory method** (p. 251)
**Specific identification** (p. 231)
**Weighted average** (p. 234)

---

## Multiple Choice Quiz            Answers on p. 269            mhhe.com/wildFAP20e

**Additional Quiz Questions are available at the book's Website.**

Use the following information from Marvel Company for the month of July to answer questions 1 through 4.

| July 1 | Beginning inventory ........ | 75 units @ $25 each |
| July 3 | Purchase ................. | 348 units @ $27 each |
| July 8 | Sale ..................... | 300 units |
| July 15 | Purchase ................. | 257 units @ $28 each |
| July 23 | Sale ..................... | 275 units |

**1.** Assume that Marvel uses a perpetual FIFO inventory system. What is the dollar value of its ending inventory?
  **a.** $2,940    **d.** $2,852
  **b.** $2,685    **e.** $2,705
  **c.** $2,625

**2.** Assume that Marvel uses a perpetual LIFO inventory system. What is the dollar value of its ending inventory?
  **a.** $2,940    **d.** $2,852
  **b.** $2,685    **e.** $2,705
  **c.** $2,625

**3.** Assume that Marvel uses a perpetual specific identification inventory system. Its ending inventory consists of 20 units from beginning inventory, 40 units from the July 3 purchase, and 45 units from the July 15 purchase. What is the dollar value of its ending inventory?
  **a.** $2,940    **d.** $2,852
  **b.** $2,685    **e.** $2,840
  **c.** $2,625

**4.^A** Assume that Marvel uses a *periodic* FIFO inventory system. What is the dollar value of its ending inventory?
  **a.** $2,940    **d.** $2,852
  **b.** $2,685    **e.** $2,705
  **c.** $2,625

**5.** A company has cost of goods sold of $85,000 and ending inventory of $18,000. Its days' sales in inventory equals:
  **a.** 49.32 days    **d.** 77.29 days
  **b.** 0.21 days    **e.** 1,723.61 days
  **c.** 4.72 days

---

*A(B)*  *Superscript letter A (B) denotes assignments based on Appendix 6A (6B).*
  Icon denotes assignments that involve decision making.

---

## Discussion Questions

**1.** Describe how costs flow from inventory to cost of goods sold for the following methods: (*a*) FIFO and (*b*) LIFO.

**2.** Where is the amount of merchandise inventory disclosed in the financial statements?

**3.** Why are incidental costs sometimes ignored in inventory costing? Under what accounting constraint is this permitted?

**4.**  If costs are declining, will the LIFO or FIFO method of inventory valuation yield the lower cost of goods sold? Why?

**5.** What does the full-disclosure principle prescribe if a company changes from one acceptable accounting method to another?

**6.** Can a company change its inventory method each accounting period? Explain.

**7.** 🔘 Does the accounting concept of consistency preclude any changes from one accounting method to another?

**8.** 🔘 If inventory errors are said to correct themselves, why are accounting users concerned when such errors are made?

**9.** Explain the following statement: "Inventory errors correct themselves."

**10.** What is the meaning of *market* as it is used in determining the lower of cost or market for inventory?

**11.** 🔘 What guidance does the accounting constraint of conservatism offer?

**12.** What factors contribute to (or cause) inventory shrinkage?

**13.**[A] What accounts are used in a periodic inventory system but not in a perpetual inventory system?

**14.** Refer to **Research In Motion**'s financial statements in Appendix A. On February 27, 2010, what percent of current assets are represented by inventory?   **RIM**

**15.** Refer to **Apple**'s financial statements in Appendix A and compute its cost of goods available for sale for the year ended September 26, 2009.   **Apple**

**16.** Refer to **Nokia**'s financial statements in Appendix A. Compute its cost of goods available for sale for the year ended December 31, 2009.   **NOKIA**

**17.** Refer to **Palm**'s financial statements in Appendix A. What percent of its current assets are inventory as of May 31, 2008 and 2009?   **Palm**

**18.**[B] When preparing interim financial statements, what two methods can companies utilize to estimate cost of goods sold and ending inventory?

## connect

A company reports the following beginning inventory and purchases for the month of January. On January 26, the company sells 360 units. What is the cost of the 155 units that remain in ending inventory at January 31, assuming costs are assigned based on a perpetual inventory system and use of FIFO? (Round per unit costs to three decimals, but inventory balances to the dollar.)

| | Units | Unit Cost |
|---|---|---|
| Beginning inventory on January 1 ......... | 320 | $6.00 |
| Purchase on January 9 ................ | 85 | 6.40 |
| Purchase on January 25 ............... | 110 | 6.60 |

**QUICK STUDY**

**QS 6-1**
Inventory costing with FIFO perpetual
P1

Refer to the information in QS 6-1 and assume the perpetual inventory system is used. Determine the costs assigned to ending inventory when costs are assigned based on LIFO. (Round per unit costs to three decimals, but inventory balances to the dollar.)

**QS 6-2**
Inventory costing with LIFO perpetual   P1

Refer to the information in QS 6-1 and assume the perpetual inventory system is used. Determine the costs assigned to ending inventory when costs are assigned based on weighted average. (Round per unit costs to three decimals, but inventory balances to the dollar.)

**QS 6-3**
Inventory costing with weighted average perpetual   P1
**Check**  $960

Segoe Company reports beginning inventory of 10 units at $50 each. Every week for four weeks it purchases an additional 10 units at respective costs of $51, $52, $55 and $60 per unit for weeks 1 through 4. Calculate the cost of goods available for sale and the units available for sale for this four-week period. Assume that no sales occur during those four weeks.

**QS 6-4**
Computing goods available for sale   P1

Mercedes Brown starts a merchandising business on December 1 and enters into three inventory purchases:

| December 7 | 10 units @ $ 9 cost |
| December 14 | 20 units @ $10 cost |
| December 21 | 15 units @ $12 cost |

Brown sells 18 units for $35 each on December 15. Seven of the sold units are from the December 7 purchase and eleven are from the December 14 purchase. Brown uses a perpetual inventory system. Determine the costs assigned to the December 31 ending inventory based on FIFO. (Round per unit costs to three decimals, but inventory balances to the dollar.)

**QS 6-5**
Assigning costs with FIFO perpetual
P1

**QS 6-6**
Inventory costing with LIFO
perpetual   P1

Refer to the information in QS 6-5 and assume the perpetual inventory system is used. Determine the costs assigned to ending inventory when costs are assigned based on LIFO. (Round per unit costs to three decimals, but inventory balances to the dollar.)

**QS 6-7**
Inventory costing with weighted
average perpetual   P1

**Check**   End. Inv. = $296

Refer to the information in QS 6-5 and assume the perpetual inventory system is used. Determine the costs assigned to ending inventory when costs are assigned based on weighted average. (Round per unit costs to three decimals, but inventory balances to the dollar.)

**QS 6-8**
Inventory costing with specific
identification perpetual   P1

Refer to the information in QS 6-5 and assume the perpetual inventory system is used. Determine the costs assigned to ending inventory when costs are assigned based on specific identification. (Round per unit costs to three decimals, but inventory balances to the dollar.)

**QS 6-9**
Contrasting inventory
costing methods

A1

Identify the inventory costing method best described by each of the following separate statements. Assume a period of increasing costs.

**1.** The preferred method when each unit of product has unique features that markedly affect cost.

**2.** Matches recent costs against net sales.

**3.** Provides a tax advantage (deferral) to a corporation when costs are rising.

**4.** Yields a balance sheet inventory amount often markedly less than its replacement cost.

**5.** Results in a balance sheet inventory amount approximating replacement cost.

**QS 6-10**
Inventory ownership

C1

Crafts Galore, a distributor of handmade gifts, operates out of owner Jenny Finn's house. At the end of the current period, Jenny reports she has 1,500 units (products) in her basement, 30 of which were damaged by water and cannot be sold. She also has another 250 units in her van, ready to deliver per a customer order, terms FOB destination, and another 70 units out on consignment to a friend who owns a retail store. How many units should Jenny include in her company's period-end inventory?

**QS 6-11**
Inventory costs

C2

A car dealer acquires a used car for $3,000, terms FOB shipping point. Additional costs in obtaining and offering the car for sale include $150 for transportation-in, $200 for import duties, $50 for insurance during shipment, $25 for advertising, and $250 for sales staff salaries. For computing inventory, what cost is assigned to the used car?

**QS 6-12**
Applying LCM to inventories

P2

Tailspin Trading Co. has the following products in its ending inventory. Compute lower of cost or market for inventory applied separately to each product.

| Product | Quantity | Cost per Unit | Market per Unit |
|---|---|---|---|
| Mountain bikes ........ | 9 | $360 | $330 |
| Skateboards .......... | 12 | 210 | 270 |
| Gliders .............. | 25 | 480 | 420 |

**QS 6-13**
Inventory errors

A2

In taking a physical inventory at the end of year 2011, Nadir Company forgot to count certain units. Explain how this error affects the following: (*a*) 2011 cost of goods sold, (*b*) 2011 gross profit, (*c*) 2011 net income, (*d*) 2012 net income, (*e*) the combined two-year income, and (*f*) income for years after 2012.

**QS 6-14**
Analyzing inventory   A3

Market Company begins the year with $200,000 of goods in inventory. At year-end, the amount in inventory has increased to $230,000. Cost of goods sold for the year is $1,600,000. Compute Market's inventory turnover and days' sales in inventory. Assume that there are 365 days in the year.

**QS 6-15**[A]
Assigning costs with FIFO
periodic   P3

Refer to the information in QS 6-1 and assume the periodic inventory system is used. Determine the costs assigned to the ending inventory when costs are assigned based on FIFO. (Round per unit costs to three decimals, but inventory balances to the dollar.)

Refer to the information in QS 6-1 and assume the periodic inventory system is used. Determine the costs assigned to ending inventory when costs are assigned based on LIFO. (Round per unit costs to three decimals, but inventory balances to the dollar.)

**QS 6-16^A**
Inventory costing with LIFO periodic  P3

Refer to the information in QS 6-1 and assume the periodic inventory system is used. Determine the costs assigned to ending inventory when costs are assigned based on weighted average. (Round per unit costs to three decimals, but inventory balances to the dollar.)

**QS 6-17^A**
Inventory costing with weighted average periodic  P3

Refer to the information in QS 6-5 and assume the periodic inventory system is used. Determine the costs assigned to the December 31 ending inventory when costs are assigned based on FIFO. (Round per unit costs to three decimals, but inventory balances to the dollar.)

**QS 6-18^A**
Inventory costing with FIFO periodic  P3

Refer to the information in QS 6-5 and assume the periodic inventory system is used. Determine the costs assigned to ending inventory when costs are assigned based on LIFO. (Round per unit costs to three decimals, but inventory balances to the dollar.)

**QS 6-19^A**
Inventory costing with LIFO periodic  P3

Refer to the information in QS 6-5 and assume the periodic inventory system is used. Determine the costs assigned to ending inventory when costs are assigned based on weighted average. (Round per unit costs to three decimals, but inventory balances to the dollar.)

**QS 6-20^A**
Inventory costing with weighted average periodic  P3

Refer to the information in QS 6-5 and assume the periodic inventory system is used. Determine the costs assigned to ending inventory when costs are assigned based on specific identification. (Round per unit costs to three decimals, but inventory balances to the dollar.)

**QS 6-21^A**
Inventory costing with specific identification periodic  P3

Dooling Store's inventory is destroyed by a fire on September 5, 2011. The following data for year 2011 are available from the accounting records. Estimate the cost of the inventory destroyed.

**QS 6-22^B**
Estimating inventories—gross profit method

P4

| | |
|---|---|
| Jan. 1 inventory .......................... | $180,000 |
| Jan. 1 through Sept. 5 purchases (net) ......... | $342,000 |
| Jan. 1 through Sept. 5 sales (net) .............. | $675,000 |
| Year 2011 estimated gross profit rate ......... | 42% |

Answer each of the following questions related to international accounting standards.

**a.** Explain how the accounting for items and costs making up merchandise inventory is different between IFRS and U.S. GAAP.

**b.** Can companies reporting under IFRS apply a cost flow assumption in assigning costs to inventory? If yes, identify at least two acceptable cost flow assumptions.

**c.** Both IFRS and U.S. GAAP apply the lower of cost or market method for reporting inventory values. If inventory is written down from applying the lower of cost or market method, explain in general terms how IFRS and U.S. GAAP differ in accounting for any subsequent period reversal of that reported decline in inventory value.

**QS 6-23**
International accounting standards

C1  C2  P2

**1.** Jolie Company has shipped $500 of goods to China Co., and China Co. has arranged to sell the goods for Jolie. Identify the consignor and the consignee. Which company should include any unsold goods as part of its inventory?

**2.** At year-end, Jolie Co. had shipped $850 of merchandise FOB destination to China Co. Which company should include the $850 of merchandise in transit as part of its year-end inventory?

**EXERCISES**

**Exercise 6-1**
Inventory ownership  C1

Duke Associates, antique dealers, purchased the contents of an estate for $37,500. Terms of the purchase were FOB shipping point, and the cost of transporting the goods to Duke Associates' warehouse was $1,200. Duke Associates insured the shipment at a cost of $150. Prior to putting the goods up for sale, they cleaned and refurbished them at a cost of $490. Determine the cost of the inventory acquired from the estate.

**Exercise 6-2**
Inventory costs

C2

**Mc Graw Hill** connect

**Exercise 6-3**
Inventory costing
methods—perpetual

**P1**

Park Company reported the following March purchases and sales data for its only product.

| Date | Activities | Units Acquired at Cost | Units Sold at Retail |
|---|---|---|---|
| Mar. 1 | Beginning inventory .......... | 150 units @ $7.00 = $1,050 | |
| Mar. 10 | Sales ..................... | | 90 units @ $15 |
| Mar. 20 | Purchase .................. | 220 units @ $6.00 = 1,320 | |
| Mar. 25 | Sales ..................... | | 145 units @ $15 |
| Mar. 30 | Purchase .................. | 90 units @ $5.00 = 450 | |
| | Totals .................... | 460 units $2,820 | 235 units |

Park uses a perpetual inventory system. Determine the cost assigned to ending inventory and to cost of goods sold using (*a*) specific identification, (*b*) weighted average, (*c*) FIFO, and (*d*) LIFO. (Round per unit costs to three decimals, but inventory balances to the dollar.) For specific identification, ending inventory consists of 225 units, where 90 are from the March 30 purchase, 80 are from the March 20 purchase, and 55 are from beginning inventory.

**Check** Ending inventory: LIFO, $1,320; WA, $1,289

**Exercise 6-4**
Income effects of
inventory methods

**A1**

Use the data in Exercise 6-3 to prepare comparative income statements for the month of January for Park Company similar to those shown in Exhibit 6.8 for the four inventory methods. Assume expenses are $1,600, and that the applicable income tax rate is 30%.

**1.** Which method yields the highest net income?

**2.** Does net income using weighted average fall between that using FIFO and LIFO?

**3.** If costs were rising instead of falling, which method would yield the highest net income?

**Exercise 6-5**
Inventory costing methods
(perpetual)—FIFO and LIFO

**P1**

Harold Co. reported the following current-year purchases and sales data for its only product.

| Date | Activities | Units Acquired at Cost | Units Sold at Retail |
|---|---|---|---|
| Jan. 1 | Beginning inventory ........ | 100 units @ $10 = $ 1,000 | |
| Jan. 10 | Sales .................... | | 90 units @ $40 |
| Mar. 14 | Purchase ................ | 250 units @ $15 = 3,750 | |
| Mar. 15 | Sales .................... | | 140 units @ $40 |
| July 30 | Purchase ................ | 400 units @ $20 = 8,000 | |
| Oct. 5 | Sales .................... | | 300 units @ $40 |
| Oct. 26 | Purchase ................ | 600 units @ $25 = 15,000 | |
| | Totals .................. | 1,350 units $27,750 | 530 units |

**Check** Ending inventory: LIFO, $18,750

Harold uses a perpetual inventory system. Determine the costs assigned to ending inventory and to cost of goods sold using (*a*) FIFO and (*b*) LIFO. Compute the gross margin for each method.

**Exercise 6-6**
Specific identification **P1**

Refer to the data in Exercise 6-5. Assume that ending inventory is made up of 100 units from the March 14 purchase, 120 units from the July 30 purchase, and all 600 units from the October 26 purchase. Using the specific identification method, calculate (*a*) the cost of goods sold and (*b*) the gross profit.

**Exercise 6-7**
Lower of cost or market

**P2**

Ripken Company's ending inventory includes the following items. Compute the lower of cost or market for ending inventory applied separately to each product.

| | | Per Unit | |
|---|---|---|---|
| Product | Units | Cost | Market |
| Helmets ......... | 22 | $50 | $54 |
| Bats ........... | 15 | 78 | 72 |
| Shoes .......... | 36 | 95 | 91 |
| Uniforms ....... | 40 | 36 | 36 |

**Check** LCM = $6,896

Ringo Company had $900,000 of sales in each of three consecutive years 2010–2012, and it purchased merchandise costing $500,000 in each of those years. It also maintained a $200,000 physical inventory from the beginning to the end of that three-year period. In accounting for inventory, it made an error at the end of year 2010 that caused its year-end 2010 inventory to appear on its statements as $180,000 rather than the correct $200,000.

**1.** Determine the correct amount of the company's gross profit in each of the years 2010–2012.

**2.** Prepare comparative income statements as in Exhibit 6.11 to show the effect of this error on the company's cost of goods sold and gross profit for each of the years 2010–2012.

**Exercise 6-8**

Analysis of inventory errors

A2

**Check** 2010 reported gross profit, $380,000

---

Chess Company uses LIFO for inventory costing and reports the following financial data. It also recomputed inventory and cost of goods sold using FIFO for comparison purposes.

|  | 2011 | 2010 |
|---|---|---|
| LIFO inventory | $150 | $100 |
| LIFO cost of goods sold | 730 | 670 |
| FIFO inventory | 220 | 125 |
| FIFO cost of goods sold | 685 | — |
| Current assets (using LIFO) | 210 | 180 |
| Current liabilities | 190 | 170 |

**1.** Compute its current ratio, inventory turnover, and days' sales in inventory for 2011 using (a) LIFO numbers and (b) FIFO numbers. (Round answers to one decimal.)

**2.** Comment on and interpret the results of part 1.

**Exercise 6-9**

Comparing LIFO numbers to FIFO numbers; ratio analysis

A1 A3

**Check** (1) FIFO: Current ratio, 1.5; Inventory turnover, 4.0 times

---

Use the following information for Ryder Co. to compute inventory turnover for 2011 and 2010, and its days' sales in inventory at December 31, 2011 and 2010. (Round answers to one decimal.) Comment on Ryder's efficiency in using its assets to increase sales from 2010 to 2011.

|  | 2011 | 2010 | 2009 |
|---|---|---|---|
| Cost of goods sold | $643,825 | $426,650 | $391,300 |
| Ending inventory | 96,400 | 86,750 | 91,500 |

**Exercise 6-10**

Inventory turnover and days' sales in inventory

A3

---

Refer to Exercise 6-3 and assume the periodic inventory system is used. Determine the costs assigned to ending inventory and to cost of goods sold using (a) specific identification, (b) weighted average, (c) FIFO, and (d) LIFO. (Round per unit costs to three decimals, but inventory balances to the dollar.)

**Exercise 6-11ᴬ**

Inventory costing— periodic system **P3**

---

Refer to Exercise 6-5 and assume the periodic inventory system is used. Determine the costs assigned to ending inventory and to cost of goods sold using (a) FIFO and (b) LIFO. Then (c) compute the gross margin for each method.

**Exercise 6-12ᴬ**

Inventory costing— periodic system **P3**

---

Lopez Co. reported the following current-year data for its only product. The company uses a periodic inventory system, and its ending inventory consists of 300 units—100 from each of the last three purchases. Determine the cost assigned to ending inventory and to cost of goods sold using (a) specific identification, (b) weighted average, (c) FIFO, and (d) LIFO. (Round per unit costs to three decimals, but inventory balances to the dollar.) Which method yields the highest net income?

**Exercise 6-13ᴬ**

Alternative cost flow assumptions—periodic

**P3**

| Jan. 1 | Beginning inventory | 200 units @ $2.00 = $ | 400 |
|---|---|---|---|
| Mar. 7 | Purchase | 440 units @ $2.25 = | 990 |
| July 28 | Purchase | 1080 units @ $2.50 = | 2,700 |
| Oct. 3 | Purchase | 960 units @ $2.80 = | 2,688 |
| Dec. 19 | Purchase | 320 units @ $2.90 = | 928 |
| | Totals | 3,000 units | $7,706 |

**Check** Inventory; LIFO, $625; FIFO, $870

**Exercise 6-14ᴬ**

Alternative cost flow
assumptions—periodic

**P3**

Candis Gifts reported the following current-year data for its only product. The company uses a periodic inventory system, and its ending inventory consists of 300 units—100 from each of the last three purchases. Determine the cost assigned to ending inventory and to cost of goods sold using (a) specific identification, (b) weighted average, (c) FIFO, and (d) LIFO. (Round per unit costs to three decimals, but inventory balances to the dollar.) Which method yields the lowest net income?

| | | | |
|---|---|---|---|
| Jan.   1 | Beginning inventory . . . . . . . . | 280 units @ $3.00 = $   840 |
| Mar.   7 | Purchase . . . . . . . . . . . . . . . . | 600 units @ $2.80 =   1,680 |
| July  28 | Purchase . . . . . . . . . . . . . . . | 800 units @ $2.50 =   2,000 |
| Oct.   3 | Purchase . . . . . . . . . . . . . . . | 1,100 units @ $2.30 =   2,530 |
| Dec. 19 | Purchase . . . . . . . . . . . . . . . | 250 units @ $2.00 =     500 |
| | Totals . . . . . . . . . . . . . . . . . | 3,030 units           $7,550 |

**Check**   Inventory: LIFO, $896;
FIFO, $615

**Exercise 6-15ᴮ**

Estimating ending inventory—
retail method

**P4**

In 2011, Wichita Company had net sales (at retail) of $130,000. The following additional information is available from its records at the end of 2011. Use the retail inventory method to estimate Wichita's 2011 ending inventory at cost.

| | At Cost | At Retail |
|---|---|---|
| Beginning inventory . . . . . . . . . . . . . | $ 31,900 | $64,200 |
| Cost of goods purchased   . . . . . . . . | 57,810 | 98,400 |

**Check**   End. Inventory, $17,930

**Exercise 6-16ᴮ**

Estimating ending inventory—
gross profit method

**P4**

On March 1, KB Shop had $450,000 of inventory at cost. In the first quarter of the year, it purchased $1,590,000 of merchandise, returned $23,100, and paid freight charges of $37,600 on purchased merchandise, terms FOB shipping point. The company's gross profit averages 30%, and the store had $2,000,000 of net sales (at retail) in the first quarter of the year. Use the gross profit method to estimate its cost of inventory at the end of the first quarter.

**Exercise 6-17**

Accounting for inventory
following IFRS

**P2**

**Samsung Electronics** reports the following regarding its accounting for inventories.

Inventories are stated at the lower of cost or net realizable value. Cost is determined using the average cost method, except for materials-in-transit which are stated at actual cost as determined using the specific identification method. Losses on valuation of inventories and losses on inventory obsolescence are recorded as part of cost of sales. As of December 31, 2008, losses on valuation of inventories amounted to ₩651,296 million (₩ is Korean won).

**1.** What cost flow assumption(s) does Samsung apply in assigning costs to its inventories?
**2.** What has Samsung recorded for 2008 as a write-down on valuation of its inventories?
**3.** If at year-end 2009 there was an increase in the value of its inventories such that there was a reversal of ₩900 million for the 2008 write-down, how would Samsung account for this under IFRS? Would Samsung's accounting be different for this reversal if it reported under U.S. GAAP? Explain.

**ᴹᶜᴳʳᵃʷ ᴴⁱˡˡ connect™**

**PROBLEM SET A**

**Problem 6-1A**

Alternative cost
flows—perpetual

**P1**

Anthony Company uses a perpetual inventory system. It entered into the following purchases and sales transactions for March.

| Date | Activities | Units Acquired at Cost | Units Sold at Retail |
|---|---|---|---|
| Mar.   1 | Beginning inventory . . . . . . . . . . | 50 units @ $50/unit | |
| Mar.   5 | Purchase . . . . . . . . . . . . . . . . . . | 200 units @ $55/unit | |
| Mar.   9 | Sales . . . . . . . . . . . . . . . . . . . . . | | 210 units @ $85/unit |
| Mar. 18 | Purchase . . . . . . . . . . . . . . . . . . | 60 units @ $60/unit | |
| Mar. 25 | Purchase . . . . . . . . . . . . . . . . . . | 100 units @ $62/unit | |
| Mar. 29 | Sales . . . . . . . . . . . . . . . . . . . . . | | 80 units @ $95/unit |
| | Totals . . . . . . . . . . . . . . . . . . . . | 410 units | 290 units |

**Required**

1. Compute cost of goods available for sale and the number of units available for sale.

2. Compute the number of units in ending inventory.

3. Compute the cost assigned to ending inventory using (*a*) FIFO, (*b*) LIFO, (*c*) weighted average, and (*d*) specific identification. (Round per unit costs to three decimals, but inventory balances to the dollar.) For specific identification, the March 9 sale consisted of 40 units from beginning inventory and 170 units from the March 5 purchase; the March 29 sale consisted of 20 units from the March 18 purchase and 60 units from the March 25 purchase.

4. Compute gross profit earned by the company for each of the four costing methods in part 3.

**Check**   (3) Ending Inventory: FIFO, $7,400; LIFO, $6,840, WA, $7,176

(4) LIFO gross profit, $8,990

Marlow Company uses a perpetual inventory system. It entered into the following calendar-year 2011 purchases and sales transactions.

**Problem 6-2A**
Alternative cost flows—perpetual

P1

| Date | Activities | Units Acquired at Cost | Units Sold at Retail |
|---|---|---|---|
| Jan.   1 | Beginning inventory . . . . . . . . . . | 600 units @ $44/unit | |
| Feb. 10 | Purchase . . . . . . . . . . . . . . . . . . | 200 units @ $40/unit | |
| Mar. 13 | Purchase . . . . . . . . . . . . . . . . . . | 100 units @ $20/unit | |
| Mar. 15 | Sales . . . . . . . . . . . . . . . . . . | | 400 units @ $75/unit |
| Aug. 21 | Purchase . . . . . . . . . . . . . . . . . . | 160 units @ $60/unit | |
| Sept. 5 | Purchase . . . . . . . . . . . . . . . . . . | 280 units @ $48/unit | |
| Sept. 10 | Sales . . . . . . . . . . . . . . . . . . | | 200 units @ $75/unit |
| | Totals . . . . . . . . . . . . . . . . . . | 1,340 units | 600 units |

**Required**

1. Compute cost of goods available for sale and the number of units available for sale.

2. Compute the number of units in ending inventory.

3. Compute the cost assigned to ending inventory using (*a*) FIFO, (*b*) LIFO, (*c*) specific identification—units sold consist of 500 units from beginning inventory and 100 units from the March 13 purchase, and (*d*) weighted average. (Round per unit costs to three decimals, but inventory balances to the dollar.)

4. Compute gross profit earned by the company for each of the four costing methods in part 3.

**Check**   (3) Ending inventory: FIFO, $33,040; LIFO, $35,440; WA, $34,055;

(4) LIFO gross profit, $21,000

**Analysis Component**

5. If the company's manager earns a bonus based on a percent of gross profit, which method of inventory costing will the manager likely prefer?

A physical inventory of Helmke Company taken at December 31 reveals the following.

**Problem 6-3A**
Lower of cost or market

P2

| | | Per Unit | |
|---|---|---|---|
| **Item** | **Units** | **Cost** | **Market** |
| Audio equipment | | | |
| Receivers | 335 | $ 90 | $ 98 |
| CD players | 250 | 111 | 100 |
| MP3 players | 316 | 86 | 95 |
| Speakers | 194 | 52 | 41 |
| Video equipment | | | |
| Handheld LCDs | 470 | 150 | 125 |
| VCRs | 281 | 93 | 84 |
| Camcorders | 202 | 310 | 322 |
| Car audio equipment | | | |
| Satellite radios | 175 | 70 | 84 |
| CD/MP3 radios | 160 | 97 | 105 |

**Required**

1. Calculate the lower of cost or market for the inventory applied separately to each item.

2. If the market amount is less than the recorded cost of the inventory, then record the LCM adjustment to the Merchandise Inventory account.

**Check**   $263,024

**Problem 6-4A**

Analysis of inventory errors

A2

mhhe.com/wildFAP20e

Doubletree Company's financial statements show the following. The company recently discovered that in making physical counts of inventory, it had made the following errors: Inventory on December 31, 2010, is understated by $50,000, and inventory on December 31, 2011, is overstated by $20,000.

| For Year Ended December 31 | | 2010 | 2011 | 2012 |
|---|---|---|---|---|
| (a) | Cost of goods sold ................ | $ 725,000 | $ 955,000 | $ 790,000 |
| (b) | Net income....................... | 268,000 | 275,000 | 250,000 |
| (c) | Total current assets ................ | 1,247,000 | 1,360,000 | 1,230,000 |
| (d) | Total equity ..................... | 1,387,000 | 1,580,000 | 1,245,000 |

**Required**

**1.** For each key financial statement figure—(a), (b), (c), and (d) above—prepare a table similar to the following to show the adjustments necessary to correct the reported amounts.

| Figure: _____ | 2010 | 2011 | 2012 |
|---|---|---|---|
| Reported amount ...................... | _____ | _____ | _____ |
| Adjustments for: 12/31/2010 error ......... | _____ | _____ | _____ |
|              12/31/2011 error ........ | _____ | _____ | _____ |
| Corrected amount .................... | _____ | _____ | _____ |

**Check** (1) Corrected net income: 2010, $318,000; 2011, $205,000; 2012, $270,000

**Analysis Component**

**2.** What is the error in total net income for the combined three-year period resulting from the inventory errors? Explain.

**3.** Explain why the understatement of inventory by $50,000 at the end of 2010 results in an understatement of equity by the same amount in that year.

**Problem 6-5A[A]**

Alternative cost flows—periodic

P3

mhhe.com/wildFAP20e

Viper Company began year 2011 with 20,000 units of product in its January 1 inventory costing $15 each. It made successive purchases of its product in year 2011 as follows. The company uses a periodic inventory system. On December 31, 2011, a physical count reveals that 35,000 units of its product remain in inventory.

| Mar. 7 ........ | 28,000 units @ $18 each |
|---|---|
| May 25 ........ | 30,000 units @ $22 each |
| Aug. 1 ........ | 20,000 units @ $24 each |
| Nov. 10 ........ | 33,000 units @ $27 each |

**Required**

**1.** Compute the number and total cost of the units available for sale in year 2011.

**Check** (2) Cost of goods sold: FIFO, $1,896,000; LIFO, $2,265,000; WA, $2,077,557

**2.** Compute the amounts assigned to the 2011 ending inventory and the cost of goods sold using (a) FIFO, (b) LIFO, and (c) weighted average. (Round per unit costs to three decimals, but inventory balances to the dollar.)

**Problem 6-6A[A]**

Income comparisons and cost flows—periodic

A1  P3

Botch Corp. sold 5,500 units of its product at $45 per unit in year 2011 and incurred operating expenses of $6 per unit in selling the units. It began the year with 600 units in inventory and made successive purchases of its product as follows.

| Jan. 1 | Beginning inventory ........ | 600 units @ $18 per unit |
|---|---|---|
| Feb. 20 | Purchase ................. | 1,500 units @ $19 per unit |
| May 16 | Purchase ................. | 700 units @ $20 per unit |
| Oct. 3 | Purchase ................. | 400 units @ $21 per unit |
| Dec. 11 | Purchase ................. | 3,300 units @ $22 per unit |
| | Total .................... | 6,500 units |

**Required**

**Check** (1) Net income: FIFO, $71,540; LIFO, $69,020; WA, $70,603

**1.** Prepare comparative income statements similar to Exhibit 6.8 for the three inventory costing methods of FIFO, LIFO, and weighted average. (Round per unit costs to three decimals, but inventory balances to the dollar.) Include a detailed cost of goods sold section as part of each statement. The company uses a periodic inventory system, and its income tax rate is 30%.

**2.** How would the financial results from using the three alternative inventory costing methods change if Botch had been experiencing declining costs in its purchases of inventory?

**3.** What advantages and disadvantages are offered by using (*a*) LIFO and (*b*) FIFO? Assume the continuing trend of increasing costs.

---

The records of Nilson Company provide the following information for the year ended December 31.

|  | At Cost | At Retail |
|---|---|---|
| January 1 beginning inventory ......... | $ 471,350 | $ 927,150 |
| Cost of goods purchased ............ | 3,276,030 | 6,279,350 |
| Sales ............................ |  | 5,495,700 |
| Sales returns ..................... |  | 44,600 |

**Problem 6-7A[B]**
Retail inventory method
**P4**

#### Required

**1.** Use the retail inventory method to estimate the company's year-end inventory at cost.

**2.** A year-end physical inventory at retail prices yields a total inventory of $1,675,800. Prepare a calculation showing the company's loss from shrinkage at cost and at retail.

**Check**   (1) Inventory, $912,808 cost;
     (2) Inventory shortage at
cost, $41,392

---

Wayman Company wants to prepare interim financial statements for the first quarter. The company wishes to avoid making a physical count of inventory. Wayman's gross profit rate averages 35%. The following information for the first quarter is available from its records.

| | |
|---|---|
| January 1 beginning inventory ......... | $ 300,260 |
| Cost of goods purchased ............ | 939,050 |
| Sales ............................ | 1,191,150 |
| Sales returns ..................... | 9,450 |

**Problem 6-8A[B]**
Gross profit method
**P4**

#### Required

Use the gross profit method to estimate the company's first quarter ending inventory.

**Check**   Estimated ending inventory,
$471,205

---

CCO Company uses a perpetual inventory system. It entered into the following purchases and sales transactions for April.

| Date | Activities | Units Acquired at Cost | Units Sold at Retail |
|---|---|---|---|
| Apr. 1 | Beginning inventory ........ | 15 units @ $3,000/unit | |
| Apr. 6 | Purchase ................ | 35 units @ $3,500/unit | |
| Apr. 9 | Sales ................... | | 18 units @ $12,000/unit |
| Apr. 17 | Purchase ................ | 8 units @ $4,500/unit | |
| Apr. 25 | Purchase ................ | 10 units @ $4,580/unit | |
| Apr. 30 | Sales ................... | _____ | 30 units @ $14,000/unit |
| | Total ................... | 68 units | 48 units |

**PROBLEM SET B**

**Problem 6-1B**
Alternative cost
flows—perpetual
**P1**

#### Required

**1.** Compute cost of goods available for sale and the number of units available for sale.

**2.** Compute the number of units in ending inventory.

**3.** Compute the cost assigned to ending inventory using (*a*) FIFO, (*b*) LIFO, (*c*) weighted average, and (*d*) specific identification. (Round per unit costs to three decimals, but inventory balances to the dollar.) For specific identification, the April 9 sale consisted of 8 units from beginning inventory and 10 units from the April 6 purchase; the April 30 sale consisted of 20 units from the April 6 purchase and 10 units from the April 25 purchase.

**4.** Compute gross profit earned by the company for each of the four costing methods in part 3.

**Check**   (3) Ending inventory: FIFO,
$88,800; LIFO, $62,500; WA,
$75,600;

     (4) LIFO gross profit,
     $449,200

**Problem 6-2B**
Alternative cost
flows—perpetual

P1

Venus Company uses a perpetual inventory system. It entered into the following calendar-year 2011 purchases and sales transactions.

| Date | Activities | Units Acquired at Cost | Units Sold at Retail |
|---|---|---|---|
| Jan. 1 | Beginning inventory ......... | 600 units @ $55/unit | |
| Jan. 10 | Purchase ................. | 450 units @ $56/unit | |
| Feb. 13 | Purchase ................. | 200 units @ $57/unit | |
| Feb. 15 | Sales .................... | | 430 units @ $90/unit |
| July 21 | Purchase ................. | 230 units @ $58/unit | |
| Aug. 5 | Purchase ................. | 345 units @ $59/unit | |
| Aug. 10 | Sales .................... | | 335 units @ $90/unit |
| | Total .................... | 1,825 units | 765 units |

**Required**

1. Compute cost of goods available for sale and the number of units available for sale.

2. Compute the number of units in ending inventory.

**Check** (3) Ending inventory: FIFO, $61,055; LIFO, $59,250; WA, $60,293;

(4) LIFO gross profit, $24,805

3. Compute the cost assigned to ending inventory using (*a*) FIFO, (*b*) LIFO, (*c*) specific identification—units sold consist of 600 units from beginning inventory and 165 units from the February 13 purchase, and (*d*) weighted average. (Round per unit costs to three decimals, but inventory balances to the dollar.)

4. Compute gross profit earned by the company for each of the four costing methods in part 3.

***Analysis Component***

5. If the company's manager earns a bonus based on a percent of gross profit, which method of inventory costing will the manager likely prefer?

**Problem 6-3B**
Lower of cost or market

P2

A physical inventory of Office Deals taken at December 31 reveals the following.

| | | Per Unit | |
|---|---|---|---|
| **Item** | **Units** | **Cost** | **Market** |
| Office furniture | | | |
|   Desks | 436 | $261 | $305 |
|   Credenzas | 295 | 227 | 256 |
|   Chairs | 587 | 49 | 43 |
|   Bookshelves | 321 | 93 | 82 |
| Filing cabinets | | | |
|   Two-drawer | 214 | 81 | 70 |
|   Four-drawer | 398 | 135 | 122 |
|   Lateral | 175 | 104 | 118 |
| Office equipment | | | |
|   Fax machines | 430 | 168 | 200 |
|   Copiers | 545 | 317 | 288 |
|   Telephones | 352 | 125 | 117 |

**Required**

**Check** $584,444

1. Compute the lower of cost or market for the inventory applied separately to each item.

2. If the market amount is less than the recorded cost of the inventory, then record the LCM adjustment to the Merchandise Inventory account.

**Problem 6-4B**
Analysis of inventory errors

A2

Watson Company's financial statements show the following. The company recently discovered that in making physical counts of inventory, it had made the following errors: Inventory on December 31, 2010, is overstated by $70,000, and inventory on December 31, 2011, is understated by $55,000.

| For Year Ended December 31 | 2010 | 2011 | 2012 |
|---|---|---|---|
| (a) Cost of goods sold ............... | $ 655,000 | $ 957,000 | $ 799,000 |
| (b) Net income ..................... | 225,000 | 277,000 | 244,000 |
| (c) Total current assets ............. | 1,251,000 | 1,360,000 | 1,200,000 |
| (d) Total equity .................... | 1,387,000 | 1,520,000 | 1,250,000 |

**Required**

1. For each key financial statement figure—(*a*), (*b*), (*c*), and (*d*) above—prepare a table similar to the following to show the adjustments necessary to correct the reported amounts.

| Figure: _____ | 2010 | 2011 | 2012 |
|---|---|---|---|
| Reported amount ..................... | _____ | _____ | _____ |
| Adjustments for: 12/31/2010 error ......... | _____ | _____ | _____ |
| 12/31/2011 error ......... | _____ | _____ | _____ |
| Corrected amount .................... | _____ | _____ | _____ |

**Check** (1) Corrected net income: 2010, $155,000; 2011, $402,000; 2012, $189,000

**Analysis Component**

2. What is the error in total net income for the combined three-year period resulting from the inventory errors? Explain.

3. Explain why the overstatement of inventory by $70,000 at the end of 2010 results in an overstatement of equity by the same amount in that year.

---

Solaris Co. began year 2011 with 6,300 units of product in its January 1 inventory costing $35 each. It made successive purchases of its product in year 2011 as follows. The company uses a periodic inventory system. On December 31, 2011, a physical count reveals that 16,500 units of its product remain in inventory.

**Problem 6-5B**[A]

Alternative cost flows—periodic

**P3**

| | | |
|---|---|---|
| Jan. 4 ........ | 10,500 units @ $33 each |
| May 18 ........ | 13,000 units @ $32 each |
| July 9 ........ | 12,000 units @ $29 each |
| Nov. 21 ........ | 15,500 units @ $26 each |

**Required**

1. Compute the number and total cost of the units available for sale in year 2011.

2. Compute the amounts assigned to the 2011 ending inventory and the cost of goods sold using (*a*) FIFO, (*b*) LIFO, and (*c*) weighted average. (Round per unit costs to three decimals, but inventory balances to the dollar.)

**Check** (2) Cost of goods sold: FIFO, $1,302,000; LIFO, $1,176,900; WA, $1,234,681

---

Rikkers Company sold 2,500 units of its product at $98 per unit in year 2011 and incurred operating expenses of $14 per unit in selling the units. It began the year with 740 units in inventory and made successive purchases of its product as follows.

**Problem 6-6B**[A]

Income comparisons and cost flows—periodic

**A1 P3**

| Jan. 1 | Beginning inventory ........ | 740 units @ $58 per unit |
|---|---|---|
| April 2 | Purchase ................ | 700 units @ $59 per unit |
| June 14 | Purchase ................ | 600 units @ $61 per unit |
| Aug. 29 | Purchase ................ | 500 units @ $64 per unit |
| Nov. 18 | Purchase ................ | 800 units @ $65 per unit |
| | Total ................ | 3,340 units |

**Required**

1. Prepare comparative income statements similar to Exhibit 6.8 for the three inventory costing methods of FIFO, LIFO, and weighted average. (Round per unit costs to three decimals, but inventory balances to the dollar.) Include a detailed cost of goods sold section as part of each statement. The company uses a periodic inventory system, and its income tax rate is 25%.

2. How would the financial results from using the three alternative inventory costing methods change if the company had been experiencing decreasing prices in its purchases of inventory?

3. What advantages and disadvantages are offered by using (*a*) LIFO and (*b*) FIFO? Assume the continuing trend of increasing costs.

**Check** (1) Net income: LIFO, $40,500; FIFO, $44,805; WA, $42,519

---

The records of Saturn Co. provide the following information for the year ended December 31.

**Problem 6-7B**[B]

Retail inventory method

**P4**

| | At Cost | At Retail |
|---|---|---|
| January 1 beginning inventory ......... | $ 81,670 | $114,610 |
| Cost of goods purchased ............ | 492,250 | 751,730 |
| Sales ............................... | | 786,120 |
| Sales returns ...................... | | 4,480 |

**Required**

1. Use the retail inventory method to estimate the company's year-end inventory.

2. A year-end physical inventory at retail prices yields a total inventory of $78,550. Prepare a calculation showing the company's loss from shrinkage at cost and at retail.

**Problem 6-8B[B]**
Gross profit method
**P4**

Ernst Equipment Co. wants to prepare interim financial statements for the first quarter. The company wishes to avoid making a physical count of inventory. Ernst's gross profit rate averages 30%. The following information for the first quarter is available from its records.

| | |
|---|---:|
| January 1 beginning inventory ......... | $ 752,880 |
| Cost of goods purchased ............ | 2,159,630 |
| Sales ............................ | 3,710,250 |
| Sales returns .................... | 74,200 |

**Required**

Use the gross profit method to estimate the company's first quarter ending inventory.

**SERIAL PROBLEM**
Business Solutions

**P2 A3**

*(This serial problem began in Chapter 1 and continues through most of the book. If previous chapter segments were not completed, the serial problem can begin at this point.)*

**SP 6**

**Part A**

Santana Rey of Business Solutions is evaluating her inventory to determine whether it must be adjusted based on lower of cost or market rules. Business Solutions has three different types of software in its inventory and the following information is available for each.

| Inventory Items | Units | Per Unit Cost | Market |
|---|:---:|:---:|:---:|
| Office productivity ........ | 3 | $ 76 | $ 74 |
| Desktop publishing ........ | 2 | 103 | 100 |
| Accounting ............. | 3 | 90 | 96 |

**Required**

1. Compute the lower of cost or market for ending inventory assuming Rey applies the lower of cost or market rule to inventory as a whole. Must Rey adjust the reported inventory value? Explain.

2. Assume that Rey had instead applied the lower of cost or market rule to each product in inventory. Under this assumption, must Rey adjust the reported inventory value? Explain.

**Part B**

Selected accounts and balances for the three months ended March 31, 2012, for Business Solutions follow.

| | |
|---|---:|
| January 1 beginning inventory ......... | $ 0 |
| Cost of goods sold ................ | 14,052 |
| March 31 ending inventory .......... | 704 |

**Required**

1. Compute inventory turnover and days' sales in inventory for the three months ended March 31, 2012.

2. Assess the company's performance if competitors average 15 times for inventory turnover and 25 days for days' sales in inventory.

## Beyond the Numbers

**REPORTING IN ACTION**

**C2 A3**

*RIM*

**BTN 6-1**   Refer to **Research In Motion**'s financial statements in Appendix A to answer the following.

**Required**

1. What amount of inventories did Research In Motion report as a current asset on February 27, 2010? On February 28, 2009?

2. Inventories represent what percent of total assets on February 27, 2010? On February 28, 2009?

3. Comment on the relative size of Research In Motion's inventories compared to its other types of assets.

4. What accounting method did Research In Motion use to compute inventory amounts on its balance sheet?

5. Compute inventory turnover for fiscal year ended February 27, 2010, and days' sales in inventory as of February 27, 2010.

### Fast Forward

6. Access Research In Motion's financial statements for fiscal years ended after February 27, 2010, from its Website (**RIM.com**) or the SEC's EDGAR database (**www.SEC.gov**). Answer questions 1 through 5 using the current RIM information and compare results to those prior years.

---

**BTN 6-2**   Comparative figures for **Research In Motion** and **Apple** follow.

**COMPARATIVE ANALYSIS**

A3

**RIM**

Apple

| ($ millions) | Research In Motion | | | Apple | | |
| --- | --- | --- | --- | --- | --- | --- |
| | Current Year | One Year Prior | Two Years Prior | Current Year | One Year Prior | Two Years Prior |
| Inventory . . . . . . . . . . . | $ 622 | $ 682 | $ 396 | $ 455 | $ 509 | $ 346 |
| Cost of sales . . . . . . . . | 8,369 | 5,968 | 2,929 | 25,683 | 24,294 | 16,426 |

### Required

1. Compute inventory turnover for each company for the most recent two years shown.

2. Compute days' sales in inventory for each company for the three years shown.

3. Comment on and interpret your findings from parts 1 and 2. Assume an industry average for inventory turnover of 10.

---

**BTN 6-3**   Golf Mart is a retail sports store carrying golf apparel and equipment. The store is at the end of its second year of operation and is struggling. A major problem is that its cost of inventory has continually increased in the past two years. In the first year of operations, the store assigned inventory costs using LIFO. A loan agreement the store has with its bank, its prime source of financing, requires the store to maintain a certain profit margin and current ratio. The store's owner is currently looking over Golf Mart's preliminary financial statements for its second year. The numbers are not favorable. The only way the store can meet the required financial ratios agreed on with the bank is to change from LIFO to FIFO. The store originally decided on LIFO because of its tax advantages. The owner recalculates ending inventory using FIFO and submits those numbers and statements to the loan officer at the bank for the required bank review. The owner thankfully reflects on the available latitude in choosing the inventory costing method.

**ETHICS CHALLENGE**

A1

### Required

1. How does Golf Mart's use of FIFO improve its net profit margin and current ratio?

2. Is the action by Golf Mart's owner ethical? Explain.

---

**BTN 6-4**   You are a financial adviser with a client in the wholesale produce business that just completed its first year of operations. Due to weather conditions, the cost of acquiring produce to resell has escalated during the later part of this period. Your client, Raphaela Gonzalez, mentions that because her business sells perishable goods, she has striven to maintain a FIFO flow of goods. Although sales are good, the increasing cost of inventory has put the business in a tight cash position. Gonzalez has expressed concern regarding the ability of the business to meet income tax obligations.

**COMMUNICATING IN PRACTICE**

A1

### Required

Prepare a memorandum that identifies, explains, and justifies the inventory method you recommend your client, Ms. Gonzalez, adopt.

---

**BTN 6-5**   Access the 2009 annual 10-K report for **Polaris Industries** (Ticker PII), filed on March 1, 2010, from the EDGAR filings at **www.SEC.gov**.

**TAKING IT TO THE NET**

A3

### Required

1. What products are manufactured by Polaris?

2. What inventory method does Polaris use? (*Hint:* See the Note 1 to its financial statements.)

3. Compute its gross margin and gross margin ratio for the 2009 calendar year. Comment on your computations—assume an industry average of 27% for the gross margin ratio.

4. Compute its inventory turnover and days' sales in inventory for the year ended December 31, 2009. Comment on your computations—assume an industry average of 5.9 for inventory turnover and 55 for days' sales in inventory.

---

## TEAMWORK IN ACTION

A1   P1  

**Point:** Step 1 allows four choices or areas for expertise. Larger teams will have some duplication of choice, but the specific identification method should not be duplicated.

**BTN 6-6**   Each team member has the responsibility to become an expert on an inventory method. This expertise will be used to facilitate teammates' understanding of the concepts relevant to that method.

1. Each learning team member should select an area for expertise by choosing one of the following inventory methods: specific identification, LIFO, FIFO, or weighted average.

2. Form expert teams made up of students who have selected the same area of expertise. The instructor will identify where each expert team will meet.

3. Using the following data, each expert team must collaborate to develop a presentation that illustrates the relevant concepts and procedures for its inventory method. Each team member must write the presentation in a format that can be shown to the learning team.

**Data**

The company uses a perpetual inventory system. It had the following beginning inventory and current year purchases of its product.

| | | | |
|---|---|---|---|
| Jan. 1 | Beginning inventory......... | 50 units @ $10 = | $ 500 |
| Jan. 14 | Purchase ................. | 150 units @ $12 = | 1,800 |
| Apr. 30 | Purchase ................. | 200 units @ $15 = | 3,000 |
| Sept. 26 | Purchase ................. | 300 units @ $20 = | 6,000 |

The company transacted sales on the following dates at a $35 per unit sales price.

| | | |
|---|---|---|
| Jan. 10 | 30 units | (specific cost: 30 @ $10) |
| Feb. 15 | 100 units | (specific cost: 100 @ $12) |
| Oct. 5 | 350 units | (specific cost: 100 @ $15 and 250 @ $20) |

**Concepts and Procedures to Illustrate in Expert Presentation**

a. Identify and compute the costs to assign to the units sold. (Round per unit costs to three decimals.)

b. Identify and compute the costs to assign to the units in ending inventory. (Round inventory balances to the dollar.)

c. How likely is it that this inventory costing method will reflect the actual physical flow of goods? How relevant is that factor in determining whether this is an acceptable method to use?

d. What is the impact of this method versus others in determining net income and income taxes?

e. How closely does the ending inventory amount reflect replacement cost?

4. Re-form learning teams. In rotation, each expert is to present to the team the presentation developed in part 3. Experts are to encourage and respond to questions.

---

## ENTREPRENEURIAL DECISION

A3  

**BTN 6-7**   Review the chapter's opening feature highlighting Randy Hetrick and his company, **Fitness Anywhere**. Assume that Fitness Anywhere consistently maintains an inventory level of $300,000, meaning that its average and ending inventory levels are the same. Also assume its annual cost of sales is $1,200,000. To cut costs, Randy proposes to slash inventory to a constant level of $150,000 with no impact on cost of sales. He plans to work with suppliers to get quicker deliveries and to order smaller quantities more often.

**Required**

1. Compute the company's inventory turnover and its days' sales in inventory under (a) current conditions and (b) proposed conditions.

2. Evaluate and comment on the merits of his proposal given your analysis for part 1. Identify any concerns you might have about the proposal.

---

## HITTING THE ROAD

C1   C2  

**BTN 6-8**   Visit four retail stores with another classmate. In each store, identify whether the store uses a bar-coding system to help manage its inventory. Try to find at least one store that does not use bar-coding. If a store does not use bar-coding, ask the store's manager or clerk whether he or she knows which type of inventory method the store employs. Create a table that shows columns for the name of store visited, type of merchandise sold, use or nonuse of bar-coding, and the inventory method used if bar-coding is not employed. You might also inquire as to what the store's inventory turnover is and how often physical inventory is taken.

**BTN 6-9** Key figures (EUR millions) for **Nokia** (**www.Nokia.com**), which is a leading global manufacturer of mobile devices and services, follow.

**GLOBAL DECISION**

A3

**NOKIA**

*RIM*

Apple

| EUR millions | Current Year | One Year Prior | Two Years Prior |
|---|---|---|---|
| Inventory . . . . . . . . . . . | 1,865 | 2,533 | 2,876 |
| Cost of sales . . . . . . . . | 27,720 | 33,337 | 33,781 |

**Required**

1. Use these data and those from BTN 6-2 to compute (*a*) inventory turnover and (*b*) days' sales in inventory for the most recent two years shown for **Nokia**, **Research In Motion**, and **Apple**.
2. Comment on and interpret your findings from part 1.

## ANSWERS TO MULTIPLE CHOICE QUIZ

**1.** a; FIFO perpetual

| Date | Goods Purchased | Cost of Goods Sold | Inventory Balance |
|---|---|---|---|
| July 1 | | | 75 units @ $25 = $ 1,875 |
| July 3 | 348 units @ $27 = $9,396 | | 75 units @ $25 <br> 348 units @ $27 } = $ 11,271 |
| July 8 | | 75 units @ $25 <br> 225 units @ $27 } = $ 7,950 | 123 units @ $27 = $ 3,321 |
| July 15 | 257 units @ $28 = $7,196 | | 123 units @ $27 <br> 257 units @ $28 } = $ 10,517 |
| July 23 | | 123 units @ $27 <br> 152 units @ $28 } = $ 7,577 | 105 units @ $28 = **$ 2,940** |
| | | $15,527 | |

**2.** b; LIFO perpetual

| Date | Goods Purchased | Cost of Goods Sold | Inventory Balance |
|---|---|---|---|
| July 1 | | | 75 units @ $25 = $ 1,875 |
| July 3 | 348 units @ $27 = $9,396 | | 75 units @ $25 <br> 348 units @ $27 } = $ 11,271 |
| July 8 | | 300 units @ $27 = $ 8,100 | 75 units @ $25 <br> 48 units @ $27 } = $ 3,171 |
| July 15 | 257 units @ $28 = $7,196 | | 75 units @ $25 <br> 48 units @ $27 <br> 257 units @ $28 } = $ 10,367 |
| July 23 | | 257 units @ $28 <br> 18 units @ $27 } = $ 7,682 | 75 units @ $25 <br> 30 units @ $27 } = **$ 2,685** |
| | | $15,782 | |

**3.** e; Specific identification perpetual—Ending inventory computation.

| | |
|---|---|
| 20 units @ $25 | $ 500 |
| 40 units @ $27 | 1,080 |
| 45 units @ $28 | 1,260 |
| 105 units | $2,840 |

**4.** a; FIFO periodic—Ending inventory computation.
105 units @ $28 each = $2,940; The FIFO periodic inventory computation is identical to the FIFO perpetual inventory computation (see question 1).

**5.** d; Days' sales in inventory = (Ending inventory/Cost of goods sold × 365)
= ($18,000/$85,000) × 365 = 77.29 days

# 7

# Accounting Information Systems

## A Look Back

Chapters 5 and 6 focused on merchandising activities and accounting for inventory. We explained inventory systems, accounting for inventory transactions, and assigning costs to inventory.

## A Look at This Chapter

This chapter emphasizes accounting information systems. We describe fundamental system principles, the system's components, use of special journals and subsidiary ledgers, and technology-based systems.

## A Look Ahead

Chapter 8 focuses on internal controls and accounting for cash and cash equivalents. We explain good internal control procedures and their importance.

## Learning Objectives

### CONCEPTUAL

**C1** Identify the principles and components of accounting information systems. (p. 272)

**C2** Explain the goals and uses of special journals. (p. 275)

**C3** Describe the use of controlling accounts and subsidiary ledgers. (p. 276)

### ANALYTICAL

**A1** Compute segment return on assets and use it to evaluate segment performance. (p. 288)

LP7

### PROCEDURAL

**P1** Journalize and post transactions using special journals. (p. 278)

**P2** Prepare and prove the accuracy of subsidiary ledgers. (p. 279)

**P3** *Appendix 7A*—Journalize and post transactions using special journals in a periodic inventory system. (p. 292)

## Decision Insight

## Successful Brew

*"It's just following your instincts, knowing the basics, and sticking with what's important"*

—KIM JORDAN

FORT COLLINS, CO—Kim Jordan's entrepreneurial roots were anything but frothy. "For about eight months, we didn't pay ourselves," explains Kim. "We borrowed money from parents and made payroll . . . looking at the bills, we had to decide which to pay." From those meager beginnings, Kim created **New Belgium Brewing Company (NewBelgium.com),** which is committed to the Belgian brewing tradition of delicious beers with loads of character.

"We did have a set of values, a purpose, and some outcomes that we wanted to achieve," says Kim. "Four things were important to us: to produce world class Belgium-style beers, to promote beer culture, to be environmental stewards, and to have fun!" To achieve those goals, Kim set up an accounting system to measure, track, summarize, and report on operations. "It is important to have the ability to read financial statements," insists Kim. "And, to understand ratios." Those expectations and priorities fundamentally shaped Kim's accounting system and controls.

"There has to be execution," explains Kim. That focus on execution includes applying internal controls, special journals,

accounting ledgers, and systems technology. Kim maintains special journals for sales, cash receipts, purchases, and cash disbursements. Developing her accounting system to capture all aspects of her operations is no easy task, but well worth the effort. "Working hard and being dedicated or committed to an outcome are keys," asserts Kim. "Our co-workers [all employees] get to see all of our financials!" Kim explains that this in turn helps shape the special journals for her business, including the control procedures applied in the brewery.

Kim's company is riding high with the right accounting systems and controls for long-run success. "Stasis is not an option," says Kim. "If we're all in the same place today that we were five years ago, that wouldn't be very interesting." Kim smiles and adds, "There's something wrong if making beer can't be fun!"

[Sources: *NewBelgium Website,* January 2011; *Entrepreneur,* November 2009; *50entrepreneurs.com,* March 2010; *CNNMoney.com,* June 2009; *Beverage World,* September 2009]

With increases in the number and complexity of business activities, the demands placed on accounting information systems increase. Accounting information systems must meet this challenge in an efficient and effective manner. In this chapter, we learn about fundamental principles guiding information systems, and we study components making up these systems. We also explain procedures that use special journals and subsidiary ledgers to make accounting information systems more efficient. An understanding of the details of accounting reports makes us better decision makers when using financial information, and it improves our ability to analyze and interpret financial statements.

**Accounting Information Systems**

| System Principles | System Components | Special Journals | System Technology |
|---|---|---|---|
| • Control<br>• Relevance<br>• Compatibility<br>• Flexibility<br>• Cost-Benefit | • Source documents<br>• Input devices<br>• Processors<br>• Storage<br>• Output devices | • Subsidiary ledgers<br>• Sales journal<br>• Cash receipts journal<br>• Purchases journal<br>• Cash disbursements journal | • Computers<br>• Data processing<br>• Networks<br>• Enterprise resource planning (ERP) |

# FUNDAMENTAL SYSTEM PRINCIPLES

**C1** Identify the principles and components of accounting information systems.

**Accounting information systems** collect and process data from transactions and events, organize them in useful reports, and communicate results to decision makers. With the increasing complexity of business and the growing need for information, accounting information systems are more important than ever. All decision makers need to have a basic knowledge of how accounting information systems work. This knowledge gives decision makers a competitive edge as they gain a better understanding of information constraints, measurement limitations, and potential applications. It allows them to make more informed decisions and to better balance the risks and returns of different strategies. This section explains five basic principles of accounting information systems, shown in Exhibit 7.1.

**EXHIBIT 7.1**

System Principles

### Control Principle

Managers need to control and monitor business activities. The **control principle** prescribes that an accounting information system have internal controls. **Internal controls** are methods and procedures allowing managers to control and monitor business activities. They include policies to direct operations toward common goals, procedures to ensure reliable financial reports, safeguards to protect company assets, and methods to achieve compliance with laws and regulations.

**Point:** A hacker stole 300,000 credit card numbers from online music retailer CDUniverse due to internal control failure.

### Relevance Principle

Decision makers need relevant information to make informed decisions. The **relevance principle** prescribes that an accounting information system report useful, understandable, timely, and pertinent information for effective decision making. The system must be designed to capture data that make a difference in decisions. To ensure this, we must consider all decision makers when identifying relevant information for disclosure.

## Compatibility Principle

Accounting information systems must be consistent with the aims of a company. The **compatibility principle** prescribes that an accounting information system conform with a company's activities, personnel, and structure. It also must adapt to a company's unique characteristics. The system must not be intrusive but must work in harmony with and be driven by company goals. Most start-up entrepreneurs require only a simple information system. **Harley-Davidson**, on the other hand, demands both a merchandising and a manufacturing information system able to assemble data from its global operations.

## Flexibility Principle

Accounting information systems must be able to adjust to changes. The **flexibility principle** prescribes that an accounting information system be able to adapt to changes in the company, business environment, and needs of decisions makers. Technological advances, competitive pressures, consumer tastes, regulations, and company activities constantly evolve. A system must be designed to adapt to these changes.

## Cost-Benefit Principle

The **cost-benefit principle** prescribes that the benefits from an activity in an accounting information system outweigh the costs of that activity. The costs and benefits of an activity such as producing a specific report will impact the decisions of both external and internal users. Decisions regarding other systems principles (control, relevance, compatibility, and flexibility) are also affected by the cost-benefit principle.

**Point:** Law requires that *all* employers destroy credit-check and other employee records *before* tossing them. A cross-cut shredder is the tool of choice.

---

### Decision Insight

**Digital Is Forever** E-communications have helped bring down many employees, including the former CEO of **Boeing**. To comply with Sarbanes-Oxley, more and more companies now archive and monitor e-mails, instant messages, blog postings, and Net-based phone calls. Using natural-language software, companies sift through digital communications in milliseconds, checking for trade secrets, bad language, porn, and pirated files. ■

---

## COMPONENTS OF ACCOUNTING SYSTEMS

Accounting information systems consist of people, records, methods, and equipment. The systems are designed to capture information about a company's transactions and to provide output including financial, managerial, and tax reports. All accounting information systems have these same goals, and thus share some basic components. These components apply whether or not a system is heavily computerized, yet the components of computerized systems usually provide more accuracy, speed, efficiency, and convenience than those of manual systems.

The five basic **components of accounting systems** are source documents, input devices, information processors, information storage, and output devices. Exhibit 7.2 shows these components as a series of steps, yet we know that much two-way communication occurs between many of these components. We briefly describe each of these key components in this section.

| Source Document | Input Devices | Information Processor | Information Storage | Output Devices |

**EXHIBIT 7.2**

Accounting System Components

## Source Documents

We introduced source documents in Chapters 1 and 2 and explained their importance for both business transactions and information collection. Source documents provide the basic information processed by an accounting system. Examples of source documents include bank statements and checks, invoices from suppliers, billings to customers, cash register files, and employee earnings records. Source documents can be paper, although they increasingly are taking the form of electronic files and Web communications. A growing number of companies are sending documents directly from their systems to their customers' and suppliers' systems. The Web is playing a major role in this transformation from paper-based to *paperless* systems.

Accurate source documents are crucial to accounting information systems. Input of faulty or incomplete information seriously impairs the reliability and relevance of the information system. We commonly refer to this as "garbage in, garbage out." Information systems are set up with attention on control procedures to limit the possibility of entering faulty data in the system.

## Input Devices

**Input devices** capture information from source documents and enable its transfer to the system's information processing component. These devices often involve converting data on source documents from written or electronic form to a form usable for the system. Journal entries, both electronic and paper based, are a type of input device. Keyboards, scanners, and modems are some of the most common input devices in practice today. For example, bar code readers capture code numbers and transfer them to the organization's computer for processing. Moreover, a scanner can capture writing samples and other input directly from source documents.

Controls are used to ensure that only authorized individuals input data to the system. Controls increase the system's reliability and allow information to be traced back to its source.

**Point:** Understanding a manual accounting system is useful in understanding an electronic system.

### Decision Insight

**Geek Chic** Cyberfashion pioneers are creating geek chic, a kind of wearable computer. Cyberfashion draws on digital cellular phones, lithium batteries, and miniature monitors. Special thread is woven into clothing to carry low-voltage signals from one part of the system to another, and fabric keyboards are sewn into clothes. These creations give new meaning to the term *software*. ■

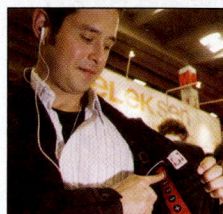

## Information Processors

**Information processors** are systems that interpret, transform, and summarize information for use in analysis and reporting. An important part of an information processor in accounting systems is professional judgment. Accounting principles are never so structured that they limit the need for professional judgment. Other parts of an information processor include journals, ledgers, working papers, and posting procedures. Each assists in transforming raw data to useful information.

Increasingly, computer technology (both computing hardware and software) is assisting manual information processors. This assistance is freeing accounting professionals to take on increased analysis, interpretive, and managerial roles. Web-based application service providers (ASPs) offer another type of information processor.

**Point:** *BusinessWeek* reported that 75% of all e-mail traffic is spam.

## Information Storage

**Information storage** is the accounting system component that keeps data in a form accessible to information processors. After being input and processed, data are stored for use in future analyses and reports. The database must be accessible to preparers of periodic financial reports. Auditors rely on this database when they audit both financial statements and a company's controls. Companies also maintain files of source documents.

Older systems consisted almost exclusively of paper documents, but most modern systems depend on electronic storage devices. Advances in information storage enable accounting systems

**Point:** A financial accounting database can be designed to support a wide range of internal reports for management.

to increasingly store more detailed data. This means managers have more data to access and work with in planning and controlling business activities. Information storage can be online, meaning that data can be accessed whenever, and from wherever, it is needed. Off-line storage means access often requires assistance and authorization. Information storage is increasingly augmented by Web sources such as SEC databases, benchmarking services, and financial and product markets.

### Decision Insight

**Direct Output**   A screenless computer display, called *virtual retinal display* (VRD), scans rows of pixels directly onto the user's retina by means of a laser. VRDs can simulate three-dimensional virtual worlds, including 3D financial graphics. ■

## Output Devices

**Output devices** are the means to take information out of an accounting system and make it available to users. Common output devices are printers, monitors, projectors, and Web communications. Output devices provide users a variety of items including graphics, analysis reports, bills to customers, checks to suppliers, employee paychecks, financial statements, and internal reports. When requests for output occur, an information processor takes the needed data from a database and prepares the necessary report, which is then sent to an output device. A special type of output is an electronic funds transfer (EFT). One example is the transfer of payroll from the company's bank account to its employees' bank accounts. This requires an interface to allow a company's accounting system to send payroll data directly to the bank's accounting system. This interface can involve a company recording its payroll data in an encrypted zip file and forwarding it to the bank. The bank then uses this output to transfer wages earned to employees' accounts.

### Decision Ethics                                                     Answer — p. 296

**Accountant**   Your client requests advice in purchasing software for its accounting system. You have been offered a 10% commission by a software company for each purchase of its system by one of your clients. Does this commission arrangement affect your evaluation of software? Do you tell your client about the commission arrangement? ■

### Quick Check                                                        Answers — p. 297

1. Identify the five primary components of an accounting information system.
2. What is the aim of information processors in an accounting system?
3. How are data in the information storage component of an accounting system used?

## SPECIAL JOURNALS IN ACCOUNTING

This section describes the underlying records of accounting information systems. Designed correctly, these records support efficiency in processing transactions and events. They are part of all systems in various forms and are increasingly electronic. Even in technologically advanced systems, a basic understanding of the records we describe in this section aids in using, interpreting, and applying accounting information. It also improves our knowledge of computer-based systems. Remember that all accounting systems have common purposes and internal workings whether or not they depend on technology.

This section focuses on special journals and subsidiary ledgers that are an important part of accounting systems. We describe how special journals are used to capture transactions, and we explain how subsidiary ledgers are set up to capture details of accounts. This section uses a *perpetual*

 **C2** Explain the goals and uses of special journals.

inventory system, and the special journals are set up using this system. Appendix 7A describes the change in special journals required for a *periodic* system. We also include a note at the bottom of each of the special journals explaining the change required if a company uses a periodic system.

## Basics of Special Journals

A **general journal** is an all-purpose journal in which we can record any transaction. Use of a general journal for all transactions is usually more costly for a business *and* is a less effective control procedure. Moreover, for less technologically advanced systems, use of a general journal requires that each debit and each credit entered be individually posted to its respective ledger account. To enhance internal control and reduce costs, transactions are organized into common groups. A **special journal** is used to record and post transactions of similar type. Most transactions of a merchandiser, for instance, can be categorized into the journals shown in Exhibit 7.3. This section assumes the use of these four special journals along with the general journal. The general journal continues to be used for transactions not covered by special journals and for adjusting, closing, and correcting entries. We show in the following discussion that special journals are *efficient tools in helping journalize and post transactions.* This is done, for instance, by accumulating debits and credits of similar transactions, which allows posting of amounts as column *totals* rather than as individual amounts. The advantage of this system increases as the number of transactions increases. Special journals allow an *efficient division of labor,* which is also an effective control procedure.

**Point:** Companies can use as many special journals as necessary given their unique business activities.

**Point:** A specific transaction is recorded in only *one* journal.

**EXHIBIT 7.3**

Using Special Journals with a General Journal

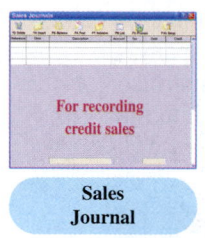
For recording credit sales

**Sales Journal**

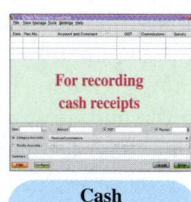
For recording cash receipts

**Cash Receipts Journal**

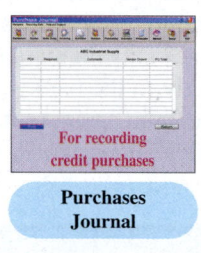
For recording credit purchases

**Purchases Journal**

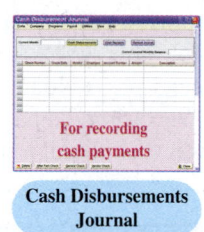
For recording cash payments

**Cash Disbursements Journal**

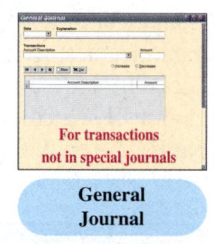
For transactions not in special journals

**General Journal**

It is important to note that special journals and subsidiary ledgers *are designed in a manner that is best suited for each business.* The most likely candidates for special journal status are recurring transactions—for many businesses those are sales, cash receipts, purchases, and cash disbursements. However, good systems design for a business could involve collapsing sales and cash receipts in one journal, or purchases and cash disbursements in another. It could also involve adding more special journals or additional subsidiary ledgers for other recurring transactions. This design decision extends to journal and ledger format. That is, the selection on number of columns, column headings, and so forth is based on what is best suited for each business. Thus, read the following sections as one example of a common systems design, but not the only design.

## Subsidiary Ledgers

**C3**  Describe the use of controlling accounts and subsidiary ledgers.

To understand special journals, it is necessary to understand the workings of a **subsidiary ledger,** which is a list of individual accounts with a common characteristic. A subsidiary ledger contains detailed information on specific accounts in the general ledger. Information systems often include several subsidiary ledgers. Two of the most important are:

- *Accounts receivable ledger*—stores transaction data of individual customers.
- *Accounts payable ledger*—stores transaction data of individual suppliers.

Individual accounts in subsidiary ledgers are often arranged alphabetically, which is the approach taken here. We describe accounts receivable and accounts payable ledgers in this section. Our discussion of special journals uses these ledgers.

**Accounts Receivable Ledger**   When we recorded credit sales in prior chapters, we debited (increased) Accounts Receivable. When a company has more than one credit customer, the accounts receivable records must show how much *each* customer purchased, paid, and has yet to pay. This information is collected by keeping a separate account receivable for each credit customer. A separate account for each customer *could* be kept in the general ledger with the other financial statement accounts, but this is uncommon. Instead, the general ledger usually has a single Accounts Receivable account, and a *subsidiary ledger* is set up to keep a separate account for each customer. This subsidiary ledger is called the **accounts receivable ledger** (also called *accounts receivable subsidiary ledger* or *customers ledger*), and it can exist in electronic or paper form.

Exhibit 7.4 shows the relation between the Accounts Receivable account and its individual accounts in the subsidiary ledger. After all items are posted, the balance in the Accounts Receivable account must equal the sum of all balances of its customers' accounts. The Accounts Receivable account is said to control the accounts receivable ledger and is called a **controlling account.** Since the accounts receivable ledger is a supplementary record controlled by an account in the general ledger, it is called a *subsidiary* ledger.

**Point:** When a general ledger account has a subsidiary ledger, any transaction that impacts one of them also impacts the other—some refer to this as *general and subsidiary ledgers kept in tandem.*

**EXHIBIT 7.4**

Accounts Receivable Controlling Account and Its Subsidiary Ledger

**Point:** A **control account** refers to any general ledger account that summarizes subsidiary ledger data.

**Accounts Payable Ledger**    There are other controlling accounts and subsidiary ledgers. We know, for example, that many companies buy on credit from several suppliers. This means that companies must keep a separate account for each supplier by keeping an Accounts Payable controlling account in the general ledger and a separate account for each supplier (creditor) in an **accounts payable ledger** (also called *accounts payable subsidiary ledger* or *creditors ledger*).

**Other Subsidiary Ledgers**    Subsidiary ledgers are common for several other accounts. A company with many classes of equipment, for example, might keep only one Equipment account in its general ledger, but its Equipment account would control a subsidiary ledger in which each class of equipment is recorded in a separate account. Similar treatment is common for investments, inventory, and any accounts needing separate detailed records. **Genmar Holdings**, which manufactures boats by Champion, Glastron, Four Winns, and Larson, reports sales information by product line in its report. Yet its accounting system keeps much more detailed sales records. Genmar Holdings, for instance, sells hundreds of different products and must be able to analyze the sales performance of each. This detail can be captured by many different general ledger sales accounts but is instead captured by using supplementary records that function like subsidiary ledgers. Overall, subsidiary ledgers are applied in many different ways to ensure that the accounting system captures sufficient details to support analyses that decision makers need. At least four benefits derive from subsidiary ledgers:

1. Removal of excessive details, and detailed accounts, from the general ledger.
2. Up-to-date information readily available on specific customers and suppliers.
3. Aid in error identification for specific accounts.
4. Potential efficiencies in recordkeeping through division of labor in posting.

## Sales Journal

A typical **sales journal** is used to record sales of inventory *on credit*. Sales of inventory for cash are not recorded in a sales journal but in a cash receipts journal. Sales of noninventory assets on credit are recorded in the general journal.

**Journalizing**   Credit sale transactions are recorded with information about each sale entered separately in a sales journal. This information is often taken from a copy of the sales ticket or invoice prepared at the time of sale. The top portion of Exhibit 7.5 shows a typical sales journal from a merchandiser. It has columns for recording the date, customer's name, invoice number, posting reference, and the retail and cost amounts of each credit sale. The sales journal in this exhibit is called a **columnar journal,** which is any journal with more than one column.

**Point:** Each transaction in the sales journal includes a debit to accounts receivable and a credit to sales.

Each transaction recorded in the sales journal yields an entry in the "Accounts Receivable Dr., Sales Cr." column. We usually need only one column for these two accounts. (An exception is when managers need more information about taxes, returns, and other sales details.) Each transaction in the sales journal also yields an entry in the "Cost of Goods Sold Dr., Inventory Cr." column. This entry reflects the perpetual inventory system of tracking costs with each sale. To illustrate, on February 2, this company sold merchandise on account to Jason Henry for $450. The invoice number is 307, and the cost of this merchandise is $315. This information is

**EXHIBIT 7.5**

Sales Journal with Posting*

| File | Edit | Maintain | Tasks | Analysis | Options | Reports | Window | Help |

**Sales Journal**                                                                                                  Page 3

| Date | Account Debited | Invoice Number | PR | Accounts Receivable Dr. Sales Cr. | Cost of Goods Sold Dr. Inventory Cr. |
|---|---|---|---|---|---|
| Feb. 2 | Jason Henry | 307 | ✓ | 450 | 315 |
| 7 | Albert Co. | 308 | ✓ | 500 | 355 |
| 13 | Kam Moore | 309 | ✓ | 350 | 260 |
| 15 | Paul Roth | 310 | ✓ | 200 | 150 |
| 22 | Jason Henry | 311 | ✓ | 225 | 155 |
| 25 | Frank Booth | 312 | ✓ | 175 | 95 |
| 28 | Albert Co. | 313 | ✓ | 250 | 170 |
| 28 | Totals | | | 2,150 | 1,500 |
| | | | | (106/413) | (502/119) |

**Totals are posted at the end of the period to General Ledger accounts.**

**Individual line item amounts in the Accounts Receivable Dr. and Sales Cr. column are posted immediately to the subsidiary ledger.**

**Customer accounts are in a subsidiary ledger and the financial statement accounts are in the General Ledger.**

**Accounts Receivable Ledger**

Customer Name **Albert Co.**

| Date | PR | Debit | Credit | Balance |
|---|---|---|---|---|
| Feb. 7 | S3 | 500 | | 500 |
| 28 | S3 | 250 | | 750 |

Customer Name **Frank Booth**

| Date | PR | Debit | Credit | Balance |
|---|---|---|---|---|
| Feb. 25 | S3 | 175 | | 175 |

Customer Name **Jason Henry**

| Date | PR | Debit | Credit | Balance |
|---|---|---|---|---|
| Feb. 2 | S3 | 450 | | 450 |
| 22 | S3 | 225 | | 675 |

Customer Name **Kam Moore**

| Date | PR | Debit | Credit | Balance |
|---|---|---|---|---|
| Feb. 13 | S3 | 350 | | 350 |

Customer Name **Paul Roth**

| Date | PR | Debit | Credit | Balance |
|---|---|---|---|---|
| Feb. 15 | S3 | 200 | | 200 |

**General Ledger**

**Accounts Receivable**     No. 106

| Date | PR | Debit | Credit | Balance |
|---|---|---|---|---|
| Feb. 28 | S3 | 2,150 | | 2,150 |

**Inventory**     No. 119

| Date | PR | Debit | Credit | Balance |
|---|---|---|---|---|
| Feb. 1 | bal. | | | 15,700 |
| 28 | S3 | | 1,500 | 14,200 |

**Sales**     No. 413

| Date | PR | Debit | Credit | Balance |
|---|---|---|---|---|
| Feb. 28 | S3 | | 2,150 | 2,150 |

**Cost of Goods Sold**     No. 502

| Date | PR | Debit | Credit | Balance |
|---|---|---|---|---|
| Feb. 28 | S3 | 1,500 | | 1,500 |

*The Sales Journal in a *periodic* system would exclude the column on the far right titled "Cost of Goods Sold Dr., Inventory Cr."  (see Exhibit 7A.1).

captured on one line in the sales journal. No further explanations or entries are necessary, saving time and effort. Moreover, this sales journal is consistent with most inventory systems that use bar codes to record both sales and costs with each sale transaction. Note that the Posting Reference (PR) column is not used when entering transactions but instead is used when posting.

**Point:** Continuously updated customer accounts provide timely information for customer inquiries on those accounts and on current amounts owed.

**Posting**   A sales journal is posted as reflected in the arrow lines of Exhibit 7.5. Two types of posting can be identified: (1) posting to the subsidiary ledger(s) and (2) posting to the general ledger.

**Posting to subsidiary ledger.**   Individual transactions in the sales journal are posted regularly (typically concurrently) to customer accounts in the accounts receivable ledger. These postings keep customer accounts up-to-date, which is important for the person granting credit to customers. When sales recorded in the sales journal are individually posted to customer accounts in the accounts receivable ledger, check marks are entered in the sales journal's PR column. Check marks are used rather than account numbers because customer accounts usually are arranged alphabetically in the accounts receivable ledger. Note that posting debits to Accounts Receivable twice—once to Accounts Receivable and once to the customer's subsidiary account—does not violate the accounting equation of debits equal credits. The equality of debits and credits is always maintained in the general ledger.

**Point:** PR column is only checked *after* the amount(s) is posted.

**Posting to general ledger.**   The sales journal's account columns are totaled at the end of each period (the month of February in this case). For the "sales" column, the $2,150 total is debited to Accounts Receivable and credited to Sales in the general ledger (see Exhibit 7.5). For the "cost" column, the $1,500 total is debited to Cost of Goods Sold and credited to Inventory in the general ledger. When totals are posted to accounts in the general ledger, the account numbers are entered below the column total in the sales journal for tracking. For example, we enter (106/413) below the total in the sales column after this amount is posted to account number 106 (Accounts Receivable) and account number 413 (Sales).

**Point:** Postings are automatic in a computerized system.

   A company identifies in the PR column of its subsidiary ledgers the journal and page number from which an amount is taken. We identify a journal by using an initial. Items posted from the sales journal carry the initial **S** before their journal page numbers in a PR column. Likewise, items from the cash receipts journal carry the initial **R**; items from the cash disbursements journal carry the initial **D**; items from the purchases journal carry the initial **P**; and items from the general journal carry the initial **G**.

**Proving the Ledgers**   Account balances in the general ledger and subsidiary ledgers are periodically proved (or reviewed) for accuracy after posting. To do this we first prepare a trial balance of the general ledger to confirm that debits equal credits. Second, we test a subsidiary ledger by preparing a *schedule* of individual accounts and amounts. A **schedule of accounts receivable** lists each customer and the balance owed. If this total equals the balance of the Accounts Receivable controlling account, the accounts in the accounts receivable ledger are assumed correct. Exhibit 7.6 shows a schedule of accounts receivable drawn from the accounts receivable ledger of Exhibit 7.5.

**P2**  Prepare and prove the accuracy of subsidiary ledgers.

| Schedule of Accounts Receivable February 28 | |
| --- | --- |
| Albert Co. .................... | $  750 |
| Frank Booth ................... | 175 |
| Jason Henry ................... | 675 |
| Kam Moore ................... | 350 |
| Paul Roth ..................... | 200 |
| Total accounts receivable ........ | $2,150 |

**EXHIBIT 7.6**

Schedule of Accounts Receivable

**Additional Issues**   We consider three additional issues with the sales journal: (1) recording sales taxes, (2) recording sales returns and allowances, and (3) using actual sales invoices as a journal.

**Point:** In accounting, the word *schedule* generally means a list.

**Sales taxes.**   Governmental agencies such as cities and states often require sellers to collect sales taxes from customers and to periodically send these taxes to the appropriate agency. When using a columnar sales journal, we can keep a record of taxes collected by adding a Sales Taxes Payable column as follows.

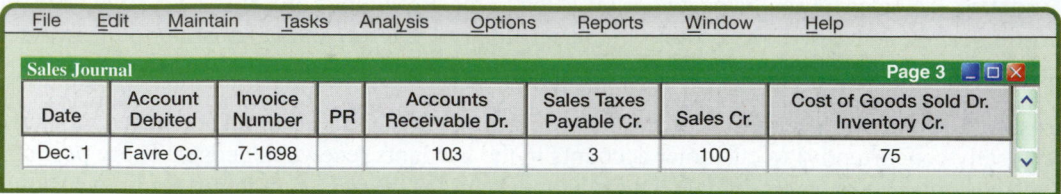

| Date | Account Debited | Invoice Number | PR | Accounts Receivable Dr. | Sales Taxes Payable Cr. | Sales Cr. | Cost of Goods Sold Dr. Inventory Cr. |
|------|----------------|----------------|----|------------------------|------------------------|-----------|--------------------------------------|
| Dec. 1 | Favre Co. | 7-1698 | | 103 | 3 | 100 | 75 |

Individual amounts in the Accounts Receivable column would continue to be posted immediately to customer accounts in the accounts receivable ledger. Individual amounts in the Sales Taxes Payable and Sales columns are not posted. Column totals would continue to be posted as usual. (A company that collects sales taxes on its cash sales can also use a Sales Taxes Payable column in its cash receipts journal.)

**Sales returns and allowances.**   A company with only a few sales returns and allowances can record them in a general journal with an entry such as the following:

| May 17 | Sales Returns and Allowances . . . . . . . . . . . . . . . . . . | 414 | 175 | |
|--------|------------------------------------------------------------------|------|-----|-----|
| | Accounts Receivable—Ray Ball . . . . . . . . . . . . . | 106/✓ | | 175 |
| | *Customer returned merchandise.* | | | |

The debit in this entry is posted to the Sales Returns and Allowances account (no. 414). The credit is posted to both the Accounts Receivable controlling account (no. 106) and to the customer's account. When we enter the account number and the check mark, 106/✓, in the PR column on the credit line, this means both the Accounts Receivable controlling account in the general ledger and the Ray Ball account in the accounts receivable ledger are credited for $175. [*Note:* If the returned goods can be resold to another customer, the company would debit (increase) the Inventory account and credit (decrease) the Cost of Goods Sold account. If the returned goods are defective (worthless), the company could simply leave their costs in the Cost of Goods Sold account (see Chapter 5).] A company with a large number of sales returns and allowances can save time by recording them in a separate sales returns and allowances journal.

**Sales invoices as a sales journal.**   To save costs, some small companies avoid using a sales journal for credit sales and instead post each sales invoice amount directly to the customer's account in the accounts receivable ledger. They then put copies of invoices in a file. At the end of the period, they total all invoices for that period and make a general journal entry to debit Accounts Receivable and credit Sales for the total amount. The file of invoice copies acts as a sales journal. This is called *direct posting of sales invoices.*

**Quick Check**                                                      Answers — p. 297

**4.** When special journals are used, where are cash payments by check recorded?

**5.** How does a columnar journal save posting time and effort?

**6.** How do debits and credits remain equal when credit sales are posted twice (once to Accounts Receivable and once to the customer's subsidiary account)?

**7.** How do we identify the journal from which an amount in a ledger account was posted?

**8.** How are sales taxes recorded in the context of special journals?

**9.** What is direct posting of sales invoices?

# Cash Receipts Journal

A **cash receipts journal** is typically used to record all receipts of cash. Exhibit 7.7 shows one common form of the cash receipts journal.

**Journalizing and Posting** Cash receipts can be separated into one of three types: (1) cash from credit customers in payment of their accounts, (2) cash from cash sales, and (3) cash from other sources. The cash receipts journal in Exhibit 7.7 has a separate credit

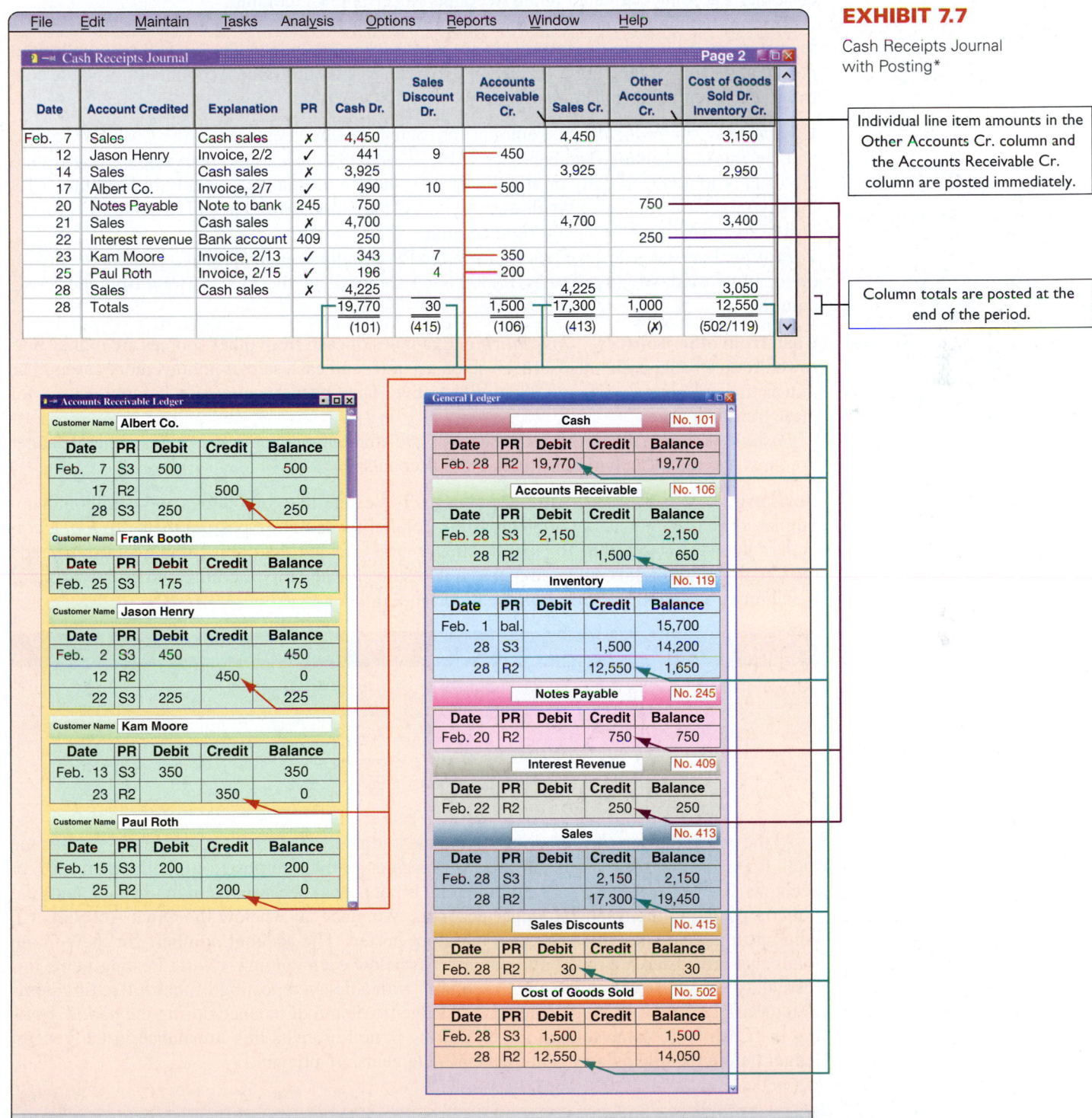

**EXHIBIT 7.7**

Cash Receipts Journal with Posting*

Individual line item amounts in the Other Accounts Cr. column and the Accounts Receivable Cr. column are posted immediately.

Column totals are posted at the end of the period.

*The Cash Receipts Journal in a *periodic* system would exclude the column on the far right titled "Cost of Goods Sold Dr., Inventory Cr." (see Exhibit 7A.2).

**Point:** Each transaction in the cash receipts journal involves a debit to Cash. Credit accounts will vary.

column for each of these three sources. We describe how to journalize transactions from each of these three sources. (An Explanation column is included in the cash receipts journal to identify the source.)

**Cash from credit customers.**   *Journalizing.* To record cash received in payment of a customer's account, the customer's name is first entered in the Account Credited column—see transactions dated February 12, 17, 23, and 25. Then the amounts debited to both Cash and the Sales Discount (if any) are entered in their respective columns, and the amount credited to the customer's account is entered in the Accounts Receivable Cr. column.

   *Posting.* Individual amounts in the Accounts Receivable Cr. column are posted immediately to customer accounts in the subsidiary accounts receivable ledger. The $1,500 column total is posted at the end of the period (month in this case) as a credit to the Accounts Receivable controlling account in the general ledger.

**Cash sales.**   *Journalizing.* The amount for each cash sale is entered in the Cash Dr. column and the Sales Cr. column. The February 7, 14, 21, and 28 transactions are examples. (Cash sales are usually journalized daily or at point of sale, but are journalized weekly in Exhibit 7.7 for brevity.) Each cash sale also yields an entry to Cost of Goods Sold Dr. and Inventory Cr. for the cost of merchandise—see the far right column.

**Point:** Some software packages put cash sales in the sales journal.

   *Posting.* For cash sales, we place an *x* in the PR column to indicate that its amount is not individually posted. We do post the $17,300 Sales Cr. total and the $12,550 total from the "cost" column.

**Cash from other sources.**   *Journalizing.* Examples of cash from other sources are money borrowed from a bank, cash interest received on account, and cash sale of noninventory assets. The transactions of February 20 and 22 are illustrative. The Other Accounts Cr. column is used for these transactions.

**Example:** Record in the cash receipts journal a $700 cash sale of land when the land carries a $700 original cost. *Answer:* Debit the Cash column for $700, and credit the Other Accounts column for $700 (the account credited is Land).

   *Posting.* Amounts from these transactions are immediately posted to their general ledger accounts and the PR column identifies those accounts.

**Footing, Crossfooting, and Posting**   To be sure that total debits and credits in a columnar journal are equal, we often crossfoot column totals before posting them. To *foot* a column of numbers is to add it. To *crossfoot* in this case is to add the Debit column totals, then add the Credit column totals, and compare the two sums for equality. Footing and crossfooting of the numbers in Exhibit 7.7 result in the report in Exhibit 7.8.

**Point:** Subsidiary ledgers and their controlling accounts are *in balance* only after all posting is complete.

**EXHIBIT 7.8**

Footing and Crossfooting Journal Totals

| Debit Columns | | Credit Columns | |
|---|---|---|---|
| Cash Dr. | $19,770 | Accounts Receivable Cr. | $ 1,500 |
| Sales Discounts Dr. | 30 | Sales Cr. | 17,300 |
| Cost of Goods Sold Dr. | 12,550 | Other Accounts Cr. | 1,000 |
| | | Inventory Cr. | 12,550 |
| Total | $32,350 | Total | $32,350 |

   At the end of the period, after crossfooting the journal to confirm that debits equal credits, the total amounts from the columns of the cash receipts journal are posted to their general ledger accounts. The Other Accounts Cr. column total is not posted because the individual amounts are directly posted to their general ledger accounts. We place an *x* below the Other Accounts Cr. column to indicate that this column total is not posted. The account numbers for the column totals that are posted are entered in parentheses below each column. (*Note:* Posting items immediately from the Other Accounts Cr. column with a delayed posting of their offsetting items in the Cash column total causes the general ledger to be out of balance during the period. Posting the Cash Dr. column total at the end of the period corrects this imbalance in the general ledger before the trial balance and financial statements are prepared.)

 **Decision Maker**           Answer — p. 297

**Entrepreneur**   You want to know how promptly customers are paying their bills. This information can help you decide whether to extend credit and to plan your cash payments. Where do you find this information? ■

## Purchases Journal

A **purchases journal** is typically used to record all credit purchases, including those for inventory. Purchases for cash are recorded in the Cash Disbursements Journal.

**Journalizing**   Entries in the purchases journal in Exhibit 7.9 reflect purchase invoices or other source documents. We use the invoice date and terms to compute the date when payment for each purchase is due. The Accounts Payable Cr. column is used to record the amounts owed to each creditor. Inventory purchases are recorded in the Inventory Dr. column.

To illustrate, inventory costing $200 is purchased from Ace Manufacturing on February 5. The creditor's name (Ace) is entered in the Account column, the invoice date is entered in the Date of Invoice column, the purchase terms are entered in the Terms column, and the $200 amount is entered in the Accounts Payable Cr. and the Inventory Dr. columns. When a purchase involves an amount recorded in the Other Accounts Dr. column, we use the Account column to identify the general ledger account debited. For example, the February 28 transaction involves purchases of inventory, office supplies, and store supplies from ITT. The journal has no column for store supplies, so the Other Accounts Dr. column is used. In this case, Store Supplies is entered in the Account column along with the creditor's name (ITT). This purchases journal also includes a separate column for credit purchases of office supplies. A separate column such as this is useful when several transactions involve debits to the same account. Each company uses its own judgment in deciding on the number of separate columns necessary.

**Posting**   The amounts in the Accounts Payable Cr. column are immediately posted to individual creditor accounts in the accounts payable subsidiary ledger. Individual amounts in the Other Accounts Dr. column are immediately posted to their general ledger accounts. At the end

**Point:** The number of special journals and the design of each are based on a company's specific needs.

**Point:** Each transaction in the purchases journal has a credit to Accounts Payable. Debit accounts will vary.

**Point:** The Other Accounts Dr. column allows the purchases journal to be used for any purchase on credit.

**EXHIBIT 7.9**

Purchases Journal with Posting*

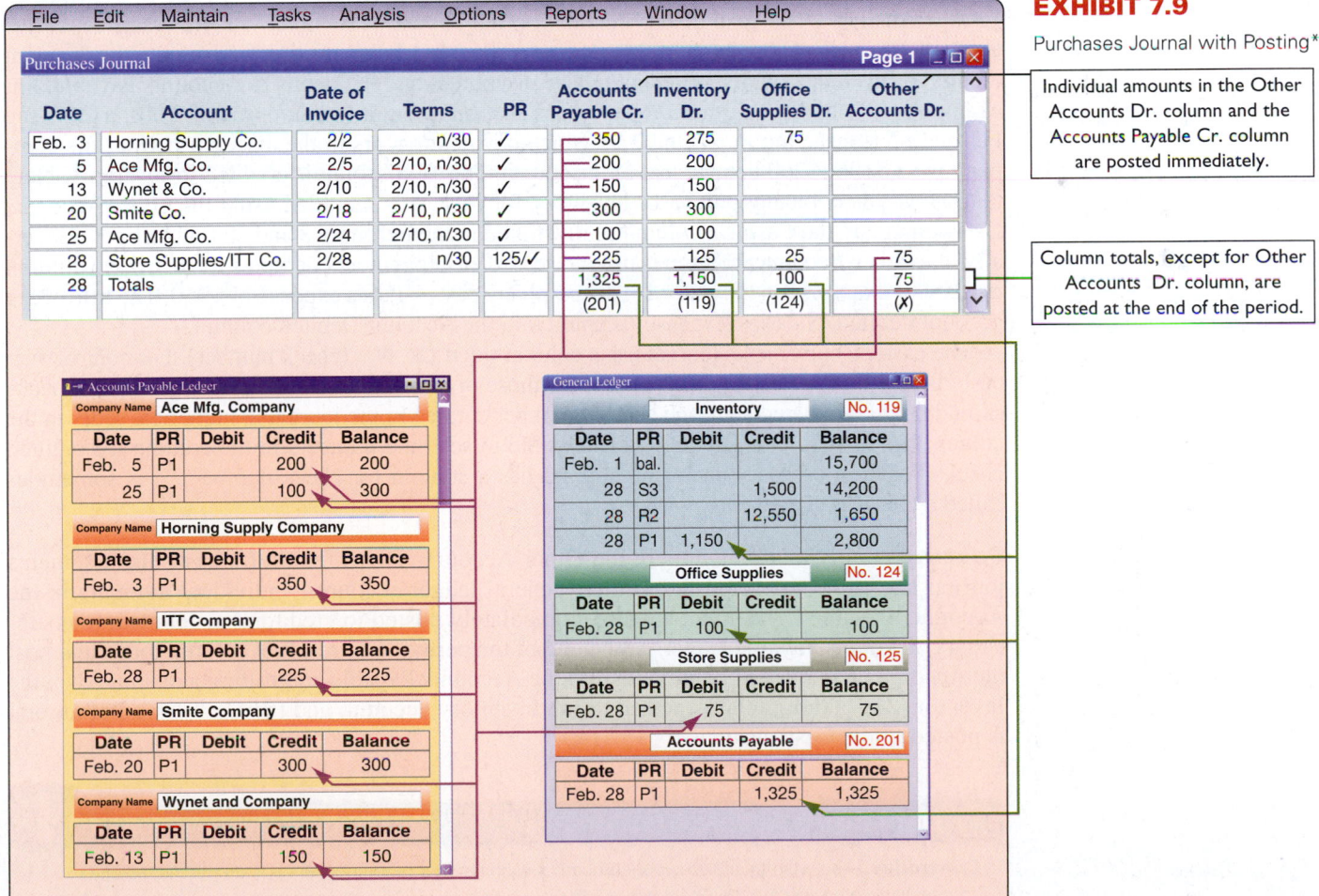

Individual amounts in the Other Accounts Dr. column and the Accounts Payable Cr. column are posted immediately.

Column totals, except for Other Accounts Dr. column, are posted at the end of the period.

*The Purchases Journal in a *periodic* system replaces "Inventory Dr." with "Purchases Dr." (see Exhibit 7A.3).

of the period, all column totals except the Other Accounts Dr. column are posted to their general ledger accounts.

**Proving the Ledger**   Accounts payable balances in the subsidiary ledger can be periodically proved after posting. We prove the subsidiary ledger by preparing a **schedule of accounts payable,** which is a list of accounts from the accounts payable ledger with their balances and the total. If this total of the individual balances equals the balance of the Accounts Payable controlling account, the accounts in the accounts payable ledger are assumed correct. Exhibit 7.10 shows a schedule of accounts payable drawn from the accounts payable ledger of Exhibit 7.9. (This schedule can be done after any posting; for example, we could prepare another schedule of accounts payable after the postings in Exhibit 7.11.)

**Point:** The balance in the Accounts Payable controlling account must equal the sum of the individual account balances in the accounts payable subsidiary ledger after posting.

**EXHIBIT 7.10**

Schedule of Accounts Payable

| Schedule of Accounts Payable February 28 | |
| --- | --- |
| Ace Mfg. Company . . . . . . . . . . . . . . | $   300 |
| Horning Supply Company . . . . . . . . . | 350 |
| ITT Company . . . . . . . . . . . . . . . . . | 225 |
| Smite Company . . . . . . . . . . . . . . . . | 300 |
| Wynet & Company . . . . . . . . . . . . . . | 150 |
| Total accounts payable . . . . . . . . . . . | $1,325 |

## Cash Disbursements Journal

A **cash disbursements journal,** also called a *cash payments journal,* is typically used to record all cash payments.

**Journalizing**   The cash disbursements journal shown in Exhibit 7.11 illustrates repetitive entries to the Cash Cr. column of this journal (reflecting cash payments). Also note the frequent credits to Inventory (which reflect purchase discounts) and the debits to Accounts Payable. For example, on February 15, the company pays Ace on account (credit terms of 2/10, n/30—see February 5 transaction in Exhibit 7.9). Since payment occurs in the discount period, the company pays $196 ($200 invoice less $4 discount). The $4 discount is credited to Inventory. Note that when this company purchases inventory for cash, it is recorded using the Other Accounts Dr. column and the Cash Cr. column as illustrated in the February 3 and 12 transactions. Generally, the Other Accounts column is used to record cash payments on items for which no column exists. For example, on February 15, the company pays salaries expense of $250. The title of the account debited (Salaries Expense) is entered in the Account Debited column.

**Point:** Each transaction in the cash disbursements journal involves a credit to Cash. The debit accounts will vary.

The cash disbursements journal has a column titled Ck. No. (check number). For control over cash disbursements, all payments except for those of small amounts are made by check. Checks should be prenumbered and each check's number entered in the journal in numerical order in the column headed Ck. No. This makes it possible to scan the numbers in the column for omitted checks. When a cash disbursements journal has a column for check numbers, it is sometimes called a **check register.**

**Posting**   Individual amounts in the Other Accounts Dr. column of a cash disbursements journal are immediately posted to their general ledger accounts. Individual amounts in the Accounts Payable Dr. column are also immediately posted to creditors' accounts in the subsidiary Accounts Payable ledger. At the end of the period, we crossfoot column totals and post the Accounts Payable Dr. column total to the Accounts Payable controlling account. Also, the Inventory Cr. column total is posted to the Inventory account, and the Cash Cr. column total is posted to the Cash account.

 **Decision Maker**        Answer — p. 297

**Controller**   You wish to analyze your company's cash payments to suppliers and its purchases discounts. Where do you find this information? ■

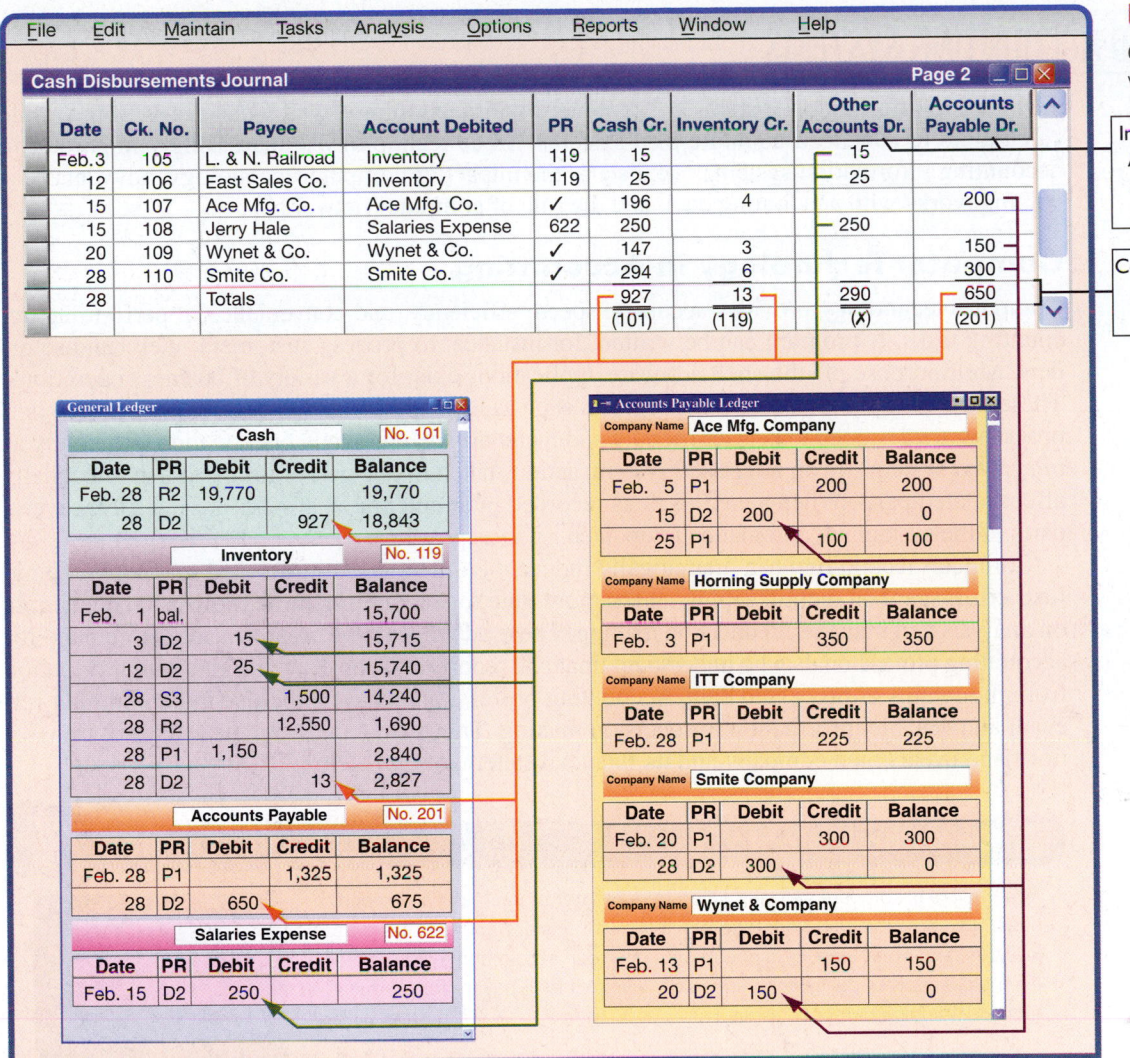

**EXHIBIT 7.11**

Cash Disbursements Journal with Posting*

Individual amounts in the Other Accounts Dr. column and the Accounts Payable Dr. column are posted immediately.

Column totals, except for Other Accounts column, are posted at the end of the period.

*The Cash Disbursements Journal in a *periodic* system replaces "Inventory Cr." with "Purchases Discounts Cr."
(see Exhibit 7A.4).

## General Journal Transactions

When special journals are used, we still need a general journal for adjusting, closing, and any other transactions for which no special journal has been set up. Examples of these other transactions might include purchases returns and allowances, purchases of plant assets by issuing a note payable, sales returns if a sales returns and allowances journal is not used, and receipt of a note receivable from a customer. We described the recording of transactions in a general journal in Chapters 2 and 3.

## Quick Check                                    Answers — p. 297

10. What are the normal recording and posting procedures when using special journals and controlling accounts with subsidiary ledgers?
11. What is the process for posting to a subsidiary ledger and its controlling account?
12. How do we prove the accuracy of account balances in the general ledger and subsidiary ledgers after posting?
13. Why does a company need a general journal when using special journals for sales, purchases, cash receipts, and cash disbursements?

# TECHNOLOGY-BASED ACCOUNTING SYSTEMS

Accounting information systems are supported with technology, which can range from simple calculators to advanced computerized systems. Since technology is increasingly important in accounting information systems, we discuss the impact of computer technology, how data processing works with accounting data, and the role of computer networks.

## Computer Technology in Accounting

Computer technology provides accuracy, speed, efficiency, and convenience in performing accounting tasks. A program can be written, for instance, to process customers' merchandise orders. Multipurpose off-the-shelf software applications exist for a variety of business operations. These include familiar accounting programs such as Peachtree® and QuickBooks®. Off-the-shelf programs are designed to be user friendly and menu driven, and many operate more efficiently as *integrated* systems. In an integrated system, actions taken in one part of the system automatically affect related parts. When a credit sale is recorded in an integrated system, for instance, several parts of the system are automatically updated, such as posting.

Computer technology can dramatically reduce the time and effort devoted to recordkeeping. Less effort spent on recordkeeping means more time for accounting professionals to concentrate on analysis and managerial decision making. These advances have created a greater demand for accounting professionals who understand financial reports and can draw insights and information from mountains of processed data. Accounting professionals have expertise in determining relevant and reliable information for decision making. They also can assess the effects of transactions and events on a company and its financial statements.

### Decision Insight

*Middleware* is software allowing different computer programs in a company or across companies to work together. It allows transfer of purchase orders, invoices, and other electronic documents between accounting systems. For example, suppliers can monitor inventory levels of their buyers for production and shipping purposes. ■

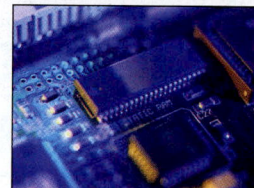

## Data Processing in Accounting

Accounting systems differ with regard to how input is entered and processed. **Online processing** enters and processes data as soon as source documents are available. This means that databases are immediately updated. **Batch processing** accumulates source documents for a period of time and then processes them all at once such as daily, weekly, or monthly. The advantage of online processing is timeliness. This often requires additional costs related to both software and hardware requirements. Companies such as **Intuit** (**Intuit.com**) are making online processing of accounting data a reality for many businesses. The advantage of batch processing is that it requires only periodic updating of databases. Records used to send bills to customers, for instance, might require updating only once a month. The disadvantage of batch processing is the lack of updated databases for management to use when making business decisions.

## Computer Networks in Accounting

Networking, or linking computers with each other, can create information advantages (and cost efficiencies). **Computer networks** are links among computers giving different users and different computers access to common databases, programs, and hardware. Many college computer labs, for instance, are networked. A small computer network is called a *local area network (LAN)*; it links machines with *hard-wire* hookups. Large computer networks extending over long distances often rely on *modem* or *wireless* communication.

Demand for information sometimes requires advanced networks such as the systems **Federal Express** and **UPS** use to track packages and bill customers and the system **Walmart** uses to monitor inventory levels in its stores. These networks include many computers and satellite communications to gather information and to provide ready access to its databases from all locations.

## Enterprise Resource Planning Software

**Enterprise resource planning (ERP) software** includes the programs that manage a company's vital operations. They extend from order taking to manufacturing to accounting. When working properly, these integrated programs can speed decision making, identify costs for reduction, and give managers control over operations with the click of a mouse. For many managers, ERP software allows them to scrutinize business, identify where inventories are piling up, and see what plants are most efficient. The software is designed to link every part of a company's operations. This software allowed **Monsanto** to slash production planning from six weeks to three, trim its inventories, and increase its bargaining power with suppliers. Monsanto estimates that this software saves the company $200 million per year.

ERP has several suppliers. **SAP** leads the market, with **Oracle**, which gobbled up PeopleSoft and J. D. Edwards, a distant second (*AMR Research*). SAP software is used by more than half of the world's 500 largest companies. It links ordering, inventory, production, purchasing, planning, tracking, and human resources. A transaction or event triggers an immediate chain reaction of events throughout the enterprise. It is making companies more efficient and profitable.

**Total ERP Market: About $30 Billion**

- Other 23%
- Infor (SSA) 7%
- Microsoft Dynamics 6%
- Sage Group 8%
- Oracle Applications 21%
- SAP 35%

ERP is pushing into cyberspace and customer relationship management (CRM). Now companies can share data with customers and suppliers. Applesauce maker **Mott's** is using SAP so that distributors can check the status of orders and place them over the Net, and the **Coca-Cola Company** uses it to ship soda on time. ERP is also increasingly used by small business. For example, **NetSuite**'s accounting services to small and medium businesses are powered by Oracle's system.

### Decision Insight

A new generation of accounting support is available. With the touch of a key, users can create real-time inventory reports showing all payments, charges, and credit limits at any point in the accounting cycle. Many services also include "alert signals" notifying the company when, for example, a large order exceeds a customer's credit limit or when purchases need to be made or when a bank balance is running low. These alerts occur via e-mail, fax, PDA, or phone. ■

### Quick Check

Answers — p. 297

14. Identify an advantage of an integrated computer-based accounting system.
15. What advantages do computer systems offer over manual systems?
16. Identify an advantage of computer networks.
17. Describe ERP software and its potential advantages to businesses.

## GLOBAL VIEW

This section discusses similarities and differences between U.S. GAAP and IFRS regarding system principles and components, and special journals.

**System Principles and Components**    Both U.S. GAAP and IFRS aim for high-quality financial reporting. That aim implies that sound information system principles and components are applied worldwide.

However, while system principles and components are fundamentally similar across the globe, culture and other realities often mean different emphases are placed on the mix of system controls. **Nokia** provides the following description of its system controls:

> Nokia's disclosure controls and procedures . . . are designed to provide reasonable assurance regarding the quality and integrity of the company's financial statements and related disclosures.

**Special Journals**   Accounting systems for recording sales, purchases, cash receipts, and cash disbursements are similar worldwide. Although the exact structure of special journals is unique to each company, the basic structure is identical. Companies desire to apply accounting in an efficient manner. Accordingly, systems that employ special journals are applied worldwide.

---

## Decision Analysis ■■■    Segment Return on Assets

**A1**  Compute segment return on assets and use it to evaluate segment performance.

Good accounting information systems collect financial data for a company's various segments. A *segment* refers to a part of a company that is separately identified by its products or services, or by the geographic market it serves. **Callaway Golf Company** reports that it operates in two business segments: (1) golf clubs and (2) golf balls. Users of financial statements are especially interested in segment information to better understand a company's activities because segments often vary on profitability, risk, and growth.

Companies must report segment information, including their sales, operating income, identifiable assets, capital expenditures, and depreciation. However, managers are reluctant to release information that can harm competitive position. Exhibit 7.12 shows survey results on the number of companies with different (reported) segments.

**EXHIBIT 7.12**

Companies Reporting Operations by Types of Segments*

*Total exceeds 100% because companies can report more than one segment.

One measure of success for business segments is the **segment return on assets** ratio defined as follows.

$$\text{Segment return on assets} = \frac{\text{Segment operating income}}{\text{Segment average assets}}$$

**EXHIBIT 7.13**

Callaway Golf's Segment Return on Assets

This ratio reflects on the profitability of a segment. Exhibit 7.13 shows the segments' operating income, average assets, and return on assets for Callaway Golf Company.

| Golf Segment* ($ thousands) | 2009 | | 2008 | | 2007 | | 2006 | |
|---|---|---|---|---|---|---|---|---|
| | Clubs | Balls | Clubs | Balls | Clubs | Balls | Clubs | Balls |
| Operating income . . . . . . . . | $ 38,934 | $(13,864) | $134,018 | $ 6,903 | $151,759 | $ 902 | $101,837 | $ (6,396) |
| Average assets . . . . . . . . . . | $406,835 | $129,796 | $429,170 | $146,855 | $413,352 | $140,730 | $419,212 | $152,282 |
| Segment return on assets . . . | 10% | n.a. | 31% | 5% | 37% | 1% | 24% | n.a. |

\* A segment's operating income is usually measured as pretax income, and assets is usually measured as identifiable assets.

The trend in Callaway's segment return on assets is up-and-down for its golf club segment, and similarly mixed for its golf balls segment. Importantly, its golf clubs segment makes up a much greater portion of its operations; for example, 2008 income of $134,018 from golf clubs make up 95% of its total income of $140,921 from both segments. Callaway should continue investments in its golf club segment vis-a-vis its golf balls segment given the greater returns and larger total income from that segment. Analysis can also be extended to geographical segments and any other segments that companies report.

| ☐ **Decision** Maker | Answer — p. 297 |  |
| --- | --- | --- |

**Banker**   A bicycle merchandiser requests a loan from you to expand operations. Its net income is $220,000, reflecting a 10% increase over the prior year. You ask about segment results. The owner reports that $160,000 of net income is from Cuban operations, reflecting a 60% increase over the prior year. The remaining $60,000 of net income is from U.S. operations, reflecting a 40% decrease. Does this segment information impact your loan decision? ■

## DEMONSTRATION PROBLEM—PERPETUAL SYSTEM

Pepper Company completed the following selected transactions and events during March of this year. (Terms of all credit sales for the company are 2/10, n/30.)

Mar.  4   Sold merchandise on credit to Jennifer Nelson, Invoice No. 954, for $16,800 (cost is $12,200).
     6   Purchased $1,220 of office supplies on credit from Mack Company. Invoice dated March 3, terms n/30.
     6   Sold merchandise on credit to Dennie Hoskins, Invoice No. 955, for $10,200 (cost is $8,100).
    11   Purchased $52,600 of merchandise, invoice dated March 6, terms 2/10, n/30, from Defore Industries.
    12   Borrowed $26,000 cash by giving Commerce Bank a long-term promissory note payable.
    14   Received cash payment from Jennifer Nelson for the March 4 sale less the discount (Invoice No. 954).
    16   Received a $200 credit memorandum from Defore Industries for unsatisfactory merchandise Pepper purchased on March 11 and later returned.
    16   Received cash payment from Dennie Hoskins for the March 6 sale less the discount (Invoice No. 955).
    18   Purchased $22,850 of store equipment on credit from Schmidt Supply, invoice dated March 15, terms n/30.
    20   Sold merchandise on credit to Marjorie Allen, Invoice No. 956, for $5,600 (cost is $3,800).
    21   Sent Defore Industries Check No. 516 in payment of its March 6 dated invoice less the return and the discount.
    22   Purchased $41,625 of merchandise, invoice dated March 18, terms 2/10, n/30, from Welch Company.
    26   Issued a $600 credit memorandum to Marjorie Allen for defective merchandise Pepper sold on March 20 and Allen later returned.
    31   Issued Check No. 517, payable to Payroll, in payment of $15,900 sales salaries for the month. Cashed the check and paid the employees.
    31   Cash sales for the month are $134,680 (cost is $67,340). (Cash sales are recorded daily but are recorded only once here to reduce repetitive entries.)

### Required

1. Open the following selected general ledger accounts: Cash (101), Accounts Receivable (106) Inventory (119), Office Supplies (124), Store Equipment (165), Accounts Payable (201), Long-Term Notes Payable (251), Sales (413), Sales Returns and Allowances (414), Sales Discounts (415), Cost of Goods Sold (502), and Sales Salaries Expense (621). Open the following accounts receivable ledger accounts: Marjorie Allen, Dennie Hoskins, and Jennifer Nelson. Open the following accounts payable ledger accounts: Defore Industries, Mack Company, Schmidt Supply, and Welch Company.

2. Enter the transactions using a sales journal, a purchases journal, a cash receipts journal, a cash disbursements journal, and a general journal similar to the ones illustrated in the chapter. Regularly post to the individual customer and creditor accounts. Also, post any amounts that should be posted as individual amounts to general ledger accounts. Foot and crossfoot the journals and make the month-end postings. *Pepper Co. uses the perpetual inventory system.*

3. Prepare a trial balance for the selected general ledger accounts in part 1 and prove the accuracy of subsidiary ledgers by preparing schedules of accounts receivable and accounts payable.

## PLANNING THE SOLUTION

- Set up the required general ledger, the subsidiary ledger accounts, and the five required journals as illustrated in the chapter.
- Read and analyze each transaction and decide in which special journal (or general journal) the transaction is recorded.
- Record each transaction in the proper journal (and post the appropriate individual amounts).
- Once you have recorded all transactions, total the journal columns. Post from each journal to the appropriate ledger accounts.
- Prepare a trial balance to prove the equality of the debit and credit balances in your general ledger.
- Prepare schedules of accounts receivable and accounts payable. Compare the totals of these schedules to the Accounts Receivable and Accounts Payable controlling account balances, making sure that they agree.

## SOLUTION TO DEMONSTRATION PROBLEM—PERPETUAL SYSTEM

**Sales Journal** — Page 2

| Date | Account Debited | Invoice Number | PR | Accounts Receivable Dr. Sales Cr. | Cost of Goods Sold Dr. Inventory Cr. |
|---|---|---|---|---|---|
| Mar. 4 | Jennifer Nelson | 954 | ✓ | 16,800 | 12,200 |
| 6 | Dennie Hoskins | 955 | ✓ | 10,200 | 8,100 |
| 20 | Marjorie Allen | 956 | ✓ | 5,600 | 3,800 |
| 31 | Totals | | | 32,600 | 24,100 |
| | | | | (106/413) | (502/119) |

**Cash Receipts Journal** — Page 3

| Date | Account Credited | Explanation | PR | Cash Dr. | Sales Discount Dr. | Accounts Receivable Cr. | Sales Cr. | Other Accounts Cr. | Cost of Goods Sold Dr. Inventory Cr. |
|---|---|---|---|---|---|---|---|---|---|
| Mar. 12 | L.T. Notes Payable | Note to bank | 251 | 26,000 | | | | 26,000 | |
| 14 | Jennifer Nelson | Invoice 954, 3/4 | ✓ | 16,464 | 336 | 16,800 | | | |
| 16 | Dennie Hoskins | Invoice 955, 3/6 | ✓ | 9,996 | 204 | 10,200 | | | |
| 31 | Sales | Cash sales | x | 134,680 | | | 134,680 | | 67,340 |
| 31 | Totals | | | 187,140 | 540 | 27,000 | 134,680 | 26,000 | 67,340 |
| | | | | (101) | (415) | (106) | (413) | (x) | (502/119) |

**Purchases Journal** — Page 3

| Date | Account | Date of Invoice | Terms | PR | Accounts Payable Cr. | Inventory Dr. | Office Supplies Dr. | Other Accounts Dr. |
|---|---|---|---|---|---|---|---|---|
| Mar. 6 | Office Supplies/Mack Co | 3/3 | n/30 | ✓ | 1,220 | | 1,220 | |
| 11 | Defore Industries | 3/6 | 2/10, n/30 | ✓ | 52,600 | 52,600 | | |
| 18 | Store Equipment/Schmidt Supp | 3/15 | n/30 | 165/✓ | 22,850 | | | 22,850 |
| 22 | Welch Company | 3/18 | 2/10, n/30 | ✓ | 41,625 | 41,625 | | |
| 31 | Totals | | | | 118,295 | 94,225 | 1,220 | 22,850 |
| | | | | | (201) | (119) | (124) | (x) |

**Cash Disbursements Journal** — Page 3

| Date | Ck. No. | Payee | Account Debited | PR | Cash Cr. | Inventory Cr. | Other Accounts Dr. | Accounts Payable Dr. |
|---|---|---|---|---|---|---|---|---|
| Mar. 21 | 516 | Defore Industries | Defore Industries | ✓ | 51,352 | 1,048 | | 52,400 |
| 31 | 517 | Payroll | Sales Salaries Expense | 621 | 15,900 | | 15,900 | |
| 31 | | Totals | | | 67,252 | 1,048 | 15,900 | 52,400 |
| | | | | | (101) | (119) | (x) | (201) |

**General Journal** — Page 2

| | | | | |
|---|---|---|---|---|
| Mar. 16 | Accounts Payable—Defore Industries | 201/✓ | 200 | |
| | Inventory | 119 | | 200 |
| | *To record credit memorandum received.* | | | |
| 26 | Sales Returns and Allowances | 414 | 600 | |
| | Accounts Receivable—Marjorie Allen | 106/✓ | | 600 |
| | *To record credit memorandum issued.* | | | |

## Accounts Receivable Ledger

**Marjorie Allen**

| Date | PR | Debit | Credit | Balance |
|---|---|---|---|---|
| Mar. 20 | S2 | 5,600 | | 5,600 |
| 26 | G2 | | 600 | 5,000 |

**Dennie Hoskins**

| Date | PR | Debit | Credit | Balance |
|---|---|---|---|---|
| Mar. 6 | S2 | 10,200 | | 10,200 |
| 16 | R3 | | 10,200 | 0 |

**Jennifer Nelson**

| Date | PR | Debit | Credit | Balance |
|---|---|---|---|---|
| Mar. 4 | S2 | 16,800 | | 16,800 |
| 14 | R3 | | 16,800 | 0 |

## Accounts Payable Ledger

**Defore Industries**

| Date | PR | Debit | Credit | Balance |
|---|---|---|---|---|
| Mar. 11 | P3 | | 52,600 | 52,600 |
| 16 | G2 | 200 | | 52,400 |
| 21 | D3 | 52,400 | | 0 |

**Mack Company**

| Date | PR | Debit | Credit | Balance |
|---|---|---|---|---|
| Mar. 6 | P3 | | 1,220 | 1,220 |

**Schmidt Supply**

| Date | PR | Debit | Credit | Balance |
|---|---|---|---|---|
| Mar. 18 | P3 | | 22,850 | 22,850 |

**Welch Company**

| Date | PR | Debit | Credit | Balance |
|---|---|---|---|---|
| Mar. 22 | P3 | | 41,625 | 41,625 |

## General Ledger (Partial Listing)

**Cash** — Acct. No. 101

| Date | PR | Debit | Credit | Balance |
|---|---|---|---|---|
| Mar. 31 | R3 | 187,140 | | 187,140 |
| 31 | D3 | | 67,252 | 119,888 |

**Accounts Receivable** — Acct. No. 106

| Date | PR | Debit | Credit | Balance |
|---|---|---|---|---|
| Mar. 26 | G2 | | 600 | (600) |
| 31 | S2 | 32,600 | | 32,000 |
| 31 | R3 | | 27,000 | 5,000 |

**Inventory** — Acct. No. 119

| Date | PR | Debit | Credit | Balance |
|---|---|---|---|---|
| Mar. 16 | G2 | | 200 | (200) |
| 21 | D3 | | 1,048 | (1,248) |
| 31 | P3 | 94,225 | | 92,977 |
| 31 | S2 | | 24,100 | 68,877 |
| 31 | R3 | | 67,340 | 1,537 |

**Office Supplies** — Acct. No. 124

| Date | PR | Debit | Credit | Balance |
|---|---|---|---|---|
| Mar. 31 | P3 | 1,220 | | 1,220 |

**Store Equipment** — Acct. No. 165

| Date | PR | Debit | Credit | Balance |
|---|---|---|---|---|
| Mar. 18 | P3 | 22,850 | | 22,850 |

**Accounts Payable** — Acct. No. 201

| Date | PR | Debit | Credit | Balance |
|---|---|---|---|---|
| Mar. 16 | G2 | 200 | | (200) |
| 31 | P3 | | 118,295 | 118,095 |
| 31 | D3 | 52,400 | | 65,695 |

**Long-Term Notes Payable** — Acct. No. 251

| Date | PR | Debit | Credit | Balance |
|---|---|---|---|---|
| Mar. 12 | R3 | | 26,000 | 26,000 |

**Sales** — Acct. No. 413

| Date | PR | Debit | Credit | Balance |
|---|---|---|---|---|
| Mar. 31 | S2 | | 32,600 | 32,600 |
| 31 | R3 | | 134,680 | 167,280 |

**Sales Returns and Allowances** — Acct. No. 414

| Date | PR | Debit | Credit | Balance |
|---|---|---|---|---|
| Mar. 26 | G2 | 600 | | 600 |

**Sales Discounts** — Acct. No. 415

| Date | PR | Debit | Credit | Balance |
|---|---|---|---|---|
| Mar. 31 | R3 | 540 | | 540 |

**Cost of Goods Sold** — Acct. No. 502

| Date | PR | Debit | Credit | Balance |
|---|---|---|---|---|
| Mar. 31 | R3 | 67,340 | | 67,340 |
| 31 | S2 | 24,100 | | 91,440 |

**Sales Salaries Expense** — Acct. No. 621

| Date | PR | Debit | Credit | Balance |
|---|---|---|---|---|
| Mar. 31 | D3 | 15,900 | | 15,900 |

**PEPPER COMPANY**
**Trial Balance (partial)**
**March 31**

| | Debit | Credit |
|---|---|---|
| Cash | $119,888 | |
| Accounts receivable | 5,000 | |
| Inventory | 1,537 | |
| Office supplies | 1,220 | |
| Store equipment | 22,850 | |
| Accounts payable | | $ 65,695 |
| Long-term notes payable | | 26,000 |
| Sales | | 167,280 |
| Sales returns and allowances | 600 | |
| Sales discounts | 540 | |
| Cost of goods sold | 91,440 | |
| Sales salaries expense | 15,900 | |
| Totals | $258,975 | $258,975 |

reconciled

reconciled

**PEPPER COMPANY**
**Schedule of Accounts Receivable**
**March 31**

| | |
|---|---|
| Marjorie Allen | $5,000 |
| Total accounts receivable | $5,000 |

**PEPPER COMPANY**
**Schedule of Accounts Payable**
**March 31**

| | |
|---|---|
| Mack Company | $ 1,220 |
| Schmidt Supply | 22,850 |
| Welch Company | 41,625 |
| Total accounts payable | $65,695 |

---

**APPENDIX**

# 7A

# Special Journals under a Periodic System

**P3** Journalize and post transactions using special journals in a periodic inventory system.

This appendix describes special journals under a periodic inventory system. Each journal is slightly impacted. The sales journal and the cash receipts journal both require one less column (namely that of Cost of Goods Sold Dr., Inventory Cr.). The Purchases Journal replaces the Inventory Dr. column with a Purchases Dr. column in a periodic system. The cash disbursements journal replaces the Inventory Cr. column with a Purchases Discounts Cr. column in a periodic system. These changes are illustrated.

**Sales Journal**   The sales journal using the periodic inventory system is shown in Exhibit 7A.1. The difference in the sales journal between the perpetual and periodic system is the exclusion of the column to record cost of goods sold and inventory amounts for each sale. The periodic system does *not* record the increase in cost of goods sold and the decrease in inventory at the time of each sale.

**EXHIBIT 7A.1**

Sales Journal—Periodic System

| Sales Journal | | | | Page 3 |
|---|---|---|---|---|
| Date | Account Debited | Invoice Number | PR | Accounts Receivable Dr. Sales Cr. |
| Feb. 2 | Jason Henry | 307 | ✓ | 450 |
| 7 | Albert Co. | 308 | ✓ | 500 |
| 13 | Kam Moore | 309 | ✓ | 350 |
| 15 | Paul Roth | 310 | ✓ | 200 |
| 22 | Jason Henry | 311 | ✓ | 225 |
| 25 | Frank Booth | 312 | ✓ | 175 |
| 28 | Albert Co. | 313 | ✓ | 250 |
| 28 | Total | | | 2,150 |
| | | | | (106/413) |

**Cash Receipts Journal**  The cash receipts journal using the periodic system is shown in Exhibit 7A.2. Note the absence of the column on the far right side to record debits to Cost of Goods Sold and credits to Inventory for the cost of merchandise sold (seen under the perpetual system). Consistent with the cash receipts journal shown in Exhibit 7.7, we show only the weekly (summary) cash sale entries.

**EXHIBIT 7A.2**

Cash Receipts Journal—Periodic System

| Cash Receipts Journal | | | | | | | | Page 2 |
|---|---|---|---|---|---|---|---|---|
| Date | Account Credited | Explanation | PR | Cash Dr. | Sales Discount Dr. | Accounts Receivable Cr. | Sales Cr. | Other Accounts Cr. |
| Feb. 7 | Sales | Cash sales | x | 4,450 | | | 4,450 | |
| 12 | Jason Henry | Invoice 307, 2/2 | ✓ | 441 | 9 | 450 | | |
| 14 | Sales | Cash sales | x | 3,925 | | | 3,925 | |
| 17 | Albert Co. | Invoice 308, 2/7 | ✓ | 490 | 10 | 500 | | |
| 20 | Notes Payable | Note to bank | 245 | 750 | | | | 750 |
| 21 | Sales | Cash sales | x | 4,700 | | | 4,700 | |
| 22 | Interest revenue | Bank account | 409 | 250 | | | | 250 |
| 23 | Kam Moore | Invoice 309, 2/13 | ✓ | 343 | 7 | 350 | | |
| 25 | Paul Roth | Invoice 310, 2/15 | ✓ | 196 | 4 | 200 | | |
| 28 | Sales | Cash sales | x | 4,225 | | | 4,225 | |
| 28 | Totals | | | 19,770 | 30 | 1,500 | 17,300 | 1,000 |
| | | | | (101) | (415) | (106) | (413) | (x) |

**Purchases Journal**  The purchases journal using the periodic system is shown in Exhibit 7A.3. This journal under a perpetual system included an Inventory column where the periodic system now has a Purchases column.

**EXHIBIT 7A.3**

Purchases Journal—Periodic System

| Purchases Journal | | | | | | | | Page 1 |
|---|---|---|---|---|---|---|---|---|
| Date | Account | Date of Invoice | Terms | PR | Accounts Payable Cr. | Purchases Dr. | Office Supplies Dr. | Other Accounts Dr. |
| Feb. 3 | Horning Supply Co. | 2/2 | n/30 | ✓ | 350 | 275 | 75 | |
| 5 | Ace Mfg. Co. | 2/5 | 2/10, n/30 | ✓ | 200 | 200 | | |
| 13 | Wynet and Co. | 2/10 | 2/10, n/30 | ✓ | 150 | 150 | | |
| 20 | Smite Co. | 2/18 | 2/10, n/30 | ✓ | 300 | 300 | | |
| 25 | Ace Mfg. Co. | 2/24 | 2/10, n/30 | ✓ | 100 | 100 | | |
| 28 | Store Supplies/ITT Co. | 2/28 | n/30 | 125/✓ | 225 | 125 | 25 | 75 |
| 28 | Totals | | | | 1,325 | 1,150 | 100 | 75 |
| | | | | | (201) | (505) | (124) | (x) |

**Cash Disbursements Journal**  The cash disbursements journal using a periodic system is shown in Exhibit 7A.4. This journal under the perpetual system included an Inventory column where the periodic system now has the Purchases Discounts column.

**EXHIBIT 7A.4**

Cash Disbursements Journal—Periodic System

| Cash Disbursements Journal | | | | | | | | Page 2 |
|---|---|---|---|---|---|---|---|---|
| Date | Ck. No. | Payee | Account Debited | PR | Cash Cr. | Purchases Discounts Cr. | Other Accounts Dr. | Accounts Payable Dr. |
| Feb. 3 | 105 | L. and N. Railroad | Purchases | 505 | 15 | | 15 | |
| 12 | 106 | East Sales Co. | Purchases | 505 | 25 | | 25 | |
| 15 | 107 | Ace Mfg. Co. | Ace Mfg. Co. | ✓ | 196 | 4 | | 200 |
| 15 | 108 | Jerry Hale | Salaries Expense | 622 | 250 | | 250 | |
| 20 | 109 | Wynet and Co. | Wynet and Co. | ✓ | 147 | 3 | | 150 |
| 28 | 110 | Smite Co. | Smite Co. | ✓ | 294 | 6 | | 300 |
| 28 | | Totals | | | 927 | 13 | 290 | 650 |
| | | | | | (101) | (507) | (x) | (201) |

# DEMONSTRATION PROBLEM—PERIODIC SYSTEM

Refer to Pepper Company's selected transactions described under the Demonstration Problem—Perpetual System to fulfill the following requirements.

**Required**

1. Open the following selected general ledger accounts: Cash (101), Accounts Receivable (106), Office Supplies (124), Store Equipment (165), Accounts Payable (201), Long-Term Notes Payable (251), Sales (413), Sales Returns and Allowances (414), Sales Discounts (415), Purchases (505), Purchases

Returns and Allowances (506), Purchases Discounts (507), and Sales Salaries Expense (621). Open the following accounts receivable ledger accounts: Marjorie Allen, Dennie Hoskins, and Jennifer Nelson. Open the following accounts payable ledger accounts: Defore Industries, Mack Company, Schmidt Supply, and Welch Company.

2. Enter the transactions using a sales journal, a purchases journal, a cash receipts journal, a cash disbursements journal, and a general journal similar to the ones illustrated in Appendix 7A. Regularly post to the individual customer and creditor accounts. Also, post any amounts that should be posted as individual amounts to general ledger accounts. Foot and crossfoot the journals and make the month-end postings. *Pepper Co. uses the periodic inventory system in this problem.*

3. Prepare a trial balance for the selected general ledger accounts in part 1 and prove the accuracy of subsidiary ledgers by preparing schedules of accounts receivable and accounts payable.

## SOLUTION TO DEMONSTRATION PROBLEM—PERIODIC SYSTEM

**Sales Journal**                                                                 Page 2

| Date | Account Debited | Invoice Number | PR | Accounts Receivable Dr. Sales Cr. |
|---|---|---|---|---|
| Mar. 4 | Jennifer Nelson | 954 | ✓ | 16,800 |
| 6 | Dennie Hoskins | 955 | ✓ | 10,200 |
| 20 | Marjorie Allen | 956 | ✓ | 5,600 |
| 31 | Totals | | | 32,600 |
| | | | | (106/413) |

**Cash Receipts Journal**                                                        Page 3

| Date | Account Credited | Explanation | PR | Cash Dr. | Sales Discount Dr. | Accounts Receivable Cr. | Sales Cr. | Other Accounts Cr. |
|---|---|---|---|---|---|---|---|---|
| Mar. 12 | L.T. Notes Payable | Note to bank | 251 | 26,000 | | | | 26,000 |
| 14 | Jennifer Nelson | Invoice 954, 3/4 | ✓ | 16,464 | 336 | 16,800 | | |
| 16 | Dennie Hoskins | Invoice 955, 3/6 | ✓ | 9,996 | 204 | 10,200 | | |
| 31 | Sales | Cash sales | x | 134,680 | | | 134,680 | |
| 31 | Totals | | | 187,140 | 540 | 27,000 | 134,680 | 26,000 |
| | | | | (101) | (415) | (106) | (413) | (x) |

**Purchases Journal**                                                            Page 3

| Date | Account | Date of Invoice | Terms | PR | Accounts Payable Cr. | Purchases Dr. | Office Supplies Dr. | Other Accounts Dr. |
|---|---|---|---|---|---|---|---|---|
| Mar. 6 | Office Supplies/Mack Co | 3/3 | n/30 | ✓ | 1,220 | | 1,220 | |
| 11 | Defore Industries | 3/6 | 2/10, n/30 | ✓ | 52,600 | 52,600 | | |
| 18 | Store Equipment/Schmidt Supp | 3/15 | n/30 | 165/✓ | 22,850 | | | 22,850 |
| 22 | Welch Company | 3/18 | 2/10, n/30 | ✓ | 41,625 | 41,625 | | |
| 31 | Totals | | | | 118,295 | 94,225 | 1,220 | 22,850 |
| | | | | | (201) | (505) | (124) | (x) |

**Cash Disbursements Journal**                                                   Page 3

| Date | Ck. No. | Payee | Account Debited | PR | Cash Cr. | Purchases Discount Cr. | Other Accounts Dr. | Accounts Payable Dr. |
|---|---|---|---|---|---|---|---|---|
| Mar. 21 | 516 | Defore Industries | Defore Industries | ✓ | 51,352 | 1,048 | | 52,400 |
| 31 | 517 | Payroll | Sales Salaries Expense | 621 | 15,900 | | 15,900 | |
| 31 | | Totals | | | 67,252 | 1,048 | 15,900 | 52,400 |
| | | | | | (101) | (507) | (x) | (201) |

**General Journal**                                                              Page 2

| | | | | |
|---|---|---|---|---|
| Mar. 16 | Accounts Payable—Defore Industries . . . . . . . . . . . . . | 201/✓ | 200 | |
| | Purchases Returns and Allowances . . . . . . . . . . . | 506 | | 200 |
| | *To record credit memorandum received.* | | | |
| 26 | Sales Returns and Allowances . . . . . . . . . . . . . . . . . . . | 414 | 600 | |
| | Accounts Receivable—Marjorie Allen . . . . . . . . . | 106/✓ | | 600 |
| | *To record credit memorandum issued.* | | | |

## Accounts Receivable Ledger

### Marjorie Allen

| Date | PR | Debit | Credit | Balance |
|---|---|---|---|---|
| Mar. 20 | S2 | 5,600 | | 5,600 |
| 26 | G2 | | 600 | 5,000 |

### Dennie Hoskins

| Date | PR | Debit | Credit | Balance |
|---|---|---|---|---|
| Mar. 6 | S2 | 10,200 | | 10,200 |
| 16 | R3 | | 10,200 | 0 |

### Jennifer Nelson

| Date | PR | Debit | Credit | Balance |
|---|---|---|---|---|
| Mar. 4 | S2 | 16,800 | | 16,800 |
| 14 | R3 | | 16,800 | 0 |

## Accounts Payable Ledger

### Defore Industries

| Date | PR | Debit | Credit | Balance |
|---|---|---|---|---|
| Mar. 11 | P3 | | 52,600 | 52,600 |
| 16 | G2 | 200 | | 52,400 |
| 21 | D3 | 52,400 | | 0 |

### Mack Company

| Date | PR | Debit | Credit | Balance |
|---|---|---|---|---|
| Mar. 6 | P3 | | 1,220 | 1,220 |

### Schmidt Supply

| Date | PR | Debit | Credit | Balance |
|---|---|---|---|---|
| Mar. 18 | P3 | | 22,850 | 22,850 |

### Welch Company

| Date | PR | Debit | Credit | Balance |
|---|---|---|---|---|
| Mar. 22 | P3 | | 41,625 | 41,625 |

## General Ledger (Partial Listing)

### Cash                                             Acct. No. 101

| Date | PR | Debit | Credit | Balance |
|---|---|---|---|---|
| Mar. 31 | R3 | 187,140 | | 187,140 |
| 31 | D3 | | 67,252 | 119,888 |

### Accounts Receivable                             Acct. No. 106

| Date | PR | Debit | Credit | Balance |
|---|---|---|---|---|
| Mar. 26 | G2 | | 600 | (600) |
| 31 | S2 | 32,600 | | 32,000 |
| 31 | R3 | | 27,000 | 5,000 |

### Office Supplies                                 Acct. No. 124

| Date | PR | Debit | Credit | Balance |
|---|---|---|---|---|
| Mar. 31 | P3 | 1,220 | | 1,220 |

### Store Equipment                                 Acct. No. 165

| Date | PR | Debit | Credit | Balance |
|---|---|---|---|---|
| Mar. 18 | P3 | 22,850 | | 22,850 |

### Accounts Payable                                Acct. No. 201

| Date | PR | Debit | Credit | Balance |
|---|---|---|---|---|
| Mar. 16 | G2 | 200 | | (200) |
| 31 | P3 | | 118,295 | 118,095 |
| 31 | D3 | 52,400 | | 65,695 |

### Long-Term Notes Payable                         Acct. No. 251

| Date | PR | Debit | Credit | Balance |
|---|---|---|---|---|
| Mar. 12 | R3 | | 26,000 | 26,000 |

### Sales                                           Acct. No. 413

| Date | PR | Debit | Credit | Balance |
|---|---|---|---|---|
| Mar. 31 | S2 | | 32,600 | 32,600 |
| 31 | R3 | | 134,680 | 167,280 |

### Sales Returns and Allowances      Acct. No. 414

| Date | PR | Debit | Credit | Balance |
|---|---|---|---|---|
| Mar. 26 | G2 | 600 | | 600 |

### Sales Discounts                                 Acct. No. 415

| Date | PR | Debit | Credit | Balance |
|---|---|---|---|---|
| Mar. 31 | R3 | 540 | | 540 |

### Purchases                                       Acct. No. 505

| Date | PR | Debit | Credit | Balance |
|---|---|---|---|---|
| Mar. 31 | P3 | 94,225 | | 94,225 |

### Purchases Returns and Allowances               Acct. No. 506

| Date | PR | Debit | Credit | Balance |
|---|---|---|---|---|
| Mar. 16 | G2 | | 200 | 200 |

### Purchases Discounts                             Acct. No. 507

| Date | PR | Debit | Credit | Balance |
|---|---|---|---|---|
| Mar. 31 | D3 | | 1,048 | 1,048 |

### Sales Salaries Expense                          Acct. No. 621

| Date | PR | Debit | Credit | Balance |
|---|---|---|---|---|
| Mar. 31 | D3 | 15,900 | | 15,900 |

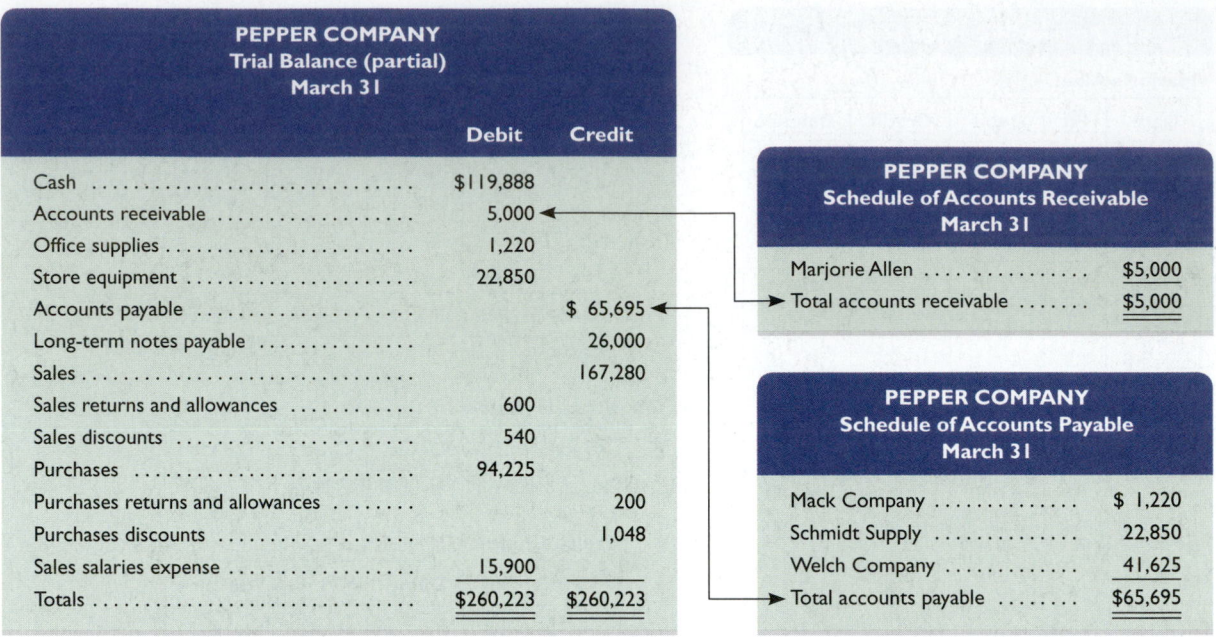

| PEPPER COMPANY Trial Balance (partial) March 31 | Debit | Credit |
|---|---|---|
| Cash | $119,888 | |
| Accounts receivable | 5,000 | |
| Office supplies | 1,220 | |
| Store equipment | 22,850 | |
| Accounts payable | | $ 65,695 |
| Long-term notes payable | | 26,000 |
| Sales | | 167,280 |
| Sales returns and allowances | 600 | |
| Sales discounts | 540 | |
| Purchases | 94,225 | |
| Purchases returns and allowances | | 200 |
| Purchases discounts | | 1,048 |
| Sales salaries expense | 15,900 | |
| Totals | $260,223 | $260,223 |

| PEPPER COMPANY Schedule of Accounts Receivable March 31 | |
|---|---|
| Marjorie Allen | $5,000 |
| Total accounts receivable | $5,000 |

| PEPPER COMPANY Schedule of Accounts Payable March 31 | |
|---|---|
| Mack Company | $ 1,220 |
| Schmidt Supply | 22,850 |
| Welch Company | 41,625 |
| Total accounts payable | $65,695 |

# Summary

**C1**   **Identify the principles and components of accounting information systems.** Accounting information systems are governed by five fundamental principles: control, relevance, compatibility, flexibility, and cost-benefit. The five basic components of an accounting information system are source documents, input devices, information processors, information storage, and output devices.

**C2**   **Explain the goals and uses of special journals.** Special journals are used for recording transactions of similar type, each meant to cover one kind of transaction. Four of the most common special journals are the sales journal, cash receipts journal, purchases journal, and cash disbursements journal. Special journals are efficient and cost-effective tools in the journalizing and posting processes.

**C3**   **Describe the use of controlling accounts and subsidiary ledgers.** A general ledger keeps controlling accounts such as Accounts Receivable and Accounts Payable, but details on individual accounts making up the controlling account are kept in subsidiary ledgers (such as an accounts receivable ledger). The balance in a controlling account must equal the sum of its subsidiary account balances after posting is complete.

**A1**   **Compute segment return on assets and use it to evaluate segment performance.** A business segment is a part of a company that is separately identified by its products or services or by the geographic market it serves. Analysis of a company's segments is aided by the segment return on assets (segment operating income divided by segment average assets).

**P1**   **Journalize and post transactions using special journals.** Each special journal is devoted to similar kinds of transactions. Transactions are journalized on one line of a special journal, with columns devoted to specific accounts, dates, names, posting references, explanations, and other necessary information. Posting is threefold: (1) individual amounts in the Other Accounts column are posted to their general ledger accounts on a regular (daily) basis, (2) individual amounts in a column whose total is *not* posted to a controlling account at the end of a period (month) are posted regularly (daily) to their general ledger accounts, and (3) total amounts for all columns except the Other Accounts column are posted at the end of a period (month) to their column's account title in the general ledger.

**P2**   **Prepare and prove the accuracy of subsidiary ledgers.** Account balances in the general ledger and its subsidiary ledgers are tested for accuracy after posting is complete. This procedure is twofold: (1) prepare a trial balance of the general ledger to confirm that debits equal credits and (2) prepare a schedule to confirm that the controlling account's balance equals the subsidiary ledger's balance.

**P3ᴬ**   **Journalize and post transactions using special journals in a periodic inventory system.** Transactions are journalized and posted using special journals in a periodic system. The methods are similar to those in a perpetual system; the primary difference is that both cost of goods sold and inventory are not adjusted at the time of each sale. This usually results in the deletion (or renaming) of one or more columns devoted to these accounts in each special journal.

---

**Guidance Answers to Decision Maker and Decision Ethics**

**Accountant**   The main issue is whether commissions have an actual or perceived impact on the integrity and objectivity of your advice. You probably should not accept a commission arrangement (the AICPA Code of Ethics prohibits it when you perform the audit or a review). In any event, you should tell the client of your commission arrangement. Also, you need to seriously examine the merits of agreeing to a commission arrangement when you are in a position to exploit it.

**Entrepreneur** The accounts receivable ledger has much of the information you need. It lists detailed information for each customer's account, including the amounts, dates for transactions, and dates of payments. It can be reorganized into an "aging schedule" to show how long customers wait before paying their bills.

**Controller** Much of the information you need is in the accounts payable ledger. It contains information for each supplier, the amounts due, and when payments are made. This subsidiary ledger along with information on credit terms should enable you to conduct your analyses.

**Banker** This merchandiser's segment information is likely to greatly impact your loan decision. The risks associated with the company's two sources of net income are quite different. While net income is up by 10%, U.S. operations are performing poorly and Cuban operations are subject to many uncertainties. These uncertainties depend on political events, legal issues, business relationships, Cuban economic conditions, and a host of other risks. Overall, net income results suggested a low-risk loan opportunity, but the segment information reveals a high-risk situation.

## Guidance Answers to Quick Checks

1. The five components are source documents, input devices, information processors, information storage, and output devices.

2. Information processors interpret, transform, and summarize the recorded accounting information so that it can be used in analysis, interpretation, and decision making.

3. Data saved in information storage are used to prepare periodic financial reports and special-purpose internal reports as well as source documentation for auditors.

4. All cash payments by check are recorded in the cash disbursements journal.

5. Columnar journals allow us to accumulate repetitive debits and credits and post them as column totals rather than as individual amounts from each entry.

6. The equality of debits and credits is kept within the general ledger. The subsidiary ledger keeps the customer's individual account and is used only for supplementary information.

7. An initial and the page number of the journal from which the amount was posted are entered in the PR column next to the amount.

8. A separate column for Sales Taxes Payable can be included in both the cash receipts journal and the sales journal.

9. This refers to a procedure of using copies of sales invoices as a sales journal. Each invoice amount is posted directly to the customer's account. All invoices are totaled at period-end for posting to the general ledger accounts.

10. The normal recording and posting procedures are threefold. First, transactions are entered in a special journal if applicable. Second, individual amounts are posted to any subsidiary ledger accounts. Third, column totals are posted to general ledger accounts if not already individually posted.

11. Controlling accounts are debited periodically for an amount or amounts equal to the sum of their respective debits in the subsidiary ledgers (equals journal column totals), and they are credited periodically for an amount or amounts equal to the sum of their respective credits in the subsidiary ledgers (from journal column totals).

12. Tests for accuracy of account balances in the general ledger and subsidiary ledgers are twofold. First, we prepare a trial balance of the general ledger to confirm that debits equal credits. Second, we prove the subsidiary ledgers by preparing schedules of accounts receivable and accounts payable.

13. The general journal is still needed for adjusting, closing, and correcting entries and for special transactions such as sales returns, purchases returns, and certain asset purchases.

14. Integrated systems can save time and minimize errors. This is so because actions taken in one part of the system automatically affect and update related parts.

15. Computer systems offer increased accuracy, speed, efficiency, and convenience.

16. Computer networks can create advantages by linking computers, and giving different users and different computers access to common databases, programs, and hardware.

17. ERP software involves integrated programs, from order taking to manufacturing to accounting. It can speed decision making, help identify costs for reduction, and aid managers in controlling operations.

## Key Terms

mhhe.com/wildFAP20e

Accounting information systems (p. 272)
Accounts payable ledger (p. 277)
Accounts receivable ledger (p. 277)
Batch processing (p. 286)
Cash disbursements journal (p. 284)
Cash receipts journal (p. 281)
Check register (p. 284)
Columnar journal (p. 278)
Compatibility principle (p. 273)

Components of accounting systems (p. 273)
Computer network (p. 286)
Control principle (p. 272)
Controlling account (p. 277)
Cost-benefit principle (p. 273)
Enterprise resource planning (ERP) software (p. 287)
Flexibility principle (p. 273)

General journal (p. 276)
Information processor (p. 274)
Information storage (p. 274)
Input device (p. 274)
Internal controls (p. 272)
Online processing (p. 286)
Output devices (p. 275)
Purchases journal (p. 283)
Relevance principle (p. 272)

Sales journal (p. 278)
Schedule of accounts payable (p. 284)

Schedule of accounts receivable (p. 279)
Segment return on assets (p. 288)

Special journal (p. 276)
Subsidiary ledger (p. 276)

## Multiple Choice Quiz          Answers on p. 313          mhhe.com/wildFAP20e

**Additional Quiz Questions are available at the book's Website.**

1. The sales journal is used to record
   a. Credit sales
   b. Cash sales
   c. Cash receipts
   d. Cash purchases
   e. Credit purchases

2. The purchases journal is used to record
   a. Credit sales
   b. Cash sales
   c. Cash receipts
   d. Cash purchases
   e. Credit purchases

3. The ledger that contains the financial statement accounts of a company is the
   a. General journal
   b. Column balance journal

   c. Special ledger
   d. General ledger
   e. Special journal

4. A subsidiary ledger that contains a separate account for each supplier (creditor) to the company is the
   a. Controlling account
   b. Accounts payable ledger
   c. Accounts receivable ledger
   d. General ledger
   e. Special journal

5. Enterprise resource planning software
   a. Refers to programs that help manage company operations.
   b. Is another name for spreadsheet programs.
   c. Uses batch processing of business information.
   d. Is substantially declining in use.
   e. Is another name for database programs.

ᴬ *Superscript letter A denotes assignments based on Appendix 7A.*
🔲 Icon denotes assignments that involve decision making.

## Discussion Questions

1. What are the five fundamental principles of accounting information systems?

2. What are five basic components of an accounting system?

3. What are source documents? Give two examples.

4. What is the purpose of an input device? Give examples of input devices for computer systems.

5. What is the difference between data that are stored off-line and data that are stored online?

6. What purpose is served by the output devices of an accounting system?

7. When special journals are used, they are usually used to record each of four different types of transactions. What are these four types of transactions?

8. What notations are entered into the Posting Reference column of a ledger account?

9. 🔲 When a general journal entry is used to record sales returns, the credit of the entry must be posted twice. Does this cause the trial balance to be out of balance? Explain.

10. Describe the procedures involving the use of copies of a company's sales invoices as a sales journal.

11. Credits to customer accounts and credits to Other Accounts are individually posted from a cash receipts journal such as the one in Exhibit 7.7. Why not put both types of credits in the same column and save journal space?

12. 🔲 Why should sales to and receipts of cash from credit customers be recorded and posted immediately?

13. 🔲 Locate the note that discusses **Research In Motion**'s operations by segments in Appendix A. In what segment does it predominantly operate?   *RIM*

14. 🔲 Does the income statement of **Palm** in Appendix A indicate the net income earned by its business segments? If so, list them.   *Palm*

15. Locate the note that discusses **Apple**'s segments from its 2009 annual report on its Website. What five reportable segments does Apple have?   *Apple*

16. 🔲 Does the balance sheet of **Nokia** in Appendix A indicate the identifiable assets owned by its business segments? If so, list them.   **NOKIA**

![connect]

*For account titles and numbers, use the Chart of Accounts at the end of the book.*

Identify the most likely role in an accounting system played by each of the numbered items 1 through 12 by assigning a letter from the list A through E on the left.

**A.** Source documents       _____    **1.** Bar code reader
**B.** Input devices          _____    **2.** Filing cabinet
**C.** Information processors    _____    **3.** Bank statement
**D.** Information storage      _____    **4.** Computer scanner
**E.** Output devices        _____    **5.** Computer keyboard
                                    _____    **6.** Zip drive
                                    _____    **7.** Computer monitor
                                    _____    **8.** Invoice from a supplier
                                    _____    **9.** Computer software
                                    _____    **10.** Computer printer
                                    _____    **11.** Digital camera
                                    _____    **12.** MP3 player

**QUICK STUDY**

**QS 7-1**
Accounting information system components
C1

---

Enter the letter of each system principle in the blank next to its best description.

**A.** Control principle          **D.** Flexibility principle
**B.** Relevance principle       **E.** Cost-benefit principle
**C.** Compatibility principle

**1.** _____ The principle prescribes the accounting information system to change in response to technological advances and competitive pressures.
**2.** _____ The principle prescribes the accounting information system to help monitor activities.
**3.** _____ The principle prescribes the accounting information system to provide timely information for effective decision making.
**4.** _____ The principle prescribes the accounting information system to adapt to the unique characteristics of the company.
**5.** _____ The principle that affects all other accounting information system principles.

**QS 7-2**
Accounting information system principles
C1

---

Fill in the blanks to complete the following descriptions.

**1.** _____ _____ _____ software comprises programs that help manage a company's vital operations, from manufacturing to accounting.
**2.** A computer _____ allows different computer users to share access to data and programs.
**3.** A _____ is an input device that captures writing and other input directly from source documents.
**4.** With _____ processing, source documents are accumulated for a period and then processed all at the same time, such as once a day, week, or month.

**QS 7-3**
Accounting information system
C1

---

General Electronics uses a sales journal, a purchases journal, a cash receipts journal, a cash disbursements journal, and a general journal as illustrated in this chapter. General recently completed the following transactions *a* through *h*. Identify the journal in which each transaction should be recorded.

**a.** Paid cash to a creditor.             **e.** Borrowed cash from the bank.
**b.** Sold merchandise on credit.       **f.** Sold merchandise for cash.
**c.** Purchased shop supplies on credit.     **g.** Purchased merchandise on credit.
**d.** Paid an employee's salary in cash.     **h.** Purchased inventory for cash.

**QS 7-4**
Identifying the special journal of entry
C2

---

Lue Gifts uses a sales journal, a purchases journal, a cash receipts journal, a cash disbursements journal, and a general journal as illustrated in this chapter. Journalize its March transactions that should be recorded in the general journal. For those not recorded in the general journal, identify the special journal where each should be recorded.

Mar.   2   The company purchased $2,900 of merchandise on credit from the Elko Co., terms 2/10, n/30.
      12   The owner, T. Lue, contributed an automobile worth $15,000 to the company.
      16   The company sold $1,100 of merchandise (cost is $700) on credit to K. Gould, terms n/30.
      19   K. Gould returned $150 of (worthless) merchandise to the company originally purchased on March 16 (assume the cost of this merchandise is left in cost of goods sold).

**QS 7-5**
Entries in the general journal
C2

**QS 7-6**

Controlling accounts and subsidiary ledgers

**C3**

Following is information from Thompson Company for its initial month of business. (1) Identify the balances listed in the accounts receivable subsidiary ledger. (2) Identify the accounts receivable balance listed in the general ledger at month's end.

| Credit Sales | | | Cash Collections | | |
|---|---|---|---|---|---|
| Jan. 10 | Boerman Company ........ | $3,000 | Jan. 20 | Boerman Company ........ | $2,000 |
| 19 | Lehman Brothers .......... | 1,600 | 28 | Lehman Brothers .......... | 1,600 |
| 23 | Finger Company ........... | 2,200 | 31 | Finger Company ........... | 1,300 |

---

**QS 7-7**

Purchases journal—perpetual

**P1**

Redmon Company uses a sales journal, a purchases journal, a cash receipts journal, a cash disbursements journal, and a general journal. The following transactions occur in the month of June.

June    1    Purchased $8,100 of merchandise on credit from Krause, Inc., terms n/30.
         8    Sold merchandise costing $900 on credit to G. Seles for $1,500 subject to a $30 sales discount if paid by the end of the month.
      14    Purchased $240 of store supplies from Chang Company on credit, terms n/30.
      17    Purchased $260 of office supplies on credit from Monder Company, terms n/30.
      24    Sold merchandise costing $400 to D. Lee for $630 cash.
      28    Purchased store supplies from Porter's for $90 cash.
      29    Paid Krause, Inc., $8,100 cash for the merchandise purchased on June 1.

Prepare headings for a purchases journal like the one in Exhibit 7.9. Journalize the June transactions that should be recorded in the purchases journal.

---

**QS 7-8**

Identifying journal of entry   **C2**

Refer to QS 7-7 and for each of the June transactions identify the journal in which it would be recorded. Assume the company uses a sales journal, purchases journal, cash receipts journal, cash disbursements journal, and general journal as illustrated in this chapter.

---

**QS 7-9ᴬ**

Purchases journal—periodic   **P3**

Prepare headings for a purchases journal like the one in Exhibit 7A.3. Journalize the June transactions from QS 7-7 that should be recorded in the purchases journal assuming the periodic inventory system is used.

---

**QS 7-10**

Accounts receivable ledger; posting from sales journal

**P2**

Winslow Company posts its sales invoices directly and then binds them into a Sales Journal. Winslow had the following credit sales to these customers during June.

| | | | |
|---|---|---|---|
| June | 2 | Joe Mack ............... | $ 3,600 |
| | 8 | Eric Horner ............ | 6,100 |
| | 10 | Tess Wilson ............ | 13,400 |
| | 14 | Hong Jiang ............. | 20,500 |
| | 20 | Tess Wilson ............ | 11,200 |
| | 29 | Joe Mack ............... | 7,300 |
| | | Total credit sales ........ | $62,100 |

*Required*

1. Open an accounts receivable subsidiary ledger having a T-account for each customer. Post the invoices to the subsidiary ledger.

2. Open an Accounts Receivable controlling T-account and a Sales T-account to reflect general ledger accounts. Post the end-of-month total from the sales journal to these accounts.

3. Prepare a schedule of accounts receivable and prove that its total equals the Accounts Receivable controlling account balance.

---

**QS 7-11**

Analyzing segment reports

**A1**

Apple

**Apple** reports the following operating income (and average assets in parentheses) for each of its geographic segments—$ millions: Americas, $6,637 ($1,882); Europe, $4,296 ($1,352); and Japan, $961 ($483). Apple also reports the following sales (only) by product segments: iPhone, $13,033; iPod, $8,091; Desktops, $4,324; Portables, $9,535; Other, $7,922. Compute Apple's return on assets for each of its geographic segments, and assess the relative performance of these segments. Compute the percentage of total sales for each of its five product segments.

Nestlé, a Switzerland-based company, uses a sales journal, a purchases journal, a cash receipts journal, a cash disbursements journal, and a general journal in a manner similar to that explained in this chapter. Journalize the following summary transactions of Nestlé transactions that should be recorded in the general journal. For those not recorded in the general journal, identify only the special journal where each should be recorded. (All amounts in millions of Swiss franc, CHF.)

1. Nestlé purchased CHF 8,000 of merchandise on credit from the suppliers.

2. Nestlé sold CHF 100,000 of merchandise (cost is CHF 44,000) on credit to customers.

3. A key customer returned CHF 900 of (worthless) merchandise to Nestlé (assume the cost of this merchandise is left in cost of goods sold).

**QS 7-12**
International accounting and special journals

C2

![McGraw Hill connect]

*For account titles and numbers, use the Chart of Accounts at the end of the book.*

**EXERCISES**

Hutton Company uses a sales journal, a purchases journal, a cash receipts journal, a cash disbursements journal, and a general journal. The following transactions occur in the month of March.

Mar. 2   Sold merchandise costing $300 to B. Fager for $450 cash, invoice no. 5703.
5   Purchased $2,300 of merchandise on credit from Marsh Corp.
7   Sold merchandise costing $800 to J. Dryer for $1,150, terms 2/10, n/30, invoice no. 5704.
8   Borrowed $8,000 cash by signing a note payable to the bank.
12   Sold merchandise costing $200 to R. Land for $320, terms n/30, invoice no. 5705.
16   Received $1,127 cash from J. Dryer to pay for the purchase of March 7.
19   Sold used store equipment for $900 cash to Malone, Inc.
25   Sold merchandise costing $350 to T. Burton for $550, terms n/30, invoice no. 5706.

Prepare headings for a sales journal like the one in Exhibit 7.5. Journalize the March transactions that should be recorded in this sales journal.

**Exercise 7-1**
Sales journal—perpetual

P1

Refer to Exercise 7-1 and for each of the March transactions identify the journal in which it would be recorded. Assume the company uses a sales journal, purchases journal, cash receipts journal, cash disbursements journal, and general journal as illustrated in this chapter.

**Exercise 7-2**
Identifying journal of entry  C2

Prepare headings for a sales journal like the one in Exhibit 7A.1. Journalize the March transactions shown in Exercise 7-1 that should be recorded in the sales journal assuming that the periodic inventory system is used.

**Exercise 7-3**[A]
Sales journal—periodic  P3

Moeder Co. uses a sales journal, a purchases journal, a cash receipts journal, a cash disbursements journal, and a general journal. The following transactions occur in the month of November.

Nov. 3   The company purchased $3,100 of merchandise on credit from Hargrave Co., terms n/20.
7   The company sold merchandise costing $840 on credit to J. York for $900, subject to an $18 sales discount if paid by the end of the month.
9   The company borrowed $2,750 cash by signing a note payable to the bank.
13   J. Emling, the owner, contributed $4,000 cash to the company.
18   The company sold merchandise costing $130 to B. Box for $230 cash.
22   The company paid Hargrave Co. $3,100 cash for the merchandise purchased on November 3.
27   The company received $882 cash from J. York in payment of the November 7 purchase.
30   The company paid salaries of $1,600 in cash.

Prepare headings for a cash receipts journal like the one in Exhibit 7.7. Journalize the November transactions that should be recorded in the cash receipts journal.

**Exercise 7-4**
Cash receipts journal—perpetual

P1

Refer to Exercise 7-4 and for each of the November transactions identify the journal in which it would be recorded. Assume the company uses a sales journal, purchases journal, cash receipts journal, cash disbursements journal, and general journal as illustrated in this chapter.

**Exercise 7-5**
Identifying journal of entry  C2

Prepare headings for a cash receipts journal like the one in Exhibit 7A.2. Journalize the November transactions shown in Exercise 7-4 that should be recorded in the cash receipts journal assuming that the periodic inventory system is used.

**Exercise 7-6**[A]
Cash receipts journal—periodic

P3

**Exercise 7-7**

Controlling accounts and subsidiary ledgers

C3

Following is information from Ryan Company for its initial month of business. (1) Identify the balances listed in the accounts payable subsidiary ledger. (2) Identify the accounts payable balance listed in the general ledger at month's end.

| Credit Purchases | | | Cash Paid | | |
|---|---|---|---|---|---|
| Jan. 9 | Boeder Company .......... | $7,000 | Jan. 19 | Boeder Company .......... | $5,100 |
| 18 | Johnson Brothers .......... | 6,600 | 27 | Johnson Brothers .......... | 6,600 |
| 22 | Padley Company ........... | 4,200 | 31 | Padley Company ........... | 3,400 |

**Exercise 7-8**

Cash disbursements journal—perpetual

P1

Pebblebrook Supply uses a sales journal, a purchases journal, a cash receipts journal, a cash disbursements journal, and a general journal. The following transactions occur in the month of April.

Apr. 3  Purchased merchandise for $2,750 on credit from Scott, Inc., terms 2/10, n/30.
     9  Issued check no. 210 to Kidman Corp. to buy store supplies for $450.
    12  Sold merchandise costing $400 on credit to C. Meyers for $670, terms n/30.
    17  Issued check no. 211 for $1,500 to pay off a note payable to City Bank.
    20  Purchased merchandise for $3,500 on credit from LeBron, terms 2/10, n/30.
    28  Issued check no. 212 to LeBron to pay the amount due for the purchase of April 20, less the discount.
    29  Paid salary of $1,700 to B. Decker by issuing check no. 213.
    30  Issued check no. 214 to Scott, Inc., to pay the amount due for the purchase of April 3.

Prepare headings for a cash disbursements journal like the one in Exhibit 7.11. Journalize the April transactions that should be recorded in the cash disbursements journal.

**Exercise 7-9**

Identifying journal of entry   C2

Refer to Exercise 7-8 and for each of the April transactions identify the journal in which it would be recorded. Assume the company uses a sales journal, purchases journal, cash receipts journal, cash disbursements journal, and general journal as illustrated in this chapter.

**Exercise 7-10^A**

Cash disbursements journal—periodic   P3

Prepare headings for a cash disbursements journal like the one in Exhibit 7A.4. Journalize the April transactions from Exercise 7-8 that should be recorded in the cash disbursements journal assuming that the periodic inventory system is used.

**Exercise 7-11**

Special journal transactions and error discovery

P1

Porter Pharmacy uses the following journals: sales journal, purchases journal, cash receipts journal, cash disbursements journal, and general journal. On June 5, Porter purchased merchandise priced at $12,000, subject to credit terms of 2/10, n/30. On June 14, the pharmacy paid the net amount due for the merchandise. In journalizing the payment, the pharmacy debited Accounts Payable for $12,000 but failed to record the cash discount on the purchases. Cash was properly credited for the actual $11,760 paid. (*a*) In what journals would the June 5 and the June 14 transactions be recorded? (*b*) What procedure is likely to discover the error in journalizing the June 14 transaction?

**Exercise 7-12**

Posting to subsidiary ledger accounts; preparing a schedule of accounts receivable

P2

At the end of May, the sales journal of Clear View appears as follows.

| Sales Journal | | | | | Page 2 |
|---|---|---|---|---|---|
| Date | Account Debited | Invoice Number | PR | Accounts Receivable Dr. Sales Cr. | Cost of Goods Sold Dr. Inventory Cr. |
| May 6 | Aaron Reckers | 190 | | 2,880 | 2,200 |
| 10 | Sara Reed | 191 | | 1,940 | 1,600 |
| 17 | Anna Page | 192 | | 850 | 500 |
| 25 | Sara Reed | 193 | | 340 | 200 |
| 31 | Totals | | | 6,010 | 4,500 |

Clear View also recorded the return of defective merchandise with the following entry.

| May 20 | Sales Returns and Allowances ..................... | 250 | |
|---|---|---|---|
| | Accounts Receivable—Anna Page ............. | | 250 |
| | *Customer returned (worthless) merchandise.* | | |

**Required**

1. Open an accounts receivable subsidiary ledger that has a T-account for each customer listed in the sales journal. Post to the customer accounts the entries in the sales journal and any portion of the general journal entry that affects a customer's account.

2. Open a general ledger that has T-accounts for Accounts Receivable, Inventory, Sales, Sales Returns and Allowances, and Cost of Goods Sold. Post the sales journal and any portion of the general journal entry that affects these accounts.

3. Prepare a schedule of accounts receivable and prove that its total equals the balance in the Accounts Receivable controlling account.

**Check**  (3) Ending Accounts Receivable, $5,760

---

A company that records credit purchases in a purchases journal and records purchases returns in a general journal made the following errors. Indicate when each error should be discovered.

1. Posted a purchases return to the Accounts Payable account and to the creditor's subsidiary account but did not post the purchases return to the Inventory account.

2. Posted a purchases return to the Inventory account and to the Accounts Payable account but did not post to the creditor's subsidiary account.

3. Correctly recorded a $4,000 purchase in the purchases journal but posted it to the creditor's subsidiary account as a $400 purchase.

4. Made an addition error in determining the balance of a creditor's subsidiary account.

5. Made an addition error in totaling the Office Supplies column of the purchases journal.

**Exercise 7-13**
Purchases journal and error identification

P1

---

Refer to Exhibit 7.13 and complete the segment return on assets table for Wolfe Company. Analyze your findings and identify the segment with the highest, and that with the lowest, segment return on assets.

**Exercise 7-14**
Computing and analyzing segment return on assets

A1

| Segment | Segment Operating Income (in $ mil.) | | Segment Assets (in $ mil.) | | Segment Return on Assets |
|---|---|---|---|---|---|
| | 2011 | 2010 | 2011 | 2010 | 2011 |
| **Specialty** | | | | | |
| Skiing Group ............. | $ 62 | $ 58 | $ 581 | $440 | |
| Skating Group ............ | 9 | 6 | 53 | 42 | |
| Specialty Footwear ........ | 22 | 19 | 155 | 136 | |
| Other Specialty ........... | 11 | 4 | 37 | 24 | |
| Subtotal ................. | 104 | 87 | 826 | 642 | |
| **General Merchandise** | | | | | |
| South America ............ | 32 | 36 | 305 | 274 | |
| United States ............. | 7 | 8 | 52 | 35 | |
| Europe ................... | 5 | 3 | 14 | 12 | |
| Subtotal ................. | 44 | 47 | 371 | 321 | |
| Total ..................... | $148 | $134 | $1197 | $963 | |

**Check**  Europe segment return, 38.5%

 connect

*For account titles and numbers, use the Chart of Accounts at the end of the book.*

**PROBLEM SET A**

Wise Company completes these transactions during April of the current year (the terms of all its credit sales are 2/10, n/30).

Apr. 2  Purchased $13,300 of merchandise on credit from Negi Company, invoice dated April 2, terms 2/10, n/60.
  3  Sold merchandise on credit to Brooke Sledd, Invoice No. 760, for $3,000 (cost is $2,000).
  3  Purchased $1,380 of office supplies on credit from Madison, Inc. Invoice dated April 2, terms n/10 EOM.
  4  Issued Check No. 587 to *U.S. View* for advertising expense, $999.
  5  Sold merchandise on credit to Paul Kohr, Invoice No. 761, for $8,000 (cost is $6,500).
  6  Received an $85 credit memorandum from Madison, Inc., for the return of some of the office supplies received on April 3.
  9  Purchased $11,125 of store equipment on credit from Ned's Supply, invoice dated April 9, terms n/10 EOM.

**Problem 7-1A**
Special journals, subsidiary ledgers, and schedule of accounts receivable—perpetual

C3 P1 P2

11   Sold merchandise on credit to Amy Nilson, Invoice No 762, for $9,500 (cost is $7,000).

12   Issued Check No. 588 to Negi Company in payment of its April 2 invoice, less the discount.

13   Received payment from Brooke Sledd for the April 3 sale, less the discount.

13   Sold $4,100 of merchandise on credit to Brooke Sledd (cost is $2,600), Invoice No. 763.

14   Received payment from Paul Kohr for the April 5 sale, less the discount.

16   Issued Check No. 589, payable to Payroll, in payment of sales salaries expense for the first half of the month, $9,750. Cashed the check and paid employees.

16   Cash sales for the first half of the month are $50,840 (cost is $33,880). (Cash sales are recorded daily from cash register data but are recorded only twice in this problem to reduce repetitive entries.)

17   Purchased $12,750 of merchandise on credit from Price Company, invoice dated April 17, terms 2/10, n/30.

18   Borrowed $50,000 cash from First State Bank by signing a long-term note payable.

20   Received payment from Amy Nilson for the April 11 sale, less the discount.

20   Purchased $730 of store supplies on credit from Ned's Supply, invoice dated April 19, terms n/10 EOM.

23   Received a $400 credit memorandum from Price Company for the return of defective merchandise received on April 17.

23   Received payment from Brooke Sledd for the April 13 sale, less the discount.

25   Purchased $10,375 of merchandise on credit from Negi Company, invoice dated April 24, terms 2/10, n/60.

26   Issued Check No. 590 to Price Company in payment of its April 17 invoice, less the return and the discount.

27   Sold $3,070 of merchandise on credit to Paul Kohr, Invoice No. 764 (cost is $2,420).

27   Sold $5,700 of merchandise on credit to Amy Nilson, Invoice No. 765 (cost is $3,305).

30   Issued Check No. 591, payable to Payroll, in payment of the sales salaries expense for the last half of the month, $9,750.

30   Cash sales for the last half of the month are $70,975 (cost is $55,900).

### Required

**1.** Prepare a sales journal like that in Exhibit 7.5 and a cash receipts journal like that in Exhibit 7.7. Number both journal pages as page 3. Then review the transactions of Wise Company and enter those that should be journalized in the sales journal and those that should be journalized in the cash receipts journal. Ignore any transactions that should be journalized in a purchases journal, a cash disbursements journal, or a general journal.

**2.** Open the following general ledger accounts: Cash, Accounts Receivable, Inventory, Long-Term Notes Payable, B. Wise, Capital, Sales, Sales Discounts, and Cost of Goods Sold. Enter the March 31 balances for Cash ($85,000), Inventory ($125,000), Long-Term Notes Payable ($110,000), and B. Wise, Capital ($100,000). Also open accounts receivable subsidiary ledger accounts for Paul Kohr, Brooke Sledd, and Amy Nilson.

**3.** Verify that amounts that should be posted as individual amounts from the journals have been posted. (Such items are immediately posted.) Foot and crossfoot the journals and make the month-end postings.

**Check**   Trial balance totals, $415,185     **4.** Prepare a trial balance of the general ledger and prove the accuracy of the subsidiary ledger by preparing a schedule of accounts receivable.

### Analysis Component

**5.** Assume that the total for the schedule of Accounts Receivable does not equal the balance of the controlling account in the general ledger. Describe steps you would take to discover the error(s).

---

### Problem 7-2A<sup>A</sup>

Special journals, subsidiary ledgers, and schedule of accounts receivable—periodic

C3   P2   P3

Assume that Wise Co. in Problem 7-1A uses the periodic inventory system.

### Required

**1.** Prepare headings for a sales journal like the one in Exhibit 7A.1. Prepare headings for a cash receipts journal like the one in Exhibit 7A.2. Journalize the April transactions shown in Problem 7-1A that should be recorded in the sales journal and the cash receipts journal assuming the *periodic* inventory system is used.

**2.** Open the general ledger accounts with balances as shown in Problem 7-1A (do not open a Cost of Goods Sold ledger account). Also open accounts receivable subsidiary ledger accounts for

Brooke Sledd, Paul Kohr, and Amy Nilson. Under the periodic system, an Inventory account exists but is inactive until its balance is updated to the correct inventory balance at year-end. In this problem, the Inventory account remains inactive but must be included to correctly complete the trial balance.

**3.** Complete parts 3, 4, and 5 of Problem 7-1A using the results of parts 1 and 2 of this problem.

**Check** Trial balance totals, $415,185

---

The April transactions of Wise Company are described in Problem 7-1A.

**Problem 7-3A**
Special journals, subsidiary ledgers, and schedule of accounts payable—perpetual

C3 P1 P2

*Required*

**1.** Prepare a general journal, a purchases journal like that in Exhibit 7.9, and a cash disbursements journal like that in Exhibit 7.11. Number all journal pages as page 3. Review the April transactions of Wise Company and enter those transactions that should be journalized in the general journal, the purchases journal, or the cash disbursements journal. Ignore any transactions that should be journalized in a sales journal or cash receipts journal.

**2.** Open the following general ledger accounts: Cash, Inventory, Office Supplies, Store Supplies, Store Equipment, Accounts Payable, Long-Term Notes Payable, B. Wise, Capital, Sales Salaries Expense, and Advertising Expense. Enter the March 31 balances of Cash ($85,000), Inventory ($125,000), Long-Term Notes Payable ($110,000), and B. Wise, Capital ($100,000). Also open accounts payable subsidiary ledger accounts for Ned's Supply, Negi Company, Price Company, and Madison, Inc.

**3.** Verify that amounts that should be posted as individual amounts from the journals have been posted. (Such items are immediately posted.) Foot and crossfoot the journals and make the month-end postings.

**4.** Prepare a trial balance of the general ledger and a schedule of accounts payable.

**Check** Trial balance totals, $233,525

---

Refer to Problem 7-1A and assume that Wise Co. uses the periodic inventory system.

**Problem 7-4A**[A]
Special journals, subsidiary ledgers, and schedule of accounts payable—periodic

C3 P2 P3

*Required*

**1.** Prepare a general journal, a purchases journal like that in Exhibit 7A.3, and a cash disbursements journal like that in Exhibit 7A.4. Number all journal pages as page 3. Review the April transactions of Wise Company (Problem 7-1A) and enter those transactions that should be journalized in the general journal, the purchases journal, or the cash disbursements journal. Ignore any transaction that should be journalized in a sales journal or cash receipts journal.

**2.** Open the following general ledger accounts: Cash, Inventory, Office Supplies, Store Supplies, Store Equipment, Accounts Payable, Long-Term Notes Payable, B. Wise, Capital, Purchases, Purchases Returns and Allowances, Purchases Discounts, Sales Salaries Expense, and Advertising Expense. Enter the March 31 balances of Cash ($85,000), Inventory ($125,000), Long-Term Notes Payable ($110,000), and B. Wise, Capital ($100,000). Also open accounts payable subsidiary ledger accounts for Ned's Supply, Negi Company, Price Company, and Madison, Inc.

**3.** Complete parts 3 and 4 of Problem 7-3A using the results of parts 1 and 2 of this problem.

**Check** Trial balance totals, $234,438

---

Bishop Company completes these transactions and events during March of the current year (terms for all its credit sales are 2/10, n/30).

**Problem 7-5A**
Special journals, subsidiary ledgers, trial balance—perpetual

C3 P1 P2

mhhe.com/wildFAP20e

Mar.  1   Purchased $42,600 of merchandise from Soy Industries, invoice dated March 1, terms 2/15, n/30.
 2   Sold merchandise on credit to Min Cho, Invoice No. 854, for $15,800 (cost is $7,900).
 3   Purchased $1,120 of office supplies on credit from Stacy Company, invoice dated March 3, terms n/10 EOM.
 3   Sold merchandise on credit to Lance Snow, Invoice No. 855, for $9,200 (cost is $4,600).
 6   Borrowed $72,000 cash from Federal Bank by signing a long-term note payable.
 9   Purchased $20,850 of office equipment on credit from Tells Supply, invoice dated March 9, terms n/10 EOM.
 10   Sold merchandise on credit to Taylor Few, Invoice No. 856, for $4,600 (cost is $2,300).
 12   Received payment from Min Cho for the March 2 sale less the discount.
 13   Sent Soy Industries Check No. 416 in payment of the March 1 invoice less the discount.
 13   Received payment from Lance Snow for the March 3 sale less the discount.
 14   Purchased $31,625 of merchandise from the JW Company, invoice dated March 13, terms 2/10, n/30.
 15   Issued Check No. 417, payable to Payroll, in payment of sales salaries expense for the first half of the month, $15,900. Cashed the check and paid the employees.

15    Cash sales for the first half of the month are $164,680 (cost is $138,000). (Cash sales are recorded daily, but are recorded only twice here to reduce repetitive entries.)

16    Purchased $1,670 of store supplies on credit from Stacy Company, invoice dated March 16, terms n/10 EOM.

17    Received a $2,425 credit memorandum from JW Company for the return of unsatisfactory merchandise purchased on March 14.

19    Received a $630 credit memorandum from Tells Supply for office equipment received on March 9 and returned for credit.

20    Received payment from Taylor Few for the sale of March 10 less the discount.

23    Issued Check No. 418 to JW Company in payment of the invoice of March 13 less the March 17 return and the discount.

27    Sold merchandise on credit to Taylor Few, Invoice No. 857, for $13,910 (cost is $6,220).

28    Sold merchandise on credit to Lance Snow, Invoice No. 858, for $5,315 (cost is $2,280).

31    Issued Check No. 419, payable to Payroll, in payment of sales salaries expense for the last half of the month, $15,900. Cashed the check and paid the employees.

31    Cash sales for the last half of the month are $174,590 (cost is $143,000).

31    Verify that amounts impacting customer and creditor accounts were posted and that any amounts that should have been posted as individual amounts to the general ledger accounts were posted. Foot and crossfoot the journals and make the month-end postings.

**Required**

1.    Open the following general ledger accounts: Cash; Accounts Receivable; Inventory (March 1 beg. bal. is $300,000); Office Supplies; Store Supplies; Office Equipment; Accounts Payable; Long-Term Notes Payable; M. Bishop, Capital (March 1 beg. bal. is $300,000); Sales; Sales Discounts; Cost of Goods Sold; and Sales Salaries Expense. Open the following accounts receivable subsidiary ledger accounts: Taylor Few, Min Cho, and Lance Snow. Open the following accounts payable subsidiary ledger accounts: Stacy Company, Soy Industries, Tells Supply, and JW Company.

2.    Enter these transactions in a sales journal like Exhibit 7.5, a purchases journal like Exhibit 7.9, a cash receipts journal like Exhibit 7.7, a cash disbursements journal like Exhibit 7.11, or a general journal. Number all journal pages as page 2.

**Check**   Trial balance totals, $783,105

3.    Prepare a trial balance of the general ledger and prove the accuracy of the subsidiary ledgers by preparing schedules of both accounts receivable and accounts payable.

---

**Problem 7-6A^A**

Special journals, subsidiary ledgers, trial balance—periodic

C3  P2  P3

mhhe.com/wildFAP20e

Assume that Bishop Company in Problem 7-5A uses the periodic inventory system.

**Required**

1.    Open the following general ledger accounts: Cash; Accounts Receivable; Inventory (March 1 beg. bal. is $300,000); Office Supplies; Store Supplies; Office Equipment; Accounts Payable; Long-Term Notes Payable; M. Bishop, Capital (March 1 beg. bal. is $300,000); Sales; Sales Discounts; Purchases; Purchases Returns and Allowances; Purchases Discounts; and Sales Salaries Expense. Open the following accounts receivable subsidiary ledger accounts: Taylor Few, Min Cho, and Lance Snow. Open the following accounts payable subsidiary ledger accounts: Stacy Company, Soy Industries, Tells Supply, and JW Company.

2.    Enter the transactions from Problem 7-5A in a sales journal like that in Exhibit 7A.1, a purchases journal like that in Exhibit 7A.3, a cash receipts journal like that in Exhibit 7A.2, a cash disbursements journal like that in Exhibit 7A.4, or a general journal. Number journal pages as page 2.

**Check**   Trial balance totals, $786,966

3.    Prepare a trial balance of the general ledger and prove the accuracy of the subsidiary ledgers by preparing schedules of both accounts receivable and accounts payable.

---

# PROBLEM SET B

For account titles and numbers, use the Chart of Accounts at the end of the book.

**Problem 7-1B**

Special journals, subsidiary ledgers, schedule of accounts receivable—perpetual

C3  P1  P2

Alcorn Industries completes these transactions during July of the current year (the terms of all its credit sales are 2/10, n/30).

July  1    Purchased $6,300 of merchandise on credit from Tahoe Company, invoice dated June 30, terms 2/10, n/30.

3    Issued Check No. 300 to *The Weekly* for advertising expense, $575.

5    Sold merchandise on credit to Kim Newsom, Invoice No. 918, for $18,400 (cost is $9,700).

6   Sold merchandise on credit to Ruth Baker, Invoice No. 919, for $7,500 (cost is $4,300).

7   Purchased $1,050 of store supplies on credit from Pryor, Inc., invoice dated July 7, terms n/10 EOM.

8   Received a $150 credit memorandum from Pryor, Inc., for the return of store supplies received on July 7.

9   Purchased $37,710 of store equipment on credit from Caro's Supply, invoice dated July 8, terms n/10 EOM.

10   Issued Check No. 301 to Tahoe Company in payment of its June 30 invoice, less the discount.

13   Sold merchandise on credit to Stephanie Meyer, Invoice No. 920, for $8,350 (cost is $5,030).

14   Sold merchandise on credit to Kim Newsom, Invoice No. 921, for $4,100 (cost is $2,800).

15   Received payment from Kim Newsom for the July 5 sale, less the discount.

15   Issued Check No. 302, payable to Payroll, in payment of sales salaries expense for the first half of the month, $30,620. Cashed the check and paid employees.

15   Cash sales for the first half of the month are $121,370 (cost is $66,330). (Cash sales are recorded daily using data from the cash registers but are recorded only twice in this problem to reduce repetitive entries.)

16   Received payment from Ruth Baker for the July 6 sale, less the discount.

17   Purchased $8,200 of merchandise on credit from Dixon Company, invoice dated July 17, terms 2/10, n/30.

20   Purchased $750 of office supplies on credit from Caro's Supply, invoice dated July 19, terms n/10 EOM.

21   Borrowed $20,000 cash from College Bank by signing a long-term note payable.

23   Received payment from Stephanie Meyer for the July 13 sale, less the discount.

24   Received payment from Kim Newsom for the July 14 sale, less the discount.

24   Received a $2,400 credit memorandum from Dixon Company for the return of defective merchandise received on July 17.

26   Purchased $9,770 of merchandise on credit from Tahoe Company, invoice dated July 26, terms 2/10, n/30.

27   Issued Check No. 303 to Dixon Company in payment of its July 17 invoice, less the return and the discount.

29   Sold merchandise on credit to Ruth Baker, Invoice No. 922, for $28,090 (cost is $22,850).

30   Sold merchandise on credit to Stephanie Meyer, Invoice No. 923, for $15,750 (cost is $9,840).

31   Issued Check No. 304, payable to Payroll, in payment of the sales salaries expense for the last half of the month, $30,620.

31   Cash sales for the last half of the month are $79,020 (cost is $51,855).

### Required

1. Prepare a sales journal like that in Exhibit 7.5 and a cash receipts journal like that in Exhibit 7.7. Number both journals as page 3. Then review the transactions of Alcorn Industries and enter those transactions that should be journalized in the sales journal and those that should be journalized in the cash receipts journal. Ignore any transactions that should be journalized in a purchases journal, a cash disbursements journal, or a general journal.

2. Open the following general ledger accounts: Cash, Accounts Receivable, Inventory, Long-Term Notes Payable, R. Alcorn, Capital, Sales, Sales Discounts, and Cost of Goods Sold. Enter the June 30 balances for Cash ($100,000), Inventory ($200,000), Long-Term Notes Payable ($200,000), and R. Alcorn, Capital ($100,000). Also open accounts receivable subsidiary ledger accounts for Kim Newsom, Stephanie Meyer, and Ruth Baker.

3. Verify that amounts that should be posted as individual amounts from the journals have been posted. (Such items are immediately posted.) Foot and crossfoot the journals and make the month-end postings.

4. Prepare a trial balance of the general ledger and prove the accuracy of the subsidiary ledger by preparing a schedule of accounts receivable.

**Check**   Trial balance totals, $602,580

### Analysis Component

5. Assume that the total for the schedule of Accounts Receivable does not equal the balance of the controlling account in the general ledger. Describe steps you would take to discover the error(s).

**Problem 7-2B$^A$**

Special journals, subsidiary ledgers, and schedule of accounts receivable—periodic

C3  P2  P3

Assume that Alcorn Industries in Problem 7-1B uses the periodic inventory system.

*Required*

1. Prepare headings for a sales journal like the one in Exhibit 7A.1. Prepare headings for a cash receipts journal like the one in Exhibit 7A.2. Journalize the July transactions shown in Problem 7-1B that should be recorded in the sales journal and the cash receipts journal assuming the periodic inventory system is used.

2. Open the general ledger accounts with balances as shown in Problem 7-1B (do not open a Cost of Goods Sold ledger account). Also open accounts receivable subsidiary ledger accounts for Ruth Baker, Stephanie Meyer, and Kim Newsom. Under the periodic system, an Inventory account exists but is inactive until its balance is updated to the correct inventory balance at year-end. In this problem, the Inventory account remains inactive but must be included to correctly complete the trial balance.

**Check** Trial balance totals, $602,580

3. Complete parts 3, 4, and 5 of Problem 7-1B using the results of parts 1 and 2 of this problem.

**Problem 7-3B**

Special journals, subsidiary ledgers, and schedule of accounts payable—perpetual

C3  P1  P2

The July transactions of Alcorn Industries are described in Problem 7-1B.

*Required*

1. Prepare a general journal, a purchases journal like that in Exhibit 7.9, and a cash disbursements journal like that in Exhibit 7.11. Number all journal pages as page 3. Review the July transactions of Alcorn Industries and enter those transactions that should be journalized in the general journal, the purchases journal, or the cash disbursements journal. Ignore any transactions that should be journalized in a sales journal or cash receipts journal.

2. Open the following general ledger accounts: Cash, Inventory, Office Supplies, Store Supplies, Store Equipment, Accounts Payable, Long-Term Notes Payable, R. Alcorn, Capital, Sales Salaries Expense, and Advertising Expense. Enter the June 30 balances of Cash ($100,000), Inventory ($200,000), Long-Term Notes Payable ($200,000), and R. Alcorn, Capital ($100,000). Also open accounts payable subsidiary ledger accounts for Caro's Supply, Tahoe Company, Dixon Company, and Pryor, Inc.

3. Verify that amounts that should be posted as individual amounts from the journals have been posted. (Such items are immediately posted.) Foot and crossfoot the journals and make the month-end postings.

**Check** Trial balance totals, $349,130

4. Prepare a trial balance of the general ledger and a schedule of accounts payable.

**Problem 7-4B$^A$**

Special journals, subsidiary ledgers, and schedule of accounts payable—periodic

C3  P2  P3

Refer to Problem 7-1B and assume that Alcorn uses the periodic inventory system.

*Required*

1. Prepare a general journal, a purchases journal like that in Exhibit 7A.3, and a cash disbursements journal like that in Exhibit 7A.4. Number all journal pages as page 3. Review the July transactions of Alcorn Company (Problem 7-1B) and enter those transactions that should be journalized in the general journal, the purchases journal, or the cash disbursements journal. Ignore any transaction that should be journalized in a sales journal or cash receipts journal.

2. Open the following general ledger accounts: Cash, Inventory, Office Supplies, Store Supplies, Store Equipment, Accounts Payable, Long-Term Notes Payable, R. Alcorn, Capital, Purchases, Purchases Returns and Allowances, Purchases Discounts, Sales Salaries Expense, and Advertising Expense. Enter the June 30 balances of Cash ($100,000), Inventory ($200,000), Long-Term Notes Payable ($200,000), and R. Alcorn, Capital ($100,000). Also open accounts payable subsidiary ledger accounts for Tahoe Company, Pryor, Inc., Caro's Supply, and Dixon Company.

**Check** Trial balance totals, $351,772

3. Complete parts 3 and 4 of Problem 7-3B using the results of parts 1 and 2 of this problem.

**Problem 7-5B**

Special journals, subsidiary ledgers, trial balance—perpetual

C3  P2  P3

Suppan Company completes these transactions during November of the current year (terms for all its credit sales are 2/10, n/30).

Nov. 1  Purchased $5,062 of office equipment on credit from Blix Supply, invoice dated November 1, terms n/10 EOM.
2  Borrowed $86,250 cash from Kansas Bank by signing a long-term note payable.
4  Purchased $11,400 of merchandise from ATM Industries, invoice dated November 3, terms 2/10, n/30.
5  Purchased $1,020 of store supplies on credit from Globe Company, invoice dated November 5, terms n/10 EOM.

  8   Sold merchandise on credit to Sid Ragan, Invoice No. 439, for $6,350 (cost is $3,710).

10   Sold merchandise on credit to Carlos Mane, Invoice No. 440, for $12,500 (cost is $7,500).

11   Purchased $2,887 of merchandise from Xu Company, invoice dated November 10, terms 2/10, n/30.

12   Sent ATM Industries Check No. 633 in payment of its November 3 invoice less the discount.

15   Issued Check No. 634, payable to Payroll, in payment of sales salaries expense for the first half of the month, $8,435. Cashed the check and paid the employees.

15   Cash sales for the first half of the month are $27,170 (cost is $17,000). (Cash sales are recorded daily but are recorded only twice in this problem to reduce repetitive entries.)

15   Sold merchandise on credit to Tony Timmons, Invoice No. 441, for $4,250 (cost is $1,450).

16   Purchased $559 of office supplies on credit from Globe Company, invoice dated November 16, terms n/10 EOM.

17   Received a $487 credit memorandum from Xu Company for the return of unsatisfactory merchandise purchased on November 11.

18   Received payment from Sid Ragan for the November 8 sale less the discount.

19   Received payment from Carlos Mane for the November 10 sale less the discount.

19   Issued Check No. 635 to Xu Company in payment of its invoice of November 10 less the return and the discount.

22   Sold merchandise on credit to Carlos Mane, Invoice No. 442, for $2,595 (cost is $1,060).

24   Sold merchandise on credit to Tony Timmons, Invoice No. 443, for $3,240 (cost is $1,090).

25   Received payment from Tony Timmons for the sale of November 15 less the discount.

26   Received a $922 credit memorandum from Blix Supply for the return of office equipment purchased on November 1.

30   Issued Check No. 636, payable to Payroll, in payment of sales salaries expense for the last half of the month, $8,435. Cashed the check and paid the employees.

30   Cash sales for the last half of the month are $35,703 (cost is $20,400).

30   Verify that amounts impacting customer and creditor accounts were posted and that any amounts that should have been posted as individual amounts to the general ledger accounts were posted. Foot and crossfoot the journals and make the month-end postings.

### *Required*

**1.** Open the following general ledger accounts: Cash; Accounts Receivable; Inventory (November 1 beg. bal. is $40,000); Office Supplies; Store Supplies; Office Equipment; Accounts Payable; Long-Term Notes Payable; J. Suppan, Capital (Nov. 1 beg. bal. is $40,000); Sales; Sales Discounts; Cost of Goods Sold; and Sales Salaries Expense. Open the following accounts receivable subsidiary ledger accounts: Carlos Mane, Tony Timmons, and Sid Ragan. Open the following accounts payable subsidiary ledger accounts: Globe Company, ATM Industries, Blix Supply, and Xu Company.

**2.** Enter these transactions in a sales journal like that in Exhibit 7.5, a purchases journal like that in Exhibit 7.9, a cash receipts journal like that in Exhibit 7.7, a cash disbursements journal like that in Exhibit 7.11, or a general journal. Number all journal pages as page 2.

**3.** Prepare a trial balance of the general ledger and prove the accuracy of the subsidiary ledgers by preparing schedules of both accounts receivable and accounts payable.

*Check   Trial balance totals, $223,777*

---

Assume that Suppan Company in Problem 7-5B uses the periodic inventory system.

**Problem 7-6B**<sup>A</sup>

Special journals, subsidiary ledgers, trial balance—periodic

**C3  P2  P3**

### *Required*

**1.** Open the following general ledger accounts: Cash; Accounts Receivable; Inventory (November 1 beg. bal. is $40,000); Office Supplies; Store Supplies; Office Equipment; Accounts Payable; Long-Term Notes Payable; J. Suppan, Capital (Nov. 1 beg. bal. is $40,000); Sales; Sales Discounts; Purchases; Purchases Returns and Allowances; Purchases Discounts; and Sales Salaries Expense. Open the following accounts receivable subsidiary ledger accounts: Carlos Mane, Tony Timmons, and Sid Ragan. Open the following accounts payable subsidiary ledger accounts: Globe Company, ATM Industries, Blix Supply, and Xu Company.

**2.** Enter the transactions from Problem 7-5B in a sales journal like that in Exhibit 7A.1, a purchases journal like that in Exhibit 7A.3, a cash receipts journal like that in Exhibit 7A.2, a cash disbursements journal like that in Exhibit 7A.4, or a general journal. Number journal pages as page 2.

**3.** Prepare a trial balance of the general ledger and prove the accuracy of the subsidiary ledgers by preparing schedules of both accounts receivable and accounts payable.

*Check   Trial balance totals, $224,540*

## SERIAL PROBLEM
Business Solutions **P1**

*(This serial problem began in Chapter 1 and continues through most of the book. If previous chapter segments were not completed, the serial problem can begin at this point. It is helpful, but not necessary, to use the Working Papers that accompany the book.)*

**SP 7**   Assume that Santana Rey expands Business Solutions' accounting system to include special journals.

### Required

1. Locate the transactions related to January through March 2012 for Business Solutions in Chapter 5.

2. Enter the Business Solutions transactions for January through March in a sales journal like that in Exhibit 7.5 (insert "n/a" in the Invoice column), a cash receipts journal like that in Exhibit 7.7, a purchases journal like that in Exhibit 7.9 (use Computer Supplies heading instead of Office Supplies), and a cash disbursements journal like that in Exhibit 7.11 (insert "n/a" in the Check Number column), or a general journal. Number journal pages as page 2. If the transaction does not specify the name of the payee, state "not specified" in the Payee column of the cash disbursements journal.

3. The transactions on the following dates should be journalized in the general journal: January 5, 11, 20, 24, and 29 (no entry required) and March 24. Do not record and post the adjusting entries for the end of March.

## COMPREHENSIVE PROBLEM
Colo Company

mhhe.com/wildFAP20e

*(If the Working Papers that accompany this book are not available, omit this comprehensive problem.)* Assume it is Monday, May 1, the first business day of the month, and you have just been hired as the accountant for Colo Company, which operates with monthly accounting periods. All of the company's accounting work is completed through the end of April and its ledgers show April 30 balances. During your first month on the job, the company experiences the following transactions and events (terms for all its credit sales are 2/10, n/30 unless stated differently):

May   1   Issued Check No. 3410 to S&P Management Co. in payment of the May rent, $3,710. (Use two lines to record the transaction. Charge 80% of the rent to Rent Expense—Selling Space and the balance to Rent Expense—Office Space.)

     2   Sold merchandise on credit to Hensel Company, Invoice No. 8785, for $6,100 (cost is $4,100).

     2   Issued a $175 credit memorandum to Knox Co., for defective (worthless) merchandise sold on April 28 and returned for credit. The total selling price (gross) was $4,725.

     3   Received a $798 credit memorandum from Peyton Products for the return of merchandise purchased on April 29.

     4   Purchased the following on credit from Gear Supply Co.: merchandise, $37,072; store supplies, $574; and office supplies, $83. Invoice dated May 4, terms n/10 EOM.

     5   Received payment from Knox Co., for the balance from the April 28 sale less the May 2 return and the discount.

     8   Issued Check No. 3411 to Peyton Products to pay for the $7,098 of merchandise purchased on April 29 less the May 3 return and a 2% discount.

     9   Sold store supplies to the merchant next door at their cost of $350 cash.

     10   Purchased $4,074 of office equipment on credit from Gear Supply Co., invoice dated May 10, terms n/10 EOM.

     11   Received payment from Hensel Company for the May 2 sale less the discount.

     11   Purchased $8,800 of merchandise from Garcia, Inc., invoice dated May 10, terms 2/10, n/30.

     12   Received an $854 credit memorandum from Gear Supply Co. for the return of defective office equipment received on May 10.

     15   Issued Check No. 3412, payable to Payroll, in payment of sales salaries, $5,320, and office salaries, $3,150. Cashed the check and paid the employees.

     15   Cash sales for the first half of the month are $59,220 (cost is $38,200). (Cash sales are recorded daily but are recorded only twice here to reduce repetitive entries.)

     15   Post to the customer and creditor accounts. Also post individual items that are not included in column totals at the end of the month to the general ledger accounts. (Such items are posted daily but are posted only twice each month because they are few in number.)

     16   Sold merchandise on credit to Hensel Company, Invoice No. 8786, for $3,990 (cost is $1,890).

     17   Purchased $13,650 of merchandise from Fink Corp., invoice dated May 14, terms 2/10, n/60.

     19   Issued Check No. 3413 to Garcia, Inc., in payment of its May 10 invoice less the discount.

     22   Sold merchandise to Lee Services, Invoice No. 8787, for $6,850 (cost is $4,990), terms 2/10, n/60.

     23   Issued Check No. 3414 to Fink Corp. in payment of its May 14 invoice less the discount.

     24   Purchased the following on credit from Gear Supply Co.: merchandise, $8,120; store supplies, $630; and office supplies, $280. Invoice dated May 24, terms n/10 EOM.

25    Purchased $3,080 of merchandise from Peyton Products, invoice dated May 23, terms 2/10, n/30.

26    Sold merchandise on credit to Crane Corp., Invoice No. 8788, for $14,210 (cost is $8,230).

26    Issued Check No. 3415 to Perennial Power in payment of the May electric bill, $1,283.

29    The owner of Colo Company, Jenny Colo, used Check No. 3416 to withdraw $7,000 cash from the business for personal use.

30    Received payment from Lee Services for the May 22 sale less the discount.

30    Issued Check No. 3417, payable to Payroll, in payment of sales salaries, $5,320, and office salaries, $3,150. Cashed the check and paid the employees.

31    Cash sales for the last half of the month are $66,052 (cost is $42,500).

31    Post to the customer and creditor accounts. Also post individual items that are not included in column totals at the end of the month to the general ledger accounts. Foot and crossfoot the journals and make the month-end postings.

### Required

1. Enter these transactions in a sales journal, a purchases journal, a cash receipts journal, a cash disbursements journal, or a general journal as illustrated in this chapter (number all journal pages as page 2). Post when instructed to do so. Assume a perpetual inventory system.

2. Prepare a trial balance in the Trial Balance columns of the work sheet form provided with the working papers. Complete the work sheet using the following information for accounting adjustments.

   **Check**  (2) Unadjusted trial balance totals, $545,020; Adjustments column totals, $2,407

   a. Expired insurance, $553.

   b. Ending store supplies inventory, $2,632.

   c. Ending office supplies inventory, $504.

   d. Depreciation of store equipment, $567.

   e. Depreciation of office equipment, $329.

   Prepare and post adjusting and closing entries.

3. Prepare a May 2011 multiple-step income statement, a May 2011 statement of owner's equity, and a May 31, 2011, classified balance sheet.

   (3) Net income, $31,647; Total assets, $385,791

4. Prepare a post-closing trial balance. Also prove the accuracy of subsidiary ledgers by preparing schedules of both accounts receivable and accounts payable.

## Beyond the Numbers

**BTN 7-1**  Refer to **Research In Motion**'s financial statements in Appendix A to answer the following.

1. Identify the note that reports on Research In Motion's business segments.

2. Describe the focus and activities of each of Research In Motion's business segments.

**REPORTING IN ACTION**

A1

RIM

### Fast Forward

3. Access Research In Motion's annual report for fiscal years ending after February 27, 2010, from its Website (**RIM.com**) or the SEC's EDGAR database (**www.SEC.gov**). Has Research In Motion changed its reporting policy regarding segment information? Explain.

**BTN 7-2**  Key figures for **Research In Motion** and **Apple** follow ($ millions).

**COMPARATIVE ANALYSIS**

A1

RIM
Apple

| RIM Segment | Current Year | | One Year Prior | | Two Years Prior | |
| --- | --- | --- | --- | --- | --- | --- |
| | Segment Revenue | Segment Assets | Segment Revenue | Segment Assets | Segment Revenue | Segment Assets |
| Domestic . . . . . . . . . . . . . . . . . | $8,620 | $4,059 | $6,968 | $2,647 | $3,529 | $1,739 |
| International . . . . . . . . . . . . . . . | 6,333 | 6,145 | 4,097 | 5,454 | 2,480 | 3,772 |

| Apple Segment | Current Year | | One Year Prior | | Two Years Prior | |
| --- | --- | --- | --- | --- | --- | --- |
| | Segment Revenue | Segment Assets | Segment Revenue | Segment Assets | Segment Revenue | Segment Assets |
| Domestic . . . . . . . . . . . . . . . . . | $22,325 | $2,698 | $20,893 | $2,269 | $14,683 | $1,752 |
| International . . . . . . . . . . . . . . | 20,580 | 495 | 16,598 | 410 | 9,895 | 260 |

***Required***

1. Compute the ratio of segment revenue divided by segment assets for each of the segments of Research In Motion and Apple for each of the two most recent years shown. (We do not compute the segment return on assets as these companies did not report their segment income.)

2. Interpret and comment on your results of part 1.

## ETHICS CHALLENGE

C1

**BTN 7-3**   Erica Gray, CPA, is a sole practitioner. She has been practicing as an auditor for 10 years. Recently a long-standing audit client asked Gray to design and implement an integrated computer-based accounting information system. The fees associated with this additional engagement with the client are very attractive. However, Gray wonders if she can remain objective on subsequent audits in her evaluation of the client's accounting system and its records if she was responsible for its design and implementation. Gray knows that professional auditing standards require her to remain independent in fact and appearance from her auditing clients.

***Required***

1. What do you believe auditing standards are mainly concerned with when they require independence in fact? In appearance?

2. Why is it important that auditors remain independent of their clients?

3. Do you think Gray can accept this engagement and remain independent? Justify your response.

## COMMUNICATING IN PRACTICE

C2   C3

**BTN 7-4**   Your friend, Wendy Geiger, owns a small retail store that sells candies and nuts. Geiger acquires her goods from a few select vendors. She generally makes purchase orders by phone and on credit. Sales are primarily for cash. Geiger keeps her own manual accounting system using a general journal and a general ledger. At the end of each business day, she records one summary entry for cash sales. Geiger recently began offering items in creative gift packages. This has increased sales substantially, and she is now receiving orders from corporate and other clients who order large quantities and prefer to buy on credit. As a result of increased credit transactions in both purchases and sales, keeping the accounting records has become extremely time consuming. Geiger wants to continue to maintain her own manual system and calls you for advice. Write a memo to her advising how she might modify her current manual accounting system to accommodate the expanded business activities. Geiger is accustomed to checking her ledger by using a trial balance. Your memo should explain the advantages of what you propose and of any other verification techniques you recommend.

## TAKING IT TO THE NET

A1

**BTN 7-5**   Access the March 18, 2010, filing of the fiscal 2010 10-K report for **Dell** (ticker DELL) at **www.SEC.gov**. Read its Note 14 that details Dell's segment information and answer the following.

1. Dell's operations are divided among which four global business segments?

2. In fiscal year 2010, which segment had the largest dollar amount of operating income? Which had the largest amount of assets?

3. Compute the return on assets for each segment for fiscal year 2010. Use operating income and average total assets by segment for your calculation. Which segment has the highest return on assets?

4. For what product groups does Dell provide segment data? What percent of Dell's net revenue is earned by each product group?

## TEAMWORK IN ACTION

C3   P1   P2

**BTN 7-6**   Each member of the team is to assume responsibility for one of the following tasks:

a. Journalizing in the purchases journal.

b. Journalizing in the cash disbursements journal.

c. Maintaining and verifying the Accounts Payable ledger.

d. Journalizing in the sales journal and the general journal.

e. Journalizing in the cash receipts journal.

f. Maintaining and verifying the Accounts Receivable ledger.

The team should abide by the following procedures in carrying out responsibilities.

***Required***

1. After tasks *a–f* are assigned, each team member is to quickly read the list of transactions in Problem 7-5A, identifying with initials the journal in which each transaction is to be recorded. Upon completion,

the team leader is to read transaction dates, and the appropriate team member is to vocalize responsibility. Any disagreement between teammates must be resolved.

2. Journalize and continually update subsidiary ledgers. Journal recorders should alert teammates assigned to subsidiary ledgers when an entry must be posted to their subsidiary.

3. Team members responsible for tasks *a*, *b*, *d*, and *e* are to summarize and prove journals; members responsible for tasks *c* and *f* are to prepare both payables and receivables schedules.

4. The team leader is to take charge of the general ledger, rotating team members to obtain amounts to be posted. The person responsible for a journal must complete posting references in that journal. Other team members should verify the accuracy of account balance computations. To avoid any abnormal account balances, post in the following order: P, S, G, R, D. (*Note:* Posting any necessary individual general ledger amounts is also done at this time.)

5. The team leader is to read out general ledger account balances while another team member fills in the trial balance form. Concurrently, one member should keep a running balance of debit account balance totals and another credit account balance totals. Verify the final total of the trial balance and the schedules. If necessary, the team must resolve any errors. Turn in the trial balance and schedules to the instructor.

---

**ENTREPRENEURIAL DECISION**

P1

**BTN 7-7** Refer to the chapter's opening feature about Kim Jordan and her company, New Belgium Brewing Company. Her manufacturing company deals with numerous suppliers and customers.

**Required**

1. Identify the special journals that New Belgium Brewing would be likely to use in its operations. Also identify any subsidiary ledgers that it would likely use.

2. New Belgium Brewing hopes to double yearly sales within five years hence from its current $100 million annual amount. Assume that its sales growth projections are as follows.

| Year | One Year Hence | Two Years Hence | Three Years Hence | Four Years Hence | Five Years Hence |
|------|------|------|------|------|------|
| Projected growth in sales (from the preceding year) . . . . . . . . . | 0% | 20% | 15% | 25% | 20% |

Estimate New Belgium Brewing's projected sales for each year (round to the nearest dollar). If this pattern of sales growth holds, will New Belgium Brewing achieve its goal of doubling sales in five years?

---

**GLOBAL DECISION**

A1

**NOKIA**

**BTN 7-8** Access and refer to the December 31, 2009, annual report for Nokia at www.Nokia.com.

**Required**

1. Identify its Note 2 (Segmental Information) to its financial statements and locate its information relating to Nokia's operating and reportable segments. Identify those three segments.

2. What financial figures does it disclose for each segment?

3. Does Nokia have a dominant segment? Explain.

---

## ANSWERS TO MULTIPLE CHOICE QUIZ

1. a
2. e
3. d

4. b
5. a

# 8

# Cash and Internal Controls

## A Look Back

Chapter 7 focused on accounting information systems. We explained the principles and components of information systems, the use of special journals and subsidiary ledgers, and technology-based systems.

## A Look at This Chapter

This chapter extends our study of accounting to internal control and the analysis of cash. We describe procedures that are good for internal control. We also explain the control of and the accounting for cash, including control features of banking activities.

## A Look Ahead

Chapter 9 focuses on receivables. We explain how to account and report on receivables and their related accounts. This includes estimating uncollectible receivables and computing interest earned.

## Learning Objectives

# CAP

### CONCEPTUAL

**C1** Define internal control and identify its purpose and principles. (p. 316)

**C2** Define cash and cash equivalents and explain how to report them. (p. 321)

### ANALYTICAL

**A1** Compute the days' sales uncollected ratio and use it to assess liquidity. (p. 335)

LP8

### PROCEDURAL

**P1** Apply internal control to cash receipts and disbursements. (p. 322)

**P2** Explain and record petty cash fund transactions. (p. 326)

**P3** Prepare a bank reconciliation. (p. 331)

**P4** *Appendix 8A*—Describe the use of documentation and verification to control cash disbursements. (p. 338)

**P5** *Appendix 8B*—Apply the net method to control purchase discounts. (p. 341)

# Candyland Biz

*"It's a creative outlet for me . . . it doesn't feel like work"*
—DYLAN LAUREN

NEW YORK—A 10-foot chocolate bunny greets you as you enter the store—that should be warning enough! This elite designer candy store, christened **Dylan's Candy Bar (DylansCandyBar.com),** is the brainchild of co-founder Dylan Lauren. Explains Dylan, "I got a business plan together and set out to make candy my livelihood."

This sweet-lovers' heaven offers more than 5,000 different choices of sweets from all over the world. It has become a hip hangout for locals and tourists—and it has made candy cool. Says Dylan, "Park Avenue women come in, and the first thing they ask for is Gummi bears. They love that it's very childhood, nostalgic."

Although marketing is an important part of its success, Dylan's management of internal controls and cash is equally impressive. Several control procedures monitor its business activities and safeguard its assets. An example is the biometric time and attendance control system using fingerprint characteristics. Says Dylan, "There's no fooling the system! It is going to help us remotely manage our employees while eliminating human error and

dishonesty. [It] is a cost-effective and important business management tool." Similar controls are applied throughout the store. Dylan explains that such controls raise productivity and cut expenses.

The store's cash management practices are equally impressive, including controls over cash receipts, disbursements, and petty cash. The use of bank reconciliations further helps with the store's control and management of cash. Dylan explains that she takes advantage of available banking services to enhance controls over cash.

Internal controls are crucial when on a busy day its stores bring in thousands of customers, and their cash. They have already expanded to three stores in New York, and one each in Houston and Orlando. Through it all, Dylan says it is "totally fun."

[Sources: *Dylan's Candy Bar Website,* January 2011; *Entrepreneur,* June 2005; *NYC Official City Guide,* July 2009; *The New York Times,* June & March 2009; *Dolce Vita Magazine,* June 2009; *Luxury Insider,* March 2009.]

We all are aware of theft and fraud. They affect us in several ways: We lock doors, chain bikes, review sales receipts, and acquire alarm systems. A company also takes actions to safeguard, control, and manage what it owns. Experience tells us that small companies are most vulnerable, usually due to weak internal controls. It is management's responsibility to set up policies and procedures to safeguard a company's assets, especially cash. To do so, management *and* employees must understand and apply principles of internal control. This chapter describes these principles and how to apply them. It focuses special attention on cash because it is easily transferable and is often at high risk of loss.

**Cash and Internal Controls**

**Internal Control**
- Purpose of controls
- Principles of controls
- Technology and controls
- Limitations of controls

**Control of Cash**
- Cash, cash equivalents, and liquidity
- Control of receipts
- Control of disbursements

**Banking Activities as Controls**
- Basic bank services
- Bank statement
- Bank reconciliation

# INTERNAL CONTROL

This section describes internal control and its fundamental principles. We also discuss the impact of technology on internal control and the limitations of control procedures.

## Purpose of Internal Control

**C1** Define internal control and identify its purpose and principles.

Managers (or owners) of small businesses often control the entire operation. These managers usually purchase all assets, hire and manage employees, negotiate all contracts, and sign all checks. They know from personal contact and observation whether the business is actually receiving the assets and services paid for. Most companies, however, cannot maintain this close personal supervision. They must delegate responsibilities and rely on formal procedures rather than personal contact in controlling business activities.

**Internal Control System**   Managers use an internal control system to monitor and control business activities. An **internal control system** consists of the policies and procedures managers use to

- Protect assets.
- Ensure reliable accounting.
- Promote efficient operations.
- Urge adherence to company policies.

A properly designed internal control system is a key part of systems design, analysis, and performance. Managers place a high priority on internal control systems because they can prevent avoidable losses, help managers plan operations, and monitor company and employee performance. Internal controls do not provide guarantees, but they lower the company's risk of loss.

**Sarbanes-Oxley Act (SOX)**   The **Sarbanes-Oxley Act (SOX)** requires the managers and auditors of companies whose stock is traded on an exchange (called *public companies*) to document and certify the system of internal controls. Following are some of the specific requirements:

- Auditors must evaluate internal controls and issue an internal control report.
- Auditors of a client are restricted as to what consulting services they can provide that client.
- The person leading an audit can serve no more than seven years without a two-year break.
- Auditors' work is overseen by the *Public Company Accounting Oversight Board* (PCAOB).
- Harsh penalties exist for violators—sentences up to 25 years in prison with severe fines.

SOX has markedly impacted companies, and the costs of its implementation are high. Importantly, **Section 404** of SOX requires that managers document and assess the effectiveness of all internal control processes that can impact financial reporting. The benefits include greater confidence in accounting systems and their related reports. However, the public continues to debate the costs versus the benefits of SOX as nearly all business activities of these companies are impacted by SOX. Section 404 of SOX requires that managers document and assess their internal controls *and* that auditors provide an opinion on managers' documentation and assessment. Costs of complying with Section 404 for companies is reported to average $4 million (source: Financial Executives Institute).

## Principles of Internal Control

Internal control policies and procedures vary from company to company according to such factors as the nature of the business and its size. Certain fundamental internal control principles apply to all companies. The **principles of internal control** are to

1. Establish responsibilities.
2. Maintain adequate records.
3. Insure assets and bond key employees.
4. Separate recordkeeping from custody of assets.
5. Divide responsibility for related transactions.
6. Apply technological controls.
7. Perform regular and independent reviews.

This section explains these seven principles and describes how internal control procedures minimize the risk of fraud and theft. These procedures also increase the reliability and accuracy of accounting records. A framework for how these seven principles improve the quality of financial reporting is provided by the **Committee of Sponsoring Organizations (COSO)** (**www.COSO.org**). Specifically, these principles link to five aspects of internal control: control activities, control environment, risk assessment, monitoring, and communication.

**Point:** Sarbanes-Oxley Act (SOX) requires that each annual report contain an *internal control report,* which must: (1) state managers' responsibility for establishing and maintaining adequate internal controls for financial reporting; and (2) assess the effectiveness of those controls.

**Establish Responsibilities**    Proper internal control means that responsibility for a task is clearly established and assigned to one person. When a problem occurs in a company where responsibility is not identified, determining who is at fault is difficult. For instance, if two sales-clerks share the same cash register and there is a cash shortage, neither clerk can be held accountable. To prevent this problem, one clerk might be given responsibility for handling all cash sales. Alternately, a company can use a register with separate cash drawers for each clerk. Most of us have waited at a retail counter during a shift change while employees swap cash drawers.

**Point:** Many companies have a mandatory vacation policy for employees who handle cash. When another employee must cover for the one on vacation, it is more difficult to hide cash frauds.

**Maintain Adequate Records**    Good recordkeeping is part of an internal control system. It helps protect assets and ensures that employees use prescribed procedures. Reliable records are also a source of information that managers use to monitor company activities. When detailed records of equipment are kept, for instance, items are unlikely to be lost or stolen without detection. Similarly, transactions are less likely to be entered in wrong accounts if a chart of accounts is set up and carefully used. Many preprinted forms and internal documents are also designed for use in a good internal control system. When sales slips are properly designed, for instance, sales personnel can record needed information efficiently with less chance of errors or delays to customers. When sales slips are prenumbered and controlled, each one issued is the responsibility of one salesperson, preventing the salesperson from pocketing cash by making a sale and destroying the sales slip. Computerized point-of-sale systems achieve the same control results.

**Insure Assets and Bond Key Employees**    Good internal control means that assets are adequately insured against casualty and that employees handling large amounts of cash and easily transferable assets are bonded. An employee is *bonded* when a company purchases an insurance policy, or a bond, against losses from theft by that employee. Bonding reduces the risk of loss. It also discourages theft because bonded employees know an independent bonding company will be involved when theft is uncovered and is unlikely to be sympathetic with an employee involved in theft.

**Point:** The Association of Certified Fraud Examiners (**cfenet.com**) estimates that employee fraud costs small companies more than $100,000 per incident.

### Separate Recordkeeping from Custody of Assets

A person who controls or has access to an asset must not keep that asset's accounting records. This principle reduces the risk of theft or waste of an asset because the person with control over it knows that another person keeps its records. Also, a recordkeeper who does not have access to the asset has no reason to falsify records. This means that to steal an asset and hide the theft from the records, two or more people must *collude*—or agree in secret to commit the fraud.

### Divide Responsibility for Related Transactions

Good internal control divides responsibility for a transaction or a series of related transactions between two or more individuals or departments. This is to ensure that the work of one individual acts as a check on the other. This principle, often called *separation of duties,* is not a call for duplication of work. Each employee or department should perform unduplicated effort. Examples of transactions with divided responsibility are placing purchase orders, receiving merchandise, and paying vendors. These tasks should not be given to one individual or department. Assigning responsibility for two or more of these tasks to one party increases mistakes and perhaps fraud. Having an independent person, for example, check incoming goods for quality and quantity encourages more care and attention to detail than having the person who placed the order do the checking. Added protection can result from identifying a third person to approve payment of the invoice. A company can even designate a fourth person with authority to write checks as another protective measure.

### Apply Technological Controls

Cash registers, check protectors, time clocks, and personal identification scanners are examples of devices that can improve internal control. Technology often improves the effectiveness of controls. A cash register with a locked-in tape or electronic file makes a record of each cash sale. A check protector perforates the amount of a check into its face and makes it difficult to alter the amount. A time clock registers the exact time an employee both arrives at and departs from the job. Mechanical change and currency counters quickly and accurately count amounts, and personal scanners limit access to only authorized individuals. Each of these and other technological controls are an effective part of many internal control systems.

### Perform Regular and Independent Reviews

Changes in personnel, stress of time pressures, and technological advances present opportunities for shortcuts and lapses. To counter these factors, regular reviews of internal control systems are needed to ensure that procedures are followed. These reviews are preferably done by internal auditors not directly involved in the activities. Their impartial perspective encourages an evaluation of the efficiency as well as the effectiveness of the internal control system. Many companies also pay for audits by independent, external auditors. These external auditors test the company's financial records to give an opinion as to whether its financial statements are presented fairly. Before external auditors decide on how much testing is needed, they evaluate the effectiveness of the internal control system. This evaluation is often helpful to a client.

**Point:** There's a new security device—a person's ECG (electrocardiogram) reading—that is as unique as a fingerprint and a lot harder to lose or steal than a PIN. ECGs can be read through fingertip touches. An ECG also shows that a living person is actually there, whereas fingerprint and facial recognition software can be fooled.

**Decision Maker**   Answer — p. 343

**Entrepreneur** As owner of a start-up information services company, you hire a systems analyst. One of her first recommendations is to require all employees to take at least one week of vacation per year. Why would she recommend a "forced vacation" policy? ■

## Technology and Internal Control

The fundamental principles of internal control are relevant no matter what the technological state of the accounting system, from purely manual to fully automated systems. Technology impacts an internal control system in several important ways. Perhaps the most obvious is that technology allows us quicker access to databases and information. Used effectively, technology greatly improves managers' abilities to monitor and control business activities. This section describes some technological impacts we must be alert to.

**Reduced Processing Errors** Technologically advanced systems reduce the number of errors in processing information. Provided the software and data entry are correct, the risk of mechanical and mathematical errors is nearly eliminated. However, we must remember that erroneous software or data entry does exist. Also, less human involvement in data processing can cause data entry errors to go undiscovered. Moreover, errors in software can produce consistent but erroneous processing of transactions. Continually checking and monitoring all types of systems are important.

**More Extensive Testing of Records** A company's review and audit of electronic records can include more extensive testing when information is easily and rapidly accessed. When accounting records are kept manually, auditors and others likely select only small samples of data to test. When data are accessible with computer technology, however, auditors can quickly analyze large samples or even the entire database.

**Limited Evidence of Processing** Many data processing steps are increasingly done by computer. Accordingly, fewer hard-copy items of documentary evidence are available for review. Yet technologically advanced systems can provide new evidence. They can, for instance, record who made the entries, the date and time, the source of the entry, and so on. Technology can also be designed to require the use of passwords or other identification before access to the system is granted. This means that internal control depends more on the design and operation of the information system and less on the analysis of its resulting documents.

**Crucial Separation of Duties** Technological advances in accounting information systems often yield some job eliminations or consolidations. While those who remain have the special skills necessary to operate advanced programs and equipment, a company with a reduced workforce risks losing its crucial separation of duties. The company must establish ways to control and monitor employees to minimize risk of error and fraud. For instance, the person who designs and programs the information system must not be the one who operates it. The company must also separate control over programs and files from the activities related to cash receipts and disbursements. For instance, a computer operator should not control check-writing activities. Achieving acceptable separation of duties can be especially difficult and costly in small companies with few employees.

**Increased E-Commerce** Technology has encouraged the growth of e-commerce. **Amazon.com** and **eBay** are examples of companies that have successfully exploited e-commerce. Most companies have some e-commerce transactions. All such transactions involve at least three risks. (1) *Credit card number theft* is a risk of using, transmitting, and storing such data online. This increases the cost of e-commerce. (2) *Computer viruses* are malicious programs that attach themselves to innocent files for purposes of infecting and harming other files and programs. (3) *Impersonation* online can result in charges of sales to bogus accounts, purchases of inappropriate materials, and the unknowing giving up of confidential information to hackers. Companies use both firewalls and encryption to

**Point:** Information on Internet fraud can be found at these Websites: **sec.gov/investor/pubs/cyberfraud.htm ftc.gov/bcp/consumer.shtm www.fraud.org**

**Point:** Evidence of any internal control failure for a company reduces user confidence in its financial statements.

**Point:** We look to several sources when assessing a company's internal controls. Sources include the auditor's report, management report on controls (if available), management discussion and analysis, and financial press.

**Point:** COSO organizes control components into five types:
- Control environment
- Control activities
- Risk assessment
- Monitoring
- Information and communication

"Worst case of identity theft I've ever seen!"

Copyright 2004 by Randy Glasbergen. www.glasbergen.com

combat some of these risks—firewalls are points of entry to a system that require passwords to continue, and encryption is a mathematical process to rearrange contents that cannot be read without the process code. Nearly 5% of Americans already report being victims of identity theft, and roughly 10 million say their privacy has been compromised.

### Decision Insight

**Cheery Fraud Victim**   Certified Fraud Examiners Website reports the following: Andrew Cameron stole Jacqueline Boanson's credit card. Cameron headed to the racetrack and promptly charged two bets for $150 on the credit card—winning $400. Unfortunately for Cameron the racetrack refused to pay him cash as its internal control policy is to credit winnings from bets made on a credit card to that same card. Cameron was later nabbed; and the racetrack let Ms. Boanson keep the winnings. ■

## Limitations of Internal Control

All internal control policies and procedures have limitations that usually arise from either (1) the human element or (2) the cost–benefit principle.

Internal control policies and procedures are applied by people. This human element creates several potential limitations that we can categorize as either (1) human error or (2) human fraud. *Human error* can occur from negligence, fatigue, misjudgment, or confusion. *Human fraud* involves intent by people to defeat internal controls, such as *management override,* for personal gain. Fraud also includes collusion to thwart the separation of duties. The human element highlights the importance of establishing an *internal control environment* to convey management's commitment to internal control policies and procedures. Human fraud is driven by the *triple-threat* of fraud:

- **Opportunity**—refers to internal control deficiencies in the workplace.
- **Pressure**—refers to financial, family, society, and other stresses to succeed.
- **Rationalization**—refers to employees justifying fraudulent behavior.

The second major limitation on internal control is the *cost–benefit principle,* which dictates that the costs of internal controls must not exceed their benefits. Analysis of costs and benefits must consider all factors, including the impact on morale. Most companies, for instance, have a legal right to read employees' e-mails, yet companies seldom exercise that right unless they are confronted with evidence of potential harm to the company. The same holds for drug testing, phone tapping, and hidden cameras. The bottom line is that managers must establish internal control policies and procedures with a net benefit to the company.

**Point:** Cybercrime.gov pursues computer and intellectual property crimes, including that of e-commerce.

| Address | www.hacker'sguidetocyberspace.com | GO |

## Hacker's Guide to Cyberspace

**Pharming**  Viruses attached to e-mails and Websites load software onto your PC that monitors keystrokes; when you sign on to financial Websites, it steals your passwords.

**Phishing**  Hackers send e-mails to you posing as banks; you are asked for information using fake Websites where they reel in your passwords and personal data.

**WI-Phishing**  Cybercrooks set up wireless networks hoping you use them to connect to the Web; your passwords and data are stolen as you use their network.

**Bot-Networking**  Hackers send remote-control programs to your PC that take control to send out spam and viruses; they even rent your bot to other cybercrooks.

**Typo-Squatting**  Hackers set up Websites with addresses similar to legit outfits; when you make a typo and hit their sites, they infect your PC with viruses or take them over as bots.

## Quick Check

Answers — p. 343

1. Principles of internal control suggest that (choose one): (*a*) Responsibility for a series of related transactions (such as placing orders, receiving and paying for merchandise) should be assigned to one employee; (*b*) Responsibility for individual tasks should be shared by more than one employee so that one serves as a check on the other; or (*c*) Employees who handle considerable cash and easily transferable assets should be bonded.
2. What are some impacts of computing technology on internal control?

# CONTROL OF CASH

*Cash* is a necessary asset of every company. Most companies also own *cash equivalents* (defined below), which are assets similar to cash. Cash and cash equivalents are the most liquid of all assets and are easily hidden and moved. An effective system of internal controls protects these assets and it should meet three basic guidelines:

1. Handling cash is separate from recordkeeping of cash.
2. Cash receipts are promptly deposited in a bank.
3. Cash disbursements are made by check.

The first guideline applies separation of duties to minimize errors and fraud. When duties are separated, two or more people must collude to steal cash and conceal this action in the accounting records. The second guideline uses immediate (say, daily) deposits of all cash receipts to produce a timely independent record of the cash received. It also reduces the likelihood of cash theft (or loss) and the risk that an employee could personally use the money before depositing it. The third guideline uses payments by check to develop an independent bank record of cash disbursements. This guideline also reduces the risk of cash theft (or loss).

This section begins with definitions of cash and cash equivalents. Discussion then focuses on controls and accounting for both cash receipts and disbursements. The exact procedures used to achieve control over cash vary across companies. They depend on factors such as company size, number of employees, volume of cash transactions, and sources of cash.

## Cash, Cash Equivalents, and Liquidity

Good accounting systems help in managing the amount of cash and controlling who has access to it. Cash is the usual means of payment when paying for assets, services, or liabilities. **Liquidity** refers to a company's ability to pay for its near-term obligations. Cash and similar assets are called **liquid assets** because they can be readily used to settle such obligations. A company needs liquid assets to effectively operate.

**Cash** includes currency and coins along with the amounts on deposit in bank accounts, checking accounts (called *demand deposits*), and many savings accounts (called *time deposits*). Cash also includes items that are acceptable for deposit in these accounts such as customer checks, cashier's checks, certified checks, and money orders. **Cash equivalents** are short-term, highly liquid investment assets meeting two criteria: (1) readily convertible to a known cash amount and (2) sufficiently close to their due date so that their market value is not sensitive to interest rate changes. Only investments purchased within three months of their due date usually satisfy these criteria. Examples of cash equivalents are short-term investments in assets such as U.S. Treasury bills and money market funds. To increase their return, many companies invest idle cash in cash equivalents. Most companies combine cash equivalents with cash as a single item on the balance sheet.

**C2** Define cash and cash equivalents and explain how to report them.

 **Point:** The most liquid assets are usually reported first on a balance sheet; the least liquid assets are reported last.

**Point: Google** reports cash and cash equivalents of $10,198 million in its balance sheet. This amount makes up nearly 25% of its total assets.

## Cash Management

When companies fail, one of the most common causes is their inability to manage cash. Companies must plan both cash receipts and cash payments. The goals of cash management are twofold:

1. Plan cash receipts to meet cash payments when due.
2. Keep a minimum level of cash necessary to operate.

The *treasurer* of the company is responsible for cash management. Effective cash management involves applying the following cash management principles.

- **Encourage collection of receivables.** The more quickly customers and others pay the company, the more quickly that company can use the money. Some companies have cash-only sales policies. Others might offer discounts for payments received early.

- **Delay payment of liabilities.** The more delayed a company is in paying others, the more time it has to use the money. Some companies regularly wait to pay their bills until the last possible day allowed—although, a company must take care not to hurt its credit standing.

- **Keep only necessary levels of assets.** The less money tied up in idle assets, the more money to invest in productive assets. Some companies maintain *just-in-time* inventory; meaning they plan inventory to be available at the same time orders are filled. Others might lease out excess warehouse space or rent equipment instead of buying it.

- **Plan expenditures.** Money should be spent only when it is available. Companies must look at seasonal and business cycles to plan expenditures.

- **Invest excess cash.** Excess cash earns no return and should be invested. Excess cash from seasonal cycles can be placed in a bank account or other short-term investment for income. Excess cash beyond what's needed for regular business should be invested in productive assets like factories and inventories.

---

**Decision Insight**

**Days' Cash Expense Coverage**   The ratio of *cash (and cash equivalents) to average daily cash expenses* indicates the number of days a company can operate without additional cash inflows. It reflects on company liquidity and on the potential of excess cash. ■

---

## Control of Cash Receipts

**P1** Apply internal control to cash receipts and disbursements.

Internal control of cash receipts ensures that cash received is properly recorded and deposited. Cash receipts can arise from transactions such as cash sales, collections of customer accounts, receipts of interest earned, bank loans, sales of assets, and owner investments. This section explains internal control over two important types of cash receipts: over-the-counter and by mail.

**Over-the-Counter Cash Receipts**   For purposes of internal control, over-the-counter cash receipts from sales should be recorded on a cash register at the time of each sale. To help ensure that correct amounts are entered, each register should be located so customers can read the amounts entered. Clerks also should be required to enter each sale before wrapping merchandise and to give the customer a receipt for each sale. The design of each cash register should provide a permanent, locked-in record of each transaction. In many systems, the register is directly linked with computing and accounting services. Less advanced registers simply print a record of each transaction on a paper tape or electronic file locked inside the register.

Proper internal control prescribes that custody over cash should be separate from its record-keeping. For over-the-counter cash receipts, this separation begins with the cash sale. The clerk who has access to cash in the register should not have access to its locked-in record. At the end of the clerk's work period, the clerk should count the cash in the register, record the amount, and turn over the cash and a record of its amount to the company cashier. The cashier, like the clerk, has access to the cash but should not have access to accounting records (or the register tape or file). A third employee, often a supervisor, compares the record of total register transactions (or the register tape or file) with the cash receipts reported by the cashier. This record is the basis for a journal entry recording over-the-counter cash receipts. The third employee has access to the records for cash but not to the actual cash. The clerk and the cashier have access to cash but not to the accounting records. None of them can make a mistake or divert cash without the difference being revealed—see the following diagram.

**Sales Department**

Clerk rings up cash sales on register; clerk prepares cash count sheet (and keeps copy) and sends to company cashier along with the cash

Supervisor reads register data, prepares register sheet (and keeps copy), and sends both to company cashier

**Cashier Department**

Cashier prepares cash records, deposit slip, and journal entry

**Cash over and short.**    Sometimes errors in making change are discovered from differences between the cash in a cash register and the record of the amount of cash receipts. Although a clerk is careful, one or more customers can be given too much or too little change. This means that at the end of a work period, the cash in a cash register might not equal the record of cash receipts. This difference is reported in the **Cash Over and Short** account, also called *Cash Short and Over,* which is an income statement account recording the income effects of cash overages and cash shortages. To illustrate, if a cash register's record shows $550 but the count of cash in the register is $555, the entry to record cash sales and its overage is

**Point:** Retailers often require cashiers to restrictively endorse checks immediately on receipt by stamping them "For deposit only."

| | | |
|---|---|---|
| Cash ........................................... | 555 | |
|     Cash Over and Short ........................ | | 5 |
|     Sales ...................................... | | 550 |
|     *To record cash sales and a cash overage.* | | |

Assets = Liabilities + Equity
+555            +   5
                         +550

On the other hand, if a cash register's record shows $625 but the count of cash in the register is $621, the entry to record cash sales and its shortage is

| | | |
|---|---|---|
| Cash ........................................... | 621 | |
| **Cash Over and Short** ......................... | 4 | |
|     Sales ...................................... | | 625 |
|     *To record cash sales and a cash shortage.* | | |

Assets = Liabilities + Equity
+621             −  4
                         +625

Since customers are more likely to dispute being shortchanged than being given too much change, the Cash Over and Short account usually has a debit balance at the end of an accounting period. A debit balance reflects an expense. It is reported on the income statement as part of general and administrative expenses. (Since the amount is usually small, it is often combined with other small expenses and reported as part of *miscellaneous expenses*—or as part of *miscellaneous revenues* if it has a credit balance.)

**Point:** Merchants begin a business day with a *change fund* in their cash register. The accounting for a change fund is similar to that for petty cash, including that for cash shortages or overages.

**Cash Receipts by Mail**    Control of cash receipts that arrive through the mail starts with the person who opens the mail. Preferably, two people are assigned the task of, and are present for, opening the mail. In this case, theft of cash receipts by mail requires collusion between these two employees. Specifically, the person(s) opening the mail enters a list (in triplicate) of money received. This list should contain a record of each sender's name, the amount, and an explanation of why the money is sent. The first copy is sent with the money to the cashier. A second copy is sent to the recordkeeper in the accounting area. A third copy is kept by the

**Point:** Collusion implies that two or more individuals are knowledgeable or involved with the activities of the other(s).

clerk(s) who opened the mail. The cashier deposits the money in a bank, and the recordkeeper records the amounts received in the accounting records.

This process reflects good internal control. That is, when the bank balance is reconciled by another person (explained later in the chapter), errors or acts of fraud by the mail clerks, the cashier, or the recordkeeper are revealed. They are revealed because the bank's record of cash deposited must agree with the records from each of the three. Moreover, if the mail clerks do not report all receipts correctly, customers will question their account balances. If the cashier does not deposit all receipts, the bank balance does not agree with the recordkeeper's cash balance. The recordkeeper and the person who reconciles the bank balance do not have access to cash and therefore have no opportunity to divert cash to themselves. This system makes errors and fraud highly unlikely. The exception is employee collusion.

### Decision Insight

**Perpetual Accounting**    **Walmart** uses a network of information links with its point-of-sale cash registers to coordinate sales, purchases, and distribution. Its supercenters, for instance, ring up 15,000 separate sales on heavy days. By using cash register information, the company can fix pricing mistakes quickly and capitalize on sales trends. ■

## Control of Cash Disbursements

Control of cash disbursements is especially important as most large thefts occur from payment of fictitious invoices. One key to controlling cash disbursements is to require all expenditures to be made by check. The only exception is small payments made from petty cash. Another key is to deny access to the accounting records to anyone other than the owner who has the authority to sign checks. A small business owner often signs checks and knows from personal contact that the items being paid for are actually received. This arrangement is impossible in large businesses. Instead, internal control procedures must be substituted for personal contact. Such procedures are designed to assure the check signer that the obligations recorded are properly incurred and should be paid. This section describes these and other internal control procedures, including the voucher system and petty cash system. A method for management of cash disbursements for purchases is described in Appendix 8B.

### Decision Insight

**Cash Budget**    Projected cash receipts and cash disbursements are often summarized in a *cash budget*. Provided that sufficient cash exists for effective operations, companies wish to minimize the cash they hold because of its risk of theft and its low return versus other investment opportunities. ■

**Voucher System of Control**    A **voucher system** is a set of procedures and approvals designed to control cash disbursements and the acceptance of obligations. The voucher system of control establishes procedures for

- Verifying, approving, and recording obligations for eventual cash disbursement.
- Issuing checks for payment of verified, approved, and recorded obligations.

A reliable voucher system follows standard procedures for every transaction. This applies even when multiple purchases are made from the same supplier.

A voucher system's control over cash disbursements begins when a company incurs an obligation that will result in payment of cash. A key factor in this system is that only approved departments and individuals are authorized to incur such obligations. The system often limits the type of obligations that a department or individual can incur. In a large retail store, for instance, only a purchasing department should be authorized to incur obligations for merchandise inventory. Another key factor is that procedures for purchasing, receiving, and paying for merchandise are divided among several departments (or individuals). These departments include the one requesting the purchase, the purchasing department, the receiving department, and the accounting department. To coordinate and control responsibilities of these departments, a company uses

**Point: MCI,** formerly **WorldCom,** paid a whopping $500 million in SEC fines for accounting fraud. Among the charges were that it inflated earnings by as much as $10 billion. Its CEO, Bernard Ebbers, was sentenced to 25 years.

**EXHIBIT 8.1**

Document Flow in a
Voucher System

several different business documents. Exhibit 8.1 shows how documents are accumulated in a **voucher,** which is an internal document (or file) used to accumulate information to control cash disbursements and to ensure that a transaction is properly recorded. This specific example begins with a *purchase requisition* and concludes with a *check* drawn against cash. Appendix 8A describes the documentation and verification necessary for a voucher system of control. It also describes the internal control objective served by each document.

A voucher system should be applied not only to purchases of inventory but to all expenditures. To illustrate, when a company receives a monthly telephone bill, it should review and verify the charges, prepare a voucher (file), and insert the bill. This transaction is then recorded with a journal entry. If the amount is currently due, a check is issued. If not, the voucher is filed for payment on its due date. If no voucher is prepared, verifying the invoice and its amount after several days or weeks can be difficult. Also, without records, a dishonest employee could collude with a dishonest supplier to get more than one payment for an obligation, payment for excessive amounts, or payment for goods and services not received. An effective voucher system helps prevent such frauds.

**Point:** A *voucher* is an internal document (or file).

**Point:** The basic purposes of paper and electronic documents are similar. However, the internal control system must change to reflect different risks, including confidential and competitive-sensitive information that is at greater risk in electronic systems.

## Decision Insight

**Cyber Setup** The FTC is on the cutting edge of cyber-sleuthing. Opportunists in search of easy money are lured to **WeMarket4U.net/SundaeStation** and **WeMarket4U.net/FatFoe**. Take the bait and you get warned. The top 5 fraud complaints as compiled by the Bureau of Consumer Protection are shown to the right. ■

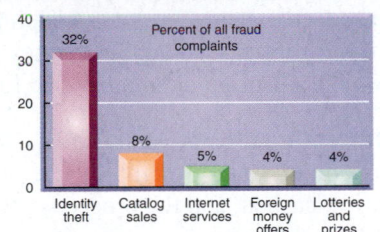

## Quick Check

Answers — p. 343

3. Why must a company hold liquid assets?
4. Why does a company hold cash equivalent assets in addition to cash?
5. Identify at least two assets that are classified as cash equivalents.
6. Good internal control procedures for cash include which of the following? (*a*) All cash disbursements, other than those for very small amounts, are made by check; (*b*) One employee counts cash received from sales and promptly deposits cash receipts; or (*c*) Cash receipts by mail are opened by one employee who is then responsible for recording and depositing them.
7. Should all companies require a voucher system? At what point in a company's growth would you recommend a voucher system?

**P2**    Explain and record petty cash fund transactions.

**Petty Cash System of Control**    A basic principle for controlling cash disbursements is that all payments must be made by check. An exception to this rule is made for *petty cash disbursements,* which are the small payments required for items such as postage, courier fees, minor repairs, and low-cost supplies. To avoid the time and cost of writing checks for small amounts, a company sets up a petty cash fund to make small payments. (**Petty cash** activities are part of an *imprest system,* which designates advance money to establish the fund, to withdraw from the fund, and to reimburse the fund.)

**Operating a petty cash fund.**    Establishing a petty cash fund requires estimating the total amount of small payments likely to be made during a short period such as a week or month. A check is then drawn by the company cashier for an amount slightly in excess of this estimate. This check is recorded with a debit to the Petty Cash account (an asset) and a credit to Cash. The check is cashed, and the currency is given to an employee designated as the *petty cashier* or *petty cash custodian.* The petty cashier is responsible for keeping this cash safe, making payments from the fund, and keeping records of it in a secure place referred to as the *petty cashbox.*

**Point:** A petty cash fund is used only for business expenses.

When each cash disbursement is made, the person receiving payment should sign a prenumbered *petty cash receipt,* also called *petty cash ticket*—see Exhibit 8.2. The petty cash receipt is then placed in the petty cashbox with the remaining money. Under this system, the sum of all receipts plus the remaining cash equals the total fund amount. A $100 petty cash fund, for instance, contains any combination of cash and petty cash receipts that totals $100 (examples are $80 cash plus $20 in receipts, or $10 cash plus $90 in receipts). Each disbursement reduces cash and increases the amount of receipts in the petty cashbox.

**EXHIBIT 8.2**

Petty Cash Receipt

**Z-Mart**    No. 9

**PETTY CASH RECEIPT**

For  Freight charges
Date  November 5, 2009                Approved by  fl Gull
Charge to  Merchandise Inventory
Amount  $6.75                Received by  Dl Zll

**Point:** Petty cash receipts with either no signature or a forged signature usually indicate misuse of petty cash. Companies respond with surprise petty cash counts for verification.

The petty cash fund should be reimbursed when it is nearing zero and at the end of an accounting period when financial statements are prepared. For this purpose, the petty cashier sorts the paid receipts by the type of expense or account and then totals the receipts. The petty cashier presents all paid receipts to the company cashier, who stamps all receipts *paid* so they cannot be reused, files them for recordkeeping, and gives the petty cashier a check for their sum. When this check is cashed and the money placed in the cashbox, the total money in the cashbox is restored to its original amount. The fund is now ready for a new cycle of petty cash payments.

**Illustrating a petty cash fund.**    To illustrate, assume Z-Mart establishes a petty cash fund on November 1 and designates one of its office employees as the petty cashier. A $75 check is drawn, cashed, and the proceeds given to the petty cashier. The entry to record the setup of this petty cash fund is

Assets = Liabilities + Equity
+75
−75

| Nov. 1 | Petty Cash ................................ | 75 | |
| | Cash ................................ | | 75 |
| | To establish a petty cash fund. | | |

**Point:** Reducing or eliminating a petty cash fund requires a credit to Petty Cash.

**Point:** Although *individual* petty cash disbursements are not evidenced by a check, the initial petty cash fund is evidenced by a check, and later petty cash expenditures are evidenced by a check to replenish them *in total.*

After the petty cash fund is established, the Petty Cash account is not debited or credited again unless the amount of the fund is changed. (A fund should be increased if it requires reimbursement too frequently. On the other hand, if the fund is too large, some of its money should be redeposited in the Cash account.)

Next, assume that Z-Mart's petty cashier makes several November payments from petty cash. Each person who received payment is required to sign a receipt. On November 27, after making a $26.50 cash payment for tile cleaning, only $3.70 cash remains in the fund. The petty cashier then summarizes and totals the petty cash receipts as shown in Exhibit 8.3.

**EXHIBIT 8.3**

Petty Cash Payments Report

| Z-MART | | |
|---|---|---|
| **Petty Cash Payments Report** | | |
| **Miscellaneous Expenses** | | |
| Nov. 2    Cleaning of LCD panels ........................... | $20.00 | |
| Nov. 27   Tile cleaning ..................................... | 26.50 | $ 46.50 |
| **Merchandise Inventory (transportation-in)** | | |
| Nov. 5    Transport of merchandise purchased ................ | 6.75 | |
| Nov. 20   Transport of merchandise purchased ............... | 8.30 | 15.05 |
| **Delivery Expense** | | |
| Nov. 18   Customer's package delivered ..................... | | 5.00 |
| **Office Supplies Expense** | | |
| Nov. 15   Purchase of office supplies immediately used ......... | | 4.75 |
| **Total** ...................................................... | | **$71.30** |

**Point:** This report can also include receipt number and names of those who approved and received cash payment (see Demo Problem 2).

The petty cash payments report and all receipts are given to the company cashier in exchange for a $71.30 check to reimburse the fund. The petty cashier cashes the check and puts the $71.30 cash in the petty cashbox. The company records this reimbursement as follows.

| Nov. 27 | Miscellaneous Expenses ......................... | 46.50 | |
| | Merchandise Inventory .......................... | 15.05 | |
| | Delivery Expense .............................. | 5.00 | |
| | Office Supplies Expense ........................ | 4.75 | |
| | Cash ..................................... | | 71.30 |
| | *To reimburse petty cash.* | | |

Assets = Liabilities + Equity
−71.30                  −46.50
                        −15.05
                        − 5.00
                        − 4.75

A petty cash fund is usually reimbursed at the end of an accounting period so that expenses are recorded in the proper period, even if the fund is not low on money. If the fund is not reimbursed at the end of a period, the financial statements would show both an overstated cash asset and understated expenses (or assets) that were paid out of petty cash. Some companies do not reimburse the petty cash fund at the end of each period under the notion that this amount is immaterial to users of financial statements.

**Point:** To avoid errors in recording petty cash reimbursement, follow these steps: (1) prepare payments report, (2) compute cash needed by subtracting cash remaining from total fund amount, (3) record entry, and (4) check "Dr. = Cr." in entry. Any difference is Cash Over and Short.

**Increasing or decreasing a petty cash fund.**   A decision to increase or decrease a petty cash fund is often made when reimbursing it. To illustrate, assume Z-Mart decides to *increase* its petty cash fund from $75 to $100 on November 27 when it reimburses the fund. The entries required are to (1) reimburse the fund as usual (see the preceding November 27 entry) and (2) increase the fund amount as follows.

| Nov. 27 | Petty Cash ................................. | 25 | |
| | Cash ..................................... | | 25 |
| | *To increase the petty cash fund amount.* | | |

Alternatively, if Z-Mart *decreases* the petty cash fund from $75 to $55 on November 27, the entry is to (1) credit Petty Cash for $20 (decreasing the fund from $75 to $55) and (2) debit Cash for $20 (reflecting the $20 transfer from Petty Cash to Cash).

**Cash over and short.**   Sometimes a petty cashier fails to get a receipt for payment or overpays for the amount due. When this occurs and the fund is later reimbursed, the petty cash payments report plus the cash remaining will not total to the fund balance. This mistake causes the fund to be *short*. This shortage is recorded as an expense in the reimbursing entry with a debit to the Cash Over and Short account. (An overage in the petty cash fund is recorded with a credit to Cash Over and Short in the reimbursing entry.) To illustrate, prepare the June 1 entry

| **Summary of Petty Cash Accounting** | | | |
|---|---|---|---|
| Event | Petty Cash | Cash | Expenses |
| Set up fund ..... | Dr. | Cr. | — |
| Reimburse fund .. | — | Cr. | Dr. |
| Increase fund.... | Dr. | Cr. | — |
| Decrease fund... | Cr. | Dr. | — |

**$200 Petty Cash Fund**

$15 Cash    $7 Short    $178 Receipts

to reimburse a $200 petty cash fund when its payments report shows $178 in miscellaneous expenses and $15 cash remains.

| | | | |
|---|---|---|---|
| June 1 | Miscellaneous Expenses ......................... | 178 | |
| | **Cash Over and Short** ....................... | **7** | |
| | Cash ...................................... | | 185 |
| | *To reimburse petty cash.* | | |

## Decision Insight

**Warning Signs** There are clues to internal control violations. Warning signs from accounting include (1) an increase in customer refunds—could be fake, (2) missing documents—could be used for fraud, (3) differences between bank deposits and cash receipts—could be cash embezzled, and (4) delayed recording—could reflect fraudulent records. Warning signs from employees include (1) lifestyle change—could be embezzlement, (2) too close with suppliers—could signal fraudulent transactions, and (3) failure to leave job, even for vacations—could conceal fraudulent activities. ■

## Quick Check

Answers — p. 343

8. Why are some cash payments made from a petty cash fund and not by check?
9. Why should a petty cash fund be reimbursed at the end of an accounting period?
10. Identify at least two results of reimbursing a petty cash fund.

# BANKING ACTIVITIES AS CONTROLS

Banks (and other financial institutions) provide many services, including helping companies control cash. Banks safeguard cash, provide detailed and independent records of cash transactions, and are a source of cash financing. This section describes these services and the documents provided by banking activities that increase managers' control over cash.

## Basic Bank Services

This section explains basic bank services—such as the bank account, the bank deposit, and checking—that contribute to the control of cash.

**Bank Account, Deposit, and Check** A *bank account* is a record set up by a bank for a customer. It permits a customer to deposit money for safekeeping and helps control withdrawals. To limit access to a bank account, all persons authorized to write checks on the account must sign a **signature card,** which bank employees use to verify signatures on checks. Many companies have more than one bank account to serve different needs and to handle special transactions such as payroll.

Each bank deposit is supported by a **deposit ticket,** which lists items such as currency, coins, and checks deposited along with their corresponding dollar amounts. The bank gives the customer a copy of the deposit ticket or a deposit receipt as proof of the deposit. Exhibit 8.4 shows one type of deposit ticket.

To withdraw money from an account, the depositor can use a **check,** which is a document signed by the depositor instructing the bank to pay a specified amount of money to a designated recipient. A check involves three parties: a *maker* who signs the check, a *payee* who is the recipient, and a *bank* (or *payer*) on which the check is drawn. The bank provides a depositor the checks that are serially numbered and imprinted with the name and address of both the depositor and bank. Both checks and deposit tickets are imprinted with identification codes in magnetic ink

**Point:** Online banking services include the ability to stop payment on a check, move money between accounts, get up-to-date balances, and identify cleared checks and deposits.

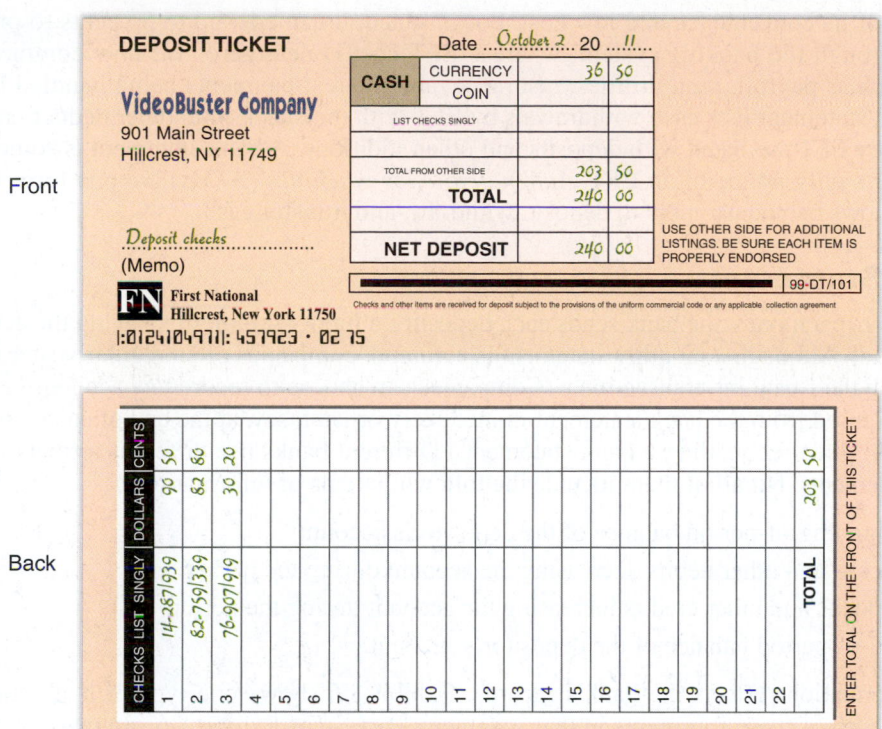

**EXHIBIT 8.4**

Deposit Ticket

for computer processing. Exhibit 8.5 shows one type of check. It is accompanied with an optional *remittance advice* explaining the payment. When a remittance advice is unavailable, the *memo* line is often used for a brief explanation.

**Electronic Funds Transfer** **Electronic funds transfer (EFT)** is the electronic transfer of cash from one party to another. No paper documents are necessary. Banks simply transfer cash from one account to another with a journal entry. Companies are increasingly using EFT

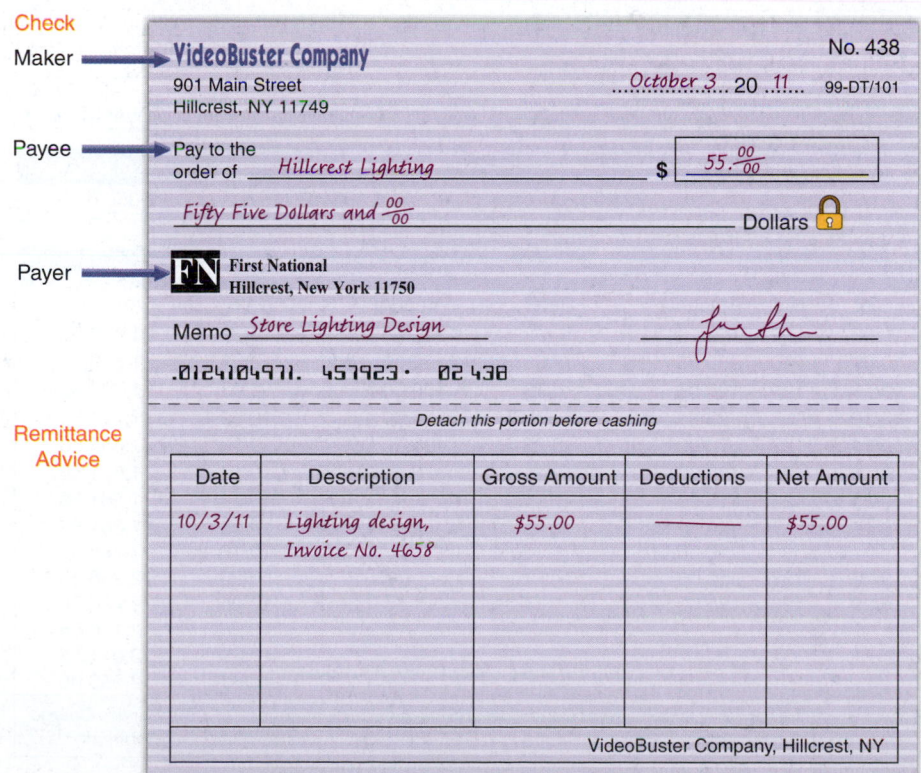

**EXHIBIT 8.5**

Check with Remittance Advice

because of its convenience and low cost. For instance, it can cost up to 50 cents to process a check through the banking system, whereas EFT cost is near zero. We now commonly see items such as payroll, rent, utilities, insurance, and interest payments being handled by EFT. The bank statement lists cash withdrawals by EFT with the checks and other deductions. Cash receipts by EFT are listed with deposits and other additions. A bank statement is sometimes a depositor's only notice of an EFT. *Automated teller machines (ATMs)* are one form of EFT, which allows bank customers to deposit, withdraw, and transfer cash.

## Bank Statement

Usually once a month, the bank sends each depositor a **bank statement** showing the activity in the account. Although a monthly statement is common, companies often regularly access information on their banking transactions. (Companies can choose to record any accounting adjustments required from the bank statement immediately or later, say, at the end of each day, week, month, or when reconciling a bank statement.) Different banks use different formats for their bank statements, but all of them include the following items of information:

1.  Beginning-of-period balance of the depositor's account.
2.  Checks and other debits decreasing the account during the period.
3.  Deposits and other credits increasing the account during the period.
4.  End-of-period balance of the depositor's account.

This information reflects the bank's records. Exhibit 8.6 shows one type of bank statement. Identify each of these four items in that statement. Part Ⓐ of Exhibit 8.6 summarizes changes in the account. Part Ⓑ lists paid checks along with other debits. Part Ⓒ lists deposits and credits to the account, and part Ⓓ shows the daily account balances.

In reading a bank statement note that a depositor's account is a liability on the bank's records. This is so because the money belongs to the depositor, not the bank. When a depositor increases

**EXHIBIT 8.6**

Bank Statement

the account balance, the bank records it with a *credit* to that liability account. This means that debit memos from the bank produce *credits* on the depositor's books, and credit memos from the bank produce *debits* on the depositor's books.

Enclosed with a bank statement is a list of the depositor's canceled checks (or the actual canceled checks) along with any debit or credit memoranda affecting the account. Increasingly, banks are showing canceled checks electronically via online access to accounts. **Canceled checks** are checks the bank has paid and deducted from the customer's account during the period. Other deductions that can appear on a bank statement include (1) service charges and fees assessed by the bank, (2) checks deposited that are uncollectible, (3) corrections of previous errors, (4) withdrawals through automated teller machines (ATMs), and (5) periodic payments arranged in advance by a depositor. (Most company checking accounts do not allow ATM withdrawals because of the company's desire to make all disbursements by check.) Except for service charges, the bank notifies the depositor of each deduction with a debit memorandum when the bank reduces the balance. A copy of each debit memorandum is usually sent with the statement (again, this information is often available earlier via online access and notifications).

Transactions that increase the depositor's account include amounts the bank collects on behalf of the depositor and the corrections of previous errors. Credit memoranda notify the depositor of all increases when they are recorded. A copy of each credit memorandum is often sent with the bank statement. Banks that pay interest on checking accounts often compute the amount of interest earned on the average cash balance and credit it to the depositor's account each period. In Exhibit 8.6, the bank credits $8.42 of interest to the account.

**Global:** If cash is in more than one currency, a company usually translates these amounts into U.S. dollars using the exchange rate as of the balance sheet date. Also, a company must disclose any restrictions on cash accounts located outside the U.S.

## Bank Reconciliation

When a company deposits all cash receipts and makes all cash payments (except petty cash) by check, it can use the bank statement for proving the accuracy of its cash records. This is done using a **bank reconciliation,** which is a report explaining any differences between the checking account balance according to the depositor's records and the balance reported on the bank statement. The figure below reflects this process, which we describe in the following sections.

**P3** Prepare a bank reconciliation.

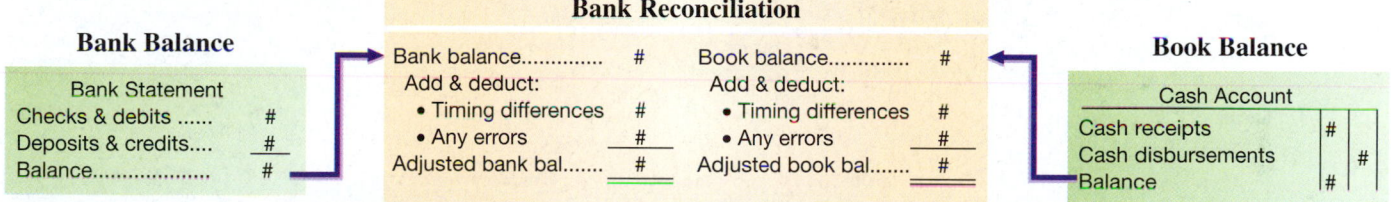

**Purpose of Bank Reconciliation** The balance of a checking account reported on the bank statement rarely equals the balance in the depositor's accounting records. This is usually due to information that one party has that the other does not. We must therefore prove the accuracy of both the depositor's records and those of the bank. This means we must *reconcile* the two balances and explain or account for any differences in them. Among the factors causing the bank statement balance to differ from the depositor's book balance are these:

- **Outstanding checks. Outstanding checks** are checks written (or drawn) by the depositor, deducted on the depositor's records, and sent to the payees but not yet received by the bank for payment at the bank statement date.
- **Deposits in transit** (also called **outstanding deposits**). **Deposits in transit** are deposits made and recorded by the depositor but not yet recorded on the bank statement. For example, companies can make deposits (in the night depository) at the end of a business day after the bank is closed. If such a deposit occurred on a bank statement date, it would not appear on this period's statement. The bank would record such a deposit on the next business day, and it would appear on the next period's bank statement. Deposits mailed to the bank near the end of a period also can be in transit and unrecorded when the statement is prepared.
- **Deductions for uncollectible items and for services.** A company sometimes deposits another party's check that is uncollectible (usually meaning the balance in that party's account is not large enough to cover the check). This check is called a *non-sufficient funds (NSF)* check. The bank would have initially credited the depositor's account for the amount of the

**Forms of Check Fraud (CkFraud.org)**
- Forged signatures—legitimate blank checks with fake payer signature
- Forged endorsements—stolen check that is endorsed and cashed by someone other than the payee
- Counterfeit checks—fraudulent checks with fake payer signature
- Altered checks—legitimate check altered (such as changed payee or amount) to benefit perpetrator
- Check kiting—deposit check from one bank account (without sufficient funds) into a second bank account

check. When the bank learns the check is uncollectible, it debits (reduces) the depositor's account for the amount of that check. The bank may also charge the depositor a fee for processing an uncollectible check and notify the depositor of the deduction by sending a debit memorandum. The depositor should record each deduction when a debit memorandum is received, but an entry is sometimes not made until the bank reconciliation is prepared. Other possible bank charges to a depositor's account that are first reported on a bank statement include printing new checks and service fees.

- **Additions for collections and for interest.** Banks sometimes act as collection agents for their depositors by collecting notes and other items. Banks can also receive electronic funds transfers to the depositor's account. When a bank collects an item, it is added to the depositor's account, less any service fee. The bank also sends a credit memorandum to notify the depositor of the transaction. When the memorandum is received, the depositor should record it; yet it sometimes remains unrecorded until the bank reconciliation is prepared. The bank statement also includes a credit for any interest earned.

- **Errors.** Both banks and depositors can make errors. Bank errors might not be discovered until the depositor prepares the bank reconciliation. Also, depositor errors are sometimes discovered when the bank balance is reconciled. Error testing includes: (a) comparing deposits on the bank statement with deposits in the accounting records and (b) comparing canceled checks on the bank statement with checks recorded in the accounting records.

**Point:** Small businesses with few employees often allow recordkeepers to both write checks and keep the general ledger. If this is done, it is essential that the owner do the bank reconciliation.

**Point:** The person preparing the bank reconciliation should not be responsible for processing cash receipts, managing checks, or maintaining cash records.

**Illustration of a Bank Reconciliation**   We follow nine steps in preparing the bank reconciliation. It is helpful to refer to the bank reconciliation in Exhibit 8.7 when studying steps ① through ⑨.

**EXHIBIT 8.7**

Bank Reconciliation

| VIDEOBUSTER Bank Reconciliation October 31, 2011 | | | | | | |
|---|---|---|---|---|---|---|
| ① | Bank statement balance .......... | | $ 2,050.00 | ⑤ | Book balance ................... | $ 1,404.58 |
| ② | Add | | | ⑥ | Add | |
| | Deposit of Oct. 31 in transit .... | | 145.00 | | Collect $500 note less $15 fee .... $485.00 | |
| | | | 2,195.00 | | Interest earned ................ 8.42 | 493.42 |
| ③ | Deduct | | | | | 1,898.00 |
| | Outstanding checks | | | ⑦ | Deduct | |
| | No. 124 .................. $150.00 | | | | Check printing charge ........... 23.00 | |
| | No. 126 .................. 200.00 | | 350.00 | | NSF check plus service fee ....... 30.00 | 53.00 |
| ④ | **Adjusted bank balance** | | **$1,845.00** | ⑧ | **Adjusted book balance** ......... | **$1,845.00** |
| | | | ⑨ Balances are equal (reconciled) | | | |

**Point:** Outstanding checks are identified by comparing canceled checks on the bank statement with checks recorded. This includes identifying any outstanding checks listed on the *previous* period's bank reconciliation that are not included in the canceled checks on this period's bank statement.

① Identify the bank statement balance of the cash account (*balance per bank*). VideoBuster's bank balance is $2,050.

② Identify and list any unrecorded deposits and any bank errors understating the bank balance. Add them to the bank balance. VideoBuster's $145 deposit placed in the bank's night depository on October 31 is not recorded on its bank statement.

③ Identify and list any outstanding checks and any bank errors overstating the bank balance. Deduct them from the bank balance. VideoBuster's comparison of canceled checks with its books shows two checks outstanding: No. 124 for $150 and No. 126 for $200.

④ Compute the *adjusted bank balance,* also called the *corrected* or *reconciled balance.*

⑤ Identify the company's book balance of the cash account (*balance per book*). VideoBuster's book balance is $1,404.58.

⑥ Identify and list any unrecorded credit memoranda from the bank, any interest earned, and errors understating the book balance. Add them to the book balance. VideoBuster's bank statement includes a credit memorandum showing the bank collected a note receivable for the company on October 23. The note's proceeds of $500 (minus a $15 collection fee) are credited to the company's account. VideoBuster's bank statement also shows a credit of $8.42 for interest earned on the average cash balance. There was no prior notification of this item, and it is not yet recorded.

⑦ Identify and list any unrecorded debit memoranda from the bank, any service charges, and errors overstating the book balance. Deduct them from the book balance. Debits on VideoBuster's bank statement that are not yet recorded include (a) a $23 charge for check printing and (b) an NSF check for $20 plus a related $10 processing fee. (The NSF check is dated October 16 and was included in the book balance.)

⑧ Compute the *adjusted book balance,* also called *corrected* or *reconciled balance.*

⑨ Verify that the two adjusted balances from steps 4 and 8 are equal. If so, they are reconciled. If not, check for accuracy and missing data to achieve reconciliation.

**Point:** Adjusting entries can be combined into one compound entry.

**Adjusting Entries from a Bank Reconciliation**   A bank reconciliation often identifies unrecorded items that need recording by the company. In VideoBuster's reconciliation, the adjusted balance of $1,845 is the correct balance as of October 31. But the company's accounting records show a $1,404.58 balance. We must prepare journal entries to adjust the book balance to the correct balance. It is important to remember that only the items reconciling the *book balance* require adjustment. A review of Exhibit 8.7 indicates that four entries are required for VideoBuster.

**Collection of note.**   The first entry is to record the proceeds of its note receivable collected by the bank less the expense of having the bank perform that service.

| Oct. 31 | Cash | 485 | |
| | Collection Expense | 15 | |
| | Notes Receivable | | 500 |
| | *To record the collection fee and proceeds for a note collected by the bank.* | | |

Assets = Liabilities + Equity
+485              −15
−500

**Interest earned.**   The second entry records interest credited to its account by the bank.

| Oct. 31 | Cash | 8.42 | |
| | Interest Revenue | | 8.42 |
| | *To record interest earned on the cash balance in the checking account.* | | |

Assets = Liabilities + Equity
+8.42             +8.42

**Check printing.**   The third entry records expenses for the check printing charge.

| Oct. 31 | Miscellaneous Expenses | 23 | |
| | Cash | | 23 |
| | *Check printing charge.* | | |

Assets = Liabilities + Equity
−23              −23

**NSF check.**   The fourth entry records the NSF check that is returned as uncollectible. The $20 check was originally received from T. Woods in payment of his account and then deposited. The bank charged $10 for handling the NSF check and deducted $30 total from VideoBuster's account. This means the entry must reverse the effects of the original entry made when the check was received and must record (add) the $10 bank fee.

**Point:** The company will try to collect the entire NSF amount of $30 from customer.

| Oct. 31 | Accounts Receivable—T. Woods | 30 | |
| | Cash | | 30 |
| | *To charge Woods' account for $20 NSF check and $10 bank fee.* | | |

Assets = Liabilities + Equity
+30
−30

**Point:** The Demo Problem 1 shows an adjusting entry for an error correction.

| Cash | | | |
|---|---|---|---|
| Unadj. bal. | 1,404.58 | | |
| ⑥ | 485.00 | ⑦ | 23.00 |
| ⑥ | 8.42 | ⑦ | 30.00 |
| Adj. bal. | 1,845.00 | | |

After these four entries are recorded, the book balance of cash is adjusted to the correct amount of $1,845 (computed as $1,404.58 + $485 + $8.42 − $23 − $30). The Cash T-account to the side shows the same computation, where entries are keyed to the numerical codes in Exhibit 8.7.

## Decision Insight

**Fraud**   A survey reports that 74% of employees had 'personally seen' or had 'firsthand knowledge of' fraud or misconduct in their company within the past year. These employees also identified factors that would drive employees and managers to engage in misconduct. They cited pressures to meet targets, lack of standards, and other root causes—see graphic (KPMG 2009). ■

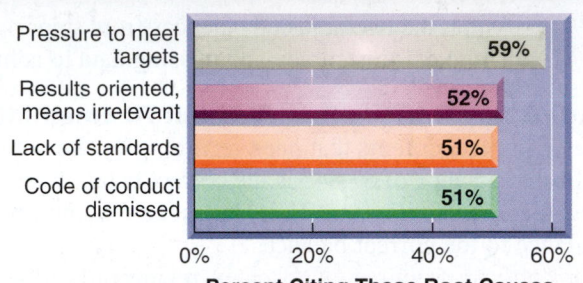

## Quick Check                                             Answers — p. 344

11. What is a bank statement?
12. What is the meaning of the phrase *to reconcile a bank balance?*
13. Why do we reconcile the bank statement balance of cash and the depositor's book balance of cash?
14. List at least two items affecting the *bank balance* side of a bank reconciliation and indicate whether the items are added or subtracted.
15. List at least three items affecting the *book balance* side of a bank reconciliation and indicate whether the items are added or subtracted.

# GLOBAL VIEW

This section discusses similarities and differences between U.S. GAAP and IFRS regarding internal controls and in the accounting and reporting of cash.

**Internal Control Purposes, Principles, and Procedures**   Both U.S. GAAP and IFRS aim for high-quality financial reporting. That aim translates into enhanced internal controls worldwide. Specifically, the purposes and principles of internal control systems are fundamentally the same across the globe. However, culture and other realities suggest different emphases on the mix of control procedures, and some sensitivity to different customs and environments when establishing that mix. Nevertheless, the discussion in this chapter applies internationally. **Nokia** provides the following description of its control activities.

**NOKIA**

> Nokia has an internal audit function that acts as an independent appraisal function by examining and evaluating the adequacy and effectiveness of the company's system of internal control.

**Control of Cash**   Accounting definitions for cash are similar for U.S. GAAP and IFRS. The need for control of cash is universal and applies globally. This means that companies worldwide desire to apply cash management procedures as explained in this chapter and aim to control both cash receipts and disbursements. Accordingly, systems that employ tools such as cash monitoring mechanisms, verification of documents, and petty cash processes are applied worldwide. The basic techniques explained in this chapter are part of those control procedures.

**Banking Activities as Controls**    There is a global demand for banking services, bank statements, and bank reconciliations. To the extent feasible, companies utilize banking services as part of their effective control procedures. Further, bank statements are similarly used along with bank reconciliations to control and monitor cash.

 **IFRS**
_____

Internal controls are crucial to companies that convert from U.S. GAAP to IFRS. Major risks include misstatement of financial information and fraud. Other risks are ineffective communication of the impact of this change for investors, creditors and others, and management's inability to certify the effectiveness of controls over financial reporting. ■

---

**Days' Sales Uncollected**        **Decision Analysis**

An important part of cash management is monitoring the receipt of cash from receivables. If customers and others who owe money to a company are delayed in payment, then that company can find it difficult to pay its obligations when they are due. A company's customers are crucial partners in its cash management. Many companies attract customers by selling to them on credit. This means that cash receipts from customers are delayed until accounts receivable are collected.

**A1**  Compute the days' sales uncollected ratio and use it to assess liquidity.

One measure of how quickly a company can convert its accounts receivable into cash is the **days' sales uncollected,** also called _days' sales in receivables_. This measure is computed by dividing the current balance of receivables by net credit sales over the year just completed and then multiplying by 365 (number of days in a year). Since net credit sales usually are not reported to external users, the net sales (or revenues) figure is commonly used in the computation as in Exhibit 8.8.

$$\text{Days' sales uncollected} = \frac{\text{Accounts receivable}}{\text{Net sales}} \times 365$$

**EXHIBIT 8.8**

Days' Sales Uncollected

We use days' sales uncollected to estimate how much time is likely to pass before the current amount of accounts receivable is received in cash. For evaluation purposes, we need to compare this estimate to that for other companies in the same industry. We also make comparisons between current and prior periods.

To illustrate, we select data from the annual reports of two toy manufacturers, **Hasbro** and **Mattel**. Their days' sales uncollected figures are shown in Exhibit 8.9.

**EXHIBIT 8.9**

Analysis Using Days' Sales Uncollected

| Company | Figure ($ millions) | 2009 | 2008 | 2007 | 2006 | 2005 |
|---------|---------------------|------|------|------|------|------|
| **Hasbro** | Accounts receivable . . . . . . . . . . | $1,039 | $612 | $655 | $556 | $523 |
|  | Net sales . . . . . . . . . . . . . . . . . | $4,068 | $4,022 | $3,838 | $3,151 | $3,088 |
|  | **Days' sales uncollected** . . . . | **93 days** | **56 days** | **62 days** | **64 days** | **62 days** |
| **Mattel** | Accounts receivable . . . . . . . . . | $749 | $874 | $991 | $944 | $761 |
|  | Net sales . . . . . . . . . . . . . . . . | $5,431 | $5,918 | $5,970 | $5,650 | $5,179 |
|  | **Days' sales uncollected** . . . . | **50 days** | **54 days** | **61 days** | **61 days** | **54 days** |

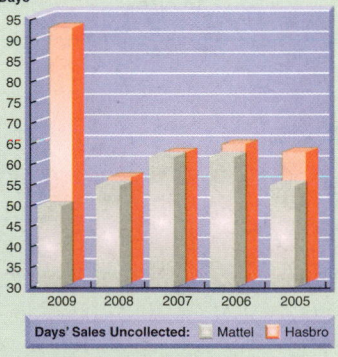

Days' sales uncollected for Hasbro in 2009 is computed as ($1,039/$4,068) × 365 days = 93 days. This means that it will take about 93 days to collect cash from ending accounts receivable. This number reflects one or more of the following factors: a company's ability to collect receivables, customer financial health, customer payment strategies, and discount terms. To further assess days' sales uncollected for Hasbro, we compare it to four prior years and to those of Mattel. We see that Hasbro's days' sales uncollected has worsened in 2009 as it takes much longer to collect its receivables relative to the prior four years. In comparison, Mattel fluctuated on days' sales uncollected for each of those years—from 54 days, to 61 days for two years, then back down to 54 days, and then down to the current 50 days. For all years, Mattel is superior to Hasbro on this measure of cash management. The less time that money is tied up in receivables often translates into increased profitability.

**Decision Maker**    Answer — p. 343

**Sales Representative**    The sales staff is told to take action to help reduce days' sales uncollected for cash management purposes. What can you, a salesperson, do to reduce days' sales uncollected? ■

## DEMONSTRATION PROBLEM 1

Prepare a bank reconciliation for Jamboree Enterprises for the month ended November 30, 2011. The following information is available to reconcile Jamboree Enterprises' book balance of cash with its bank statement balance as of November 30, 2011:

a. After all posting is complete on November 30, the company's book balance of Cash has a $16,380 debit balance, but its bank statement shows a $38,520 balance.

b. Checks No. 2024 for $4,810 and No. 2026 for $5,000 are outstanding.

c. In comparing the canceled checks on the bank statement with the entries in the accounting records, it is found that Check No. 2025 in payment of rent is correctly drawn for $1,000 but is erroneously entered in the accounting records as $880.

d. The November 30 deposit of $17,150 was placed in the night depository after banking hours on that date, and this amount does not appear on the bank statement.

e. In reviewing the bank statement, a check written by Jumbo Enterprises in the amount of $160 was erroneously drawn against Jamboree's account.

f. A credit memorandum enclosed with the bank statement indicates that the bank collected a $30,000 note and $900 of related interest on Jamboree's behalf. This transaction was not recorded by Jamboree prior to receiving the statement.

g. A debit memorandum for $1,100 lists a $1,100 NSF check received from a customer, Marilyn Welch. Jamboree had not recorded the return of this check before receiving the statement.

h. Bank service charges for November total $40. These charges were not recorded by Jamboree before receiving the statement.

### PLANNING THE SOLUTION

● Set up a bank reconciliation with a bank side and a book side (as in Exhibit 8.7). Leave room to both add and deduct items. Each column will result in a reconciled, equal balance.

● Examine each item *a* through *h* to determine whether it affects the book or the bank balance and whether it should be added or deducted from the bank or book balance.

● After all items are analyzed, complete the reconciliation and arrive at a reconciled balance between the bank side and the book side.

● For each reconciling item on the book side, prepare an adjusting entry. Additions to the book side require an adjusting entry that debits Cash. Deductions on the book side require an adjusting entry that credits Cash.

### SOLUTION TO DEMONSTRATION PROBLEM 1

**JAMBOREE ENTERPRISES**
**Bank Reconciliation**
**November 30, 2011**

| Bank statement balance ..... | | $ 38,520 | Book balance ............. | | $ 16,380 |
|---|---|---|---|---|---|
| Add | | | Add | | |
| Deposit of Nov. 30 ....... | $17,150 | | Collection of note ........ | $30,000 | |
| Bank error (Jumbo) ....... | 160 | 17,310 | Interest earned .......... | 900 | 30,900 |
| | | 55,830 | | | 47,280 |
| Deduct | | | Deduct | | |
| Outstanding checks | | | NSF check (M. Welch) .... | 1,100 | |
| No. 2024 ............. | 4,810 | | Recording error (# 2025) ... | 120 | |
| No. 2026 ............. | 5,000 | 9,810 | Service charge ........... | 40 | 1,260 |
| **Adjusted bank balance** ... | | **$46,020** | **Adjusted book balance** .... | | **$46,020** |

**Required Adjusting Entries for Jamboree**

| | | | |
|---|---|---:|---:|
| Nov. 30 | Cash . . . . . . . . . . . . . . . . . . . . . . . . . . . . . . . . . . . . . . . . . | 30,900 | |
| | Notes Receivable . . . . . . . . . . . . . . . . . . . . . . . . . . | | 30,000 |
| | Interest Earned . . . . . . . . . . . . . . . . . . . . . . . . . . . | | 900 |
| | *To record collection of note with interest.* | | |
| Nov. 30 | Accounts Receivable—M. Welch . . . . . . . . . . . . . . . . . . | 1,100 | |
| | Cash . . . . . . . . . . . . . . . . . . . . . . . . . . . . . . . . . . . . | | 1,100 |
| | *To reinstate account due from an NSF check.* | | |
| Nov. 30 | Rent Expense . . . . . . . . . . . . . . . . . . . . . . . . . . . . . . . . | 120 | |
| | Cash . . . . . . . . . . . . . . . . . . . . . . . . . . . . . . . . . . . . | | 120 |
| | *To correct recording error on check no. 2025.* | | |
| Nov. 30 | Bank Service Charges . . . . . . . . . . . . . . . . . . . . . . . . . | 40 | |
| | Cash . . . . . . . . . . . . . . . . . . . . . . . . . . . . . . . . . . . . | | 40 |
| | *To record bank service charges.* | | |

**Point:** Error correction can alternatively involve (1) reversing the error entry, and (2) recording the correct entry.

# DEMONSTRATION PROBLEM 2

Bacardi Company established a $150 petty cash fund with Dean Martin as the petty cashier. When the fund balance reached $19 cash, Martin prepared a petty cash payment report, which follows.

| Petty Cash Payments Report | | | | |
|---|---|---|---|---|
| **Receipt No.** | **Account Charged** | | **Approved by** | **Received by** |
| 12 | Delivery Expense . . . . . . . . . . . . . | $ 29 | Martin | A. Smirnoff |
| 13 | Merchandise Inventory . . . . . . . . . | 18 | Martin | J. Daniels |
| 15 | (Omitted) . . . . . . . . . . . . . . . . . . . | 32 | Martin | C. Carlsberg |
| 16 | Miscellaneous Expense . . . . . . . . . | 41 | (Omitted) | J. Walker |
| | Total . . . . . . . . . . . . . . . . . . . . . . | $120 | | |

**Required**

1. Identify four internal control weaknesses from the payment report.
2. Prepare general journal entries to record:
   **a.** Establishment of the petty cash fund.
   **b.** Reimbursement of the fund. (Assume for this part only that petty cash receipt no. 15 was issued for miscellaneous expenses.)
3. What is the Petty Cash account balance immediately before reimbursement? Immediately after reimbursement?

## SOLUTION TO DEMONSTRATION PROBLEM 2

1. Four internal control weaknesses are
   **a.** Petty cash ticket no. 14 is missing. Its omission raises questions about the petty cashier's management of the fund.
   **b.** The $19 cash balance means that $131 has been withdrawn ($150 − $19 = $131). However, the total amount of the petty cash receipts is only $120 ($29 + $18 + $32 + $41). The fund is $11 short of cash ($131 − $120 = $11). Was petty cash receipt no. 14 issued for $11? Management should investigate.
   **c.** The petty cashier (Martin) did not sign petty cash receipt no. 16. This omission could have been an oversight on his part or he might not have authorized the payment. Management should investigate.
   **d.** Petty cash receipt no. 15 does not indicate which account to charge. This omission could have been an oversight on the petty cashier's part. Management could check with C. Carlsberg and the petty cashier (Martin) about the transaction. Without further information, debit Miscellaneous Expense.

**2.** Petty cash general journal entries.

    **a.** Entry to establish the petty cash fund.

    **b.** Entry to reimburse the fund.

| Petty Cash | 150 | |
|---|---|---|
| Cash | | 150 |

| Delivery Expense | 29 | |
|---|---|---|
| Merchandise Inventory | 18 | |
| Miscellaneous Expense ($41 + $32) | 73 | |
| Cash Over and Short | 11 | |
| Cash | | 131 |

**3.** The Petty Cash account balance *always* equals its fund balance, in this case $150. This account balance does not change unless the fund is increased or decreased.

# 8A   Documentation and Verification

This appendix describes the important business documents of a voucher system of control.

**P4** Describe the use of documentation and verification to control cash disbursements.

**Purchase Requisition**   Department managers are usually not allowed to place orders directly with suppliers for control purposes. Instead, a department manager must inform the purchasing department of its needs by preparing and signing a **purchase requisition,** which lists the merchandise needed and requests that it be purchased—see Exhibit 8A.1. Two copies of the purchase requisition are sent to the purchasing department, which then sends one copy to the accounting department. When the accounting department receives a purchase requisition, it creates and maintains a voucher for this transaction. The requesting department keeps the third copy.

**EXHIBIT 8A.1**

Purchase Requisition

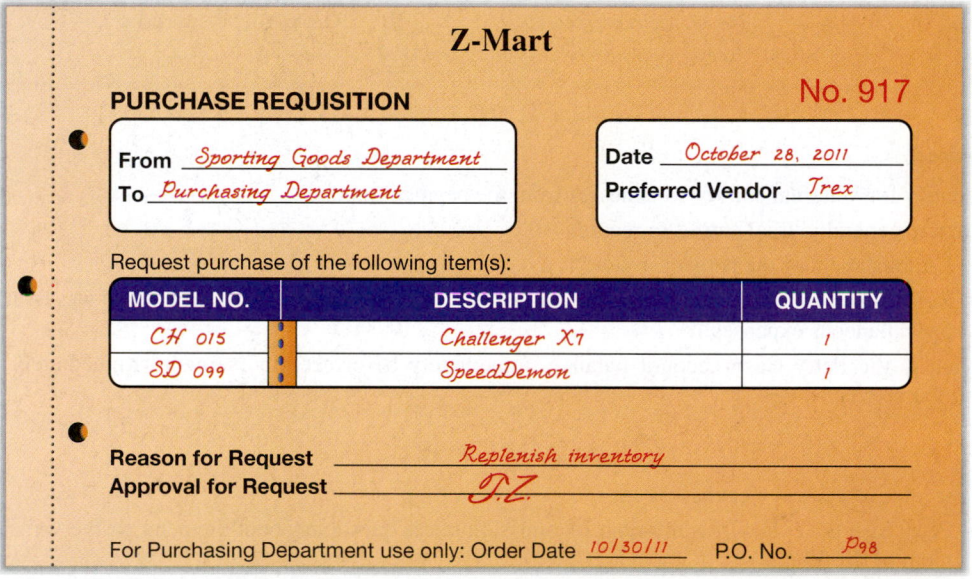

**Point:** A voucher system is designed to uniquely meet the needs of a specific business. Thus, we should read this appendix as one example of a common voucher system design, but *not* the only design.

**Purchase Order**   A **purchase order** is a document the purchasing department uses to place an order with a **vendor** (seller or supplier). A purchase order authorizes a vendor to ship ordered merchandise at the stated price and terms—see Exhibit 8A.2. When the purchasing department receives a purchase requisition, it prepares at least five copies of a purchase order. The copies are distributed as follows: *copy 1* to the vendor as a purchase request and as authority to ship merchandise; *copy 2,* along with a copy of the purchase requisition, to the accounting department, where it is entered in the voucher and used in approving payment of the invoice; *copy 3* to the requesting department to inform its manager that action is being taken; *copy 4* to the receiving department without order quantity so it can compare with goods received and provide independent count of goods received; and *copy 5* retained on file by the purchasing department.

**EXHIBIT 8A.2**

Purchase Order

**Z-Mart**
10 Michigan Street
Chicago, Illinois 60521

**PURCHASE ORDER**

No. P98

| Date | 10/30/11 |
|---|---|
| FOB | Destination |
| Ship by | As soon as possible |
| Terms | 2/15, n/30 |

To: Trex
W9797 Cherry Road
Antigo, Wisconsin 54409

Request shipment of the following item(s):

| Model No. | Description | Quantity | Price | Amount | |
|---|---|---|---|---|---|
| CH 015 | Challenger X7 | 1 | 490 | 490 | |
| SD 099 | SpeedDemon | 1 | 710 | 710 | |

All shipments and invoices must include purchase order number

*J. W.*

**ORDERED BY**

**EXHIBIT 8A.2**

Purchase Order

**Invoice** An **invoice** is an itemized statement of goods prepared by the vendor listing the customer's name, items sold, sales prices, and terms of sale. An invoice is also a bill sent to the buyer from the supplier. From the vendor's point of view, it is a *sales invoice*. The buyer, or **vendee,** treats it as a *purchase invoice*. When receiving a purchase order, the vendor ships the ordered merchandise to the buyer and includes or mails a copy of the invoice covering the shipment to the buyer. The invoice is sent to the buyer's accounting department where it is placed in the voucher. (Refer back to Exhibit 5.5, which shows Z-Mart's purchase invoice.)

**Receiving Report** Many companies maintain a separate department to receive all merchandise and purchased assets. When each shipment arrives, this receiving department counts the goods and checks them for damage and agreement with the purchase order. It then prepares four or more copies of a **receiving report,** which is used within the company to notify the appropriate persons that ordered goods have been received and to describe the quantities and condition of the goods. One copy is sent to accounting and placed in the voucher. Copies are also sent to the requesting department and the purchasing department to notify them that the goods have arrived. The receiving department retains a copy in its files.

**Invoice Approval** When a receiving report arrives, the accounting department should have copies of the following documents in the voucher: purchase requisition, purchase order, and invoice. With the information in these documents, the accounting department can record the purchase and approve its payment. In approving an invoice for payment, it checks and compares information across all documents. To facilitate this checking and to ensure that no step is omitted, it often uses an **invoice approval,** also called *check authorization*—see Exhibit 8A.3. An invoice approval is a checklist of steps necessary for approving an invoice for recording and payment. It is a separate document either filed in the voucher or preprinted (or stamped) on the voucher.

**EXHIBIT 8A.3**

Invoice Approval

**INVOICE APPROVAL**

| DOCUMENT | | | BY | DATE |
|---|---|---|---|---|
| Purchase requisition | | 917 | TZ | 10/28/11 |
| Purchase order | | P98 | JW | 10/30/11 |
| Receiving report | | R85 | SK | 11/03/11 |
| Invoice: | | 4657 | | 11/12/11 |
| Price | | | JK | 11/12/11 |
| Calculations | | | JK | 11/12/11 |
| Terms | | | JK | 11/12/11 |
| Approved for payment | | | BC | |

**EXHIBIT 8A.3**

Invoice Approval

As each step in the checklist is approved, the person initials the invoice approval and records the current date. Final approval implies the following steps have occurred:

1. **Requisition check:** Items on invoice are requested per purchase requisition.
2. **Purchase order check:** Items on invoice are ordered per purchase order.
3. **Receiving report check:** Items on invoice are received per receiving report.
4. **Invoice check: Price:** Invoice prices are as agreed with the vendor.
    **Calculations:** Invoice has no mathematical errors.
    **Terms:** Terms are as agreed with the vendor.

**Voucher**   Once an invoice has been checked and approved, the voucher is complete. A complete voucher is a record summarizing a transaction. Once the voucher certifies a transaction, it authorizes recording an obligation. A voucher also contains approval for paying the obligation on an appropriate date. The physical form of a voucher varies across companies. Many are designed so that the invoice and other related source documents are placed inside the voucher, which can be a folder.

Completion of a voucher usually requires a person to enter certain information on both the inside and outside of the voucher. Typical information required on the inside of a voucher is shown in Exhibit 8A.4, and that for the outside is shown in Exhibit 8A.5. This information is taken from the invoice and the supporting documents filed in the voucher. A complete voucher is sent to an authorized individual (often called an *auditor*). This person performs a final review, approves the accounts and amounts for debiting (called the *accounting distribution*), and authorizes recording of the voucher.

**EXHIBIT 8A.4**

Inside of a Voucher

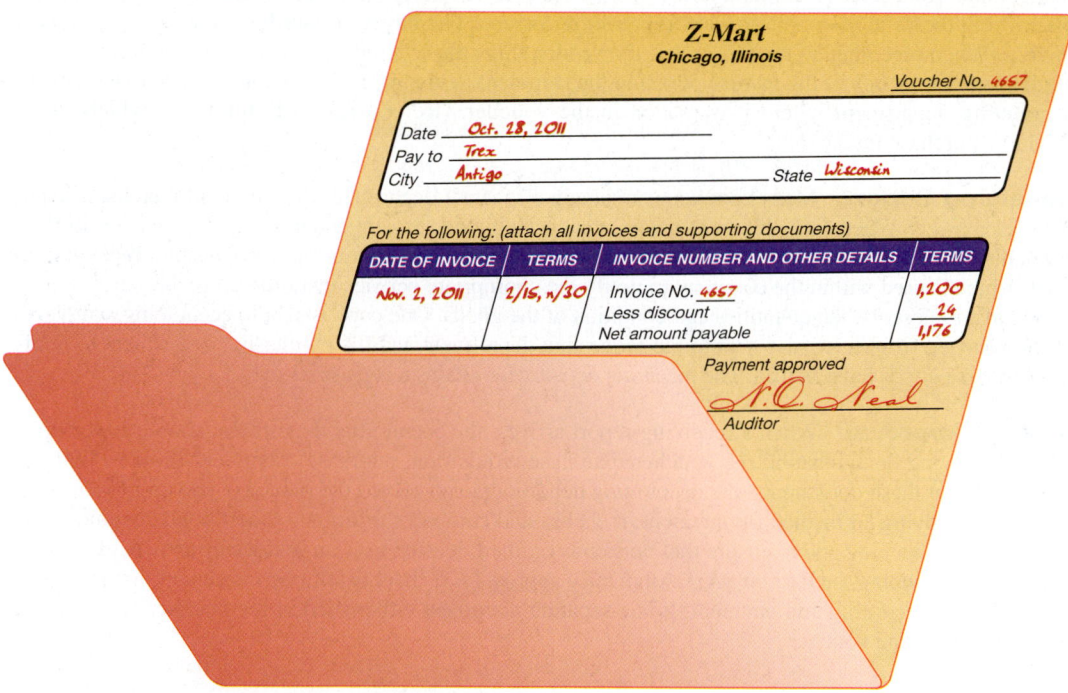

After a voucher is approved and recorded (in a journal called a **voucher register**), it is filed by its due date. A check is then sent on the payment date from the cashier, the voucher is marked "paid," and the voucher is sent to the accounting department and recorded (in a journal called the **check register**). The person issuing checks relies on the approved voucher and its signed supporting documents as proof that an obligation has been incurred and must be paid. The purchase requisition and purchase order confirm the purchase was authorized. The receiving report shows that items have been received, and the invoice approval form verifies that the invoice has been checked for errors. There is little chance for error and even less chance for fraud without collusion unless all the documents and signatures are forged.

**EXHIBIT 8A.5**

Outside of a Voucher

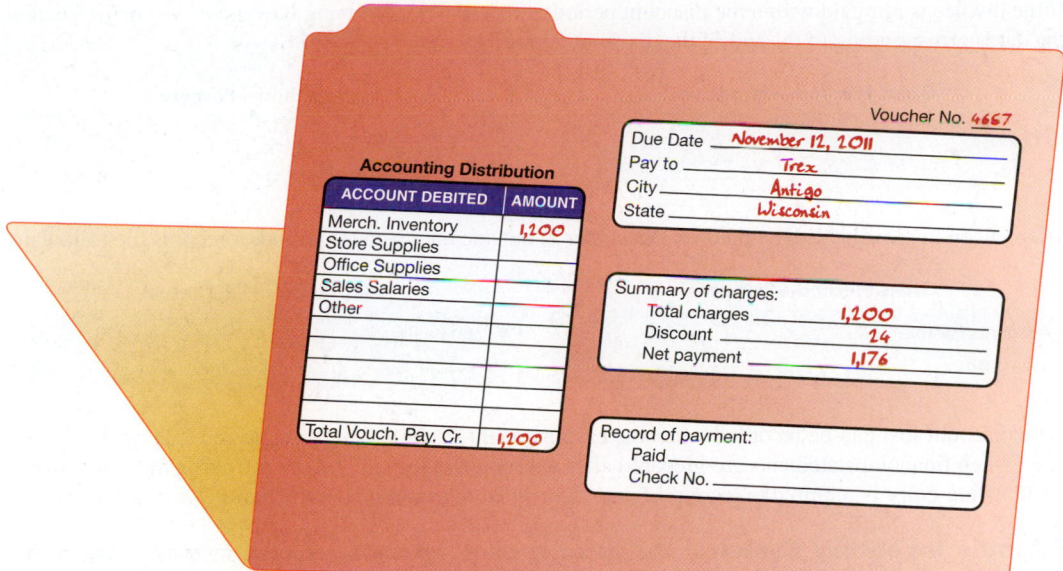

**EXHIBIT 8A.5**

Outside of a Voucher

---

**APPENDIX**

# Control of Purchase Discounts

## 8B

This appendix explains how a company can better control its cash *disbursements* to take advantage of favorable purchases discounts. Chapter 5 described the entries to record the receipt and payment of an invoice for a merchandise purchase with and without discount terms. Those entries were prepared under what is called the **gross method** of recording purchases, which initially records the invoice at its *gross* amount ignoring any cash discount.

The **net method** is another means of recording purchases, which initially records the invoice at its *net* amount of any cash discount. The net method gives management an advantage in controlling and monitoring cash payments involving purchase discounts.

To explain, when invoices are recorded at *gross* amounts, the amount of any discounts taken is deducted from the balance of the Merchandise Inventory account when cash payment is made. This means that the amount of any discounts lost is not reported in any account or on the income statement. Lost discounts recorded in this way are unlikely to come to the attention of management. When purchases are recorded at *net* amounts, a **Discounts Lost** expense account is recorded and brought to management's attention. Management can then seek to identify the reason for discounts lost such as oversight, carelessness, or unfavorable terms. (Chapter 5 explains how managers assess whether a discount is favorable or not.)

**P5** Apply the net method to control purchase discounts.

**Perpetual Inventory System**   To illustrate, assume that a company purchases merchandise on November 2 at a $1,200 invoice price with terms of 2/10, n/30. Its November 2 entries under the gross and net methods are

| **Gross Method—Perpetual** | | | | **Net Method—Perpetual** | | |
|---|---|---|---|---|---|---|
| Merchandise Inventory ............ | 1,200 | | | Merchandise Inventory ............ | 1,176 | |
| Accounts Payable ............. | | 1,200 | | Accounts Payable ............. | | 1,176 |

If the invoice is paid on November 12 within the discount period, it records the following:

| **Gross Method—Perpetual** | | | | **Net Method—Perpetual** | | |
|---|---|---|---|---|---|---|
| Accounts Payable ............... | 1,200 | | | Accounts Payable ................. | 1,176 | |
| Merchandise Inventory ........ | | 24 | | Cash ...................... | | 1,176 |
| Cash ..................... | | 1,176 | | | | |

If the invoice is *not* paid within the discount period, it records the following November 12 entry (which is the date corresponding to the end of the discount period):

| Gross Method—Perpetual | | | Net Method—Perpetual | | |
|---|---|---|---|---|---|
| No entry | | | Discounts Lost ................ | 24 | |
| | | |     Accounts Payable ............. | | 24 |

Then, when the invoice is later paid on December 2, outside the discount period, it records the following:

| Gross Method—Perpetual | | | Net Method—Perpetual | | |
|---|---|---|---|---|---|
| Accounts Payable ............... | 1,200 | | Accounts Payable ................ | 1,200 | |
|     Cash....................... | | 1,200 |     Cash ...................... | | 1,200 |

(The discount lost can be recorded when the cash payment is made with a single entry. However, in this case, when financial statements are prepared after a discount is lost and before the cash payment is made, an adjusting entry is required to recognize any unrecorded discount lost in the period when incurred.)

**Periodic Inventory System**    The preceding entries assume a perpetual inventory system. If a company is using a periodic system, its November 2 entries under the gross and net methods are

| Gross Method—Periodic | | | Net Method—Periodic | | |
|---|---|---|---|---|---|
| Purchases ...................... | 1,200 | | Purchases ...................... | 1,176 | |
|     Accounts Payable ............. | | 1,200 |     Accounts Payable ............. | | 1,176 |

If the invoice is paid on November 12 within the discount period, it records the following:

| Gross Method—Periodic | | | Net Method—Periodic | | |
|---|---|---|---|---|---|
| Accounts Payable ............... | 1,200 | | Accounts Payable ................ | 1,176 | |
|     Purchases Discounts .......... | | 24 |     Cash ...................... | | 1,176 |
|     Cash....................... | | 1,176 | | | |

If the invoice is *not* paid within the discount period, it records the following November 12 entry:

| Gross Method—Periodic | | | Net Method—Periodic | | |
|---|---|---|---|---|---|
| No entry | | | Discounts Lost ................ | 24 | |
| | | |     Accounts Payable ............. | | 24 |

Then, when the invoice is later paid on December 2, outside the discount period, it records the following:

| Gross Method—Periodic | | | Net Method—Periodic | | |
|---|---|---|---|---|---|
| Accounts Payable ............... | 1,200 | | Accounts Payable ................ | 1,200 | |
|     Cash ...................... | | 1,200 |     Cash ...................... | | 1,200 |

# Summary

**C1**   **Define internal control and identify its purpose and principles.** An internal control system consists of the policies and procedures managers use to protect assets, ensure reliable accounting, promote efficient operations, and urge adherence to company policies. It can prevent avoidable losses and help managers both plan operations and monitor company and human performance. Principles of good internal control include establishing responsibilities, maintaining adequate records, insuring assets and bonding employees, separating recordkeeping from custody of assets, dividing responsibilities for related transactions, applying technological controls, and performing regular independent reviews.

**C2**   **Define cash and cash equivalents and explain how to report them.** Cash includes currency, coins, and amounts on (or acceptable for) deposit in checking and savings accounts. Cash equivalents are short-term, highly liquid investment assets readily convertible to a known cash amount and sufficiently close to their maturity date so that market value is not sensitive to interest rate changes. Cash and cash equivalents are liquid assets because they are readily converted into other assets or can be used to pay for goods, services, or liabilities.

**A1** **Compute the days' sales uncollected ratio and use it to assess liquidity.** Many companies attract customers by selling to them on credit. This means that cash receipts from customers are delayed until accounts receivable are collected. Users want to know how quickly a company can convert its accounts receivable into cash. The days' sales uncollected ratio, one measure reflecting company liquidity, is computed by dividing the ending balance of receivables by annual net sales, and then multiplying by 365.

**P1** **Apply internal control to cash receipts and disbursements.** Internal control of cash receipts ensures that all cash received is properly recorded and deposited. Attention focuses on two important types of cash receipts: over-the-counter and by mail. Good internal control for over-the-counter cash receipts includes use of a cash register, customer review, use of receipts, a permanent transaction record, and separation of the custody of cash from its record-keeping. Good internal control for cash receipts by mail includes at least two people assigned to open mail and a listing of each sender's name, amount, and explanation. (Banks offer several services that promote the control and safeguarding of cash.)

**P2** **Explain and record petty cash fund transactions.** Petty cash disbursements are payments of small amounts for items such as postage, courier fees, minor repairs, and supplies. A company usually sets up one or more petty cash funds. A petty cash fund cashier is responsible for safekeeping the cash, making payments from this fund, and keeping receipts and records. A Petty Cash account

is debited only when the fund is established or increased in amount. When the fund is replenished, petty cash disbursements are recorded with debits to expense (or asset) accounts and a credit to cash.

**P3** **Prepare a bank reconciliation.** A bank reconciliation proves the accuracy of the depositor's and the bank's records. The bank statement balance is adjusted for items such as outstanding checks and unrecorded deposits made on or before the bank statement date but not reflected on the statement. The book balance is adjusted for items such as service charges, bank collections for the depositor, and interest earned on the account.

**P4ᴬ** **Describe the use of documentation and verification to control cash disbursements.** A voucher system is a set of procedures and approvals designed to control cash disbursements and acceptance of obligations. The voucher system of control relies on several important documents, including the voucher and its supporting files. A key factor in this system is that only approved departments and individuals are authorized to incur certain obligations.

**P5ᴮ** **Apply the net method to control purchase discounts.** The net method aids management in monitoring and controlling purchase discounts. When invoices are recorded at gross amounts, the amount of discounts taken is deducted from the balance of the Inventory account. This means that the amount of any discounts lost is not reported in any account and is unlikely to come to the attention of management. When purchases are recorded at net amounts, a Discounts Lost account is brought to management's attention as an operating expense. Management can then seek to identify the reason for discounts lost, such as oversight, carelessness, or unfavorable terms.

---

## Guidance Answers to Decision Maker and Decision Ethics

**Entrepreneur** A forced vacation policy is part of a good system of internal controls. When employees are forced to take vacations, their ability to hide any fraudulent behavior decreases because others must perform the vacationers' duties. A replacement employee potentially can uncover fraudulent behavior or falsified records. A forced vacation policy is especially important for employees in sensitive positions of handling money or in control of easily transferable assets.

**Sales Representative** A salesperson can take several steps to reduce days' sales uncollected. These include (1) decreasing the ratio of sales on account to total sales by encouraging more cash sales, (2) identifying customers most delayed in their payments and encouraging earlier payments or cash sales, and (3) applying stricter credit policies to eliminate credit sales to customers that never pay.

---

## Guidance Answers to Quick Checks

1. (c)
2. Technology reduces processing errors. It also allows more extensive testing of records, limits the amount of hard evidence, and highlights the importance of separation of duties.
3. A company holds liquid assets so that it can purchase other assets, buy services, and pay obligations.
4. It owns cash equivalents because they yield a return greater than what cash earns (and are readily exchanged for cash).
5. Examples of cash equivalents are 90-day (or less) U.S. Treasury bills, money market funds, and commercial paper (notes).
6. (a)
7. A voucher system is used when an owner/manager can no longer control purchasing procedures through personal supervision and direct participation.
8. If all cash payments are made by check, numerous checks for small amounts must be written. Since this practice is expensive and time-consuming, a petty cash fund is often established for making small (immaterial) cash payments.
9. If the petty cash fund is not reimbursed at the end of an accounting period, the transactions involving petty cash are not yet recorded and the petty cash asset is overstated.
10. First, petty cash transactions are recorded when the petty cash fund is reimbursed. Second, reimbursement provides cash to allow the fund to continue being used. Third, reimbursement identifies any cash shortage or overage in the fund.
11. A bank statement is a report prepared by the bank describing the activities in a depositor's account.

12. To reconcile a bank balance means to explain the difference between the cash balance in the depositor's accounting records and the cash balance on the bank statement.

13. The purpose of the bank reconciliation is to determine whether the bank or the depositor has made any errors and whether the bank has entered any transactions affecting the account that the depositor has not recorded.

14. Unrecorded deposits—added
Outstanding checks—subtracted

15. Interest earned—added     Debit memos—subtracted
Credit memos—added     NSF checks—subtracted
                           Bank service charges—subtracted

## Key Terms                                mhhe.com/wildFAP20e

Bank reconciliation (p. 331)
Bank statement (p. 330)
Canceled checks (p. 331)
Cash (p. 321)
Cash equivalents (p. 321)
Cash Over and Short (p. 323)
Check (p. 328)
Check register (p. 340)
Committee of Sponsoring Organizations (COSO) (p. 317)
Days' sales uncollected (p. 335)
Deposit ticket (p. 328)

Deposits in transit (p. 331)
Discounts lost (p. 341)
Electronic funds transfer (EFT) (p. 329)
Gross method (p. 341)
Internal control system (p. 316)
Invoice (p. 339)
Invoice approval (p. 339)
Liquid assets (p. 321)
Liquidity (p. 321)
Net method (p. 341)
Outstanding checks (p. 331)
Petty cash (p. 326)

Principles of internal control (p. 317)
Purchase order (p. 338)
Purchase requisition (p. 338)
Receiving report (p. 339)
Sarbanes-Oxley Act (p. 316)
Section 404 (of SOX) (p. 317)
Signature card (p. 328)
Vendee (p. 339)
Vendor (p. 338)
Voucher (p. 325)
Voucher register (p. 340)
Voucher system (p. 324)

## Multiple Choice Quiz          Answers on p. 391          mhhe.com/wildFAP20e

*Additional Quiz Questions are available at the book's Website.*

1. A company needs to replenish its $500 petty cash fund. Its petty cash box has $75 cash and petty cash receipts of $420. The journal entry to replenish the fund includes
   a. A debit to Cash for $75.
   b. A credit to Cash for $75.
   c. A credit to Petty Cash for $420.
   d. A credit to Cash Over and Short for $5.
   e. A debit to Cash Over and Short for $5.

2. The following information is available for Hapley Company:
   - The November 30 bank statement shows a $1,895 balance.
   - The general ledger shows a $1,742 balance at November 30.
   - A $795 deposit placed in the bank's night depository on November 30 does not appear on the November 30 bank statement.
   - Outstanding checks amount to $638 at November 30.
   - A customer's $335 note was collected by the bank in November. A collection fee of $15 was deducted by the bank and the difference deposited in Hapley's account.
   - A bank service charge of $10 is deducted by the bank and appears on the November 30 bank statement.

   How will the customer's note appear on Hapley's November 30 bank reconciliation?
   a. $320 appears as an addition to the book balance of cash.
   b. $320 appears as a deduction from the book balance of cash.
   c. $320 appears as an addition to the bank balance of cash.

   d. $320 appears as a deduction from the bank balance of cash.
   e. $335 appears as an addition to the bank balance of cash.

3. Using the information from question 2, what is the reconciled balance on Hapley's November 30 bank reconciliation?
   a. $2,052
   b. $1,895
   c. $1,742
   d. $2,201
   e. $1,184

4. A company had net sales of $84,000 and accounts receivable of $6,720. Its days' sales uncollected is
   a. 3.2 days
   b. 18.4 days
   c. 230.0 days
   d. 29.2 days
   e. 12.5 days

5.[B] A company records its purchases using the net method. On August 1, it purchases merchandise on account for $6,000 with terms of 2/10, n/30. The August 1 journal entry to record this transaction includes a
   a. Debit to Merchandise Inventory for $6,000.
   b. Debit to Merchandise Inventory for $5,880.
   c. Debit to Merchandise Inventory for $120.
   d. Debit to Accounts Payable for $5,880.
   e. Credit to Accounts Payable for $6,000.

**A(B)** *Superscript letter A(B) denotes assignments based on Appendix 8A (8B).*

⬛ Icon denotes assignments that involve decision making.

## Discussion Questions

**1.** List the seven broad principles of internal control.

**2.** ⬛ Internal control procedures are important in every business, but at what stage in the development of a business do they become especially critical?

**3.** ⬛ Why should responsibility for related transactions be divided among different departments or individuals?

**4.** ⬛ Why should the person who keeps the records of an asset not be the person responsible for its custody?

**5.** ⬛ When a store purchases merchandise, why are individual departments not allowed to directly deal with suppliers?

**6.** What are the limitations of internal controls?

**7.** Which of the following assets is most liquid? Which is least liquid? Inventory, building, accounts receivable, or cash.

**8.** What is a petty cash receipt? Who should sign it?

**9.** Why should cash receipts be deposited on the day of receipt?

**10.** **Research In Motion**'s statement of cash flows in Appendix A describes changes in cash and cash *RIM*

equivalents for the year ended February 27, 2010. What total amount is provided (used) by investing activities? What amount is provided (used) by financing activities?

**11.** Refer to **Apple**'s financial statements in Appendix A. *Apple* Identify Apple's net income for the year ended December 31, 2009. Is its net income equal to the increase in cash and cash equivalents for the year? Explain the difference between net income and the increase in cash and cash equivalents.

**12.** ⬛ Refer to **Nokia**'s balance sheet in Appendix A. **NOKIA** How does its cash (titled "bank and cash") compare with its other current assets (both in amount and percent) as of December 31, 2009? Compare and assess its cash at December 31, 2009, with its cash at December 31, 2008.

**13.** ⬛ **Palm**'s balance sheet in Appendix A reports that *Palm* cash and equivalents decreased during the fiscal year ended May, 31, 2009. Identify the cash generated (or used) by operating activities, by investing activities, and by financing activities.

---

## connect

An internal control system consists of all policies and procedures used to protect assets, ensure reliable accounting, promote efficient operations, and urge adherence to company policies.

**1.** What is the main objective of internal control procedures? How is that objective achieved?

**2.** Why should recordkeeping for assets be separated from custody over those assets?

**3.** Why should the responsibility for a transaction be divided between two or more individuals or departments?

**QUICK STUDY**

**QS 8-1**
Internal control objectives

C1 ⬛

---

A good system of internal control for cash provides adequate procedures for protecting both cash receipts and cash disbursements.

**1.** What are three basic guidelines that help achieve this protection?

**2.** Identify two control systems or procedures for cash disbursements.

**QS 8-2**
Internal control for cash

P1

---

Good accounting systems help in managing cash and controlling who has access to it.

**1.** What items are included in the category of cash?

**2.** What items are included in the category of cash equivalents?

**3.** What does the term *liquidity* refer to?

**QS 8-3**
Cash and equivalents

C2

---

**1.** The petty cash fund of the Rio Agency is established at $75. At the end of the current period, the fund contained $14 and had the following receipts: film rentals, $19, refreshments for meetings, $23 (both expenditures to be classified as Entertainment Expense); postage, $6; and printing, $13. Prepare journal entries to record (a) establishment of the fund and (b) reimbursement of the fund at the end of the current period.

**2.** Identify the two events that cause a Petty Cash account to be credited in a journal entry.

**QS 8-4**
Petty cash accounting

P2

---

**1.** For each of the following items, indicate whether its amount (i) affects the bank or book side of a bank reconciliation and (ii) represents an addition or a subtraction in a bank reconciliation.

  **a.** Outstanding checks    **d.** Unrecorded deposits    **g.** Bank service charges

  **b.** Debit memos    **e.** Interest on cash balance

  **c.** NSF checks    **f.** Credit memos

**2.** Which of the items in part 1 require an adjusting journal entry?

**QS 8-5**
Bank reconciliation

P3

**QS 8-6**

Bank reconciliation

P3

Cruz Company deposits all cash receipts on the day when they are received and it makes all cash payments by check. At the close of business on June 30, 2011, its Cash account shows an $11,352 debit balance. Cruz's June 30 bank statement shows $10,332 on deposit in the bank. Prepare a bank reconciliation for Cruz Company using the following information.

**a.** Outstanding checks as of June 30 total $1,713.

**b.** The June 30 bank statement included a $23 debit memorandum for bank services; Cruz has not yet recorded the cost of these services.

**c.** In reviewing the bank statement, a $90 check written by Cruz Company was mistakenly recorded in Cruz Company's books at $99.

**d.** June 30 cash receipts of $2,724 were placed in the bank's night depository after banking hours and were not recorded on the June 30 bank statement.

**e.** The bank statement included a $5 credit for interest earned on the cash in the bank.

**QS 8-7**

Days' sales uncollected

A1

The following annual account balances are taken from ProTeam Sports at December 31.

|  | 2011 | 2010 |
|---|---|---|
| Accounts receivable ........ | $ 75,692 | $ 70,484 |
| Net sales ................ | 2,591,933 | 2,296,673 |

What is the change in the number of days' sales uncollected between years 2010 and 2011? According to this analysis, is the company's collection of receivables improving? Explain.

**QS 8-8ᴬ**

Documents in a voucher system

P4

Management uses a voucher system to help control and monitor cash disbursements. Identify and describe at least four key documents that are part of a voucher system of control.

**QS 8-9ᴮ**

Purchase discounts    P5

An important part of cash management is knowing when, and if, to take purchase discounts.

**a.** Which accounting method uses a Discounts Lost account?

**b.** What is the advantage of this method for management?

**QS 8-10**

International accounting and internal controls

C1  P1

Answer each of the following related to international accounting standards.

**a.** Explain how the purposes and principles of internal controls are different between accounting systems reporting under IFRS versus U.S. GAAP.

**b.** Cash presents special internal control challenges. How do internal controls for cash differ for accounting systems reporting under IFRS versus U.S. GAAP? How do the procedures applied differ across those two accounting systems?

**QS 8-11**

Reviewing bank statements

P3

An entrepreneur commented that a bank reconciliation may not be necessary as she regularly reviews her online bank statement for any unusual items and errors.

**a.** Describe how a bank reconciliation and an online review (or reading) of the bank statement are not equivalent.

**b.** Identify and explain at least two frauds or errors that would be uncovered through a bank reconciliation and that would *not* be uncovered through an online review of the bank statement.

## EXERCISES

**Exercise 8-1**

Internal control recommendations

C1

What internal control procedures would you recommend in each of the following situations?

**1.** A concession company has one employee who sells towels, coolers, and sunglasses at the beach. Each day, the employee is given enough towels, coolers, and sunglasses to last through the day and enough cash to make change. The money is kept in a box at the stand.

**2.** An antique store has one employee who is given cash and sent to garage sales each weekend. The employee pays cash for any merchandise acquired that the antique store resells.

Cantu Company is a rapidly growing start-up business. Its recordkeeper, who was hired nine months ago, left town after the company's manager discovered that a large sum of money had disappeared over the past three months. An audit disclosed that the recordkeeper had written and signed several checks made payable to her fiancé and then recorded the checks as salaries expense. The fiancé, who cashed the checks but never worked for the company, left town with the recordkeeper. As a result, the company incurred an uninsured loss of $84,000. Evaluate Cantu's internal control system and indicate which principles of internal control appear to have been ignored.

**Exercise 8-2**
Analyzing internal control
C1

Some of Chester Company's cash receipts from customers are received by the company with the regular mail. Chester's recordkeeper opens these letters and deposits the cash received each day. (*a*) Identify any internal control problem(s) in this arrangement. (*b*) What changes to its internal control system do you recommend?

**Exercise 8-3**
Control of cash receipts by mail
P1

Good accounting systems help with the management and control of cash and cash equivalents.

1.  Define and contrast the terms *liquid asset* and *cash equivalent*.
2.  Why would companies invest their idle cash in cash equivalents?
3.  Identify five principles of effective cash management.

**Exercise 8-4**
Cash, liquidity, and return
C2

Hawk Company establishes a $400 petty cash fund on September 9. On September 30, the fund shows $166 in cash along with receipts for the following expenditures: transportation-in, $32; postage expenses, $113; and miscellaneous expenses, $87. The petty cashier could not account for a $2 shortage in the fund. Hawk uses the perpetual system in accounting for merchandise inventory. Prepare (1) the September 9 entry to establish the fund, (2) the September 30 entry to reimburse the fund, and (3) an October 1 entry to decrease the fund to $300.

**Exercise 8-5**
Petty cash fund with a shortage
P2

**Check**   (2) Cr. Cash $234 and (3) Dr. Cash $100

NetPerks Co. establishes a $200 petty cash fund on January 1. On January 8, the fund shows $28 in cash along with receipts for the following expenditures: postage, $64; transportation-in, $19; delivery expenses, $36; and miscellaneous expenses, $53. NetPerks uses the perpetual system in accounting for merchandise inventory. Prepare journal entries to (1) establish the fund on January 1, (2) reimburse it on January 8, and (3) both reimburse the fund and increase it to $500 on January 8, assuming no entry in part 2. (*Hint*: Make two separate entries for part 3.)

**Exercise 8-6**
Petty cash fund accounting
P2

**Check**   (3) Cr. Cash $472 (total)

Prepare a table with the following headings for a monthly bank reconciliation dated September 30.

**Exercise 8-7**
Bank reconciliation and adjusting entries
P3

| Bank Balance | | Book Balance | | | Not Shown on the Reconciliation |
| --- | --- | --- | --- | --- | --- |
| Add | Deduct | Add | Deduct | Adjust | |

For each item 1 through 12, place an *x* in the appropriate column to indicate whether the item should be added to or deducted from the book or bank balance, or whether it should not appear on the reconciliation. If the book balance is to be adjusted, place a *Dr.* or *Cr.* in the Adjust column to indicate whether the Cash balance should be debited or credited. At the left side of your table, number the items to correspond to the following list.

1.  Bank service charge for September.
2.  Checks written and mailed to payees on October 2.
3.  Checks written by another depositor but charged against this company's account.
4.  Principal and interest on a note receivable to this company is collected by the bank but not yet recorded by the company.
5.  Special bank charge for collection of note in part 4 on this company's behalf.
6.  Check written against the company's account and cleared by the bank; erroneously not recorded by the company's recordkeeper.
7.  Interest earned on the September cash balance in the bank.
8.  Night deposit made on September 30 after the bank closed.
9.  Checks outstanding on August 31 that cleared the bank in September.
10. NSF check from customer is returned on September 25 but not yet recorded by this company.
11. Checks written by the company and mailed to payees on September 30.
12. Deposit made on September 5 and processed by the bank on September 6.

**Exercise 8-8**

Voucher system

**P1**

The voucher system of control is designed to control cash disbursements and the acceptance of obligations.
1. The voucher system of control establishes procedures for what two processes?
2. What types of expenditures should be overseen by a voucher system of control?
3. When is the voucher initially prepared? Explain.

**Exercise 8-9**

Bank reconciliation

**P3**

Frederick Clinic deposits all cash receipts on the day when they are received and it makes all cash payments by check. At the close of business on June 30, 2011, its Cash account shows a $15,141 debit balance. Frederick Clinic's June 30 bank statement shows $14,275 on deposit in the bank. Prepare a bank reconciliation for Frederick Clinic using the following information:

a. Outstanding checks as of June 30 total $2,500.

b. The June 30 bank statement included a $125 debit memorandum for bank services.

c. Check No. 919, listed with the canceled checks, was correctly drawn for $645 in payment of a utility bill on June 15. Frederick Clinic mistakenly recorded it with a debit to Utilities Expense and a credit to Cash in the amount of $654.

**Check**    Reconciled bal., $15,025

d. The June 30 cash receipts of $3,250 were placed in the bank's night depository after banking hours and were not recorded on the June 30 bank statement.

**Exercise 8-10**

Adjusting entries from bank reconciliation    **P3**

Prepare the adjusting journal entries that Frederick Clinic must record as a result of preparing the bank reconciliation in Exercise 8-9.

**Exercise 8-11**

Bank reconciliation

**P3**

Chung Company deposits all cash receipts on the day when they are received and it makes all cash payments by check. At the close of business on May 31, 2011, its Cash account shows a $15,500 debit balance. Chung's May 31 bank statement shows $13,800 on deposit in the bank. Prepare a bank reconciliation for Chung Company using the following information.

a. May 31 cash receipts of $2,200 were placed in the bank's night depository after banking hours and were not recorded on the May 31 bank statement.

b. Outstanding checks as of May 31 total $1,600.

c. The May 31 bank statement included a $100 debit memorandum for bank services; Chung has not yet recorded the cost of these services.

d. In reviewing the bank statement, a $400 check written by Wald Company was mistakenly drawn against Chung's account.

**Check**    Reconciled bal., $14,800

e. A debit memorandum for $600 refers to a $600 NSF check from a customer; Chung has not yet recorded this NSF check.

**Exercise 8-12**

Liquid assets and accounts receivable

**A1**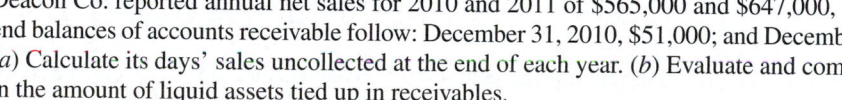

Deacon Co. reported annual net sales for 2010 and 2011 of $565,000 and $647,000, respectively. Its year-end balances of accounts receivable follow: December 31, 2010, $51,000; and December 31, 2011, $83,000. (*a*) Calculate its days' sales uncollected at the end of each year. (*b*) Evaluate and comment on any changes in the amount of liquid assets tied up in receivables.

**Exercise 8-13<sup>A</sup>**

Documents in a voucher system

**P4**

Match each document in a voucher system in column one with its description in column two.

**Document**
1. Voucher
2. Invoice approval
3. Receiving report
4. Invoice
5. Purchase order
6. Purchase requisition

**Description**

A. A document used to notify the appropriate persons that ordered goods have arrived, including a description of the quantities and condition of goods.

B. An internal file used to store documents and information to control cash disbursements and to ensure that a transaction is properly authorized and recorded.

C. A document used to place an order with a vendor that authorizes the vendor to ship ordered merchandise at the stated price and terms.

D. A checklist of steps necessary for the approval of an invoice for recording and payment; also known as a check authorization.

E. A document used by department managers to inform the purchasing department to place an order with a vendor.

F. An itemized statement of goods prepared by the vendor listing the customer's name, items sold, sales prices, and terms of sale.

USA Imports uses the perpetual system in accounting for merchandise inventory and had the following transactions during the month of October. Prepare entries to record these transactions assuming that USA Imports records invoices (*a*) at gross amounts and (*b*) at net amounts.

Oct.  2  Purchased merchandise at a $4,000 price, invoice dated October 2, terms 2/10, n/30.
     10  Received a $400 credit memorandum (at full invoice price) for the return of merchandise that it purchased on October 2.
     17  Purchased merchandise at a $4,400 price, invoice dated October 16, terms 2/10, n/30.
     26  Paid for the merchandise purchased on October 17, less the discount.
     31  Paid for the merchandise purchased on October 2. Payment was delayed because the invoice was mistakenly filed for payment today. This error caused the discount to be lost.

**Exercise 8-14[B]**
Record invoices at gross or net amounts
**P5**

**connect**

For each of these five separate cases, identify the principle(s) of internal control that is violated. Recommend what the business should do to ensure adherence to principles of internal control.

1. Heather Flat records all incoming customer cash receipts for her employer and posts the customer payments to their respective accounts.
2. At Netco Company, Jeff and Jose alternate lunch hours. Jeff is the petty cash custodian, but if someone needs petty cash when he is at lunch, Jose fills in as custodian.
3. Nadine Cox posts all patient charges and payments at the Dole Medical Clinic. Each night Nadine backs up the computerized accounting system to a tape and stores the tape in a locked file at her desk.
4. Barto Sayles prides himself on hiring quality workers who require little supervision. As office manager, Barto gives his employees full discretion over their tasks and for years has seen no reason to perform independent reviews of their work.
5. Desi West's manager has told her to reduce costs. Desi decides to raise the deductible on the plant's property insurance from $5,000 to $10,000. This cuts the property insurance premium in half. In a related move, she decides that bonding the plant's employees is a waste of money since the company has not experienced any losses due to employee theft. Desi saves the entire amount of the bonding insurance premium by dropping the bonding insurance.

**PROBLEM SET A**

**Problem 8-1A**
Analyzing internal control
**C1**

Shawnee Co. set up a petty cash fund for payments of small amounts. The following transactions involving the petty cash fund occurred in May (the last month of the company's fiscal year).

May  1  Prepared a company check for $250 to establish the petty cash fund.
     15  Prepared a company check to replenish the fund for the following expenditures made since May 1.
         *a.*  Paid $78 for janitorial services.
         *b.*  Paid $63.68 for miscellaneous expenses.
         *c.*  Paid postage expenses of $43.50.
         *d.*  Paid $57.15 to *The County Gazette* (the local newspaper) for an advertisement.
         *e.*  Counted $11.15 remaining in the petty cash box.
     16  Prepared a company check for $200 to increase the fund to $450.
     31  The petty cashier reports that $293.39 cash remains in the fund. A company check is drawn to replenish the fund for the following expenditures made since May 15.
         *f.*  Paid postage expenses of $48.36.
         *g.*  Reimbursed the office manager for business mileage, $38.50.
         *h.*  Paid $39.75 to deliver merchandise to a customer, terms FOB destination.
     31  The company decides that the May 16 increase in the fund was too large. It reduces the fund by $50, leaving a total of $400.

**Problem 8-2A**
Establish, reimburse, and adjust petty cash
**P2**

**Required**

1. Prepare journal entries to establish the fund on May 1, to replenish it on May 15 and on May 31, and to reflect any increase or decrease in the fund balance on May 16 and May 31.

**Check**  (1) Cr. to Cash: May 15, $238.85; May 16, $200.00

**Analysis Component**

2. Explain how the company's financial statements are affected if the petty cash fund is not replenished and no entry is made on May 31.

**Problem 8-3A**

Establish, reimburse, and increase petty cash

P2

Shelton Gallery had the following petty cash transactions in February of the current year.

Feb. 2  Wrote a $300 check, cashed it, and gave the proceeds and the petty cashbox to Bo Brown, the petty cashier.
5  Purchased bond paper for the copier for $10.13 that is immediately used.
9  Paid $22.50 COD shipping charges on merchandise purchased for resale, terms FOB shipping point. Shelton uses the perpetual system to account for merchandise inventory.
12  Paid $9.95 postage to express mail a contract to a client.
14  Reimbursed Alli Buck, the manager, $58 for business mileage on her car.
20  Purchased stationery for $77.76 that is immediately used.
23  Paid a courier $18 to deliver merchandise sold to a customer, terms FOB destination.
25  Paid $15.10 COD shipping charges on merchandise purchased for resale, terms FOB shipping point.
27  Paid $64 for postage expenses.
28  The fund had $21.23 remaining in the petty cash box. Sorted the petty cash receipts by accounts affected and exchanged them for a check to reimburse the fund for expenditures.
28  The petty cash fund amount is increased by $100 to a total of $400.

**Required**

**1.** Prepare the journal entry to establish the petty cash fund.

**2.** Prepare a petty cash payments report for February with these categories: delivery expense, mileage expense, postage expense, merchandise inventory (for transportation-in), and office supplies expense. Sort the payments into the appropriate categories and total the expenditures in each category.

**Check** (3a & 3b) Total Cr. to Cash $378.77

**3.** Prepare the journal entries for part 2 to both (a) reimburse and (b) increase the fund amount.

**Problem 8-4A**

Prepare a bank reconciliation and record adjustments

P3

mhhe.com/wildFAP20e

The following information is available to reconcile Clark Company's book balance of cash with its bank statement cash balance as of July 31, 2011.

**a.** On July 31, the company's Cash account has a $26,193 debit balance, but its July bank statement shows a $28,020 cash balance.

**b.** Check No. 3031 for $1,380 and Check No. 3040 for $552 were outstanding on the June 30 bank reconciliation. Check No. 3040 is listed with the July canceled checks, but Check No. 3031 is not. Also, Check No. 3065 for $336 and Check No. 3069 for $2,148, both written in July, are not among the canceled checks on the July 31 statement.

**c.** In comparing the canceled checks on the bank statement with the entries in the accounting records, it is found that Check No. 3056 for July rent was correctly written and drawn for $1,250 but was erroneously entered in the accounting records as $1,230.

**d.** A credit memorandum enclosed with the July bank statement indicates the bank collected $9,000 cash on a non-interest-bearing note for Clark, deducted a $45 collection fee, and credited the remainder to its account. Clark had not recorded this event before receiving the statement.

**e.** A debit memorandum for $805 lists a $795 NSF check plus a $10 NSF charge. The check had been received from a customer, Jim Shaw. Clark has not yet recorded this check as NSF.

**f.** Enclosed with the July statement is a $15 debit memorandum for bank services. It has not yet been recorded because no previous notification had been received.

**g.** Clark's July 31 daily cash receipts of $10,152 were placed in the bank's night depository on that date, but do not appear on the July 31 bank statement.

**Required**

**1.** Prepare the bank reconciliation for this company as of July 31, 2011.

**Check** (1) Reconciled balance, $34,308; (2) Cr. Note Receivable $9,000

**2.** Prepare the journal entries necessary to bring the company's book balance of cash into conformity with the reconciled cash balance as of July 31, 2011.

**Analysis Component**

**3.** Assume that the July 31, 2011, bank reconciliation for this company is prepared and some items are treated incorrectly. For each of the following errors, explain the effect of the error on (i) the adjusted bank statement cash balance and (ii) the adjusted cash account book balance.

**a.** The company's unadjusted cash account balance of $26,193 is listed on the reconciliation as $26,139.

**b.** The bank's collection of the $9,000 note less the $45 collection fee is added to the bank statement cash balance on the reconciliation.

Els Company most recently reconciled its bank statement and book balances of cash on August 31 and it reported two checks outstanding, No. 5888 for $1,038.05 and No. 5893 for $484.25. The following information is available for its September 30, 2011, reconciliation.

**Problem 8-5A**
Prepare a bank reconciliation and record adjustments

**P3**

mhhe.com/wildFAP20e

### From the September 30 Bank Statement

| PREVIOUS BALANCE | TOTAL CHECKS AND DEBITS | TOTAL DEPOSITS AND CREDITS | CURRENT BALANCE |
|---|---|---|---|
| 16,800.45 | 9,620.05 | 11,182.85 | 18,363.25 |

| CHECKS AND DEBITS | | | DEPOSITS AND CREDITS | | DAILY BALANCE | |
|---|---|---|---|---|---|---|
| Date | No. | Amount | Date | Amount | Date | Amount |
| 09/03 | 5888 | 1,038.05 | 09/05 | 1,103.75 | 08/31 | 16,800.45 |
| 09/04 | 5902 | 731.90 | 09/12 | 2,226.90 | 09/03 | 15,762.40 |
| 09/07 | 5901 | 1,824.25 | 09/21 | 4,093.00 | 09/04 | 15,030.50 |
| 09/17 | | 588.25 NSF | 09/25 | 2,351.70 | 09/05 | 16,134.25 |
| 09/20 | 5905 | 937.00 | 09/30 | 22.50 IN | 09/07 | 14,310.00 |
| 09/22 | 5903 | 399.10 | 09/30 | 1,385.00 CM | 09/12 | 16,536.90 |
| 09/22 | 5904 | 2,080.00 | | | 09/17 | 15,948.65 |
| 09/28 | 5907 | 213.85 | | | 09/20 | 15,011.65 |
| 09/29 | 5909 | 1,807.65 | | | 09/21 | 19,104.65 |
| | | | | | 09/22 | 16,625.55 |
| | | | | | 09/25 | 18,977.25 |
| | | | | | 09/28 | 18,763.40 |
| | | | | | 09/29 | 16,955.75 |
| | | | | | 09/30 | 18,363.25 |

### From Els Company's Accounting Records

| Cash Receipts Deposited | | | |
|---|---|---|---|
| Date | | | Cash Debit |
| Sept. | 5 | | 1,103.75 |
| | 12 | | 2,226.90 |
| | 21 | | 4,093.00 |
| | 25 | | 2,351.70 |
| | 30 | | 1,582.75 |
| | | | 11,358.10 |

| Cash Disbursements | | |
|---|---|---|
| Check No. | | Cash Credit |
| 5901 | | 1,824.25 |
| 5902 | | 731.90 |
| 5903 | | 399.10 |
| 5904 | | 2,050.00 |
| 5905 | | 937.00 |
| 5906 | | 859.30 |
| 5907 | | 213.85 |
| 5908 | | 276.00 |
| 5909 | | 1,807.65 |
| | | 9,099.05 |

| Cash | | | | | | Acct. No. 101 |
|---|---|---|---|---|---|---|
| Date | | Explanation | PR | Debit | Credit | Balance |
| Aug. | 31 | Balance | | | | 15,278.15 |
| Sept. | 30 | Total receipts | R12 | 11,358.10 | | 26,636.25 |
| | 30 | Total disbursements | D23 | | 9,099.05 | 17,537.20 |

### Additional Information

Check No. 5904 is correctly drawn for $2,080 to pay for computer equipment; however, the recordkeeper misread the amount and entered it in the accounting records with a debit to Computer Equipment and a credit to Cash of $2,050. The NSF check shown in the statement was originally received from a customer, S. Nilson, in payment of her account. Its return has not yet been recorded by the company. The credit memorandum is from the collection of a $1,400 note for Els Company by the bank. The bank deducted a $15 collection fee. The collection and fee are not yet recorded.

**Required**

**Check**   (1) Reconciled balance, $18,326.45 (2) Cr. Note Receivable $1,400

1. Prepare the September 30, 2011, bank reconciliation for this company.
2. Prepare the journal entries to adjust the book balance of cash to the reconciled balance.

**Analysis Component**

3. The bank statement reveals that some of the prenumbered checks in the sequence are missing. Describe three situations that could explain this.

# PROBLEM SET B

**Problem 8-1B**

Analyzing internal control

C1

For each of these five separate cases, identify the principle(s) of internal control that is violated. Recommend what the business should do to ensure adherence to principles of internal control.

1. Latoya Tally is the company's computer specialist and oversees its computerized payroll system. Her boss recently asked her to put password protection on all office computers. Latoya has put a password in place that allows only the boss access to the file where pay rates are changed and personnel are added or deleted from the payroll.

2. Lake Theater has a computerized order-taking system for its tickets. The system is active all week and backed up every Friday night.

3. X2U Company has two employees handling acquisitions of inventory. One employee places purchase orders and pays vendors. The second employee receives the merchandise.

4. The owner of Super-Aid Pharmacy uses a check protector to perforate checks, making it difficult for anyone to alter the amount of the check. The check protector is on the owner's desk in an office that contains company checks and is normally unlocked.

5. LeAnn Company is a small business that has separated the duties of cash receipts and cash disbursements. The employee responsible for cash disbursements reconciles the bank account monthly.

**Problem 8-2B**

Establishing, reimbursing, and adjusting petty cash

P2

Pepco Co. establishes a petty cash fund for payments of small amounts. The following transactions involving the petty cash fund occurred in January (the last month of the company's fiscal year).

Jan.   3    A company check for $150 is written and made payable to the petty cashier to establish the petty cash fund.

     14    A company check is written to replenish the fund for the following expenditures made since January 3.
        *a.*   Purchased office supplies for $16.29 that are immediately used up.
        *b.*   Paid $17.60 COD shipping charges on merchandise purchased for resale, terms FOB shipping point. Pepco uses the perpetual system to account for inventory.
        *c.*   Paid $36.57 to All-Tech for minor repairs to a computer.
        *d.*   Paid $14.82 for items classified as miscellaneous expenses.
        *e.*   Counted $62.28 remaining in the petty cash box.

     15    Prepared a company check for $25 to increase the fund to $175.

     31    The petty cashier reports that $17.35 remains in the fund. A company check is written to replenish the fund for the following expenditures made since January 14.
        *f.*   Paid $40 to *The Smart Shopper* for an advertisement in January's newsletter.
        *g.*   Paid $38.19 for postage expenses.
        *h.*   Paid $58 to Take-You-There for delivery of merchandise, terms FOB destination.

     31    The company decides that the January 15 increase in the fund was too little. It increases the fund by another $75, leaving a total of $250.

**Required**

**Check**   (1) Cr. to Cash: Jan. 14, $87.72; Jan. 31 (total), $232.65

1. Prepare journal entries to establish the fund on January 3, to replenish it on January 14 and January 31, and to reflect any increase or decrease in the fund balance on January 15 and 31.

**Analysis Component**

2. Explain how the company's financial statements are affected if the petty cash fund is not replenished and no entry is made on January 31.

RPM Music Center had the following petty cash transactions in March of the current year.

**Problem 8-3B**
Establish, reimburse, and
increase petty cash

P2

March  5  Wrote a $200 check, cashed it, and gave the proceeds and the petty cashbox to Liz Buck, the petty cashier.

6  Paid $14.50 COD shipping charges on merchandise purchased for resale, terms FOB shipping point. RPM uses the perpetual system to account for merchandise inventory.

11  Paid $8.75 delivery charges on merchandise sold to a customer, terms FOB destination.

12  Purchased file folders for $12.13 that are immediately used.

14  Reimbursed Will Nelson, the manager, $9.65 for office supplies purchased and used.

18  Purchased printer paper for $22.54 that is immediately used.

27  Paid $47.10 COD shipping charges on merchandise purchased for resale, terms FOB shipping point.

28  Paid postage expenses of $16.

30  Reimbursed Nelson $58.80 for business car mileage.

31  Cash of $11.53 remained in the fund. Sorted the petty cash receipts by accounts affected and exchanged them for a check to reimburse the fund for expenditures.

31  The petty cash fund amount is increased by $50 to a total of $250.

**Required**

1. Prepare the journal entry to establish the petty cash fund.

2. Prepare a petty cash payments report for March with these categories: delivery expense, mileage expense, postage expense, merchandise inventory (for transportation-in), and office supplies expense. Sort the payments into the appropriate categories and total the expenses in each category.

3. Prepare the journal entries for part 2 to both (*a*) reimburse and (*b*) increase the fund amount.

**Check**   (2) Total expenses $189.47

(3a & 3b) Total Cr. to Cash
$238.47

---

The following information is available to reconcile Style Co.'s book balance of cash with its bank statement cash balance as of December 31, 2011.

**Problem 8-4B**
Prepare a bank reconciliation
and record adjustments

P3

a. The December 31 cash balance according to the accounting records is $31,743.70, and the bank statement cash balance for that date is $45,091.80.

b. Check No. 1273 for $1,084.20 and Check No. 1282 for $390, both written and entered in the accounting records in December, are not among the canceled checks. Two checks, No. 1231 for $2,289 and No. 1242 for $370.50, were outstanding on the most recent November 30 reconciliation. Check No. 1231 is listed with the December canceled checks, but Check No. 1242 is not.

c. When the December checks are compared with entries in the accounting records, it is found that Check No. 1267 had been correctly drawn for $2,435 to pay for office supplies but was erroneously entered in the accounting records as $2,453.

d. Two debit memoranda are enclosed with the statement and are unrecorded at the time of the reconciliation. One debit memorandum is for $749.50 and dealt with an NSF check for $732 received from a customer, Titus Industries, in payment of its account. The bank assessed a $17.50 fee for processing it. The second debit memorandum is a $79 charge for check printing. Style did not record these transactions before receiving the statement.

e. A credit memorandum indicates that the bank collected $20,000 cash on a note receivable for the company, deducted a $20 collection fee, and credited the balance to the company's Cash account. Style did not record this transaction before receiving the statement.

f. Style's December 31 daily cash receipts of $7,666.10 were placed in the bank's night depository on that date, but do not appear on the December 31 bank statement.

**Required**

1. Prepare the bank reconciliation for this company as of December 31, 2011.

2. Prepare the journal entries necessary to bring the company's book balance of cash into conformity with the reconciled cash balance as of December 31, 2011.

**Check**   (1) Reconciled balance,
$50,913.20; (2) Cr. Note Receivable
$20,000

**Analysis Component**

3. Explain the nature of the communications conveyed by a bank when the bank sends the depositor (*a*) a debit memorandum and (*b*) a credit memorandum.

**Problem 8-5B**
Prepare a bank reconciliation
and record adjustments

P3

Safe Systems most recently reconciled its bank balance on April 30 and reported two checks outstanding at that time, No. 1771 for $781 and No. 1780 for $1,325.90. The following information is available for its May 31, 2011, reconciliation.

### From the May 31 Bank Statement

| PREVIOUS BALANCE | TOTAL CHECKS AND DEBITS | TOTAL DEPOSITS AND CREDITS | CURRENT BALANCE |
|---|---|---|---|
| 18,290.70 | 12,898.90 | 16,416.80 | 21,808.60 |

| CHECKS AND DEBITS | | | DEPOSITS AND CREDITS | | DAILY BALANCE | |
|---|---|---|---|---|---|---|
| Date | No. | Amount | Date | Amount | Date | Amount |
| 05/01 | 1771 | 781.00 | 05/04 | 2,438.00 | 04/30 | 18,290.70 |
| 05/02 | 1783 | 195.30 | 05/14 | 2,898.00 | 05/01 | 17,509.70 |
| 05/04 | 1782 | 1,285.50 | 05/22 | 1,801.80 | 05/02 | 17,314.40 |
| 05/11 | 1784 | 1,449.60 | 05/25 | 7,200.00 CM | 05/04 | 18,466.90 |
| 05/18 | | 431.80 NSF | 05/26 | 2,079.00 | 05/11 | 17,017.30 |
| 05/25 | 1787 | 8,032.50 | | | 05/14 | 19,915.30 |
| 05/26 | 1785 | 157.20 | | | 05/18 | 19,483.50 |
| 05/29 | 1788 | 554.00 | | | 05/22 | 21,285.30 |
| 05/31 | | 12.00 SC | | | 05/25 | 20,452.80 |
| | | | | | 05/26 | 22,374.60 |
| | | | | | 05/29 | 21,820.60 |
| | | | | | 05/31 | 21,808.60 |

### From Safe Systems' Accounting Records

| Cash Receipts Deposited | | |
|---|---|---|
| Date | | Cash Debit |
| May 4 | | 2,438.00 |
| 14 | | 2,898.00 |
| 22 | | 1,801.80 |
| 26 | | 2,079.00 |
| 31 | | 2,526.30 |
| | | 11,743.10 |

| Cash Disbursements | | |
|---|---|---|
| Check No. | | Cash Credit |
| 1782 | | 1,285.50 |
| 1783 | | 195.30 |
| 1784 | | 1,449.60 |
| 1785 | | 157.20 |
| 1786 | | 353.10 |
| 1787 | | 8,032.50 |
| 1788 | | 544.00 |
| 1789 | | 639.50 |
| | | 12,656.70 |

| Cash | | | | | | Acct. No. 101 |
|---|---|---|---|---|---|---|
| Date | | Explanation | PR | Debit | Credit | Balance |
| Apr. | 30 | Balance | | | | 16,183.80 |
| May | 31 | Total receipts | R7 | 11,743.10 | | 27,926.90 |
| | 31 | Total disbursements | D8 | | 12,656.70 | 15,270.20 |

**Additional Information**

Check No. 1788 is correctly drawn for $554 to pay for May utilities; however, the recordkeeper misread the amount and entered it in the accounting records with a debit to Utilities Expense and a credit to Cash for $544. The bank paid and deducted the correct amount. The NSF check shown in the statement was originally received from a customer, S. Bax, in payment of her account. The company has not yet recorded its return. The credit memorandum is from a $7,300 note that the bank collected for the company. The bank deducted a $100 collection fee and deposited the remainder in the company's account. The collection and fee have not yet been recorded.

**Required**

1. Prepare the May 31, 2011, bank reconciliation for Safe Systems.
2. Prepare the journal entries to adjust the book balance of cash to the reconciled balance.

**Check** (1) Reconciled balance, $22,016.40; (2) Cr. Note Receivable $7,300

**Analysis Component**

3. The bank statement reveals that some of the prenumbered checks in the sequence are missing. Describe three possible situations to explain this.

---

*(This serial problem began in Chapter 1 and continues through most of the book. If previous chapter segments were not completed, the serial problem can begin at this point. It is helpful, but not necessary, to use the Working Papers that accompany the book.)*

**SERIAL PROBLEM**
Business Solutions

P3

**SP 8** Santana Rey receives the March bank statement for Business Solutions on April 11, 2012. The March 31 bank statement shows an ending cash balance of $67,566. A comparison of the bank statement with the general ledger Cash account, No. 101, reveals the following.

a. S. Rey notices that the bank erroneously cleared a $500 check against her account in March that she did not issue. The check documentation included with the bank statement shows that this check was actually issued by a company named Business Systems.

b. On March 25, the bank issued a $50 debit memorandum for the safety deposit box that Business Solutions agreed to rent from the bank beginning March 25.

c. On March 26, the bank issued a $102 debit memorandum for printed checks that Business Solutions ordered from the bank.

d. On March 31, the bank issued a credit memorandum for $33 interest earned on Business Solutions' checking account for the month of March.

e. S. Rey notices that the check she issued for $128 on March 31, 2012, has not yet cleared the bank.

f. S. Rey verifies that all deposits made in March do appear on the March bank statement.

g. The general ledger Cash account, No. 101, shows an ending cash balance per books of $68,057 as of March 31 (prior to any reconciliation).

**Required**

1. Prepare a bank reconciliation for Business Solutions for the month ended March 31, 2012.
2. Prepare any necessary adjusting entries. Use Miscellaneous Expenses, No. 677, for any bank charges. Use Interest Revenue, No. 404, for any interest earned on the checking account for the month of March.

**Check** (1) Adj. bank bal. $67,938

---

## Beyond the Numbers

**BTN 8-1** Refer to **Research In Motion**'s financial statements in Appendix A to answer the following.

1. For both fiscal year-ends February 27, 2010, and February 28, 2009, identify the total amount of cash and cash equivalents. Determine the percent this amount represents of total current assets, total current liabilities, total shareholders' equity, and total assets for both years. Comment on any trends.

2. For fiscal years ended February 27, 2010, and February 28, 2009, use the information in the statement of cash flows to determine the percent change between the beginning and ending year amounts of cash and cash equivalents.

3. Compute the days' sales uncollected as of February 27, 2010, and February 28, 2009. Has the collection of receivables improved? Are accounts receivable an important asset for Research In Motion? Explain.

**REPORTING IN ACTION**

C2 A1

**RIM**

**Fast Forward**

4. Access Research In Motion's financial statements for fiscal years ending after February 27, 2010, from its Website (**RIM.com**) or the SEC's EDGAR database (**www.sec.gov**). Recompute its days' sales uncollected for fiscal years ending after February 27, 2010. Compare this to the days' sales uncollected for 2010 and 2009.

## COMPARATIVE ANALYSIS

A1

### RIM

Apple

**BTN 8-2**   Key comparative figures for **Research In Motion** and **Apple** follow.

| ($ millions) | Research In Motion Current Year | Research In Motion Prior Year | Apple Current Year | Apple Prior Year |
|---|---|---|---|---|
| Accounts receivable ......... | $ 2,594 | $ 2,112 | $ 3,361 | $ 2,422 |
| Net sales ................. | 14,953 | 11,065 | 42,905 | 37,491 |

**Required**

Compute days' sales uncollected for these companies for each of the two years shown. Comment on any trends for the companies. Which company has the largest percent change in days' sales uncollected?

## ETHICS CHALLENGE

C1

**BTN 8-3**   Carol Benton, Sue Knox, and Marcia Diamond work for a family physician, Dr. Gwen Conrad, who is in private practice. Dr. Conrad is knowledgeable about office management practices and has segregated the cash receipt duties as follows. Benton opens the mail and prepares a triplicate list of money received. She sends one copy of the list to Knox, the cashier, who deposits the receipts daily in the bank. Diamond, the recordkeeper, receives a copy of the list and posts payments to patients' accounts. About once a month the office clerks have an expensive lunch they pay for as follows. First, Knox endorses a patient's check in Dr. Conrad's name and cashes it at the bank. Benton then destroys the remittance advice accompanying the check. Finally, Diamond posts payment to the customer's account as a miscellaneous credit. The three justify their actions by their relatively low pay and knowledge that Dr. Conrad will likely never miss the money.

**Required**

1. Who is the best person in Dr. Conrad's office to reconcile the bank statement?
2. Would a bank reconciliation uncover this office fraud?
3. What are some procedures to detect this type of fraud?
4. Suggest additional internal controls that Dr. Conrad could implement.

## COMMUNICATING IN PRACTICE

P5

**BTN 8-4**[B]   Assume you are a business consultant. The owner of a company sends you an e-mail expressing concern that the company is not taking advantage of its discounts offered by vendors. The company currently uses the gross method of recording purchases. The owner is considering a review of all invoices and payments from the previous period. Due to the volume of purchases, however, the owner recognizes that this is time-consuming and costly. The owner seeks your advice about monitoring purchase discounts in the future. Provide a response in memorandum form.

## TAKING IT TO THE NET

C1  P1

**BTN 8-5**   Visit the Association of Certified Fraud Examiners Website at **cfenet.com**. Find and open the file "2008 Report to the Nation." Read the two-page Executive Summary and fill in the following blanks. (The report is under its *Fraud Resources* tab or under its *About the ACFE* tab [under Press Room]; we can also use the *Search* tab.)

1. The median loss caused by occupational frauds was $_____.
2. More than _____ of fraud cases caused at least $1 million in losses.
3. Companies lose ___% of their annual revenues to fraud; this figure translates to $_____ billion in fraud losses.
4. The typical length of fraud schemes was _____ years from the time the fraud began until it was detected.
5. Companies that conducted surprise audits suffered a median loss of $_____, whereas those without surprise audits had a median loss of $_____.
6. The median loss suffered by companies with fewer than 100 employees was $_____ per scheme.
7. _____ and _____ were the most common small business fraud schemes.
8. ___% of respondents cited inadequate internal controls as the primary contributing factor in the frauds investigated.
9. Only ___% of the perpetrators had convictions prior to committing their frauds.

**BTN 8-6**    Organize the class into teams. Each team must prepare a list of 10 internal controls a consumer could observe in a typical retail department store. When called upon, the team's spokesperson must be prepared to share controls identified by the team that have not been shared by another team's spokesperson.

**TEAMWORK IN ACTION**

C1

**BTN 8-7**    Review the opening feature of this chapter that highlights Dylan Lauren and her company **Dylan's Candy Bar**.

**ENTREPRENEURIAL DECISION**

C1  P1

**Required**

**1.** List the seven principles of internal control and explain how Dylan could implement each of them in her retail stores.

**2.** Do you believe that Dylan will need to add controls as her business expands? Explain.

**BTN 8-8**    Visit an area of your college that serves the student community with either products or services. Some examples are food services, libraries, and bookstores. Identify and describe between four and eight internal controls being implemented.

**HITTING THE ROAD**

C1

**BTN 8-9**    The following information is from **Nokia** (**www.Nokia.com**), which is a leading global manufacturer of mobile devices and services.

**GLOBAL DECISION**

C2  A1

 **NOKIA**

| EUR millions | Current Year | Prior Year |
|---|---|---|
| Cash ................... | 1,142 | 1,706 |
| Accounts receivable ........ | 7,981 | 9,444 |
| Current assets ............ | 23,613 | 24,470 |
| Total assets ............... | 35,738 | 39,582 |
| Current liabilities .......... | 15,188 | 20,355 |
| Shareholders' equity ........ | 14,749 | 16,510 |
| Net sales ................. | 40,984 | 50,710 |

**Required**

**1.** For each year, compute the percentage that cash represents of current assets, total assets, current liabilities, and shareholders' equity. Comment on any trends in these percentages.

**2.** Determine the percentage change between the current and prior year cash balances.

**3.** Compute the days' sales uncollected at the end of both the current year and the prior year. Has the collection of receivables improved? Explain.

## ANSWERS TO MULTIPLE CHOICE QUIZ

**1.** e; The entry follows.

| | | |
|---|---|---|
| Debits to expenses (or assets) ......... | 420 | |
| Cash Over and Short ............... | 5 | |
| Cash ......................... | | 425 |

**2.** a; recognizes cash collection of note by bank.

**3.** a; the bank reconciliation follows.

**4.** d; ($6,720/$84,000) × 365 = <u>29.2 days</u>

**5.** b; The entry follows.

| | | |
|---|---|---|
| Merchandise Inventory* ........ | 5,880 | |
| Accounts Payable .......... | | 5,880 |

*$6,000 × 98%

| Bank Reconciliation<br>November 30 | | | |
|---|---|---|---|
| Balance per bank statement ...... | $1,895 | Balance per books ............. | $1,742 |
| Add: Deposit in transit .......... | 795 | Add: Note collected less fee ...... | 320 |
| Deduct: Outstanding checks ...... | (638) | Deduct: Service charge .......... | (10) |
| Reconciled balance ............ | $2,052 | Reconciled balance ............ | $2,052 |

# 9

# Accounting for Receivables

## A Look Back

Chapter 8 focused on internal control and reporting for cash. We described internal control procedures and the accounting for and management of cash.

## A Look at This Chapter

This chapter emphasizes receivables. We explain that they are liquid assets and describe how companies account for and report them. We also discuss the importance of estimating uncollectibles.

## A Look Ahead

Chapter 10 focuses on plant assets, natural resources, and intangible assets. We explain how to account for, report, and analyze these long-term assets.

## Learning Objectives

### CAP

#### CONCEPTUAL

**C1** Describe accounts receivable and how they occur and are recorded. (p. 360)

**C2** Describe a note receivable, the computation of its maturity date, and the recording of its existence. (p. 370)

**C3** Explain how receivables can be converted to cash before maturity. (p. 373)

#### ANALYTICAL

**A1** Compute accounts receivable turnover and use it to help assess financial condition. (p. 375)

LP9

#### PROCEDURAL

**P1** Apply the direct write-off method to account for accounts receivable. (p. 363)

**P2** Apply the allowance method and estimate uncollectibles based on sales and accounts receivable. (p. 366)

**P3** Record the honoring and dishonoring of a note and adjustments for interest. (p. 372)

# Monk E-Business

*"We are not wearing bling . . . I mean, we are still monks"*
—BROTHER BERNARD MCCOY

SPARTA, WI—"My printer ran out of toner," recalls Brother Bernard McCoy. "I was just appalled at the cost of the black dust . . . the markup on toner is sinfully high!" So, Bernard, who is part of a handful of monks living at and trying to keep a remote monastery in rural Wisconsin going, started thinking. "Nine hundred years ago, my brothers were copying manuscripts and making their own paper and ink," explains Bernard. His response was to launch **LaserMonks** (**LaserMonks.com**), a supplier of toner and ink products (and other goods).

Sales quickly soared, and Bernard, along with what he calls his monk-helper angels, had to contend with accounting activities, receivables management, and other day-to-day recordkeeping needs. Special attention was focused on monitoring receivables. Decisions on credit sales and policies for extending credit can make or break a start-up, and Bernard was determined to succeed in spite of the demands of a monk's life. "We spend about five hours a day in Gregorian chant, and another couple of hours in prayers," explains Bernard. "We're monks . . . we do monk things!"

Nevertheless, Bernard and his angels ensured that credit sales were extended to customers in good credit standing. Further, his team knows their customers, including who pays and when. Explains Bernard, we understand our customers—inside and out—including cash payment patterns that allow them to estimate uncollectibles and minimize bad debts. Bernard points out, however, that "we use the money for good works and to support monks who dedicate their lives to serving God and neighbor."

A commitment to quality customers and products is propelling LaserMonks' sales and shattering Bernard's most optimistic goals. "The results have been beyond anything we could imagine," affirms Bernard. Both accounts and notes receivables receive his attention. Bernard and his team's financial focus includes reviewing the allowance for doubtful accounts monthly. "We're scrambling to keep up with growth," adds Bernard. "[We're] continuing to negotiate with suppliers . . . processing orders between our times of prayer."

Bernard's focus on serving people is unwavering. "Our customer service is following our order's tradition of hospitality," explains Bernard. "We try to transfer monastic hospitality into commerce hospitality . . . we try to treat every single customer with kid gloves." Bernard says he wishes that all customers "be abundantly blessed with prosperity of soul."

[Sources: *LaserMonks Website,* January 2011; *Entrepreneur,* September 2009; *CBS Broadcasting,* August 2006; *Religion & Ethics Newsweekly,* September 2009; *Consumer Reports,* February 2010]

This chapter focuses on accounts receivable and short-term notes receivable. We describe each of these assets, their uses, and how they are accounted for and reported in financial statements. This knowledge helps us use accounting information to make better business decisions. It can also help in predicting future company performance and financial condition as well as in managing one's own business.

**Accounting for Receivables**

| **Accounts Receivable** | **Notes Receivable** | **Disposal of Receivables** |
|---|---|---|
| • Recognizing accounts receivable<br>• Valuing accounts receivable<br>• Estimating bad debts | • Computing maturity and interest<br>• Recognizing notes receivable<br>• Valuing and settling notes | • Selling receivables<br>• Pledging receivables |

## ACCOUNTS RECEIVABLE

A *receivable* is an amount due from another party. The two most common receivables are accounts receivable and notes receivable. Other receivables include interest receivable, rent receivable, tax refund receivable, and receivables from employees. **Accounts receivable** are amounts due from customers for credit sales. This section begins by describing how accounts receivable occur. It includes receivables that occur when customers use credit cards issued by third parties and when a company gives credit directly to customers. When a company does extend credit directly to customers, it (1) maintains a separate account receivable for each customer and (2) accounts for bad debts from credit sales.

### Recognizing Accounts Receivable

**C1** Describe accounts receivable and how they occur and are recorded.

Accounts receivable occur from credit sales to customers. The amount of credit sales has increased in recent years, reflecting several factors including an efficient financial system. Retailers such as **Costco** and **Best Buy** hold millions of dollars in accounts receivable. Similar amounts are held by wholesalers such as **SUPERVALU** and **SYSCO**. Exhibit 9.1 shows recent dollar amounts of receivables and their percent of total assets for four well-known companies.

**EXHIBIT 9.1**

Accounts Receivable for Selected Companies

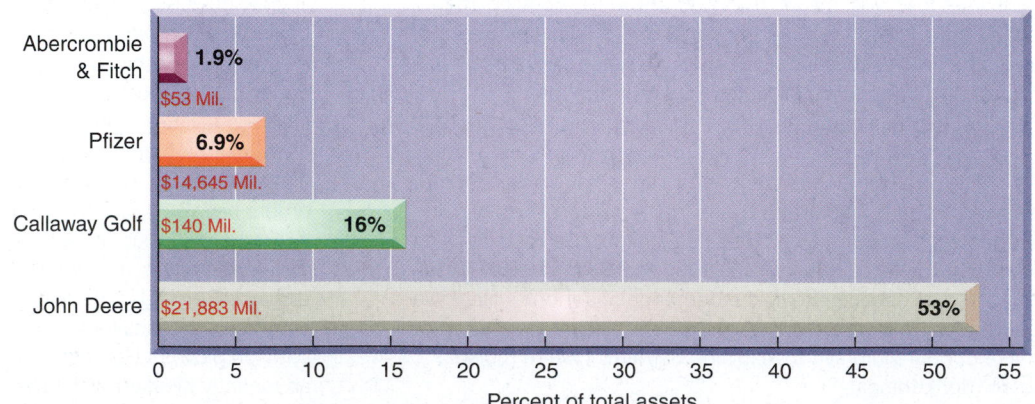

**Sales on Credit** Credit sales are recorded by increasing (debiting) Accounts Receivable. A company must also maintain a separate account for each customer that tracks how much that customer purchases, has already paid, and still owes. This information provides the basis for sending bills to customers and for other business analyses. To maintain this information, companies that extend credit directly to their customers keep a separate account receivable for each one of them. The general ledger continues to have a single Accounts Receivable account along with the other financial statement accounts, but a supplementary record is created to maintain a separate account for each customer. This supplementary record is called the *accounts receivable ledger*.

Exhibit 9.2 shows the relation between the Accounts Receivable account in the general ledger and its individual customer accounts in the accounts receivable ledger for TechCom, a small electronics wholesaler. This exhibit reports a $3,000 ending balance of TechCom's accounts receivable for June 30. TechCom's transactions are mainly in cash, but it has two major credit customers: CompStore and RDA Electronics. Its *schedule of accounts receivable* shows that the $3,000 balance of the Accounts Receivable account in the general ledger equals the total of its two customers' balances in the accounts receivable ledger.

**EXHIBIT 9.2**

General Ledger and the Accounts Receivable Ledger (before July 1 transactions)

To see how accounts receivable from credit sales are recognized in the accounting records, we look at two transactions on July 1 between TechCom and its credit customers—see Exhibit 9.3. The first is a credit sale of $950 to CompStore. A credit sale is posted with both a debit to the Accounts Receivable account in the general ledger and a debit to the customer account in the accounts receivable ledger. The second transaction is a collection of $720 from RDA Electronics from a prior credit sale. Cash receipts from a credit customer are posted with a credit to the Accounts Receivable account in the general ledger and flow through to credit the customer account in the accounts receivable ledger. (Posting debits or credits to Accounts Receivable in two separate ledgers does not violate the requirement that debits equal credits. The equality of debits and credits is maintained in the general ledger. The accounts receivable ledger is a *supplementary* record providing information on each customer.)

**EXHIBIT 9.3**

Accounts Receivable Transactions

| July 1 | Accounts Receivable—CompStore | 950 | |
| | Sales | | 950 |
| | *To record credit sales** | | |
| July 1 | Cash | 720 | |
| | Accounts Receivable—RDA Electronics | | 720 |
| | *To record collection of credit sales.* | | |

Assets = Liabilities + Equity
+ 950                             +950

Assets = Liabilities + Equity
+720
−720

* We omit the entry to Dr. Cost of Sales and Cr. Merchandise Inventory to focus on sales and receivables.

Exhibit 9.4 shows the general ledger and the accounts receivable ledger after recording the two July 1 transactions. The general ledger shows the effects of the sale, the collection, and the resulting balance of $3,230. These events are also reflected in the individual customer accounts: RDA Electronics has an ending balance of $280, and CompStore's ending balance is $2,950.

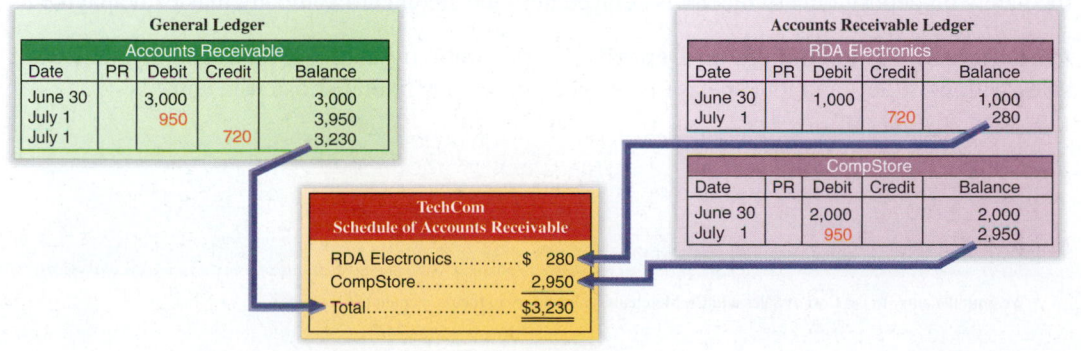

**EXHIBIT 9.4**

General Ledger and the Accounts Receivable Ledger (after July 1 transactions)

The $3,230 sum of the individual accounts equals the debit balance of the Accounts Receivable account in the general ledger.

Like TechCom, many large retailers such as **Sears** and **JCPenney** sell on credit. Many also maintain their own credit cards to grant credit to approved customers and to earn interest on any balance not paid within a specified period of time. This allows them to avoid the fee charged by credit card companies. The entries in this case are the same as those for TechCom except for the possibility of added interest revenue. If a customer owes interest on a bill, we debit Interest Receivable and credit Interest Revenue for that amount.

**Credit Card Sales**   Many companies allow their customers to pay for products and services using third-party credit cards such as **Visa**, **MasterCard**, or **American Express**, and debit cards (also called ATM or bank cards). This practice gives customers the ability to make purchases without cash or checks. Once credit is established with a credit card company or bank, the customer does not have to open an account with each store. Customers using these cards can make single monthly payments instead of several payments to different creditors and can defer their payments.

Many sellers allow customers to use third-party credit cards and debit cards instead of granting credit directly for several reasons. First, the seller does not have to evaluate each customer's credit standing or make decisions about who gets credit and how much. Second, the seller avoids the risk of extending credit to customers who cannot or do not pay. This risk is transferred to the card company. Third, the seller typically receives cash from the card company sooner than had it granted credit directly to customers. Fourth, a variety of credit options for customers offers a potential increase in sales volume. **Sears** historically offered credit only to customers using a Sears card but later changed its policy to permit customers to charge purchases to third-party credit card companies in a desire to increase sales. It reported: "SearsCharge increased its share of Sears retail sales even as the company expanded the payment options available to its customers with the acceptance . . . of Visa, MasterCard, and American Express in addition to the [Sears] Card."

There are guidelines in how companies account for credit card and debit card sales. Some credit cards, but nearly all debit cards, credit a seller's Cash account immediately upon deposit. In this case the seller deposits a copy of each card sales receipt in its bank account just as it deposits a customer's check. The majority of credit cards, however, require the seller to remit a copy (often electronically) of each receipt to the card company. Until payment is received, the seller has an account receivable from the card company. In both cases, the seller pays a fee for services provided by the card company, often ranging from 1% to 5% of card sales. This charge is deducted from the credit to the seller's account or the cash payment to the seller.

### Decision Insight

**Debit Card vs. Credit Card**   A buyer's debit card purchase reduces the buyer's cash account balance at the card company, which is often a bank. Since the buyer's cash account balance is a liability (with a credit balance) for the card company to the buyer, the card company would debit that account for a buyer's purchase—hence, the term *debit card*. A credit card reflects authorization by the card company of a line of credit for the buyer with preset interest rates and payment terms—hence, the term *credit card*. Most card companies waive interest charges if the buyer pays its balance each month. ∎

The procedures used in accounting for credit card sales depend on whether cash is received immediately on deposit or cash receipt is delayed until the credit card company makes the payment.

**Cash Received Immediately on Deposit**   To illustrate, if TechCom has $100 of credit card sales with a 4% fee, and its $96 cash is received immediately on deposit, the entry is

Assets = Liabilities + Equity
+96                 +100
                    −4

| July 15 | Cash ................................................. | 96 | |
| | Credit Card Expense .................................. | 4 | |
| | Sales ........................................... | | 100 |
| | *To record credit card sales less a 4% credit card expense.*\* | | |

\* We omit the entry to Dr. Cost of Sales and Cr. Merchandise Inventory to focus on credit card expense.

**Cash Received Some Time after Deposit**   However, if instead TechCom must remit electronically the credit card sales receipts to the credit card company and wait for the $96 cash payment, the entry on the date of sale is

| July 15 | **Accounts Receivable—Credit Card Co.** ................ | 96 | |
| | Credit Card Expense ................................ | 4 | |
| | Sales ........................................... | | 100 |
| | *To record credit card sales less 4% credit card expense.** | | |

Assets = Liabilities + Equity
+96                    +100
                        −4

\* We omit the entry to Dr. Cost of Sales and Cr. Merchandise Inventory to focus on credit card expense.

When cash is later received from the credit card company, usually through electronic funds transfer, the entry is

| July 20 | Cash ............................................. | 96 | |
| | Accounts Receivable—Credit Card Co. ................ | | 96 |
| | *To record cash receipt.* | | |

Assets = Liabilities + Equity
+96
−96

Some firms report credit card expense in the income statement as a type of discount deducted from sales to get net sales. Other companies classify it as a selling expense or even as an administrative expense. Arguments can be made for each approach.

**Point:** Third-party credit card costs can be large. JCPenney reported third-party credit card costs exceeding $10 million.

**Installment Sales and Receivables**   Many companies allow their credit customers to make periodic payments over several months. For example, **Ford Motor Company** reports more than $75 billion in installment receivables. The seller refers to such assets as *installment accounts* (or *finance) receivable,* which are amounts owed by customers from credit sales for which payment is required in periodic amounts over an extended time period. Source documents for installment accounts receivable include sales slips or invoices describing the sales transactions. The customer is usually charged interest. Although installment accounts receivable can have credit periods of more than one year, they are classified as current assets if the seller regularly offers customers such terms.

  **Decision Maker**                                   Answer — p. 378

**Entrepreneur**   As a small retailer, you are considering allowing customers to buy merchandise using credit cards. Until now, your store accepted only cash and checks. What analysis do you use to make this decision? ■

 **Quick Check**                                   Answers — p. 379

1. In recording credit card sales, when do you debit Accounts Receivable and when do you debit Cash?
2. A company accumulates sales receipts and remits them to the credit card company for payment. When are the credit card expenses recorded? When are these expenses incurred?

## Valuing Accounts Receivable—Direct Write-Off Method

When a company directly grants credit to its customers, it expects that some customers will not pay what they promised. The accounts of these customers are *uncollectible accounts,* commonly called **bad debts.** The total amount of uncollectible accounts is an expense of selling on credit. Why do companies sell on credit if they expect some accounts to be uncollectible? The answer is that companies believe that granting credit will increase total sales and net income enough to offset bad debts. Companies use two methods to account for uncollectible accounts: (1) direct write-off method and (2) allowance method. We describe both.

 **P1**   Apply the direct write-off method to account for accounts receivable.

**Recording and Writing Off Bad Debts**   The **direct write-off method** of accounting for bad debts records the loss from an uncollectible account receivable when it is determined to

**Point:** Managers realize that some portion of credit sales will be uncollectible, but which credit sales are uncollectible is unknown.

be uncollectible. No attempt is made to predict bad debts expense. To illustrate, if TechCom determines on January 23 that it cannot collect $520 owed to it by its customer J. Kent, it recognizes the loss using the direct write-off method as follows:

Assets = Liabilities + Equity<br>−520                −520

| Jan. 23 | Bad Debts Expense ............................... | 520 | |
|---------|--------------------------------------------------|-----|-----|
| | Accounts Receivable—J. Kent ................. | | 520 |
| | *To write off an uncollectible account.* | | |

The debit in this entry charges the uncollectible amount directly to the current period's Bad Debts Expense account. The credit removes its balance from the Accounts Receivable account in the general ledger (and its subsidiary ledger).

**Point:** If a customer fails to pay within the credit period, most companies send out repeated billings and make other efforts to collect.

**Recovering a Bad Debt**    Although uncommon, sometimes an account written off is later collected. This can be due to factors such as continual collection efforts or a customer's good fortune. If the account of J. Kent that was written off directly to Bad Debts Expense is later collected in full, the following two entries record this recovery.

Assets = Liabilities + Equity<br>+520                +520

Assets = Liabilities + Equity<br>+520               <br>−520

| Mar. 11 | Accounts Receivable—J. Kent ..................... | 520 | |
|---------|---------------------------------------------------|-----|-----|
| | Bad Debts Expense ......................... | | 520 |
| | *To reinstate account previously written off.* | | |
| Mar. 11 | Cash ......................................... | 520 | |
| | Accounts Receivable—J. Kent ................. | | 520 |
| | *To record full payment of account.* | | |

**Assessing the Direct Write-Off Method**    Examples of companies that use the direct write-off method include **Rand Medical Billing**, **Gateway Distributors**, **Microwave Satellite Technologies**, **First Industrial Realty**, **New Frontier Energy**, and **Sub Surface Waste Management**. The following disclosure by **Pharma-Bio Serv** is typical of the justification for this method: Bad debts are accounted for using the direct write-off method whereby an expense is recognized only when a specific account is determined to be uncollectible. The effect of using this method approximates that of the allowance method. Companies must weigh at least two accounting concepts when considering the use of the direct write-off method: the (1) matching principle and (2) materiality constraint.

**Matching principle applied to bad debts.**    The **matching (expense recognition) principle** requires expenses to be reported in the same accounting period as the sales they helped produce. This means that if extending credit to customers helped produce sales, the bad debts expense linked to those sales is matched and reported in the same period. The direct write-off method usually does *not* best match sales and expenses because bad debts expense is not recorded until an account becomes uncollectible, which often occurs in a period after that of the credit sale. To match bad debts expense with the sales it produces therefore requires a company to estimate future uncollectibles.

**Point:** Harley-Davidson reports $169 million of credit losses matched against $4,782 million of total revenues.

**Materiality constraint applied to bad debts.**    The **materiality constraint** states that an amount can be ignored if its effect on the financial statements is unimportant to users' business decisions. The materiality constraint permits the use of the direct write-off method when bad debts expenses are very small in relation to a company's other financial statement items such as sales and net income.

## Valuing Accounts Receivable—Allowance Method

The **allowance method** of accounting for bad debts matches the *estimated* loss from uncollectible accounts receivable against the sales they helped produce. We must use estimated losses because when sales occur, management does not know which customers will not pay their bills. This means that at the end of each period, the allowance method requires an estimate of the total bad debts expected to result from that period's sales. This method has two advantages over the direct write-off method: (1) it records estimated bad debts expense in the period when the related sales are recorded and (2) it reports accounts receivable on the balance sheet at the estimated amount of cash to be collected.

**Point:** Under direct write-off, expense is recorded each time an account is written off. Under the allowance method, expense is recorded with an adjusting entry equal to the total estimated uncollectibles for that period's sales.

**Recording Bad Debts Expense** The allowance method estimates bad debts expense at the end of each accounting period and records it with an adjusting entry. TechCom, for instance, had credit sales of $300,000 during its first year of operations. At the end of the first year, $20,000 of credit sales remained uncollected. Based on the experience of similar businesses, TechCom estimated that $1,500 of its accounts receivable would be uncollectible. This estimated expense is recorded with the following adjusting entry.

| Dec. 31 | Bad Debts Expense ............................ | 1,500 | |
| | Allowance for Doubtful Accounts .............. | | 1,500 |
| | *To record estimated bad debts.* | | |

Assets = Liabilities + Equity
−1,500            −1,500

The estimated Bad Debts Expense of $1,500 is reported on the income statement (as either a selling expense or an administrative expense) and offsets the $300,000 credit sales it helped produce. The **Allowance for Doubtful Accounts** is a contra asset account. A contra account is used instead of reducing accounts receivable directly because at the time of the adjusting entry, the company does not know which customers will not pay. After the bad debts adjusting entry is posted, TechCom's account balances (in T-account form) for Accounts Receivable and its Allowance for Doubtful Accounts are as shown in Exhibit 9.5.

**Point:** Credit approval is usually not assigned to the selling dept. because its goal is to increase sales, and it may approve customers at the cost of increased bad debts. Instead, approval is assigned to a separate credit-granting or administrative dept.

| Accounts Receivable | | | Allowance for Doubtful Accounts | | |
|---|---|---|---|---|---|
| Dec. 31 | 20,000 | | | Dec. 31 | 1,500 |

**EXHIBIT 9.5**

General Ledger Entries after Bad Debts Adjusting Entry

The Allowance for Doubtful Accounts credit balance of $1,500 has the effect of reducing accounts receivable to its estimated realizable value. **Realizable value** refers to the expected proceeds from converting an asset into cash. Although credit customers owe $20,000 to TechCom, only $18,500 is expected to be realized in cash collections from these customers. In the balance sheet, the Allowance for Doubtful Accounts is subtracted from Accounts Receivable and is often reported as shown in Exhibit 9.6.

**Point:** Bad Debts Expense is also called *Uncollectible Accounts Expense.* The Allowance for Doubtful Accounts is also called *Allowance for Uncollectible Accounts.*

**EXHIBIT 9.6**

Balance Sheet Presentation of the Allowance for Doubtful Accounts

| Current assets | | |
|---|---|---|
| **Accounts receivable**............................. | **$20,000** | |
| **Less allowance for doubtful accounts** .............. | **1,500** | **$18,500** |

Sometimes the Allowance for Doubtful Accounts is not reported separately. This alternative presentation is shown in Exhibit 9.7 (also see Appendix A).

**EXHIBIT 9.7**

Alternative Presentation of the Allowance for Doubtful Accounts

| Current assets | |
|---|---|
| **Accounts receivable (net of $1,500 doubtful accounts)** ......... | **$18,500** |

**Writing Off a Bad Debt** When specific accounts are identified as uncollectible, they are written off against the Allowance for Doubtful Accounts. To illustrate, TechCom decides that J. Kent's $520 account is uncollectible and makes the following entry to write it off.

| Jan. 23 | Allowance for Doubtful Accounts ................. | 520 | |
| | Accounts Receivable—J. Kent ................. | | 520 |
| | *To write off an uncollectible account.* | | |

Assets = Liabilities + Equity
+520
−520

Posting this write-off entry to the Accounts Receivable account removes the amount of the bad debt from the general ledger (it is also posted to the accounts receivable subsidiary ledger). The general ledger accounts now appear as in Exhibit 9.8 (assuming no other transactions affecting these accounts).

**Point:** The Bad Debts Expense account is not debited in the write-off entry because it was recorded in the period when sales occurred.

| Accounts Receivable | | | Allowance for Doubtful Accounts | | |
|---|---|---|---|---|---|
| Dec. 31 | 20,000 | | | Dec. 31 | 1,500 |
| | | Jan. 23 | **520** | Jan. 23 | **520** |

**EXHIBIT 9.8**

General Ledger Entries after Write-Off

**Point:** In posting a write-off, the ledger's Explanation column indicates the reason for this credit so it is not misinterpreted as payment in full.

The write-off does *not* affect the realizable value of accounts receivable as shown in Exhibit 9.9. Neither total assets nor net income is affected by the write-off of a specific account. Instead, both assets and net income are affected in the period when bad debts expense is predicted and recorded with an adjusting entry.

**EXHIBIT 9.9**

Realizable Value before and after Write-Off of a Bad Debt

|  | Before Write-Off | After Write-Off |
|---|---|---|
| Accounts receivable ............................... | $ 20,000 | $ 19,480 |
| Less allowance for doubtful accounts ................. | 1,500 | 980 |
| **Estimated realizable accounts receivable** ........ | **$18,500** | **$18,500** |

**Recovering a Bad Debt**    When a customer fails to pay and the account is written off as uncollectible, his or her credit standing is jeopardized. To help restore credit standing, a customer sometimes volunteers to pay all or part of the amount owed. A company makes two entries when collecting an account previously written off by the allowance method. The first is to reverse the write-off and reinstate the customer's account. The second entry records the collection of the reinstated account. To illustrate, if on March 11 Kent pays in full his account previously written off, the entries are

Assets = Liabilities + Equity
+520
−520

Assets = Liabilities + Equity
+520
−520

| Mar. 11 | Accounts Receivable—J. Kent...................... | 520 | |
| | Allowance for Doubtful Accounts .............. | | 520 |
| | *To reinstate account previously written off.* | | |
| Mar. 11 | Cash .......................................... | 520 | |
| | Accounts Receivable—J. Kent ................. | | 520 |
| | *To record full payment of account.* | | |

**Example:** If TechCom used a collection agency and paid a 35% commission on $520 collected from Kent, how is this recorded? *Answer:*
Cash ................... 338
Collection Expense ...... 182
    Accts. Recble.—J. Kent ...... 520

In this illustration, Kent paid the entire amount previously written off, but sometimes a customer pays only a portion of the amount owed. A question then arises as to whether the entire balance of the account or just the amount paid is returned to accounts receivable. This is a matter of judgment. If we believe this customer will later pay in full, we return the entire amount owed to accounts receivable, but if we expect no further collection, we return only the amount paid.

**Decision Insight**

**PayPal**    PayPal is legally just a money transfer agent, but it is increasingly challenging big credit card brands—see chart. PayPal is successful because: (1) online credit card processing fees often exceed $0.15 per dollar, but PayPal's fees are under $0.10 per dollar. (2) PayPal's merchant fraud losses are under 0.2% of revenues, which compares to nearly 2% for online merchants using credit cards. ■

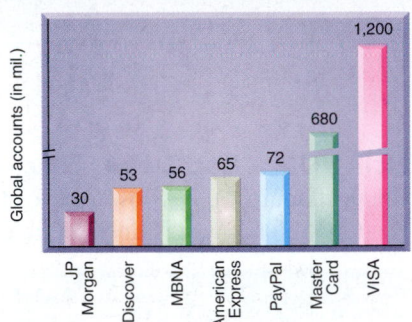

## Estimating Bad Debts—Percent of Sales Method

**P2**    Apply the allowance method and estimate uncollectibles based on sales and accounts receivable.

The allowance method requires an estimate of bad debts expense to prepare an adjusting entry at the end of each accounting period. There are two common methods. One is based on the income statement relation between bad debts expense and sales. The second is based on the balance sheet relation between accounts receivable and the allowance for doubtful accounts.

The *percent of sales method,* also referred to as the *income statement method,* is based on the idea that a given percent of a company's credit sales for the period is uncollectible. To illustrate, assume that Musicland has credit sales of $400,000 in year 2011. Based on past experience,

Musicland estimates 0.6% of credit sales to be uncollectible. This implies that Musicland expects $2,400 of bad debts expense from its sales (computed as $400,000 × 0.006). The adjusting entry to record this estimated expense is

| Dec. 31 | Bad Debts Expense .......................... | 2,400 | |
| | Allowance for Doubtful Accounts ............. | | 2,400 |
| | *To record estimated bad debts.* | | |

Assets = Liabilities + Equity
−2,400                         −2,400

The allowance account ending balance on the balance sheet for this method would rarely equal the bad debts expense on the income statement. This is so because unless a company is in its first period of operations, its allowance account has a zero balance only if the prior amounts written off as uncollectible *exactly* equal the prior estimated bad debts expenses. (When computing bad debts expense as a percent of sales, managers monitor and adjust the percent so it is not too high or too low.)

**Point:** When using the *percent of sales method* for estimating uncollectibles, the estimate of bad debts is the number used in the adjusting entry.

## Estimating Bad Debts—Percent of Receivables Method

The *accounts receivable methods,* also referred to as *balance sheet methods,* use balance sheet relations to estimate bad debts—mainly the relation between accounts receivable and the allowance amount. The goal of the bad debts adjusting entry for these methods is to make the Allowance for Doubtful Accounts balance equal to the portion of accounts receivable that is estimated to be uncollectible. The estimated balance for the allowance account is obtained in one of two ways: (1) computing the percent uncollectible from the total accounts receivable or (2) aging accounts receivable.

The *percent of accounts receivable method* assumes that a given percent of a company's receivables is uncollectible. This percent is based on past experience and is impacted by current conditions such as economic trends and customer difficulties. The total dollar amount of all receivables is multiplied by this percent to get the estimated dollar amount of uncollectible accounts—reported in the balance sheet as the Allowance for Doubtful Accounts.

To illustrate, assume that Musicland has $50,000 of accounts receivable on December 31, 2011. Experience suggests 5% of its receivables is uncollectible. This means that *after* the adjusting entry is posted, we want the Allowance for Doubtful Accounts to show a $2,500 credit balance (5% of $50,000). We are also told that its beginning balance is $2,200, which is 5% of the $44,000 accounts receivable on December 31, 2010—see Exhibit 9.10.

**Point:** When using an accounts receivable method for estimating uncollectibles, the allowance account balance is adjusted to equal the estimate of uncollectibles.

**EXHIBIT 9.10**

Allowance for Doubtful Accounts after Bad Debts Adjusting Entry

During 2011, accounts of customers are written off on February 6, July 10, and November 20. Thus, the account has a $200 credit balance *before* the December 31, 2011, adjustment. The adjusting entry to give the allowance account the estimated $2,500 balance is

| Dec. 31 | Bad Debts Expense ........................... | 2,300 | |
| | Allowance for Doubtful Accounts ............. | | 2,300 |
| | *To record estimated bad debts.* | | |

Assets = Liabilities + Equity
−2,300                         −2,300

**Decision Insight**

**Aging Pains**  Experience shows that the longer a receivable is past due, the lower is the likelihood of its collection. An *aging schedule* uses this knowledge to estimate bad debts. The chart here is from a survey that reported estimates of bad debts for receivables grouped by how long they were past their due dates. Each company sets its own estimates based on its customers and its experiences with those customers' payment patterns. ■

## Estimating Bad Debts—Aging of Receivables Method

The **aging of accounts receivable** method uses both past and current receivables information to estimate the allowance amount. Specifically, each receivable is classified by how long it is past its due date. Then estimates of uncollectible amounts are made assuming that the longer an amount is past due, the more likely it is to be uncollectible. Classifications are often based on 30-day periods. After the amounts are classified (or aged), experience is used to estimate the percent of each uncollectible class. These percents are applied to the amounts in each class and then totaled to get the estimated balance of the Allowance for Doubtful Accounts. This computation is performed by setting up a schedule such as Exhibit 9.11.

**EXHIBIT 9.11**

Aging of Accounts Receivable

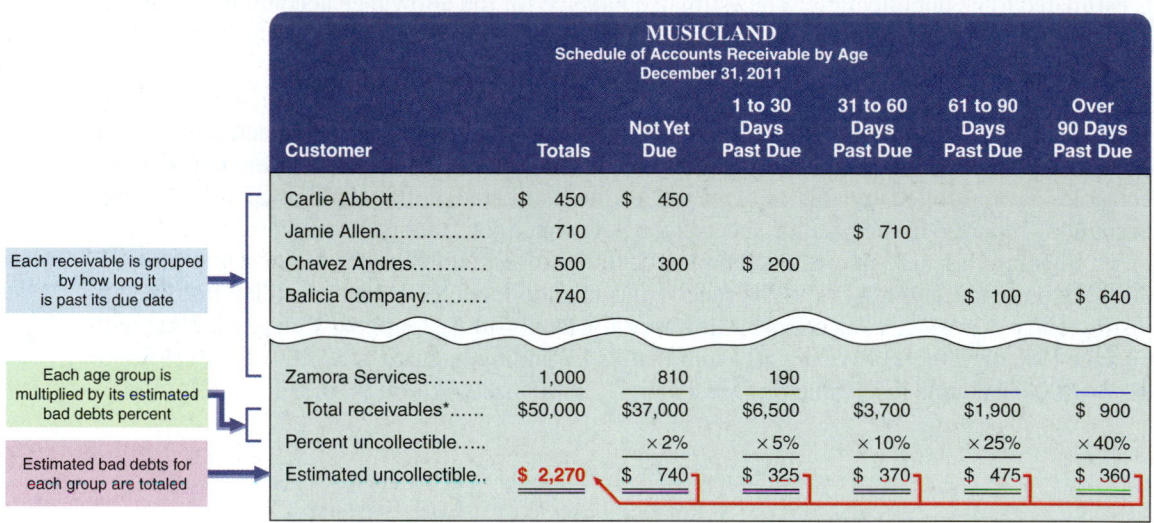

*The "white line break" means that additional customer accounts are not shown in the table but are included in each column's total.

Exhibit 9.11 lists each customer's individual balances assigned to one of five classes based on its days past due. The amounts in each class are totaled and multiplied by the estimated percent of uncollectible accounts for each class. The percents used are regularly reviewed to reflect changes in the company and economy.

To explain, Musicland has $3,700 in accounts receivable that are 31 to 60 days past due. Its management estimates 10% of the amounts in this age class are uncollectible, or a total of $370 (computed as $3,700 × 10%). Similar analysis is done for each of the other four classes. The final total of $2,270 ($740 + $325 + 370 + $475 + $360) shown in the first column is the estimated balance for the Allowance for Doubtful Accounts. Exhibit 9.12 shows that since the allowance

**EXHIBIT 9.12**

Computation of the Required Adjustment for the Accounts Receivable Method

| | |
|---|---|
| Unadjusted balance | $   200 credit |
| Estimated balance | 2,270 credit |
| **Required adjustment** | **$2,070 credit** |

account has an unadjusted credit balance of $200, the required adjustment to the Allowance for Doubtful Accounts is $2,070. (We could also use a T-account for this analysis as shown in the margin.) This yields the following end-of-period adjusting entry.

| Dec. 31 | Bad Debts Expense ............................. | 2,070 | |
|---------|------------------------------------------------|-------|-------|
| | Allowance for Doubtful Accounts .............. | | 2,070 |
| | *To record estimated bad debts.* | | |

Alternatively, if the allowance account had an unadjusted *debit* balance of $500 (instead of the $200 credit balance), its required adjustment would be computed as follows. (Again, a T-account can be used for this analysis as shown in the margin.)

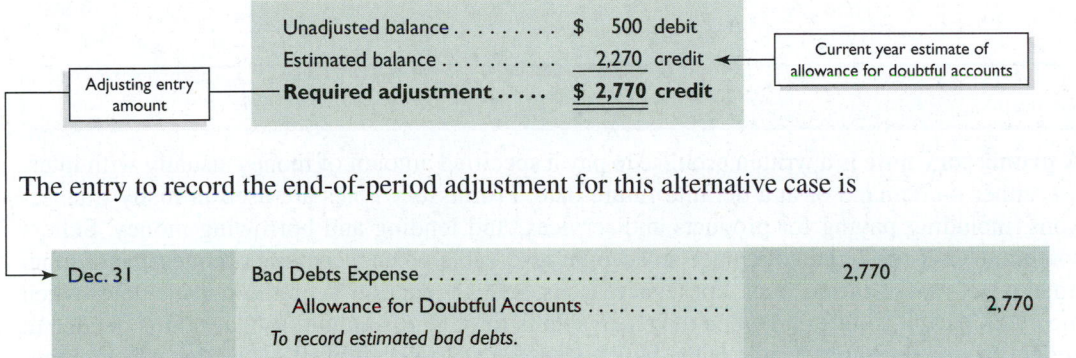

The entry to record the end-of-period adjustment for this alternative case is

| Dec. 31 | Bad Debts Expense ............................. | 2,770 | |
|---------|------------------------------------------------|-------|-------|
| | Allowance for Doubtful Accounts .............. | | 2,770 |
| | *To record estimated bad debts.* | | |

The aging of accounts receivable method is an examination of specific accounts and is usually the most reliable of the estimation methods.

**Estimating Bad Debts—Summary of Methods**  Exhibit 9.13 summarizes the principles guiding all three estimation methods and their focus of analysis. Percent of sales, with its income statement focus, does a good job at matching bad debts expense with sales. The accounts receivable methods, with their balance sheet focus, do a better job at reporting accounts receivable at realizable value.

**Allowance for Doubtful Accounts**

| | | Unadj. bal. | 200 |
|---|---|---|---|
| | | **Req. adj.** | **2,070** |
| | | Estim. bal. | 2,270 |

Assets = Liabilities + Equity
−2,070                   −2,070

**Point:** A debit balance implies that write-offs for that period exceed the total allowance.

**Allowance for Doubtful Accounts**

| Unadj. bal. | 500 | | |
|---|---|---|---|
| | | **Req. adj.** | **2,770** |
| | | Estim. bal. | 2,270 |

Assets = Liabilities + Equity
−2,770                   −2,770

**EXHIBIT 9.13**

Methods to Estimate Bad Debts

**Decision Maker**                              Answer — p. 379

**Labor Union Chief**  One week prior to labor contract negotiations, financial statements are released showing no income growth. A 10% growth was predicted. Your analysis finds that the company increased its allowance for uncollectibles from 1.5% to 4.5% of receivables. Without this change, income would show a 9% growth. Does this analysis impact negotiations? ■

3. Why must bad debts expense be estimated if such an estimate is possible?

4. What term describes the balance sheet valuation of Accounts Receivable less the Allowance for Doubtful Accounts?

5. Why is estimated bad debts expense credited to a contra account (Allowance for Doubtful Accounts) rather than to the Accounts Receivable account?

6. SnoBoard Company's year-end balance in its Allowance for Doubtful Accounts is a credit of $440. By aging accounts receivable, it estimates that $6,142 is uncollectible. Prepare SnoBoard's year-end adjusting entry for bad debts.

7. Record entries for these transactions assuming the allowance method is used:

   Jan. 10  The $300 account of customer Cool Jam is determined uncollectible.

   April 12  Cool Jam unexpectedly pays in full the account deemed uncollectible on Jan. 10.

# NOTES RECEIVABLE

**C2** Describe a note receivable, the computation of its maturity date, and the recording of its existence.

A **promissory note** is a written promise to pay a specified amount of money, usually with interest, either on demand or at a definite future date. Promissory notes are used in many transactions, including paying for products and services, and lending and borrowing money. Sellers sometimes ask for a note to replace an account receivable when a customer requests additional time to pay a past-due account. For legal reasons, sellers generally prefer to receive notes when the credit period is long and when the receivable is for a large amount. If a lawsuit is needed to collect from a customer, a note is the buyer's written acknowledgment of the debt, its amount, and its terms.

Exhibit 9.14 shows a simple promissory note dated July 10, 2011. For this note, Julia Browne promises to pay TechCom or to its order (according to TechCom's instructions) a specified amount of money ($1,000), called the **principal of a note,** at a definite future date (October 8, 2011). As the one who signed the note and promised to pay it at maturity, Browne is the **maker of the note.** As the person to whom the note is payable, TechCom is the **payee of the note.** To Browne, the note is a liability called a *note payable*. To TechCom, the same note is an asset called a *note receivable*. This note bears interest at 12%, as written on the note. **Interest** is the charge for using the money until its due date. To a borrower, interest is an expense. To a lender, it is revenue.

**EXHIBIT 9.14**

Promissory Note

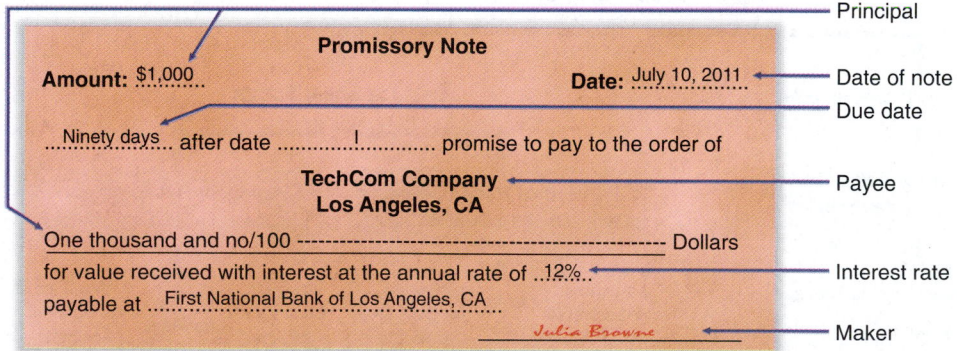

## Computing Maturity and Interest

This section describes key computations for notes including the determination of maturity date, period covered, and interest computation.

**Maturity Date and Period**   The **maturity date of a note** is the day the note (principal and interest) must be repaid. The *period* of a note is the time from the note's (contract) date to its maturity date. Many notes mature in less than a full year, and the period they cover is often expressed in days. When the time of a note is expressed in days, its maturity date is the specified number of days after the note's date. As an example, a five-day note dated June 15 matures and is due on June 20. A 90-day note dated July 10 matures on October 8. This October 8 due date is computed as shown in Exhibit 9.15. The period of a note is sometimes expressed in months or years. When months are used, the note matures and is payable in the month of its maturity on the *same day of the month* as its original date. A nine-month note dated July 10, for instance, is payable on April 10. The same analysis applies when years are used.

| | |
|---|---|
| Days in July . . . . . . . . . . . . . . . . . . . . . . . . . . . . . . . . . . . . . . . . . . . . . . | 31 |
| Minus the date of the note . . . . . . . . . . . . . . . . . . . . . . . . . . . . . . . . . | 10 |
| Days remaining in July . . . . . . . . . . . . . . . . . . . . . . . . . . . . . . . . . . . . . | 21 ← July 11–31 |
| Add days in August . . . . . . . . . . . . . . . . . . . . . . . . . . . . . . . . . . . . . . . . | 31 ← Aug. 1–31 |
| Add days in September . . . . . . . . . . . . . . . . . . . . . . . . . . . . . . . . . . . . . | 30 ← Sept. 1–30 |
| Days to equal 90 days, or **maturity date of October 8** . . . . . . . . . | 8 ← Oct. 1–8 |
| Period of the note in days . . . . . . . . . . . . . . . . . . . . . . . . . . . . . . . . . | 90 |

**EXHIBIT 9.15**

Maturity Date Computation

**Interest Computation**  *Interest* is the cost of borrowing money for the borrower or, alternatively, the profit from lending money for the lender. Unless otherwise stated, the rate of interest on a note is the rate charged for the use of the principal for one year. The formula for computing interest on a note is shown in Exhibit 9.16.

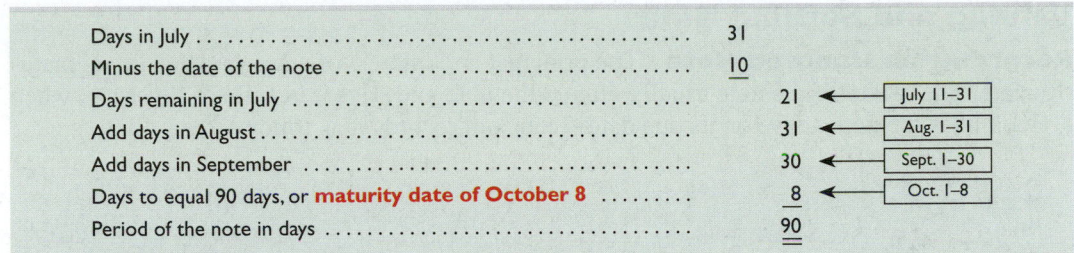

$$\begin{array}{ccccccc} \textbf{Principal} & & \textbf{Annual} & & \textbf{Time expressed} & & \\ \textbf{of the note} & \times & \textbf{interest rate} & \times & \textbf{in fraction of year} & = & \textbf{Interest} \end{array}$$

**EXHIBIT 9.16**

Computation of Interest Formula

To simplify interest computations, a year is commonly treated as having 360 days (called the *banker's rule* in the business world and widely used in commercial transactions). **We treat a year as having 360 days for interest computations in the examples and assignments**. Using the promissory note in Exhibit 9.14 where we have a 90-day, 12%, $1,000 note, the total interest is computed as follows.

$$\$1,000 \times 12\% \times \frac{90}{360} = \$1,000 \times 0.12 \times 0.25 = \$30$$

## Recognizing Notes Receivable

Notes receivable are usually recorded in a single Notes Receivable account to simplify record-keeping. The original notes are kept on file, including information on the maker, rate of interest, and due date. (When a company holds a large number of notes, it sometimes sets up a controlling account and a subsidiary ledger for notes. This is similar to the handling of accounts receivable.) To illustrate the recording for the receipt of a note, we use the $1,000, 90-day, 12% promissory note in Exhibit 9.14. TechCom received this note at the time of a product sale to Julia Browne. This transaction is recorded as follows.

| July 10* | | | |
|---|---|---|---|
| | Notes Receivable . . . . . . . . . . . . . . . . . . . . . . . . . . . . | 1,000 | |
| | Sales . . . . . . . . . . . . . . . . . . . . . . . . . . . . . . . . . . . . . . | | 1,000 |
| | *Sold goods in exchange for a 90-day, 12% note.* | | |

Assets = Liabilities + Equity
+1,000              +1,000

* We omit the entry to Dr. Cost of Sales and Cr. Merchandise Inventory to focus on sales and receivables.

When a seller accepts a note from an overdue customer as a way to grant a time extension on a past-due account receivable, it will often collect part of the past-due balance in cash. This partial payment forces a concession from the customer, reduces the customer's debt (and the seller's risk), and produces a note for a smaller amount. To illustrate, assume that Tech-Com agreed to accept $232 in cash along with a $600, 60-day, 15% note from Jo Cook to

**Point:** Notes receivable often are a major part of a company's assets. Likewise, notes payable often are a large part of a company's liabilities.

settle her $832 past-due account. TechCom made the following entry to record receipt of this cash and note.

Assets = Liabilities + Equity
+232
+600
−832

| Oct. 5 | Cash .......................................... | 232 | |
| | Notes Receivable ............................... | 600 | |
| |       Accounts Receivable—J. Cook ................. | | 832 |
| | *Received cash and note to settle account.* | | |

## Valuing and Settling Notes

**P3**   Record the honoring and dishonoring of a note and adjustments for interest.

**Recording an Honored Note**   The principal and interest of a note are due on its maturity date. The maker of the note usually *honors* the note and pays it in full. To illustrate, when J. Cook pays the note above on its due date, TechCom records it as follows.

Assets = Liabilities + Equity
+615                        +15
−600

| Dec. 4 | Cash .......................................... | 615 | |
| |       Notes Receivable ......................... | | 600 |
| |       Interest Revenue ......................... | | 15 |
| | *Collect note with interest of $600 × 15% × 60/360.* | | |

Interest Revenue, also called *Interest Earned,* is reported on the income statement.

**Recording a Dishonored Note**   When a note's maker is unable or refuses to pay at maturity, the note is *dishonored.* The act of dishonoring a note does not relieve the maker of the obligation to pay. The payee should use every legitimate means to collect. How do companies report this event? The balance of the Notes Receivable account should include only those notes that have not matured. Thus, when a note is dishonored, we remove the amount of this note from the Notes Receivable account and charge it back to an account receivable from its maker. To illustrate, TechCom holds an $800, 12%, 60-day note of Greg Hart. At maturity, Hart dishonors the note. TechCom records this dishonoring of the note as follows.

**Point:** When posting a dishonored note to a customer's account, an explanation is included so as not to misinterpret the debit as a sale on account.

Assets = Liabilities + Equity
+816                        +16
−800

| Oct. 14 | Accounts Receivable—G. Hart ................... | 816 | |
| |       Interest Revenue ......................... | | 16 |
| |       Notes Receivable ......................... | | 800 |
| | *To charge account of G. Hart for a dishonored note and interest of $800 × 12% × 60/360.* | | |

**Point:** Reporting the details of notes is consistent with the **full disclosure principle,** which requires financial statements (including footnotes) to report all relevant information.

Charging a dishonored note back to the account of its maker serves two purposes. First, it removes the amount of the note from the Notes Receivable account and records the dishonored note in the maker's account. Second, and more important, if the maker of the dishonored note applies for credit in the future, his or her account will reveal all past dealings, including the dishonored note. Restoring the account also reminds the company to continue collection efforts from Hart for both principal and interest. The entry records the full amount, including interest, to ensure that it is included in collection efforts.

**Recording End-of-Period Interest Adjustment**   When notes receivable are outstanding at the end of a period, any accrued interest earned is computed and recorded. To illustrate, on December 16, TechCom accepts a $3,000, 60-day, 12% note from a customer in granting an extension on a past-due account. When TechCom's accounting period ends on December 31, $15 of interest has accrued on this note ($3,000 × 12% × 15/360). The following adjusting entry records this revenue.

Assets = Liabilities + Equity
+15                         +15

| Dec. 31 | Interest Receivable ............................ | 15 | |
| |       Interest Revenue ......................... | | 15 |
| | *To record accrued interest earned.* | | |

Interest Revenue appears on the income statement, and Interest Receivable appears on the balance sheet as a current asset. When the December 16 note is collected on February 14, TechCom's entry to record the cash receipt is

| Feb. 14 | Cash ........................................ | 3,060 | |
| | Interest Revenue ........................... | | 45 |
| | Interest Receivable ........................ | | 15 |
| | Notes Receivable ......................... | | 3,000 |
| | *Received payment of note and its interest.* | | |

Assets = Liabilities + Equity
+3,060          +45
−15
−3,000

Total interest earned on the 60-day note is $60. The $15 credit to Interest Receivable on February 14 reflects the collection of the interest accrued from the December 31 adjusting entry. The $45 interest earned reflects TechCom's revenue from holding the note from January 1 to February 14 of the current period.

## Quick Check
Answers — p. 379

8. Irwin purchases $7,000 of merchandise from Stamford on December 16, 2011. Stamford accepts Irwin's $7,000, 90-day, 12% note as payment. Stamford's accounting period ends on December 31, and it does not make reversing entries. Prepare entries for Stamford on December 16, 2011, and December 31, 2011.
9. Using the information in Quick Check 8, prepare Stamford's March 16, 2012, entry if Irwin dishonors the note.

# DISPOSAL OF RECEIVABLES

Companies can convert receivables to cash before they are due. Reasons for this include the need for cash or the desire not to be involved in collection activities. Converting receivables is usually done either by (1) selling them or (2) using them as security for a loan. A recent survey shows that about 20% of companies obtain cash from either selling receivables or pledging them as security. In some industries such as textiles, apparel and furniture, this is common practice.

**C3** Explain how receivables can be converted to cash before maturity.

## Selling Receivables

A company can sell all or a portion of its receivables to a finance company or bank. The buyer, called a *factor,* charges the seller a *factoring fee* and then the buyer takes ownership of the receivables and receives cash when they come due. By incurring a factoring fee, the seller receives cash earlier and can pass the risk of bad debts to the factor. The seller can also choose to avoid costs of billing and accounting for the receivables. To illustrate, if TechCom sells $20,000 of its accounts receivable and is charged a 4% factoring fee, it records this sale as follows.

**Global:** Firms in export sales increasingly sell their receivables to factors.

| Aug. 15 | Cash ........................................ | 19,200 | |
| | Factoring Fee Expense ..................... | 800 | |
| | Accounts Receivable ...................... | | 20,000 |
| | *Sold accounts receivable for cash, less 4% fee.* | | |

Assets = Liabilities + Equity
+19,200          −800
−20,000

The accounting for sales of notes receivable is similar to that for accounts receivable. The detailed entries are covered in advanced courses.

## Pledging Receivables

A company can raise cash by borrowing money and *pledging* its receivables as security for the loan. Pledging receivables does not transfer the risk of bad debts to the lender because the borrower retains ownership of the receivables. If the borrower defaults on the loan, the lender has a right to be paid from the cash receipts of the receivable when collected. To illustrate, when TechCom borrows $35,000 and pledges its receivables as security, it records this transaction as follows.

Assets = Liabilities + Equity
+35,000    +35,000

| Aug. 20 | Cash .......................................... | 35,000 | |
| | Notes Payable ............................ | | 35,000 |
| | *Borrowed money with a note secured by pledging receivables.* | | |

Since pledged receivables are committed as security for a specific loan, the borrower's financial statements disclose the pledging of them. TechCom, for instance, includes the following note with its statements: Accounts receivable of $40,000 are pledged as security for a $35,000 note payable.

### Decision Insight

**What's the Proper Allowance?**   How can we assess whether a company has properly estimated its allowance for uncollectibles? One way is to compute the ratio of the allowance account to the gross accounts receivable. When this ratio is analyzed over several consecutive periods, trends often emerge that reflect on the adequacy of the allowance amount. ■

# GLOBAL VIEW

This section discusses similarities and differences between U.S. GAAP and IFRS regarding the recognition, measurement, and disposition of receivables.

**Recognition of Receivables**   Both U.S. GAAP and IFRS have similar asset criteria that apply to recognition of receivables. Further, receivables that arise from revenue-generating activities are subject to broadly similar criteria for U.S. GAAP and IFRS. Specifically, both refer to the realization principle and an earnings process. The realization principle under U.S. GAAP implies an *arm's-length transaction* occurs, whereas under IFRS this notion is applied in terms of reliable measurement and likelihood of economic benefits. Regarding U.S. GAAP's reference to an earnings process, IFRS instead refers to risk transfer and ownership reward. While these criteria are broadly similar, differences do exist, and they arise mainly from industry-specific guidance under U.S. GAAP, which is very limited under IFRS.

**Valuation of Receivables**   Both U.S. GAAP and IFRS require that receivables be reported net of estimated uncollectibles. Further, both systems require that the expense for estimated uncollectibles be recorded in the same period when any revenues from those receivables are recorded. This means that for accounts receivable, both U.S. GAAP and IFRS require the allowance method for uncollectibles (unless uncollectibles are immaterial). The allowance method using percent of sales, percent of receivables, and aging was explained in this chapter. **Nokia** reports the following for its allowance for uncollectibles:

**NOKIA**

Management specifically analyzes accounts receivables and historical bad debt, customer concentrations, customer creditworthiness, current economic trends and changes in our customer payment terms when evaluating the adequacy of the allowance.

**Disposition of Receivables**   Both U.S. GAAP and IFRS apply broadly similar rules in recording dispositions of receivables. Those rules are discussed in this chapter. We should be aware of an important difference in terminology. Companies reporting under U.S. GAAP disclose Bad Debts Expense, which is also referred to as Provision for Bad Debts or the Provision for Uncollectible Accounts. For U.S. GAAP, *provision* here refers to expense. Under IFRS, the term *provision* usually refers to a liability whose amount or timing (or both) is uncertain.

For a company selling on credit, we want to assess both the quality and liquidity of its accounts receivable. *Quality* of receivables refers to the likelihood of collection without loss. Experience shows that the longer receivables are outstanding beyond their due date, the lower the likelihood of collection. *Liquidity* of receivables refers to the speed of collection. **Accounts receivable turnover** is a measure of both the quality and liquidity of accounts receivable. It indicates how often, on average, receivables are received and collected during the period. The formula for this ratio is shown in Exhibit 9.17.

 **A1** Compute accounts receivable turnover and use it to help assess financial condition.

$$\text{Accounts receivable turnover} = \frac{\text{Net sales}}{\text{Average accounts receivable, net}}$$

**EXHIBIT 9.17**

Accounts Receivable Turnover

We prefer to use net *credit* sales in the numerator because cash sales do not create receivables. However, since financial statements rarely report net credit sales, our analysis uses net sales. The denominator is the *average* accounts receivable balance, computed as (Beginning balance + Ending balance) ÷ 2. TechCom has an accounts receivable turnover of 5.1. This indicates its average accounts receivable balance is converted into cash 5.1 times during the period. Exhibit 9.18 shows graphically this turnover activity for TechCom.

5.1 times per year

| Jan. | Feb. | March | Apr. | May | June | July | Aug. | Sept. | Oct. | Nov. | Dec. |

**EXHIBIT 9.18**

Rate of Accounts Receivable Turnover for TechCom

Accounts receivable turnover also reflects how well management is doing in granting credit to customers in a desire to increase sales. A high turnover in comparison with competitors suggests that management should consider using more liberal credit terms to increase sales. A low turnover suggests management should consider stricter credit terms and more aggressive collection efforts to avoid having its resources tied up in accounts receivable.

To illustrate, we take fiscal year data from two competitors: **Dell** and **Apple**. Exhibit 9.19 shows accounts receivable turnover for both companies.

**Point: Credit risk ratio** is computed by dividing the Allowance for Doubtful Accounts by Accounts Receivable. The higher this ratio, the higher is credit risk.

**EXHIBIT 9.19**

Analysis Using Accounts Receivable Turnover

| Company | Figure ($ millions) | 2008 | 2007 | 2006 | 2005 |
|---------|---------------------|------|------|------|------|
| **Dell** | Net sales .......................... | $61,101 | $61,133 | $57,420 | $55,788 |
| | Average accounts receivable, net ........... | $ 5,346 | $ 5,292 | $ 4,352 | $ 3,826 |
| | **Accounts receivable turnover** .......... | 11.4 | 11.6 | 13.2 | 14.6 |
| **Apple** | Net sales .......................... | $32,479 | $24,006 | $19,315 | $13,931 |
| | Average accounts receivable, net ........... | $ 2,030 | $ 1,445 | $ 1,074 | $ 835 |
| | **Accounts receivable turnover** .......... | 16.0 | 16.6 | 18.0 | 16.7 |

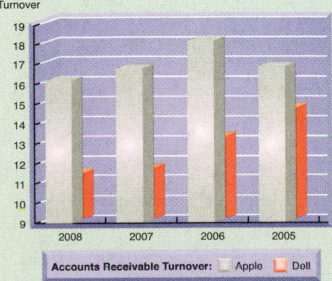

Dell's 2008 turnover is 11.4, computed as $61,101/$5,346 ($ millions). This means that Dell's average accounts receivable balance was converted into cash 11.4 times in 2008. Its turnover declined in 2008, as it has for each of the past 3 years. Apple's turnover exceeds that for Dell in each of the past 4 years. Is either company's turnover too high? Since sales are stable or markedly growing over this time period, each company's turnover rate does not appear to be too high. Instead, both Dell and Apple seem to be doing well in managing receivables. This is especially true given the recession-ary period of 2008 and 2009. Turnover for competitors is generally in the range of 7 to 12 for this same period.[1]

**Decision Maker**                                              Answer — p. 379

**Family Physician**   Your medical practice is barely profitable, so you hire a health care analyst. The ana-lyst highlights several points including the following: *"Accounts receivable turnover is too low. Tighter credit policies are recommended along with discontinuing service to those most delayed in payments."* How do you interpret these recommendations? What actions do you take? ■

## DEMONSTRATION PROBLEM

Clayco Company completes the following selected transactions during year 2011.

July  14   Writes off a $750 account receivable arising from a sale to Briggs Company that dates to 10 months ago. (Clayco Company uses the allowance method.)

     30   Clayco Company receives a $1,000, 90-day, 10% note in exchange for merchandise sold to Sumrell Company (the merchandise cost $600).

Aug. 15   Receives $2,000 cash plus a $10,000 note from JT Co. in exchange for merchandise that sells for $12,000 (its cost is $8,000). The note is dated August 15, bears 12% interest, and matures in 120 days.

Nov.  1   Completed a $200 credit card sale with a 4% fee (the cost of sales is $150). The cash is received immediately from the credit card company.

     3   Sumrell Company refuses to pay the note that was due to Clayco Company on October 28. Prepare the journal entry to charge the dishonored note plus accrued interest to Sumrell Com-pany's accounts receivable.

     5   Completed a $500 credit card sale with a 5% fee (the cost of sales is $300). The payment from the credit card company is received on Nov. 9.

     15   Received the full amount of $750 from Briggs Company that was previously written off on July 14. Record the bad debts recovery.

Dec. 13   Received payment of principal plus interest from JT for the August 15 note.

### Required

**1.** Prepare journal entries to record these transactions on Clayco Company's books.

**2.** Prepare an adjusting journal entry as of December 31, 2011, assuming the following:

   **a.** Bad debts are estimated to be $20,400 by aging accounts receivable. The unadjusted balance of the Allowance for Doubtful Accounts is $1,000 debit.

   **b.** Alternatively, assume that bad debts are estimated using the percent of sales method. The Allowance for Doubtful Accounts had a $1,000 debit balance before adjustment, and the company estimates bad debts to be 1% of its credit sales of $2,000,000.

### PLANNING THE SOLUTION

● Examine each transaction to determine the accounts affected, and then record the entries.

● For the year-end adjustment, record the bad debts expense for the two approaches.

---

[1] As an estimate of *average days' sales uncollected,* we compute how many days (*on average*) it takes to collect receivables as follows: 365 days ÷ accounts receivable turnover. An increase in this *average collection period* can signal a decline in customers' financial condition.

## SOLUTION TO DEMONSTRATION PROBLEM

1.

| | | | |
|---|---|---|---|
| July 14 | Allowance for Doubtful Accounts ................. | 750 | |
| |     Accounts Receivable—Briggs Co. .............. | | 750 |
| | *Wrote off an uncollectible account.* | | |
| July 30 | Notes Receivable—Sumrell Co. .................... | 1,000 | |
| |     Sales ...................................... | | 1,000 |
| | *Sold merchandise for a 90-day, 10% note.* | | |
| July 30 | Cost of Goods Sold .......................... | 600 | |
| |     Merchandise Inventory ..................... | | 600 |
| | *To record the cost of July 30 sale.* | | |
| Aug. 15 | Cash ...................................... | 2,000 | |
| | Notes Receivable—JT Co. ...................... | 10,000 | |
| |     Sales ...................................... | | 12,000 |
| | *Sold merchandise to customer for $2,000* *cash and $10,000 note.* | | |
| Aug. 15 | Cost of Goods Sold .......................... | 8,000 | |
| |     Merchandise Inventory ..................... | | 8,000 |
| | *To record the cost of Aug. 15 sale.* | | |
| Nov. 1 | Cash ...................................... | 192 | |
| | Credit Card Expense ......................... | 8 | |
| |     Sales ...................................... | | 200 |
| | *To record credit card sale less a 4% credit* *card expense.* | | |
| Nov. 1 | Cost of Goods Sold .......................... | 150 | |
| |     Merchandise Inventory ..................... | | 150 |
| | *To record the cost of Nov. 1 sale.* | | |
| Nov. 3 | Accounts Receivable—Sumrell Co. ................ | 1,025 | |
| |     Interest Revenue .......................... | | 25 |
| |     Notes Receivable—Sumrell Co. ............... | | 1,000 |
| | *To charge account of Sumrell Company for* *a $1,000 dishonored note and interest of* *$1,000 × 10% × 90/360.* | | |
| Nov. 5 | Accounts Receivable—Credit Card Co. .............. | 475 | |
| | Credit Card Expense ......................... | 25 | |
| |     Sales ...................................... | | 500 |
| | *To record credit card sale less a 5% credit card expense.* | | |
| Nov. 5 | Cost of Goods Sold .......................... | 300 | |
| |     Merchandise Inventory ..................... | | 300 |
| | *To record the cost of Nov. 5 sale.* | | |
| Nov. 9 | Cash ...................................... | 475 | |
| |     Accounts Receivable—Credit Card Co. .......... | | 475 |
| | *To record cash receipt from Nov. 5 sale.* | | |
| Nov. 15 | Accounts Receivable—Briggs Co. ................ | 750 | |
| |     Allowance for Doubtful Accounts .............. | | 750 |
| | *To reinstate the account of Briggs Company* *previously written off.* | | |
| Nov. 15 | Cash ...................................... | 750 | |
| |     Accounts Receivable—Briggs Co. ............. | | 750 |
| | *Cash received in full payment of account.* | | |
| Dec. 13 | Cash ...................................... | 10,400 | |
| |     Interest Revenue .......................... | | 400 |
| |     Note Receivable—JT Co. .................... | | 10,000 |
| | *Collect note with interest of* *$10,000 × 12% × 120/360.* | | |

**2a.** Aging of accounts receivable method.

| Dec. 31 | Bad Debts Expense . . . . . . . . . . . . . . . . . . . . . . . . . . . . . | 21,400 | |
|---|---|---|---|
| |      Allowance for Doubtful Accounts . . . . . . . . . . . . . . | | 21,400 |
| | *To adjust allowance account from a $1,000* | | |
| | *debit balance to a $20,400 credit balance.* | | |

**2b.** Percent of sales method.*

| Dec. 31 | Bad Debts Expense . . . . . . . . . . . . . . . . . . . . . . . . . . . . . | 20,000 | |
|---|---|---|---|
| |      Allowance for Doubtful Accounts . . . . . . . . . . . . . . | | 20,000 |
| | *To provide for bad debts as 1% × $2,000,000* | | |
| | *in credit sales.* | | |

\* For the income statement approach, which requires estimating bad debts as a percent of sales or credit sales, the Allowance account balance is *not* considered when making the adjusting entry.

# Summary

**C1 Describe accounts receivable and how they occur and are recorded.** Accounts receivable are amounts due from customers for credit sales. A subsidiary ledger lists amounts owed by each customer. Credit sales arise from at least two sources: (1) sales on credit and (2) credit card sales. *Sales on credit* refers to a company's granting credit directly to customers. Credit card sales involve customers' use of third-party credit cards.

**C2 Describe a note receivable, the computation of its maturity date, and the recording of its existence.** A note receivable is a written promise to pay a specified amount of money at a definite future date. The maturity date is the day the note (principal and interest) must be repaid. Interest rates are normally stated in annual terms. The amount of interest on the note is computed by expressing time as a fraction of one year and multiplying the note's principal by this fraction and the annual interest rate. A note received is recorded at its principal amount by debiting the Notes Receivable account. The credit amount is to the asset, product, or service provided in return for the note.

**C3 Explain how receivables can be converted to cash before maturity.** Receivables can be converted to cash before maturity in three ways. First, a company can sell accounts receivable to a factor, who charges a factoring fee. Second, a company can borrow money by signing a note payable that is secured by pledging the accounts receivable. Third, notes receivable can be discounted at (sold to) a financial institution.

**A1 Compute accounts receivable turnover and use it to help assess financial condition.** Accounts receivable turnover is a measure of both the quality and liquidity of accounts receivable.

The accounts receivable turnover measure indicates how often, on average, receivables are received and collected during the period. Accounts receivable turnover is computed as net sales divided by average accounts receivable.

**P1 Apply the direct write-off method to account for accounts receivable.** The direct write-off method charges Bad Debts Expense when accounts are written off as uncollectible. This method is acceptable only when the amount of bad debts expense is immaterial.

**P2 Apply the allowance method and estimate uncollectibles based on sales and accounts receivable.** Under the allowance method, bad debts expense is recorded with an adjustment at the end of each accounting period that debits the Bad Debts Expense account and credits the Allowance for Doubtful Accounts. The uncollectible accounts are later written off with a debit to the Allowance for Doubtful Accounts. Uncollectibles are estimated by focusing on either (1) the income statement relation between bad debts expense and credit sales or (2) the balance sheet relation between accounts receivable and the allowance for doubtful accounts. The first approach emphasizes the matching principle using the income statement. The second approach emphasizes realizable value of accounts receivable using the balance sheet.

**P3 Record the honoring and dishonoring of a note and adjustments for interest.** When a note is honored, the payee debits the money received and credits both Notes Receivable and Interest Revenue. Dishonored notes are credited to Notes Receivable and debited to Accounts Receivable (to the account of the maker in an attempt to collect), and Interest Revenue is recorded for interest earned for the time the note is held.

## Guidance Answers to Decision Maker and Decision Ethics

**Entrepreneur** Analysis of credit card sales should weigh the benefits against the costs. The primary benefit is the potential to increase sales by attracting customers who prefer the convenience of credit cards. The primary cost is the fee charged by the credit card company for providing this service. Analysis should therefore estimate the expected increase in dollar sales from allowing credit card sales and then subtract (1) the normal costs and expenses and (2) the credit card fees associated with this expected increase in dollar sales. If your analysis shows an increase in profit from allowing credit card sales, your store should probably accept them.

**Labor Union Chief**  Yes, this information is likely to impact your negotiations. The obvious question is why the company markedly increased this allowance. The large increase in this allowance means a substantial increase in bad debts expense *and* a decrease in earnings. This change (coming immediately prior to labor contract discussions) also raises concerns since it reduces the union's bargaining power for increased compensation. You want to ask management for supporting documentation justifying this increase. You also want data for two or three prior years and similar data from competitors.

These data should give you some sense of whether the change in the allowance for uncollectibles is justified.

**Family Physician**  The recommendations are twofold. First, the analyst suggests more stringent screening of patients' credit standing. Second, the analyst suggests dropping patients who are most overdue in payments. You are likely bothered by both suggestions. They are probably financially wise recommendations, but you are troubled by eliminating services to those less able to pay. One alternative is to follow the recommendations while implementing a care program directed at patients less able to pay for services. This allows you to continue services to patients less able to pay and lets you discontinue services to patients able but unwilling to pay.

## Guidance Answers to Quick Checks

1. If cash is immediately received when credit card sales receipts are deposited, the company debits Cash at the time of sale. If the company does not receive payment until after it submits receipts to the credit card company, it debits Accounts Receivable at the time of sale. (Cash is later debited when payment is received from the credit card company.)

2. Credit card expenses are usually *recorded* and *incurred* at the time of their related sales, not when cash is received from the credit card company.

3. If possible, bad debts expense must be matched with the sales that gave rise to the accounts receivable. This requires that companies estimate future bad debts at the end of each period before they learn which accounts are uncollectible.

4. Realizable value (also called *net realizable value*).

5. The estimated amount of bad debts expense cannot be credited to the Accounts Receivable account because the specific customer accounts that will prove uncollectible cannot yet be identified and removed from the accounts receivable subsidiary ledger. Moreover, if only the Accounts Receivable account is credited, its balance would not equal the sum of its subsidiary account balances.

6.

| Dec. 31 | Bad Debts Expense | 5,702 | |
| |     Allowance for Doubtful Accounts | | 5,702 |

7.

| Jan. 10 | Allowance for Doubtful Accounts | 300 | |
| |     Accounts Receivable—Cool Jam | | 300 |
| Apr. 12 | Accounts Receivable—Cool Jam | 300 | |
| |     Allowance for Doubtful Accounts | | 300 |
| Apr. 12 | Cash | 300 | |
| |     Accounts Receivable—Cool Jam | | 300 |

8.

| Dec. 16 | Note Receivable—Irwin | 7,000 | |
| |     Sales | | 7,000 |
| Dec. 31 | Interest Receivable | 35 | |
| |     Interest Revenue | | 35 |
| | ($7,000 × 12% × 15/360) | | |

9.

| Mar. 16 | Accounts Receivable—Irwin | 7,210 | |
| |     Interest Revenue | | 175 |
| |     Interest Receivable | | 35 |
| |     Notes Receivable—Irwin | | 7,000 |

## Key Terms

mhhe.com/wildFAP20e

Accounts receivable (p. 360)
Accounts receivable turnover (p. 375)
Aging of accounts receivable (p. 368)
Allowance for Doubtful Accounts (p. 365)
Allowance method (p. 364)
Bad debts (p. 363)

Direct write-off method (p. 363)
Interest (p. 370)
Maker of the note (p. 370)
Matching (expense recognition) principle (p. 364)
Materiality constraint (p. 364)

Maturity date of a note (p. 370)
Payee of the note (p. 370)
Principal of a note (p. 370)
Promissory note (or note) (p. 370)
Realizable value (p. 365)

## Multiple Choice Quiz

Answers on p. 391

**mhhe.com/wildFAP20e**

Additional Quiz Questions are available at the book's Website.

1. A company's Accounts Receivable balance at its December 31 year-end is $125,650, and its Allowance for Doubtful Accounts has a credit balance of $328 before year-end adjustment. Its net sales are $572,300. It estimates that 4% of outstanding accounts receivable are uncollectible. What amount of Bad Debts Expense is recorded at December 31?
   a. $5,354
   b. $328
   c. $5,026
   d. $4,698
   e. $34,338

2. A company's Accounts Receivable balance at its December 31 year-end is $489,300, and its Allowance for Doubtful Accounts has a debit balance of $554 before year-end adjustment. Its net sales are $1,300,000. It estimates that 6% of outstanding accounts receivable are uncollectible. What amount of Bad Debts Expense is recorded at December 31?
   a. $29,912
   b. $28,804
   c. $78,000
   d. $29,358
   e. $554

3. Total interest to be earned on a $7,500, 5%, 90-day note is
   a. $93.75
   b. $375.00
   c. $1,125.00
   d. $31.25
   e. $125.00

4. A company receives a $9,000, 8%, 60-day note. The maturity value of the note is
   a. $120
   b. $9,000
   c. $9,120
   d. $720
   e. $9,720

5. A company has net sales of $489,600 and average accounts receivable of $40,800. What is its accounts receivable turnover?
   a. 0.08
   b. 30.41
   c. 1,341.00
   d. 12.00
   e. 111.78

🔒 Icon denotes assignments that involve decision making.

## Discussion Questions

1. 🔒 How do sellers benefit from allowing their customers to use credit cards?

2. 🔒 Why does the direct write-off method of accounting for bad debts usually fail to match revenues and expenses?

3. Explain the accounting constraint of materiality.

4. Explain why writing off a bad debt against the Allowance for Doubtful Accounts does not reduce the estimated realizable value of a company's accounts receivable.

5. 🔒 Why does the Bad Debts Expense account usually not have the same adjusted balance as the Allowance for Doubtful Accounts?

6. Why might a business prefer a note receivable to an account receivable?

7. 🔒 Refer to the financial statements and notes of **Research In Motion** in Appendix A. In its presentation of accounts receivable on the balance sheet, how does it   **RIM**

title accounts receivable? What does it report for its allowance as of February 27, 2010?

8. 🔒 Refer to the balance sheet of **Apple** in Appendix A. Does it use the direct write-off method or allowance method in accounting for its Accounts Receivable? What is the realizable value of its receivable's balance as of September 26, 2009?    **Apple**

9. Refer to the financial statements of **Palm** in Appendix A. What are Palm's gross accounts receivable at May 31, 2009? What percentage of its accounts receivable does it believe to be uncollectible at this date?    **Palm**

10. Refer to the December 31, 2009, financial statements of **Nokia** in Appendix A. What does it title its accounts receivable on its statement of financial position? What percent of its accounts receivable does it believe to be uncollectible?    **NOKIA**

**connect**

## QUICK STUDY

**QS 9-1**
Credit card sales

C1

Prepare journal entries for the following credit card sales transactions (the company uses the perpetual inventory system).

1. Sold $10,000 of merchandise, that cost $7,500, on MasterCard credit cards. The net cash receipts from sales are immediately deposited in the seller's bank account. MasterCard charges a 5% fee.

2. Sold $3,000 of merchandise, that cost $1,500, on an assortment of credit cards. Net cash receipts are received 7 days later, and a 4% fee is charged.

Milner Corp. uses the allowance method to account for uncollectibles. On October 31, it wrote off a $1,000 account of a customer, C. Schaub. On December 9, it receives a $200 payment from Schaub.

**1.** Prepare the journal entry or entries for October 31.

**2.** Prepare the journal entry or entries for December 9; assume no additional money is expected from Schaub.

**QS 9-2**
Allowance method for bad debts
**P2**

---

Wecker Company's year-end unadjusted trial balance shows accounts receivable of $89,000, allowance for doubtful accounts of $500 (credit), and sales of $270,000. Uncollectibles are estimated to be 1.5% of accounts receivable.

**1.** Prepare the December 31 year-end adjusting entry for uncollectibles.

**2.** What amount would have been used in the year-end adjusting entry if the allowance account had a year-end unadjusted debit balance of $200?

**QS 9-3**
Percent of accounts receivable method
**P2**

---

Assume the same facts as in QS 9-3, except that Wecker estimates uncollectibles as 1.0% of sales. Prepare the December 31 year-end adjusting entry for uncollectibles.

**QS 9-4**
Percent of sales method  **P2**

---

On August 2, 2011, JLK Co. receives a $5,500, 90-day, 12% note from customer Tom Menke as payment on his $9,000 account. (1) Compute the maturity date for this note. (2) Prepare JLK's journal entry for August 2.

**QS 9-5**
Note receivable  **C2**

---

Refer to the information in QS 9-5 and prepare the journal entry assuming the note is honored by the customer on October 31, 2011.

**QS 9-6**
Note receivable  **P3**

---

Dekon Company's December 31 year-end unadjusted trial balance shows a $8,000 balance in Notes Receivable. This balance is from one 6% note dated December 1, with a period of 45 days. Prepare any necessary journal entries for December 31 and for the note's maturity date assuming it is honored.

**QS 9-7**
Note receivable  **P3**

---

Record the sale by Kroll Company of $1,000 in accounts receivable on May 1. Kroll is charged a 3% factoring fee.

**QS 9-8**
Disposing receivables  **C3**

---

Krugg Company determines on May 1 that it cannot collect $1,000 of its accounts receivable from its customer P. Carroll. Apply the direct write-off method to record this loss as of May 1.

**QS 9-9**
Direct write-off method  **P1**

---

Refer to the information in QS 9-9. On May 30, P. Carroll unexpectedly paid his account in full to Krugg Company. Record Krugg's entry(ies) to reflect this recovery of this bad debt.

**QS 9-10**
Recovering a bad debt  **P1**

---

The following data are taken from the comparative balance sheets of Fulton Company. Compute and interpret its accounts receivable turnover for year 2011 (competitors average a turnover of 7.5).

**QS 9-11**
Accounts receivable turnover

**A1**

|  | 2011 | 2010 |
|---|---|---|
| Accounts receivable, net ......... | $152,900 | $133,700 |
| Net sales ..................... | 754,200 | 810,600 |

---

Answer each of the following related to international accounting standards.

**a.** Explain (in general terms) how the accounting for recognition of receivables is different between IFRS and U.S. GAAP.

**b.** Explain (in general terms) how the accounting for valuation of receivables is different between IFRS and U.S. GAAP.

**QS 9-12**
International accounting standards

**C1**

## EXERCISES

**Exercise 9-1**

Accounting for credit card sales

C1

Petri Company uses the perpetual inventory system and allows customers to use two credit cards in charging purchases. With the Omni Bank Card, Petri receives an immediate credit to its account when it deposits sales receipts. Omni assesses a 4% service charge for credit card sales. The second credit card that Petri accepts is the Continental Card. Petri sends its accumulated receipts to Continental on a weekly basis and is paid by Continental about a week later. Continental assesses a 2.5% charge on sales for using its card. Prepare journal entries to record the following selected credit card transactions of Petri Company.

Apr. 8   Sold merchandise for $9,200 (that had cost $6,800) and accepted the customer's Omni Bank Card. The Omni receipts are immediately deposited in Petri's bank account.

    12   Sold merchandise for $5,400 (that had cost $3,500) and accepted the customer's Continental Card. Transferred $5,400 of credit card receipts to Continental, requesting payment.

    20   Received Continental's check for the April 12 billing, less the service charge.

---

**Exercise 9-2**

Accounts receivable subsidiary ledger; schedule of accounts receivable

C1

Sami Company recorded the following selected transactions during November 2011.

| | | | |
|---|---|---|---|
| Nov. 5 | Accounts Receivable—Surf Shop ................... | 4,417 | |
| | Sales ...................................... | | 4,417 |
| 10 | Accounts Receivable—Yum Enterprises ............ | 1,250 | |
| | Sales ...................................... | | 1,250 |
| 13 | Accounts Receivable—Matt Albin.................. | 733 | |
| | Sales ...................................... | | 733 |
| 21 | Sales Returns and Allowances .................... | 189 | |
| | Accounts Receivable—Matt Albin .............. | | 189 |
| 30 | Accounts Receivable—Surf Shop ................. | 2,606 | |
| | Sales ...................................... | | 2,606 |

1. Open a general ledger having T-accounts for Accounts Receivable, Sales, and Sales Returns and Allowances. Also open an accounts receivable subsidiary ledger having a T-account for each customer. Post these entries to both the general ledger and the accounts receivable ledger.

**Check**   Accounts Receivable ending balance, $8,817

2. Prepare a schedule of accounts receivable (see Exhibit 9.4) and compare its total with the balance of the Accounts Receivable controlling account as of November 30.

---

**Exercise 9-3**

Direct write-off method

P1

Diablo Company applies the direct write-off method in accounting for uncollectible accounts. Prepare journal entries to record the following selected transactions of Diablo.

June 11   Diablo determines that it cannot collect $9,000 of its accounts receivable from its customer Chaffey Company.

    29   Chaffey Company unexpectedly pays its account in full to Diablo Company. Diablo records its recovery of this bad debt.

---

**Exercise 9-4**

Percent of sales method; write-off

P2

At year-end (December 31), Alvare Company estimates its bad debts as 0.5% of its annual credit sales of $875,000. Alvare records its Bad Debts Expense for that estimate. On the following February 1, Alvare decides that the $420 account of P. Coble is uncollectible and writes it off as a bad debt. On June 5, Coble unexpectedly pays the amount previously written off. Prepare the journal entries of Alvare to record these transactions and events of December 31, February 1, and June 5.

---

**Exercise 9-5**

Percent of accounts receivable method

P2

At each calendar year-end, Cabool Supply Co. uses the percent of accounts receivable method to estimate bad debts. On December 31, 2011, it has outstanding accounts receivable of $53,000, and it estimates that 4% will be uncollectible. Prepare the adjusting entry to record bad debts expense for year 2011 under the assumption that the Allowance for Doubtful Accounts has (*a*) a $915 credit balance before the adjustment and (*b*) a $1,332 debit balance before the adjustment.

---

**Exercise 9-6**

Aging of receivables method

P2

Hecter Company estimates uncollectible accounts using the allowance method at December 31. It prepared the following aging of receivables analysis.

| | | | Days Past Due | | | |
|---|---|---|---|---|---|---|
| | Total | 0 | 1 to 30 | 31 to 60 | 61 to 90 | Over 90 |
| Accounts receivable ......... | $190,000 | $132,000 | $30,000 | $12,000 | $6,000 | $10,000 |
| Percent uncollectible ........ | | 1% | 2% | 4% | 7% | 12% |

a. Estimate the balance of the Allowance for Doubtful Accounts using the aging of accounts receivable method.

b. Prepare the adjusting entry to record Bad Debts Expense using the estimate from part *a*. Assume the unadjusted balance in the Allowance for Doubtful Accounts is a $600 credit.

c. Prepare the adjusting entry to record Bad Debts Expense using the estimate from part *a*. Assume the unadjusted balance in the Allowance for Doubtful Accounts is a $400 debit.

---

Refer to the information in Exercise 9-6 to complete the following requirements.

a. Estimate the balance of the Allowance for Doubtful Accounts assuming the company uses 3.5% of total accounts receivable to estimate uncollectibles, instead of the aging of receivables method.

b. Prepare the adjusting entry to record Bad Debts Expense using the estimate from part *a*. Assume the unadjusted balance in the Allowance for Doubtful Accounts is a $300 credit.

c. Prepare the adjusting entry to record Bad Debts Expense using the estimate from part *a*. Assume the unadjusted balance in the Allowance for Doubtful Accounts is a $200 debit.

**Exercise 9-7**
Percent of receivables method

**P2**

---

Refer to the information in Exercise 9-6 to complete the following requirements.

a. On February 1 of the next period, the company determined that $1,900 in customer accounts is uncollectible; specifically, $400 for Oxford Co. and $1,500 for Brookes Co. Prepare the journal entry to write off those accounts.

b. On June 5 of that next period, the company unexpectedly received a $400 payment on a customer account, Oxford Company, that had previously been written off in part *a*. Prepare the entries necessary to reinstate the account and to record the cash received.

**Exercise 9-8**
Writing off receivables

**P2**

---

At December 31, GreenTea Company reports the following results for its calendar-year.

| | |
|---|---|
| Cash sales ............ | $1,200,000 |
| Credit sales .......... | 900,000 |

Its year-end unadjusted trial balance includes the following items.

| | |
|---|---|
| Accounts receivable ..................... | $195,000 debit |
| Allowance for doubtful accounts ........... | 3,000 debit |

a. Prepare the adjusting entry to record Bad Debts Expense assuming uncollectibles are estimated to be 1.5% of credit sales.

b. Prepare the adjusting entry to record Bad Debts Expense assuming uncollectibles are estimated to be 0.5% of total sales.

c. Prepare the adjusting entry to record Bad Debts Expense assuming uncollectibles are estimated to be 6% of year-end accounts receivable.

**Exercise 9-9**
Estimating bad debts

**P2**

**Check** Dr. Bad Debts Expense.
(a) $13,500

(c) $14,700

---

On June 30, Roman Co. has $125,900 of accounts receivable. Prepare journal entries to record the following selected July transactions. Also prepare any footnotes to the July 31 financial statements that result from these transactions. (The company uses the perpetual inventory system.)

| | | |
|---|---|---|
| July | 4 | Sold $6,295 of merchandise (that had cost $4,000) to customers on credit. |
| | 9 | Sold $18,000 of accounts receivable to Center Bank. Center charges a 4% factoring fee. |
| | 17 | Received $3,436 cash from customers in payment on their accounts. |
| | 27 | Borrowed $10,000 cash from Center Bank, pledging $13,000 of accounts receivable as security for the loan. |

**Exercise 9-10**
Selling and pledging accounts receivable

**C3**

---

Prepare journal entries to record these selected transactions for Eduardo Company.

| | | |
|---|---|---|
| Nov. | 1 | Accepted a $5,000, 180-day, 6% note dated November 1 from Melosa Allen in granting a time extension on her past-due account receivable. |
| Dec. | 31 | Adjusted the year-end accounts for the accrued interest earned on the Allen note. |
| Apr. | 30 | Allen honors her note when presented for payment; February has 28 days for the current year. |

**Exercise 9-11**
Honoring a note

**P3**

---

**Exercise 9-12**

Dishonoring a note

**P3**

Prepare journal entries to record the following selected transactions of Paloma Company.

Mar. 21   Accepted a $3,100, 180-day, 10% note dated March 21 from Salma Hernandez in granting a time extension on her past-due account receivable.

Sept. 17   Hernandez dishonors her note when it is presented for payment.

Dec. 31   After exhausting all legal means of collection, Paloma Company writes off Hernandez's account against the Allowance for Doubtful Accounts.

---

**Exercise 9-13**

Notes receivable transactions

**C2**

**Check**   Dec. 31, Cr. Interest Revenue $40

Prepare journal entries for the following selected transactions of Deshawn Company for 2010.

**2010**

Dec. 13   Accepted a $10,000, 45-day, 8% note dated December 13 in granting Latisha Clark a time extension on her past-due account receivable.

     31   Prepared an adjusting entry to record the accrued interest on the Clark note.

---

**Exercise 9-14**

Notes receivable transactions

**P3**

**Check**   Jan. 27, Dr. Cash $10,100

 

June 1, Dr. Cash $4,100

Refer to the information in Exercise 9-13 and prepare the journal entries for the following selected transactions of Deshawn Company for 2011.

**2011**

Jan. 27   Received Clark's payment for principal and interest on the note dated December 13.

Mar. 3   Accepted a $4,000, 10%, 90-day note dated March 3 in granting a time extension on the past-due account receivable of Shandi Company.

     17   Accepted a $2,000, 30-day, 9% note dated March 17 in granting Juan Torres a time extension on his past-due account receivable.

Apr. 16   Torres dishonors his note when presented for payment.

May 1   Wrote off the Torres account against the Allowance for Doubtful Accounts.

June 1   Received the Shandi payment for principal and interest on the note dated March 3.

---

**Exercise 9-15**

Accounts receivable turnover

**A1**

The following information is from the annual financial statements of Waseem Company. Compute its accounts receivable turnover for 2010 and 2011. Compare the two years results and give a possible explanation for any change (competitors average a turnover of 11).

| | 2011 | 2010 | 2009 |
|---|---|---|---|
| Net sales ............................. | $305,000 | $236,000 | $288,000 |
| Accounts receivable, net (year-end) ......... | 22,900 | 20,700 | 17,400 |

---

**Exercise 9-16**

Accounting for bad debts following IFRS

**P2**

**Hitachi, Ltd.**, reports total revenues of ¥10,000,369 million for its fiscal year ending March 31, 2009, and its March 31, 2009, unadjusted trial balance reports a debit balance for trade receivables (gross) of ¥2,179,764 million.

**a.** Prepare the adjusting entry to record its Bad Debts Expense assuming uncollectibles are estimated to be 0.4% of total revenues and its unadjusted trial balance reports a credit balance of ¥10,000 million.

**b.** Prepare the adjusting entry to record Bad Debts Expense assuming uncollectibles are estimated to be 2.1% of year-end trade receivables (gross) and its unadjusted trial balance reports a credit balance of ¥10,000 million.

---

Mc Graw Hill **connect**

---

# PROBLEM SET A

**Problem 9-1A**

Sales on account and credit card sales

**C1**

Atlas Co. allows select customers to make purchases on credit. Its other customers can use either of two credit cards: Zisa or Access. Zisa deducts a 3% service charge for sales on its credit card and credits the bank account of Atlas immediately when credit card receipts are deposited. Atlas deposits the Zisa credit card receipts each business day. When customers use Access credit cards, Atlas accumulates the receipts for several days before submitting them to Access for payment. Access deducts a 2% service charge and usually pays within one week of being billed. Atlas completes the following transactions in June. (The terms of all credit sales are 2/15, n/30, and all sales are recorded at the gross price.)

June 4   Sold $750 of merchandise (that had cost $500) on credit to Anne Cianci.

     5   Sold $5,900 of merchandise (that had cost $3,200) to customers who used their Zisa cards.

6 Sold $4,800 of merchandise (that had cost $2,800) to customers who used their Access cards.

8 Sold $3,200 of merchandise (that had cost $1,900) to customers who used their Access cards.

10 Submitted Access card receipts accumulated since June 6 to the credit card company for payment.

13 Wrote off the account of Nakia Wells against the Allowance for Doubtful Accounts. The $329 balance in Wells's account stemmed from a credit sale in October of last year.

17 Received the amount due from Access.

18 Received Cianci's check in full payment for the purchase of June 4.

**Check** June 17, Dr. Cash $7,840

### Required

Prepare journal entries to record the preceding transactions and events. (The company uses the perpetual inventory system. Round amounts to the nearest dollar.)

---

Lopez Company began operations on January 1, 2010. During its first two years, the company completed a number of transactions involving sales on credit, accounts receivable collections, and bad debts. These transactions are summarized as follows.

**Problem 9-2A**
Accounts receivable transactions and bad debts adjustments

C1 P2

### 2010

**a.** Sold $1,803,750 of merchandise (that had cost $1,475,000) on credit, terms n/30.

**b.** Wrote off $20,300 of uncollectible accounts receivable.

**c.** Received $789,200 cash in payment of accounts receivable.

**d.** In adjusting the accounts on December 31, the company estimated that 1.5% of accounts receivable will be uncollectible.

**Check** (*d*) Dr. Bad Debts Expense $35,214

### 2011

**e.** Sold $1,825,700 of merchandise (that had cost $1,450,000) on credit, terms n/30.

**f.** Wrote off $28,800 of uncollectible accounts receivable.

**g.** Received $1,304,800 cash in payment of accounts receivable.

**h.** In adjusting the accounts on December 31, the company estimated that 1.5% of accounts receivable will be uncollectible.

(*h*) Dr. Bad Debts Expense $36,181

### Required

Prepare journal entries to record Lopez's 2010 and 2011 summarized transactions and its year-end adjustments to record bad debts expense. (The company uses the perpetual inventory system. Round amounts to the nearest dollar.)

---

At December 31, 2011, Ethan Company reports the following results for its calendar-year.

**Problem 9-3A**
Estimating and reporting bad debts

P2

| | |
|---|---|
| Cash sales .......... | $1,803,750 |
| Credit sales ......... | 3,534,000 |

In addition, its unadjusted trial balance includes the following items.

| | |
|---|---|
| Accounts receivable .................. | $1,070,100 debit |
| Allowance for doubtful accounts ........ | 15,750 debit |

### Required

**1.** Prepare the adjusting entry for this company to recognize bad debts under each of the following independent assumptions.

  **a.** Bad debts are estimated to be 2% of credit sales.

  **b.** Bad debts are estimated to be 1% of total sales.

  **c.** An aging analysis estimates that 5% of year-end accounts receivable are uncollectible.

**2.** Show how Accounts Receivable and the Allowance for Doubtful Accounts appear on its December 31, 2011, balance sheet given the facts in part 1a.

**3.** Show how Accounts Receivable and the Allowance for Doubtful Accounts appear on its December 31, 2011, balance sheet given the facts in part 1c.

**Check** Bad Debts Expense: (1*a*) $70,680, (1*c*) $69,255

**Problem 9-4A**

Aging accounts receivable and
accounting for bad debts

P2

Carmack Company has credit sales of $2.6 million for year 2011. On December 31, 2011, the company's
Allowance for Doubtful Accounts has an unadjusted credit balance of $13,400. Carmack prepares a schedule
of its December 31, 2011, accounts receivable by age. On the basis of past experience, it estimates the percent
of receivables in each age category that will become uncollectible. This information is summarized here.

| December 31, 2011 Accounts Receivable | Age of Accounts Receivable | Expected Percent Uncollectible |
|---|---|---|
| $730,000 | Not yet due | 1.25% |
| 354,000 | 1 to 30 days past due | 2.00 |
| 76,000 | 31 to 60 days past due | 6.50 |
| 48,000 | 61 to 90 days past due | 32.75 |
| 12,000 | Over 90 days past due | 68.00 |

**Required**

**1.** Estimate the required balance of the Allowance for Doubtful Accounts at December 31, 2011, using
the aging of accounts receivable method.

**Check**  (2) Dr. Bad Debts Expense
$31,625

**2.** Prepare the adjusting entry to record bad debts expense at December 31, 2011.

**Analysis Component**

**3.** On June 30, 2012, Carmack Company concludes that a customer's $3,750 receivable (created in 2011)
is uncollectible and that the account should be written off. What effect will this action have on
Carmack's 2012 net income? Explain.

---

**Problem 9-5A**

Analyzing and journalizing notes
receivable transactions

C2  C3  P3

**Check**  Feb. 14, Cr. Interest
Revenue $108

The following selected transactions are from Ohlde Company.

**2010**

Dec. 16   Accepted a $9,600, 60-day, 9% note dated this day in granting Todd Duke a time extension on
his past-due account receivable.

     31   Made an adjusting entry to record the accrued interest on the Duke note.

**2011**

Feb. 14   Received Duke's payment of principal and interest on the note dated December 16.

Mar.  2   Accepted an $4,120, 8%, 90-day note dated this day in granting a time extension on the past-
due account receivable from Mare Co.

     17   Accepted a $2,400, 30-day, 7% note dated this day in granting Jolene Halaam a time extension
on her past-due account receivable.

Apr. 16   Halaam dishonored her note when presented for payment.

June  2   Mare Co. refuses to pay the note that was due to Ohlde Co. on May 31. Prepare the journal entry
to charge the dishonored note plus accrued interest to Mare Co.'s accounts receivable.

July 17   Received payment from Mare Co. for the maturity value of its dishonored note plus interest for
46 days beyond maturity at 8%.

Aug.  7   Accepted an $5,440, 90-day, 10% note dated this day in granting a time extension on the past-
due account receivable of Birch and Byer Co.

Sept. 3   Accepted a $2,080, 60-day, 10% note dated this day in granting Kevin York a time extension on
his past-due account receivable.

Nov.  2   Received payment of principal plus interest from York for the September 3 note.

Nov.  5   Received payment of principal plus interest from Birch and Byer for the August 7 note.

Dec.  1   Wrote off the Jolene Halaam account against Allowance for Doubtful Accounts.

June 2, Cr. Interest
Revenue $82

Nov. 2, Cr. Interest
Revenue $35

**Required**

**1.** Prepare journal entries to record these transactions and events. (Round amounts to the nearest dollar.)

**Analysis Component**

**2.** What reporting is necessary when a business pledges receivables as security for a loan and the loan is
still outstanding at the end of the period? Explain the reason for this requirement and the accounting
principle being satisfied.

Able Co. allows select customers to make purchases on credit. Its other customers can use either of two credit cards: Commerce Bank or Aztec. Commerce Bank deducts a 3% service charge for sales on its credit card and immediately credits the bank account of Able when credit card receipts are deposited. Able deposits the Commerce Bank credit card receipts each business day. When customers use the Aztec card, Able accumulates the receipts for several days and then submits them to Aztec for payment. Aztec deducts a 2% service charge and usually pays within one week of being billed. Able completed the following transactions in August (terms of all credit sales are 2/10, n/30; and all sales are recorded at the gross price).

**PROBLEM SET B**

**Problem 9-1B**
Sales on account and credit card sales

C1

Aug. 4  Sold $2,780 of merchandise (that had cost $1,750) on credit to Stacy Dalton.
10  Sold $3,248 of merchandise (that had cost $2,456) to customers who used their Commerce Bank credit cards.
11  Sold $1,575 of merchandise (that had cost $1,150) to customers who used their Aztec cards.
14  Received Dalton's check in full payment for the purchase of August 4.
15  Sold $2,960 of merchandise (that had cost $1,758) to customers who used their Aztec cards.
18  Submitted Aztec card receipts accumulated since August 11 to the credit card company for payment.
22  Wrote off the account of Ness City against the Allowance for Doubtful Accounts. The $398 balance in Ness City's account stemmed from a credit sale in November of last year.
25  Received the amount due from Aztec.

**Check**  Aug. 25, Dr. Cash $4,444

**Required**

Prepare journal entries to record the preceding transactions and events. (The company uses the perpetual inventory system. Round amounts to the nearest dollar.)

---

Crist Co. began operations on January 1, 2010, and completed several transactions during 2010 and 2011 that involved sales on credit, accounts receivable collections, and bad debts. These transactions are summarized as follows.

**Problem 9-2B**
Accounts receivable transactions and bad debts adjustments

C1  P2

**2010**

**a.** Sold $673,490 of merchandise (that had cost $500,000) on credit, terms n/30.
**b.** Received $437,250 cash in payment of accounts receivable.
**c.** Wrote off $8,330 of uncollectible accounts receivable.
**d.** In adjusting the accounts on December 31, the company estimated that 1% of accounts receivable will be uncollectible.

**Check**  (d) Dr. Bad Debts Expense $10,609

**2011**

**e.** Sold $930,100 of merchandise (that had cost $650,000) on credit, terms n/30.
**f.** Received $890,220 cash in payment of accounts receivable.
**g.** Wrote off $10,090 of uncollectible accounts receivable.
**h.** In adjusting the accounts on December 31, the company estimated that 1% of accounts receivable will be uncollectible.

(h) Dr. Bad Debts Expense $10,388

**Required**

Prepare journal entries to record Crist's 2010 and 2011 summarized transactions and its year-end adjusting entry to record bad debts expense. (The company uses the perpetual inventory system. Round amounts to the nearest dollar.)

---

At December 31, 2011, Klimek Company reports the following results for the year.

**Problem 9-3B**
Estimating and reporting bad debts

P2

| Cash sales . . . . . . . . | $1,015,000 |
|---|---|
| Credit sales . . . . . . . . | 1,241,000 |

In addition, its unadjusted trial balance includes the following items.

| Accounts receivable . . . . . . . . . . . . . . . . . . | $475,000 debit |
|---|---|
| Allowance for doubtful accounts . . . . . . . . | 5,200 credit |

**Required**

1. Prepare the adjusting entry for Klimek Co. to recognize bad debts under each of the following independent assumptions.

   **a.** Bad debts are estimated to be 2.5% of credit sales.

   **b.** Bad debts are estimated to be 1.5% of total sales.

   **c.** An aging analysis estimates that 6% of year-end accounts receivable are uncollectible.

**Check**   Bad debts expense:
(1*b*) $33,840, (1*c*) $23,300

2. Show how Accounts Receivable and the Allowance for Doubtful Accounts appear on its December 31, 2011, balance sheet given the facts in part 1*a*.

3. Show how Accounts Receivable and the Allowance for Doubtful Accounts appear on its December 31, 2011, balance sheet given the facts in part 1*c*.

---

**Problem 9-4B**

Aging accounts receivable and accounting for bad debts

P2

Quisp Company has credit sales of $3.5 million for year 2011. At December 31, 2011, the company's Allowance for Doubtful Accounts has an unadjusted debit balance of $4,100. Quisp prepares a schedule of its December 31, 2011, accounts receivable by age. On the basis of past experience, it estimates the percent of receivables in each age category that will become uncollectible. This information is summarized here.

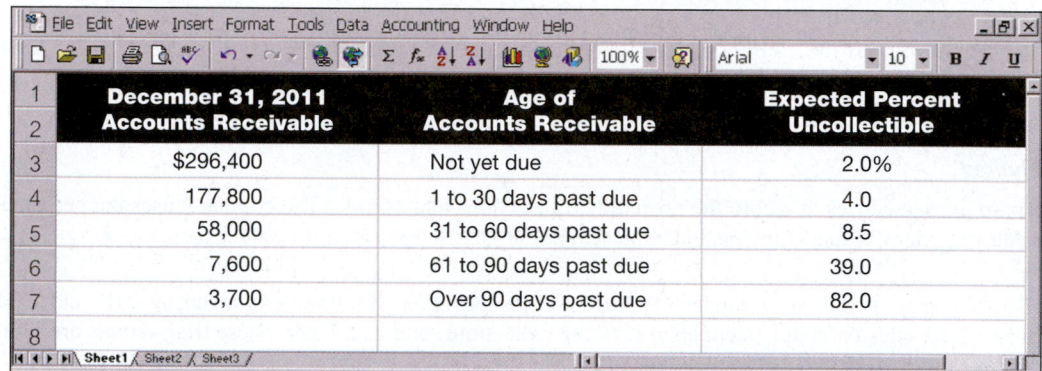

| December 31, 2011 Accounts Receivable | Age of Accounts Receivable | Expected Percent Uncollectible |
|---|---|---|
| $296,400 | Not yet due | 2.0% |
| 177,800 | 1 to 30 days past due | 4.0 |
| 58,000 | 31 to 60 days past due | 8.5 |
| 7,600 | 61 to 90 days past due | 39.0 |
| 3,700 | Over 90 days past due | 82.0 |

**Required**

1. Compute the required balance of the Allowance for Doubtful Accounts at December 31, 2011, using the aging of accounts receivable method.

**Check**   (2) Dr. Bad Debts Expense
$28,068

2. Prepare the adjusting entry to record bad debts expense at December 31, 2011.

**Analysis Component**

3. On July 31, 2012, Quisp concludes that a customer's $2,345 receivable (created in 2011) is uncollectible and that the account should be written off. What effect will this action have on Quisp's 2012 net income? Explain.

---

**Problem 9-5B**

Analyzing and journalizing notes receivable transactions

C2  C3  P3

The following selected transactions are from Seeker Company.

**2010**

Nov.  1   Accepted a $4,800, 90-day, 8% note dated this day in granting Julie Stephens a time extension on her past-due account receivable.

Dec.  31   Made an adjusting entry to record the accrued interest on the Stephens note.

**2011**

**Check**   Jan. 30, Cr. Interest
Revenue $32

Jan.  30   Received Stephens's payment for principal and interest on the note dated November 1.

Feb.  28   Accepted a $12,600, 6%, 30-day note dated this day in granting a time extension on the past-due account receivable from Kramer Co.

Mar.  1   Accepted a $6,200, 60-day, 8% note dated this day in granting Shelly Myers a time extension on her past-due account receivable.

      30   The Kramer Co. dishonored its note when presented for payment.

April 30, Cr. Interest
Revenue $83

April  30   Received payment of principal plus interest from Myers for the March 1 note.

June  15   Accepted a $2,000, 60-day, 10% note dated this day in granting a time extension on the past-due account receivable of Rhonda Rye.

      21   Accepted a $9,500, 90-day, 12% note dated this day in granting J. Striker a time extension on his past-due account receivable.

Aug.  14   Received payment of principal plus interest from R. Rye for the note of June 15.

Sep. 19, Cr. Interest
Revenue $285

Sep.  19   Received payment of principal plus interest from J. Striker for the June 21 note.

Nov.  30   Wrote off Kramer's account against Allowance for Doubtful Accounts.

**Required**

1. Prepare journal entries to record these transactions and events. (Round amounts to the nearest dollar.)

*Analysis Component*

2. What reporting is necessary when a business pledges receivables as security for a loan and the loan is still outstanding at the end of the period? Explain the reason for this requirement and the accounting principle being satisfied.

---

*(This serial problem began in Chapter 1 and continues through most of the book. If previous chapter segments were not completed, the serial problem can begin at this point. It is helpful, but not necessary, to use the Working Papers that accompany the book.)*

**SP 9**  Santana Rey, owner of Business Solutions, realizes that she needs to begin accounting for bad debts expense. Assume that Business Solutions has total revenues of $44,000 during the first three months of 2012, and that the Accounts Receivable balance on March 31, 2012, is $22,867.

**SERIAL PROBLEM**
Business Solutions
P1  P2

**Required**

1. Prepare the adjusting entry needed for Business Solutions to recognize bad debts expense on March 31, 2012, under each of the following independent assumptions (assume a zero unadjusted balance in the Allowance for Doubtful Accounts at March 31).

   **a.** Bad debts are estimated to be 1% of total revenues. (Round amounts to the dollar.)

   **b.** Bad debts are estimated to be 2% of accounts receivable. (Round amounts to the dollar.)

2. Assume that Business Solutions' Accounts Receivable balance at June 30, 2012, is $20,250 and that one account of $100 has been written off against the Allowance for Doubtful Accounts since March 31, 2012. If S. Rey uses the method prescribed in Part 1b, what adjusting journal entry must be made to recognize bad debts expense on June 30, 2012?

**Check**  (2) Bad Debts Expense, $48

3. Should S. Rey consider adopting the direct write-off method of accounting for bad debts expense rather than one of the allowance methods considered in part 1? Explain.

---

## Beyond the Numbers

**BTN 9-1**  Refer to **Research In Motion**'s financial statements in Appendix A to answer the following.
1. What is the amount of Research In Motion's accounts receivable as of February 27, 2010?
2. Compute Research In Motion's accounts receivable turnover as of February 27, 2010.
3. How long does it take, *on average*, for the company to collect receivables? Do you believe that customers actually pay the amounts due within this short period? Explain.
4. Research In Motion's most liquid assets include (*a*) cash and cash equivalents, (*b*) short-term investments, and (*c*) receivables. Compute the percentage that these liquid assets make up of current liabilities as of February 27, 2010. Do the same computations for February 28, 2009. Comment on the company's ability to satisfy its current liabilities as of its 2010 fiscal year-end compared to its 2009 fiscal year-end.
5. What criteria did Research In Motion use to classify items as cash equivalents?

**REPORTING IN ACTION**
A1

*RIM*

*Fast Forward*

6. Access Research In Motion's financial statements for fiscal years after February 27, 2010, at its Website (**www.RIM.com**) or the SEC's EDGAR database (**www.SEC.gov**). Recompute parts 2 and 4 and comment on any changes since February 27, 2010.

---

**BTN 9-2**  Comparative figures for **Research In Motion** and **Apple** follow.

**COMPARATIVE ANALYSIS**
A1  P2

*RIM*
Apple

| ($ millions) | Research In Motion | | | Apple | | |
| --- | --- | --- | --- | --- | --- | --- |
| | Current Year | One Year Prior | Two Years Prior | Current Year | One Year Prior | Two Years Prior |
| Accounts receivable, net ........ | $ 2,594 | $ 2,112 | $1,175 | $ 3,361 | $ 2,422 | $ 1,637 |
| Net sales ............. | 14,953 | 11,065 | 6,009 | 42,905 | 37,491 | 24,578 |

**Required**

**Hint:** Average collection period equals 365 divided by the accounts receivable turnover.

1. Compute the accounts receivable turnover for Research In Motion and Apple for each of the two most recent years using the data shown.
2. Using results from part 1, compute how many days it takes each company, *on average,* to collect receivables. Compare the collection periods for RIM and Apple, and suggest at least one explanation for the difference.
3. Which company is more efficient in collecting its accounts receivable? Explain.

## ETHICS CHALLENGE
P2

**BTN 9-3** Kelly Steinman is the manager of a medium-size company. A few years ago, Steinman persuaded the owner to base a part of her compensation on the net income the company earns each year. Each December she estimates year-end financial figures in anticipation of the bonus she will receive. If the bonus is not as high as she would like, she offers several recommendations to the accountant for year-end adjustments. One of her favorite recommendations is for the controller to reduce the estimate of doubtful accounts.

**Required**

1. What effect does lowering the estimate for doubtful accounts have on the income statement and balance sheet?
2. Do you believe Steinman's recommendation to adjust the allowance for doubtful accounts is within her right as manager, or do you believe this action is an ethics violation? Justify your response.
3. What type of internal control(s) might be useful for this company in overseeing the manager's recommendations for accounting changes?

## COMMUNICATING IN PRACTICE
P2

**BTN 9-4** As the accountant for Pure-Air Distributing, you attend a sales managers' meeting devoted to a discussion of credit policies. At the meeting, you report that bad debts expense is estimated to be $59,000 and accounts receivable at year-end amount to $1,750,000 less a $43,000 allowance for doubtful accounts. Sid Omar, a sales manager, expresses confusion over why bad debts expense and the allowance for doubtful accounts are different amounts. Write a one-page memorandum to him explaining why a difference in bad debts expense and the allowance for doubtful accounts is not unusual. The company estimates bad debts expense as 2% of sales.

## TAKING IT TO THE NET
C1

**BTN 9-5** Access **eBay**'s, February 17, 2010, filing of its 10-K report for the year ended December 31, 2009, at **www.SEC.gov**.

**Required**

1. What is the amount of eBay's net accounts receivable at December 31, 2009, and at December 31, 2008?
2. "Financial Statement Schedule II" to its financial statements lists eBay's allowance for doubtful accounts (including authorized credits). For the two years ended December 31, 2009 and 2008, compute its allowance for doubtful accounts (including authorized credits) as a percent of gross accounts receivable.
3. Do you believe that these percentages are reasonable based on what you know about eBay? Explain.

## TEAMWORK IN ACTION
P2

**BTN 9-6** Each member of a team is to participate in estimating uncollectibles using the aging schedule and percents shown in Problem 9-4A. The division of labor is up to the team. Your goal is to accurately complete this task as soon as possible. After estimating uncollectibles, check your estimate with the instructor. If the estimate is correct, the team then should prepare the adjusting entry and the presentation of accounts receivable (net) for the December 31, 2011, balance sheet.

## ENTREPRENEURIAL DECISION
C1

**BTN 9-7** Bernard McCoy of **LaserMonks** is introduced in the chapter's opening feature. Bernard currently sells his products through multiple outlets. Assume that he is considering two new selling options.

**Plan A.** LaserMonks would begin selling additional products online directly to customers, which are only currently sold directly to outlet stores. These new online customers would use their credit cards. It currently has the capability of selling through its Website with no additional investment in hardware or software. Credit sales are expected to increase by $250,000 per year. Costs associated with this plan are: cost of these sales will be $135,500, credit card fees will be 4.75% of sales, and additional recordkeeping and shipping costs will be 6% of sales. These online sales will reduce the sales to stores by $35,000 because some customers will now purchase items online. Sales to stores have a 25% gross margin percentage.

**Plan B.** LaserMonks would expand its market to more outlet stores. It would make additional credit sales of $500,000 to those stores. Costs associated with those sales are: cost of sales will be $375,000, additional recordkeeping and shipping will be 4% of sales, and uncollectible accounts will be 6.2% of sales.

#### Required

1. Compute the additional annual net income or loss expected under (a) Plan A and (b) Plan B.
2. Should LaserMonks pursue either plan? Discuss both the financial and nonfinancial factors relevant to this decision.

**Check** (1*b*) Net income, $74,000

---

**BTN 9-8**  Many commercials include comments similar to the following: "We accept **VISA**" or "We do not accept **American Express**." Conduct your own research by contacting at least five companies via interviews, phone calls, or the Internet to determine the reason(s) companies discriminate in their use of credit cards. Collect information on the fees charged by the different cards for the companies contacted. (The instructor can assign this as a team activity.)

**HITTING THE ROAD**

C1

---

**BTN 9-9**  Key information from Nokia (<u>www.Nokia.com</u>), which is a leading global manufacturer of mobile devices and services, follows.

| EUR millions | Current Year | Prior Year |
|---|---|---|
| Accounts receivable, net* ........ | 7,981 | 9,444 |
| Sales ........................ | 40,984 | 50,710 |

*Nokia refers to it as "Accounts receivable, net of allowance for doubtful accounts."

1. Compute the accounts receivable turnover for the current year.
2. How long does it take on average for Nokia to collect receivables?
3. Refer to BTN 9-2. How does Nokia compare to Research In Motion and Apple in terms of its accounts receivable turnover and its collection period?
4. Nokia reports an aging analysis of its receivables, based on due dates, as follows (in EUR millions) as of December 31, 2009. Compute the percent of receivables in each category.

| EUR millions | Total Receivables |
|---|---|
| Current ................... | 7,302 |
| Past due 1–30 days .......... | 393 |
| Past due 31–180 days ........ | 170 |
| More than 180 days ......... | 116 |

**GLOBAL DECISION**

C1  P2

**NOKIA**

**RIM**

Apple

---

### ANSWERS TO MULTIPLE CHOICE QUIZ

1. d; Desired balance in Allowance for Doubtful Accounts  = $ 5,026  cr.
   ($125,650 × 0.04)
   Current balance in Allowance for Doubtful Accounts =    (328) cr.
   Bad Debts Expense to be recorded            = $ 4,698
2. a; Desired balance in Allowance for Doubtful Accounts  = $29,358  cr.
   ($489,300 × 0.06)
   Current balance in Allowance for Doubtful Accounts  =     554  dr.
   Bad Debts Expense to be recorded            = $29,912
3. a; $7,500 × 0.05 × 90/360 = $93.75

4. c; Principal amount ............ $9,000
   Interest accrued ............    120 ($9,000 × 0.08 × 60/360)
   Maturity value .............. $9,120
5. d; $489,600/$40,800 = 12

# 10

# Plant Assets, Natural Resources, and Intangibles

## A Look Back

Chapters 8 and 9 focused on short-term assets: cash, cash equivalents, and receivables. We explained why they are known as liquid assets and described how companies account and report for them.

## A Look at This Chapter

This chapter introduces us to long-term assets. We explain how to account for a long-term asset's cost, the allocation of an asset's cost to periods benefiting from it, the recording of additional costs after an asset is purchased, and the disposal of an asset.

## A Look Ahead

Chapter 11 focuses on current liabilities. We explain how they are computed, recorded, and reported in financial statements. We also explain the accounting for company payroll and contingencies.

## Learning Objectives

### CONCEPTUAL

**C1** Explain the cost principle for computing the cost of plant assets. (p. 395)

**C2** Explain depreciation for partial years and changes in estimates. (p. 402)

**C3** Distinguish between revenue and capital expenditures, and account for them. (p. 404)

### ANALYTICAL

**A1** Compute total asset turnover and apply it to analyze a company's use of assets. (p. 413)

LP10

### PROCEDURAL

**P1** Compute and record depreciation using the straight-line, units-of-production, and declining-balance methods. (p. 398)

**P2** Account for asset disposal through discarding or selling an asset. (p. 406)

**P3** Account for natural resource assets and their depletion. (p. 408)

**P4** Account for intangible assets. (p. 409)

**P5** *Appendix 10A—Account for asset exchanges.* (p. 416)

# Gaming Assets

*"We want the average kid to have a party like a rock star"*
—DAVID PIKOFF

AUSTIN, TX—Fun and games are the common bond for brothers Stuart and David Pikoff. That bond was also the driving force for an excursion into business. "We're both fun guys, we love kids, and we love games," explains David. "So we thought, 'Why not create our own game franchise?'" What they did was create **Games2U (Games2U.com),** a business focused on bringing fun and games to children and adults, using vans and trailers outfitted with state-of-the-art games and activities.

The brothers started operations by scraping up just enough money. However, long-term assets such as mobile vehicles outfitted with video games, large flat-screen displays, high-quality sound systems, and laser-light and fog machines for effects, are very expensive. David explains that financing such equipment, machinery, and similar assets is a struggle. "We would be much bigger, much quicker, if we didn't have that challenge." The owners had to work out depreciation schedules and estimate payback for different games and accessories.

Games2U is now rocking—employing nearly 20 workers, offering franchise agreements to others interested in mimicking their fun and games business, and generating several million in annual sales. Still, a constant challenge for the brothers is maintaining the right kind and amount of assets to meet people's demands and be profitable. "That made us hone in on product development," explains David. "How do we provide unique entertainment at your doorstep?" Games2U's success depends on monitoring and controlling those asset costs, which range from a mobile 4-D movie theater to decked-out trailers to a patented seven-foot tall kid-controlled robot.

Each of these tangible and intangible assets commands Stuart and David's attention. The brothers account for, manage, and focus on recovering all costs of these long-term assets. "We're never done," says David. "We're always challenging ourselves." Their success in asset management permits them to pursue further expansion and new ideas for gaming experiences. They have expanded into outdoor laser tag, human gyros, air cannons, and a version of capture-the-flag called "Booger Wars." "We have a unique concept, a solid infrastructure," explains David. "We provide unique entertainment."

[Sources: *Games2U Website,* January 2011; *Entrepreneur,* June 2009; *The Wall Street Journal,* March 2010; *Inc.com* October 2009; *The Monitor,* September 2009; *Franchise Update,* August 2009]

This chapter focuses on long-term assets, which can be grouped into plant assets, natural resource assets, and intangible assets. Plant assets make up a large part of assets on most balance sheets, and they yield depreciation, often one of the largest expenses on income statements. The acquisition or building of a plant asset is often referred to as a *capital expenditure*. Capital expenditures are important events because they impact both the short- and long-term success of a company. Natural resource assets and intangible assets have similar impacts. This chapter describes the purchase and use of these assets. We also explain what distinguishes these assets from other types of assets, how to determine their cost, how to allocate their costs to periods benefiting from their use, and how to dispose of them.

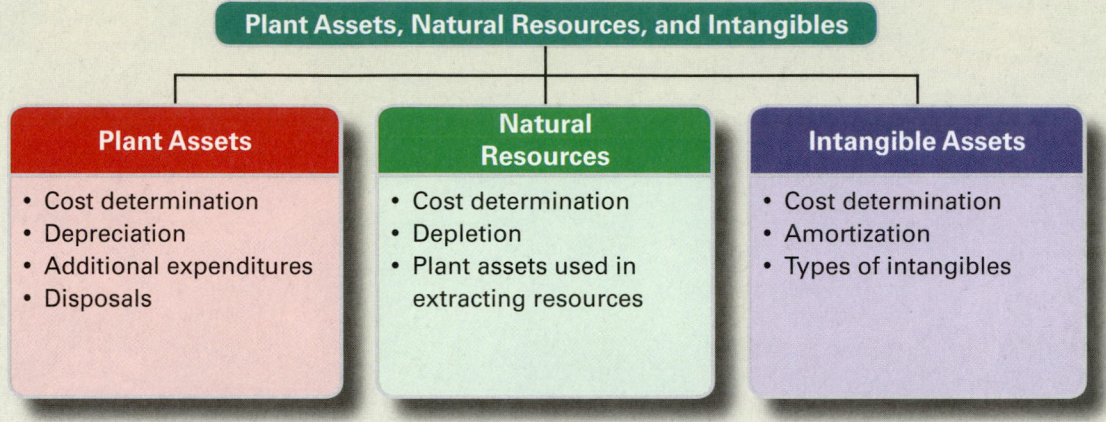

**Plant Assets, Natural Resources, and Intangibles**

**Plant Assets**
- Cost determination
- Depreciation
- Additional expenditures
- Disposals

**Natural Resources**
- Cost determination
- Depletion
- Plant assets used in extracting resources

**Intangible Assets**
- Cost determination
- Amortization
- Types of intangibles

# Section 1—Plant Assets

**Plant assets** are tangible assets used in a company's operations that have a useful life of more than one accounting period. Plant assets are also called *plant and equipment; property, plant, and equipment;* or *fixed assets.* For many companies, plant assets make up the single largest class of assets they own. Exhibit 10.1 shows plant assets as a percent of total assets for several companies. Not only do they make up a large percent of many companies' assets, but their dollar values are large. **McDonald's** plant assets, for instance, are reported at more than $20 billion, and **Walmart** reports plant assets of more than $92 billion.

**EXHIBIT 10.1**

Plant Assets of Selected Companies

eBay $1,120 mil. **7%**

Walmart $92,856 mil. **57%**

Boston Beer $148 mil. **67%**

McDonald's $20,255 mil. **71%**

0    20    40    60    80

**As a Percent of Total Assets**

Plant assets are set apart from other assets by two important features. First, *plant assets are used in operations.* This makes them different from, for instance, inventory that is held for sale and not used in operations. The distinctive feature here is use, not type of asset. A company that purchases a computer to resell it reports it on the balance sheet as inventory. If the same company purchases this computer to use in operations, however, it is a plant asset. Another example is land held for future expansion, which is reported as a long-term investment. However, if this land holds a factory used in operations, the land is part of plant assets. Another example is equipment held for use in the event of a breakdown or for peak periods of production, which is reported in plant assets. If this same equipment is removed from use and held for sale, however, it is not reported in plant assets.

The second important feature is that *plant assets have useful lives extending over more than one accounting period.* This makes plant assets different from current assets such as supplies that are normally consumed in a short time period after they are placed in use.

The accounting for plant assets reflects these two features. Since plant assets are used in operations, we try to match their costs against the revenues they generate. Also, since their useful lives extend over more than one period, our matching of costs and revenues must extend over several periods. Specifically, we value plant assets (balance sheet effect) and then, for many of them, we allocate their costs to periods benefiting from their use (income statement effect). An important exception is land; land cost is not allocated to expense when we expect it to have an indefinite life.

**Point:** It can help to view plant assets as prepaid expenses that benefit several future accounting periods.

Exhibit 10.2 shows four main issues in accounting for plant assets: (1) computing the costs of plant assets, (2) allocating the costs of most plant assets (less any salvage amounts) against revenues for the periods they benefit, (3) accounting for expenditures such as repairs and improvements to plant assets, and (4) recording the disposal of plant assets. The following sections discuss these issues.

**EXHIBIT 10.2**

Issues in Accounting for Plant Assets

Decline in asset value over its useful life

| Acquisition | Use | Disposal |
|---|---|---|
| 1. Compute cost | 2. Allocate cost to periods benefited<br>3. Account for subsequent expenditures | 4. Record disposal |

## COST DETERMINATION

Plant assets are recorded at cost when acquired. This is consistent with the *cost principle.* **Cost** includes all normal and reasonable expenditures necessary to get the asset in place and ready for its intended use. The cost of a factory machine, for instance, includes its invoice cost less any cash discount for early payment, plus any necessary freight, unpacking, assembling, installing, and testing costs. Examples are the costs of building a base or foundation for a machine, providing electrical hookups, and testing the asset before using it in operations.

 **C1** Explain the cost principle for computing the cost of plant assets.

To be recorded as part of the cost of a plant asset, an expenditure must be normal, reasonable, and necessary in preparing it for its intended use. If an asset is damaged during unpacking, the repairs are not added to its cost. Instead, they are charged to an expense account. Nor is a paid traffic fine for moving heavy machinery on city streets without a proper permit part of the machinery's cost; but payment for a proper permit is included in the cost of machinery. Charges are sometimes incurred to modify or customize a new plant asset. These charges are added to the asset's cost. We explain in this section how to determine the cost of plant assets for each of its four major classes.

### Land

When land is purchased for a building site, its cost includes the total amount paid for the land, including any real estate commissions, title insurance fees, legal fees, and any accrued property taxes paid by the purchaser. Payments for surveying, clearing, grading, and draining also are included in the cost of land. Other costs include government assessments, whether incurred at the time of purchase or later, for items such as public roadways, sewers, and sidewalks. These assessments are included because they permanently add to the land's value. Land purchased as a building site sometimes includes structures that must be removed. In such cases, the total purchase price is charged to the Land account as is the cost of removing the structures, less any amounts recovered through sale of salvaged materials. To illustrate, assume that **Starbucks** paid $167,000 cash to acquire land for a retail store. This land had an old service garage that was removed at a net cost of

**EXHIBIT 10.3**

Computing Cost of Land

| | |
|---|---:|
| Cash price of land | $ 167,000 |
| Net cost of garage removal | 13,000 |
| Closing costs | 10,000 |
| **Cost of land** | **$190,000** |

$13,000 ($15,000 in costs less $2,000 proceeds from salvaged materials). Additional closing costs total $10,000, consisting of brokerage fees ($8,000), legal fees ($1,500), and title costs ($500). The cost of this land to Starbucks is $190,000 and is computed as shown in Exhibit 10.3.

## Land Improvements

Land has an indefinite (unlimited) life and is not usually used up over time. **Land improvements** such as parking lot surfaces, driveways, fences, shrubs, and lighting systems, however, have limited useful lives and are used up. While the costs of these improvements increase the usefulness of the land, they are charged to a separate Land Improvement account so that their costs can be allocated to the periods they benefit.

## Buildings

A Building account is charged for the costs of purchasing or constructing a building that is used in operations. When purchased, a building's costs usually include its purchase price, brokerage

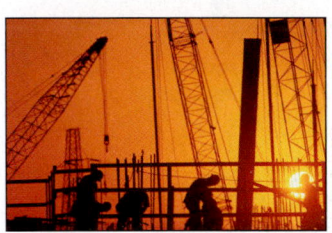

fees, taxes, title fees, and attorney fees. Its costs also include all expenditures to ready it for its intended use, including any necessary repairs or renovations such as wiring, lighting, flooring, and wall coverings. When a company constructs a building or any plant asset for its own use, its costs include materials and labor plus a reasonable amount of indirect overhead cost. Overhead includes the costs of items such as heat, lighting, power, and depreciation on machinery used to construct the asset. Costs of construction also include design fees, building permits, and insurance during construction. However, costs such as insurance to cover the asset *after* it is placed in use are operating expenses.

## Machinery and Equipment

The costs of machinery and equipment consist of all costs normal and necessary to purchase them and prepare them for their intended use. These include the purchase price, taxes, transportation charges, insurance while in transit, and the installing, assembling, and testing of the machinery and equipment.

## Lump-Sum Purchase

Plant assets sometimes are purchased as a group in a single transaction for a lump-sum price. This transaction is called a *lump-sum purchase,* or *group, bulk,* or *basket purchase.* When this occurs, we allocate the cost of the purchase among the different types of assets acquired based on their *relative market values,* which can be estimated by appraisal or by using the tax-assessed valuations of the assets. To illustrate, assume **CarMax** paid $90,000 cash to acquire a group of items consisting of land appraised at $30,000, land improvements appraised at $10,000, and a building appraised at $60,000. The $90,000 cost is allocated on the basis of these appraised values as shown in Exhibit 10.4.

**EXHIBIT 10.4**

Computing Costs in a Lump-Sum Purchase

| | Appraised Value | Percent of Total | Apportioned Cost |
|---|---|---|---|
| Land | $ 30,000 | 30% ($30,000/$100,000) | **$27,000** ($90,000 × 30%) |
| Land improvements | 10,000 | 10   ($10,000/$100,000) | **9,000** ($90,000 × 10%) |
| Building | 60,000 | 60   ($60,000/$100,000) | **54,000** ($90,000 × 60%) |
| Totals | $100,000 | 100% | $ 90,000 |

## Quick Check

Answers — p. 419

1. Identify the asset class for each of the following: (*a*) supplies, (*b*) office equipment, (*c*) inventory, (*d*) land for future expansion, and (*e*) trucks used in operations.

2. Identify the account charged for each of the following: (*a*) the purchase price of a vacant lot to be used in operations and (*b*) the cost of paving that same vacant lot.

3. Compute the amount recorded as the cost of a new machine given the following payments related to its purchase: gross purchase price, $700,000; sales tax, $49,000; purchase discount taken, $21,000; freight cost—terms FOB shipping point, $3,500; normal assembly costs, $3,000; cost of necessary machine platform, $2,500; cost of parts used in maintaining machine, $4,200.

# DEPRECIATION

**Depreciation** is the process of allocating the cost of a plant asset to expense in the accounting periods benefiting from its use. Depreciation does not measure the decline in the asset's market value each period, nor does it measure the asset's physical deterioration. Since depreciation reflects the cost of using a plant asset, depreciation charges are only recorded when the asset is actually in service. This section describes the factors we must consider in computing depreciation, the depreciation methods used, revisions in depreciation, and depreciation for partial periods.

## Factors in Computing Depreciation

Factors that determine depreciation are (1) cost, (2) salvage value, and (3) useful life.

**Cost**    The **cost** of a plant asset consists of all necessary and reasonable expenditures to acquire it and to prepare it for its intended use.

**Salvage Value**    The total amount of depreciation to be charged off over an asset's benefit period equals the asset's cost minus its salvage value. **Salvage value,** also called *residual value* or *scrap value,* is an estimate of the asset's value at the end of its benefit period. This is the amount the owner expects to receive from disposing of the asset at the end of its benefit period. If the asset is expected to be traded in on a new asset, its salvage value is the expected trade-in value.

**Point:** If we expect additional costs in preparing a plant asset for disposal, the salvage value equals the expected amount from disposal less any disposal costs.

**Useful Life**    The **useful life** of a plant asset is the length of time it is productively used in a company's operations. Useful life, also called *service life,* might not be as long as the asset's total productive life. For example, the productive life of a computer can be eight years or more. Some companies, however, trade in old computers for new ones every two years. In this case, these computers have a two-year useful life, meaning the cost of these computers (less their expected trade-in values) is charged to depreciation expense over a two-year period.

**Point:** Useful life and salvage value are estimates. Estimates require judgment based on all available information.

Several variables often make the useful life of a plant asset difficult to predict. A major variable is the wear and tear from use in operations. Two other variables, inadequacy and obsolescence, also require consideration. **Inadequacy** refers to the insufficient capacity of a company's plant assets to meet its growing productive demands. **Obsolescence** refers to the condition of a plant asset that is no longer useful in producing goods or services with a competitive advantage because of new inventions and improvements. Both inadequacy and obsolescence are difficult to predict because of demand changes, new inventions, and improvements. A company usually disposes of an inadequate or obsolete asset before it wears out.

A company is often able to better predict a new asset's useful life when it has past experience with a similar asset. When it has no such experience, a company relies on the experience of others or on engineering studies and judgment. In note 1 of its annual report, **Tootsie Roll**, a snack food manufacturer, reports the following useful lives:

| | |
|---|---|
| Buildings . . . . . . . . . . . . . . . . . . . . . . | 20–35 years |
| Machinery and Equipment . . . . . . . . | 5–20 years |

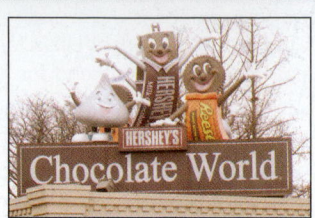

**Decision Insight**

**Life Line** Life expectancy of plant assets is often in the eye of the beholder. For instance, **Hershey Foods** and **Tootsie Roll** are competitors and apply similar manufacturing processes, yet their equipment's life expectancies are different. Hershey depreciates equipment over 3 to 15 years, but Tootsie Roll depreciates them over 5 to 20 years. Such differences markedly impact financial statements. ■

## Depreciation Methods

| | |
|---|---|
| **P1** | Compute and record depreciation using the straight-line, units-of-production, and declining-balance methods. |

Depreciation methods are used to allocate a plant asset's cost over the accounting periods in its useful life. The most frequently used method of depreciation is the straight-line method. Another common depreciation method is the units-of-production method. We explain both of these methods in this section. This section also describes accelerated depreciation methods, with a focus on the declining-balance method.

The computations in this section use information about a machine that inspects athletic shoes before packaging. Manufacturers such as **Converse**, **Reebok**, **adidas**, and **Fila** use this machine. Data for this machine are in Exhibit 10.5.

**EXHIBIT 10.5**

Data for Athletic Shoe-Inspecting Machine

| | |
|---|---|
| Cost ....................... | $10,000 |
| Salvage value ............... | 1,000 |
| Depreciable cost ............. | $ 9,000 |
| Useful life | |
| Accounting periods ......... | 5 years |
| Units inspected ............ | 36,000 shoes |

**Straight-Line Method** **Straight-line depreciation** charges the same amount of expense to each period of the asset's useful life. A two-step process is used. We first compute the *depreciable cost* of the asset, also called the *cost to be depreciated*. It is computed by subtracting the asset's salvage value from its total cost. Second, depreciable cost is divided by the number of accounting periods in the asset's useful life. The formula for straight-line depreciation, along with its computation for the inspection machine just described, is shown in Exhibit 10.6.

**EXHIBIT 10.6**

Straight-Line Depreciation Formula and Example

$$\frac{\text{Cost} - \text{Salvage value}}{\text{Useful life in periods}} = \frac{\$10,000 - \$1,000}{5 \text{ years}} = \$1,800 \text{ per year}$$

If this machine is purchased on December 31, 2010, and used throughout its predicted useful life of five years, the straight-line method allocates an equal amount of depreciation to each of the years 2011 through 2015. We make the following adjusting entry at the end of each of the five years to record straight-line depreciation of this machine.

| Assets | = | Liabilities | + | Equity |
|---|---|---|---|---|
| −1,800 | | | | −1,800 |

| Dec. 31 | Depreciation Expense .......................... | 1,800 | |
|---|---|---|---|
| | Accumulated Depreciation—Machinery ........ | | 1,800 |
| | *To record annual depreciation.* | | |

**Example:** If the salvage value of the machine is $2,500, what is the annual depreciation? *Answer:* ($10,000 − $2,500)/5 years = $1,500

The $1,800 Depreciation Expense is reported on the income statement among operating expenses. The $1,800 Accumulated Depreciation is a contra asset account to the Machinery account in the balance sheet. The graph on the left in Exhibit 10.7 shows the $1,800 per year expenses reported in each of the five years. The graph on the right shows the amounts reported on each of the six December 31 balance sheets.

**EXHIBIT 10.7**

Financial Statement Effects of Straight-Line Depreciation

The net balance sheet amount is the **asset book value,** or simply *book value,* and is computed as the asset's total cost less its accumulated depreciation. For example, at the end of year 2 (December 31, 2012), its book value is $6,400 and is reported in the balance sheet as follows:

| | | |
|---|---|---|
| Machinery ......................... | $10,000 | |
| Less accumulated depreciation ........ | 3,600 | $6,400 |

The book value of this machine declines by $1,800 each year due to depreciation. From the graphs in Exhibit 10.7 we can see why this method is called straight-line.

We also can compute the *straight-line depreciation rate,* defined as 100% divided by the number of periods in the asset's useful life. For the inspection machine, this rate is 20% (100% ÷ 5 years, or 1/5 per period). We use this rate, along with other information, to compute the machine's *straight-line depreciation schedule* shown in Exhibit 10.8. Note three points in this exhibit. First, depreciation expense is the same each period. Second, accumulated depreciation is the sum of current and prior periods' depreciation expense. Third, book value declines each period until it equals salvage value at the end of the machine's useful life.

**Point:** Depreciation requires estimates for salvage value and useful life. Ethics are relevant when managers might be tempted to choose estimates to achieve desired results on financial statements.

| | Depreciation for the Period | | | End of Period | |
|---|---|---|---|---|---|
| Annual Period | Depreciable Cost* | Depreciation Rate | Depreciation Expense | Accumulated Depreciation | Book Value† |
| 2010 | — | — | — | — | $10,000 |
| 2011 | $9,000 | 20% | **$1,800** | $1,800 | 8,200 |
| 2012 | 9,000 | 20 | **1,800** | 3,600 | 6,400 |
| 2013 | 9,000 | 20 | **1,800** | 5,400 | 4,600 |
| 2014 | 9,000 | 20 | **1,800** | 7,200 | 2,800 |
| 2015 | 9,000 | 20 | **1,800** | 9,000 | **1,000** |

\* $10,000 − $1,000.    † Book value is total cost minus accumulated depreciation.

**EXHIBIT 10.8**

Straight-Line Depreciation Schedule

**Units-of-Production Method**   The straight-line method charges an equal share of an asset's cost to each period. If plant assets are used up in about equal amounts each accounting period, this method produces a reasonable matching of expenses with revenues. However, the use of some plant assets varies greatly from one period to the next. A builder, for instance, might use a piece of construction equipment for a month and then not use it again for several months. When equipment use varies from period to period, the units-of-production depreciation method can better match expenses with revenues. **Units-of-production depreciation** charges a varying amount to expense for each period of an asset's useful life depending on its usage.

A two-step process is used to compute units-of-production depreciation. We first compute *depreciation per unit* by subtracting the asset's salvage value from its total cost and then dividing by the total number of units expected to be produced during its useful life. Units of production can be expressed in product or other units such as hours used or miles driven. The second step is to compute depreciation expense for the period by multiplying the units produced in the period by the depreciation per unit. The formula for units-of-production depreciation, along with its computation for the machine described in Exhibit 10.5, is shown in Exhibit 10.9. (7,000 shoes are inspected and sold in its first year.)

**EXHIBIT 10.9**

Units-of-Production Depreciation Formula and Example

*Step 1*

$$\text{Depreciation per unit} = \frac{\text{Cost} - \text{Salvage value}}{\text{Total units of production}} = \frac{\$10,000 - \$1,000}{36,000 \text{ shoes}} = \$0.25 \text{ per shoe}$$

*Step 2*

$$\text{Depreciation expense} = \text{Depreciation per unit} \times \text{Units produced in period}$$
$$\$0.25 \text{ per shoe} \times 7,000 \text{ shoes} = \$1,750$$

Using data on the number of shoes inspected by the machine, we can compute the *units-of-production depreciation schedule* shown in Exhibit 10.10. For example, depreciation for the first year is $1,750 (7,000 shoes at $0.25 per shoe). Depreciation for the second year is $2,000 (8,000 shoes at $0.25 per shoe). Other years are similarly computed. Exhibit 10.10 shows that (1) depreciation expense depends on unit output, (2) accumulated depreciation is the sum of current and prior periods' depreciation expense, and (3) book value declines each period until it equals salvage value at the end of the asset's useful life. **Deltic Timber** is one of many companies using the units-of-production depreciation method. It reports that depreciation "is calculated over the estimated useful lives of the assets by using the units of production method for machinery and equipment."

**Example:** Refer to Exhibit 10.10. If the number of shoes inspected in 2015 is 5,500, what is depreciation for 2015? *Answer:* $1,250 (never depreciate below salvage value)

**EXHIBIT 10.10**

Units-of-Production Depreciation Schedule

| Annual Period | Depreciation for the Period | | | End of Period | |
| | Number of Units | Depreciation per Unit | Depreciation Expense | Accumulated Depreciation | Book Value |
| --- | --- | --- | --- | --- | --- |
| 2010 | — | — | — | — | $10,000 |
| 2011 | 7,000 | $0.25 | **$1,750** | $1,750 | 8,250 |
| 2012 | 8,000 | 0.25 | **2,000** | 3,750 | 6,250 |
| 2013 | 9,000 | 0.25 | **2,250** | 6,000 | 4,000 |
| 2014 | 7,000 | 0.25 | **1,750** | 7,750 | 2,250 |
| 2015 | 5,000 | 0.25 | **1,250** | 9,000 | **1,000** |

**Declining-Balance Method**   An **accelerated depreciation method** yields larger depreciation expenses in the early years of an asset's life and less depreciation in later years. The most common accelerated method is the **declining-balance method** of depreciation, which uses a depreciation rate that is a multiple of the straight-line rate and applies it to the asset's beginning-of-period book value. The amount of depreciation declines each period because book value declines each period.

A common depreciation rate for the declining-balance method is double the straight-line rate. This is called the *double-declining-balance (DDB)* method. This method is applied in three steps: (1) compute the asset's straight-line depreciation rate, (2) double the straight-line rate, and (3) compute depreciation expense by multiplying this rate by the asset's beginning-of-period book value. To illustrate, let's return to the machine in Exhibit 10.5 and apply the double-declining-balance method to compute depreciation expense. Exhibit 10.11 shows the first-year depreciation computation for the machine. The three-step process is to (1) divide 100% by five years to determine the straight-line rate of 20%, or 1/5, per year, (2) double this 20% rate to get the

**Point:** In the DDB method, *double* refers to the rate and *declining balance* refers to book value. The rate is applied to beginning book value each period.

declining-balance rate of 40%, or 2/5, per year, and (3) compute depreciation expense as 40%, or 2/5, multiplied by the beginning-of-period book value.

**EXHIBIT 10.11**

Double-Declining-Balance
Depreciation Formula*

**Step 1**

    **Straight-line rate = 100% ÷ Useful life = 100% ÷ 5 years = 20%**

**Step 2**

    **Double-declining-balance rate = 2 × Straight-line rate = 2 × 20% = 40%**

**Step 3**

    **Depreciation expense = Double-declining-balance rate × Beginning-period book value**

                    40% × $10,000 = $4,000 (for 2011)

\* To simplify: DDB depreciation = (2 × Beginning-period book value)/Useful life.

The *double-declining-balance depreciation schedule* is shown in Exhibit 10.12. The schedule follows the formula except for year 2015, when depreciation expense is $296. This $296 is not equal to 40% × $1,296, or $518.40. If we had used the $518.40 for depreciation expense in 2015, the ending book value would equal $777.60, which is less than the $1,000 salvage value. Instead, the $296 is computed by subtracting the $1,000 salvage value from the $1,296 book value at the beginning of the fifth year (the year when DDB depreciation cuts into salvage value).

**Example:** What is the DDB depreciation expense in year 2014 if the salvage value is $2,000?
*Answer:* $2,160 − $2,000 = $160

**EXHIBIT 10.12**

Double-Declining-Balance
Depreciation Schedule

| Annual Period | Depreciation for the Period | | | End of Period | |
| --- | --- | --- | --- | --- | --- |
| | Beginning of Period Book Value | Depreciation Rate | Depreciation Expense | Accumulated Depreciation | Book Value |
| 2010 | — | — | — | — | $10,000 |
| 2011 | $10,000 | 40% | $4,000 | $4,000 | 6,000 |
| 2012 | 6,000 | 40 | 2,400 | 6,400 | 3,600 |
| 2013 | 3,600 | 40 | 1,440 | 7,840 | 2,160 |
| 2014 | 2,160 | 40 | 864 | 8,704 | 1,296 |
| 2015 | 1,296 | 40 | 296* | 9,000 | 1,000 |

\* Year 2015 depreciation is $1,296 − $1,000 = $296 (never depreciate book value below salvage value).

**Comparing Depreciation Methods**    Exhibit 10.13 shows depreciation expense for each year of the machine's useful life under each of the three depreciation methods. While depreciation expense per period differs for different methods, total depreciation expense of $9,000 is the same over the machine's useful life.

**EXHIBIT 10.13**

Depreciation Expense for the
Different Methods

| Period | Straight-Line | Units-of-Production | Double-Declining-Balance |
| --- | --- | --- | --- |
| 2011 | $1,800 | $1,750 | $4,000 |
| 2012 | 1,800 | 2,000 | 2,400 |
| 2013 | 1,800 | 2,250 | 1,440 |
| 2014 | 1,800 | 1,750 | 864 |
| 2015 | 1,800 | 1,250 | 296 |
| Totals | $9,000 | $9,000 | $9,000 |

Each method starts with a total cost of $10,000 and ends with a salvage value of $1,000. The difference is the pattern in depreciation expense over the useful life. The book value of the asset when using straight-line is always greater than the book value from using double-declining-balance, except at the beginning and end of the asset's useful life, when it is the same. Also,

**Point:** Depreciation is higher and income lower in the short run when using accelerated versus straight-line methods.

the straight-line method yields a steady pattern of depreciation expense while the units-of-production depreciation depends on the number of units produced. Each of these methods is acceptable because it allocates cost in a systematic and rational manner.

**Decision Insight**

**In Vogue**  About 87% of companies use straight-line depreciation for plant assets, 4% use units-of-production, and 4% use declining-balance. Another 5% use an unspecified accelerated method—most likely declining-balance. ■

**Depreciation for Tax Reporting**   The records a company keeps for financial accounting purposes are usually separate from the records it keeps for tax accounting purposes. This is so because financial accounting aims to report useful information on financial performance and position, whereas tax accounting reflects government objectives in raising revenues. Differences between these two accounting systems are normal and expected. Depreciation is a common example of how the records differ. For example, many companies use accelerated depreciation in computing taxable income. Reporting higher depreciation expense in the early years of an asset's life reduces the company's taxable income in those years and increases it in later years, when the depreciation expense is lower. The company's goal here is to *postpone* its tax payments.

**Point:** Understanding depreciation for financial accounting will help in learning MACRS for tax accounting. Rules for MACRS are available from www.IRS.gov.

The U.S. federal income tax law has rules for depreciating assets. These rules include the **Modified Accelerated Cost Recovery System (MACRS),** which allows straight-line depreciation for some assets but requires accelerated depreciation for most kinds of assets. MACRS separates depreciable assets into different classes and defines the depreciable life and rate for each class. MACRS is *not* acceptable for financial reporting because it often allocates costs over an arbitrary period that is less than the asset's useful life and it fails to estimate salvage value. Details of MACRS are covered in tax accounting courses.

## Partial-Year Depreciation

**C2**  Explain depreciation for partial years and changes in estimates.

Plant assets are purchased and disposed of at various times. When an asset is purchased (or disposed of) at a time other than the beginning or end of an accounting period, depreciation is recorded for part of a year. This is done so that the year of purchase or the year of disposal is charged with its share of the asset's depreciation.

To illustrate, assume that the machine in Exhibit 10.5 is purchased and placed in service on October 8, 2010, and the annual accounting period ends on December 31. Since this machine is purchased and used for nearly three months in 2010, the calendar-year income statement should report depreciation expense on the machine for that part of the year. Normally, depreciation assumes that the asset is purchased on the first day of the month nearest the actual date of purchase. In this case, since the purchase occurred on October 8, we assume an October 1 purchase date. This means that three months' depreciation is recorded in 2010. Using straight-line depreciation, we compute three months' depreciation of $450 as follows.

$$\frac{\$10,000 - \$1,000}{5 \text{ years}} \times \frac{3}{12} = \$450$$

A similar computation is necessary when an asset disposal occurs during a period. To illustrate, assume that the machine is sold on June 24, 2015. Depreciation is recorded for the period January 1 through June 24 when it is disposed of. This partial year's depreciation, computed to the nearest whole month, is

**Example:** If the machine's salvage value is zero and purchase occurs on Oct. 8, 2010, how much depreciation is recorded at Dec. 31, 2010?
*Answer:* $10,000/5 × 3/12 = $500

$$\frac{\$10,000 - \$1,000}{5 \text{ years}} \times \frac{6}{12} = \$900$$

## Change in Estimates for Depreciation

Depreciation is based on estimates of salvage value and useful life. During the useful life of an asset, new information may indicate that these estimates are inaccurate. If our estimate of an asset's useful life and/or salvage value changes, what should we do? The answer is to use the new estimate to compute depreciation for current and future periods. This means that we revise the depreciation expense computation by spreading the cost yet to be depreciated over the remaining useful life. This approach is used for all depreciation methods.

Let's return to the machine described in Exhibit 10.8 using straight-line depreciation. At the beginning of this asset's third year, its book value is $6,400, computed as $10,000 minus $3,600. Assume that at the beginning of its third year, the estimated number of years remaining in its useful life changes from three to four years *and* its estimate of salvage value changes from $1,000 to $400. Straight-line depreciation for each of the four remaining years is computed as shown in Exhibit 10.14.

$$\frac{\text{Book value} - \text{Revised salvage value}}{\text{Revised remaining useful life}} = \frac{\$6,400 - \$400}{4 \text{ years}} = \$1,500 \text{ per year}$$

Thus, $1,500 of depreciation expense is recorded for the machine at the end of the third through sixth years—each year of its remaining useful life. Since this asset was depreciated at $1,800 per year for the first two years, it is tempting to conclude that depreciation expense was overstated in the first two years. However, these expenses reflected the best information available at that time. We do not go back and restate prior years' financial statements for this type of new information. Instead, we adjust the current and future periods' statements to reflect this new information. Revising an estimate of the useful life or salvage value of a plant asset is referred to as a **change in an accounting estimate** and is reflected in current and future financial statements, not in prior statements.

## Reporting Depreciation

Both the cost and accumulated depreciation of plant assets are reported on the balance sheet or in its notes. **Dale Jarrett Racing Adventure**, for instance, reports the following.

| | |
|---|---:|
| Office furniture and equipment . . . . . . . . . | $ 54,593 |
| Shop and track equipment . . . . . . . . . . . . . | 202,973 |
| Race vehicles and other . . . . . . . . . . . . . . . | 975,084 |
| Property and equipment, gross . . . . . . . . | 1,232,650 |
| Less accumulated depreciation . . . . . . . . . | 628,355 |
| Property and equipment, net . . . . . . . . . | $ 604,295 |

Many companies also show plant assets on one line with the net amount of cost less accumulated depreciation. When this is done, the amount of accumulated depreciation is disclosed in a note. **Apple** reports only the net amount of its property, plant and equipment in its balance sheet in Appendix A. To satisfy the full-disclosure principle, Apple describes its depreciation methods in its Note 1 and the amounts comprising plant assets in its Note 5—see its 10-K at **www.SEC.gov**.

Reporting both the cost and accumulated depreciation of plant assets helps users compare the assets of different companies. For example, a company holding assets costing $50,000 and accumulated depreciation of $40,000 is likely in a situation different from a company with new assets costing $10,000. While the net undepreciated cost of $10,000 is the same in both cases, the first company may have more productive capacity available but likely is facing the need to replace older assets. These insights are not provided if the two balance sheets report only the $10,000 book values.

Users must remember that plant assets are reported on a balance sheet at their undepreciated costs (book value), not at fair (market) values. This emphasis on costs rather than fair values is based on the *going-concern assumption* described in Chapter 1. This assumption states that, unless there is evidence to the contrary, we assume that a company continues in business. This implies

**Point:** Remaining depreciable cost equals book value less revised salvage value at the point of revision.

**Point:** Income is overstated (and depreciation understated) when useful life is too high; when useful life is too low, the opposite results.

**EXHIBIT 10.14**

Computing Revised Straight-Line Depreciation

**Example:** If at the beginning of its second year the machine's remaining useful life changes from four to three years and salvage value from $1,000 to $400, how much straight-line depreciation is recorded in remaining years?
*Answer:* Revised depreciation = ($8,200 − $400)/3 = $2,600.

**Point:** A company usually keeps records for each asset showing its cost and depreciation to date. The combined records for individual assets are a type of *plant asset subsidiary ledger.*

that plant assets are held and used long enough to recover their cost through the sale of products and services. Because plant assets are not for sale, their fair values are not reported. An exception is when there is a *permanent decline* in the fair value of an asset relative to its book value, called an asset **impairment.** In this case the company writes the asset down to this fair value (details for the two-step process for assessing and computing the impairment loss are in advanced courses).

Accumulated Depreciation is a contra asset account with a normal credit balance. It does *not* reflect funds accumulated to buy new assets when the assets currently owned are replaced. If a company has funds available to buy assets, the funds are shown on the balance sheet among liquid assets such as Cash or Investments.

---

### ■ Decision Ethics  Answer — p. 418

**Controller**   You are the controller for a struggling company. Its operations require regular investments in equipment, and depreciation is its largest expense. Its competitors frequently replace equipment—often depreciated over three years. The company president instructs you to revise useful lives of equipment from three to six years and to use a six-year life on all new equipment. What actions do you take? ■

---

### Quick Check  Answers — p. 419

4. On January 1, 2011, a company pays $77,000 to purchase office furniture with a zero salvage value. The furniture's useful life is somewhere between 7 and 10 years. What is the year 2011 straight-line depreciation on the furniture using (*a*) a 7-year useful life and (*b*) a 10-year useful life?

5. What does the term *depreciation* mean in accounting?

6. A company purchases a machine for $96,000 on January 1, 2011. Its useful life is five years or 100,000 units of product, and its salvage value is $8,000. During 2011, 10,000 units of product are produced. Compute the book value of this machine on December 31, 2011, assuming (*a*) straight-line depreciation and (*b*) units-of-production depreciation.

7. In early January 2011, a company acquires equipment for $3,800. The company estimates this equipment to have a useful life of three years and a salvage value of $200. Early in 2013, the company changes its estimates to a total four-year useful life and zero salvage value. Using the straight-line method, what is depreciation for the year ended 2013?

---

## ADDITIONAL EXPENDITURES

 **C3** Distinguish between revenue and capital expenditures, and account for them.

After a company acquires a plant asset and puts it into service, it often makes additional expenditures for that asset's operation, maintenance, repair, and improvement. In recording these expenditures, it must decide whether to capitalize or expense them (to capitalize an expenditure is to debit the asset account). The issue is whether these expenditures are reported as current period expenses or added to the plant asset's cost and depreciated over its remaining useful life.

**Revenue expenditures,** also called *income statement expenditures,* are additional costs of plant assets that do not materially increase the asset's life or productive capabilities. They are recorded as expenses and deducted from revenues in the current period's income statement. Examples of revenue expenditures are cleaning, repainting, adjustments, and lubricants. **Capital expenditures,** also called *balance sheet expenditures,* are additional costs of plant assets that provide benefits extending beyond the current period. They are debited to asset accounts and reported on the balance sheet. Capital expenditures increase or improve the type or amount of service an asset provides. Examples are roofing replacement, plant expansion, and major overhauls of machinery and equipment.

Financial statements are affected for several years by the accounting choice of recording costs as either revenue expenditures or capital expenditures. This decision is based on whether the expenditures are identified as ordinary repairs or as betterments and extraordinary repairs.

| | Financial Statement Effect | |
|---|---|---|
| | **Accounting** | **Expense Timing** |
| Revenue expenditure | Income stmt. account debited | Expensed currently |
| Capital expenditure | Balance sheet account debited | Expensed in future |

### Ordinary Repairs

**Ordinary repairs** are expenditures to keep an asset in normal, good operating condition. They are necessary if an asset is to perform to expectations over its useful life. Ordinary repairs do not extend an asset's useful life beyond its original estimate or increase its productivity beyond original expectations. Examples are normal costs of cleaning, lubricating, adjusting, and replacing small parts of a machine. Ordinary repairs are treated as *revenue expenditures*. This means their costs are reported as expenses on the current period income statement. Following this rule, **Brunswick** reports that "maintenance and repair costs are expensed as incurred." If Brunswick's current year repair costs are $9,500, it makes the following entry.

| Dec. 31 | Repairs Expense .............................. | 9,500 | |
| | Cash ........................................ | | 9,500 |
| | *To record ordinary repairs of equipment.* | | |

**Point:** Many companies apply the *materiality constraint* to treat *low-cost plant assets* (say, less than $500) as revenue expenditures. This practice is referred to as a "capitalization policy."

Assets  = Liabilities + Equity
−9,500                        −9,500

## Betterments and Extraordinary Repairs

Accounting for betterments and extraordinary repairs is similar—both are treated as *capital expenditures*.

**Betterments (Improvements)**   **Betterments,** also called *improvements,* are expenditures that make a plant asset more efficient or productive. A betterment often involves adding a component to an asset or replacing one of its old components with a better one, and does not always increase an asset's useful life. An example is replacing manual controls on a machine with automatic controls. One special type of betterment is an *addition,* such as adding a new wing or dock to a warehouse. Since a betterment benefits future periods, it is debited to the asset account as a capital expenditure. The new book value (less salvage value) is then depreciated over the asset's remaining useful life. To illustrate, suppose a company pays $8,000 for a machine with an eight-year useful life and no salvage value. After three years and $3,000 of depreciation, it adds an automated control system to the machine at a cost of $1,800. This results in reduced labor costs in future periods. The cost of the betterment is added to the Machinery account with this entry.

**Example:** Assume a firm owns a Web server. Identify each cost as a revenue or capital expenditure: (1) purchase price, (2) necessary wiring, (3) platform for operation, (4) circuits to increase capacity, (5) cleaning after each month of use, (6) repair of a faulty switch, and (7) replaced a worn fan. *Answer:* Capital expenditures: 1, 2, 3, 4; revenue expenditures: 5, 6, 7.

| Jan. 2 | Machinery ...................................... | 1,800 | |
| | Cash ....................................... | | 1,800 |
| | *To record installation of automated system.* | | |

Assets  = Liabilities + Equity
+1,800
−1,800

After the betterment is recorded, the remaining cost to be depreciated is $6,800, computed as $8,000 − $3,000 + $1,800. Depreciation expense for the remaining five years is $1,360 per year, computed as $6,800/5 years.

**Point:** Both extraordinary repairs and betterments require revising future depreciation.

**Extraordinary Repairs (Replacements)**   **Extraordinary repairs** are expenditures extending the asset's useful life beyond its original estimate. Extraordinary repairs are *capital expenditures* because they benefit future periods. Their costs are debited to the asset account (or to accumulated depreciation). For example, **Delta Air Lines** reports, "modifications that . . . extend the useful lives of airframes or engines are capitalized and amortized [depreciated] over the remaining estimated useful life of the asset."

**Decision Maker**                                    Answer — p. 419

**Entrepreneur**  Your start-up Internet services company needs cash, and you are preparing financial statements to apply for a short-term loan. A friend suggests that you treat as many expenses as possible as capital expenditures. What are the impacts on financial statements of this suggestion? What do you think is the aim of this suggestion? ■

## DISPOSALS OF PLANT ASSETS

Plant assets are disposed of for several reasons. Some are discarded because they wear out or become obsolete. Others are sold because of changing business plans. Regardless of the reason, disposals of plant assets occur in one of three basic ways: discarding, sale, or exchange. The general steps in accounting for a disposal of plant assets are described in Exhibit 10.15.

**EXHIBIT 10.15**

Accounting for Disposals of Plant Assets

1. Record depreciation up to the date of disposal—this also updates Accumulated Depreciation.
2. Record the removal of the disposed asset's account balances—including its Accumulated Depreciation.
3. Record any cash (and/or other assets) received or paid in the disposal.
4. Record any gain or loss—computed by comparing the disposed asset's book value with the market value of any assets received.*

*\* An exception to step 4 is the case of an exchange that lacks commercial substance—see Appendix 10A.*

## Discarding Plant Assets

**P2** Account for asset disposal through discarding or selling an asset.

A plant asset is *discarded* when it is no longer useful to the company and it has no market value. To illustrate, assume that a machine costing $9,000 with accumulated depreciation of $9,000 is discarded. When accumulated depreciation equals the asset's cost, it is said to be *fully depreciated* (zero book value). The entry to record the discarding of this asset is

Assets = Liabilities + Equity
+9,000
−9,000

| June 5 | Accumulated Depreciation—Machinery ............. | 9,000 | |
| | Machinery ................................. | | 9,000 |
| | *To discard fully depreciated machinery.* | | |

This entry reflects all four steps of Exhibit 10.15. Step 1 is unnecessary since the machine is fully depreciated. Step 2 is reflected in the debit to Accumulated Depreciation and credit to Machinery. Since no other asset is involved, step 3 is irrelevant. Finally, since book value is zero and no other asset is involved, no gain or loss is recorded in step 4.

How do we account for discarding an asset that is not fully depreciated or one whose depreciation is not up-to-date? To answer this, consider equipment costing $8,000 with accumulated depreciation of $6,000 on December 31 of the prior fiscal year-end. This equipment is being depreciated using the straight-line method over eight years with zero salvage. On July 1 of the current year it is discarded. Step 1 is to bring depreciation up-to-date.

**Point:** Recording depreciation expense up-to-date gives an up-to-date book value for determining gain or loss.

Assets = Liabilities + Equity
−500                     −500

| July 1 | Depreciation Expense .......................... | 500 | |
| | Accumulated Depreciation—Equipment ........ | | 500 |
| | *To record 6 months' depreciation ($1,000 × 6/12).* | | |

Steps 2 through 4 of Exhibit 10.15 are reflected in the second (and final) entry.

Assets = Liabilities + Equity
+6,500                   −1,500
−8,000

| July 1 | Accumulated Depreciation—Equipment ............ | 6,500 | |
| | Loss on Disposal of Equipment .................... | 1,500 | |
| | Equipment ................................. | | 8,000 |
| | *To discard equipment with a $1,500 book value.* | | |

**Point:** Gain or loss is determined by comparing "value given" (book value) to "value received."

This loss is computed by comparing the equipment's $1,500 book value ($8,000 − $6,000 − $500) with the zero net cash proceeds. The loss is reported in the Other Expenses and Losses section of the income statement. Discarding an asset can sometimes require a cash payment that would increase the loss.

## Selling Plant Assets

Companies often sell plant assets when they restructure or downsize operations. To illustrate the accounting for selling plant assets, we consider BTO's March 31 sale of equipment that cost $16,000 and has accumulated depreciation of $12,000 at December 31 of the prior calendar year-end. Annual depreciation on this equipment is $4,000 computed using straight-line depreciation. Step 1 of this sale is to record depreciation expense and update accumulated depreciation to March 31 of the current year.

| March 31 | Depreciation Expense ........................... | 1,000 | |
| | Accumulated Depreciation—Equipment ........ | | 1,000 |
| | *To record 3 months' depreciation ($4,000 × 3/12).* | | |

Assets = Liabilities + Equity
−1,000                         −1,000

Steps 2 through 4 of Exhibit 10.15 can be reflected in one final entry that depends on the amount received from the asset's sale. We consider three different possibilities.

**Sale at Book Value**  If BTO receives $3,000 cash, an amount equal to the equipment's book value as of March 31 (book value = $16,000 − $12,000 − $1,000), no gain or loss occurs on disposal. The entry is

Sale price = Book value → No gain or loss

| March 31 | Cash ......................................... | 3,000 | |
| | Accumulated Depreciation—Equipment ............ | 13,000 | |
| | Equipment .................................. | | 16,000 |
| | *To record sale of equipment for no gain or loss.* | | |

Assets = Liabilities + Equity
+3,000
+13,000
−16,000

**Sale above Book Value**  If BTO receives $7,000, an amount that is $4,000 above the equipment's $3,000 book value as of March 31, a gain on disposal occurs. The entry is

Sale price > Book value → Gain

| March 31 | Cash ......................................... | 7,000 | |
| | Accumulated Depreciation—Equipment ............ | 13,000 | |
| | Gain on Disposal of Equipment ............... | | 4,000 |
| | Equipment .................................. | | 16,000 |
| | *To record sale of equipment for a $4,000 gain.* | | |

Assets = Liabilities + Equity
+7,000                         +4,000
+13,000
−16,000

**Sale below Book Value**  If BTO receives $2,500, an amount that is $500 below the equipment's $3,000 book value as of March 31, a loss on disposal occurs. The entry is

Sale price < Book value → Loss

| March 31 | Cash ......................................... | 2,500 | |
| | Loss on Disposal of Equipment ................... | 500 | |
| | Accumulated Depreciation—Equipment ............ | 13,000 | |
| | Equipment .................................. | | 16,000 |
| | *To record sale of equipment for a $500 loss.* | | |

Assets = Liabilities + Equity
+2,500                         −500
+13,000
−16,000

 **IFRS** _____

Unlike U.S. GAAP, IFRS requires an annual review of useful life and salvage value estimates. IFRS also permits revaluation of plant assets to market value if market value is reliably determined. ■

## Quick Check                                                                 Answers — p. 419

8.  Early in the fifth year of a machine's six-year useful life, it is overhauled, and its useful life is extended to nine years. This machine originally cost $108,000 and the overhaul cost is $12,000. Prepare the entry to record the overhaul cost.

9.  Explain the difference between revenue expenditures and capital expenditures and how both are recorded.

10. What is a betterment? How is a betterment recorded?

11. A company acquires equipment on January 10, 2011, at a cost of $42,000. Straight-line depreciation is used with a five-year life and $7,000 salvage value. On June 27, 2012, the company sells this equipment for $32,000. Prepare the entry(ies) for June 27, 2012.

# Section 2—Natural Resources

| | |
|---|---|
| **P3** | Account for natural resource assets and their depletion. |

**Natural resources** are assets that are physically consumed when used. Examples are standing timber, mineral deposits, and oil and gas fields. Since they are consumed when used, they are often called *wasting assets*. These assets represent soon-to-be inventories of raw materials that will be converted into one or more products by cutting, mining, or pumping. Until that conversion takes place, they are noncurrent assets and are shown in a balance sheet using titles such as timberlands, mineral deposits, or oil reserves. Natural resources are reported under either plant assets or their own separate category. **Alcoa**, for instance, reports its natural resources under the balance sheet title *Properties, plants and equipment*. In a note to its financial statements, Alcoa reports a separate amount for *Land and land rights, including mines*. **Weyerhaeuser**, on the other hand, reports its timber holdings in a separate balance sheet category titled *Timber and timberlands*.

## Cost Determination and Depletion

Natural resources are recorded at cost, which includes all expenditures necessary to acquire the resource and prepare it for its intended use. **Depletion** is the process of allocating the cost of a natural resource to the period when it is consumed. Natural resources are reported on the balance sheet at cost less *accumulated depletion*. The depletion expense per period is usually based on units extracted from cutting, mining, or pumping. This is similar to units-of-production depreciation. **Exxon Mobil** uses this approach to amortize the costs of discovering and operating its oil wells.

To illustrate depletion of natural resources, let's consider a mineral deposit with an estimated 250,000 tons of available ore. It is purchased for $500,000, and we expect zero salvage value. The depletion charge per ton of ore mined is $2, computed as $500,000 ÷ 250,000 tons. If 85,000 tons are mined and sold in the first year, the depletion charge for that year is $170,000. These computations are detailed in Exhibit 10.16.

**EXHIBIT 10.16**

Depletion Formula and Example

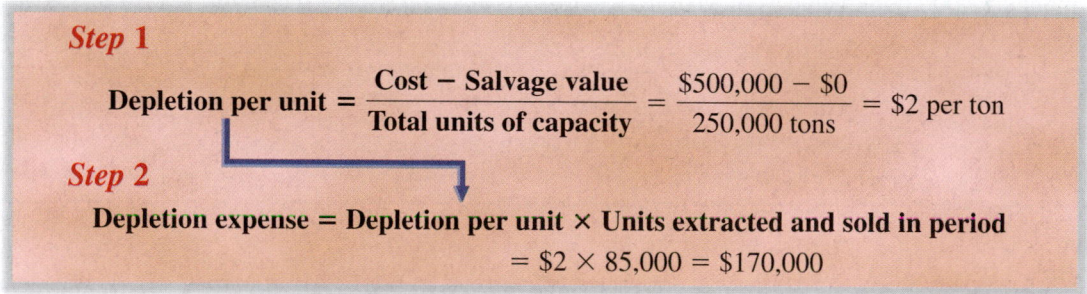

*Step 1*

$$\text{Depletion per unit} = \frac{\text{Cost} - \text{Salvage value}}{\text{Total units of capacity}} = \frac{\$500,000 - \$0}{250,000 \text{ tons}} = \$2 \text{ per ton}$$

*Step 2*

$$\text{Depletion expense} = \text{Depletion per unit} \times \text{Units extracted and sold in period}$$
$$= \$2 \times 85,000 = \$170,000$$

Depletion expense for the first year is recorded as follows.

| Assets = Liabilities + Equity | | | |
|---|---|---|---|
| −170,000           −170,000 | | | |

| Dec. 31 | Depletion Expense—Mineral Deposit .............. | 170,000 | |
|---|---|---|---|
| | Accumulated Depletion—Mineral Deposit ...... | | 170,000 |
| | *To record depletion of the mineral deposit.* | | |

The period-end balance sheet reports the mineral deposit as shown in Exhibit 10.17.

**EXHIBIT 10.17**

Balance Sheet Presentation of Natural Resources

| | | |
|---|---|---|
| Mineral deposit ..................... | $500,000 | |
| **Less accumulated depletion** ........ | 170,000 | $330,000 |

Since all 85,000 tons of the mined ore are sold during the year, the entire $170,000 of depletion is reported on the income statement. If some of the ore remains unsold at year-end, however, the depletion related to the unsold ore is carried forward on the balance sheet and reported as

Ore Inventory, a current asset. To illustrate, and continuing with our example, assume that 40,000 tons are mined in the second year, but only 34,000 tons are sold. We record depletion of $68,000 (34,000 tons × $2 depletion per unit) and the remaining Ore Inventory of $12,000 (6,000 tons × $2 depletion per unit) as follows.

| Dec. 31 | Depletion Expense—Mineral Deposit .............. | 68,000 | |
|---|---|---|---|
| | Ore Inventory ................................. | 12,000 | |
| | Accumulated Depletion—Mineral Deposit ...... | | 80,000 |
| | *To record depletion and inventory of mineral deposit.* | | |

Assets = Liabilities + Equity
−80,000                         −68,000
+12,000

## Plant Assets Used in Extracting

The conversion of natural resources by mining, cutting, or pumping usually requires machinery, equipment, and buildings. When the usefulness of these plant assets is directly related to the depletion of a natural resource, their costs are depreciated using the units-of-production method in proportion to the depletion of the natural resource. For example, if a machine is permanently installed in a mine and 10% of the ore is mined and sold in the period, then 10% of the machine's cost (less any salvage value) is allocated to depreciation expense. The same procedure is used when a machine is abandoned once resources have been extracted. If, however, a machine will be moved to and used at another site when extraction is complete, the machine is depreciated over its own useful life.

**Decision Insight**

**Asset Control**   Long-term assets must be safeguarded against theft, misuse, and other damages. Controls take many forms depending on the asset, including use of security tags, the legal monitoring of rights infringements, and approvals of all asset disposals. A study reports that 44% of employees in operations and service areas witnessed the wasting, mismanaging, or abusing of assets in the past year (KPMG 2009). Another 21% in general management and administration observed stealing or misappropriation of assets. ■

# Section 3—Intangible Assets

Intangible assets are nonphysical assets (used in operations) that confer on their owners long-term rights, privileges, or competitive advantages. Examples are patents, copyrights, licenses, leaseholds, franchises, goodwill, and trademarks. Lack of physical substance does not necessarily imply an intangible asset. Notes and accounts receivable, for instance, lack physical substance, but they are not intangibles. This section identifies the more common types of intangible assets and explains the accounting for them.

**P4** Account for intangible assets.

## Cost Determination and Amortization

An intangible asset is recorded at cost when purchased. Intangibles are then separated into those with limited lives or indefinite lives. If an intangible has a **limited life,** its cost is systematically allocated to expense over its estimated useful life through the process of **amortization.** If an intangible asset has an **indefinite life**—meaning that no legal, regulatory, contractual, competitive, economic, or other factors limit its useful life—it should not be amortized. (If an intangible with an indefinite life is later judged to have a limited life, it is amortized over that limited life.) Amortization of intangible assets is similar to depreciation of plant assets and the depletion of natural resources in that it is a process of cost allocation. However, only the straight-line method is used for amortizing intangibles *unless* the company can show that another method is preferred. The effects of amortization are recorded in a contra account (Accumulated Amortization). The gross acquisition cost of intangible assets is disclosed in the balance sheet along with their accumulated amortization (these disclosures are new). The eventual disposal of an intangible asset involves removing its book value, recording any other asset(s) received or given up, and recognizing any gain or loss for the difference.

**Point:** The cost to acquire a Website address is an intangible asset.

**Point:** Goodwill is not amortized; instead, it is annually tested for impairment.

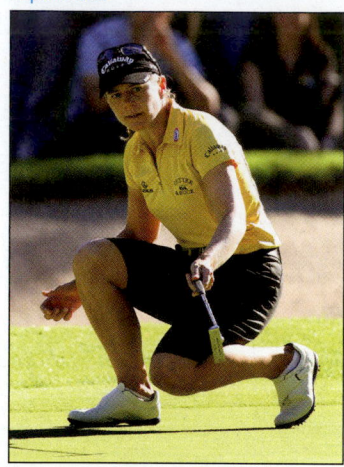

Many intangibles have limited lives due to laws, contracts, or other asset characteristics. Examples are patents, copyrights, and leaseholds. Other intangibles such as goodwill, trademarks, and trade names have lives that cannot be easily determined. The cost of intangible assets is amortized over the periods expected to benefit by their use, but in no case can this period be longer than the asset's legal existence. The values of some intangible assets such as goodwill continue indefinitely into the future and are not amortized. (An intangible asset that is not amortized is tested annually for **impairment**—if necessary, an impairment loss is recorded. Details for this test are in advanced courses.)

Intangible assets are often shown in a separate section of the balance sheet immediately after plant assets. **Callaway Golf**, for instance, follows this approach in reporting nearly $150 million of intangible assets in its balance sheet. Companies usually disclose their amortization periods for intangibles. The remainder of our discussion focuses on accounting for specific types of intangible assets.

## Types of Intangibles

**Patents**   The federal government grants patents to encourage the invention of new technology, mechanical devices, and production processes. A **patent** is an exclusive right granted to its owner to manufacture and sell a patented item or to use a process for 20 years. When patent rights are purchased, the cost to acquire the rights is debited to an account called Patents. If the owner engages in lawsuits to successfully defend a patent, the cost of lawsuits is debited to the Patents account. However, the costs of research and development leading to a new patent are expensed when incurred.

A patent's cost is amortized over its estimated useful life (not to exceed 20 years). If we purchase a patent costing $25,000 with a useful life of 10 years, we make the following adjusting entry at the end of each of the 10 years to amortize one-tenth of its cost.

Assets = Liabilities + Equity
−2,500                   −2,500

| Dec. 31 | Amortization Expense—Patents . . . . . . . . . . . . . . . . . . | 2,500 | |
| | Accumulated Amortization—Patents . . . . . . . . . . | | 2,500 |
| | *To amortize patent costs over its useful life.* | | |

The $2,500 debit to Amortization Expense appears on the income statement as a cost of the product or service provided under protection of the patent. The Accumulated Amortization—Patents account is a contra asset account to Patents.

### Decision Insight

Mention "drug war" and most people think of illegal drug trade. But another drug war is under way: Brand-name drugmakers are fighting to stop generic copies of their products from hitting the market once patents expire. Delaying a generic rival can yield millions in extra sales. ■

**Percent of Prescriptions That Specify Generics**

*(line graph showing Percent on y-axis (0, 20, 40, 60) and years 1980, 1990, 2000, 2005, 2010 on x-axis)*

**Copyrights**   A **copyright** gives its owner the exclusive right to publish and sell a musical, literary, or artistic work during the life of the creator plus 70 years, although the useful life of most copyrights is much shorter. The costs of a copyright are amortized over its useful life. The only identifiable cost of many copyrights is the fee paid to the Copyright Office of the federal government or international agency granting the copyright. If this fee is immaterial, it is charged directly to an expense account; but if the identifiable costs of a copyright are material, they are capitalized (recorded in an asset account) and periodically amortized by debiting an account called Amortization Expense—Copyrights.

**Franchises and Licenses**   **Franchises** and **licenses** are rights that a company or government grants an entity to deliver a product or service under specified conditions. Many organizations grant franchise and license rights—**McDonald's**, **Pizza Hut**, and **Major**

**League Baseball** are just a few examples. The costs of franchises and licenses are debited to a Franchises and Licenses asset account and are amortized over the lives of the agreements. If an agreement is for an indefinite or perpetual period, those costs are not amortized.

**Trademarks and Trade Names**  Companies often adopt unique symbols or select unique names and brands in marketing their products. A **trademark** or **trade (brand) name** is a symbol, name, phrase, or jingle identified with a company, product, or service. Examples are Nike swoosh, Marlboro Man, Big Mac, Coca-Cola, and Corvette. Ownership and exclusive right to use a trademark or trade name is often established by showing that one company used it before another. Ownership is best established by registering a trademark or trade name with the government's Patent Office. The cost of developing, maintaining, or enhancing the value of a trademark or trade name (such as advertising) is charged to expense when incurred. If a trademark or trade name is purchased, however, its cost is debited to an asset account and then amortized over its expected life. If the company plans to renew indefinitely its right to the trademark or trade name, the cost is not amortized.

**Point:** McDonald's "golden arches" are one of the world's most valuable trademarks, yet this asset is not shown on McDonald's balance sheet.

**Goodwill**  **Goodwill** has a specific meaning in accounting. Goodwill is the amount by which a company's value exceeds the value of its individual assets and liabilities. This usually implies that the company as a whole has certain valuable attributes not measured among its individual assets and liabilities. These can include superior management, skilled workforce, good supplier or customer relations, quality products or services, good location, or other competitive advantages.

To keep accounting information from being too subjective, goodwill is not recorded unless an entire company or business segment is purchased. Purchased goodwill is measured by taking the purchase price of the company and subtracting the market value of its individual net assets (excluding goodwill). For instance, **Yahoo!** paid nearly $3.0 billion to acquire **GeoCities**; about $2.8 of the $3.0 billion was for goodwill and other intangibles.

Goodwill is measured as the excess of the cost of an acquired entity over the value of the acquired net assets. Goodwill is recorded as an asset, and it is *not* amortized. Instead, goodwill is annually tested for impairment. If the book value of goodwill does not exceed its fair (market) value, goodwill is not impaired. However, if the book value of goodwill does exceed its fair value, an impairment loss is recorded equal to that excess. (Details of this test are in advanced courses.)

**Point:** Amortization of goodwill is different for financial accounting and tax accounting. The IRS requires the amortization of goodwill over 15 years.

**Example:** Assume goodwill carries a book value of $500 and has an implied fair value of $475, *and* this $25 decline in value meets the 2-step impairment test. The entry to record this impairment is:
Impairment Loss . . . . . . . . .   $25
 Goodwill . . . . . . . . . . . .       $25

**Leaseholds**  Property is rented under a contract called a **lease.** The property's owner, called the **lessor,** grants the lease. The one who secures the right to possess and use the property is called the **lessee.** A **leasehold** refers to the rights the lessor grants to the lessee under the terms of the lease. A leasehold is an intangible asset for the lessee.

Certain leases require no advance payment from the lessee but require monthly rent payments. In this case, we do not set up a Leasehold account. Instead, the monthly payments are debited to a Rent Expense account. If a long-term lease requires the lessee to pay the final period's rent in advance when the lease is signed, the lessee records this advance payment with a debit to the Leasehold account. Since the advance payment is not used until the final period, the Leasehold account balance remains intact until that final period when its balance is transferred to Rent Expense. (Some long-term leases give the lessee essentially the same rights as a purchaser. This results in a tangible asset and a liability reported by the lessee. Chapter 14 describes these so-called *capital leases*.)

A long-term lease can increase in value when current rental rates for similar property rise while the required payments under the lease remain constant. This increase in value of a lease is not reported on the lessee's balance sheet. However, if the property is subleased and the new tenant makes a cash payment to the original lessee for the rights under the old lease, the new tenant debits this payment to a Leasehold account, which is amortized to Rent Expense over the remaining life of the lease.

**Point:** A leasehold account implies existence of future benefits that the lessee controls because of a prepayment. It also meets the definition of an asset.

**Leasehold Improvements**  A lessee sometimes pays for alterations or improvements to the leased property such as partitions, painting, and storefronts. These alterations and improvements are called **leasehold improvements,** and the lessee debits these costs to a Leasehold Improvements account. Since leasehold improvements become part of the property and revert to the lessor at the end of the lease, the lessee amortizes these costs over the life of the lease or the life of the improvements, whichever is shorter. The amortization entry debits

Amortization Expense—Leasehold Improvements and credits Accumulated Amortization—Leasehold Improvements.

**Other Intangibles**  There are other types of intangible assets such as *software, noncompete covenants, customer lists,* and so forth. Our accounting for them is the same. First, we record the intangible asset's costs. Second, we determine whether the asset has a limited or indefinite life. If limited, we allocate its costs over that period. If indefinite, its costs are not amortized.

| **Quick Check** | Answers — p. 419 |
|---|---|

**12.** Give an example of a natural resource and of an intangible asset.

**13.** A company pays $650,000 for an ore deposit. The deposit is estimated to have 325,000 tons of ore that will be mined over the next 10 years. During the first year, it mined, processed, and sold 91,000 tons. What is that year's depletion expense?

**14.** On January 6, 2011, a company pays $120,000 for a patent with a remaining 17-year legal life to produce a toy expected to be marketable for three years. Prepare entries to record its acquisition and the December 31, 2011, amortization entry.

# GLOBAL VIEW

This section discusses similarities and differences between U.S. GAAP and IFRS in accounting and reporting for plant assets and intangible assets.

**Accounting for Plant Assets**  Issues involving cost determination, depreciation, additional expenditures, and disposals of plant assets are subject to broadly similar guidance for both U.S. GAAP and IFRS. Although differences exist, the similarities vastly outweigh the differences. **Nokia** describes its accounting for plant assets as follows:

**NOKIA**

> Property, plant and equipment are stated at cost less accumulated depreciation. Depreciation is recorded on a straight-line basis over the expected useful lives of the assets. Maintenance, repairs and renewals are generally charged to expense during the financial period in which they are incurred. However, major renovations are capitalized and included in the carrying amount of the asset . . . Major renovations are depreciated over the remaining useful life of the related asset.

One area where notable differences exist is in accounting for changes in the value of plant assets (between the time they are acquired and when disposed of). Namely, how does IFRS and U.S. GAAP treat decreases and increases in the value of plant assets subsequent to acquisition?

**Decreases in the Value of Plant Assets**  When the value of plant assets declines after acquisition, but before disposition, both U.S. GAAP and IFRS require companies to record those decreases as *impairment losses*. While the *test for impairment* uses a different base between U.S. GAAP and IFRS, a more fundamental difference is that U.S. GAAP revalues impaired plant assets to *fair value* whereas IFRS revalues them to a *recoverable amount* (defined as fair value less costs to sell).

**Increases in the Value of Plant Assets**  U.S. GAAP prohibits companies from recording increases in the value of plant assets. However, IFRS permits upward *asset revaluations*. Namely, under IFRS, if an impairment was previously recorded, a company would reverse that impairment to the extent necessary and record that increase in income. If the increase is beyond the original cost, that increase is recorded in comprehensive income.

**Accounting for Intangible Assets**  For intangible assets, the accounting for cost determination, amortization, additional expenditures, and disposals is subject to broadly similar guidance for U.S. GAAP and IFRS. Although differences exist, the similarities vastly outweigh differences. Again, and consistent with the accounting for plant assets, U.S. GAAP and IFRS handle decreases and increases in the value of intangible assets differently. However, IFRS requirements for recording increases in the value of intangible assets are so restrictive that such increases are rare. **Nokia** describes its accounting for intangible assets as follows:

> [Intangible assets] are capitalized and amortized using the straight-line method over their useful lives. Where an indication of impairment exists, the carrying amount of any intangible asset is assessed and written down to its recoverable amount.

---

**Total Asset Turnover**      **Decision Analysis**

A company's assets are important in determining its ability to generate sales and earn income. Managers devote much attention to deciding what assets a company acquires, how much it invests in assets, and how to use assets most efficiently and effectively. One important measure of a company's ability to use its assets is **total asset turnover,** defined in Exhibit 10.18.

$$\text{Total asset turnover} = \frac{\text{Net sales}}{\text{Average total assets}}$$

**A1** Compute total asset turnover and apply it to analyze a company's use of assets.

**EXHIBIT 10.18**

Total Asset Turnover

The numerator reflects the net amounts earned from the sale of products and services. The denominator reflects the average total resources devoted to operating the company and generating sales.

To illustrate, let's look at total asset turnover in Exhibit 10.19 for two competing companies: **Molson Coors** and **Boston Beer**.

| Company | Figure ($ millions) | 2009 | 2008 | 2007 | 2006 | 2005 |
|---|---|---|---|---|---|---|
| Molson Coors | Net sales | $ 3,032.4 | $ 4,774.3 | $ 6,190.6 | $ 5,845.0 | $ 5,506.9 |
| | Average total assets | $11,203.9 | $11,934.1 | $12,527.5 | $11,701.4 | $ 8,228.4 |
| | **Total asset turnover** | **0.27** | **0.40** | **0.49** | **0.50** | **0.67** |
| Boston Beer | Net sales | $ 415.053 | $ 398.400 | $ 341.647 | $ 285.431 | $238.304 |
| | Average total assets | $ 241.347 | $ 208.856 | $ 176.215 | $ 136.765 | $113.258 |
| | **Total asset turnover** | **1.72** | **1.91** | **1.94** | **2.09** | **2.10** |

**EXHIBIT 10.19**

Analysis Using Total Asset Turnover

To show how we use total asset turnover, let's look at Molson Coors. We express Molson Coors's use of assets in generating net sales by saying "it turned its assets over 0.27 times during 2009." This means that each $1.00 of assets produced $0.27 of net sales. Is a total asset turnover of 0.27 good or bad? It is safe to say that all companies desire a high total asset turnover. Like many ratio analyses, however, a company's total asset turnover must be interpreted in comparison with those of prior years and of its competitors. Interpreting the total asset turnover also requires an understanding of the company's operations. Some operations are capital intensive, meaning that a relatively large amount is invested in assets to generate sales. This suggests a relatively lower total asset turnover. Other companies' operations are labor intensive, meaning that they generate sales more by the efforts of people than the use of assets. In that case, we expect a higher total asset turnover. Companies with low total asset turnover require higher profit margins (examples are hotels and real estate); companies with high total asset turnover can succeed with lower profit margins (examples are food stores and toy merchandisers). Molson Coors's turnover recently declined and is now much lower than that for Boston Beer and many other competitors. Total asset turnover for Molson Coors's competitors, available in industry publications such as Dun & Bradstreet, is generally in the range of 0.5 to 1.0 over this same period. Overall, Molson Coors must improve relative to its competitors on total asset turnover.

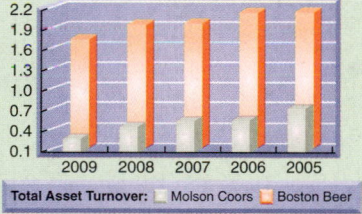

**Point:** An estimate of **plant asset useful life** equals the plant asset cost divided by depreciation expense.

**Point:** The **plant asset age** is estimated by dividing accumulated depreciation by depreciation expense. Older plant assets can signal needed asset replacements; they may also signal less efficient assets.

**Decision Maker**      Answer — p. 419

**Environmentalist**   A paper manufacturer claims it cannot afford more environmental controls. It points to its low total asset turnover of 1.9 and argues that it cannot compete with companies whose total asset turnover is much higher. Examples cited are food stores (5.5) and auto dealers (3.8). How do you respond? ∎

# DEMONSTRATION PROBLEM

On July 14, 2011, Tulsa Company pays $600,000 to acquire a fully equipped factory. The purchase involves the following assets and information.

| Asset | Appraised Value | Salvage Value | Useful Life | Depreciation Method |
|---|---|---|---|---|
| Land ...................... | $160,000 | | | Not depreciated |
| Land improvements ......... | 80,000 | $      0 | 10 years | Straight-line |
| Building .................. | 320,000 | 100,000 | 10 years | Double-declining-balance |
| Machinery ............... | 240,000 | 20,000 | 10,000 units | Units-of-production* |
| Total .................... | $800,000 | | | |

\* The machinery is used to produce 700 units in 2011 and 1,800 units in 2012.

**Required**

1. Allocate the total $600,000 purchase cost among the separate assets.
2. Compute the 2011 (six months) and 2012 depreciation expense for each asset, and compute the company's total depreciation expense for both years.
3. On the last day of calendar year 2013, Tulsa discarded machinery that had been on its books for five years. The machinery's original cost was $12,000 (estimated life of five years) and its salvage value was $2,000. No depreciation had been recorded for the fifth year when the disposal occurred. Journalize the fifth year of depreciation (straight-line method) and the asset's disposal.
4. At the beginning of year 2013, Tulsa purchased a patent for $100,000 cash. The company estimated the patent's useful life to be 10 years. Journalize the patent acquisition and its amortization for the year 2013.
5. Late in the year 2013, Tulsa acquired an ore deposit for $600,000 cash. It added roads and built mine shafts for an additional cost of $80,000. Salvage value of the mine is estimated to be $20,000. The company estimated 330,000 tons of available ore. In year 2013, Tulsa mined and sold 10,000 tons of ore. Journalize the mine's acquisition and its first year's depletion.
6.ᴬ On the first day of 2013, Tulsa exchanged the machinery that was acquired on July 14, 2011, along with $5,000 cash for machinery with a $210,000 market value. Journalize the exchange of these assets assuming the exchange lacked commercial substance. (Refer to background information in parts 1 and 2.)

## PLANNING THE SOLUTION

- Complete a three-column table showing the following amounts for each asset: appraised value, percent of total value, and apportioned cost.
- Using allocated costs, compute depreciation for 2011 (only one-half year) and 2012 (full year) for each asset. Summarize those computations in a table showing total depreciation for each year.
- Remember that depreciation must be recorded up-to-date before discarding an asset. Calculate and record depreciation expense for the fifth year using the straight-line method. Since salvage value is not received at the end of a discarded asset's life, the amount of any salvage value becomes a loss on disposal. Record the loss on the disposal as well as the removal of the discarded asset and its related accumulated depreciation.
- Record the patent (an intangible asset) at its purchase price. Use straight-line amortization over its useful life to calculate amortization expense.
- Record the ore deposit (a natural resource asset) at its cost, including any added costs to ready the mine for use. Calculate depletion per ton using the depletion formula. Multiply the depletion per ton by the amount of tons mined and sold to calculate depletion expense for the year.
- Remember that gains and losses on asset exchanges that lack commercial substance are not recognized. Make a journal entry to add the acquired machinery to the books and to remove the old machinery, along with its accumulated depreciation, and to record the cash given in the exchange.

## SOLUTION TO DEMONSTRATION PROBLEM

1. Allocation of the total cost of $600,000 among the separate assets.

| Asset | Appraised Value | Percent of Total Value | Apportioned Cost |
|---|---|---|---|
| Land ..................... | $160,000 | 20% | **$120,000** ($600,000 × 20%) |
| Land improvements ......... | 80,000 | 10 | **60,000** ($600,000 × 10%) |
| Building ................. | 320,000 | 40 | **240,000** ($600,000 × 40%) |
| Machinery ............... | 240,000 | 30 | **180,000** ($600,000 × 30%) |
| Total ................... | $800,000 | 100% | $ 600,000 |

**2.** Depreciation for each asset. (Land is not depreciated.)

**Land Improvements**

| | |
|---|---|
| Cost ......................................... | $ 60,000 |
| Salvage value ................................. | 0 |
| Depreciable cost ............................. | $ 60,000 |
| Useful life .................................... | 10 years |
| Annual depreciation expense ($60,000/10 years) ........... | $   6,000 |
| **2011 depreciation** ($6,000 × 6/12) ................... | **$   3,000** |
| **2012 depreciation** ............................. | **$   6,000** |

**Building**

Straight-line rate = 100%/10 years = 10%
Double-declining-balance rate = 10% × 2 = 20%

| | |
|---|---|
| **2011 depreciation** ($240,000 × 20% × 6/12) ............ | **$ 24,000** |
| **2012 depreciation** [($240,000 − $24,000) × 20%] ......... | **$ 43,200** |

**Machinery**

| | |
|---|---|
| Cost ......................................... | $180,000 |
| Salvage value ................................. | 20,000 |
| Depreciable cost ............................. | $160,000 |
| Total expected units of production ...................... | 10,000 units |
| Depreciation per unit ($160,000/10,000 units) ............. | $      16 |
| **2011 depreciation** ($16 × 700 units) ................... | **$ 11,200** |
| **2012 depreciation** ($16 × 1,800 units) ................. | **$ 28,800** |

Total depreciation expense for each year:

| | 2011 | 2012 |
|---|---|---|
| Land improvements ......... | $   3,000 | $   6,000 |
| Building ................. | 24,000 | 43,200 |
| Machinery ............... | 11,200 | 28,800 |
| Total .................... | $38,200 | $78,000 |

**3.** Record the depreciation up-to-date on the discarded asset.

| | | |
|---|---|---|
| Depreciation Expense—Machinery ............................... | 2,000 | |
| Accumulated Depreciation—Machinery ...................... | | 2,000 |
| *To record depreciation on date of disposal: ($12,000 − $2,000)/5* | | |

Record the removal of the discarded asset and its loss on disposal.

| | | |
|---|---|---|
| Accumulated Depreciation—Machinery ........................... | 10,000 | |
| Loss on Disposal of Machinery ...................................... | 2,000 | |
| Machinery ...................................................... | | 12,000 |
| *To record the discarding of machinery with a $2,000 book value.* | | |

**4.**

| | | |
|---|---|---|
| Patent ........................................ | 100,000 | |
|     Cash ........................................ | | 100,000 |
| *To record patent acquisition.* | | |

| | | |
|---|---|---|
| Amortization Expense—Patent ..................... | 10,000 | |
|     Accumulated Amortization—Patent ............... | | 10,000 |
| *To record amortization expense: $100,000/10 years = $10,000.* | | |

**5.**

| | | |
|---|---|---|
| Ore Deposit ................................... | 680,000 | |
|     Cash ........................................ | | 680,000 |
| *To record ore deposit acquisition and its related costs.* | | |

| | | |
|---|---|---|
| Depletion Expense—Ore Deposit .................. | 20,000 | |
|     Accumulated Depletion—Ore Deposit ............ | | 20,000 |
| *To record depletion expense: ($680,000 − $20,000)/330,000 tons = $2 per ton. 10,000 tons mined and sold × $2 = $20,000 depletion.* | | |

**6.** Record the asset exchange: The book value on the exchange date is $180,000 (cost) − $40,000 (accumulated depreciation). The book value of the machinery given up in the exchange ($140,000) plus the $5,000 cash paid is less than the $210,000 value of the machine acquired. The entry to record this exchange of assets that lacks commercial substance does not recognize the $65,000 "gain."

| | | |
|---|---|---|
| Machinery (new) ............................... | 145,000* | |
| Accumulated Depreciation—Machinery (old) ......... | 40,000 | |
|     Machinery (old) ............................... | | 180,000 |
|     Cash ........................................ | | 5,000 |
| *To record asset exchange that lacks commercial substance.* | | |

* Market value of the acquired asset of $210,000 minus $65,000 "gain."

---

# 10A

# Exchanging Plant Assets

**P5A** Account for asset exchanges.

Many plant assets such as machinery, automobiles, and office equipment are disposed of by exchanging them for newer assets. In a typical exchange of plant assets, a *trade-in allowance* is received on the old asset and the balance is paid in cash. Accounting for the exchange of assets depends on whether the transaction has *commercial substance* (per *SFAS 153,* commercial substance implies that it alters the company's future cash flows). If an asset exchange has commercial substance, a gain or loss is recorded based on the difference between the book value of the asset(s) given up and the market value of the asset(s) received. If an asset exchange lacks commercial substance, no gain or loss is recorded, and the asset(s) received is recorded based on the book value of the asset(s) given up. An exchange has commercial substance if the company's future cash flows change as a result of the transaction. This section describes the accounting for the exchange of assets.

**Exchange with Commercial Substance: A Loss**   A company acquires $42,000 in new equipment. In exchange, the company pays $33,000 cash and trades in old equipment. The old equipment originally cost $36,000 and has accumulated depreciation of $20,000, which implies a $16,000 book value at the time of exchange. We are told this exchange has commercial substance and that the old equipment has a trade-in allowance of $9,000. This exchange yields a loss as computed in the middle (Loss) columns of Exhibit 10A.1; the loss is computed as Asset received − Assets given = $42,000 − $49,000 = $(7,000). We can also compute the loss as Trade-in allowance − Book value of asset given = $9,000 − $16,000 = $(7,000).

| Asset Exchange Has Commercial Substance | Loss | | Gain | |
|---|---|---|---|---|
| Market value of asset received . . . . . . . . . . . . . . . . . . . . . | | $42,000 | | $52,000 |
| Book value of assets given: | | | | |
| Equipment ($36,000 − $20,000) . . . . . . . . . . . . . . . . . . | $16,000 | | $16,000 | |
| Cash . . . . . . . . . . . . . . . . . . . . . . . . . . . . . . . . . . . . . . | 33,000 | 49,000 | 33,000 | 49,000 |
| **Gain (loss) on exchange** . . . . . . . . . . . . . . . . . . . . . . . . | | $(7,000) | | $ 3,000 |

**EXHIBIT 10A.1**

Computing Gain or Loss on Asset Exchange with Commercial Substance

The entry to record this asset exchange is

| Jan. 3 | Equipment (**new**). . . . . . . . . . . . . . . . . . . . . . . . . . . . . . | 42,000 | |
|---|---|---|---|
| | Loss on Exchange of Assets . . . . . . . . . . . . . . . . . . . . | 7,000 | |
| | Accumulated Depreciation—Equipment (**old**) . . . . . . . . | 20,000 | |
| |     Equipment (**old**) . . . . . . . . . . . . . . . . . . . . . . . . . . | | 36,000 |
| |     Cash . . . . . . . . . . . . . . . . . . . . . . . . . . . . . . . . . . . | | 33,000 |
| | *To record exchange (with commercial substance) of old equipment and cash for new equipment.* | | |

Assets = Liabilities + Equity
+42,000           −7,000
+20,000
−36,000
−33,000

**Point:** Parenthetical notes to "new" and "old" equipment are for illustration only. Both the debit and credit are to the same Equipment account.

**Exchange with Commercial Substance: A Gain** Let's assume the same facts as in the preceding asset exchange *except* that the new equipment received has a market value of $52,000 instead of $42,000. We are told that this exchange has commercial substance and that the old equipment has a trade-in allowance of $19,000. This exchange yields a gain as computed in the right-most (Gain) columns of Exhibit 10A.1; the gain is computed as Asset received − Assets given = $52,000 − $49,000 = $3,000. We can also compute the gain as Trade-in allowance − Book value of asset given = $19,000 − $16,000 = $3,000. The entry to record this asset exchange is

| Jan. 3 | Equipment (**new**) . . . . . . . . . . . . . . . . . . . . . . . . . . . . | 52,000 | |
|---|---|---|---|
| | Accumulated Depreciation—Equipment (**old**) . . . . . . . . | 20,000 | |
| |     Equipment (**old**) . . . . . . . . . . . . . . . . . . . . . . . . . . | | 36,000 |
| |     Cash . . . . . . . . . . . . . . . . . . . . . . . . . . . . . . . . . . . | | 33,000 |
| |     Gain on Exchange of Assets . . . . . . . . . . . . . . . . . . | | 3,000 |
| | *To record exchange (with commercial substance) of old equipment and cash for new equipment.* | | |

Assets = Liabilities + Equity
+52,000           +3,000
+20,000
−36,000
−33,000

**Exchanges without Commercial Substance** Let's assume the same facts as in the preceding asset exchange involving new equipment received with a market value of $52,000, but let's instead assume the transaction *lacks commercial substance*. The entry to record this asset exchange is

| Jan. 3 | Equipment (**new**) . . . . . . . . . . . . . . . . . . . . . . . . . . . . | 49,000 | |
|---|---|---|---|
| | Accumulated Depreciation—Equipment (**old**) . . . . . . . . | 20,000 | |
| |     Equipment (**old**) . . . . . . . . . . . . . . . . . . . . . . . . . . | | 36,000 |
| |     Cash . . . . . . . . . . . . . . . . . . . . . . . . . . . . . . . . . . . | | 33,000 |
| | *To record exchange (without commercial substance) of old equipment and cash for new equipment.* | | |

Assets = Liabilities + Equity
+49,000
+20,000
−36,000
−33,000

**Point:** No gain or loss is recorded for exchanges *without* commercial substance.

The $3,000 gain recorded when the transaction has commercial substance is *not* recognized in this entry because of the rule prohibiting recording a gain or loss on asset exchanges without commercial substance. The $49,000 recorded for the new equipment equals its cash price ($52,000) less the unrecognized gain ($3,000) on the exchange. The $49,000 cost recorded is called the *cost basis* of the new machine. This cost basis is the amount we use to compute depreciation and its book value. The cost basis of the new asset also can be computed by summing the book values of the assets given up as shown in Exhibit 10A.2. The same analysis and approach are taken for a loss on an asset exchange without commercial substance.

| Cost of old equipment . . . . . . . . . . . . . | $ 36,000 |
|---|---|
| Less accumulated depreciation . . . . . . . | 20,000 |
| Book value of old equipment . . . . . . . . | 16,000 |
| Cash paid in the exchange . . . . . . . . . | 33,000 |
| **Cost recorded for new equipment** . . . . . . . . . . . . . . . . . . | **$49,000** |

**EXHIBIT 10A.2**

Cost Basis of New Asset When Gain Not Recorded on Asset Exchange without Commercial Substance

# Summary

**C1  Explain the cost principle for computing the cost of plant assets.** Plant assets are set apart from other tangible assets by two important features: use in operations and useful lives longer than one period. Plant assets are recorded at cost when purchased. Cost includes all normal and reasonable expenditures necessary to get the asset in place and ready for its intended use. The cost of a lump-sum purchase is allocated among its individual assets.

**C2  Explain depreciation for partial years and changes in estimates.** Partial-year depreciation is often required because assets are bought and sold throughout the year. Depreciation is revised when changes in estimates such as salvage value and useful life occur. If the useful life of a plant asset changes, for instance, the remaining cost to be depreciated is spread over the remaining (revised) useful life of the asset.

**C3  Distinguish between revenue and capital expenditures, and account for them.** Revenue expenditures expire in the current period and are debited to expense accounts and matched with current revenues. Ordinary repairs are an example of revenue expenditures. Capital expenditures benefit future periods and are debited to asset accounts. Examples of capital expenditures are extraordinary repairs and betterments.

**A1  Compute total asset turnover and apply it to analyze a company's use of assets.** Total asset turnover measures a company's ability to use its assets to generate sales. It is defined as net sales divided by average total assets. While all companies desire a high total asset turnover, it must be interpreted in comparison with those for prior years and its competitors.

**P1  Compute and record depreciation using the straight-line, units-of-production, and declining-balance methods.** *Depreciation* is the process of allocating to expense the cost of a plant asset over the accounting periods that benefit from its use. Depreciation does not measure the decline in a plant asset's market value or its physical deterioration. Three factors determine depreciation:

cost, salvage value, and useful life. Salvage value is an estimate of the asset's value at the end of its benefit period. Useful (service) life is the length of time an asset is productively used. The straight-line method divides cost less salvage value by the asset's useful life to determine depreciation expense per period. The units-of-production method divides cost less salvage value by the estimated number of units the asset will produce over its life to determine depreciation per unit. The declining-balance method multiplies the asset's beginning-of-period book value by a factor that is often double the straight-line rate.

**P2  Account for asset disposal through discarding or selling an asset.** When a plant asset is discarded or sold, its cost and accumulated depreciation are removed from the accounts. Any cash proceeds from discarding or selling an asset are recorded and compared to the asset's book value to determine gain or loss.

**P3  Account for natural resource assets and their depletion.** The cost of a natural resource is recorded in a noncurrent asset account. Depletion of a natural resource is recorded by allocating its cost to depletion expense using the units-of-production method. Depletion is credited to an Accumulated Depletion account.

**P4  Account for intangible assets.** An intangible asset is recorded at the cost incurred to purchase it. The cost of an intangible asset with a definite useful life is allocated to expense using the straight-line method, and is called *amortization*. Goodwill and intangible assets with an indefinite useful life are not amortized— they are annually tested for impairment. Intangible assets include patents, copyrights, leaseholds, goodwill, and trademarks.

**P5A  Account for asset exchanges.** For an asset exchange with commercial substance, a gain or loss is recorded based on the difference between the book value of the asset given up and the market value of the asset received. For an asset exchange without commercial substance, no gain or loss is recorded, and the asset received is recorded based on the book value of the asset given up.

## Guidance Answers to Decision Maker and Decision Ethics

**Controller**   The president's instructions may reflect an honest and reasonable prediction of the future. Since the company is struggling financially, the president may have concluded that the normal pattern of replacing assets every three years cannot continue. Perhaps the strategy is to avoid costs of frequent replacements and stretch use of equipment a few years longer until financial conditions improve.

However, if you believe the president's decision is unprincipled, you might confront the president with your opinion that it is unethical to change the estimate to increase income. Another possibility is to wait and see whether the auditor will prohibit this change in estimate. In either case, you should insist that the statements be based on reasonable estimates.

**Entrepreneur**  Treating an expense as a capital expenditure means that reported expenses will be lower and income higher in the short run. This is so because a capital expenditure is not expensed immediately but is spread over the asset's useful life. Treating an expense as a capital expenditure also means that asset and equity totals are reported at larger amounts in the short run. This continues until the asset is fully depreciated. Your friend is probably trying to help, but the suggestion is misguided. Only an expenditure benefiting future periods is a capital expenditure.

**Environmentalist**  The paper manufacturer's comparison of its total asset turnover with food stores and auto dealers is misdirected. These other industries' turnovers are higher because their profit margins are lower (about 2%). Profit margins for the paper industry are usually 3% to 3.5%. You need to collect data from competitors in the paper industry to show that a 1.9 total asset turnover is about the norm for this industry. You might also want to collect data on this company's revenues and expenses, along with compensation data for its high-ranking officers and employees.

## Guidance Answers to Quick Checks

**1.** **a.** Supplies—current assets

   **b.** Office equipment—plant assets

   **c.** Inventory—current assets

   **d.** Land for future expansion—long-term investments

   **e.** Trucks used in operations—plant assets

**2.** **a.** Land     **b.** Land Improvements

**3.** $700,000 + $49,000 − $21,000 + $3,500 + $3,000 + $2,500 = $737,000

**4.** **a.** Straight-line with 7-year life: ($77,000/7) = $11,000

   **b.** Straight-line with 10-year life: ($77,000/10) = $7,700

**5.** Depreciation is a process of allocating the cost of plant assets to the accounting periods that benefit from the assets' use.

**6.** **a.** Book value using straight-line depreciation:
    $96,000 − [($96,000 − $8,000)/5] = $78,400

   **b.** Book value using units of production:
    $96,000 − [($96,000 − $8,000) × (10,000/100,000)]
    = $87,200

**7.** ($3,800 − $200)/3 = $1,200 (original depreciation per year)
$1,200 × 2 = $2,400 (accumulated depreciation)
($3,800 − $2,400)/2 = $700 (revised depreciation)

**8.**

| | | |
|---|---|---|
| Machinery | 12,000 | |
|   Cash | | 12,000 |

**9.** A revenue expenditure benefits only the current period and should be charged to expense in the current period. A capital expenditure yields benefits that extend beyond the end of the current period and should be charged to an asset.

**10.** A betterment involves modifying an existing plant asset to make it more efficient, usually by replacing part of the asset with an improved or superior part. The cost of a betterment is debited to the asset account.

**11.**

| | | |
|---|---|---|
| Depreciation Expense | 3,500 | |
|   Accumulated Depreciation | | 3,500 |
| | | |
| Cash | 32,000 | |
| Accumulated Depreciation | 10,500 | |
|   Gain on Sale of Equipment | | 500 |
|   Equipment | | 42,000 |

**12.** Examples of natural resources are timberlands, mineral deposits, and oil reserves. Examples of intangible assets are patents, copyrights, leaseholds, leasehold improvements, goodwill, trademarks, and licenses.

**13.** ($650,000/325,000 tons) × 91,000 tons = $182,000

**14.**

| | | | |
|---|---|---|---|
| Jan.  6 | Patents | 120,000 | |
| |   Cash | | 120,000 |
| Dec. 31 | Amortization Expense | 40,000* | |
| |   Accumulated | | |
| |     Amortization—Patents | | 40,000 |

\* $120,000/3 years = $40,000.

**15.**

| | | | |
|---|---|---|---|
| (a) Equipment (new) | 45,000 | |
| Loss on Exchange of Assets | 3,600 | |
| Accumulated Depreciation—Equipment (old) | 23,400 | |
|   Equipment (old) | | 30,000 |
|   Cash ($45,000 − $3,000) | | 42,000 |

| | | | |
|---|---|---|---|
| (b) Equipment (new)* | 44,600 | |
| Accumulated Depreciation—Equipment (old) | 23,400 | |
|   Equipment (old) | | 30,000 |
|   Cash ($45,000 − $7,000) | | 38,000 |

\* Includes $400 unrecognized gain.

## Key Terms        mhhe.com/wildFAP20e

Land improvements (p. 396)
Lease (p. 411)
Leasehold (p. 411)
Leasehold improvements (p. 411)
Lessee (p. 411)
Lessor (p. 411)
Licenses (p. 410)
Limited life (p. 409)

Modified Accelerated Cost Recovery System (MACRS) (p. 402)
Natural resources (p. 408)
Obsolescence (p. 397)
Ordinary repairs (p. 404)
Patent (p. 410)
Plant asset age (p. 413)
Plant assets (p. 394)

Revenue expenditures (p. 404)
Salvage value (p. 397)
Straight-line depreciation (p. 398)
Total asset turnover (p. 413)
Trademark or trade (brand) name (p. 411)
Units-of-production depreciation (p. 399)
Useful life (p. 397)

## Multiple Choice Quiz   Answers on p. 433   mhhe.com/wildFAP20e

**Additional Quiz Questions are available at the book's Website.**

1. A company paid $326,000 for property that included land, land improvements, and a building. The land was appraised at $175,000, the land improvements were appraised at $70,000, and the building was appraised at $105,000. What is the allocation of property costs to the three assets purchased?
   a. Land, $150,000; Land Improvements, $60,000; Building, $90,000
   b. Land, $163,000; Land Improvements, $65,200; Building, $97,800
   c. Land, $150,000; Land Improvements, $61,600; Building, $92,400
   d. Land, $159,000; Land Improvements, $65,200; Building, $95,400
   e. Land, $175,000; Land Improvements, $70,000; Building, $105,000

2. A company purchased a truck for $35,000 on January 1, 2011. The truck is estimated to have a useful life of four years and an estimated salvage value of $1,000. Assuming that the company uses straight-line depreciation, what is the depreciation expense on the truck for the year ended December 31, 2012?
   a. $8,750
   b. $17,500
   c. $8,500
   d. $17,000
   e. $25,500

3. A company purchased machinery for $10,800,000 on January 1, 2011. The machinery has a useful life of 10 years and an

estimated salvage value of $800,000. What is the depreciation expense on the machinery for the year ended December 31, 2012, assuming that the double-declining-balance method is used?
   a. $2,160,000
   b. $3,888,000
   c. $1,728,000
   d. $2,000,000
   e. $1,600,000

4. A company sold a machine that originally cost $250,000 for $120,000 when accumulated depreciation on the machine was $100,000. The gain or loss recorded on the sale of this machine is
   a. $0 gain or loss.
   b. $120,000 gain.
   c. $30,000 loss.
   d. $30,000 gain.
   e. $150,000 loss.

5. A company had average total assets of $500,000, gross sales of $575,000, and net sales of $550,000. The company's total asset turnover is
   a. 1.15
   b. 1.10
   c. 0.91
   d. 0.87
   e. 1.05

---

$^A$ *Superscript letter A denotes assignments based on Appendix 10A.*

🔵 Icon denotes assignments that involve decision making.

## Discussion Questions

1. 🔵 What characteristics of a plant asset make it different from other assets?

2. What is the general rule for cost inclusion for plant assets?

3. What is different between land and land improvements?

4. Why is the cost of a lump-sum purchase allocated to the individual assets acquired?

5. 🔵 Does the balance in the Accumulated Depreciation—Machinery account represent funds to replace the machinery when it wears out? If not, what does it represent?

6. Why is the Modified Accelerated Cost Recovery System not generally accepted for financial accounting purposes?

**7.** 🛈 What accounting concept justifies charging low-cost plant asset purchases immediately to an expense account?

**8.** What is the difference between ordinary repairs and extra-ordinary repairs? How should each be recorded?

**9.** 🛈 Identify events that might lead to disposal of a plant asset.

**10.** What is the process of allocating the cost of natural resources to expense as they are used?

**11.** Is the declining-balance method an acceptable way to compute depletion of natural resources? Explain.

**12.** What are the characteristics of an intangible asset?

**13.** What general procedures are applied in accounting for the acquisition and potential cost allocation of intangible assets?

**14.** 🛈 When do we know that a company has goodwill? When can goodwill appear in a company's balance sheet?

**15.** 🛈 Assume that a company buys another business and pays for its goodwill. If the company plans to incur costs each year to maintain the value of the goodwill, must it also amortize this goodwill?

**16.** 🛈 How is total asset turnover computed? Why would a financial statement user be interested in total asset turnover?

**17.** Refer to **Research In Motion**'s balance sheet in Appendix A. What property, plant and equipment assets does RIM list on its balance sheet? What is the book value of its total net property, plant and equipment assets at February 27, 2010?  **RIM**

**18.** **Apple** lists its plant assets as "Property, plant and equipment, net." What does "net" mean in this title?  **Apple**

**19.** 🛈 Refer to **Nokia**'s balance sheet in Appendix A. What does it title its plant assets? What is the book value of its plant assets at December 31, 2009?  **NOKIA**

**20.** Refer to the May 31, 2009, balance sheet of **Palm** in Appendix A. What long-term assets discussed in this chapter are reported by the company?  **Palm**

---

McGraw Hill **connect**

**Strike Bowling** installs automatic scorekeeping equipment with an invoice cost of $180,000. The electrical work required for the installation costs $8,000. Additional costs are $3,000 for delivery and $12,600 for sales tax. During the installation, a component of the equipment is carelessly left on a lane and hit by the automatic lane-cleaning machine. The cost of repairing the component is $2,250. What is the total recorded cost of the automatic scorekeeping equipment?

**QUICK STUDY**

**QS 10-1**
Cost of plant assets  C1

---

Identify the main difference between (1) plant assets and inventory, (2) plant assets and current assets, and (3) plant assets and long-term investments.

**QS 10-2**
Defining assets  C1

---

On January 2, 2011, the Crossover Band acquires sound equipment for concert performances at a cost of $55,900. The band estimates it will use this equipment for four years, during which time it anticipates performing about 120 concerts. It estimates that after four years it can sell the equipment for $1,900. During year 2011, the band performs 40 concerts. Compute the year 2011 depreciation using the straight-line method.

**QS 10-3**
Straight-line depreciation
P1

---

Refer to the information in QS 10-3. Compute the year 2011 depreciation using the units-of-production method.

**QS 10-4**
Units-of-production depreciation
P1

---

Refer to the facts in QS 10-3. Assume that the Crossover Band uses straight-line depreciation but realizes at the start of the second year that due to concert bookings beyond expectations, this equipment will last only a total of three years. The salvage value remains unchanged. Compute the revised depreciation for both the second and third years.

**QS 10-5**
Computing revised depreciation
C2

---

A fleet of refrigerated delivery trucks is acquired on January 5, 2011, at a cost of $930,000 with an estimated useful life of eight years and an estimated salvage value of $150,000. Compute the depreciation expense for the first three years using the double-declining-balance method.

**QS 10-6**
Double-declining-balance method  P1

---

Assume a company's equipment carries a book value of $4,000 ($4,500 cost less $500 accumulated depreciation) and a fair value of $3,750, *and* that the $250 decline in fair value in comparison to the book value meets the 2-step impairment test. Prepare the entry to record this $250 impairment.

**QS 10-7**
Recording plant asset impairment  C2

**QS 10-8**

Revenue and capital expenditures

C3

1. Classify the following as either revenue or capital expenditures.
   a. Completed an addition to an office building for $250,000 cash.
   b. Paid $160 for the monthly cost of replacement filters on an air-conditioning system.
   c. Paid $300 cash per truck for the cost of their annual tune-ups.
   d. Paid $50,000 cash to replace a compressor on a refrigeration system that extends its useful life by four years.
2. Prepare the journal entries to record transactions a and d of part 1.

---

**QS 10-9**

Disposal of assets  P2

Horizon Co. owns equipment that cost $138,750, with accumulated depreciation of $81,000. Horizon sells the equipment for cash. Record the sale of the equipment assuming Horizon sells the equipment for (1) $63,000 cash, (2) $57,750 cash, and (3) $46,500 cash.

---

**QS 10-10**

Natural resources and depletion

P3

Diamond Company acquires an ore mine at a cost of $1,300,000. It incurs additional costs of $200,000 to access the mine, which is estimated to hold 500,000 tons of ore. The estimated value of the land after the ore is removed is $150,000.

1. Prepare the entry(ies) to record the cost of the ore mine.
2. Prepare the year-end adjusting entry if 90,000 tons of ore are mined and sold the first year.

---

**QS 10-11**

Classify assets

P3  P4

Which of the following assets are reported on the balance sheet as intangible assets? Which are reported as natural resources? (a) timberland, (b) patent, (c) leasehold, (d) Oil well, (e) equipment, (f) copyright, (g) franchise, (h) gold mine.

---

**QS 10-12**

Intangible assets and amortization  P4

On January 4 of this year, Larsen Boutique incurs a $95,000 cost to modernize its store. Improvements include new floors, ceilings, wiring, and wall coverings. These improvements are estimated to yield benefits for 10 years. Larsen leases its store and has eight years remaining on the lease. Prepare the entry to record (1) the cost of modernization and (2) amortization at the end of this current year.

---

**QS 10-13**

Computing total asset turnover

A1

Eastman Company reports the following ($ 000s): net sales of $13,557 for 2011 and $12,670 for 2010; end-of-year total assets of $14,968 for 2011 and $18,810 for 2010. Compute its total asset turnover for 2011, and assess its level if competitors average a total asset turnover of 2.0 times.

---

**QS 10-14ᴬ**

Asset exchange

P5

Esteban Co. owns a machine that costs $38,400 with accumulated depreciation of $20,400. Esteban exchanges the machine for a newer model that has a market value of $48,000. (1) Record the exchange assuming Esteban paid $32,000 cash and the exchange has commercial substance. (2) Record the exchange assuming Esteban pays $24,000 cash and the exchange lacks commercial substance.

---

**QS 10-15**

International accounting standards

C1  C3

Answer each of the following related to international accounting standards.
a. Accounting for plant assets involves cost determination, depreciation, additional expenditures, and disposals. Is plant asset accounting broadly similar or dissimilar between IFRS and U.S. GAAP? Identify one notable difference between IFRS and U.S. GAAP in accounting for plant assets.
b. Describe how IFRS and U.S. GAAP treat increases in the value of plant assets subsequent to their acquisition (but before their disposition).

---

connect

## EXERCISES

**Exercise 10-1**

Cost of plant assets

C1

Farha Co. purchases a machine for $11,500, terms 2/10, n/60, FOB shipping point. The seller prepaid the $260 freight charges, adding the amount to the invoice and bringing its total to $11,760. The machine requires special steel mounting and power connections costing $795. Another $375 is paid to assemble the machine and get it into operation. In moving the machine to its steel mounting, $190 in damages occurred. Materials costing $30 are used in adjusting the machine to produce a satisfactory product. The adjustments are normal for this machine and are not the result of the damages. Compute the cost recorded for this machine. (Farha pays for this machine within the cash discount period.)

Cerner Manufacturing purchases a large lot on which an old building is located as part of its plans to build a new plant. The negotiated purchase price is $225,000 for the lot plus $120,000 for the old building. The company pays $34,500 to tear down the old building and $51,000 to fill and level the lot. It also pays a total of $1,440,000 in construction costs—this amount consists of $1,354,500 for the new building and $85,500 for lighting and paving a parking area next to the building. Prepare a single journal entry to record these costs incurred by Cerner, all of which are paid in cash.

**Exercise 10-2**
Recording costs of assets
C1

Ming Yue Company pays $368,250 for real estate plus $19,600 in closing costs. The real estate consists of land appraised at $166,320; land improvements appraised at $55,440; and a building appraised at $174,240. Allocate the total cost among the three purchased assets and prepare the journal entry to record the purchase.

**Exercise 10-3**
Lump-sum purchase of plant assets   C1

In early January 2011, LabTech purchases computer equipment for $147,000 to use in operating activities for the next four years. It estimates the equipment's salvage value at $30,000. Prepare a table showing depreciation and book value for each of the four years assuming straight-line depreciation.

**Exercise 10-4**
Straight-line depreciation   P1

Refer to the information in Exercise 10-4. Prepare a table showing depreciation and book value for each of the four years assuming double-declining-balance depreciation.

**Exercise 10-5**
Double-declining-balance depreciation   P1

Feng Company installs a computerized manufacturing machine in its factory at the beginning of the year at a cost of $42,300. The machine's useful life is estimated at 10 years, or 363,000 units of product, with a $6,000 salvage value. During its second year, the machine produces 35,000 units of product. Determine the machine's second-year depreciation under the straight-line method.

**Exercise 10-6**
Straight-line depreciation
P1

Refer to the information in Exercise 10-6. Determine the machine's second-year depreciation using the units-of-production method.

**Exercise 10-7**
Units-of-production depreciation
P1

Refer to the information in Exercise 10-6. Determine the machine's second-year depreciation using the double-declining-balance method.

**Exercise 10-8**
Double-declining-balance depreciation   P1

On April 1, 2010, Stone's Backhoe Co. purchases a trencher for $250,000. The machine is expected to last five years and have a salvage value of $25,000. Compute depreciation expense for both 2010 and 2011 assuming the company uses the straight-line method.

**Exercise 10-9**
Straight-line, partial-year depreciation   C2

Refer to the information in Exercise 10-9. Compute depreciation expense for both 2010 and 2011 assuming the company uses the double-declining-balance method.

**Exercise 10-10**
Double-declining-balance, partial-year depreciation   C2

Supreme Fitness Club uses straight-line depreciation for a machine costing $21,750, with an estimated four-year life and a $2,250 salvage value. At the beginning of the third year, Supreme determines that the machine has three more years of remaining useful life, after which it will have an estimated $1,800 salvage value. Compute (1) the machine's book value at the end of its second year and (2) the amount of depreciation for each of the final three years given the revised estimates.

**Exercise 10-11**
Revising depreciation
C2

**Check**   (2) $3,400

Mulan Enterprises pays $235,200 for equipment that will last five years and have a $52,500 salvage value. By using the equipment in its operations for five years, the company expects to earn $85,500 annually, after deducting all expenses except depreciation. Prepare a table showing income before depreciation, depreciation expense, and net (pretax) income for each year and for the total five-year period, assuming straight-line depreciation.

**Exercise 10-12**
Straight-line depreciation and income effects   P1 🔲

Refer to the information in Exercise 10-12. Prepare a table showing income before depreciation, depreciation expense, and net (pretax) income for each year and for the total five-year period, assuming double-declining-balance depreciation is used.

**Exercise 10-13**
Double-declining-balance depreciation   P1 🔲

**Check**   Year 3 NI, $53,328

**Exercise 10-14**

Extraordinary repairs;
plant asset age

C3

**Check**  (3) $207,450

Passat Company owns a building that appears on its prior year-end balance sheet at its original $561,000 cost less $420,750 accumulated depreciation. The building is depreciated on a straight-line basis assuming a 20-year life and no salvage value. During the first week in January of the current calendar year, major structural repairs are completed on the building at a $67,200 cost. The repairs extend its useful life for 7 years beyond the 20 years originally estimated.

1. Determine the building's age (plant asset age) as of the prior year-end balance sheet date.
2. Prepare the entry to record the cost of the structural repairs that are paid in cash.
3. Determine the book value of the building immediately after the repairs are recorded.
4. Prepare the entry to record the current calendar year's depreciation.

---

**Exercise 10-15**

Ordinary repairs, extraordinary
repairs and betterments

C3

Patterson Company pays $262,500 for equipment expected to last four years and have a $30,000 salvage value. Prepare journal entries to record the following costs related to the equipment.

1. During the second year of the equipment's life, $21,000 cash is paid for a new component expected to increase the equipment's productivity by 10% a year.
2. During the third year, $5,250 cash is paid for normal repairs necessary to keep the equipment in good working order.
3. During the fourth year, $13,950 is paid for repairs expected to increase the useful life of the equipment from four to five years.

---

**Exercise 10–16**

Disposal of assets

P2

Millworks Company owns a milling machine that cost $125,000 and has accumulated depreciation of $91,000. Prepare the entry to record the disposal of the milling machine on January 5 under each of the following independent situations.

1. The machine needed extensive repairs, and it was not worth repairing. Millworks disposed of the machine, receiving nothing in return.
2. Millworks sold the machine for $17,500 cash.
3. Millworks sold the machine for $34,000 cash.
4. Millworks sold the machine for $40,000 cash.

---

**Exercise 10-17**

Partial-year depreciation;
disposal of plant asset

P2

Finesse Co. purchases and installs a machine on January 1, 2011, at a total cost of $92,750. Straight-line depreciation is taken each year for four years assuming a seven-year life and no salvage value. The machine is disposed of on July 1, 2015, during its fifth year of service. Prepare entries to record the partial year's depreciation on July 1, 2015, and to record the disposal under the following separate assumptions: (1) the machine is sold for $35,000 cash and (2) Finesse receives an insurance settlement of $30,000 resulting from the total destruction of the machine in a fire.

---

**Exercise 10-18**

Depletion of natural resources

P1  P3

On April 2, 2011, Idaho Mining Co. pays $3,633,750 for an ore deposit containing 1,425,000 tons. The company installs machinery in the mine costing $171,000, with an estimated seven-year life and no salvage value. The machinery will be abandoned when the ore is completely mined. Idaho begins mining on May 1, 2011, and mines and sells 156,200 tons of ore during the remaining eight months of 2011. Prepare the December 31, 2011, entries to record both the ore deposit depletion and the mining machinery depreciation. Mining machinery depreciation should be in proportion to the mine's depletion.

---

**Exercise 10-19**

Amortization of intangible assets

P4

Busch Gallery purchases the copyright on an oil painting for $236,700 on January 1, 2011. The copyright legally protects its owner for 12 more years. The company plans to market and sell prints of the original for 15 years. Prepare entries to record the purchase of the copyright on January 1, 2011, and its annual amortization on December 31, 2011.

---

**Exercise 10-20**

Goodwill

P4

On January 1, 2011, Timothy Company purchased Macys Company at a price of $3,750,000. The fair market value of the net assets purchased equals $2,700,000.

1. What is the amount of goodwill that Timothy records at the purchase date?
2. Explain how Timothy would determine the amount of goodwill amortization for the year ended December 31, 2011.
3. Timothy Company believes that its employees provide superior customer service, and through their efforts, Timothy Company believes it has created $1,350,000 of goodwill. How would Timothy Company record this goodwill?

Refer to the statement of cash flows for **Apple** in Appendix A for the fiscal year ended September 26, 2009, to answer the following.

1. What amount of cash is used to purchase property, plant, and equipment?
2. How much depreciation, amortization, and accretion are recorded?
3. What total amount of net cash is used in investing activities?

**Exercise 10-21**
Cash flows related to assets

C1

Apple

---

Joy Co. reports net sales of $4,862,000 for 2010 and $7,542,000 for 2011. End-of-year balances for total assets are 2009, $1,586,000; 2010, $1,700,000; and 2011, $1,882,000. (*a*) Compute Joy's total asset turnover for 2010 and 2011. (*b*) Comment on Joy's efficiency in using its assets if its competitors average a total asset turnover of 3.0.

**Exercise 10-22**
Evaluating efficient use of assets

A1

---

Ramond Construction trades in an old tractor for a new tractor, receiving a $31,850 trade-in allowance and paying the remaining $93,275 in cash. The old tractor had cost $107,900, and straight-line accumulated depreciation of $58,500 had been recorded to date under the assumption that it would last eight years and have a $14,300 salvage value. Answer the following questions assuming the exchange has commercial substance.

1. What is the book value of the old tractor at the time of exchange?
2. What is the loss on this asset exchange?
3. What amount should be recorded (debited) in the asset account for the new tractor?

**Exercise 10-23ᴬ**
Exchanging assets

P5

**Check** (2) $17,550

---

On January 5, 2011, Holstrom Co. disposes of a machine costing $65,500 with accumulated depreciation of $35,284. Prepare the entries to record the disposal under each of the following separate assumptions.

1. The machine is sold for $25,343 cash.
2. The machine is traded in for a newer machine having an $86,125 cash price. A $31,912 trade-in allowance is received, and the balance is paid in cash. Assume the asset exchange lacks commercial substance.
3. The machine is traded in for a newer machine having an $86,125 cash price. A $23,393 trade-in allowance is received, and the balance is paid in cash. Assume the asset exchange has commercial substance.

**Exercise 10-24ᴬ**
Recording plant asset disposals

P2 P5

**Check** (2) Dr. Machinery (new), $84,429

---

**Volkswagen Group** reports the following information for property, plant and equipment as of December 31, 2008, along with additions, disposals, depreciation, and impairments for the year ended December 31, 2008 (euros in millions):

| | |
|---|---:|
| Property, plant and equipment, net . . . . . . . . . . . . . . . . . . . | €23,121 |
| Additions to property, plant and equipment . . . . . . . . . . . | 6,651 |
| Disposals of property, plant and equipment . . . . . . . . . . . . | 2,322 |
| Depreciation on property, plant and equipment . . . . . . . . . | 4,625 |
| Impairments to property, plant and equipment . . . . . . . . . | 184 |

**Exercise 10-25**
Accounting for plant assets under IFRS

C2 P1 P2

1. Prepare Volkswagen's journal entry to record its depreciation for 2008.
2. Prepare Volkswagen's journal entry to record its additions for 2008 assuming they are paid in cash and are treated as "betterments (improvements)" to the assets.
3. Prepare Volkswagen's journal entry to record its €2,322 in disposals for 2008 assuming it receives €700 cash in return and the accumulated depreciation on the disposed assets totals €1,322.
4. Volkswagen reports €184 of impairments. Do these impairments increase or decrease the property, plant and equipment account? And, by what amount?

---

**McGraw Hill connect**

Xavier Construction negotiates a lump-sum purchase of several assets from a company that is going out of business. The purchase is completed on January 1, 2011, at a total cash price of $787,500 for a building, land, land improvements, and four vehicles. The estimated market values of the assets are building, $408,000; land, $289,000; land improvements, $42,500; and four vehicles, $110,500. The company's fiscal year ends on December 31.

**PROBLEM SET A**

**Problem 10-1A**
Plant asset costs; depreciation methods C1 P1

mhhe.com/wildFAP20e

*Required*

1. Prepare a table to allocate the lump-sum purchase price to the separate assets purchased (round percents to the nearest 1%). Prepare the journal entry to record the purchase.

**Check**    (2) $23,490

(3) $15,750

mhhe.com/wildFAP20e

2. Compute the depreciation expense for year 2011 on the building using the straight-line method, assuming a 15-year life and a $25,650 salvage value.

3. Compute the depreciation expense for year 2011 on the land improvements assuming a five-year life and double-declining-balance depreciation.

**Analysis Component**

4. Defend or refute this statement: Accelerated depreciation results in payment of less taxes over the asset's life.

---

## Problem 10-2A
Asset cost allocation; straight-line depreciation

C1 P1

In January 2011, Keona Co. pays $2,800,000 for a tract of land with two buildings on it. It plans to demolish Building 1 and build a new store in its place. Building 2 will be a company office; it is appraised at $641,300, with a useful life of 20 years and an $80,000 salvage value. A lighted parking lot near Building 1 has improvements (Land Improvements 1) valued at $408,100 that are expected to last another 14 years with no salvage value. Without the buildings and improvements, the tract of land is valued at $1,865,600. The company also incurs the following additional costs:

| | |
|---|---|
| Cost to demolish Building 1 ............................................. | $ 422,600 |
| Cost of additional land grading ......................................... | 167,200 |
| Cost to construct new building (Building 3), having a useful life of 25 years and a $390,100 salvage value ................................ | 2,019,000 |
| Cost of new land improvements (Land Improvements 2) near Building 2 having a 20-year useful life and no salvage value ...................... | 158,000 |

**Required**

**Check**    (1) Land costs, $2,381,800; Building 2 costs, $616,000

1. Prepare a table with the following column headings: Land, Building 2, Building 3, Land Improvements 1, and Land Improvements 2. Allocate the costs incurred by Keona to the appropriate columns and total each column (round percents to the nearest 1%).

2. Prepare a single journal entry to record all the incurred costs assuming they are paid in cash on January 1, 2011.

(3) Depr.—Land Improv. 1 and 2, $28,000 and $7,900

3. Using the straight-line method, prepare the December 31 adjusting entries to record depreciation for the 12 months of 2011 when these assets were in use.

---

## Problem 10-3A
Computing and revising depreciation; revenue and capital expenditures

C1 C2 C3

Clarion Contractors completed the following transactions and events involving the purchase and operation of equipment in its business.

**2010**

Jan.   1   Paid $255,440 cash plus $15,200 in sales tax and $2,500 in transportation (FOB shipping point) for a new loader. The loader is estimated to have a four-year life and a $34,740 salvage value. Loader costs are recorded in the Equipment account.

Jan.   3   Paid $3,660 to enclose the cab and install air conditioning in the loader to enable operations under harsher conditions. This increased the estimated salvage value of the loader by another $1,110.

**Check**    Dec. 31, 2010, Dr. Depr. Expense—Equip., $60,238

Dec. 31   Recorded annual straight-line depreciation on the loader.

**2011**

Jan.   1   Paid $4,500 to overhaul the loader's engine, which increased the loader's estimated useful life by two years.

Feb. 17   Paid $920 to repair the loader after the operator backed it into a tree.

**Check**    Dec. 31, 2011, Dr. Depr. Expense—Equip., $37,042

Dec. 31   Recorded annual straight-line depreciation on the loader.

**Required**

Prepare journal entries to record these transactions and events.

---

## Problem 10-4A
Computing and revising depreciation; selling plant assets

C2 P1 P2

Chen Company completed the following transactions and events involving its delivery trucks.

**2010**

Jan.   1   Paid $19,415 cash plus $1,165 in sales tax for a new delivery truck estimated to have a five-year life and a $3,000 salvage value. Delivery truck costs are recorded in the Trucks account.

Dec. 31   Recorded annual straight-line depreciation on the truck.

**2011**

Dec. 31   Due to new information obtained earlier in the year, the truck's estimated useful life was changed from five to four years, and the estimated salvage value was increased to $3,500. Recorded annual straight-line depreciation on the truck.

**Check**   Dec. 31, 2011, Dr. Depr. Expense—Trucks, $4,521

**2012**

Dec. 31   Recorded annual straight-line depreciation on the truck.
Dec. 31   Sold the truck for $6,200 cash.

Dec. 31, 2012, Dr. Loss on Disposal of Trucks, $1,822

**Required**

Prepare journal entries to record these transactions and events.

---

A machine costing $210,000 with a four-year life and an estimated $20,000 salvage value is installed in Calhoon Company's factory on January 1. The factory manager estimates the machine will produce 475,000 units of product during its life. It actually produces the following units: year 1, 121,400; year 2, 122,400; year 3, 119,600; and year 4, 118,200. The total number of units produced by the end of year 4 exceeds the original estimate—this difference was not predicted. (The machine must not be depreciated below its estimated salvage value.)

**Problem 10-5A**
Depreciation methods
**P1**

**Required**

Prepare a table with the following column headings and compute depreciation for each year (and total depreciation of all years combined) for the machine under each depreciation method.

| Year | Straight-Line | Units-of-Production | Double-Declining-Balance |
|------|---------------|---------------------|--------------------------|
|      |               |                     |                          |

**Check**   Year 4: units-of-production depreciation, $44,640; DDB depreciation, $6,250

---

Saturn Co. purchases a used machine for $167,000 cash on January 2 and readies it for use the next day at an $3,420 cost. On January 3, it is installed on a required operating platform costing $1,080, and it is further readied for operations. The company predicts the machine will be used for six years and have a $14,600 salvage value. Depreciation is to be charged on a straight-line basis. On December 31, at the end of its fifth year in operations, it is disposed of.

**Problem 10-6A**
Disposal of plant assets
**C1   P1   P2**

**Required**

1. Prepare journal entries to record the machine's purchase and the costs to ready and install it. Cash is paid for all costs incurred.
2. Prepare journal entries to record depreciation of the machine at December 31 of (a) its first year in operations and (b) the year of its disposal.
3. Prepare journal entries to record the machine's disposal under each of the following separate assumptions: (a) it is sold for $13,500 cash; (b) it is sold for $45,000 cash; and (c) it is destroyed in a fire and the insurance company pays $24,000 cash to settle the loss claim.

**Check**   (2b) Depr. Exp., $26,150

(3c) Dr. Loss from Fire, $16,750

---

On July 23 of the current year, Dakota Mining Co. pays $4,836,000 for land estimated to contain 7,800,000 tons of recoverable ore. It installs machinery costing $390,000 that has a 10-year life and no salvage value and is capable of mining the ore deposit in eight years. The machinery is paid for on July 25, seven days before mining operations begin. The company removes and sells 400,000 tons of ore during its first five months of operations ending on December 31. Depreciation of the machinery is in proportion to the mine's depletion as the machinery will be abandoned after the ore is mined.

**Problem 10-7A**
Natural resources
**P3**

**Required**

Prepare entries to record (a) the purchase of the land, (b) the cost and installation of machinery, (c) the first five months' depletion assuming the land has a net salvage value of zero after the ore is mined, and (d) the first five months' depreciation on the machinery.

**Check**   (c) Depletion, $248,000
(d) Depreciation, $20,000

**Analysis Component**

Describe both the similarities and differences in amortization, depletion, and depreciation.

**Problem 10-8A**

Intangible assets

P4

On July 1, 2006, Sweetman Company signed a contract to lease space in a building for 15 years. The lease contract calls for annual (prepaid) rental payments of $70,000 on each July 1 throughout the life of the lease and for the lessee to pay for all additions and improvements to the leased property. On June 25, 2011, Sweetman decides to sublease the space to Kirk & Associates for the remaining 10 years of the lease—Kirk pays $185,000 to Sweetman for the right to sublease and it agrees to assume the obligation to pay the $70,000 annual rent to the building owner beginning July 1, 2011. After taking possession of the leased space, Kirk pays for improving the office portion of the leased space at a $129,840 cost. The improvements are paid for by Kirk on July 5, 2011, and are estimated to have a useful life equal to the 16 years remaining in the life of the building.

**Required**

1. Prepare entries for Kirk to record (*a*) its payment to Sweetman for the right to sublease the building space, (*b*) its payment of the 2011 annual rent to the building owner, and (*c*) its payment for the office improvements.

2. Prepare Kirk's year-end adjusting entries required at December 31, 2011, to (*a*) amortize the $185,000 cost of the sublease, (*b*) amortize the office improvements, and (*c*) record rent expense.

**Check**   Dr. Rent Expense for (2*a*) $9,250, (2*c*) $35,000

---

## PROBLEM SET B

**Problem 10-1B**

Plant asset costs; depreciation methods

C1 P1

**Check**   (2) $52,000

(3) $41,860

Racerback Company negotiates a lump-sum purchase of several assets from a contractor who is relocating. The purchase is completed on January 1, 2011, at a total cash price of $1,610,000 for a building, land, land improvements, and six trucks. The estimated market values of the assets are building, $784,800; land, $540,640; land improvements, $226,720; and six trucks, $191,840. The company's fiscal year ends on December 31.

**Required**

1. Prepare a table to allocate the lump-sum purchase price to the separate assets purchased (round percents to the nearest 1%). Prepare the journal entry to record the purchase.

2. Compute the depreciation expense for year 2011 on the building using the straight-line method, assuming a 12-year life and a $100,500 salvage value.

3. Compute the depreciation expense for year 2011 on the land improvements assuming a 10-year life and double-declining-balance depreciation.

**Analysis Component**

4. Defend or refute this statement: Accelerated depreciation results in payment of more taxes over the asset's life.

---

**Problem 10-2B**

Asset cost allocation; straight-line depreciation

C1 P1

In January 2011, InTech Co. pays $1,350,000 for a tract of land with two buildings. It plans to demolish Building A and build a new shop in its place. Building B will be a company office; it is appraised at $472,770, with a useful life of 15 years and a $90,000 salvage value. A lighted parking lot near Building B has improvements (Land Improvements B) valued at $125,145 that are expected to last another six years with no salvage value. Without the buildings and improvements, the tract of land is valued at $792,585. The company also incurs the following additional costs.

| | |
|---|---:|
| Cost to demolish Building A . . . . . . . . . . . . . . . . . . . . . . . . . . . . . . . . . . . . . . . . . . . . | $ 117,000 |
| Cost of additional land grading . . . . . . . . . . . . . . . . . . . . . . . . . . . . . . . . . . . . . . . . . | 172,500 |
| Cost to construct new building (Building C), having a useful life of 20 years and a $295,500 salvage value . . . . . . . . . . . . . . . . . . . . . . . . . . . . . . . . . . . . . . . | 1,356,000 |
| Cost of new land improvements (Land Improvements C) near Building C, having a 10-year useful life and no salvage value . . . . . . . . . . . . . . . . . . . . . . . . . | 101,250 |

**Required**

**Check**   (1) Land costs, $1,059,000; Building B costs, $459,000

1. Prepare a table with the following column headings: Land, Building B, Building C, Land Improvements B, and Land Improvements C. Allocate the costs incurred by InTech to the appropriate columns and total each column (round percents to the nearest 1%).

2. Prepare a single journal entry to record all incurred costs assuming they are paid in cash on January 1, 2011.

(3) Depr.—Land Improv. B and C, $20,250 and $10,125

3. Using the straight-line method, prepare the December 31 adjusting entries to record depreciation for the 12 months of 2011 when these assets were in use.

Xpress Delivery Service completed the following transactions and events involving the purchase and operation of equipment for its business.

**2010**

Jan.  1   Paid $24,950 cash plus $1,950 in sales tax for a new delivery van that was estimated to have a five-year life and a $3,400 salvage value. Van costs are recorded in the Equipment account.

Jan.  3   Paid $1,550 to install sorting racks in the van for more accurate and quicker delivery of packages. This increases the estimated salvage value of the van by another $200.

Dec. 31   Recorded annual straight-line depreciation on the van.

**2011**

Jan.  1   Paid $1,970 to overhaul the van's engine, which increased the van's estimated useful life by two years.

May 10   Paid $600 to repair the van after the driver backed it into a loading dock.

Dec. 31   Record annual straight-line depreciation on the van. (Round to the nearest dollar.)

**Required**

Prepare journal entries to record these transactions and events.

**Problem 10-3B**
Computing and revising depreciation; revenue and capital expenditures

C1  C2  C3

**Check**  Dec. 31, 2010, Dr. Depr. Expense—Equip., $4,970

**Check**  Dec. 31, 2011, Dr. Depr. Expense—Equip., $3,642

---

Field Instruments completed the following transactions and events involving its machinery.

**2010**

Jan.  1   Paid $106,600 cash plus $6,400 in sales tax for a new machine. The machine is estimated to have a six-year life and a $9,800 salvage value.

Dec. 31   Recorded annual straight-line depreciation on the machinery.

**2011**

Dec. 31   Due to new information obtained earlier in the year, the machine's estimated useful life was changed from six to four years, and the estimated salvage value was increased to $13,050. Recorded annual straight-line depreciation on the machinery.

**2012**

Dec. 31   Recorded annual straight-line depreciation on the machinery.

Dec. 31   Sold the machine for $25,240 cash.

**Required**

Prepare journal entries to record these transactions and events.

**Problem 10-4B**
Computing and revising depreciation; selling plant assets

C2  P1  P2

**Check**  Dec. 31, 2011, Dr. Depr. Expense—Machinery, $27,583

Dec. 31, 2012, Dr. Loss on Disposal of Machinery, $15,394

---

On January 2, Gannon Co. purchases and installs a new machine costing $312,000 with a five-year life and an estimated $28,000 salvage value. Management estimates the machine will produce 1,136,000 units of product during its life. Actual production of units is as follows: year 1, 245,600; year 2, 230,400; year 3, 227,000; year 4, 232,600; and year 5, 211,200. The total number of units produced by the end of year 5 exceeds the original estimate—this difference was not predicted. (The machine must not be depreciated below its estimated salvage value.)

**Required**

Prepare a table with the following column headings and compute depreciation for each year (and total depreciation of all years combined) for the machine under each depreciation method.

**Problem 10-5B**
Depreciation methods

P1

| Year | Straight-Line | Units-of-Production | Double-Declining-Balance |
|------|---------------|---------------------|--------------------------|
|      |               |                     |                          |

**Check**  DDB Depreciation, Year 3, $44,928; U-of-P Depreciation, Year 4, $58,150

---

On January 1, Jefferson purchases a used machine for $130,000 and readies it for use the next day at a cost of $3,390. On January 4, it is mounted on a required operating platform costing $4,800, and it is further readied for operations. Management estimates the machine will be used for seven years and have an $18,000 salvage value. Depreciation is to be charged on a straight-line basis. On December 31, at the end of its sixth year of use, the machine is disposed of.

**Problem 10-6B**
Disposal of plant assets

C1  P1  P2

*Required*

1. Prepare journal entries to record the machine's purchase and the costs to ready and install it. Cash is paid for all costs incurred.

**Check** (2*b*) Depr. Exp., $17,170

(3*c*) Dr. Loss from Fire,
$15,170

2. Prepare journal entries to record depreciation of the machine at December 31 of (*a*) its first year in operations and (*b*) the year of its disposal.

3. Prepare journal entries to record the machine's disposal under each of the following separate assumptions: (*a*) it is sold for $30,000 cash; (*b*) it is sold for $50,000 cash; and (*c*) it is destroyed in a fire and the insurance company pays $20,000 cash to settle the loss claim.

**Problem 10-7B**
Natural resources
P3

On February 19 of the current year, Rock Chalk Co. pays $4,450,000 for land estimated to contain 5 million tons of recoverable ore. It installs machinery costing $200,000 that has a 16-year life and no salvage value and is capable of mining the ore deposit in 12 years. The machinery is paid for on March 21, eleven days before mining operations begin. The company removes and sells 352,000 tons of ore during its first nine months of operations ending on December 31. Depreciation of the machinery is in proportion to the mine's depletion as the machinery will be abandoned after the ore is mined.

*Required*

**Check** (*c*) Depletion, $313,280;
(*d*) Depreciation, $14,080

Prepare entries to record (*a*) the purchase of the land, (*b*) the cost and installation of the machinery, (*c*) the first nine months' depletion assuming the land has a net salvage value of zero after the ore is mined, and (*d*) the first nine months' depreciation on the machinery.

*Analysis Component*

Describe both the similarities and differences in amortization, depletion, and depreciation.

**Problem 10-8B**
Intangible assets
P4

On January 1, 2004, Liberty Co. entered into a 12-year lease on a building. The lease contract requires (1) annual (prepaid) rental payments of $26,400 each January 1 throughout the life of the lease and (2) for the lessee to pay for all additions and improvements to the leased property. On January 1, 2011, Liberty decides to sublease the space to Moberly Co. for the remaining five years of the lease—Moberly pays $30,000 to Liberty for the right to sublease and agrees to assume the obligation to pay the $26,400 annual rent to the building owner beginning January 1, 2011. After taking possession of the leased space, Moberly pays for improving the office portion of the leased space at an $18,000 cost. The improvements are paid for by Moberly on January 3, 2011, and are estimated to have a useful life equal to the 13 years remaining in the life of the building.

*Required*

1. Prepare entries for Moberly to record (*a*) its payment to Liberty for the right to sublease the building space, (*b*) its payment of the 2011 annual rent to the building owner, and (*c*) its payment for the office improvements.

**Check** Dr. Rent Expense:
(2*a*) $6,000, (2*c*) $26,400

2. Prepare Moberly's year-end adjusting entries required on December 31, 2011, to (*a*) amortize the $30,000 cost of the sublease, (*b*) amortize the office improvements, and (*c*) record rent expense.

**SERIAL PROBLEM**
Business Solutions
P1　A1

*(This serial problem began in Chapter 1 and continues through most of the book. If previous chapter segments were not completed, the serial problem can begin at this point. It is helpful, but not necessary, to use the Working Papers that accompany the book.)*

**SP 10**　Selected ledger account balances for Business Solutions follow.

|  | For Three Months Ended December 31, 2011 | For Three Months Ended March 31, 2012 |
| --- | --- | --- |
| Office equipment | $ 8,000 | $ 8,000 |
| Accumulated depreciation— Office equipment | 400 | 800 |
| Computer equipment | 20,000 | 20,000 |
| Accumulated depreciation— Computer equipment | 1,250 | 2,500 |
| Total revenue | 31,284 | 44,000 |
| Total assets | 83,460 | 120,268 |

*Required*

1. Assume that Business Solutions does not acquire additional office equipment or computer equipment in 2012. Compute amounts for *the year ended* December 31, 2012, for Depreciation Expense—Office Equipment and for Depreciation Expense—Computer Equipment (assume use of the straight-line method).

2. Given the assumptions in part 1, what is the book value of both the office equipment and the computer equipment as of December 31, 2012?

3. Compute the three-month total asset turnover for Business Solutions as of March 31, 2012. Use total revenue for the numerator and average the December 31, 2011, total assets and the March 31, 2012, total assets for the denominator. Interpret its total asset turnover if competitors average 2.5 for annual periods. (Round turnover to two decimals.)

**Check**   (3) Three-month (annual)
turnover = 0.43 (1.73 annual)

## Beyond the Numbers

**BTN 10-1**   Refer to the financial statements of **Research In Motion** in Appendix A to answer the following.

1. What percent of the original cost of RIM's property, plant and equipment remains to be depreciated as of February 27, 2010, and at February 28, 2009? Assume these assets have no salvage value.

2. Over what length(s) of time is RIM depreciating its major categories of property, plant and equipment?

3. What is the change in total property, plant and equipment (before accumulated depreciation) for the year ended February 27, 2010? What is the amount of cash provided (used) by investing activities for property, plant and equipment for the year ended February 27, 2010? What is one possible explanation for the difference between these two amounts?

4. Compute its total asset turnover for the year ended February 27, 2010, and the year ended February 28, 2009. Assume total assets at March 1, 2008, are $5,511 ($ millions).

**REPORTING IN ACTION**

A1

*RIM*

*Fast Forward*

5. Access RIM's financial statements for fiscal years ending after February 27, 2010, at its Website (**RIM.com**) or the SEC's EDGAR database (**www.SEC.gov**). Recompute RIM's total asset turnover for the additional years' data you collect. Comment on any differences relative to the turnover computed in part 4.

---

**BTN 10-2**   Comparative figures for **Research In Motion** and **Apple** follow.

**COMPARATIVE ANALYSIS**

A1

*RIM*

Apple

| ($ millions) | Research In Motion | | | Apple | | |
| | Current Year | One Year Prior | Two Years Prior | Current Year | One Year Prior | Two Years Prior |
| --- | --- | --- | --- | --- | --- | --- |
| Total assets ........... | $10,204 | $ 8,101 | $5,511 | $47,501 | $36,171 | $25,347 |
| Net sales ............. | 14,953 | 11,065 | 6,009 | 42,905 | 37,491 | 24,578 |

*Required*

1. Compute total asset turnover for the most recent two years for Research In Motion and Apple using the data shown.

2. Which company is more efficient in generating net sales given the total assets it employs? Assume an industry average of 1.0 for asset turnover.

---

**BTN 10-3**   Flo Choi owns a small business and manages its accounting. Her company just finished a year in which a large amount of borrowed funds was invested in a new building addition as well as in equipment and fixture additions. Choi's banker requires her to submit semiannual financial statements so he can monitor the financial health of her business. He has warned her that if profit margins erode, he might raise the interest rate on the borrowed funds to reflect the increased loan risk from the bank's point of view. Choi knows profit margin is likely to decline this year. As she prepares year-end adjusting entries, she decides to apply the following depreciation rule: All asset additions are considered to be in use on the first day of the following month. (The previous rule assumed assets are in use on the first day of the month nearest to the purchase date.)

**ETHICS CHALLENGE**

C1

*Required*

1. Identify decisions that managers like Choi must make in applying depreciation methods.
2. Is Choi's rule an ethical violation, or is it a legitimate decision in computing depreciation?
3. How will Choi's new depreciation rule affect the profit margin of her business?

---

**COMMUNICATING
IN PRACTICE**

A1

**BTN 10-4**   Teams are to select an industry, and each team member is to select a different company in that industry. Each team member is to acquire the financial statements (Form 10-K) of the company selected—see the company's Website or the SEC's EDGAR database (www.SEC.gov). Use the financial statements to compute total asset turnover. Communicate with teammates via a meeting, e-mail, or telephone to discuss the meaning of this ratio, how different companies compare to each other, and the industry norm. The team must prepare a one-page report that describes the ratios for each company and identifies the conclusions reached during the team's discussion.

---

**TAKING IT TO
THE NET**

P4

**BTN 10-5**   Access the Yahoo! (ticker: YHOO) 10-K report for the year ended December 31, 2009, filed on February 26, 2010, at www.SEC.gov.

*Required*

1. What amount of goodwill is reported on Yahoo!'s balance sheet? What percentage of total assets does its goodwill represent? Is goodwill a major asset for Yahoo!? Explain.
2. Locate Note 5 to its financial statements. Identify the change in goodwill from December 31, 2008, to December 31, 2009. Comment on the change in goodwill over this period.
3. Locate Note 6 to its financial statements. What are the three categories of intangible assets that Yahoo! reports at December 31, 2009? What proportion of total assets do the intangibles represent?
4. What does Yahoo! indicate is the life of "Trade names, trademarks, and domain names" according to its Note 6? Comment on the difference between the estimated useful life and the legal life of Yahoo!'s trademark.

---

**TEAMWORK IN
ACTION**

P1

**BTN 10-6**   Each team member is to become an expert on one depreciation method to facilitate teammates' understanding of that method. Follow these procedures:

a. Each team member is to select an area for expertise from one of the following depreciation methods: straight-line, units-of-production, or double-declining-balance.
b. Expert teams are to be formed from those who have selected the same area of expertise. The instructor will identify the location where each expert team meets.
c. Using the following data, expert teams are to collaborate and develop a presentation answering the requirements. Expert team members must write the presentation in a format they can show to their learning teams.

**Point:** This activity can follow an overview of each method. Step 1 allows for three areas of expertise. Larger teams will have some duplication of areas, but the straight-line choice should not be duplicated. Expert teams can use the book and consult with the instructor.

**Data and Requirements**   On January 8, 2009, Waverly Riders purchases a van to transport rafters back to the point of departure at the conclusion of the rafting adventures they operate. The cost of the van is $44,000. It has an estimated salvage value of $2,000 and is expected to be used for four years and driven 60,000 miles. The van is driven 12,000 miles in 2009, 18,000 miles in 2010, 21,000 in 2011, and 10,000 in 2012.

1. Compute the annual depreciation expense for each year of the van's estimated useful life.
2. Explain when and how annual depreciation is recorded.
3. Explain the impact on income of this depreciation method versus others over the van's life.
4. Identify the van's book value for each year of its life and illustrate the reporting of this amount for any one year.

d. Re-form original learning teams. In rotation, experts are to present to their teams the results from part *c*. Experts are to encourage and respond to questions.

---

**ENTREPRENEURIAL
DECISION**

A1

**BTN 10-7**   Review the chapter's opening feature involving Games2U. Assume that the company currently has net sales of $8,000,000, and that it is planning an expansion that will increase net sales by $4,000,000. To accomplish this expansion, Games2U must increase its average total assets from $2,500,000 to $3,000,000.

*Required*

1. Compute the company's total asset turnover under (*a*) current conditions and (*b*) proposed conditions.
2. Evaluate and comment on the merits of the proposal given your analysis in part 1. Identify any concerns you would express about the proposal.

**BTN 10-8**   Team up with one or more classmates for this activity. Identify companies in your community or area that must account for at least one of the following assets: natural resource; patent; lease; leasehold improvement; copyright; trademark; or goodwill. You might find a company having more than one type of asset. Once you identify a company with a specific asset, describe the accounting this company uses to allocate the cost of that asset to the periods benefited from its use.

**HITTING THE ROAD**

P3   P4

**BTN 10-9**   **Nokia** (www.Nokia.com), **Research In Motion**, and **Apple** are all competitors in the global marketplace. Comparative figures for these companies' recent annual accounting periods follow.

**GLOBAL DECISION**

A1

**NOKIA**

*RIM*

Apple

| (in millions, except turnover) | Nokia (EUR millions) | | | Research In Motion | | Apple | |
|---|---|---|---|---|---|---|---|
| | Current Year | Prior Year | Two Years Prior | Current Year | Prior Year | Current Year | Prior Year |
| Total assets | 35,738 | 39,582 | 37,599 | $10,204 | $ 8,101 | $47,501 | $36,171 |
| Net sales | 40,984 | 50,710 | 51,058 | 14,953 | 11,065 | 42,905 | 37,491 |
| Total asset turnover | ? | ? | — | 1.63 | 1.63 | 1.03 | 1.22 |

*Required*

1. Compute total asset turnover for the most recent two years for Nokia using the data shown.
2. Which company is most efficient in generating net sales given the total assets it employs?

## ANSWERS TO MULTIPLE CHOICE QUIZ

**1.** b;

| | Appraisal Value | % | Total Cost | Allocated |
|---|---|---|---|---|
| Land | $175,000 | 50% | $326,000 | $163,000 |
| Land improvements | 70,000 | 20 | 326,000 | 65,200 |
| Building | 105,000 | 30 | 326,000 | 97,800 |
| Totals | $350,000 | | | $326,000 |

**2.** c; ($35,000 − $1,000)/4 years = $8,500 per year.
**3.** c; 2011: $10,800,000 × (2 × 10%) = $2,160,000
     2012: ($10,800,000 − $2,160,000) × (2 × 10%) = $1,728,000
**4.** c;

| | |
|---|---|
| Cost of machine | $250,000 |
| Accumulated depreciation | 100,000 |
| Book value | 150,000 |
| Cash received | 120,000 |
| Loss on sale | $ 30,000 |

**5.** b; $550,000/$500,000 = 1.10

# 11

# Current Liabilities and Payroll Accounting

## A Look Back

Chapter 10 focused on long-term assets including plant assets, natural resources, and intangibles. We showed how to account for and analyze those assets.

## A Look at This Chapter

This chapter explains how to identify, compute, record, and report current liabilities in financial statements. We also analyze and interpret these liabilities, including those related to employee costs.

## A Look Ahead

Chapter 12 explains the partnership form of organization. It also describes the accounting concepts and procedures for partnership transactions.

## Learning Objectives

### CONCEPTUAL

**C1** Describe current and long-term liabilities and their characteristics. (p. 436)

**C2** Identify and describe known current liabilities. (p. 438)

**C3** Explain how to account for contingent liabilities. (p. 448)

### ANALYTICAL

**A1** Compute the times interest earned ratio and use it to analyze liabilities. (p. 450)

LP11

### PROCEDURAL

**P1** Prepare entries to account for short-term notes payable. (p. 439)

**P2** Compute and record *employee* payroll deductions and liabilities. (p. 441)

**P3** Compute and record *employer* payroll expenses and liabilities. (p. 443)

**P4** Account for estimated liabilities, including warranties and bonuses. (p. 445)

**P5** *Appendix 11A*—Identify and describe the details of payroll reports, records, and procedures. (p. 453)

## No Stuffed Shirts

*"Part of the fun is the journey . . . working til 2 am every day"*
—MATT WALLS

ATLANTA, GA—Brothers Matt and Bryan Walls never planned to be entrepreneurs in the T-shirt business. "[It was] an idea we had while hanging out in our parents' basement," explains Matt. "We were naive and, like many first-time entrepreneurs, just dove right in." Matt and Bryan's plans involved making T-shirts with visual humor and pop culture themes. Their company, **SnorgTees (SnorgTees.com),** had a shaky start but soon found its groove with best-selling T-shirts such as "With a shirt like this, who needs pants?" "Don't act like you're not impressed," and "I'm kind of a big deal."

"We dreamed it would be successful overnight," recalls Matt. "But when things first started we had a huge reality check, and at that point I don't know if I believed." Today their business is thriving. Their commitment to success carries over to the financial side. They especially focus on the important task of managing liabilities for payroll, supplies, employee wages, training, and taxes. Both insist that effective management of liabilities, especially payroll and employee benefits, is crucial. They stress that monitoring and controlling liabilities are a must.

To help control liabilities, Matt and Bryan describe how they began by working out of their parents' home to reduce liabilities. "Most people think all we do is sit around and think up funny ideas," explains Matt. "In reality most of the time is spent on executing projects and managing the business . . . [including] order fulfillment, supply chain management, marketing, and accounting." In short, creative reduction of liabilities can mean success or failure.

The two continue to monitor liabilities and their payment patterns. "I'm pretty conservative about spending money," admits Matt. "If you want to run a successful company, you can't forget all the details." The two insist that accounting for and monitoring liabilities are one key to a successful start-up. Their company now generates sufficient income to pay for liabilities and produces revenue growth for expansion. "We plan to keep having fun," insists Matt. "We do business with people all over the world."

Sources: *SnorgTees Website,* January 2011; *Entrepreneur,* September 2009; *RetireAt21.com,* October 2008; *Business to Business,* January 2008; *WannaBeMogul.com,* November 2007.

Previous chapters introduced liabilities such as accounts payable, notes payable, wages payable, and unearned revenues. This chapter further explains these liabilities and additional ones such as warranties, taxes, payroll, vacation pay, and bonuses. It also describes contingent liabilities and introduces long-term liabilities. The focus is on how to define, classify, measure, report, and analyze these liabilities so that this information is useful to business decision makers.

**Current Liabilities and Payroll Accounting**

| Liability Characteristics | Known Liabilities | Estimated Liabilities | Contingent Liabilities |
|---|---|---|---|
| • Definition<br>• Classification<br>• Uncertainty | • Accounts payable<br>• Sales taxes payable<br>• Unearned revenues<br>• Short-term notes<br>• Payroll liabilities | • Health and pension benefits<br>• Vacation benefits<br>• Bonus plans<br>• Warranty liabilities | • Accounting for contingencies<br>• Reasonably possible contingencies |

# CHARACTERISTICS OF LIABILITIES

This section discusses important characteristics of liabilities and how liabilities are classified and reported.

## Defining Liabilities

**C1** Describe current and long-term liabilities and their characteristics.

A *liability* is a probable future payment of assets or services that a company is presently obligated to make as a result of past transactions or events. This definition includes three crucial factors:

1. A past transaction or event.
2. A present obligation.
3. A future payment of assets or services.

These three important elements are portrayed visually in Exhibit 11.1. Liabilities reported in financial statements exhibit those characteristics. No liability is reported when one or more of those characteristics is absent. For example, most companies expect to pay wages to their employees in upcoming months and years, but these future payments are *not* liabilities because no past event such as employee work resulted in a present obligation. Instead, such liabilities arise when employees perform their work and earn the wages.

**EXHIBIT 11.1**

Characteristics of a Liability

Due to a past event ...

Company has a present obligation

... For future sacrifices

Past — Present — Future

## Classifying Liabilities

Information about liabilities is more useful when the balance sheet identifies them as either current or long term. Decision makers need to know when obligations are due so they can plan for them and take appropriate action.

**Current Liabilities** **Current liabilities,** also called *short-term liabilities,* are obligations due within one year or the company's operating cycle, whichever is longer. They are expected to be paid using current assets or by creating other current liabilities. Common examples of current liabilities are accounts payable, short-term notes payable, wages payable, warranty liabilities, lease liabilities, taxes payable, and unearned revenues.

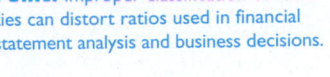
**Point:** Improper classification of liabilities can distort ratios used in financial statement analysis and business decisions.

Current liabilities differ across companies because they depend on the type of company operations. **MGM Mirage**, for instance, included the following current liabilities related to its gaming, hospitality and entertainment operations ($000s):

| | |
|---|---|
| Advance deposits and ticket sales | $104,911 |
| Casino outstanding chip liability | 83,957 |
| Casino front money deposits | 80,944 |

**Harley-Davidson** reports a much different set of current liabilities. It discloses current liabilities made up of items such as warranty, recall, and dealer incentive liabilities.

**Long-Term Liabilities** A company's obligations not expected to be paid within the longer of one year or the company's operating cycle are reported as **long-term liabilities.** They can include long-term notes payable, warranty liabilities, lease liabilities, and bonds payable. They are sometimes reported on the balance sheet in a single long-term liabilities total or in multiple categories. **Domino's Pizza**, for instance, reports long-term liabilities of $1,555 million. They are reported after current liabilities. A single liability also can be divided between the current and noncurrent sections if a company expects to make payments toward it in both the short and long term. Domino's reports ($ millions) long-term debt, $1,522; and current portion of long-term debt, $50. The second item is reported in current liabilities. We sometimes see liabilities that do not have a fixed due date but instead are payable on the creditor's demand. These are reported as current liabilities because of the possibility of payment in the near term. Exhibit 11.2 shows amounts of current liabilities and as a percent of total liabilities for selected companies.

**Point:** The current ratio is overstated if a company fails to classify any portion of long-term debt due next period as a current liability.

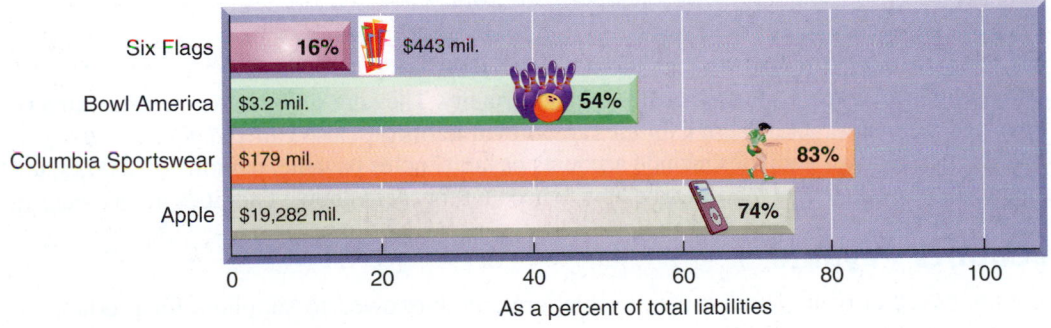

**EXHIBIT 11.2**

Current Liabilities of Selected Companies

| | |
|---|---|
| Six Flags | 16% $443 mil. |
| Bowl America | $3.2 mil. 54% |
| Columbia Sportswear | $179 mil. 83% |
| Apple | $19,282 mil. 74% |

As a percent of total liabilities

## Uncertainty in Liabilities

Accounting for liabilities involves addressing three important questions: Whom to pay? When to pay? How much to pay? Answers to these questions are often decided when a liability is incurred. For example, if a company has a $100 account payable to a specific individual, payable on March 15, the answers are clear. The company knows whom to pay, when to pay, and how much to pay. However, the answers to one or more of these questions are uncertain for some liabilities.

**Uncertainty in Whom to Pay** Liabilities can involve uncertainty in whom to pay. For instance, a company can create a liability with a known amount when issuing a note that is payable to its holder. In this case, a specific amount is payable to the note's holder at a specified date, but the company does not know who the holder is until that date. Despite this uncertainty, the company reports this liability on its balance sheet.

**Point:** An *accrued expense* is an unpaid expense, and is also called an *accrued liability.*

**Uncertainty in When to Pay** A company can have an obligation of a known amount to a known creditor but not know when it must be paid. For example, a legal services firm can accept fees in advance from a client who plans to use the firm's services in the future. This means that the firm has a liability that it settles by providing services at an unknown future date. Although this uncertainty exists, the legal firm's balance sheet must report this liability. These types of obligations are reported as current liabilities because they are likely to be settled in the short term.

**Uncertainty in How Much to Pay** A company can be aware of an obligation but not know how much will be required to settle it. For example, a company using electrical power is billed only after the meter has been read. This cost is incurred and the liability created before a bill is received. A liability to the power company is reported as an estimated amount if the balance sheet is prepared before a bill arrives.

 **IFRS** _____

IFRS records a contingent liability when an obligation exists from a past event if there is a 'probable' outflow of resources and the amount can be estimated reliably. However, IFRS defines probable as 'more likely than not' while U.S. GAAP defines it as 'likely to occur.' ■

---

**Quick Check** Answers — p. 461

1. What is a liability? Identify its crucial characteristics.
2. Is every expected future payment a liability?
3. If a liability is payable in 15 months, is it classified as current or long term?

---

# KNOWN LIABILITIES

 **C2** Identify and describe known current liabilities.

Most liabilities arise from situations with little uncertainty. They are set by agreements, contracts, or laws and are measurable. These liabilities are **known liabilities,** also called _definitely determinable liabilities._ Known liabilities include accounts payable, notes payable, payroll, sales taxes, unearned revenues, and leases. We describe how to account for these known liabilities in this section.

## Accounts Payable

Accounts payable, or trade accounts payable, are amounts owed to suppliers for products or services purchased on credit. Accounting for accounts payable is primarily explained and illustrated in our discussion of merchandising activities in Chapters 5 and 6.

## Sales Taxes Payable

Nearly all states and many cities levy taxes on retail sales. Sales taxes are stated as a percent of selling prices. The seller collects sales taxes from customers when sales occur and remits these collections (often monthly) to the proper government agency. Since sellers currently owe these collections to the government, this amount is a current liability. **Home Depot**, for instance, reports sales taxes payable of $362 million in its recent annual report. To illustrate, if Home Depot sells materials on August 31 for $6,000 cash that are subject to a 5% sales tax, the revenue portion of this transaction is recorded as follows:

Assets = Liabilities + Equity
+6,300    +300      +6,000

| Aug. 31 | Cash ........................................ | 6,300 | |
|---------|----------------------------------------------|-------|-------|
|         | Sales ...................................... | | 6,000 |
|         | Sales Taxes Payable ($6,000 × 0.05) .......... | | 300 |
|         | _To record cash sales and 5% sales tax._ | | |

Sales Taxes Payable is debited and Cash credited when it remits these collections to the government. Sales Taxes Payable
is not an expense. It arises because laws require sellers to
collect this cash from customers for the government.[1]

## Unearned Revenues

*Unearned revenues* (also called *deferred revenues, collections
in advance,* and *prepayments*) are amounts received in advance from customers for future products or services. Advance ticket sales for sporting events or music concerts are
examples. **Beyonce**, for instance, has "deferred revenues"
from advance ticket sales. To illustrate, assume that Beyonce
sells $5 million in tickets for eight concerts; the entry is

**Point:** To *defer* a revenue means to
postpone recognition of a revenue collected in advance until it is earned. Sport
teams must defer recognition of ticket
sales until games are played.

| June 30 | Cash .......................................... | 5,000,000 | |
| | Unearned Ticket Revenue ..................... | | 5,000,000 |
| | *To record sale of concert tickets.* | | |

|  Assets  | = | Liabilities | + | Equity |
|---|---|---|---|---|
| +5,000,000 | | +5,000,000 | | |

When a concert is played, Beyonce would record revenue for the portion earned.

| Oct. 31 | Unearned Ticket Revenue ......................... | 625,000 | |
| | Ticket Revenue ............................. | | 625,000 |
| | *To record concert ticket revenues earned.* | | |

| Assets | = | Liabilities | + | Equity |
|---|---|---|---|---|
| | | −625,000 | | +625,000 |

Unearned Ticket Revenue is an unearned revenue account and is reported as a current liability.
Unearned revenues also arise with airline ticket sales, magazine subscriptions, construction
projects, hotel reservations, and custom orders.

---

### 🔲 Decision **Insight**

**Reward Programs**   Gift card sales now exceed $100 billion annually, and reward (also called loyalty)
programs are growing. There are no exact rules for how retailers account for rewards. When **Best Buy**
launched its "Reward Zone," shoppers earned $5 on each $125 spent and had 90 days to spend it. Retailers make assumptions about how many reward program dollars will be spent and how to report it. Best
Buy sets up a liability and reduces revenue by the same amount. **Talbots** does not reduce revenue but
instead increases selling expense. **Men's Wearhouse** records rewards in cost of goods sold, whereas
**Neiman Marcus** subtracts them from revenue. The FASB continues to review reward programs. ■

---

## Short-Term Notes Payable

A **short-term note payable** is a written promise to pay a specified amount on a definite future
date within one year or the company's operating cycle, whichever is longer. These promissory
notes are negotiable (as are checks), meaning they can be transferred from party to party by
endorsement. The written documentation provided by notes is helpful in resolving disputes and
for pursuing legal actions involving these liabilities. Most notes payable bear interest to compensate for use of the money until payment is made. Short-term notes payable can arise from
many transactions. A company that purchases merchandise on credit can sometimes extend the
credit period by signing a note to replace an account payable. Such notes also can arise when
money is borrowed from a bank. We describe both of these cases.

**P1** Prepare entries to
account for short-term
notes payable.

**Point:** Required characteristics for
negotiability of a note: (1) unconditional
promise, (2) in writing, (3) specific
amount, and (4) definite due date.

---

[1] Sales taxes can be computed from total sales receipts when sales taxes are not separately identified on the register. To
illustrate, assume a 5% sales tax and $420 in total sales receipts (which includes sales taxes). Sales are computed as
follows:

$$\text{Sales} = \text{Total sales receipts}/(1 + \text{Sales tax percentage}) = \$420/1.05 = \$400$$

Thus, the sales tax amount equals total sales receipts minus sales, or $420 − $400 = $20.

**Note Given to Extend Credit Period**   A company can replace an account payable with a note payable. A common example is a creditor that requires the substitution of an interest-bearing note for an overdue account payable that does not bear interest. A less common situation occurs when a debtor's weak financial condition motivates the creditor to accept a note, sometimes for a lesser amount, and to close the account to ensure that this customer makes no additional credit purchases.

To illustrate, let's assume that on August 23, Brady Company asks to extend its past-due $600 account payable to McGraw. After some negotiations, McGraw agrees to accept $100 cash and a 60-day, 12%, $500 note payable to replace the account payable. Brady records the transaction with this entry:

Assets = Liabilities + Equity
−100        −600
            +500

| Aug. 23 | Accounts Payable—McGraw | 600 | |
|---|---|---|---|
| | Cash | | 100 |
| | Notes Payable—McGraw | | 500 |
| | *Gave $100 cash and a 60-day, 12% note for* | | |
| | *payment on account.* | | |

**Point:** Accounts payable are detailed in a subsidiary ledger, but notes payable are sometimes not. A file with copies of notes can serve as a subsidiary ledger.

Signing the note does not resolve Brady's debt. Instead, the form of debt is changed from an account payable to a note payable. McGraw prefers the note payable over the account payable because it earns interest and it is written documentation of the debt's existence, term, and amount. When the note comes due, Brady pays the note and interest by giving McGraw a check for $510. Brady records that payment with this entry:

Assets = Liabilities + Equity
−510        −500        −10

| Oct. 22 | Notes Payable—McGraw | 500 | |
|---|---|---|---|
| | Interest Expense | 10 | |
| | Cash | | 510 |
| | *Paid note with interest ($500 × 12% × 60/360).* | | |

**Point:** Commercial companies commonly compute interest using a 360-day year. This is known as the *banker's rule*.

Interest expense is computed by multiplying the principal of the note ($500) by the annual interest rate (12%) for the fraction of the year the note is outstanding (60 days/360 days).

**Note Given to Borrow from Bank**   A bank nearly always requires a borrower to sign a promissory note when making a loan. When the note matures, the borrower repays the note with an amount larger than the amount borrowed. The difference between the amount borrowed and the amount repaid is *interest*. This section considers a type of note whose signer promises to pay *principal* (the amount borrowed) plus interest. In this case, the *face value* of the note equals principal. Face value is the value shown on the face (front) of the note. To illustrate, assume that a company needs $2,000 for a project and borrows this money from a bank at 12% annual interest. The loan is made on September 30, 2011, and is due in 60 days. Specifically, the borrowing company signs a note with a face value equal to the amount borrowed. The note includes a statement similar to this: *"I promise to pay $2,000 plus interest at 12% within 60 days after September 30."* This simple note is shown in Exhibit 11.3.

**Point:** When money is borrowed from a bank, the loan is reported as an asset (receivable) on the bank's balance sheet.

**EXHIBIT 11.3**

Note with Face Value Equal to Amount Borrowed

The borrower records its receipt of cash and the new liability with this entry:

| Sept. 30 | Cash ........................................... | 2,000 | |
|---|---|---|---|
| | Notes Payable ............................ | | 2,000 |
| | *Borrowed $2,000 cash with a 60-day, 12%, $2,000 note.* | | |

Assets = Liabilities + Equity
+2,000    +2,000

When principal and interest are paid, the borrower records payment with this entry:

| Nov. 29 | Notes Payable .............................. | 2,000 | |
|---|---|---|---|
| | Interest Expense ............................ | 40 | |
| | Cash ..................................... | | 2,040 |
| | *Paid note with interest ($2,000 × 12% × 60/360).* | | |

Assets = Liabilities + Equity
−2,040    −2,000    −40

**End-of-period interest adjustment.**   When the end of an accounting period occurs between the signing of a note payable and its maturity date, the *matching principle* requires us to record the accrued but unpaid interest on the note. To illustrate, let's return to the note in Exhibit 11.3, but assume that the company borrows $2,000 cash on December 16, 2011, instead of September 30. This 60-day note matures on February 14, 2012, and the company's fiscal year ends on December 31. Thus, we need to record interest expense for the final 15 days in December. This means that one-fourth (15 days/60 days) of the $40 total interest is an expense of year 2011. The borrower records this expense with the following adjusting entry:

| 2011 | | | |
|---|---|---|---|
| Dec. 31 | Interest Expense ............................. | 10 | |
| | Interest Payable ........................... | | 10 |
| | *To record accrued interest on note ($2,000 × 12% × 15/360).* | | |

Assets = Liabilities + Equity
+10    −10

When this note matures on February 14, the borrower must recognize 45 days of interest expense for year 2012 and remove the balances of the two liability accounts:

| 2012 | | | |
|---|---|---|---|
| Feb. 14 | Interest Expense* ............................. | 30 | |
| | Interest Payable ............................. | 10 | |
| | Notes Payable ............................. | 2,000 | |
| | Cash ..................................... | | 2,040 |
| | *Paid note with interest. *($2,000 × 12% × 45/360)* | | |

**Example:** If this note is dated Dec. 1 instead of Dec. 16, how much expense is recorded on Dec. 31? *Answer:* $2,000 × 12% × 30/360 = $20

Assets = Liabilities + Equity
−2,040    −10    −30
          −2,000

### Decision Insight

Many franchisors such as **Baskin-Robbins**, **Dunkin' Donuts**, and **Cold Stone Creamery**, use notes to help entrepreneurs acquire their own franchises, including using notes to pay for the franchise fee and any equipment. Payments on these notes are usually collected monthly and often are secured by the franchisees' assets. ■

## Payroll Liabilities

An employer incurs several expenses and liabilities from having employees. These expenses and liabilities are often large and arise from salaries and wages earned, from employee benefits, and from payroll taxes levied on the employer. **Boston Beer**, for instance, reports payroll-related current liabilities of more than $6.6 million from accrued "employee wages, benefits and reimbursements." We discuss payroll liabilities and related accounts in this section. Appendix 11A describes details about payroll reports, records, and procedures.

**Employee Payroll Deductions**    **Gross pay** is the total compensation an employee earns including wages, salaries, commissions, bonuses, and any compensation earned before deductions such as taxes. (*Wages* usually refer to payments to employees at an hourly rate. *Salaries* usually refer to payments to employees at a monthly or yearly rate.) **Net pay,** also called *take-home pay,* is gross pay less all deductions. **Payroll deductions,** commonly called *withholdings,* are amounts withheld from an employee's gross pay, either required or voluntary. Required deductions result from laws and include income taxes and Social Security taxes. Voluntary deductions, at an employee's option, include pension and health contributions, health and life insurance premiums, union dues, and charitable giving. Exhibit 11.4 shows the typical payroll deductions of an employee. The employer withholds payroll deductions from employees' pay and is obligated to transmit this money to the designated organization. The employer records payroll deductions as current liabilities until these amounts are transmitted. This section discusses the major payroll deductions.

**Point:** Deductions at some companies, such as those for insurance coverage, are "required" under its own labor contracts.

**EXHIBIT 11.4**

Payroll Deductions

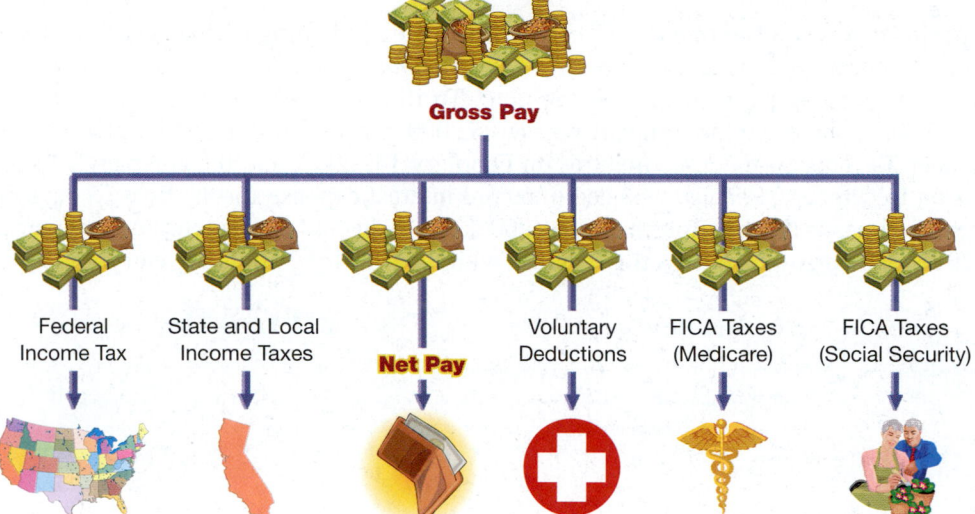

**Employee FICA taxes.**    The federal Social Security system provides retirement, disability, survivorship, and medical benefits to qualified workers. Laws *require* employers to withhold **Federal Insurance Contributions Act (FICA) taxes** from employees' pay to cover costs of the system. Employers usually separate FICA taxes into two groups: (1) retirement, disability, and survivorship and (2) medical. For the first group, the Social Security system provides monthly cash payments to qualified retired workers for the rest of their lives. These payments are often called *Social Security benefits.* Taxes related to this group are often called *Social Security taxes.* For the second group, the system provides monthly payments to deceased workers' surviving families and to disabled workers who qualify for assistance. These payments are commonly called *Medicare benefits;* like those in the first group, they are paid with *Medicare taxes* (part of FICA taxes).

Law requires employers to withhold FICA taxes from each employee's salary or wages on each payday. The taxes for Social Security and Medicare are computed separately. For example, for the year 2010, the amount withheld from each employee's pay for Social Security tax was 6.2% of the first $106,800 the employee earns in the calendar year, or a maximum of $6,621.60. The Medicare tax was 1.45% of *all* amounts the employee earns; there is no maximum limit to Medicare tax.

Employers must pay withheld taxes to the Internal Revenue Service (IRS) on specific filing dates during the year. Employers who fail to send the withheld taxes to the IRS on time can be assessed substantial penalties. Until all the taxes are sent to the IRS, they are included in employers' current liabilities. For any changes in rates or with the maximum earnings level, check the IRS Website at **www.IRS.gov** or the SSA Website at **www.SSA.gov**.

**Point:** The sources of U.S. tax receipts are roughly as follows:

| | |
|---|---|
| 50% | Personal income tax |
| 35 | FICA and FUTA taxes |
| 10 | Corporate income tax |
| 5 | Other taxes |

**Point:** Part-time employees may claim "exempt from withholding" if they did not have any income tax liability in the prior year and do not expect any in the current year.

**Employee income tax.**    Most employers are required to withhold federal income tax from each employee's paycheck. The amount withheld is computed using tables published by the IRS. The amount depends on the employee's annual earnings rate and the number of *withholding allowances* the employee claims. Allowances reduce the amount of taxes one owes the government. The more allowances one claims, the less tax the employer will withhold. Employees can claim allowances for themselves and their dependents. They also can claim additional allowances if they expect major declines in their taxable income for medical expenses. (An employee who claims more allowances than appropriate is subject to a fine.) Most states and many local governments require employers to withhold income taxes from employees' pay and to remit them promptly to the proper government agency. Until they are paid, withholdings are reported as a current liability on the employer's balance sheet.

**Point:** IRS withholding tables are based on projecting weekly (or other period) pay into an annual figure.

**Employee voluntary deductions.**   Beyond Social Security, Medicare, and income taxes, employers often withhold other amounts from employees' earnings. These withholdings arise from employee requests, contracts, unions, or other agreements. They can include amounts for charitable giving, medical and life insurance premiums, pension contributions, and union dues. Until they are paid, such withholdings are reported as part of employers' current liabilities.

**Recording employee payroll deductions.**   Employers must accrue payroll expenses and liabilities at the end of each pay period. To illustrate, assume that an employee earns a salary of $2,000 per month. At the end of January, the employer's entry to accrue payroll expenses and liabilities for this employee is

| Jan. 31 | Salaries Expense ............................... | 2,000 | |
|---|---|---|---|
| | FICA—Social Security Taxes Payable (6.2%) ...... | | 124 |
| | FICA—Medicare Taxes Payable (1.45%) ......... | | 29 |
| | Employee Federal Income Taxes Payable* ........ | | 213 |
| | Employee Medical Insurance Payable* .......... | | 85 |
| | Employee Union Dues Payable* .............. | | 25 |
| | Salaries Payable ........................... | | 1,524 |
| | *To record accrued payroll for January.* | | |

\* Amounts taken from employer's accounting records.

| Assets | = | Liabilities | + | Equity |
|---|---|---|---|---|
| | | +124 | | −2,000 |
| | | +29 | | |
| | | +213 | | |
| | | +85 | | |
| | | +25 | | |
| | | +1,524 | | |

Salaries Expense (debit) shows that the employee earns a gross salary of $2,000. The first five payables (credits) show the liabilities the employer owes on behalf of this employee to cover FICA taxes, income taxes, medical insurance, and union dues. The Salaries Payable account (credit) records the $1,524 net pay the employee receives from the $2,000 gross pay earned. When the employee is paid, another entry (or a series of entries) is required to record the check written and distributed (or funds transferred). The entry to record cash payment to this employee is to debit Salaries Payable and credit Cash for $1,524.

| Salaries Payable .... | 1,524 | |
|---|---|---|
| Cash ........... | | 1,524 |

---

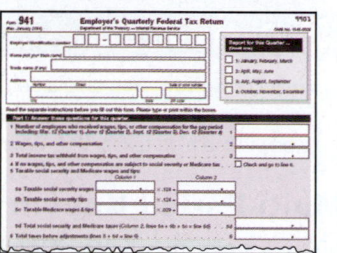

### Decision Insight

A company's delay or failure to pay withholding taxes to the government has severe consequences. For example, a 100% penalty can be levied, with interest, on the unpaid balance. The government can even close a company, take its assets, and pursue legal actions against those involved.

---

**Employer Payroll Taxes**   Employers must pay payroll taxes in addition to those required of employees. Employer taxes include FICA and unemployment taxes.

**Employer FICA tax.**   Employers must pay FICA taxes *equal in amount to* the FICA taxes withheld from their employees. An employer's tax is credited to the same FICA Taxes Payable accounts used to record the Social Security and Medicare taxes withheld from employees. (A self-employed person must pay both the employee and employer FICA taxes.)

**P3**   Compute and record *employer* payroll expenses and liabilities.

**Federal and state unemployment taxes.** The federal government participates with states in a joint federal and state unemployment insurance program. Each state administers its program. These programs provide unemployment benefits to qualified workers. The federal government approves state programs and pays a portion of their administrative expenses.

*Federal Unemployment Taxes (FUTA).* Employers are subject to a federal unemployment tax on wages and salaries paid to their employees. For the year 2010, employers were required to pay FUTA taxes of as much as 6.2% of the first $7,000 earned by each employee. This federal tax can be reduced by a credit of up to 5.4% for taxes paid to a state program. As a result, the net federal unemployment tax is often only 0.8%.

*State Unemployment Taxes (SUTA).* All states support their unemployment insurance programs by placing a payroll tax on employers. (A few states require employees to make a contribution. In the book's assignments, we assume that this tax is only on the employer.) In most states, the base rate for SUTA taxes is 5.4% of the first $7,000 paid each employee. This base rate is adjusted according to an employer's merit rating. The state assigns a **merit rating** that reflects a company's stability or instability in employing workers. A good rating reflects stability in employment and means an employer can pay less than the 5.4% base rate. A low rating reflects high turnover or seasonal hirings and layoffs. To illustrate, an employer with 50 employees each of whom earns $7,000 or more per year saves $15,400 annually if it has a merit rating of 1.0% versus 5.4%. This is computed by comparing taxes of $18,900 at the 5.4% rate to only $3,500 at the 1.0% rate.

**Recording employer payroll taxes.** Employer payroll taxes are an added expense beyond the wages and salaries earned by employees. These taxes are often recorded in an entry separate from the one recording payroll expenses and deductions. To illustrate, assume that the $2,000 recorded salaries expense from the previous example is earned by an employee whose earnings have not yet reached $5,000 for the year. This means the entire salaries expense for this period is subject to tax because year-to-date pay is under $7,000. Also assume that the federal unemployment tax rate is 0.8% and the state unemployment tax rate is 5.4%. Consequently, the FICA portion of the employer's tax is $153, computed by multiplying both the 6.2% and 1.45% by the $2,000 gross pay. Moreover, state unemployment (SUTA) taxes are $108 (5.4% of the $2,000 gross pay), and federal unemployment (FUTA) taxes are $16 (0.8% of $2,000). The entry to record the employer's payroll tax expense and related liabilities is

**Example:** If the employer's merit rating in this example reduces its SUTA rate to 2.9%, what is its SUTA liability?
*Answer:* SUTA payable = $2,000 × 2.9% = $58

Assets = Liabilities + Equity
+124     −277
+29
+108
+16

| Jan. 31 | Payroll Taxes Expense | 277 | |
|---------|----------------------|-----|-----|
| | FICA—Social Security Taxes Payable (6.2%) | | 124 |
| | FICA—Medicare Taxes Payable (1.45%) | | 29 |
| | State Unemployment Taxes Payable | | 108 |
| | Federal Unemployment Taxes Payable | | 16 |
| | *To record employer payroll taxes.* | | |

**Point:** Internal control is important for payroll accounting. Managers must monitor (1) employee hiring, (2) time-keeping, (3) payroll listings, and (4) payroll payments. Poor controls led the U.S. Army to pay nearly $10 million to deserters, fictitious soldiers, and other unauthorized entities.

 **Decision Ethics**      Answer — p. 460

**Web Designer** You take a summer job working for a family friend who runs a small IT service. On your first payday, the owner slaps you on the back, gives you full payment in cash, winks, and adds: "No need to pay those high taxes, eh." What action, if any, do you take? ■

## Multi-Period Known Liabilities

Many known liabilities extend over multiple periods. These often include unearned revenues and notes payable. For example, if **Sports Illustrated** sells a four-year magazine subscription, it records amounts received for this subscription in an Unearned Subscription Revenues account. Amounts in this account are liabilities, but are they current or long term? They are *both*. The portion of the Unearned Subscription Revenues account that will be fulfilled in the next year is reported as a current liability. The remaining portion is reported as a long-term liability.

The same analysis applies to notes payable. For example, a borrower reports a three-year note payable as a long-term liability in the first two years it is outstanding. In the third year, the borrower reclassifies this note as a current liability since it is due within one year or the operating cycle, whichever is longer. The **current portion of long-term debt** refers to that part of long-term debt due within one year or the operating cycle, whichever is longer. Long-term debt is reported under long-term liabilities, but the *current portion due* is reported under current liabilities. To illustrate, assume that a $7,500 debt is paid in installments of $1,500 per year for five years. The $1,500 due within the year is reported as a current liability. No journal entry is necessary for this reclassification. Instead, we simply classify the amounts for debt as either current or long term when the balance sheet is prepared.

Some known liabilities are rarely reported in long-term liabilities. These include accounts payable, sales taxes, and wages and salaries.

**Point:** Some accounting systems do make an entry to transfer the current amount due out of Long-Term Debt and into the Current Portion of Long-Term Debt as follows:

Long-Term Debt .......... 1,500
  Current Portion of L-T Debt ... 1,500

### Decision Insight

**Liability Limits**  Probably the greatest number of frauds involve payroll. Companies must safeguard payroll activities. Controls include proper approvals and processes for employee additions, deletions, and pay rate changes. A common fraud is a manager adding a fictitious employee to the payroll and then cashing the fictitious employee's check. A study reports that 28% of employees in operations and service areas witnessed violations of employee wage, overtime, or benefit rules in the past year (KPMG 2009). Another 21% observed falsifying of time and expense reports. ■

### Quick Check

Answers — p. 461

4. Why does a creditor prefer a note payable to a past-due account payable?
5. A company pays its one employee $3,000 per month. This company's FUTA rate is 0.8% on the first $7,000 earned; its SUTA rate is 4.0% on the first $7,000; its Social Security tax rate is 6.2% of the first $106,800; and its Medicare tax rate is 1.45% of all amounts earned. The entry to record this company's March payroll includes what amount for total payroll taxes expense?
6. Identify whether the employer or employee or both incurs each of the following: (*a*) FICA taxes, (*b*) FUTA taxes, (*c*) SUTA taxes, and (*d*) withheld income taxes.

## ESTIMATED LIABILITIES

An **estimated liability** is a known obligation that is of an uncertain amount but that can be reasonably estimated. Common examples are employee benefits such as pensions, health care and vacation pay, and warranties offered by a seller. We discuss each of these in this section. Other examples of estimated liabilities include property taxes and certain contracts to provide future services.

**P4** Account for estimated liabilities, including warranties and bonuses.

### Health and Pension Benefits

Many companies provide **employee benefits** beyond salaries and wages. An employer often pays all or part of medical, dental, life, and disability insurance. Many employers also contribute to *pension plans,* which are agreements by employers to provide benefits (payments) to employees after retirement. Many companies also provide medical care and insurance benefits to their retirees. When payroll taxes and charges for employee benefits are totaled, payroll cost often exceeds employees' gross earnings by 25% or more.

To illustrate, assume that an employer agrees to (1) pay an amount for medical insurance equal to $8,000 and (2) contribute an additional 10% of the employees' $120,000 gross salary to a retirement program. The entry to record these accrued benefits is

| | | | |
|---|---|---|---|
| Dec. 31 | Employee Benefits Expense ....................... | 20,000 | |
| | Employee Medical Insurance Payable .......... | | 8,000 |
| | Employee Retirement Program Payable ........ | | 12,000 |
| | *To record costs of employee benefits.* | | |

Assets = Liabilities + Equity
    +8,000  −20,000
    +12,000

## Decision Insight

**Postgame Spoils** Baseball was the first pro sport to set up a pension, originally up to $100 per month depending on years played. Many former players now take home six-figure pensions. Cal Ripken Jr.'s pension when he reaches 62 is estimated at $160,000 per year (he played 21 seasons). The requirement is only 43 games for a full pension and just one game for full medical benefits. ■

## Vacation Benefits

Many employers offer paid vacation benefits, also called *paid absences*. To illustrate, assume that salaried employees earn 2 weeks' vacation per year. This benefit increases employers' payroll expenses because employees are paid for 52 weeks but work for only 50 weeks. Total annual salary is the same, but the cost per week worked is greater than the amount paid per week. For example, if an employee is paid $20,800 for 52 weeks but works only 50 weeks, the total weekly expense to the employer is $416 ($20,800/50 weeks) instead of the $400 cash paid weekly to the employee ($20,800/52 weeks). The $16 difference between these two amounts is recorded weekly as follows:

Assets = Liabilities + Equity
+16              −16

| | | |
|---|---|---|
| Vacation Benefits Expense . . . . . . . . . . . . . . . . . . . . . . . | 16 | |
| Vacation Benefits Payable . . . . . . . . . . . . . . . . . . . . . | | 16 |
| *To record vacation benefits accrued.* | | |

Vacation Benefits Payable . . . . #
  Cash . . . . . . . . . . . . . . . . . . . . #

Vacation Benefits Expense is an operating expense, and Vacation Benefits Payable is a current liability. When the employee takes a vacation, the employer reduces (debits) the Vacation Benefits Payable and credits Cash (no additional expense is recorded).

## Bonus Plans

Many companies offer bonuses to employees, and many of the bonuses depend on net income. To illustrate, assume that an employer offers a bonus to its employees equal to 5% of the company's annual net income (to be equally shared by all). The company's expected annual net income is $210,000. The year-end adjusting entry to record this benefit is

Assets = Liabilities + Equity
+10,000         −10,000

| Dec. 31 | Employee Bonus Expense* . . . . . . . . . . . . . . . . . . . . . . | 10,000 | |
|---|---|---|---|
| | Bonus Payable . . . . . . . . . . . . . . . . . . . . . . . . . . . . . | | 10,000 |
| | *To record expected bonus costs.* | | |

\* Bonus Expense (B) equals 5% of net income, which equals $210,000 minus the bonus; this is computed as:

$$B = 0.05 (\$210,000 − B)$$
$$B = \$10,500 − 0.05B$$
$$1.05B = \$10,500$$
$$\mathbf{B = \$10,500/1.05 = \$10,000}$$

When the bonus is paid, Bonus Payable is debited and Cash is credited for $10,000.

## Warranty Liabilities

**Point: Kodak** recently reported $60 million in warranty obligations.

A **warranty** is a seller's obligation to replace or correct a product (or service) that fails to perform as expected within a specified period. Most new cars, for instance, are sold with a warranty covering parts for a specified period of time. **Ford Motor Company** reported more than $15 billion in "dealer and customer allowances and claims" in its annual report. To comply with the *full disclosure* and *matching principles,* the seller reports the expected warranty expense in the period when revenue from the sale of the product or service is reported. The seller reports this warranty obligation as a liability, although the existence, amount, payee, and date of future sacrifices are uncertain. This is because such warranty costs are probable and the amount can be estimated using, for instance, past experience with warranties.

To illustrate, a dealer sells a used car for $16,000 on December 1, 2011, with a maximum one-year or 12,000-mile warranty covering parts. This dealer's experience shows that warranty expense averages about 4% of a car's selling price, or $640 in this case ($16,000 × 4%). The dealer records the estimated expense and liability related to this sale with this entry:

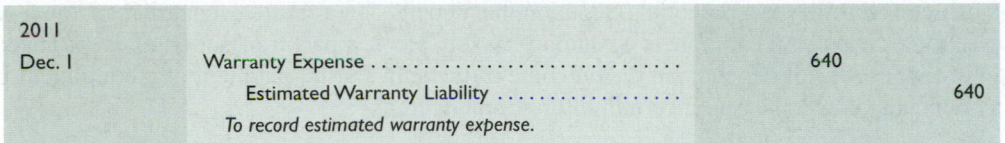

| 2011 | | | |
|------|---|---|---|
| Dec. 1 | Warranty Expense . . . . . . . . . . . . . . . . . . . . . . . . . . . . . | 640 | |
| | Estimated Warranty Liability . . . . . . . . . . . . . . . . . | | 640 |
| | *To record estimated warranty expense.* | | |

Assets = Liabilities + Equity
+640          −640

This entry alternatively could be made as part of end-of-period adjustments. Either way, the estimated warranty expense is reported on the 2011 income statement and the warranty liability on the 2011 balance sheet. To further extend this example, suppose the customer returns the car for warranty repairs on January 9, 2012. The dealer performs this work by replacing parts costing $200. The entry to record partial settlement of the estimated warranty liability is

**Point:** Recognition of warranty liabilities is necessary to comply with the matching and full disclosure principles.

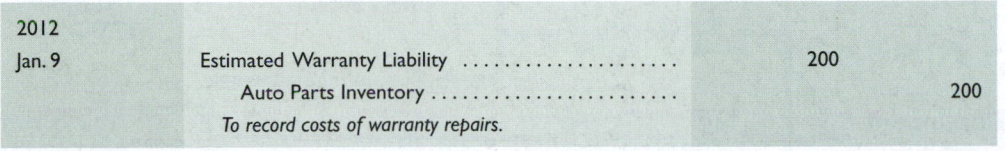

| 2012 | | | |
|------|---|---|---|
| Jan. 9 | Estimated Warranty Liability . . . . . . . . . . . . . . . . . . . . | 200 | |
| | Auto Parts Inventory . . . . . . . . . . . . . . . . . . . . . . . | | 200 |
| | *To record costs of warranty repairs.* | | |

Assets = Liabilities + Equity
−200          −200

This entry reduces the balance of the estimated warranty liability. Warranty expense was previously recorded in 2011, the year the car was sold with the warranty. Finally, what happens if total warranty expenses are more or less than the estimated 4%, or $640? The answer is that management should monitor actual warranty expenses to see whether the 4% rate is accurate. If experience reveals a large difference from the estimate, the rate for current and future sales should be changed. Differences are expected, but they should be small.

**Point:** Both U.S. GAAP and IFRS account for restructuring costs in a manner similar to accounting for warranties.

### Decision Insight

**Guaranteed Profits**  **Best Buy** earns a 60% profit margin on its warranty contracts, and those contracts are a large part of its profit—see table to the side [*BusinessWeek*]. ■

| | |
|---|---|
| Warranty contracts as a percentage of sales . . . . | 4% |
| Warranty contracts as a percentage of operating profit . . . . . . . . . . . . . . . . . . . . . . | 45% |
| Profit margin on warranty contracts . . . . . . . . . . | 60% |

## Multi-Period Estimated Liabilities

Estimated liabilities can be both current and long term. For example, pension liabilities to employees are long term to workers who will not retire within the next period. For employees who are retired or will retire within the next period, a portion of pension liabilities is current. Other examples include employee health benefits and warranties. Specifically, many warranties are for 30 or 60 days in length. Estimated costs under these warranties are properly reported in current liabilities. Many other automobile warranties are for three years or 36,000 miles. A portion of these warranties is reported as long term.

### Quick Check                                         Answers — p. 461

7. Estimated liabilities involve an obligation to pay which of these? (*a*) An uncertain but reasonably estimated amount owed on a known obligation or (*b*) A known amount to a specific entity on an uncertain due date.

8. A car is sold for $15,000 on June 1, 2011, with a one-year warranty on parts. Warranty expense is estimated at 1.5% of selling price at each calendar year-end. On March 1, 2012, the car is returned for warranty repairs costing $135. The amount recorded as warranty expense on March 1 is (*a*) $0; (*b*) $60; (*c*) $75; (*d*) $135; (*e*) $225.

## CONTINGENT LIABILITIES

 **C3** Explain how to account for contingent liabilities.

A **contingent liability** is a potential obligation that depends on a future event arising from a past transaction or event. An example is a pending lawsuit. Here, a past transaction or event leads to a lawsuit whose result depends on the outcome of the suit. Future payment of a contingent liability depends on whether an uncertain future event occurs.

### Accounting for Contingent Liabilities

Accounting for contingent liabilities depends on the likelihood that a future event will occur and the ability to estimate the future amount owed if this event occurs. Three different possibilities are identified in the following chart: record liability, disclose in notes, or no disclosure.

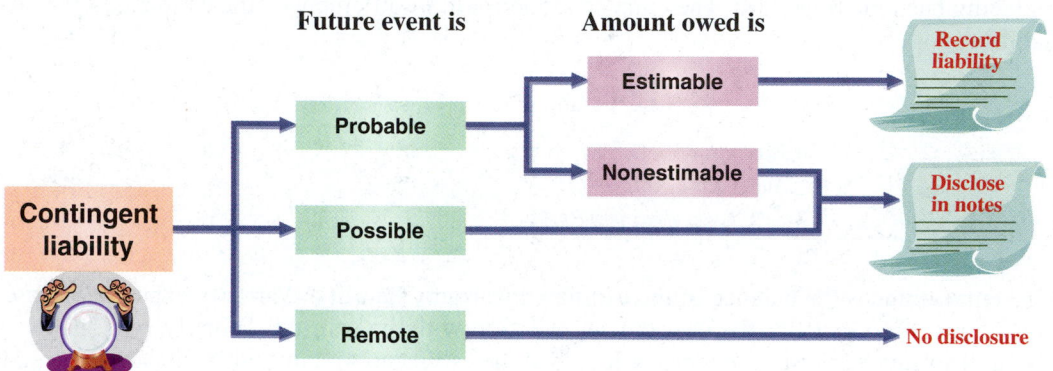

The conditions that determine each of these three possibilities follow:

1. The future event is *probable* (likely) and the amount owed can be *reasonably estimated.* We then record this amount as a liability. Examples are the estimated liabilities described earlier such as warranties, vacation pay, and income taxes.
2. The future event is *reasonably possible* (could occur). We disclose information about this type of contingent liability in notes to the financial statements.
3. The future event is *remote* (unlikely). We do not record or disclose information on remote contingent liabilities.

**Point:** A contingency is an *if*. Namely, if a future event occurs, then financial consequences are likely for the entity.

### Reasonably Possible Contingent Liabilities

This section identifies and discusses contingent liabilities that commonly fall in the second category—when the future event is reasonably possible. Disclosing information about contingencies in this category is motivated by the *full-disclosure principle,* which requires information relevant to decision makers be reported and not ignored.

**Point:** A sale of a note receivable is often a contingent liability. It becomes a liability if the original signer of the note fails to pay it at maturity.

**Potential Legal Claims**   Many companies are sued or at risk of being sued. The accounting issue is whether the defendant should recognize a liability on its balance sheet or disclose a contingent liability in its notes while a lawsuit is outstanding and not yet settled. The answer is that a potential claim is recorded in the accounts *only* if payment for damages is probable and the amount can be reasonably estimated. If the potential claim cannot be reasonably estimated or is less than probable but reasonably possible, it is disclosed. **Ford Motor Company**, for example, includes the following note in its annual report: "Various legal actions, governmental investigations and proceedings and claims are pending . . . arising out of alleged defects in our products."

**Debt Guarantees**   Sometimes a company guarantees the payment of debt owed by a supplier, customer, or another company. The guarantor usually discloses the guarantee in its financial statement notes as a contingent liability. If it is probable that the debtor will default, the guarantor needs to record and report the guarantee in its financial statements as a liability. The **Boston Celtics** report a unique guarantee when it comes to coaches and players: "Certain of the contracts provide for guaranteed payments which must be paid even if the employee [player] is injured or terminated."

**Other Contingencies**   Other examples of contingencies include environmental damages, possible tax assessments, insurance losses, and government investigations. **Sunoco**, for instance, reports that "federal, state and local laws . . . result in liabilities and loss contingencies. Sunoco accrues . . . cleanup costs [that] are probable and reasonably estimable. Management believes it is reasonably possible (i.e., less than probable but greater than remote) that additional . . . losses will be incurred." Many of Sunoco's contingencies are revealed only in notes.

**Point:** Auditors and managers often have different views about whether a contingency is recorded, disclosed, or omitted.

### Decision Insight

**Pricing Priceless**   What's it worth to see from one side of the Grand Canyon to the other? What's the cost when gulf coast beaches are closed due to an oil well disaster? A method to measure environmental liabilities is *contingent valuation*, by which people answer such questions. Regulators use their answers to levy fines and assess punitive damages. ■

## Uncertainties that Are Not Contingencies

All organizations face uncertainties from future events such as natural disasters and the development of new competing products or services. These uncertainties are not contingent liabilities because they are future events *not* arising from past transactions. Accordingly, they are not disclosed.

### Quick Check                                         Answers — p. 461

9. A future payment is reported as a liability on the balance sheet if payment is contingent on a future event that (a) is reasonably possible but the payment cannot be reasonably estimated; (b) is probable and the payment can be reasonably estimated; or (c) is not probable but the payment is known.

10. Under what circumstances is a future payment reported in the notes to the financial statements as a contingent liability?

## GLOBAL VIEW

This section discusses similarities and differences between U.S. GAAP and IFRS in accounting and reporting for current liabilities.

**Characteristics of Liabilities**   The definitions and characteristics of current liabilities are broadly similar for both U.S. GAAP and IFRS. Although differences exist, the similarities vastly outweigh any differences. Remembering that "provision" is typically used under IFRS to refer to what is titled "liability" under U.S. GAAP, **Nokia** describes its recognition of liabilities as follows:

> Provisions are recognized when the Group has a present legal or constructive obligation as a result of past events, it is probable that an outflow of resources will be required to settle the obligation and a reliable estimate of the amount can be made.

**NOKIA**

**Known (Determinable) Liabilities**   When there is little uncertainty surrounding current liabilities, both U.S. GAAP and IFRS require companies to record them in a similar manner. This correspondence in accounting applies to accounts payable, sales taxes payable, unearned revenues, short-term notes, and payroll liabilities. Of course, tax regulatory systems of countries are different, which implies use of different rates and levels. Still, the basic approach is the same.

**Estimated Liabilities**   When there is a known current obligation that involves an uncertain amount, but one that can be reasonably estimated, both U.S. GAAP and IFRS require similar treatment. This treatment extends to many obligations such as those arising from vacations, warranties, restructurings, pensions, and health care. Both accounting systems require that companies record estimated expenses related to these obligations when they can reasonably estimate the amounts. **Nokia** reports wages, salaries and bonuses of €5,658 million. It also reports pension expenses of €427 million.

## Decision Analysis ▉▉▉                                          Times Interest Earned Ratio

 **A1** Compute the times interest earned ratio and use it to analyze liabilities.

A company incurs interest expense on many of its current and long-term liabilities. Examples extend from its short-term notes and the current portion of long-term liabilities to its long-term notes and bonds. Interest expense is often viewed as a *fixed expense* because the amount of these liabilities is likely to remain in one form or another for a substantial period of time. This means that the amount of interest is unlikely to vary due to changes in sales or other operating activities. While fixed expenses can be advantageous when a company is growing, they create risk. This risk stems from the possibility that a company might be unable to pay fixed expenses if sales decline. To illustrate, consider Diego Co.'s results for 2011 and two possible outcomes for year 2012 in Exhibit 11.5.

**EXHIBIT 11.5**

Actual and Projected Results

| ($ thousands) | 2011 | 2012 Projections | |
| --- | --- | --- | --- |
| | | Sales Increase | Sales Decrease |
| Sales ........................ | $600 | $900 | $300 |
| Expenses (75% of sales) ......... | 450 | 675 | 225 |
| Income before interest ......... | 150 | 225 | 75 |
| Interest expense (fixed) ......... | 60 | 60 | 60 |
| Net income ................. | $ 90 | $165 | $ 15 |

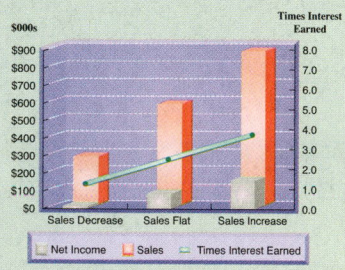

Expenses excluding interest are at, and expected to remain at, 75% of sales. Expenses such as these that change with sales volume are called *variable expenses*. However, interest expense is at, and expected to remain at, $60,000 per year due to its fixed nature.

The middle numerical column of Exhibit 11.5 shows that Diego's income increases by 83% to $165,000 if sales increase by 50% to $900,000. In contrast, the far right column shows that income decreases by 83% if sales decline by 50%. These results reveal that the amount of fixed interest expense affects a company's risk of its ability to pay interest, which is numerically reflected in the **times interest earned** ratio in Exhibit 11.6.

**EXHIBIT 11.6**

Times Interest Earned

$$\text{Times interest earned} = \frac{\text{Income before interest expense and income taxes}}{\text{Interest expense}}$$

For 2011, Diego's times interest earned is computed as $150,000/$60,000, or 2.5 times. This ratio suggests that Diego faces low to moderate risk because its sales must decline sharply before it would be unable to cover its interest expenses. (Diego is an LLC and does not pay income taxes.)

Experience shows that when times interest earned falls below 1.5 to 2.0 and remains at that level or lower for several periods, the default rate on liabilities increases sharply. This reflects increased risk for companies and their creditors. We also must interpret the times interest earned ratio in light of information about the variability of a company's income before interest. If income is stable from year to year or if it is growing, the company can afford to take on added risk by borrowing. If its income greatly varies from year to year, fixed interest expense can increase the risk that it will not earn enough income to pay interest.

■ **Decision Maker**                                              Answer — p. 461

**Entrepreneur**   You wish to invest in a franchise for either one of two national chains. Each franchise has an expected annual net income *after* interest and taxes of $100,000. Net income for the first franchise includes a regular fixed interest charge of $200,000. The fixed interest charge for the second franchise is $40,000. Which franchise is riskier to you if sales forecasts are not met? Does your decision change if the first franchise has more variability in its income stream? ■

## DEMONSTRATION PROBLEM

The following transactions and events took place at Kern Company during its recent calendar-year reporting period (Kern does not use reversing entries).

**a.** In September 2011, Kern sold $140,000 of merchandise covered by a 180-day warranty. Prior experience shows that costs of the warranty equal 5% of sales. Compute September's warranty expense and prepare the adjusting journal entry for the warranty liability as recorded at September 30. Also prepare the journal entry on October 8 to record a $300 cash expenditure to provide warranty service on an item sold in September.

**b.** On October 12, 2011, Kern arranged with a supplier to replace Kern's overdue $10,000 account payable by paying $2,500 cash and signing a note for the remainder. The note matures in 90 days and has a 12% interest rate. Prepare the entries recorded on October 12, December 31, and January 10, 2012, related to this transaction.

**c.** In late December, Kern learns it is facing a product liability suit filed by an unhappy customer. Kern's lawyer advises that although it will probably suffer a loss from the lawsuit, it is not possible to estimate the amount of damages at this time.

**d.** Sally Bline works for Kern. For the pay period ended November 30, her gross earnings are $3,000. Bline has $800 deducted for federal income taxes and $200 for state income taxes from each paycheck. Additionally, a $35 premium for her health care insurance and a $10 donation for the United Way are deducted. Bline pays FICA Social Security taxes at a rate of 6.2% and FICA Medicare taxes at a rate of 1.45%. She has not earned enough this year to be exempt from any FICA taxes. Journalize the accrual of salaries expense of Bline's wages by Kern.

**e.** On November 1, Kern borrows $5,000 cash from a bank in return for a 60-day, 12%, $5,000 note. Record the note's issuance on November 1 and its repayment with interest on December 31.

**f.**[B] Kern has estimated and recorded its quarterly income tax payments. In reviewing its year-end tax adjustments, it identifies an additional $5,000 of income tax expense that should be recorded. A portion of this additional expense, $1,000, is deferrable to future years. Record this year-end income taxes expense adjusting entry.

**g.** For this calendar-year, Kern's net income is $1,000,000, its interest expense is $275,000, and its income taxes expense is $225,000. Calculate Kern's times interest earned ratio.

### PLANNING THE SOLUTION

● For *a,* compute the warranty expense for September and record it with an estimated liability. Record the October expenditure as a decrease in the liability.

● For *b,* eliminate the liability for the account payable and create the liability for the note payable. Compute interest expense for the 80 days that the note is outstanding in 2011 and record it as an additional liability. Record the payment of the note, being sure to include the interest for the 10 days in 2012.

● For *c,* decide whether the company's contingent liability needs to be disclosed or accrued (recorded) according to the two necessary criteria: probable loss and reasonably estimable.

● For *d,* set up payable accounts for all items in Bline's paycheck that require deductions. After deducting all necessary items, credit the remaining amount to Salaries Payable.

● For *e,* record the issuance of the note. Calculate 60 days' interest due using the 360-day convention in the interest formula.

● For *f,* determine how much of the income taxes expense is payable in the current year and how much needs to be deferred.

● For *g,* apply and compute times interest earned.

## SOLUTION TO DEMONSTRATION PROBLEM

**a.** Warranty expense = 5% × $140,000 = $7,000

| | | | |
|---|---|---|---|
| Sept. 30 | Warranty Expense . . . . . . . . . . . . . . . . . . . . . . . . . . . . . . | 7,000 | |
| | Estimated Warranty Liability . . . . . . . . . . . . . . . . . . | | 7,000 |
| | *To record warranty expense for the month.* | | |
| Oct.  8 | Estimated Warranty Liability . . . . . . . . . . . . . . . . . . . . | 300 | |
| | Cash . . . . . . . . . . . . . . . . . . . . . . . . . . . . . . . . . . . . . . | | 300 |
| | *To record the cost of the warranty service.* | | |

**b.** Interest expense for 2011 = 12% × $7,500 × 80/360 = $200
Interest expense for 2012 = 12% × $7,500 × 10/360 = $25

| | | | |
|---|---|---|---|
| Oct. 12 | Accounts Payable . . . . . . . . . . . . . . . . . . . . . . . . . . . . . | 10,000 | |
| | Notes Payable . . . . . . . . . . . . . . . . . . . . . . . . . . . . . | | 7,500 |
| | Cash . . . . . . . . . . . . . . . . . . . . . . . . . . . . . . . . . . . . . . | | 2,500 |
| | *Paid $2,500 cash and gave a 90-day, 12% note* | | |
| | *to extend the due date on the account.* | | |
| Dec. 31 | Interest Expense . . . . . . . . . . . . . . . . . . . . . . . . . . . . . | 200 | |
| | Interest Payable . . . . . . . . . . . . . . . . . . . . . . . . . . . . | | 200 |
| | *To accrue interest on note payable.* | | |
| Jan.  10 | Interest Expense . . . . . . . . . . . . . . . . . . . . . . . . . . . . . | 25 | |
| | Interest Payable . . . . . . . . . . . . . . . . . . . . . . . . . . . . . | 200 | |
| | Notes Payable . . . . . . . . . . . . . . . . . . . . . . . . . . . . . . | 7,500 | |
| | Cash . . . . . . . . . . . . . . . . . . . . . . . . . . . . . . . . . . . . . . | | 7,725 |
| | *Paid note with interest, including the accrued* | | |
| | *interest payable.* | | |

**c.** Disclose the pending lawsuit in the financial statement notes. Although the loss is probable, no liability can be accrued since the loss cannot be reasonably estimated.

**d.**

| | | | |
|---|---|---|---|
| Nov. 30 | Salaries Expense . . . . . . . . . . . . . . . . . . . . . . . . . . . . . | 3,000.00 | |
| | FICA—Social Security Taxes Payable (6.2%) . . . . . | | 186.00 |
| | FICA—Medicare Taxes Payable (1.45%) . . . . . . . . . | | 43.50 |
| | Employee Federal Income Taxes Payable . . . . . . . . | | 800.00 |
| | Employee State Income Taxes Payable . . . . . . . . . . | | 200.00 |
| | Employee Medical Insurance Payable . . . . . . . . . . . | | 35.00 |
| | Employee United Way Payable . . . . . . . . . . . . . . . . | | 10.00 |
| | Salaries Payable . . . . . . . . . . . . . . . . . . . . . . . . . . . . | | 1,725.50 |
| | *To record Bline's accrued payroll.* | | |

**e.**

| | | | |
|---|---|---|---|
| Nov.  1 | Cash . . . . . . . . . . . . . . . . . . . . . . . . . . . . . . . . . . . . . . . | 5,000 | |
| | Notes Payable . . . . . . . . . . . . . . . . . . . . . . . . . . . . . | | 5,000 |
| | *Borrowed cash with a 60-day, 12% note.* | | |

When the note and interest are paid 60 days later, Kern Company records this entry:

| | | | |
|---|---|---|---|
| Dec. 31 | Notes Payable . . . . . . . . . . . . . . . . . . . . . . . . . . . . . . | 5,000 | |
| | Interest Expense . . . . . . . . . . . . . . . . . . . . . . . . . . . . . | 100 | |
| | Cash . . . . . . . . . . . . . . . . . . . . . . . . . . . . . . . . . . . . . . | | 5,100 |
| | *Paid note with interest ($5,000 × 12% × 60/360).* | | |

**f.**

| Dec. 31 | Income Taxes Expense . . . . . . . . . . . . . . . . . . . . . . . . . . . | 5,000 | |
|---|---|---|---|
| | Income Taxes Payable . . . . . . . . . . . . . . . . . . . . . . | | 4,000 |
| | Deferred Income Tax Liability . . . . . . . . . . . . . . . . | | 1,000 |
| | *To record added income taxes expense and the* | | |
| | *deferred tax liability.* | | |

**g.** Times interest earned $= \dfrac{\$1,000,000 + \$275,000 + \$225,000}{\$275,000} = \underline{5.45\ \text{times}}$

# Payroll Reports, Records, and Procedures

## 11A

Understanding payroll procedures and keeping adequate payroll reports and records are essential to a company's success. This appendix focuses on payroll accounting and its reports, records, and procedures.

**Payroll Reports**   Most employees and employers are required to pay local, state, and federal payroll taxes. Payroll expenses involve liabilities to individual employees, to federal and state governments, and to other organizations such as insurance companies. Beyond paying these liabilities, employers are required to prepare and submit reports explaining how they computed these payments.

**P5** Identify and describe the details of payroll reports, records, and procedures.

**Reporting FICA Taxes and Income Taxes**   The Federal Insurance Contributions Act (FICA) requires each employer to file an Internal Revenue Service (IRS) **Form 941,** the *Employer's Quarterly Federal Tax Return,* within one month after the end of each calendar quarter. A sample Form 941 is shown in Exhibit 11A.1 for Phoenix Sales & Service, a landscape design company. Accounting information and software are helpful in tracking payroll transactions and reporting the accumulated information on Form 941. Specifically, the employer reports total wages subject to income tax withholding on line 2 of Form 941. (For simplicity, this appendix uses *wages* to refer to both wages and salaries.) The income tax withheld is reported on line 3. The combined amount of employee and employer FICA (Social Security) taxes for Phoenix Sales & Service is reported on line 5a (taxable Social Security wages, $36,599 × 12.4% = $4,538.28). The 12.4% is the sum of the Social Security tax withheld, computed as 6.2% tax withheld from the employee wages for the quarter plus the 6.2% tax levied on the employer. The combined amount of employee Medicare wages is reported on line 5c. The 2.9% is the sum of 1.45% withheld from employee wages for the quarter plus 1.45% tax levied on the employer. Total FICA taxes are reported on line 5d and are added to the total income taxes withheld of $3,056.47 to yield a total of $8,656.12. For this year, assume that income up to $106,800 is subject to Social Security tax. There is no income limit on amounts subject to Medicare tax. Congress sets annual limits on the amount owed for Social Security tax.

**Federal depository banks** are authorized to accept deposits of amounts payable to the federal government. Deposit requirements depend on the amount of tax owed. For example, when the sum of FICA taxes plus the employee income taxes is less than $2,500 for a quarter, the taxes can be paid when Form 941 is filed. Companies with large payrolls are often required to pay monthly or even semiweekly.

**Reporting FUTA Taxes and SUTA Taxes**   An employer's federal unemployment taxes (FUTA) are reported on an annual basis by filing an *Annual Federal Unemployment Tax Return,* IRS **Form 940.** It must be mailed on or before January 31 following the end of each tax year. Ten more days are allowed if all required tax deposits are filed on a timely basis and the full amount of tax is paid on or before January 31. FUTA payments are made quarterly to a federal depository bank if the total amount due exceeds $500. If $500 or less is due, the taxes are remitted annually. Requirements for paying and reporting state unemployment taxes (SUTA) vary depending on the laws of each state. Most states require quarterly payments and reports.

**Form 941**

**Employer's QUARTERLY Federal Tax Return**

Department of the Treasury — Internal Revenue Service

(EIN) Employer identification number: 8 6 – 3 2 7 4 5 8 7

Name (not your trade name): *Phoenix Sales & Service*

Trade name (if any):

Address: 1214 *Mill Road*
Number · Street · Suite or room number

City: *Phoenix* · State: AZ · ZIP code: 85621

**Report for this Quarter ...**
(Check one.)

- [ ] 1: January, February, March
- [ ] 2: April, May, June
- [ ] 3: July, August, September
- [X] 4: October, November, December

**Part 1: Answer these questions for this quarter.**

| | | |
|---|---|---|
| 1 Number of employees who received wages, tips, or other compensation for the pay period including: *Mar. 12* (Quarter 1), *June 12* (Quarter 2), *Sept. 12* (Quarter 3), *Dec. 12* (Quarter 4) | 1 | 1 |
| 2 Wages, tips, and other compensation | 2 | 36,599.00 |
| 3 Total income tax withheld from wages, tips, and other compensation | 3 | 3,056.47 |

4 If no wages, tips, and other compensation are subject to social security or Medicare tax . [ ] Check and go to line 6.

5 Taxable social security and Medicare wages and tips:

| | Column 1 | | Column 2 |
|---|---|---|---|
| 5a Taxable social security wages | 36,599.00 | × .124 = | 4,538.28 |
| 5b Taxable social security tips | | × .124 = | |
| 5c Taxable Medicare wages & tips | 36,599.00 | × .029 = | 1,061.37 |

| | | |
|---|---|---|
| 5d Total social security and Medicare taxes (*Column 2, lines 5a + 5b + 5c = line 5d*) | 5d | 5,599.65 |
| 6 Total taxes before adjustments (lines 3 + 5d = line 6) | 6 | 8,656.12 |

7 TAX ADJUSTMENTS (Read the instructions for line 7 before completing lines 7a through 7h.):

| | | |
|---|---|---|
| 7a Current quarter's fractions of cents | | . |
| 7b Current quarter's sick pay | | . |
| 7c Current quarter's adjustments for tips and group-term life insurance | | . |
| 7d Current year's income tax withholding (attach Form 941c) | | . |
| 7e Prior quarters' social security and Medicare taxes (attach Form 941c) | | . |
| 7f Special additions to federal income tax (attach Form 941c) | | . |
| 7g Special additions to social security and Medicare (attach Form 941c) | | . |
| 7h TOTAL ADJUSTMENTS (Combine all amounts: lines 7a through 7g.) | 7h | 0.00 |
| 8 Total taxes after adjustments (Combine lines 6 and 7h.) | 8 | 8,656.12 |
| 9 Advance earned income credit (EIC) payments made to employees | 9 | . |
| 10 Total taxes after adjustment for advance EIC (lines 8 – line 9 = line 10) | 10 | 8,656.12 |
| 11 Total deposits for this quarter, including overpayment applied from a prior quarter | 11 | 8,656.12 |
| 12 Balance due (If line 10 is more than line 11, write the difference here.) Make checks payable to *United States Treasury*. | 12 | 0.00 |
| 13 Overpayment (If line 11 is more than line 10, write the difference here.) | | 0.00 |

Line 13 Check one: [ ] Apply to next return. [ ] Send a refund.

**Part 2: Tell us about your deposit schedule and tax liability for this quarter.**

If you are unsure about whether you are a monthly schedule depositor or a semiweekly schedule depositor, see *Pub. 15 (Circular E)*, section 11.

14 [A][Z] Write the state abbreviation for the state where you made your deposits OR write "MU" if you made your deposits in *multiple* states.

15 Check one: [ ] Line 10 is less than $2,500. Go to Part 3.

[X] You were a monthly schedule depositor for the entire quarter. Fill out your tax liability for each month. Then go to Part 3.

| Tax liability: | Month 1 | 3,079.11 |
|---|---|---|
| | Month 2 | 2,049.77 |
| | Month 3 | 3,527.24 |
| | Total liability for quarter | 8,656.12 |

Total must equal line 10.

[ ] You were a semiweekly schedule depositor for any part of this quarter. Fill out *Schedule B (Form 941): Report of Tax Liability for Semiweekly Schedule Depositors*, and attach it to this form.

**Part 3: Tell us about your business. If a question does NOT apply to your business, leave it blank.**

16 If your business has closed or you stopped paying wages . . . . . . . . [ ] Check here, and

enter the final date you paid wages [ / / ]

17 If you are a seasonal employer and you do not have to file a return for every quarter of the year . [ ] Check here.

**Part 4: May we speak with your third-party designee?**

Do you want to allow an employee, a paid tax preparer, or another person to discuss this return with the IRS? See the instructions for details.

[ ] Yes. Designee's name

Phone ( ) –       Personal Identification Number (PIN) [ ][ ][ ][ ][ ]

[X] No.

**Part 5: Sign here. You MUST fill out both sides of this form and SIGN it.**

Under penalties of perjury, I declare that I have examined this return, including accompanying schedules and statements, and to the best of my knowledge and belief, it is true, correct, and complete.

Sign your name here

Print name and title

Date [ / / ]   Phone ( ) –

**Reporting Wages and Salaries**    Employers are required to give each employee an annual report of his or her wages subject to FICA and federal income taxes along with the amounts of these taxes withheld. This report is called a *Wage and Tax Statement,* or **Form W-2.** It must be given to employees before January 31 following the year covered by the report. Exhibit 11A.2 shows Form W-2 for one of the employees at Phoenix Sales & Service. Copies of the W-2 Form must be sent to the Social Security Administration, where the amount of the employee's wages subject to FICA taxes and FICA taxes withheld are posted to each employee's Social Security account. These posted amounts become the basis for determining an employee's retirement and survivors' benefits. The Social Security Administration also transmits to the IRS the amount of each employee's wages subject to federal income taxes and the amount of taxes withheld.

**EXHIBIT 11A.2**

Form W-2

| Form **W-2** Wage and Tax Statement | | Department of Treasury—Internal Revenue Service | |
|---|---|---|---|
| Copy 1–For State, City, or Local Tax Department | | | |

| **a** Control number  AR101  22222 | | OMB No. 1545-0006 | |
|---|---|---|---|
| **b** Employer identification number (EIN)  86-3214587 | | **1** Wages, tips, other compensation  4,910.00 | **2** Federal income tax withheld  333.37 |
| **c** Employer's name, address and ZIP code  Phoenix Sales & Service  1214 Mill Road  Phoenix, AZ  85621 | | **3** Social security wages  4,910.00 | **4** Social security tax withheld  304.42 |
| | | **5** Medicare wages and tips  4,910.00 | **6** Medicare tax withheld  71.20 |
| | | **7** Social security tips | **8** Allocated tips |
| **d** Employee's social security number  333-22-9999 | | **9** Advance EIC payment | **10** Dependent care benefits |
| **e** Employee's first name and initial  Robert J.     Last name  Austin | | **11** Nonqualified plans | **12a** Code |
| **f** Employee's address and ZIP code  18 Roosevelt Blvd., Apt. C  Tempe, AZ  86322 | | **13** Statutory employee  Retirement plan  Third-party sick pay | **12b** Code |
| | | **14** Other | **12c** Code |
| | | | **12d** Code |

| **15** State  AZ   Employer's state ID number  13-902319 | **16** State wages, tips, etc.  4,910.00 | **17** State income tax  26.68 | **18** Local wages, tips, etc. | **19** Local income tax | **20** Locality name |
|---|---|---|---|---|---|

**Payroll Records**    Employers must keep payroll records in addition to reporting and paying taxes. These records usually include a payroll register and an individual earnings report for each employee.

**Payroll Register**    A **payroll register** usually shows the pay period dates, hours worked, gross pay, deductions, and net pay of each employee for each pay period. Exhibit 11A.3 shows a payroll register for Phoenix Sales & Service. It is organized into nine columns:

Col. 1    Employee identification (ID); Employee name; Social Security number (SS No.); Reference (check number); and Date (date check issued)
Col. 2    Pay Type (regular and overtime)
Col. 3    Pay Hours (number of hours worked as regular and overtime)
Col. 4    Gross Pay (amount of gross pay)[2]
Col. 5    FIT (federal income taxes withheld); FUTA (federal unemployment taxes)
Col. 6    SIT (state income taxes withheld); SUTA (state unemployment taxes)
Col. 7    FICA-SS_EE (social security taxes withheld, employee); FICA-SS_ER (social security taxes, employer)
Col. 8    FICA-Med_EE (medicare tax withheld, employee); FICA-Med_ER (medicare tax, employer)
Col. 9    Net pay (Gross pay less amounts withheld from employees)

---

[2] The Gross Pay column shows regular hours worked on the first line multiplied by the regular pay rate—this equals regular pay. Overtime hours multiplied by the overtime premium rate equals overtime premium pay reported on the second line. If employers are engaged in interstate commerce, federal law sets a minimum overtime rate of pay to employees. For this company, workers earn 150% of their regular rate for hours in excess of 40 per week.

**EXHIBIT 11A.3**

Payroll Register

| Accounting System: Exhibit A.3 | | | | | | | | | _ □ ✕ |
|---|---|---|---|---|---|---|---|---|---|
| File  Edit  Maintain  Tasks  Analysis  Options  Reports  Window  Help | | | | | | | | | |

**Phoenix Sales & Service**
**Payroll Register**
**For Week Ended Oct. 8, 2011**

| Employee ID Employee SS No. Refer., Date | Gross Pay | | | FIT [blank] FUTA | SIT [blank] SUTA | FICA-SS_EE [blank] FICA-SS_ER | FICA-Med_EE [blank] FICA-Med_ER | Net Pay |
|---|---|---|---|---|---|---|---|---|
| | Pay Type | Pay Hours | Gross Pay | | | | | |
| AR101 Robert Austin 333-22-9999 9001, 10/8/11 | Regular Overtime | 40.00 0.00 | 400.00 0.00 400.00 | −28.99 −3.20 | −2.32 −10.80 | −24.80 −24.80 | −5.80 −5.80 | 338.09 |
| CJ102 Judy Cross 299-11-9201 9002, 10/8/11 | Regular Overtime | 40.00 1.00 | 560.00 21.00 581.00 | −52.97 −4.65 | −4.24 −15.69 | −36.02 −36.02 | −8.42 −8.42 | 479.35 |
| DJ103 John Diaz 444-11-9090 9003, 10/8/11 | Regular Overtime | 40.00 2.00 | 560.00 42.00 602.00 | −48.33 −4.82 | −3.87 −16.25 | −37.32 −37.32 | −8.73 −8.73 | 503.75 |
| KK104 Kay Keife 909-11-3344 9004, 10/8/11 | Regular Overtime | 40.00 0.00 | 560.00 0.00 560.00 | −68.57 −4.48 | −5.49 −15.12 | −34.72 −34.72 | −8.12 −8.12 | 443.10 |
| ML105 Lee Miller 444-56-3211 9005, 10/8/11 | Regular Overtime | 40.00 0.00 | 560.00 0.00 560.00 | −34.24 −4.48 | −2.74 −15.12 | −34.72 −34.72 | −8.12 −8.12 | 480.18 |
| SD106 Dale Sears 909-33-1234 9006, 10/8/11 | Regular Overtime | 40.00 0.00 | 560.00 0.00 560.00 | −68.57 −4.48 | −5.49 −15.12 | −34.72 −34.72 | −8.12 −8.12 | 443.10 |
| Totals | Regular Overtime | 240.00 3.00 | 3,200.00 63.00 3,263.00 | −301.67 −26.11 | −24.15 −88.10 | −202.30 −202.30 | −47.31 −47.31 | 2,687.57 |

| Sales | Purchases | General Ledger | Payroll | Inventory | Company | Analysis |
|---|---|---|---|---|---|---|

Net pay for each employee is computed as gross pay minus the items on the first line of columns 5–8. The employer's payroll tax for each employee is computed as the sum of items on the third line of columns 5–8. A payroll register includes all data necessary to record payroll. In some software programs the entries to record payroll are made in a special *payroll journal.*

**Payroll Check**    Payment of payroll is usually done by check or electronic funds transfer. Exhibit 11A.4 shows a *payroll check* for a Phoenix employee. This check is accompanied with a detachable *statement of earnings* (at top) showing gross pay, deductions, and net pay.

**Employee Earnings Report**    An **employee earnings report** is a cumulative record of an employee's hours worked, gross earnings, deductions, and net pay. Payroll information on this report is taken from the payroll register. The employee earnings report for R. Austin at Phoenix Sales & Service is shown in Exhibit 11A.5. An employee earnings report accumulates information that can show when an employee's earnings reach the tax-exempt points for FICA, FUTA, and SUTA taxes. It also gives data an employer needs to prepare Form W-2.

**Payroll Procedures**    Employers must be able to compute federal income tax for payroll purposes. This section explains how we compute this tax and how to use a payroll bank account.

**Computing Federal Income Taxes**    To compute the amount of taxes withheld from each employee's wages, we need to determine both the employee's wages earned and the employee's number of *withholding*

**EXHIBIT 11A.4**

Check and Statement of Earnings

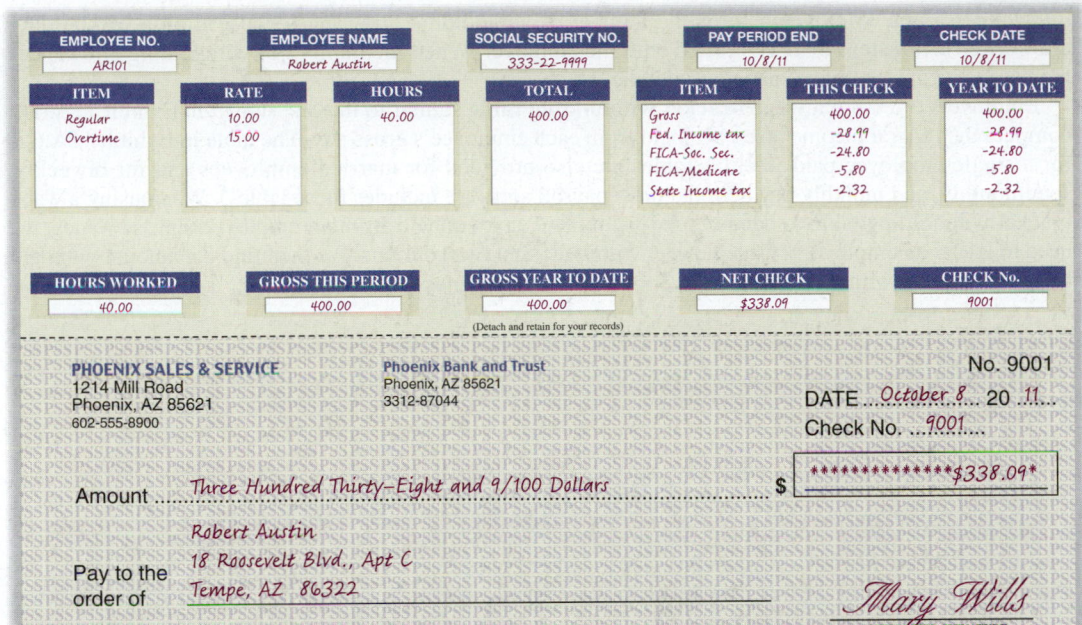

**EXHIBIT 11A.5**

Employee Earnings Report

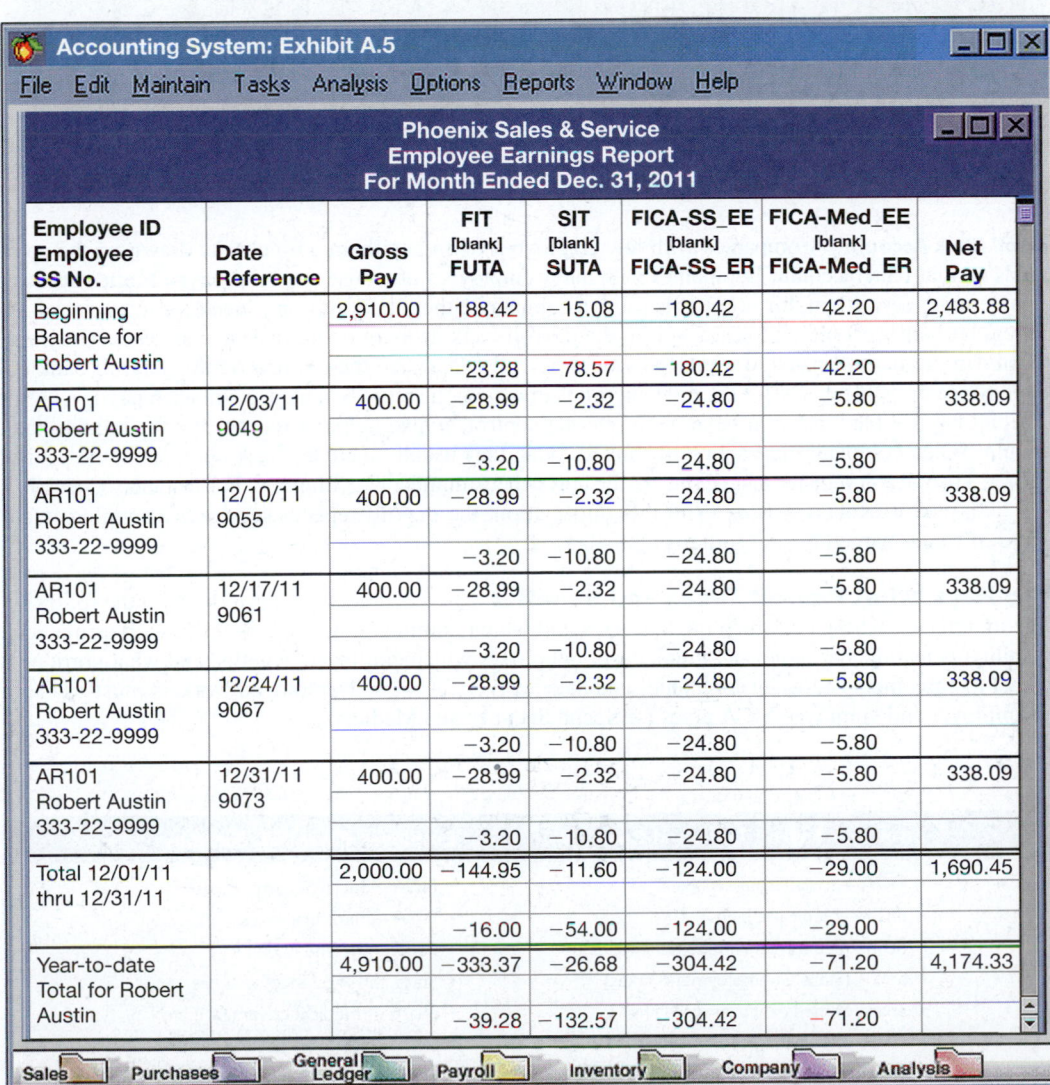

*allowances.* Each employee records the number of withholding allowances claimed on a withholding allowance certificate, **Form W-4,** filed with the employer. When the number of withholding allowances increases, the amount of income taxes withheld decreases.

Employers often use a **wage bracket withholding table** similar to the one shown in Exhibit 11A.6 to compute the federal income taxes withheld from each employee's gross pay. The table in Exhibit 11A.6 is for a single employee paid weekly. Tables are also provided for married employees and for biweekly, semimonthly, and monthly pay periods (most payroll software includes these tables). When using a wage bracket withholding table to compute federal income tax withheld from an employee's gross wages, we need to locate an employee's wage bracket within the first two columns. We then find the amount withheld by looking in the withholding allowance column for that employee.

**EXHIBIT 11A.6**

Wage Bracket Withholding Table

### SINGLE Persons—WEEKLY Payroll Period

| If the wages are— | | And the number of withholding allowances claimed is— | | | | | | | | | | |
|---|---|---|---|---|---|---|---|---|---|---|---|---|
| At least | But less than | 0 | 1 | 2 | 3 | 4 | 5 | 6 | 7 | 8 | 9 | 10 |
| | | The amount of income tax to be withheld is— | | | | | | | | | | |
| $600 | $610 | $76 | $67 | $58 | $49 | $39 | $30 | $21 | $12 | $6 | $0 | $0 |
| 610 | 620 | 79 | 69 | 59 | 50 | 41 | 32 | 22 | 13 | 7 | 1 | 0 |
| 620 | 630 | 81 | 70 | 61 | 52 | 42 | 33 | 24 | 15 | 8 | 2 | 0 |
| 630 | 640 | 84 | 72 | 62 | 53 | 44 | 35 | 25 | 16 | 9 | 3 | 0 |
| 640 | 650 | 86 | 73 | 64 | 55 | 45 | 36 | 27 | 18 | 10 | 4 | 0 |
| 650 | 660 | 89 | 75 | 65 | 56 | 47 | 38 | 28 | 19 | 11 | 5 | 0 |
| 660 | 670 | 91 | 76 | 67 | 58 | 48 | 39 | 30 | 21 | 12 | 6 | 0 |
| 670 | 680 | 94 | 78 | 68 | 59 | 50 | 41 | 31 | 22 | 13 | 7 | 1 |
| 680 | 690 | 96 | 81 | 70 | 61 | 51 | 42 | 33 | 24 | 14 | 8 | 2 |
| 690 | 700 | 99 | 83 | 71 | 62 | 53 | 44 | 34 | 25 | 16 | 9 | 3 |
| 700 | 710 | 101 | 86 | 73 | 64 | 54 | 45 | 35 | 27 | 17 | 10 | 4 |
| 710 | 720 | 104 | 88 | 74 | 65 | 56 | 47 | 37 | 28 | 19 | 11 | 5 |
| 720 | 730 | 106 | 91 | 76 | 67 | 57 | 48 | 39 | 30 | 20 | 12 | 6 |
| 730 | 740 | 109 | 93 | 78 | 68 | 59 | 50 | 40 | 31 | 22 | 13 | 7 |
| 740 | 750 | 111 | 96 | 80 | 70 | 60 | 51 | 42 | 33 | 23 | 14 | 8 |

**Payroll Bank Account**    Companies with few employees often pay them with checks drawn on the company's regular bank account. Companies with many employees often use a special **payroll bank account** to pay employees. When this account is used, a company either (1) draws one check for total payroll on the regular bank account and deposits it in the payroll bank account or (2) executes an *electronic funds transfer* to the payroll bank account. Individual payroll checks are then drawn on this payroll bank account. Since only one check for the total payroll is drawn on the regular bank account each payday, use of a special payroll bank account helps with internal control. It also helps in reconciling the regular bank account. When companies use a payroll bank account, they usually include check numbers in the payroll register. The payroll register in Exhibit 11A.3 shows check numbers in column 1. For instance, Check No. 9001 is issued to Robert Austin. With this information, the payroll register serves as a supplementary record of wages earned by and paid to employees.

### Who Pays What Payroll Taxes and Benefits

We conclude this appendix with the following table identifying who pays which payroll taxes and which common employee benefits such as medical, disability, pension, charitable, and union costs. Who pays which employee benefits, and what portion, is subject to agreements between companies and their workers. Also, self-employed workers must pay both the employer and employee FICA taxes for Social Security and Medicare.

| Employer Payroll Taxes and Costs | Employee Payroll Deductions |
|---|---|
| • FICA—Social Security Taxes | • FICA—Social Security taxes |
| • FICA—Medicare Taxes | • FICA—Medicare taxes |
| • FUTA (Federal Unemployment Taxes) | • Federal Income taxes |
| • SUTA (State Unemployment Taxes) | • State and local income taxes |
| • Share of medical coverage, if any | • Share of medical coverage, if any |
| • Share of pension coverage, if any | • Share of pension coverage, if any |
| • Share of other benefits, if any | • Share of other benefits, if any |

## Quick Check

Answers — p. 461

**11.** What three items determine the amount deducted from an employee's wages for federal income taxes?

**12.** What amount of income tax is withheld from the salary of an employee who is single with three withholding allowances and earnings of $675 in a week? (*Hint:* Use the wage bracket withholding table in Exhibit 11A.6.)

**13.** Which of the following steps are executed when a company draws one check for total payroll and deposits it in a special payroll bank account? (*a*) Write a check to the payroll bank account for the total payroll and record it with a debit to Salaries Payable and a credit to Cash. (*b*) Deposit a check (or transfer funds) for the total payroll in the payroll bank account. (*c*) Issue individual payroll checks drawn on the payroll bank account. (*d*) All of the above.

---

**APPENDIX**

# Corporate Income Taxes

# 11B

This appendix explains current liabilities involving income taxes for corporations.

**Income Tax Liabilities**    Corporations are subject to income taxes and must estimate their income tax liability when preparing financial statements. Since income tax expense is created by earning income, a liability is incurred when income is earned. This tax must be paid quarterly under federal regulations. To illustrate, consider a corporation that prepares monthly financial statements. Based on its income in January 2011, this corporation estimates that it owes income taxes of $12,100. The following adjusting entry records this estimate:

| Jan. 31 | Income Taxes Expense ........................... | 12,100 | |
| | Income Taxes Payable ...................... | | 12,100 |
| | *To accrue January income taxes.* | | |

Assets = Liabilities + Equity
        +12,100   −12,100

The tax liability is recorded each month until the first quarterly payment is made. If the company's estimated taxes for this first quarter total $30,000, the entry to record its payment is

| Apr. 10 | Income Taxes Payable ........................... | 30,000 | |
| | Cash ..................................... | | 30,000 |
| | *Paid estimated quarterly income taxes based on first quarter income.* | | |

Assets = Liabilities + Equity
−30,000   −30,000

This process of accruing and then paying estimated income taxes continues through the year. When annual financial statements are prepared at year-end, the corporation knows its actual total income and the actual amount of income taxes it must pay. This information allows it to properly record income taxes expense for the fourth quarter so that the total of the four quarters' expense amounts equals the actual taxes paid to the government.

**Deferred Income Tax Liabilities**    An income tax liability for corporations can arise when the amount of income before taxes that the corporation reports on its income statement is not the same as the amount of income reported on its income tax return. This difference occurs because income tax laws and GAAP measure income differently. (Differences between tax laws and GAAP arise because Congress uses tax laws to generate receipts, stimulate the economy, and influence behavior, whereas GAAP are intended to provide financial information useful for business decisions. Also, tax accounting often follows the cash basis, whereas GAAP follows the accrual basis.)

Some differences between tax laws and GAAP are temporary. *Temporary differences* arise when the tax return and the income statement report a revenue or expense in different years. As an example, companies are often able to deduct higher amounts of depreciation in the early years of an asset's life and smaller amounts in later years for tax reporting in comparison to GAAP. This means that in the early years, depreciation for tax reporting is often more than depreciation on the income statement. In later years, depreciation for tax reporting is often less than depreciation on the income statement. When temporary differences exist between taxable income on the tax return and the income before taxes on the income statement, corporations compute income taxes expense based on the income reported on the income statement. The result is that income taxes expense reported in the income statement is often different from the amount of income taxes payable to the government. This difference is the **deferred income tax liability.**

To illustrate, assume that in recording its usual quarterly income tax payments, a corporation computes $25,000 of income taxes expense. It also determines that only $21,000 is currently due and $4,000 is deferred to future years (a timing difference). The entry to record this end-of-period adjustment is

Assets = Liabilities + Equity
+21,000    −25,000
+4,000

| Dec. 31 | Income Taxes Expense | 25,000 | |
|---|---|---|---|
| | Income Taxes Payable | | 21,000 |
| | Deferred Income Tax Liability | | 4,000 |
| | *To record tax expense and deferred tax liability.* | | |

The credit to Income Taxes Payable reflects the amount currently due to be paid. The credit to Deferred Income Tax Liability reflects tax payments deferred until future years when the temporary difference reverses.

Temporary differences also can cause a company to pay income taxes *before* they are reported on the income statement as expense. If so, the company reports a *Deferred Income Tax Asset* on its balance sheet.

# Summary

**C1** **Describe current and long-term liabilities and their characteristics.** Liabilities are probable future payments of assets or services that past transactions or events obligate an entity to make. Current liabilities are due within one year or the operating cycle, whichever is longer. All other liabilities are long term.

**C2** **Identify and describe known current liabilities.** Known (determinable) current liabilities are set by agreements or laws and are measurable with little uncertainty. They include accounts payable, sales taxes payable, unearned revenues, notes payable, payroll liabilities, and the current portion of long-term debt.

**C3** **Explain how to account for contingent liabilities.** If an uncertain future payment depends on a probable future event and the amount can be reasonably estimated, the payment is recorded as a liability. The uncertain future payment is reported as a contingent liability (in the notes) if (*a*) the future event is reasonably possible but not probable or (*b*) the event is probable but the payment amount cannot be reasonably estimated.

**A1** **Compute the times interest earned ratio and use it to analyze liabilities.** Times interest earned is computed by dividing a company's net income before interest expense and income taxes by the amount of interest expense. The times interest earned ratio reflects a company's ability to pay interest obligations.

**P1** **Prepare entries to account for short-term notes payable.** Short-term notes payable are current liabilities; most bear

interest. When a short-term note's face value equals the amount borrowed, it identifies a rate of interest to be paid at maturity.

**P2** **Compute and record *employee* payroll deductions and liabilities.** Employee payroll deductions include FICA taxes, income taxes, and voluntary deductions such as for pensions and charities. They make up the difference between gross and net pay.

**P3** **Compute and record *employer* payroll expenses and liabilities.** An employer's payroll expenses include employees' gross earnings, any employee benefits, and the payroll taxes levied on the employer. Payroll liabilities include employees' net pay amounts, withholdings from employee wages, any employer-promised benefits, and the employer's payroll taxes.

**P4** **Account for estimated liabilities, including warranties and bonuses.** Liabilities for health and pension benefits, warranties, and bonuses are recorded with estimated amounts. These items are recognized as expenses when incurred and matched with revenues generated.

**P5ᴬ** **Identify and describe the details of payroll reports, records, and procedures.** Employers report FICA taxes and federal income tax withholdings using Form 941. FUTA taxes are reported on Form 940. Earnings and deductions are reported to each employee and the federal government on Form W-2. An employer's payroll records often include a payroll register for each pay period, payroll checks and statements of earnings, and individual employee earnings reports.

## Guidance Answers to Decision Maker and Decision Ethics

**Web Designer**    You need to be concerned about being an accomplice to unlawful payroll activities. Not paying federal and state taxes on wages earned is illegal and unethical. Such payments also will not provide the employee with Social Security and some Medicare credits. The best course of action is to request payment by check. If this fails to change the owner's payment practices, you must consider quitting this job.

**Entrepreneur**    Risk is partly reflected by the times interest earned ratio. This ratio for the first franchise is 1.5 [($100,000 +

$200,000)/$200,000], whereas the ratio for the second franchise is 3.5 [($100,000 + $40,000)/$40,000]. This analysis shows that the first franchise is more at risk of incurring a loss if its sales decline. The second question asks about variability of income. If income greatly varies, this increases the risk an owner will not earn sufficient income to cover interest. Since the first franchise has the greater variability, it is a riskier investment.

## Guidance Answers to Quick Checks

1. A liability involves a probable future payment of assets or services that an entity is presently obligated to make as a result of past transactions or events.

2. No, an expected future payment is not a liability unless an existing obligation was created by a past event or transaction.

3. In most cases, a liability due in 15 months is classified as long term. It is classified as a current liability if the company's operating cycle is 15 months or longer.

4. A creditor prefers a note payable instead of a past-due account payable so as to (a) charge interest and/or (b) have evidence of the debt and its terms for potential litigation or disputes.

5. $1,000* × (.008) + $1,000* × (.04) + $3,000 × (.062) + $3,000 × (.0145) = $277.50

   _____
   * $1,000 of the $3,000 March pay is subject to FUTA and SUTA—the entire $6,000 pay from January and February was subject to them.

6. (a) FICA taxes are incurred by both employee and employer.
   (b) FUTA taxes are incurred by the employer.
   (c) SUTA taxes are incurred by the employer.
   (d) Withheld income taxes are incurred by the employee.

7. (a)

8. (a) Warranty expense was previously estimated and recorded.

9. (b)

10. A future payment is reported in the notes as a contingent liability if (a) the uncertain future event is probable but the amount of payment cannot be reasonably estimated or (b) the uncertain future event is not probable but has a reasonable possibility of occurring.

11. An employee's marital status, gross earnings and number of withholding allowances determine the deduction for federal income taxes.

12. $59

13. (d)

## Key Terms

mhhe.com/wildFAP20e

Contingent liability (p. 448)

Current liabilities (p. 437)

Current portion of long-term debt (p. 445)

Deferred income tax liability (p. 460)

Employee benefits (p. 445)

Employee earnings report (p. 456)

Estimated liability (p. 445)

Federal depository bank (p. 453)

Federal Insurance Contributions Act (FICA) Taxes (p. 442)

Federal Unemployment Taxes (FUTA) (p. 444)

Form 940 (p. 453)

Form 941 (p. 453)

Form W-2 (p. 455)

Form W-4 (p. 458)

Gross pay (p. 442)

Known liabilities (p. 438)

Long-term liabilities (p. 437)

Merit rating (p. 444)

Net pay (p. 442)

Payroll bank account (p. 458)

Payroll deductions (p. 442)

Payroll register (p. 455)

Short-term note payable (p. 439)

State Unemployment Taxes (SUTA) (p. 444)

Times interest earned (p. 450)

Wage bracket withholding table (p. 458)

Warranty (p. 446)

## Multiple Choice Quiz          Answers on p. 477          mhhe.com/wildFAP20e

**Additional Quiz Questions are available at the book's Website.**

1. On December 1, a company signed a $6,000, 90-day, 5% note payable, with principal plus interest due on March 1 of the following year. What amount of interest expense should be accrued at December 31 on the note?
   a. $300
   b. $25
   c. $100
   d. $75
   e. $0

2. An employee earned $50,000 during the year. FICA tax for social security is 6.2% and FICA tax for Medicare is 1.45%. The employer's share of FICA taxes is
   a. Zero, since the employee's pay exceeds the FICA limit.
   b. Zero, since FICA is not an employer tax.
   c. $3,100
   d. $725
   e. $3,825

3. Assume the FUTA tax rate is 0.8% and the SUTA tax rate is 5.4%. Both taxes are applied to the first $7,000 of an employee's pay. What is the total unemployment tax an employer must pay on an employee's annual wages of $40,000?
   a. $2,480
   b. $434
   c. $56
   d. $378
   e. Zero; the employee's wages exceed the $7,000 maximum.

4. A company sells big screen televisions for $3,000 each. Each television has a two-year warranty that covers the replacement of defective parts. It is estimated that 1% of all televisions sold will be returned under warranty at an average cost of $250 each. During July, the company sold 10,000 big screen televisions, and 80 were serviced under the warranty during July at a total cost of $18,000. The credit balance in the Estimated

Warranty Liability account at July 1 was $26,000. What is the company's warranty expense for the month of July?

a. $51,000
b. $1,000
c. $25,000
d. $33,000
e. $18,000

5. Employees earn vacation pay at the rate of 1 day per month. During October, 150 employees qualify for one vacation day

each. Their average daily wage is $175 per day. What is the amount of vacation benefit expense for October?

a. $26,250
b. $175
c. $2,100
d. $63,875
e. $150

---

A(B) *Superscript letter A (B) denotes assignments based on Appendix 11A (11B).*

Icon denotes assignments that involve decision making.

## Discussion Questions

1. What are the three important questions concerning the uncertainty of liabilities?

2. What is the difference between a current and a long-term liability?

3. What is an estimated liability?

4. If $988 is the total of a sale that includes its sales tax of 4%, what is the selling price of the item only?

5. What is the combined amount (in percent) of the employee and employer Social Security tax rate?

6. What is the current Medicare tax rate? This rate is applied to what maximum level of salary and wages?

7. What determines the amount deducted from an employee's wages for federal income taxes?

8. Which payroll taxes are the employee's responsibility and which are the employer's responsibility?

9. What is an employer's unemployment merit rating? How are these ratings assigned to employers?

10. Why are warranty liabilities usually recognized on the balance sheet as liabilities even when they are uncertain?

11. Suppose that a company has a facility located where disastrous weather conditions often occur. Should it report a probable loss from a future disaster as a liability on its balance sheet? Explain.

12.A What is a wage bracket withholding table?

13.A What amount of income tax is withheld from the salary of an employee who is single with two withholding allowances and earning $725 per week? What if the employee earned $625 and has no withholding allowances? (Use Exhibit 11A.6.)

14. Refer to **Research In Motion**'s balance sheet in Appendix A. What revenue-related liability does Research In Motion report at February 27, 2010? **RIM**

15. Refer to **Apple**'s balance sheet in Appendix A. What is the amount of Apple's accounts payable as of September 26, 2009? **Apple**

16. Refer to **Nokia**'s balance sheet in Appendix A. List Nokia's current liabilities as of December 31, 2009. **NOKIA**

17. Refer to **Palm**'s balance sheet in Appendix A. What current liabilities related to income taxes are on its balance sheet? Explain the meaning of each income tax account identified. **Palm**

---

 connect™

## QUICK STUDY

**QS 11-1**

Classifying liabilities C1

Which of the following items are normally classified as a current liability for a company that has a 15-month operating cycle?

1. Salaries payable.
2. Note payable due in 19 months.
3. FICA taxes payable.
4. Note payable maturing in 3 years.
5. Note payable due in 10 months.
6. Portion of long-term note due in 15 months.

**QS 11-2**

Accounting for sales taxes

C2

Wrecker Computing sells merchandise for $5,000 cash on September 30 (cost of merchandise is $2,900). The sales tax law requires Wrecker to collect 4% sales tax on every dollar of merchandise sold. Record the entry for the $5,000 sale and its applicable sales tax. Also record the entry that shows the remittance of the 4% tax on this sale to the state government on October 15.

**QS 11-3**

Unearned revenue C2

Tickets, Inc., receives $5,500,000 cash in advance ticket sales for a four-date tour of Bruce Springsteen. Record the advance ticket sales on October 31. Record the revenue earned for the first concert date of November 8, assuming it represents one-fourth of the advance ticket sales.

The following legal claims exist for Kalamazoo Co. Identify the accounting treatment for each claim as either (*a*) a liability that is recorded or (*b*) an item described in notes to its financial statements.

**1.** Kalamazoo (defendant) estimates that a pending lawsuit could result in damages of $1,000,000; it is reasonably possible that the plaintiff will win the case.

**2.** Kalamazoo faces a probable loss on a pending lawsuit; the amount is not reasonably estimable.

**3.** Kalamazoo estimates damages in a case at $2,500,000 with a high probability of losing the case.

**QS 11-4**
Accounting for contingent liabilities
C3

---

On November 7, 2011, Ortez Company borrows $150,000 cash by signing a 90-day, 8% note payable with a face value of $150,000. (1) Compute the accrued interest payable on December 31, 2011, (2) prepare the journal entry to record the accrued interest expense at December 31, 2011, and (3) prepare the journal entry to record payment of the note at maturity.

**QS 11-5**
Interest-bearing note transactions P1

---

On January 14, the end of the first bi-weekly pay period of the year, Rockin Company's payroll register showed that its employees earned $14,000 of sales salaries. Withholdings from the employees' salaries include FICA Social Security taxes at the rate of 6.2%, FICA Medicare taxes at the rate of 1.45%, $2,600 of federal income taxes, $309 of medical insurance deductions, and $120 of union dues. No employee earned more than $7,000 in this first period. Prepare the journal entry to record Rockin Company's January 14 (employee) payroll expenses and liabilities.

**QS 11-6**
Record employee payroll taxes
P2

---

Merger Co. has ten employees, each of whom earns $2,000 per month and has been employed since January 1. FICA Social Security taxes are 6.2% of the first $106,800 paid to each employee, and FICA Medicare taxes are 1.45% of gross pay. FUTA taxes are 0.8% and SUTA taxes are 5.4% of the first $7,000 paid to each employee. Prepare the March 31 journal entry to record the March payroll taxes expense.

**QS 11-7**
Record employer payroll taxes
P3

---

On September 11, 2010, Home Store sells a mower for $400 with a one-year warranty that covers parts. Warranty expense is estimated at 5% of sales. On July 24, 2011, the mower is brought in for repairs covered under the warranty requiring $35 in materials taken from the Repair Parts Inventory. Prepare the July 24, 2011, entry to record the warranty repairs.

**QS 11-8**
Recording warranty repairs
P4

---

Paris Company offers an annual bonus to employees if the company meets certain net income goals. Prepare the journal entry to record a $10,000 bonus owed to its workers (to be shared equally) at calendar year-end.

**QS 11-9**
Accounting for bonuses P4

---

Chester Co.'s salaried employees earn four weeks vacation per year. It pays $192,000.12 in total employee salaries for 52 weeks but its employees work only 48 weeks. This means Chester's total weekly expense is $4,000 ($192,000/48 weeks) instead of the $3,692.31 cash paid weekly to the employees ($192,000/52 weeks). Record Chester's weekly vacation benefits expense.

**QS 11-10**
Accounting for vacations
P4

---

Compute the times interest earned for Weltin Company, which reports income before interest expense and income taxes of $2,044,000, and interest expense of $350,000. Interpret its times interest earned (assume that its competitors average a times interest earned of 4.0).

**QS 11-11**
Times interest earned A1

---

The payroll records of Clix Software show the following information about Trish Farqua, an employee, for the weekly pay period ending September 30, 2011. Farqua is single and claims one allowance. Compute her Social Security tax (6.2%), Medicare tax (1.45%), federal income tax withholding, state income tax (1.0%), and net pay for the current pay period. (Use the withholding table in Exhibit 11A.6 and round tax amounts to the nearest cent.)

**QS 11-12^A**
Net pay and tax computations
P5

| | |
|---|---|
| Total (gross) earnings for current pay period . . . . . . . . . | $ 735 |
| Cumulative earnings of previous pay periods . . . . . . . . . | 9,700 |

**Check** Net pay, $578.42

---

Cather Corporation has made and recorded its quarterly income tax payments. After a final review of taxes for the year, the company identifies an additional $30,000 of income tax expense that should be recorded. A portion of this additional expense, $8,000, is deferred for payment in future years. Record Cather's year-end adjusting entry for income tax expense.

**QS 11-13^B**
Record deferred income tax liability P4

---

Answer each of the following related to international accounting standards.

**a.** In general, how similar or different are the definitions and characteristics of current liabilities between IFRS and U.S. GAAP?

**b.** Companies reporting under IFRS often reference a set of current liabilities with the title *financial liabilities*. Identify two current liabilities that would be classified under financial liabilities per IFRS. (*Hint:* **Nokia** provides examples in this chapter and in Appendix A.)

**QS 11-14**
International accounting standards
C1 C2

# EXERCISES

**Exercise 11-1**
Classifying liabilities

C1

The following items appear on the balance sheet of a company with a two-month operating cycle. Identify the proper classification of each item as follows: *C* if it is a current liability, *L* if it is a long-term liability, or *N* if it is not a liability.

_____ **1.** Sales taxes payable.              _____ **6.** Notes payable (due in 6 to 12 months).

_____ **2.** FUTA taxes payable.            _____ **7.** Notes payable (due in 120 days).

_____ **3.** Accounts receivable.            _____ **8.** Current portion of long-term debt.

_____ **4.** Wages payable.                      _____ **9.** Notes payable (mature in five years).

_____ **5.** Salaries payable.                   _____ **10.** Notes payable (due in 13 to 24 months).

---

**Exercise 11-2**
Recording known
current liabilities

C2

Prepare any necessary adjusting entries at December 31, 2011, for Yacht Company's year-end financial statements for each of the following separate transactions and events.

**1.** Yacht Company records an adjusting entry for $2,000,000 of previously unrecorded cash sales (costing $1,000,000) and its sales taxes at a rate of 5%.

**2.** The company earned $40,000 of $100,000 previously received in advance for services.

---

**Exercise 11-3**
Accounting for contingent
liabilities

C3

Prepare any necessary adjusting entries at December 31, 2011, for Moor Company's year-end financial statements for each of the following separate transactions and events.

**1.** A disgruntled employee is suing Moor Company. Legal advisers believe that the company will probably need to pay damages, but the amount cannot be reasonably estimated.

**2.** Moor Company guarantees the $5,000 debt of a supplier. The supplier will probably not default on the debt.

---

**Exercise 11-4**
Accounting for note payable

P1

**Check** (2b) Interest expense, $1,880

Perfect Systems borrows $94,000 cash on May 15, 2011, by signing a 60-day, 12% note.

**1.** On what date does this note mature?

**2.** Suppose the face value of the note equals $94,000, the principal of the loan. Prepare the journal entries to record (*a*) issuance of the note and (*b*) payment of the note at maturity.

---

**Exercise 11-5**
Interest-bearing notes payable
with year-end adjustments

P1

**Check** (2) $2,250
(3) $1,125

Kwon Co. borrows $150,000 cash on November 1, 2011, by signing a 90-day, 9% note with a face value of $150,000.

**1.** On what date does this note mature? (Assume that February of 2011 has 28 days.)

**2.** How much interest expense results from this note in 2011? (Assume a 360-day year.)

**3.** How much interest expense results from this note in 2012? (Assume a 360-day year.)

**4.** Prepare journal entries to record (*a*) issuance of the note, (*b*) accrual of interest at the end of 2011, and (*c*) payment of the note at maturity.

---

**Exercise 11-6**
Computing payroll taxes

P2  P3

**Check** (*a*) FUTA, $4.80; SUTA, $17.40

MRI Company has one employee. FICA Social Security taxes are 6.2% of the first $106,800 paid to its employee, and FICA Medicare taxes are 1.45% of gross pay. For MRI, its FUTA taxes are 0.8% and SUTA taxes are 2.9% of the first $7,000 paid to its employee. Compute MRI's amounts for each of these four taxes as applied to the employee's gross earnings for September under each of three separate situations (*a*), (*b*), and (*c*).

| | Gross Pay through August | Gross Pay for September |
|---|---|---|
| **a.** | $ 6,400 | $ 800 |
| **b.** | 18,200 | 2,100 |
| **c.** | 100,500 | 8,000 |

---

**Exercise 11-7**
Payroll-related journal entries   P2

Using the data in situation *a* of Exercise 11-6, prepare the employer's September 30 journal entries to record salary expense and its related payroll liabilities for this employee. The employee's federal income taxes withheld by the employer are $135 for this pay period.

---

**Exercise 11-8**
Payroll-related journal entries   P3

Using the data in situation *a* of Exercise 11-6, prepare the employer's September 30 journal entries to record the *employer's* payroll taxes expense and its related liabilities.

For the year ended December 31, 2011, Winter Company has implemented an employee bonus program equal to 3% of Winter's net income, which employees will share equally. Winter's net income (prebonus) is expected to be $1,000,000, and bonus expense is deducted in computing net income.

1. Compute the amount of the bonus payable to the employees at year-end (use the method described in the chapter and round to the nearest dollar).
2. Prepare the journal entry at December 31, 2011, to record the bonus due the employees.
3. Prepare the journal entry at January 19, 2012, to record payment of the bonus to employees.

**Exercise 11-9**
Computing and recording bonuses **P4**

**Check** (1) $29,126

---

Prepare any necessary adjusting entries at December 31, 2011, for Jester Company's year-end financial statements for each of the following separate transactions and events.

1. During December, Jester Company sold 3,000 units of a product that carries a 60-day warranty. December sales for this product total $120,000. The company expects 8% of the units to need warranty repairs, and it estimates the average repair cost per unit will be $15.
2. Employees earn vacation pay at a rate of one day per month. During December, 20 employees qualify for one vacation day each. Their average daily wage is $120 per employee.

**Exercise 11-10**
Accounting for estimated liabilities
**P4**

---

Chang Co. sold a copier costing $3,800 with a two-year parts warranty to a customer on August 16, 2011, for $5,500 cash. Chang uses the perpetual inventory system. On November 22, 2012, the copier requires on-site repairs that are completed the same day. The repairs cost $199 for materials taken from the Repair Parts Inventory. These are the only repairs required in 2012 for this copier. Based on experience, Chang expects to incur warranty costs equal to 4% of dollar sales. It records warranty expense with an adjusting entry at the end of each year.

1. How much warranty expense does the company report in 2011 for this copier?
2. How much is the estimated warranty liability for this copier as of December 31, 2011?
3. How much warranty expense does the company report in 2012 for this copier?
4. How much is the estimated warranty liability for this copier as of December 31, 2012?
5. Prepare journal entries to record (a) the copier's sale; (b) the adjustment on December 31, 2011, to recognize the warranty expense; and (c) the repairs that occur in November 2012.

**Exercise 11-11**
Warranty expense and liability computations and entries
**P4**

**Check** (1) $220

(4) $21

---

Use the following information from separate companies a through f to compute times interest earned. Which company indicates the strongest ability to pay interest expense as it comes due?

**Exercise 11-12**
Computing and interpreting times interest earned

**A1**

| | Net Income (Loss) | Interest Expense | Income Taxes |
|---|---|---|---|
| a. | $140,000 | $48,000 | $ 35,000 |
| b. | 140,000 | 15,000 | 50,000 |
| c. | 140,000 | 8,000 | 70,000 |
| d. | 265,000 | 12,000 | 130,000 |
| e. | 79,000 | 12,000 | 30,000 |
| f. | (4,000) | 12,000 | 0 |

**Check** (b) 13.67

---

Tony Newbern, an unmarried employee, works 48 hours in the week ended January 12. His pay rate is $12 per hour, and his wages are subject to no deductions other than FICA—Social Security, FICA—Medicare, and federal income taxes. He claims two withholding allowances. Compute his regular pay, overtime pay (for this company, workers earn 150% of their regular rate for hours in excess of 40 per week), and gross pay. Then compute his FICA tax deduction (use 6.2% for the Social Security portion and 1.45% for the Medicare portion), income tax deduction (use the wage bracket withholding table of Exhibit 11A.6), total deductions, and net pay. (Round tax amounts to the nearest cent.)

**Exercise 11-13[A]**
Gross and net pay computation
**P5**

**Check** Net pay, $515.26

---

Ming Corporation prepares financial statements for each month-end. As part of its accounting process, estimated income taxes are accrued each month for 30% of the current month's net income. The income taxes are paid in the first month of each quarter for the amount accrued for the prior quarter. The following information is available for the fourth quarter of year 2011. When tax computations are completed on January 20, 2012, Ming determines that the quarter's Income Taxes Payable account balance should be $29,100 on December 31, 2011 (its unadjusted balance is $23,640).

**Exercise 11-14[B]**
Accounting for income taxes
**P4**

| | |
|---|---|
| October 2011 net income .......... | $27,900 |
| November 2011 net income ........ | 18,200 |
| December 2011 net income ........ | 32,700 |

**Check**   (1) $5,460

1. Determine the amount of the accounting adjustment (dated as of December 31, 2011) to produce the proper ending balance in the Income Taxes Payable account.

2. Prepare journal entries to record (a) the December 31, 2011, adjustment to the Income Taxes Payable account and (b) the January 20, 2012, payment of the fourth-quarter taxes.

---

**Exercise 11-15**

Accounting for current liabilities under IFRS

**P4**

**Volvo Group** reports the following information for its product warranty costs as of December 31, 2008, along with provisions and utilizations of warranty liabilities for the year ended December 31, 2008 (SEK in millions).

***Product warranty costs***

Estimated costs for product warranties are charged to cost of sales when the products are sold. Estimated warranty costs include contractual warranty and goodwill warranty. Warranty provisions are estimated with consideration of historical claims statistics, the warranty period, the average time-lag between faults occurring and claims to the company, and anticipated changes in quality indexes. Differences between actual warranty claims and the estimated claims generally affect the recognized expense and provisions in future periods. At December 31, 2008, warranty cost provisions amounted to 10,354.

| | |
|---|---|
| Product warranty liabilities, December 31, 2007 ................ | SEK 9,373 |
| Additional provisions to product warranty liabilities ............. | 6,201 |
| Utilizations and reductions of product warranty liabilities ........ | (5,220) |
| Product warranty liabilities, December 31, 2008 ................ | 10,354 |

1. Prepare Volvo's journal entry to record its estimated warranty liabilities (provisions) for 2008.

2. Prepare Volvo's journal entry to record its costs (utilizations) related to its warranty program for 2008. Assume those costs involve replacements taken out of Inventory, with no cash involved.

3. How much warranty expense does Volvo report for 2008?

---

**Exercise 11-16**

Recording payroll

**P2   P3**

The following monthly data are taken from Nunez Company at July 31: Sales salaries, $120,000; Office salaries, $60,000; Federal income taxes withheld, $45,000; State income taxes withheld, $10,000; Social security taxes withheld, $11,160; Medicare taxes withheld, $2,610; Medical insurance premiums, $7,000; Life insurance premiums, $4,000; Union dues deducted, $1,000; and Salaries subject to unemployment taxes, $50,000. The employee pays forty percent of medical and life insurance premiums.

Prepare journal entries to record: (1) accrued payroll, including employee deductions, for July; (2) cash payment of the net payroll (salaries payable) for July; (3) accrued employer payroll taxes, and other related employment expenses, for July—assume that FICA taxes are identical to those on employees and that SUTA taxes are 5.4% and FUTA taxes are 0.8%; and (4) cash payment of all liabilities related to the July payroll.

---

**Exercise 11-17**

Computing payroll taxes

**P2   P3**

Madison Company has nine employees. FICA Social Security taxes are 6.2% of the first $106,800 paid to each employee, and FICA Medicare taxes are 1.45% of gross pay. FUTA taxes are 0.8% and SUTA taxes are 5.4% of the first $7,000 paid to each employee. Cumulative pay for the current year for each of its employees follows.

| Employee | Cumulative Pay | Employee | Cumulative Pay | Employee | Cumulative Pay |
|---|---|---|---|---|---|
| Steve S. ....... | $ 6,000 | Christina S. .... | $156,800 | Dana W. ........ | $116,800 |
| Tim V. ......... | 60,000 | Michelle H. .... | 106,800 | Stewart M. ...... | 36,800 |
| Brent G. ....... | 87,000 | Kathleen K. .... | 110,000 | Sankha B. ....... | 4,000 |

a. Prepare a table with the following column headings: Employee; Cumulative Pay; Pay Subject to FICA Social Security Taxes; Pay Subject to FICA Medicare Taxes; Pay Subject to FUTA Taxes; Pay Subject to SUTA Taxes. Compute the amounts in this table for each employee and total the columns.

b. For the company, compute each total for: FICA Social Security taxes, FICA Medicare taxes, FUTA taxes, and SUTA taxes. (*Hint:* Remember to include in those totals any employee share of taxes that the company must collect.)

---

**Exercise 11-18**

Preparing payroll register and related entries   **P5**

SP Company has five employees. Employees paid by the hour receive a $10 per hour pay rate for the regular 40-hour work week plus one and one-half times the hourly rate for each overtime hour beyond the 40-hours per week. Hourly employees are paid every two weeks, but salaried employees are paid monthly on the last biweekly payday of each month. FICA Social Security taxes are 6.2% of the first $106,800 paid to each employee, and FICA Medicare taxes are 1.45% of gross pay. FUTA taxes are 0.8% and SUTA taxes are 5.4% of the first $7,000 paid to each employee. The company has a benefits plan that includes medical insurance, life insurance, and retirement funding for employees. Under this plan, employees must contribute 5 percent of their gross income as a payroll withholding, which the company matches with double the amount. Following is the partially completed payroll register for the biweekly period ending August 31, which is the last payday of August.

| Employee | Cumulative Pay (Excludes Current Period) | Current Period Gross Pay | | | FIT | FUTA | FICA-SS_EE | FICA-Med_EE | EE-Ben_Plan Withholding | Employee Net Pay |
| | | Pay Type | Pay Hours | Gross Pay | SIT | SUTA | FICA-SS_ER | FICA-Med_ER | ER-Ben_Plan Withholding | |
|---|---|---|---|---|---|---|---|---|---|---|
| Kathleen | $105,000.00 | Salary | --- | $7,000.00 | $2,000.00 | | | | | |
| | | | | | 300.00 | | | | | |
| Nichole | 6,800.00 | Salary | --- | 500.00 | 80.00 | | | | | |
| | | | | | 20.00 | | | | | |
| Anthony | 15,000.00 | Regular | 80 | | 110.00 | | | | | |
| | | Overtime | 8 | | 25.00 | | | | | |
| Zoey | 6,500.00 | Regular | 80 | | 100.00 | | | | | |
| | | Overtime | 4 | | 22.00 | | | | | |
| Gracie | 5,000.00 | Regular | 74 | 740.00 | 90.00 | | | | | |
| | | Overtime | 0 | 0.00 | 21.00 | | | | | |
| Totals | 138,300.00 | | | | 2,380.00 | | | | | |
| | | | | | 388.00 | | | | | |

* Table abbreviations follow those in Exhibit 11A.3 (see pages 455–456); and, "Ben_Plan" refers to employee (EE) or employer (ER) withholding for the benefits plan.

**a.** Complete this payroll register by filling in all cells for the pay period ended August 31. *Hint:* See Exhibit 11A.3 for guidance. (Round amounts to cents.)

**b.** Prepare the August 31 journal entry to record the accrued biweekly payroll and related liabilities for deductions.

**c.** Prepare the August 31 journal entry to record the employer's cash payment of the net payroll of part *b.*

**d.** Prepare the August 31 journal entry to record the employer's payroll taxes including the contribution to the benefits plan.

**e.** Prepare the August 31 journal entry to pay all liabilities (expect net payroll in part *c*) for this biweekly period.

**connect**

Tytus Co. entered into the following transactions involving short-term liabilities in 2010 and 2011.

**2010**

Apr. 20   Purchased $38,500 of merchandise on credit from Frier, terms are 1/10, n/30. Tytus uses the perpetual inventory system.

May 19   Replaced the April 20 account payable to Frier with a 90-day, $30,000 note bearing 9% annual interest along with paying $8,500 in cash.

July 8   Borrowed $60,000 cash from Community Bank by signing a 120-day, 10% interest-bearing note with a face value of $60,000.

?   Paid the amount due on the note to Frier at the maturity date.

?   Paid the amount due on the note to Community Bank at the maturity date.

Nov. 28   Borrowed $21,000 cash from UMB Bank by signing a 60-day, 8% interest-bearing note with a face value of $21,000.

Dec. 31   Recorded an adjusting entry for accrued interest on the note to UMB Bank.

**2011**

?   Paid the amount due on the note to UMB Bank at the maturity date.

**Required**

**1.** Determine the maturity date for each of the three notes described.

**2.** Determine the interest due at maturity for each of the three notes. (Assume a 360-day year.)

**3.** Determine the interest expense to be recorded in the adjusting entry at the end of 2010.

**4.** Determine the interest expense to be recorded in 2011.

**5.** Prepare journal entries for all the preceding transactions and events for years 2010 and 2011.

**PROBLEM SET A**

**Problem 11-1A**
Short-term notes payable transactions and entries

P1

mhhe.com/wildFAP20e

**Check**   (2) Frier, $675
(3) $154
(4) $126

**Problem 11-2A**

Warranty expense and
liability estimation

P4

On October 29, 2010, Lue Co. began operations by purchasing razors for resale. Lue uses the perpetual inventory method. The razors have a 90-day warranty that requires the company to replace any nonworking razor. When a razor is returned, the company discards it and mails a new one from Merchandise Inventory to the customer. The company's cost per new razor is $18 and its retail selling price is $80 in both 2010 and 2011. The manufacturer has advised the company to expect warranty costs to equal 7% of dollar sales. The following transactions and events occurred.

*2010*

Nov. 11   Sold 75 razors for $6,000 cash.
      30   Recognized warranty expense related to November sales with an adjusting entry.
Dec.   9   Replaced 15 razors that were returned under the warranty.
      16   Sold 210 razors for $16,800 cash.
      29   Replaced 30 razors that were returned under the warranty.
      31   Recognized warranty expense related to December sales with an adjusting entry.

*2011*

Jan.   5   Sold 130 razors for $10,400 cash.
      17   Replaced 50 razors that were returned under the warranty.
      31   Recognized warranty expense related to January sales with an adjusting entry.

**Required**

1. Prepare journal entries to record these transactions and adjustments for 2010 and 2011.
2. How much warranty expense is reported for November 2010 and for December 2010?

**Check**  (3) $728
3. How much warranty expense is reported for January 2011?

          (4) $786 Cr.
4. What is the balance of the Estimated Warranty Liability account as of December 31, 2010?

          (5) $614 Cr.
5. What is the balance of the Estimated Warranty Liability account as of January 31, 2011?

---

**Problem 11-3A**

Computing and analyzing times
interest earned

A1

Shown here are condensed income statements for two different companies (both are organized as LLCs and pay no income taxes).

| Ace Company | |
| --- | --- |
| Sales . . . . . . . . . . . . . . . . . . . . . . . | $500,000 |
| Variable expenses (80%) . . . . . . . . . | 400,000 |
| Income before interest . . . . . . . . . . | 100,000 |
| Interest expense (fixed) . . . . . . . . . | 30,000 |
| Net income . . . . . . . . . . . . . . . . . . | $ 70,000 |

| Deuce Company | |
| --- | --- |
| Sales . . . . . . . . . . . . . . . . . . . . . . . | $500,000 |
| Variable expenses (60%) . . . . . . . . . | 300,000 |
| Income before interest . . . . . . . . . . | 200,000 |
| Interest expense (fixed) . . . . . . . . . | 130,000 |
| Net income . . . . . . . . . . . . . . . . . . | $ 70,000 |

**Required**

1. Compute times interest earned for Ace Company.
2. Compute times interest earned for Deuce Company.

**Check**  (3) Ace net income,
$100,000 (43% increase)
3. What happens to each company's net income if sales increase by 30%?
4. What happens to each company's net income if sales increase by 50%?
5. What happens to each company's net income if sales increase by 80%?

          (6) Deuce net income,
$50,000 (29% decrease)
6. What happens to each company's net income if sales decrease by 10%?
7. What happens to each company's net income if sales decrease by 20%?
8. What happens to each company's net income if sales decrease by 40%?

**Analysis Component**

9. Comment on the results from parts 3 through 8 in relation to the fixed-cost strategies of the two companies and the ratio values you computed in parts 1 and 2.

---

**Problem 11-4A**

Payroll expenses, withholdings,
and taxes

P2  P3

Legal Stars has four employees. FICA Social Security taxes are 6.2% of the first $106,800 paid to each employee, and FICA Medicare taxes are 1.45% of gross pay. Also, its FUTA taxes are 0.8% and SUTA taxes are 2.15% of the first $7,000 paid to each employee. The company is preparing its payroll calculations for the week ended August 25. Payroll records show the following information for the company's four employees.

mhhe.com/wildFAP20e

In addition to gross pay, the company must pay one-half of the $32 per employee weekly health insurance; each employee pays the remaining one-half. The company also contributes an extra 8% of each employee's gross pay (at no cost to employees) to a pension fund.

*Required*

Compute the following for the week ended August 25 (round amounts to the nearest cent):

1. Each employee's FICA withholdings for Social Security.
2. Each employee's FICA withholdings for Medicare.
3. Employer's FICA taxes for Social Security.
4. Employer's FICA taxes for Medicare.
5. Employer's FUTA taxes.
6. Employer's SUTA taxes.
7. Each employee's net (take-home) pay.
8. Employer's total payroll-related expense for each employee.

**Check**  (3) $201.50

(4) $54.38

(5) $5.20

(7) Total net pay, $2,989.12

On January 8, the end of the first weekly pay period of the year, Royal Company's payroll register showed that its employees earned $11,380 of office salaries and $32,920 of sales salaries. Withholdings from the employees' salaries include FICA Social Security taxes at the rate of 6.2%, FICA Medicare taxes at the rate of 1.45%, $6,340 of federal income taxes, $670 of medical insurance deductions, and $420 of union dues. No employee earned more than $7,000 in this first period.

**Problem 11-5A**
Entries for payroll transactions

**P2   P3**

*Required*

1. Calculate FICA Social Security taxes payable and FICA Medicare taxes payable. Prepare the journal entry to record Royal Company's January 8 (employee) payroll expenses and liabilities.
2. Prepare the journal entry to record Royal's (employer) payroll taxes resulting from the January 8 payroll. Royal's merit rating reduces its state unemployment tax rate to 4% of the first $7,000 paid each employee. The federal unemployment tax rate is 0.8%.

**Check**  (1) Cr. Salaries Payable, $33,481.05

(2) Dr. Payroll Taxes Expense, $5,515.35

Polo Company has 10 employees, each of whom earns $2,600 per month and is paid on the last day of each month. All 10 have been employed continuously at this amount since January 1. Polo uses a payroll bank account and special payroll checks to pay its employees. On March 1, the following accounts and balances exist in its general ledger:

**Problem 11-6A**<sup>A</sup>
Entries for payroll transactions

**P2   P3   P5**

a. FICA—Social Security Taxes Payable, $3,224; FICA—Medicare Taxes Payable, $754. (The balances of these accounts represent total liabilities for *both* the employer's and employees' FICA taxes for the February payroll only.)
b. Employees' Federal Income Taxes Payable, $3,900 (liability for February only).
c. Federal Unemployment Taxes Payable, $416 (liability for January and February together).
d. State Unemployment Taxes Payable, $2,080 (liability for January and February together).

During March and April, the company had the following payroll transactions.

Mar. 15   Issued check payable to Fleet Bank, a federal depository bank authorized to accept employers' payments of FICA taxes and employee income tax withholdings. The $7,878 check is in payment of the February FICA and employee income taxes.

31   Recorded the March payroll and transferred funds from the regular bank account to the payroll bank account. Issued checks payable to each employee in payment of the March payroll. The payroll register shows the following summary totals for the March pay period.

**Check**   March 31: Cr. Salaries Payable, $20,111

| | Salaries and Wages | | | | Federal | |
|---|---|---|---|---|---|---|
| | Office Salaries | Shop Wages | Gross Pay | FICA Taxes* | Income Taxes | Net Pay |
| | $10,400 | $15,600 | $26,000 | $1,612 | $3,900 | $20,111 |
| | | | | $ 377 | | |

* FICA taxes are Social Security and Medicare, respectively.

March 31: Dr. Payroll Taxes
Expenses, $2,853

April 15: Cr. Cash, $7,878
(Fleet Bank)

31   Recorded the employer's payroll taxes resulting from the March payroll. The company has a merit rating that reduces its state unemployment tax rate to 4.0% of the first $7,000 paid each employee. The federal rate is 0.8%.

Apr. 15   Issued check to Fleet Bank in payment of the March FICA and employee income taxes.

15   Issued check to the State Tax Commission for the January, February, and March state unemployment taxes. Mailed the check and the first quarter tax return to the Commission.

30   Issued check payable to Fleet Bank in payment of the employer's FUTA taxes for the first quarter of the year.

30   Mailed Form 941 to the IRS, reporting the FICA taxes and the employees' federal income tax withholdings for the first quarter.

**Required**

Prepare journal entries to record the transactions and events for both March and April.

## PROBLEM SET B

### Problem 11-1B
Short-term notes payable transactions and entries

**P1**

Bargen Co. entered into the following transactions involving short-term liabilities in 2010 and 2011.

**2010**

Apr. 22   Purchased $4,000 of merchandise on credit from Quinn Products, terms are 1/10, n/30. Bargen uses the perpetual inventory system.

May 23   Replaced the April 22 account payable to Quinn Products with a 60-day, $3,600 note bearing 15% annual interest along with paying $400 in cash.

July 15   Borrowed $9,000 cash from Blackhawk Bank by signing a 120-day, 10% interest-bearing note with a face value of $9,000.

___?___   Paid the amount due on the note to Quinn Products at maturity.

___?___   Paid the amount due on the note to Blackhawk Bank at maturity.

Dec. 6   Borrowed $16,000 cash from City Bank by signing a 45-day, 9% interest-bearing note with a face value of $16,000.

31   Recorded an adjusting entry for accrued interest on the note to City Bank.

**2011**

___?___   Paid the amount due on the note to City Bank at maturity.

**Required**

Check   (2) Quinn, $90
       (3) $100
       (4) $80

**1.** Determine the maturity date for each of the three notes described.

**2.** Determine the interest due at maturity for each of the three notes. (Assume a 360-day year.)

**3.** Determine the interest expense to be recorded in the adjusting entry at the end of 2010.

**4.** Determine the interest expense to be recorded in 2011.

**5.** Prepare journal entries for all the preceding transactions and events for years 2010 and 2011.

### Problem 11-2B
Warranty expense and liability estimation

**P4**

On November 10, 2011, Byung Co. began operations by purchasing coffee grinders for resale. Byung uses the perpetual inventory method. The grinders have a 60-day warranty that requires the company to replace any nonworking grinder. When a grinder is returned, the company discards it and mails a new one from Merchandise Inventory to the customer. The company's cost per new grinder is $14 and its retail selling price is $35 in both 2011 and 2012. The manufacturer has advised the company to expect warranty costs to equal 10% of dollar sales. The following transactions and events occurred.

**2011**

Nov. 16   Sold 50 grinders for $1,750 cash.

30   Recognized warranty expense related to November sales with an adjusting entry.

Dec. 12   Replaced six grinders that were returned under the warranty.

18   Sold 150 grinders for $5,250 cash.

28   Replaced 17 grinders that were returned under the warranty.

31   Recognized warranty expense related to December sales with an adjusting entry.

**2012**

Jan. 7 Sold 60 grinders for $2,100 cash.
　21 Replaced 38 grinders that were returned under the warranty.
　31 Recognized warranty expense related to January sales with an adjusting entry.

**Required**

1. Prepare journal entries to record these transactions and adjustments for 2011 and 2012.
2. How much warranty expense is reported for November 2011 and for December 2011?
3. How much warranty expense is reported for January 2012?
4. What is the balance of the Estimated Warranty Liability account as of December 31, 2011?
5. What is the balance of the Estimated Warranty Liability account as of January 31, 2012?

**Check** (3) $210
　(4) $378 Cr.
　(5) $56 Cr.

---

Shown here are condensed income statements for two different companies (both are organized as LLCs and pay no income taxes).

**Problem 11-3B**
Computing and analyzing times interest earned

A1

| Virgo Company | |
|---|---|
| Sales . . . . . . . . . . . . . . . . . . . . . . . | $120,000 |
| Variable expenses (50%) . . . . . . . . | 60,000 |
| Income before interest . . . . . . . . . . | 60,000 |
| Interest expense (fixed) . . . . . . . . . | 45,000 |
| Net income . . . . . . . . . . . . . . . . . | $ 15,000 |

| Zodiac Company | |
|---|---|
| Sales . . . . . . . . . . . . . . . . . . . . . . . | $120,000 |
| Variable expenses (75%) . . . . . . . . . | 90,000 |
| Income before interest . . . . . . . . . . | 30,000 |
| Interest expense (fixed) . . . . . . . . . | 15,000 |
| Net income . . . . . . . . . . . . . . . . . | $ 15,000 |

**Required**

1. Compute times interest earned for Virgo Company.
2. Compute times interest earned for Zodiac Company.
3. What happens to each company's net income if sales increase by 10%?
4. What happens to each company's net income if sales increase by 40%?
5. What happens to each company's net income if sales increase by 90%?
6. What happens to each company's net income if sales decrease by 20%?
7. What happens to each company's net income if sales decrease by 50%?
8. What happens to each company's net income if sales decrease by 80%?

**Check** (4) Virgo net income, $39,000 (160% increase)

　(6) Zodiac net income, $9,000 (40% decrease)

**Analysis Component**

9. Comment on the results from parts 3 through 8 in relation to the fixed-cost strategies of the two companies and the ratio values you computed in parts 1 and 2.

---

Sea Biz Co. has four employees. FICA Social Security taxes are 6.2% of the first $106,800 paid to each employee, and FICA Medicare taxes are 1.45% of gross pay. Also, its FUTA taxes are 0.8% and SUTA taxes are 1.75% of the first $7,000 paid to each employee. The company is preparing its payroll calculations for the week ended September 30. Payroll records show the following information for the company's four employees.

**Problem 11-4B**
Payroll expenses, withholdings, and taxes

P2　P3

| | | File Edit View Insert Format Tools Data Accounting Window Help | | _|8|x| |
|---|---|---|---|---|
| | | | Σ ƒ× ↓ ↓   100% ▾   Arial ▾ 10 ▾ B I U | |
| 1 | | **Gross Pay** | **Current Week** | |
| 2 | **Name** | **through 9/23** | **Gross Pay** | **Income Tax Withholding** |
| 3 | Alli | $104,300 | $2,500 | $198 |
| 4 | Eve | 36,650 | 1,515 | 182 |
| 5 | Hong | 6,650 | 475 | 52 |
| 6 | Juan | 22,200 | 600 | 48 |
| 7 | | | | |

Sheet1 / Sheet2 / Sheet3

In addition to gross pay, the company must pay one-half of the $44 per employee weekly health insurance; each employee pays the remaining one-half. The company also contributes an extra 5% of each employee's gross pay (at no cost to employees) to a pension fund.

### Required

Compute the following for the week ended September 30 (round amounts to the nearest cent):

1. Each employee's FICA withholdings for Social Security.
2. Each employee's FICA withholdings for Medicare.
3. Employer's FICA taxes for Social Security.
4. Employer's FICA taxes for Medicare.
5. Employer's FUTA taxes.
6. Employer's SUTA taxes.
7. Each employee's net (take-home) pay.
8. Employer's total payroll-related expense for each employee.

## Problem 11-5B
Entries for payroll transactions
**P2  P3**

Palmer Company's first weekly pay period of the year ends on January 8. On that date, the column totals in Palmer's payroll register indicate its sales employees earned $69,490, its office employees earned $42,450, and its delivery employees earned $2,060. The employees are to have withheld from their wages FICA Social Security taxes at the rate of 6.2%, FICA Medicare taxes at the rate of 1.45%, $17,250 of federal income taxes, $2,320 of medical insurance deductions, and $275 of union dues. No employee earned more than $7,000 in the first pay period.

### Required

1. Calculate FICA Social Security taxes payable and FICA Medicare taxes payable. Prepare the journal entry to record Palmer Company's January 8 (employee) payroll expenses and liabilities.
2. Prepare the journal entry to record Palmer's (employer) payroll taxes resulting from the January 8 payroll. Palmer's merit rating reduces its state unemployment tax rate to 3.4% of the first $7,000 paid each employee. The federal unemployment tax rate is 0.8%.

## Problem 11-6B[A]
Entries for payroll transactions
**P2  P3  P5**

JLK Company has five employees, each of whom earns $1,200 per month and is paid on the last day of each month. All five have been employed continuously at this amount since January 1. JLK uses a payroll bank account and special payroll checks to pay its employees. On June 1, the following accounts and balances exist in its general ledger:

a. FICA—Social Security Taxes Payable, $744; FICA—Medicare Taxes Payable, $174. (The balances of these accounts represent total liabilities for *both* the employer's and employees' FICA taxes for the May payroll only.)
b. Employees' Federal Income Taxes Payable, $900 (liability for May only).
c. Federal Unemployment Taxes Payable, $96 (liability for April and May together).
d. State Unemployment Taxes Payable, $480 (liability for April and May together).

During June and July, the company had the following payroll transactions.

June   15   Issued check payable to Security Bank, a federal depository bank authorized to accept employers' payments of FICA taxes and employee income tax withholdings. The $1,818 check is in payment of the May FICA and employee income taxes.
       30   Recorded the June payroll and transferred funds from the regular bank account to the payroll bank account. Issued checks payable to each employee in payment of the June payroll. The payroll register shows the following summary totals for the June pay period.

| Salaries and Wages | | | | Federal | |
| Office Salaries | Shop Wages | Gross Pay | FICA Taxes* | Income Taxes | Net Pay |
|---|---|---|---|---|---|
| $2,000 | $4,000 | $6,000 | $372 | $900 | $4,641 |
|  |  |  | $ 87 |  |  |

\* FICA taxes are Social Security and Medicare, respectively.

       30   Recorded the employer's payroll taxes resulting from the June payroll. The company has a merit rating that reduces its state unemployment tax rate to 4.0% of the first $7,000 paid each employee. The federal rate is 0.8%.
July   15   Issued check payable to Security Bank in payment of the June FICA and employee income taxes.
       15   Issued check to the State Tax Commission for the April, May and June state unemployment taxes. Mailed the check and the second quarter tax return to the State Tax Commission.
       31   Issued check payable to Security Bank in payment of the employer's FUTA taxes for the first quarter of the year.
       31   Mailed Form 941 to the IRS, reporting the FICA taxes and the employees' federal income tax withholdings for the second quarter.

**Required**

Prepare journal entries to record the transactions and events for both June and July.

SERIAL PROBLEM
Business Solutions
P2 P3 C2

*(This serial problem began in Chapter 1 and continues through most of the book. If previous chapter segments were not completed, the serial problem can begin at this point. It is helpful, but not necessary, to use the Working Papers that accompany the book.)*

**SP 11** Review the February 26 and March 25 transactions for Business Solutions (SP 5) from Chapter 5.

**Required**

1. Assume that Lyn Addie is an unmarried employee. Her $1,000 of wages are subject to no deductions other than FICA Social Security taxes, FICA Medicare taxes, and federal income taxes. Her federal income taxes for this pay period total $159. Compute her net pay for the eight days' work paid on February 26. (Round amounts to the nearest cent.)

2. Record the journal entry to reflect the payroll payment to Lyn Addie as computed in part 1.

3. Record the journal entry to reflect the (employer) payroll tax expenses for the February 26 payroll payment. Assume Lyn Addie has not met earnings limits for FUTA and SUTA—the FUTA rate is 0.8% and the SUTA rate is 4% for Business Solutions. (Round amounts to the nearest cent.)

4. Record the entry(ies) for the merchandise sold on March 25 if a 4% sales tax rate applies.

COMPREHENSIVE PROBLEM
Bug-Off Exterminators
(Review of Chapters 1–11)

**CP 11** Bug-Off Exterminators provides pest control services and sells extermination products manufactured by other companies. The following six-column table contains the company's unadjusted trial balance as of December 31, 2011.

**BUG-OFF EXTERMINATORS**
**December 31, 2011**

| | Unadjusted Trial Balance | | Adjustments | | Adjusted Trial Balance | |
|---|---|---|---|---|---|---|
| Cash | $ 17,000 | | | | | |
| Accounts receivable | 4,000 | | | | | |
| Allowance for doubtful accounts | | $ 828 | | | | |
| Merchandise inventory | 11,700 | | | | | |
| Trucks | 32,000 | | | | | |
| Accum. depreciation—Trucks | | 0 | | | | |
| Equipment | 45,000 | | | | | |
| Accum. depreciation—Equipment | | 12,200 | | | | |
| Accounts payable | | 5,000 | | | | |
| Estimated warranty liability | | 1,400 | | | | |
| Unearned services revenue | | 0 | | | | |
| Interest payable | | 0 | | | | |
| Long-term notes payable | | 15,000 | | | | |
| D. Buggs, Capital | | 59,700 | | | | |
| D. Buggs, Withdrawals | 10,000 | | | | | |
| Extermination services revenue | | 60,000 | | | | |
| Interest revenue | | 872 | | | | |
| Sales (of merchandise) | | 71,026 | | | | |
| Cost of goods sold | 46,300 | | | | | |
| Depreciation expense—Trucks | 0 | | | | | |
| Depreciation expense—Equipment | 0 | | | | | |
| Wages expense | 35,000 | | | | | |
| Interest expense | 0 | | | | | |
| Rent expense | 9,000 | | | | | |
| Bad debts expense | 0 | | | | | |
| Miscellaneous expense | 1,226 | | | | | |
| Repairs expense | 8,000 | | | | | |
| Utilities expense | 6,800 | | | | | |
| Warranty expense | 0 | | | | | |
| Totals | $226,026 | $226,026 | | | | |

The following information in *a* through *h* applies to the company at the end of the current year.

**a.** The bank reconciliation as of December 31, 2011, includes the following facts.

| | |
|---|---:|
| Cash balance per bank ........................... | $15,100 |
| Cash balance per books .......................... | 17,000 |
| Outstanding checks .............................. | 1,800 |
| Deposit in transit .............................. | 2,450 |
| Interest earned (on bank account) ............... | 52 |
| Bank service charges (miscellaneous expense) ........ | 15 |

Reported on the bank statement is a canceled check that the company failed to record. (Information from the bank reconciliation allows you to determine the amount of this check, which is a payment on an account payable.)

**b.** An examination of customers' accounts shows that accounts totaling $679 should be written off as uncollectible. Using an aging of receivables, the company determines that the ending balance of the Allowance for Doubtful Accounts should be $700.

**c.** A truck is purchased and placed in service on January 1, 2011. Its cost is being depreciated with the straight-line method using the following facts and estimates.

| | |
|---|---:|
| Original cost ................ | $32,000 |
| Expected salvage value ........ | 8,000 |
| Useful life (years) ............ | 4 |

**d.** Two items of equipment (a sprayer and an injector) were purchased and put into service in early January 2009. They are being depreciated with the straight-line method using these facts and estimates.

| | Sprayer | Injector |
|---|---:|---:|
| Original cost ................ | $27,000 | $18,000 |
| Expected salvage value ........ | 3,000 | 2,500 |
| Useful life (years) ............ | 8 | 5 |

**e.** On August 1, 2011, the company is paid $3,840 cash in advance to provide monthly service for an apartment complex for one year. The company began providing the services in August. When the cash was received, the full amount was credited to the Extermination Services Revenue account.

**f.** The company offers a warranty for the services it sells. The expected cost of providing warranty service is 2.5% of the extermination services revenue of $57,760 for 2011. No warranty expense has been recorded for 2011. All costs of servicing warranties in 2011 were properly debited to the Estimated Warranty Liability account.

**g.** The $15,000 long-term note is an 8%, five-year, interest-bearing note with interest payable annually on December 31. The note was signed with First National Bank on December 31, 2011.

**h.** The ending inventory of merchandise is counted and determined to have a cost of $11,700. Bug-Off uses a perpetual inventory system.

### Required

**1.** Use the preceding information to determine amounts for the following items.

**a.** Correct (reconciled) ending balance of Cash, and the amount of the omitted check.

**b.** Adjustment needed to obtain the correct ending balance of the Allowance for Doubtful Accounts.

**c.** Depreciation expense for the truck used during year 2011.

**d.** Depreciation expense for the two items of equipment used during year 2011.

**e.** The adjusted 2011 ending balances of the Extermination Services Revenue and Unearned Services Revenue accounts.

**f.** The adjusted 2011 ending balances of the accounts for Warranty Expense and Estimated Warranty Liability.

**g.** The adjusted 2011 ending balances of the accounts for Interest Expense and Interest Payable. (Round amounts to nearest whole dollar.)

**Check** (1*a*) Cash bal. $15,750
(1*b*) $551 credit

(1*f*) Estim. warranty liability, $2,844 Cr.

**2.** Use the results of part 1 to complete the six-column table by first entering the appropriate adjustments for items *a* through *g* and then completing the adjusted trial balance columns. (*Hint:* Item *b* requires two adjustments.)

**3.** Prepare journal entries to record the adjustments entered on the six-column table. Assume Bug-Off's adjusted balance for Merchandise Inventory matches the year-end physical count.

**4.** Prepare a single-step income statement, a statement of owner's equity (cash withdrawals during 2011 were $10,000), and a classified balance sheet.

(2) Adjusted trial balance totals, $238,207

(4) Net income, $9,274; Total assets, $82,771

## Beyond the Numbers

**BTN 11-1**   Refer to the financial statements of **Research In Motion** in Appendix A to answer the following.

**1.** Compute times interest earned for the fiscal years ended 2010, 2009, and 2008. Comment on RIM's ability to cover its interest expense for this period. Assume interest expense of $1, $502, and $31 for fiscal years ended 2010, 2009, and 2008 ($ thousands); and, assume an industry average of 18.1 for times interest earned.

**2.** RIM's current liabilities include "deferred revenue"; assume that this account reflects "Unredeemed gift card liabilities." Explain how this liability is created and how RIM satisfies this liability.

**3.** Does RIM have any commitments or contingencies? Briefly explain them.

*Fast Forward*

**4.** Access RIM's financial statements for fiscal years ending after February 27, 2010, at its Website (**RIM.com**) or the SEC's EDGAR database (**www.sec.gov**). Compute its times interest earned for years ending after February 27, 2010, and compare your results to those in part 1.

**REPORTING IN ACTION**

A1  P4

*RIM*

**BTN 11-2**   Key figures for **Research In Motion** and **Apple** follow. (Interest expense figures for Apple are assumed as it has no interest expense for these years.)

| ($ millions) | Research In Motion | | | Apple | | |
| | Current Year | One Year Prior | Two Years Prior | Current Year | One Year Prior | Two Years Prior |
| --- | --- | --- | --- | --- | --- | --- |
| Net income | $2,457.144 | $1,892.616 | $1,293.867 | $8,235 | $6,119 | $3,495 |
| Income taxes | 809.366 | 907.747 | 516.653 | 3,831 | 2,828 | 1,511 |
| Interest expense | .001 | .502 | .031 | 3 | 2 | 1 |

**COMPARATIVE ANALYSIS**

A1

*RIM*
Apple

*Required*

**1.** Compute times interest earned for the three years' data shown for each company.

**2.** Comment on which company appears stronger in its ability to pay interest obligations if income should decline. Assume an industry average of 18.1.

**BTN 11-3**   Connor Bly is a sales manager for an automobile dealership. He earns a bonus each year based on revenue from the number of autos sold in the year less related warranty expenses. Actual warranty expenses have varied over the prior 10 years from a low of 3% of an automobile's selling price to a high of 10%. In the past, Bly has tended to estimate warranty expenses on the high end to be conservative. He must work with the dealership's accountant at year-end to arrive at the warranty expense accrual for cars sold each year.

**1.** Does the warranty accrual decision create any ethical dilemma for Bly?

**2.** Since warranty expenses vary, what percent do you think Bly should choose for the current year? Justify your response.

**ETHICS CHALLENGE**

P4

**BTN 11-4**   Dustin Clemens is the accounting and finance manager for a manufacturer. At year-end, he must determine how to account for the company's contingencies. His manager, Madeline Pretti, objects to Clemens's proposal to recognize an expense and a liability for warranty service on units of a new product introduced in the fourth quarter. Pretti comments, "There's no way we can estimate this warranty cost. We don't owe anyone anything until a product fails and it is returned. Let's report an expense if and when we do any warranty work."

**COMMUNICATING IN PRACTICE**

C3

*Required*

Prepare a one-page memorandum for Clemens to send to Pretti defending his proposal.

## TAKING IT TO THE NET

C1   A1  

**BTN 11-5**   Access the February 26, 2010, filing of the December 31, 2009, annual 10-K report of **McDonald's Corporation** (Ticker: MCD), which is available from **www.sec.gov**.

**Required**

1. Identify the current liabilities on McDonald's balance sheet as of December 31, 2009.
2. What portion (in percent) of McDonald's long-term debt matures within the next 12 months?
3. Use the consolidated statement of income for the year ended December 31, 2009, to compute McDonald's times interest earned ratio. Comment on the result. Assume an industry average of 12.0.

## TEAMWORK IN ACTION

C2   P1

**BTN 11-6**   Assume that your team is in business and you must borrow $6,000 cash for short-term needs. You have been shopping banks for a loan, and you have the following two options.

**A.** Sign a $6,000, 90-day, 10% interest-bearing note dated June 1.
**B.** Sign a $6,000, 120-day, 8% interest-bearing note dated June 1.

**Required**

1. Discuss these two options and determine the best choice. Ensure that all teammates concur with the decision and understand the rationale.
2. Each member of the team is to prepare *one* of the following journal entries.
    **a.** Option A—at date of issuance.
    **b.** Option B—at date of issuance.
    **c.** Option A—at maturity date.
    **d.** Option B—at maturity date.
3. In rotation, each member is to explain the entry he or she prepared in part 2 to the team. Ensure that all team members concur with and understand the entries.
4. Assume that the funds are borrowed on December 1 (instead of June 1) and your business operates on a calendar-year reporting period. Each member of the team is to prepare *one* of the following entries.
    **a.** Option A—the year-end adjustment.
    **b.** Option B—the year-end adjustment.
    **c.** Option A—at maturity date.
    **d.** Option B—at maturity date.
5. In rotation, each member is to explain the entry he or she prepared in part 4 to the team. Ensure that all team members concur with and understand the entries.

## ENTREPRENEURIAL DECISION

A1  

**BTN 11-7**   Review the chapter's opening feature about Matt and Bryan Walls, and their start-up company, **SnorgTees**. Assume that these young entrepreneurs are considering expanding their business to open an outlet in Europe. Assume their current income statement is as follows.

| SNORGTEES<br>Income Statement<br>For Year Ended December 31, 2011 | |
|---|---:|
| Sales . . . . . . . . . . . . . . . . . . . . . . . . . . | $1,000,000 |
| Cost of goods sold (30%) . . . . . . . . . . | 300,000 |
| Gross profit . . . . . . . . . . . . . . . . . . . . | 700,000 |
| Operating expenses (25%) . . . . . . . . | 250,000 |
| Net income . . . . . . . . . . . . . . . . . . . | $ 450,000 |

SnorgTees currently has no interest-bearing debt. If it expands to open a European location, it will require a $300,000 loan. SnorgTees has found a bank that will loan it the money on a 7% note payable. The company believes that, at least for the first few years, sales at its European location will be $250,000, and that all expenses (including cost of goods sold) will follow the same patterns as its current locations.

*Required*

1. Prepare an income statement (showing three separate columns for current operations, European, and total) for SnorgTees assuming that it borrows the funds and expands to Europe. Annual revenues for current operations are expected to remain at $1,000,000.

2. Compute SnorgTees' times interest earned under the expansion assumptions in part 1.

3. Assume sales at its European location are $400,000. Prepare an income statement (with columns for current operations, European, and total) for the company and compute times interest earned.

4. Assume sales at its European location are $100,000. Prepare an income statement (with columns for current operations, European, and total) for the company and compute times interest earned.

5. Comment on your results from parts 1 through 4.

---

**BTN 11-8**   Check your phone book or the Social Security Administration Website (www.ssa.gov) to locate the Social Security office near you. Visit the office to request a personal earnings and estimate form. Fill out the form and mail according to the instructions. You will receive a statement from the Social Security Administration regarding your earnings history and future Social Security benefits you can receive. (Formerly the request could be made online. The online service has been discontinued and is now under review by the Social Security Administration due to security concerns.) It is good to request an earnings and benefit statement every 5 to 10 years to make sure you have received credit for all wages earned and for which you and your employer have paid taxes into the system.

**HITTING THE ROAD**

P2

---

**BTN 11-9**   Nokia, Research In Motion, and Apple are all competitors in the global marketplace. Comparative figures for Nokia (www.Nokia.com), along with selected figures from Research In Motion and Apple, follow.

**GLOBAL DECISION**

A1

**NOKIA**

*RIM*

Apple

| Key Figures | Nokia (EUR millions) Current Year | Prior Year | Research In Motion Current Year | Prior Year | Apple Current Year | Prior Year |
|---|---|---|---|---|---|---|
| Net income ................ | 260 | 3,889 | — | — | — | — |
| Income taxes .............. | 702 | 1,081 | — | — | — | — |
| Interest expense ........... | 243 | 185 | — | — | — | — |
| Times interest earned ....... | ? | ? | 3,267 | 5,579 | 4,023 | 4,475 |

*Required*

1. Compute the times interest earned ratio for the most recent two years for Nokia using the data shown.

2. Which company of the three presented provides the best coverage of interest expense? Explain.

---

**ANSWERS TO MULTIPLE CHOICE QUIZ**

1. b; $6,000 × 0.05 × 30/360 = $25
2. e; $50,000 × (.062 + .0145) = $3,825
3. b; $7,000 × (.008 + .054) = $434

4. c; 10,000 television sets × .01 × $250 = $25,000
5. a; 150 employees × $175 per day × 1 vacation day earned = $26,250

# 12

# Accounting for Partnerships

## A Look Back

Chapter 11 focused on how current liabilities are identified, computed, recorded, and reported. Attention was directed at notes, payroll, sales taxes, warranties, employee benefits, and contingencies.

## A Look at This Chapter

This chapter explains the partnership form of organization. Important partnership characteristics are described along with the accounting concepts and procedures for its most fundamental transactions.

## A Look Ahead

Chapter 13 extends our discussion to the corporate form of organization. We describe the accounting and reporting for stock issuances, dividends, and other equity transactions.

## Learning Objectives

### CAP

**CONCEPTUAL**

**C1** Identify characteristics of partnerships and similar organizations. (p. 480)

**ANALYTICAL**

**A1** Compute partner return on equity and use it to evaluate partnership performance. (p. 492)

LP12

**PROCEDURAL**

**P1** Prepare entries for partnership formation. (p. 483)

**P2** Allocate and record income and loss among partners. (p. 483)

**P3** Account for the admission and withdrawal of partners. (p. 486)

**P4** Prepare entries for partnership liquidation. (p. 490)

## Decision Insight

# Let's Do Eco-Lunch

*"We are making a difference"*
—**CHANCE CLAXTON AND LYNN JULIAN**

PHOENIX—Believe it or not, nearly 20,000 pounds of trash is generated annually from the typical elementary school. "When we researched it," explains Chance Claxton, "We discovered that 67 pounds of lunchtime trash is created by each schoolage child each school year." Armed with that evidence, and as mothers of young children, Chance, along with partner Lynn Julian, felt an urgent need to respond. The result is **Kids Konserve (KidsKonserve.com),** a start-up partnership that sells reusable and recycled food kits. "With waste from snack and lunch breaks at an all-time high," says Chance, "Kids Konserve is empowering parents and kids with information and a reusable product that will help . . . decrease waste in community landfills."

While Chance focuses on the design and sales side, Lynn's focus is on the accounting, marketing, and financial side of Kids Konserve. Her knowledge of partnerships and their financial implications are important to Kid Konserve's success. Lynn explains that she is working on a model for fund-raising opportunities to further expand their product opportunities. Both partners stress the importance of attending to partnership

formation, partnership agreements, and financial reports to stay afloat. They refer to the partners' return on equity and establishing the proper organizational form as key inputs to partnership strategies and decisions.

Success is causing their partnership to evolve, but the partners adhere to an eco-focused mentality. "The best part of being a 'mompreneur' is that I am doing something for myself, for others, for my family, and for the earth," insists Chance. "It is a great feeling to have my children watch me work."

The partners continue to apply strict accounting fundamentals. Lynn explains that their partnership cannot survive unless the business is profitable, even with their noble agenda. To that end, both partners review their accounting results and regularly assess the partnership's costs and revenues. Nevertheless, Lynn emphasizes their greater goal: "We're delivering a program that reduces waste on campus. I'd say that deserves an A+."

[Sources: *Kids Konserve Website,* January 2011; *Entrepreneur,* October 2009; *MomBites.com,* September 2009; *Daily Grommet,* September 2009]

The three basic types of business organizations are proprietorships, partnerships, and corporations. Partnerships are similar to proprietorships, except they have more than one owner. This chapter explains partnerships and looks at several variations of them such as limited partnerships, limited liability partnerships, S corporations, and limited liability companies. Understanding the advantages and disadvantages of the partnership form of business organization is important for making informed business decisions.

### Accounting for Partnerships

| Partnership Organization | Basic Partnership Accounting | Partner Admission and Withdrawal | Partnership Liquidation |
|---|---|---|---|
| • Characteristics<br>• Organizations with partnership characteristics<br>• Choice of business form | • Organizing a partnership<br>• Dividing income or loss<br>• Partnership financial statements | • Admission of partner<br>• Withdrawal of partner<br>• Death of partner | • No capital deficiency<br>• Capital deficiency |

# PARTNERSHIP FORM OF ORGANIZATION

**C1** Identify characteristics of partnerships and similar organizations.

A **partnership** is an unincorporated association of two or more people to pursue a business for profit as co-owners. Many businesses are organized as partnerships. They are especially common in small retail and service businesses. Many professional practitioners, including physicians, lawyers, investors, and accountants, also organize their practices as partnerships.

## Characteristics of Partnerships

Partnerships are an important type of organization because they offer certain advantages with their unique characteristics. We describe these characteristics in this section.

**Voluntary Association** A partnership is a voluntary association between partners. Joining a partnership increases the risk to one's personal financial position. Some courts have ruled that partnerships are created by the actions of individuals even when there is no *express agreement* to form one.

**Partnership Agreement** Forming a partnership requires that two or more legally competent people (who are of age and of sound mental capacity) agree to be partners. Their agreement becomes a **partnership contract,** also called *articles of copartnership.* Although it should be in writing, the contract is binding even if it is only expressed verbally. Partnership agreements normally include details of the partners' (1) names and contributions, (2) rights and duties, (3) sharing of income and losses, (4) withdrawal arrangement, (5) dispute procedures, (6) admission and withdrawal of partners, and (7) rights and duties in the event a partner dies.

**Point:** When a new partner is admitted, all parties usually must agree to the admission.

**Limited Life** The life of a partnership is limited. Death, bankruptcy, or any event taking away the ability of a partner to enter into or fulfill a contract ends a partnership. Any one of the partners can also terminate a partnership at will.

**Point:** The end of a partnership is referred to as its *dissolution.*

**Taxation** A partnership is not subject to taxes on its income. The income or loss of a partnership is allocated to the partners according to the partnership agreement, and it is included in determining the taxable income for each partner's tax return. Partnership income or loss is allocated each year whether or not cash is distributed to partners.

**Point:** Partners are taxed on their share of partnership income, not on their withdrawals.

**Mutual Agency** Mutual agency implies that each partner is a fully authorized agent of the partnership. As its agent, a partner can commit or bind the partnership to any contract within the scope of the partnership business. For instance, a partner in a merchandising business can sign contracts binding the partnership to buy merchandise, lease a store building, borrow money, or hire employees. These activities are all within the scope of a merchandising firm. A partner in a law firm, acting alone, however, cannot bind the other partners to a contract to buy snowboards for resale or rent an apartment for parties. These actions are outside the normal scope of a law firm's business. Partners also can agree to limit the power of any one or more of the partners to negotiate contracts for the partnership. This agreement is binding on the partners and on outsiders who know it exists. It is not binding on outsiders who do not know it exists. Outsiders unaware of the agreement have the right to assume each partner has normal agency powers for the partnership. Mutual agency exposes partners to the risk of unwise actions by any one partner.

**Point:** The majority of states adhere to the Uniform Partnership Act for the basic rules of partnership formation, operation, and dissolution.

**Unlimited Liability**  **Unlimited liability** implies that each partner can be called on to pay a partnership's debts. When a partnership cannot pay its debts, creditors usually can apply their claims to partners' *personal* assets. If a partner does not have enough assets to meet his or her share of the partnership debt, the creditors can apply their claims to the assets of the other partners. A partnership in which all partners have *mutual agency* and *unlimited liability* is called a **general partnership.** Mutual agency and unlimited liability are two main reasons that most general partnerships have only a few members.

**Point:** Limited life, mutual agency, and unlimited liability are disadvantages of a partnership.

**Co-Ownership of Property**  Partnership assets are owned jointly by all partners. Any investment by a partner becomes the joint property of all partners. Partners have a claim on partnership assets based on their capital account and the partnership contract.

## Organizations with Partnership Characteristics

Organizations exist that combine certain characteristics of partnerships with other forms of organizations. We discuss several of these forms in this section.

**Limited Partnerships**  Some individuals who want to invest in a partnership are unwilling to accept the risk of unlimited liability. Their needs can be met with a **limited partnership.** This type of organization is identified in its name with the words "Limited Partnership" or "Ltd." or "LP." A limited partnership has two classes of partners, general and limited. At least one partner must be a **general partner,** who assumes management duties and unlimited liability for the debts of the partnership. The **limited partners** have no personal liability beyond the amounts they invest in the partnership. Limited partners have no active role except as specified in the partnership agreement. A limited partnership agreement often specifies unique procedures for allocating income and losses between general and limited partners. The accounting procedures are similar for both limited and general partnerships.

### Decision **Insight**

**Nutty Partners**   The Hawaii-based **ML Macadamia Orchards LP** is one of the world's largest growers of macadamia nuts. It reported the following partners' capital balances ($ 000s) in its balance sheet: ■

| | |
|---|---|
| General Partner . . . . . . | $    81 |
| Limited Partners . . . . . . | $43,560 |

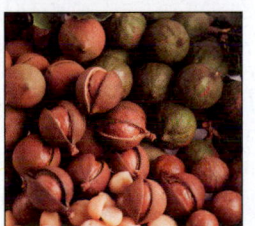

**Limited Liability Partnerships**  Most states allow individuals to form a **limited liability partnership.** This is identified in its name with the words "Limited Liability Partnership" or by "LLP." This type of partnership is designed to protect innocent partners from malpractice or negligence claims resulting from the acts of another partner. When a partner provides service resulting in a malpractice claim, that partner has personal liability for the claim. The remaining partners who were not responsible for the actions resulting in the claim are not personally liable for it. However, most states hold all partners personally liable for other partnership debts. Accounting for a limited liability partnership is the same as for a general partnership.

**Point:** Many accounting services firms are set up as LLPs.

**S Corporations**   Certain corporations with 100 or fewer stockholders can elect to be treated as a partnership for income tax purposes. These corporations are called *Sub-Chapter S* or simply **S corporations.** This distinguishes them from other corporations, called *Sub-Chapter C* or simply **C corporations.** S corporations provide stockholders the same limited liability feature that C corporations do. The advantage of an S corporation is that it does not pay income taxes. If stockholders work for an S corporation, their salaries are treated as expenses of the corporation. The remaining income or loss of the corporation is allocated to stockholders for inclusion on their personal tax returns. Except for C corporations having to account for income tax expenses and liabilities, the accounting procedures are the same for both S and C corporations.

**Point:** The majority of proprietorships and partnerships that are organized today are set up as LLCs.

**Limited Liability Companies**   A relatively new form of business organization is the **limited liability company.** The names of these businesses usually include the words "Limited Liability Company" or an abbreviation such as "LLC" or "LC." This form of business has certain features similar to a corporation and others similar to a limited partnership. The owners, who are called *members,* are protected with the same limited liability feature as owners of corporations. While limited partners cannot actively participate in the management of a limited partnership, the members of a limited liability company can assume an active management role. A limited liability company usually has a limited life. For income tax purposes, a limited liability company is typically treated as a partnership. This treatment depends on factors such as whether the members' equity interests are freely transferable and whether the company has continuity of life. A limited liability company's accounting system is designed to help management comply with the dictates of the articles of organization and company regulations adopted by its members. The accounting system also must provide information to support the company's compliance with state and federal laws, including taxation.

**Point:** Accounting for LLCs is similar to that for partnerships (and proprietorships). One difference is that Owner (Partner), Capital is usually called *Members, Capital* for LLCs.

## Choosing a Business Form

Choosing the proper business form is crucial. Many factors should be considered, including taxes, liability risk, tax and fiscal year-end, ownership structure, estate planning, business risks, and earnings and property distributions. The following table summarizes several important characteristics of business organizations:

|  | Proprietorship | Partnership | LLP | LLC | S Corp. | Corporation |
|---|---|---|---|---|---|---|
| Business entity ......... | Yes | Yes | Yes | Yes | Yes | Yes |
| Legal entity ............ | No | No | No | Yes | Yes | Yes |
| Limited liability ......... | No | No | Limited* | Yes | Yes | Yes |
| Business taxed .......... | No | No | No | No | No | Yes |
| One owner allowed ..... | Yes | No | No | Yes | Yes | Yes |

\* A partner's personal liability for LLP debts is limited. Most LLPs carry insurance to protect against malpractice.

**Point:** The Small Business Administration provides suggestions and information on setting up the proper form for your organization—see **SBA.gov**.

We must remember that this table is a summary, not a detailed list. Many details underlie each of these business forms, and several details differ across states. Also, state and federal laws change, and a body of law is still developing around LLCs. Business owners should look at these details and consider unique business arrangements such as organizing various parts of their businesses in different forms.

### Quick Check

Answers — p. 495

1. A partnership is terminated in the event (*a*) a partnership agreement is not in writing, (*b*) a partner dies, (*c*) a partner exercises mutual agency.
2. What does the term *unlimited liability* mean when applied to a general partnership?
3. Which of the following forms of organization do not provide limited liability to *all* of its owners? (*a*) S corporation, (*b*) limited liability company, (*c*) limited partnership.

## BASIC PARTNERSHIP ACCOUNTING

Since ownership rights in a partnership are divided among partners, partnership accounting

- Uses a capital account for each partner.
- Uses a withdrawals account for each partner.
- Allocates net income or loss to partners according to the partnership agreement.

This section describes partnership accounting for organizing a partnership, distributing income and loss, and preparing financial statements.

### Organizing a Partnership

When partners invest in a partnership, their capital accounts are credited for the invested amounts. Partners can invest both assets and liabilities. Each partner's investment is recorded at an agreed-on value, normally the market values of the contributed assets and liabilities at the date of contribution. To illustrate, Kayla Zayn and Hector Perez organize a partnership on January 11 called BOARDS that offers year-round facilities for skateboarding and snowboarding. Zayn's initial net investment in BOARDS is $30,000, made up of cash ($7,000), boarding facilities ($33,000), and a note payable reflecting a bank loan for the new business ($10,000). Perez's initial investment is cash of $10,000. These amounts are the values agreed on by both partners. The entries to record these investments follow.

**P1** Prepare entries for partnership formation.

**Zayn's Investment**

| Jan. 11 | Cash .......................................... | 7,000 | |
| | Boarding facilities ............................. | 33,000 | |
| |     Note payable ............................. | | 10,000 |
| |     K. Zayn, Capital ........................... | | 30,000 |
| | *To record the investment of Zayn.* | | |

Assets  = Liabilities +  Equity
+7,000    +10,000    +30,000
+33,000

**Perez's Investment**

| Jan. 11 | Cash .......................................... | 10,000 | |
| |   H. Perez, Capital ........................... | | 10,000 |
| | *To record the investment of Perez.* | | |

Assets  = Liabilities +  Equity
+10,000            +10,000

In accounting for a partnership, the following additional relations hold true: (1) Partners' withdrawals are debited to their own separate withdrawals accounts. (2) Partners' capital accounts are credited (or debited) for their shares of net income (or net loss) when closing the accounts at the end of a period. (3) Each partner's withdrawals account is closed to that partner's capital account. Separate capital and withdrawals accounts are kept for each partner.

**Point:** Both equity and cash are reduced when a partner withdraws cash from a partnership.

### Decision Insight

**Broadway Partners** **Big River Productions** is a partnership that owns the rights to the play *Big River*. The play is performed on tour and periodically on Broadway. For a recent year-end, its Partners' Capital was approximately $300,000, and it was distributed in its entirety to the partners. ■

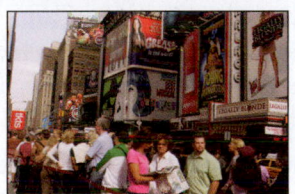

### Dividing Income or Loss

Partners are not employees of the partnership but are its owners. If partners devote their time and services to their partnership, they are understood to do so for profit, not for salary. This means there are no salaries to partners that are reported as expenses on the partnership income statement. However, when net income or loss of a partnership is allocated among partners, the partners can agree to allocate "salary allowances" reflecting the relative value of services

**P2** Allocate and record income and loss among partners.

provided. Partners also can agree to allocate "interest allowances" based on the amount invested. For instance, since Zayn contributes three times the investment of Perez, it is only fair that this be considered when allocating income between them. Like salary allowances, these interest allowances are not expenses on the income statement.

Partners can agree to any method of dividing income or loss. In the absence of an agreement, the law says that the partners share income or loss of a partnership equally. If partners agree on how to share income but say nothing about losses, they share losses the same way they share income. Three common methods to divide income or loss use (1) a stated ratio basis, (2) the ratio of capital balances, or (3) salary and interest allowances and any remainder according to a fixed ratio. We explain each of these methods in this section.

**Allocation on Stated Ratios**    The *stated ratio* (also called the *income-and-loss-sharing ratio*, the *profit and loss ratio,* or the *P&L ratio*) method of allocating partnership income or loss gives each partner a fraction of the total. Partners must agree on the fractional share each receives. To illustrate, assume the partnership agreement of K. Zayn and H. Perez says Zayn receives two-thirds and Perez one-third of partnership income and loss. If their partnership's net income is $60,000, it is allocated to the partners when the Income Summary account is closed as follows.

**Point:** Partners can agree on a ratio to divide income and another ratio to divide a loss.

**Point:** The fractional basis can be stated as a proportion, ratio, or percent. For example, a 3:2 basis is the same as ⅗ and ⅖, or 60% and 40%.

Assets = Liabilities + Equity
          −60,000
          +40,000
          +20,000

| Dec. 31 | Income Summary .......................... | 60,000 | |
| | K. Zayn, Capital .......................... | | 40,000 |
| | H. Perez, Capital .......................... | | 20,000 |
| | *To allocate income and close Income Summary.* | | |

**Allocation on Capital Balances**    The *capital balances* method of allocating partnership income or loss assigns an amount based on the ratio of each partner's relative capital balance. If Zayn and Perez agree to share income and loss on the ratio of their beginning capital balances—Zayn's $30,000 and Perez's $10,000—Zayn receives three-fourths of any income or loss ($30,000/$40,000) and Perez receives one-fourth ($10,000/$40,000). The journal entry follows the same format as that using stated ratios (see the preceding entries).

**Point:** To determine the percent of income received by each partner, divide an individual partner's share by total net income.

**Allocation on Services, Capital, and Stated Ratios**    The *services, capital, and stated ratio* method of allocating partnership income or loss recognizes that service and capital contributions of partners often are not equal. Salary allowances can make up for differences in service contributions. Interest allowances can make up for unequal capital contributions. Also, the allocation of income and loss can include *both* salary and interest allowances. To illustrate, assume that the partnership agreement of K. Zayn and H. Perez reflects differences in service and capital contributions as follows: (1) annual salary allowances of $36,000 to Zayn and $24,000 to Perez, (2) annual interest allowances of 10% of a partner's beginning-year capital balance, and (3) equal share of any remaining balance of income or loss. These salaries and interest allowances are *not* reported as expenses on the income statement. They are simply a means of dividing partnership income or loss. The remainder of this section provides two illustrations using this three-point allocation agreement.

**Illustration when income exceeds allowance.**    If BOARDS has first-year net income of $70,000, and Zayn and Perez apply the three-point partnership agreement described in the prior paragraph, income is allocated as shown in Exhibit 12.1. Zayn gets $42,000 and Perez gets $28,000 of the $70,000 total.

**Point:** When allowances exceed income, the amount of this negative balance often is referred to as a *sharing agreement loss* or *deficit.*

**Illustration when allowances exceed income.**    The sharing agreement between Zayn and Perez must be followed even if net income is less than the total of the allowances. For example, if BOARDS' first-year net income is $50,000 instead of $70,000, it is allocated to the partners as shown in Exhibit 12.2. Computations for salaries and interest are identical to those in Exhibit 12.1. However, when we apply the total allowances against income, the balance of income is negative. This $(14,000) negative balance is allocated equally to the partners per their sharing agreement. This means that a negative $(7,000) is allocated to each partner. In this case, Zayn ends up with $32,000 and Perez with $18,000. If BOARDS had experienced a net loss, Zayn and Perez would share it in the same manner as the $50,000 income. The only difference is that they would have begun with a negative amount because of the loss. Specifically, the partners would still have been

**Point:** Check to make sure the sum of the dollar amounts allocated to each partner equals net income or loss.

|  | Zayn | Perez | Total |
|---|---|---|---|
| Net income .................. |  |  | **$70,000** |
| **Salary allowances** |  |  |  |
| Zayn ..................... | $ 36,000 |  |  |
| Perez ..................... |  | $ 24,000 |  |
| **Interest allowances** |  |  |  |
| Zayn (10% × $30,000) ......... | 3,000 |  |  |
| Perez (10% × $10,000) ........ |  | 1,000 |  |
| Total salaries and interest ......... | 39,000 | 25,000 | 64,000 |
| **Balance of income** ........... |  |  | 6,000 |
| Balance allocated equally |  |  |  |
| Zayn ..................... | 3,000 ← |  |  |
| Perez ..................... |  | 3,000 ← |  |
| Total allocated ............... |  |  | 6,000 |
| **Balance of income** ........... |  |  | $      0 |
| Income of each partner ......... | **$42,000** | **$28,000** |  |

**EXHIBIT 12.1**

Dividing Income When Income Exceeds Allowances

|  | Zayn | Perez | Total |
|---|---|---|---|
| Net income .................. |  |  | **$50,000** |
| **Salary allowances** |  |  |  |
| Zayn ..................... | $ 36,000 |  |  |
| Perez ..................... |  | $ 24,000 |  |
| **Interest allowances** |  |  |  |
| Zayn (10% × $30,000) ......... | 3,000 |  |  |
| Perez (10% × $10,000) ........ |  | 1,000 |  |
| Total salaries and interest ......... | 39,000 | 25,000 | 64,000 |
| **Balance of income** ........... |  |  | (14,000) |
| Balance allocated equally |  |  |  |
| Zayn ..................... | (7,000) ← |  |  |
| Perez ..................... |  | (7,000) ← |  |
| Total allocated ............... |  |  | (14,000) |
| **Balance of income** ........... |  |  | $      0 |
| Income of each partner ......... | **$32,000** | **$18,000** |  |

**EXHIBIT 12.2**

Dividing Income When Allowances Exceed Income

allocated their salary and interest allowances, further adding to the negative balance of the loss. This *total* negative balance *after* salary and interest allowances would have been allocated equally between the partners. These allocations would have been applied against the positive numbers from any allowances to determine each partner's share of the loss.

**Point:** When a loss occurs, it is possible for a specific partner's capital to increase (when closing income summary) if that partner's allowance is in excess of his or her share of the negative balance. This implies that decreases to the capital balances of other partners exceed the partnership's loss amount.

## Quick Check
Answer — p. 495

4. Denzel and Shantell form a partnership by contributing $70,000 and $35,000, respectively. They agree to an interest allowance equal to 10% of each partner's capital balance at the beginning of the year, with the remaining income shared equally. Allocate first-year income of $40,000 to each partner.

## Partnership Financial Statements

Partnership financial statements are similar to those of other organizations. The **statement of partners' equity,** also called *statement of partners' capital,* is one exception. It shows *each* partner's beginning capital balance, additional investments, allocated income or loss, withdrawals, and ending capital balance. To illustrate, Exhibit 12.3 shows the statement of partners' equity for BOARDS prepared using the sharing agreement of Exhibit 12.1. Recall that BOARDS' income was $70,000; also, assume that Zayn withdrew $20,000 and Perez $12,000 at year-end.

**EXHIBIT 12.3**

Statement of Partners' Equity

| BOARDS<br>Statement of Partners' Equity<br>For Year Ended December 31, 2011 | | | | |
|---|---|---|---|---|
| | **Zayn** | | **Perez** | **Total** |
| Beginning capital balances . . . . . . . . . . | | $    0 | $    0 | $    0 |
| Plus | | | | |
|   Investments by owners . . . . . . . . . . | | 30,000 | 10,000 | 40,000 |
|   Net income | | | | |
|     Salary allowances . . . . . . . . . . . . | $36,000 | | $24,000 | |
|     Interest allowances . . . . . . . . . . . | 3,000 | | 1,000 | |
|     Balance allocated . . . . . . . . . . . | 3,000 | | 3,000 | |
|     Total net income . . . . . . . . . . . . . | | 42,000 | 28,000 | 70,000 |
| | | 72,000 | 38,000 | 110,000 |
| Less partners' withdrawals . . . . . . . . . | | (20,000) | (12,000) | (32,000) |
| **Ending capital balances** . . . . . . . . | | **$52,000** | **$26,000** | **$78,000** |

The equity section of the balance sheet of a partnership usually shows the separate capital account balance of each partner. In the case of BOARDS, both K. Zayn, Capital, and H. Perez, Capital, are listed in the equity section along with their balances of $52,000 and $26,000, respectively.

### Decision Insight

**Gambling Partners**   **Trump Entertainment Resorts LP** and subsidiaries operate three casino hotel properties in Atlantic City: Trump Taj Mahal Casino Resort ("Trump Taj Mahal"), Trump Plaza Hotel and Casino ("Trump Plaza"), and Trump Marina Hotel Casino ("Trump Marina"). Its recent statement of partners' equity reports $1,020,000 in partners' withdrawals, leaving $605,314,000 in partners' capital balances. ■

## ADMISSION AND WITHDRAWAL OF PARTNERS

**P3**  Account for the admission and withdrawal of partners.

A partnership is based on a contract between individuals. When a partner is admitted or withdraws, the present partnership ends. Still, the business can continue to operate as a new partnership consisting of the remaining partners. This section considers how to account for the admission and withdrawal of partners.

### Admission of a Partner

A new partner is admitted in one of two ways: by purchasing an interest from one or more current partners or by investing cash or other assets in the partnership.

**Purchase of Partnership Interest**   The purchase of partnership interest is a *personal transaction between one or more current partners and the new partner.* To become a partner, the current partners must accept the purchaser. Accounting for the purchase of partnership interest involves reallocating current partners' capital to reflect the transaction. To illustrate, at the end of BOARDS' first year, H. Perez sells one-half of his partnership interest to Tyrell Rasheed for $18,000. This means that Perez gives up a $13,000 recorded interest ($26,000 × 1/2) in the partnership (see the ending capital balance in Exhibit 12.3). The partnership records this January 4 transaction as follows.

Assets = Liabilities + Equity
−13,000
+13,000

| Jan. 4 | H. Perez, Capital . . . . . . . . . . . . . . . . . . . . . . . . . . . . | 13,000 | |
| | T. Rasheed, Capital . . . . . . . . . . . . . . . . . . . . . . | | 13,000 |
| | *To record admission of Rasheed by purchase.* | | |

After this entry is posted, BOARDS' equity shows K. Zayn, Capital; H. Perez, Capital; and T. Rasheed, Capital, and their respective balances of $52,000, $13,000, and $13,000.

Two aspects of this transaction are important. First, the partnership does *not* record the $18,000 Rasheed paid Perez. The partnership's assets, liabilities, and *total equity* are unaffected by this transaction among partners. Second, Zayn and Perez must agree that Rasheed is to become a partner. If they agree to accept Rasheed, a new partnership is formed and a new contract with a new income-and-loss-sharing agreement is prepared. If Zayn or Perez refuses to accept Rasheed as a partner, then (under the Uniform Partnership Act) Rasheed gets Perez's sold share of partnership income and loss. If the partnership is liquidated, Rasheed gets Perez's sold share of partnership assets. Rasheed gets no voice in managing the company unless Rasheed is admitted as a partner.

**Point:** Partners' withdrawals are not constrained by the partnership's annual income or loss.

**Investing Assets in a Partnership**   Admitting a partner by accepting assets is a *transaction between the new partner and the partnership*. The invested assets become partnership property. To illustrate, if Zayn (with a $52,000 interest) and Perez (with a $26,000 interest) agree to accept Rasheed as a partner in BOARDS after an investment of $22,000 cash, this is recorded as follows.

| Jan. 4 | Cash........................................ | 22,000 | |
| | T. Rasheed, Capital ........................ | | 22,000 |
| | *To record admission of Rasheed by investment.* | | |

Assets  = Liabilities +  Equity
+22,000                          +22,000

After this entry is posted, both assets (cash) and equity (T. Rasheed, Capital) increase by $22,000. Rasheed now has a 22% equity in the assets of the business, computed as $22,000 divided by the entire partnership equity ($52,000 + $26,000 + $22,000). Rasheed does not necessarily have a right to 22% of income. Dividing income and loss is a separate matter on which partners must agree.

**Bonus to old partners.**   When the current value of a partnership is greater than the recorded amounts of equity, the partners usually require a new partner to pay a bonus for the privilege of joining. To illustrate, assume that Zayn and Perez agree to accept Rasheed as a partner with a 25% interest in BOARDS if Rasheed invests $42,000. Recall that the partnership's accounting records show that Zayn's recorded equity in the business is $52,000 and Perez's recorded equity is $26,000 (see Exhibit 12.3). Rasheed's equity is determined as follows.

| Equities of existing partners ($52,000 + $26,000) ....... | $ 78,000 |
| Investment of new partner .......................... | 42,000 |
| Total partnership equity ........................... | $120,000 |
| Equity of Rasheed (25% × $120,000) ................. | $ 30,000 |

Although Rasheed invests $42,000, the equity attributed to Rasheed in the new partnership is only $30,000. The $12,000 difference is called a *bonus* and is allocated to existing partners (Zayn and Perez) according to their income-and-loss-sharing agreement. A bonus is shared in this way because it is viewed as reflecting a higher value of the partnership that is not yet reflected in income. The entry to record this transaction follows.

| Jan. 4 | Cash........................................ | 42,000 | |
| | T. Rasheed, Capital ........................ | | 30,000 |
| | K. Zayn, Capital ($12,000 × ½) .............. | | 6,000 |
| | H. Perez, Capital ($12,000 × ½) .............. | | 6,000 |
| | *To record admission of Rasheed and bonus.* | | |

Assets  = Liabilities +  Equity
+42,000                          +30,000
                                 +6,000
                                 +6,000

**Bonus to new partner.**   Alternatively, existing partners can grant a bonus to a new partner. This usually occurs when they need additional cash or the new partner has exceptional talents. The bonus to the new partner is in the form of a larger share of equity than the amount invested. To illustrate, assume that Zayn and Perez agree to accept Rasheed as a partner with a

25% interest in the partnership, but they require Rasheed to invest only $18,000. Rasheed's equity is determined as follows.

| | |
|---|---:|
| Equities of existing partners ($52,000 + $26,000) . . . . . . . . . | $78,000 |
| Investment of new partner . . . . . . . . . . . . . . . . . . . . . . . . | 18,000 |
| Total partnership equity . . . . . . . . . . . . . . . . . . . . . . . . . . . . . | $96,000 |
| Equity of Rasheed (25% × $96,000) . . . . . . . . . . . . . . . . . . . | $24,000 |

The old partners contribute the $6,000 bonus (computed as $24,000 minus $18,000) to Rasheed according to their income-and-loss-sharing ratio. Moreover, Rasheed's 25% equity does not necessarily entitle Rasheed to 25% of future income or loss. This is a separate matter for agreement by the partners. The entry to record the admission and investment of Rasheed is

Assets = Liabilities + Equity
+18,000
−3,000
−3,000
+24,000

| Jan. 4 | Cash . . . . . . . . . . . . . . . . . . . . . . . . . . . . . . . . . . . . . . . | 18,000 | |
|---|---|---|---|
| | K. Zayn, Capital ($6,000 × ½) . . . . . . . . . . . . . . . . . . | 3,000 | |
| | H. Perez, Capital ($6,000 × ½) . . . . . . . . . . . . . . . . . . | 3,000 | |
| | T. Rasheed, Capital . . . . . . . . . . . . . . . . . . . . . . . . | | 24,000 |
| | *To record Rasheed's admission and bonus.* | | |

## Withdrawal of a Partner

A partner generally withdraws from a partnership in one of two ways. (1) First, the withdrawing partner can sell his or her interest to another person who pays for it in cash or other assets. For this, we need only debit the withdrawing partner's capital account and credit the new partner's capital account. (2) The second case is when cash or other assets of the partnership are distributed to the withdrawing partner in settlement of his or her interest. To illustrate these cases, assume that Perez withdraws from the partnership of BOARDS in some future period. The partnership shows the following capital balances at the date of Perez's withdrawal: K. Zayn, $84,000; H. Perez, $38,000; and T. Rasheed, $38,000. The partners (Zayn, Perez, and Rasheed) share income and loss equally. Accounting for Perez's withdrawal depends on whether a bonus is paid. We describe three possibilities.

**No Bonus**    If Perez withdraws and takes cash equal to Perez's capital balance, the entry is

Assets = Liabilities + Equity
−38,000         −38,000

| Oct. 31 | H. Perez, Capital . . . . . . . . . . . . . . . . . . . . . . . . . . . . | 38,000 | |
|---|---|---|---|
| | Cash . . . . . . . . . . . . . . . . . . . . . . . . . . . . . . . . . . . | | 38,000 |
| | *To record withdrawal of Perez from partnership* | | |
| | *with no bonus.* | | |

Perez can take any combination of assets to which the partners agree to settle Perez's equity. Perez's withdrawal creates a new partnership between the remaining partners. A new partnership contract and a new income-and-loss-sharing agreement are required.

**Bonus to Remaining Partners**    A withdrawing partner is sometimes willing to take less than the recorded value of his or her equity to get out of the partnership or because the recorded value is overstated. Whatever the reason, when this occurs, the withdrawing partner in effect gives the remaining partners a bonus equal to the equity left behind. The remaining partners share this unwithdrawn equity according to their income-and-loss-sharing ratio. To illustrate, if Perez withdraws and agrees to take $34,000 cash in settlement of Perez's capital balance, the entry is

Assets = Liabilities + Equity
−34,000         −38,000
+2,000
+2,000

| Oct. 31 | H. Perez, Capital . . . . . . . . . . . . . . . . . . . . . . . . . . . . | 38,000 | |
|---|---|---|---|
| | Cash . . . . . . . . . . . . . . . . . . . . . . . . . . . . . . . . . . . | | 34,000 |
| | K. Zayn, Capital . . . . . . . . . . . . . . . . . . . . . . . . . . | | 2,000 |
| | T. Rasheed, Capital . . . . . . . . . . . . . . . . . . . . . . . | | 2,000 |
| | *To record withdrawal of Perez and bonus to* | | |
| | *remaining partners.* | | |

Perez withdrew $4,000 less than Perez's recorded equity of $38,000. This $4,000 is divided between Zayn and Rasheed according to their income-and-loss-sharing ratio.

**Bonus to Withdrawing Partner**   A withdrawing partner may be able to receive more than his or her recorded equity for at least two reasons. First, the recorded equity may be understated. Second, the remaining partners may agree to remove this partner by giving assets of greater value than this partner's recorded equity. In either case, the withdrawing partner receives a bonus. The remaining partners reduce their equity by the amount of this bonus according to their income-and-loss-sharing ratio. To illustrate, if Perez withdraws and receives $40,000 cash in settlement of Perez's capital balance, the entry is

| Oct. 31 | H. Perez, Capital | 38,000 | |
| | K. Zayn, Capital | 1,000 | |
| | T. Rasheed, Capital | 1,000 | |
| | Cash | | 40,000 |
| | *To record Perez's withdrawal from partnership with a bonus to Perez.* | | |

Assets  = Liabilities +  Equity
−40,000                    −38,000
                           −1,000
                           −1,000

**Falcon Cable Communications** set up a partnership withdrawal agreement. Falcon owns and operates cable television systems and had two managing general partners. The partnership agreement stated that either partner "can offer to sell to the other partner the offering partner's entire partnership interest . . . for a negotiated price. If the partner receiving such an offer rejects it, the offering partner may elect to cause [the partnership] . . . to be liquidated and dissolved."

## Death of a Partner

A partner's death dissolves a partnership. A deceased partner's estate is entitled to receive his or her equity. The partnership contract should contain provisions for settlement in this case. These provisions usually require (1) closing the books to determine income or loss since the end of the previous period and (2) determining and recording current market values for both assets and liabilities. The remaining partners and the deceased partner's estate then must agree to a settlement of the deceased partner's equity. This can involve selling the equity to remaining partners or to an outsider, or it can involve withdrawing assets.

**■ Decision Ethics**                         Answer — p. 495

**Financial Planner**   You are hired by the two remaining partners of a three-member partnership after the third partner's death. The partnership agreement states that a deceased partner's estate is entitled to a "share of partnership assets equal to the partner's relative equity balance" (partners' equity balances are equal). The estate argues that it is entitled to one-third of the current value of partnership assets. The remaining partners say the distribution should use asset book values, which are 75% of current value. They also point to partnership liabilities, which equal 40% of total asset book value and 30% of current value. How would you resolve this situation? ■

## LIQUIDATION OF A PARTNERSHIP

When a partnership is liquidated, its business ends and four concluding steps are required.

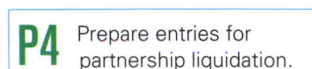

1. Record the sale of noncash assets for cash and any gain or loss from their liquidation.
2. Allocate any gain or loss from liquidation of the assets in step 1 to the partners *using their income-and-loss-sharing ratio.*
3. Pay or settle all partner liabilities.
4. Distribute any remaining cash to partners *based on their capital balances.*

**Partnership liquidation** usually falls into one of two cases, as described in this section.

## No Capital Deficiency

*No capital deficiency* means that all partners have a zero or credit balance in their capital accounts for final distribution of cash. To illustrate, assume that Zayn, Perez, and Rasheed operate their partnership in BOARDS for several years, sharing income and loss equally. The partners then decide to liquidate. On the liquidation date, the current period's income or loss is transferred to the partners' capital accounts according to the sharing agreement. After that transfer, assume the partners' recorded account balances (immediately prior to liquidation) are:

| | | | | | |
|---|---|---|---|---|---|
| Cash ....... | $178,000 | Accounts payable ....... | $20,000 | H. Perez, Capital ......... | $66,000 |
| Land ........ | 40,000 | K. Zayn, Capital ........ | 70,000 | T. Rasheed, Capital ....... | 62,000 |

We apply three steps for liquidation. ① *The partnership sells its noncash assets, and any losses or gains from liquidation are shared among partners according to their income-and-loss-sharing agreement* (equal for these partners). Assume that BOARDS sells its noncash assets consisting of $40,000 in land for $46,000 cash, yielding a net gain of $6,000. In a liquidation, gains or losses usually result from the sale of noncash assets, which are called *losses and gains from liquidation*. The entry to sell its assets for $46,000 follows.

Assets = Liabilities + Equity
−40,000            +6,000
+46,000

| Jan. 15 | Cash .......................................... | 46,000 | |
|---|---|---|---|
| | Land ......................................... | | 40,000 |
| | Gain from Liquidation ....................... | | 6,000 |
| | *Sold noncash assets at a gain.* | | |

Allocation of the gain from liquidation per the partners' income-and-loss-sharing agreement follows.

Assets = Liabilities + Equity
              −6,000
              +2,000
              +2,000
              +2,000

| Jan. 15 | Gain from Liquidation ......................... | 6,000 | |
|---|---|---|---|
| | K. Zayn, Capital ........................... | | 2,000 |
| | H. Perez, Capital .......................... | | 2,000 |
| | T. Rasheed, Capital ........................ | | 2,000 |
| | *To allocate liquidation gain to partners.* | | |

② *The partnership pays its liabilities, and any losses or gains from liquidation of liabilities are shared among partners according to their income-and-loss-sharing agreement.* BOARDS' only liability is $20,000 in accounts payable, and no gain or loss occurred.

Assets = Liabilities + Equity
−20,000    −20,000

| Jan. 15 | Accounts Payable ............................. | 20,000 | |
|---|---|---|---|
| | Cash ........................................ | | 20,000 |
| | *To pay claims of creditors.* | | |

After step 2, we have the following capital balances along with the remaining cash balance.

| K. Zayn | | |
|---|---|---|
| | Bal. | 70,000 |
| | (2) | 2,000 |
| | Bal. | 72,000 |

| H. Perez, Capital | | |
|---|---|---|
| | Bal. | 66,000 |
| | (2) | 2,000 |
| | Bal. | 68,000 |

| T. Rasheed, Capital | | |
|---|---|---|
| | Bal. | 62,000 |
| | (2) | 2,000 |
| | Bal. | 64,000 |

| Cash | | | | |
|---|---|---|---|---|
| Bal. | 178,000 | (3) | 20,000 |
| (1) | 46,000 | | |
| Bal. | 204,000 | | |

③ *Any remaining cash is divided among the partners* **according to their capital account balances.** The entry to record the final distribution of cash to partners follows.

Assets = Liabilities + Equity
−204,000          −72,000
                  −68,000
                  −64,000

| Jan. 15 | K. Zayn, Capital ............................. | 72,000 | |
|---|---|---|---|
| | H. Perez, Capital ............................ | 68,000 | |
| | T. Rasheed, Capital .......................... | 64,000 | |
| | Cash ........................................ | | 204,000 |
| | *To distribute remaining cash to partners.* | | |

It is important to remember that the final cash payment is distributed to partners according to their capital account balances, whereas gains and losses from liquidation are allocated according to the income-and-loss-sharing ratio. The following *statement of liquidation* summarizes the three steps in this section.

| Statement of Liquidation | Cash | Noncash Assets | = | Liabilities | K. Zayn, Capital | H. Perez, Capital | T. Rasheed, Capital |
|---|---|---|---|---|---|---|---|
| Balances prior to liquidation. . . . | $178,000 | $ 40,000 | | $ 20,000 | $ 70,000 | $66,000 | $62,000 |
| ① Sale of noncash assets . . . . . . . . | 46,000 | (40,000) | | | 2,000 | 2,000 | 2,000 |
| ② Payment of liabilities . . . . . . . . . | (20,000) | | | (20,000) | 0 | 0 | 0 |
| Balances for distribution . . . . . . | 204,000 | | | | 72,000 | 68,000 | 64,000 |
| ③ Distribution of cash to partners | (204,000) | | | | (72,000) | (68,000) | (64,000) |

## Capital Deficiency

*Capital deficiency* means that at least one partner has a debit balance in his or her capital account at the point of final cash distribution (during step ③ as explained in the prior section). This can arise from liquidation losses, excessive withdrawals before liquidation, or recurring losses in prior periods. A partner with a capital deficiency must, if possible, cover the deficit by paying cash into the partnership.

To illustrate, assume that Zayn, Perez, and Rasheed operate their partnership in BOARDS for several years, sharing income and losses equally. The partners then decide to liquidate. Immediately prior to the final distribution of cash, the partners' recorded capital balances are Zayn, $19,000; Perez, $8,000; and Rasheed, $(3,000). Rasheed's capital deficiency means that Rasheed owes the partnership $3,000. Both Zayn and Perez have a legal claim against Rasheed's personal assets. The final distribution of cash in this case depends on how this capital deficiency is handled. Two possibilities exist: the partner pays the deficiency or the partner cannot pay the deficiency.

**Partner Pays Deficiency**   Rasheed is obligated to pay $3,000 into the partnership to cover the deficiency. If Rasheed is willing and able to pay, the entry to record receipt of payment from Rasheed follows.

| Jan. 15 | Cash . . . . . . . . . . . . . . . . . . . . . . . . . . . . . . . . . . . . . . . . . . . . . . . . | 3,000 | |
|---|---|---|---|
| |     T. Rasheed, Capital  . . . . . . . . . . . . . . . . . . . . . . . . . . | | 3,000 |
| | *To record payment of deficiency by Rasheed.* | | |

Assets = Liabilities + Equity
+3,000                          +3,000

After the $3,000 payment, the partners' capital balances are Zayn, $19,000; Perez, $8,000; and Rasheed, $0. The entry to record the final cash distributions to partners is

| Jan. 15 | K. Zayn, Capital . . . . . . . . . . . . . . . . . . . . . . . . . . . . . . . . . . . | 19,000 | |
|---|---|---|---|
| | H. Perez, Capital  . . . . . . . . . . . . . . . . . . . . . . . . . . . . . | 8,000 | |
| |     Cash . . . . . . . . . . . . . . . . . . . . . . . . . . . . . . . . . . . . . . . | | 27,000 |
| | *To distribute remaining cash to partners.* | | |

Assets = Liabilities + Equity
−27,000                          −19,000
                                 −8,000

**Partner Cannot Pay Deficiency**   The remaining partners with credit balances absorb any partner's unpaid deficiency according to their income-and-loss-sharing ratio. To illustrate, if Rasheed is unable to pay the $3,000 deficiency, Zayn and Perez absorb it. Since they share income and loss equally, Zayn and Perez each absorb $1,500 of the deficiency. This is recorded as follows.

| Jan. 15 | K. Zayn, Capital  . . . . . . . . . . . . . . . . . . . . . . . . . . . . . | 1,500 | |
|---|---|---|---|
| | H. Perez, Capital  . . . . . . . . . . . . . . . . . . . . . . . . . . . . . | 1,500 | |
| |     T. Rasheed, Capital  . . . . . . . . . . . . . . . . . . . . . . . . | | 3,000 |
| | *To transfer Rasheed deficiency to Zayn and Perez.* | | |

Assets = Liabilities + Equity
                                 −1,500
                                 −1,500
                                 +3,000

After Zayn and Perez absorb Rasheed's deficiency, the capital accounts of the partners are Zayn, $17,500; Perez, $6,500; and Rasheed, $0. The entry to record the final cash distribution to the partners is

| Jan. 15 | K. Zayn, Capital  . . . . . . . . . . . . . . . . . . . . . . . . . . . . . | 17,500 | |
|---|---|---|---|
| | H. Perez, Capital  . . . . . . . . . . . . . . . . . . . . . . . . . . . . . | 6,500 | |
| |     Cash . . . . . . . . . . . . . . . . . . . . . . . . . . . . . . . . . . . . . . . | | 24,000 |
| | *To distribute remaining cash to partners.* | | |

Assets = Liabilities + Equity
−24,000                          −17,500
                                 −6,500

Rasheed's inability to cover this deficiency does not relieve Rasheed of the liability. If Rasheed becomes able to pay at a future date, Zayn and Perez can each collect $1,500 from Rasheed.

# GLOBAL VIEW

Partnership accounting according to U.S. GAAP is similar, but not identical, to that under IFRS. This section discusses broad differences in partnership accounting, organization, admission, withdrawal, and liquidation.

Both U.S. GAAP and IFRS include broad and similar guidance for partnership accounting. Further, partnership organization is similar worldwide; however, different legal and tax systems dictate different implications and motivations for how a partnership is effectively set up.

The accounting for partnership admission, withdrawal, and liquidation is likewise similar worldwide. Specifically, procedures for admission, withdrawal, and liquidation depend on the partnership agreements constructed by all parties involved. However, different legal and tax systems impact those agreements and their implications to the parties.

**Decision Analysis**                                     Partner Return on Equity

**A1** Compute partner return on equity and use it to evaluate partnership performance.

An important role of partnership financial statements is to aid current and potential partners in evaluating partnership success compared with other opportunities. One measure of this success is the **partner return on equity** ratio:

$$\text{Partner return on equity} = \frac{\text{Partner net income}}{\text{Average partner equity}}$$

This measure is separately computed for each partner. To illustrate, Exhibit 12.4 reports selected data from the **Boston Celtics LP**. The return on equity for the *total* partnership is computed as $216/[(\$85 + \$253)/2] = 127.8\%$. However, return on equity is quite different across the partners. For example, the **Boston Celtics LP I** partner return on equity is computed as $\$44/[(\$122 + \$166)/2] = 30.6\%$, whereas the **Celtics LP** partner return on equity is computed as $\$111/[(\$270 + \$333)/2] = 36.8\%$. Partner return on equity provides *each* partner an assessment of its return on its equity invested in the partnership. A specific partner often uses this return to decide whether additional investment or withdrawal of resources is best for that partner. Exhibit 12.4 reveals that the year shown produced good returns for all partners (the Boston Celtics LP II return is not computed because its average equity is negative due to an unusual and large distribution in the prior year).

**EXHIBIT 12.4**

Selected Data from Boston Celtics LP

| ($ thousands) | Total* | Boston Celtics LP I | Boston Celtics LP II | Celtics LP |
|---|---|---|---|---|
| Beginning-year balance .............. | $ 85 | $122 | $(307) | $270 |
| Net income (loss) for year .......... | 216 | 44 | 61 | 111 |
| Cash distribution ................. | (48) | — | — | (48) |
| Ending-year balance .............. | $253 | $166 | $(246) | $333 |
| **Partner return on equity** ........ | **127.8%** | **30.6%** | **n.a.** | **36.8%** |

\* Totals may not add up due to rounding.

# DEMONSTRATION PROBLEM

The following transactions and events affect the partners' capital accounts in several successive partnerships. Prepare a table with six columns, one for each of the five partners along with a total column to show the effects of the following events on the five partners' capital accounts.

## Part 1

4/13/2009    Ries and Bax create R&B Company. Each invests $10,000, and they agree to share income and losses equally.

12/31/2009    R&B Co. earns $15,000 in income for its first year. Ries withdraws $4,000 from the partnership, and Bax withdraws $7,000.

1/1/2010    Royce is made a partner in RB&R Company after contributing $12,000 cash. The partners agree that a 10% interest allowance will be given on each partner's beginning-year capital balance. In addition, Bax and Royce are to receive $5,000 salary allowances. The remainder of the income or loss is to be divided evenly.

| | |
|---|---|
| 12/31/2010 | The partnership's income for the year is $40,000, and withdrawals at year-end are Ries, $5,000; Bax, $12,500; and Royce, $11,000. |
| 1/1/2011 | Ries sells her interest for $20,000 to Murdock, whom Bax and Royce accept as a partner in the new BR&M Co. Income or loss is to be shared equally after Bax and Royce receive $25,000 salary allowances. |
| 12/31/2011 | The partnership's income for the year is $35,000, and year-end withdrawals are Bax, $2,500, and Royce, $2,000. |
| 1/1/2012 | Elway is admitted as a partner after investing $60,000 cash in the new Elway & Associates partnership. He is given a 50% interest in capital after the other partners transfer $3,000 to his account from each of theirs. A 20% interest allowance (on the beginning-year capital balances) will be used in sharing any income or loss, there will be no salary allowances, and Elway will receive 40% of the remaining balance—the other three partners will each get 20%. |
| 12/31/2012 | Elway & Associates earns $127,600 in income for the year, and year-end withdrawals are Bax, $25,000; Royce, $27,000; Murdock, $15,000; and Elway, $40,000. |
| 1/1/2013 | Elway buys out Bax and Royce for the balances of their capital accounts after a revaluation of the partnership assets. The revaluation gain is $50,000, which is divided in using a 1:1:1:2 ratio (Bax:Royce:Murdock:Elway). Elway pays the others from personal funds. Murdock and Elway will share income on a 1:9 ratio. |
| 2/28/2013 | The partnership earns $10,000 of income since the beginning of the year. Murdock retires and receives partnership cash equal to her capital balance. Elway takes possession of the partnership assets in his own name, and the partnership is dissolved. |

## Part 2

Journalize the events affecting the partnership for the year ended December 31, 2010.

## PLANNING THE SOLUTION

- Evaluate each transaction's effects on the capital accounts of the partners.
- Each time a new partner is admitted or a partner withdraws, allocate any bonus based on the income-or-loss-sharing agreement.
- Each time a new partner is admitted or a partner withdraws, allocate subsequent net income or loss in accordance with the new partnership agreement.
- Prepare entries to (1) record Royce's initial investment; (2) record the allocation of interest, salaries, and remainder; (3) show the cash withdrawals from the partnership; and (4) close the withdrawal accounts on December 31, 2010.

## SOLUTION TO DEMONSTRATION PROBLEM

### Part 1

| Event | Ries | Bax | Royce | Murdock | Elway | Total |
|---|---|---|---|---|---|---|
| **4/13/2009** | | | | | | |
| Initial investment . . . . . . . . . . | $10,000 | $10,000 | | | | $ 20,000 |
| **12/31/2009** | | | | | | |
| Income (equal) . . . . . . . . . . . | 7,500 | 7,500 | | | | 15,000 |
| Withdrawals . . . . . . . . . . . . . | (4,000) | (7,000) | | | | (11,000) |
| Ending balance . . . . . . . . . . . | $13,500 | $10,500 | | | | $ 24,000 |
| **1/1/2010** | | | | | | |
| New investment . . . . . . . . . . | | | $12,000 | | | $ 12,000 |
| **12/31/2010** | | | | | | |
| 10% interest . . . . . . . . . . . . . | 1,350 | 1,050 | 1,200 | | | 3,600 |
| Salaries . . . . . . . . . . . . . . . . | | 5,000 | 5,000 | | | 10,000 |
| Remainder (equal) . . . . . . . . . | 8,800 | 8,800 | 8,800 | | | 26,400 |
| Withdrawals . . . . . . . . . . . . . | (5,000) | (12,500) | (11,000) | | | (28,500) |
| Ending balance . . . . . . . . . . . | $18,650 | $12,850 | $16,000 | | | $ 47,500 |

[continued on next page]

[continued from previous page]

| Event | Ries | Bax | Royce | Murdock | Elway | Total |
|---|---|---|---|---|---|---|
| **1/1/2011** | | | | | | |
| Transfer interest .......... | (18,650) | | | $18,650 | | $ 0 |
| **12/31/2011** | | | | | | |
| Salaries ................ | | 25,000 | 25,000 | | | 50,000 |
| Remainder (equal) ........ | | (5,000) | (5,000) | (5,000) | | (15,000) |
| Withdrawals ............ | | (2,500) | (2,000) | | | (4,500) |
| Ending balance ........... | $ 0 | $30,350 | $34,000 | $13,650 | | $ 78,000 |
| **1/1/2012** | | | | | | |
| New investment .......... | | | | | $ 60,000 | 60,000 |
| Bonuses to Elway ......... | | (3,000) | (3,000) | (3,000) | 9,000 | 0 |
| Adjusted balance .......... | | $27,350 | $31,000 | $10,650 | $ 69,000 | $138,000 |
| **12/31/2012** | | | | | | |
| 20% interest.............. | | 5,470 | 6,200 | 2,130 | 13,800 | 27,600 |
| Remainder (1:1:1:2) ........ | | 20,000 | 20,000 | 20,000 | 40,000 | 100,000 |
| Withdrawals.............. | | (25,000) | (27,000) | (15,000) | (40,000) | (107,000) |
| Ending balance ........... | | $27,820 | $30,200 | $17,780 | $ 82,800 | $158,600 |
| **1/1/2013** | | | | | | |
| Gain (1:1:1:2) ............. | | 10,000 | 10,000 | 10,000 | 20,000 | 50,000 |
| Adjusted balance .......... | | $37,820 | $40,200 | $27,780 | $102,800 | $208,600 |
| Transfer interests ......... | | (37,820) | (40,200) | | 78,020 | 0 |
| Adjusted balance .......... | | $ 0 | $ 0 | $27,780 | $180,820 | $208,600 |
| **2/28/2013** | | | | | | |
| Income (1:9)............. | | | | 1,000 | 9,000 | 10,000 |
| Adjusted balance .......... | | | | $28,780 | $189,820 | $218,600 |
| Settlements .............. | | | | (28,780) | (189,820) | (218,600) |
| Final balance............. | | | | $ 0 | $ 0 | $ 0 |

## Part 2

| 2010 | | | |
|---|---|---|---|
| Jan. 1 | Cash ........................................ | 12,000 | |
| |     Royce, Capital ............................ | | 12,000 |
| | *To record investment of Royce.* | | |
| Dec. 31 | Income Summary ............................ | 40,000 | |
| |     Ries, Capital ............................... | | 10,150 |
| |     Bax, Capital ............................... | | 14,850 |
| |     Royce, Capital ............................. | | 15,000 |
| | *To allocate interest, salaries, and remainders.* | | |
| Dec. 31 | Ries, Withdrawals ............................ | 5,000 | |
| | Bax, Withdrawals ............................ | 12,500 | |
| | Royce, Withdrawals .......................... | 11,000 | |
| |     Cash ..................................... | | 28,500 |
| | *To record cash withdrawals by partners.* | | |
| Dec. 31 | Ries, Capital ................................ | 5,000 | |
| | Bax, Capital ................................ | 12,500 | |
| | Royce, Capital .............................. | 11,000 | |
| |     Ries, Withdrawals ......................... | | 5,000 |
| |     Bax, Withdrawals ......................... | | 12,500 |
| |     Royce, Withdrawals ........................ | | 11,000 |
| | *To close withdrawal accounts.* | | |

# Summary

**C1** **Identify characteristics of partnerships and similar organizations.** Partnerships are voluntary associations, involve partnership agreements, have limited life, are not subject to income tax, include mutual agency, and have unlimited liability. Organizations that combine selected characteristics of partnerships and corporations include limited partnerships, limited liability partnerships, S corporations, and limited liability companies.

**A1** **Compute partner return on equity and use it to evaluate partnership performance.** Partner return on equity provides each partner an assessment of his or her return on equity invested in the partnership.

**P1** **Prepare entries for partnership formation.** A partner's initial investment is recorded at the market value of the assets contributed to the partnership.

**P2** **Allocate and record income and loss among partners.** A partnership agreement should specify how to allocate partnership income or loss among partners. Allocation can be based on a stated ratio, capital balances, or salary and interest allowances to

compensate partners for differences in their service and capital contributions.

**P3** **Account for the admission and withdrawal of partners.** When a new partner buys a partnership interest directly from one or more existing partners, the amount of cash paid from one partner to another does not affect the partnership total recorded equity. When a new partner purchases equity by investing additional assets in the partnership, the new partner's investment can yield a bonus either to existing partners or to the new partner. The entry to record a withdrawal can involve payment from either (1) the existing partners' personal assets or (2) partnership assets. The latter can yield a bonus to either the withdrawing or remaining partners.

**P4** **Prepare entries for partnership liquidation.** When a partnership is liquidated, losses and gains from selling partnership assets are allocated to the partners according to their income-and-loss-sharing ratio. If a partner's capital account has a deficiency that the partner cannot pay, the other partners share the deficit according to their relative income-and-loss-sharing ratio.

---

## Guidance Answers to Decision Ethics

**Financial Planner**   The partnership agreement apparently fails to mention liabilities or use the term *net assets*. To give the estate one-third of total assets is not fair to the remaining partners because if the partner had lived and the partners had decided to liquidate, the liabilities would need to be paid out of assets before any liquidation. Also, a settlement based on the deceased partner's recorded equity would fail to recognize excess of current value over book value. This value increase would be realized if the partnership were liquidated. A fair settlement would seem to be a payment to the estate for the balance of the deceased partner's equity based on the *current value of net assets.*

---

## Guidance Answers to Quick Checks

**1.** (*b*)

**2.** *Unlimited liability* means that the creditors of a partnership require each partner to be personally responsible for all partnership debts.

**3.** (*c*)

**4.**

|  | Denzel | Shantell | Total |
|---|---|---|---|
| Net income . . . . . . . . . . . . . . . . |  |  | $40,000 |
| Interest allowance (10%) . . . . . . | $ 7,000 | $ 3,500 | 10,500 |
| **Balance of income** . . . . . . . . . |  |  | **$29,500** |
| Balance allocated equally . . . . . . | 14,750 | 14,750 | 29,500 |
| Balance of income . . . . . . . . . . . |  |  | $     0 |
| **Income of partners** . . . . . . . . | **$21,750** | **$18,250** |  |

---

## Multiple Choice Quiz     Answers on p. 505     mhhe.com/wildFAP20e

**Additional Quiz Questions are available at the book's Website.**

1. Stokely and Leder are forming a partnership. Stokely invests a building that has a market value of $250,000; and the partnership assumes responsibility for a $50,000 note secured by a mortgage on that building. Leder invests $100,000 cash. For the partnership, the amounts recorded for the building and for Stokely's Capital account are these:
   a. Building, $250,000; Stokely, Capital, $250,000.
   b. Building, $200,000; Stokely, Capital, $200,000.
   c. Building, $200,000; Stokely, Capital, $100,000.
   d. Building, $200,000; Stokely, Capital, $250,000.
   e. Building, $250,000; Stokely, Capital, $200,000.

2. Katherine, Alliah, and Paulina form a partnership. Katherine contributes $150,000, Alliah contributes $150,000, and Paulina contributes $100,000. Their partnership agreement calls for the income or loss division to be based on the ratio of capital invested. If the partnership reports income of $90,000 for its first year of operations, what amount of income is credited to Paulina's capital account?
   a. $22,500
   b. $25,000
   c. $45,000
   d. $30,000
   e. $90,000

3. Jamison and Blue form a partnership with capital contributions of $600,000 and $800,000, respectively. Their partnership agreement calls for Jamison to receive $120,000 per year in salary. Also, each partner is to receive an interest allowance equal to 10% of the partner's beginning capital contributions, with any remaining income or loss divided equally. If net income for its initial year is $270,000, then Jamison's and Blue's respective shares are
   a. $135,000; $135,000.
   b. $154,286; $115,714.
   c. $120,000; $150,000.
   d. $185,000; $85,000.
   e. $85,000; $185,000.

4. Hansen and Fleming are partners and share equally in income or loss. Hansen's current capital balance in the partnership is $125,000 and Fleming's is $124,000. Hansen and Fleming agree to accept Black with a 20% interest. Black invests $75,000 in the partnership. The bonus granted to Hansen and Fleming equals
   a. $13,000 each.
   b. $5,100 each.
   c. $4,000 each.
   d. $5,285 to Hansen; $4,915 to Fleming.
   e. $0; Hansen and Fleming grant a bonus to Black.

5. Mee Su is a partner in Hartford Partners, LLC. Her partnership capital balance at the beginning of the current year was $110,000, and her ending balance was $124,000. Her share of the partnership income is $10,500. What is her partner return on equity?
   a. 8.97%
   b. 1060.00%
   c. 9.54%
   d. 1047.00%
   e. 8.47%

[i] Icon denotes assignments that involve decision making.

## Discussion Questions

1. [i] If a partnership contract does not state the period of time the partnership is to exist, when does the partnership end?

2. What does the term *mutual agency* mean when applied to a partnership?

3. [i] Can partners limit the right of a partner to commit their partnership to contracts? Would such an agreement be binding (*a*) on the partners and (*b*) on outsiders?

4. [i] Assume that Amey and Lacey are partners. Lacey dies, and her son claims the right to take his mother's place in the partnership. Does he have this right? Why or why not?

5. [i] Assume that the Barnes and Ardmore partnership agreement provides for a two-third/one-third sharing of income but says nothing about losses. The first year of partnership operation resulted in a loss, and Barnes argues that the loss should be shared equally because the partnership agreement said nothing about sharing losses. Is Barnes correct? Explain.

6. Allocation of partnership income among the partners appears on what financial statement?

7. What does the term *unlimited liability* mean when it is applied to partnership members?

8. How does a general partnership differ from a limited partnership?

9. [i] George, Burton, and Dillman have been partners for three years. The partnership is being dissolved. George is leaving the firm, but Burton and Dillman plan to carry on the business. In the final settlement, George places a $75,000 salary claim against the partnership. He contends that he has a claim for a salary of $25,000 for each year because he devoted all of his time for three years to the affairs of the partnership. Is his claim valid? Why or why not?

10. [i] Kay, Kat, and Kim are partners. In a liquidation, Kay's share of partnership losses exceeds her capital account balance. Moreover, she is unable to meet the deficit from her personal assets, and her partners shared the excess losses. Does this relieve Kay of liability?

11. After all partnership assets have been converted to cash and all liabilities paid, the remaining cash should equal the sum of the balances of the partners' capital accounts. Why?

12. Assume a partner withdraws from a partnership and receives assets of greater value than the book value of his equity. Should the remaining partners share the resulting reduction in their equities in the ratio of their relative capital balances or according to their income-and-loss-sharing ratio?

Kent and Davis are partners in operating a store. Without consulting Kent, Davis enters into a contract to purchase merchandise for the store. Kent contends that he did not authorize the order and refuses to pay for it. The vendor sues the partners for the contract price of the merchandise. (*a*) Must the partnership pay for the merchandise? Why? (*b*) Does your answer differ if Kent and Davis are partners in a public accounting firm? Explain.

**QUICK STUDY**

**QS 12-1**
Partnership liability

C1

---

Lamb organized a limited partnership and is the only general partner. Maxi invested $20,000 in the partnership and was admitted as a limited partner with the understanding that she would receive 10% of the profits. After two unprofitable years, the partnership ceased doing business. At that point, partnership liabilities were $85,000 larger than partnership assets. How much money can the partnership's creditors obtain from Maxi's personal assets to satisfy the unpaid partnership debts?

**QS 12-2**
Liability in limited partnerships

P1

---

Ann Keeley and Susie Norton are partners in a business they started two years ago. The partnership agreement states that Keeley should receive a salary allowance of $40,000 and that Norton should receive a $30,000 salary allowance. Any remaining income or loss is to be shared equally. Determine each partner's share of the current year's net income of $210,000.

**QS 12-3**
Partnership income allocation

P2

---

Jake and Ness are partners who agree that Jake will receive a $60,000 salary allowance and that any remaining income or loss will be shared equally. If Ness's capital account is credited for $1,000 as his share of the net income in a given period, how much net income did the partnership earn in that period?

**QS 12-4**
Partnership income allocation

P2

---

Jones and Bordan are partners, each with $30,000 in their partnership capital accounts. Holly is admitted to the partnership by investing $30,000 cash. Make the entry to show Holly's admission to the partnership.

**QS 12-5**
Admission of a partner

P3

---

Mintz agrees to pay Bogg and Heyer $10,000 each for a one-third (33⅓%) interest in the Bogg and Heyer partnership. Immediately prior to Mintz's admission, each partner had a $30,000 capital balance. Make the journal entry to record Mintz's purchase of the partners' interest.

**QS 12-6**
Partner admission through purchase of interest

P3

---

The Red, White & Blue partnership was begun with investments by the partners as follows: Red, $175,000; White, $220,000; and Blue, $205,000. The operations did not go well, and the partners eventually decided to liquidate the partnership, sharing all losses equally. On August 31, after all assets were converted to cash and all creditors were paid, only $60,000 in partnership cash remained.

1. Compute the capital account balance of each partner after the liquidation of assets and the payment of creditors.
2. Assume that any partner with a deficit agrees to pay cash to the partnership to cover the deficit. Present the journal entries on August 31 to record (*a*) the cash receipt from the deficient partner(s) and (*b*) the final disbursement of cash to the partners.
3. Assume that any partner with a deficit is not able to reimburse the partnership. Present journal entries (*a*) to transfer the deficit of any deficient partners to the other partners and (*b*) to record the final disbursement of cash to the partners.

**QS 12-7**
Liquidation of partnership

P4

**Check**   (1) Red, $(5,000)

---

Gilson and Lott's company is organized as a partnership. At the prior year-end, partnership equity totaled $300,000 ($200,000 from Gilson and $100,000 from Lott). For the current year, partnership net income is $50,000 ($40,000 allocated to Gilson and $10,000 allocated to Lott), and year-end total partnership equity is $400,000 ($280,000 from Gilson and $120,000 from Lott). Compute the total partnership return on equity *and* the individual partner return on equity ratios.

**QS 12-8**
Partner return on equity

A1

## EXERCISES

**Exercise 12-1**

Forms of organization

C1

For each of the following separate cases, recommend a form of business organization. With each recommendation, explain how business income would be taxed if the owners adopt the form of organization recommended. Also list several advantages that the owners will enjoy from the form of business organization that you recommend.

**a.** Milan has been out of school for about six years and has become quite knowledgeable about the residential real estate market. He would like to organize a company that buys and sells real estate. Milan believes he has the expertise to manage the company but needs funds to invest in residential property.

**b.** Dr. Langholz and Dr. Clark are recent graduates from medical residency programs. Both are family practice physicians and would like to open a clinic in an underserved rural area. Although neither has any funds to bring to the new venture, an investor has expressed interest in making a loan to provide start-up funds for their practice.

**c.** Ross, Jenks and Keim are recent college graduates in computer science. They want to start a Website development company. They all have college debts and currently do not own any substantial computer equipment needed to get the company started.

**Exercise 12-2**

Characteristics of partnerships

C1

Next to the following list of eight characteristics of business organizations, enter a brief description of how each characteristic applies to general partnerships.

| Characteristic | Application to General Partnerships |
| --- | --- |
| 1. Ease of formation  . . . . . . . . . . . . . . . . . . . . . . . . . . | |
| 2. Transferability of ownership  . . . . . . . . . . . . . . . . . | |
| 3. Ability to raise large amounts of capital  . . . . . . . . | |
| 4. Life . . . . . . . . . . . . . . . . . . . . . . . . . . . . . . . . . . . . | |
| 5. Owners' liability . . . . . . . . . . . . . . . . . . . . . . . . . . . | |
| 6. Legal status  . . . . . . . . . . . . . . . . . . . . . . . . . . . . . | |
| 7. Tax status of income  . . . . . . . . . . . . . . . . . . . . . . | |
| 8. Owners' authority . . . . . . . . . . . . . . . . . . . . . . . . . | |

**Exercise 12-3**

Journalizing partnership formation

P2

Anita Kroll and Aaron Rogers organize a partnership on January 1. Kroll's initial net investment is $60,000, consisting of cash ($14,000), equipment ($66,000), and a note payable reflecting a bank loan for the new business ($20,000). Rogers's initial investment is cash of $25,000. These amounts are the values agreed on by both partners. Prepare journal entries to record (1) Kroll's investment and (2) Rogers's investment.

**Exercise 12-4**

Journalizing partnership transactions

P2

On March 1, 2011, Abbey and Dames formed a partnership. Abbey contributed $88,000 cash and Dames contributed land valued at $70,000 and a building valued at $100,000. The partnership also assumed responsibility for Dames's $80,000 long-term note payable associated with the land and building. The partners agreed to share income as follows: Abbey is to receive an annual salary allowance of $30,000, both are to receive an annual interest allowance of 10% of their beginning-year capital investment, and any remaining income or loss is to be shared equally. On October 20, 2011, Abbey withdrew $32,000 cash and Dames withdrew $25,000 cash. After the adjusting and closing entries are made to the revenue and expense accounts at December 31, 2011, the Income Summary account had a credit balance of $79,000.

**1.** Prepare journal entries to record (*a*) the partners' initial capital investments, (*b*) their cash withdrawals, and (*c*) the December 31 closing of both the Withdrawals and Income Summary accounts.

**Check**   (2) Dames, $89,600

**2.** Determine the balances of the partners' capital accounts as of December 31, 2011.

**Exercise 12-5**

Income allocation in a partnership

P2

Cosmo and Ellis began a partnership by investing $50,000 and $75,000, respectively. During its first year, the partnership earned $165,000. Prepare calculations showing how the $165,000 income should be allocated to the partners under each of the following three separate plans for sharing income and loss: (1) the partners failed to agree on a method to share income; (2) the partners agreed to share income and loss in proportion to their initial investments (round amounts to the nearest dollar); and (3) the partners agreed to share income by granting a $55,000 per year salary allowance to Cosmo, a $45,000 per year salary allowance to Ellis, 10% interest on their initial capital investments, and the remaining balance shared equally.

**Check**   Plan 3, Cosmo, $86,250

Assume that the partners of Exercise 12-5 agreed to share net income and loss by granting annual salary allowances of $55,000 to Cosmo and $45,000 to Ellis, 10% interest allowances on their investments, and any remaining balance shared equally.

**1.** Determine the partners' shares of Cosmo and Ellis given a first-year net income of $94,400.

**2.** Determine the partners' shares of Cosmo and Ellis given a first-year net loss of $15,700.

**Exercise 12-6**
Income allocation in a partnership
P2

**Check**  (2) Cosmo, $(4,100)

---

The partners in the Biz Partnership have agreed that partner Mona may sell her $90,000 equity in the partnership to Seal, for which Seal will pay Mona $75,000. Present the partnership's journal entry to record the sale of Mona's interest to Seal on September 30.

**Exercise 12-7**
Sale of partnership interest
P3

---

The Treed Partnership has total partners' equity of $510,000, which is made up of Elm, Capital, $400,000, and Oak, Capital, $110,000. The partners share net income and loss in a ratio of 80% to Elm and 20% to Oak. On November 1, Ash is admitted to the partnership and given a 15% interest in equity and a 15% share in any income and loss. Prepare the journal entry to record the admission of Ash under each of the following separate assumptions: Ash invests cash of (1) $90,000; (2) $125,000; and (3) $60,000.

**Exercise 12-8**
Admission of new partner
P3

---

Holland, Flowers, and Tulip have been partners while sharing net income and loss in a 5:3:2 ratio. On January 31, the date Tulip retires from the partnership, the equities of the partners are Holland, $350,000; Flowers, $240,000; and Tulip, $180,000. Present journal entries to record Tulip's retirement under each of the following separate assumptions: Tulip is paid for her equity using partnership cash of (1) $180,000; (2) $200,000; and (3) $150,000.

**Exercise 12-9**
Retirement of partner
P3

---

Tuttle, Ritter, and Lee are partners who share income and loss in a 1:4:5 ratio. After lengthy disagreements among the partners and several unprofitable periods, the partners decide to liquidate the partnership. Immediately before liquidation, the partnership balance sheet shows total assets, $116,000; total liabilities, $88,000; Tuttle, Capital, $1,200; Ritter, Capital, $11,700; and Lee, Capital, $15,100. The cash proceeds from selling the assets were sufficient to repay all but $24,000 to the creditors. (a) Calculate the loss from selling the assets. (b) Allocate the loss to the partners. (c) Determine how much of the remaining liability should be paid by each partner.

**Exercise 12-10**
Liquidation of partnership
P4

**Check**  (b) Lee, Capital after allocation, $(10,900)

---

Assume that the Tuttle, Ritter, and Lee partnership of Exercise 12-10 is a limited partnership. Tuttle and Ritter are general partners and Lee is a limited partner. How much of the remaining $24,000 liability should be paid by each partner? (Round amounts to the nearest dollar.)

**Exercise 12-11**
Liquidation of limited partnership
P4

---

Hunt Sports Enterprises LP is organized as a limited partnership consisting of two individual partners: Soccer LP and Football LP. Both partners separately operate a minor league soccer team and a semipro football team. Compute partner return on equity for each limited partnership (and the total) for the year ended June 30, 2011, using the following selected data on partner capital balances from Hunt Sports Enterprises LP.

**Exercise 12-12**
Partner return on equity
A1

|  | Soccer LP | Football LP | Total |
|---|---|---|---|
| Balance at 6/30/2010 . . . . . . . . | $378,000 | $1,516,000 | $1,894,000 |
| Annual net income . . . . . . . . . . | 44,268 | 891,796 | 936,064 |
| Cash distribution . . . . . . . . . . . | — | (100,000) | (100,000) |
| Balance at 6/30/2011 . . . . . . . . | $422,268 | $2,307,796 | $2,730,064 |

## PROBLEM SET A

### Problem 12-1A
Allocating partnership income

P2

**Check** (3) Thomas, Capital, $48,900

Kim Ries, Tere Bax, and Josh Thomas invested $40,000, $56,000, and $64,000, respectively, in a partnership. During its first calendar year, the firm earned $124,500.

**Required**

Prepare the entry to close the firm's Income Summary account as of its December 31 year-end and to allocate the $124,500 net income to the partners under each of the following separate assumptions: The partners (1) have no agreement on the method of sharing income and loss; (2) agreed to share income and loss in the ratio of their beginning capital investments; and (3) agreed to share income and loss by providing annual salary allowances of $33,000 to Ries, $28,000 to Bax, and $40,000 to Thomas; granting 10% interest on the partners' beginning capital investments; and sharing the remainder equally.

### Problem 12-2A
Allocating partnership income and loss; sequential years

P2

mhhe.com/wildFAP20e

Rex Baker and Ty Farney are forming a partnership to which Baker will devote one-half time and Farney will devote full time. They have discussed the following alternative plans for sharing income and loss: (*a*) in the ratio of their initial capital investments, which they have agreed will be $21,000 for Baker and $31,500 for Farney; (*b*) in proportion to the time devoted to the business; (*c*) a salary allowance of $3,000 per month to Farney and the balance in accordance with the ratio of their initial capital investments; or (*d*) a salary allowance of $3,000 per month to Farney, 10% interest on their initial capital investments, and the balance shared equally. The partners expect the business to perform as follows: year 1, $18,000 net loss; year 2, $45,000 net income; and year 3, $75,000 net income.

**Required**

Prepare three tables with the following column headings.

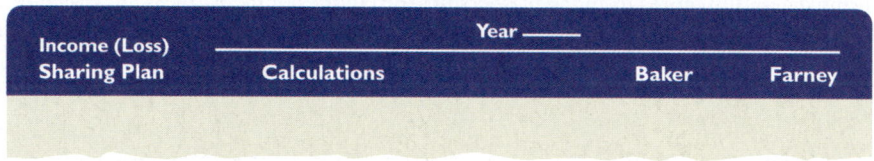

| Income (Loss) Sharing Plan | Calculations | Year ——— Baker | Farney |
|---|---|---|---|
| | | | |

**Check** Plan d, year 1, Farney's share, $9,525

Complete the tables, one for each of the first three years, by showing how to allocate partnership income or loss to the partners under each of the four plans being considered. (Round answers to the nearest whole dollar.)

### Problem 12-3A
Partnership income allocation, statement of partners' equity, and closing entries

P2

mhhe.com/wildFAP20e

Will Beck, Ron Beck, and Barb Beck formed the BBB Partnership by making capital contributions of $183,750, $131,250, and $210,000, respectively. They predict annual partnership net income of $225,000 and are considering the following alternative plans of sharing income and loss: (*a*) equally; (*b*) in the ratio of their initial capital investments; or (*c*) salary allowances of $40,000 to Will, $30,000 to Ron, and $45,000 to Barb; interest allowances of 10% on their initial capital investments; and the balance shared equally.

**Required**

**1.** Prepare a table with the following column headings.

| Income (Loss) Sharing Plan | Calculations | Will | Ron | Barb | Total |
|---|---|---|---|---|---|
| | | | | | |

**Check** (2) Barb, Ending Capital, $223,000

Use the table to show how to distribute net income of $225,000 for the calendar year under each of the alternative plans being considered. (Round answers to the nearest whole dollar.)

**2.** Prepare a statement of partners' equity showing the allocation of income to the partners assuming they agree to use plan (*c*), that income earned is $104,500, and that Will, Ron, and Barb withdraw $17,000, $24,000, and $32,000, respectively, at year-end.

**3.** Prepare the December 31 journal entry to close Income Summary assuming they agree to use plan (*c*) and that net income is $104,500. Also close the withdrawals accounts.

**Part 1.** Goering, Zarcus, and Schmit are partners and share income and loss in a 3:2:5 ratio. The partnership's capital balances are as follows: Goering, $84,000; Zarcus, $69,000; and Schmit, $147,000. Zarcus decides to withdraw from the partnership, and the partners agree to not have the assets revalued upon Zarcus's retirement. Prepare journal entries to record Zarcus's February 1 withdrawal from the partnership under each of the following separate assumptions: Zarcus (a) sells her interest to Getz for $80,000 after Goering and Schmit approve the entry of Getz as a partner; (b) gives her interest to a son-in-law, Swanson, and thereafter Goering and Schmit accept Swanson as a partner; (c) is paid $69,000 in partnership cash for her equity; (d) is paid $107,000 in partnership cash for her equity; and (e) is paid $15,000 in partnership cash plus equipment recorded on the partnership books at $35,000 less its accumulated depreciation of $11,600.

**Part 2.** Assume that Zarcus does not retire from the partnership described in Part 1. Instead, Ford is admitted to the partnership on February 1 with a 25% equity. Prepare journal entries to record Ford's entry into the partnership under each of the following separate assumptions: Ford invests (a) $100,000; (b) $74,000; and (c) $131,000.

**Problem 12-4A**
Partner withdrawal
and admission
**P3**

**Check** (1*e*) Cr. Schmit, Capital,
$19,125

(2*c*) Cr. Zarcus, Capital,
$4,650

---

Quick, Drake, and Sage share income and loss in a 3:2:1 ratio. The partners have decided to liquidate their partnership. On the day of liquidation their balance sheet appears as follows.

**Problem 12-5A**
Liquidation of a partnership
**P4**

| QUICK, DRAKE, AND SAGE | | | |
|---|---|---|---|
| Balance Sheet | | | |
| May 31 | | | |
| **Assets** | | **Liabilities and Equity** | |
| Cash ............. | $ 90,400 | Accounts payable ............... | $122,750 |
| Inventory ......... | 268,600 | Quick, Capital .................. | 46,500 |
| | | Drake, Capital ................. | 106,250 |
| | | Sage, Capital .................. | 83,500 |
| Total assets ........ | $359,000 | Total liabilities and equity ......... | $359,000 |

**Required**

Prepare journal entries for (a) the sale of inventory, (b) the allocation of its gain or loss, (c) the payment of liabilities at book value, and (d) the distribution of cash in each of the following separate cases: Inventory is sold for (1) $300,000; (2) $250,000; (3) $160,000 and any partners with capital deficits pay in the amount of their deficits; and (4) $125,000 and the partners have no assets other than those invested in the partnership. (Round to the nearest dollar.)

**Check** (4) Cash distribution: Sage,
$51,134

---

Matt Albin, Ryan Peters and Seth Ramsey invested $82,000, $49,200 and $32,800, respectively, in a partnership. During its first calendar year, the firm earned $135,000.

**Required**

Prepare the entry to close the firm's Income Summary account as of its December 31 year-end and to allocate the $135,000 net income to the partners under each of the following separate assumptions. (Round answers to whole dollars.) The partners (1) have no agreement on the method of sharing income and loss; (2) agreed to share income and loss in the ratio of their beginning capital investments; and (3) agreed to share income and loss by providing annual salary allowances of $48,000 to Albin, $36,000 to Peters, and $25,000 to Ramsey; granting 10% interest on the partners' beginning capital investments; and sharing the remainder equally.

**PROBLEM SET B**

**Problem 12-1B**
Allocating partnership income
**P2**

**Check** (3) Ramsey, Capital,
$31,480

---

Maria Karto and J.R. Black are forming a partnership to which Karto will devote one-third time and Black will devote full time. They have discussed the following alternative plans for sharing income and loss: (a) in the ratio of their initial capital investments, which they have agreed will be $52,000 for Karto and $78,000 for Black; (b) in proportion to the time devoted to the business; (c) a salary allowance of $2,000 per month to Black and the balance in accordance with the ratio of their initial capital investments; or

**Problem 12-2B**
Allocating partnership income
and loss; sequential years
**P2**

(d) a salary allowance of $2,000 per month to Black, 10% interest on their initial capital investments, and the balance shared equally. The partners expect the business to perform as follows: year 1, $18,000 net loss; year 2, $38,000 net income; and year 3, $94,000 net income.

**Required**

Prepare three tables with the following column headings.

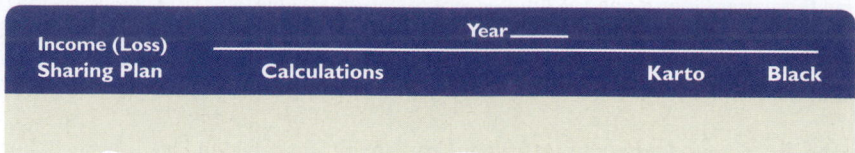

| Income (Loss) Sharing Plan | Calculations | Year_____ | | |
|---|---|---|---|---|
| | | | Karto | Black |

Complete the tables, one for each of the first three years, by showing how to allocate partnership income or loss to the partners under each of the four plans being considered. (Round answers to the nearest whole dollar.)

**Check** Plan d, year 1, Black's share, $4,300

---

**Problem 12-3B**
Partnership income allocation, statement of partners' equity, and closing entries

P2

Staci Cook, Lin Xi, and Kevin Schwartz formed the CXS Partnership by making capital contributions of $72,000, $108,000, and $60,000, respectively. They predict annual partnership net income of $120,000 and are considering the following alternative plans of sharing income and loss: (a) equally; (b) in the ratio of their initial capital investments; or (c) salary allowances of $20,000 to Cook, $15,000 to Xi, and $40,000 to Schwartz; interest allowances of 12% on their initial capital investments; and the balance shared equally.

**Required**

**1.** Prepare a table with the following column headings.

| Income (Loss) Sharing Plan | Calculations | Cook | Xi | Schwartz | Total |
|---|---|---|---|---|---|
| | | | | | |

Use the table to show how to distribute net income of $120,000 for the calendar year under each of the alternative plans being considered. (Round answers to the nearest whole dollar.)

**Check** (2) Schwartz, Ending Capital, $75,200

**2.** Prepare a statement of partners' equity showing the allocation of income to the partners assuming they agree to use plan (c), that income earned is $43,800, and that Cook, Xi, and Schwartz withdraw $9,000, $19,000, and $12,000, respectively, at year-end.

**3.** Prepare the December 31 journal entry to close Income Summary assuming they agree to use plan (c) and that net income is $43,800. Also close the withdrawals accounts.

---

**Problem 12-4B**
Partner withdrawal and admission

P3

**Part 1.** Gibbs, Mier, and Hill are partners and share income and loss in a 5:1:4 ratio. The partnership's capital balances are as follows: Gibbs, $303,000; Mier, $74,000; and Hill, $223,000. Gibbs decides to withdraw from the partnership, and the partners agree not to have the assets revalued upon Gibbs's retirement. Prepare journal entries to record Gibbs's April 30 withdrawal from the partnership under each of the following separate assumptions: Gibbs (a) sells her interest to Brady for $250,000 after Mier and Hill approve the entry of Brady as a partner; (b) gives her interest to a daughter-in-law, Cannon, and thereafter Mier and Hill accept Cannon as a partner; (c) is paid $303,000 in partnership cash for her equity; (d) is paid $175,000 in partnership cash for her equity; and (e) is paid $100,000 in partnership cash plus manufacturing equipment recorded on the partnership books at $269,000 less its accumulated depreciation of $168,000.

**Check** (1e) Cr. Hill, Capital, $81,600

**Part 2.** Assume that Gibbs does not retire from the partnership described in Part 1. Instead, Brise is admitted to the partnership on April 30 with a 20% equity. Prepare journal entries to record the entry of Brise under each of the following separate assumptions: Brise invests (a) $150,000; (b) $98,000; and (c) $213,000.

**Check** (2c) Cr. Mier, Capital, $5,040

Asure, Ramirez, and Soney, who share income and loss in a 2:1:2 ratio, plan to liquidate their partnership. At liquidation, their balance sheet appears as follows.

**Problem 12-5B**
Liquidation of a partnership
**P4**

| ASURE, RAMIREZ, AND SONEY | | | |
|---|---|---|---|
| Balance Sheet | | | |
| January 18 | | | |
| **Assets** | | **Liabilities and Equity** | |
| Cash . . . . . . . . . . . . | $174,300 | Accounts payable . . . . . . . . . . . . . . | $171,300 |
| Equipment . . . . . . . . | 308,600 | Asure, Capital . . . . . . . . . . . . . . . . . | 150,200 |
| | | Ramirez, Capital . . . . . . . . . . . . . . | 97,900 |
| | | Soney, Capital . . . . . . . . . . . . . . . . | 63,500 |
| Total assets . . . . . . . . | $482,900 | Total liabilities and equity . . . . . . . . | $482,900 |

**Required**

Prepare journal entries for (*a*) the sale of equipment, (*b*) the allocation of its gain or loss, (*c*) the payment of liabilities at book value, and (*d*) the distribution of cash in each of the following separate cases: Equipment is sold for (1) $325,000; (2) $265,000; (3) $100,000 and any partners with capital deficits pay in the amount of their deficits; and (4) $75,000 and the partners have no assets other than those invested in the partnership. (Round amounts to the nearest dollar.)

**Check** (4) Cash distribution: Asure, $36,800

---

(*This serial problem began in Chapter 1 and continues through most of the book. If previous chapter segments were not completed, the serial problem can begin at this point. It is helpful, but not necessary, to use the Working Papers that accompany the book.*)

**SERIAL PROBLEM**
Business Solutions
**P3**

**SP 12** At the start of 2012, Santana Rey is considering adding a partner to her business. She envisions the new partner taking the lead in generating sales of both services and merchandise for Business Solutions. S. Rey's equity in Business Solutions as of January 1, 2012, is reflected in the following capital balance.

| S. Rey, Capital . . . . . . . . . . . . | $80,360 |
|---|---|

**Required**

1. S. Rey is evaluating whether the prospective partner should be an equal partner with respect to capital investment and profit sharing (1:1) or whether the agreement should be 4:1 with Rey retaining four-fifths interest with rights to four-fifths of the net income or loss. What factors should she consider in deciding which partnership agreement to offer?

2. Prepare the January 1, 2012, journal entry(ies) necessary to admit a new partner to Business Solutions through the purchase of a partnership interest for each of the following two separate cases: (*a*) 1:1 sharing agreement and (*b*) 4:1 sharing agreement.

3. Prepare the January 1, 2012, journal entry(ies) required to admit a new partner if the new partner invests cash of $20,090.

4. After posting the entry in part 3, what would be the new partner's equity percentage?

## Beyond the Numbers

**BTN 12-1** Take a step back in time and imagine **Research In Motion** in its infancy as a company. The year is 1984.

**REPORTING IN ACTION**
**C1**
**RIM**

**Required**

1. Read the history of Research In Motion at **www.RIM.com**. Identify the two partners that founded the company.

2. Assume that Research In Motion was originally organized as a partnership. RIM's income statement in Appendix A varies in several key ways from what it would look like for a partnership. Identify at least two ways in which a corporate income statement differs from a partnership income statement.

3. Compare the Research In Motion balance sheet in Appendix A to what a partnership balance sheet would have shown. Identify and explain any account differences we would anticipate.

**COMPARATIVE ANALYSIS**

C1

*RIM*

Apple

**BTN 12-2** Over the years **Research In Motion** and **Apple** have evolved into large corporations. Today it is difficult to imagine them as fledgling start-ups. Research each company's history online.

*Required*

1. Which company is older?
2. In what years did each company first achieve $1,000,000,000 in sales?
3. In what years did each company have its first public offering of stock?

---

**ETHICS CHALLENGE**

P2

**BTN 12-3** Doctors Maben, Orlando, and Clark have been in a group practice for several years. Maben and Orlando are family practice physicians, and Clark is a general surgeon. Clark receives many referrals for surgery from his family practice partners. Upon the partnership's original formation, the three doctors agreed to a two-part formula to share income. Every month each doctor receives a salary allowance of $3,000. Additional income is divided according to a percent of patient charges the doctors generate for the month. In the current month, Maben generated 10% of the billings, Orlando 30%, and Clark 60%. The group's income for this month is $50,000. Clark has expressed dissatisfaction with the income-sharing formula and asks that income be split entirely on patient charge percents.

*Required*

1. Compute the income allocation for the current month using the original agreement.
2. Compute the income allocation for the current month using Clark's proposed agreement.
3. Identify the ethical components of this partnership decision for the doctors.

---

**COMMUNICATING IN PRACTICE**

C1

**BTN 12-4** Assume that you are studying for an upcoming accounting exam with a good friend. Your friend says that she has a solid understanding of general partnerships but is less sure that she understands organizations that combine certain characteristics of partnerships with other forms of business organization. You offer to make some study notes for your friend to help her learn about limited partnerships, limited liability partnerships, S corporations, and limited liability companies. Prepare a one-page set of well-organized, complete study notes on these four forms of business organization.

---

**TAKING IT TO THE NET**

P1   P2

**BTN 12-5** Access the March 29, 2010, filing of the December 31, 2009, 10-K of **America First Tax Exempt Investors LP**. This company deals with tax-exempt mortgage revenue bonds that, among other things, finance student housing properties.

1. Locate its December 31, 2009, balance sheet and list the account titles reported in the equity section of the balance sheet.
2. Locate its statement of partners' capital and comprehensive income (loss). How many units of limited partnership (known as "beneficial unit certificate holders") are outstanding at December 31, 2009?
3. What is the partnership's largest asset and its amount at December 31, 2009?

---

**TEAMWORK IN ACTION**

P2

**BTN 12-6** This activity requires teamwork to reinforce understanding of accounting for partnerships.

*Required*

1. Assume that Baker, Warner, and Rice form the BWR Partnership by making capital contributions of $200,000, $300,000, and $500,000, respectively. BWR predicts annual partnership net income of $600,000. The partners are considering various plans for sharing income and loss. Assign a different team member to compute how the projected $600,000 income would be shared under each of the following separate plans:

   **a.** Shared equally.

   **b.** In the ratio of the partners' initial capital investments.

   **c.** Salary allowances of $50,000 to Baker, $60,000 to Warner, and $70,000 to Rice, with the remaining balance shared equally.

   **d.** Interest allowances of 10% on the partners' initial capital investments, with the remaining balance shared equally.

2. In sequence, each member is to present his or her income-sharing calculations with the team.

3. As a team, identify and discuss at least one other possible way that income could be shared.

**BTN 12-7**  Recall the chapter's opening feature involving Chance Claxton and Lynn Julian, and their company, **Kids Konserve**. Assume that Chance and Lynn, partners in Kids Konserve, decide to expand their business with the help of general partners.

**ENTREPRENEURIAL DECISION**

C1

### Required

1. What details should Chance, Lynn, and their future partners specify in the general partnership agreements?

2. What advantages should Chance, Lynn, and their future partners be aware of with respect to organizing as a general partnership?

3. What disadvantages should Chance, Lynn, and their future partners be aware of with respect to organizing as a general partnership?

**BTN 12-8**  Access **Nokia**'s Website (www.Nokia.com) and research the company's history.

1. When was the company founded?

2. What three companies merged to create Nokia Corporation?

3. What are some of the companies that are part of Nokia?

**GLOBAL DECISION**

C1

**NOKIA**

## ANSWERS TO MULTIPLE CHOICE QUIZ

1. e; Capital = $250,000 − $50,000

2. a; $90,000 × [$100,000/($150,000 + $150,000 + $100,000)]
   = $22,500

3. d;

| | Jamison | Blue | Total |
|---|---|---|---|
| Net income ................. | | | $ 270,000 |
| Salary allowance .............. | $120,000 | | (120,000) |
| Interest allowance ............ | 60,000 | $80,000 | (140,000) |
| Balance of income ............ | | | 10,000 |
| Balance divided equally ........ | 5,000 | 5,000 | (10,000) |
| Totals ..................... | $185,000 | $85,000 | $      0 |

4. b; Total partnership equity = $125,000 + $124,000 + $75,000
   = $324,000
   Equity of Black = $324,000 × 20% = $64,800
   Bonus to old partners = $75,000 − $64,800 = $10,200, split equally

5. a; $10,500/[($110,000 + $124,000)/2] = 8.97%

# 13

# Accounting for Corporations

## A Look Back

Chapter 12 focused on the partnership form of organization. We described crucial characteristics of partnerships and the accounting and reporting of their important transactions.

## A Look at This Chapter

This chapter emphasizes details of the corporate form of organization. The accounting concepts and procedures for equity transactions are explained. We also describe how to report and analyze income, earnings per share, and retained earnings.

## A Look Ahead

Chapter 14 focuses on long-term liabilities. We explain how to value, record, amortize, and report these liabilities in financial statements.

## Learning Objectives

**CAP**

### CONCEPTUAL

**C1** Identify characteristics of corporations and their organization. (p. 508)

**C2** Explain characteristics of, and distribute dividends between, common and preferred stock. (p. 519)

**C3** Explain the items reported in retained earnings. (p. 524)

### ANALYTICAL

**A1** Compute earnings per share and describe its use. (p. 527)

**A2** Compute price-earnings ratio and describe its use in analysis. (p. 527)

**A3** Compute dividend yield and explain its use in analysis. (p. 528)

**A4** Compute book value and explain its use in analysis. (p. 528)

LP13

### PROCEDURAL

**P1** Record the issuance of corporate stock. (p. 512)

**P2** Record transactions involving cash dividends, stock dividends, and stock splits. (p. 515)

**P3** Record purchases and sales of treasury stock and the retirement of stock. (p. 522)

## Decision Insight

# Greener Lawns

*"Every part of our business is . . . profitable"*
—KELLY GIARD

FORT COLLINS, CO—According to the U.S. Environmental Protection Agency, a gas-powered lawn mower produces as much air pollution as 43 new cars each driven 12,000 miles. "At least 5 percent of pollution is caused by gas-powered maintenance equipment," explains Kelly Giard, owner of **Clean Air Lawn Care** (**CleanAirLawnCare.com**). "This is one of the last dirty frontiers in America that can be easily solved."

Kelly launched his business four years ago, which is a full-service sustainable lawn care company dedicated to using clean electrical and biodiesel powered equipment. His equipment is charged by solar panels during the day and by wind power overnight. "I started [it] out of my garage mostly for fun," says Kelly. "And business took off."

Kelly explains that his success would not have been possible without equity financing and knowledge of business operations. To make it happen, says Kelly, he studied corporate formation, equity issuance, stock types, retaining earnings, and dividend policies. After that analysis, Kelly set up Clean Air Lawn Care as a corporation, which had several benefits given his business

goals and strategies. With his corporate structure in place, Kelly was ready to attack the market. "Only about 1% of the country uses an electrical mower," says Kelly. "That's awful, and that's something we're committed to changing."

The success of Kelly's corporate structure and his equity financing brings both opportunities and challenges. The positive is being part of the green movement, yielding "a ripple effect where there's profit, happy customers and an environmental benefit." The challenge is effectively using accounting for equity as a tool to achieve those objectives. That includes his knowledge of corporate formation, stock types, and equity transactions. "This is critical to us doing well in the long term," explains Kelly. Still, the focus remains on the environment. "We want [consumers] to have a choice when they hire a service: sustainable vs. dirty."

[Sources: *Clean Air Lawn Care Website,* January 2011; *Entrepreneur,* January 2010; *Lawn & Landscape,* April 2010; *Charles & Hudson Website,* 2010]

This chapter focuses on equity transactions. The first part of the chapter describes the basics of the corporate form of organization and explains the accounting for common and preferred stock. We then focus on several special financing transactions, including cash and stock dividends, stock splits, and treasury stock. The final section considers accounting for retained earnings, including prior period adjustments, retained earnings restrictions, and reporting guidelines.

# CORPORATE FORM OF ORGANIZATION

**C1** Identify characteristics of corporations and their organization.

A **corporation** is an entity created by law that is separate from its owners. It has most of the rights and privileges granted to individuals. Owners of corporations are called *stockholders* or *shareholders*. Corporations can be separated into two types. A *privately held* (or *closely held*) corporation does not offer its stock for public sale and usually has few stockholders. A *publicly held* corporation offers its stock for public sale and can have thousands of stockholders. *Public sale* usually refers to issuance and trading on an organized stock market.

## Characteristics of Corporations

Corporations represent an important type of organization. Their unique characteristics offer advantages and disadvantages.

### Advantages of Corporate Characteristics

- **Separate legal entity:** A corporation conducts its affairs with the same rights, duties, and responsibilities of a person. It takes actions through its agents, who are its officers and managers.

- **Limited liability of stockholders:** Stockholders are liable for neither corporate acts nor corporate debt.

**Point:** The *business entity assumption* requires a corporation to be accounted for separately from its owners (shareholders).

- **Transferable ownership rights:** The transfer of shares from one stockholder to another usually has no effect on the corporation or its operations except when this causes a change in the directors who control or manage the corporation.

- **Continuous life:** A corporation's life continues indefinitely because it is not tied to the physical lives of its owners.

**Global:** U.S., U.K., and Canadian corporations finance much of their operations with stock issuances, but companies in countries such as France, Germany, and Japan finance mainly with note and bond issuances.

- **Lack of mutual agency for stockholders:** A corporation acts through its agents, who are its officers and managers. Stockholders, who are not its officers and managers, do not have the power to bind the corporation to contracts—referred to as *lack of mutual agency*.

- **Ease of capital accumulation:** Buying stock is attractive to investors because (1) stockholders are not liable for the corporation's acts and debts, (2) stocks usually are transferred easily, (3) the life of the corporation is unlimited, and (4) stockholders are not corporate agents. These advantages enable corporations to accumulate large amounts of capital from the combined investments of many stockholders.

## Disadvantages of Corporate Characteristics

- **Government regulation:** A corporation must meet requirements of a state's incorporation laws, which subject the corporation to state regulation and control. Proprietorships and partnerships avoid many of these regulations and governmental reports.
- **Corporate taxation:** Corporations are subject to the same property and payroll taxes as proprietorships and partnerships plus *additional* taxes. The most burdensome of these are federal and state income taxes that together can take 40% or more of corporate pretax income. Moreover, corporate income is usually taxed a second time as part of stockholders' personal income when they receive cash distributed as dividends. This is called *double taxation.* (The usual dividend tax is 15%; however, it is less than 15% for lower income taxpayers, and in some cases zero.)

**Point:** Proprietorships and partnerships are not subject to income taxes. Their income is taxed as the personal income of their owners.

**Point:** Double taxation is less severe when a corporation's owner-manager collects a salary that is taxed only once as part of his or her personal income.

---

### Decision Insight

**Stock Financing**   Marc Andreessen cofounded **Netscape** at age 22, only four months after earning his degree. One year later, he and friends issued Netscape shares to the public. The stock soared, making Andreessen a multimillionaire. ∎

---

## Corporate Organization and Management

This section describes the incorporation, costs, and management of corporate organizations.

**Incorporation**   A corporation is created by obtaining a charter from a state government. A charter application usually must be signed by the prospective stockholders called *incorporators* or *promoters* and then filed with the proper state official. When the application process is complete and fees paid, the charter is issued and the corporation is formed. Investors then purchase the corporation's stock, meet as stockholders, and elect a board of directors. Directors oversee a corporation's affairs.

**Point:** A corporation is not required to have an office in its state of incorporation.

**Organization Expenses**   **Organization expenses** (also called *organization costs*) are the costs to organize a corporation; they include legal fees, promoters' fees, and amounts paid to obtain a charter. The corporation records (debits) these costs to an expense account called *Organization Expenses*. Organization costs are expensed as incurred because it is difficult to determine the amount and timing of their future benefits.

**Management of a Corporation**   The ultimate control of a corporation rests with stockholders who control a corporation by electing its *board of directors,* or simply, *directors.* Each stockholder usually has one vote for each share of stock owned. This control relation is shown in Exhibit 13.1. Directors are responsible for and have final authority for managing corporate activities. A board can act only as a collective body and usually limits its actions to setting general policy.

A corporation usually holds a stockholder meeting at least once a year to elect directors and transact business as its bylaws require. A group of stockholders owning or controlling votes of more than a 50% share of a corporation's stock can elect the board and control the corporation. Stockholders who do not attend stockholders' meetings must have an opportunity to delegate their voting rights to an agent by signing a **proxy,** a document that gives a designated agent the right to vote the stock.

Day-to-day direction of corporate business is delegated to executive officers appointed by the board. A corporation's chief executive officer (CEO) is often its president. Several vice presidents, who report to the president, are commonly assigned specific areas of management responsibility such as finance, production, and marketing. One person often has the dual role

**EXHIBIT 13.1**

Corporate Structure

**Point:** *Bylaws* are guidelines that govern the behavior of individuals employed by and managing the corporation.

of chairperson of the board of directors and CEO. In this case, the president is usually designated the chief operating officer (COO).

### Decision Insight

**Seed Money**   Sources for start-up money include (1) "angel" investors such as family, friends, or anyone who believes in a company, (2) employees, investors, and even suppliers who can be paid with stock, and (3) venture capitalists (investors) who have a record of entrepreneurial success. See the National Venture Capital Association (**NVCA.org**) for information. ■

## Stockholders of Corporations

This section explains stockholder rights, stock purchases and sales, and the role of registrar and transfer agents.

**Rights of Stockholders**   When investors buy stock, they acquire all *specific* rights the corporation's charter grants to stockholders. They also acquire *general* rights granted stockholders by the laws of the state in which the company is incorporated. When a corporation has only one class of stock, it is identified as **common stock.** State laws vary, but common stockholders usually have the general right to

1.  Vote at stockholders' meetings.
2.  Sell or otherwise dispose of their stock.
3.  Purchase their proportional share of any common stock later issued by the corporation. This **preemptive right** protects stockholders' proportionate interest in the corporation. For example, a stockholder who owns 25% of a corporation's common stock has the first opportunity to buy 25% of any new common stock issued.
4.  Receive the same dividend, if any, on each common share of the corporation.
5.  Share in any assets remaining after creditors and preferred stockholders are paid when, and if, the corporation is liquidated. Each common share receives the same amount.

Stockholders also have the right to receive timely financial reports.

**Stock Certificates and Transfer**   Investors who buy a corporation's stock, sometimes receive a *stock certificate* as proof of share ownership. Many corporations issue only one certificate for each block of stock purchased. A certificate can be for any number of shares. Exhibit 13.2 shows a stock certificate of the **Green Bay Packers**. A certificate shows the company name, stockholder name, number of shares, and other crucial information. Issuance of certificates is becoming less common. Instead, many stockholders maintain accounts with the corporation or their stockbrokers and never receive actual certificates.

**EXHIBIT 13.2**

Stock Certificate

**Registrar and Transfer Agents**   If a corporation's stock is traded on a major stock exchange, the corporation must have a registrar and a transfer agent. A *registrar* keeps stockholder records and prepares official lists of stockholders for stockholder meetings and dividend payments. A *transfer agent* assists with purchases and sales of shares by receiving and issuing certificates as necessary. Registrars and transfer agents are usually large banks or trust companies with computer facilities and staff to do this work.

## Decision Insight

**Pricing Stock** A prospectus accompanies a stock's initial public offering (IPO), giving financial information about the company issuing the stock. A prospectus should help answer these questions to price an IPO: (1) Is the underwriter reliable? (2) Is there growth in revenues, profits, and cash flows? (3) What is management's view of operations? (4) Are current owners selling? (5) What are the risks? ■

## Basics of Capital Stock

**Capital stock** is a general term that refers to any shares issued to obtain capital (owner financing). This section introduces terminology and accounting for capital stock.

**Authorized Stock**    **Authorized stock** is the number of shares that a corporation's charter allows it to sell. The number of authorized shares usually exceeds the number of shares issued (and outstanding), often by a large amount. (*Outstanding stock* refers to issued stock held by stockholders.) No formal journal entry is required for stock authorization. A corporation must apply to the state for a change in its charter if it wishes to issue more shares than previously authorized. A corporation discloses the number of shares authorized in the equity section of its balance sheet or notes. **Apple**'s balance sheet in Appendix A reports 1.8 billion common shares authorized as of the start of its 2010 fiscal year.

**Subcategories of Authorized Stock**

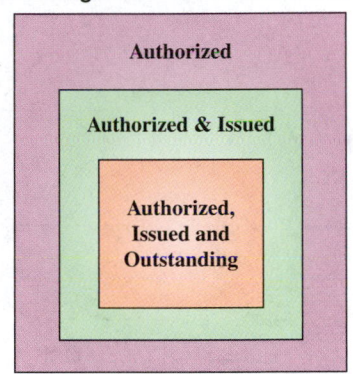

**Selling (Issuing) Stock**    A corporation can sell stock directly or indirectly. To *sell directly,* it advertises its stock issuance to potential buyers. This type of issuance is most common with privately held corporations. To *sell indirectly,* a corporation pays a brokerage house (investment banker) to issue its stock. Some brokerage houses *underwrite* an indirect issuance of stock; that is, they buy the stock from the corporation and take all gains or losses from its resale.

**Market Value of Stock**    **Market value per share** is the price at which a stock is bought and sold. Expected future earnings, dividends, growth, and other company and economic factors influence market value. Traded stocks' market values are available daily in newspapers such as *The Wall Street Journal* and online. The current market value of previously issued shares (for example, the price of stock in trades between investors) does not impact the issuing corporation's stockholders' equity.

**Classes of Stock**    When all authorized shares have the same rights and characteristics, the stock is called *common stock*. A corporation is sometimes authorized to issue more than one class of stock, including preferred stock and different classes of common stock. **American Greetings**, for instance, has two types of common stock: Class A stock has 1 vote per share and Class B stock has 10 votes per share.

**Par Value Stock**    **Par value stock** is stock that is assigned a **par value,** which is an amount assigned per share by the corporation in its charter. For example, **Palm**'s common stock has a par value of $0.001. Other commonly assigned par values are $10, $5, $1 and $0.01. There is no restriction on the assigned par value. In many states, the par value of a stock establishes **minimum legal capital,** which refers to the least amount that the buyers of stock must contribute to the corporation or be subject to paying at a future date. For example, if a corporation issues 1,000 shares of $10 par value stock, the corporation's minimum legal capital in these states would be $10,000. Minimum legal capital is intended to protect a corporation's creditors. Since creditors cannot demand payment from stockholders' personal assets, their claims are limited to the corporation's assets and any minimum legal capital. At liquidation, creditor claims are paid before any amounts are distributed to stockholders.

**No-Par Value Stock**    **No-par value stock,** or simply *no-par stock,* is stock *not* assigned a value per share by the corporate charter. Its advantage is that it can be issued at any price without the possibility of a minimum legal capital deficiency.

**Point:** Managers are motivated to set a low par value when minimum legal capital or state issuance taxes are based on par value.

**Point:** Minimum legal capital was intended to protect creditors by requiring a minimum level of net assets.

**Point:** Par, no-par, and stated value do *not* set the stock's market value.

**EXHIBIT 13.3**

Equity Composition

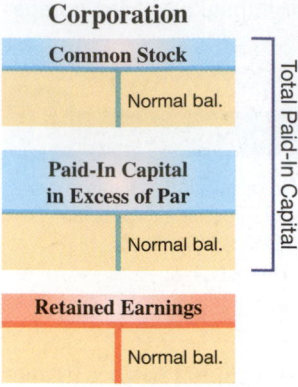

**Point:** Paid-in capital comes from stock-related transactions, whereas retained earnings comes from operations.

**Stated Value Stock**   Stated value stock is no-par stock to which the directors assign a "stated" value per share. Stated value per share becomes the minimum legal capital per share in this case.

**Stockholders' Equity**   A corporation's equity is known as **stockholders' equity,** also called *shareholders' equity* or *corporate capital*. Stockholders' equity consists of (1) paid-in (or contributed) capital and (2) retained earnings; see Exhibit 13.3. **Paid-in capital** is the total amount of cash and other assets the corporation receives from its stockholders in exchange for its stock. **Retained earnings** is the cumulative net income (and loss) not distributed as dividends to its stockholders.

**Decision Insight**

**Stock Quote**   The **Best Buy** stock quote is interpreted as (left to right):
**Hi,** highest price in past 52 weeks;
**Lo,** lowest price in past 52 weeks;

| 52 Weeks | | | | Yld | | Vol | | | | Net |
|---|---|---|---|---|---|---|---|---|---|---|
| Hi | Lo | Sym | Div | % | PE | mil. | Hi | Lo | Close | Chg |
| 54.15 | 41.85 | BBY | 0.13 | 0.98 | 19 | 7.2 | 53.14 | 52.36 | 52.91 | +0.20 |

**Sym,** company exchange symbol; **Div,** dividends paid per share in past year; **Yld %,** dividend divided by closing price; **PE,** stock price per share divided by earnings per share; **Vol mil.,** number (in millions) of shares traded; **Hi,** highest price for the day; **Lo,** lowest price for the day; **Close,** closing price for the day; **Net Chg,** change in closing price from prior day. ■

**Quick Check**      Answers — p. 533

1. Which of the following is *not* a characteristic of the corporate form of business? (*a*) Ease of capital accumulation, (*b*) Stockholder responsibility for corporate debts, (*c*) Ease in transferability of ownership rights, or (*d*) Double taxation.
2. Why is a corporation's income said to be taxed twice?
3. What is a proxy?

## COMMON STOCK

**P1** Record the issuance of corporate stock.

Accounting for the issuance of common stock affects only paid-in (contributed) capital accounts; no retained earnings accounts are affected.

### Issuing Par Value Stock

Par value stock can be issued at par, at a premium (above par), or at a discount (below par). In each case, stock can be exchanged for either cash or noncash assets.

**Issuing Par Value Stock at Par**   When common stock is issued at par value, we record amounts for both the asset(s) received and the par value stock issued. To illustrate, the entry to record Dillon Snowboards' issuance of 30,000 shares of $10 par value stock for $300,000 cash on June 5, 2011, follows.

Assets = Liabilities + Equity
+300,000          +300,000

$10 par value × 30,000 shares

| June 5 | Cash .......................................... | 300,000 | |
| |      Common Stock, $10 Par Value ................ | | 300,000 |
| | *Issued 30,000 shares of $10 par value* | | |
| | *common stock at par.* | | |

Exhibit 13.4 shows the stockholders' equity of Dillon Snowboards at year-end 2011 (its first year of operations) after income of $65,000 and no dividend payments.

**EXHIBIT 13.4**

Stockholders' Equity for Stock Issued at Par

| Stockholders' Equity | |
| --- | --- |
| Common Stock—$10 par value; 50,000 shares authorized; | |
| 30,000 shares issued and outstanding ............................................ | $300,000 |
| Retained earnings .................................................................. | 65,000 |
| Total stockholders' equity ........................................................ | $365,000 |

### Issuing Par Value Stock at a Premium

**A premium on stock** occurs when a corporation sells its stock for more than par (or stated) value. To illustrate, if Dillon Snowboards issues its $10 par value common stock at $12 per share, its stock is sold at a $2 per share premium. The premium, known as **paid-in capital in excess of par value,** is reported as part of equity; it is not revenue and is not listed on the income statement. The entry to record Dillon Snowboards' issuance of 30,000 shares of $10 par value stock for $12 per share on June 5, 2011, follows

**Point:** A *premium* is the amount by which issue price exceeds par (or stated) value. It is recorded in the "Paid-In Capital in Excess of Par Value, Common Stock" account; also called "Additional Paid-In Capital, Common Stock."

The Paid-In Capital in Excess of Par Value account is added to the par value of the stock in the equity section of the balance sheet as shown in Exhibit 13.5.

**Point:** The *Paid-In Capital* terminology is interchangeable with *Contributed Capital.*

**EXHIBIT 13.5**

Stockholders' Equity for Stock Issued at a Premium

| Stockholders' Equity | |
| --- | --- |
| Common Stock—$10 par value; 50,000 shares authorized; | |
| 30,000 shares issued and outstanding ............................................ | $300,000 |
| **Paid-in capital in excess of par value, common stock** ........................ | **60,000** |
| Retained earnings .................................................................. | 65,000 |
| Total stockholders' equity ........................................................ | $425,000 |

### Issuing Par Value Stock at a Discount

**A discount on stock** occurs when a corporation sells its stock for less than par (or stated) value. Most states prohibit the issuance of stock at a discount. In states that allow stock to be issued at a discount, its buyers usually become contingently liable to creditors for the discount. If stock is issued at a discount, the amount by which issue price is less than par is debited to a *Discount on Common Stock* account, a contra to the common stock account, and its balance is subtracted from the par value of stock in the equity section of the balance sheet. This discount is not an expense and does not appear on the income statement.

**Point:** Retained earnings can be negative, reflecting accumulated losses. Amazon.com had an accumulated deficit of $730 million at the start of 2009.

## Issuing No-Par Value Stock

When no-par stock is issued and is not assigned a stated value, the amount the corporation receives becomes legal capital and is recorded as Common Stock. This means that the entire proceeds are credited to a no-par stock account. To illustrate, a corporation records its October 20 issuance of 1,000 shares of no-par stock for $40 cash per share as follows.

**Frequency of Stock Types**

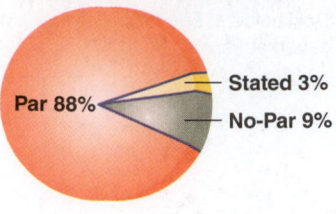

Par 88%
Stated 3%
No-Par 9%

## Issuing Stated Value Stock

When no-par stock is issued and assigned a stated value, its stated value becomes legal capital and is credited to a stated value stock account. Assuming that stated value stock is issued at an amount in excess of stated value (the usual case), the excess is credited to Paid-In Capital in Excess of Stated Value, Common Stock, which is reported in the stockholders' equity section. To illustrate, a corporation that issues 1,000 shares of no-par common stock having a stated value of $40 per share in return for $50 cash per share records this as follows.

Assets = Liabilities + Equity
+50,000           +40,000
                  +10,000

$40 stated value × 1,000 shares

[$50 issue price − $40 stated value] × 1,000 shares

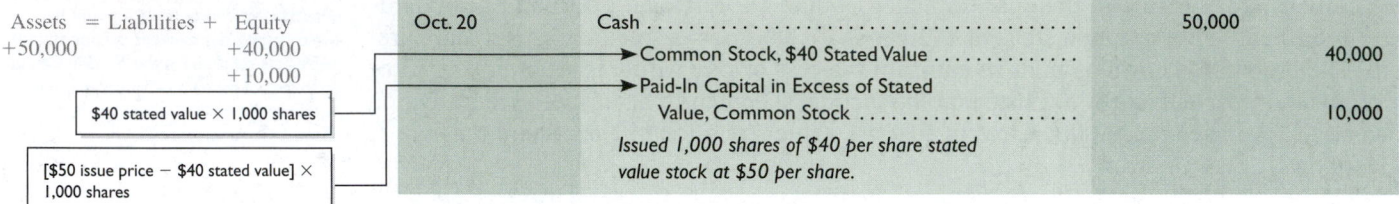

| Oct. 20 | Cash ........................................... | 50,000 | |
| |     Common Stock, $40 Stated Value .............. | | 40,000 |
| |     Paid-In Capital in Excess of Stated | | |
| |         Value, Common Stock ...................... | | 10,000 |
| |     *Issued 1,000 shares of $40 per share stated* | | |
| |     *value stock at $50 per share.* | | |

## Issuing Stock for Noncash Assets

**Point:** Stock issued for noncash assets should be recorded at the market value of either the stock or the noncash asset, whichever is more clearly determinable.

A corporation can receive assets other than cash in exchange for its stock. (It can also assume liabilities on the assets received such as a mortgage on property received.) The corporation records the assets received at their market values as of the date of the transaction. The stock given in exchange is recorded at its par (or stated) value with any excess recorded in the Paid-In Capital in Excess of Par (or Stated) Value account. (If no-par stock is issued, the stock is recorded at the assets' market value.) To illustrate, the entry to record receipt of land valued at $105,000 in return for issuance of 4,000 shares of $20 par value common stock on June 10 is

Assets = Liabilities + Equity
+105,000         +80,000
                +25,000

$20 par value × 4,000 shares

$105,000 asset value − $80,000 stock value

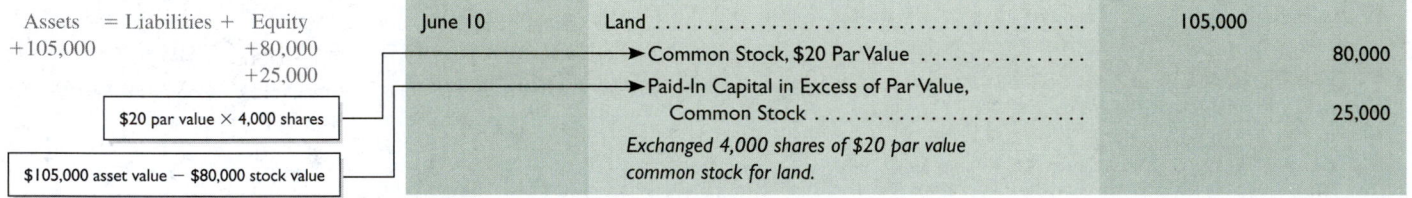

| June 10 | Land ........................................... | 105,000 | |
| |     Common Stock, $20 Par Value ............... | | 80,000 |
| |     Paid-In Capital in Excess of Par Value, | | |
| |         Common Stock .......................... | | 25,000 |
| |     *Exchanged 4,000 shares of $20 par value* | | |
| |     *common stock for land.* | | |

**Point:** Any type of stock can be issued for noncash assets.

A corporation sometimes gives shares of its stock to promoters in exchange for their services in organizing the corporation, which the corporation records as **Organization Expenses.** The entry to record receipt of services valued at $12,000 in organizing the corporation in return for 600 shares of $15 par value common stock on June 5 is

Assets = Liabilities + Equity
                −12,000
                +9,000
                +3,000

$15 par value × 600 shares

$12,000 services value − $9,000 stock value

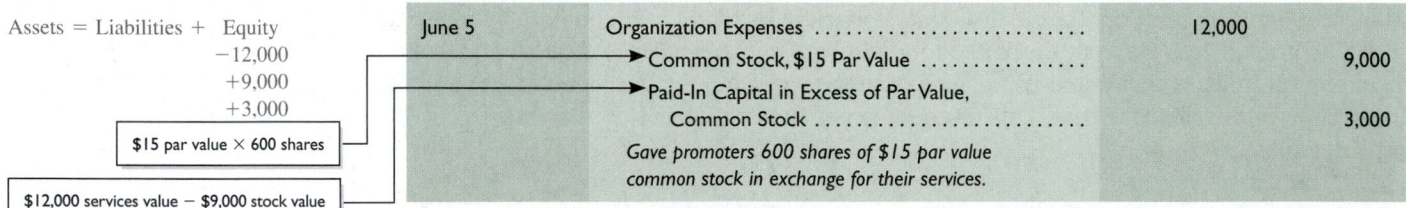

| June 5 | Organization Expenses ......................... | 12,000 | |
| |     Common Stock, $15 Par Value ............... | | 9,000 |
| |     Paid-In Capital in Excess of Par Value, | | |
| |         Common Stock .......................... | | 3,000 |
| |     *Gave promoters 600 shares of $15 par value* | | |
| |     *common stock in exchange for their services.* | | |

## Quick Check

Answers — p. 533

4. A company issues 7,000 shares of its $10 par value common stock in exchange for equipment valued at $105,000. The entry to record this transaction includes a credit to (a) Paid-In Capital in Excess of Par Value, Common Stock, for $35,000. (b) Retained Earnings for $35,000. (c) Common Stock, $10 Par Value, for $105,000.

5. What is a premium on stock issuance?

6. Who is intended to be protected by minimum legal capital?

# DIVIDENDS

This section describes both cash and stock dividend transactions.

## Cash Dividends

The decision to pay cash dividends rests with the board of directors and involves more than evaluating the amounts of retained earnings and cash. The directors, for instance, may decide to keep the cash to invest in the corporation's growth, to meet emergencies, to take advantage of unexpected opportunities, or to pay off debt. Alternatively, many corporations pay cash dividends to their stockholders at regular dates. These cash flows provide a return to investors and almost always affect the stock's market value.

**P2** Record transactions involving cash dividends, stock dividends, and stock splits.

**Accounting for Cash Dividends**   Dividend payment involves three important dates: declaration, record, and payment. **Date of declaration** is the date the directors vote to declare and pay a dividend. This creates a legal liability of the corporation to its stockholders. **Date of record** is the future date specified by the directors for identifying those stockholders listed in the corporation's records to receive dividends. The date of record usually follows the date of declaration by at least two weeks. Persons who own stock on the date of record receive dividends. **Date of payment** is the date when the corporation makes payment; it follows the date of record by enough time to allow the corporation to arrange checks, money transfers, or other means to pay dividends.

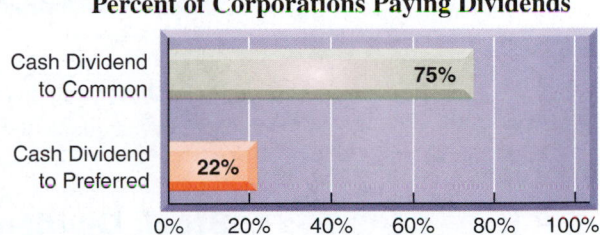

**Percent of Corporations Paying Dividends**

To illustrate, the entry to record a January 9 declaration of a $1 per share cash dividend by the directors of Z-Tech, Inc., with 5,000 outstanding shares is

**Date of Declaration**

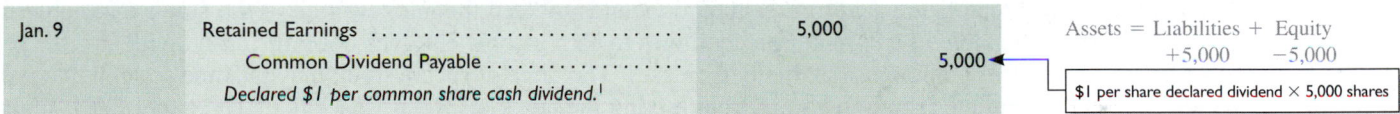

| Jan. 9 | Retained Earnings . . . . . . . . . . . . . . . . . . . . . . . . . . . . . . | 5,000 | |
| | Common Dividend Payable . . . . . . . . . . . . . . . . . . . | | 5,000 |
| | *Declared $1 per common share cash dividend.*[1] | | |

Assets = Liabilities + Equity
       +5,000    −5,000

$1 per share declared dividend × 5,000 shares

Common Dividend Payable is a current liability. The date of record for the Z-Tech dividend is January 22. *No formal journal entry is needed on the date of record.* The February 1 date of payment requires an entry to record both the settlement of the liability and the reduction of the cash balance, as follows:

**Date of Payment**

| Feb. 1 | Common Dividend Payable . . . . . . . . . . . . . . . . . . . . . . . | 5,000 | |
| | Cash . . . . . . . . . . . . . . . . . . . . . . . . . . . . . . . . . . . . . | | 5,000 |
| | *Paid $1 per common share cash dividend.* | | |

Assets = Liabilities + Equity
−5,000    −5,000

**Deficits and Cash Dividends**   A corporation with a debit (abnormal) balance for retained earnings is said to have a **retained earnings deficit,** which arises when a company incurs cumulative losses and/or pays more dividends than total earnings from current and prior years. A deficit is reported as a deduction on the balance sheet, as shown in Exhibit 13.6. Most states prohibit a corporation with a deficit from paying a cash dividend to its stockholders. This legal restriction is designed to protect creditors by preventing distribution of assets to stockholders when the company may be in financial difficulty.

**Point:** It is often said a dividend is a distribution of retained earnings, but it is more precise to describe a dividend as a distribution of assets to satisfy stockholder claims.

**Point:** The Retained Earnings Deficit account is also called *Accumulated Deficit.*

---

[1] An alternative entry is to debit Dividends instead of Retained Earnings. The balance in Dividends is then closed to Retained Earnings at the end of the reporting period. The effect is the same: Retained Earnings is decreased and a Dividend Payable is increased. For simplicity, all assignments in this chapter use the Retained Earnings account to record dividend declarations.

**EXHIBIT 13.6**

Stockholders' Equity
with a Deficit

| | |
|---|---|
| Common stock—$10 par value, 5,000 shares authorized, issued, and outstanding ......... | $50,000 |
| **Retained earnings deficit** .................................................. | **(6,000)** |
| Total stockholders' equity ................................................... | $44,000 |

**Point: Amazon.com** has never
declared a cash dividend.

Some state laws allow cash dividends to be paid by returning a portion of the capital contributed by stockholders. This type of dividend is called a **liquidating cash dividend,** or simply *liquidating dividend,* because it returns a part of the original investment back to the stockholders. This requires a debit entry to one of the contributed capital accounts instead of Retained Earnings at the declaration date.

---

## Quick Check
Answers — p. 534

**7.** What type of an account is the Common Dividend Payable account?

**8.** What three crucial dates are involved in the process of paying a cash dividend?

**9.** When does a dividend become a company's legal obligation?

---

## Stock Dividends

A **stock dividend,** declared by a corporation's directors, is a distribution of additional shares of the corporation's own stock to its stockholders without the receipt of any payment in return. Stock dividends and cash dividends are different. A stock dividend does not reduce assets and equity but instead transfers a portion of equity from retained earnings to contributed capital.

**Reasons for Stock Dividends**   Stock dividends exist for at least two reasons. First, directors are said to use stock dividends to keep the market price of the stock affordable. For example, if a corporation continues to earn income but does not issue cash dividends, the price of its common stock likely increases. The price of such a stock may become so high that it discourages some investors from buying the stock (especially in lots of 100 and 1,000). When a corporation has a stock dividend, it increases the number of outstanding shares and lowers the per share stock price. Another reason for a stock dividend is to provide evidence of management's confidence that the company is doing well and will continue to do well.

**Accounting for Stock Dividends**   A stock dividend affects the components of equity by transferring part of retained earnings to contributed capital accounts, sometimes described as *capitalizing* retained earnings. Accounting for a stock dividend depends on whether it is a small or large stock dividend. A **small stock dividend** is a distribution of 25% or less of previously outstanding shares. It is recorded by capitalizing retained earnings for an amount equal to the market value of the shares to be distributed. A **large stock dividend** is a distribution of more than 25% of previously outstanding shares. A large stock dividend is recorded by capitalizing retained earnings for the minimum amount required by state law governing the corporation. Most states require capitalizing retained earnings equal to the par or stated value of the stock.

To illustrate stock dividends, we use the equity section of Quest's balance sheet shown in Exhibit 13.7 just *before* its declaration of a stock dividend on December 31.

**EXHIBIT 13.7**

Stockholders' Equity *before*
Declaring a Stock Dividend

| **Stockholders' Equity (before dividend)** | |
|---|---|
| Common stock—$10 par value, 15,000 shares authorized, 10,000 shares issued and outstanding ....................................... | $100,000 |
| Paid-in capital in excess of par value, common stock .............................. | 8,000 |
| Retained earnings .................................................... | 35,000 |
| Total stockholders' equity .............................................. | $143,000 |

**Recording a small stock dividend.**   Assume that Quest's directors declare a 10% stock dividend on December 31. This stock dividend of 1,000 shares, computed as 10% of its 10,000 issued and outstanding shares, is to be distributed on January 20 to the stockholders of record on January 15. Since the market price of Quest's stock on December 31 is $15 per share, this small stock dividend declaration is recorded as follows:

**Point:** Small stock dividends are recorded at market value.

**Date of Declaration—Small Stock Dividend**

| Dec. 31 | Retained Earnings ............................. | 15,000 | |
| | Common Stock Dividend Distributable ......... | | 10,000 |
| | Paid-In Capital in Excess of Par Value, | | |
| | Common Stock ......................... | | 5,000 |
| | *Declared a 1,000-share (10%) stock dividend.* | | |

Assets = Liabilities + Equity
−15,000
+10,000
+5,000

10% dividend × 10,000 issued shares × $10 par value

10% dividend × 10,000 issued shares × [$15 market price − $10 par value]

The $10,000 credit in the declaration entry equals the par value of the shares and is recorded in *Common Stock Dividend Distributable,* an equity account. Its balance exists only until the shares are issued. The $5,000 credit equals the amount by which market value exceeds par value. This amount increases the Paid-In Capital in Excess of Par Value account in anticipation of the issuance of shares. In general, the balance sheet changes in three ways when a stock dividend is declared. First, the amount of equity attributed to common stock increases; for Quest, from $100,000 to $110,000 for 1,000 additional declared shares. Second, paid-in capital in excess of par increases by the excess of market value over par value for the declared shares. Third, retained earnings decreases, reflecting the transfer of amounts to both common stock and paid-in capital in excess of par. The stockholders' equity of Quest is shown in Exhibit 13.8 *after* its 10% stock dividend is declared on December 31—the items impacted are in bold.

**Point:** The term *Distributable* (not *Payable*) is used for stock dividends. A stock dividend is never a liability because it never reduces assets.

**Point:** The credit to Paid-In Capital in Excess of Par Value is recorded when the stock dividend is declared. This account is not affected when stock is later distributed.

| Stockholders' Equity (after dividend) | |
| --- | --- |
| Common stock—$10 par value, 15,000 shares authorized, 10,000 shares issued and outstanding ........................ | $100,000 |
| **Common stock dividend distributable—1,000 shares** ........ | **10,000** |
| **Paid-in capital in excess of par value, common stock** ......... | **13,000** |
| **Retained earnings** ....................................... | **20,000** |
| Total stockholders' equity ................................... | $143,000 |

**EXHIBIT 13.8**

Stockholders' Equity *after* Declaring a Stock Dividend

No entry is made on the date of record for a stock dividend. On January 20, the date of payment, Quest distributes the new shares to stockholders and records this entry:

**Date of Payment—Small Stock Dividend**

| Jan. 20 | Common Stock Dividend Distributable ............. | 10,000 | |
| | Common Stock, $10 Par Value ................ | | 10,000 |
| | *To record issuance of common stock dividend.* | | |

Assets = Liabilities + Equity
−10,000
+10,000

The combined effect of these stock dividend entries is to transfer (or capitalize) $15,000 of retained earnings to paid-in capital accounts. The amount of capitalized retained earnings equals the market value of the 1,000 issued shares ($15 × 1,000 shares). A stock dividend has no effect on the ownership percent of individual stockholders.

**Point:** A stock dividend does not affect assets.

**Recording a large stock dividend.**   A corporation capitalizes retained earnings equal to the minimum amount required by state law for a large stock dividend. For most states, this amount is the par or stated value of the newly issued shares. To illustrate, suppose Quest's board declares a stock dividend of 30% instead of 10% on December 31. Since this dividend is more

**Point:** Large stock dividends are recorded at par or stated value.

than 25%, it is treated as a large stock dividend. Thus, the par value of the 3,000 dividend shares is capitalized at the date of declaration with this entry:

Assets = Liabilities + Equity
                        −30,000
                        +30,000

30% dividend × 10,000 issued shares × $10 par value

**Date of Declaration—Large Stock Dividend**

| Dec. 31 | Retained Earnings ............................... | 30,000 | |
|---------|---------------------------------------------------|--------|--------|
| | Common Stock Dividend Distributable ......... | | 30,000 |
| | *Declared a 3,000-share (30%) stock dividend.* | | |

This transaction decreases retained earnings and increases contributed capital by $30,000. On the date of payment the company debits Common Stock Dividend Distributable and credits Common Stock for $30,000. The effects from a large stock dividend on balance sheet accounts are similar to those for a small stock dividend except for the absence of any effect on paid-in capital in excess of par.

## Stock Splits

Before 5:1 Split: 1 share, $50 par

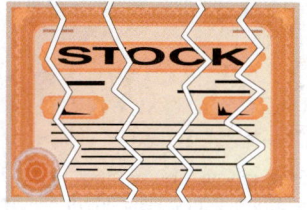

After 5:1 Split: 5 shares, $10 par

A **stock split** is the distribution of additional shares to stockholders according to their percent ownership. When a stock split occurs, the corporation "calls in" its outstanding shares and issues more than one new share in exchange for each old share. Splits can be done in any ratio, including 2-for-1, 3-for-1, or higher. Stock splits reduce the par or stated value per share. The reasons for stock splits are similar to those for stock dividends.

To illustrate, CompTec has 100,000 outstanding shares of $20 par value common stock with a current market value of $88 per share. A 2-for-1 stock split cuts par value in half as it replaces 100,000 shares of $20 par value stock with 200,000 shares of $10 par value stock. Market value is reduced from $88 per share to about $44 per share. The split does not affect any equity amounts reported on the balance sheet or any individual stockholder's percent ownership. Both the Paid-In Capital and Retained Earnings accounts are unchanged by a split, and *no journal entry is made*. The only effect on the accounts is a change in the stock account description. CompTec's 2-for-1 split on its $20 par value stock means that after the split, it changes its stock account title to Common Stock, $10 Par Value. This stock's description on the balance sheet also changes to reflect the additional authorized, issued, and outstanding shares and the new par value.

**Point:** Berkshire Hathaway has resisted a stock split. Its recent stock price was $150,000 per share.

**Point:** A reverse stock split is the opposite of a stock split. It increases both the market value per share and the par or stated value per share with a split ratio less than 1-for-1, such as 1-for-2. A reverse split results in fewer shares.

The difference between stock splits and large stock dividends is often blurred. Many companies report stock splits in their financial statements without calling in the original shares by simply changing their par value. This type of "split" is really a large stock dividend and results in additional shares issued to stockholders by capitalizing retained earnings or transferring other paid-in capital to Common Stock. This approach avoids administrative costs of splitting the stock. **Harley-Davidson** recently declared a 2-for-1 stock split executed in the form of a 100% stock dividend.

**Decision Maker**      Answer — p. 533

**Entrepreneur**   A company you cofounded and own stock in announces a 50% stock dividend. Has the value of your stock investment increased, decreased, or remained the same? Would it make a difference if it was a 3-for-2 stock split executed in the form of a dividend? ■

**Quick Check**      Answers — p. 534

**10.** How does a stock dividend impact assets and retained earnings?
**11.** What distinguishes a large stock dividend from a small stock dividend?
**12.** What amount of retained earnings is capitalized for a small stock dividend?

# PREFERRED STOCK

 **C2**   Explain characteristics of, and distribute dividends between, common and preferred stock.

A corporation can issue two basic kinds of stock, common and preferred. **Preferred stock** has special rights that give it priority (or senior status) over common stock in one or more areas. Special rights typically include a preference for receiving dividends and for the distribution of assets if the corporation is liquidated. Preferred stock carries all rights of common stock unless the corporate charter nullifies them. Most preferred stock, for instance, does not confer the right to vote. Exhibit 13.9 shows that preferred stock is issued by about one-fourth of corporations. All corporations issue common stock.

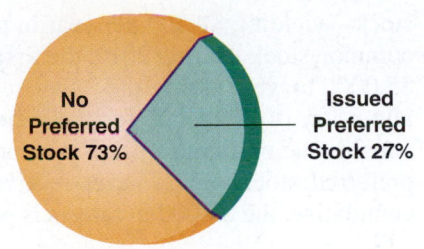

Issued Preferred Stock 27%

**EXHIBIT 13.9**

Corporations and Preferred Stock

## Issuance of Preferred Stock

Preferred stock usually has a par value. Like common stock, it can be sold at a price different from par. Preferred stock is recorded in its own separate capital accounts. To illustrate, if Dillon Snowboards issues 50 shares of $100 par value preferred stock for $6,000 cash on July 1, 2011, the entry is

| July 1 | Cash .......................................... | 6,000 | |
| | Preferred Stock, $100 Par Value .............. | | 5,000 |
| | Paid-In Capital in Excess of Par Value, | | |
| | Preferred Stock ......................... | | 1,000 |
| | *Issued preferred stock for cash.* | | |

Assets = Liabilities + Equity
+6,000            +5,000
                  +1,000

$100 par value × 50 shares

$6,000 cash − [$100 par value × 50 shares]

The equity section of the year-end balance sheet for Dillon Snowboards, including preferred stock, is shown in Exhibit 13.10. (This exhibit assumes that common stock was issued at par.) Issuing no-par preferred stock is similar to issuing no-par common stock. Also, the entries for issuing preferred stock for noncash assets are similar to those for common stock.

| **Stockholders' Equity** | |
| --- | --- |
| Common stock—$10 par value; 50,000 shares authorized; | |
| 30,000 shares issued and outstanding ............................ | $300,000 |
| **Preferred stock—$100 par value; 1,000 shares authorized;** | |
| **50 shares issued and outstanding** ............................ | **5,000** |
| **Paid-in capital in excess of par value, preferred stock** .............. | **1,000** |
| Retained earnings ................................................ | 65,000 |
| Total stockholders' equity ........................................ | $371,000 |

**EXHIBIT 13.10**

Stockholders' Equity with Common and Preferred Stock

## Dividend Preference of Preferred Stock

Preferred stock usually carries a preference for dividends, meaning that preferred stockholders are allocated their dividends before any dividends are allocated to common stockholders. The dividends allocated to preferred stockholders are usually expressed as a dollar amount per share or a percent applied to par value. A preference for dividends does *not* ensure dividends. If the directors do not declare a dividend, neither the preferred nor the common stockholders receive one.

**Cumulative or Noncumulative Dividend**   Most preferred stocks carry a cumulative dividend right. **Cumulative preferred stock** has a right to be paid both the current and all prior periods' unpaid dividends before any dividend is paid to common stockholders. When preferred stock is cumulative and the directors either do not declare a dividend to preferred stockholders or declare one that does not cover the total amount of cumulative dividend, the unpaid dividend amount is called **dividend in arrears.** Accumulation of dividends in arrears on cumulative preferred stock does not guarantee they will be paid. **Noncumulative preferred stock** confers no right to prior periods' unpaid dividends if they were not declared in those prior periods.

To illustrate the difference between cumulative and noncumulative preferred stock, assume that a corporation's outstanding stock includes (1) 1,000 shares of $100 par, 9% preferred

**Point:** Dividend preference does not imply that preferred stockholders receive more dividends than common stockholders, nor does it guarantee a dividend.

stock—yielding $9,000 per year in potential dividends, and (2) 4,000 shares of $50 par value common stock. During 2010, the first year of operations, the directors declare cash dividends of $5,000. In year 2011, they declare cash dividends of $42,000. See Exhibit 13.11 for the allocation of dividends for these two years. Allocation of year 2011 dividends depends on whether the preferred stock is noncumulative or cumulative. With noncumulative preferred, the preferred stockholders never receive the $4,000 skipped in 2010. If the preferred stock is cumulative, the $4,000 in arrears is paid in 2011 before any other dividends are paid.

**EXHIBIT 13.11**

Allocation of Dividends (noncumulative vs. cumulative preferred stock)

**Example:** What dividends do cumulative preferred stockholders receive in 2011 if the corporation paid only $2,000 of dividends in 2010? How does this affect dividends to common stockholders in 2011? *Answers:* $16,000 ($7,000 dividends in arrears, plus $9,000 current preferred dividends). Dividends to common stockholders decrease to $26,000.

|  | Preferred | Common |
|---|---|---|
| **Preferred Stock Is Noncumulative** | | |
| Year 2010 .................................... | $ 5,000 | $ 0 |
| Year 2011 | | |
|     Step 1: Current year's preferred dividend ........ | $ 9,000 | |
|     Step 2: Remainder to common ................. | | $33,000 |
| **Preferred Stock Is Cumulative** | | |
| Year 2010 .................................... | $ 5,000 | $ 0 |
| Year 2011 | | |
|     Step 1: Dividend in arrears .................... | $ 4,000 | |
|     Step 2: Current year's preferred dividend ........ | 9,000 | |
|     Step 3: Remainder to common ................. | | $29,000 |
| Totals for year 2011 ........................... | $13,000 | $29,000 |

A liability for a dividend does not exist until the directors declare a dividend. If a preferred dividend date passes and the corporation's board fails to declare the dividend on its cumulative preferred stock, the dividend in arrears is not a liability. The *full-disclosure principle* requires a corporation to report (usually in a note) the amount of preferred dividends in arrears as of the balance sheet date.

**Participating or Nonparticipating Dividend**   **Nonparticipating preferred stock** has a feature that limits dividends to a maximum amount each year. This maximum is often stated as a percent of the stock's par value or as a specific dollar amount per share. Once preferred stockholders receive this amount, the common stockholders receive any and all additional dividends. **Participating preferred stock** has a feature allowing preferred stockholders to share with common stockholders in any dividends paid in excess of the percent or dollar amount stated on the preferred stock. This participation feature does not apply until common stockholders receive dividends equal to the preferred stock's dividend percent. Many corporations are authorized to issue participating preferred stock but rarely do, and most managers never expect to issue it.[2]

## Convertible Preferred Stock

Preferred stock is more attractive to investors if it carries a right to exchange preferred shares for a fixed number of common shares. **Convertible preferred stock** gives holders the option to

---

[2] Participating preferred stock is usually authorized as a defense against a possible corporate *takeover* by an "unfriendly" investor (or a group of investors) who intends to buy enough voting common stock to gain control. Taking a term from spy novels, the financial world refers to this type of plan as a *poison pill* that a company swallows if enemy investors threaten its capture. A poison pill usually works as follows: A corporation's common stockholders on a given date are granted the right to purchase a large amount of participating preferred stock at a very low price. This right to purchase preferred shares is *not* transferable. If an unfriendly investor buys a large block of common shares (whose right to purchase participating preferred shares does *not* transfer to this buyer), the board can issue preferred shares at a low price to the remaining common shareholders who retained the right to purchase. Future dividends are then divided between the newly issued participating preferred shares and the common shares. This usually transfers value from common shares to preferred shares, causing the unfriendly investor's common stock to lose much of its value and reduces the potential benefit of a hostile takeover.

exchange their preferred shares for common shares at a specified rate. When a company prospers and its common stock increases in value, convertible preferred stockholders can share in this success by converting their preferred stock into more valuable common stock.

## Callable Preferred Stock

**Callable preferred stock** gives the issuing corporation the right to purchase (retire) this stock from its holders at specified future prices and dates. The amount paid to call and retire a preferred share is its **call price,** or *redemption value,* and is set when the stock is issued. The call price normally includes the stock's par value plus a premium giving holders additional return on their investment. When the issuing corporation calls and retires a preferred stock, the terms of the agreement often require it to pay the call price *and* any dividends in arrears.

**Point:** The issuing corporation has the right, or option, to retire its callable preferred stock.

 **IFRS**

Like U.S. GAAP, IFRS requires that preferred stocks be classified as debt or equity based on analysis of the stock's contractual terms. However, IFRS uses different criteria for such classification. ∎

## Reasons for Issuing Preferred Stock

Corporations issue preferred stock for several reasons. One is to raise capital without sacrificing control. For example, suppose a company's organizers have $100,000 cash to invest and organize a corporation that needs $200,000 of capital to start. If they sell $200,000 worth of common stock (with $100,000 to the organizers), they would have only 50% control and would need to negotiate extensively with other stockholders in making policy. However, if they issue $100,000 worth of common stock to themselves and sell outsiders $100,000 of 8%, cumulative preferred stock with no voting rights, they retain control.

A second reason to issue preferred stock is to boost the return earned by common stockholders. To illustrate, suppose a corporation's organizers expect to earn an annual after-tax income of $24,000 on an investment of $200,000. If they sell and issue $200,000 worth of common stock, the $24,000 income produces a 12% return on the $200,000 of common stockholders' equity. However, if they issue $100,000 of 8% preferred stock to outsiders and $100,000 of common stock to themselves, their own return increases to 16% per year, as shown in Exhibit 13.12.

| | |
|---|---|
| Net (after-tax) income | $24,000 |
| Less preferred dividends at 8% | (8,000) |
| Balance to common stockholders | $16,000 |
| Return to common stockholders ($16,000/$100,000) | 16% |

**EXHIBIT 13.12**

Return to Common Stockholders When Preferred Stock Is Issued

Common stockholders earn 16% instead of 12% because assets contributed by preferred stockholders are invested to earn $12,000 while the preferred dividend is only $8,000. Use of preferred stock to increase return to common stockholders is an example of **financial leverage** (also called *trading on the equity*). As a general rule, when the dividend rate on preferred stock is less than the rate the corporation earns on its assets, the effect of issuing preferred stock is to increase (or *lever*) the rate earned by common stockholders.

**Point:** Financial leverage also occurs when debt is issued and the interest rate paid on it is less than the rate earned from using the assets the creditors lend the company.

Other reasons for issuing preferred stock include its appeal to some investors who believe that the corporation's common stock is too risky or that the expected return on common stock is too low.

 **Decision Maker** Answer — p. 533

**Concert Organizer** Assume that you alter your business strategy from organizing concerts targeted at under 1,000 people to those targeted at between 5,000 to 20,000 people. You also incorporate because of increased risk of lawsuits and a desire to issue stock for financing. It is important that you control the company for decisions on whom to schedule. What types of stock do you offer? ∎

# TREASURY STOCK

**P3**  Record purchases and sales of treasury stock and the retirement of stock.

Corporations acquire shares of their own stock for several reasons: (1) to use their shares to acquire another corporation, (2) to purchase shares to avoid a hostile takeover of the company, (3) to reissue them to employees as compensation, and (4) to maintain a strong market for their stock or to show management confidence in the current price.

A corporation's reacquired shares are called **treasury stock,** which is similar to unissued stock in several ways: (1) neither treasury stock nor unissued stock is an asset, (2) neither receives cash dividends or stock dividends, and (3) neither allows the exercise of voting rights. However, treasury stock does differ from unissued stock in one major way: The corporation can resell treasury stock at less than par without having the buyers incur a liability, provided it was originally issued at par value or higher. Treasury stock purchases also require management to exercise ethical sensitivity because funds are being paid to specific stockholders instead of all stockholders. Managers must be sure the purchase is in the best interest of all stockholders. These concerns cause companies to fully disclose treasury stock transactions.

**Corporations and Treasury Stock**

With Treasury Stock 62%

No Treasury Stock 38%

## Purchasing Treasury Stock

Purchasing treasury stock reduces the corporation's assets and equity by equal amounts. (We describe the *cost method* of accounting for treasury stock, which is the most widely used method. The *par value* method is another method explained in advanced courses.) To illustrate, Exhibit 13.13 shows Cyber Corporation's account balances *before* any treasury stock purchase (Cyber has no liabilities).

**EXHIBIT 13.13**

Account Balances *before* Purchasing Treasury Stock

| Assets | | Stockholders' Equity | |
|---|---|---|---|
| Cash .............. | $ 30,000 | Common stock—$10 par; 10,000 shares | |
| Other assets ........ | 95,000 | authorized, issued, and outstanding ........... | $100,000 |
| | | Retained earnings ......................... | 25,000 |
| Total assets ......... | $125,000 | Total stockholders' equity .................... | $125,000 |

Cyber then purchases 1,000 of its own shares for $11,500 on May 1, which is recorded as follows.

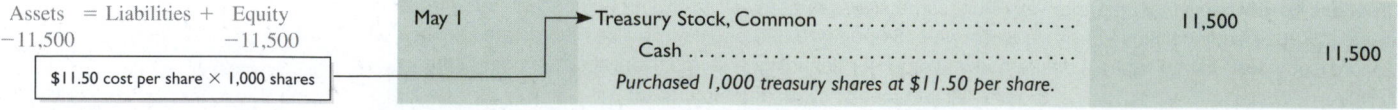

Assets = Liabilities + Equity
−11,500                −11,500

$11.50 cost per share × 1,000 shares

| May 1 | Treasury Stock, Common ...................... | 11,500 | |
|---|---|---|---|
| | Cash ...................................... | | 11,500 |
| | *Purchased 1,000 treasury shares at $11.50 per share.* | | |

This entry reduces equity through the debit to the Treasury Stock account, which is a contra equity account. Exhibit 13.14 shows account balances *after* this transaction.

| Assets | | Stockholders' Equity | |
|---|---|---|---|
| Cash ........... | $ 18,500 | Common stock—$10 par; 10,000 shares authorized and issued; 1,000 shares in treasury ...... | $100,000 |
| Other assets ..... | 95,000 | Retained earnings, $11,500 restricted by treasury stock purchase ...................... | 25,000 |
| | | **Less cost of treasury stock** .................... | **(11,500)** |
| Total assets ...... | $113,500 | Total stockholders' equity ...................... | $113,500 |

**EXHIBIT 13.14**

Account Balances *after* Purchasing Treasury Stock

The treasury stock purchase reduces Cyber's cash, total assets, and total equity by $11,500 but does not reduce the balance of either the Common Stock or the Retained Earnings account. The equity reduction is reported by deducting the cost of treasury stock in the equity section. Also, two disclosures are evident. First, the stock description reveals that 1,000 issued shares are in treasury, leaving only 9,000 shares still outstanding. Second, the description for retained earnings reveals that it is partly restricted.

**Point:** The Treasury Stock account is *not* an asset. Treasury stock does not carry voting or dividend rights.

**Point:** A treasury stock purchase is also called a *stock buyback*.

## Reissuing Treasury Stock

Treasury stock can be reissued by selling it at cost, above cost, or below cost.

**Selling Treasury Stock at Cost** If treasury stock is reissued at cost, the entry is the reverse of the one made to record the purchase. For instance, if on May 21 Cyber reissues 100 of the treasury shares purchased on May 1 at the same $11.50 per share cost, the entry is

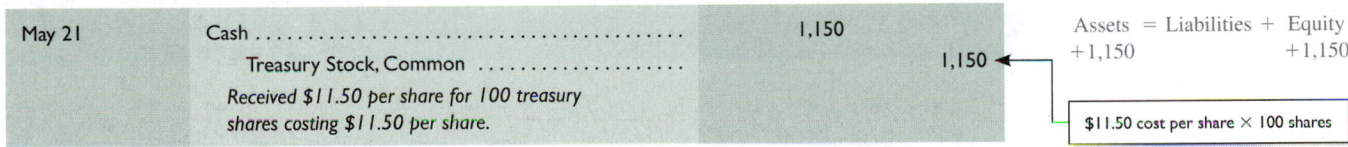

| May 21 | Cash ........................................... | 1,150 | |
|---|---|---|---|
| | Treasury Stock, Common ................... | | 1,150 |
| | *Received $11.50 per share for 100 treasury shares costing $11.50 per share.* | | |

Assets = Liabilities + Equity
+1,150            +1,150

$11.50 cost per share × 100 shares

**Selling Treasury Stock *above* Cost** If treasury stock is sold for more than cost, the amount received in excess of cost is credited to the Paid-In Capital, Treasury Stock account. This account is reported as a separate item in the stockholders' equity section. No gain is ever reported from the sale of treasury stock. To illustrate, if Cyber receives $12 cash per share for 400 treasury shares costing $11.50 per share on June 3, the entry is

**Point:** Treasury stock does not represent ownership. A company cannot own a part of itself.

| June 3 | Cash ........................................... | 4,800 | |
|---|---|---|---|
| | Treasury Stock, Common ................... | | 4,600 |
| | **Paid-In Capital, Treasury Stock** ........... | | 200 |
| | *Received $12 per share for 400 treasury shares costing $11.50 per share.* | | |

Assets = Liabilities + Equity
+4,800            +4,600
                  +200

$11.50 cost per share × 400 shares

[$12 issue price − $11.50 cost per share] × 400 shares

**Selling Treasury Stock *below* Cost** When treasury stock is sold below cost, the entry to record the sale depends on whether the Paid-In Capital, Treasury Stock account has a credit balance. If it has a zero balance, the excess of cost over the sales price is debited to Retained Earnings. If the Paid-In Capital, Treasury Stock account has a credit balance, it is debited for the excess of the cost over the selling price but not to exceed the balance in this account. When the credit balance in this paid-in capital account is eliminated, any remaining difference between the cost and selling price is debited to Retained Earnings. To illustrate, if Cyber sells its remaining 500 shares of treasury stock at $10 per share on July 10, equity is

**Point:** The phrase *treasury stock* is believed to arise from the fact that reacquired stock is held in a corporation's treasury.

**Point:** The Paid-In Capital, Treasury Stock account can have a zero or credit balance but never a debit balance.

reduced by $750 (500 shares × $1.50 per share excess of cost over selling price), as shown in this entry:

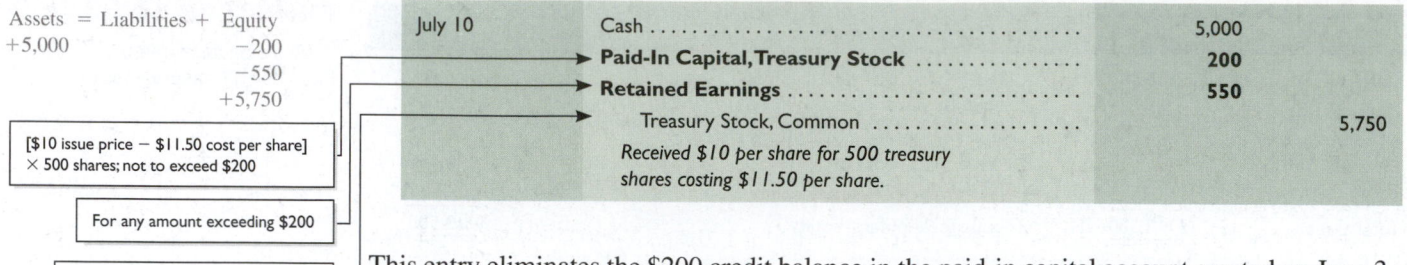

Assets = Liabilities + Equity
+5,000　　　　　　　−200
　　　　　　　　　　−550
　　　　　　　　　　+5,750

[$10 issue price − $11.50 cost per share] × 500 shares; not to exceed $200

For any amount exceeding $200

$11.50 cost per share × 500 shares

| July 10 | Cash ............................................... | 5,000 | |
| | Paid-In Capital, Treasury Stock ................ | 200 | |
| | Retained Earnings ............................ | 550 | |
| | 　Treasury Stock, Common ..................... | | 5,750 |
| | 　*Received $10 per share for 500 treasury* | | |
| | 　*shares costing $11.50 per share.* | | |

This entry eliminates the $200 credit balance in the paid-in capital account created on June 3 and then reduces the Retained Earnings balance by the remaining $550 excess of cost over selling price. A company never reports a loss (or gain) from the sale of treasury stock.

## Retiring Stock

**Point:** Recording stock retirement results in canceling the equity from the original issuance of the shares.

A corporation can purchase its own stock and retire it. Retiring stock reduces the number of is-sued shares. Retired stock is the same as authorized and unissued shares. Purchases and retire-ments of stock are permissible under state law only if they do not jeopardize the interests of creditors and stockholders. When stock is purchased for retirement, we remove all capital amounts related to the retired shares. If the purchase price exceeds the net amount removed, this excess is debited to Retained Earnings. If the net amount removed from all capital accounts exceeds the purchase price, this excess is credited to the Paid-In Capital from Retirement of Stock account. A company's assets and equity are always reduced by the amount paid for the retiring stock.

### Quick Check
Answers — p. 534

16. Purchase of treasury stock (*a*) has no effect on assets; (*b*) reduces total assets and total equity by equal amounts; or (*c*) is recorded with a debit to Retained Earnings.
17. Southern Co. purchases shares of Northern Corp. Should either company classify these shares as treasury stock?
18. How does treasury stock affect the authorized, issued, and outstanding shares?
19. When a company purchases treasury stock, (*a*) retained earnings are restricted by the amount paid; (*b*) Retained Earnings is credited; or (*c*) it is retired.

# REPORTING OF EQUITY

**C3**　Explain the items reported in retained earnings.

## Statement of Retained Earnings

Retained earnings generally consist of a company's cumulative net income less any net losses and dividends declared since its inception. Retained earnings are part of stockholders' claims on the company's net assets, but this does *not* imply that a certain amount of cash or other assets is available to pay stockholders. For example, **Research In Motion** has $5,274,365 thousand in retained earnings, but only $1,550,861 thousand in cash. This section describes events and transactions affecting retained earnings and how retained earnings are reported.

**Restrictions and Appropriations**　The term **restricted retained earnings** refers to both statutory and contractual restrictions. A common *statutory* (or *legal*) *restriction* is to limit treasury stock purchases to the amount of retained earnings. The balance sheet in Exhibit 13.14 provides an example. A common *contractual restriction* involves loan agreements that restrict paying dividends beyond a specified amount or percent of retained earnings. Restrictions are usually described in the notes. The term **appropriated retained earnings** refers to a voluntary transfer of amounts from the Retained Earnings account to the Appropriated Retained Earnings account to inform users of special activities that require funds.

**Prior Period Adjustments**　**Prior period adjustments** are corrections of material errors in prior period financial statements. These errors include arithmetic mistakes, unacceptable accounting, and missed facts. Prior period adjustments are reported in the *statement of retained earnings* (or the statement of stockholders' equity), net of any income tax effects. Prior period adjustments result in changing the beginning balance of retained earnings for events occurring prior to the earliest period reported in the current set of financial statements. To illustrate, assume that ComUS makes an error in a 2009 journal entry for the purchase of land by incorrectly debiting an expense account. When this is discovered in 2011, the statement of retained earnings includes a prior period adjustment, as shown in Exhibit 13.15. This exhibit also shows the usual format of the statement of retained earnings.

**Point:** If a year 2009 error is discovered in 2010, the company records the adjustment in 2010. But if the financial statements include 2009 and 2010 figures, the statements report the correct amounts for 2009, and a note describes the correction.

| ComUS<br>Statement of Retained Earnings<br>For Year Ended December 31, 2011 | |
|---|---:|
| Retained earnings, Dec. 31, 2010, as previously reported .......................... | $4,745,000 |
| Prior period adjustment | |
|    **Cost of land incorrectly expensed (net of $63,000 income taxes)** ......... | **147,000** |
| Retained earnings, Dec. 31, 2010, as adjusted .................................... | 4,892,000 |
| Plus net income ..................................................... | 1,224,300 |
| Less cash dividends declared .......................................... | (301,800) |
| Retained earnings, Dec. 31, 2011 ....................................... | $5,814,500 |

**EXHIBIT 13.15**

Statement of Retained Earnings with a Prior Period Adjustment

Many items reported in financial statements are based on estimates. Future events are certain to reveal that some of these estimates were inaccurate even when based on the best data available at the time. These inaccuracies are *not* considered errors and are *not* reported as prior period adjustments. Instead, they are identified as **changes in accounting estimates** and are accounted for in current and future periods. To illustrate, we know that depreciation is based on estimated useful lives and salvage values. As time passes and new information becomes available, managers may need to change these estimates and the resulting depreciation expense for current and future periods.

**Point:** Accounting for changes in estimates is sometimes criticized as two wrongs to make a right. Consider a change in an asset's life. Depreciation neither before nor after the change is the amount computed if the revised estimate were originally selected. Regulators chose this approach to avoid restating prior period numbers.

**Closing Process**　The closing process was explained earlier in the book as: (1) Close credit balances in revenue accounts to Income Summary, (2) Close debit balances in expense accounts to Income Summary, and (3) Close Income Summary to Retained Earnings. If dividends are recorded in a Dividends account, and not as an immediate reduction to Retained Earnings (as shown in this chapter), a fourth step is necessary to close the Dividends account to Retained Earnings.

## Statement of Stockholders' Equity

Instead of a separate statement of retained earnings, companies commonly report a statement of stockholders' equity that includes changes in retained earnings. A **statement of stockholders' equity** lists the beginning and ending balances of key equity accounts and describes the changes that occur during the period. The companies in Appendix A report such a statement. The usual format is to provide a column for each component of equity and use the rows to describe events occurring in the period. Exhibit 13.16 shows a condensed statement for **Apple**.

## Reporting Stock Options

The majority of corporations whose shares are publicly traded issue **stock options,** which are rights to purchase common stock at a fixed price over a specified period. As the stock's price rises, the option's value increases. **Starbucks** and **Home Depot** offer stock options to both full- and part-time employees. Stock options are said to motivate managers and employees to

**EXHIBIT 13.16**

Statement of Stockholders' Equity

Apple

| APPLE<br>Statement of Stockholders' Equity | | | | | |
|---|---|---|---|---|---|
| ($ millions, shares in thousands) | Common<br>Stock<br>Shares | Common<br>Stock<br>Amount | Retained<br>Earnings | Other | Total<br>Equity |
| Balance, Sept. 27, 2008 ................ | 888,326 | $7,177 | $15,129 | $(9) | $22,297 |
| Net income ......................... | — | — | 8,235 | — | 8,235 |
| Issuance of Common Stock ............... | 11,480 | 404 | (11) | — | 393 |
| Other ............................. | — | 629 | — | 86 | 715 |
| Cash Dividends ($0.00 per share) ......... | — | — | — | — | — |
| Balance, Sept. 26, 2009 ............... | 899,806 | $8,210 | $23,353 | $77 | $31,640 |

(1) focus on company performance, (2) take a long-run perspective, and (3) remain with the company. A stock option is like having an investment with no risk ("a carrot with no stick").

To illustrate, Quantum grants each of its employees the option to purchase 100 shares of its $1 par value common stock at its current market price of $50 per share anytime within the next 10 years. If the stock price rises to $70 per share, an employee can exercise the option at a gain of $20 per share (acquire a $70 stock at the $50 option price). With 100 shares, a single employee would have a total gain of $2,000, computed as $20 × 100 shares. Companies report the cost of stock options in the income statement. Measurement of this cost is explained in advanced courses.

## GLOBAL VIEW

This section discusses similarities and differences between U.S. GAAP and IFRS in accounting and reporting for equity.

**Accounting for Common Stock**   The accounting for and reporting of common stock under U.S. GAAP and IFRS are similar. Specifically, procedures for issuing common stock at par, at a premium, at a discount, and for noncash assets are similar across the two systems. However, we must be aware of legal and cultural differences across the world that can impact the rights and responsibilities of common shareholders. **Nokia**'s terminology is a bit different as it uses the phrase "share capital" in reference to what U.S. GAAP would title "common shares" (see Appendix A). It also discloses that it has issued (and outstanding) shares of 3,744,956,052.

NOKIA

**Accounting for Dividends**   Accounting for and reporting of dividends under U.S. GAAP and IFRS are consistent. This applies to cash dividends, stock dividends, and stock splits. For **Nokia**, a "dividend of EUR 0.40 per share is to be paid out on the shares of the Company." Nokia, like many other companies, follows a dividend policy set by management and its board.

**Accounting for Preferred Stock**   Accounting and reporting for preferred stock are similar for U.S. GAAP and IFRS, but there are some important differences. First, preferred stock that is redeemable at the option of the preferred stockholders is reported *between* liabilities and equity in U.S. GAAP balance sheets. However, that same stock is reported as a liability in IFRS balance sheets. Second, the issue price of convertible preferred stock (and bonds) is recorded entirely under preferred stock (or bonds) *and none is assigned to the conversion feature* under U.S. GAAP. However, IFRS requires that a portion of the issue price be allocated to the conversion feature when it exists. Nokia has no preferred stock.

**Accounting for Treasury Stock**   Both U.S. GAAP and IFRS apply the principle that companies do not record gains or losses on transactions involving their own stock. This applies to purchases, reissuances, and retirements of treasury stock. Consequently, the accounting for treasury stock explained in this chapter is consistent with that under IFRS. However, IFRS in this area is less detailed than that of U.S. GAAP. **Nokia**'s policy regarding treasury stock follows: "[It] recognizes acquired treasury shares as a deduction from equity at their acquisition cost."

Earnings per Share, Price-Earnings Ratio, Dividend Yield, and
Book Value per Share

**Decision Analysis**

## Earnings per Share

The income statement reports **earnings per share,** also called *EPS* or *net income per share,* which is the amount of income earned per each share of a company's outstanding common stock. The **basic earnings per share** formula is shown in Exhibit 13.17. When a company has no preferred stock, then preferred dividends are zero. The weighted-average common shares outstanding is measured over the income reporting period; its computation is explained in advanced courses.

 **A1** Compute earnings per share and describe its use.

$$\text{Basic earnings per share} = \frac{\text{Net income} - \text{Preferred dividends}}{\text{Weighted-average common shares outstanding}}$$

**EXHIBIT 13.17**

Basic Earnings per Share

To illustrate, assume that Quantum Co. earns $40,000 net income in 2011 and declares dividends of $7,500 on its noncumulative preferred stock. (If preferred stock is *non*cumulative, the income available [numerator] is the current period net income less any preferred dividends *declared* in that same period. If preferred stock is cumulative, the income available [numerator] is the current period net income less the preferred dividends whether declared or not.) Quantum has 5,000 weighted-average common shares outstanding during 2011. Its basic EPS[3] is

$$\text{Basic earnings per share} = \frac{\$40,000 - \$7,500}{5,000 \text{ shares}} = \$6.50$$

## Price-Earnings Ratio

A stock's market value is determined by its *expected* future cash flows. A comparison of a company's EPS and its market value per share reveals information about market expectations. This comparison is traditionally made using a **price-earnings** (or **PE**) **ratio,** expressed also as *price earnings, price to earnings,* or *PE.* Some analysts interpret this ratio as what price the market is willing to pay for a company's current earnings stream. Price-earnings ratios can differ across companies that have similar earnings because of either higher or lower expectations of future earnings. The price-earnings ratio is defined in Exhibit 13.18.

**A2** Compute price-earnings ratio and describe its use in analysis.

**Point:** The average PE ratio of stocks in the 1950–2010 period is about 14.

$$\text{Price-earnings ratio} = \frac{\text{Market value (price) per share}}{\text{Earnings per share}}$$

**EXHIBIT 13.18**

Price-Earnings Ratio

This ratio is often computed using EPS from the most recent period (for Amazon, its PE is 52; for Altria, its PE is 13). However, many users compute this ratio using *expected* EPS for the next period.

Some analysts view stocks with high PE ratios (higher than 20 to 25) as more likely to be overpriced and stocks with low PE ratios (less than 5 to 8) as more likely to be underpriced. These investors prefer to sell or avoid buying stocks with high PE ratios and to buy or hold stocks with low PE ratios. However, investment decision making is rarely so simple as to rely on a single ratio. For instance, a stock with a high PE ratio can prove to be a good investment if its earnings continue to increase beyond current expectations. Similarly, a stock with a low PE ratio can prove to be a poor investment if its earnings decline below expectations.

**Point:** Average PE ratios for U.S. stocks increased over the past two decades. Some analysts interpret this as a signal the market is overpriced. But higher ratios can at least partly reflect accounting changes that have reduced reported earnings.

[3] A corporation can be classified as having either a simple or complex capital structure. The term **simple capital structure** refers to a company with only common stock and nonconvertible preferred stock outstanding. The term **complex capital structure** refers to companies with dilutive securities. **Dilutive securities** include options, rights to purchase common stock, and any bonds or preferred stock that are convertible into common stock. A company with a complex capital structure must often report two EPS figures: basic and diluted. **Diluted earnings per share** is computed by adding all dilutive securities to the denominator of the basic EPS computation. It reflects the decrease in basic EPS *assuming* that all dilutive securities are converted into common shares.

■ Decision **Maker**                                                          Answer — p. 533

**Money Manager**   You plan to invest in one of two companies identified as having identical future prospects. One has a PE of 19 and the other a PE of 25. Which do you invest in? Does it matter if your *estimate* of PE for these two companies is 29 as opposed to 22? ■

## Dividend Yield

**A3** Compute dividend yield and explain its use in analysis.

Investors buy shares of a company's stock in anticipation of receiving a return from either or both cash dividends and stock price increases. Stocks that pay large dividends on a regular basis, called *income stocks,* are attractive to investors who want recurring cash flows from their investments. In contrast, some stocks pay little or no dividends but are still attractive to investors because of their expected stock price increases. The stocks of companies that distribute little or no cash but use their cash to finance expansion are called *growth stocks.* One way to help identify whether a stock is an income stock or a growth stock is to analyze its dividend yield. **Dividend yield,** defined in Exhibit 13.19, shows the annual amount of cash dividends distributed to common shares relative to their market value.

**EXHIBIT 13.19**

Dividend Yield

$$\text{Dividend yield} = \frac{\text{Annual cash dividends per share}}{\text{Market value per share}}$$

Dividend yield can be computed for current and prior periods using actual dividends and stock prices and for future periods using expected values. Exhibit 13.20 shows recent dividend and stock price data for **Amazon** and **Altria Group** to compute dividend yield.

**EXHIBIT 13.20**

Dividend and Stock Price Information

| Company | Cash Dividends per Share | Market Value per Share | Dividend Yield |
|---|---|---|---|
| Amazon . . . . . . . . . . . | $0.00 | $80 | 0.0% |
| Altria Group. . . . . . . . | 1.68 | 20 | 8.4 |

**Point:** The *payout ratio* equals cash dividends declared on common stock divided by net income. A low payout ratio suggests that a company is retaining earnings for future growth.

Dividend yield is zero for Amazon, implying it is a growth stock. An investor in Amazon would look for increases in stock prices (and eventual cash from the sale of stock). Altria has a dividend yield of 8.4%, implying it is an income stock for which dividends are important in assessing its value.

## Book Value per Share

**A4** Compute book value and explain its use in analysis.

*Case 1: Common Stock (Only) Outstanding.* **Book value per common share,** defined in Exhibit 13.21, reflects the amount of equity applicable to *common* shares on a per share basis. To illustrate, we use Dillon Snowboards' data from Exhibit 13.4. Dillon has 30,000 outstanding common shares, and the stockholders' equity applicable to common shares is $365,000. Dillon's book value per common share is $12.17, computed as $365,000 divided by 30,000 shares.

**EXHIBIT 13.21**

Book Value per Common Share

$$\text{Book value per common share} = \frac{\text{Stockholders' equity applicable to common shares}}{\text{Number of common shares outstanding}}$$

**Point:** Book value per share is also referred to as *stockholders' claim to assets on a per share basis.*

*Case 2: Common and Preferred Stock Outstanding.* To compute book value when both common and preferred shares are outstanding, we allocate total equity between the two types of shares. The **book value per preferred share** is computed first; its computation is shown in Exhibit 13.22.

**EXHIBIT 13.22**

Book Value per Preferred Share

$$\text{Book value per preferred share} = \frac{\text{Stockholders' equity applicable to preferred shares}}{\text{Number of preferred shares outstanding}}$$

The equity applicable to preferred shares equals the preferred share's call price (or par value if the preferred is not callable) plus any cumulative dividends in arrears. The remaining equity is the portion applicable to common shares. To illustrate, consider LTD's equity in Exhibit 13.23. Its preferred stock is callable at $108 per share, and two years of cumulative preferred dividends are in arrears.

**EXHIBIT 13.23**

Stockholders' Equity with
Preferred and Common Stock

**Stockholders' Equity**

| | |
|---|---|
| Preferred stock—$100 par value, 7% cumulative, | |
|   2,000 shares authorized, 1,000 shares issued and outstanding . . . . . . . . . . . . . . . . . . . . . | $100,000 |
| Common stock—$25 par value, 12,000 shares authorized, | |
|   10,000 shares issued and outstanding . . . . . . . . . . . . . . . . . . . . . . . . . . . . . . . . . . . . | 250,000 |
| Paid-in capital in excess of par value, common stock . . . . . . . . . . . . . . . . . . . . . . . . . | 15,000 |
| Retained earnings . . . . . . . . . . . . . . . . . . . . . . . . . . . . . . . . . . . . . . . . . . . . . . . . . . | 82,000 |
| Total stockholders' equity . . . . . . . . . . . . . . . . . . . . . . . . . . . . . . . . . . . . . . . . . . . | $447,000 |

The book value computations are in Exhibit 13.24. Equity is first allocated to preferred shares before the book value of common shares is computed.

**EXHIBIT 13.24**

Computing Book Value per
Preferred and Common Share

| | | |
|---|---|---|
| Total stockholders' equity . . . . . . . . . . . . . . . . . . . . . . . . . . . . . . . . . . . | | $447,000 |
| Less equity applicable to preferred shares | | |
|   Call price (1,000 shares × $108) . . . . . . . . . . . . . . . . . . . . . . . . . . . . | $108,000 | |
|   Dividends in arrears ($100,000 × 7% × 2 years) . . . . . . . . . . . . . . . . . | 14,000 | (122,000) |
| Equity applicable to common shares . . . . . . . . . . . . . . . . . . . . . . . . . . . . | | $325,000 |
| **Book value per preferred share ($122,000/1,000 shares)** . . . . . . . . . . | | **$ 122.00** |
| **Book value per common share ($325,000/10,000 shares)** . . . . . . . . . | | **$ 32.50** |

Book value per share reflects the value per share if a company is liquidated at balance sheet amounts. Book value is also the starting point in many stock valuation models, merger negotiations, price setting for public utilities, and loan contracts. The main limitation in using book value is the potential difference between recorded value and market value for assets and liabilities. Investors often adjust their analysis for estimates of these differences.

 **Decision Maker**    Answer — p. 533

**Investor**   You are considering investing in **BMX**, whose book value per common share is $4 and price per common share on the stock exchange is $7. From this information, are BMX's net assets priced higher or lower than its recorded values? ■

## DEMONSTRATION PROBLEM 1

Barton Corporation began operations on January 1, 2010. The following transactions relating to stockholders' equity occurred in the first two years of the company's operations.

**2010**

Jan. 1   Authorized the issuance of 2 million shares of $5 par value common stock and 100,000 shares of $100 par value, 10% cumulative, preferred stock.

Jan. 2   Issued 200,000 shares of common stock for $12 cash per share.

Jan. 3   Issued 100,000 shares of common stock in exchange for a building valued at $820,000 and merchandise inventory valued at $380,000.

Jan. 4   Paid $10,000 cash to the company's founders for organization activities.

Jan. 5   Issued 12,000 shares of preferred stock for $110 cash per share.

**2011**

June 4   Issued 100,000 shares of common stock for $15 cash per share.

**Required**

1. Prepare journal entries to record these transactions.

2. Prepare the stockholders' equity section of the balance sheet as of December 31, 2010, and December 31, 2011, based on these transactions.

3. Prepare a table showing dividend allocations and dividends per share for 2010 and 2011 assuming Barton declares the following cash dividends: 2010, $50,000, and 2011, $300,000.

4. Prepare the January 2, 2010, journal entry for Barton's issuance of 200,000 shares of common stock for $12 cash per share assuming
   a. Common stock is no-par stock without a stated value.
   b. Common stock is no-par stock with a stated value of $10 per share.

## PLANNING THE SOLUTION

● Record journal entries for the transactions for 2010 and 2011.
● Determine the balances for the 2010 and 2011 equity accounts for the balance sheet.
● Prepare the contributed capital portion of the 2010 and 2011 balance sheets.
● Prepare a table similar to Exhibit 13.11 showing dividend allocations for 2010 and 2011.
● Record the issuance of common stock under both specifications of no-par stock.

## SOLUTION TO DEMONSTRATION PROBLEM 1

**1.** Journal entries.

| 2010 | | | |
|---|---|---|---|
| Jan. 2 | Cash | 2,400,000 | |
| | Common Stock, $5 Par Value | | 1,000,000 |
| | Paid-In Capital in Excess of Par Value, Common Stock | | 1,400,000 |
| | *Issued 200,000 shares of common stock.* | | |
| Jan. 3 | Building | 820,000 | |
| | Merchandise Inventory | 380,000 | |
| | Common Stock, $5 Par Value | | 500,000 |
| | Paid-In Capital in Excess of Par Value, Common Stock | | 700,000 |
| | *Issued 100,000 shares of common stock.* | | |
| Jan. 4 | Organization Expenses | 10,000 | |
| | Cash | | 10,000 |
| | *Paid founders for organization costs.* | | |
| Jan. 5 | Cash | 1,320,000 | |
| | Preferred Stock, $100 Par Value | | 1,200,000 |
| | Paid-In Capital in Excess of Par Value, Preferred Stock | | 120,000 |
| | *Issued 12,000 shares of preferred stock.* | | |
| 2011 | | | |
| June 4 | Cash | 1,500,000 | |
| | Common Stock, $5 Par Value | | 500,000 |
| | Paid-In Capital in Excess of Par Value, Common Stock | | 1,000,000 |
| | *Issued 100,000 shares of common stock.* | | |

**2.** Balance sheet presentations (at December 31 year-end).

| | 2011 | 2010 |
|---|---|---|
| **Stockholders' Equity** | | |
| Preferred stock—$100 par value, 10% cumulative, 100,000 shares authorized, 12,000 shares issued and outstanding | $1,200,000 | $1,200,000 |
| Paid-in capital in excess of par value, preferred stock | 120,000 | 120,000 |
| Total paid-in capital by preferred stockholders | 1,320,000 | 1,320,000 |
| Common stock—$5 par value, 2,000,000 shares authorized, 300,000 shares issued and outstanding in 2010, and 400,000 shares issued and outstanding in 2011 | 2,000,000 | 1,500,000 |
| Paid-in capital in excess of par value, common stock | 3,100,000 | 2,100,000 |
| Total paid-in capital by common stockholders | 5,100,000 | 3,600,000 |
| Total paid-in capital | $6,420,000 | $4,920,000 |

**3.** Dividend allocation table.

| | Common | Preferred |
|---|---|---|
| **2010 ($50,000)** | | |
| Preferred—current year (12,000 shares × $10 = $120,000) ............ | $ 0 | $ 50,000 |
| Common—remainder (300,000 shares outstanding) ................... | 0 | 0 |
| Total for the year ...... | $ 0 | $ 50,000 |
| **2011 ($300,000)** | | |
| Preferred—dividend in arrears from 2010 ($120,000 − $50,000) ........ | $ 0 | $ 70,000 |
| Preferred—current year ...................................... | 0 | 120,000 |
| Common—remainder (400,000 shares outstanding) ................. | 110,000 | 0 |
| Total for the year ...... | $110,000 | $190,000 |
| **Dividends per share** | | |
| 2010 ........ | $ 0.00 | $ 4.17 |
| 2011 ........ | $ 0.28 | $ 15.83 |

**4.** Journal entries.

**a.** For 2010 (no-par stock without a stated value):

| Jan. 2 | Cash ......................................... | 2,400,000 | |
|---|---|---|---|
| | Common Stock, No-Par Value ................ | | 2,400,000 |
| | *Issued 200,000 shares of no-par common stock at $12 per share.* | | |

**b.** For 2010 (no-par stock with a stated value):

| Jan. 2 | Cash ......................................... | 2,400,000 | |
|---|---|---|---|
| | Common Stock, $10 Stated Value .............. | | 2,000,000 |
| | Paid-In Capital in Excess of Stated Value, Common Stock ............... | | 400,000 |
| | *Issued 200,000 shares of $10 stated value common stock at $12 per share.* | | |

## DEMONSTRATION PROBLEM 2

Precision Company began year 2011 with the following balances in its stockholders' equity accounts.

| | |
|---|---|
| Common stock—$10 par, 500,000 shares authorized, 200,000 shares issued and outstanding ................... | $2,000,000 |
| Paid-in capital in excess of par, common stock .............. | 1,000,000 |
| Retained earnings ....................................... | 5,000,000 |
| Total ...................................................... | $8,000,000 |

All outstanding common stock was issued for $15 per share when the company was created. Prepare journal entries to account for the following transactions during year 2011.

Jan. 10 The board declared a $0.10 cash dividend per share to shareholders of record Jan. 28.
Feb. 15 Paid the cash dividend declared on January 10.
Mar. 31 Declared a 20% stock dividend. The market value of the stock is $18 per share.
May 1 Distributed the stock dividend declared on March 31.
July 1 Purchased 30,000 shares of treasury stock at $20 per share.
Sept. 1 Sold 20,000 treasury shares at $26 cash per share.
Dec. 1 Sold the remaining 10,000 shares of treasury stock at $7 cash per share.

## PLANNING THE SOLUTION

- Calculate the total cash dividend to record by multiplying the cash dividend declared by the number of shares as of the date of record.
- Decide whether the stock dividend is a small or large dividend. Then analyze each event to determine the accounts affected and the appropriate amounts to be recorded.

## SOLUTION TO DEMONSTRATION PROBLEM 2

| Date | Account | Debit | Credit |
|---|---|---|---|
| Jan. 10 | Retained Earnings | 20,000 | |
| |     Common Dividend Payable | | 20,000 |
| | *Declared a $0.10 per share cash dividend.* | | |
| Feb. 15 | Common Dividend Payable | 20,000 | |
| |     Cash | | 20,000 |
| | *Paid $0.10 per share cash dividend.* | | |
| Mar. 31 | Retained Earnings | 720,000 | |
| |     Common Stock Dividend Distributable | | 400,000 |
| |     Paid-In Capital in Excess of | | |
| |        Par Value, Common Stock | | 320,000 |
| | *Declared a small stock dividend of 20% or* | | |
| | *40,000 shares; market value is $18 per share.* | | |
| May 1 | Common Stock Dividend Distributable | 400,000 | |
| |     Common Stock | | 400,000 |
| | *Distributed 40,000 shares of common stock.* | | |
| July 1 | Treasury Stock, Common | 600,000 | |
| |     Cash | | 600,000 |
| | *Purchased 30,000 common shares at $20 per share.* | | |
| Sept. 1 | Cash | 520,000 | |
| |     Treasury Stock, Common | | 400,000 |
| |     Paid-In Capital, Treasury Stock | | 120,000 |
| | *Sold 20,000 treasury shares at $26 per share.* | | |
| Dec. 1 | Cash | 70,000 | |
| | Paid-In Capital, Treasury Stock | 120,000 | |
| | Retained Earnings | 10,000 | |
| |     Treasury Stock, Common | | 200,000 |
| | *Sold 10,000 treasury shares at $7 per share.* | | |

# Summary

**C1**   **Identify characteristics of corporations and their organization.** Corporations are legal entities whose stockholders are not liable for its debts. Stock is easily transferred, and the life of a corporation does not end with the incapacity of a stockholder. A corporation acts through its agents, who are its officers and managers. Corporations are regulated and subject to income taxes. Authorized stock is the stock that a corporation's charter authorizes it to sell. Issued stock is the portion of authorized shares sold. Par value stock is a value per share assigned by the charter. No-par value stock is stock *not* assigned a value per share by the charter. Stated value stock is no-par stock to which the directors assign a value per share.

**C2**   **Explain characteristics of, and distribute dividends between, common and preferred stock.** Preferred stock has a priority (or senior status) relative to common stock in one or more areas, usually (1) dividends and (2) assets in case of liquidation. Preferred stock usually does not carry voting rights and can be

convertible or callable. Convertibility permits the holder to convert preferred to common. Callability permits the issuer to buy back preferred stock under specified conditions. Preferred stockholders usually hold the right to dividend distributions before common stockholders. When preferred stock is cumulative and in arrears, the amount in arrears must be distributed to preferred before any dividends are distributed to common.

**C3**   **Explain the items reported in retained earnings.** Stockholders' equity is made up of (1) paid-in capital and (2) retained earnings. Paid-in capital consists of funds raised by stock issuances. Retained earnings consists of cumulative net income (losses) not distributed. Many companies face statutory and contractual restrictions on retained earnings. Corporations can voluntarily appropriate retained earnings to inform others about their disposition. Prior period adjustments are corrections of errors in prior financial statements.

**A1**  **Compute earnings per share and describe its use.** A company with a simple capital structure computes basic EPS by dividing net income less any preferred dividends by the weighted-average number of outstanding common shares. A company with a complex capital structure must usually report both basic and diluted EPS.

**A2**  **Compute price-earnings ratio and describe its use in analysis.** A common stock's price-earnings (PE) ratio is computed by dividing the stock's market value (price) per share by its EPS. A stock's PE is based on expectations that can prove to be better or worse than eventual performance.

**A3**  **Compute dividend yield and explain its use in analysis.** Dividend yield is the ratio of a stock's annual cash dividends per share to its market value (price) per share. Dividend yield can be compared with the yield of other companies to determine whether the stock is expected to be an income or growth stock.

**A4**  **Compute book value and explain its use in analysis.** Book value per common share is equity applicable to common shares divided by the number of outstanding common shares. Book value per preferred share is equity applicable to preferred shares divided by the number of outstanding preferred shares.

**P1**  **Record the issuance of corporate stock.** When stock is issued, its par or stated value is credited to the stock account and any excess is credited to a separate contributed capital account. If a stock has neither par nor stated value, the entire proceeds are credited to the stock account. Stockholders must contribute assets equal to minimum legal capital or be potentially liable for the deficiency.

**P2**  **Record transactions involving cash dividends, stock dividends, and stock splits.** Cash dividends involve three events. On the date of declaration, the directors bind the company to pay the dividend. A dividend declaration reduces retained earnings and creates a current liability. On the date of record, recipients of the dividend are identified. On the date of payment, cash is paid to stockholders and the current liability is removed. Neither a stock dividend nor a stock split alters the value of the company. However, the value of each share is less due to the distribution of additional shares. The distribution of additional shares is according to individual stockholders' ownership percent. Small stock dividends ($\leq 25\%$) are recorded by capitalizing retained earnings equal to the market value of distributed shares. Large stock dividends ($>25\%$) are recorded by capitalizing retained earnings equal to the par or stated value of distributed shares. Stock splits do not necessitate journal entries but do necessitate changes in the description of stock.

**P3**  **Record purchases and sales of treasury stock and the retirement of stock.** When a corporation purchases its own previously issued stock, it debits the cost of these shares to Treasury Stock. Treasury stock is subtracted from equity in the balance sheet. If treasury stock is reissued, any proceeds in excess of cost are credited to Paid-In Capital, Treasury Stock. If the proceeds are less than cost, they are debited to Paid-In Capital, Treasury Stock to the extent a credit balance exists. Any remaining amount is debited to Retained Earnings. When stock is retired, all accounts related to the stock are removed.

## Guidance Answers to Decision Maker and Decision Ethics

**Entrepreneur**  The 50% stock dividend provides you no direct income. A stock dividend often reveals management's optimistic expectations about the future and can improve a stock's marketability by making it affordable to more investors. Accordingly, a stock dividend usually reveals "good news" and because of this, it likely increases (slightly) the market value for your stock. The same conclusions apply to the 3-for-2 stock split.

**Concert Organizer**  You have two basic options: (1) different classes of common stock or (2) common and preferred stock. Your objective is to issue to yourself stock that has all or a majority of the voting power. The other class of stock would carry limited or no voting rights. In this way, you maintain control and are able to raise the necessary funds.

**Money Manager**  Since one company requires a payment of $19 for each $1 of earnings, and the other requires $25, you would prefer the stock with the PE of 19; it is a better deal given identical prospects. You should make sure these companies' earnings computations are roughly the same, for example, no extraordinary items, unusual events, and so forth. Also, your PE estimates for these companies do matter. If you are willing to pay $29 for each $1 of earnings for these companies, you obviously expect both to exceed current market expectations.

**Investor**  Book value reflects recorded values. BMX's book value is $4 per common share. Stock price reflects the market's expectation of net asset value (both tangible and intangible items). BMX's market value is $7 per common share. Comparing these figures suggests BMX's market value of net assets is higher than its recorded values (by an amount of $7 versus $4 per share).

## Guidance Answers to Quick Checks

1. (*b*)

2. A corporation pays taxes on its income, and its stockholders normally pay personal income taxes (at the 15% rate or lower) on any cash dividends received from the corporation.

3. A proxy is a legal document used to transfer a stockholder's right to vote to another person.

4. (*a*)

5. A stock premium is an amount in excess of par (or stated) value paid by purchasers of newly issued stock.

6. Minimum legal capital intends to protect creditors of a corporation by obligating stockholders to some minimum level of

equity financing and by constraining a corporation from excessive payments to stockholders.

**7.** Common Dividend Payable is a current liability account.

**8.** The date of declaration, date of record, and date of payment.

**9.** A dividend is a legal liability at the date of declaration, on which date it is recorded as a liability.

**10.** A stock dividend does not transfer assets to stockholders, but it does require an amount of retained earnings to be transferred to a contributed capital account(s).

**11.** A small stock dividend is 25% or less of the previous outstanding shares. A large stock dividend is more than 25%.

**12.** Retained earnings equal to the distributable shares' market value should be capitalized for a small stock dividend.

**13.** Typically, preferred stock has a preference in receipt of dividends and in distribution of assets.

**14.** (a)

**15.** (b)

| | |
|---|---:|
| Total cash dividend | $288,000 |
| To preferred shareholders | 135,000* |
| Remainder to common shareholders | $153,000 |

\* 9,000 × $50 × 10% × 3 years = $135,000.

**16.** (b)

**17.** No. The shares are an investment for Southern Co. and are issued and outstanding shares for Northern Corp.

**18.** Treasury stock does not affect the number of authorized or issued shares, but it reduces the outstanding shares.

**19.** (a)

## Key Terms

Appropriated retained earnings (p. 525)
Authorized stock (p. 511)
Basic earnings per share (p. 527)
Book value per common share (p. 528)
Book value per preferred share (p. 528)
Call price (p. 521)
Callable preferred stock (p. 521)
Capital stock (p. 511)
Changes in accounting estimates (p. 525)
Common stock (p. 510)
Complex capital structure (p. 527)
Convertible preferred stock (p. 520)
Corporation (p. 508)
Cumulative preferred stock (p. 519)
Date of declaration (p. 515)
Date of payment (p. 515)
Date of record (p. 515)
Diluted earnings per share (p. 527)
Dilutive securities (p. 527)

Discount on stock (p. 513)
Dividend in arrears (p. 519)
Dividend yield (p. 528)
Earnings per share (EPS) (p. 527)
Financial leverage (p. 521)
Large stock dividend (p. 516)
Liquidating cash dividend (p. 516)
Market value per share (p. 511)
Minimum legal capital (p. 511)
Noncumulative preferred stock (p. 519)
Nonparticipating preferred stock (p. 520)
No-par value stock (p. 511)
Organization expenses (p. 509)
Paid-in capital (p. 512)
Paid-in capital in excess of par value (p. 513)
Participating preferred stock (p. 520)
Par value (p. 511)
Par value stock (p. 511)

Preemptive right (p. 510)
Preferred stock (p. 518)
Premium on stock (p. 513)
Price-earnings (PE) ratio (p. 527)
Prior period adjustments (p. 525)
Proxy (p. 509)
Restricted retained earnings (p. 524)
Retained earnings (p. 512)
Retained earnings deficit (p. 515)
Reverse stock split (p. 518)
Simple capital structure (p. 527)
Small stock dividend (p. 516)
Stated value stock (p. 512)
Statement of stockholders' equity (p. 525)
Stock dividend (p. 516)
Stock options (p. 525)
Stock split (p. 518)
Stockholders' equity (p. 512)
Treasury stock (p. 522)

## Multiple Choice Quiz

Answers on p. 549

Additional Quiz Questions are available at the book's Website.

**1.** A corporation issues 6,000 shares of $5 par value common stock for $8 cash per share. The entry to record this transaction includes:
  **a.** A debit to Paid-In Capital in Excess of Par Value for $18,000.
  **b.** A credit to Common Stock for $48,000.
  **c.** A credit to Paid-In Capital in Excess of Par Value for $30,000.
  **d.** A credit to Cash for $48,000.
  **e.** A credit to Common Stock for $30,000.

**2.** A company reports net income of $75,000. Its weighted-average common shares outstanding is 19,000. It has no other stock outstanding. Its earnings per share is:
  **a.** $4.69
  **b.** $3.95
  **c.** $3.75
  **d.** $2.08
  **e.** $4.41

**3.** A company has 5,000 shares of $100 par preferred stock and 50,000 shares of $10 par common stock outstanding. Its total stockholders' equity is $2,000,000. Its book value per common share is:
  **a.** $100.00
  **b.** $ 10.00
  **c.** $ 40.00
  **d.** $ 30.00
  **e.** $ 36.36

**4.** A company paid cash dividends of $0.81 per share. Its earnings per share is $6.95 and its market price per share is $45.00. Its dividend yield is:
  **a.** 1.8%
  **b.** 11.7%

  **c.** 15.4%
  **d.** 55.6%
  **e.** 8.6%

**5.** A company's shares have a market value of $85 per share. Its net income is $3,500,000, and its weighted-average common shares outstanding is 700,000. Its price-earnings ratio is:
  **a.** 5.9
  **b.** 425.0
  **c.** 17.0
  **d.** 10.4
  **e.** 41.2

 Icon denotes assignments that involve decision making.

## Discussion Questions

**1.** What are organization expenses? Provide examples.
**2.** How are organization expenses reported?
**3.** Who is responsible for directing a corporation's affairs?
**4.** What is the preemptive right of common stockholders?
**5.** List the general rights of common stockholders.
**6.** What is the difference between authorized shares and outstanding shares?
**7.** Why would an investor find convertible preferred stock attractive?
**8.** What is the difference between the market value per share and the par value per share?
**9.** What is the difference between the par value and the call price of a share of preferred stock?
**10.** Identify and explain the importance of the three dates relevant to corporate dividends.
**11.** Why is the term *liquidating dividend* used to describe cash dividends debited against paid-in capital accounts?
**12.** How does declaring a stock dividend affect the corporation's assets, liabilities, and total equity? What are the effects of the eventual distribution of that stock?
**13.** What is the difference between a stock dividend and a stock split?
**14.** Courts have ruled that a stock dividend is not taxable income to stockholders. What justifies this decision?

**15.** How does the purchase of treasury stock affect the purchaser's assets and total equity?
**16.** Why do laws place limits on treasury stock purchases?
**17.** How are EPS results computed for a corporation with a simple capital structure?
**18.** What is a stock option?
**19.** How is book value per share computed for a corporation with no preferred stock? What is the main limitation of using book value per share to value a corporation?
**20.** Review the 2009 balance sheet for **Nokia** in Appendix A and list the amounts for treasury shares and retained earnings.
**21.** Refer to **Research In Motion**'s 2010 balance sheet in Appendix A. How many shares of common stock are authorized? How many shares of voting common stock are issued?
**22.** Refer to the 2009 balance sheet for **Palm** in Appendix A. What is the par value per share of its common stock? Suggest a rationale for the amount of par value it assigned.
**23.** Refer to the financial statements for **Apple** in Appendix A. What are its cash proceeds from issuance of common stock *and* its cash repurchases of common stock for the year ended September 26, 2009? Explain.

## connect

Of the following statements, which are true for the corporate form of organization?
**1.** Owners are not agents of the corporation.
**2.** It is a separate legal entity.
**3.** It has a limited life.
**4.** Capital is more easily accumulated than with most other forms of organization.
**5.** Corporate income that is distributed to shareholders is usually taxed twice.
**6.** Owners have unlimited liability for corporate debts.
**7.** Ownership rights cannot be easily transferred.

**QUICK STUDY**

**QS 13-1**
Characteristics of corporations
C1

**QS 13-2**

Issuance of common stock

P1

Prepare the journal entry to record Channel One Company's issuance of 100,000 shares of $0.50 par value common stock assuming the shares sell for:

**a.** $0.50 cash per share.

**b.** $2 cash per share.

---

**QS 13-3**

Issuance of no-par common stock

P1

Prepare the journal entry to record Selectist Company's issuance of 104,000 shares of no-par value common stock assuming the shares:

**a.** Sell for $15 cash per share.

**b.** Are exchanged for land valued at $1,560,000.

---

**QS 13-4**

Issuance of par and stated value common stock

P1

Prepare the journal entry to record Typist Company's issuance of 250,000 shares of its common stock assuming the shares have a:

**a.** $1 par value and sell for $10 cash per share.

**b.** $1 stated value and sell for $10 cash per share.

---

**QS 13-5**

Issuance of common stock

P1

Prepare the issuer's journal entry for each separate transaction. (*a*) On March 1, Edgar Co. issues 44,500 shares of $4 par value common stock for $255,000 cash. (*b*) On April 1, GT Co. issues no-par value common stock for $50,000 cash. (*c*) On April 6, MTV issues 2,000 shares of $20 par value common stock for $35,000 of inventory, $135,000 of machinery, and acceptance of an $84,000 note payable.

---

**QS 13-6**

Issuance of preferred stock

P1  P2

**a.** Prepare the journal entry to record Stefan Company's issuance of 12,000 shares of $50 par value 6% cumulative preferred stock for $75 cash per share.

**b.** Assuming the facts in part 1, if Stefan declares a year-end cash dividend, what is the amount of dividend paid to preferred shareholders? (Assume no dividends in arrears.)

---

**QS 13-7**

Accounting for cash dividends

P2

Prepare journal entries to record the following transactions for Emerson Corporation.

April 15    Declared a cash dividend payable to common stockholders of $40,000.

May 15    Date of record is May 15 for the cash dividend declared on April 15.

May 31    Paid the dividend declared on April 15.

---

**QS 13-8**

Dividend allocation between classes of shareholders

C2

Stockholders' equity of STIX Company consists of 75,000 shares of $5 par value, 8% cumulative preferred stock and 200,000 shares of $1 par value common stock. Both classes of stock have been outstanding since the company's inception. STIX did not declare any dividends in the prior year, but it now declares and pays a $108,000 cash dividend at the current year-end. Determine the amount distributed to each class of stockholders for this two-year-old company.

---

**QS 13-9**

Accounting for small stock dividend

P2

The stockholders' equity section of Zacman Company's balance sheet as of April 1 follows. On April 2, Zacman declares and distributes a 10% stock dividend. The stock's per share market value on April 2 is $25 (prior to the dividend). Prepare the stockholders' equity section immediately after the stock dividend.

| | |
|---|---|
| Common stock—$5 par value, 375,000 shares authorized, 150,000 shares issued and outstanding ......... | $ 750,000 |
| Paid-in capital in excess of par value, common stock ......... | 352,500 |
| Retained earnings ...................................... | 633,000 |
| Total stockholders' equity ............................. | $1,735,500 |

---

**QS 13-10**

Accounting for changes in estimates; error adjustments

C3

Answer the following questions related to a company's activities for the current year:

**1.** After using an expected useful life of 20 years and no salvage value to depreciate its office equipment over the preceding 15 years, the company decided early this year that the equipment will last only two more years. How should the effects of this decision be reported in the current year financial statements?

**2.** A review of the notes payable files discovers that two years ago the company reported the entire amount of a payment (principal and interest) on an installment note payable as interest expense. This mistake had a material effect on the amount of income in that year. How should the correction be reported in the current year financial statements?

On May 3, Lassman Corporation purchased 3,000 shares of its own stock for $27,000 cash. On November 4, Lassman reissued 750 shares of this treasury stock for $7,080. Prepare the May 3 and November 4 journal entries to record Lassman's purchase and reissuance of treasury stock.

**QS 13-11**
Purchase and sale of
treasury stock  P3

Barnes Company earned net income of $450,000 this year. The number of common shares outstanding during the entire year was 200,000, and preferred shareholders received a $10,000 cash dividend. Compute Barnes Company's basic earnings per share.

**QS 13-12**
Basic earnings per share  A1

Campbell Company reports net income of $1,200,000 for the year. It has no preferred stock, and its weighted-average common shares outstanding is 300,000 shares. Compute its basic earnings per share.

**QS 13-13**
Basic earnings per share  A1

Compute Fox Company's price-earnings ratio if its common stock has a market value of $30.75 per share and its EPS is $4.10. Would an analyst likely consider this stock potentially over- or underpriced? Explain.

**QS 13-14**
Price-earnings ratio  A2

Fiona Company expects to pay a $2.10 per share cash dividend this year on its common stock. The current market value of Fiona stock is $28.50 per share. Compute the expected dividend yield on the Fiona stock. Would you classify the Fiona stock as a growth or an income stock? Explain.

**QS 13-15**
Dividend yield  A3

The stockholders' equity section of Axel Company's balance sheet follows. The preferred stock's call price is $30. Determine the book value per share of the common stock.

**QS 13-16**
Book value per common share

A4

| | |
|---|---|
| Preferred stock—5% cumulative, $10 par value, | |
| 10,000 shares authorized, issued and outstanding .......... | $100,000 |
| Common stock—$5 par value, 100,000 shares | |
| authorized, 75,000 shares issued and outstanding .......... | 375,000 |
| Retained earnings ..................................... | 445,000 |
| Total stockholders' equity ............................ | $920,000 |

**Air France-KLM** reports the following equity information for its fiscal year ended March 31, 2009 (euros in millions). Prepare its journal entry, using its account titles, to record the issuance of capital stock assuming that its entire par value stock was issued on March 31, 2009, for cash.

**QS 13-17**
International equity disclosures

P1

| March 31 | 2009 |
|---|---|
| Issued capital .................. | €2,552 |
| Additional paid-in capital ........ | 765 |

**connect**

Describe how each of the following characteristics of organizations applies to corporations.

**EXERCISES**

| | |
|---|---|
| 1. Duration of life | 5. Owner authority and control |
| 2. Owner liability | 6. Ease of formation |
| 3. Legal status | 7. Transferability of ownership |
| 4. Tax status of income | 8. Ability to raise large capital amounts |

**Exercise 13-1**
Characteristics of corporations

C1

Aloha Corporation issues 6,000 shares of its common stock for $144,000 cash on February 20. Prepare journal entries to record this event under each of the following separate situations.
1. The stock has neither par nor stated value.
2. The stock has a $20 par value.
3. The stock has an $8 stated value.

**Exercise 13-2**
Accounting for par, stated, and no-par stock issuances

P1

---

**Exercise 13-3**
Recording stock issuances
P1

Prepare journal entries to record the following four separate issuances of stock.

**1.** A corporation issued 2,000 shares of no-par common stock to its promoters in exchange for their efforts, estimated to be worth $30,000. The stock has no stated value.

**2.** A corporation issued 2,000 shares of no-par common stock to its promoters in exchange for their efforts, estimated to be worth $30,000. The stock has a $1 per share stated value.

**3.** A corporation issued 4,000 shares of $10 par value common stock for $70,000 cash.

**4.** A corporation issued 1,000 shares of $100 par value preferred stock for $120,000 cash.

---

**Exercise 13-4**
Stock issuance for noncash assets
P1

Soku Company issues 36,000 shares of $9 par value common stock in exchange for land and a building. The land is valued at $225,000 and the building at $360,000. Prepare the journal entry to record issuance of the stock in exchange for the land and building.

---

**Exercise 13-5**
Identifying characteristics of preferred stock
C2

Match each description 1 through 6 with the characteristic of preferred stock that it best describes by writing the letter of that characteristic in the blank next to each description.

**A.** Cumulative     **B.** Noncumulative     **C.** Convertible

**D.** Callable     **E.** Nonparticipating     **F.** Participating

_____ **1.** Holders of the stock lose any dividends that are not declared in the current year.

_____ **2.** The issuing corporation can retire the stock by paying a prespecified price.

_____ **3.** Holders of the stock can receive dividends exceeding the stated rate under certain conditions.

_____ **4.** Holders of the stock are not entitled to receive dividends in excess of the stated rate.

_____ **5.** Holders of this stock can exchange it for shares of common stock.

_____ **6.** Holders of the stock are entitled to receive current and all past dividends before common stockholders receive any dividends.

---

**Exercise 13-6**
Stock dividends and splits
P2

On June 30, 2011, Quinn Corporation's common stock is priced at $31 per share before any stock dividend or split, and the stockholders' equity section of its balance sheet appears as follows.

| | |
|---|---|
| Common stock—$10 par value, 60,000 shares authorized, 25,000 shares issued and outstanding . . . . . . . . . . | $250,000 |
| Paid-in capital in excess of par value, common stock . . . . . . . . . | 100,000 |
| Retained earnings . . . . . . . . . . . . . . . . . . . . . . . . . . . . . . . . . . | 330,000 |
| Total stockholders' equity . . . . . . . . . . . . . . . . . . . . . . . . . . . . | $680,000 |

**1.** Assume that the company declares and immediately distributes a 100% stock dividend. This event is recorded by capitalizing retained earnings equal to the stock's par value. Answer these questions about stockholders' equity as it exists *after* issuing the new shares.

    **a.** What is the retained earnings balance?

**Check**   (1*b*) $680,000                **b.** What is the amount of total stockholders' equity?

    **c.** How many shares are outstanding?

**2.** Assume that the company implements a 2-for-1 stock split instead of the stock dividend in part 1. Answer these questions about stockholders' equity as it exists *after* issuing the new shares.

(2*a*) $330,000                 **a.** What is the retained earnings balance?

    **b.** What is the amount of total stockholders' equity?

    **c.** How many shares are outstanding?

**3.** Explain the difference, if any, to a stockholder from receiving new shares distributed under a large stock dividend versus a stock split.

---

**Exercise 13-7**
Stock dividends and per share book values
P2

The stockholders' equity of Whiz.com Company at the beginning of the day on February 5 follows.

| | |
|---|---|
| Common stock—$25 par value, 150,000 shares authorized, 60,000 shares issued and outstanding . . . . . . . . . . | $1,500,000 |
| Paid-in capital in excess of par value, common stock . . . . . . . . . | 525,000 |
| Retained earnings . . . . . . . . . . . . . . . . . . . . . . . . . . . . . . . . . . | 675,000 |
| Total stockholders' equity . . . . . . . . . . . . . . . . . . . . . . . . . . . . | $2,700,000 |

On February 5, the directors declare a 20% stock dividend distributable on February 28 to the February 15 stockholders of record. The stock's market value is $40 per share on February 5 before the stock dividend. The stock's market value is $34 per share on February 28.

**1.** Prepare entries to record both the dividend declaration and its distribution.

**2.** One stockholder owned 750 shares on February 5 before the dividend. Compute the book value per share and total book value of this stockholder's shares immediately before *and* after the stock dividend of February 5.

**Check** (2) Book value per share: before, $45; after, $37.50

**3.** Compute the total market value of the investor's shares in part 2 as of February 5 and February 28.

---

Wade's outstanding stock consists of 40,000 shares of *noncumulative* 7.5% preferred stock with a $10 par value and also 100,000 shares of common stock with a $1 par value. During its first four years of operation, the corporation declared and paid the following total cash dividends.

**Exercise 13-8**
Dividends on common and noncumulative preferred stock
**C2**

| | |
|---|---|
| 2011 ......................... | $ 10,000 |
| 2012 ......................... | 24,000 |
| 2013 ......................... | 100,000 |
| 2014 ......................... | 196,000 |

Determine the amount of dividends paid each year to each of the two classes of stockholders: preferred and common. Also compute the total dividends paid to each class for the four years combined.

**Check** 4-year total paid to preferred, $94,000

---

Use the data in Exercise 13-8 to determine the amount of dividends paid each year to each of the two classes of stockholders assuming that the preferred stock is *cumulative*. Also determine the total dividends paid to each class for the four years combined.

**Exercise 13-9**
Dividends on common and cumulative preferred stock **C2**

---

On October 10, the stockholders' equity of Noble Systems appears as follows.

**Exercise 13-10**
Recording and reporting treasury stock transactions

**P3**

| | |
|---|---|
| Common stock—$10 par value, 36,000 shares | |
| authorized, issued, and outstanding ..................... | $360,000 |
| Paid-in capital in excess of par value, common stock .......... | 108,000 |
| Retained earnings ...................................... | 432,000 |
| Total stockholders' equity ............................. | $900,000 |

**1.** Prepare journal entries to record the following transactions for Noble Systems.

**a.** Purchased 4,500 shares of its own common stock at $30 per share on October 11.

**b.** Sold 1,200 treasury shares on November 1 for $36 cash per share.

**c.** Sold all remaining treasury shares on November 25 for $25 cash per share.

**Check** (1c) Dr. Retained Earnings, $9,300

**2.** Explain how the company's equity section changes after the October 11 treasury stock purchase, and prepare the revised equity section of its balance sheet at that date.

---

The following information is available for Ballard Company for the year ended December 31, 2011.
**a.** Balance of retained earnings, December 31, 2010, prior to discovery of error, $850,000.
**b.** Cash dividends declared and paid during 2011, $15,000.
**c.** It neglected to record 2009 depreciation expense of $55,600, which is net of $5,500 in income taxes.
**d.** The company earned $205,000 in 2011 net income.
Prepare a 2011 statement of retained earnings for Ballard Company.

**Exercise 13-11**
Preparing a statement of retained earnings
**C3**

---

Guess Company reports $648,500 of net income for 2011 and declares $102,500 of cash dividends on its preferred stock for 2011. At the end of 2011, the company had 260,000 weighted-average shares of common stock.

**Exercise 13-12**
Earnings per share
**A1**

**1.** What amount of net income is available to common stockholders for 2011?

**2.** What is the company's basic EPS for 2011?

**Check** (2) $2.10

**Exercise 13-13**

Earnings per share

**A1**

**Check**   (2) $3.56

Franklin Company reports $698,000 of net income for 2011 and declares $75,500 of cash dividends on its preferred stock for 2011. At the end of 2011, the company had 175,000 weighted-average shares of common stock.

**1.** What amount of net income is available to common stockholders for 2011?

**2.** What is the company's basic EPS for 2011? Round your answer to the nearest whole cent.

**Exercise 13-14**

Dividend yield computation and interpretation

**A3**

Compute the dividend yield for each of these four separate companies. Which company's stock would probably *not* be classified as an income stock? Explain.

| Company | Annual Cash Dividend per Share | Market Value per Share |
|---------|-------------------------------|------------------------|
| 1 | $15.00 | $216.00 |
| 2 | 12.00 | 128.00 |
| 3 | 6.00 | 61.00 |
| 4 | 1.20 | 86.00 |

**Exercise 13-15**

Price-earnings ratio computation and interpretation

**A2**

Compute the price-earnings ratio for each of these four separate companies. Which stock might an analyst likely investigate as being potentially undervalued by the market? Explain.

| Company | Earnings per Share | Market Value per Share |
|---------|-------------------|------------------------|
| 1 | $10.00 | $166.00 |
| 2 | 9.00 | 90.00 |
| 3 | 6.50 | 84.50 |
| 4 | 40.00 | 240.00 |

**Exercise 13-16**

Book value per share

**A4**

The equity section of Webster Corporation's balance sheet shows the following.

| | |
|---|---|
| Preferred stock—5% cumulative, $10 par value, $15 call price, 10,000 shares issued and outstanding ................. | $100,000 |
| Common stock—$10 par value, 55,000 shares issued and outstanding .................................... | 550,000 |
| Retained earnings ......................................... | 267,500 |
| Total stockholders' equity ................................ | $917,500 |

Determine the book value per share of the preferred and common stock under two separate situations.

**Check**   (1) Book value of common, $13.95

**1.** No preferred dividends are in arrears.

**2.** Three years of preferred dividends are in arrears.

**Exercise 13-17**

Accounting for equity under IFRS

**C3  P1**

**Unilever Group** reports the following equity information for the years ended December 31, 2007 and 2008 (euros in millions).

| December 31 | 2008 | 2007 |
|-------------|------|------|
| Share capital .............. | € 484 | € 484 |
| Share premium ............ | 121 | 153 |
| Other reserves ............ | (6,469) | (3,412) |
| Retained profit ............ | 15,812 | 15,162 |
| Shareholders' equity ........ | € 9,948 | €12,387 |

1. For each of the three account titles *share capital*, *share premium*, and *retained profit*, match it with the usual account title applied under U.S. GAAP from the following options:

   a. Paid-in capital in excess of par value, common stock

   b. Retained earnings

   c. Common stock, par value

2. Prepare Unilever's journal entry, using its account titles, to record the issuance of capital stock assuming that its entire par value stock was issued on December 31, 2007, for cash.

3. What were Unilever's 2008 dividends assuming that only dividends and income impacted retained profit for 2008 and that its 2008 income totaled €2,692?

---

Kroll Corporation reports the following components of stockholders' equity on December 31, 2011.

**Exercise 13-18**
Cash dividends, treasury stock, and statement of retained earnings

C3 P2 P3

| | |
|---|---|
| Common stock—$25 par value, 40,000 shares authorized, 30,000 shares issued and outstanding .................. | $ 750,000 |
| Paid-in capital in excess of par value, common stock ......... | 50,000 |
| Retained earnings ....................................... | 260,000 |
| Total stockholders' equity ............................. | $1,060,000 |

In year 2012, the following transactions affected its stockholders' equity accounts.

Jan. 2 Purchased 2,000 shares of its own stock at $25 cash per share.
Jan. 7 Directors declared a $2 per share cash dividend payable on Feb. 28 to the Feb. 9 stockholders of record.
Feb. 28 Paid the dividend declared on January 7.
July 9 Sold 500 of its treasury shares at $30 cash per share.
Aug. 27 Sold 1,500 of its treasury shares at $23 cash per share.
Sept. 9 Directors declared a $2 per share cash dividend payable on October 22 to the September 23 stockholders of record.
Oct. 22 Paid the dividend declared on September 9.
Dec. 31 Closed the $8,000 credit balance (from net income) in the Income Summary account to Retained Earnings.

**Required**

1. Prepare journal entries to record each of these transactions for 2012.

2. Prepare a statement of retained earnings for the year ended December 31, 2012.

3. Prepare the stockholders' equity section of the company's balance sheet as of December 31, 2012.

---

**connect**

Oxygen Co. is incorporated at the beginning of this year and engages in a number of transactions. The following journal entries impacted its stockholders' equity during its first year of operations.

**PROBLEM SET A**

**Problem 13-1A**
Stockholders' equity transactions and analysis

C2 P1

| | | | |
|---|---|---|---|
| a. | Cash ........................................ | 150,000 | |
| | Common Stock, $25 Par Value ................ | | 125,000 |
| | Paid-In Capital in Excess of Par Value, Common Stock ................... | | 25,000 |
| b. | Organization Expenses ......................... | 75,000 | |
| | Common Stock, $25 Par Value ................ | | 62,500 |
| | Paid-In Capital in Excess of Par Value, Common Stock ................. | | 12,500 |
| c. | Cash ...................................... | 21,500 | |
| | Accounts Receivable ........................... | 7,500 | |
| | Building ..................................... | 30,000 | |
| | Notes Payable .............................. | | 19,000 |
| | Common Stock, $25 Par Value ................ | | 25,000 |
| | Paid-In Capital in Excess of Par Value, Common Stock ................. | | 15,000 |

[continued on next page]

[continued from previous page]

| | | | |
|---|---|---|---|
| d. | Cash ..................................... | 60,000 | |
| | Common Stock, $25 Par Value ................ | | 37,500 |
| | Paid-In Capital in Excess of Par Value, Common Stock .................. | | 22,500 |

**Required**

**Check** (2) 10,000 shares

(3) $250,000

(4) $325,000

1. Explain the transaction(s) underlying each journal entry (*a*) through (*d*).
2. How many shares of common stock are outstanding at year-end?
3. What is the amount of minimum legal capital (based on par value) at year-end?
4. What is the total paid-in capital at year-end?
5. What is the book value per share of the common stock at year-end if total paid-in capital plus retained earnings equals $347,500?

---

## Problem 13-2A

Cash dividends, treasury stock, and statement of retained earnings

C3 P2 P3

Context Corporation reports the following components of stockholders' equity on December 31, 2011.

| | |
|---|---|
| Common stock—$10 par value, 50,000 shares authorized, 20,000 shares issued and outstanding ........................... | $200,000 |
| Paid-in capital in excess of par value, common stock ................ | 30,000 |
| Retained earnings ............................................... | 135,000 |
| Total stockholders' equity ...................................... | $365,000 |

In year 2012, the following transactions affected its stockholders' equity accounts.

| | | |
|---|---|---|
| Jan. | 1 | Purchased 2,000 shares of its own stock at $20 cash per share. |
| Jan. | 5 | Directors declared a $2 per share cash dividend payable on Feb. 28 to the Feb. 5 stockholders of record. |
| Feb. | 28 | Paid the dividend declared on January 5. |
| July | 6 | Sold 750 of its treasury shares at $24 cash per share. |
| Aug. | 22 | Sold 1,250 of its treasury shares at $17 cash per share. |
| Sept. | 5 | Directors declared a $2 per share cash dividend payable on October 28 to the September 25 stockholders of record. |
| Oct. | 28 | Paid the dividend declared on September 5. |
| Dec. | 31 | Closed the $194,000 credit balance (from net income) in the Income Summary account to Retained Earnings. |

**Required**

**Check** (2) Retained earnings, Dec. 31, 2012, $252,250.

1. Prepare journal entries to record each of these transactions for 2012.
2. Prepare a statement of retained earnings for the year ended December 31, 2012.
3. Prepare the stockholders' equity section of the company's balance sheet as of December 31, 2012.

---

## Problem 13-3A

Equity analysis—journal entries and account balances

P2

At September 30, the end of Excel Company's third quarter, the following stockholders' equity accounts are reported.

| | |
|---|---|
| Common stock, $12 par value ........................... | $720,000 |
| Paid-in capital in excess of par value, common stock ......... | 180,000 |
| Retained earnings ..................................... | 640,000 |

In the fourth quarter, the following entries related to its equity are recorded.

| | | | |
|---|---|---|---|
| Oct. 2 | Retained Earnings ............................. | 120,000 | |
| | Common Dividend Payable .................. | | 120,000 |
| Oct. 25 | Common Dividend Payable ...................... | 120,000 | |
| | Cash ...................................... | | 120,000 |
| Oct. 31 | Retained Earnings ............................ | 150,000 | |
| | Common Stock Dividend Distributable ......... | | 72,000 |
| | Paid-In Capital in Excess of Par Value, Common Stock .................. | | 78,000 |

[continued on next page]

[continued from previous page]

| | | | |
|---|---|---|---|
| Nov. 5 | Common Stock Dividend Distributable . . . . . . . . . . . . | 72,000 | |
| | Common Stock, $12 Par Value . . . . . . . . . . . . . . . | | 72,000 |
| Dec. 1 | Memo—Change the title of the common stock account to reflect the new par value of $4. | | |
| Dec. 31 | Income Summary . . . . . . . . . . . . . . . . . . . . . . . . | 420,000 | |
| | Retained Earnings . . . . . . . . . . . . . . . . . . . . . . | | 420,000 |

**Required**

1. Explain the transaction(s) underlying each journal entry.
2. Complete the following table showing the equity account balances at each indicated date (include the balances from September 30).

| | Oct. 2 | Oct. 25 | Oct. 31 | Nov. 5 | Dec. 1 | Dec. 31 |
|---|---|---|---|---|---|---|
| Common stock . . . . . . . . . . . . . . . . . . . . | $____ | $____ | $____ | $____ | $____ | $____ |
| Common stock dividend distributable . . . . . . . . . . . . . . . . . . . . | ____ | ____ | ____ | ____ | ____ | ____ |
| Paid-in capital in excess of par, common stock . . . . . . . . | ____ | ____ | ____ | ____ | ____ | ____ |
| Retained earnings . . . . . . . . . . . . . . . . . . | ____ | ____ | ____ | ____ | ____ | ____ |
| Total equity . . . . . . . . . . . . . . . . . . . . . . . | $____ | $____ | $____ | $____ | $____ | $____ |

**Check** Total equity: Oct. 2, $1,420,000; Dec. 31, $1,840,000

---

The equity sections from Salazar Group's 2011 and 2012 year-end balance sheets follow.

| **Stockholders' Equity (December 31, 2011)** | |
|---|---|
| Common stock—$4 par value, 50,000 shares authorized, 20,000 shares issued and outstanding . . . . . . . . . . . . . . . | $ 80,000 |
| Paid-in capital in excess of par value, common stock . . . . . . . . . . . . . . | 60,000 |
| Retained earnings . . . . . . . . . . . . . . . . . . . . . . . . . . . . . . . . . . . . . . . | 160,000 |
| Total stockholders' equity . . . . . . . . . . . . . . . . . . . . . . . . . . . . . . . . . | $300,000 |

| **Stockholders' Equity (December 31, 2012)** | |
|---|---|
| Common stock—$4 par value, 50,000 shares authorized, 23,700 shares issued, 1,500 shares in treasury . . . . . . . . . | $ 94,800 |
| Paid-in capital in excess of par value, common stock . . . . . . . . . . . . . . | 89,600 |
| Retained earnings ($15,000 restricted by treasury stock) . . . . . . . . . . | 200,000 |
| | 384,400 |
| Less cost of treasury stock . . . . . . . . . . . . . . . . . . . . . . . . . . . . . . . . . | (15,000) |
| Total stockholders' equity . . . . . . . . . . . . . . . . . . . . . . . . . . . . . . . . . | $369,400 |

**Problem 13-4A**
Analysis of changes in stockholders' equity accounts

C3 P2 P3

The following transactions and events affected its equity during year 2012.

Jan.   5   Declared a $0.50 per share cash dividend, date of record January 10.
Mar. 20   Purchased treasury stock for cash.
Apr.   5   Declared a $0.50 per share cash dividend, date of record April 10.
July   5   Declared a $0.50 per share cash dividend, date of record July 10.
July 31   Declared a 20% stock dividend when the stock's market value is $12 per share.
Aug. 14   Issued the stock dividend that was declared on July 31.
Oct.   5   Declared a $0.50 per share cash dividend, date of record October 10.

**Required**

1. How many common shares are outstanding on each cash dividend date?
2. What is the total dollar amount for each of the four cash dividends?
3. What is the amount of the capitalization of retained earnings for the stock dividend?
4. What is the per share cost of the treasury stock purchased?
5. How much net income did the company earn during year 2012?

**Check** (3) $44,400

(4) $10

(5) $124,000

**Problem 13-5A**
Computation of book values and
dividend allocations

C2 A4

Razz Corporation's common stock is currently selling on a stock exchange at $170 per share, and its current balance sheet shows the following stockholders' equity section.

| | |
|---|---|
| Preferred stock—5% cumulative, $___ par value, 1,000 shares authorized, issued, and outstanding | $100,000 |
| Common stock—$___ par value, 4,000 shares authorized, issued, and outstanding | 160,000 |
| Retained earnings | 300,000 |
| Total stockholders' equity | $560,000 |

**Required** (Round per share amounts to cents.)

1. What is the current market value (price) of this corporation's common stock?
2. What are the par values of the corporation's preferred stock and its common stock?
3. If no dividends are in arrears, what are the book values per share of the preferred stock and the common stock?

**Check** (4) Book value of common, $112.50

(5) Book value of common, $110

(6) Dividends per common share, $1.25

4. If two years' preferred dividends are in arrears, what are the book values per share of the preferred stock and the common stock?
5. If two years' preferred dividends are in arrears and the preferred stock is callable at $110 per share, what are the book values per share of the preferred stock and the common stock?
6. If two years' preferred dividends are in arrears and the board of directors declares cash dividends of $20,000, what total amount will be paid to the preferred and to the common shareholders? What is the amount of dividends per share for the common stock?

**Analysis Component**

7. What are some factors that can contribute to a difference between the book value of common stock and its market value (price)?

---

## PROBLEM SET B

**Problem 13-1B**
Stockholders' equity
transactions and analysis

C2 P1

Nilson Company is incorporated at the beginning of this year and engages in a number of transactions. The following journal entries impacted its stockholders' equity during its first year of operations.

| | | | |
|---|---|---|---|
| a. | Cash | 60,000 | |
| |     Common Stock, $1 Par Value | | 1,500 |
| |     Paid-In Capital in Excess of Par Value, Common Stock | | 58,500 |
| b. | Organization Expenses | 20,000 | |
| |     Common Stock, $1 Par Value | | 500 |
| |     Paid-In Capital in Excess of Par Value, Common Stock | | 19,500 |
| c. | Cash | 6,650 | |
| | Accounts Receivable | 4,000 | |
| | Building | 12,500 | |
| |     Notes Payable | | 3,150 |
| |     Common Stock, $1 Par Value | | 400 |
| |     Paid-In Capital in Excess of Par Value, Common Stock | | 19,600 |
| d. | Cash | 30,000 | |
| |     Common Stock, $1 Par Value | | 600 |
| |     Paid-In Capital in Excess of Par Value, Common Stock | | 29,400 |

**Required**

1. Explain the transaction(s) underlying each journal entry (a) through (d).

**Check** (2) 3,000 shares

(3) $3,000

2. How many shares of common stock are outstanding at year-end?
3. What is the amount of minimum legal capital (based on par value) at year-end?

**4.** What is the total paid-in capital at year-end?

(4) $130,000

**5.** What is the book value per share of the common stock at year-end if total paid-in capital plus retained earnings equals $141,500?

---

Baycore Corp. reports the following components of stockholders' equity on December 31, 2011.

**Problem 13-2B**
Cash dividends, treasury stock, and statement of retained earnings

C3  P2  P3

| | |
|---|---|
| Common stock—$1 par value, 160,000 shares authorized, 100,000 shares issued and outstanding ..................... | $  100,000 |
| Paid-in capital in excess of par value, common stock ............. | 700,000 |
| Retained earnings ........................................ | 1,080,000 |
| Total stockholders' equity ................................. | $1,880,000 |

It completed the following transactions related to stockholders' equity in year 2012.

Jan. 10  Purchased 20,000 shares of its own stock at $12 cash per share.
Mar.  2  Directors declared a $1.50 per share cash dividend payable on March 31 to the March 15 stockholders of record.
Mar. 31  Paid the dividend declared on March 2.
Nov. 11  Sold 12,000 of its treasury shares at $13 cash per share.
Nov. 25  Sold 8,000 of its treasury shares at $9.50 cash per share.
Dec.  1  Directors declared a $2.50 per share cash dividend payable on January 2 to the December 10 stockholders of record.
Dec. 31  Closed the $536,000 credit balance (from net income) in the Income Summary account to Retained Earnings.

**Required**

**1.** Prepare journal entries to record each of these transactions for 2012.
**2.** Prepare a statement of retained earnings for the year ended December 31, 2012.
**3.** Prepare the stockholders' equity section of the company's balance sheet as of December 31, 2012.

**Check**  (2) Retained earnings, Dec. 31, 2012, $1,238,000

---

At December 31, the end of Intertec Communication's third quarter, the following stockholders' equity accounts are reported.

**Problem 13-3B**
Equity analysis—journal entries and account balances

P2

| | |
|---|---|
| Common stock, $10 par value ......................... | $480,000 |
| Paid-in capital in excess of par value, common stock ......... | 192,000 |
| Retained earnings .................................... | 800,000 |

In the fourth quarter, the following entries related to its equity are recorded.

| | | | |
|---|---|---|---|
| Jan. 17 | Retained Earnings ............................. | 48,000 | |
| | Common Dividend Payable ................... | | 48,000 |
| Feb.  5 | Common Dividend Payable ..................... | 48,000 | |
| | Cash ...................................... | | 48,000 |
| Feb. 28 | Retained Earnings ............................. | 126,000 | |
| | Common Stock Dividend Distributable ......... | | 60,000 |
| | Paid-In Capital in Excess of Par Value, Common Stock .......................... | | 66,000 |
| Mar. 14 | Common Stock Dividend Distributable ............ | 60,000 | |
| | Common Stock, $10 Par Value ............... | | 60,000 |
| Mar. 25 | Memo—Change the title of the common stock account to reflect the new par value of $5. | | |
| Mar. 31 | Income Summary ............................. | 360,000 | |
| | Retained Earnings ......................... | | 360,000 |

**Required**

1. Explain the transaction(s) underlying each journal entry.
2. Complete the following table showing the equity account balances at each indicated date (include the balances from December 31).

| | Jan. 17 | Feb. 5 | Feb. 28 | Mar. 14 | Mar. 25 | Mar. 31 |
|---|---|---|---|---|---|---|
| Common stock .................... | $_____ | $_____ | $_____ | $_____ | $_____ | $_____ |
| Common stock dividend distributable .................... | _____ | _____ | _____ | _____ | _____ | _____ |
| Paid-in capital in excess of par, common stock ........ | _____ | _____ | _____ | _____ | _____ | _____ |
| Retained earnings ................. | _____ | _____ | _____ | _____ | _____ | _____ |
| Total equity ..................... | $_____ | $_____ | $_____ | $_____ | $_____ | $_____ |

**Check** Total equity: Jan. 17, $1,424,000; Mar. 31, $1,784,000

---

**Problem 13-4B**

Analysis of changes in stockholders' equity accounts

C3 P2 P3

The equity sections from Jetta Corporation's 2011 and 2012 balance sheets follow.

**Stockholders' Equity (December 31, 2011)**

| | |
|---|---|
| Common stock—$20 par value, 15,000 shares authorized, 8,500 shares issued and outstanding ......................... | $170,000 |
| Paid-in capital in excess of par value, common stock .............. | 30,000 |
| Retained earnings ...................................... | 135,000 |
| Total stockholders' equity .................................. | $335,000 |

**Stockholders' Equity (December 31, 2012)**

| | |
|---|---|
| Common stock—$20 par value, 15,000 shares authorized, 9,500 shares issued, 500 shares in treasury ................... | $190,000 |
| Paid-in capital in excess of par value, common stock ............. | 52,000 |
| Retained earnings ($20,000 restricted by treasury stock) .......... | 147,600 |
| | 389,600 |
| Less cost of treasury stock ................................. | (20,000) |
| Total stockholders' equity .................................. | $369,600 |

The following transactions and events affected its equity during year 2012.

Feb. 15 Declared a $0.40 per share cash dividend, date of record five days later.
Mar. 2 Purchased treasury stock for cash.
May 15 Declared a $0.40 per share cash dividend, date of record five days later.
Aug. 15 Declared a $0.40 per share cash dividend, date of record five days later.
Oct. 4 Declared a 12.5% stock dividend when the stock's market value is $42 per share.
Oct. 20 Issued the stock dividend that was declared on October 4.
Nov. 15 Declared a $0.40 per share cash dividend, date of record five days later.

**Required**

1. How many common shares are outstanding on each cash dividend date?
2. What is the total dollar amount for each of the four cash dividends?
3. What is the amount of the capitalization of retained earnings for the stock dividend?
4. What is the per share cost of the treasury stock purchased?
5. How much net income did the company earn during year 2012?

**Check** (3) $42,000

(4) $40

(5) $68,000

---

**Problem 13-5B**

Computation of book values and dividend allocations

C2 A4

Scotch Company's common stock is currently selling on a stock exchange at $45 per share, and its current balance sheet shows the following stockholders' equity section.

| | |
|---|---|
| Preferred stock—8% cumulative, $___ par value, 1,500 shares authorized, issued, and outstanding ............................ | $ 187,500 |
| Common stock—$___ par value, 18,000 shares authorized, issued, and outstanding ............................ | 450,000 |
| Retained earnings ...................................... | 562,500 |
| Total stockholders' equity ................................. | $1,200,000 |

**Required** (Round per share amounts to cents.)

1. What is the current market value (price) of this corporation's common stock?
2. What are the par values of the corporation's preferred stock and its common stock?
3. If no dividends are in arrears, what are the book values per share of the preferred stock and the common stock? (Round per share values to the nearest cent.)
4. If two years' preferred dividends are in arrears, what are the book values per share of the preferred stock and the common stock? (Round per share values to the nearest cent.)
5. If two years' preferred dividends are in arrears and the preferred stock is callable at $140 per share, what are the book values per share of the preferred stock and the common stock? (Round per share values to the nearest cent.)
6. If two years' preferred dividends are in arrears and the board of directors declares cash dividends of $50,000, what total amount will be paid to the preferred and to the common shareholders? What is the amount of dividends per share for the common stock? (Round per share values to the nearest cent.)

**Check** (4) Book value of common, $54.58

(5) Book value of common, $53.33

(6) Dividends per common share, $0.28

*Analysis Component*

7. Discuss why the book value of common stock is not always a good estimate of its market value.

---

*(This serial problem began in Chapter 1 and continues through most of the book. If previous chapter segments were not completed, the serial problem can begin at this point. It is helpful, but not necessary, to use the Working Papers that accompany the book.)*

**SERIAL PROBLEM**
Business Solutions
**P1 C1 C2**

**SP 13** Santana Rey created Business Solutions on October 1, 2011. The company has been successful, and Santana plans to expand her business. She believes that an additional $86,000 is needed and is investigating three funding sources.

a. Santana's sister Cicely is willing to invest $86,000 in the business as a common shareholder. Since Santana currently has about $129,000 invested in the business, Cicely's investment will mean that Santana will maintain about 60% ownership, and Cicely will have 40% ownership of Business Solutions.

b. Santana's uncle Marcello is willing to invest $86,000 in the business as a preferred shareholder. Marcello would purchase 860 shares of $100 par value, 7% preferred stock.

c. Santana's banker is willing to lend her $86,000 on a 7%, 10-year note payable. She would make monthly payments of $1,000 per month for 10 years.

**Required**

1. Prepare the journal entry to reflect the initial $86,000 investment under each of the options (a), (b), and (c).
2. Evaluate the three proposals for expansion, providing the pros and cons of each option.
3. Which option do you recommend Santana adopt? Explain.

---

## Beyond the Numbers

**BTN 13-1** Refer to **Research In Motion**'s financial statements in Appendix A to answer the following.

1. How many shares of common stock are issued and outstanding at February 27, 2010, and February 28, 2009? How do these numbers compare with the basic weighted-average common shares outstanding at February 27, 2010, and February 28, 2009?
2. What is the book value of its entire common stock at February 27, 2010?
3. What is the total amount of cash dividends paid to common stockholders for the years ended February 27, 2010, and February 28, 2009?
4. Identify and compare basic EPS amounts across fiscal years 2010, 2009, and 2008. Identify and comment on any notable changes.
5. How many shares does Research In Motion hold in treasury stock, if any, as of February 27, 2010? As of February 28, 2009?

**REPORTING IN ACTION**

**C2 A1 A4**

**RIM**

*Fast Forward*

6. Access Research In Motion's financial statements for fiscal years ending after February 27, 2010, from its Website (**RIM.com**) or the SEC's EDGAR database (**www.sec.gov**). Has the number of common shares outstanding increased since that date? Has the company increased the total amount of cash dividends paid compared to the total amount for fiscal year 2010?

**COMPARATIVE ANALYSIS**

A1  A2  A3  A4

*RIM*

**Palm**

Apple

**BTN 13-2**   Key comparative figures for **Research In Motion**, **Palm**, and **Apple** follow.

| Key Figures | Research In Motion | Palm | Apple |
|---|---|---|---|
| Net income (in millions) ................................... | $2,457 | $ (753) | $8,235 |
| Cash dividends declared per common share .................. | $  — | $  — | $  — |
| Common shares outstanding (in millions) ..................... | 557 | 140 | 900 |
| Weighted-average common shares outstanding (in mil.) ......... | 564 | 116 | 893 |
| Market value (price) per share ............................ | $69.76 | $12.19 | $184.40 |
| Equity applicable to common shares (in millions) ............. | $7,603 | $ (414) | $31,640 |

**Required**

1. Compute the book value per common share for each company using these data.
2. Compute the basic EPS for each company using these data.
3. Compute the dividend yield for each company using these data. Does the dividend yield of any of the companies characterize it as an income or growth stock? Explain.
4. Compute, compare, and interpret the price-earnings ratio for each company using these data.

**ETHICS CHALLENGE**

C3

**BTN 13-3**   Gianna Tuck is an accountant for Post Pharmaceuticals. Her duties include tracking research and development spending in the new product development division. Over the course of the past six months, Gianna notices that a great deal of funds have been spent on a particular project for a new drug. She hears "through the grapevine" that the company is about to patent the drug and expects it to be a major advance in antibiotics. Gianna believes that this new drug will greatly improve company performance and will cause the company's stock to increase in value. Gianna decides to purchase shares of Post in order to benefit from this expected increase.

**Required**

What are Gianna's ethical responsibilities, if any, with respect to the information she has learned through her duties as an accountant for Post Pharmaceuticals? What are the implications to her planned purchase of Post shares?

**COMMUNICATING IN PRACTICE**

A1  A2

Hint: Make a transparency of each team's memo for a class discussion.

**BTN 13-4**   Teams are to select an industry, and each team member is to select a different company in that industry. Each team member then is to acquire the selected company's financial statements (or Form 10-K) from the SEC site (**www.SEC.gov**). Use these data to identify basic EPS. Use the financial press (or **finance.yahoo.com**) to determine the market price of this stock, and then compute the price-earnings ratio. Communicate with teammates via a meeting, e-mail, or telephone to discuss the meaning of this ratio, how companies compare, and the industry norm. The team must prepare a single memorandum reporting the ratio for each company and identifying the team conclusions or consensus of opinion. The memorandum is to be duplicated and distributed to the instructor and teammates.

**TAKING IT TO THE NET**

C1  C3

**BTN 13-5**   Access the February 26, 2010, filing of the 2009 calendar-year 10-K report of **McDonald's**, (ticker MCD) from **www.SEC.gov**.

**Required**

1. Review McDonald's balance sheet and identify how many classes of stock it has issued.
2. What are the par values, number of authorized shares, and issued shares of the classes of stock you identified in part 1?
3. Review its statement of cash flows and identify what total amount of cash it paid in 2009 to purchase treasury stock.
4. What amount did McDonald's pay out in common stock cash dividends for 2009?

**TEAMWORK IN ACTION**

P3

Hint: Instructor should be sure each team accurately completes part 1 before proceeding.

**BTN 13-6**   This activity requires teamwork to reinforce understanding of accounting for treasury stock.

1. Write a brief team statement (*a*) generalizing what happens to a corporation's financial position when it engages in a stock "buyback" and (*b*) identifying reasons why a corporation would engage in this activity.
2. Assume that an entity acquires 100 shares of its $100 par value common stock at a cost of $134 cash per share. Discuss the entry to record this acquisition. Next, assign *each* team member to prepare *one* of the following entries (assume each entry applies to all shares):
   a. Reissue treasury shares at cost.
   b. Reissue treasury shares at $150 per share.

**c.** Reissue treasury shares at $120 per share; assume the paid-in capital account from treasury shares has a $1,500 balance.

**d.** Reissue treasury shares at $120 per share; assume the paid-in capital account from treasury shares has a $1,000 balance.

**e.** Reissue treasury shares at $120 per share; assume the paid-in capital account from treasury shares has a zero balance.

**3.** In sequence, each member is to present his/her entry to the team and explain the *similarities* and *differences* between that entry and the previous entry.

---

**BTN 13-7**  Assume that Kelly Giard of **Clean Air Lawn Care** decides to launch a new retail chain to market electrical mowers. This chain, named Mow Green, requires $500,000 of start-up capital. Kelly contributes $375,000 of personal assets in return for 15,000 shares of common stock, but he must raise another $125,000 in cash. There are two alternative plans for raising the additional cash. *Plan A* is to sell 3,750 shares of common stock to one or more investors for $125,000 cash. *Plan B* is to sell 1,250 shares of cumulative preferred stock to one or more investors for $125,000 cash (this preferred stock would have a $100 par value, an annual 8% dividend rate, and be issued at par).

**ENTREPRENEURIAL DECISION**

C2  P2

**1.** If the new business is expected to earn $72,000 of after-tax net income in the first year, what rate of return on beginning equity will Kelly earn under each alternative plan? Which plan will provide the higher expected return?

**2.** If the new business is expected to earn $16,800 of after-tax net income in the first year, what rate of return on beginning equity will Kelly earn under each alternative plan? Which plan will provide the higher expected return?

**3.** Analyze and interpret the differences between the results for parts 1 and 2.

---

**BTN 13-8**  Review 30 to 60 minutes of financial news programming on television. Take notes on companies that are catching analysts' attention. You might hear reference to over- and undervaluation of firms and to reports about PE ratios, dividend yields, and earnings per share. Be prepared to give a brief description to the class of your observations.

**HITTING THE ROAD**

A1  A2  A3

---

**BTN 13-9**  Financial information for **Nokia Corporation** (www.nokia.com) follows.

**GLOBAL DECISION**

A1  C3

**NOKIA**

| | |
|---|---|
| Net income (in millions) | € 260 |
| Cash dividends declared (in millions) | € 1,481 |
| Cash dividends declared per share | € 0.40 |
| Number of shares outstanding (in millions)* | 3,708 |
| Equity applicable to shares (in millions) | €14,749 |

\* Assume that for Nokia the year-end number of shares outstanding approximates the weighted-average shares outstanding.

**Required**

**1.** Compute book value per share for Nokia.

**2.** Compute earnings per share (EPS) for Nokia.

**3.** Compare Nokia's dividends per share with its EPS. Is Nokia paying out a large or small amount of its income as dividends? Explain.

---

## ANSWERS TO MULTIPLE CHOICE QUIZ

**1.** e; Entry to record this stock issuance is:

| | | |
|---|---|---|
| Cash (6,000 × $8) | 48,000 | |
| Common Stock (6,000 × $5) | | 30,000 |
| Paid-In Capital in Excess of Par Value, Common Stock | | 18,000 |

**2.** b; $75,000/19,000 shares = $3.95 per share

**3.** d; Preferred stock = 5,000 × $100 = $500,000
Book value per share = ($2,000,000 − $500,000)/50,000 shares = $30 per common share

**4.** a; $0.81/$45.00 = 1.8%

**5.** c; Earnings per share = $3,500,000/700,000 shares = $5 per share
PE ratio = $85/$5 = 17.0

# 14

# Long-Term Liabilities

## A Look Back

Chapter 13 focused on corporate equity transactions, including stock issuances and dividends. We also explained how to report and analyze income, earnings per share, and retained earnings.

## A Look at This Chapter

This chapter describes the accounting for and analysis of bonds and notes. We explain their characteristics, payment patterns, interest computations, retirement, and reporting requirements. An appendix to this chapter introduces leases and pensions.

## A Look Ahead

Chapter 15 focuses on how to classify, account for, and report investments in both debt and equity securities. We also describe accounting for transactions listed in a foreign currency.

## Learning Objectives

## CAP

### CONCEPTUAL

**C1** Explain the types and payment patterns of notes. (p. 562)

**C2** *Appendix 14A*—Explain and compute the present value of an amount(s) to be paid at a future date(s). (p. 570)

**C3** *Appendix 14C*—Describe interest accrual when bond payment periods differ from accounting periods. (p. 574)

**C4** *Appendix 14D*—Describe accounting for leases and pensions. (p. 576)

### ANALYTICAL

**A1** Compare bond financing with stock financing. (p. 552)

**A2** Assess debt features and their implications. (p. 566)

**A3** Compute the debt-to-equity ratio and explain its use. (p. 566)

LP14

### PROCEDURAL

**P1** Prepare entries to record bond issuance and interest expense. (p. 554)

**P2** Compute and record amortization of bond discount. (p. 555)

**P3** Compute and record amortization of bond premium. (p. 558)

**P4** Record the retirement of bonds. (p. 561)

**P5** Prepare entries to account for notes. (p. 564)

## Love At First Bite

*"Each individual problem you face is totally surmountable"*
—WARREN BROWN

WASHINGTON, DC—Warren Brown started baking cakes in his apartment after work each evening. He sold his sweet concoctions mostly to coworkers and friends, and even held a cake open house at the local art gallery. But Warren was determined to grow his business. He took a course in entrepreneurship at his local community college, and there he discovered the importance of financial reporting and accounting.

Launching his fledgling cake business presented Warren with many challenges. He needed to especially focus on the important task of managing liabilities for payroll, baking supplies, employee benefits, training, and taxes. Warren insists that effective management of liabilities, especially long-term financing from sources such as bonds and notes, is crucial to business success. "Everything feels like a disaster when it's right in your face," says Warren. "You just have to be calm, look at what you're doing, and fix the problem."

Warren fixed the problems and unveiled his business called **Cake Love (CakeLove.com),** funded with short- and long-term notes. "I opened up this tiny retail, walk-up bakery . . . [to sell] goodies that are baked from scratch," Warren explains. Today Cake Love entices the neighborhood with a gentle scent of fresh bakery and a sidewalk view into the kitchen. Warmly painted walls, comfy window seats, and free wireless Internet encourage customers to lounge for hours. "I want it to be relaxed and comfortable," says Warren. "People can bring their work, their kids, their friends, and just relax."

Warren continues to monitor liabilities and their payment patterns, and he is not shy about striving to better learn the accounting side. "I'm always getting better, improving my skills," he explains. Warren insists that accounting for and monitoring liabilities of long-term financing are important ingredients to a successful start-up. His company now generates sufficient income to pay for liabilities of interest and principal on long-term debt and still produces revenue growth for expansion. He shows a keen appetite for using accounting information to make good business decisions. "But," says Warren, "I love eating what I make more."

"The bigger message of Cake Love is finding your passion and working to reach your goals," explains Warren. That's a slice of advice worth more than any amount of dough.

[Sources: *Cake Love Website,* January 2011; *Black Enterprise,* September 2004; *Georgetown Voice,* March 2005; *National Public Radio (NPR) Website,* May 2005; *Inc.com,* April 2005]

Individuals, companies, and governments issue bonds to finance their activities. In return for financing, bonds promise to repay the lender with interest. This chapter explains the basics of bonds and the accounting for their issuance and retirement. The chapter also describes long-term notes as another financing source. We explain how present value concepts impact both the accounting for and reporting of bonds and notes. Appendixes to this chapter discuss present value concepts applicable to liabilities, effective interest amortization, and the accounting for leases and pensions.

**Long-Term Liabilities**

| Bond Basics | Bond Issuances | Bond Retirement | Long-Term Notes |
|---|---|---|---|
| • Bond financing<br>• Bond trading<br>• Issuance procedures | • Issuance at par<br>• Issuance at a discount<br>• Issuance at a premium<br>• Bond pricing | • At maturity<br>• Before maturity<br>• By conversion | • Installment notes<br>• Mortgage terms |

# BASICS OF BONDS

This section explains the basics of bonds and a company's motivation for issuing them.

## Bond Financing

**A1** Compare bond financing with stock financing.

Projects that demand large amounts of money often are funded from bond issuances. (Both for-profit and nonprofit companies, as well as governmental units, such as nations, states, cities, and school districts, issue bonds.) A **bond** is its issuer's written promise to pay an amount identified as the par value of the bond with interest. The **par value of a bond,** also called the *face amount* or *face value,* is paid at a specified future date known as the bond's *maturity date.* Most bonds also require the issuer to make semiannual interest payments. The amount of interest paid each period is determined by multiplying the par value of the bond by the bond's contract rate of interest for that same period. This section explains both advantages and disadvantages of bond financing.

**Advantages of Bonds**  There are three main advantages of bond financing:

1.  *Bonds do not affect owner control.* Equity financing reflects ownership in a company, whereas bond financing does not. A person who contributes $1,000 of a company's $10,000 equity financing typically controls one-tenth of all owner decisions. A person who owns a $1,000, 11%, 20-year bond has no ownership right. This person, or bondholder, is to receive from the bond issuer 11% interest, or $110, each year the bond is outstanding and $1,000 when it matures in 20 years.

2.  *Interest on bonds is tax deductible.* Bond interest payments are tax deductible for the issuer, but equity payments (distributions) to owners are not. To illustrate, assume that a corporation with no bond financing earns $15,000 in income *before* paying taxes at a 40% tax rate, which amounts to $6,000 ($15,000 × 40%) in taxes. If a portion of its financing is in bonds, however, the resulting bond interest is deducted in computing taxable income. That is, if bond interest expense is $10,000, the taxes owed would be $2,000 ([$15,000 − $10,000] × 40%), which is less than the $6,000 owed with no bond financing.

3.  *Bonds can increase return on equity.* A company that earns a higher return with borrowed funds than it pays in interest on those funds increases its return on equity. This process is called *financial leverage* or *trading on the equity.*

**Point:** Financial leverage reflects issuance of bonds, notes, or preferred stock.

To illustrate the third point, consider Magnum Co., which has $1 million in equity and is planning a $500,000 expansion to meet increasing demand for its product. Magnum predicts the

$500,000 expansion will yield $125,000 in additional income before paying any interest. It currently earns $100,000 per year and has no interest expense. Magnum is considering three plans. Plan A is to not expand. Plan B is to expand and raise $500,000 from equity financing. Plan C is to expand and issue $500,000 of bonds that pay 10% annual interest ($50,000). Exhibit 14.1 shows how these three plans affect Magnum's net income, equity, and return on equity (net income/equity). The owner(s) will earn a higher return on equity if expansion occurs. Moreover, the preferred expansion plan is to issue bonds. Projected net income under Plan C ($175,000) is smaller than under Plan B ($225,000), but the return on equity is larger because of less equity investment. Plan C has another advantage if income is taxable. This illustration reflects a general rule: *Return on equity increases when the expected rate of return from the new assets is higher than the rate of interest expense on the debt financing.*

**Example:** Compute return on equity for all three plans if Magnum currently earns $150,000 instead of $100,000. Answer ($ 000s):

Plan A = 15%    ($150/$1,000)
Plan B = 18.3%    ($275/$1,500)
Plan C = 22.5%    ($225/$1,000)

**EXHIBIT 14.1**

Financing with Bonds versus Equity

| | Plan A: Do Not Expand | Plan B: Equity Financing | Plan C: Bond Financing |
|---|---|---|---|
| Income before interest expense ........ | $ 100,000 | $ 225,000 | $ 225,000 |
| Interest expense ..................... | — | — | (50,000) |
| Net income ..................... | $ 100,000 | $ 225,000 | $ 175,000 |
| Equity ......................... | $1,000,000 | $1,500,000 | $1,000,000 |
| Return on equity ................. | 10.0% | 15.0% | 17.5% |

**Disadvantages of Bonds**    The two main disadvantages of bond financing are these:

1. *Bonds can decrease return on equity.* When a company earns a lower return with the borrowed funds than it pays in interest, it decreases its return on equity. This downside risk of financial leverage is more likely to arise when a company has periods of low income or net losses.

2. *Bonds require payment of both periodic interest and the par value at maturity.* Bond payments can be especially burdensome when income and cash flow are low. Equity financing, in contrast, does not require any payments because cash withdrawals (dividends) are paid at the discretion of the owner (or board).

A company must weigh the risks and returns of the disadvantages and advantages of bond financing when deciding whether to issue bonds to finance operations.

**Point:** Debt financing is desirable when interest is tax deductible, when owner control is preferred, and when return on equity exceeds the debt's interest rate.

## Bond Trading

Bonds are securities that can be readily bought and sold. A large number of bonds trade on both the New York Exchange and the American Exchange. A bond *issue* consists of a number of bonds, usually in denominations of $1,000 or $5,000, and is sold to many different lenders. After bonds are issued, they often are bought and sold by investors, meaning that any particular bond probably has a number of owners before it matures. Since bonds are exchanged (bought and sold) in the market, they have a market value (price). For convenience, bond market values are expressed as a percent of their par (face) value. For example, a company's bonds might be trading at 103½, meaning they can be bought or sold for 103.5% of their par value. Bonds can also trade below par value. For instance, if a company's bonds are trading at 95, they can be bought or sold at 95% of their par value.

**Decision Insight**

**Quotes**    The **IBM** bond quote here is interpreted (left to right) as **Bonds,** issuer name; **Rate,** contract interest rate (7%); **Mat,** matures in year 2025 when

| Bonds | Rate | Mat | Yld | Vol | Close | Chg |
|---|---|---|---|---|---|---|
| IBM | 7 | 25 | 5.9 | 130 | 119¼ | +1¼ |

principal is paid; **Yld,** yield rate (5.9%) of bond at current price; **Vol,** daily dollar worth ($130,000) of trades (in 1,000s); **Close,** closing price (119.25) for the day as percentage of par value; **Chg,** change (+1.25) in closing price from prior day's close. ■

## Bond-Issuing Procedures

State and federal laws govern bond issuances. Bond issuers also want to ensure that they do not violate any of their existing contractual agreements when issuing bonds. Authorization of bond issuances includes the number of bonds authorized, their par value, and the contract interest rate. The legal document identifying the rights and obligations of both the bondholders and the issuer is called the **bond indenture,** which is the legal contract between the issuer and the bondholders. A bondholder may also receive a bond certificate as evidence of the company's debt. A **bond certificate,** such as that shown in Exhibit 14.2, includes specifics such as the issuer's name, the par value, the contract interest rate, and the maturity date. Many companies reduce costs by not issuing paper certificates to bondholders.[1]

**EXHIBIT 14.2**

Bond Certificate

**Point:** *Indenture* refers to a bond's legal contract; *debenture* refers to an unsecured bond.

---

# BOND ISSUANCES

This section explains accounting for bond issuances at par, below par (discount), and above par (premium). It also describes how to amortize a discount or premium and record bonds issued between interest payment dates.

### Issuing Bonds at Par

 **P1** Prepare entries to record bond issuance and interest expense.

To illustrate an issuance of bonds at par value, suppose a company receives authorization to issue $800,000 of 9%, 20-year bonds dated January 1, 2011, that mature on December 31, 2030, and pay interest semiannually on each June 30 and December 31. After accepting the bond indenture on behalf of the bondholders, the trustee can sell all or a portion of the bonds to an underwriter. If all bonds are sold at par value, the issuer records the sale as follows.

Assets = Liabilities + Equity
+800,000    +800,000

| 2011 | | | |
|---|---|---|---|
| Jan. 1 | Cash ........................................ | 800,000 | |
| | Bonds Payable ............................. | | 800,000 |
| | *Sold bonds at par.* | | |

This entry reflects increases in the issuer's cash *and* long-term liabilities.

The issuer records the first semiannual interest payment as follows.

Assets = Liabilities + Equity
−36,000             −36,000

| 2011 | | | |
|---|---|---|---|
| June 30 | Bond Interest Expense ........................ | 36,000 | |
| | Cash ..................................... | | 36,000 |
| | *Paid semiannual interest (9% × $800,000 × ½ year).* | | |

---

**Point:** The *spread* between the dealer's cost and what buyers pay can be huge. Dealers earn more than $25 billion in annual spread revenue.

**Global:** In the United Kingdom, government bonds are called *gilts*—short for gilt-edged investments.

[1] The issuing company normally sells its bonds to an investment firm called an *underwriter,* which resells them to the public. An issuing company can also sell bonds directly to investors. When an underwriter sells bonds to a large number of investors, a *trustee* represents and protects the bondholders' interests. The trustee monitors the issuer to ensure that it complies with the obligations in the bond indenture. Most trustees are large banks or trust companies. The trustee writes and accepts the terms of a bond indenture before it is issued. When bonds are offered to the public, called *floating an issue,* they must be registered with the Securities and Exchange Commission (SEC). SEC registration requires the issuer to file certain financial information. Most company bonds are issued in par value units of $1,000 or $5,000. *A baby bond* has a par value of less than $1,000, such as $100.

The issuer pays and records its semiannual interest obligation every six months until the bonds mature. When they mature, the issuer records its payment of principal as follows.

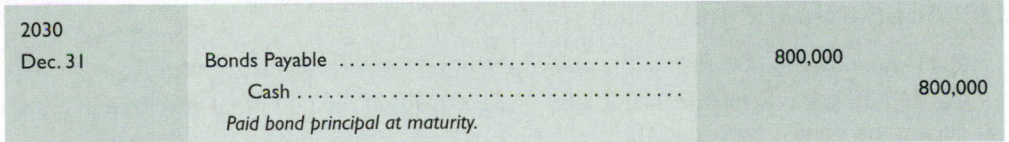

| 2030 | | | | |
|---|---|---|---|---|
| Dec. 31 | Bonds Payable ................................ | 800,000 | |
| | Cash ...................................... | | 800,000 |
| | *Paid bond principal at maturity.* | | |

Assets  =  Liabilities  +  Equity
−800,000      −800,000

## Bond Discount or Premium

The bond issuer pays the interest rate specified in the indenture, the **contract rate,** also referred to as the *coupon rate, stated rate,* or *nominal rate.* The annual interest paid is determined by multiplying the bond par value by the contract rate. The contract rate is usually stated on an annual basis, even if interest is paid semiannually. For example, if a company issues a $1,000, 8% bond paying interest semiannually, it pays annual interest of $80 (8% × $1,000) in two semiannual payments of $40 each.

The contract rate sets the amount of interest the issuer pays in *cash,* which is not necessarily the *bond interest expense* actually incurred by the issuer. Bond interest expense depends on the bond's market value at issuance, which is determined by market expectations of the risk of lending to the issuer. The bond's **market rate** of interest is the rate that borrowers are willing to pay and lenders are willing to accept for a particular bond and its risk level. As the risk level increases, the rate increases to compensate purchasers for the bonds' increased risk. Also, the market rate is generally higher when the time period until the bond matures is longer due to the risk of adverse events occurring over a longer time period.

Many bond issuers try to set a contract rate of interest equal to the market rate they expect as of the bond issuance date. When the contract rate and market rate are equal, a bond sells at par value, but when they are not equal, a bond does not sell at par value. Instead, it is sold at a *premium* above par value or at a *discount* below par value. Exhibit 14.3 shows the relation between the contract rate, market rate, and a bond's issue price.

**EXHIBIT 14.3**

Relation between Bond Issue Price, Contract Rate, and Market Rate

| Bond Sets | Market Sets | Bond Price Determined | |
|---|---|---|---|
| Contract rate | Market rate | Contract rate > Market rate | Bond sells at premium |
| | | Contract rate = Market rate | Bond sells at par |
| | | Contract rate < Market rate | Bond sells at discount |

## Quick Check                    Answers — p. 579

1. A company issues $10,000 of 9%, 5-year bonds dated January 1, 2011, that mature on December 31, 2015, and pay interest semiannually on each June 30 and December 31. Prepare the entry to record this bond issuance and the first semiannual interest payment.
2. How do you compute the amount of interest a bond issuer pays in cash each year?
3. When the contract rate is above the market rate, do bonds sell at a premium or a discount? Do purchasers pay more or less than the par value of the bonds?

## Issuing Bonds at a Discount

A **discount on bonds payable** occurs when a company issues bonds with a contract rate less than the market rate. This means that the issue price is less than par value. To illustrate, assume that **Fila** announces an offer to issue bonds with a $100,000 par value, an 8% annual contract rate (paid semiannually), and a two-year life. Also assume that the market rate for Fila bonds is

**P2** Compute and record amortization of bond discount.

**Point:** The difference between the con-tract rate and the market rate of interest on a new bond issue is usually a fraction of a percent. We use a difference of 2% to emphasize the effects.

10%. These bonds then will sell at a discount since the contract rate is less than the market rate. The exact issue price for these bonds is stated as 96.454 (implying 96.454% of par value, or $96,454); we show how to compute this issue price later in the chapter. These bonds obligate the issuer to pay two separate types of future cash flows:

1. Par value of $100,000 cash at the end of the bonds' two-year life.
2. Cash interest payments of $4,000 (4% × $100,000) at the end of each semiannual period during the bonds' two-year life.

The exact pattern of cash flows for the Fila bonds is shown in Exhibit 14.4.

**EXHIBIT 14.4**

Cash Flows for Fila Bonds

When Fila accepts $96,454 cash for its bonds on the issue date of December 31, 2011, it records the sale as follows.

Assets  = Liabilities + Equity
+96,454    +100,000
           −3,546

| Dec. 31 | Cash ..................................................... | 96,454 | |
| | Discount on Bonds Payable ..................... | 3,546 | |
| | Bonds Payable ............................. | | 100,000 |
| | *Sold bonds at a discount on their issue date.* | | |

**Point:** Book value at issuance always equals the issuer's cash borrowed.

These bonds are reported in the long-term liability section of the issuer's December 31, 2011, balance sheet as shown in Exhibit 14.5. A discount is deducted from the par value of bonds to yield the **carrying (book) value of bonds.** Discount on Bonds Payable is a contra liability account.

**EXHIBIT 14.5**

Balance Sheet Presentation of Bond Discount

| Long-term liabilities | | |
| Bonds payable, 8%, due December 31, 2013 ......... | $100,000 | |
| **Less discount on bonds payable** .............. | **3,546** | **$96,454** |

**Amortizing a Bond Discount**   Fila receives $96,454 for its bonds; in return it must pay bondholders $100,000 after two years (plus semiannual interest payments). The $3,546 discount is paid to bondholders at maturity and is part of the cost of using the $96,454 for two years. The upper portion of panel A in Exhibit 14.6 shows that total bond interest expense of $19,546 is the difference between the total amount repaid to bondholders ($116,000) and the amount borrowed from bondholders ($96,454). Alternatively, we can compute total bond interest expense as the sum of the four interest payments and the bond discount. This alternative computation is shown in the lower portion of panel A.

**Point:** *Zero-coupon bonds* do not pay periodic interest (contract rate is zero). These bonds always sell at a discount because their 0% contract rate is always below the market rate.

   The total $19,546 bond interest expense must be allocated across the four semiannual periods in the bonds' life, and the bonds' carrying value must be updated at each balance sheet date. This is accomplished using the straight-line method (or the effective interest method in Appendix 14B). Both methods systematically reduce the bond discount to zero over the two-year life. This process is called *amortizing a bond discount.*

**Straight-Line Method**   The **straight-line bond amortization** method allocates an equal portion of the total bond interest expense to each interest period. To apply the straight-line method to Fila's bonds, we divide the total bond interest expense of $19,546 by 4 (the number of semiannual periods in the bonds' life). This gives a bond interest expense of $4,887 per period, which is $4,886.5 rounded to the nearest dollar per period (all computations, including those for assignments, are rounded to the nearest whole dollar). Alternatively, we can find this number by first dividing the $3,546 discount by 4, which yields the $887 amount of discount to be amortized each interest period. When the $887 is added to the $4,000 cash payment, the bond

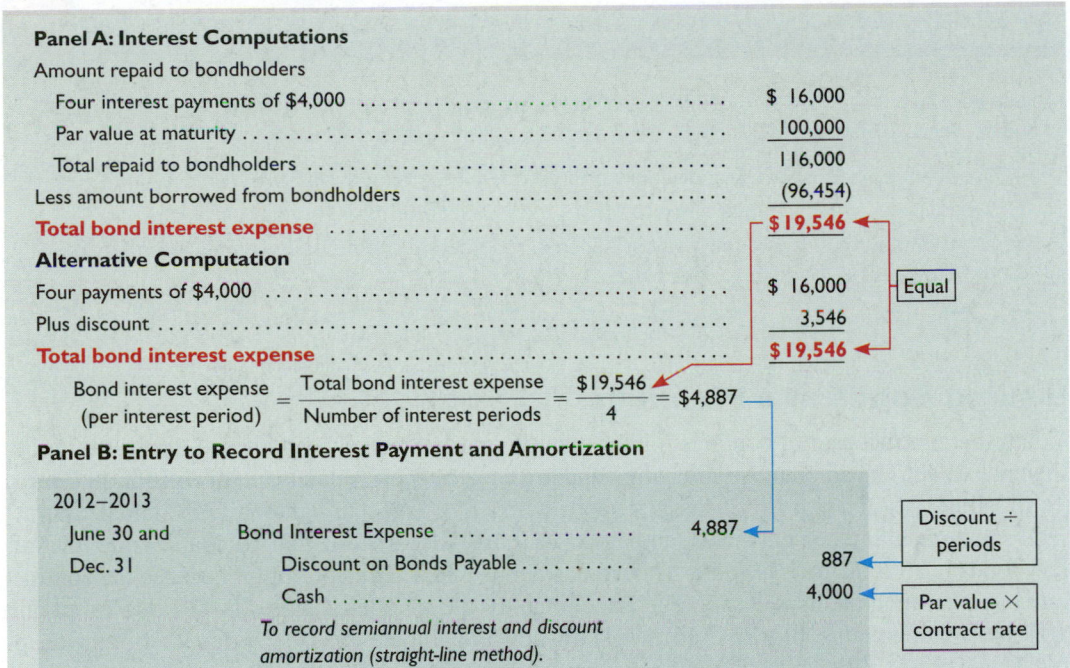

**EXHIBIT 14.6**

Interest Computation and Entry for Bonds Issued at a Discount

**Panel A: Interest Computations**

| | |
|---|---|
| Amount repaid to bondholders | |
| Four interest payments of $4,000 | $ 16,000 |
| Par value at maturity | 100,000 |
| Total repaid to bondholders | 116,000 |
| Less amount borrowed from bondholders | (96,454) |
| **Total bond interest expense** | **$19,546** |
| **Alternative Computation** | |
| Four payments of $4,000 | $ 16,000 |
| Plus discount | 3,546 |
| **Total bond interest expense** | **$19,546** |

Equal

$$\frac{\text{Bond interest expense}}{\text{(per interest period)}} = \frac{\text{Total bond interest expense}}{\text{Number of interest periods}} = \frac{\$19,546}{4} = \$4,887$$

**Panel B: Entry to Record Interest Payment and Amortization**

| 2012–2013 | | | |
|---|---|---|---|
| June 30 and | Bond Interest Expense | 4,887 | |
| Dec. 31 | Discount on Bonds Payable | | 887 |
| | Cash | | 4,000 |

Discount ÷ periods

Par value × contract rate

To record semiannual interest and discount amortization (straight-line method).

interest expense for each period is $4,887. Panel B of Exhibit 14.6 shows how the issuer records bond interest expense and updates the balance of the bond liability account at the end of *each* of the four semiannual interest periods (June 30, 2012, through December 31, 2013).

Exhibit 14.7 shows the pattern of decreases in the Discount on Bonds Payable account and the pattern of increases in the bonds' carrying value. The following points summarize the discount bonds' straight-line amortization:

1. At issuance, the $100,000 par value consists of the $96,454 cash received by the issuer plus the $3,546 discount.

2. During the bonds' life, the (unamortized) discount decreases each period by the $887 amortization ($3,546/4), and the carrying value (par value less unamortized discount) increases each period by $887.

3. At maturity, the unamortized discount equals zero, and the carrying value equals the $100,000 par value that the issuer pays the holder.

**EXHIBIT 14.7**

Straight-Line Amortization of Bond Discount

| Semiannual Period-End | Unamortized Discount* | Carrying Value† |
|---|---|---|
| (0) 12/31/2011 | $3,546 | $ 96,454 |
| (1) 6/30/2012 | 2,659 | 97,341 |
| (2) 12/31/2012 | 1,772 | 98,228 |
| (3) 6/30/2013 | 885 | 99,115 |
| (4) 12/31/2013 | 0‡ | 100,000 |

The two columns always sum to par value for a discount bond.

\* Total bond discount (of $3,546) less accumulated periodic amortization ($887 per semiannual interest period).

† Bond par value (of $100,000) less unamortized discount.

‡ Adjusted for rounding.

We see that the issuer incurs a $4,887 bond interest expense each period but pays only $4,000 cash. The $887 unpaid portion of this expense is added to the bonds' carrying value. (The total $3,546 unamortized discount is "paid" when the bonds mature; $100,000 is paid at maturity but only $96,454 was received at issuance.)

**Decision Insight**

**Ratings Game** Many bond buyers rely on rating services to assess bond risk. The best known are **Standard & Poor's, Moody's**, and **Fitch**. These services focus on the issuer's financial statements and other factors in setting ratings. Standard & Poor's ratings, from best quality to default, are AAA, AA, A, BBB, BB, B, CCC, CC, C, and D. Ratings can include a plus (+) or minus (−) to show relative standing within a category. ■

Five-year, 6% bonds with a $100,000 par value are issued at a price of $91,893. Interest is paid semiannually, and the bonds' market rate is 8% on the issue date. Use this information to answer the following questions:

**4.** Are these bonds issued at a discount or a premium? Explain your answer.

**5.** What is the issuer's journal entry to record the issuance of these bonds?

**6.** What is the amount of bond interest expense recorded at the first semiannual period using the straight-line method?

## Issuing Bonds at a Premium

**P3** Compute and record amortization of bond premium.

When the contract rate of bonds is higher than the market rate, the bonds sell at a price higher than par value. The amount by which the bond price exceeds par value is the **premium on bonds.** To illustrate, assume that **Adidas** issues bonds with a $100,000 par value, a 12% annual contract rate, semiannual interest payments, and a two-year life. Also assume that the market rate for Adidas bonds is 10% on the issue date. The Adidas bonds will sell at a premium because the contract rate is higher than the market rate. The issue price for these bonds is stated as 103.546 (implying 103.546% of par value, or $103,546); we show how to compute this issue price later in the chapter. These bonds obligate the issuer to pay out two separate future cash flows:

1. Par value of $100,000 cash at the end of the bonds' two-year life.
2. Cash interest payments of $6,000 (6% × $100,000) at the end of each semiannual period during the bonds' two-year life.

The exact pattern of cash flows for the Adidas bonds is shown in Exhibit 14.8.

**EXHIBIT 14.8**

Cash Flows for Adidas Bonds

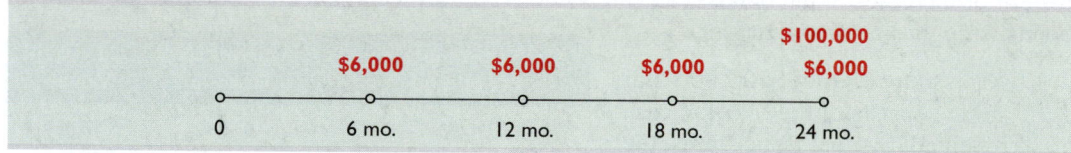

When Adidas accepts $103,546 cash for its bonds on the issue date of December 31, 2011, it records this transaction as follows.

| Dec. 31 | Cash ............................................... | 103,546 | |
| | Premium on Bonds Payable .................... | | 3,546 |
| | Bonds Payable .............................. | | 100,000 |
| | *Sold bonds at a premium on their issue date.* | | |

These bonds are reported in the long-term liability section of the issuer's December 31, 2011, balance sheet as shown in Exhibit 14.9. A premium is added to par value to yield the carrying (book) value of bonds. Premium on Bonds Payable is an adjunct (also called *accretion*) liability account.

**EXHIBIT 14.9**

Balance Sheet Presentation of Bond Premium

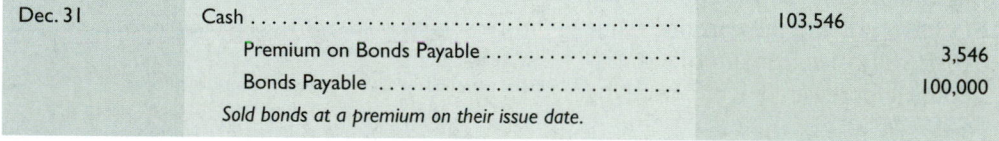

**Amortizing a Bond Premium**  Adidas receives $103,546 for its bonds; in return, it pays bondholders $100,000 after two years (plus semiannual interest payments). The $3,546 premium not repaid to issuer's bondholders at maturity goes to reduce the issuer's expense of using the $103,546 for two years. The upper portion of panel A of Exhibit 14.10 shows that total bond interest expense of $20,454 is the difference between the total amount repaid to bondholders ($124,000) and the amount borrowed from bondholders ($103,546). Alternatively, we can compute total bond interest expense as the sum of the four interest payments less the bond premium. The premium is

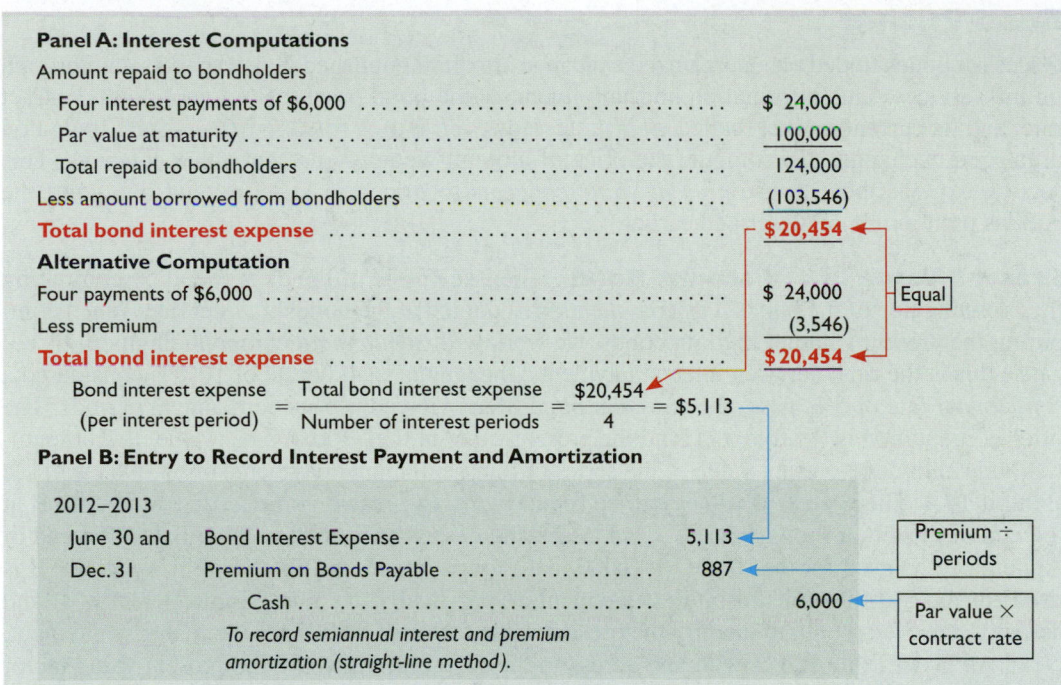

**EXHIBIT 14.10**

Interest Computation and Entry for Bonds Issued at a Premium

subtracted because it will not be paid to bondholders when the bonds mature; see the lower portion of panel A. Total bond interest expense must be allocated over the four semiannual periods using the straight-line method (or the effective interest method in Appendix 14B).

**Straight-Line Method**   The straight-line method allocates an equal portion of total bond interest expense to each of the bonds' semiannual interest periods. To apply this method to Adidas bonds, we divide the two years' total bond interest expense of $20,454 by 4 (the number of semiannual periods in the bonds' life). This gives a total bond interest expense of $5,113 per period, which is $5,113.5 rounded down so that the journal entry balances and for simplicity in presentation (alternatively, one could carry cents). Panel B of Exhibit 14.10 shows how the issuer records bond interest expense and updates the balance of the bond liability account for *each* semiannual period (June 30, 2012, through December 31, 2013).

**Point:** A premium decreases Bond Interest Expense; a discount increases it.

Exhibit 14.11 shows the pattern of decreases in the unamortized Premium on Bonds Payable account and in the bonds' carrying value. The following points summarize straight-line amortization of the premium bonds:

| Semiannual Period-End | Unamortized Premium* | Carrying Value† |
|---|---|---|
| (0)  12/31/2011 ........ | $3,546 | $103,546 |
| (1)  6/30/2012 ........ | 2,659 | 102,659 |
| (2)  12/31/2012 ........ | 1,772 | 101,772 |
| (3)  6/30/2013 ........ | 885 | 100,885 |
| (4)  12/31/2013 ........ | 0‡ | 100,000 |

**EXHIBIT 14.11**

Straight-Line Amortization of Bond Premium

During the bond life, carrying value is adjusted to par and the amortized premium to zero.

\* Total bond premium (of $3,546) less accumulated periodic amortization ($887 per semiannual interest period).

† Bond par value (of $100,000) plus unamortized premium.

‡ Adjusted for rounding.

1. At issuance, the $100,000 par value plus the $3,546 premium equals the $103,546 cash received by the issuer.

2. During the bonds' life, the (unamortized) premium decreases each period by the $887 amortization ($3,546/4), and the carrying value decreases each period by the same $887.

3. At maturity, the unamortized premium equals zero, and the carrying value equals the $100,000 par value that the issuer pays the holder.

*The next section describes bond pricing. An instructor can choose to cover bond pricing or not. Assignments requiring the next section are Quick Study 14-5, and Exercises 14-9 & 14-10.*

## Bond Pricing

Prices for bonds traded on an organized exchange are often published in newspapers and through online services. This information normally includes the bond price (called *quote*), its contract rate, and its current market (called *yield*) rate. However, only a fraction of bonds are traded on organized exchanges. To compute the price of a bond, we apply present value concepts. This section explains how to use *present value concepts* to price the Fila discount bond and the Adidas premium bond described earlier.

**Present Value of a Discount Bond**   The issue price of bonds is found by computing the present value of the bonds' cash payments, discounted at the bonds' market rate. When computing the present value of the Fila bonds, we work with *semiannual* compounding periods because this is the time between interest payments; the annual market rate of 10% is considered a semiannual rate of 5%. Also, the two-year bond life is viewed as four semiannual periods. The price computation is twofold: (1) Find the present value of the $100,000 par value paid at maturity and (2) find the present value of the series of four semiannual payments of $4,000 each; see Exhibit 14.4. These present values can be found by using *present value tables*. Appendix B at the end of this book shows present value tables and describes their use. Table B.1 at the end of Appendix B is used for the single $100,000 maturity payment, and Table B.3 in Appendix B is used for the $4,000 series of interest payments. Specifically, we go to Table B.1, row 4, and across to the 5% column to identify the present value factor of 0.8227 for the maturity payment. Next, we go to Table B.3, row 4, and across to the 5% column, where the present value factor is 3.5460 for the series of interest payments. We compute bond price by multiplying the cash flow payments by their corresponding present value factors and adding them together; see Exhibit 14.12.

**Point:** A bond's market value (price) at issuance equals the present value of its future cash payments, where the interest (discount) rate used is the bond's market rate.

**Point:** Many calculators have present value functions for computing bond prices.

**EXHIBIT 14.12**

Computing Issue Price for the Fila Discount Bonds

| Cash Flow | Table | Present Value Factor | Amount | Present Value |
|---|---|---|---|---|
| $100,000 par (maturity) value ......... | B.1 | 0.8227 | × $100,000 = | $ 82,270 |
| $4,000 interest payments ............. | B.3 | 3.5460 | × 4,000 = | 14,184 |
| Price of bond ..................... | | | | **$96,454** |

**Present Value of a Premium Bond**   We find the issue price of the Adidas bonds by using the market rate to compute the present value of the bonds' future cash flows. When computing the present value of these bonds, we again work with *semiannual* compounding periods because this is the time between interest payments. The annual 10% market rate is applied as a semiannual rate of 5%, and the two-year bond life is viewed as four semiannual periods. The computation is twofold: (1) Find the present value of the $100,000 par value paid at maturity and (2) find the present value of the series of four payments of $6,000 each; see Exhibit 14.8. These present values can be found by using present value tables. First, go to Table B.1, row 4, and across to the 5% column where the present value factor is 0.8227 for the maturity payment. Second, go to Table B.3, row 4, and across to the 5% column, where the present value factor is 3.5460 for the series of interest payments. The bonds' price is computed by multiplying the cash flow payments by their corresponding present value factors and adding them together; see Exhibit 14.13.

**Point:** There are nearly 5 million individual U.S. bond issues, ranging from huge treasuries to tiny municipalities. This compares to about 12,000 individual U.S. stocks that are traded.

**EXHIBIT 14.13**

Computing Issue Price for the Adidas Premium Bonds

| Cash Flow | Table | Present Value Factor | Amount | Present Value |
|---|---|---|---|---|
| $100,000 par (maturity) value ......... | B.1 | 0.8227 | × $100,000 = | $ 82,270 |
| $6,000 interest payments ............. | B.3 | 3.5460 | × 6,000 = | 21,276 |
| Price of bond ..................... | | | | **$103,546** |

## Quick Check

Answers — p. 579

On December 31, 2010, a company issues 16%, 10-year bonds with a par value of $100,000. Interest is paid on June 30 and December 31. The bonds are sold to yield a 14% annual market rate at an issue price of $110,592. Use this information to answer questions 7 through 9:

**7.** Are these bonds issued at a discount or a premium? Explain your answer.

**8.** Using the straight-line method to allocate bond interest expense, the issuer records the second interest payment (on December 31, 2011) with a debit to Premium on Bonds Payable in the amount of (a) $7,470, (b) $530, (c) $8,000, or (d) $400.

**9.** How are these bonds reported in the long-term liability section of the issuer's balance sheet as of December 31, 2011?

# BOND RETIREMENT

This section describes the retirement of bonds (1) at maturity, (2) before maturity, and (3) by conversion to stock.

**P4** Record the retirement of bonds.

## Bond Retirement at Maturity

The carrying value of bonds at maturity always equals par value. For example, both Exhibits 14.7 (a discount) and 14.11 (a premium) show that the carrying value of bonds at the end of their lives equals par value ($100,000). The retirement of these bonds at maturity, assuming interest is already paid and entered, is recorded as follows:

| 2013 | | | |
|---|---|---|---|
| Dec. 31 | Bonds Payable ............................ | 100,000 | |
| | Cash ..................................... | | 100,000 |
| | *To record retirement of bonds at maturity.* | | |

| Assets | = | Liabilities | + | Equity |
|---|---|---|---|---|
| −100,000 | = | −100,000 | | |

## Bond Retirement before Maturity

Issuers sometimes wish to retire some or all of their bonds prior to maturity. For instance, if interest rates decline greatly, an issuer may wish to replace high-interest-paying bonds with new low-interest bonds. Two common ways to retire bonds before maturity are to (1) exercise a call option or (2) purchase them on the open market. In the first instance, an issuer can reserve the right to retire bonds early by issuing callable bonds. The bond indenture can give the issuer an option to *call* the bonds before they mature by paying the par value plus a *call premium* to bondholders. In the second case, the issuer retires bonds by repurchasing them on the open market at their current price. Whether bonds are called or repurchased, the issuer is unlikely to pay a price that exactly equals their carrying value. When a difference exists between the bonds' carrying value and the amount paid, the issuer records a gain or loss equal to the difference.

To illustrate the accounting for retiring callable bonds, assume that a company issued callable bonds with a par value of $100,000. The call option requires the issuer to pay a call premium of $3,000 to bondholders in addition to the par value. Next, assume that after the June 30, 2011, interest payment, the bonds have a carrying value of $104,500. Then on July 1, 2011, the issuer calls these bonds and pays $103,000 to bondholders. The issuer recognizes a $1,500 gain from the difference between the bonds' carrying value of $104,500 and the retirement price of $103,000. The issuer records this bond retirement as follows.

**Point:** Bond retirement is also referred to as *bond redemption.*

**Point:** Gains and losses from retiring bonds were *previously* reported as extraordinary items. New standards require that they now be judged by the "unusual and infrequent" criteria for reporting purposes.

| July 1 | Bonds Payable ............................ | 100,000 | |
|---|---|---|---|
| | Premium on Bonds Payable ...................... | 4,500 | |
| | Gain on Bond Retirement ................... | | 1,500 |
| | Cash ..................................... | | 103,000 |
| | *To record retirement of bonds before maturity.* | | |

| Assets | = | Liabilities | + | Equity |
|---|---|---|---|---|
| −103,000 | = | −100,000 | | +1,500 |
| | | −4,500 | | |

An issuer usually must call all bonds when it exercises a call option. However, to retire as many or as few bonds as it desires, an issuer can purchase them on the open market. If it retires less than the entire class of bonds, it recognizes a gain or loss for the difference between the carrying value of those bonds retired and the amount paid to acquire them.

## Bond Retirement by Conversion

**Convertible Bond**

Holders of convertible bonds have the right to convert their bonds to stock. When conversion occurs, the bonds' carrying value is transferred to equity accounts and no gain or loss is recorded. (We further describe convertible bonds in the Decision Analysis section of this chapter.)

To illustrate, assume that on January 1 the $100,000 par value bonds of **Converse**, with a carrying value of $100,000, are converted to 15,000 shares of $2 par value common stock. The entry to record this conversion follows (the market prices of the bonds and stock are *not* relevant to this entry; the material in Chapter 13 is helpful in understanding this transaction):

| Assets | = | Liabilities | + | Equity |
|---|---|---|---|---|
| −100,000 | | | | +30,000 |
| | | | | +70,000 |

| Jan. 1 | Bonds Payable . . . . . . . . . . . . . . . . . . . . . . . . . . . . . | 100,000 | |
|---|---|---|---|
| | Common Stock . . . . . . . . . . . . . . . . . . . . . . . . . . . | | 30,000 |
| | Paid-In Capital in Excess of Par Value . . . . . . . . . . . | | 70,000 |
| | *To record retirement of bonds by conversion.* | | |

### Decision **Insight**

**Junk Bonds**  Junk bonds are company bonds with low credit ratings due to a higher than average likelihood of default. On the upside, the high risk of junk bonds can yield high returns if the issuer survives and repays its debt. ■

### Quick Check                                Answer — p. 579

10. Six years ago, a company issued $500,000 of 6%, eight-year bonds at a price of 95. The current carrying value is $493,750. The company decides to retire 50% of these bonds by buying them on the open market at a price of 102½. What is the amount of gain or loss on the retirement of these bonds?

# LONG-TERM NOTES PAYABLE

**C1**  Explain the types and payment patterns of notes.

Like bonds, notes are issued to obtain assets such as cash. Unlike bonds, notes are typically transacted with a *single* lender such as a bank. An issuer initially records a note at its selling price—that is, the note's face value minus any discount or plus any premium. Over the note's life, the amount of interest expense allocated to each period is computed by multiplying the market rate (at issuance of the note) by the beginning-of-period note balance. The note's carrying (book) value at any time equals its face value minus any unamortized discount or plus any unamortized premium; carrying value is also computed as the present value of all remaining payments, discounted using the market rate at issuance.

## Installment Notes

An **installment note** is an obligation requiring a series of payments to the lender. Installment notes are common for franchises and other businesses when lenders and borrowers agree to spread payments over several periods. To illustrate, assume that Foghog borrows $60,000 from a bank to purchase equipment. It signs an 8% installment note requiring six annual payments of principal plus interest and it records the note's issuance at January 1, 2011, as follows.

| Jan. 1 | Cash ........................................... | 60,000 | |
| | Notes Payable ............................. | | 60,000 |
| | *Borrowed $60,000 by signing an 8%, six-year* | | |
| | *installment note.* | | |

Assets = Liabilities + Equity
+60,000        +60,000

Payments on an installment note normally include the accrued interest expense plus a portion of the amount borrowed (the *principal*). This section describes an installment note with equal payments.

The equal total payments pattern consists of changing amounts of both interest and principal. To illustrate, assume that Foghog borrows $60,000 by signing a $60,000 note that requires six *equal payments* of $12,979 at the end of each year. (The present value of an annuity of six annual payments of $12,979, discounted at 8%, equals $60,000; we show this computation in footnote 2 on the next page.) The $12,979 includes both interest and principal, the amounts of which change with each payment. Exhibit 14.14 shows the pattern of equal total payments and its two parts, interest and principal. Column A shows the note's beginning balance. Column B shows accrued interest for each year at 8% of the beginning note balance. Column C shows the impact on the note's principal, which equals the difference between the total payment in column D and the interest expense in column B. Column E shows the note's year-end balance.

**Years**

2011 2012 2013 2014 2015 2016

**Point:** Most consumer notes are installment notes that require equal total payments.

**EXHIBIT 14.14**

Installment Note: Equal Total Payments

| Period Ending Date | (A) Beginning Balance | (B) Debit Interest Expense 8% × (A) | + | (C) Debit Notes Payable (D) − (B) | = | (D) Credit Cash (computed) | (E) Ending Balance (A) − (C) |
|---|---|---|---|---|---|---|---|
| (1) 12/31/2011 | $60,000 | $ 4,800 | | $ 8,179 | | $12,979 | $51,821 |
| (2) 12/31/2012 | 51,821 | 4,146 | | 8,833 | | 12,979 | 42,988 |
| (3) 12/31/2013 | 42,988 | 3,439 | | 9,540 | | 12,979 | 33,448 |
| (4) 12/31/2014 | 33,448 | 2,676 | | 10,303 | | 12,979 | 23,145 |
| (5) 12/31/2015 | 23,145 | 1,852 | | 11,127 | | 12,979 | 12,018 |
| (6) 12/31/2016 | 12,018 | 961 | | 12,018 | | 12,979 | 0 |
| | | $17,874 | | $60,000 | | $77,874 | |

**P5** Prepare entries to account for notes.

Although the six cash payments are equal, accrued interest decreases each year because the principal balance of the note declines. As the amount of interest decreases each year, the portion of each payment applied to principal increases. This pattern is graphed in the lower part of Exhibit 14.14. Foghog uses the amounts in Exhibit 14.14 to record its first two payments (for years 2011 and 2012) as follows:

Assets = Liabilities + Equity
−12,979  −8,179  −4,800

| 2011 | | | |
|---|---|---|---|
| Dec. 31 | Interest Expense .............................. | 4,800 | |
| | Notes Payable .................................. | 8,179 | |
| | Cash ...................................... | | 12,979 |
| | *To record first installment payment.* | | |

Assets = Liabilities + Equity
−12,979  −8,833  −4,146

| 2012 | | | |
|---|---|---|---|
| Dec. 31 | Interest Expense .............................. | 4,146 | |
| | Notes Payable .................................. | 8,833 | |
| | Cash ...................................... | | 12,979 |
| | *To record second installment payment.* | | |

Foghog records similar entries but with different amounts for each of the remaining four payments. After six years, the Notes Payable account balance is zero.[2]

## Mortgage Notes and Bonds

**Point:** The Truth-in-Lending Act requires lenders to provide information about loan costs including finance charges and interest rate.

A **mortgage** is a legal agreement that helps protect a lender if a borrower fails to make required payments on notes or bonds. A mortgage gives the lender a right to be paid from the cash proceeds of the sale of a borrower's assets identified in the mortgage. A legal document, called a *mortgage contract,* describes the mortgage terms.

**Global:** Countries vary in the preference given to debtholders vs. stockholders when a company is in financial distress. Some countries such as Germany, France, and Japan give preference to stockholders over debtholders.

*Mortgage notes* carry a mortgage contract pledging title to specific assets as security for the note. Mortgage notes are especially popular in the purchase of homes and the acquisition of plant assets. Less common *mortgage bonds* are backed by the issuer's assets. Accounting for mortgage notes and bonds is similar to that for unsecured notes and bonds, except that the mortgage agreement must be disclosed. For example, **TIBCO Software** reports that its "**mortgage note payable ... is collateralized by the commercial real property acquired [corporate headquarters].**"

**Example:** Suppose the $60,000 installment loan has an 8% interest rate with eight equal annual payments. What is the annual payment? *Answer* (using Table B.3): $60,000/5.7466 = $10,441

[2] Table B.3 in Appendix B is used to compute the dollar amount of the six payments that equal the initial note balance of $60,000 at 8% interest. We go to Table B.3, row 6, and across to the 8% column, where the present value factor is 4.6229. The dollar amount is then computed by solving this relation:

| Table | Present Value Factor | Dollar Amount | | Present Value |
|---|---|---|---|---|
| B.3 | 4.6229 | × ? | = | $60,000 |

The dollar amount is computed by dividing $60,000 by 4.6229, yielding $12,979.

**Decision Maker** Answer — p. 579

**Entrepreneur** You are an electronics retailer planning a holiday sale on a custom stereo system that requires no payments for two years. At the end of two years, buyers must pay the full amount. The system's suggested retail price is $4,100, but you are willing to sell it today for $3,000 cash. What is your holiday sale price if payment will not occur for two years and the market interest rate is 10%? ∎

## Quick Check
Answers — p. 579

11. Which of the following is true for an installment note requiring a series of equal total cash payments? (*a*) Payments consist of increasing interest and decreasing principal; (*b*) payments consist of changing amounts of principal but constant interest; or (*c*) payments consist of decreasing interest and increasing principal.
12. How is the interest portion of an installment note payment computed?
13. When a borrower records an interest payment on an installment note, how are the balance sheet and income statement affected?

# GLOBAL VIEW

This section discusses similarities and differences between U.S. GAAP and IFRS in accounting and reporting for long-term liabilities such as bonds and notes.

**Accounting for Bonds and Notes** The definitions and characteristics of bonds and notes are broadly similar for both U.S. GAAP and IFRS. Although slight differences exist, accounting for bonds and notes under U.S. GAAP and IFRS is similar. Specifically, the accounting for issuances (including recording discounts and premiums), market pricing, and retirement of both bonds and notes follows the procedures in this chapter. **Nokia** describes its accounting for bonds, which follows the amortized cost approach explained in this chapter (and in Appendix 14B), as follows: Loans payable [bonds] are recognized initially at fair value, net of transaction costs incurred. In the subsequent periods, they are stated at amortized cost.

**NOKIA**

Both U.S. GAAP and IFRS allow companies to account for bonds and notes using fair value (different from the amortized value described in this chapter). This method is referred to as the **fair value option.** This method is similar to that applied in measuring and accounting for debt and equity securities. *Fair value* is the amount a company would receive if it settled a liability (or sold an asset) in an orderly transaction as of the balance sheet date. Companies can use several sources of inputs to determine fair value, and those inputs fall into three classes (ranked in order of preference):

Level 1: Observable quoted market prices in active markets for identical items.
Level 2: Observable inputs other than those in Level 1 such as prices from inactive markets or from similar, but not identical, items.
Level 3: Unobservable inputs reflecting a company's assumptions about value.

The exact procedures for marking liabilities to fair value at each balance sheet date are in advanced courses.

**Accounting for Leases and Pensions** Both U.S. GAAP and IFRS require companies to distinguish between operating leases and capital leases; the latter is referred to as *finance leases* under IFRS. The accounting and reporting for leases are broadly similar for both U.S. GAAP and IFRS. The main difference is the criteria for identifying a lease as a capital lease are more general under IFRS. However, the basic approach applies. **Nokia** describes its accounting for operating leases as follows: the payments . . . are treated as rentals and recognized in the profit and loss account.

For pensions, both U.S. GAAP and IFRS require companies to record costs of retirement benefits as employees work and earn them. The basic methods are similar in accounting and reporting for pensions.

**Decision Analysis**  Debt Features and the Debt-to-Equity Ratio

*Collateral agreements* can reduce the risk of loss for both bonds and notes. Unsecured bonds and notes are riskier because the issuer's obligation to pay interest and principal has the same priority as all other unsecured liabilities in the event of bankruptcy. If a company is unable to pay its debts in full, the unsecured creditors (including the holders of debentures) lose all or a portion of their balances. These types of legal agreements and other characteristics of long-term liabilities are crucial for effective business decisions. The first part of this section describes the different types of features sometimes included with bonds and notes. The second part explains and applies the debt-to-equity ratio.

 **A2** Assess debt features and their implications.

## Features of Bonds and Notes

This section describes common features of debt securities.

**Secured Debt**          **Unsecured Debt**

**Secured or Unsecured**   **Secured bonds** (and notes) have specific assets of the issuer pledged (or *mortgaged*) as collateral. This arrangement gives holders added protection against the issuer's default. If the issuer fails to pay interest or par value, the secured holders can demand that the collateral be sold and the proceeds used to pay the obligation. **Unsecured bonds** (and notes), also called *debentures,* are backed by the issuer's general credit standing. Unsecured debt is riskier than secured debt. *Subordinated debentures* are liabilities that are not repaid until the claims of the more senior, unsecured (and secured) liabilities are settled.

**Term or Serial**   **Term bonds** (and notes) are scheduled for maturity on one specified date. **Serial bonds** (and notes) mature at more than one date (often in series) and thus are usually repaid over a number of periods. For instance, $100,000 of serial bonds might mature at the rate of $10,000 each year from 6 to 15 years after they are issued. Many bonds are **sinking fund bonds,** which to reduce the holder's risk require the issuer to create a *sinking fund* of assets set aside at specified amounts and dates to repay the bonds.

**Registered or Bearer**   Bonds issued in the names and addresses of their holders are **registered bonds.** The issuer makes bond payments by sending checks (or cash transfers) to registered holders. A registered holder must notify the issuer of any ownership change. Registered bonds offer the issuer the practical advantage of not having to actually issue bond certificates. Bonds payable to whoever holds them (the *bearer*) are called **bearer bonds** or *unregistered bonds*. Sales or exchanges might not be recorded, so the holder of a bearer bond is presumed to be its rightful owner. As a result, lost bearer bonds are difficult to replace. Many bearer bonds are also **coupon bonds.** This term reflects interest coupons that are attached to the bonds. When each coupon matures, the holder presents it to a bank or broker for collection. At maturity, the holder follows the same process and presents the bond certificate for collection. Issuers of coupon bonds cannot deduct the related interest expense for taxable income. This is to prevent abuse by taxpayers who own coupon bonds but fail to report interest income on their tax returns.

**Convertible Debt**      **Callable Debt**

**Convertible and/or Callable**   **Convertible bonds** (and notes) can be exchanged for a fixed number of shares of the issuing corporation's common stock. Convertible debt offers holders the potential to participate in future increases in stock price. Holders still receive periodic interest while the debt is held and the par value if they hold the debt to maturity. In most cases, the holders decide whether and when to convert debt to stock. **Callable bonds** (and notes) have an option exercisable by the issuer to retire them at a stated dollar amount before maturity.

🟨 **Decision Insight**

**Munis**   More than a million municipal bonds, or "munis," exist, and many are tax exempt. Munis are issued by state, city, town, and county governments to pay for public projects including schools, libraries, roads, bridges, and stadiums. ■

 **A3** Compute the debt-to-equity ratio and explain its use.

## Debt-to-Equity Ratio

Beyond assessing different characteristics of debt as just described, we want to know the level of debt, especially in relation to total equity. Such knowledge helps us assess the risk of a company's financing structure. A company financed mainly with debt is more risky because liabilities must be repaid—usually with periodic interest—whereas equity financing does not. A measure to assess the risk of a company's financing structure is the **debt-to-equity ratio** (see Exhibit 14.15).

$$\text{Debt-to-equity} = \frac{\text{Total liabilities}}{\text{Total equity}}$$

**EXHIBIT 14.15**

Debt-to-Equity Ratio

The debt-to-equity ratio varies across companies and industries. Industries that are more variable tend to have lower ratios, while more stable industries are less risky and tend to have higher ratios. To apply the debt-to-equity ratio, let's look at this measure for **Cedar Fair** in Exhibit 14.16.

| ($ millions) | 2009 | 2008 | 2007 | 2006 | 2005 |
|---|---|---|---|---|---|
| Total liabilities ................ | $2,017.577 | $2,079.297 | $2,133.576 | $2,100.306 | $590.560 |
| Total equity .................. | $ 127.862 | $ 106.786 | $ 285.092 | $ 410.615 | $434.234 |
| **Debt-to-equity** .............. | 15.8 | 19.5 | 7.5 | 5.1 | 1.4 |
| Industry debt-to-equity ........ | 11.4 | 10.3 | 5.7 | 3.2 | 1.2 |

**EXHIBIT 14.16**

Cedar Fair's Debt-to-Equity Ratio

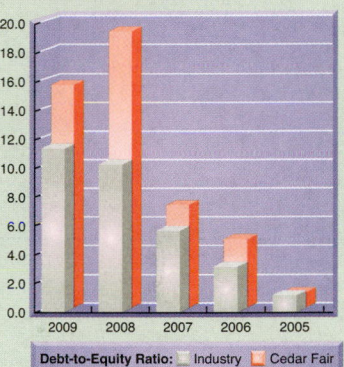

Cedar Fair's 2009 debt-to-equity ratio is 15.8, meaning that debtholders contributed $15.8 for each $1 contributed by equityholders. This implies a fairly risky financing structure for Cedar Fair. A similar concern is drawn from a comparison of Cedar Fair with its competitors, where the 2009 industry ratio is 11.4. Analysis across the years shows that Cedar Fair's financing structure has grown increasingly risky in recent years. Given its sluggish revenues and increasing operating expenses in recent years (see its annual report), Cedar Fair is increasingly at risk of financial distress.

**Decision Maker**                                         Answer – p. 579

**Bond Investor**   You plan to purchase debenture bonds from one of two companies in the same industry that are similar in size and performance. The first company has $350,000 in total liabilities, and $1,750,000 in equity. The second company has $1,200,000 in total liabilities, and $1,000,000 in equity. Which company's debenture bonds are less risky based on the debt-to-equity ratio? ■

# DEMONSTRATION PROBLEM

Water Sports Company (WSC) patented and successfully test-marketed a new product. To expand its ability to produce and market the new product, WSC needs to raise $800,000 of financing. On January 1, 2011, the company obtained the money in two ways:

**a.** WSC signed a $400,000, 10% installment note to be repaid with five equal annual installments to be made on December 31 of 2011 through 2015.

**b.** WSC issued five-year bonds with a par value of $400,000. The bonds have a 12% annual contract rate and pay interest on June 30 and December 31. The bonds' annual market rate is 10% as of January 1, 2011.

**Required**

**1.** For the installment note, (*a*) compute the size of each annual payment, (*b*) prepare an amortization table such as Exhibit 14.14, and (*c*) prepare the journal entry for the first payment.

**2.** For the bonds, (*a*) compute their issue price; (*b*) prepare the January 1, 2011, journal entry to record their issuance; (*c*) prepare an amortization table using the straight-line method; (*d*) prepare the June 30, 2011, journal entry to record the first interest payment; and (*e*) prepare a journal entry to record retiring the bonds at a $416,000 call price on January 1, 2013.

**3.**[B]Redo parts 2(*c*), 2(*d*), and 2(*e*) assuming the bonds are amortized using the effective interest method.

## PLANNING THE SOLUTION

- For the installment note, divide the borrowed amount by the annuity factor (from Table B.3) using the 10% rate and five payments to compute the amount of each payment. Prepare a table similar to Exhibit 14.14 and use the numbers in the table's first line for the journal entry.
- Compute the bonds' issue price by using the market rate to find the present value of their cash flows (use tables found in Appendix B). Then use this result to record the bonds' issuance. Next, prepare an amortization table like Exhibit 14.11 (and Exhibit 14B.2) and use it to get the numbers needed for the journal entry. Also use the table to find the carrying value as of the date of the bonds' retirement that you need for the journal entry.

## SOLUTION TO DEMONSTRATION PROBLEM

### Part 1: Installment Note

**a.** Annual payment = Note balance/Annuity factor = $400,000/3.7908 = $105,519 (The annuity factor is for five payments and a rate of 10%.)

**b.** An amortization table follows.

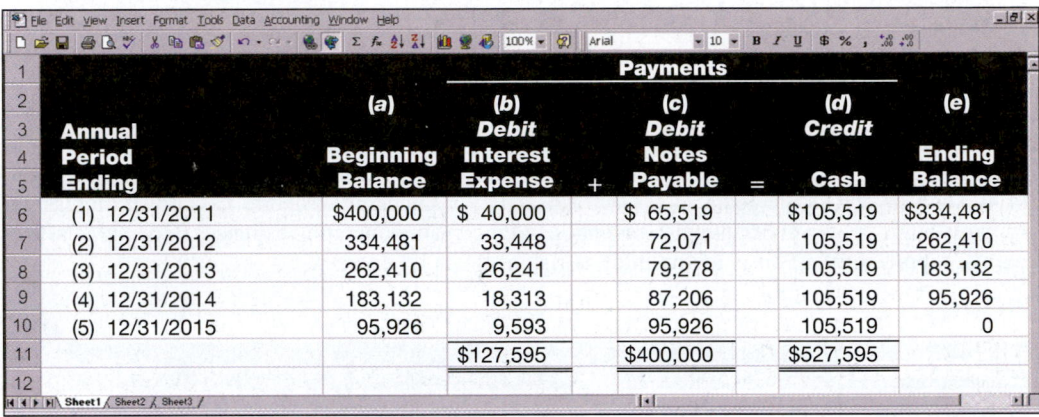

| Annual Period Ending | (a) Beginning Balance | (b) Debit Interest Expense + | (c) Debit Notes Payable = | (d) Credit Cash | (e) Ending Balance |
|---|---|---|---|---|---|
| | | | **Payments** | | |
| (1) 12/31/2011 | $400,000 | $ 40,000 | $ 65,519 | $105,519 | $334,481 |
| (2) 12/31/2012 | 334,481 | 33,448 | 72,071 | 105,519 | 262,410 |
| (3) 12/31/2013 | 262,410 | 26,241 | 79,278 | 105,519 | 183,132 |
| (4) 12/31/2014 | 183,132 | 18,313 | 87,206 | 105,519 | 95,926 |
| (5) 12/31/2015 | 95,926 | 9,593 | 95,926 | 105,519 | 0 |
| | | $127,595 | $400,000 | $527,595 | |

**c.** Journal entry for December 31, 2011, payment.

| Dec. 31 | Interest Expense | 40,000 | |
| | Notes Payable | 65,519 | |
| | Cash | | 105,519 |
| | *To record first installment payment.* | | |

### Part 2: Bonds (Straight-Line Amortization)

**a.** Compute the bonds' issue price.

| Cash Flow | Table | Present Value Factor* | Amount | Present Value |
|---|---|---|---|---|
| Par (maturity) value | B.1 in App. B (PV of 1) | 0.6139 | × 400,000 = | $245,560 |
| Interest payments | B.3 in App. B (PV of annuity) | 7.7217 | × 24,000 = | 185,321 |
| Price of bond | | | | $430,881 |

\* Present value factors are for 10 payments using a semiannual market rate of 5%.

**b.** Journal entry for January 1, 2011, issuance.

| Jan. 1 | Cash | 430,881 | |
| | Premium on Bonds Payable | | 30,881 |
| | Bonds Payable | | 400,000 |
| | *Sold bonds at a premium.* | | |

c. Straight-line amortization table for premium bonds.

| Semiannual Period-End | Unamortized Premium | Carrying Value |
|---|---|---|
| (0) 1/1/2011 ........ | $30,881 | $430,881 |
| (1) 6/30/2011 ........ | 27,793 | 427,793 |
| (2) 12/31/2011 ........ | 24,705 | 424,705 |
| (3) 6/30/2012 ........ | 21,617 | 421,617 |
| (4) 12/31/2012 ........ | 18,529 | 418,529 |
| (5) 6/30/2013 ........ | 15,441 | 415,441 |
| (6) 12/31/2013 ........ | 12,353 | 412,353 |
| (7) 6/30/2014 ........ | 9,265 | 409,265 |
| (8) 12/31/2014 ........ | 6,177 | 406,177 |
| (9) 6/30/2015 ........ | 3,089 | 403,089 |
| (10) 12/31/2015 ........ | 0* | 400,000 |

* Adjusted for rounding.

d. Journal entry for June 30, 2011, bond payment.

| June 30 | Bond Interest Expense ......................... | 20,912 | |
| | Premium on Bonds Payable ..................... | 3,088 | |
| | Cash ..................................... | | 24,000 |
| | *Paid semiannual interest on bonds.* | | |

e. Journal entry for January 1, 2013, bond retirement.

| Jan. 1 | Bonds Payable ............................... | 400,000 | |
| | Premium on Bonds Payable ..................... | 18,529 | |
| | Cash ..................................... | | 416,000 |
| | Gain on Retirement of Bonds ............... | | 2,529 |
| | *To record bond retirement (carrying value as of Dec. 31, 2012).* | | |

## Part 3: Bonds (Effective Interest Amortization)[B]

c. The effective interest amortization table for premium bonds.

| | (A) Cash Interest Paid 6% × $400,000 | (B) Interest Expense 5% × Prior (E) | (C) Premium Amortization (A) − (B) | (D) Unamortized Premium Prior (D) − (C) | (E) Carrying Value $400,000 + (D) |
|---|---|---|---|---|---|
| (0) 1/1/2011 | | | | $30,881 | $430,881 |
| (1) 6/30/2011 | $ 24,000 | $ 21,544 | $ 2,456 | 28,425 | 428,425 |
| (2) 12/31/2011 | 24,000 | 21,421 | 2,579 | 25,846 | 425,846 |
| (3) 6/30/2012 | 24,000 | 21,292 | 2,708 | 23,138 | 423,138 |
| (4) 12/31/2012 | 24,000 | 21,157 | 2,843 | 20,295 | 420,295 |
| (5) 6/30/2013 | 24,000 | 21,015 | 2,985 | 17,310 | 417,310 |
| (6) 12/31/2013 | 24,000 | 20,866 | 3,134 | 14,176 | 414,176 |
| (7) 6/30/2014 | 24,000 | 20,709 | 3,291 | 10,885 | 410,885 |
| (8) 12/31/2014 | 24,000 | 20,544 | 3,456 | 7,429 | 407,429 |
| (9) 6/30/2015 | 24,000 | 20,371 | 3,629 | 3,800 | 403,800 |
| (10) 12/31/2015 | 24,000 | 20,200* | 3,800 | 0 | 400,000 |
| | $240,000 | $209,119 | $30,881 | | |

* Adjusted for rounding

**d.** Journal entry for June 30, 2011, bond payment.

| June 30 | Bond Interest Expense ......................... | 21,544 | |
|---|---|---|---|
| | Premium on Bonds Payable ...................... | 2,456 | |
| | Cash ....................................... | | 24,000 |
| | *Paid semiannual interest on bonds.* | | |

**e.** Journal entry for January 1, 2013, bond retirement.

| Jan. 1 | Bonds Payable ................................. | 400,000 | |
|---|---|---|---|
| | Premium on Bonds Payable ...................... | 20,295 | |
| | Cash ....................................... | | 416,000 |
| | Gain on Retirement of Bonds ................. | | 4,295 |
| | *To record bond retirement (carrying value as of December 31, 2012).* | | |

**APPENDIX**

# 14A

# Present Values of Bonds and Notes

This appendix explains how to apply present value techniques to measure a long-term liability when it is created and to assign interest expense to the periods until it is settled. Appendix B at the end of the book provides additional discussion of present value concepts.

**C2** Explain and compute the present value of an amount(s) to be paid at a future date(s).

**Present Value Concepts** The basic present value concept is that cash paid (or received) in the future has less value now than the same amount of cash paid (or received) today. To illustrate, if we must pay $1 one year from now, its present value is less than $1. To see this, assume that we borrow $0.9259 today that must be paid back in one year with 8% interest. Our interest expense for this loan is computed as $0.9259 × 8%, or $0.0741. When the $0.0741 interest is added to the $0.9259 borrowed, we get the $1 payment necessary to repay our loan with interest. This is formally computed in Exhibit 14A.1. The $0.9259 borrowed is the present value of the $1 future payment. More generally, an amount borrowed equals the present value of the future payment. (This same interpretation applies to an investment. If $0.9259 is invested at 8%, it yields $0.0741 in revenue after one year. This amounts to $1, made up of principal and interest.)

**EXHIBIT 14A.1**

Components of a One-Year Loan

| Amount borrowed .............. | $0.9259 |
|---|---|
| Interest for one year at 8% ........ | 0.0741 |
| Amount owed after 1 year ........ | $ 1.0000 |

**Point:** Benjamin Franklin is said to have described compounding as "the money, money makes, makes more money."

To extend this example, assume that we owe $1 two years from now instead of one year, and the 8% interest is compounded annually. *Compounded* means that interest during the second period is based on the total of the amount borrowed plus the interest accrued from the first period. The second period's interest is then computed as 8% multiplied by the sum of the amount borrowed plus interest earned in the first period. Exhibit 14A.2 shows how we compute the present value of $1 to be paid in two years. This amount is $0.8573. The first year's interest of $0.0686 is added to the principal so that the second year's interest is based on $0.9259. Total interest for this two-year period is $0.1427, computed as $0.0686 plus $0.0741.

**EXHIBIT 14A.2**

Components of a Two-Year Loan

| Amount borrowed ...................... | $0.8573 |
|---|---|
| Interest for first year ($0.8573 × 8%) .......... | 0.0686 |
| Amount owed after 1 year .................. | 0.9259 |
| Interest for second year ($0.9259 × 8%) ......... | 0.0741 |
| Amount owed after 2 years .................. | $ 1.0000 |

**Present Value Tables**   The present value of $1 that we must repay at some future date can be computed by using this formula: $1/(1 + i)^n$. The symbol $i$ is the interest rate per period and $n$ is the number of periods until the future payment must be made. Applying this formula to our two-year loan, we get $1/(1.08)^2$, or $0.8573. This is the same value shown in Exhibit 14A.2. We can use this formula to find any present value. However, a simpler method is to use a *present value table,* which lists present values computed with this formula for various interest rates and time periods. Many people find it helpful in learning present value concepts to first work with the table and then move to using a calculator.

Exhibit 14A.3 shows a present value table for a future payment of 1 for up to 10 periods at three different interest rates. Present values in this table are rounded to four decimal places. This table is drawn from the larger and more complete Table B.1 in Appendix B at the end of the book. Notice that the first value in the 8% column is 0.9259, the value we computed earlier for the present value of a $1 loan for one year at 8% (see Exhibit 14A.1). Go to the second row in the same 8% column and find the present value of 1 discounted at 8% for two years, or 0.8573. This $0.8573 is the present value of our obligation to repay $1 after two periods at 8% interest (see Exhibit 14A.2).

**EXHIBIT 14A.3**

Present Value of 1

| | Rate | | |
|---|---|---|---|
| Periods | 6% | 8% | 10% |
| 1 | 0.9434 | **0.9259** | 0.9091 |
| 2 | 0.8900 | **0.8573** | 0.8264 |
| 3 | 0.8396 | 0.7938 | 0.7513 |
| 4 | 0.7921 | 0.7350 | 0.6830 |
| 5 | 0.7473 | 0.6806 | 0.6209 |
| 6 | 0.7050 | 0.6302 | 0.5645 |
| 7 | 0.6651 | 0.5835 | 0.5132 |
| 8 | 0.6274 | 0.5403 | 0.4665 |
| 9 | 0.5919 | 0.5002 | 0.4241 |
| 10 | 0.5584 | 0.4632 | 0.3855 |

**Example:** Use Exhibit 14A.3 to find the present value of $1 discounted for 2 years at 6%. *Answer:* $0.8900

**Applying a Present Value Table**   To illustrate how to measure a liability using a present value table, assume that a company plans to borrow cash and repay it as follows: $2,000 after one year, $3,000 after two years, and $5,000 after three years. How much does this company receive today if the interest rate on this loan is 10%? To answer, we need to compute the present value of the three future payments, discounted at 10%. This computation is shown in Exhibit 14A.4 using present values from Exhibit 14A.3. The company can borrow $8,054 today at 10% interest in exchange for its promise to make these three payments at the scheduled dates.

**EXHIBIT 14A.4**

Present Value of a Series of Unequal Payments

| Periods | Payments | Present Value of 1 at 10% | Present Value of Payments |
|---|---|---|---|
| 1 | $2,000 | 0.9091 | $ 1,818 |
| 2 | 3,000 | 0.8264 | 2,479 |
| 3 | 5,000 | 0.7513 | 3,757 |
| Present value of all payments ....... | | | $8,054 |

**Present Value of an Annuity**   The $8,054 present value for the loan in Exhibit 14A.4 equals the sum of the present values of the three payments. When payments are not equal, their combined present value is best computed by adding the individual present values as shown in Exhibit 14A.4. Sometimes payments follow an **annuity,** which is a series of *equal* payments at equal time intervals. The present value of an annuity is readily computed.

To illustrate, assume that a company must repay a 6% loan with a $5,000 payment at each year-end for the next four years. This loan amount equals the present value of the four payments discounted at 6%. Exhibit 14A.5 shows how to compute this loan's present value of $17,326 by multiplying each payment by its matching present value factor taken from Exhibit 14A.3.

However, the series of $5,000 payments is an annuity, so we can compute its present value with either of two shortcuts. First, the third column of Exhibit 14A.5 shows that the sum of the present values of 1 at 6% for periods 1 through 4 equals 3.4651. One shortcut is to multiply this total of 3.4651 by the $5,000 annual payment to get the combined present value of $17,326. It requires one multiplication instead of four.

**EXHIBIT 14A.5**

Present Value of a Series of Equal Payments (Annuity) by Discounting Each Payment

| Periods | Payments | Present Value of 1 at 6% | Present Value of Payments |
|---|---|---|---|
| 1 | $5,000 | 0.9434 | $ 4,717 |
| 2 | 5,000 | 0.8900 | 4,450 |
| 3 | 5,000 | 0.8396 | 4,198 |
| 4 | 5,000 | 0.7921 | 3,961 |
| Present value of all payments ....... | | 3.4651 | $17,326 |

**EXHIBIT 14A.6**

Present Value of an Annuity of 1

| Periods | Rate | | |
|---|---|---|---|
| | 6% | 8% | 10% |
| 1 | 0.9434 | 0.9259 | 0.9091 |
| 2 | 1.8334 | 1.7833 | 1.7355 |
| 3 | 2.6730 | 2.5771 | 2.4869 |
| 4 | **3.4651** | 3.3121 | 3.1699 |
| 5 | 4.2124 | 3.9927 | 3.7908 |
| 6 | 4.9173 | 4.6229 | 4.3553 |
| 7 | 5.5824 | 5.2064 | 4.8684 |
| 8 | 6.2098 | 5.7466 | 5.3349 |
| 9 | 6.8017 | 6.2469 | 5.7590 |
| 10 | 7.3601 | 6.7101 | 6.1446 |

**Example:** Use Exhibit 14A.6 to find the present value of an annuity of eight $15,000 payments with an 8% interest rate. *Answer:* $15,000 × 5.7466 = $86,199

The second shortcut uses an *annuity table* such as the one shown in Exhibit 14A.6, which is drawn from the more complete Table B.3 in Appendix B. We go directly to the annuity table to get the present value factor for a specific number of payments and interest rate. We then multiply this factor by the amount of the payment to find the present value of the annuity. Specifically, find the row for four periods and go across to the 6% column, where the factor is 3.4651. This factor equals the present value of an annuity with four payments of 1, discounted at 6%. We then multiply 3.4651 by $5,000 to get the $17,326 present value of the annuity.

## Compounding Periods Shorter Than a Year

The present value examples all involved periods of one year. In many situations, however, interest is compounded over shorter periods. For example, the interest rate on bonds is usually stated as an annual rate but interest is often paid every six months (semiannually). This means that the present value of interest payments from such bonds must be computed using interest periods of six months.

Assume that a borrower wants to know the present value of a series of 10 *semiannual payments* of $4,000 made over five years at an *annual interest rate* of 12%. The interest rate is stated as an annual rate of 12%, but it is actually a rate of 6% per semiannual interest period. To compute the present value of this series of $4,000 payments, go to row 10 of Exhibit 14A.6 and across to the 6% column to find the factor 7.3601. The present value of this annuity is $29,440 (7.3601 × $4,000).

**Example:** If this borrower makes five semiannual payments of $8,000, what is the present value of this annuity at a 12% rate? *Answer:* 4.2124 × $8,000 = $33,699

*Appendix B further describes present value concepts and includes more complete present value tables and assignments.*

## Quick Check

Answers — p. 579

14. A company enters into an agreement to make four annual year-end payments of $1,000 each, starting one year from now. The annual interest rate is 8%. The present value of these four payments is (*a*) $2,923, (*b*) $2,940, or (*c*) $3,312.

15. Suppose a company has an option to pay either (*a*) $10,000 after one year or (*b*) $5,000 after six months and another $5,000 after one year. Which choice has the lower present value?

## APPENDIX

# 14B

# Effective Interest Amortization

**Effective Interest Amortization of a Discount Bond**   The straight-line method yields changes in the bonds' carrying value while the amount for bond interest expense remains constant. This gives the impression of a changing interest rate when users divide a constant bond interest expense over a changing carrying value. As a result, accounting standards allow use of the straight-line method only when its results do not differ materially from those obtained using the effective interest method. The **effective interest method,** or simply *interest method,* allocates total bond interest expense over the bonds' life in a way that yields a constant rate of interest. This constant rate of interest is the market rate at the issue date. Thus, bond interest expense for a period equals the carrying value of the bond at the beginning of that period multiplied by the market rate when issued.

**Point:** The effective interest method computes bond interest expense using the market rate at issuance. This rate is applied to a changing carrying value.

Exhibit 14B.1 shows an effective interest amortization table for the Fila bonds (as described in Exhibit 14.4). The key difference between the effective interest and straight-line methods lies in computing bond interest expense. Instead of assigning an equal amount of bond interest expense to each period, the effective interest method assigns a bond interest expense amount that increases over the life of a discount bond. **Both methods allocate the *same* $19,546 of total bond interest expense to the bonds' life, but in different patterns.** Specifically, the amortization table in Exhibit 14B.1 shows that the balance of the discount (column D) is amortized until it reaches zero. Also, the bonds' carrying value (column E) changes each period until it equals par value at maturity. Compare columns D and E to the corresponding columns in Exhibit 14.7 to see the amortization patterns. Total bond interest expense is $19,546, consisting of $16,000 of semiannual cash payments and $3,546 of the original bond discount, the same for both methods.

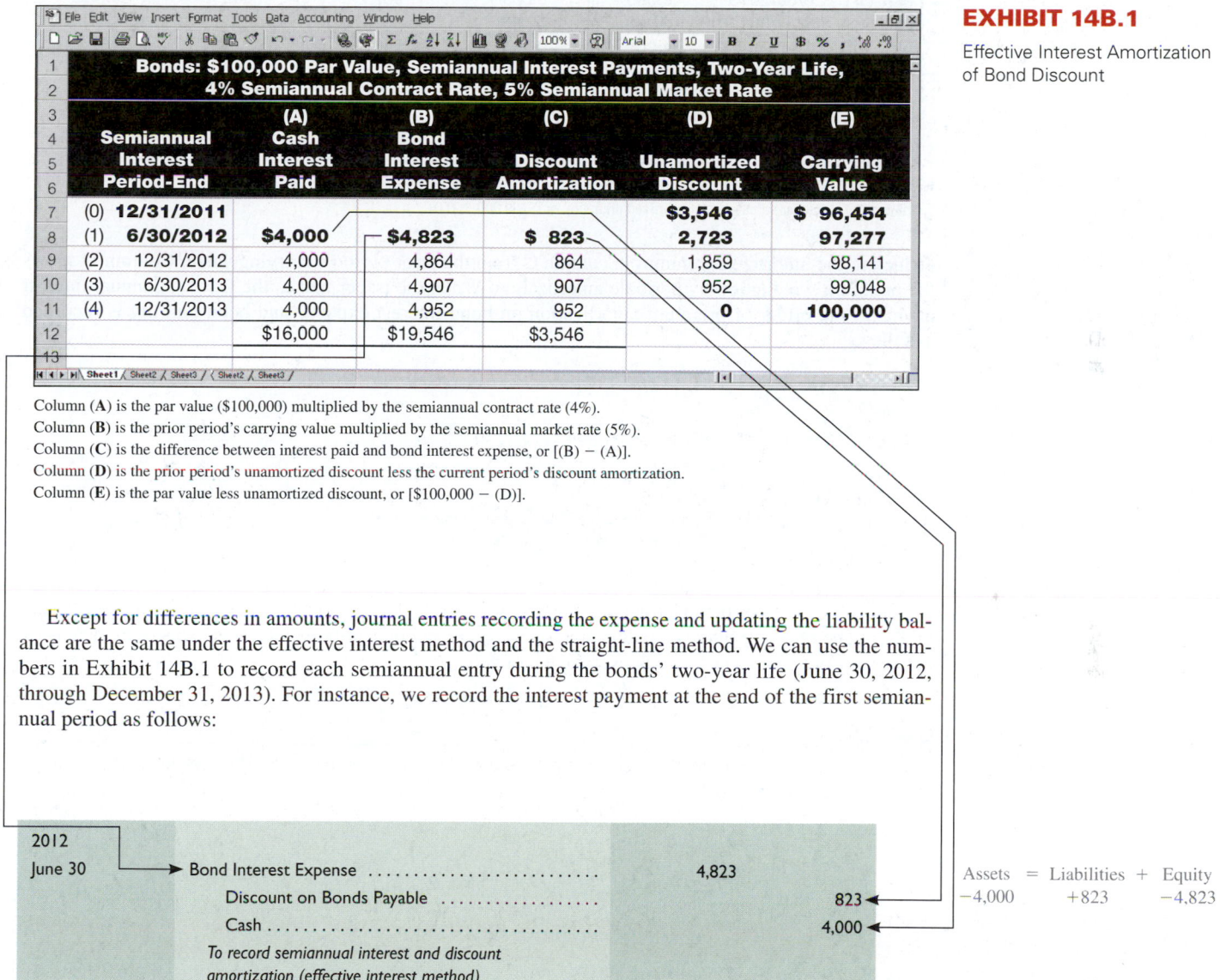

**EXHIBIT 14B.1**

Effective Interest Amortization of Bond Discount

Bonds: $100,000 Par Value, Semiannual Interest Payments, Two-Year Life,
4% Semiannual Contract Rate, 5% Semiannual Market Rate

| | | (A) Cash Interest Paid | (B) Bond Interest Expense | (C) Discount Amortization | (D) Unamortized Discount | (E) Carrying Value |
|---|---|---|---|---|---|---|
| Semiannual Interest Period-End | | | | | | |
| (0) | 12/31/2011 | | | | $3,546 | $ 96,454 |
| (1) | 6/30/2012 | $4,000 | $4,823 | $ 823 | 2,723 | 97,277 |
| (2) | 12/31/2012 | 4,000 | 4,864 | 864 | 1,859 | 98,141 |
| (3) | 6/30/2013 | 4,000 | 4,907 | 907 | 952 | 99,048 |
| (4) | 12/31/2013 | 4,000 | 4,952 | 952 | 0 | 100,000 |
| | | $16,000 | $19,546 | $3,546 | | |

Column (**A**) is the par value ($100,000) multiplied by the semiannual contract rate (4%).
Column (**B**) is the prior period's carrying value multiplied by the semiannual market rate (5%).
Column (**C**) is the difference between interest paid and bond interest expense, or [(B) − (A)].
Column (**D**) is the prior period's unamortized discount less the current period's discount amortization.
Column (**E**) is the par value less unamortized discount, or [$100,000 − (D)].

Except for differences in amounts, journal entries recording the expense and updating the liability balance are the same under the effective interest method and the straight-line method. We can use the numbers in Exhibit 14B.1 to record each semiannual entry during the bonds' two-year life (June 30, 2012, through December 31, 2013). For instance, we record the interest payment at the end of the first semiannual period as follows:

| 2012 | | | |
|---|---|---|---|
| June 30 | Bond Interest Expense ........................... | 4,823 | |
| | Discount on Bonds Payable .................. | | 823 |
| | Cash .................................... | | 4,000 |
| | *To record semiannual interest and discount* | | |
| | *amortization (effective interest method).* | | |

| Assets | = | Liabilities | + | Equity |
|---|---|---|---|---|
| −4,000 | | +823 | | −4,823 |

**Effective Interest Amortization of a Premium Bond**   Exhibit 14B.2 shows the amortization table using the effective interest method for the Adidas bonds (as described in Exhibit 14.8). Column A lists the semiannual cash payments. Column B shows the amount of bond interest expense, computed as the 5% semiannual market rate at issuance multiplied by the beginning-of-period carrying value. The amount of cash paid in column A is larger than the bond interest expense because the cash payment is based on the higher 6% semiannual contract rate. The excess cash payment over the interest expense reduces the principal. These amounts are shown in column C. Column E shows the carrying value after

**EXHIBIT 14B.2**

Effective Interest Amortization
of Bond Premium

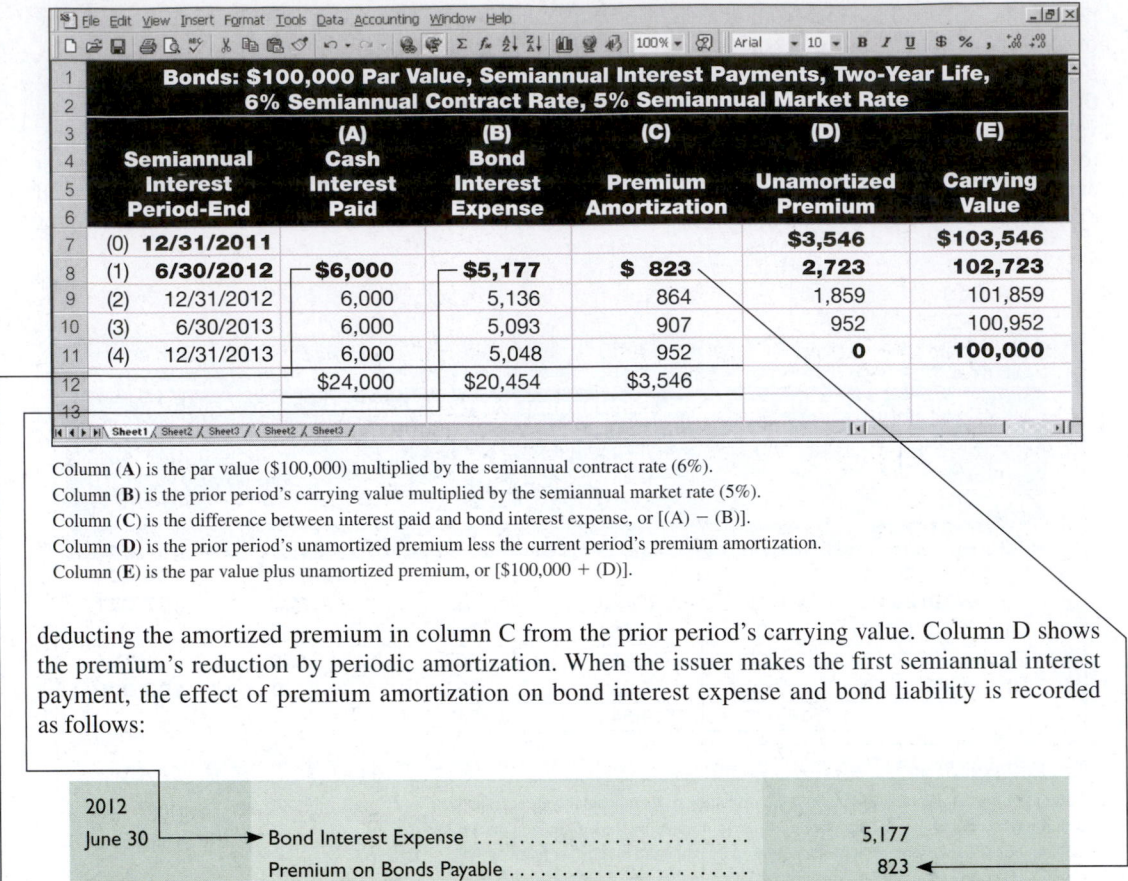

Column (**A**) is the par value ($100,000) multiplied by the semiannual contract rate (6%).
Column (**B**) is the prior period's carrying value multiplied by the semiannual market rate (5%).
Column (**C**) is the difference between interest paid and bond interest expense, or [(A) − (B)].
Column (**D**) is the prior period's unamortized premium less the current period's premium amortization.
Column (**E**) is the par value plus unamortized premium, or [$100,000 + (D)].

deducting the amortized premium in column C from the prior period's carrying value. Column D shows the premium's reduction by periodic amortization. When the issuer makes the first semiannual interest payment, the effect of premium amortization on bond interest expense and bond liability is recorded as follows:

Assets = Liabilities + Equity
−6,000    −823      −5,177

| 2012 | | | |
|---|---|---|---|
| June 30 | Bond Interest Expense ........................... | 5,177 | |
| | Premium on Bonds Payable ...................... | 823 | |
| | Cash ................................. | | 6,000 |
| | *To record semiannual interest and premium amortization (effective interest method).* | | |

Similar entries with different amounts are recorded at each payment date until the bond matures at the end of 2013. The effective interest method yields decreasing amounts of bond interest expense and increasing amounts of premium amortization over the bonds' life.

 **IFRS**

Unlike U.S. GAAP, IFRS requires that interest expense be computed using the effective interest method with *no exemptions*. ■

---

**APPENDIX**

# 14C

**C3** Describe interest accrual when bond payment periods differ from accounting periods.

# Issuing Bonds between Interest Dates

An issuer can sell bonds at a date other than an interest payment date. When this occurs, the buyers normally pay the issuer the purchase price plus any interest accrued since the prior interest payment date. This accrued interest is then repaid to these buyers on the next interest payment date. To illustrate, suppose **Avia** sells $100,000 of its 9% bonds at par on March 1, 2011, 60 days after the stated issue date. The interest on Avia bonds is payable semiannually on each June 30 and December 31. Since 60 days have passed, the issuer collects accrued interest from the buyers at the time of issuance. This amount is $1,500 ($100,000 × 9% × 60/360 year). This case is reflected in Exhibit 14C.1.

**EXHIBIT 14C.1**

Accruing Interest between Interest Payment Dates

Avia records the issuance of these bonds on March 1, 2011, as follows:

| Mar. 1 | Cash .......................................... | 101,500 | |
| | Interest Payable ............................ | | 1,500 |
| | Bonds Payable.............................. | | 100,000 |
| | *Sold bonds at par with accrued interest.* | | |

Assets  = Liabilities + Equity
+101,500     +100,000
                +1,500

Liabilities for interest payable and bonds payable are recorded in separate accounts. When the June 30, 2011, semiannual interest date arrives, Avia pays the full semiannual interest of $4,500 ($100,000 × 9% × ½ year) to the bondholders. This payment includes the four months' interest of $3,000 earned by the bondholders from March 1 to June 30 *plus* the repayment of the 60 days' accrued interest collected by Avia when the bonds were sold. Avia records this first semiannual interest payment as follows:

**Example:** How much interest is collected from a buyer of $50,000 of Avia bonds sold at par 150 days after the contract issue date? *Answer:* $1,875 (computed as $50,000 × 9% × $^{150}/_{360}$ year)

| June 30 | Interest Payable ............................. | 1,500 | |
| | Bond Interest Expense....................... | 3,000 | |
| | Cash ....................................... | | 4,500 |
| | *Paid semiannual interest on the bonds.* | | |

Assets  = Liabilities + Equity
−4,500      −1,500      −3,000

The practice of collecting and then repaying accrued interest with the next interest payment is to simplify the issuer's administrative efforts. To explain, suppose an issuer sells bonds on 15 or 20 different dates between the stated issue date and the first interest payment date. If the issuer does not collect accrued interest from buyers, it needs to pay different amounts of cash to each of them according to the time that passed after purchasing the bonds. The issuer needs to keep detailed records of buyers and the dates they bought bonds. Issuers avoid this recordkeeping by having each buyer pay accrued interest at purchase. Issuers then pay the full semiannual interest to all buyers, regardless of when they bought bonds.

**Accruing Bond Interest Expense**    If a bond's interest period does not coincide with the issuer's accounting period, an adjusting entry is needed to recognize bond interest expense accrued since the most recent interest payment. To illustrate, assume that the stated issue date for Adidas bonds described in Exhibit 14.10 is September 1, 2011, instead of December 31, 2011, and that the bonds are sold on September 1, 2011. As a result, four months' interest (and premium amortization) accrue before the end of the 2011 calendar year. Interest for this period equals $3,409, or ⅔ of the first six months' interest of $5,113. Also, the premium amortization is $591, or ⅔ of the first six months' amortization of $887. The sum of the bond interest expense and the amortization is $4,000 ($3,409 + $591), which equals ⅔ of the $6,000 cash payment due on February 28, 2012. Adidas records these effects with an adjusting entry at December 31, 2011.

**Point:** Computation of accrued bond interest may use months instead of days for simplicity purposes. For example, the accrued interest computation for the Adidas bonds is based on months.

| Dec. 31 | Bond Interest Expense ......................... | 3,409 | |
| | Premium on Bonds Payable ...................... | 591 | |
| | Interest Payable ............................ | | 4,000 |
| | *To record four months' accrued interest and premium amortization.* | | |

Assets  = Liabilities + Equity
                −591      −3,409
               +4,000

Similar entries are made on each December 31 throughout the bonds' two-year life. When the $6,000 cash payment occurs on each February 28 interest payment date, Adidas must recognize bond interest expense and amortization for January and February. It must also eliminate the interest payable liability created by the December 31 adjusting entry. For example, Adidas records its payment on February 28, 2012, as follows:

| Assets | = Liabilities | + Equity |
|--------|--------------|---------|
| −6,000 | −4,000 | −1,704 |
| | −296 | |

| Feb. 28 | Interest Payable ................................. | 4,000 | |
|---------|-----------------------------------------------|-------|-------|
| | Bond Interest Expense ($5,113 × ⅔) .............. | 1,704 | |
| | Premium on Bonds Payable ($887 × ⅔) ........... | 296 | |
| | Cash ...................................... | | 6,000 |
| | *To record 2 months' interest and amortization, and eliminate accrued interest liability.* | | |

The interest payments made each August 31 are recorded as usual because the entire six-month interest period is included within this company's calendar-year reporting period.

## Decision Maker     Answer — p. 579

**Bond Rater**   You must assign a rating to a bond that reflects its risk to bondholders. Identify factors you consider in assessing bond risk. Indicate the likely levels (relative to the norm) for the factors you identify for a bond that sells at a discount. ■

## Quick Check     Answer — p. 579

**16.** On May 1, a company sells 9% bonds with a $500,000 par value that pay semiannual interest on each January 1 and July 1. The bonds are sold at par plus interest accrued since January 1. The issuer records the first semiannual interest payment on July 1 with (*a*) a debit to Interest Payable for $15,000, (*b*) a debit to Bond Interest Expense for $22,500, or (*c*) a credit to Interest Payable for $7,500.

---

## APPENDIX

# 14D                    Leases and Pensions

This appendix briefly explains the accounting and analysis for both leases and pensions.

| **C4** | Describe accounting for leases and pensions. |
|--------|---------------------------------------------|

**Lease Liabilities**   A **lease** is a contractual agreement between a *lessor* (asset owner) and a *lessee* (asset renter or tenant) that grants the lessee the right to use the asset for a period of time in return for cash (rent) payments. Nearly one-fourth of all equipment purchases are financed with leases. The advantages of lease financing include the lack of an immediate large cash payment and the potential to deduct rental payments in computing taxable income. From an accounting perspective, leases can be classified as either operating or capital leases.

**Point:** Home Depot reports that its rental expenses from operating leases total more than $900 million.

**Operating Leases**   **Operating leases** are short-term (or cancelable) leases in which the lessor retains the risks and rewards of ownership. Examples include most car and apartment rental agreements. The lessee records such lease payments as expenses; the lessor records them as revenue. The lessee does not report the leased item as an asset or a liability (it is the lessor's asset). To illustrate, if an employee of Amazon leases a car for $300 at an airport while on company business, Amazon (lessee) records this cost as follows:

| Assets | = Liabilities | + Equity |
|--------|--------------|---------|
| −300 | | −300 |

| July 4 | Rental Expense ................................. | 300 | |
|--------|-----------------------------------------------|-----|-----|
| | Cash ...................................... | | 300 |
| | *To record lease rental payment.* | | |

**Capital Leases**   **Capital leases** are long-term (or noncancelable) leases by which the lessor transfers substantially all risks and rewards of ownership to the lessee.[3] Examples include most leases of airplanes and department store buildings. The lessee records the leased item as its own asset along with a lease liability at the start of the lease term; the amount recorded equals the present value of all lease payments. To illustrate, assume that K2 Co. enters into a six-year lease of a building in which it will sell sporting equipment. The lease transfers all building ownership risks and rewards to K2 (the present value of its $12,979 annual lease payments is $60,000). K2 records this transaction as follows:

| 2011 | | | |
|---|---|---|---|
| Jan. 1 | Leased Asset—Building .......................... | 60,000 | |
| | Lease Liability ............................. | | 60,000 |
| | *To record leased asset and lease liability.* | | |

Assets = Liabilities + Equity
+60,000    +60,000

K2 reports the leased asset as a plant asset and the lease liability as a long-term liability. The portion of the lease liability expected to be paid in the next year is reported as a current liability.[4] At each year-end, K2 records depreciation on the leased asset (assume straight-line depreciation, six-year lease term, and no salvage value) as follows:

**Point:** Home Depot reports *"certain locations ... are leased under capital leases."* The net present value of this Lease Liability is about $400 million.

| | | | |
|---|---|---|---|
| Dec. 31 | Depreciation Expense—Building .................. | 10,000 | |
| | Accumulated Depreciation—Building .......... | | 10,000 |
| | *To record depreciation on leased asset.* | | |

Assets = Liabilities + Equity
−10,000                  −10,000

K2 also accrues interest on the lease liability at each year-end. Interest expense is computed by multiplying the remaining lease liability by the interest rate on the lease. Specifically, K2 records its annual interest expense as part of its annual lease payment ($12,979) as follows (for its first year):

| 2011 | | | |
|---|---|---|---|
| Dec. 31 | Interest Expense ............................ | 4,800 | |
| | Lease Liability ............................. | 8,179 | |
| | Cash ....................................... | | 12,979 |
| | *To record first annual lease payment.** | | |

Assets = Liabilities + Equity
−12,979    −8,179    −4,800

\* These numbers are computed from a *lease payment schedule*. For simplicity, we use the same numbers from Exhibit 14.14 for this lease payment schedule—with different headings as follows:

| | (A) | Payments | | | (E) |
|---|---|---|---|---|---|
| | | (B) Debit | (C) Debit | (D) Credit | |
| | | | | | Ending |
| | Beginning | Interest | | | Balance |
| Period | Balance | on Lease + | Lease = | Cash | of Lease |
| Ending | of Lease | Liability | Liability | Lease | Liability |
| Date | Liability | 8% × (A) | (D) − (B) | Payment | (A) − (C) |
| 12/31/2011 ......... | $60,000 | $ 4,800 | $ 8,179 | $12,979 | $51,821 |
| 12/31/2012 ......... | 51,821 | 4,146 | 8,833 | 12,979 | 42,988 |
| 12/31/2013 ......... | 42,988 | 3,439 | 9,540 | 12,979 | 33,448 |
| 12/31/2014 ......... | 33,448 | 2,676 | 10,303 | 12,979 | 23,145 |
| 12/31/2015 ......... | 23,145 | 1,852 | 11,127 | 12,979 | 12,018 |
| 12/31/2016 ......... | 12,018 | 961 | 12,018 | 12,979 | 0 |
| | | $17,874 | $60,000 | $77,874 | |

---

[3] A *capital lease* meets any one or more of four criteria: (1) transfers title of leased asset to lessee, (2) contains a bargain purchase option, (3) has a lease term that is 75% or more of the leased asset's useful life, or (4) has a present value of lease payments that is 90% or more of the leased asset's market value.

[4] Most lessees try to keep leased assets and lease liabilities off their balance sheets by failing to meet any one of the four criteria of a capital lease. This is because a lease liability increases a company's total liabilities, making it more difficult to obtain additional financing. The acquisition of assets without reporting any related liabilities (or other asset outflows) on the balance sheet is called **off-balance-sheet financing.**

**Pension Liabilities**    A **pension plan** is a contractual agreement between an employer and its employees for the employer to provide benefits (payments) to employees after they retire. Most employers pay the full cost of the pension, but sometimes employees pay part of the cost. An employer records its payment into a pension plan with a debit to Pension Expense and a credit to Cash. A *plan administrator* receives payments from the employer, invests them in pension assets, and makes benefit payments to *pension recipients* (retired employees). Insurance and trust companies often serve as pension plan administrators.

Many pensions are known as *defined benefit plans* that define future benefits; the employer's contributions vary, depending on assumptions about future pension assets and liabilities. Several disclosures are necessary in this case. Specifically, a pension liability is reported when the accumulated benefit obligation is *more than* the plan assets, a so-called *underfunded plan*. The accumulated benefit obligation is the present value of promised future pension payments to retirees. *Plan assets* refer to the market value of assets the plan administrator holds. A pension asset is reported when the accumulated benefit obligation is *less than* the plan assets, a so-called *overfunded plan*. An employer reports pension expense when it receives the benefits from the employees' services, which is sometimes decades before it pays pension benefits to employees. (*Other Postretirement Benefits* refer to nonpension benefits such as health care and life insurance benefits. Similar to a pension, costs of these benefits are estimated and liabilities accrued when the employees earn them.)

# Summary

**C1    Explain the types and payment patterns of notes.** Notes repaid over a period of time are called *installment notes* and usually follow one of two payment patterns: (1) decreasing payments of interest plus equal amounts of principal or (2) equal total payments. Mortgage notes also are common.

**C2^A    Explain and compute the present value of an amount(s) to be paid at a future date(s).** The basic concept of present value is that an amount of cash to be paid or received in the future is worth less than the same amount of cash to be paid or received today. Another important present value concept is that interest is compounded, meaning interest is added to the balance and used to determine interest for succeeding periods. An annuity is a series of equal payments occurring at equal time intervals. An annuity's present value can be computed using the present value table for an annuity (or a calculator).

**C3^C    Describe interest accrual when bond payment periods differ from accounting periods.** Issuers and buyers of debt record the interest accrued when issue dates or accounting periods do not coincide with debt payment dates.

**C4^D    Describe accounting for leases and pensions.** A lease is a rental agreement between the lessor and the lessee. When the lessor retains the risks and rewards of asset ownership (an *operating lease*), the lessee debits Rent Expense and credits Cash for its lease payments. When the lessor substantially transfers the risks and rewards of asset ownership to the lessee (a *capital lease*), the lessee capitalizes the leased asset and records a lease liability. Pension agreements can result in either pension assets or pension liabilities.

**A1    Compare bond financing with stock financing.** Bond financing is used to fund business activities. Advantages of bond financing versus stock include (1) no effect on owner control, (2) tax savings, and (3) increased earnings due to financial leverage. Disadvantages include (1) interest and principal payments and (2) amplification of poor performance.

**A2    Assess debt features and their implications.** Certain bonds are secured by the issuer's assets; other bonds, called *debentures,* are unsecured. Serial bonds mature at different points in time;

term bonds mature at one time. Registered bonds have each bondholder's name recorded by the issuer; bearer bonds are payable to the holder. Convertible bonds are exchangeable for shares of the issuer's stock. Callable bonds can be retired by the issuer at a set price. Debt features alter the risk of loss for creditors.

**A3    Compute the debt-to-equity ratio and explain its use.** Both creditors and equity holders are concerned about the relation between the amount of liabilities and the amount of equity. A company's financing structure is at less risk when the debt-to-equity ratio is lower, as liabilities must be paid and usually with periodic interest.

**P1    Prepare entries to record bond issuance and interest expense.** When bonds are issued at par, Cash is debited and Bonds Payable is credited for the bonds' par value. At bond interest payment dates (usually semiannual), Bond Interest Expense is debited and Cash credited—the latter for an amount equal to the bond par value multiplied by the bond contract rate.

**P2    Compute and record amortization of bond discount.** Bonds are issued at a discount when the contract rate is less than the market rate, making the issue (selling) price less than par. When this occurs, the issuer records a credit to Bonds Payable (at par) and debits both Discount on Bonds Payable and Cash. The amount of bond interest expense assigned to each period is computed using either the straight-line or effective interest method.

**P3    Compute and record amortization of bond premium.** Bonds are issued at a premium when the contract rate is higher than the market rate, making the issue (selling) price greater than par. When this occurs, the issuer records a debit to Cash and credits both Premium on Bonds Payable and Bonds Payable (at par). The amount of bond interest expense assigned to each period is computed using either the straight-line or effective interest method. The Premium on Bonds Payable is allocated to reduce bond interest expense over the life of the bonds.

**P4    Record the retirement of bonds.** Bonds are retired at maturity with a debit to Bonds Payable and a credit to Cash at par value. The issuer can retire the bonds early by exercising a call option or purchasing them in the market. Bondholders can also re-tire bonds early by exercising a conversion feature on convertible bonds. The issuer recognizes a gain or loss for the difference be-tween the amount paid and the bond carrying value.

**P5**  **Prepare entries to account for notes.** Interest is allocated to each period in a note's life by multiplying its beginning-period carrying value by its market rate at issuance. If a note is repaid with equal payments, the payment amount is computed by dividing the borrowed amount by the present value of an annuity factor (taken from a present value table) using the market rate and the number of payments.

## Guidance Answers to Decision Maker

**Entrepreneur**  This is a "present value" question. The market interest rate (10%) and present value ($3,000) are known, but the payment required two years later is unknown. This amount ($3,630) can be computed as $3,000 \times 1.10 \times 1.10$. Thus, the sale price is $3,630 when no payments are received for two years. The $3,630 received two years from today is equivalent to $3,000 cash today.

**Bond Investor**  The debt-to-equity ratio for the first company is 0.2 ($350,000/$1,750,000) and for the second company is 1.2 ($1,200,000/$1,000,000), suggesting that the financing structure of the second company is more risky than that of the first company. Consequently, as a buyer of unsecured debenture bonds, you prefer the first company (all else equal).

**Bond Rater**  Bonds with longer repayment periods (life) have higher risk. Also, bonds issued by companies in financial difficulties or facing higher than normal uncertainties have higher risk. More-over, companies with higher than normal debt and large fluctuations in earnings are considered of higher risk. Discount bonds are more risky on one or more of these factors.

## Guidance Answers to Quick Checks

**1.**

| 2011 | | | |
|---|---|---|---|
| Jan. 1 | Cash ...................................... | 10,000 | |
| | Bonds Payable .................... | | 10,000 |
| June 30 | Bond Interest Expense ................. | 450 | |
| | Cash ........................... | | 450 |

**2.** Multiply the bond's par value by its contract rate of interest.

**3.** Bonds sell at a premium when the contract rate exceeds the market rate and the purchasers pay more than their par value.

**4.** The bonds are issued at a discount, meaning that issue price is less than par value. A discount occurs because the bond contract rate (6%) is less than the market rate (8%).

**5.**

| Cash ...................................... | 91,893 | |
|---|---|---|
| Discount on Bonds Payable ................... | 8,107 | |
| Bonds Payable ......................... | | 100,000 |

**6.** $3,811 (total bond interest expense of $38,107 divided by 10 periods; or the $3,000 semiannual cash payment plus the $8,107 discount divided by 10 periods).

**7.** The bonds are issued at a premium, meaning issue price is higher than par value. A premium occurs because the bonds' contract rate (16%) is higher than the market rate (14%).

**8.** (*b*) For each semiannual period: $10,592/20 periods = $530 premium amortization.

**9.**

| Bonds payable, 16%, due 12/31/2020 ......... | $100,000 | |
|---|---|---|
| Plus premium on bonds payable ............. | 9,532* | $109,532 |

\* Original premium balance of $10,592 less $530 and $530 amortized on 6/30/2011 and 12/31/2011, respectively.

**10.** $9,375 loss, computed as the difference between the repurchase price of $256,250 [50% of ($500,000 × 102.5%)] and the car-rying value of $246,875 (50% of $493,750).

**11.** (*c*)

**12.** The interest portion of an installment payment equals the peri-od's beginning loan balance multiplied by the market interest rate at the time of the note's issuance.

**13.** On the balance sheet, the account balances of the related liabil-ity (note payable) and asset (cash) accounts are decreased. On the income statement, interest expense is recorded.

**14.** (*c*), computed as 3.3121 × $1,000 = $3,312.

**15.** The option of paying $10,000 after one year has a lower present value. It postpones paying the first $5,000 by six months. More generally, the present value of a further delayed payment is always lower than a less delayed payment.

**16.** (*a*) Reflects payment of accrued interest recorded back on May 1; $500,000 × 9% × ⁴/₁₂ = $15,000.

## Key Terms

mhhe.com/wildFAP20e

| | | |
|---|---|---|
| **Annuity** (p. 571) | **Bond certificate** (p. 554) | **Capital leases** (p. 577) |
| **Bearer bonds** (p. 566) | **Bond indenture** (p. 554) | **Carrying (book) value of bonds** (p. 556) |
| **Bond** (p. 552) | **Callable bonds** (p. 566) | **Contract rate** (p. 555) |

| | | |
|---|---|---|
| Convertible bonds (p. 566) | Market rate (p. 555) | Secured bonds (p. 566) |
| Coupon bonds (p. 566) | Mortgage (p. 564) | Serial bonds (p. 566) |
| Debt-to-equity ratio (p. 567) | Off-balance-sheet financing (p. 577) | Sinking fund bonds (p. 566) |
| Discount on bonds payable (p. 555) | Operating leases (p. 576) | Straight-line bond amortization (p. 556) |
| Effective interest method (p. 572) | Par value of a bond (p. 552) | Term bonds (p. 566) |
| Fair value option (p. 565) | Pension plan (p. 578) | Unsecured bonds (p. 566) |
| Installment note (p. 562) | Premium on bonds (p. 558) | |
| Lease (p. 576) | Registered bonds (p. 566) | |

## Multiple Choice Quiz    Answers on p. 593    mhhe.com/wildFAP20e

**Additional Quiz Questions are available at the book's Website.**

1. A bond traded at 97½ means that
   a. The bond pays 97½% interest.
   b. The bond trades at $975 per $1,000 bond.
   c. The market rate of interest is below the contract rate of interest for the bond.
   d. The bonds can be retired at $975 each.
   e. The bond's interest rate is 2½%.

2. A bondholder that owns a $1,000, 6%, 15-year bond has
   a. The right to receive $1,000 at maturity.
   b. Ownership rights in the bond issuing entity.
   c. The right to receive $60 per month until maturity.
   d. The right to receive $1,900 at maturity.
   e. The right to receive $600 per year until maturity.

3. A company issues 8%, 20-year bonds with a par value of $500,000. The current market rate for the bonds is 8%. The amount of interest owed to the bondholders for each semiannual interest payment is
   a. $40,000.
   b. $0.
   c. $20,000.

   d. $800,000.
   e. $400,000.

4. A company issued 5-year, 5% bonds with a par value of $100,000. The company received $95,735 for the bonds. Using the straight-line method, the company's interest expense for the first semiannual interest period is
   a. $2,926.50.
   b. $5,853.00.
   c. $2,500.00.
   d. $5,000.00.
   e. $9,573.50.

5. A company issued 8-year, 5% bonds with a par value of $350,000. The company received proceeds of $373,745. Interest is payable semiannually. The amount of premium amortized for the first semiannual interest period, assuming straight-line bond amortization, is
   a. $2,698.
   b. $23,745.
   c. $8,750.
   d. $9,344.
   e. $1,484.

B(C,D) *Superscript letter B(C, D) denotes assignments based on Appendix 14B (14C, 14D).*

🔢 Icon denotes assignments that involve decision making.

## Discussion Questions

1. What is the main difference between a bond and a share of stock?

2. What is the main difference between notes payable and bonds payable?

3. 🔢 What is the advantage of issuing bonds instead of obtaining financing from the company's owners?

4. What are the duties of a trustee for bondholders?

5. What is a bond indenture? What provisions are usually included in it?

6. What are the *contract* rate and the *market* rate for bonds?

7. 🔢 What factors affect the market rates for bonds?

8.ᴮ 🔢 Does the straight-line or effective interest method produce an interest expense allocation that yields a constant rate of interest over a bond's life? Explain.

9.ᶜ Why does a company that issues bonds between interest dates collect accrued interest from the bonds' purchasers?

10. 🔢 If you know the par value of bonds, the contract rate, and the market rate, how do you compute the bonds' price?

11. What is the issue price of a $2,000 bond sold at 98¼? What is the issue price of a $6,000 bond sold at 101½?

12. Describe the debt-to-equity ratio and explain how creditors and owners would use this ratio to evaluate a company's risk.

**13.** 🔲 What obligation does an entrepreneur (owner) have to investors that purchase bonds to finance the business?

**14.** Refer to **Research In Motion**'s annual report in Appendix A. Is there any indication that RIM has issued bonds?   *RIM*

**15.** By what amount did **Palm**'s long-term debt increase or decrease in 2009?   **Palm**

**16.** Refer to the statement of cash flows for **Nokia** in Appendix A. For the year ended December 31, 2009, what was the amount for repayment of bank loans?   **NOKIA**

**17.** Refer to the annual report for **Apple** in Appendix A. For the year ended September 26, 2009, what is its debt-to-equity ratio? What does this ratio tell us?   Apple

**18.ᴰ** When can a lease create both an asset and a liability for the lessee?

**19.ᴰ** Compare and contrast an operating lease with a capital lease.

**20.ᴰ** Describe the two basic types of pension plans.

---

**connect**

*Round dollar amounts to the nearest whole dollar.*

**QUICK STUDY**

**QS 14-1**
Bond features and terminology
A2

Enter the letter of the description A through H that best fits each term or phrase 1 through 8.

**A.** Records and tracks the bondholders' names.
**B.** Is unsecured; backed only by the issuer's credit standing.
**C.** Has varying maturity dates for amounts owed.
**D.** Identifies rights and responsibilities of the issuer and the bondholders.
**E.** Can be exchanged for shares of the issuer's stock.
**F.** Is unregistered; interest is paid to whoever possesses them.
**G.** Maintains a separate asset account from which bondholders are paid at maturity.
**H.** Pledges specific assets of the issuer as collateral.

**1.** _____ Debenture
**2.** _____ Bond indenture
**3.** _____ Bearer bond
**4.** _____ Registered bond
**5.** _____ Sinking fund bond
**6.** _____ Convertible bond
**7.** _____ Secured bond
**8.** _____ Serial bond

---

Alberto Company issues 8%, 10-year bonds with a par value of $350,000 and semiannual interest payments. On the issue date, the annual market rate for these bonds is 10%, which implies a selling price of 87½. The straight-line method is used to allocate interest expense.

**1.** What are the issuer's cash proceeds from issuance of these bonds?
**2.** What total amount of bond interest expense will be recognized over the life of these bonds?
**3.** What is the amount of bond interest expense recorded on the first interest payment date?

**QS 14-2**
Bond computations—
straight-line
P1   P2

---

Sanchez Company issues 10%, 15-year bonds with a par value of $120,000 and semiannual interest payments. On the issue date, the annual market rate for these bonds is 8%, which implies a selling price of 117¼. The effective interest method is used to allocate interest expense.

**1.** What are the issuer's cash proceeds from issuance of these bonds?
**2.** What total amount of bond interest expense will be recognized over the life of these bonds?
**3.** What amount of bond interest expense is recorded on the first interest payment date?

**QS 14-3ᴮ**
Bond computations—
effective interest
P1   P3

---

Prepare the journal entries for the issuance of the bonds in both QS 14-2 and QS 14-3. Assume that both bonds are issued for cash on January 1, 2011.

**QS 14-4**
Journalize bond issuance   P1

---

Using the bond details in both QS 14-2 and QS 14-3, confirm that the bonds' selling prices given in each problem are approximately correct. Use the present value tables B.1 and B.3 in Appendix B.

**QS 14-5**
Computing bond price   P2   P3

**QS 14-6**

Recording bond issuance and discount amortization  **P1  P2**

Bellvue Company issues 10%, five-year bonds, on December 31, 2010, with a par value of $100,000 and semiannual interest payments. Use the following straight-line bond amortization table and prepare journal entries to record (*a*) the issuance of bonds on December 31, 2010; (*b*) the first interest payment on June 30, 2011; and (*c*) the second interest payment on December 31, 2011.

| Semiannual Period-End | Unamortized Discount | Carrying Value |
|---|---|---|
| (0)  12/31/2010 . . . . . . . . . . . . . | $7,360 | $92,640 |
| (1)   6/30/2011 . . . . . . . . . . . . . | 6,624 | 93,376 |
| (2)  12/31/2011 . . . . . . . . . . . . . | 5,888 | 94,112 |

**QS 14-7**

Bond retirement by call option

**P4**

On July 1, 2011, Jackson Company exercises a $5,000 call option (plus par value) on its outstanding bonds that have a carrying value of $208,000 and par value of $200,000. The company exercises the call option after the semiannual interest is paid on June 30, 2011. Record the entry to retire the bonds.

**QS 14-8**

Bond retirement by stock conversion  **P4**

On January 1, 2011, the $1,000,000 par value bonds of Gruden Company with a carrying value of $1,000,000 are converted to 500,000 shares of $0.50 par value common stock. Record the entry for the conversion of the bonds.

**QS 14-9**

Computing payments for an installment note  **C1**

Valdez Company borrows $170,000 cash from a bank and in return signs an installment note for five annual payments of equal amount, with the first payment due one year after the note is signed. Use Table B.3 in Appendix B to compute the amount of the annual payment for each of the following annual market rates: (*a*) 4%, (*b*) 8%, and (*c*) 12%.

**QS 14-10**

Debt-to-equity ratio

**A2**

Compute the debt-to-equity ratio for each of the following companies. Which company appears to have a riskier financing structure? Explain.

|  | Canal Company | Sears Company |
|---|---|---|
| Total liabilities . . . . . . . . | $492,000 | $ 384,000 |
| Total equity . . . . . . . . . | 656,000 | 1,200,000 |

**QS 14-11<sup>C</sup>**

Issuing bonds between interest dates  **P1**

Kemper Company plans to issue 6% bonds on January 1, 2011, with a par value of $1,000,000. The company sells $900,000 of the bonds on January 1, 2011. The remaining $100,000 sells at par on March 1, 2011. The bonds pay interest semiannually as of June 30 and December 31. Record the entry for the March 1 cash sale of bonds.

**QS 14-12<sup>D</sup>**

Recording operating leases  **C4**

Lauren Wright, an employee of ETrain.com, leases a car at O'Hare airport for a three-day business trip. The rental cost is $350. Prepare the entry by ETrain.com to record Lauren's short-term car lease cost.

**QS 14-13<sup>D</sup>**

Recording capital leases  **C4**

Juicyfruit, Inc., signs a five-year lease for office equipment with Office Solutions. The present value of the lease payments is $20,859. Prepare the journal entry that Juicyfruit records at the inception of this capital lease.

**QS 14-14**

International liabilities disclosures

**P1  P2**

**Vodafone Group Plc** reports the following information among its bonds payable as of March 31, 2009 (pounds in millions).

| Financial Long-Term Liabilities Measured at Amortised Cost | | | |
|---|---|---|---|
| (£ millions) | Nominal (par) Value | Carrying Value | Fair Value |
| 4.625% (US dollar 500 million) bond due July 2018 . . . . . . . . . . . . . . . . . . . . . . . | £350 | £392 | £315 |

**a.** What is the par value of the 4.625% bond issuance? What is its book (carrying) value?

**b.** Was the 4.625% bond sold at a discount or a premium? Explain.

Refer to the information in QS 14-14 for **Vodafone Group Plc**. The following price quotes (from Yahoo! Finance Bond Center) relate to its bonds payable as of late 2009. For example, the price quote indicates that the 4.625% bonds have a market price of 98.0 (98.0% of par value), resulting in a yield to maturity of 4.899%.

**QS 14-15**
International liabilities disclosures and interpretations

**P1   P2**

| Price | Contract Rate (coupon) | Maturity Date | Market Rate (YTM) |
|-------|------------------------|---------------|-------------------|
| 98.0 ......... | 4.625% | 15-Jul-2018 | 4.899% |

**a.** Assuming that the 4.625% bonds were originally issued at par value, what does the market price reveal about interest rate changes since bond issuance? (Assume that Vodafone's credit rating has remained the same.)

**b.** Does the change in market rates since the issuance of these bonds affect the amount of interest expense reported on Vodafone's income statement? Explain.

**c.** How much cash would Vodafone need to pay to repurchase the 4.625% bonds at the quoted market price of 98.0? (Assume no interest is owed when the bonds are repurchased.)

**d.** Assuming that the 4.625% bonds remain outstanding until maturity, at what market price will the bonds sell on the due date in 2018?

**connect**

---

**EXERCISES**

Round dollar amounts to the nearest whole dollar. Assume no reversing entries are used.

On January 1, 2011, Kidman Enterprises issues bonds that have a $1,700,000 par value, mature in 20 years, and pay 9% interest semiannually on June 30 and December 31. The bonds are sold at par.

**1.** How much interest will Kidman pay (in cash) to the bondholders every six months?

**2.** Prepare journal entries to record (*a*) the issuance of bonds on January 1, 2011; (*b*) the first interest payment on June 30, 2011; and (*c*) the second interest payment on December 31, 2011.

**3.** Prepare the journal entry for issuance assuming the bonds are issued at (*a*) 98 and (*b*) 102.

**Exercise 14-1**
Recording bond issuance and interest

**P1**

Moss issues bonds with a par value of $90,000 on January 1, 2011. The bonds' annual contract rate is 8%, and interest is paid semiannually on June 30 and December 31. The bonds mature in three years. The annual market rate at the date of issuance is 10%, and the bonds are sold for $85,431.

**1.** What is the amount of the discount on these bonds at issuance?

**2.** How much total bond interest expense will be recognized over the life of these bonds?

**3.** Prepare an amortization table like the one in Exhibit 14.7 for these bonds; use the straight-line method to amortize the discount.

**Exercise 14-2**
Straight-line amortization of bond discount

**P2**

Welch issues bonds dated January 1, 2011, with a par value of $250,000. The bonds' annual contract rate is 9%, and interest is paid semiannually on June 30 and December 31. The bonds mature in three years. The annual market rate at the date of issuance is 12%, and the bonds are sold for $231,570.

**1.** What is the amount of the discount on these bonds at issuance?

**2.** How much total bond interest expense will be recognized over the life of these bonds?

**3.** Prepare an amortization table like the one in Exhibit 14B.1 for these bonds; use the effective interest method to amortize the discount.

**Exercise 14-3**[B]
Effective interest amortization of bond discount

**P2**

Prairie Dunes Co. issues bonds dated January 1, 2011, with a par value of $800,000. The bonds' annual contract rate is 13%, and interest is paid semiannually on June 30 and December 31. The bonds mature in three years. The annual market rate at the date of issuance is 12%, and the bonds are sold for $819,700.

**1.** What is the amount of the premium on these bonds at issuance?

**2.** How much total bond interest expense will be recognized over the life of these bonds?

**3.** Prepare an amortization table like the one in Exhibit 14.11 for these bonds; use the straight-line method to amortize the premium.

**Exercise 14-4**
Straight-line amortization of bond premium

**P3**

**Exercise 14-5ᴮ**
Effective interest amortization of bond premium   P3

Refer to the bond details in Exercise 14-4 and prepare an amortization table like the one in Exhibit 14B.2 for these bonds using the effective interest method to amortize the premium.

**Exercise 14-6**
Recording bond issuance and premium amortization
P1   P3

Jobbs Company issues 10%, five-year bonds, on December 31, 2010, with a par value of $100,000 and semiannual interest payments. Use the following straight-line bond amortization table and prepare journal entries to record (a) the issuance of bonds on December 31, 2010; (b) the first interest payment on June 30, 2011; and (c) the second interest payment on December 31, 2011.

| Semiannual Period-End | Unamortized Premium | Carrying Value |
|---|---|---|
| (0)   12/31/2010 ................. | $8,111 | $108,111 |
| (1)    6/30/2011 ................. | 7,300 | 107,300 |
| (2)   12/31/2011 ................. | 6,489 | 106,489 |

**Exercise 14-7**
Recording bond issuance and discount amortization
P1   P2

Matchbox Company issues 6%, four-year bonds, on December 31, 2011, with a par value of $100,000 and semiannual interest payments. Use the following straight-line bond amortization table and prepare journal entries to record (a) the issuance of bonds on December 31, 2011; (b) the first interest payment on June 30, 2012; and (c) the second interest payment on December 31, 2012.

| Semiannual Period-End | Unamortized Discount | Carrying Value |
|---|---|---|
| (0)   12/31/2011 ................. | $6,733 | $93,267 |
| (1)    6/30/2012 ................. | 5,891 | 94,109 |
| (2)   12/31/2012 ................. | 5,049 | 94,951 |

**Exercise 14-8**
Recording bond issuance and discount amortization
P1   P2

Oneil Company issues 5%, two-year bonds, on December 31, 2011, with a par value of $100,000 and semi-annual interest payments. Use the following straight-line bond amortization table and prepare journal entries to record (a) the issuance of bonds on December 31, 2011; (b) the first through fourth interest payments on each June 30 and December 31; and (c) the maturity of the bond on December 31, 2013.

| Semiannual Period-End | Unamortized Discount | Carrying Value |
|---|---|---|
| (0)   12/31/2011 ................. | $6,000 | $ 94,000 |
| (1)    6/30/2012 ................. | 4,500 | 95,500 |
| (2)   12/31/2012 ................. | 3,000 | 97,000 |
| (3)    6/30/2013 ................. | 1,500 | 98,500 |
| (4)   12/31/2013 ................. | 0 | 100,000 |

**Exercise 14-9**
Computing bond interest and price; recording bond issuance

P2

Jester Company issues bonds with a par value of $600,000 on their stated issue date. The bonds mature in 10 years and pay 6% annual interest in semiannual payments. On the issue date, the annual market rate for the bonds is 8%.

1. What is the amount of each semiannual interest payment for these bonds?
2. How many semiannual interest payments will be made on these bonds over their life?
3. Use the interest rates given to determine whether the bonds are issued at par, at a discount, or at a premium.

**Check**   (4) $518,465

4. Compute the price of the bonds as of their issue date.
5. Prepare the journal entry to record the bonds' issuance.

**Exercise 14-10**
Computing bond interest and price; recording bond issuance

P3

Metro Company issues bonds with a par value of $75,000 on their stated issue date. The bonds mature in five years and pay 10% annual interest in semiannual payments. On the issue date, the annual market rate for the bonds is 8%.

1. What is the amount of each semiannual interest payment for these bonds?
2. How many semiannual interest payments will be made on these bonds over their life?
3. Use the interest rates given to determine whether the bonds are issued at par, at a discount, or at a premium.

**4.** Compute the price of the bonds as of their issue date.

**5.** Prepare the journal entry to record the bonds' issuance.

**Check**   (4) $81,086

---

On January 1, 2011, Steadman issues $350,000 of 10%, 15-year bonds at a price of 97¾. Six years later, on January 1, 2017, Steadman retires 20% of these bonds by buying them on the open market at 104½. All interest is accounted for and paid through December 31, 2016, the day before the purchase. The straight-line method is used to amortize any bond discount.

**1.** How much does the company receive when it issues the bonds on January 1, 2011?

**2.** What is the amount of the discount on the bonds at January 1, 2011?

**3.** How much amortization of the discount is recorded on the bonds for the entire period from January 1, 2011, through December 31, 2016?

**4.** What is the carrying (book) value of the bonds as of the close of business on December 31, 2016? What is the carrying value of the 20% soon-to-be-retired bonds on this same date?

**5.** How much did the company pay on January 1, 2017, to purchase the bonds that it retired?

**6.** What is the amount of the recorded gain or loss from retiring the bonds?

**7.** Prepare the journal entry to record the bond retirement at January 1, 2017.

**Exercise 14-11**
Bond computations, straight-line amortization, and bond retirement
**P2  P4**

**Check**   (6) $4,095 loss

---

On May 1, 2011, Fellenger Enterprises issues bonds dated January 1, 2011, that have a $1,700,000 par value, mature in 20 years, and pay 9% interest semiannually on June 30 and December 31. The bonds are sold at par plus four months' accrued interest.

**1.** How much accrued interest do the bond purchasers pay Fellenger on May 1, 2011?

**2.** Prepare Fellenger's journal entries to record (*a*) the issuance of bonds on May 1, 2011; (*b*) the first interest payment on June 30, 2011; and (*c*) the second interest payment on December 31, 2011.

**Exercise 14-12<sup>C</sup>**
Recording bond issuance with accrued interest
**C4  P1**

**Check**   (1) $51,000

---

Simon issues four-year bonds with a $50,000 par value on June 1, 2011, at a price of $47,974. The annual contract rate is 7%, and interest is paid semiannually on November 30 and May 31.

**1.** Prepare an amortization table like the one in Exhibit 14.7 for these bonds. Use the straight-line method of interest amortization.

**2.** Prepare journal entries to record the first two interest payments and to accrue interest as of December 31, 2011.

**Exercise 14-13**
Straight-line amortization and accrued bond interest expense
**P1  P2**

---

On January 1, 2011, Randa borrows $25,000 cash by signing a four-year, 7% installment note. The note requires four equal total payments of accrued interest and principal on December 31 of each year from 2011 through 2014.

**1.** Compute the amount of each of the four equal total payments.

**2.** Prepare an amortization table for this installment note like the one in Exhibit 14.14.

**Exercise 14-14**
Installment note with equal total payments **C1  P5**

**Check**   (1) $7,381

---

Use the information in Exercise 14-14 to prepare the journal entries for Randa to record the loan on January 1, 2011, and the four payments from December 31, 2011, through December 31, 2014.

**Exercise 14-15**
Installment note entries  **P5**

---

Ramirez Company is considering a project that will require a $500,000 loan. It presently has total liabilities of $220,000, and total assets of $620,000.

**1.** Compute Ramirez's (*a*) present debt-to-equity ratio and (*b*) the debt-to-equity ratio assuming it borrows $500,000 to fund the project.

**2.** Evaluate and discuss the level of risk involved if Ramirez borrows the funds to pursue the project.

**Exercise 14-16**
Applying debt-to-equity ratio
**A3**

---

Indicate whether the company in each separate case 1 through 3 has entered into an operating lease or a capital lease.

**1.** The present value of the lease payments is 95% of the leased asset's market value, and the lease term is 70% of the leased asset's useful life.

**2.** The title is transferred to the lessee, the lessee can purchase the asset for $1 at the end of the lease, and the lease term is five years. The leased asset has an expected useful life of six years.

**3.** The lessor retains title to the asset, and the lease term is three years on an asset that has a five-year useful life.

**Exercise 14-17<sup>D</sup>**
Identifying capital and operating leases
**C4**

---

**Exercise 14-18^D**
Accounting for capital lease

**C4**

Flyer (lessee) signs a five-year capital lease for office equipment with a $20,000 annual lease payment. The present value of the five annual lease payments is $82,000, based on a 7% interest rate.

1. Prepare the journal entry Flyer will record at inception of the lease.
2. If the leased asset has a five-year useful life with no salvage value, prepare the journal entry Flyer will record each year to recognize depreciation expense related to the leased asset.

---

**Exercise 14-19^D**
Analyzing lease options

**C2  C3  C4**

**General Motors** advertised three alternatives for a 25-month lease on a new Blazer: (1) zero dollars down and a lease payment of $1,750 per month for 25 months, (2) $5,000 down and $1,500 per month for 25 months, or (3) $38,500 down and no payments for 25 months. Use the present value Table B.3 in Appendix B to determine which is the best alternative (assume you have enough cash to accept any alternative and the annual interest rate is 12% compounded monthly).

---

**Exercise 14-20**
Accounting for long-term liabilities under IFRS

**P1  P2  P3**

**Heineken N.V.** reports the following information for its Loans and Borrowings as of December 31, 2008, including proceeds and repayments for the year ended December 31, 2008 (euros in millions).

| **Loans and borrowings (noncurrent liabilities)** | |
| --- | --- |
| Loans and borrowings, December 31, 2008 . . . . . . . . . . . . . . . . . . . . | € 9,084 |
| Proceeds (cash) from issuances of loans and borrowings . . . . . . . . . | 6,361 |
| Repayments (in cash) of loans and borrowings . . . . . . . . . . . . . . . . | (2,532) |

1. Prepare Heineken's journal entry to record its cash proceeds from issuances of its loans and borrowings for 2008. Assume that the par value of these issuances is €6,000.
2. Prepare Heineken's journal entry to record its cash repayments of its loans and borrowings for 2008. Assume that the par value of these issuances is €2,400, and the premium on them is €32.
3. Compute the discount or premium on its loans and borrowings as of December 31, 2008, assuming that the par value of these liabilities is €9,000.
4. Given the facts in part 3 and viewing the entirety of loans and borrowings as one issuance, was the contract rate on these loans and borrowings higher or lower than the market rate at the time of issuance? Explain. (Assume that Heineken's credit rating has remained the same.)

---

<sup>Mc Graw Hill</sup> **connect**™

## PROBLEM SET A

**Problem 14-1A**
Computing bond price and recording issuance

**P1  P2  P3**

**Check** (1) Premium, $2,718

(3) Discount, $2,294

| Round dollar amounts to the nearest whole dollar. Assume no reversing entries are used. |
| --- |

Stowers Research issues bonds dated January 1, 2011, that pay interest semiannually on June 30 and December 31. The bonds have a $20,000 par value and an annual contract rate of 10%, and they mature in 10 years.

**Required**

For each of the following three separate situations, (a) determine the bonds' issue price on January 1, 2011, and (b) prepare the journal entry to record their issuance.

1. The market rate at the date of issuance is 8%.
2. The market rate at the date of issuance is 10%.
3. The market rate at the date of issuance is 12%.

---

**Problem 14-2A**
Straight-line amortization of bond discount

**P1  P2**

mhhe.com/wildFAP20e

**Check** (3) $2,071,776

(4) 12/31/2012 carrying value, $1,764,460

Heathrow issues $2,000,000 of 6%, 15-year bonds dated January 1, 2011, that pay interest semiannually on June 30 and December 31. The bonds are issued at a price of $1,728,224.

**Required**

1. Prepare the January 1, 2011, journal entry to record the bonds' issuance.
2. For each semiannual period, compute (a) the cash payment, (b) the straight-line discount amortization, and (c) the bond interest expense.
3. Determine the total bond interest expense to be recognized over the bonds' life.
4. Prepare the first two years of an amortization table like Exhibit 14.7 using the straight-line method.
5. Prepare the journal entries to record the first two interest payments.

Refer to the bond details in Problem 14-2A, *except* assume that the bonds are issued at a price of $2,447,990.

**Problem 14-3A**
Straight-line amortization of bond premium

P1  P3

**Required**

1. Prepare the January 1, 2011, journal entry to record the bonds' issuance.
2. For each semiannual period, compute (*a*) the cash payment, (*b*) the straight-line premium amortization, and (*c*) the bond interest expense.
3. Determine the total bond interest expense to be recognized over the bonds' life.
4. Prepare the first two years of an amortization table like Exhibit 14.7 using the straight-line method.
5. Prepare the journal entries to record the first two interest payments.

**Check**  (3) $1,352,010

(4) 12/31/2012 carrying value, $2,388,258

---

Saturn issues 6.5%, five-year bonds dated January 1, 2011, with a $500,000 par value. The bonds pay interest on June 30 and December 31 and are issued at a price of $510,666. The annual market rate is 6% on the issue date.

**Problem 14-4A**
Straight-line amortization of bond premium

P1  P3

e**X**cel

mhhe.com/wildFAP20e

**Required**

1. Calculate the total bond interest expense over the bonds' life.
2. Prepare a straight-line amortization table like Exhibit 14.11 for the bonds' life.
3. Prepare the journal entries to record the first two interest payments.

**Check**  (2) 6/30/2013 carrying value, $505,331

---

Refer to the bond details in Problem 14-4A.

**Problem 14-5A**[B]
Effective interest amortization of bond premium; computing bond price  P1  P3

**Required**

1. Compute the total bond interest expense over the bonds' life.
2. Prepare an effective interest amortization table like the one in Exhibit 14B.2 for the bonds' life.
3. Prepare the journal entries to record the first two interest payments.
4. Use the market rate at issuance to compute the present value of the remaining cash flows for these bonds as of December 31, 2013. Compare your answer with the amount shown on the amortization table as the balance for that date (from part 2) and explain your findings.

**Check**  (2) 6/30/2013 carrying value, $505,728

(4) $504,653

---

Patton issues $650,000 of 5%, four-year bonds dated January 1, 2011, that pay interest semiannually on June 30 and December 31. They are issued at $584,361 and their market rate is 8% at the issue date.

**Problem 14-6A**
Straight-line amortization of bond discount

P1  P2

**Required**

1. Prepare the January 1, 2011, journal entry to record the bonds' issuance.
2. Determine the total bond interest expense to be recognized over the bonds' life.
3. Prepare a straight-line amortization table like the one in Exhibit 14.7 for the bonds' first two years.
4. Prepare the journal entries to record the first two interest payments.

**Check**  (2) $195,639

(3) 12/31/2012 carrying value, $617,181

**Analysis Component**

5. Assume the market rate on January 1, 2011, is 4% instead of 8%. Without providing numbers, describe how this change affects the amounts reported on Patton's financial statements.

---

Refer to the bond details in Problem 14-6A.

**Problem 14-7A**[B]
Effective interest amortization of bond discount  P1  P2

**Required**

1. Prepare the January 1, 2011, journal entry to record the bonds' issuance.
2. Determine the total bond interest expense to be recognized over the bonds' life.
3. Prepare an effective interest amortization table like the one in Exhibit 14B.1 for the bonds' first two years.
4. Prepare the journal entries to record the first two interest payments.

**Check**  (2) $195,639

(3) 12/31/2012 carrying value, $614,614

mhhe.com/wildFAP20e

## Problem 14-8Aᴮ
Effective interest amortization of bond premium; retiring bonds

P1  P3  P4

**Check** (3) 6/30/2012 carrying value, $91,224

(5) $2,635 gain

mhhe.com/wildFAP20e

McFad issues $90,000 of 11%, three-year bonds dated January 1, 2011, that pay interest semiannually on June 30 and December 31. They are issued at $92,283. Their market rate is 10% at the issue date.

**Required**

1. Prepare the January 1, 2011, journal entry to record the bonds' issuance.
2. Determine the total bond interest expense to be recognized over the bonds' life.
3. Prepare an effective interest amortization table like Exhibit 14B.2 for the bonds' first two years.
4. Prepare the journal entries to record the first two interest payments.
5. Prepare the journal entry to record the bonds' retirement on January 1, 2013, at 98.

**Analysis Component**

6. Assume that the market rate on January 1, 2011, is 12% instead of 10%. Without presenting numbers, describe how this change affects the amounts reported on McFad's financial statements.

---

## Problem 14-9A
Installment notes

C1  P5

**Check** (2) 10/31/2015 ending balance, $92,759

On November 1, 2011, Leetch Ltd. borrows $400,000 cash from a bank by signing a five-year installment note bearing 8% interest. The note requires equal total payments each year on October 31.

**Required**

1. Compute the total amount of each installment payment.
2. Complete an amortization table for this installment note similar to the one in Exhibit 14.14.
3. Prepare the journal entries in which Leetch records (a) accrued interest as of December 31, 2011 (the end of its annual reporting period), and (b) the first annual payment on the note.

---

## Problem 14-10A
Applying the debt-to-equity ratio

A3

At the end of the current year, the following information is available for both Kumar Company and Asher Company.

|                      | Kumar Company | Asher Company |
|----------------------|---------------|---------------|
| Total assets ........... | $2,254,500 | $1,123,500 |
| Total liabilities ........ | 904,500 | 598,500 |
| Total equity .......... | 1,350,000 | 525,000 |

**Required**

1. Compute the debt-to-equity ratios for both companies.
2. Comment on your results and discuss the riskiness of each company's financing structure.

---

## Problem 14-11Aᴰ
Capital lease accounting

C4

**Check** (1) $79,854

(3) Year 3 ending balance, $35,664

Montana Company signs a five-year capital lease with Elway Company for office equipment. The annual lease payment is $20,000, and the interest rate is 8%.

**Required**

1. Compute the present value of Montana's five-year lease payments.
2. Prepare the journal entry to record Montana's capital lease at its inception.
3. Complete a lease payment schedule for the five years of the lease with the following headings. Assume that the beginning balance of the lease liability (present value of lease payments) is $79,854. (*Hint:* To find the amount allocated to interest in year 1, multiply the interest rate by the beginning-of-year lease liability. The amount of the annual lease payment not allocated to interest is allocated to principal. Reduce the lease liability by the amount allocated to principal to update the lease liability at each year-end.)

| Period Ending Date | Beginning Balance of Lease Liability | Interest on Lease Liability | Reduction of Lease Liability | Cash Lease Payment | Ending Balance of Lease Liability |
|---|---|---|---|---|---|
|  |  |  |  |  |  |

4. Use straight-line depreciation and prepare the journal entry to depreciate the leased asset at the end of year 1. Assume zero salvage value and a five-year life for the office equipment.

Sedona Systems issues bonds dated January 1, 2011, that pay interest semiannually on June 30 and December 31. The bonds have a $45,000 par value and an annual contract rate of 12%, and they mature in five years.

**Required**

For each of the following three separate situations, (*a*) determine the bonds' issue price on January 1, 2011, and (*b*) prepare the journal entry to record their issuance.

**1.** The market rate at the date of issuance is 10%.
**2.** The market rate at the date of issuance is 12%.
**3.** The market rate at the date of issuance is 14%.

**PROBLEM SET B**

**Problem 14-1B**
Computing bond price and recording issuance
P1 P2 P3

**Check** (1) Premium, $3,475

(3) Discount, $3,162

---

ParFour issues $1,700,000 of 10%, 10-year bonds dated January 1, 2011, that pay interest semiannually on June 30 and December 31. The bonds are issued at a price of $1,505,001.

**Required**

**1.** Prepare the January 1, 2011, journal entry to record the bonds' issuance.
**2.** For each semiannual period, compute (*a*) the cash payment, (*b*) the straight-line discount amortization, and (*c*) the bond interest expense.
**3.** Determine the total bond interest expense to be recognized over the bonds' life.
**4.** Prepare the first two years of an amortization table like Exhibit 14.7 using the straight-line method.
**5.** Prepare the journal entries to record the first two interest payments.

**Problem 14-2B**
Straight-line amortization of bond discount
P1 P2

**Check** (3) $1,894,999

(4) 6/30/2012 carrying value, $1,534,251

---

Refer to the bond details in Problem 14-2B, *except* assume that the bonds are issued at a price of $2,096,466.

**Required**

**1.** Prepare the January 1, 2011, journal entry to record the bonds' issuance.
**2.** For each semiannual period, compute (*a*) the cash payment, (*b*) the straight-line premium amortization, and (*c*) the bond interest expense.
**3.** Determine the total bond interest expense to be recognized over the bonds' life.
**4.** Prepare the first two years of an amortization table like Exhibit 14.7 using the straight-line method.
**5.** Prepare the journal entries to record the first two interest payments.

**Problem 14-3B**
Straight-line amortization of bond premium
P1 P3

**Check** (3) $1,303,534

(4) 6/30/2012 carrying value, $2,036,997

---

Zooba Company issues 9%, five-year bonds dated January 1, 2011, with a $160,000 par value. The bonds pay interest on June 30 and December 31 and are issued at a price of $166,494. Their annual market rate is 8% on the issue date.

**Required**

**1.** Calculate the total bond interest expense over the bonds' life.
**2.** Prepare a straight-line amortization table like Exhibit 14.11 for the bonds' life.
**3.** Prepare the journal entries to record the first two interest payments.

**Problem 14-4B**
Straight-line amortization of bond premium
P1 P3

**Check** (2) 6/30/2013 carrying value, $163,249

---

Refer to the bond details in Problem 14-4B.

**Required**

**1.** Compute the total bond interest expense over the bonds' life.
**2.** Prepare an effective interest amortization table like the one in Exhibit 14B.2 for the bonds' life.
**3.** Prepare the journal entries to record the first two interest payments.
**4.** Use the market rate at issuance to compute the present value of the remaining cash flows for these bonds as of December 31, 2013. Compare your answer with the amount shown on the amortization table as the balance for that date (from part 2) and explain your findings.

**Problem 14-5B[B]**
Effective interest amortization of bond premium; computing bond price P1 P3

**Check** (2) 6/30/2013 carrying value, $163,568

(4) $162,903

## Problem 14-6B
Straight-line amortization of bond discount

P1  P2

**Check** (2) $128,753

(3) 6/30/2012 carrying value, $101,323

Roney issues $120,000 of 6%, 15-year bonds dated January 1, 2011, that pay interest semiannually on June 30 and December 31. They are issued at $99,247, and their market rate is 8% at the issue date.

**Required**

1. Prepare the January 1, 2011, journal entry to record the bonds' issuance.
2. Determine the total bond interest expense to be recognized over the life of the bonds.
3. Prepare a straight-line amortization table like the one in Exhibit 14.7 for the bonds' first two years.
4. Prepare the journal entries to record the first two interest payments.

## Problem 14-7B[B]
Effective interest amortization of bond discount

P1  P2

**Check** (2) $128,753;

(3) 6/30/2012 carrying value, $100,402

Refer to the bond details in Problem 14-6B.

**Required**

1. Prepare the January 1, 2011, journal entry to record the bonds' issuance.
2. Determine the total bond interest expense to be recognized over the bonds' life.
3. Prepare an effective interest amortization table like the one in Exhibit 14B.1 for the bonds' first two years.
4. Prepare the journal entries to record the first two interest payments.

## Problem 14-8B[B]
Effective interest amortization of bond premium; retiring bonds

P1  P3  P4

**Check** (3) 6/30/2012 carrying value, $958,406

(5) $6,174 loss

Hutton issues $900,000 of 13%, four-year bonds dated January 1, 2011, that pay interest semiannually on June 30 and December 31. They are issued at $987,217, and their market rate is 10% at the issue date.

**Required**

1. Prepare the January 1, 2011, journal entry to record the bonds' issuance.
2. Determine the total bond interest expense to be recognized over the bonds' life.
3. Prepare an effective interest amortization table like the one in Exhibit 14B.2 for the bonds' first two years.
4. Prepare the journal entries to record the first two interest payments.
5. Prepare the journal entry to record the bonds' retirement on January 1, 2013, at 106.

### Analysis Component

6. Assume that the market rate on January 1, 2011, is 14% instead of 10%. Without presenting numbers, describe how this change affects the amounts reported on Hutton's financial statements.

## Problem 14-9B
Installment notes

C1  P5

**Check** (2) 9/30/2013 ending balance, $109,673

On October 1, 2011, Milan Enterprises borrows $300,000 cash from a bank by signing a three-year installment note bearing 10% interest. The note requires equal total payments each year on September 30.

**Required**

1. Compute the total amount of each installment payment.
2. Complete an amortization table for this installment note similar to the one in Exhibit 14.14.
3. Prepare the journal entries to record (a) accrued interest as of December 31, 2011 (the end of its annual reporting period) and (b) the first annual payment on the note.

## Problem 14-10B
Applying the debt-to-equity ratio

A3

At the end of the current year, the following information is available for both West Elm Company and East Park Company.

|  | West Elm Company | East Park Company |
|---|---|---|
| Total assets .......... | $396,396 | $1,650,000 |
| Total liabilities ........ | 178,596 | 1,237,500 |
| Total equity .......... | 217,800 | 412,500 |

**Required**

1. Compute the debt-to-equity ratios for both companies.
2. Comment on your results and discuss what they imply about the relative riskiness of these companies.

Preston Company signs a five-year capital lease with Starbuck Company for office equipment. The annual lease payment is $10,000, and the interest rate is 10%.

**Required**

1. Compute the present value of Preston's lease payments.
2. Prepare the journal entry to record Preston's capital lease at its inception.
3. Complete a lease payment schedule for the five years of the lease with the following headings. Assume that the beginning balance of the lease liability (present value of lease payments) is $37,908. (*Hint:* To find the amount allocated to interest in year 1, multiply the interest rate by the beginning-of-year lease liability. The amount of the annual lease payment not allocated to interest is allocated to principal. Reduce the lease liability by the amount allocated to principal to update the lease liability at each year-end.)

| Period Ending Date | Beginning Balance of Lease Liability | Interest on Lease Liability | Reduction of Lease Liability | Cash Lease Payment | Ending Balance of Lease Liability |
|---|---|---|---|---|---|
| | | | | | |

4. Use straight-line depreciation and prepare the journal entry to depreciate the leased asset at the end of year 1. Assume zero salvage value and a five-year life for the office equipment.

**Problem 14-11B**ᴰ
Capital lease accounting
C4

**Check** (1) $37,908

(3) Year 3 ending balance, $17,356

---

(*This serial problem began in Chapter 1 and continues through most of the book. If previous chapter segments were not completed, the serial problem can begin at this point. It is helpful, but not necessary, to use the Working Papers that accompany the book.*)

**SP 14** Santana Rey has consulted with her local banker and is considering financing an expansion of her business by obtaining a long-term bank loan. Selected account balances at March 31, 2012, for Business Solutions follow.

| Total assets ........ | $120,268 | Total liabilities ....... | $875 | Total equity ....... | $119,393 |
|---|---|---|---|---|---|

**Required**

1. The bank has offered a long-term secured note to Business Solutions. The bank's loan procedures require that a client's debt-to-equity ratio not exceed 0.8. As of March 31, 2012, what is the maximum amount that Business Solutions could borrow from this bank (rounded to nearest dollar)?
2. If Business Solutions borrows the maximum amount allowed from the bank, what percentage of assets would be financed (*a*) by debt and (*b*) by equity?
3. What are some factors Santana Rey should consider before borrowing the funds?

**SERIAL PROBLEM**
Business Solutions
A1 A3

**Check** (1) $94,639

---

**Beyond the Numbers**

**BTN 14-1** Refer to **Research In Motion**'s financial statements in Appendix A to answer the following.

1. Identify the items, if any, that make up RIM's long-term debt as reported on its balance sheet at February 27, 2010.
2. Assume that RIM has $402,000 thousand in convertible debentures that carry a 2.25% contract rate of interest. How much annual cash interest must be paid on those convertible debentures?
3. How much cash did it generate from issuance of debt for the year-ended February 27, 2010? How much cash did it use for repayments of debt for that same year?

**REPORTING IN ACTION**
A1 A2

*RIM*

**Fast Forward**

4. Access Research In Motion's financial statements for the years ending after February 27, 2010, from its Website (**RIM.com**) or the SEC's EDGAR database (**www.sec.gov**). Has it issued additional long-term debt since the year-end February 27, 2010? If yes, identify the amount(s).

**COMPARATIVE ANALYSIS**

A3

*RIM*

Apple

**BTN 14-2**  Key figures for **Research In Motion** and **Apple** follow.

| ($ millions) | Research In Motion | | Apple | |
|---|---|---|---|---|
| | Current Year | Prior Year | Current Year | Prior Year |
| Total assets ........... | $10,204 | $8,101 | $47,501 | $36,171 |
| Total liabilities ......... | 2,602 | 2,227 | 15,861 | 13,874 |
| Total equity ........... | 7,603 | 5,874 | 31,640 | 22,297 |

**Required**

1. Compute the debt-to-equity ratios for Research In Motion and Apple for both the current year and the prior year.

2. Use the ratios you computed in part 1 to determine which company's financing structure is least risky. Assume an industry average of 0.64 for debt-to-equity.

**ETHICS CHALLENGE**

C4 A1

**BTN 14-3**  Holly County needs a new county government building that would cost $24 million. The politicians feel that voters will not approve a municipal bond issue to fund the building since it would increase taxes. They opt to have a state bank issue $24 million of tax-exempt securities to pay for the building construction. The county then will make yearly lease payments (of principal and interest) to repay the obligation. Unlike conventional municipal bonds, the lease payments are not binding obligations on the county and, therefore, require no voter approval.

**Required**

1. Do you think the actions of the politicians and the bankers in this situation are ethical?

2. How do the tax-exempt securities used to pay for the building compare in risk to a conventional municipal bond issued by Holly County?

**COMMUNICATING IN PRACTICE**

P3

**BTN 14-4**  Your business associate mentions that she is considering investing in corporate bonds currently selling at a premium. She says that since the bonds are selling at a premium, they are highly valued and her investment will yield more than the going rate of return for the risk involved. Reply with a memorandum to confirm or correct your associate's interpretation of premium bonds.

**TAKING IT TO THE NET**

A2

**BTN 14-5**  Access the March 25, 2010, filing of the 10-K report of **Home Depot** for the year ended January 31, 2010, from **www.sec.gov** (Ticker: HD). Refer to Home Depot's balance sheet, including its note 4 (on debt).

**Required**

1. Identify Home Depot's long-term liabilities and the amounts for those liabilities from Home Depot's balance sheet at January 31, 2010.

2. Review Home Depot's note 5. The note reports that as of January 31, 2010, it had $2.96 billion of "5.875% Senior Notes; due December 16, 2036; interest payable semiannually on June 16 and December 16." These notes have a face value of $3.0 billion and were originally issued at $2.958 billion.

   a. Why would Home Depot issue $3.0 billion of its notes for only $2.958 billion?

   b. How much cash interest must Home Depot pay each June 16 and December 16 on these notes?

**TEAMWORK IN ACTION**

P2 P3

**BTN 14-6ᴮ**  Break into teams and complete the following requirements related to effective interest amortization for a premium bond.

1. Each team member is to independently prepare a blank table with proper headings for amortization of a bond premium. When all have finished, compare tables and ensure that all are in agreement.

*Parts 2 and 3 require use of these facts:* On January 1, 2010, Caleb issues $100,000, 9%, five-year bonds at 104.1. The market rate at issuance is 8%. Caleb pays interest semiannually on June 30 and December 31.

2. In rotation, *each* team member must explain how to complete *one* line of the bond amortization table, including all computations for his or her line. (Round amounts to the nearest dollar.) All members are to fill in their tables during this process. You need not finish the table; stop after all members have explained a line.

**3.** In rotation, *each* team member is to identify a separate column of the table and indicate what the final number in that column will be and explain the reasoning.

**4.** Reach a team consensus as to what the total bond interest expense on this bond issue will be if the bond is not retired before maturity.

**5.** As a team, prepare a list of similarities and differences between the amortization table just prepared and the amortization table if the bond had been issued at a discount.

**Hint:** Rotate teams to report on parts 4 and 5. Consider requiring entries for issuance and interest payments.

---

**BTN 14-7**   Warren Brown is the founder of Cake Love. Assume that his company currently has $250,000 in equity, and he is considering a $100,000 expansion to meet increased demand. The $100,000 expansion would yield $16,000 in additional annual income before interest expense. Assume that the business currently earns $40,000 annual income before interest expense of $10,000, yielding a return on equity of 12% ($30,000/$250,000). To fund the expansion, he is considering the issuance of a 10-year, $100,000 note with annual interest payments (the principal due at the end of 10 years).

**ENTREPRENEURIAL DECISION**

A1

*Required*

**1.** Using return on equity as the decision criterion, show computations to support or reject the expansion if interest on the $100,000 note is (*a*) 10%, (*b*) 15%, (*c*) 16%, (*d*) 17%, and (*e*) 20%.

**2.** What general rule do the results in part 1 illustrate?

---

**BTN 14-8**   Visit your city or county library. Ask the librarian to help you locate the recent financial records of your city or county government. Examine those records.

**HITTING THE ROAD**

A1

*Required*

**1.** Determine the amount of long-term bonds and notes currently outstanding.

**2.** Read the supporting information to your municipality's financial statements and record

   **a.** The market interest rate(s) when the bonds and/or notes were issued.

   **b.** The date(s) when the bonds and/or notes will mature.

   **c.** Any rating(s) on the bonds and/or notes received from Moody's, Standard & Poor's, or another rating agency.

---

**BTN 14-9**   Nokia (www.Nokia.com), Research In Motion, and Apple are competitors in the global marketplace. Selected results from these companies follow.

**GLOBAL DECISION**

A3

**NOKIA**

**RIM**

Apple

| Key Figures | Nokia (EURm) Current Year | Nokia (EURm) Prior Year | Research In Motion ($ millions) Current Year | Research In Motion ($ millions) Prior Year | Apple ($ millions) Current Year | Apple ($ millions) Prior Year |
|---|---|---|---|---|---|---|
| Total assets . . . . . . . . . . . . . . . | €35,738 | €39,582 | $10,204 | $8,101 | $47,501 | $36,171 |
| Total liabilities . . . . . . . . . . . . . | 20,989 | 23,072 | 2,602 | 2,227 | 15,861 | 13,874 |
| Total equity . . . . . . . . . . . . . . | 14,749 | 16,510 | 7,603 | 5,874 | 31,640 | 22,297 |
| Debt-to-equity ratio . . . . . . . . | ? | ? | 0.34 | 0.38 | 0.50 | 0.62 |

*Required*

**1.** Compute Nokia's debt-to-equity ratios for the current year and the prior year.

**2.** Use the data provided and the ratios computed in part 1 to determine which company's financing structure is least risky.

---

## ANSWERS TO MULTIPLE CHOICE QUIZ

**1.** b

**2.** a

**3.** c; $500,000 × 0.08 × ½ year = $20,000

**4.** a; Cash interest paid = $100,000 × 5% × ½ year = $2,500
Discount amortization = ($100,000 − $95,735)/10 periods = $426.50
Interest expense = $2,500.00 + $426.50 = $2,926.50

**5.** e; ($373,745 − $350,000)/16 periods = $1,484

# 15

# Investments and International Operations

## A Look Back

Chapter 14 focused on long-term liabilities—a main part of most companies' financing. We explained how to value, record, amortize, and report these liabilities in financial statements.

## A Look at This Chapter

This chapter focuses on investments in securities. We explain how to identify, account for, and report investments in both debt and equity securities. We also explain accounting for transactions listed in a foreign currency.

## A Look Ahead

Chapter 16 focuses on reporting and analyzing a company's cash flows. Special emphasis is directed at the statement of cash flows reported under the indirect method.

## Learning Objectives

### CONCEPTUAL

**C1** Distinguish between debt and equity securities and between short-term and long-term investments. (p. 596)

**C2** Describe how to report equity securities with controlling influence. (p. 603)

**C3** *Appendix 15A*—Explain foreign exchange rates and record transactions listed in a foreign currency. (p. 610)

### ANALYTICAL

**A1** Compute and analyze the components of return on total assets. (p. 605)

LP15

### PROCEDURAL

**P1** Account for trading securities. (p. 599)

**P2** Account for held-to-maturity securities. (p. 600)

**P3** Account for available-for-sale securities. (p. 600)

**P4** Account for equity securities with significant influence. (p. 602)

# Schooling the Market

*"There's this whole new emerging category of academic technology"*

—**MICHAEL CHASEN**

WASHINGTON, DC—Michael Chasen and Matthew Pittinsky had just finished college—Michael earning a degree in accounting and Matthew Pittinsky in education. Both took jobs at KPMG. "Matthew and I had decided to leave KPMG and start an e-learning business, which we called **Blackboard (Blackboard.com),**" explains Michael. "Campuses nationwide were beginning to connect to the Internet but had no way to put courses online."

What Michael and Matthew did was leverage online technology to enhance education and learning for both students and instructors. "[Students and instructors] want improved ease of use," insists Michael. "They want the teaching and learning kept not just inside the class, but outside the classroom." Michael and Matthew have been so successful that their company's operations now extend over many countries. "We not only continue to expand within higher education but we are expanding internationally," says Michael. "I travel all over the world for Blackboard."

This broad reach has led to business challenges involving both investments and international operations. "I am asked a lot of questions about . . . education on the Internet," explains Michael. "[Investments are] often one of the better ways to deploy capital."

Blackboard's annual report states: "[We] pursue strategic relationships with, acquisitions of, and investments in, companies that would enhance the technological features of our products, offer complementary products, services and technologies, or broaden the scope of our product offerings." Also, investments in international operations require them to translate their performance into U.S. dollars for financial reporting. Those tasks require knowledge of accounting and reporting requirements for investments, including investments in securities of other companies.

Blackboard's annual report reveals that it has "a variety of marketable investments." It reports that "for those investments in entities where the Company has significant influence over operations . . . [it] follows the equity method of accounting." It also explains that Blackboard "consolidates investments where it has a controlling financial interest." Still, Michael insists that their investment in the future of learning is the key. "We are very much focused on innovation," says Michael. "[The market's] ripe for a technology explosion in e-learning."

[Sources: *Blackboard Website,* January 2011; *Entrepreneur,* March 2009; *The New York Times,* November 2009; *The Washington Post,* August 2007; *Washington Business Journal,* October 2008]

This chapter's main focus is investments in securities. Many companies have investments, and many of these are in the form of debt and equity securities issued by other companies. We describe investments in these securities and how to account for them. An increasing number of companies also invest in international operations. We explain how to account for and report international transactions listed in foreign currencies.

**Investments and International Operations**

| Basics of Investments | Noninfluential Investments | Influential Investments |
|---|---|---|
| • Motivation for investments<br>• Short-term versus long-term<br>• Classification and reporting<br>• Accounting basics | • Trading securities<br>• Held-to-maturity securities<br>• Available-for-sale securities | • Securities with significant influence<br>• Securities with controlling influence<br>• Accounting summary |

# BASICS OF INVESTMENTS

**C1** Distinguish between debt and equity securities and between short-term and long-term investments.

This section describes the motivation for investments, the distinction between short- and long-term investments, and the different classes of investments.

## Motivation for Investments

Companies make investments for at least three reasons. First, companies transfer *excess cash* into investments to produce higher income. Second, some entities, such as mutual funds and pension funds, are set up to produce income from investments. Third, companies make investments for strategic reasons. Examples are investments in competitors, suppliers, and even customers. Exhibit 15.1 shows short-term (S-T) and long-term (L-T) investments as a percent of total assets for several companies.

**EXHIBIT 15.1**

Investments of Selected Companies

Percent of total assets

**Short-Term Investments** Cash equivalents are investments that are both readily converted to known amounts of cash and mature within three months. Many investments, however, mature between 3 and 12 months. These investments are **short-term investments,** also called *temporary investments* and *marketable securities*. Specifically, short-term investments are securities that (1) management intends to convert to cash within one year or the operating cycle, whichever is longer, and (2) are readily convertible to cash. Short-term investments are reported under current assets and serve a purpose similar to cash equivalents.

**Long-Term Investments** **Long-term investments** in securities are defined as those securities that are not readily convertible to cash or are not intended to be converted into cash in the short term. Long-term investments can also include funds earmarked for a special purpose, such as bond sinking funds and investments in land or other assets not used in the company's operations. Long-term investments are reported in the noncurrent section of the balance sheet, often in its own separate line titled *Long-Term Investments*.

**Debt Securities versus Equity Securities** Investments in securities can include both debt and equity securities. *Debt securities* reflect a creditor relationship such as investments in notes, bonds, and certificates of deposit; they are issued by governments, companies, and individuals. *Equity securities* reflect an owner relationship such as shares of stock issued by companies.

## Classification and Reporting

Accounting for investments in securities depends on three factors: (1) security type, either debt or equity, (2) the company's intent to hold the security either short term or long term, and (3) the company's (investor's) percent ownership in the other company's (investee's) equity securities. Exhibit 15.2 identifies five classes of securities using these three factors. It describes each of these five classes of securities and the standard reporting required under each class.

**EXHIBIT 15.2**

Investments in Securities

**Class**

| Trading | Held-to-Maturity | Available-for-Sale | Significant Influence | Controlling Influence |
|---|---|---|---|---|
| [Debt and noninfluential equity[a] securities that are actively traded] | [Debt securities intended to be held until maturity] | [Debt and noninfluential equity[a] securities] | [Equity securities with significant influence[b]] | [Equity securities with controlling influence[c]] |

**Reporting**

| Fair Value* | Amortized Cost | Fair Value** | Equity Method | Consolidation |
|---|---|---|---|---|

[a] Holding less than 20% of voting stock (equity securities only).   [b] Holding 20% or more, but not more than 50%, of voting stock.
[c] Holding more than 50% of voting stock.
\* Unrealized gains and losses reported on the income statement.
\*\* Unrealized gains and losses reported in the equity section of the balance sheet and in comprehensive income.

## Debt Securities: Accounting Basics

This section explains the accounting basics for *debt securities,* including that for acquisition, disposition, and any interest.

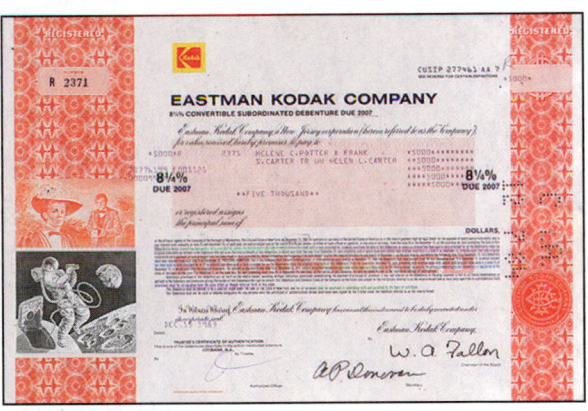

**Acquisition.**   Debt securities are recorded at cost when purchased. To illustrate, assume that Music City paid $29,500 plus a $500 brokerage fee on September 1, 2010, to buy Dell's 7%, two-year bonds payable with a $30,000 par value. The bonds pay interest semiannually on August 31 and February 28. Music City intends to hold the bonds until they mature on August 31, 2012; consequently, they are classified as held-to-maturity (HTM) securities. The entry to record this purchase follows. (If the maturity of the securities was short term, and management's intent was to hold them until they mature, then they would be classified as Short-Term Investments—HTM.)

| 2010 | | | |
|---|---|---|---|
| Sept. 1 | Long-Term Investments—HTM (Dell) . . . . . . . . . . . . . | 30,000 | |
| | Cash . . . . . . . . . . . . . . . . . . . . . . . . . . . . . . . . . . . . . | | 30,000 |
| | *Purchased bonds to be held to maturity.* | | |

Assets = Liabilities + Equity
+30,000
−30,000

**Interest earned.**   Interest revenue for investments in debt securities is recorded when earned. To illustrate, on December 31, 2010, at the end of its accounting period, Music City accrues interest receivable as follows.

| Dec. 31 | Interest Receivable . . . . . . . . . . . . . . . . . . . . . . . . . . . | 700 | |
|---|---|---|---|
| | Interest Revenue . . . . . . . . . . . . . . . . . . . . . . . . . . | | 700 |
| | *Accrued interest earned ($30,000 × 7% × 1/12).* | | |

Assets = Liabilities + Equity
+700            +700

The $700 reflects 4/6 of the semiannual cash receipt of interest—the portion Music City earned as of December 31. Relevant sections of Music City's financial statements at December 31, 2010, are shown in Exhibit 15.3.

**EXHIBIT 15.3**

Financial Statement Presentation
of Debt Securities

| On the income statement for year 2010: | |
|---|---|
| **Interest revenue** ................................................................. | **$   700** |
| On the December 31, 2010, balance sheet: | |
| **Long-term investments—Held-to-maturity securities (at amortized cost)** ......... | **$30,000** |

On February 28, 2011, Music City records receipt of semiannual interest.

Assets  =  Liabilities +  Equity
+1,050                        +350
−700

| Feb. 28 | Cash ......................................... | 1,050 | |
|---|---|---|---|
| | Interest Receivable ......................... | | 700 |
| | Interest Revenue ........................... | | 350 |
| | *Received six months' interest on Dell bonds.* | | |

**Disposition.**   When the bonds mature, the proceeds (not including the interest entry) are recorded as:

Assets  =  Liabilities +  Equity
+30,000
−30,000

| 2012 | | | |
|---|---|---|---|
| Aug. 31 | Cash ........................................ | 30,000 | |
| | Long-Term Investments—HTM (Dell)........... | | 30,000 |
| | *Received cash from matured bonds.* | | |

The cost of a debt security can be either higher or lower than its maturity value. When the investment is long term, the difference between cost and maturity value is amortized over the remaining life of the security. We assume for ease of computations that the cost of a long-term debt security equals its maturity value.

Example: What is cost per share?
*Answer:* Cost per share is the total cost
of acquisition, including broker fees,
divided by number of shares acquired.

## Equity Securities: Accounting Basics

This section explains the accounting basics for *equity securities,* including that for acquisition, dividends, and disposition.

**Acquisition.**   Equity securities are recorded at cost when acquired, including commissions or brokerage fees paid. To illustrate, assume that Music City purchases 1,000 shares of Intex common stock at par value for $86,000 on October 10, 2010. It records this purchase of available-for-sale (AFS) securities as follows.

Assets  =  Liabilities +  Equity
+86,000
−86,000

| Oct. 10 | Long-Term Investments—AFS (Intex) .............. | 86,000 | |
|---|---|---|---|
| | Cash ..................................... | | 86,000 |
| | *Purchased 1,000 shares of Intex.* | | |

**Dividend earned.**   Any cash dividends received are credited to Dividend Revenue and reported in the income statement. To illustrate, on November 2, Music City receives a $1,720 quarterly cash dividend on the Intex shares, which it records as:

Assets  =  Liabilities +  Equity
+1,720                        +1,720

| Nov. 2 | Cash ......................................... | 1,720 | |
|---|---|---|---|
| | Dividend Revenue .......................... | | 1,720 |
| | *Received dividend of $1.72 per share.* | | |

**Disposition.**   When the securities are sold, sale proceeds are compared with the cost, and any gain or loss is recorded. To illustrate, on December 20, Music City sells 500 of the Intex shares for $45,000 cash and records this sale as:

Assets  =  Liabilities +  Equity
+45,000                       +2,000
−43,000

| Dec. 20 | Cash ......................................... | 45,000 | |
|---|---|---|---|
| | Long-Term Investments—AFS (Intex) .......... | | 43,000 |
| | Gain on Sale of Long-Term Investments ........ | | 2,000 |
| | *Sold 500 Intex shares ($86,000 × 500/1,000).* | | |

## REPORTING OF NONINFLUENTIAL INVESTMENTS

Companies must value and report most noninfluential investments at *fair value*. The exact reporting requirements depend on whether the investments are classified as (1) trading, (2) held-to-maturity, or (3) available-for-sale.

### Trading Securities

**Trading securities** are *debt and equity securities* that the company intends to actively manage and trade for profit. Frequent purchases and sales are expected and are made to earn profits on short-term price changes. Trading securities are *always* reported as current assets.

| **P1** | Account for trading securities. |
|---|---|

**Valuing and reporting trading securities.**   The entire portfolio of trading securities is reported at its fair value; this requires a "fair value adjustment" from the cost of the portfolio. The term *portfolio* refers to a group of securities. Any unrealized gain (or loss) from a change in the fair value of the portfolio of trading securities is reported on the income statement. Most users believe accounting reports are more useful when changes in fair value for trading securities are reported in income.

To illustrate, TechCom's portfolio of trading securities had a total cost of $11,500 and a fair value of $13,000 on December 31, 2010, the first year it held trading securities. The difference between the $11,500 cost and the $13,000 fair value reflects a $1,500 gain. It is an unrealized gain because it is not yet confirmed by actual sales. The fair value adjustment for trading securities is recorded with an adjusting entry at the end of each period to equal the difference between the portfolio's cost and its fair value. TechCom records this gain as follows.

**Point:** '*Unrealized gain (or loss)*' refers to a change in fair value that is not yet realized through actual sale.

**Point:** 'Fair Value Adjustment—Trading' is a *permanent account*, shown as a deduction or addition to 'Short-Term Investments—Trading.'

| Dec. 31 | Fair Value Adjustment—Trading ................... | 1,500 | |
|---|---|---|---|
| | Unrealized Gain—Income .................... | | 1,500 |
| | *To reflect an unrealized gain in fair values of trading securities.* | | |

Assets = Liabilities + Equity
+1,500                          +1,500

The **Unrealized Gain (or Loss)** is reported in the Other Revenues and Gains (or Expenses and Losses) section on the income statement. Unrealized Gain (or Loss)—Income is a *temporary* account that is closed to Income Summary at the end of each period. Fair Value Adjustment—Trading is a *permanent* account, which adjusts the reported value of the trading securities portfolio from its prior period fair value to the current period fair value. The total cost of the trading securities portfolio is maintained in one account, and the fair value adjustment is recorded in a separate account. For example, TechCom's investment in trading securities is reported in the current assets section of its balance sheet as follows.

**Example:** If TechCom's trading securities have a cost of $14,800 and a fair value of $16,100 at Dec. 31, 2011, its adjusting entry is
Unrealized Loss—Income ..... 200
    Fair Value Adj.—Trading..... 200
This is computed as: $1,500 Beg. Dr. bal. + $200 Cr. = $1,300 End. Dr. bal.

| **Current Assets** | | |
|---|---|---|
| Short-term investments—Trading (at cost) ........................ | $11,500 | |
| Fair Value adjustment—Trading ................................ | 1,500 | |
| Short-term investments—Trading (at fair value) ................... | | $13,000 |
| **or simply** | | |
| Short-term investments—Trading (at fair value; cost is $11,500) ....... | | $13,000 |

**Selling trading securities.**   When individual trading securities are sold, the difference between the net proceeds (sale price less fees) and the cost of the individual trading securities that are sold is recognized as a gain or a loss. Any prior period fair value adjustment to the portfolio is *not* used to compute the gain or loss from sale of individual trading securities. For example, if TechCom sold some of its trading securities that had cost $1,000 for $1,200 cash on January 9, 2011, it would record the following.

**Point:** Reporting securities at fair value is referred to as *mark-to-market* accounting.

| Jan. 9 | Cash .......................................... | 1,200 | |
| | Short-Term Investments—Trading ............. | | 1,000 |
| | Gain on Sale of Short-Term Investments ........ | | 200 |
| | *Sold trading securities costing $1,000 for $1,200 cash.* | | |

A gain is reported in the Other Revenues and Gains section on the income statement, whereas a loss is shown in Other Expenses and Losses. When the period-end fair value adjustment for the portfolio of trading securities is computed, it excludes the cost and fair value of any securities sold.

## Held-to-Maturity Securities

**P2** Account for held-to-maturity securities.

**Held-to-maturity (HTM) securities** are *debt* securities a company intends and is able to hold until maturity. They are reported in current assets if their maturity dates are within one year or the operating cycle, whichever is longer. HTM securities are reported in long-term assets when the maturity dates extend beyond one year or the operating cycle, whichever is longer. All HTM securities are recorded at cost when purchased, and interest revenue is recorded when earned.

The portfolio of HTM securities is usually reported at (amortized) cost, which is explained in advanced courses. There is no fair value adjustment to the portfolio of HTM securities—neither to the short-term nor long-term portfolios. The basics of accounting for HTM securities were described earlier in this chapter.

**Point:** Only debt securities can be classified as *held-to-maturity*; equity securities have no maturity date.

**Decision Maker**                                      Answer — p. 613

**Money Manager**   You expect interest rates to sharply fall within a few weeks and remain at this lower rate. What is your strategy for holding investments in fixed-rate bonds and notes? ■

## Available-for-Sale Securities

**P3** Account for available-for-sale securities.

**Available-for-sale (AFS) securities** are *debt and equity securities* not classified as trading or held-to-maturity securities. AFS securities are purchased to yield interest, dividends, or increases in fair value. They are not actively managed like trading securities. If the intent is to sell AFS securities within the longer of one year or operating cycle, they are classified as short-term investments. Otherwise, they are classified as long-term.

**Valuing and reporting available-for-sale securities.**   As with trading securities, companies adjust the cost of the portfolio of AFS securities to reflect changes in fair value. This is done with a fair value adjustment to its total portfolio cost. However, any unrealized gain or loss for the portfolio of AFS securities is *not* reported on the income statement. Instead, it is reported in the equity section of the balance sheet (and is part of *comprehensive income,* explained later). To illustrate, assume that Music City had no prior period investments in available-for-sale securities other than those purchased in the current period. Exhibit 15.4 shows both the cost and fair value of those investments on December 31, 2010, the end of its reporting period.

**Example:** If fair value in Exhibit 15.4 is $70,000 (instead of $74,550), what entry is made? *Answer:*
Unreal. Loss—Equity .... 3,000
    Fair Value Adj.—AFS. . .        3,000

**EXHIBIT 15.4**

Cost and Fair Value of Available-for-Sale Securities

| | Cost | Fair Value | Unrealized Gain (Loss) |
| --- | --- | --- | --- |
| Improv bonds ...................... | $30,000 | $29,050 | $ (950) |
| Intex common stock, 500 shares ........ | 43,000 | 45,500 | 2,500 |
| Total .............................. | $73,000 | $74,550 | **$1,550** |

The year-end adjusting entry to record the fair value of these investments follows.

| Dec. 31 | Fair Value Adjustment—Available-for-Sale (LT) ....... | 1,550 | |
| | Unrealized Gain—Equity .................... | | 1,550 |
| | *To record adjustment to fair value of* | | |
| | *available-for-sale securities.* | | |

Exhibit 15.5 shows the December 31, 2010, balance sheet presentation—it assumes these investments are long term, but they can also be short term. It is also common to combine the cost of investments with the balance in the Fair Value Adjustment account and report the net as a single amount.

**Point:** 'Unrealized Loss—Equity' and 'Unrealized Gain—Equity' are *permanent* (balance sheet) equity *accounts*.

**EXHIBIT 15.5**

Balance Sheet Presentation of Available-for-Sale Securities

Reconciled

**Assets**

| | | |
|---|---|---|
| Long-term investments—Available-for-sale (at cost) .......................... | $73,000 | |
| Fair value adjustment— Available-for-sale ................................... | 1,550 | |
| Long-term investments—Available-for-sale (at fair value) ....................... | | $74,550 |

or simply

| | |
|---|---|
| Long-term investments—Available-for-sale (at fair value; cost is $73,000) ........... | $74,550 |

**Equity**

... consists of usual equity accounts ...

| | |
|---|---|
| Add unrealized gain on available-for-sale securities* ......................... | $ 1,550 |

\* Often included under the caption Accumulated Other Comprehensive Income.

Let's extend this illustration and assume that at the end of its next calendar year (December 31, 2011), Music City's portfolio of long-term AFS securities has an $81,000 cost and an $82,000 fair value. It records the adjustment to fair value as follows.

**Point:** Income can be window-dressed upward by selling AFS securities with unrealized gains; income is reduced by selling those with unrealized losses.

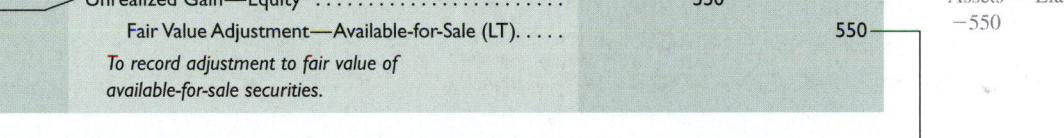

| Dec. 31 | Unrealized Gain—Equity ........................ | 550 | |
|---|---|---|---|
| | Fair Value Adjustment—Available-for-Sale (LT)..... | | 550 |
| | *To record adjustment to fair value of available-for-sale securities.* | | |

Assets = Liabilities + Equity
−550　　　　　　　　　−550

The effects of the 2010 and 2011 securities transactions are reflected in the following T-accounts.

| Unrealized Gain—Equity | | | | Fair Value Adjustment—Available-for-Sale (LT) | | | |
|---|---|---|---|---|---|---|---|
| Adj. 12/31/11 | 550 | Bal. 12/31/10 | 1,550 | Bal. 12/31/10 | 1,550 | Adj. 12/31/11 | 550 |
| | | **Bal. 12/31/11** | **1,000** | **Bal. 12/31/11** | **1,000** | | |

Amounts reconcile.

**Example:** If cost is $83,000 and fair value is $82,000 at Dec. 31, 2011, it records the following adjustment:
Unreal. Gain—Equity ..... 1,550
Unreal. Loss—Equity ..... 1,000
　Fair Value Adj.—AFS .. 　2,550

**Selling available-for-sale securities.** Accounting for the sale of individual AFS securities is identical to that described for the sale of trading securities. When individual AFS securities are sold, the difference between the cost of the individual securities sold and the net proceeds (sale price less fees) is recognized as a gain or loss.

**Point:** 'Fair Value Adjustment— Available-for-Sale' is a permanent account, shown as a deduction or addition to the Investment account.

**Quick Check**　　　　　　　　　　Answers — p. 613

1. How are short-term held-to-maturity securities reported (valued) on the balance sheet?
2. How are trading securities reported (valued) on the balance sheet?
3. Where are unrealized gains and losses on available-for-sale securities reported?
4. Where are unrealized gains and losses on trading securities reported?

**Alert**　*Both U.S. GAAP (and IFRS) permit companies to use fair value in reporting financial assets (referred to as the fair value option). This option allows companies to report any financial asset at fair value and recognize value changes in income. This method was previously reserved only for trading securities, but is now an option for available-for-sale and held-to-maturity securities (and other 'financial assets and liabilities' such as accounts and notes receivable, accounts and notes payable, and bonds). U.S. standards also set a 3-level system to determine fair value:*
*—Level 1: Use quoted market values*
*—Level 2: Use observable values from related assets or liabilities*
*—Level 3: Use unobservable values from estimates or assumptions*
*To date, a fairly small set of companies has chosen to broadly apply the fair value option—but, we continue to monitor its use...*

## REPORTING OF INFLUENTIAL INVESTMENTS

### Investment in Securities with Significant Influence

**P4** Account for equity securities with significant influence.

A long-term investment classified as **equity securities with significant influence** implies that the investor can exert significant influence over the investee. An investor that owns 20% or more (but not more than 50%) of a company's voting stock is usually presumed to have a significant influence over the investee. In some cases, however, the 20% test of significant influence is overruled by other, more persuasive, evidence. This evidence can either lower the 20% requirement or increase it. The **equity method** of accounting and reporting is used for long-term investments in equity securities with significant influence, which is explained in this section.

Long-term investments in equity securities with significant influence are recorded at cost when acquired. To illustrate, Micron Co. records the purchase of 3,000 shares (30%) of Star Co. common stock at a total cost of $70,650 on January 1, 2010, as follows.

Assets = Liabilities + Equity
+70,650
−70,650

| Jan. 1 | Long-Term Investments—Star .................... | 70,650 | |
|---|---|---|---|
| | Cash ...................................... | | 70,650 |
| | *To record purchase of 3,000 Star shares.* | | |

The investee's (Star) earnings increase both its net assets and the claim of the investor (Micron) on the investee's net assets. Thus, when the investee reports its earnings, the investor records its share of those earnings in its investment account. To illustrate, assume that Star reports net income of $20,000 for 2010. Micron then records its 30% share of those earnings as follows.

Assets = Liabilities + Equity
+6,000              +6,000

| Dec. 31 | Long-Term Investments—Star .................... | 6,000 | |
|---|---|---|---|
| | Earnings from Long-Term Investment ........... | | 6,000 |
| | *To record 30% equity in investee earnings.* | | |

The debit reflects the increase in Micron's equity in Star. The credit reflects 30% of Star's net income. Earnings from Long-Term Investment is a *temporary* account (closed to Income Summary at each period-end) and is reported on the investor's (Micron's) income statement. If the investee incurs a net loss instead of a net income, the investor records its share of the loss and reduces (credits) its investment account. The investor closes this earnings or loss account to Income Summary.

The receipt of cash dividends is not revenue under the equity method because the investor has already recorded its share of the investee's earnings. Instead, cash dividends received by an investor from an investee are viewed as a conversion of one asset to another; that is, dividends reduce the balance of the investment account. To illustrate, Star declares and pays $10,000 in cash dividends on its common stock. Micron records its 30% share of these dividends received on January 9, 2011, as:

Assets = Liabilities + Equity
+3,000
−3,000

| Jan. 9 | Cash ......................................... | 3,000 | |
|---|---|---|---|
| | Long-Term Investments—Star ............... | | 3,000 |
| | *To record share of dividend paid by Star.* | | |

The book value of an investment under the equity method equals the cost of the investment plus (minus) the investor's equity in the *undistributed* (*distributed*) earnings of the investee. Once Micron records these transactions, its Long-Term Investments account appears as in Exhibit 15.6.

**EXHIBIT 15.6**

Investment in Star Common Stock (Ledger Account)

| Long-Term Investment—Star | | | | |
|---|---|---|---|---|
| 1/ 1/2010 Investment acquisition | 70,650 | | | |
| 12/31/2010 Share of earnings | 6,000 | | | |
| 12/31/2010 Balance | 76,650 | | | |
| | | 1/ 9/2011 Share of dividend | 3,000 | |
| 1/ 9/2011 Balance | 73,650 | | | |

Micron's account balance on January 9, 2011, for its investment in Star is $73,650. This is the investment's cost *plus* Micron's equity in Star's earnings since its purchase *less* Micron's equity in Star's cash dividends since its purchase. When an investment in equity securities is sold, the gain or loss is computed by comparing proceeds from the sale with the book value of the investment on the date of sale. If Micron sells its Star stock for $80,000 on January 10, 2011, it records the sale as:

**Point:** Security prices are sometimes listed in fractions. For example, a debt security with a price of $22\frac{1}{4}$ is the same as $22.25.

| Jan. 10 | Cash ......................................... | 80,000 | |
| | Long-Term Investments—Star ............... | | 73,650 |
| | Gain on Sale of Investment .................. | | 6,350 |
| | *Sold 3,000 shares of stock for $80,000.* | | |

Assets  =  Liabilities  +  Equity
+80,000                        +6,350
−73,650

## Investment in Securities with Controlling Influence

A long-term investment classified as **equity securities with controlling influence** implies that the investor can exert a controlling influence over the investee. An investor who owns more than 50% of a company's voting stock has control over the investee. This investor can dominate all other shareholders in electing the corporation's board of directors and has control over the investee's management. In some cases, controlling influence can extend to situations of less than 50% ownership. Exhibit 15.7 summarizes the accounting for investments in equity securities based on an investor's ownership in the stock.

 Describe how to report equity securities with controlling influence.

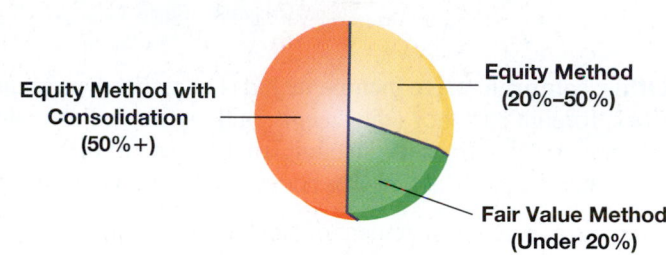

**Equity Method with Consolidation (50%+)**

**Equity Method (20%–50%)**

**Fair Value Method (Under 20%)**

**EXHIBIT 15.7**

Accounting for Equity Investments by Percent of Ownership

The *equity method with consolidation* is used to account for long-term investments in equity securities with controlling influence. The investor reports *consolidated financial statements* when owning such securities. The controlling investor is called the **parent**, and the investee is called the **subsidiary**. Many companies are parents with subsidiaries. Examples are (1) **McGraw-Hill**, the parent of J.D. Power and Associates, Standard & Poor's, and Platt's; (2) **Gap, Inc.**, the parent of Gap, Old Navy, and Banana Republic; and (3) **Brunswick**, the parent of Mercury Marine, Sea Ray, and U.S. Marine. A company owning all the outstanding stock of a subsidiary can, if it desires, take over the subsidiary's assets, retire the subsidiary's stock, and merge the subsidiary into the parent. However, there often are financial, legal, and tax advantages if a business operates as a parent controlling one or more subsidiaries. When a company operates as a parent with subsidiaries, each entity maintains separate accounting records. From a legal viewpoint, the parent and each subsidiary are separate entities with all rights, duties, and responsibilities of individual companies.

**Consolidated financial statements** show the financial position, results of operations, and cash flows of all entities under the parent's control, including all subsidiaries. These statements are prepared as if the business were organized as one entity. The parent uses the equity method in its accounts, but the investment account is *not* reported on the parent's financial statements. Instead, the individual assets and liabilities of the parent and its subsidiaries are combined on one balance sheet. Their revenues and expenses also are combined on one income statement, and their cash flows are combined on one statement of cash flows. The procedures for preparing consolidated financial statements are in advanced courses.

 **IFRS** _____

Unlike U.S. GAAP, IFRS requires uniform accounting policies be used throughout the group of consolidated subsidiaries. Also, unlike U.S. GAAP, IFRS offers no detailed guidance on valuation procedures. ■

## Accounting Summary for Investments in Securities

Exhibit 15.8 summarizes the standard accounting for investments in securities. Recall that many investment securities are classified as either short term or long term depending on management's intent and ability to convert them in the future. Understanding the accounting for these investments enables us to draw better conclusions from financial statements in making business decisions.

**EXHIBIT 15.8**

Accounting for Investments in Securities

| Classification | Accounting |
|---|---|
| **Short-Term Investment in Securities** | |
| Held-to-maturity (debt) securities . . . . . . . . . . . . . . . | **Cost** (without any discount or premium amortization) |
| Trading (debt and equity) securities . . . . . . . . . . . . . . | **Fair value** (with fair value adjustment to income) |
| Available-for-sale (debt and equity) securities . . . . . . . | **Fair value** (with fair value adjustment to equity) |
| **Long-Term Investment in Securities** | |
| Held-to-maturity (debt) securities . . . . . . . . . . . . . . . | **Cost** (with any discount or premium amortization) |
| Available-for-sale (debt and equity) securities . . . . . . . | **Fair value** (with fair value adjustment to equity) |
| Equity securities with significant influence . . . . . . . . . | Equity method |
| Equity securities with controlling influence . . . . . . . . . | Equity method (with consolidation) |

**Comprehensive Income**    Comprehensive income is defined as all changes in equity during a period except those from owners' investments and dividends. Specifically, comprehensive income is computed by adding or subtracting *other comprehensive income* to net income:

| | |
|---|---|
| Net income . . . . . . . . . . . . . . . . . . . . . . | $ # |
| Other comprehensive income . . . . . . . . | # |
| Comprehensive income . . . . . . . . . . . . | $ # |

**Other comprehensive income** includes unrealized gains and losses on available-for-sale securities, foreign currency adjustments, and pension adjustments. (*Accumulated other comprehensive income* is defined as the cumulative impact of *other comprehensive income*.)

Comprehensive income can be reported in financial statements:

1. As part of the statement of stockholders' equity
2. On the income statement
3. In a statement of comprehensive income

Apple    Option 1 is the most common. **Apple**, for example, reports comprehensive income as part of its statement of shareholders' equity in Appendix A near the end of the book as follows ($ millions):

| | |
|---|---|
| Net income . . . . . . . . . . . . . . . . . . . . . . . . . . . . . . | $8,235 |
| Change in foreign currency translation . . . . . . . . . . . . . | (14) |
| Change in unrealized loss on AFS securities . . . . . . . . | 118 |
| Change in unrealized gain on derivatives . . . . . . . . . . | (18) |
| Comprehensive income . . . . . . . . . . . . . . . . . . . . . . | $8,321 |

Other comprehensive income

The 2009 *cumulative* total of Apple's *other comprehensive income* from all prior periods is $77, which is reported in its statement of shareholders' equity and is its *accumulated other comprehensive income*. That total is carried over to the equity section of its balance sheet as follows:

| | |
|---|---|
| Common stock . . . . . . . . . . . . . . . . . . . . . . . . . . . . . | $ 8,210 |
| Retained earnings . . . . . . . . . . . . . . . . . . . . . . . . . . . | 23,353 |
| Accumulated other comprehensive income . . . . . . . . | 77 |
| Total shareholders' equity . . . . . . . . . . . . . . . . . . . . . | $31,640 |

**Point:** Some users believe that since AFS securities are not actively traded, reporting fair value changes in income would unnecessarily increase income variability and decrease usefulness.

## Quick Check                                    Answers – p. 613

5. Give at least two examples of assets classified as long-term investments.
6. What are the requirements for an equity security to be listed as a long-term investment?
7. Identify similarities and differences in accounting for long-term investments in debt securities that are held-to-maturity versus those available-for-sale.
8. What are the three possible classifications of long-term equity investments? Describe the criteria for each class and the method used to account for each.

## GLOBAL VIEW

This section discusses similarities and differences for the accounting and reporting of investments when financial statements are prepared under U.S. GAAP vis-à-vis IFRS.

**Accounting for Noninfluential Securities**  The accounting for noninfluential securities is broadly similar between U.S. GAAP and IFRS. *Trading securities* are accounted for using fair values with unrealized gains and losses reported in net income as fair values change. *Available-for-sale securities* are accounted for using fair values with unrealized gains and losses reported in other comprehensive income as fair values change (and later in net income when realized). *Held-to-maturity securities* are accounted for using amortized cost. Similarly, companies have the option under both systems to apply the fair value option for available-for-sale and held-to-maturity securities. Also, both systems review held-to-maturity securities for impairment. There are some differences in terminology under IFRS: (1) trading securities are commonly referred to as *financial assets at fair value through profit and loss,* and (2) available-for-sale securities are commonly referred to as *available-for-sale financial assets.*  NOKIA reports the following categories for noninfluential securities: (1) *Financial assets at fair value through profit or loss,* consisting of financial assets held for trading and financial assets designated upon initial recognition as at fair value through profit or loss, (2) *Available-for-sale financial assets,* which are measured at fair value.

**Accounting for Influential Securities**  The accounting for influential securities is broadly similar across U.S. GAAP and IFRS. Specifically, under the *equity method,* the share of investee's net income is reported in the investor's income in the same period the investee earns that income; also, the investment account equals the acquisition cost plus the share of investee income less the share of investee dividends (minus amortization of excess on purchase price above fair value of identifiable, limited-life assets). Under the *consolidation method,* investee and investor revenues and expenses are combined, absent intercompany transactions, and subtracting noncontrolling interests. Also, nonintercompany assets and liabilities are similarly combined (eliminating the need for an investment account), and noncontrolling interests are subtracted from equity. There are some differences in terminology: (1) U.S. GAAP companies commonly refer to earnings from long-term investments as *equity in earnings of affiliates* whereas IFRS companies commonly use *equity in earnings of associated (or associate) companies,* (2) U.S. GAAP companies commonly refer to noncontrolling interests in consolidated subsidiaries as *minority interests* whereas IFRS companies commonly use *noncontrolling interests.*

---

Components of Return on Total Assets  **Decision Analysis**

A company's **return on total assets** (or simply *return on assets*) is important in assessing financial performance. The return on total assets can be separated into two components, profit margin and total asset turnover, for additional analyses. Exhibit 15.9 shows how these two components determine return on total assets.

**A1** Compute and analyze the components of return on total assets.

$$\text{Return on total assets} = \text{Profit margin} \times \text{Total asset turnover}$$

$$\frac{\text{Net income}}{\text{Average total assets}} = \frac{\text{Net income}}{\text{Net sales}} \times \frac{\text{Net sales}}{\text{Average total assets}}$$

**EXHIBIT 15.9**

Components of Return on Total Assets

Profit margin reflects the percent of net income in each dollar of net sales. Total asset turnover reflects a company's ability to produce net sales from total assets. All companies desire a high return on total assets. By considering these two components, we can often discover strengths and weaknesses not revealed by return on total assets alone. This improves our ability to assess future performance and company strategy.

To illustrate, consider return on total assets and its components for **Gap Inc.** in Exhibit 15.10.

**EXHIBIT 15.10**

Gap's Components of Return on
Total Assets

| Fiscal Year | Return on Total Assets | = | Profit Margin | × | Total Asset Turnover |
|---|---|---|---|---|---|
| 2009 | 12.6% | = | 6.66% | × | 1.89 |
| 2008 | 10.2* | = | 5.28 | × | 1.92 |
| 2007 | 9.0 | = | 4.9 | × | 1.84 |
| 2006 | 11.8* | = | 6.9 | × | 1.70 |
| 2005 | 11.1 | = | 7.1 | × | 1.57 |

* Differences due to rounding.

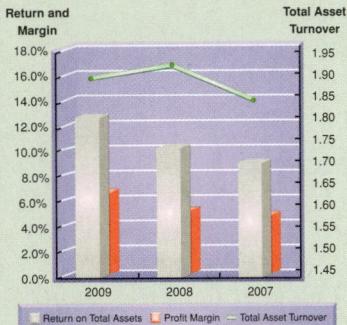

At least three findings emerge. First, Gap's return on total assets improved from 9.0% in 2007 to 12.6% in 2009. Second, total asset turnover has slightly improved over this period, from 1.84 to 1.89. Third, Gap's profit margin steadily increased over this period, from 4.9% in 2007 to 6.66% in 2009. These components reveal the dual role of profit margin and total asset turnover in determining return on total assets. They also reveal that the driver of Gap's recent improvement in return on total assets is not total asset turnover but profit margin.

Generally, if a company is to maintain or improve its return on total assets, it must meet any decline in either profit margin or total asset turnover with an increase in the other. If not, return on assets will decline. Companies consider these components in planning strategies. A component analysis can also reveal where a company is weak and where changes are needed, especially in a competitor analysis. If asset turnover is lower than the industry norm, for instance, a company should focus on raising asset turnover at least to the norm. The same applies to profit margin.

**◻ Decision Maker**                                    Answer — p. 613

**Retailer**   You are an entrepreneur and owner of a retail sporting goods store. The store's recent annual performance reveals (industry norms in parentheses): return on total assets = 11% (11.2%); profit margin = 4.4% (3.5%); and total asset turnover = 2.5 (3.2). What does your analysis of these figures reveal? ◼

# DEMONSTRATION PROBLEM—1

Garden Company completes the following selected transactions related to its short-term investments during 2011.

May  8    Purchased 300 shares of FedEx stock as a short-term investment in available-for-sale securities at $40 per share plus $975 in broker fees.

Sept. 2    Sold 100 shares of its investment in FedEx stock at $47 per share and held the remaining 200 shares; broker's commission was $225.

Oct.  2    Purchased 400 shares of Ajay stock for $60 per share plus $1,600 in commissions. The stock is held as a short-term investment in available-for-sale securities.

**Required**

1. Prepare journal entries for the above transactions of Garden Company for 2011.
2. Prepare an adjusting journal entry as of December 31, 2011, if the fair values of the equity securities held by Garden Company are $48 per share for FedEx and $55 per share for Ajay. (Year 2011 is the first year Garden Company acquired short-term investments.)

## SOLUTION TO DEMONSTRATION PROBLEM—1

**1.**

| | | | |
|---|---|---|---|
| May 8 | Short-Term Investments—AFS (FedEx) . . . . . . . . . . . . . | 12,975 | |
| | Cash . . . . . . . . . . . . . . . . . . . . . . . . . . . . . . . . . . . . . . | | 12,975 |
| | *Purchased 300 shares of FedEx stock* | | |
| | *(300 × $40) + $975.* | | |

[continued on next page]

[continued from previous page]

| | | | |
|---|---|---|---|
| Sept. 2 | Cash ........................................ | 4,475 | |
| | Gain on Sale of Short-Term Investment ......... | | 150 |
| | Short-Term Investments—AFS (FedEx) ......... | | 4,325 |
| | *Sold 100 shares of FedEx for $47 per share less* *a $225 commission. The original cost is* *($12,975 × 100/300).* | | |
| Oct. 2 | Short-Term Investments—AFS (Ajay) ............. | 25,600 | |
| | Cash ...................................... | | 25,600 |
| | *Purchased 400 shares of Ajay for $60 per share* *plus $1,600 in commissions.* | | |

2. Computation of unrealized gain or loss follows.

| Short-Term Investments in Available-for-Sale Securities | Shares | Cost per Share | Total Cost | Fair Value per Share | Total Fair Value | Unrealized Gain (Loss) |
|---|---|---|---|---|---|---|
| FedEx ..................... | 200 | $43.25 | $ 8,650 | $48.00 | $ 9,600 | |
| Ajay ...................... | 400 | 64.00 | 25,600 | 55.00 | 22,000 | |
| Totals .................... | | | $34,250 | | $31,600 | $(2,650) |

The adjusting entry follows.

| | | | |
|---|---|---|---|
| Dec. 31 | Unrealized Loss—Equity .......................... | 2,650 | |
| | Fair Value Adjustment—Available-for-Sale (ST) .... | | 2,650 |
| | *To reflect an unrealized loss in fair values* *of available-for-sale securities.* | | |

# DEMONSTRATION PROBLEM—2

The following transactions relate to Brown Company's long-term investments during 2010 and 2011. Brown did not own any long-term investments prior to 2010. Show (1) the appropriate journal entries and (2) the relevant portions of each year's balance sheet and income statement that reflect these transactions for both 2010 and 2011.

## 2010

Sept.  9   Purchased 1,000 shares of Packard, Inc., common stock for $80,000 cash. These shares represent 30% of Packard's outstanding shares.

Oct.  2   Purchased 2,000 shares of AT&T common stock for $60,000 cash as a long-term investment. These shares represent less than a 1% ownership in AT&T.

17   Purchased as a long-term investment 1,000 shares of Apple Computer common stock for $40,000 cash. These shares are less than 1% of Apple's outstanding shares.

Nov.  1   Received $5,000 cash dividend from Packard.

30   Received $3,000 cash dividend from AT&T.

Dec.  15   Received $1,400 cash dividend from Apple.

31   Packard's net income for this year is $70,000.

31   Fair values for the investments in equity securities are Packard, $84,000; AT&T, $48,000; and Apple Computer, $45,000.

31   For preparing financial statements, note the following post-closing account balances: Common Stock, $500,000, and Retained Earnings, $350,000.

## 2011

Jan.  1   Sold Packard, Inc., shares for $108,000 cash.

May  30   Received $3,100 cash dividend from AT&T.

June  15   Received $1,600 cash dividend from Apple.

Aug. 17  Sold the AT&T stock for $52,000 cash.
   19  Purchased 2,000 shares of Coca-Cola common stock for $50,000 cash as a long-term invest-
       ment. The stock represents less than a 5% ownership in Coca-Cola.
Dec. 15  Received $1,800 cash dividend from Apple.
   31  Fair values of the investments in equity securities are Apple, $39,000, and Coca-Cola,
       $48,000.
   31  For preparing financial statements, note the following post-closing account balances: Common
       Stock, $500,000, and Retained Earnings, $410,000.

## PLANNING THE SOLUTION

- Account for the investment in Packard under the equity method.
- Account for the investments in AT&T, Apple, and Coca-Cola as long-term investments in available-for-
  sale securities.
- Prepare the information for the two years' balance sheets by including the relevant asset and equity
  accounts, and the two years' income statements by identifying the relevant revenues, earnings, gains,
  and losses.

## SOLUTION TO DEMONSTRATION PROBLEM–2

**1.** Journal entries for 2010.

| | | | |
|---|---|---|---|
| Sept. 9 | Long-Term Investments—Packard | 80,000 | |
| | Cash | | 80,000 |
| | *Acquired 1,000 shares, representing a 30% equity in Packard.* | | |
| Oct. 2 | Long-Term Investments—AFS (AT&T) | 60,000 | |
| | Cash | | 60,000 |
| | *Acquired 2,000 shares as a long-term investment in available-for-sale securities.* | | |
| Oct. 17 | Long-Term Investments—AFS (Apple) | 40,000 | |
| | Cash | | 40,000 |
| | *Acquired 1,000 shares as a long-term investment in available-for-sale securities.* | | |
| Nov. 1 | Cash | 5,000 | |
| | Long-Term Investments—Packard | | 5,000 |
| | *Received dividend from Packard.* | | |
| Nov. 30 | Cash | 3,000 | |
| | Dividend Revenue | | 3,000 |
| | *Received dividend from AT&T.* | | |
| Dec. 15 | Cash | 1,400 | |
| | Dividend Revenue | | 1,400 |
| | *Received dividend from Apple.* | | |
| Dec. 31 | Long-Term Investments—Packard | 21,000 | |
| | Earnings from Investment (Packard) | | 21,000 |
| | *To record 30% share of Packard's annual earnings of $70,000.* | | |
| Dec. 31 | Unrealized Loss—Equity | 7,000 | |
| | Fair Value Adjustment—Available-for-Sale (LT)* | | 7,000 |
| | *To record change in fair value of long-term available-for-sale securities.* | | |

\* Fair value adjustment computations:

| | Cost | Fair Value | Unrealized Gain (Loss) |
|---|---|---|---|
| AT&T | $ 60,000 | $48,000 | $(12,000) |
| Apple | 40,000 | 45,000 | 5,000 |
| Total | $100,000 | $93,000 | $ (7,000) |

Required balance of the Fair Value
   Adjustment—Available-for-Sale
   (LT) account (credit) . . . . . . . . . . .  $(7,000)
Existing balance . . . . . . . . . . . . . . . .        0
Necessary adjustment (credit)  . . . . . .  $(7,000)

**2.** The December 31, 2010, selected balance sheet items appear as follows.

| Assets | |
|---|---|
| Long-term investments | |
| Available-for-sale securities (at fair value; cost is $100,000) . . . . . . . . | $ 93,000 |
| Investment in equity securities . . . . . . . . . . . . . . . . . . . . . . . . . . . . | 96,000 |
| Total long-term investments . . . . . . . . . . . . . . . . . . . . . . . . . . . . . | 189,000 |
| **Stockholders' Equity** | |
| Common stock . . . . . . . . . . . . . . . . . . . . . . . . . . . . . . . . . . . . . . . . . | 500,000 |
| Retained earnings . . . . . . . . . . . . . . . . . . . . . . . . . . . . . . . . . . . . . | 350,000 |
| Unrealized loss—Equity . . . . . . . . . . . . . . . . . . . . . . . . . . . . . . . . . | (7,000) |

The relevant income statement items for the year ended December 31, 2010, follow.

| Dividend revenue . . . . . . . . . . . . . . | $ 4,400 |
|---|---|
| Earnings from investment . . . . . . . . | 21,000 |

**1.** Journal entries for 2011.

| Jan. 1 | Cash . . . . . . . . . . . . . . . . . . . . . . . . . . . . . . . . . . . . . . . . . . . . | 108,000 | |
|---|---|---|---|
| | Long-Term Investments—Packard . . . . . . . . . . . . . | | 96,000 |
| | Gain on Sale of Long-Term Investments . . . . . . . . . | | 12,000 |
| | *Sold 1,000 shares for cash.* | | |
| May 30 | Cash . . . . . . . . . . . . . . . . . . . . . . . . . . . . . . . . . . . . . . . . . . | 3,100 | |
| | Dividend Revenue . . . . . . . . . . . . . . . . . . . . . . . . | | 3,100 |
| | *Received dividend from AT&T.* | | |
| June 15 | Cash . . . . . . . . . . . . . . . . . . . . . . . . . . . . . . . . . . . . . . . . . . | 1,600 | |
| | Dividend Revenue . . . . . . . . . . . . . . . . . . . . . . . . | | 1,600 |
| | *Received dividend from Apple.* | | |
| Aug. 17 | Cash . . . . . . . . . . . . . . . . . . . . . . . . . . . . . . . . . . . . . . . . . . | 52,000 | |
| | Loss on Sale of Long-Term Investments . . . . . . . . . . . . | 8,000 | |
| | Long-Term Investments—AFS (AT&T) . . . . . . . . . | | 60,000 |
| | *Sold 2,000 shares for cash.* | | |
| Aug. 19 | Long-Term Investments—AFS (Coca-Cola) . . . . . . . . . | 50,000 | |
| | Cash . . . . . . . . . . . . . . . . . . . . . . . . . . . . . . . . . . . . | | 50,000 |
| | *Acquired 2,000 shares as a long-term investment in available-for-sale securities.* | | |
| Dec. 15 | Cash . . . . . . . . . . . . . . . . . . . . . . . . . . . . . . . . . . . . . . . . . . | 1,800 | |
| | Dividend Revenue . . . . . . . . . . . . . . . . . . . . . . . . | | 1,800 |
| | *Received dividend from Apple.* | | |
| Dec. 31 | Fair Value Adjustment—Available-for-Sale (LT)* . . . . . . . | 4,000 | |
| | Unrealized Loss—Equity . . . . . . . . . . . . . . . . . . | | 4,000 |
| | *To record change in fair value of long-term available-for-sale securities.* | | |

\* Fair value adjustment computations:

| | Cost | Fair Value | Unrealized Gain (Loss) |
|---|---|---|---|
| Apple | $40,000 | $39,000 | $(1,000) |
| Coca-Cola | 50,000 | 48,000 | (2,000) |
| Total | $90,000 | $87,000 | $(3,000) |

| Required balance of the Fair Value Adjustment—Available-for-Sale (LT) account (credit) . . . . . . . . . . . | $(3,000) |
|---|---|
| Existing balance (credit) . . . . . . . . . . . | (7,000) |
| Necessary adjustment (debit) . . . . . . . | $ 4,000 |

**2.** The December 31, 2011, balance sheet items appear as follows.

| | |
|---|---|
| **Assets** | |
| Long-term investments | |
| Available-for-sale securities (at fair value; cost is $90,000) . . . . . . . | $ 87,000 |
| **Stockholders' Equity** | |
| Common stock . . . . . . . . . . . . . . . . . . . . . . . . . . . . . . . . . . . . . . . . . | 500,000 |
| Retained earnings . . . . . . . . . . . . . . . . . . . . . . . . . . . . . . . . . . . . . . | 410,000 |
| Unrealized loss—Equity . . . . . . . . . . . . . . . . . . . . . . . . . . . . . . . . . | (3,000) |

The relevant income statement items for the year ended December 31, 2011, follow.

| | |
|---|---|
| Dividend revenue . . . . . . . . . . . . . . . . . . . . . . . . . . | $ 6,500 |
| Gain on sale of long-term investments . . . . . . . . . . | 12,000 |
| Loss on sale of long-term investments . . . . . . . . . . | (8,000) |

# 15A

# Investments in International Operations

Many entities from small entrepreneurs to large corporations conduct business internationally. Some entities' operations occur in so many different countries that the companies are called **multinationals.** Many of us think of **Coca-Cola** and **McDonald's**, for example, as primarily U.S. companies, but most of their sales occur outside the United States. Exhibit 15A.1 shows the percent of international sales and income for selected U.S. companies. Managing and accounting for multinationals present challenges. This section describes some of these challenges and how to account for and report these activities.

**EXHIBIT 15A.1**

International Sales and Income as a Percent of Their Totals

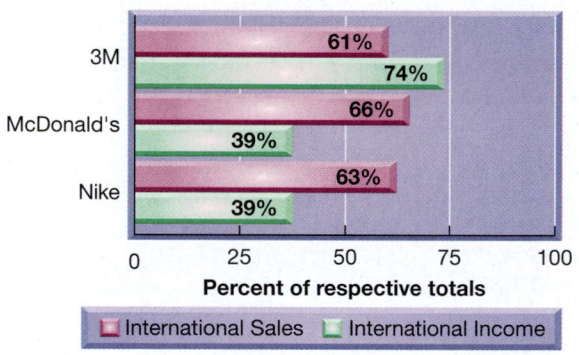

Two major accounting challenges that arise when companies have international operations relate to transactions that involve more than one currency. The first is to account for sales and purchases listed in a foreign currency. The second is to prepare consolidated financial statements with international subsidiaries. For ease in this discussion, we use companies with a U.S. base of operations and assume the need to prepare financial statements in U.S. dollars. This means the *reporting currency* of these companies is the U.S. dollar.

**Point:** Transactions *listed* or *stated* in a foreign currency are said to be *denominated* in that currency.

 **C3**  Explain foreign exchange rates and record transactions listed in a foreign currency.

**Exchange Rates between Currencies**    Markets for the purchase and sale of foreign currencies exist all over the world. In these markets, U.S. dollars can be exchanged for Canadian dollars, British pounds, Japanese yen, Euros, or any other legal currencies. The price of one currency stated in terms of another currency is called a **foreign exchange rate.** Exhibit 15A.2 lists recent exchange rates for selected currencies. The exchange rate for British pounds and U.S. dollars is $1.8980, meaning 1 British pound could be purchased for $1.8980. On that same day, the exchange rate between Mexican pesos and U.S. dollars is $0.0925, or 1 Mexican peso can be purchased for $0.0925. Exchange rates fluctuate due to changing economic and political conditions, including the supply and demand for currencies and expectations about future events.

**Point:** To convert currency, see XE.com

## Decision Insight

**Rush to Russia**    Investors are still eager to buy Russian equities even in the face of rampant crime, corruption, and slow economic growth. Why? Many argue Russia remains a bargain-priced, if risky, bet on future growth. Some analysts argue that natural-resource-rich Russia is one of the least expensive emerging markets. ■

| Source (unit) | Price in $U.S. | Source (unit) | Price in $U.S. |
|---|---|---|---|
| Britain (pound) ........ | $1.8980 | Canada (dollar) ........ | $0.9793 |
| Mexico (peso) ......... | 0.0925 | Japan (yen) ........... | 0.0090 |
| Taiwan (dollar) ........ | 0.0305 | Europe (Euro) ........ | 1.2920 |

**EXHIBIT 15A.2**

Foreign Exchange Rates for Selected Currencies*

* Rates will vary over time based on economic, political, and other changes.

### Sales and Purchases Listed in a Foreign Currency

When a U.S. company makes a credit sale to an international customer, accounting for the sale and the account receivable is straightforward if sales terms require the international customer's payment in U.S. dollars. If sale terms require (or allow) payment in a foreign currency, however, the U.S. company must account for the sale and the account receivable in a different manner.

**Sales in a Foreign Currency**    To illustrate, consider the case of the U.S.-based manufacturer Boston Company, which makes credit sales to London Outfitters, a British retail company. A sale occurs on December 12, 2010, for a price of £10,000 with payment due on February 10, 2011. Boston Company keeps its accounting records in U.S. dollars. To record the sale, Boston Company must translate the sales price from pounds to dollars. This is done using the exchange rate on the date of the sale. Assuming the exchange rate on December 12, 2010, is $1.80, Boston records this sale as follows.

| Dec. 12 | Accounts Receivable—London Outfitters ........... | 18,000 | |
| | Sales* .................................. | | 18,000 |
| | *To record a sale at £10,000, when the exchange rate equals $1.80.* * (£10,000 × $1.80/£) | | |

Assets = Liabilities + Equity
+18,000                  +18,000

When Boston Company prepares its annual financial statements on December 31, 2010, the current exchange rate is $1.84. Thus, the current dollar value of Boston Company's receivable is $18,400 (£10,000 × $1.84/£). This amount is $400 higher than the amount recorded on December 12. Accounting principles require a receivable to be reported in the balance sheet at its current dollar value. Thus, Boston Company must make the following entry to record the increase in the dollar value of this receivable at year-end.

| Dec. 31 | Accounts Receivable—London Outfitters ........... | 400 | |
| | Foreign Exchange Gain ...................... | | 400 |
| | *To record the increased value of the British pound for the receivable.* | | |

Assets = Liabilities + Equity
+400                     +400

On February 10, 2011, Boston Company receives London Outfitters' payment of £10,000. It immediately exchanges the pounds for U.S. dollars. On this date, the exchange rate for pounds is $1.78. Thus, Boston Company receives only $17,800 (£10,000 × $1.78/£). It records the cash receipt and the loss associated with the decline in the exchange rate as follows.

**Point:** Foreign exchange gains are credits, and foreign exchange losses are debits.

| Feb. 10 | Cash ......................................... | 17,800 | |
| | Foreign Exchange Loss ........................ | 600 | |
| | Accounts Receivable—London Outfitters ....... | | 18,400 |
| | *Received foreign currency payment of an account and converted it into dollars.* | | |

Assets = Liabilities + Equity
+17,800                  −600
−18,400

Gains and losses from foreign exchange transactions are accumulated in the Foreign Exchange Gain (or Loss) account. After year-end adjustments, the balance in the Foreign Exchange Gain (or Loss) account is reported on the income statement and closed to the Income Summary account.

**Purchases in a Foreign Currency**    Accounting for credit purchases from an international seller is similar to the case of a credit sale to an international customer. In particular, if the U.S. company is required to make payment in a foreign currency, the account payable must be translated into dollars before the U.S. company can record it. If the exchange rate is different when preparing financial statements and when paying for the purchase, the U.S. company must recognize a foreign exchange gain or loss at those dates. To illustrate, assume NC Imports, a U.S. company, purchases products costing €20,000 (euros) from

**Example:** Assume that a U.S. company makes a credit purchase from a British company for £10,000 when the exchange rate is $1.62. At the balance sheet date, this rate is $1.72. Does this imply a gain or loss for the U.S. company? *Answer:* A loss.

Hamburg Brewing on January 15, when the exchange rate is $1.20 per euro. NC records this transaction as follows.

| Assets | = | Liabilities | + | Equity |
|--------|---|-------------|---|--------|
| +24,000 | | +24,000 | | |

| Jan. 15 | Inventory ........................................ | 24,000 | |
|---------|------------------------------------------------|--------|--------|
| |     Accounts Payable—Hamburg Brewing .......... | | 24,000 |
| | *To record a €20,000 purchase when exchange rate* | | |
| | *is $1.20 (€20,000 × $1.20/€)* | | |

NC Imports makes payment in full on February 14 when the exchange rate is $1.25 per euro, which is recorded as follows.

| Assets | = | Liabilities | + | Equity |
|--------|---|-------------|---|--------|
| −25,000 | | −24,000 | | −1,000 |

| Feb. 14 | Accounts Payable—Hamburg Brewing .............. | 24,000 | |
|---------|------------------------------------------------|--------|--------|
| | Foreign Exchange Loss .......................... | 1,000 | |
| |     Cash ...................................... | | 25,000 |
| | *To record cash payment towards €20,000 account* | | |
| | *when exchange rate is $1.25 (€20,000 × $1.25/€).* | | |

## Decision Insight

**Global Greenback**   What do changes in foreign exchange rates mean? A decline in the price of the U.S. dollar against other currencies usually yields increased international sales for U.S. companies, without hiking prices or cutting costs, and puts them on a stronger competitive footing abroad. At home, they can raise prices without fear that foreign rivals will undercut them. ∎

### Consolidated Statements with International Subsidiaries

A second challenge in accounting for international operations involves preparing consolidated financial statements when the parent company has one or more international subsidiaries. Consider a U.S.-based company that owns a controlling interest in a French subsidiary. The reporting currency of the U.S. parent is the dollar. The French subsidiary maintains its financial records in euros. Before preparing consolidated statements, the parent must translate financial statements of the French company into U.S. dollars. After this translation is complete (including that for accounting differences), it prepares consolidated statements the same as for domestic subsidiaries. Procedures for translating an international subsidiary's account balances depend on the nature of the subsidiary's operations. The process requires the parent company to select appropriate foreign exchange rates and to apply those rates to the foreign subsidiary's account balances. This is described in advanced courses.

**Global:** A weaker U.S. dollar often increases global sales for U.S. companies.

## Decision Maker

Answer — p. 613

**Entrepreneur**   You are a U.S. home builder that purchases lumber from mills in both the U.S. and Canada. The price of the Canadian dollar in terms of the U.S. dollar jumps from US$0.70 to US$0.80. Are you now more or less likely to buy lumber from Canadian or U.S. mills? ∎

# Summary

**C1**   **Distinguish between debt and equity securities and between short-term and long-term investments.** *Debt securities* reflect a creditor relationship and include investments in notes, bonds, and certificates of deposit. *Equity securities* reflect an owner relationship and include shares of stock issued by other companies. Short-term investments in securities are current assets that meet two criteria: (1) They are expected to be converted into cash within one year or the current operating cycle of the business, whichever is longer and (2) they are readily convertible to cash, or *marketable*. All other investments in securities are long-term. Long-term investments also include assets not used in operations and those held for special purposes, such as land for expansion.

Investments in securities are classified into one of five groups: (1) trading securities, which are always short-term, (2) debt securities held-to-maturity, (3) debt and equity securities available-for-sale, (4) equity securities in which an investor has a significant influence over the investee, and (5) equity securities in which an investor has a controlling influence over the investee.

**C2**   **Describe how to report equity securities with controlling influence.** If an investor owns more than 50% of another company's voting stock and controls the investee, the investor's financial reports are prepared on a consolidated basis. These reports are prepared as if the company were organized as one entity.

**C3A** **Explain foreign exchange rates and record transactions listed in a foreign currency.** A foreign exchange rate is the price of one currency stated in terms of another. An entity with transactions in a foreign currency when the exchange rate changes between the transaction dates and their settlement will experience exchange gains or losses. When a company makes a credit sale to a foreign customer and sales terms call for payment in a foreign currency, the company must translate the foreign currency into dollars to record the receivable. If the exchange rate changes before payment is received, exchange gains or losses are recognized in the year they occur. The same treatment is used when a company makes a credit purchase from a foreign supplier and is required to make payment in a foreign currency.

**A1** **Compute and analyze the components of return on total assets.** Return on total assets has two components: profit margin and total asset turnover. A decline in one component must be met with an increase in another if return on assets is to be maintained. Component analysis is helpful in assessing company performance compared to that of competitors and its own past.

**P1** **Account for trading securities.** Investments are initially recorded at cost, and any dividend or interest from these investments is recorded in the income statement. Investments classified as trading securities are reported at fair value. Unrealized gains and losses on trading securities are reported in income. When investments are sold, the difference between the net proceeds from the sale and the cost of the securities is recognized as a gain or loss.

**P2** **Account for held-to-maturity securities.** Debt securities held-to-maturity are reported at cost when purchased. Interest revenue is recorded as it accrues. The cost of long-term held-to-maturity securities is adjusted for the amortization of any difference between cost and maturity value.

**P3** **Account for available-for-sale securities.** Debt and equity securities available-for-sale are recorded at cost when purchased. Available-for-sale securities are reported at their fair values on the balance sheet with unrealized gains or losses shown in the equity section. Gains and losses realized on the sale of these investments are reported in the income statement.

**P4** **Account for equity securities with significant influence.** The equity method is used when an investor has a significant influence over an investee. This usually exists when an investor owns 20% or more of the investee's voting stock but not more than 50%. The equity method means an investor records its share of investee earnings with a debit to the investment account and a credit to a revenue account. Dividends received reduce the investment account balance.

## Guidance Answers to Decision Maker

**Money Manager**   If you have investments in fixed-rate bonds and notes when interest rates fall, the value of your investments increases. This is so because the bonds and notes you hold continue to pay the same (high) rate while the market is demanding a new lower interest rate. Your strategy is to continue holding your investments in bonds and notes, and, potentially, to increase these holdings through additional purchases.

**Retailer**   Your store's return on assets is 11%, which is similar to the industry norm of 11.2%. However, disaggregation of return on assets reveals that your store's profit margin of 4.4% is much higher than the norm of 3.5%, but your total asset turnover of 2.5 is much lower than the norm of 3.2. These results suggest that, as compared with competitors, you are less efficient in using assets. You need to

focus on increasing sales or reducing assets. You might consider reducing prices to increase sales, provided such a strategy does not reduce your return on assets. For instance, you could reduce your profit margin to 4% to increase sales. If total asset turnover increases to more than 2.75 when profit margin is lowered to 4%, your overall return on assets is improved.

**Entrepreneur**   You are now less likely to buy Canadian lumber because it takes more U.S. money to buy a Canadian dollar (and lumber). For instance, the purchase of lumber from a Canadian mill with a $1,000 (Canadian dollars) price would have cost the U.S. builder $700 (U.S. dollars, computed as C$1,000 × US$0.70) before the rate change, and $800 (US dollars, computed as C$1,000 × US$0.80) after the rate change.

## Guidance Answers to Quick Checks

1. Short-term held-to-maturity securities are reported at cost.
2. Trading securities are reported at fair value.
3. The equity section of the balance sheet (and in comprehensive income).
4. The income statement.
5. Long-term investments include (1) long-term funds earmarked for a special purpose, (2) debt and equity securities that do not meet current asset requirements, and (3) long-term assets not used in the regular operations of the business.
6. An equity investment is classified as long term if it is not marketable or, if marketable, it is not held as an available source of cash to meet the needs of current operations.

7. Debt securities held-to-maturity and debt securities available-for-sale are both recorded at cost. Also, interest on both is accrued as earned. However, only long-term securities held-to-maturity require amortization of the difference between cost and maturity value. In addition, only securities available-for-sale require a period-end adjustment to fair value.
8. Long-term equity investments are placed in one of three categories and accounted for as follows: (a) **available-for-sale** (noninfluential, less than 20% of outstanding stock)—fair value; (b) **significant influence** (20% to 50% of outstanding stock)—equity method; and (c) **controlling influence** (holding more than 50% of outstanding stock)—equity method with consolidation.

## Key Terms

mhhe.com/wildFAP20e

Available-for-sale (AFS) securities (p. 600)

Comprehensive income (p. 604)

Consolidated financial statements (p. 603)

Equity method (p. 602)

Equity securities with controlling influence (p. 603)

Equity securities with significant influence (p. 602)

Foreign exchange rate (p. 610)

Held-to-maturity (HTM) securities (p. 600)

Long-term investments (p. 596)

Multinational (p. 610)

Other comprehensive income (p. 604)

Parent (p. 603)

Return on total assets (p. 605)

Short-term investments (p. 596)

Subsidiary (p. 603)

Trading securities (p. 599)

Unrealized gain (loss) (p. 599)

## Multiple Choice Quiz            Answers on p. 629            mhhe.com/wildFAP20e

**Additional Quiz Questions are available at the book's Website.**

1. A company purchased $30,000 of 5% bonds for investment purposes on May 1. The bonds pay interest on February 1 and August 1. The amount of interest revenue accrued at December 31 (the company's year-end) is:
   a. $1,500
   b. $1,375
   c. $1,000
   d. $625
   e. $300

2. Earlier this period, Amadeus Co. purchased its only available-for-sale investment in the stock of Bach Co. for $83,000. The period-end fair value of this stock is $84,500. Amadeus records a:
   a. Credit to Unrealized Gain—Equity for $1,500.
   b. Debit to Unrealized Loss—Equity for $1,500.
   c. Debit to Investment Revenue for $1,500.
   d. Credit to Fair Value Adjustment—Available-for-Sale for $3,500.
   e. Credit to Cash for $1,500.

3. Mozart Co. owns 35% of Melody Inc. Melody pays $50,000 in cash dividends to its shareholders for the period. Mozart's entry to record the Melody dividend includes a:
   a. Credit to Investment Revenue for $50,000.
   b. Credit to Long-Term Investments for $17,500.

   c. Credit to Cash for $17,500.
   d. Debit to Long-Term Investments for $17,500.
   e. Debit to Cash for $50,000.

4. A company has net income of $300,000, net sales of $2,500,000, and total assets of $2,000,000. Its return on total assets equals:
   a. 6.7%
   b. 12.0%
   c. 8.3%
   d. 80.0%
   e. 15.0%

5. A company had net income of $80,000, net sales of $600,000, and total assets of $400,000. Its profit margin and total asset turnover are:

|       | Profit Margin | Total Asset Turnover |
|-------|---------------|----------------------|
| a.    | 1.5%          | 13.3                 |
| b.    | 13.3%         | 1.5                  |
| c.    | 13.3%         | 0.7                  |
| d.    | 7.0%          | 13.3                 |
| e.    | 10.0%         | 26.7                 |

## Discussion Questions

1. Under what two conditions should investments be classified as current assets?

2. 🔲 On a balance sheet, what valuation must be reported for short-term investments in trading securities?

3. If a short-term investment in available-for-sale securities costs $6,780 and is sold for $7,500, how should the difference between these two amounts be recorded?

4. Identify the three classes of noninfluential and two classes of influential investments in securities.

5. Under what conditions should investments be classified as current assets? As long-term assets?

6. If a company purchases its only long-term investments in available-for-sale debt securities this period and their fair value is below cost at the balance sheet date, what entry is required to recognize this unrealized loss?

7. On a balance sheet, what valuation must be reported for debt securities classified as available-for-sale?

8. Under what circumstances are long-term investments in debt securities reported at cost and adjusted for amortization of any difference between cost and maturity value?

9. For investments in available-for-sale securities, how are unrealized (holding) gains and losses reported?

10. In accounting for investments in equity securities, when should the equity method be used?

11. Under what circumstances does a company prepare consolidated financial statements?

12.ᴬ What are two major challenges in accounting for international operations?

13.ᴬ Assume a U.S. company makes a credit sale to a foreign customer that is required to make payment in its foreign currency. In the current period, the exchange rate is $1.40 on the date of the sale and is $1.30 on the date the customer pays the receivable. Will the U.S. company record an exchange gain or loss?

14.ᴬ If a U.S. company makes a credit sale to a foreign customer required to make payment in U.S. dollars, can the U.S. company have an exchange gain or loss on this sale?

15. Refer to **Apple**'s statement of changes in shareholders' equity in Appendix A. What is the amount of foreign currency translation adjustment for the year ended September 26, 2009? Is this adjustment an unrealized gain or an unrealized loss? **Apple**

16. Refer to **Palm**'s statement of stockholders' equity. What was the amount of its fiscal 2009 unrealized gain or loss on securities? **Palm**

17. Refer to the balance sheet of **Nokia** in Appendix A. How can you tell that Nokia uses the consolidated method of accounting? **NOKIA**

18. Refer to the financial statements of **Research In Motion** in Appendix A. Compute its return on total assets for the year ended February 27, 2010. **RIM**

---

**connect**

Complete the following descriptions by filling in the blanks.

1. Accrual of interest on bonds held as long-term investments requires a credit to _____ _____.

2. The controlling investor (more than 50% ownership) is called the _____, and the investee company is called the _____.

3. Trading securities are classified as _____ assets.

4. Equity securities giving an investor significant influence are accounted for using the _____ _____.

5. Available-for-sale debt securities are reported on the balance sheet at _____ _____.

**QUICK STUDY**

**QS 15-1**
Describing investments in securities
**C1 C2**

---

Which of the following statements are true of long-term investments?

a. They can include investments in trading securities.

b. They are always easily sold and therefore qualify as being marketable.

c. They can include debt and equity securities available-for-sale.

d. They are held as an investment of cash available for current operations.

e. They can include debt securities held-to-maturity.

f. They can include bonds and stocks not intended to serve as a ready source of cash.

g. They can include funds earmarked for a special purpose, such as bond sinking funds.

**QS 15-2**
Identifying long-term investments
**C1**

---

On April 18, Dice Co. made a short-term investment in 500 common shares of XLT Co. The purchase price is $45 per share and the broker's fee is $150. The intent is to actively manage these shares for profit. On May 30, Dice Co. receives $1 per share from XLT in dividends. Prepare the April 18 and May 30 journal entries to record these transactions.

**QS 15-3**
Short-term equity investments **P1**

---

Fender Co. purchased short-term investments in available-for-sale securities at a cost of $100,000 on November 25, 2011. At December 31, 2011, these securities had a fair value of $94,000. This is the first and only time the company has purchased such securities.

1. Prepare the December 31, 2011, year-end adjusting entry for the securities' portfolio.

2. For each account in the entry for part 1, explain how it is reported in financial statements.

3. Prepare the April 6, 2012, entry when Fender sells one-half of these securities for $52,000.

**QS 15-4**
Available-for-sale securities
**P3**

---

Prepare Hoffman Company's journal entries to reflect the following transactions for the current year.

May 7   Purchases 100 shares of Lov stock as a short-term investment in available-for-sale securities at a cost of $25 per share plus $200 in broker fees.

June 6   Sells 100 shares of its investment in Lov stock at $28 per share. The broker's commission on this sale is $75.

**QS 15-5**
Available-for-sale securities
**P3**

**QS 15-6**

Available-for-sale securities

P3

Galaxy Company completes the following transactions during the current year.

May   9   Purchases 400 shares of X&O stock as a short-term investment in available-for-sale securities at a cost of $50 per share plus $400 in broker fees.

June   2   Sells 200 shares of its investment in X&O stock at $56 per share. The broker's commission on this sale is $180.

Dec. 31   The closing market price (fair value) of the X&O stock is $46 per share.

Prepare the May 9 and June 2 journal entries and the December 31 adjusting entry. This is the first and only time the company purchased such securities.

---

**QS 15-7**

Recording equity securities

P3

On May 20, 2011, Alexis Co. paid $750,000 to acquire 25,000 common shares (10%) of TKR Corp. as a long-term investment. On August 5, 2012, Alexis sold one-half of these shares for $475,000. What valuation method should be used to account for this stock investment? Prepare entries to record both the acquisition and the sale of these shares.

---

**QS 15-8**

Equity method transactions

P4

Assume the same facts as in QS 15-7 except that the stock acquired represents 40% of TKR Corp.'s outstanding stock. Also assume that TKR Corp. paid a $125,000 dividend on November 1, 2011, and reported a net income of $550,000 for 2011. Prepare the entries to record (*a*) the receipt of the dividend and (*b*) the December 31, 2011, year-end adjustment required for the investment account.

---

**QS 15-9**

Debt securities transactions

P2

On February 1, 2011, Charo Mendez purchased 6% bonds issued by CR Utilities at a cost of $30,000, which is their par value. The bonds pay interest semiannually on July 31 and January 31. For 2011, prepare entries to record Mendez's July 31 receipt of interest and its December 31 year-end interest accrual.

---

**QS 15-10**

Recording fair value adjustment for securities

P3

During the current year, Patton Consulting Group acquired long-term available-for-sale securities at a $35,000 cost. At its December 31 year-end, these securities had a fair value of $29,000. This is the first and only time the company purchased such securities.

**1.** Prepare the necessary year-end adjusting entry related to these securities.

**2.** Explain how each account used in part 1 is reported in the financial statements.

---

**QS 15-11**

Return on total assets   A1

The return on total assets is the focus of analysts, creditors, and other users of financial statements.

**1.** How is the return on total assets computed?

**2.** What does this important ratio reflect?

---

**QS 15-12**

Component return on total assets   A1

Return on total assets can be separated into two important components.

**1.** Write the formula to separate the return on total assets into its two basic components.

**2.** Explain how these components of the return on total assets are helpful to financial statement users for business decisions.

---

**QS 15-13<sup>A</sup>**

Foreign currency transactions

C3

A U.S. company sells a product to a British company with the transaction listed in British pounds. On the date of the sale, the transaction total of $16,000 is billed as £10,000, reflecting an exchange rate of 1.60 (that is, $1.60 per pound). Prepare the entry to record (1) the sale and (2) the receipt of payment in pounds when the exchange rate is 1.50.

---

**QS 15-14<sup>A</sup>**

Foreign currency transactions

C3

On March 1, 2011, a U.S. company made a credit sale requiring payment in 30 days from a Malaysian company, Hamac Sdn. Bhd., in 20,000 Malaysian ringgits. Assuming the exchange rate between Malaysian ringgits and U.S. dollars is $0.6811 on March 1 and $0.6985 on March 31, prepare the entries to record the sale on March 1 and the cash receipt on March 31.

---

**QS 15-15**

Equity securities with controlling influence

C2

Complete the following descriptions by filling in the blanks.

**1.** A long-term investment classified as equity securities with controlling influence implies that the investor can exert a _____ influence over the investee.

**2.** The controlling investor is called the _____, and the investee is called the _____.

The **Carrefour Group** reports the following description of its trading securities (titled "financial assets reported at fair value in the income statement").

> These are financial assets held by the Group in order to make a short-term profit on the sale. These assets are valued at their fair value with variations in value recognized in the income statement.

Note 10 to Carrefour's 2008 financial statements reports €117 million in unrealized gains for 2008 and €63 million in unrealized losses for 2008, both included in the fair value of those financial assets held for trading. What amount of these unrealized gains and unrealized losses, if any, are reported in its 2008 income statement? Explain.

**QS 15-16**
International accounting for investments

P1

 **connect** _____

Prepare journal entries to record the following transactions involving the short-term securities investments of Maxwell Co., all of which occurred during year 2011.

**a.** On February 15, paid $100,000 cash to purchase FTR's 90-day short-term debt securities ($100,000 principal), dated February 15, that pay 8% interest (categorized as held-to-maturity securities).

**b.** On May 16, received a check from FTR in payment of the principal and 90 days' interest on the debt securities purchased in transaction a.

**EXERCISES**

**Exercise 15-1**
Accounting for short-term held-to-maturity securities   P2

Prepare journal entries to record the following transactions involving the short-term securities investments of Smart Co., all of which occurred during year 2011.

**a.** On March 22, purchased 700 shares of FIX Company stock at $30 per share plus a $150 brokerage fee. These shares are categorized as trading securities.

**b.** On September 1, received a $1.00 per share cash dividend on the FIX Company stock purchased in transaction a.

**c.** On October 8, sold 350 shares of FIX Co. stock for $40 per share, less a $140 brokerage fee.

**Exercise 15-2**
Accounting for short-term trading securities

P1

(c) Dr. Cash $13,860

Prepare journal entries to record the following transactions involving the short-term securities investments of Prairie Co., all of which occurred during year 2011.

**a.** On August 1, paid $60,000 cash to purchase Better Buy's 10% debt securities ($60,000 principal), dated July 30, 2011, and maturing January 30, 2012 (categorized as available-for-sale securities).

**b.** On October 30, received a check from Better Buy for 90 days' interest on the debt securities purchased in transaction a.

**Exercise 15-3**
Accounting for short-term available-for-sale securities

P3

Complete the following descriptions by filling in the blanks.

**1.** Short-term investments are securities that (1) management intends to convert to cash within ___ ___ or the ___ ___ whichever is longer, and (2) are readily convertible to _____.

**2.** Long-term investments in securities are defined as those securities that are ___ ___ convertible to cash or are ___ ___ to be converted into cash in the short term.

**3.** Debt securities reflect a _____ relationship such as investments in notes, bonds, and certificates of deposit.

**4.** Equity securities reflect an _____ relationship such as shares of stock issued by companies.

**Exercise 15-4**
Debt and equity securities and short- and long-term investments

C1

Complete the following descriptions by filling in the blanks.

**1.** The equity method with _____ is used to account for long-term investments in equity securities with controlling influence.

**2.** Consolidated _____ _____ show the financial position, results of operations, and cash flows of all entities under the parent's control, including all subsidiaries.

**Exercise 15-5**
Equity securities with controlling influence

C2

Forex Co. purchases various investments in trading securities at a cost of $56,000 on December 27, 2011. (This is its first and only purchase of such securities.) At December 31, 2011, these securities had a fair value of $66,000.

**1.** Prepare the December 31, 2011, year-end adjusting entry for the trading securities' portfolio.

**2.** Explain how each account in the entry of part 1 is reported in financial statements.

**3.** Prepare the January 3, 2012, entry when Forex sells a portion of its trading securities (that had originally cost $28,000) for $30,000.

**Exercise 15-6**
Accounting for trading securities

P1

**Check** (3) Gain, $2,000

**Exercise 15-7**

Adjusting available-for-sale
securities to fair value

P3

On December 31, 2011, Rollo Company held the following short-term investments in its portfolio of available-for-sale securities. Rollo had no short-term investments in its prior accounting periods. Prepare the December 31, 2011, adjusting entry to report these investments at fair value.

|  | Cost | Fair Value |
|---|---|---|
| Vicks Corporation bonds payable ............. | $79,600 | $90,600 |
| Pace Corporation notes payable .............. | 60,600 | 52,900 |
| Lake Lugano Company common stock ......... | 85,500 | 82,100 |

**Check**   Unrealized loss, $100

**Exercise 15-8**

Transactions in short-term and
long-term investments

P1  P2  P3

Prepare journal entries to record the following transactions involving both the short-term and long-term investments of Sophia Corp., all of which occurred during calendar year 2011. Use the account Short-Term Investments for any transactions that you determine are short term.

**a.** On February 15, paid $150,000 cash to purchase American General's 120-day short-term notes at par, which are dated February 15 and pay 10% interest (classified as held-to-maturity).

**b.** On March 22, bought 700 shares of Frain Industries common stock at $25 cash per share plus a $250 brokerage fee (classified as long-term available-for-sale securities).

**c.** On June 15, received a check from American General in payment of the principal and 120 days' interest on the notes purchased in transaction *a*.

**d.** On July 30, paid $50,000 cash to purchase MP3 Electronics' 8% notes at par, dated July 30, 2011, and maturing on January 30, 2012 (classified as trading securities).

**e.** On September 1, received a $0.50 per share cash dividend on the Frain Industries common stock purchased in transaction *b*.

**f.** On October 8, sold 350 shares of Frain Industries common stock for $32 cash per share, less a $175 brokerage fee.

**g.** On October 30, received a check from MP3 Electronics for three months' interest on the notes purchased in transaction *d*.

**Exercise 15-9**

Fair value adjustment to
available-for-sale securities

P3

On December 31, 2011, Manhattan Co. held the following short-term available-for-sale securities.

|  | Cost | Fair Value |
|---|---|---|
| Nintendo Co. common stock ............. | $68,900 | $75,300 |
| Atlantic bonds payable .................. | 24,500 | 22,800 |
| Kellogg Co. notes payable ................ | 50,000 | 47,200 |
| McDonald's Corp. common stock ......... | 91,400 | 86,600 |

Manhattan had no short-term investments prior to the current period. Prepare the December 31, 2011, year-end adjusting entry to record the fair value adjustment for these securities.

**Exercise 15-10**

Fair value adjustment to
available-for-sale securities

P3

Berroa Co. began operations in 2010. The cost and fair values for its long-term investments portfolio in available-for-sale securities are shown below. Prepare Berroa's December 31, 2011, adjusting entry to reflect any necessary fair value adjustment for these investments.

|  | Cost | Fair Value |
|---|---|---|
| December 31, 2010 ......... | $79,483 | $72,556 |
| December 31, 2011 ......... | 85,120 | 90,271 |

**Exercise 15-11**

Multiyear fair value adjustments
to available-for-sale securities

P3

Ticker Services began operations in 2009 and maintains long-term investments in available-for-sale securities. The year-end cost and fair values for its portfolio of these investments follow. Prepare journal entries to record each year-end fair value adjustment for these securities.

|  | Cost | Fair Value |
|---|---|---|
| December 31, 2009 ............ | $374,000 | $362,560 |
| December 31, 2010 ............ | 426,900 | 453,200 |
| December 31, 2011 ............ | 580,700 | 686,450 |
| December 31, 2012 ............ | 875,500 | 778,800 |

Information regarding Central Company's individual investments in securities during its calendar-year 2011, along with the December 31, 2011, fair values, follows.

**a.** Investment in Beeman Company bonds: $418,500 cost, $455,000 fair value. Central intends to hold these bonds until they mature in 2016.

**b.** Investment in Baybridge common stock: 29,500 shares; $332,450 cost; $361,375 fair value. Central owns 32% of Baybridge's voting stock and has a significant influence over Baybridge.

**c.** Investment in Carroll common stock: 12,000 shares; $169,750 cost; $183,000 fair value. This investment amounts to 3% of Carroll's outstanding shares, and Central's goal with this investment is to earn dividends over the next few years.

**d.** Investment in Newtech common stock: 3,500 shares; $95,300 cost; $93,625 fair value. Central's goal with this investment is to reap an increase in fair value of the stock over the next three to five years. Newtech has 30,000 common shares outstanding.

**e.** Investment in Flock common stock: 16,300 shares; $102,860 cost; $109,210 fair value. This stock is marketable and is held as an investment of cash available for operations.

**Required**

**1.** Identify whether each investment should be classified as a short-term or long-term investment. For each long-term investment, indicate in which of the long-term investment classifications it should be placed.

**2.** Prepare a journal entry dated December 31, 2011, to record the fair value adjustment of the long-term investments in available-for-sale securities. Central had no long-term investments prior to year 2011.

**Exercise 15-12**
Classifying investments in securities; recording fair values
C1 P2 P3 P4

**Check** (2) Unrealized gain, $11,575

---

Prepare journal entries to record the following transactions and events of Kash Company.

**2011**

Jan. 2  Purchased 30,000 shares of Bushtex Co. common stock for $204,000 cash plus a broker's fee of $3,480 cash. Bushtex has 90,000 shares of common stock outstanding and its policies will be significantly influenced by Kash.
Sept. 1  Bushtex declared and paid a cash dividend of $3.10 per share.
Dec. 31  Bushtex announced that net income for the year is $624,900.

**2012**

June 1  Bushtex declared and paid a cash dividend of $3.60 per share.
Dec. 31  Bushtex announced that net income for the year is $699,750.
Dec. 31  Kash sold 10,000 shares of Bushtex for $162,500 cash.

**Exercise 15-13**
Securities transactions; equity method
P4

---

The following information is available from the financial statements of Wright Industries. Compute Wright's return on total assets for 2011 and 2012. (Round returns to one-tenth of a percent.) Comment on the company's efficiency in using its assets in 2011 and 2012.

**Exercise 15-14**
Return on total assets
A1

| | 2010 | 2011 | 2012 |
|---|---|---|---|
| Total assets, December 31 | $190,000 | $320,000 | $750,000 |
| Net income | 28,200 | 36,400 | 58,300 |

---

Desi of New York sells its products to customers in the United States and the United Kingdom. On December 16, 2011, Desi sold merchandise on credit to Bronson Ltd. of London at a price of 17,000 pounds. The exchange rate on that day for £1 was $1.5238. On December 31, 2011, when Desi prepared its financial statements, the rate was £1 for $1.4990. Bronson paid its bill in full on January 15, 2012, at which time the exchange rate was £1 for $1.5156. Desi immediately exchanged the 17,000 pounds for U.S. dollars. Prepare Desi's journal entries on December 16, December 31, and January 15 (round to the nearest dollar).

**Exercise 15-15**[A]
Foreign currency transactions
C3

**Exercise 15-16^A**
Computing foreign exchange gains and losses on receivables
**C3**

On May 8, 2011, Jett Company (a U.S. company) made a credit sale to Lopez (a Mexican company). The terms of the sale required Lopez to pay 800,000 pesos on February 10, 2012. Jett prepares quarterly financial statements on March 31, June 30, September 30, and December 31. The exchange rates for pesos during the time the receivable is outstanding follow.

| | |
|---|---|
| May 8, 2011 . . . . . . . . . . . . . . . . | $0.1984 |
| June 30, 2011 . . . . . . . . . . . . . . . | 0.2013 |
| September 30, 2011 . . . . . . . . . | 0.2029 |
| December 31, 2011 . . . . . . . . . . | 0.1996 |
| February 10, 2012 . . . . . . . . . . | 0.2047 |

Compute the foreign exchange gain or loss that Jett should report on each of its quarterly income statements for the last three quarters of 2011 and the first quarter of 2012. Also compute the amount reported on Jett's balance sheets at the end of each of its last three quarters of 2011.

**Exercise 15-17**
International accounting for investments
**P3**

The **Carrefour Group** reports the following description of its financial assets available-for-sale.

> Assets available for sale are . . . valued at fair value. Unrealized . . . gains or losses are recorded as shareholders' equity until they are sold.

Note 10 to Carrefour's 2008 financial statements reports €6 million in *net* unrealized losses (net of unrealized gains) for 2008, which is included in the fair value of its available-for-sale securities reported on the balance sheet.

**1.** What amount of the €6 million net unrealized losses, if any, is reported in its 2008 income statement? Explain.

**2.** If the €6 million net unrealized losses are not reported in the income statement, in which statement are they reported, if any? Explain.

# PROBLEM SET A

Ryder Company, which began operations in 2011, invests its idle cash in trading securities. The following transactions are from its short-term investments in its trading securities.

**Problem 15-1A**
Recording transactions and fair value adjustments for trading securities
**P1**

**2011**

Jan.  20   Purchased 900 shares of Ford Motor Co. at $36 per share plus a $125 commission.
Feb.   9   Purchased 4,400 shares of Lucent at $10 per share plus a $200 commission.
Oct.  12   Purchased 500 shares of Z-Seven at $8 per share plus a $100 commission.

**2012**

Apr. 15   Sold 900 shares of Ford Motor Co. at $39 per share less a $185 commission.
July   5   Sold 500 shares of Z-Seven at $10.25 per share less a $100 commission.
July  22   Purchased 800 shares of Hunt Corp. at $30 per share plus a $225 commission.
Aug. 19   Purchased 1,000 shares of Donna Karan at $12 per share plus a $100 commission.

**2013**

Feb.  27   Purchased 3,400 shares of HCA at $22 per share plus a $220 commission.
Mar.   3   Sold 800 shares of Hunt at $25 per share less a $125 commission.
June 21   Sold 4,400 shares of Lucent at $8 per share less a $180 commission.
June 30   Purchased 1,000 shares of Black & Decker at $47.50 per share plus a $195 commission.
Nov.   1   Sold 1,000 shares of Donna Karan at $22 per share less a $208 commission.

**Required**

**1.** Prepare journal entries to record these short-term investment activities for the years shown. (Ignore any year-end adjusting entries.)

**Check** (2) Dr. Fair Value Adjustment—Trading $2,385

**2.** On December 31, 2013, prepare the adjusting entry to record any necessary fair value adjustment for the portfolio of trading securities when HCA's share price is $24 and Black & Decker's share price is $43.50. (Assume the Fair Value Adjustment—Trading account had an unadjusted balance of zero.)

Perry Company had no short-term investments prior to year 2011. It had the following transactions involving short-term investments in available-for-sale securities during 2011.

**Problem 15-2A**
Recording, adjusting, and reporting short-term available-for-sale securities

P3

Apr. 16   Purchased 8,000 shares of Gem Co. stock at $24.25 per share plus a $360 brokerage fee.

May  1   Paid $200,000 to buy 90-day U.S. Treasury bills (debt securities): $200,000 principal amount, 6% interest, securities dated May 1.

July  7   Purchased 4,000 shares of PepsiCo stock at $49.25 per share plus a $350 brokerage fee.

    20   Purchased 2,000 shares of Xerox stock at $16.75 per share plus a $410 brokerage fee.

Aug.  3   Received a check for principal and accrued interest on the U.S. Treasury bills that matured on July 29.

    15   Received an $0.85 per share cash dividend on the Gem Co. stock.

    28   Sold 4,000 shares of Gem Co. stock at $30 per share less a $450 brokerage fee.

Oct.  1   Received a $1.90 per share cash dividend on the PepsiCo shares.

Dec. 15   Received a $1.05 per share cash dividend on the remaining Gem Co. shares.

    31   Received a $1.30 per share cash dividend on the PepsiCo shares.

### Required

1. Prepare journal entries to record the preceding transactions and events.
2. Prepare a table to compare the year-end cost and fair values of Perry's short-term investments in available-for-sale securities. The year-end fair values per share are: Gem Co., $26.50; PepsiCo, $46.50; and Xerox, $13.75.
3. Prepare an adjusting entry, if necessary, to record the year-end fair value adjustment for the portfolio of short-term investments in available-for-sale securities.

**Check**  (2) Cost = $328,440

(3) Dr. Unrealized Loss—Equity $8,940

### Analysis Component

4. Explain the balance sheet presentation of the fair value adjustment for Perry's short-term investments.
5. How do these short-term investments affect Perry's (*a*) income statement for year 2011 and (*b*) the equity section of its balance sheet at year-end 2011?

---

Shaq Security, which began operations in 2011, invests in long-term available-for-sale securities. Following is a series of transactions and events determining its long-term investment activity.

**Problem 15-3A**
Recording, adjusting, and reporting long-term available-for-sale securities

P3

### 2011

Jan. 20   Purchased 900 shares of Johnson & Johnson at $18.75 per share plus a $590 commission.

Feb.  9   Purchased 2,200 shares of Sony at $46.88 per share plus a $2,578 commission.

June 12   Purchased 500 shares of Mattel at $55.50 per share plus an $832 commission.

Dec. 31   Per share fair values for stocks in the portfolio are Johnson & Johnson, $20.38; Mattel, $57.25; Sony, $39.

### 2012

Apr. 15   Sold 900 shares of Johnson & Johnson at $21.75 per share less a $685 commission.

July  5   Sold 500 shares of Mattel at $49.13 per share less a $491 commission.

July 22   Purchased 1,600 shares of Sara Lee at $36.25 per share plus a $1,740 commission.

Aug. 19   Purchased 1,800 shares of Eastman Kodak at $28 per share plus a $1,260 commission.

Dec. 31   Per share fair values for stocks in the portfolio are: Kodak, $31.75; Sara Lee, $30.00; Sony, $36.50.

### 2013

Feb. 27   Purchased 3,400 shares of Microsoft at $23.63 per share plus a $1,606 commission.

June 21   Sold 2,200 shares of Sony at $40.00 per share less a $2,640 commission.

June 30   Purchased 1,200 shares of Black & Decker at $47.50 per share plus a $1,995 commission.

Aug.  3   Sold 1,600 shares of Sara Lee at $31.25 per share less a $1,750 commission.

Nov.  1   Sold 1,800 shares of Eastman Kodak at $42.75 per share less a $2,309 commission.

Dec. 31   Per share fair values for stocks in the portfolio are: Black & Decker, $56.50; Microsoft, $28.

### Required

1. Prepare journal entries to record these transactions and events and any year-end fair value adjustments to the portfolio of long-term available-for-sale securities.

2. Prepare a table that summarizes the (*a*) total cost, (*b*) total fair value adjustment, and (*c*) total fair value of the portfolio of long-term available-for-sale securities at each year-end.

3. Prepare a table that summarizes (*a*) the realized gains and losses and (*b*) the unrealized gains or losses for the portfolio of long-term available-for-sale securities at each year-end.

---

**Problem 15-4A**
Long-term investment transactions; unrealized and realized gains and losses

C2   P3   P4

Park Co.'s long-term available-for-sale portfolio at December 31, 2010, consists of the following.

| Available-for-Sale Securities | Cost | Fair Value |
|---|---|---|
| 80,000 shares of Company A common stock ......... | $1,070,600 | $ 980,000 |
| 14,000 shares of Company B common stock ......... | 318,750 | 308,000 |
| 35,000 shares of Company C common stock ......... | 1,325,500 | 1,281,875 |

Park enters into the following long-term investment transactions during year 2011.

Jan. 29   Sold 7,000 shares of Company B common stock for $158,375 less a brokerage fee of $3,100.
Apr. 17   Purchased 20,000 shares of Company W common stock for $395,000 plus a brokerage fee of $3,500. The shares represent a 30% ownership in Company W.
July  6   Purchased 9,000 shares of Company X common stock for $253,125 plus a brokerage fee of $3,500. The shares represent a 10% ownership in Company X.
Aug. 22   Purchased 100,000 shares of Company Y common stock for $750,000 plus a brokerage fee of $8,200. The shares represent a 51% ownership in Company Y.
Nov. 13   Purchased 17,000 shares of Company Z common stock for $533,800 plus a brokerage fee of $6,900. The shares represent a 5% ownership in Company Z.
Dec.  9   Sold 80,000 shares of Company A common stock for $1,030,000 less a brokerage fee of $4,100.

The fair values of its investments at December 31, 2011, are: B, $162,750; C, $1,220,625; W, $382,500; X, $236,250; Y, $1,062,500; and Z, $557,600.

**Required**

1. Determine the amount Park should report on its December 31, 2011, balance sheet for its long-term investments in available-for-sale securities.

2. Prepare any necessary December 31, 2011, adjusting entry to record the fair value adjustment for the long-term investments in available-for-sale securities.

3. What amount of gains or losses on transactions relating to long-term investments in available-for-sale securities should Park report on its December 31, 2011, income statement?

---

**Problem 15-5A**
Accounting for long-term investments in securities; with and without significant influence

P3   P4

Pillar Steel Co., which began operations on January 4, 2011, had the following subsequent transactions and events in its long-term investments.

**2011**

Jan.   5   Pillar purchased 30,000 shares (20% of total) of Kildaire's common stock for $780,000.
Oct. 23   Kildaire declared and paid a cash dividend of $1.60 per share.
Dec. 31   Kildaire's net income for 2011 is $582,000, and the fair value of its stock at December 31 is $27.75 per share.

**2012**

Oct. 15   Kildaire declared and paid a cash dividend of $1.30 per share.
Dec. 31   Kildaire's net income for 2012 is $738,000, and the fair value of its stock at December 31 is $30.45 per share.

**2013**

Jan.   2   Pillar sold all of its investment in Kildaire for $947,000 cash.

**Part 1**

Assume that Pillar has a significant influence over Kildaire with its 20% share of stock.

**Required**

1. Prepare journal entries to record these transactions and events for Pillar.

2. Compute the carrying (book) value per share of Pillar's investment in Kildaire common stock as reflected in the investment account on January 1, 2013.

3. Compute the net increase or decrease in Pillar's equity from January 5, 2011, through January 2, 2013, resulting from its investment in Kildaire.

## Part 2

Assume that although Pillar owns 20% of Kildaire's outstanding stock, circumstances indicate that it does not have a significant influence over the investee and that it is classified as an available-for-sale security investment.

**Required**

1. Prepare journal entries to record the preceding transactions and events for Pillar. Also prepare an entry dated January 2, 2013, to remove any balance related to the fair value adjustment.

2. Compute the cost per share of Pillar's investment in Kildaire common stock as reflected in the investment account on January 1, 2013.

3. Compute the net increase or decrease in Pillar's equity from January 5, 2011, through January 2, 2013, resulting from its investment in Kildaire.

(1) 1/2/2013 Dr. Unrealized Gain—Equity $133,500

(3) Net increase, $254,000

---

Roundtree Company, a U.S. corporation with customers in several foreign countries, had the following selected transactions for 2011 and 2012.

**Problem 15-6A^A**
Foreign currency transactions
**C3**

### 2011

| | | |
|---|---|---|
| Apr. 8 | Sold merchandise to Salinas & Sons of Mexico for $7,938 cash. The exchange rate for pesos is $0.1323 on this day. |
| July 21 | Sold merchandise on credit to Sumito Corp. in Japan. The price of 1.5 million yen is to be paid 120 days from the date of sale. The exchange rate for yen is $0.0096 on this day. |
| Oct. 14 | Sold merchandise for 19,000 pounds to Smithers Ltd. of Great Britain, payment in full to be received in 90 days. The exchange rate for pounds is $1.5181 on this day. |
| Nov. 18 | Received Sumito's payment in yen for its July 21 purchase and immediately exchanged the yen for dollars. The exchange rate for yen is $0.0091 on this day. |
| Dec. 20 | Sold merchandise for 17,000 ringgits to Hamid Albar of Malaysia, payment in full to be received in 30 days. On this day, the exchange rate for ringgits is $0.6852. |
| Dec. 31 | Recorded adjusting entries to recognize exchange gains or losses on Roundtree's annual financial statements. Rates for exchanging foreign currencies on this day follow. |

| | |
|---|---|
| Pesos (Mexico) . . . . . . . . . | $0.1335 |
| Yen (Japan) . . . . . . . . . . . . . | 0.0095 |
| Pounds (Britain) . . . . . . . . | 1.5235 |
| Ringgits (Malaysia) . . . . . . . . | 0.6807 |

### 2012

| | | |
|---|---|---|
| Jan. 12 | Received full payment in pounds from Smithers for the October 14 sale and immediately exchanged the pounds for dollars. The exchange rate for pounds is $1.5314 on this day. |
| Jan. 19 | Received Hamid Albar's full payment in ringgits for the December 20 sale and immediately exchanged the ringgits for dollars. The exchange rate for ringgits is $0.6771 on this day. |

**Required**

1. Prepare journal entries for the Roundtree transactions and adjusting entries (round amounts to the nearest dollar).

2. Compute the foreign exchange gain or loss to be reported on Roundtree's 2011 income statement.

**Check** (2) 2011 total foreign exchange loss, $723

**Analysis Component**

3. What actions might Roundtree consider to reduce its risk of foreign exchange gains or losses?

---

Deal Company, which began operations in 2011, invests its idle cash in trading securities. The following transactions relate to its short-term investments in its trading securities.

## PROBLEM SET B

**Problem 15-1B**
Recording transactions and fair value adjustments for trading securities **P1**

### 2011

| | | |
|---|---|---|
| Mar. 10 | Purchased 1,200 shares of AOL at $59.15 per share plus a $773 commission. |
| May 7 | Purchased 2,500 shares of MTV at $36.25 per share plus a $1,428 commission. |
| Sept. 1 | Purchased 600 shares of UPS at $57.25 per share plus a $625 commission. |

### 2012

| | | |
|---|---|---|
| Apr. 26 | Sold 2,500 shares of MTV at $34.50 per share less a $1,025 commission. |
| Apr. 27 | Sold 600 shares of UPS at $60.50 per share less an $894 commission. |

June   2   Purchased 1,800 shares of SPW at $172 per share plus a $1,625 commission.
June  14   Purchased 450 shares of Walmart at $50.25 per share plus a $541.50 commission.

**2013**

Jan.  28   Purchased 1,000 shares of PepsiCo at $43 per share plus a $1,445 commission.
Jan.  31   Sold 1,800 shares of SPW at $168 per share less a $1,020 commission.
Aug. 22   Sold 1,200 shares of AOL at $56.75 per share less a $1,240 commission.
Sept.  3   Purchased 750 shares of Vodaphone at $40.50 per share plus an $840 commission.
Oct.   9   Sold 450 shares of Walmart at $53.75 per share less a $610.50 commission.

**Required**

1. Prepare journal entries to record these short-term investment activities for the years shown. (Ignore any year-end adjusting entries.)

**Check**  (2) Cr. Fair Value
Adjustment—Trading $6,910

2. On December 31, 2013, prepare the adjusting entry to record any necessary fair value adjustment for the portfolio of trading securities when PepsiCo's share price is $41 and Vodaphone's share price is $37. (Assume the Fair Value Adjustment—Trading account had an unadjusted balance of zero.)

---

**Problem 15-2B**

Recording, adjusting, and reporting short-term available-for-sale securities

P3

Day Systems had no short-term investments prior to 2011. It had the following transactions involving short-term investments in available-for-sale securities during 2011.

Feb.   6   Purchased 1,700 shares of Nokia stock at $41.25 per share plus a $1,500 brokerage fee.
       15   Paid $10,000 to buy six-month U.S. Treasury bills (debt securities): $10,000 principal amount, 6% interest, securities dated February 15.
Apr.   7   Purchased 600 shares of Dell Co. stock at $39.50 per share plus a $627 brokerage fee.
June   2   Purchased 1,250 shares of Merck stock at $72.50 per share plus a $1,945 brokerage fee.
       30   Received a $0.19 per share cash dividend on the Nokia shares.
Aug.  11   Sold 425 shares of Nokia stock at $46 per share less a $525 brokerage fee.
       16   Received a check for principal and accrued interest on the U.S. Treasury bills purchased February 15.
       24   Received a $0.10 per share cash dividend on the Dell shares.
Nov.   9   Received a $0.20 per share cash dividend on the remaining Nokia shares.
Dec.  18   Received a $0.15 per share cash dividend on the Dell shares.

**Required**

1. Prepare journal entries to record the preceding transactions and events.

**Check**   (2) Cost = $170,616

2. Prepare a table to compare the year-end cost and fair values of the short-term investments in available-for-sale securities. The year-end fair values per share are: Nokia, $40.25; Dell, $41; and Merck, $59.

(3) Dr. Unrealized Loss—
Equity, $20,947

3. Prepare an adjusting entry, if necessary, to record the year-end fair value adjustment for the portfolio of short-term investments in available-for-sale securities.

**Analysis Component**

4. Explain the balance sheet presentation of the fair value adjustment to Day's short-term investments.

5. How do these short-term investments affect (*a*) its income statement for year 2011 and (*b*) the equity section of its balance sheet at the 2011 year-end?

---

**Problem 15-3B**

Recording, adjusting, and reporting long-term available-for-sale securities

P3

Venice Enterprises, which began operations in 2011, invests in long-term available-for-sale securities. Following is a series of transactions and events involving its long-term investment activity.

**2011**

Mar. 10   Purchased 2,400 shares of Apple at $33.25 per share plus $1,995 commission.
Apr.   7   Purchased 5,000 shares of Ford at $17.50 per share plus $2,625 commission.
Sept.  1   Purchased 1,200 shares of Polaroid at $49.00 per share plus $1,176 commission.
Dec.  31   Per share fair values for stocks in the portfolio are: Apple, $35.50; Ford, $17.00; Polaroid, $51.75.

**2012**

Apr.  26   Sold 5,000 shares of Ford at $16.38 per share less a $2,237 commission.
June   2   Purchased 3,600 shares of Duracell at $18.88 per share plus a $2,312 commission.
June  14   Purchased 900 shares of Sears at $24.50 per share plus a $541 commission.
Nov.  27   Sold 1,200 shares of Polaroid at $52 per share less a $1,672 commission.
Dec.  31   Per share fair values for stocks in the portfolio are: Apple, $35.50; Duracell, $18.00; Sears, $26.00.

**2013**

Jan.  28   Purchased 2,000 shares of Coca-Cola Co. at $41 per share plus a $3,280 commission.
Aug. 22   Sold 2,400 shares of Apple at $29.75 per share less a $2,339 commission.
Sept.  3   Purchased 1,500 shares of Motorola at $29 per share plus a $870 commission.
Oct.   9   Sold 900 shares of Sears at $27.50 per share less a $619 commission.
Oct.  31   Sold 3,600 shares of Duracell at $16.00 per share less a $1,496 commission.
Dec.  31   Per share fair values for stocks in the portfolio are: Coca-Cola, $46.00; Motorola, $22.00.

**Required**

1. Prepare journal entries to record these transactions and events and any year-end fair value adjustments to the portfolio of long-term available-for-sale securities.
2. Prepare a table that summarizes the (*a*) total cost, (*b*) total fair value adjustment, and (*c*) total fair value for the portfolio of long-term available-for-sale securities at each year-end.
3. Prepare a table that summarizes (*a*) the realized gains and losses and (*b*) the unrealized gains or losses for the portfolio of long-term available-for-sale securities at each year-end.

**Check**   (2b) Fair Value Adjustment bal.: 12/31/11, $404; 12/31/12, $(1,266)

(3b) Unrealized Loss at 12/31/2013, $4,650

Capollo's long-term available-for-sale portfolio at December 31, 2010, consists of the following.

| Available-for-Sale Securities | Cost | Fair Value |
|---|---|---|
| 45,000 shares of Company R common stock ......... | $1,118,250 | $1,198,125 |
| 17,000 shares of Company S common stock .......... | 616,760 | 586,500 |
| 22,000 shares of Company T common stock .......... | 294,470 | 303,600 |

**Problem 15-4B**
Long-term investment transactions; unrealized and realized gains and losses

C2  P3  P4

Capollo enters into the following long-term investment transactions during year 2011.

Jan.  13   Sold 4,250 shares of Company S stock for $144,500 less a brokerage fee of $2,390.
Mar. 24   Purchased 31,000 shares of Company U common stock for $565,750 plus a brokerage fee of $9,900. The shares represent a 62% ownership interest in Company U.
Apr.   5   Purchased 85,000 shares of Company V common stock for $267,750 plus a brokerage fee of $4,500. The shares represent a 10% ownership in Company V.
Sept.  2   Sold 22,000 shares of Company T common stock for $313,500 less a brokerage fee of $5,400.
Sept. 27   Purchased 5,000 shares of Company W common stock for $101,000 plus a brokerage fee of $2,100. The shares represent a 25% ownership interest in Company W.
Oct. 30   Purchased 10,000 shares of Company X common stock for $97,500 plus a brokerage fee of $2,340. The shares represent a 13% ownership interest in Company X.

The fair values of its investments at December 31, 2011, are: R, $1,136,250; S, $420,750; U, $545,600; V, $269,875; W, $109,375; and X, $91,250.

**Required**

1. Determine the amount Capollo should report on its December 31, 2011, balance sheet for its long-term investments in available-for-sale securities.
2. Prepare any necessary December 31, 2011, adjusting entry to record the fair value adjustment of the long-term investments in available-for-sale securities.
3. What amount of gains or losses on transactions relating to long-term investments in available-for-sale securities should Capollo report on its December 31, 2011, income statement?

**Check**   (2) Dr. Unrealized Loss—Equity, $34,785; Cr. Fair Value Adjustment—AFS (LT), $93,530

Bengal Company, which began operations on January 3, 2011, had the following subsequent transactions and events in its long-term investments.

**Problem 15-5B**
Accounting for long-term investments in securities; with and without significant influence

P3  P4

**2011**

Jan.   5   Bengal purchased 15,000 shares (25% of total) of Bloch's common stock for $187,500.
Aug.   1   Bloch declared and paid a cash dividend of $0.95 per share.
Dec.  31   Bloch's net income for 2011 is $92,000, and the fair value of its stock is $12.90 per share.

**2012**

Aug.   1   Bloch declared and paid a cash dividend of $1.25 per share.
Dec.  31   Bloch's net income for 2012 is $76,000, and the fair value of its stock is $13.55 per share.

*2013*

Jan.    8    Bengal sold all of its investment in Bloch for $204,750 cash.

### Part 1

Assume that Bengal has a significant influence over Bloch with its 25% share.

### Required

1. Prepare journal entries to record these transactions and events for Bengal.

**Check**    (2) Carrying value per share, $13.10

2. Compute the carrying (book) value per share of Bengal's investment in Bloch common stock as reflected in the investment account on January 7, 2013.

3. Compute the net increase or decrease in Bengal's equity from January 5, 2011, through January 8, 2013, resulting from its investment in Bloch.

### Part 2

Assume that although Bengal owns 25% of Bloch's outstanding stock, circumstances indicate that it does not have a significant influence over the investee and that it is classified as an available-for-sale security investment.

### Required

(1) 1/8/2013 Dr. Unrealized Gain—Equity $15,750

1. Prepare journal entries to record these transactions and events for Bengal. Also prepare an entry dated January 8, 2013, to remove any balance related to the fair value adjustment.

2. Compute the cost per share of Bengal's investment in Bloch common stock as reflected in the investment account on January 7, 2013.

(3) Net increase, $50,250

3. Compute the net increase or decrease in Bengal's equity from January 5, 2011, through January 8, 2013, resulting from its investment in Bloch.

---

### Problem 15-6B[A]

Foreign currency transactions

**C3**

Datamix, a U.S. corporation with customers in several foreign countries, had the following selected transactions for 2011 and 2012.

*2011*

May 26    Sold merchandise for 6.5 million yen to Fuji Company of Japan, payment in full to be received in 60 days. On this day, the exchange rate for yen is $0.0094.

June    1    Sold merchandise to Fordham Ltd. of Great Britain for $72,613 cash. The exchange rate for pounds is $1.5277 on this day.

July 25    Received Fuji's payment in yen for its May 26 purchase and immediately exchanged the yen for dollars. The exchange rate for yen is $0.0090 on this day.

Oct.  15    Sold merchandise on credit to Martinez Brothers of Mexico. The price of 373,000 pesos is to be paid 90 days from the date of sale. On this day, the exchange rate for pesos is $0.1340.

Dec.   6    Sold merchandise for 242,000 yuans to Chi-Ying Company of China, payment in full to be received in 30 days. The exchange rate for yuans is $0.1975 on this day.

Dec. 31    Recorded adjusting entries to recognize exchange gains or losses on Datamix's annual financial statements. Rates of exchanging foreign currencies on this day follow.

| | |
|---|---|
| Yen (Japan) . . . . . . . . . . . . | $0.0094 |
| Pounds (Britain) . . . . . . . . | 1.5318 |
| Pesos (Mexico) . . . . . . . . . | 0.1560 |
| Yuans (China) . . . . . . . . . . | 0.2000 |

*2012*

Jan.    5    Received Chi-Ying's full payment in yuans for the December 6 sale and immediately exchanged the yuans for dollars. The exchange rate for yuans is $0.2060 on this day.

Jan.  13    Received full payment in pesos from Martinez for the October 15 sale and immediately exchanged the pesos for dollars. The exchange rate for pesos is $0.1420 on this day.

### Required

1. Prepare journal entries for the Datamix transactions and adjusting entries.

**Check**    (2) 2011 total foreign exchange gain, $6,211

2. Compute the foreign exchange gain or loss to be reported on Datamix's 2011 income statement.

### Analysis Component

3. What actions might Datamix consider to reduce its risk of foreign exchange gains or losses?

*(This serial problem began in Chapter 1 and continues through most of the book. If previous chapter segments were not completed, the serial problem can begin at this point. It is helpful, but not necessary, to use the Working Papers that accompany the book.)*

**SP 15**   While reviewing the March 31, 2012, balance sheet of Business Solutions, Santana Rey notes that the business has built a large cash balance of $68,057. Its most recent bank money market statement shows that the funds are earning an annualized return of 0.75%. S. Rey decides to make several investments with the desire to earn a higher return on the idle cash balance. Accordingly, in April 2012, Business Solutions makes the following investments in trading securities:

April 16   Purchases 400 shares of Johnson & Johnson stock at $50 per share plus $300 commission.
April 30   Purchases 200 shares of Starbucks Corporation at $22 per share plus $250 commission.

On June 30, 2012, the per share market price (fair value) of the Johnson & Johnson shares is $55 and the Starbucks shares is $19.

**Required**

1. Prepare journal entries to record the April purchases of trading securities by Business Solutions.
2. On June 30, 2012, prepare the adjusting entry to record any necessary fair value adjustment to its portfolio of trading securities.

## Beyond the Numbers

**BTN 15-1**   Refer to **Research In Motion**'s financial statements in Appendix A to answer the following.
1. Are Research In Motion's financial statements consolidated? How can you tell?
2. What is Research In Motion's *comprehensive income* for the year ended February 27, 2010?
3. Does Research In Motion have any foreign operations? How can you tell?
4. Compute Research In Motion's return on total assets for the year ended February 27, 2010.

*Fast Forward*

5. Access Research In Motion's annual report for a fiscal year ending after February 27, 2010, from either its Website (**RIM.com**) or the SEC's database (**www.sec.gov**). Recompute Research In Motion's return on total assets for the years subsequent to February 27, 2010.

---

**BTN 15-2**   Key figures for **Research In Motion** and **Apple** follow.

| ($ millions) | Research In Motion | | | Apple | | |
| --- | --- | --- | --- | --- | --- | --- |
| | Current Year | 1 Year Prior | 2 Years Prior | Current Year | 1 Year Prior | 2 Years Prior |
| Net income ........ | $ 2,457 | $1,893 | $1,294 | $ 8,235 | $ 6,119 | $ 3,495 |
| Net sales .......... | 12,536 | 9,411 | 4,914 | 42,905 | 37,491 | 24,578 |
| Total assets ....... | 10,204 | 8,101 | 5,511 | 47,501 | 36,171 | 25,347 |

**Required**

1. Compute return on total assets for Research In Motion and Apple for the two most recent years.
2. Separate the return on total assets computed in part 1 into its components for both companies and both years according to the formula in Exhibit 15.9.
3. Which company has the highest total return on assets? The highest profit margin? The highest total asset turnover? What does this comparative analysis reveal? (Assume an industry average of 10.0% for return on assets.)

---

**BTN 15-3**   Kendra Wecker is the controller for Wildcat Company, which has numerous long-term investments in debt securities. Wildcat's investments are mainly in 10-year bonds. Wecker is preparing its year-end financial statements. In accounting for long-term debt securities, she knows that each long-term investment must be designated as a held-to-maturity or an available-for-sale security. Interest rates rose sharply this past year causing the portfolio's fair value to substantially decline. The company does not intend to hold the bonds for the entire 10 years. Wecker also earns a bonus each year, which is computed as a percent of net income.

**Required**

1.  Will Wecker's bonus depend in any way on the classification of the debt securities? Explain.
2.  What criteria must Wecker use to classify the securities as held-to-maturity or available-for-sale?
3.  Is there likely any company oversight of Wecker's classification of the securities? Explain.

---

**COMMUNICATING IN PRACTICE**

P4

**BTN 15-4**   Assume that you are Jackson Company's accountant. Company owner Abel Terrio has reviewed the 2011 financial statements you prepared and questions the $6,000 loss reported on the sale of its investment in Blackhawk Co. common stock. Jackson acquired 50,000 shares of Blackhawk's common stock on December 31, 2009, at a cost of $500,000. This stock purchase represented a 40% interest in Blackhawk. The 2010 income statement reported that earnings from all investments were $126,000. On January 3, 2011, Jackson Company sold the Blackhawk stock for $575,000. Blackhawk did not pay any dividends during 2010 but reported a net income of $202,500 for that year. Terrio believes that because the Blackhawk stock purchase price was $500,000 and was sold for $575,000, the 2011 income statement should report a $75,000 gain on the sale.

**Required**

Draft a one-half page memorandum to Terrio explaining why the $6,000 loss on sale of Blackhawk stock is correctly reported.

---

**TAKING IT TO THE NET**

C1

**BTN 15-5**   Access the July 30, 2009, 10-K filing (for year-end June 30, 2009) of **Microsoft** (MSFT) at **www.SEC.gov**. Review its note 4, "Investments."

**Required**

1.  How does the "cost-basis" total amount for its investments as of June 30, 2009, compare to the prior year-end amount?
2.  Identify at least eight types of short-term investments held by Microsoft as of June 30, 2009.
3.  What were Microsoft's unrealized gains and its unrealized losses from its investments for 2009?
4.  Was the cost or fair value ("recorded basis") of the investments higher as of June 30, 2009?

---

**TEAMWORK IN ACTION**

C1  C2  P1  P2  P3  P4

**BTN 15-6**   Each team member is to become an expert on a specific classification of long-term investments. This expertise will be used to facilitate other teammates' understanding of the concepts and procedures relevent to the classification chosen.

1.  Each team member must select an area for expertise by choosing one of the following classifications of long-term investments.
    a.  Held-to-maturity debt securities
    b.  Available-for-sale debt and equity securities
    c.  Equity securities with significant influence
    d.  Equity securities with controlling influence
2.  Learning teams are to disburse and expert teams are to be formed. Expert teams are made up of those who select the same area of expertise. The instructor will identify the location where each expert team will meet.
3.  Expert teams will collaborate to develop a presentation based on the following requirements. Students must write the presentation in a format they can show to their learning teams in part (4).

**Requirements for Expert Presentation**

a.  Write a transaction for the acquisition of this type of investment security. The transaction description is to include all necessary data to reflect the chosen classification.
b.  Prepare the journal entry to record the acquisition.

[*Note:* The expert team on equity securities with controlling influence will substitute requirements (*d*) and (*e*) with a discussion of the reporting of these investments.]

    **c.** Identify information necessary to complete the end-of-period adjustment for this investment.

    **d.** Assuming that this is the only investment owned, prepare any necessary year-end entries.

    **e.** Present the relevant balance sheet section(s).

**4.** Re-form learning teams. In rotation, experts are to present to their teams the presentations they developed in part 3. Experts are to encourage and respond to questions.

---

**BTN 15-7<sup>A</sup>**    Refer to the opening feature in this chapter about Michael Chasen and Matthew Pittinsky and their company, **Blackboard**. Assume that they must acquire the Japanese rights to certain educational software that will then be produced for sale to U.S. consumers. Assume Blackboard acquires those rights on January 1, 2011, from a Japanese distributor and agrees to pay 12,000,000 yen per year for those rights. Quarterly payments are due March 31, June 30, September 30, and December 31 each year. On January 1, 2011, the yen is worth $0.00891.

*Required*

**1.** Prepare the journal entry to record the rights purchased on January 1, 2011.

**2.** Prepare the journal entries to record the payments on March 31, June 30, September 30, and December 31, 2011. The value of the yen on those dates follows.

| | |
|---|---|
| March 31 ............ | $0.00893 |
| June 30 ............. | 0.00901 |
| September 30 ........ | 0.00902 |
| December 31 ........ | 0.00897 |

**3.** How can Blackboard protect itself from unanticipated gains and losses from currency translation if all of the payments are specified to be paid in yen?

---

**BTN 15-8<sup>A</sup>**    Assume that you are planning a spring break trip to Europe. Identify three locations where you can find exchange rates for the dollar relative to the Euro or other currencies.

---

**BTN 15-9**    **Nokia**, **Research In Motion**, and **Apple** are competitors in the global marketplace. Following are selected data from each company.

| Key Figure | Nokia (Euro millions) | | | Research In Motion | | Apple | |
|---|---|---|---|---|---|---|---|
| | Current Year | One Year Prior | Two Years Prior | Current Year | Prior Year | Current Year | Prior Year |
| Net income ............. | € 260 | € 3,889 | € 6,746 | — | — | — | — |
| Net sales ............... | 40,984 | 50,710 | 51,058 | — | — | — | — |
| Total assets ............. | 35,738 | 39,582 | 37,599 | — | — | — | — |
| Profit margin ............ | ? | ? | — | 19.6% | 20.1% | 19.2% | 16.3% |
| Total asset turnover ....... | ? | ? | — | 1.37 | 1.38 | 1.03 | 1.22 |

*Required*

**1.** Compute Nokia's return on total assets, and its components of profit margin and total asset turnover, for the most recent two years using the data provided.

**2.** Which of these three companies has the highest return on total assets? Highest profit margin? Highest total asset turnover? Interpret these results.

---

## ANSWERS TO MULTIPLE CHOICE QUIZ

**1.** d; $30,000 × 5% × 5/12 = $625

**2.** a; Unrealized gain = $84,500 − $83,000 = $1,500

**3.** b; $50,000 × 35% = $17,500

**4.** e; $300,000/$2,000,000 = 15%

**5.** b; Profit margin = $80,000/$600,000 = 13.3%
        Total asset turnover = $600,000/$400,000 = 1.5

# 16

# Reporting the Statement of Cash Flows

## A Look Back

Chapter 15 focused on how to identify, account for, and report investments in securities. We also accounted for transactions listed in a foreign currency.

## A Look at This Chapter

This chapter focuses on reporting and analyzing cash inflows and cash outflows. We emphasize how to prepare and interpret the statement of cash flows.

## A Look Ahead

Chapter 17 focuses on tools to help us analyze financial statements. We also describe comparative analysis and the application of ratios for financial analysis.

## Learning Objectives

**CAP**

### CONCEPTUAL

**C1** Distinguish between operating, investing, and financing activities, and describe how noncash investing and financing activities are disclosed. (p. 633)

### ANALYTICAL

**A1** Analyze the statement of cash flows and apply the cash flow on total assets ratio. (p. 650)

LP16

### PROCEDURAL

**P1** Prepare a statement of cash flows. (p. 636)

**P2** Compute cash flows from operating activities using the indirect method. (p. 639)

**P3** Determine cash flows from both investing and financing activities. (p. 645)

**P4** *Appendix 16A*—Illustrate use of a spreadsheet to prepare a statement of cash flows. (p. 654)

**P5** *Appendix 16B*—Compute cash flows from operating activities using the direct method. (p. 657)

## Decision Insight

# Shape Up Your Images

NEW YORK—"I don't know about you, but I get shown so many boring slideshows of my friends' trips," admits Jason Hsiao. "It's like 20 minutes, and you're like, 'Kill me now.'" However, unlike the rest of us, Jason decided to do something about it. He, along with childhood buddies Brad Jefferson, Stevie Clifton, and Tom Clifton, launched **Animoto (Animoto.com).** Its Website describes their service as "a web application that automatically . . . analyzes and combines user-selected images, video clips, and music."

"We want to help users create professional-quality content," explains Jason. "So it doesn't matter what you give us, we'll take that and put it in our magic black box, and in a couple minutes, we'll deliver something that . . . you never could have dreamed of doing on your own." The owners point out that they can create a 30-second video for free. This has cash flow implications. "We decided that we would make a *freemium* model, which allows people to get a taste of the Animoto service for free," says Brad. However, longer videos and videos with more user-options require cash payments, which generate positive cash inflows.

User traffic at Animoto has grown to over 1 million per month. That type of growth has obvious cash implications for technology support, accounting, and other operating and investing cash outflows. The owners emphasize the importance of monitoring and tracking cash inflows and cash outflows. Jason admits, "There's

no possible way we could handle [growth] . . . without quickly digging ourselves into a multimillion dollar hole!"

Accordingly, the young owners learned to monitor and control cash flows for each of their operating, investing, and financing activities. Their focus on controlling cash flows led them to apply *cloud computing,* which is a pay-as-you-go model. "[We] could not have existed . . . without cloud computing," admits Jason. A review of Animoto's statement of cash flows, and its individual cash inflows and outflows, led them to this cash flow model. Explains Brad, "We use Amazon . . . for all IT infrastructure . . . PayPal and Google . . . for billing/payment . . . SaaS for email and sales." This model highlights those activities that generate the most cash and those that are cash drains. Adds Jason, "The only real asset we have in our office [is] . . . a fancy espresso machine!"

Yet cash management has not curtailed the team's fun-loving approach. Their Website describes themselves as "a bunch of techies . . . who decided to lock themselves in a room together and nerd out!" Adds Brad, "We're going through the process of figuring out where we want the future to take us."

[Sources: *Animoto Website,* January 2011; *Entrepreneur,* January 2009; *Fast Company,* September 2008; *Bellevue Reporter,* May 2008]

A company cannot achieve or maintain profits without carefully managing cash. Managers and other users of information pay attention to a company's cash position and the events and transactions affecting cash. This chapter explains how we prepare, analyze, and interpret a statement of cash flows. It also discusses the importance of cash flow information for predicting future performance and making managerial decisions. More generally, effectively using the statement of cash flows is crucial for managing and analyzing the operating, investing, and financing activities of businesses.

### Reporting the Statement of Cash Flows

| Basics of Cash Flow Reporting | Cash Flows from Operating | Cash Flows from Investing | Cash Flows from Financing |
|---|---|---|---|
| • Purpose<br>• Importance<br>• Measurement<br>• Classification<br>• Noncash activities<br>• Format and preparation | • Indirect and direct methods of reporting<br>• Application of indirect method of reporting<br>• Summary of indirect method adjustments | • Three-stage process of analysis<br>• Analysis of noncurrent assets<br>• Analysis of other assets | • Three-stage process of analysis<br>• Analysis of non-current liabilities<br>• Analysis of equity |

# BASICS OF CASH FLOW REPORTING

This section describes the basics of cash flow reporting, including its purpose, measurement, classification, format, and preparation.

## Purpose of the Statement of Cash Flows

The purpose of the **statement of cash flows** is to report cash receipts (inflows) and cash payments (outflows) during a period. This includes separately identifying the cash flows related to operating, investing, and financing activities. The statement of cash flows does more than simply report changes in cash. It is the detailed disclosure of individual cash flows that makes this statement useful to users. Information in this statement helps users answer questions such as these:

● How does a company obtain its cash?
● Where does a company spend its cash?
● What explains the change in the cash balance?

**Point:** Internal users rely on the statement of cash flows to make investing and financing decisions. External users rely on this statement to assess the amount and timing of a company's cash flows.

The statement of cash flows addresses important questions such as these by summarizing, classifying, and reporting a company's cash inflows and cash outflows for each period.

## Importance of Cash Flows

Information about cash flows can influence decision makers in important ways. For instance, we look more favorably at a company that is financing its expenditures with cash from operations than one that does it by selling its assets. Information about cash flows helps users decide whether a company has enough cash to pay its existing debts as they mature. It is also relied upon to evaluate a company's ability to meet unexpected obligations and pursue unexpected opportunities. External information users especially want to assess a company's ability to take advantage of new business opportunities. Internal users such as managers use cash flow information to plan day-to-day operating activities and make long-term investment decisions.

**Macy's** striking turnaround is an example of how analysis and management of cash flows can lead to improved financial stability. Several years ago Macy's obtained temporary protection from bankruptcy, at which time it desperately needed to improve its cash flows. It did so by engaging in aggressive cost-cutting measures. As a result, Macy's annual cash flow rose to $210 million, up from a negative cash flow of $38.9 million in the prior year. Macy's eventually met its financial obligations and then successfully merged with **Federated Department Stores**.

The case of **W. T. Grant Co.** is a classic example of the importance of cash flow information in predicting a company's future performance and financial strength. Grant reported net income of more than $40 million per year for three consecutive years. At that same time, it was experiencing an alarming decrease in cash provided by operations. For instance, net cash outflow was more than $90 million by the end of that three-year period. Grant soon went bankrupt. Users who relied solely on Grant's income numbers were unpleasantly surprised. This reminds us that cash flows as well as income statement and balance sheet information are crucial in making business decisions.

## Decision Insight

**Cash Savvy**   "A lender must have a complete understanding of a borrower's cash flows to assess both the borrowing needs and repayment sources. This requires information about the major types of cash inflows and outflows. I have seen many companies, whose financial statements indicate good profitability, experience severe financial problems because the owners or managers lacked a good understanding of cash flows."—Mary E. Garza, **Bank of America** ■

## Measurement of Cash Flows

Cash flows are defined to include both *cash* and *cash equivalents*. The statement of cash flows explains the difference between the beginning and ending balances of cash and cash equivalents. We continue to use the phrases *cash flows* and the *statement of cash flows,* but we must remember that both phrases refer to cash and cash equivalents. Recall that a cash equivalent must satisfy two criteria: (1) be readily convertible to a known amount of cash and (2) be sufficiently close to its maturity so its market value is unaffected by interest rate changes. In most cases, a debt security must be within three months of its maturity to satisfy these criteria. Companies must disclose and follow a clear policy for determining cash and cash equivalents and apply it consistently from period to period. **American Express**, for example, defines its cash equivalents as "time deposits and other highly liquid investments with original maturities of 90 days or less."

## Classification of Cash Flows

Since cash and cash equivalents are combined, the statement of cash flows does not report transactions between cash and cash equivalents such as cash paid to purchase cash equivalents and cash received from selling cash equivalents. However, all other cash receipts and cash payments are classified and reported on the statement as operating, investing, or financing activities. Individual cash receipts and payments for each of these three categories are labeled to identify their originating transactions or events. A net cash inflow (source) occurs when the receipts in a category exceed the payments. A net cash outflow (use) occurs when the payments in a category exceed the receipts.

> **C1** Distinguish between operating, investing, and financing activities, and describe how noncash investing and financing activities are disclosed.

**Operating Activities**   **Operating activities** include those transactions and events that determine net income. Examples are the production and purchase of merchandise, the sale of goods and services to customers, and the expenditures to administer the business. Not all items in income, such as unusual gains and losses, are operating activities (we discuss these exceptions later in the chapter). Exhibit 16.1 lists the more common cash inflows and outflows from operating activities. (Although cash receipts and cash payments from buying and selling trading

**EXHIBIT 16.1**

Cash Flows from Operating Activities

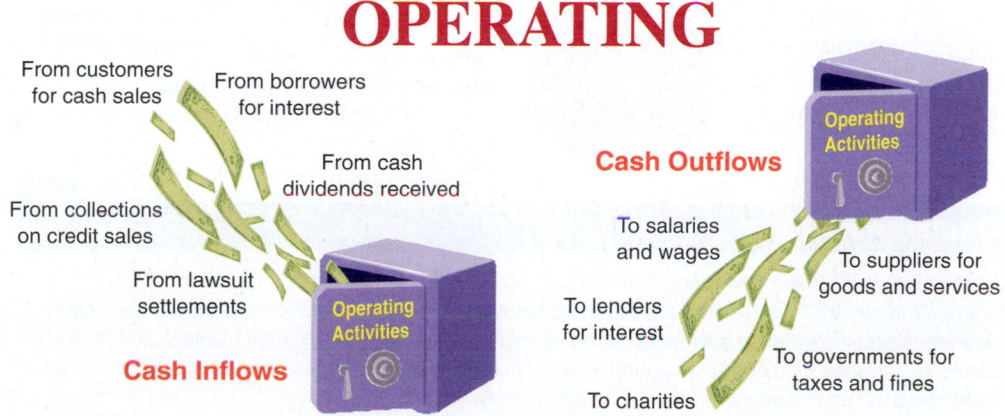

securities are often reported under operating activities, new standards require that these receipts and payments be classified based on the nature and purpose of those securities.)

**Investing Activities**   **Investing activities** generally include those transactions and events that affect long-term assets—namely, the purchase and sale of long-term assets. They also include (1) the purchase and sale of short-term investments in the securities of other entities, other than cash equivalents and trading securities and (2) lending and collecting money for notes receivable. Exhibit 16.2 lists examples of cash flows from investing activities. Proceeds from collecting the principal amounts of notes deserve special mention. If the note results from sales to customers, its cash receipts are classed as operating activities whether short-term or long-term. If the note results from a loan to another party apart from sales, however, the cash receipts from collecting the note principal are classed as an investing activity. The FASB requires that the collection of interest on loans be reported as an operating activity.

**Point:** The FASB requires that *cash dividends received* and *cash interest received* be reported as operating activities.

**EXHIBIT 16.2**

Cash Flows from
Investing Activities

**Financing Activities**   **Financing activities** include those transactions and events that affect long-term liabilities and equity. Examples are (1) obtaining cash from issuing debt and repaying the amounts borrowed and (2) receiving cash from or distributing cash to owners. These activities involve transactions with a company's owners and creditors. They also often involve borrowing and repaying principal amounts relating to both short- and long-term debt. GAAP requires that payments of interest expense be classified as operating activities. Also, cash payments to settle credit purchases of merchandise, whether on account or by note, are operating activities. Exhibit 16.3 lists examples of cash flows from financing activities.

**EXHIBIT 16.3**

Cash Flows from
Financing Activities

## FINANCING

From issuing its own
equity stock

From contributions
by owners

From issuing short-
and long-term debt

From issuing
notes and bonds

**Financing
Activities**

**Cash Inflows**

**Cash Outflows**

**Financing
Activities**

To repay
cash loans

To pay
withdrawals
by owners

To pay dividends
to shareholders

To purchase
treasury stock

**Point:** Interest payments on a loan are classified as operating activities, but payments of loan principal are financing activities.

---

**Decision Insight**

**Cash Monitoring**   Cash flows can be delayed or accelerated at the end of a period to improve or reduce current period cash flows. Also, cash flows can be misclassified. Cash outflows reported under operations are interpreted as expense payments. However, cash outflows reported under investing activities are interpreted as a positive sign of growth potential. Thus, managers face incentives to misclassify cash flows. For these reasons, cash flow reporting warrants our scrutiny. ■

# Noncash Investing and Financing

When important investing and financing activities do not affect cash receipts or payments, they are still disclosed at the bottom of the statement of cash flows or in a note to the statement because of their importance and the *full-disclosure principle*. One example of such a transaction is the purchase of long-term assets using a long-term note payable (loan). This transaction involves both investing and financing activities but does not affect any cash inflow or outflow and is not reported in any of the three sections of the statement of cash flows. This disclosure rule also extends to transactions with partial cash receipts or payments.

To illustrate, assume that Goorin purchases land for $12,000 by paying $5,000 cash and trading in used equipment worth $7,000. The investing section of the statement of cash flows reports only the $5,000 cash outflow for the land purchase. The $12,000 investing transaction is only partially described in the body of the statement of cash flows, yet this information is potentially important to users because it changes the makeup of assets. Goorin could either describe the transaction in a footnote or include information at the bottom of its statement that lists the $12,000 land purchase along with the cash financing of $5,000 and a $7,000 trade-in of equipment. As another example, Borg Co. acquired $900,000 of assets in exchange for $200,000 cash and a $700,000 long-term note, which should be reported as follows:

**Point:** A stock dividend transaction involving a transfer from retained earnings to common stock or a credit to contributed capital is *not* considered a noncash investing and financing activity because the company receives no consideration for shares issued.

| | |
|---|---|
| Fair value of assets acquired .......... | $900,000 |
| Less cash paid ..................... | 200,000 |
| Liabilities incurred or assumed ........ | $700,000 |

Exhibit 16.4 lists transactions commonly disclosed as noncash investing and financing activities.

- Retirement of debt by issuing equity stock.
- Conversion of preferred stock to common stock.
- Lease of assets in a capital lease transaction.
- Purchase of long-term assets by issuing a note or bond.
- Exchange of noncash assets for other noncash assets.
- Purchase of noncash assets by issuing equity or debt.

**EXHIBIT 16.4**

Examples of Noncash Investing and Financing Activities

# Format of the Statement of Cash Flows

Accounting standards require companies to include a statement of cash flows in a complete set of financial statements. This statement must report information about a company's cash receipts and cash payments during the period. Exhibit 16.5 shows the usual format. A company must report cash flows from three activities: operating, investing, and financing. The statement

**EXHIBIT 16.5**

Format of the Statement of Cash Flows

| **COMPANY NAME** Statement of Cash Flows For *period* Ended *date* | | |
|---|---|---|
| **Cash flows from operating activities** | | |
| [List of individual inflows and outflows] | | |
| Net cash provided (used) by operating activities .................. | $ # | |
| **Cash flows from investing activities** | | |
| [List of individual inflows and outflows] | | |
| Net cash provided (used) by investing activities ................... | # | |
| **Cash flows from financing activities** | | |
| [List of individual inflows and outflows] | | |
| Net cash provided (used) by financing activities .................. | # | |
| **Net increase (decrease) in cash** ............................. | $ # | |
| Cash (and equivalents) balance at prior period-end ........... | # | |
| Cash (and equivalents) balance at current period-end ......... | $ # | |

> Separate schedule or note disclosure of any "noncash investing and financing transactions" is required.

explains how transactions and events impact the prior period-end cash (and cash equivalents) balance to produce its current period-end balance.

### Decision Maker                                                   Answer — p. 662

**Entrepreneur**   You are considering purchasing a start-up business that recently reported a $110,000 annual net loss and a $225,000 annual net cash inflow. How are these results possible? ■

### Quick Check                                                      Answers — p. 662

1. Does a statement of cash flows report the cash payments to purchase cash equivalents? Does it report the cash receipts from selling cash equivalents?
2. Identify the three categories of cash flows reported separately on the statement of cash flows.
3. Identify the cash activity category for each transaction: (*a*) purchase equipment for cash, (*b*) cash payment of wages, (*c*) sale of common stock for cash, (*d*) receipt of cash dividends from stock investment, (*e*) cash collection from customers, (*f*) notes issued for cash.

## Preparing the Statement of Cash Flows

**P1**   Prepare a statement of cash flows.

Preparing a statement of cash flows involves five steps: 1 compute the net increase or decrease in cash; 2 compute and report the net cash provided or used by operating activities (using either the direct or indirect method; both are explained); 3 compute and report the net cash provided or used by investing activities; 4 compute and report the net cash provided or used by financing activities; and 5 compute the net cash flow by combining net cash provided or used by operating, investing, and financing activities and then *prove it* by adding it to the beginning cash balance to show that it equals the ending cash balance.

Step 1 Compute net increase or decrease in cash

Step 2 Compute net cash from operating activities

Step 3 Compute net cash from investing activities

Step 4 Compute net cash from financing activities

Step 5 Prove and report beginning and ending cash balances

Computing the net increase or net decrease in cash is a simple but crucial computation. It equals the current period's cash balance minus the prior period's cash balance. This is the *bottom-line* figure for the statement of cash flows and is a check on accuracy. The information we need to prepare a statement of cash flows comes from various sources including comparative balance sheets at the beginning and end of the period, and an income statement for the period. There are two alternative approaches to preparing the statement: (1) analyzing the Cash account and (2) analyzing noncash accounts.

**Point:** View the change in cash as a *target* number that we will fully explain and prove in the statement of cash flows.

**Analyzing the Cash Account**   A company's cash receipts and cash payments are recorded in the Cash account in its general ledger. The Cash account is therefore a natural place to look for information about cash flows from operating, investing, and financing activities. To illustrate, review the summarized Cash T-account of Genesis, Inc., in Exhibit 16.6. Individual cash transactions are summarized in this Cash account according to the major types of cash receipts and cash payments. For instance, only the total of cash receipts from all customers is listed. Individual cash transactions underlying these totals can number in the thousands. Accounting software is available to provide summarized cash accounts.

Preparing a statement of cash flows from Exhibit 16.6 requires determining whether an individual cash inflow or outflow is an operating, investing, or financing activity, and then listing each by

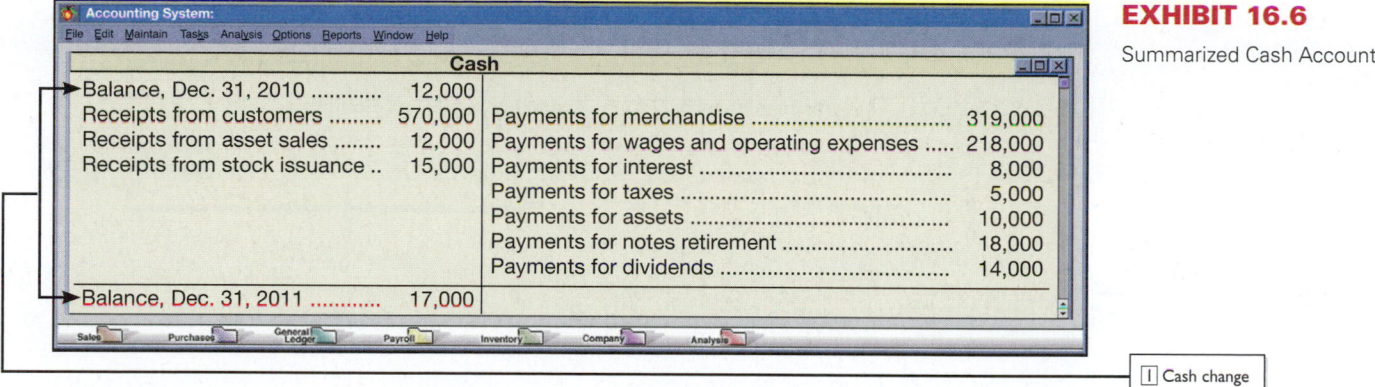

**EXHIBIT 16.6**

Summarized Cash Account

activity. This yields the statement shown in Exhibit 16.7. However, preparing the statement of cash flows from an analysis of the summarized Cash account has two limitations. First, most companies have many individual cash receipts and payments, making it difficult to review them all. Accounting software minimizes this burden, but it is still a task requiring professional judgment for many transactions. Second, the Cash account does not usually carry an adequate description of each cash transaction, making assignment of all cash transactions according to activity difficult.

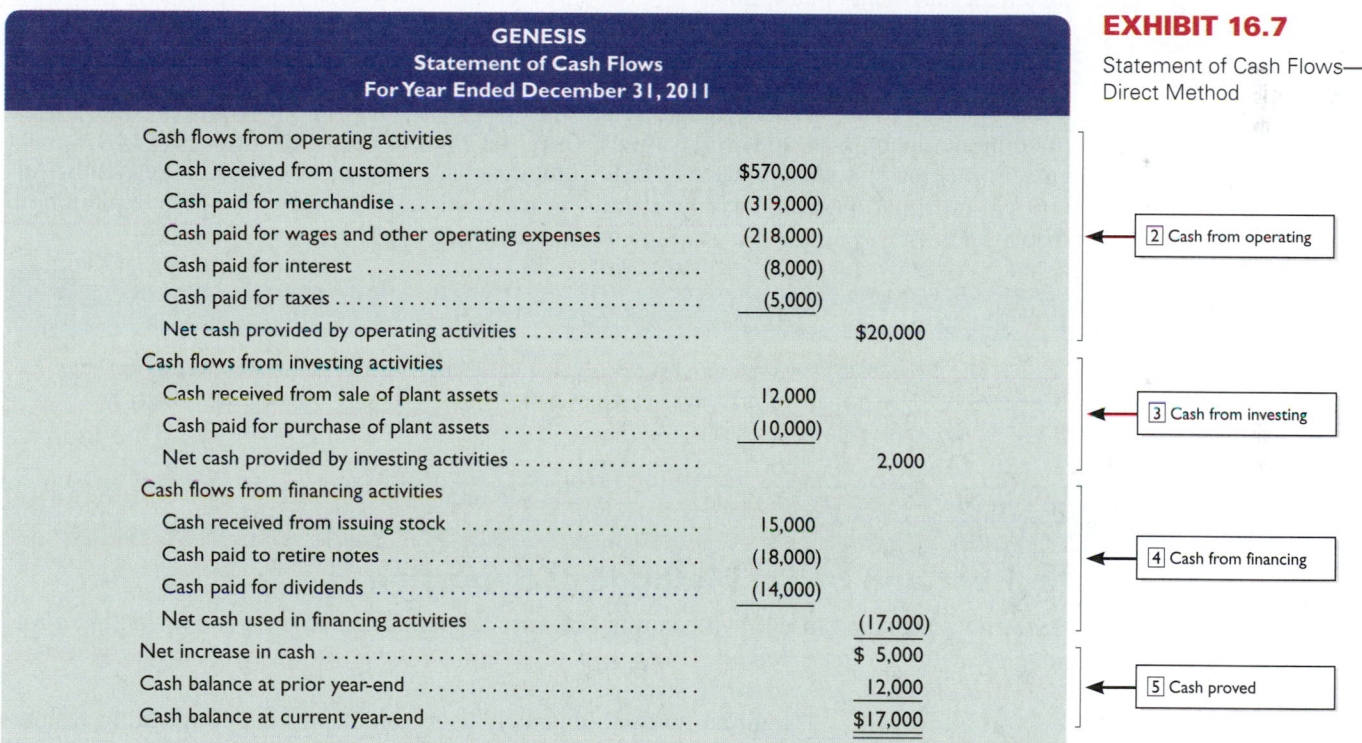

**EXHIBIT 16.7**

Statement of Cash Flows—
Direct Method

**Analyzing Noncash Accounts**    A second approach to preparing the statement of cash flows is analyzing noncash accounts. This approach uses the fact that when a company records cash inflows and outflows with debits and credits to the Cash account (see Exhibit 16.6), it also records credits and debits in noncash accounts (reflecting double-entry accounting). Many of these noncash accounts are balance sheet accounts—for instance, from the sale of land for cash. Others are revenue and expense accounts that are closed to equity. For instance, the sale of services for cash yields a credit to Services Revenue that is closed to Retained Earnings for a corporation. In sum, *all cash transactions eventually affect noncash balance sheet accounts*. Thus, we can determine cash inflows and outflows by analyzing changes in noncash balance sheet accounts.

Exhibit 16.8 uses the accounting equation to show the relation between the Cash account and the noncash balance sheet accounts. This exhibit starts with the accounting equation at the

**EXHIBIT 16.8**

Relation between Cash and Noncash Accounts

Information on changes in cash is obtained from studying *either* the Cash account OR the noncash accounts

top. It is then expanded in line (2) to separate cash from noncash asset accounts. Line (3) moves noncash asset accounts to the right-hand side of the equality where they are subtracted. This shows that cash equals the sum of the liability and equity accounts *minus* the noncash asset accounts. Line (4) points out that *changes* on one side of the accounting equation equal *changes* on the other side. It shows that we can explain changes in cash by analyzing changes in the noncash accounts consisting of liability accounts, equity accounts, and noncash asset accounts. By analyzing noncash balance sheet accounts and any related income statement accounts, we can prepare a statement of cash flows.

**Information to Prepare the Statement**    Information to prepare the statement of cash flows usually comes from three sources: (1) comparative balance sheets, (2) the current income statement, and (3) additional information. Comparative balance sheets are used to compute changes in noncash accounts from the beginning to the end of the period. The current income statement is used to help compute cash flows from operating activities. Additional information often includes details on transactions and events that help explain both the cash flows and noncash investing and financing activities.

---

**Decision Insight**

**e-Cash**    Every credit transaction on the Net leaves a trail that a hacker or a marketer can pick up. Enter e-cash—or digital money. The encryption of e-cash protects your money from snoops and thieves and cannot be traced, even by the issuing bank. ■

---

## CASH FLOWS FROM OPERATING

### Indirect and Direct Methods of Reporting

Cash flows provided (used) by operating activities are reported in one of two ways: the *direct method* or the *indirect method*. **These two different methods apply only to the operating activities section.**

The **direct method** separately lists each major item of operating cash receipts (such as cash received from customers) and each major item of operating cash payments (such as cash paid for merchandise). The cash payments are subtracted from cash receipts to determine the net cash provided (used) by operating activities. The operating activities section of Exhibit 16.7 reflects the direct method of reporting operating cash flows.

The **indirect method** reports net income and then adjusts it for items necessary to obtain net cash provided or used by operating activities. It does *not* report individual items of cash inflows and cash outflows from operating activities. Instead, the indirect method reports the necessary adjustments to reconcile net income to net cash provided or used by operating activities. The operating activities section for Genesis prepared under the indirect method is shown in Exhibit 16.9. **The net cash amount provided by operating activities is *identical* under both the direct and indirect methods.**

**EXHIBIT 16.9**

Operating Activities Section—
Indirect Method

| Cash flows from operating activities | | |
|---|---:|---:|
| Net income | | $ 38,000 |
| Adjustments to reconcile net income to net | | |
| cash provided by operating activities | | |
| Increase in accounts receivable | (20,000) | |
| Increase in merchandise inventory | (14,000) | |
| Increase in prepaid expenses | (2,000) | |
| Decrease in accounts payable | (5,000) | |
| Decrease in interest payable | (1,000) | |
| Increase in income taxes payable | 10,000 | |
| Depreciation expense | 24,000 | |
| Loss on sale of plant assets | 6,000 | |
| Gain on retirement of notes | (16,000) | |
| **Net cash provided by operating activities** | | **$20,000** |

This equality always exists. The difference in these methods is with the computation and presentation of this amount. The FASB recommends the direct method, but because it is not required and the indirect method is arguably easier to compute, nearly all companies report operating cash flows using the indirect method.

    To illustrate, we prepare the operating activities section of the statement of cash flows for Genesis. Exhibit 16.10 shows the December 31, 2010 and 2011, balance sheets of Genesis along with its 2011 income statement. We use this information to prepare a statement of cash flows that explains the $5,000 increase in cash for 2011 as reflected in its balance sheets. This $5,000 is computed as Cash of $17,000 at the end of 2011 minus Cash of $12,000 at the end of 2010. Genesis discloses additional information on its 2011 transactions:

**a.** The accounts payable balances result from merchandise inventory purchases.

**b.** Purchased $70,000 in plant assets by paying $10,000 cash and issuing $60,000 of notes payable.

**c.** Sold plant assets with an original cost of $30,000 and accumulated depreciation of $12,000 for $12,000 cash, yielding a $6,000 loss.

**d.** Received $15,000 cash from issuing 3,000 shares of common stock.

**e.** Paid $18,000 cash to retire notes with a $34,000 book value, yielding a $16,000 gain.

**f.** Declared and paid cash dividends of $14,000.

*The next section describes the indirect method. Appendix 16B describes the direct method. An instructor can choose to cover either one or both methods. Neither section depends on the other.*

**Point:** To better understand the direct and indirect methods of reporting operating cash flows, identify similarities and differences between Exhibits 16.7 and 16.11.

## Application of the Indirect Method of Reporting

Net income is computed using accrual accounting, which recognizes revenues when earned and expenses when incurred. Revenues and expenses do not necessarily reflect the receipt and payment of cash. The indirect method of computing and reporting net cash flows from operating activities involves adjusting the net income figure to obtain the net cash provided or used by operating activities. This includes subtracting noncash increases (credits) from net income and adding noncash charges (debits) back to net income.

    To illustrate, the indirect method begins with Genesis's net income of $38,000 and adjusts it to obtain net cash provided by operating activities of $20,000. Exhibit 16.11 shows the results of the indirect method of reporting operating cash flows, which adjusts net income for three types of adjustments. There are adjustments ① to reflect changes in noncash current assets and current liabilities related to operating activities, ② to income statement items involving operating activities that do not affect cash inflows or outflows, and ③ to eliminate gains and losses resulting from investing and financing activities (not part of operating activities). This section describes each of these adjustments.

**P2** Compute cash flows from operating activities using the indirect method.

**Point:** *Noncash credits* refer to *revenue* amounts reported on the income statement that are *not collected in cash* this period. *Noncash charges* refer to *expense* amounts reported on the income statement that are *not paid* this period.

## EXHIBIT 16.10

Financial Statements

| GENESIS<br>Income Statement<br>For Year Ended December 31, 2011 | | |
| --- | --- | --- |
| Sales ............................ | | $590,000 |
| Cost of goods sold ................ | $300,000 | |
| Wages and other operating expenses .. | 216,000 | |
| Interest expense ................... | 7,000 | |
| Depreciation expense .............. | 24,000 | (547,000) |
| | | 43,000 |
| Other gains (losses) | | |
|    Gain on retirement of notes ...... | 16,000 | |
|    Loss on sale of plant assets ........ | (6,000) | 10,000 |
| Income before taxes ............... | | 53,000 |
| Income taxes expense ............. | | (15,000) |
| Net income ...................... | | $ 38,000 |

| GENESIS<br>Balance Sheets<br>December 31, 2011 and 2010 | | |
| --- | --- | --- |
| | **2011** | **2010** |
| **Assets** | | |
| Current assets | | |
|    Cash ......................... | $ 17,000 | $ 12,000 |
|    Accounts receivable ............. | 60,000 | 40,000 |
|    Merchandise inventory ........... | 84,000 | 70,000 |
|    Prepaid expenses ............... | 6,000 | 4,000 |
|    Total current assets ............. | 167,000 | 126,000 |
| Long-term assets | | |
|    Plant assets .................... | 250,000 | 210,000 |
|    Accumulated depreciation ........ | (60,000) | (48,000) |
| Total assets ...................... | $357,000 | $288,000 |
| **Liabilities** | | |
| Current liabilities | | |
|    Accounts payable ............... | $ 35,000 | $ 40,000 |
|    Interest payable ................. | 3,000 | 4,000 |
|    Income taxes payable ........... | 22,000 | 12,000 |
|    Total current liabilities ........... | 60,000 | 56,000 |
| Long-term notes payable ........... | 90,000 | 64,000 |
| Total liabilities .................... | 150,000 | 120,000 |
| **Equity** | | |
| Common stock, $5 par ............. | 95,000 | 80,000 |
| Retained earnings ................. | 112,000 | 88,000 |
| Total equity ..................... | 207,000 | 168,000 |
| Total liabilities and equity .......... | $357,000 | $288,000 |

① **Adjustments for Changes in Current Assets and Current Liabilities**   This section describes adjustments for changes in noncash current assets and current liabilities.

**Point:** Operating activities are typically those that determine income, which are often reflected in changes in current assets and current liabilities.

**Adjustments for changes in noncash current assets.**   Changes in noncash current assets normally result from operating activities. Examples are sales affecting accounts receivable and building usage affecting prepaid rent. Decreases in noncash current assets yield the following adjustment:

**Decreases in noncash current assets are added to net income.**

To see the logic for this adjustment, consider that a decrease in a noncash current asset such as accounts receivable suggests more available cash at the end of the period compared to the beginning. This is so because a decrease in accounts receivable implies higher cash receipts than reflected in sales. We add these higher cash receipts (from decreases in noncash current assets) to net income when computing cash flow from operations.

     In contrast, an increase in noncash current assets such as accounts receivable implies less cash receipts than reflected in sales. As another example, an increase in prepaid rent indicates that more cash is paid for rent than is deducted as rent expense. Increases in noncash current assets yield the following adjustment:

**Increases in noncash current assets are subtracted from net income.**

To illustrate, these adjustments are applied to the noncash current assets in Exhibit 16.10.

     *Accounts receivable.* Accounts receivable *increase* $20,000, from a beginning balance of $40,000 to an ending balance of $60,000. This increase implies that Genesis collects less cash than is reported in sales. That is, some of these sales were in the form of accounts receivable and that amount increased during the period. To see this it is helpful to use *account analysis.* This usually involves setting up a T-account and reconstructing its major entries to compute cash receipts or payments. The following reconstructed Accounts Receivable T-account reveals that cash receipts are less than sales:

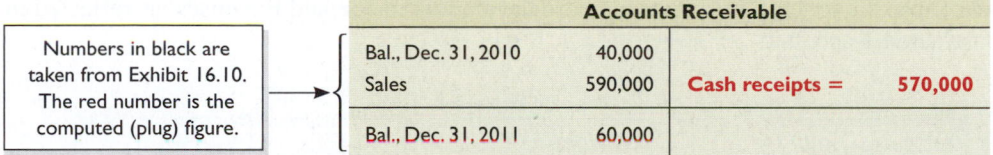

| Accounts Receivable | | | |
|---|---|---|---|
| Bal., Dec. 31, 2010 | 40,000 | | |
| Sales | 590,000 | **Cash receipts =** | **570,000** |
| Bal., Dec. 31, 2011 | 60,000 | | |

Numbers in black are taken from Exhibit 16.10. The red number is the computed (plug) figure.

We see that sales are $20,000 greater than cash receipts. This $20,000—as reflected in the $20,000 increase in Accounts Receivable—is subtracted from net income when computing cash provided by operating activities (see Exhibit 16.11).

*Merchandise inventory.* Merchandise inventory *increases* by $14,000, from a $70,000 beginning balance to an $84,000 ending balance. This increase implies that Genesis had greater cash purchases than cost of goods sold. This larger amount of cash purchases is in the form of inventory, as reflected in the following account analysis:

| Merchandise Inventory | | | |
|---|---|---|---|
| Bal., Dec. 31, 2010 | 70,000 | | |
| **Purchases =** | **314,000** | Cost of goods sold | 300,000 |
| Bal., Dec. 31, 2011 | 84,000 | | |

| GENESIS |
|---|
| Statement of Cash Flows |
| For Year Ended December 31, 2011 |

| | | |
|---|---|---|
| Cash flows from operating activities | | |
| Net income . . . . . . . . . . . . . . . . . . . . . . . . . . . . . . . . | $ 38,000 | |
| Adjustments to reconcile net income to net | | |
| cash provided by operating activities | | |
| Increase in accounts receivable. . . . . . . . . . . . . . . . | (20,000) | |
| Increase in merchandise inventory . . . . . . . . . . . . . | (14,000) | |
| Increase in prepaid expenses . . . . . . . . . . . . . . . . . | (2,000) | |
| Decrease in accounts payable. . . . . . . . . . . . . . . . . | (5,000) | |
| Decrease in interest payable. . . . . . . . . . . . . . . . . . | (1,000) | |
| Increase in income taxes payable . . . . . . . . . . . . . . | 10,000 | |
| Depreciation expense . . . . . . . . . . . . . . . . . . . . . . . | 24,000 | |
| Loss on sale of plant assets. . . . . . . . . . . . . . . . . . . | 6,000 | |
| Gain on retirement of notes. . . . . . . . . . . . . . . . . . | (16,000) | |
| Net cash provided by operating activities . . . . . . . . . . . | | $20,000 |
| Cash flows from investing activities | | |
| Cash received from sale of plant assets . . . . . . . . . . . . . | 12,000 | |
| Cash paid for purchase of plant assets . . . . . . . . . . . . . . | (10,000) | |
| Net cash provided by investing activities . . . . . . . . . . . . | | 2,000 |
| Cash flows from financing activities | | |
| Cash received from issuing stock . . . . . . . . . . . . . . . . . . | 15,000 | |
| Cash paid to retire notes . . . . . . . . . . . . . . . . . . . . . . . | (18,000) | |
| Cash paid for dividends. . . . . . . . . . . . . . . . . . . . . . . . . | (14,000) | |
| Net cash used in financing activities . . . . . . . . . . . . . . . . | | (17,000) |
| Net increase in cash . . . . . . . . . . . . . . . . . . . . . . . . . . . | | $ 5,000 |
| Cash balance at prior year-end. . . . . . . . . . . . . . . . . . . . | | 12,000 |
| Cash balance at current year-end . . . . . . . . . . . . . . . . . . | | $17,000 |

Labels: ① (operating adjustments), ② { Depreciation expense, ③ { Loss on sale of plant assets / Gain on retirement of notes

**EXHIBIT 16.11**

Statement of Cash Flows—Indirect Method

**Point:** Refer to Exhibit 16.10 and identify the $5,000 change in cash. This change is what the statement of cash flows explains; it serves as a check.

The amount by which purchases exceed cost of goods sold—as reflected in the $14,000 increase in inventory—is subtracted from net income when computing cash provided by operating activities (see Exhibit 16.11).

*Prepaid expenses.* Prepaid Expenses *increase* $2,000, from a $4,000 beginning balance to a $6,000 ending balance, implying that Genesis's cash payments exceed its recorded prepaid expenses. These higher cash payments increase the amount of Prepaid Expenses, as reflected in its reconstructed T-account:

| Prepaid Expenses | | | |
|---|---|---|---|
| Bal., Dec. 31, 2010 | 4,000 | | |
| **Cash payments =** | **218,000** | Wages and other operating exp. | 216,000 |
| Bal., Dec. 31, 2011 | 6,000 | | |

The amount by which cash payments exceed the recorded operating expenses—as reflected in the $2,000 increase in Prepaid Expenses—is subtracted from net income when computing cash provided by operating activities (see Exhibit 16.11).

**Adjustments for changes in current liabilities.** Changes in current liabilities normally result from operating activities. An example is a purchase that affects accounts payable. Increases in current liabilities yield the following adjustment to net income when computing operating cash flows:

**Increases in current liabilities are added to net income.**

To see the logic for this adjustment, consider that an increase in the Accounts Payable account suggests that cash payments are less than the related (cost of goods sold) expense. As another example, an increase in wages payable implies that cash paid for wages is less than the recorded wages expense. Since the recorded expense is greater than the cash paid, we add the increase in wages payable to net income to compute net cash flow from operations.

Conversely, when current liabilities decrease, the following adjustment is required:

**Decreases in current liabilities are subtracted from net income.**

To illustrate, these adjustments are applied to the current liabilities in Exhibit 16.10.

*Accounts payable.* Accounts payable *decrease* $5,000, from a beginning balance of $40,000 to an ending balance of $35,000. This decrease implies that cash payments to suppliers exceed purchases by $5,000 for the period, which is reflected in the reconstructed Accounts Payable T-account:

| Accounts Payable | | | |
|---|---|---|---|
| | | Bal., Dec. 31, 2010 | 40,000 |
| **Cash payments =** | **319,000** | Purchases | 314,000 |
| | | Bal., Dec. 31, 2011 | 35,000 |

The amount by which cash payments exceed purchases—as reflected in the $5,000 decrease in Accounts Payable—is subtracted from net income when computing cash provided by operating activities (see Exhibit 16.11).

*Interest payable.* Interest payable *decreases* $1,000, from a $4,000 beginning balance to a $3,000 ending balance. This decrease indicates that cash paid for interest exceeds interest expense by $1,000, which is reflected in the Interest Payable T-account:

| Interest Payable | | | |
|---|---|---|---|
| | | Bal., Dec. 31, 2010 | 4,000 |
| **Cash paid for interest =** | **8,000** | Interest expense | 7,000 |
| | | Bal., Dec. 31, 2011 | 3,000 |

The amount by which cash paid exceeds recorded expense—as reflected in the $1,000 decrease in Interest Payable—is subtracted from net income (see Exhibit 16.11).

*Income taxes payable.* Income taxes payable *increase* $10,000, from a $12,000 beginning balance to a $22,000 ending balance. This increase implies that reported income taxes exceed the cash paid for taxes, which is reflected in the Income Taxes Payable T-account:

| Income Taxes Payable | | | |
|---|---|---|---|
| | | Bal., Dec. 31, 2010 | 12,000 |
| **Cash paid for taxes =** | **5,000** | Income taxes expense | 15,000 |
| | | Bal., Dec. 31, 2011 | 22,000 |

The amount by which cash paid falls short of the reported taxes expense—as reflected in the $10,000 increase in Income Taxes Payable—is added to net income when computing cash provided by operating activities (see Exhibit 16.11).

② **Adjustments for Operating Items Not Providing or Using Cash** The income statement usually includes some expenses that do not reflect cash outflows in the period. Examples are depreciation, amortization, depletion, and bad debts expense. The indirect method for reporting operating cash flows requires that

**Expenses with no cash outflows are added back to net income.**

To see the logic of this adjustment, recall that items such as depreciation, amortization, depletion, and bad debts originate from debits to expense accounts and credits to noncash accounts. These entries have *no* cash effect, and we add them back to net income when computing net cash flows from operations. Adding them back cancels their deductions.

Similarly, when net income includes revenues that do not reflect cash inflows in the period, the indirect method for reporting operating cash flows requires that

**Revenues with no cash inflows are subtracted from net income.**

We apply these adjustments to the Genesis operating items that do not provide or use cash.

**Depreciation.** Depreciation expense is the only Genesis operating item that has no effect on cash flows in the period. We must add back the $24,000 depreciation expense to net income when computing cash provided by operating activities. (We later explain that any cash outflow to acquire a plant asset is reported as an investing activity.)

③ **Adjustments for Nonoperating Items** Net income often includes losses that are not part of operating activities but are part of either investing or financing activities. Examples are a loss from the sale of a plant asset and a loss from retirement of notes payable. The indirect method for reporting operating cash flows requires that

**Nonoperating losses are added back to net income.**

To see the logic, consider that items such as a plant asset sale and a notes retirement are normally recorded by recognizing the cash, removing all plant asset or notes accounts, and recognizing any loss or gain. The cash received or paid is not part of operating activities but is part of either investing or financing activities. *No* operating cash flow effect occurs. However, because the nonoperating loss is a deduction in computing net income, we need to add it back to net income when computing cash flow from operations. Adding it back cancels the deduction.

Similarly, when net income includes gains not part of operating activities, the indirect method for reporting operating cash flows requires that

**Nonoperating gains are subtracted from net income.**

To illustrate these adjustments, we consider the nonoperating items of Genesis.

**Summary Adjustments for Changes in Current Assets and Current Liabilities**

| Account | Increases | Decreases |
|---|---|---|
| Noncash current assets . . . . . . . | Deduct from NI | Add to NI |
| Current liabilities . . . . . . | Add to NI | Deduct from NI |

**Point:** An income statement reports revenues, gains, expenses, and losses on an accrual basis. The statement of cash flows reports cash received and cash paid for operating, financing, and investing activities.

**Loss on sale of plant assets.**   Genesis reports a $6,000 loss on sale of plant assets as part of net income. This loss is a proper deduction in computing income, but it is *not part of operating activities*. Instead, a sale of plant assets is part of investing activities. Thus, the $6,000 nonoperating loss is added back to net income (see Exhibit 16.11). Adding it back cancels the loss. We later explain how to report the cash inflow from the asset sale in investing activities.

**Gain on retirement of debt.**   A $16,000 gain on retirement of debt is properly included in net income, but it is *not part of operating activities*. This means the $16,000 nonoperating gain must be subtracted from net income to obtain net cash provided by operating activities (see Exhibit 16.11). Subtracting it cancels the recorded gain. We later describe how to report the cash outflow to retire debt.

## Summary of Adjustments for Indirect Method

Exhibit 16.12 summarizes the most common adjustments to net income when computing net cash provided or used by operating activities under the indirect method.

**EXHIBIT 16.12**

Summary of Selected Adjustments for Indirect Method

\* Excludes current portion of long-term debt and any (nonsales-related) short-term notes payable—both are financing activities.

The computations in determining cash provided or used by operating activities are different for the indirect and direct methods, but the result is identical. Both methods yield the same $20,000 figure for cash from operating activities for Genesis; see Exhibits 16.7 and 16.11.

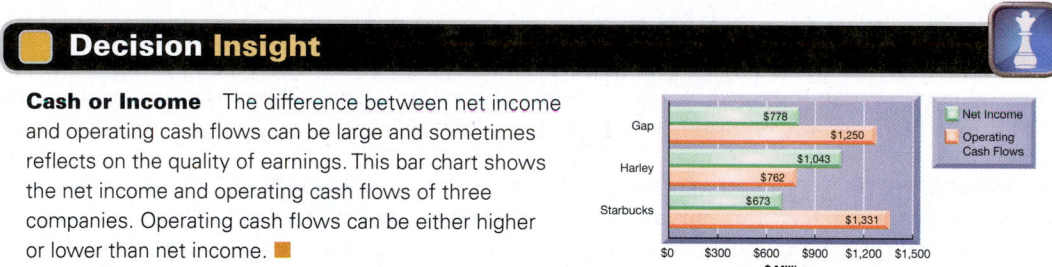

**Decision Insight**

**Cash or Income**   The difference between net income and operating cash flows can be large and sometimes reflects on the quality of earnings. This bar chart shows the net income and operating cash flows of three companies. Operating cash flows can be either higher or lower than net income.

**Quick Check**                                    Answers — p. 662

4. Determine the net cash provided or used by operating activities using the following data: net income, $74,900; decrease in accounts receivable, $4,600; increase in inventory, $11,700; decrease in accounts payable, $1,000; loss on sale of equipment, $3,400; payment of cash dividends, $21,500.

5. Why are expenses such as depreciation and amortization added to net income when cash flow from operating activities is computed by the indirect method?

6. A company reports net income of $15,000 that includes a $3,000 gain on the sale of plant assets. Why is this gain subtracted from net income in computing cash flow from operating activities using the indirect method?

## CASH FLOWS FROM INVESTING

The third major step in preparing the statement of cash flows is to compute and report cash flows from investing activities. We normally do this by identifying changes in (1) all noncurrent asset accounts and (2) the current accounts for both notes receivable and investments in securities (excluding trading securities). We then analyze changes in these accounts to determine their effect, if any, on cash and report the cash flow effects in the investing activities section of the statement of cash flows. **Reporting of investing activities is identical under the direct method and indirect method.**

### Three-Stage Process of Analysis

Information to compute cash flows from investing activities is usually taken from beginning and ending balance sheets and the income statement. We use a three-stage process to determine cash provided or used by investing activities: (1) identify changes in investing-related accounts, (2) explain these changes using reconstruction analysis, and (3) report their cash flow effects.

**P3** Determine cash flows from both investing and financing activities.

### Analysis of Noncurrent Assets

Information about the Genesis transactions provided earlier reveals that the company both purchased and sold plant assets during the period. Both transactions are investing activities and are analyzed for their cash flow effects in this section.

**Plant Asset Transactions** The first stage in analyzing the Plant Assets account and its related Accumulated Depreciation is to identify any changes in these accounts from comparative balance sheets in Exhibit 16.10. This analysis reveals a $40,000 increase in plant assets from $210,000 to $250,000 and a $12,000 increase in accumulated depreciation from $48,000 to $60,000.

The second stage is to explain these changes. Items *b* and *c* of the additional information for Genesis (page 639) are relevant in this case. Recall that the Plant Assets account is affected by both asset purchases and sales, while its Accumulated Depreciation account is normally increased from depreciation and decreased from the removal of accumulated depreciation in asset sales. To explain changes in these accounts and to identify their cash flow effects, we prepare *reconstructed entries* from prior transactions; *they are not the actual entries by the preparer.*

To illustrate, item *b* reports that Genesis purchased plant assets of $70,000 by issuing $60,000 in notes payable to the seller and paying $10,000 in cash. The reconstructed entry for analysis of item *b* follows:

**Point:** Investing activities include (1) purchasing and selling long-term assets, (2) lending and collecting on notes receivable, and (3) purchasing and selling short-term investments other than cash equivalents and trading securities.

**Point:** Financing and investing info is available in ledger accounts to help explain changes in comparative balance sheets. Post references lead to relevant entries and explanations.

| Reconstruction | Plant Assets ................................... | 70,000 | |
|---|---|---|---|
| | Notes Payable .......................... | | 60,000 |
| | **Cash** ..................................... | | **10,000** |

This entry reveals a $10,000 cash outflow for plant assets and a $60,000 noncash investing and financing transaction involving notes exchanged for plant assets.

Next, item *c* reports that Genesis sold plant assets costing $30,000 (with $12,000 of accumulated depreciation) for $12,000 cash, resulting in a $6,000 loss. The reconstructed entry for analysis of item *c* follows:

| Reconstruction | **Cash** ....................................... | **12,000** | |
|---|---|---|---|
| | Accumulated Depreciation ...................... | 12,000 | |
| | Loss on Sale of Plant Assets .................... | 6,000 | |
| | Plant Assets ............................. | | 30,000 |

This entry reveals a $12,000 cash inflow from assets sold. The $6,000 loss is computed by comparing the asset book value to the cash received and does not reflect any cash inflow or outflow. We also reconstruct the entry for Depreciation Expense using information from the income statement.

| Reconstruction | Depreciation Expense . . . . . . . . . . . . . . . . . . . . . . . . . . . . | 24,000 | |
|---|---|---|---|
| | Accumulated Depreciation . . . . . . . . . . . . . . . . . . | | 24,000 |

This entry shows that Depreciation Expense results in no cash flow effect. These three reconstructed entries are reflected in the following plant asset and related T-accounts.

| Plant Assets | | | | | Accumulated Depreciation—Plant Assets | | | |
|---|---|---|---|---|---|---|---|---|
| Bal., Dec. 31, 2010 | 210,000 | | | | | | Bal., Dec. 31, 2010 | 48,000 |
| Purchase | 70,000 | Sale | 30,000 | Sale | 12,000 | Depr. expense | | 24,000 |
| Bal., Dec. 31, 2011 | 250,000 | | | | | | Bal., Dec. 31, 2011 | 60,000 |

This reconstruction analysis is complete in that the change in plant assets from $210,000 to $250,000 is fully explained by the $70,000 purchase and the $30,000 sale. Also, the change in accumulated depreciation from $48,000 to $60,000 is fully explained by depreciation expense of $24,000 and the removal of $12,000 in accumulated depreciation from an asset sale. (Preparers of the statement of cash flows have the entire ledger and additional information at their disposal, but for brevity reasons only the information needed for reconstructing accounts is given.)

**Example:** If a plant asset costing $40,000 with $37,000 of accumulated depreciation is sold at a $1,000 loss, what is the cash flow? What is the cash flow if this asset is sold at a gain of $3,000? *Answers:* +$2,000; +$6,000.

The third stage looks at the reconstructed entries for identification of cash flows. The two identified cash flow effects are reported in the investing section of the statement as follows (also see Exhibit 16.7 or 16.11):

| Cash flows from investing activities | |
|---|---|
| Cash received from sale of plant assets . . . . . . . . . . . . . . . | $12,000 |
| Cash paid for purchase of plant assets . . . . . . . . . . . . . . . | (10,000) |

The $60,000 portion of the purchase described in item *b* and financed by issuing notes is a noncash investing and financing activity. It is reported in a note or in a separate schedule to the statement as follows:

| Noncash investing and financing activity | |
|---|---|
| Purchased plant assets with issuance of notes . . . . . . . . . . | $60,000 |

## Analysis of Other Assets

Many other asset transactions (including those involving current notes receivable and investments in certain securities) are considered investing activities and can affect a company's cash flows. Since Genesis did not enter into other investing activities impacting assets, we do not need to extend our analysis to these other assets. If such transactions did exist, we would analyze them using the same three-stage process illustrated for plant assets.

| **Quick Check** | Answer — p. 662 |
|---|---|

> **7.** Equipment costing $80,000 with accumulated depreciation of $30,000 is sold at a loss of $10,000. What is the cash receipt from this sale? In what section of the statement of cash flows is this transaction reported?

## CASH FLOWS FROM FINANCING

The fourth major step in preparing the statement of cash flows is to compute and report  cash flows from financing activities. We normally do this by identifying changes in all noncurrent liability accounts (including the current portion of any notes and bonds) and the equity accounts. These accounts include long-term debt, notes payable, bonds payable, common stock, and retained earnings. Changes in these accounts are then analyzed using available information to determine their effect, if any, on cash. Results are reported in the financing activities section of the statement. **Reporting of financing activities is identical under the direct method and indirect method.**

### Three-Stage Process of Analysis

We again use a three-stage process to determine cash provided or used by financing activities: (1) identify changes in financing-related accounts, (2) explain these changes using reconstruction analysis, and (3) report their cash flow effects.

### Analysis of Noncurrent Liabilities

Information about Genesis provided earlier reveals two transactions involving noncurrent liabilities. We analyzed one of those, the $60,000 issuance of notes payable to purchase plant assets. This transaction is reported as a significant noncash investing and financing activity in a footnote or a separate schedule to the statement of cash flows. The other remaining transaction involving noncurrent liabilities is the cash retirement of notes payable.

**Point:** Financing activities generally refer to changes in the noncurrent liability and the equity accounts. Examples are (1) receiving cash from issuing debt or repaying amounts borrowed and (2) receiving cash from or distributing cash to owners.

**Notes Payable Transactions**    The first stage in analysis of notes is to review the comparative balance sheets from Exhibit 16.10. This analysis reveals an increase in notes payable from $64,000 to $90,000.

The second stage explains this change. Item *e* of the additional information for Genesis (page 639) reports that notes with a carrying value of $34,000 are retired for $18,000 cash, resulting in a $16,000 gain. The reconstructed entry for analysis of item *e* follows:

| Reconstruction | Notes Payable ............................... | 34,000 | |
|---|---|---|---|
| | Gain on retirement of debt .................. | | 16,000 |
| | **Cash** ...................................... | | **18,000** |

This entry reveals an $18,000 cash outflow for retirement of notes and a $16,000 gain from comparing the notes payable carrying value to the cash received. This gain does not reflect any cash inflow or outflow. Also, item *b* of the additional information reports that Genesis purchased plant assets costing $70,000 by issuing $60,000 in notes payable to the seller and paying $10,000 in cash. We reconstructed this entry when analyzing investing activities: It showed a $60,000 increase to notes payable that is reported as a noncash investing and financing transaction. The Notes Payable account reflects (and is fully explained by) these reconstructed entries as follows:

| Notes Payable | | | |
|---|---|---|---|
| | | Bal., Dec. 31, 2010 | 64,000 |
| **Retired notes** | 34,000 | **Issued notes** | **60,000** |
| | | Bal., Dec. 31, 2011 | 90,000 |

The third stage is to report the cash flow effect of the notes retirement in the financing section of the statement as follows (also see Exhibit 16.7 or 16.11):

| **Cash flows from financing activities** | |
|---|---|
| Cash paid to retire notes ................. | $(18,000) |

## Analysis of Equity

The Genesis information reveals two transactions involving equity accounts. The first is the issuance of common stock for cash. The second is the declaration and payment of cash dividends. We analyze both.

**Common Stock Transactions**    The first stage in analyzing common stock is to review the comparative balance sheets from Exhibit 16.10, which reveal an increase in common stock from $80,000 to $95,000.

The second stage explains this change. Item *d* of the additional information (page 639) reports that 3,000 shares of common stock are issued at par for $5 per share. The reconstructed entry for analysis of item *d* follows:

| Reconstruction | Cash ........................................ | 15,000 | |
| | Common Stock ........................... | | 15,000 |

This entry reveals a $15,000 cash inflow from stock issuance and is reflected in (and explains) the Common Stock account as follows:

| Common Stock | | |
|---|---|---|
| | Bal., Dec. 31, 2010 | 80,000 |
| | Issued stock | 15,000 |
| | Bal., Dec. 31, 2011 | 95,000 |

The third stage discloses the cash flow effect from stock issuance in the financing section of the statement as follows (also see Exhibit 16.7 or 16.11):

| Cash flows from financing activities | |
|---|---|
| Cash received from issuing stock ............. | $15,000 |

**Retained Earnings Transactions**    The first stage in analyzing the Retained Earnings account is to review the comparative balance sheets from Exhibit 16.10. This reveals an increase in retained earnings from $88,000 to $112,000.

The second stage explains this change. Item *f* of the additional information (page 639) reports that cash dividends of $14,000 are paid. The reconstructed entry follows:

| Reconstruction | Retained Earnings ............................. | 14,000 | |
| | Cash ..................................... | | 14,000 |

This entry reveals a $14,000 cash outflow for cash dividends. Also see that the Retained Earnings account is impacted by net income of $38,000. (Net income was analyzed under the operating section of the statement of cash flows.) The reconstructed Retained Earnings account follows:

| Retained Earnings | | | | |
|---|---|---|---|---|
| | | | Bal., Dec. 31, 2010 | 88,000 |
| Cash dividend | 14,000 | | Net income | 38,000 |
| | | | Bal., Dec. 31, 2011 | 112,000 |

**Point:** Financing activities not affecting cash flow include *declaration* of a cash dividend, *declaration* of a stock dividend, payment of a stock dividend, and a stock split.

The third stage reports the cash flow effect from the cash dividend in the financing section of the statement as follows (also see Exhibit 16.7 or 16.11):

| Cash flows from financing activities | |
|---|---|
| Cash paid for dividends..................... | $(14,000) |

**Global:** There are no requirements to separate domestic and international cash flows, leading some users to ask, "Where in the world is cash flow?"

We now have identified and explained all of the Genesis cash inflows and cash outflows and one noncash investing and financing transaction. Specifically, our analysis has reconciled changes in all noncash balance sheet accounts.

## Proving Cash Balances

The fifth and final step in preparing the statement is to report the beginning and ending cash balances and prove that the *net change in cash* is explained by operating, investing, and financing cash flows. This step is shown here for Genesis.

| | |
|---|---|
| Net cash provided by operating activities ........ | $20,000 |
| Net cash provided by investing activities ......... | 2,000 |
| Net cash used in financing activities ............ | (17,000) |
| **Net increase in cash** ...................... | **$ 5,000** |
| Cash balance at 2010 year-end ................ | 12,000 |
| Cash balance at 2011 year-end ................ | $17,000 |

The preceding table shows that the $5,000 net increase in cash, from $12,000 at the beginning of the period to $17,000 at the end, is reconciled by net cash flows from operating ($20,000 inflow), investing ($2,000 inflow), and financing ($17,000 outflow) activities. This is formally reported at the bottom of the statement of cash flows as shown in both Exhibits 16.7 and 16.11.

**Decision Maker**    Answer — p. 662

**Reporter**   Management is in labor contract negotiations and grants you an interview. It highlights a recent $600,000 net loss that involves a $930,000 extraordinary loss and a total net cash outflow of $550,000 (which includes net cash outflows of $850,000 for investing activities and $350,000 for financing activities). What is your assessment of this company? ∎

## GLOBAL VIEW

The statement of cash flows, which explains changes in cash (including cash equivalents) from period to period, is required under both U.S. GAAP and IFRS. This section discusses similarities and differences between U.S. GAAP and IFRS in reporting that statement.

**Reporting Cash Flows from Operating**   Both U.S. GAAP and IFRS permit the reporting of cash flows from operating activities using either the direct or indirect method. Further, the basic requirements underlying the application of both methods are fairly consistent across these two accounting systems. Appendix A shows that Nokia reports its cash flows from operating activities using the indirect method, and in a manner similar to that explained in this chapter. Further, the definition of cash and cash equivalents is roughly similar for U.S. GAAP and IFRS.

NOKIA

There are, however, some differences between U.S. GAAP and IFRS in reporting operating cash flows. We mention two of the more notable. First, U.S. GAAP requires cash inflows from interest revenue and dividend revenue be classified as operating, whereas IFRS permits classification under operating or investing provided that this classification is consistently applied across periods. Nokia reports its cash from interest received under operating, consistent with U.S. GAAP (no mention is made of any dividends received). Second, U.S. GAAP requires cash outflows for interest expense be classified as operating, whereas IFRS again permits classification under operating or financing provided that it is consistently applied across periods. (Some believe that interest payments, like dividends payments, are better classified as financing because they represent payments to financiers.) Nokia reports cash outflows for interest under operating, which is consistent with U.S. GAAP and acceptable under IFRS.

**Reporting Cash Flows from Investing and Financing**   U.S. GAAP and IFRS are broadly similar in computing and classifying cash flows from investing and financing activities. A quick review of these two sections for Nokia's statement of cash flows shows a structure similar to that explained in this chapter. One notable exception is that U.S. GAAP requires cash outflows for income tax be classified as operating, whereas IFRS permits the splitting of those cash flows among operating, investing, and financing depending on the sources of that tax. Nokia reports its cash outflows for income tax under operating, which is similar to U.S. GAAP.

## Decision Analysis 　　　Cash Flow Analysis

### Analyzing Cash Sources and Uses

**A1** Analyze the statement of cash flows and apply the cash flow on total assets ratio.

Most managers stress the importance of understanding and predicting cash flows for business decisions. Creditors evaluate a company's ability to generate cash before deciding whether to lend money. Investors also assess cash inflows and outflows before buying and selling stock. Information in the statement of cash flows helps address these and other questions such as (1) How much cash is generated from or used in operations? (2) What expenditures are made with cash from operations? (3) What is the source of cash for debt payments? (4) What is the source of cash for distributions to owners? (5) How is the increase in investing activities financed? (6) What is the source of cash for new plant assets? (7) Why is cash flow from operations different from income? (8) How is cash from financing used?

To effectively answer these questions, it is important to separately analyze investing, financing, and operating activities. To illustrate, consider data from three different companies in Exhibit 16.13. These companies operate in the same industry and have been in business for several years.

**EXHIBIT 16.13**

Cash Flows of Competing Companies

| ($ thousands) | BMX | ATV | Trex |
|---|---|---|---|
| Cash provided (used) by operating activities . . . . . . . . . | $90,000 | $40,000 | $(24,000) |
| Cash provided (used) by investing activities | | | |
|   Proceeds from sale of plant assets . . . . . . . . . . . . . . | | | 26,000 |
|   Purchase of plant assets . . . . . . . . . . . . . . . . . . . . . . | (48,000) | (25,000) | |
| Cash provided (used) by financing activities | | | |
|   Proceeds from issuance of debt . . . . . . . . . . . . . . . . | | | 13,000 |
|   Repayment of debt . . . . . . . . . . . . . . . . . . . . . . . . . . | (27,000) | | |
| Net increase (decrease) in cash . . . . . . . . . . . . . . . . . . | $15,000 | $15,000 | $ 15,000 |

Each company generates an identical $15,000 net increase in cash, but its sources and uses of cash flows are very different. BMX's operating activities provide net cash flows of $90,000, allowing it to purchase plant assets of $48,000 and repay $27,000 of its debt. ATV's operating activities provide $40,000 of cash flows, limiting its purchase of plant assets to $25,000. Trex's $15,000 net cash increase is due to selling plant assets and incurring additional debt. Its operating activities yield a net cash outflow of $24,000. Overall, analysis of these cash flows reveals that BMX is more capable of generating future cash flows than is ATV or Trex.

### Decision Insight

**Free Cash Flows**　Many investors use cash flows to value company stock. However, cash-based valuation models often yield different stock values due to differences in measurement of cash flows. Most models require cash flows that are "free" for distribution to shareholders. These *free cash flows* are defined as cash flows available to shareholders after operating asset reinvestments and debt payments. Knowledge of the statement of cash flows is key to proper computation of free cash flows. A company's growth and financial flexibility depend on adequate free cash flows. ■

### Cash Flow on Total Assets

Cash flow information has limitations, but it can help measure a company's ability to meet its obligations, pay dividends, expand operations, and obtain financing. Users often compute and analyze a cash-based ratio similar to return on total assets except that its numerator is net cash flows from operating activities. The **cash flow on total assets** ratio is in Exhibit 16.14.

**EXHIBIT 16.14**

Cash Flow on Total Assets

$$\text{Cash flow on total assets} = \frac{\text{Cash flow from operations}}{\text{Average total assets}}$$

This ratio reflects actual cash flows and is not affected by accounting income recognition and measurement. It can help business decision makers estimate the amount and timing of cash flows when planning and analyzing operating activities.

To illustrate, the 2009 cash flow on total assets ratio for **Nike** is 13.5%—see Exhibit 16.15. Is a 13.5% ratio good or bad? To answer this question, we compare this ratio with the ratios of prior years (we could also compare its ratio with those of its competitors and the market). Nike's cash flow on total assets ratio for several prior years is in the second column of Exhibit 16.15. Results show that its 13.5% return is the lowest return over the past several years. This is probably reflective of the recent recessionary period.

| Year | Cash Flow on Total Assets | Return on Total Assets |
|---|---|---|
| 2009......... | 13.5% | 11.6% |
| 2008........ | 16.7 | 16.3 |
| 2007......... | 18.3 | 14.5 |
| 2006........ | 17.9 | 14.9 |
| 2005........ | 18.8 | 14.5 |

**EXHIBIT 16.15**

Nike's Cash Flow on Total Assets

As an indicator of *earnings quality,* some analysts compare the cash flow on total assets ratio to the return on total assets ratio. Nike's return on total assets is provided in the third column of Exhibit 16.15. Nike's cash flow on total assets ratio exceeds its return on total assets in each of the five years, leading some analysts to infer that Nike's earnings quality is high for that period because more earnings are realized in the form of cash.

## Decision Insight

**Cash Flow Ratios**  Analysts use various other cash-based ratios, including the following two:

(1) $$\text{Cash coverage of growth} = \frac{\text{Operating cash flow}}{\text{Cash outflow for plant assets}}$$

where a low ratio (less than 1) implies cash inadequacy to meet asset growth, whereas a high ratio implies cash adequacy for asset growth.

(2) $$\text{Operating cash flow to sales} = \frac{\text{Operating cash flow}}{\text{Net sales}}$$

When this ratio substantially and consistently differs from the operating income to net sales ratio, the risk of accounting improprieties increases. ■

**Point:** The following ratio helps assess whether operating cash flow is adequate to meet long-term obligations:
**Cash coverage of debt** = Cash flow from operations ÷ Noncurrent liabilities. A low ratio suggests a higher risk of insolvency; a high ratio suggests a greater ability to meet long-term obligations.

# DEMONSTRATION PROBLEM

Umlauf's comparative balance sheets, income statement, and additional information follow.

**UMLAUF COMPANY**
**Balance Sheets**
**December 31, 2011 and 2010**

| | 2011 | 2010 |
|---|---|---|
| **Assets** | | |
| Cash ...................... | $ 43,050 | $ 23,925 |
| Accounts receivable ................ | 34,125 | 39,825 |
| Merchandise inventory ............... | 156,000 | 146,475 |
| Prepaid expenses ................... | 3,600 | 1,650 |
| Equipment ........................ | 135,825 | 146,700 |
| Accum. depreciation—Equipment ........ | (61,950) | (47,550) |
| Total assets ...................... | $310,650 | $311,025 |
| **Liabilities and Equity** | | |
| Accounts payable ................... | $ 28,800 | $ 33,750 |
| Income taxes payable ............... | 5,100 | 4,425 |
| Dividends payable ................... | 0 | 4,500 |
| Bonds payable ..................... | 0 | 37,500 |
| Common stock, $10 par .............. | 168,750 | 168,750 |
| Retained earnings .................. | 108,000 | 62,100 |
| Total liabilities and equity ............. | $310,650 | $311,025 |

**UMLAUF COMPANY**
**Income Statement**
**For Year Ended December 31, 2011**

| | | |
|---|---|---|
| Sales ....................... | | $446,100 |
| Cost of goods sold ............ | $222,300 | |
| Other operating expenses ...... | 120,300 | |
| Depreciation expense .......... | 25,500 | (368,100) |
| | | 78,000 |
| Other gains (losses) | | |
| Loss on sale of equipment .... | 3,300 | |
| Loss on retirement of bonds .. | 825 | (4,125) |
| Income before taxes ........... | | 73,875 |
| Income taxes expense ......... | | (13,725) |
| Net income ................... | | $ 60,150 |

### Additional Information

a. Equipment costing $21,375 with accumulated depreciation of $11,100 is sold for cash.

b. Equipment purchases are for cash.

c. Accumulated Depreciation is affected by depreciation expense and the sale of equipment.

d. The balance of Retained Earnings is affected by dividend declarations and net income.

e. All sales are made on credit.

f. All merchandise inventory purchases are on credit.

g. Accounts Payable balances result from merchandise inventory purchases.

h. Prepaid expenses relate to "other operating expenses."

### Required

1. Prepare a statement of cash flows using the indirect method for year 2011.

2.<sup>B</sup> Prepare a statement of cash flows using the direct method for year 2011.

## PLANNING THE SOLUTION

- Prepare two blank statements of cash flows with sections for operating, investing, and financing activities using the (1) indirect method format and (2) direct method format.

- Compute the cash paid for equipment and the cash received from the sale of equipment using the additional information provided along with the amount for depreciation expense and the change in the balances of equipment and accumulated depreciation. Use T-accounts to help chart the effects of the sale and purchase of equipment on the balances of the Equipment account and the Accumulated Depreciation account.

- Compute the effect of net income on the change in the Retained Earnings account balance. Assign the difference between the change in retained earnings and the amount of net income to dividends declared. Adjust the dividends declared amount for the change in the Dividends Payable balance.

- Compute cash received from customers, cash paid for merchandise, cash paid for other operating expenses, and cash paid for taxes as illustrated in the chapter.

- Enter the cash effects of reconstruction entries to the appropriate section(s) of the statement.

- Total each section of the statement, determine the total net change in cash, and add it to the beginning balance to get the ending balance of cash.

## SOLUTION TO DEMONSTRATION PROBLEM

Supporting computations for cash receipts and cash payments.

| | |
|---|---:|
| (1) *Cost of equipment sold ............................. | $ 21,375 |
|     Accumulated depreciation of equipment sold ........... | (11,100) |
|     Book value of equipment sold ....................... | 10,275 |
|     Loss on sale of equipment .......................... | (3,300) |
|     Cash received from sale of equipment ............... | **$ 6,975** |
|     Cost of equipment sold ............................. | $ 21,375 |
|     Less decrease in the equipment account balance ........ | (10,875) |
|     Cash paid for new equipment ....................... | **$ 10,500** |
| (2)  Loss on retirement of bonds ........................ | $ 825 |
|     Carrying value of bonds retired ..................... | 37,500 |
|     Cash paid to retire bonds ......................... | **$ 38,325** |
| (3)  Net income ........................................ | $ 60,150 |
|     Less increase in retained earnings .................... | 45,900 |
|     Dividends declared ............................... | 14,250 |
|     Plus decrease in dividends payable ................... | 4,500 |
|     Cash paid for dividends ........................... | **$ 18,750** |
| (4)<sup>B</sup> Sales ............................................. | $ 446,100 |
|     Add decrease in accounts receivable ................ | 5,700 |
|     Cash received from customers .................... | **$451,800** |

[continued on next page]

[continued from previous page]

| | | |
|---|---|---|
| (5)B Cost of goods sold | | $ 222,300 |
| Plus increase in merchandise inventory | | 9,525 |
| Purchases | | 231,825 |
| Plus decrease in accounts payable | | 4,950 |
| Cash paid for merchandise | | **$236,775** |
| (6)B Other operating expenses | | $ 120,300 |
| Plus increase in prepaid expenses | | 1,950 |
| Cash paid for other operating expenses | | **$122,250** |
| (7)B Income taxes expense | | $ 13,725 |
| Less increase in income taxes payable | | (675) |
| Cash paid for income taxes | | **$ 13,050** |

\* Supporting T-account analysis for part 1 follows:

| Equipment | | | | |
|---|---|---|---|---|
| Bal., Dec. 31, 2010 | 146,700 | | | |
| Cash purchase | 10,500 | Sale | 21,375 | |
| Bal., Dec. 31, 2011 | 135,825 | | | |

| Accumulated Depreciation—Equipment | | | | |
|---|---|---|---|---|
| | | Bal., Dec. 31, 2010 | 47,550 | |
| Sale | 11,100 | Depr. expense | 25,500 | |
| | | Bal., Dec. 31, 2011 | 61,950 | |

## UMLAUF COMPANY
### Statement of Cash Flows (Indirect Method)
### For Year Ended December 31, 2011

| | | |
|---|---|---|
| Cash flows from operating activities | | |
| Net income | $60,150 | |
| Adjustments to reconcile net income to net cash provided by operating activities | | |
| Decrease in accounts receivable | 5,700 | |
| Increase in merchandise inventory | (9,525) | |
| Increase in prepaid expenses | (1,950) | |
| Decrease in accounts payable | (4,950) | |
| Increase in income taxes payable | 675 | |
| Depreciation expense | 25,500 | |
| Loss on sale of plant assets | 3,300 | |
| Loss on retirement of bonds | 825 | |
| Net cash provided by operating activities | | $79,725 |
| Cash flows from investing activities | | |
| Cash received from sale of equipment | 6,975 | |
| Cash paid for equipment | (10,500) | |
| Net cash used in investing activities | | (3,525) |
| Cash flows from financing activities | | |
| Cash paid to retire bonds payable | (38,325) | |
| Cash paid for dividends | (18,750) | |
| Net cash used in financing activities | | (57,075) |
| Net increase in cash | | $19,125 |
| Cash balance at prior year-end | | 23,925 |
| Cash balance at current year-end | | $43,050 |

**UMLAUF COMPANY**
**Statement of Cash Flows (Direct Method)**
**For Year Ended December 31, 2011**

| | | |
|---|---:|---:|
| Cash flows from operating activities | | |
| Cash received from customers | $451,800 | |
| Cash paid for merchandise | (236,775) | |
| Cash paid for other operating expenses | (122,250) | |
| Cash paid for income taxes | (13,050) | |
| Net cash provided by operating activities | | $79,725 |
| Cash flows from investing activities | | |
| Cash received from sale of equipment | 6,975 | |
| Cash paid for equipment | (10,500) | |
| Net cash used in investing activities | | (3,525) |
| Cash flows from financing activities | | |
| Cash paid to retire bonds payable | (38,325) | |
| Cash paid for dividends | (18,750) | |
| Net cash used in financing activities | | (57,075) |
| Net increase in cash | | $19,125 |
| Cash balance at prior year-end | | 23,925 |
| Cash balance at current year-end | | $43,050 |

---

**APPENDIX**

# 16A

# Spreadsheet Preparation of the Statement of Cash Flows

This appendix explains how to use a spreadsheet to prepare the statement of cash flows under the indirect method.

**P4** Illustrate use of a spreadsheet to prepare a statement of cash flows.

**Preparing the Indirect Method Spreadsheet**  Analyzing noncash accounts can be challenging when a company has a large number of accounts and many operating, investing, and financing transactions. A *spreadsheet,* also called *work sheet* or *working paper,* can help us organize the information needed to prepare a statement of cash flows. A spreadsheet also makes it easier to check the accuracy of our work. To illustrate, we return to the comparative balance sheets and income statement shown in Exhibit 16.10. We use the following identifying letters *a* through *g* to code changes in accounts, and letters *h* through *m* for additional information, to prepare the statement of cash flows:

**a.** Net income is $38,000.

**b.** Accounts receivable increase by $20,000.

**c.** Merchandise inventory increases by $14,000.

**d.** Prepaid expenses increase by $2,000.

**e.** Accounts payable decrease by $5,000.

**f.** Interest payable decreases by $1,000.

**g.** Income taxes payable increase by $10,000.

**h.** Depreciation expense is $24,000.

**i.** Plant assets costing $30,000 with accumulated depreciation of $12,000 are sold for $12,000 cash. This yields a loss on sale of assets of $6,000.

**j.** Notes with a book value of $34,000 are retired with a cash payment of $18,000, yielding a $16,000 gain on retirement.

**k.** Plant assets costing $70,000 are purchased with a cash payment of $10,000 and an issuance of notes payable for $60,000.

**l.** Issued 3,000 shares of common stock for $15,000 cash.

**m.** Paid cash dividends of $14,000.

Exhibit 16A.1 shows the indirect method spreadsheet for Genesis. We enter both beginning and ending balance sheet amounts on the spreadsheet. We also enter information in the Analysis of Changes columns (keyed to the additional information items *a* through *m*) to explain changes in the accounts and determine the cash flows for operating, investing, and financing activities. Information about noncash investing and financing activities is reported near the bottom.

**EXHIBIT 16A.1**

Spreadsheet for Preparing Statement of Cash Flows—Indirect Method

| | Dec. 31, 2010 | Analysis of Changes Debit | | Analysis of Changes Credit | | Dec. 31, 2011 |
|---|---|---|---|---|---|---|
| **GENESIS** — Spreadsheet for Statement of Cash Flows—Indirect Method — For Year Ended December 31, 2011 | | | | | | |
| **Balance Sheet—Debit Bal. Accounts** | | | | | | |
| Cash | $ 12,000 | | | | | $ 17,000 |
| Accounts receivable | 40,000 | (b) | $ 20,000 | | | 60,000 |
| Merchandise inventory | 70,000 | (c) | 14,000 | | | 84,000 |
| Prepaid expenses | 4,000 | (d) | 2,000 | | | 6,000 |
| Plant assets | 210,000 | (k1) | 70,000 | (i) | $ 30,000 | 250,000 |
| | $336,000 | | | | | $417,000 |
| | | | | | | |
| **Balance Sheet—Credit Bal. Accounts** | | | | | | |
| Accumulated depreciation | $ 48,000 | (i) | 12,000 | (h) | 24,000 | $ 60,000 |
| Accounts payable | 40,000 | (e) | 5,000 | | | 35,000 |
| Interest payable | 4,000 | (f) | 1,000 | | | 3,000 |
| Income taxes payable | 12,000 | | | (g) | 10,000 | 22,000 |
| Notes payable | 64,000 | (j) | 34,000 | (k2) | 60,000 | 90,000 |
| Common stock, $5 par value | 80,000 | | | (l) | 15,000 | 95,000 |
| Retained earnings | 88,000 | (m) | 14,000 | (a) | 38,000 | 112,000 |
| | $336,000 | | | | | $417,000 |
| | | | | | | |
| **Statement of Cash Flows** | | | | | | |
| Operating activities | | | | | | |
| Net income | | (a) | 38,000 | | | |
| Increase in accounts receivable | | | | (b) | 20,000 | |
| Increase in merchandise inventory | | | | (c) | 14,000 | |
| Increase in prepaid expenses | | | | (d) | 2,000 | |
| Decrease in accounts payable | | | | (e) | 5,000 | |
| Decrease in interest payable | | | | (f) | 1,000 | |
| Increase in income taxes payable | | (g) | 10,000 | | | |
| Depreciation expense | | (h) | 24,000 | | | |
| Loss on sale of plant assets | | (i) | 6,000 | | | |
| Gain on retirement of notes | | | | (j) | 16,000 | |
| Investing activities | | | | | | |
| Receipts from sale of plant assets | | (i) | 12,000 | | | |
| Payment for purchase of plant assets | | | | (k1) | 10,000 | |
| Financing activities | | | | | | |
| Payment to retire notes | | | | (j) | 18,000 | |
| Receipts from issuing stock | | (l) | 15,000 | | | |
| Payment of cash dividends | | | | (m) | 14,000 | |
| | | | | | | |
| **Noncash Investing and Financing Activities** | | | | | | |
| Purchase of plant assets with notes | | (k2) | 60,000 | (k1) | 60,000 | |
| | | | $337,000 | | $337,000 | |

**Entering the Analysis of Changes on the Spreadsheet** The following sequence of procedures is used to complete the spreadsheet after the beginning and ending balances of the balance sheet accounts are entered:

① Enter net income as the first item in the Statement of Cash Flows section for computing operating cash inflow (debit) and as a credit to Retained Earnings.

② In the Statement of Cash Flows section, adjustments to net income are entered as debits if they increase cash flows and as credits if they decrease cash flows. Applying this same rule, adjust net income for the change in each noncash current asset and current liability account related to operating activities. For each adjustment to net income, the offsetting debit or credit must help reconcile the beginning and ending balances of a current asset or current liability account.

③ Enter adjustments to net income for income statement items not providing or using cash in the period. For each adjustment, the offsetting debit or credit must help reconcile a noncash balance sheet account.

④ Adjust net income to eliminate any gains or losses from investing and financing activities. Because the cash from a gain must be excluded from operating activities, the gain is entered as a credit in the operating activities section. Losses are entered as debits. For each adjustment, the related debit and/or credit must help reconcile balance sheet accounts and involve reconstructed entries to show the cash flow from investing or financing activities.

⑤ After reviewing any unreconciled balance sheet accounts and related information, enter the remaining reconciling entries for investing and financing activities. Examples are purchases of plant assets, issuances of long-term debt, stock issuances, and dividend payments. Some of these may require entries in the noncash investing and financing section of the spreadsheet (reconciled).

⑥ Check accuracy by totaling the Analysis of Changes columns and by determining that the change in each balance sheet account has been explained (reconciled).

**Point:** Analysis of the changes on the spreadsheet are summarized here:

1. Cash flows from operating activities generally affect net income, current assets, and current liabilities.
2. Cash flows from investing activities generally affect noncurrent asset accounts.
3. Cash flows from financing activities generally affect noncurrent liability and equity accounts.

We illustrate these steps in Exhibit 16A.1 for Genesis:

| Step | Entries |
|---|---|
| ①......... | (a) |
| ②......... | (b) through (g) |
| ③......... | (h) |
| ④......... | (i) through (j) |
| ⑤......... | (k) through (m) |

Since adjustments *i, j,* and *k* are more challenging, we show them in the following debit and credit format. These entries are for purposes of our understanding; they are *not* the entries actually made in the journals. Changes in the Cash account are identified as sources or uses of cash.

| | | | |
|---|---|---|---|
| *i.* | Loss from sale of plant assets ................................... | 6,000 | |
| | Accumulated depreciation ..................................... | 12,000 | |
| | Receipt from sale of plant assets **(source of cash)** ............... | 12,000 | |
| | Plant assets ......................................... | | 30,000 |
| | *To describe sale of plant assets.* | | |
| *j.* | Notes payable ............................................ | 34,000 | |
| | Payments to retire notes **(use of cash)** ................... | | 18,000 |
| | Gain on retirement of notes ............................. | | 16,000 |
| | *To describe retirement of notes.* | | |
| *k1.* | Plant assets ............................................ | 70,000 | |
| | Payment to purchase plant assets **(use of cash)** ............ | | 10,000 |
| | Purchase of plant assets financed by notes ................. | | 60,000 |
| | *To describe purchase of plant assets.* | | |
| *k2.* | Purchase of plant assets financed by notes ..................... | 60,000 | |
| | Notes payable ........................................ | | 60,000 |
| | *To issue notes for purchase of assets.* | | |

# Direct Method of Reporting Operating Cash Flows

16B

We compute cash flows from operating activities under the direct method by adjusting accrual-based income statement items to the cash basis. The usual approach is to adjust income statement accounts related to operating activities for changes in their related balance sheet accounts as follows:

> **P5** Compute cash flows from operating activities using the direct method.

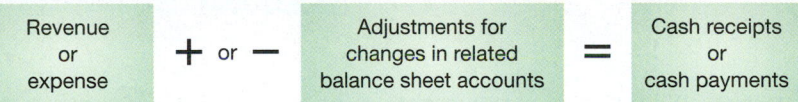

| Revenue or expense | **+ or −** | Adjustments for changes in related balance sheet accounts | **=** | Cash receipts or cash payments |

The framework for reporting cash receipts and cash payments for the operating section of the cash flow statement under the direct method is shown in Exhibit 16B.1. We consider cash receipts first and then cash payments.

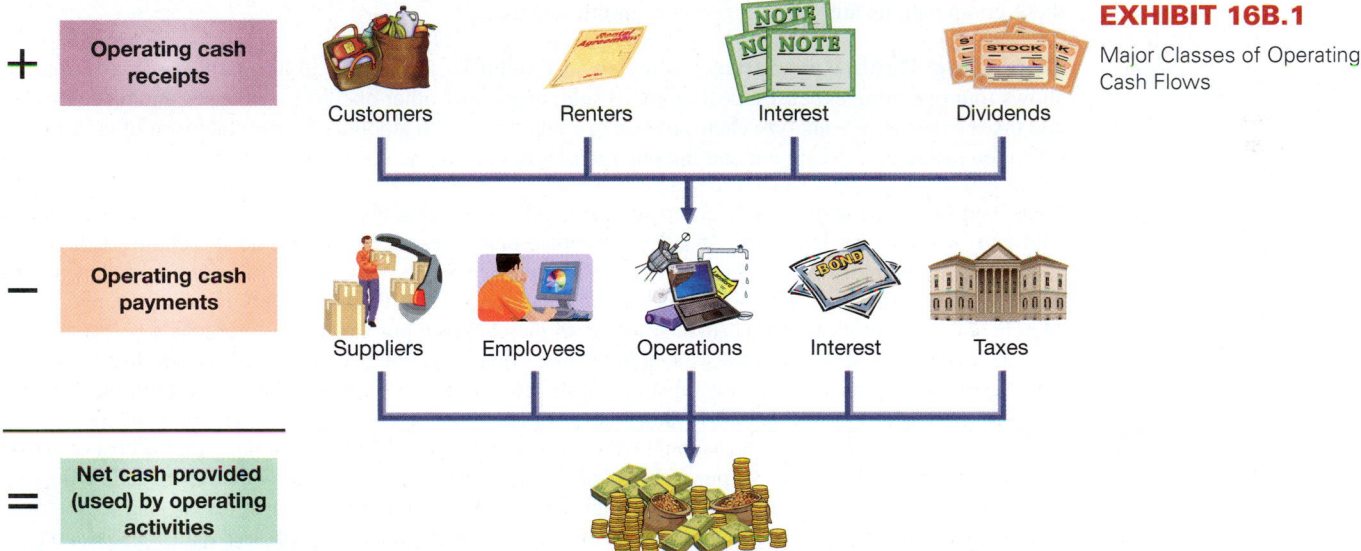

**EXHIBIT 16B.1**

Major Classes of Operating Cash Flows

**Operating Cash Receipts**   A review of Exhibit 16.10 and the additional information reported by Genesis suggests only one potential cash receipt: sales to customers. This section, therefore, starts with sales to customers as reported on the income statement and then adjusts it as necessary to obtain cash received from customers to report on the statement of cash flows.

**Cash Received from Customers**   If all sales are for cash, the amount received from customers equals the sales reported on the income statement. When some or all sales are on account, however, we must adjust the amount of sales for the change in Accounts Receivable. It is often helpful to use *account analysis* to do this. This usually involves setting up a T-account and reconstructing its major entries, with emphasis on cash receipts and payments. To illustrate, we use a T-account that includes accounts receivable balances for Genesis on December 31, 2010 and 2011. The beginning balance is $40,000 and the ending balance is $60,000. Next, the income statement shows sales of $590,000, which we enter on the debit side of this account. We now can reconstruct the Accounts Receivable account to determine the amount of cash received from customers as follows:

> **Point:** An accounts receivable increase implies that cash received from customers is less than sales (the converse is also true).

| Accounts Receivable | | | |
|---|---|---|---|
| Bal., Dec. 31, 2010 | 40,000 | | |
| Sales | 590,000 | **Cash receipts =** | **570,000** |
| Bal., Dec. 31, 2011 | 60,000 | | |

This T-account shows that the Accounts Receivable balance begins at $40,000 and increases to $630,000 from sales of $590,000, yet its ending balance is only $60,000. This implies that cash receipts from customers are $570,000, computed as $40,000 + $590,000 − [?] = $60,000. This computation can be rearranged to express cash received as equal to sales of $590,000 minus a $20,000 increase in accounts receivable. This computation is summarized as a general rule in Exhibit 16B.2. The statement of cash flows in Exhibit 16.7 reports the $570,000 cash received from customers as a cash inflow from operating activities.

## EXHIBIT 16B.2

Formula to Compute Cash Received from Customers—Direct Method

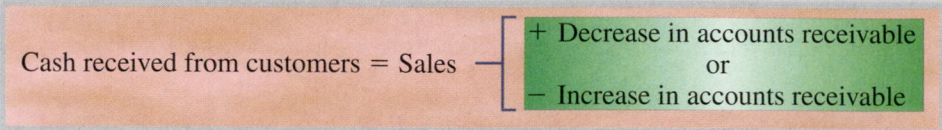

Cash received from customers = Sales − [ + Decrease in accounts receivable / or / − Increase in accounts receivable ]

**Other Cash Receipts**    While Genesis's cash receipts are limited to collections from customers, we often see other types of cash receipts, most commonly cash receipts involving rent, interest, and dividends. We compute cash received from these items by subtracting an increase in their respective receivable or adding a decrease. For instance, if rent receivable increases in the period, cash received from renters is less than rent revenue reported on the income statement. If rent receivable decreases, cash received is more than reported rent revenue. The same logic applies to interest and dividends. The formulas for these computations are summarized later in this appendix.

**Operating Cash Payments**    A review of Exhibit 16.10 and the additional Genesis information shows four operating expenses: cost of goods sold; wages and other operating expenses; interest expense; and taxes expense. We analyze each expense to compute its cash amounts for the statement of cash flows. (We then examine depreciation and the other losses and gains.)

**Cash Paid for Merchandise**    We compute cash paid for merchandise by analyzing both cost of goods sold and merchandise inventory. If all merchandise purchases are for cash and the ending balance of Merchandise Inventory is unchanged from the beginning balance, the amount of cash paid for merchandise equals cost of goods sold—an uncommon situation. Instead, there normally is some change in the Merchandise Inventory balance. Also, some or all merchandise purchases are often made on credit, and this yields changes in the Accounts Payable balance. When the balances of both Merchandise Inventory and Accounts Payable change, we must adjust the cost of goods sold for changes in both accounts to compute cash paid for merchandise. This is a two-step adjustment.

First, we use the change in the account balance of Merchandise Inventory, along with the cost of goods sold amount, to compute cost of purchases for the period. An increase in merchandise inventory implies that we bought more than we sold, and we add this inventory increase to cost of goods sold to compute cost of purchases. A decrease in merchandise inventory implies that we bought less than we sold, and we subtract the inventory decrease from cost of goods sold to compute purchases. We illustrate the *first step* by reconstructing the Merchandise Inventory account of Genesis:

| Merchandise Inventory | | | |
|---|---|---|---|
| Bal., Dec. 31, 2010 | 70,000 | | |
| Purchases = | 314,000 | Cost of goods sold | 300,000 |
| Bal., Dec. 31, 2011 | 84,000 | | |

The beginning balance is $70,000, and the ending balance is $84,000. The income statement shows that cost of goods sold is $300,000, which we enter on the credit side of this account. With this information, we determine the amount for cost of purchases to be $314,000. This computation can be rearranged to express cost of purchases as equal to cost of goods sold of $300,000 plus the $14,000 increase in inventory.

The second step uses the change in the balance of Accounts Payable, and the amount of cost of purchases, to compute cash paid for merchandise. A decrease in accounts payable implies that we paid for more goods than we acquired this period, and we would then add the accounts payable decrease to cost of purchases to compute cash paid for merchandise. An increase in accounts payable implies that we paid for less than the amount of goods acquired, and we would subtract the accounts payable increase from purchases to compute cash paid for merchandise. The *second step* is applied to Genesis by reconstructing its Accounts Payable account:

| Accounts Payable | | | |
|---|---|---|---|
| | | Bal., Dec. 31, 2010 | 40,000 |
| **Cash payments =** | **319,000** | Purchases | 314,000 |
| | | Bal., Dec. 31, 2011 | 35,000 |

Its beginning balance of $40,000 plus purchases of $314,000 minus an ending balance of $35,000 yields cash paid of $319,000 (or $40,000 + $314,000 − [?] = $35,000). Alternatively, we can express cash paid for merchandise as equal to purchases of $314,000 plus the $5,000 decrease in accounts payable. The $319,000 cash paid for merchandise is reported on the statement of cash flows in Exhibit 16.7 as a cash outflow under operating activities.

We summarize this two-step adjustment to cost of goods sold to compute cash paid for merchandise inventory in Exhibit 16B.3.

**Example:** If the ending balances of Inventory and Accounts Payable are $60,000 and $50,000, respectively (instead of $84,000 and $35,000), what is cash paid for merchandise? *Answer:* $280,000

### EXHIBIT 16B.3

Two Steps to Compute Cash Paid for Merchandise—Direct Method

**Cash Paid for Wages and Operating Expenses (Excluding Depreciation)**   The income statement of Genesis shows wages and other operating expenses of $216,000 (see Exhibit 16.10). To compute cash paid for wages and other operating expenses, we adjust this amount for any changes in their related balance sheet accounts. We begin by looking for any prepaid expenses and accrued liabilities related to wages and other operating expenses in the balance sheets of Genesis in Exhibit 16.10. The balance sheets show prepaid expenses but no accrued liabilities. Thus, the adjustment is limited to the change in prepaid expenses. The amount of adjustment is computed by assuming that all cash paid for wages and other operating expenses is initially debited to Prepaid Expenses. This assumption allows us to reconstruct the Prepaid Expenses account:

| Prepaid Expenses | | | |
|---|---|---|---|
| Bal., Dec. 31, 2010 | 4,000 | | |
| **Cash payments =** | **218,000** | Wages and other operating exp. | 216,000 |
| Bal., Dec. 31, 2011 | 6,000 | | |

Prepaid Expenses increase by $2,000 in the period, meaning that cash paid for wages and other operating expenses exceeds the reported expense by $2,000. Alternatively, we can express cash paid for wages and other operating expenses as equal to its reported expenses of $216,000 plus the $2,000 increase in prepaid expenses.[1]

Exhibit 16B.4 summarizes the adjustments to wages (including salaries) and other operating expenses. The Genesis balance sheet did not report accrued liabilities, but we include them in the formula to explain the adjustment to cash when they do exist. A decrease in accrued liabilities implies that we paid cash for more goods or services than received this period, so we add the decrease in accrued liabilities to the expense amount to obtain cash paid for these goods or services. An increase in accrued liabilities implies that we paid cash for less than what was acquired, so we subtract this increase in accrued liabilities from the expense amount to get cash paid.

**Point:** A decrease in prepaid expenses implies that reported expenses include an amount(s) that did not require a cash outflow in the period.

---

[1] The assumption that all cash payments for wages and operating expenses are initially debited to Prepaid Expenses is not necessary for our analysis to hold. If cash payments are debited directly to the expense account, the total amount of cash paid for wages and other operating expenses still equals the $216,000 expense plus the $2,000 increase in Prepaid Expenses (which arise from end-of-period adjusting entries).

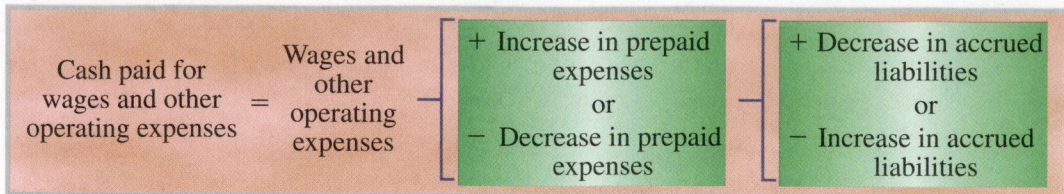

**Cash paid for interest and income taxes**   Computing operating cash flows for interest and taxes is similar to that for operating expenses. Both require adjustments to their amounts reported on the income statement for changes in their related balance sheet accounts. We begin with the Genesis income statement showing interest expense of $7,000 and income taxes expense of $15,000. To compute the cash paid, we adjust interest expense for the change in interest payable and then the income taxes expense for the change in income taxes payable. These computations involve reconstructing both liability accounts:

| Interest Payable | | |
|---|---|---|
| | Bal., Dec. 31, 2010 | 4,000 |
| **Cash paid for interest =**   **8,000** | Interest expense | 7,000 |
| | Bal., Dec. 31, 2011 | 3,000 |

| Income Taxes Payable | | |
|---|---|---|
| | Bal., Dec. 31, 2010 | 12,000 |
| **Cash paid for taxes =**   **5,000** | Income taxes expense | 15,000 |
| | Bal., Dec. 31, 2011 | 22,000 |

These accounts reveal cash paid for interest of $8,000 and cash paid for income taxes of $5,000. The formulas to compute these amounts are in Exhibit 16B.5. Both of these cash payments are reported as operating cash outflows on the statement of cash flows in Exhibit 16.7.

**Analysis of Additional Expenses, Gains, and Losses**   Genesis has three additional items reported on its income statement: depreciation, loss on sale of assets, and gain on retirement of debt. We must consider each for its potential cash effects.

***Depreciation Expense***   Depreciation expense is $24,000. It is often called a *noncash expense* because depreciation has no cash flows. Depreciation expense is an allocation of an asset's depreciable cost. The cash outflow with a plant asset is reported as part of investing activities when it is paid for. Thus, depreciation expense is *never* reported on a statement of cash flows using the direct method; nor is depletion or amortization expense.

***Loss on Sale of Assets***   Sales of assets frequently result in gains and losses reported as part of net income, but the amount of recorded gain or loss does *not* reflect any cash flows in these transactions. Asset sales result in cash inflow equal to the cash amount received, regardless of whether the asset was sold at a gain or a loss. This cash inflow is reported under investing activities. Thus, the loss or gain on a sale of assets is *never* reported on a statement of cash flows using the direct method.

***Gain on Retirement of Debt***   Retirement of debt usually yields a gain or loss reported as part of net income, but that gain or loss does *not* reflect cash flow in this transaction. Debt retirement results in cash outflow equal to the cash paid to settle the debt, regardless of whether the debt is retired at a gain or loss.

This cash outflow is reported under financing activities; the loss or gain from retirement of debt is *never* reported on a statement of cash flows using the direct method.

**Summary of Adjustments for Direct Method**  Exhibit 16B.6 summarizes common adjustments for net income to yield net cash provided (used) by operating activities under the direct method.

**EXHIBIT 16B.6**

Summary of Selected Adjustments for Direct Method

| Item | From Income Statement | Adjustments to Obtain Cash Flow Numbers | |
|---|---|---|---|
| **Receipts** | | | |
| From sales | Sales Revenue | +Decrease in Accounts Receivable<br>−Increase in Accounts Receivable | |
| From rent | Rent Revenue | +Decrease in Rent Receivable<br>−Increase in Rent Receivable | |
| From interest | Interest Revenue | +Decrease in Interest Receivable<br>−Increase in Interest Receivable | |
| From dividends | Dividend Revenue | +Decrease in Dividends Receivable<br>−Increase in Dividends Receivable | |
| **Payments** | | | |
| To suppliers | Cost of Goods Sold | +Increase in Inventory<br>−Decrease in Inventory | +Decrease in Accounts Payable<br>−Increase in Accounts Payable |
| For operations | Operating Expense | +Increase in Prepaids<br>−Decrease in Prepaids | +Decrease in Accrued Liabilities<br>−Increase in Accrued Liabilities |
| To employees | Wages (Salaries) Expense | +Decrease in Wages (Salaries) Payable<br>−Increase in Wages (Salaries) Payable | |
| For interest | Interest Expense | +Decrease in Interest Payable<br>−Increase in Interest Payable | |
| For taxes | Income Tax Expense | +Decrease in Income Tax Payable<br>−Increase in Income Tax Payable | |

**Direct Method Format of Operating Activities Section**  Exhibit 16.7 shows the Genesis statement of cash flows using the direct method. Major items of cash inflows and cash outflows are listed separately in the operating activities section. The format requires that operating cash outflows be subtracted from operating cash inflows to get net cash provided (used) by operating activities. The FASB recommends that the operating activities section of the statement of cash flows be reported using the direct method, which is considered more useful to financial statement users. *However, the FASB requires a reconciliation of net income to net cash provided (used) by operating activities when the direct method is used* (which can be reported in the notes). This reconciliation is similar to preparation of the operating activities section of the statement of cash flows using the indirect method.

**Point:** Some preparers argue that it is easier to prepare a statement of cash flows using the indirect method. This likely explains its greater frequency in financial statements.

 **IFRS** _____

Like U.S. GAAP, IFRS allows cash flows from operating activities to be reported using either the indirect method or the direct method. ■

**Quick Check**  Answers — p. 662

8. Net sales in a period are $590,000, beginning accounts receivable are $120,000, and ending accounts receivable are $90,000. What cash amount is collected from customers in the period?

9. The Merchandise Inventory account balance decreases in the period from a beginning balance of $32,000 to an ending balance of $28,000. Cost of goods sold for the period is $168,000. If the Accounts Payable balance increases $2,400 in the period, what is the cash amount paid for merchandise inventory?

10. This period's wages and other operating expenses total $112,000. Beginning-of-period prepaid expenses totaled $1,200, and its ending balance is $4,200. There were no beginning-of-period accrued liabilities, but end-of-period wages payable equal $5,600. How much cash is paid for wages and other operating expenses?

# Summary

**C1** **Distinguish between operating, investing, and financing activities, and describe how noncash investing and financing activities are disclosed.** The purpose of the statement of cash flows is to report major cash receipts and cash payments relating to operating, investing, or financing activities. Operating activities include transactions and events that determine net income. Investing activities include transactions and events that mainly affect long-term assets. Financing activities include transactions and events that mainly affect long-term liabilities and equity. Noncash investing and financing activities must be disclosed in either a note or a separate schedule to the statement of cash flows. Examples are the retirement of debt by issuing equity and the exchange of a note payable for plant assets.

**A1** **Analyze the statement of cash flows and apply the cash flow on total assets ratio.** To understand and predict cash flows, users stress identification of the sources and uses of cash flows by operating, investing, and financing activities. Emphasis is on operating cash flows since they derive from continuing operations. The cash flow on total assets ratio is defined as operating cash flows divided by average total assets. Analysis of current and past values for this ratio can reflect a company's ability to yield regular and positive cash flows. It is also viewed as a measure of earnings quality.

**P1** **Prepare a statement of cash flows.** Preparation of a statement of cash flows involves five steps: (1) Compute the net increase or decrease in cash; (2) compute net cash provided or used by operating activities (*using either the direct or indirect method*); (3) compute net cash provided or used by investing activities; (4) compute net cash

provided or used by financing activities; and (5) report the beginning and ending cash balance and prove that it is explained by net cash flows. Noncash investing and financing activities are also disclosed.

**P2** **Compute cash flows from operating activities using the indirect method.** The indirect method for reporting net cash provided or used by operating activities starts with net income and then adjusts it for three items: (1) changes in noncash current assets and current liabilities related to operating activities, (2) revenues and expenses not providing or using cash, and (3) gains and losses from investing and financing activities.

**P3** **Determine cash flows from both investing and financing activities.** Cash flows from both investing and financing activities are determined by identifying the cash flow effects of transactions and events affecting each balance sheet account related to these activities. All cash flows from these activities are identified when we can explain changes in these accounts from the beginning to the end of the period.

**P4<sup>A</sup>** **Illustrate use of a spreadsheet to prepare a statement of cash flows.** A spreadsheet is a useful tool in preparing a statement of cash flows. Six key steps (see Appendix 16A) are applied when using the spreadsheet to prepare the statement.

**P5<sup>B</sup>** **Compute cash flows from operating activities using the direct method.** The direct method for reporting net cash provided or used by operating activities lists major operating cash inflows less cash outflows to yield net cash inflow or outflow from operations.

---

## Guidance Answers to Decision Maker

**Entrepreneur** Several factors might explain an increase in net cash flows when a net loss is reported, including (1) early recognition of expenses relative to revenues generated (such as research and development), (2) cash advances on long-term sales contracts not yet recognized in income, (3) issuances of debt or equity for cash to finance expansion, (4) cash sale of assets, (5) delay of cash payments, and (6) cash prepayment on sales. Analysis needs to focus on the components of both the net loss and the net cash flows and their implications for future performance.

**Reporter** Your initial reaction based on the company's $600,000 loss with a $550,000 decrease in net cash flows is not positive. However, closer scrutiny reveals a more positive picture of this company's performance. Cash flow from operating activities is $650,000, computed as [?] − $850,000 − $350,000 = $(550,000). You also note that net income *before* the extraordinary loss is $330,000, computed as [?] − $930,000 = $(600,000).

---

## Guidance Answers to Quick Checks

1. No to both. The statement of cash flows reports changes in the sum of cash plus cash equivalents. It does not report transfers between cash and cash equivalents.

2. The three categories of cash inflows and outflows are operating activities, investing activities, and financing activities.

3. **a.** Investing    **c.** Financing    **e.** Operating
       **b.** Operating    **d.** Operating    **f.** Financing

4. $74,900 + $4,600 − $11,700 − $1,000 + $3,400 = $70,200

5. Expenses such as depreciation and amortization do not require current cash outflows. Therefore, adding these expenses back to

    net income eliminates these noncash items from the net income number, converting it to a cash basis.

6. A gain on the sale of plant assets is subtracted from net income because a sale of plant assets is not an operating activity; it is an investing activity for the amount of cash received from its sale. Also, such a gain yields no cash effects.

7. $80,000 − $30,000 − $10,000 = $40,000 cash receipt. The $40,000 cash receipt is reported as an investing activity.

8. $590,000 + ($120,000 − $90,000) = $620,000

9. $168,000 − ($32,000 − $28,000) − $2,400 = $161,600

10. $112,000 + ($4,200 − $1,200) − $5,600 = $109,400

## Key Terms

mhhe.com/wildFAP20e

Cash flow on total assets (p. 650)
Direct method (p. 638)
Financing activities (p. 634)

Indirect method (p. 638)
Investing activities (p. 634)

Operating activities (p. 633)
Statement of cash flows (p. 632)

## Multiple Choice Quiz

Answers on p. 683

mhhe.com/wildFAP20e

Additional Quiz Questions are available at the book's Website.

1. A company uses the indirect method to determine its cash flows from operating activities. Use the following information to determine its net cash provided or used by operating activities.

| | |
|---|---|
| Net income .............................. | $15,200 |
| Depreciation expense ................. | 10,000 |
| Cash payment on note payable ......... | 8,000 |
| Gain on sale of land ................. | 3,000 |
| Increase in inventory ................ | 1,500 |
| Increase in accounts payable .......... | 2,850 |

   a. $23,550 used by operating activities
   b. $23,550 provided by operating activities
   c. $15,550 provided by operating activities
   d. $42,400 provided by operating activities
   e. $20,850 provided by operating activities

2. A machine with a cost of $175,000 and accumulated depreciation of $94,000 is sold for $87,000 cash. The amount reported as a source of cash under cash flows from investing activities is
   a. $81,000.
   b. $6,000.
   c. $87,000.
   d. Zero; this is a financing activity.
   e. Zero; this is an operating activity.

3. A company settles a long-term note payable plus interest by paying $68,000 cash toward the principal amount and $5,440 cash for interest. The amount reported as a use of cash under cash flows from financing activities is
   a. Zero; this is an investing activity.
   b. Zero; this is an operating activity.

   c. $73,440.
   d. $68,000.
   e. $5,440.

4. The following information is available regarding a company's annual salaries and wages. What amount of cash is paid for salaries and wages?

| | |
|---|---|
| Salaries and wages expense .................... | $255,000 |
| Salaries and wages payable, prior year-end ........ | 8,200 |
| Salaries and wages payable, current year-end ...... | 10,900 |

   a. $252,300
   b. $257,700
   c. $255,000
   d. $274,100
   e. $235,900

5. The following information is available for a company. What amount of cash is paid for merchandise for the current year?

| | |
|---|---|
| Cost of goods sold .......................... | $545,000 |
| Merchandise inventory, prior year-end ........... | 105,000 |
| Merchandise inventory, current year-end ......... | 112,000 |
| Accounts payable, prior year-end ............... | 98,500 |
| Accounts payable, current year-end ............. | 101,300 |

   a. $545,000
   b. $554,800
   c. $540,800
   d. $535,200
   e. $549,200

A(B) *Superscript letter A (B) denotes assignments based on Appendix 16A (16B).*
[i] Icon denotes assignments that involve decision making.

## Discussion Questions

1. What is the reporting purpose of the statement of cash flows? Identify at least two questions that this statement can answer.
2. Describe the direct method of reporting cash flows from operating activities.
3. When a statement of cash flows is prepared using the direct method, what are some of the operating cash flows?

4. Describe the indirect method of reporting cash flows from operating activities.
5. What are some investing activities reported on the statement of cash flows?
6. What are some financing activities reported on the statement of cash flows?

**7.** Where on the statement of cash flows is the payment of cash dividends reported?

**8.**  Assume that a company purchases land for $100,000, paying $20,000 cash and borrowing the remainder with a long-term note payable. How should this transaction be reported on a statement of cash flows?

**9.**  On June 3, a company borrows $50,000 cash by giving its bank a 160-day, interest-bearing note. On the statement of cash flows, where should this be reported?

**10.**  If a company reports positive net income for the year, can it also show a net cash outflow from operating activities? Explain.

**11.**  Is depreciation a source of cash flow?

**12.**  Refer to **Research In Motion**'s statement of cash flows in Appendix A. (*a*) Which method is used *RIM* to compute its net cash provided by operating activities?

(*b*) While its balance sheet shows an increase in working capital (current assets less current liabilities) from fiscal years 2009 to 2010, why is this increase in working capital subtracted when computing net cash provided by operating activities for the year ended February 27, 2010?

**13.**  Refer to **Palm**'s statement of cash flows in Appendix A. What are its cash flows from financing *Palm* activities for the year ended May 31, 2009? List items and amounts.

**14.**  Refer to **Nokia**'s statement of cash flows in Appendix A. List its cash flows from operating *NOKIA* activities, investing activities, and financing activities.

**15.**  Refer to **Apple**'s statement of cash flows in Appendix A. What investing activities result in cash *Apple* outflows for the year ended September 26, 2009? List items and amounts.

---

**connect**

## QUICK STUDY

**QS 16-1**

Transaction classification by activity

C1

Classify the following cash flows as operating, investing, or financing activities.

**1.** Paid cash for property taxes on building.
**2.** Paid cash dividends.
**3.** Paid cash for wages and salaries.
**4.** Purchased inventories for cash.
**5.** Received cash payments from customers.
**6.** Received cash from sale of land at a loss.
**7.** Received cash interest on a note.
**8.** Paid cash interest on outstanding notes.
**9.** Issued common stock for cash.
**10.** Sold long-term investments for cash.

---

**QS 16-2**

Statement of cash flows

C1

The statement of cash flows is one of the four primary financial statements.

**1.** Describe the content and layout of a statement of cash flows, including its three sections.
**2.** List at least three transactions classified as significant noncash financing and investing activities in the statement of cash flows.
**3.** List at least three transactions classified as financing activities in a statement of cash flows.
**4.** List at least three transactions classified as investing activities in a statement of cash flows.

---

**QS 16-3**

Computing cash from operations (indirect)

P2

Use the following information to determine this company's cash flows from operating activities using the indirect method.

**LING COMPANY**
**Selected Balance Sheet Information**
**December 31, 2011 and 2010**

| | 2011 | 2010 |
|---|---|---|
| Current assets | | |
| Cash .................... | $338,600 | $107,200 |
| Accounts receivable ......... | 100,000 | 128,000 |
| Inventory ................. | 240,000 | 216,400 |
| Current liabilities | | |
| Accounts payable ........... | 121,600 | 102,800 |
| Income taxes payable ........ | 8,200 | 8,800 |

**LING COMPANY**
**Income Statement**
**For Year Ended December 31, 2011**

| | | |
|---|---|---|
| Sales ......................... | | $2,060,000 |
| Cost of goods sold ............. | | 1,326,400 |
| Gross profit ................... | | 733,600 |
| Operating expenses | | |
| Depreciation expense ......... | $144,000 | |
| Other expenses ............. | 486,000 | 630,000 |
| Income before taxes ............ | | 103,600 |
| Income taxes expense .......... | | 30,800 |
| Net income .................... | | $ 72,800 |

The following selected information is from Mooney Company's comparative balance sheets.

| At December 31 | 2011 | 2010 |
|---|---|---|
| Furniture ............................ | $155,000 | $ 260,000 |
| Accumulated depreciation—Furniture ......... | (74,400) | (121,400) |

The income statement reports depreciation expense for the year of $36,000. Also, furniture costing $105,000 was sold for its book value. Compute the cash received from the sale of furniture.

**QS 16-4**
Computing cash from asset sales
P3

The following selected information is from the Teeter Company's comparative balance sheets.

| At December 31 | 2011 | 2010 |
|---|---|---|
| Common stock, $10 par value ......... | $ 310,000 | $300,000 |
| Paid-in capital in excess of par ......... | 1,134,000 | 684,000 |
| Retained earnings ................... | 627,000 | 575,000 |

The company's net income for the year ended December 31, 2011, was $196,000.

**1.** Compute the cash received from the sale of its common stock during 2011.

**2.** Compute the cash paid for dividends during 2011.

**QS 16-5**
Computing financing cash flows
P3

For each of the following separate cases, compute cash flows from operations. The list includes all balance sheet accounts related to operating activities.

| | Case A | Case B | Case C |
|---|---|---|---|
| Net income ............................. | $ 20,000 | $125,000 | $105,000 |
| Depreciation expense ...................... | 60,000 | 16,000 | 48,000 |
| Accounts receivable increase (decrease) ........ | 80,000 | 40,000 | (8,000) |
| Inventory increase (decrease) ................ | (40,000) | (20,000) | 21,000 |
| Accounts payable increase (decrease) .......... | 28,000 | (44,000) | 16,000 |
| Accrued liabilities increase (decrease) .......... | (88,000) | 10,000 | (16,000) |

**QS 16-6**
Computing cash flows from operations (indirect)
P2

Compute cash flows from investing activities using the following company information.

| | |
|---|---|
| Sale of short-term investments .......... | $16,000 |
| Cash collections from customers ......... | 44,000 |
| Purchase of used equipment ............. | 10,000 |
| Depreciation expense ................. | 6,000 |

**QS 16-7**
Computing cash flows from investing
P3

Compute cash flows from financing activities using the following company information.

| | |
|---|---|
| Additional short-term borrowings .......... | $88,000 |
| Purchase of short-term investments ........ | 25,000 |
| Cash dividends paid ................... | 32,000 |
| Interest paid ......................... | 17,000 |

**QS 16-8**
Computing cash flows from financing
P3

**QS 16-9**
Computing cash from
operations (indirect) P2

**Use the following balance sheets and income statement to answer QS 16-9 through QS 16-14.**

Use the indirect method to prepare the cash provided or used from operating activities section only of the statement of cash flows for this company.

### ORWELL, INC.
### Comparative Balance Sheets
### December 31, 2011

| | 2011 | 2010 |
|---|---|---|
| **Assets** | | |
| Cash ............................. | $ 95,800 | $ 25,000 |
| Accounts receivable, net ............... | 42,000 | 52,000 |
| Inventory ......................... | 86,800 | 96,800 |
| Prepaid expenses ................... | 6,400 | 5,200 |
| Furniture ......................... | 110,000 | 120,000 |
| Accum. depreciation—Furniture ........ | (18,000) | (10,000) |
| Total assets ....................... | $323,000 | $289,000 |
| | | |
| **Liabilities and Equity** | | |
| Accounts payable ................... | $ 16,000 | $ 22,000 |
| Wages payable ...................... | 10,000 | 6,000 |
| Income taxes payable ................ | 2,400 | 3,600 |
| Notes payable (long-term) ............. | 30,000 | 70,000 |
| Common stock, $5 par value ........... | 230,000 | 180,000 |
| Retained earnings ................... | 34,600 | 7,400 |
| Total liabilities and equity ............. | $323,000 | $289,000 |

### ORWELL, INC.
### Income Statement
### For Year Ended December 31, 2011

| | | |
|---|---|---|
| Sales ........................... | | $468,000 |
| Cost of goods sold .............. | | 312,000 |
| Gross profit ..................... | | 156,000 |
| Operating expenses | | |
| Depreciation expense .......... | $38,600 | |
| Other expenses .............. | 57,000 | 95,600 |
| Income before taxes ............. | | 60,400 |
| Income taxes expense ........... | | 24,600 |
| Net income .................... | | $ 35,800 |

---

**QS 16-10**
Computing cash from asset sales
P3

Refer to the data in QS 16-9.
Furniture costing $54,000 is sold at its book value in 2011. Acquisitions of furniture total $44,000 cash, on which no depreciation is necessary because it is acquired at year-end. What is the cash inflow related to the sale of furniture?

---

**QS 16-11**
Computing financing cash outflows P3

Refer to the data in QS 16-9.
1. Assume that all common stock is issued for cash. What amount of cash dividends is paid during 2011?
2. Assume that no additional notes payable are issued in 2011. What cash amount is paid to reduce the notes payable balance in 2011?

---

**QS 16-12**[B]
Computing cash received from customers P5

Refer to the data in QS 16-9.
1. How much cash is received from sales to customers for year 2011?
2. What is the net increase or decrease in cash for year 2011?

---

**QS 16-13**[B]
Computing operating cash outflows P5

Refer to the data in QS 16-9.
1. How much cash is paid to acquire merchandise inventory during year 2011?
2. How much cash is paid for operating expenses during year 2011?

---

**QS 16-14**[B]
Computing cash from operations (direct) P5

Refer to the data in QS 16-9.
Use the direct method to prepare the cash provided or used from operating activities section only of the statement of cash flows for this company.

---

**QS 16-15**
Analyses of sources and uses of cash A1

Financial data from three competitors in the same industry follow.
1. Which of the three competitors is in the strongest position as shown by its statement of cash flows?
2. Analyze and compare the strength of Z-Best's cash flow on total assets ratio to that of Lopez.

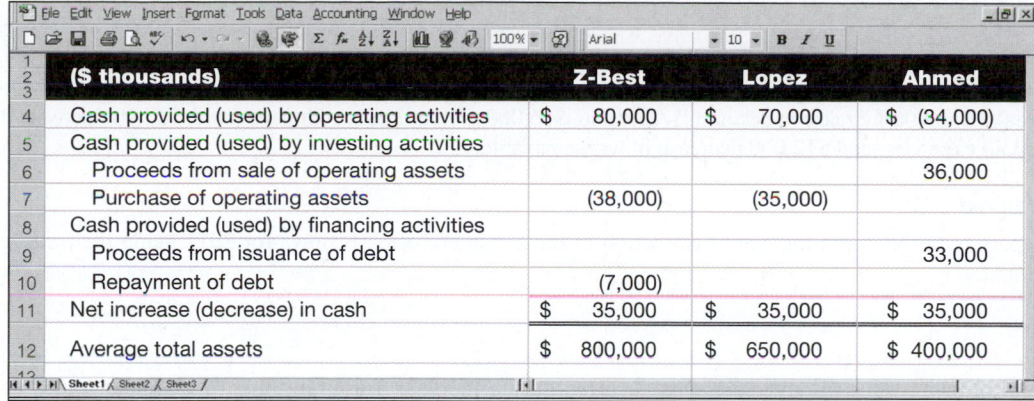

| ($ thousands) | Z-Best | Lopez | Ahmed |
|---|---|---|---|
| Cash provided (used) by operating activities | $ 80,000 | $ 70,000 | $ (34,000) |
| Cash provided (used) by investing activities | | | |
| Proceeds from sale of operating assets | | | 36,000 |
| Purchase of operating assets | (38,000) | (35,000) | |
| Cash provided (used) by financing activities | | | |
| Proceeds from issuance of debt | | | 33,000 |
| Repayment of debt | (7,000) | | |
| Net increase (decrease) in cash | $ 35,000 | $ 35,000 | $ 35,000 |
| Average total assets | $ 800,000 | $ 650,000 | $ 400,000 |

When a spreadsheet for a statement of cash flows is prepared, all changes in noncash balance sheet accounts are fully explained on the spreadsheet. Explain how these noncash balance sheet accounts are used to fully account for cash flows on a spreadsheet.

**QS 16-16^A**
Noncash accounts
on a spreadsheet **P4**

Use the following financial statements and additional information to (1) prepare a statement of cash flows for the year ended December 31, 2012, using the *indirect method,* and (2) analyze and briefly discuss the statement prepared in part 1 with special attention to operating activities and to the company's cash level.

**QS 16-17**
Preparation of statement
of cash flows (indirect)
**P1**

### KRUG INC.
#### Comparative Balance Sheets
#### December 31, 2012 and 2011

| | 2012 | 2011 |
|---|---|---|
| **Assets** | | |
| Cash | $ 26,400 | $ 30,550 |
| Accounts receivable, net | 14,050 | 12,150 |
| Inventory | 90,100 | 70,150 |
| Equipment | 49,900 | 44,500 |
| Accum. depreciation—Equipment | (22,500) | (18,300) |
| Total assets | $157,950 | $139,050 |
| | | |
| **Liabilities and Equity** | | |
| Accounts payable | $ 23,350 | $ 25,400 |
| Salaries payable | 1,050 | 600 |
| Common stock, no par value | 107,000 | 100,000 |
| Retained earnings | 26,550 | 13,050 |
| Total liabilities and equity | $157,950 | $139,050 |

### KRUG INC.
#### Income Statement
#### For Year Ended December 31, 2012

| | | |
|---|---|---|
| Sales | | $47,575 |
| Cost of goods sold | | (17,950) |
| Gross profit | | 29,625 |
| Operating expenses | | |
| Depreciation expense | $4,200 | |
| Other expenses | 8,550 | |
| Total operating expense | | 12,750 |
| Income before taxes | | 16,875 |
| Income tax expense | | 3,375 |
| Net income | | $13,500 |

**Additional Information**

**a.** No dividends are declared or paid in 2012.

**b.** Issued additional stock for $7,000 cash in 2012.

**c.** Purchased equipment for cash in 2012; no equipment was sold in 2012.

Answer each of the following related to international accounting standards.

**1.** Which method, indirect or direct, is acceptable for reporting operating cash flows under IFRS?

**2.** For each of the following four cash flows, identify whether it is reported under the operating, investing, or financing section (or some combination) within the indirect format of the statement of cash flows reported under IFRS and under U.S. GAAP.

**QS 16-18**
International cash flow
disclosures
**C1**

| Cash Flow Source | US GAAP Reporting | IFRS Reporting |
|---|---|---|
| **a.** Interest paid | | |
| **b.** Dividends paid | | |
| **c.** Interest received | | |
| **d.** Dividends received | | |

## EXERCISES

**Exercise 16-1**

Cash flow from operations (indirect)

P2

Rasheed Company reports net income of $390,000 for the year ended December 31, 2011. It also reports $70,000 depreciation expense and a $10,000 gain on the sale of machinery. Its comparative balance sheets reveal a $30,000 increase in accounts receivable, $16,000 increase in accounts payable, $8,000 decrease in prepaid expenses, and $12,000 decrease in wages payable.

**Required**

Prepare only the operating activities section of the statement of cash flows for 2011 using the *indirect method*.

---

**Exercise 16-2**

Cash flow classification (indirect)

C1

The following transactions and events occurred during the year. Assuming that this company uses the *indirect method* to report cash provided by operating activities, indicate where each item would appear on its statement of cash flows by placing an *x* in the appropriate column.

| | Statement of Cash Flows | | | Noncash Investing and Financing Activities | Not Reported on Statement or in Notes |
|---|---|---|---|---|---|
| | Operating Activities | Investing Activities | Financing Activities | | |
| a. Accounts receivable decreased in the year ......... | ___ | ___ | ___ | ___ | ___ |
| b. Purchased land by issuing common stock ........... | ___ | ___ | ___ | ___ | ___ |
| c. Paid cash to purchase inventory .................. | ___ | ___ | ___ | ___ | ___ |
| d. Sold equipment for cash, yielding a loss ........... | ___ | ___ | ___ | ___ | ___ |
| e. Accounts payable decreased in the year ........... | ___ | ___ | ___ | ___ | ___ |
| f. Income taxes payable increased in the year ......... | ___ | ___ | ___ | ___ | ___ |
| g. Declared and paid a cash dividend ................ | ___ | ___ | ___ | ___ | ___ |
| h. Recorded depreciation expense ................... | ___ | ___ | ___ | ___ | ___ |
| i. Paid cash to settle long-term note payable ......... | ___ | ___ | ___ | ___ | ___ |
| j. Prepaid expenses increased in the year ........... | ___ | ___ | ___ | ___ | ___ |

---

**Exercise 16-3[B]**

Cash flow classification (direct)

C1   P5

The following transactions and events occurred during the year. Assuming that this company uses the *direct method* to report cash provided by operating activities, indicate where each item would appear on the statement of cash flows by placing an *x* in the appropriate column.

| | Statement of Cash Flows | | | Noncash Investing and Financing Activities | Not Reported on Statement or in Notes |
|---|---|---|---|---|---|
| | Operating Activities | Investing Activities | Financing Activities | | |
| a. Accepted six-month note receivable in exchange for plant assets ..................... | ___ | ___ | ___ | ___ | ___ |
| b. Recorded depreciation expense .................. | ___ | ___ | ___ | ___ | ___ |
| c. Paid cash to acquire treasury stock .............. | ___ | ___ | ___ | ___ | ___ |
| d. Collected cash from sales ...................... | ___ | ___ | ___ | ___ | ___ |
| e. Borrowed cash from bank by signing a nine-month note payable .............. | ___ | ___ | ___ | ___ | ___ |
| f. Paid cash to purchase a patent .................. | ___ | ___ | ___ | ___ | ___ |
| g. Retired long-term notes payable by issuing common stock ...................... | ___ | ___ | ___ | ___ | ___ |
| h. Paid cash toward accounts payable .............. | ___ | ___ | ___ | ___ | ___ |
| i. Sold inventory for cash ........................ | ___ | ___ | ___ | ___ | ___ |
| j. Paid cash dividend that was declared in a prior period .......................... | ___ | ___ | ___ | ___ | ___ |

Roney Company's calendar-year 2011 income statement shows the following: Net Income, $364,000; Depreciation Expense, $45,000; Amortization Expense, $8,200; Gain on Sale of Plant Assets, $7,000. An examination of the company's current assets and current liabilities reveals the following changes (all from operating activities): Accounts Receivable decrease, $18,100; Merchandise Inventory decrease, $52,000; Prepaid Expenses increase, $3,700; Accounts Payable decrease, $9,200; Other Payables increase, $1,400. Use the *indirect method* to compute cash flow from operating activities.

**Exercise 16-4**
Cash flows from operating activities (indirect)
P2

For each of the following three separate cases, use the information provided about the calendar-year 2012 operations of Sahim Company to compute the required cash flow information.

**Exercise 16-5**[B]
Computation of cash flows (direct)
P5

**Case A:** Compute cash received from customers:

| | |
|---|---|
| Sales | $510,000 |
| Accounts receivable, December 31, 2011 | 25,200 |
| Accounts receivable, December 31, 2012 | 34,800 |

**Case B:** Compute cash paid for rent:

| | |
|---|---|
| Rent expense | $140,800 |
| Rent payable, December 31, 2011 | 8,800 |
| Rent payable, December 31, 2012 | 7,200 |

**Case C:** Compute cash paid for merchandise:

| | |
|---|---|
| Cost of goods sold | $528,000 |
| Merchandise inventory, December 31, 2011 | 159,600 |
| Accounts payable, December 31, 2011 | 67,800 |
| Merchandise inventory, December 31, 2012 | 131,400 |
| Accounts payable, December 31, 2012 | 84,000 |

Use the following income statement and information about changes in noncash current assets and current liabilities to prepare only the cash flows from operating activities section of the statement of cash flows using the *indirect* method.

**Exercise 16-6**
Cash flows from operating activities (indirect)
P2

| BEKHAM COMPANY<br>Income Statement<br>For Year Ended December 31, 2011 | | |
|---|---|---|
| Sales | | $1,818,000 |
| Cost of goods sold | | 891,000 |
| Gross profit | | 927,000 |
| Operating expenses | | |
| Salaries expense | $248,535 | |
| Depreciation expense | 43,200 | |
| Rent expense | 48,600 | |
| Amortization expenses—Patents | 5,400 | |
| Utilities expense | 19,125 | 364,860 |
| | | 562,140 |
| Gain on sale of equipment | | 7,200 |
| Net income | | $ 569,340 |

Changes in current asset and current liability accounts for the year that relate to operations follow.

| | | | |
|---|---|---|---|
| Accounts receivable | $40,500 increase | Accounts payable | $13,500 decrease |
| Merchandise inventory | 27,000 increase | Salaries payable | 4,500 decrease |

Refer to the information about Bekham Company in Exercise 16-6.
Use the *direct method* to prepare only the cash provided or used by operating activities section of the statement of cash flows for this company.

**Exercise 16-7**[B]
Cash flows from operating activities (direct) P5

**Exercise 16-8**

Cash flows from investing activities

P3

Use the following information to determine this company's cash flows from investing activities.

**a.** Sold land costing $315,000 for $400,000 cash, yielding a gain of $15,000.

**b.** Paid $106,000 cash for a new truck.

**c.** Equipment with a book value of $80,500 and an original cost of $165,000 was sold at a loss of $34,000.

**d.** Long-term investments in stock were sold for $94,700 cash, yielding a gain of $15,750.

**Exercise 16-9**

Cash flows from financing activities

P3

Use the following information to determine this company's cash flows from financing activities.

**a.** Net income was $472,000.

**b.** Issued common stock for $75,000 cash.

**c.** Paid cash dividend of $13,000.

**d.** Paid $120,000 cash to settle a note payable at its $120,000 maturity value.

**e.** Paid $118,000 cash to acquire its treasury stock.

**f.** Purchased equipment for $92,000 cash.

**Exercise 16-10**

Preparation of statement of cash flows (indirect) P1

Use the following financial statements and additional information to (1) prepare a statement of cash flows for the year ended June 30, 2011, using the *indirect method,* and (2) compute the company's cash flow on total assets ratio for its fiscal year 2011.

| GECKO INC. Income Statement For Year Ended June 30, 2011 | | |
|---|---:|---:|
| Sales ............................ | | $668,000 |
| Cost of goods sold ................. | | 412,000 |
| Gross profit ....................... | | 256,000 |
| Operating expenses | | |
|   Depreciation expense ............. | $58,600 | |
|   Other expenses ................ | 67,000 | |
| Total operating expenses ............ | | 125,600 |
| | | 130,400 |
| Other gains (losses) | | |
|   Gain on sale of equipment ......... | | 2,000 |
| Income before taxes ................ | | 132,400 |
| Income taxes expense .............. | | 45,640 |
| Net income ....................... | | $ 86,760 |

| GECKO INC. Comparative Balance Sheets June 30, 2011 and 2010 | | |
|---|---:|---:|
| | **2011** | **2010** |
| **Assets** | | |
| Cash ..................... | $ 85,800 | $ 45,000 |
| Accounts receivable, net ................ | 70,000 | 52,000 |
| Inventory .......................... | 66,800 | 96,800 |
| Prepaid expenses .................... | 5,400 | 5,200 |
| Equipment .......................... | 130,000 | 120,000 |
| Accum. depreciation—Equipment ........ | (28,000) | (10,000) |
| Total assets ......................... | $330,000 | $309,000 |
| **Liabilities and Equity** | | |
| Accounts payable ..................... | $ 26,000 | $ 32,000 |
| Wages payable ....................... | 7,000 | 16,000 |
| Income taxes payable ................. | 2,400 | 3,600 |
| Notes payable (long term) ............. | 40,000 | 70,000 |
| Common stock, $5 par value ........... | 230,000 | 180,000 |
| Retained earnings .................... | 24,600 | 7,400 |
| Total liabilities and equity .............. | $330,000 | $309,000 |

**Additional Information**

**a.** A $30,000 note payable is retired at its $30,000 carrying (book) value in exchange for cash.

**b.** The only changes affecting retained earnings are net income and cash dividends paid.

**c.** New equipment is acquired for $58,600 cash.

**d.** Received cash for the sale of equipment that had cost $48,600, yielding a $2,000 gain.

**e.** Prepaid Expenses and Wages Payable relate to Other Expenses on the income statement.

**f.** All purchases and sales of merchandise inventory are on credit.

Refer to the data in Exercise 16-10.
Using the *direct method,* prepare the statement of cash flows for the year ended June 30, 2011.

**Exercise 16-11ᴮ**
Preparation of statement of cash flows (direct)

P1

Use the following information about the cash flows of Kansas Company to prepare a complete statement of cash flows (*direct method*) for the year ended December 31, 2011. Use a note disclosure for any noncash investing and financing activities.

**Exercise 16-12ᴮ**
Preparation of statement of cash flows (direct) and supporting note

P1

| | |
|---|---:|
| Cash and cash equivalents balance, December 31, 2010 | $ 25,000 |
| Cash and cash equivalents balance, December 31, 2011 | 70,000 |
| Cash received as interest | 2,500 |
| Cash paid for salaries | 72,500 |
| Bonds payable retired by issuing common stock (no gain or loss on retirement) | 187,500 |
| Cash paid to retire long-term notes payable | 125,000 |
| Cash received from sale of equipment | 61,250 |
| Cash received in exchange for six-month note payable | 25,000 |
| Land purchased by issuing long-term note payable | 106,250 |
| Cash paid for store equipment | 23,750 |
| Cash dividends paid | 15,000 |
| Cash paid for other expenses | 40,000 |
| Cash received from customers | 485,000 |
| Cash paid for merchandise | 252,500 |

The following summarized Cash T-account reflects the total debits and total credits to the Cash account of Texas Corporation for calendar year 2011.

(1) Use this information to prepare a complete statement of cash flows for year 2011. The cash provided or used by operating activities should be reported using the *direct method.*

(2) Refer to the statement of cash flows prepared for part 1 to answer the following questions *a* through *d*: (*a*) Which section—operating, investing, or financing—shows the largest cash (i) inflow and (ii) outflow? (*b*) What is the largest individual item among the investing cash outflows? (*c*) Are the cash proceeds larger from issuing notes or issuing stock? (*d*) Does the company have a net cash inflow or outflow from borrowing activities?

**Exercise 16-13ᴮ**
Preparation of statement of cash flows (direct) from Cash T-account

P1

| **Accounting System:** | | _ □ × |
|---|---|---|
| File  Edit  Maintain  Tasks  Analysis  Options  Reports  Window  Help | | |

| | | Cash | | _ □ × |
|---|---:|---|---:|---|
| Balance, Dec. 31, 2010 | 135,200 | | | |
| Receipts from customers | 6,000,000 | Payments for merchandise | 1,590,000 | |
| Receipts from dividends | 208,400 | Payments for wages | 550,000 | |
| Receipts from land sale | 220,000 | Payments for rent | 320,000 | |
| Receipts from machinery sale | 710,000 | Payments for interest | 218,000 | |
| Receipts from issuing stock | 1,540,000 | Payments for taxes | 450,000 | |
| Receipts from borrowing | 2,600,000 | Payments for machinery | 2,236,000 | |
| | | Payments for long-term investments | 2,260,000 | |
| | | Payments for note payable | 386,000 | |
| | | Payments for dividends | 500,000 | |
| | | Payments for treasury stock | 218,000 | |
| Balance, Dec. 31, 2011 | $        ? | | | |

Sales    Purchases    General Ledger    Payroll    Inventory    Company    Analysis

**Exercise 16-14**

Reporting cash flows from operations (indirect)

P2

Harold Company reports the following information for its recent calendar year.

| | |
|---|---:|
| Sales .......................... | $70,000 |
| Expenses | |
|    Cost of goods sold ............. | 40,000 |
|    Salaries expense ............... | 12,000 |
|    Depreciation expense ........... | 6,000 |
| Net income ..................... | $12,000 |
| | |
| Accounts receivable increase ........ | $ 9,000 |
| Inventory decrease ............... | 3,000 |
| Salaries payable increase ........... | 800 |

**Required**

Prepare the operating activities section of the statement of cash flows for Harold Company using the indirect method.

**Exercise 16-15**

Reporting and interpreting cash flows from operations (indirect)

P2

Oregon Company disclosed the following information for its recent calendar year.

| | |
|---|---:|
| Revenues ......................... | $100,000 |
| Expenses | |
|    Salaries expense .................. | 68,000 |
|    Utilities expense .................. | 28,000 |
|    Depreciation expense .............. | 29,200 |
|    Other expenses ................... | 6,800 |
| Net loss ......................... | $ (32,000) |
| | |
| Accounts receivable decrease .......... | $ 28,000 |
| Purchased a machine ................. | 20,000 |
| Salaries payable increase .............. | 26,000 |
| Other accrued liabilities decrease ........ | 16,000 |

**Required**

1. Prepare the operating activities section of the statement of cash flows using the indirect method.
2. What were the major reasons that this company was able to report a net loss but positive cash flow from operations?
3. Of the potential causes of differences between cash flow from operations and net income, which are the most important to investors?

**Exercise 16-16**

Analyses of cash flow on total assets    A1

A company reported average total assets of $248,000 in 2010 and $302,000 in 2011. Its net operating cash flow in 2010 was $20,575 and $27,750 in 2011. Calculate its cash flow on total assets ratio for both years. Comment on the results and any change in performance.

**Exercise 16-17**

Cash flows spreadsheet (indirect method)

P4

Complete the following spreadsheet in preparation of the statement of cash flows. (The statement of cash flows is not required.) Prepare the spreadsheet as in Exhibit 16A.1; report operating activities under the indirect method. Identify the debits and credits in the Analysis of Changes columns with letters that correspond to the following transactions *a* through *e*.

**a.** Net income for the year was $30,000.

**b.** Dividends of $10,000 cash were declared and paid.

**c.** Stylish's only noncash expense was $50,000 of depreciation.

**d.** The company purchased plant assets for $70,000 cash.

**e.** Notes payable of $40,000 were issued for $40,000 cash.

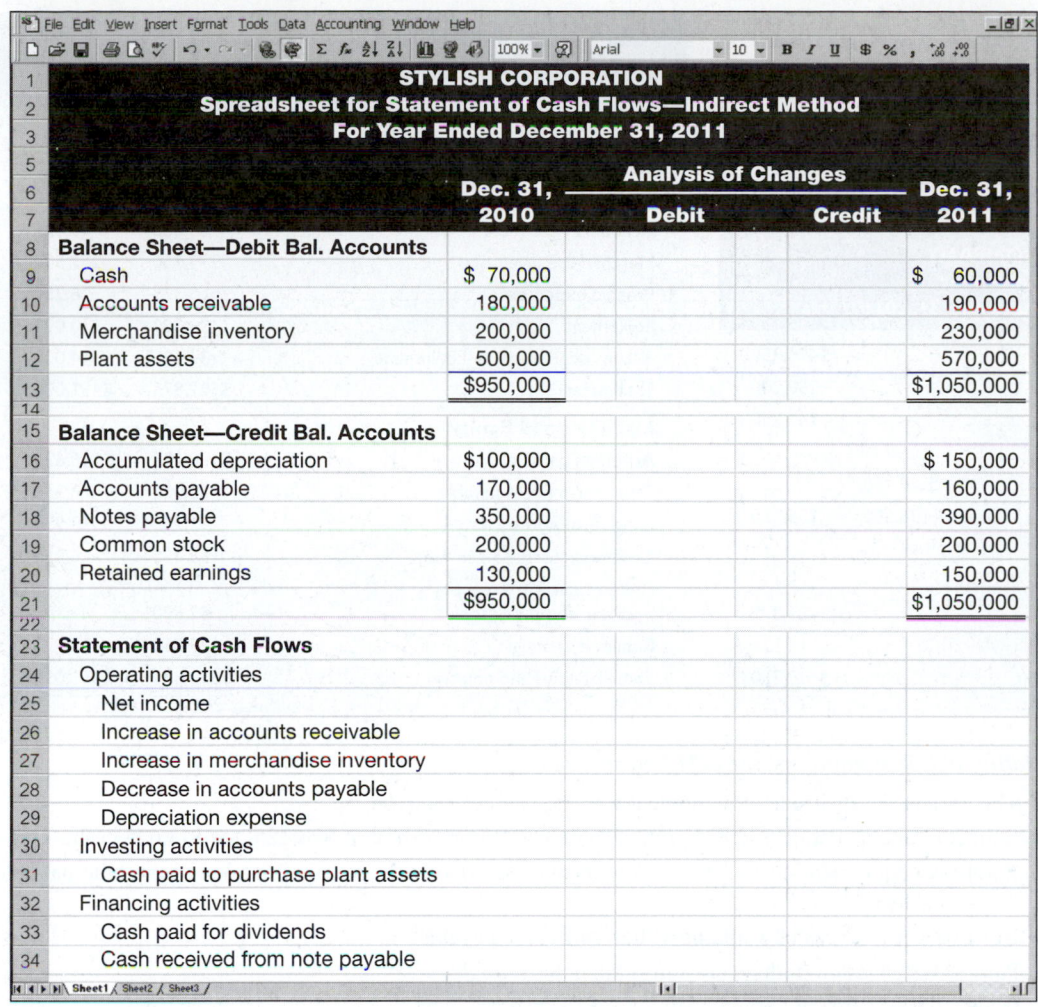

File Edit View Insert Format Tools Data Accounting Window Help

| | STYLISH CORPORATION<br>Spreadsheet for Statement of Cash Flows—Indirect Method<br>For Year Ended December 31, 2011 | | | | |
|---|---|---|---|---|---|
| | | **Dec. 31,<br>2010** | **Analysis of Changes** | | **Dec. 31,<br>2011** |
| | | | **Debit** | **Credit** | |
| 8 | **Balance Sheet—Debit Bal. Accounts** | | | | |
| 9 | Cash | $ 70,000 | | | $ 60,000 |
| 10 | Accounts receivable | 180,000 | | | 190,000 |
| 11 | Merchandise inventory | 200,000 | | | 230,000 |
| 12 | Plant assets | 500,000 | | | 570,000 |
| 13 | | $950,000 | | | $1,050,000 |
| 15 | **Balance Sheet—Credit Bal. Accounts** | | | | |
| 16 | Accumulated depreciation | $100,000 | | | $ 150,000 |
| 17 | Accounts payable | 170,000 | | | 160,000 |
| 18 | Notes payable | 350,000 | | | 390,000 |
| 19 | Common stock | 200,000 | | | 200,000 |
| 20 | Retained earnings | 130,000 | | | 150,000 |
| 21 | | $950,000 | | | $1,050,000 |
| 23 | **Statement of Cash Flows** | | | | |
| 24 | Operating activities | | | | |
| 25 | Net income | | | | |
| 26 | Increase in accounts receivable | | | | |
| 27 | Increase in merchandise inventory | | | | |
| 28 | Decrease in accounts payable | | | | |
| 29 | Depreciation expense | | | | |
| 30 | Investing activities | | | | |
| 31 | Cash paid to purchase plant assets | | | | |
| 32 | Financing activities | | | | |
| 33 | Cash paid for dividends | | | | |
| 34 | Cash received from note payable | | | | |

Sheet1 / Sheet2 / Sheet3 /

**Peugeot S.A.** reports the following financial information for the year ended December 31, 2008 (euros in millions). Prepare its statement of cash flows under the indirect method.

**Exercise 16-18**
Statement of cash flows under IFRS (indirect)

**P1**

| | | | |
|---|---|---|---|
| Net loss ........................ | € 500 | Cash from sales of treasury stock and other ....... | € 812 |
| Depreciation and amortization ..... | 3,679 | Cash paid for dividends ....................... | 361 |
| Gains on disposals and other ...... | (362) | Cash from disposal of plant assets and intangibles .... | 88 |
| Net increase in current assets ..... | (417) | Cash paid for plant assets and intangibles ......... | (3,331) |
| Net decrease in current liabilities ... | (2,338) | Cash and cash equivalents, December 31, 2007 ...... | 5,937 |

**connect**

Kazaam Company, a merchandiser, recently completed its calendar-year 2011 operations. For the year, (1) all sales are credit sales, (2) all credits to Accounts Receivable reflect cash receipts from customers, (3) all purchases of inventory are on credit, (4) all debits to Accounts Payable reflect cash payments for inventory, and (5) Other Expenses are paid in advance and are initially debited to Prepaid Expenses. The company's balance sheets and income statement follow.

**PROBLEM SET A**

**Problem 16-1A**
Statement of cash flows (indirect method)

**A1  P1  P2  P3**

### KAZAAM COMPANY
### Income Statement
### For Year Ended December 31, 2011

| | | |
|---|---:|---:|
| Sales ............................. | | $496,250 |
| Cost of goods sold ................ | | 250,000 |
| Gross profit ...................... | | 246,250 |
| Operating expenses | | |
|    Depreciation expense ............ | $ 18,750 | |
|    Other expenses................. | 136,500 | 155,250 |
| Other gains (losses) | | |
|    Loss on sale of equipment ........ | | 5,125 |
| Income before taxes ............... | | 85,875 |
| Income taxes expense ............. | | 12,125 |
| Net income ...................... | | $ 73,750 |

### KAZAAM COMPANY
### Comparative Balance Sheets
### December 31, 2011 and 2010

| | 2011 | 2010 |
|---|---:|---:|
| **Assets** | | |
| Cash ................................. | $ 53,875 | $ 76,625 |
| Accounts receivable .................... | 65,000 | 49,625 |
| Merchandise inventory ................. | 273,750 | 252,500 |
| Prepaid expenses .................... | 5,375 | 6,250 |
| Equipment .......................... | 159,500 | 110,000 |
| Accum. depreciation—Equipment ......... | (34,625) | (44,000) |
| Total assets ......................... | $522,875 | $451,000 |
| **Liabilities and Equity** | | |
| Accounts payable ..................... | $ 88,125 | $116,625 |
| Short-term notes payable .............. | 10,000 | 6,250 |
| Long-term notes payable .............. | 93,750 | 53,750 |
| Common stock, $5 par value ............ | 168,750 | 156,250 |
| Paid-in capital in excess | | |
|   of par, common stock ............... | 32,500 | 0 |
| Retained earnings ................... | 129,750 | 118,125 |
| Total liabilities and equity .............. | $522,875 | $451,000 |

**Additional Information on Year 2011 Transactions**

**a.** The loss on the cash sale of equipment was $5,125 (details in *b*).

**b.** Sold equipment costing $46,875, with accumulated depreciation of $28,125, for $13,625 cash.

**c.** Purchased equipment costing $96,375 by paying $25,000 cash and signing a long-term note payable for the balance.

**d.** Borrowed $3,750 cash by signing a short-term note payable.

**e.** Paid $31,375 cash to reduce the long-term notes payable.

**f.** Issued 2,500 shares of common stock for $18 cash per share.

**g.** Declared and paid cash dividends of $62,125.

**Required**

**Check**   Cash from operating activities, $33,375

**1.** Prepare a complete statement of cash flows; report its operating activities using the *indirect method*. Disclose any noncash investing and financing activities in a note.

**Analysis Component**

**2.** Analyze and discuss the statement of cash flows prepared in part 1, giving special attention to the wisdom of the cash dividend payment.

---

**Problem 16-2A**[B]

Statement of cash flows (direct method)   P1   P3   P5

**Check**   Cash used in financing activities, $(44,750)

Refer to Kazaam Company's financial statements and related information in Problem 16-1A.

**Required**

Prepare a complete statement of cash flows; report its operating activities according to the *direct method*. Disclose any noncash investing and financing activities in a note.

---

**Problem 16-3A**[A]

Cash flows spreadsheet (indirect method)

P1   P2   P3   P4

Refer to the information reported about Kazaam Company in Problem 16-1A.

**Required**

Prepare a complete statement of cash flows using a spreadsheet as in Exhibit 16A.1; report its operating activities using the indirect method. Identify the debits and credits in the Analysis of Changes columns with letters that correspond to the following list of transactions and events.

   **a.** Net income was $73,750.

   **b.** Accounts receivable increased.

   **c.** Merchandise inventory increased.

**d.** Prepaid expenses decreased.

**e.** Accounts payable decreased.

**f.** Depreciation expense was $18,750.

**g.** Sold equipment costing $46,875, with accumulated depreciation of $28,125, for $13,625 cash. This yielded a loss of $5,125.

**h.** Purchased equipment costing $96,375 by paying $25,000 cash and **(i.)** by signing a long-term note payable for the balance.

**j.** Borrowed $3,750 cash by signing a short-term note payable.

**k.** Paid $31,375 cash to reduce the long-term notes payable.

**l.** Issued 2,500 shares of common stock for $18 cash per share.

**m.** Declared and paid cash dividends of $62,125.

**Check**  Analysis of Changes column totals, $515,375

Galley Corp., a merchandiser, recently completed its 2011 operations. For the year, (1) all sales are credit sales, (2) all credits to Accounts Receivable reflect cash receipts from customers, (3) all purchases of inventory are on credit, (4) all debits to Accounts Payable reflect cash payments for inventory, (5) Other Expenses are all cash expenses, and (6) any change in Income Taxes Payable reflects the accrual and cash payment of taxes. The company's balance sheets and income statement follow.

**Problem 16-4A**
Statement of cash flows (indirect method)
P1  P2  P3

mhhe.com/wildFAP20e

### GALLEY CORPORATION
### Comparative Balance Sheets
### December 31, 2011 and 2010

| Assets | 2011 | 2010 |
|---|---|---|
| Cash | $ 174,000 | $117,000 |
| Accounts receivable | 93,000 | 81,000 |
| Merchandise inventory | 609,000 | 534,000 |
| Equipment | 333,000 | 297,000 |
| Accum. depreciation—Equipment | (156,000) | (102,000) |
| Total assets | $1,053,000 | $927,000 |
| **Liabilities and Equity** | | |
| Accounts payable | $ 69,000 | $ 96,000 |
| Income taxes payable | 27,000 | 24,000 |
| Common stock, $2 par value | 582,000 | 558,000 |
| Paid-in capital in excess of par value, common stock | 198,000 | 162,000 |
| Retained earnings | 177,000 | 87,000 |
| Total liabilities and equity | $1,053,000 | $927,000 |

### GALLEY CORPORATION
### Income Statement
### For Year Ended December 31, 2011

| | | |
|---|---|---|
| Sales | | $1,992,000 |
| Cost of goods sold | | 1,194,000 |
| Gross profit | | 798,000 |
| Operating expenses | | |
| Depreciation expense | $ 54,000 | |
| Other expenses | 501,000 | 555,000 |
| Income before taxes | | 243,000 |
| Income taxes expense | | 42,000 |
| Net income | | $ 201,000 |

**Additional Information on Year 2011 Transactions**

**a.** Purchased equipment for $36,000 cash.

**b.** Issued 12,000 shares of common stock for $5 cash per share.

**c.** Declared and paid $111,000 in cash dividends.

**Required**

Prepare a complete statement of cash flows; report its cash inflows and cash outflows from operating activities according to the *indirect method*.

**Check**  Cash from operating activities, $144,000

Refer to Galley Corporation's financial statements and related information in Problem 16-4A.

**Required**

Prepare a complete statement of cash flows; report its cash flows from operating activities according to the *direct method*.

**Problem 16-5A**[B]
Statement of cash flows (direct method)  P1  P3  P5

mhhe.com/wildFAP20e

**Check**  Cash used in financing activities, $(51,000)

**Problem 16-6A^A**

Cash flows spreadsheet
(indirect method)

P1 P2 P3 P4

mhhe.com/wildFAP20e

Refer to the information reported about Galley Corporation in Problem 16-4A.

***Required***

Prepare a complete statement of cash flows using a spreadsheet as in Exhibit 16A.1; report operating activities under the indirect method. Identify the debits and credits in the Analysis of Changes columns with letters that correspond to the following list of transactions and events.

**a.** Net income was $201,000.

**b.** Accounts receivable increased.

**c.** Merchandise inventory increased.

**d.** Accounts payable decreased.

**e.** Income taxes payable increased.

**f.** Depreciation expense was $54,000.

**g.** Purchased equipment for $36,000 cash.

**h.** Issued 12,000 shares at $5 cash per share.

**i.** Declared and paid $111,000 of cash dividends.

**Check** Analysis of Changes column totals, $579,000

---

**Problem 16-7A**

Computing cash flows from operations (indirect)

P2

Rapture Company's 2011 income statement and selected balance sheet data at December 31, 2010 and 2011, follow ($ thousands).

**RAPTURE COMPANY**
**Selected Balance Sheet Accounts**

| At December 31 | 2011 | 2010 |
|---|---|---|
| Accounts receivable | $380 | $390 |
| Inventory | 99 | 77 |
| Accounts payable | 120 | 130 |
| Salaries payable | 44 | 35 |
| Utilities payable | 11 | 8 |
| Prepaid insurance | 13 | 14 |
| Prepaid rent | 11 | 9 |

**RAPTURE COMPANY**
**Income Statement**
**For Year Ended December 31, 2011**

| | |
|---|---|
| Sales revenue | $58,600 |
| Expenses | |
| Cost of goods sold | 21,000 |
| Depreciation expense | 6,000 |
| Salaries expense | 11,000 |
| Rent expense | 2,500 |
| Insurance expense | 1,900 |
| Interest expense | 1,800 |
| Utilities expense | 1,400 |
| Net income | $13,000 |

***Required***

Prepare the cash flows from operating activities section only of the company's 2011 statement of cash flows using the indirect method.

**Check** Cash from operating activities, $18,989

---

**Problem 16-8A^B**

Computing cash flows from operations (direct)

P5

Refer to the information in Problem 16-7A.

***Required***

Prepare the cash flows from operating activities section only of the company's 2011 statement of cash flows using the direct method.

---

## PROBLEM SET B

**Problem 16-1B**

Statement of cash flows
(indirect method)

A1 P1 P2 P3

Kite Corporation, a merchandiser, recently completed its calendar-year 2011 operations. For the year, (1) all sales are credit sales, (2) all credits to Accounts Receivable reflect cash receipts from customers, (3) all purchases of inventory are on credit, (4) all debits to Accounts Payable reflect cash payments for inventory, and (5) Other Expenses are paid in advance and are initially debited to Prepaid Expenses. The company's balance sheets and income statement follow.

### KITE CORPORATION
### Comparative Balance Sheets
### December 31, 2011 and 2010

| | 2011 | 2010 |
|---|---|---|
| **Assets** | | |
| Cash ................................ | $136,500 | $ 71,550 |
| Accounts receivable ................... | 74,100 | 90,750 |
| Merchandise inventory ................ | 454,500 | 490,200 |
| Prepaid expenses .................... | 17,100 | 19,200 |
| Equipment ......................... | 278,250 | 216,000 |
| Accum. depreciation—Equipment ........ | (108,750) | (93,000) |
| Total assets ......................... | $851,700 | $794,700 |
| **Liabilities and Equity** | | |
| Accounts payable .................... | $117,450 | $123,450 |
| Short-term notes payable .............. | 17,250 | 11,250 |
| Long-term notes payable .............. | 112,500 | 82,500 |
| Common stock, $5 par ................ | 465,000 | 450,000 |
| Paid-in capital in excess | | |
| of par, common stock ............... | 18,000 | 0 |
| Retained earnings .................... | 121,500 | 127,500 |
| Total liabilities and equity ............. | $851,700 | $794,700 |

### KITE CORPORATION
### Income Statement
### For Year Ended December 31, 2011

| | | |
|---|---|---|
| Sales............................ | | $1,083,000 |
| Cost of goods sold ................ | | 585,000 |
| Gross profit....................... | | 498,000 |
| Operating expenses | | |
| Depreciation expense ............ | $ 36,600 | |
| Other expenses ................ | 392,850 | |
| Total operating expenses ........... | | 429,450 |
| | | 68,550 |
| Other gains (losses) | | |
| Loss on sale of equipment ........ | | 2,100 |
| Income before taxes ............... | | 66,450 |
| Income taxes expense ............. | | 9,450 |
| Net income ...................... | | $ 57,000 |

### Additional Information on Year 2011 Transactions

**a.** The loss on the cash sale of equipment was $2,100 (details in *b*).

**b.** Sold equipment costing $51,000, with accumulated depreciation of $20,850, for $28,050 cash.

**c.** Purchased equipment costing $113,250 by paying $38,250 cash and signing a long-term note payable for the balance.

**d.** Borrowed $6,000 cash by signing a short-term note payable.

**e.** Paid $45,000 cash to reduce the long-term notes payable.

**f.** Issued 3,000 shares of common stock for $11 cash per share.

**g.** Declared and paid cash dividends of $63,000.

### Required

**1.** Prepare a complete statement of cash flows; report its operating activities using the *indirect method*. Disclose any noncash investing and financing activities in a note.

**Check**  Cash from operating activities, $144,150

### Analysis Component

**2.** Analyze and discuss the statement of cash flows prepared in part 1, giving special attention to the wisdom of the cash dividend payment.

---

Refer to Kite Corporation's financial statements and related information in Problem 16-1B.

**Problem 16-2B**[B]

Statement of cash flows (direct method)  P1  P3  P5

### Required

Prepare a complete statement of cash flows; report its operating activities according to the *direct method*. Disclose any noncash investing and financing activities in a note.

**Check**  Cash used in financing activities, $(69,000)

---

Refer to the information reported about Kite Corporation in Problem 16-1B.

**Problem 16-3B**[A]

Cash flows spreadsheet (indirect method)

P1  P2  P3  P4

### Required

Prepare a complete statement of cash flows using a spreadsheet as in Exhibit 16A.1; report its operating activities using the *indirect method*. Identify the debits and credits in the Analysis of Changes columns with letters that correspond to the following list of transactions and events.

a. Net income was $57,000.

b. Accounts receivable decreased.

c. Merchandise inventory decreased.

d. Prepaid expenses decreased.

e. Accounts payable decreased.

f. Depreciation expense was $36,600.

g. Sold equipment costing $51,000, with accumulated depreciation of $20,850, for $28,050 cash. This yielded a loss of $2,100.

h. Purchased equipment costing $113,250 by paying $38,250 cash and **(i.)** by signing a long-term note payable for the balance.

j. Borrowed $6,000 cash by signing a short-term note payable.

k. Paid $45,000 cash to reduce the long-term notes payable.

l. Issued 3,000 shares of common stock for $11 cash per share.

m. Declared and paid cash dividends of $63,000.

**Check** Analysis of Changes column totals, $540,300

---

**Problem 16-4B**
Statement of cash flows
(indirect method)
P1  P2  P3

Taurasi Company, a merchandiser, recently completed its 2011 operations. For the year, (1) all sales are credit sales, (2) all credits to Accounts Receivable reflect cash receipts from customers, (3) all purchases of inventory are on credit, (4) all debits to Accounts Payable reflect cash payments for inventory, (5) Other Expenses are cash expenses, and (6) any change in Income Taxes Payable reflects the accrual and cash payment of taxes. The company's balance sheets and income statement follow.

### TAURASI COMPANY
### Comparative Balance Sheets
### December 31, 2011 and 2010

|  | 2011 | 2010 |
|---|---|---|
| **Assets** | | |
| Cash | $ 53,925 | $ 31,800 |
| Accounts receivable | 19,425 | 23,250 |
| Merchandise inventory | 175,350 | 139,875 |
| Equipment | 105,450 | 76,500 |
| Accum. depreciation—Equipment | (48,300) | (30,600) |
| Total assets | $305,850 | $240,825 |
| **Liabilities and Equity** | | |
| Accounts payable | $ 38,475 | $ 35,625 |
| Income taxes payable | 4,500 | 6,750 |
| Common stock, $2 par value | 165,000 | 150,000 |
| Paid-in capital in excess of par, common stock | 42,000 | 15,000 |
| Retained earnings | 55,875 | 33,450 |
| Total liabilities and equity | $305,850 | $240,825 |

### TAURASI COMPANY
### Income Statement
### For Year Ended December 31, 2011

| | | |
|---|---|---|
| Sales | | $609,750 |
| Cost of goods sold | | 279,000 |
| Gross profit | | 330,750 |
| Operating expenses | | |
| Depreciation expense | $ 17,700 | |
| Other expenses | 179,775 | 197,475 |
| Income before taxes | | 133,275 |
| Income taxes expense | | 44,850 |
| Net income | | $ 88,425 |

**Additional Information on Year 2011 Transactions**

a. Purchased equipment for $28,950 cash.

b. Issued 3,000 shares of common stock for $14 cash per share.

c. Declared and paid $66,000 of cash dividends.

**Required**

**Check** Cash from operating activities, $75,075

Prepare a complete statement of cash flows; report its cash inflows and cash outflows from operating activities according to the *indirect method*.

---

**Problem 16-5B**[B]
Statement of cash flows
(direct method)  P1  P3  P5

Refer to Taurasi Company's financial statements and related information in Problem 16-4B.

**Required**

**Check** Cash used by financing activities, $(24,000)

Prepare a complete statement of cash flows; report its cash flows from operating activities according to the *direct method*.

Refer to the information reported about Taurasi Company in Problem 16-4B.

**Problem 16-6B**[A]

Cash flows spreadsheet
(indirect method)

**P1  P2  P3  P4**

*Required*

Prepare a complete statement of cash flows using a spreadsheet as in Exhibit 16A.1; report operating activities under the *indirect method*. Identify the debits and credits in the Analysis of Changes columns with letters that correspond to the following list of transactions and events.

**a.** Net income was $88,425.

**b.** Accounts receivable decreased.

**c.** Merchandise inventory increased.

**d.** Accounts payable increased.

**e.** Income taxes payable decreased.

**f.** Depreciation expense was $17,700.

**g.** Purchased equipment for $28,950 cash.

**h.** Issued 3,000 shares at $14 cash per share.

**i.** Declared and paid $66,000 of cash dividends.

**Check**  Analysis of Changes
column totals, $287,475

---

Tyra Company's 2011 income statement and selected balance sheet data at December 31, 2010 and 2011, follow ($ thousands).

**Problem 16-7B**

Computing cash flows from
operations (indirect)

**P2**

**TYRA COMPANY**
**Income Statement**
**For Year Ended December 31, 2011**

| | |
|---|---|
| Sales revenue | $412,000 |
| Expenses | |
| Cost of goods sold | 244,000 |
| Depreciation expense | 64,000 |
| Salaries expense | 30,000 |
| Rent expense | 20,000 |
| Insurance expense | 5,200 |
| Interest expense | 4,800 |
| Utilities expense | 4,000 |
| Net income | $ 40,000 |

**TYRA COMPANY**
**Selected Balance Sheet Accounts**

| At December 31 | 2011 | 2010 |
|---|---|---|
| Accounts receivable | $820 | $700 |
| Inventory | 272 | 296 |
| Accounts payable | 480 | 520 |
| Salaries payable | 280 | 220 |
| Utilities payable | 40 | 0 |
| Prepaid insurance | 28 | 36 |
| Prepaid rent | 40 | 60 |

*Required*

Prepare the cash flows from operating activities section only of the company's 2011 statement of cash flows using the indirect method.

**Check**  Cash from operating
activities, $103,992

---

Refer to the information in Problem 16-7B.

**Problem 16-8B**[B]

Computing cash flows from
operations (direct)

**P5**

*Required*

Prepare the cash flows from operating activities section only of the company's 2011 statement of cash flows using the direct method.

---

*(This serial problem began in Chapter 1 and continues through most of the book. If previous chapter segments were not completed, the serial problem can begin at this point. It is helpful, but not necessary, to use the Working Papers that accompany the book.)*

**SERIAL PROBLEM**
Business Solutions

**P1  P2  P3**

**SP 16**  Santana Rey, owner of Business Solutions, decides to prepare a statement of cash flows for her business. (Although the serial problem allowed for various ownership changes in earlier chapters, we will prepare the statement of cash flows using the following financial data.)

### BUSINESS SOLUTIONS
### Income Statement
### For Three Months Ended March 31, 2012

| | | |
|---|---:|---:|
| Computer services revenue | | $25,307 |
| Net sales | | 18,693 |
| Total revenue | | 44,000 |
| Cost of goods sold | $14,052 | |
| Depreciation expense— Office equipment | 400 | |
| Depreciation expense— Computer equipment | 1,250 | |
| Wages expense | 3,250 | |
| Insurance expense | 555 | |
| Rent expense | 2,475 | |
| Computer supplies expense | 1,305 | |
| Advertising expense | 600 | |
| Mileage expense | 320 | |
| Repairs expense—Computer | 960 | |
| Total expenses | | 25,167 |
| Net income | | $18,833 |

### BUSINESS SOLUTIONS
### Comparative Balance Sheets
### December 31, 2011, and March 31, 2012

| | 2012 | 2011 |
|---|---:|---:|
| **Assets** | | |
| Cash | $ 68,057 | $48,372 |
| Accounts receivable | 22,867 | 5,668 |
| Merchandise inventory | 704 | 0 |
| Computer supplies | 2,005 | 580 |
| Prepaid insurance | 1,110 | 1,665 |
| Prepaid rent | 825 | 825 |
| Office equipment | 8,000 | 8,000 |
| Accumulated depreciation—Office equipment | (800) | (400) |
| Computer equipment | 20,000 | 20,000 |
| Accumulated depreciation— Computer equipment | (2,500) | (1,250) |
| Total assets | $120,268 | $83,460 |
| **Liabilities and Equity** | | |
| Accounts payable | $    0 | $ 1,100 |
| Wages payable | 875 | 500 |
| Unearned computer service revenue | 0 | 1,500 |
| Common stock | 98,000 | 73,000 |
| Retained earnings | 21,393 | 7,360 |
| Total liabilities and equity | $120,268 | $83,460 |

**Required**

**Check**  Cash flows used by operations: $(515)

Prepare a statement of cash flows for Business Solutions using the *indirect method* for the three months ended March 31, 2012. Recall that the owner Santana Rey contributed $25,000 to the business in exchange for additional stock in the first quarter of 2012 and has received $4,800 in cash dividends.

---

## Beyond the Numbers

**REPORTING IN ACTION**

A1

**RIM**

**BTN 16-1**   Refer to **Research In Motion**'s financial statements in Appendix A to answer the following.

1. Is Research In Motion's statement of cash flows prepared under the direct method or the indirect method? How do you know?

2. For each fiscal year 2010, 2009, and 2008, is the amount of cash provided by operating activities more or less than the cash paid for dividends?

3. What is the largest amount in reconciling the difference between net income and cash flow from operating activities in 2010? In 2009? In 2008?

4. Identify the largest cash inflow and outflow for investing *and* for financing activities in 2010 and in 2009.

*Fast Forward*

5. Obtain Research In Motion's financial statements for a fiscal year ending after February 27, 2010, from either its Website (**RIM.com**) or the SEC's database (**www.sec.gov**). Since February 27, 2010, what are Research In Motion's largest cash outflows and cash inflows in the investing and in the financing sections of its statement of cash flows?

**BTN 16-2**    Key figures for **Research In Motion** and **Apple** follow.

| ($ millions) | Research In Motion | | | Apple | | |
|---|---|---|---|---|---|---|
| | Current Year | 1 Year Prior | 2 Years Prior | Current Year | 1 Year Prior | 2 Years Prior |
| Operating cash flows . . . . . . . . . | $ 3,035 | $1,452 | $1,577 | $10,159 | $ 9,596 | $ 5,470 |
| Total assets . . . . . . . . . . . . . . . . | 10,204 | 8,101 | 5,511 | 47,501 | 36,171 | 25,347 |

COMPARATIVE
ANALYSIS

A1

*RIM*

Apple

**Required**

1. Compute the recent two years' cash flow on total assets ratios for Research In Motion and Apple.
2. What does the cash flow on total assets ratio measure?
3. Which company has the highest cash flow on total assets ratio for the periods shown?
4. Does the cash flow on total assets ratio reflect on the quality of earnings? Explain.

**BTN 16-3**    Lisa Gish is preparing for a meeting with her banker. Her business is finishing its fourth year of operations. In the first year, it had negative cash flows from operations. In the second and third years, cash flows from operations were positive. However, inventory costs rose significantly in year 4, and cash flows from operations will probably be down 25%. Gish wants to secure a line of credit from her banker as a financing buffer. From experience, she knows the banker will scrutinize operating cash flows for years 1 through 4 and will want a projected number for year 5. Gish knows that a steady progression upward in operating cash flows for years 1 through 4 will help her case. She decides to use her discretion as owner and considers several business actions that will turn her operating cash flow in year 4 from a decrease to an increase.

ETHICS CHALLENGE

C1  A1

**Required**

1. Identify two business actions Gish might take to improve cash flows from operations.
2. Comment on the ethics and possible consequences of Gish's decision to pursue these actions.

**BTN 16-4**    Your friend, Jessica Willard, recently completed the second year of her business and just received annual financial statements from her accountant. Willard finds the income statement and balance sheet informative but does not understand the statement of cash flows. She says the first section is especially confusing because it contains a lot of additions and subtractions that do not make sense to her. Willard adds, "The income statement tells me the business is more profitable than last year and that's most important. If I want to know how cash changes, I can look at comparative balance sheets."

COMMUNICATING
IN PRACTICE

C1

**Required**

Write a half-page memorandum to your friend explaining the purpose of the statement of cash flows. Speculate as to why the first section is so confusing and how it might be rectified.

**BTN 16-5**    Access the March 19, 2010, filing of the 10-K report (for fiscal year ending January 30, 2010) of **J. Crew Group, Inc.** (ticker JCG), at **WWW.SEC.GOV**.

TAKING IT TO
THE NET

A1

**Required**

1. Does J. Crew use the direct or indirect method to construct its consolidated statement of cash flows?
2. For the fiscal year ended January 30, 2010, what is the largest item in reconciling the net income to net cash provided by operating activities?
3. In the recent three years, has the company been more successful in generating operating cash flows or in generating net income? Identify the figures to support the answer.
4. In the year ended January 30, 2010, what was the largest cash outflow for investing activities *and* for financing activities?
5. What item(s) does J. Crew report as supplementary cash flow information?
6. Does J. Crew report any noncash financing activities for fiscal year 2010? Identify them, if any.

**TEAMWORK IN ACTION**

C1  A1  P2  P5

**BTN 16-6**   Team members are to coordinate and independently answer one question within each of the following three sections. Team members should then report to the team and confirm or correct teammates' answers.

1. Answer *one* of the following questions about the statement of cash flows.
   a. What are this statement's reporting objectives?
   b. What two methods are used to prepare it? Identify similarities and differences between them.
   c. What steps are followed to prepare the statement?
   d. What types of analyses are often made from this statement's information?
2. Identify and explain the adjustment from net income to obtain cash flows from operating activities using the indirect method for *one* of the following items.
   a. Noncash operating revenues and expenses.
   b. Nonoperating gains and losses.
   c. Increases and decreases in noncash current assets.
   d. Increases and decreases in current liabilities.
3.ᴮIdentify and explain the formula for computing cash flows from operating activities using the direct method for *one* of the following items.
   a. Cash receipts from sales to customers.
   b. Cash paid for merchandise inventory.
   c. Cash paid for wages and operating expenses.
   d. Cash paid for interest and taxes.

**Note:** For teams of more than four, some pairing within teams is necessary. Use as an in-class activity or as an assignment. If used in class, specify a time limit on each part. Conclude with reports to the entire class, using team rotation. Each team can prepare responses on a transparency.

**ENTREPRENEURIAL DECISION**

C1  A1

**BTN 16-7**   Review the chapter's opener involving **Animoto** and its four young entrepreneurial owners.

*Required*

1. In a business such as Animoto, monitoring cash flow is always a priority. Even though Animoto now has thousands in annual sales and earns a positive net income, explain how cash flow can lag behind earnings.
2. Animoto is a closely held corporation. What are potential sources of financing for its future expansion?

C1  A1

**BTN 16-8**   Jenna and Matt Wilder are completing their second year operating Mountain High, a downhill ski area and resort. Mountain High reports a net loss of $(10,000) for its second year, which includes an $85,000 extraordinary loss from fire. This past year also involved major purchases of plant assets for renovation and expansion, yielding a year-end total asset amount of $800,000. Mountain High's net cash outflow for its second year is $(5,000); a summarized version of its statement of cash flows follows:

| | |
|---|---|
| Net cash flow provided by operating activities ......... | $295,000 |
| Net cash flow used by investing activities ............. | (310,000) |
| Net cash flow provided by financing activities .......... | 10,000 |

*Required*

Write a one-page memorandum to the Wilders evaluating Mountain High's current performance and assessing its future. Give special emphasis to cash flow data and their interpretation.

**HITTING THE ROAD**

C1

**BTN 16-9**   Visit **The Motley Fool**'s Website (**Fool.com**). Enter the *Fool's School* (at *Fool.com/School*). Identify and select the link *How to Value Stocks*.

*Required*

1. Click on *Introduction to Valuation Methods,* and then *Cash-Flow-Based Valuations.* How does the Fool's school define cash flow? What is the school's reasoning for this definition?
2. Per the school's instruction, why do analysts focus on earnings before interest and taxes (EBIT)?
3. Visit other links at this Website that interest you such as "How to Read a Balance Sheet," or find out what the "Fool's Ratio" is. Write a half-page report on what you find.

**BTN 16-10**    Key comparative information for Nokia (www.Nokia.com), which is a leading global manufacturer of mobile devices and services, follows (in EUR).

**GLOBAL DECISION**

C1

NOKIA

*RIM*

Apple

| (Euro millions) | Current Year | I Year Prior | 2 Years Prior |
|---|---|---|---|
| Operating cash flows ........ | 3,247 | 3,197 | 7,882 |
| Total assets ............... | 35,738 | 39,582 | 37,599 |

*Required*

1. Compute the recent two years' cash flow on total assets ratio for Nokia.
2. How does Nokia's ratio compare to Research In Motion's and Apple's ratios from BTN 16-2?

## ANSWERS TO MULTIPLE CHOICE QUIZ

**1.** b;

| | |
|---|---|
| Net income ......................... | $15,200 |
| Depreciation expense ................. | 10,000 |
| Gain on sale of land .................. | (3,000) |
| Increase in inventory ................. | (1,500) |
| Increase in accounts payable ............ | 2,850 |
| Net cash provided by operations ......... | $23,550 |

**2.** c; cash received from sale of machine is reported as an investing activity.

**3.** d; FASB requires cash interest paid to be reported under operating.

**4.** a; Cash paid for salaries and wages = $255,000 + $8,200 − $10,900 = $252,300

**5.** e; Increase in inventory = $112,000 − $105,000 = $7,000
Increase in accounts payable = $101,300 − $98,500 = $2,800
Cash paid for merchandise = $545,000 + $7,000 − $2,800 = $549,200

# 17

# Analysis of Financial Statements

## A Look Back

Chapter 16 focused on reporting and analyzing cash inflows and cash outflows. We explained how to prepare, analyze, and interpret the statement of cash flows.

## A Look at This Chapter

This chapter emphasizes the analysis and interpretation of financial statement information. We learn to apply horizontal, vertical, and ratio analyses to better understand company performance and financial condition.

## Learning Objectives

### CAP

**CONCEPTUAL**

**C1** Explain the purpose and identify the building blocks of analysis. (p. 686)

**C2** Describe standards for comparisons in analysis. (p. 688)

**ANALYTICAL**

**A1** Summarize and report results of analysis. (p. 706)

**A2** *Appendix 17A*—Explain the form and assess the content of a complete income statement. (p. 710)

LP17

**PROCEDURAL**

**P1** Explain and apply methods of horizontal analysis. (p. 688)

**P2** Describe and apply methods of vertical analysis. (p. 693)

**P3** Define and apply ratio analysis. (p. 696)

## Decision Insight

# Motley Fool

*"What goes on at The Motley Fool . . . is similar to what goes on in a library"*

—**TOM GARDNER** (DAVID GARDNER ON LEFT)

ALEXANDRIA, VA—In Shakespeare's Elizabethan comedy *As You Like It,* only the fool could speak truthfully to the King without getting his head lopped off. Inspired by Shakespeare's stage character, Tom and David Gardner vowed to become modern-day fools who tell it like it is. With under $10,000 in start-up money, the brothers launched **The Motley Fool (Fool.com).** And befitting of a Shakespearean play, the two say they are "dedicated to educating, amusing, and enriching individuals in search of the truth."

The Gardners do not fear the wrath of any King, real or fictional. They are intent on exposing the truth, as they see it, "that the financial world preys on ignorance and fear." As Tom explains, "There is such a great need in the general populace for financial information." Who can argue, given their brilliant success through practically every medium, including their Website, radio shows, newspaper columns, online store, investment newsletters, and global expansion.

Despite the brothers' best efforts, however, ordinary people still do not fully use information contained in financial state-

ments. For instance, discussions keep appearing on The Motley Fool's online bulletin board that can be easily resolved using reliable and available accounting data. So, it would seem that the Fools must continue their work of "educating and enriching" individuals and showing them the advantages of financial statement analysis.

Following The Motley Fool's objectives, this chapter introduces horizontal and vertical analyses—tools used to reveal crucial trends and insights from financial information. It also expands on ratio analysis, which gives insight into a company's financial condition and performance. By arming ourselves with the information contained in this chapter and the investment advice of The Motley Fool, *we* can be sure to not play the fool in today's financial world.

[Sources: *Motley Fool Website,* January 2011; *Entrepreneur,* July 1997; *What to Do with Your Money Now,* June 2002; *USA Weekend,* July 2004; *Washington Post,* November 2007; *Money after 40,* April 2007]

This chapter shows how we use financial statements to evaluate a company's financial performance and condition. We explain financial statement analysis, its basic building blocks, the information available, standards for comparisons, and tools of analysis. Three major analysis tools are presented: horizontal analysis, vertical analysis, and ratio analysis. We apply each of these tools using **Research In Motion**'s financial statements, and we introduce comparative analysis using **Apple** and **Nokia** (and sometimes **Palm**). This chapter expands and organizes the ratio analyses introduced at the end of each chapter.

### Analysis of Financial Statements

| Basics of Analysis | Horizontal Analysis | Vertical Analysis | Ratio Analysis |
|---|---|---|---|
| • Purpose<br>• Building blocks<br>• Information<br>• Standards for comparisons<br>• Tools | • Comparative balance sheets<br>• Comparative income statements<br>• Trend analysis | • Common-size balance sheet<br>• Common-size income statement<br>• Common-size graphics | • Liquidity and efficiency<br>• Solvency<br>• Profitability<br>• Market prospects<br>• Ratio summary |

# BASICS OF ANALYSIS

**C1** Explain the purpose and identify the building blocks of analysis.

**Financial statement analysis** applies analytical tools to general-purpose financial statements and related data for making business decisions. It involves transforming accounting data into more useful information. Financial statement analysis reduces our reliance on hunches, guesses, and intuition as well as our uncertainty in decision making. It does not lessen the need for expert judgment; instead, it provides us an effective and systematic basis for making business decisions. This section describes the purpose of financial statement analysis, its information sources, the use of comparisons, and some issues in computations.

## Purpose of Analysis

Internal users of accounting information are those involved in strategically managing and operating the company. They include managers, officers, internal auditors, consultants, budget directors, and market researchers. The purpose of financial statement analysis for these users is to provide strategic information to improve company efficiency and effectiveness in providing products and services.

**Point:** Financial statement analysis tools are also used for personal financial investment decisions.

External users of accounting information are *not* directly involved in running the company. They include shareholders, lenders, directors, customers, suppliers, regulators, lawyers, brokers, and the press. External users rely on financial statement analysis to make better and more informed decisions in pursuing their own goals.

We can identify other uses of financial statement analysis. Shareholders and creditors assess company prospects to make investing and lending decisions. A board of directors analyzes financial statements in monitoring management's decisions. Employees and unions use financial statements in labor negotiations. Suppliers use financial statement information in establishing credit terms. Customers analyze financial statements in deciding whether to establish supply relationships. Public utilities set customer rates by analyzing financial statements. Auditors use financial statements in assessing the "fair presentation" of their clients' financial results. Analyst services such as **Dun & Bradstreet**, **Moody's**, and **Standard & Poor's** use financial statements in making buy-sell recommendations and in setting credit ratings. The common goal of these users is to evaluate company performance and financial condition. This includes evaluating (1) past and current performance, (2) current financial position, and (3) future performance and risk.

**Point:** Financial statement analysis is a topic on the CPA, CMA, CIA, and CFA exams.

# Building Blocks of Analysis

Financial statement analysis focuses on one or more elements of a company's financial condition or performance. Our analysis emphasizes four areas of inquiry—with varying degrees of importance. These four areas are described and illustrated in this chapter and are considered the *building blocks* of financial statement analysis:

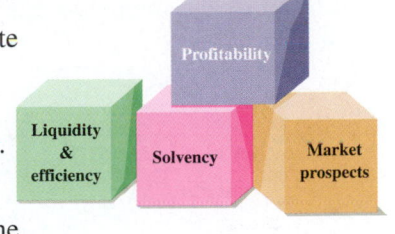

- **Liquidity** and **efficiency**—ability to meet short-term obligations and to efficiently generate revenues.
- **Solvency**—ability to generate future revenues and meet long-term obligations.
- **Profitability**—ability to provide financial rewards sufficient to attract and retain financing.
- **Market prospects**—ability to generate positive market expectations.

Applying the building blocks of financial statement analysis involves determining (1) the objectives of analysis and (2) the relative emphasis among the building blocks. We distinguish among these four building blocks to emphasize the different aspects of a company's financial condition or performance, yet we must remember that these areas of analysis are interrelated. For instance, a company's operating performance is affected by the availability of financing and short-term liquidity conditions. Similarly, a company's credit standing is not limited to satisfactory short-term liquidity but depends also on its profitability and efficiency in using assets. Early in our analysis, we need to determine the relative emphasis of each building block. Emphasis and analysis can later change as a result of evidence collected.

---

## ♟ Decision **Insight**

**Chips and Brokers**   The phrase *blue chips* refers to stock of big, profitable companies. The phrase comes from poker; where the most valuable chips are blue. The term *brokers* refers to those who execute orders to buy or sell stock. The term comes from wine retailers—individuals who broach (break) wine casks. ■

---

# Information for Analysis

Some users, such as managers and regulatory authorities, are able to receive special financial reports prepared to meet their analysis needs. However, most users must rely on **general-purpose financial statements** that include the (1) income statement, (2) balance sheet, (3) statement of stockholders' equity (or statement of retained earnings), (4) statement of cash flows, and (5) notes to these statements.

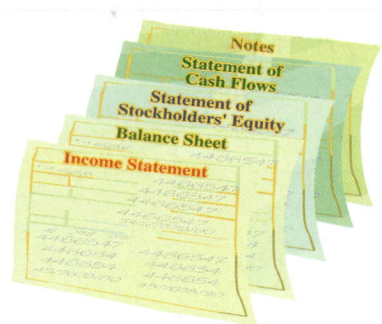

   **Financial reporting** refers to the communication of financial information useful for making investment, credit, and other business decisions. Financial reporting includes not only general-purpose financial statements but also information from SEC 10-K or other filings, press releases, shareholders' meetings, forecasts, management letters, auditors' reports, and Webcasts.

   Management's Discussion and Analysis (MD&A) is one example of useful information outside traditional financial statements. **Research In Motion**'s MD&A (available at <u>RIM.com</u>), for example, begins with an overview, followed by critical accounting policies and restatements of previous statements. It then discusses operating results followed by financial condition (liquidity, capital resources, and cash flows). The final few parts discuss legal proceedings, market risk of financial instruments, disclosure controls, and internal controls. The MD&A is an excellent starting point in understanding a company's business activities.

---

## ♟ Decision **Insight**

**Analysis Online**   Many Websites offer free access and screening of companies by key numbers such as earnings, sales, and book value. For instance, **Standard & Poor's** has information for more than 10,000 stocks (<u>www.standardandpoors.com</u>). ■

## Standards for Comparisons

 **C2** Describe standards for comparisons in analysis.

When interpreting measures from financial statement analysis, we need to decide whether the measures indicate good, bad, or average performance. To make such judgments, we need standards (benchmarks) for comparisons that include the following:

- *Intracompany*—The company under analysis can provide standards for comparisons based on its own prior performance and relations between its financial items. **Research In Motion**'s current net income, for instance, can be compared with its prior years' net income and in relation to its revenues or total assets.
- *Competitor*—One or more direct competitors of the company being analyzed can provide standards for comparisons. **Coca-Cola**'s profit margin, for instance, can be compared with **PepsiCo**'s profit margin.
- *Industry*—Industry statistics can provide standards of comparisons. Such statistics are available from services such as **Dun & Bradstreet**, **Standard & Poor's**, and **Moody's**.
- *Guidelines (rules of thumb)*—General standards of comparisons can develop from experience. Examples are the 2:1 level for the current ratio or 1:1 level for the acid-test ratio. Guidelines, or rules of thumb, must be carefully applied because context is crucial.

**Point:** Each chapter's *Reporting in Action* problems engage students in *intracompany* analysis, whereas *Comparative Analysis* problems require competitor analysis (RIM vs. Apple and often vs. Palm).

All of these comparison standards are useful when properly applied, yet measures taken from a selected competitor or group of competitors are often best. Intracompany and industry measures are also important. Guidelines or rules of thumb should be applied with care, and then only if they seem reasonable given past experience and industry norms.

## Tools of Analysis

Three of the most common tools of financial statement analysis are

1. **Horizontal analysis**—Comparison of a company's financial condition and performance across time.
2. **Vertical analysis**—Comparison of a company's financial condition and performance to a base amount.
3. **Ratio analysis**—Measurement of key relations between financial statement items.

The remainder of this chapter describes these analysis tools and how to apply them.

### Quick Check                                                    Answers — p. 713

1. Who are the intended users of general-purpose financial statements?
2. General-purpose financial statements consist of what information?
3. Which of the following is *least* useful as a basis for comparison when analyzing ratios? (a) Company results from a different economic setting. (b) Standards from past experience. (c) Rule-of-thumb standards. (d) Industry averages.
4. What is the preferred basis of comparison for ratio analysis?

# HORIZONTAL ANALYSIS

Analysis of any single financial number is of limited value. Instead, much of financial statement analysis involves identifying and describing relations between numbers, groups of numbers, and changes in those numbers. Horizontal analysis refers to examination of financial statement data *across time*. [The term *horizontal analysis* arises from the left-to-right (or right-to-left) movement of our eyes as we review comparative financial statements across time.]

## Comparative Statements

**P1** Explain and apply methods of horizontal analysis.

Comparing amounts for two or more successive periods often helps in analyzing financial statements. **Comparative financial statements** facilitate this comparison by showing financial amounts in side-by-side columns on a single statement, called a *comparative format*. Using figures from **Research In Motion**'s financial statements, this section explains how to compute dollar changes and percent changes for comparative statements.

**Computation of Dollar Changes and Percent Changes**  Comparing financial statements over relatively short time periods—two to three years—is often done by analyzing changes in line items. A change analysis usually includes analyzing absolute dollar amount changes and percent changes. Both analyses are relevant because dollar changes can yield large percent changes inconsistent with their importance. For instance, a 50% change from a base figure of $100 is less important than the same percent change from a base amount of $100,000 in the same statement. Reference to dollar amounts is necessary to retain a proper perspective and to assess the importance of changes. We compute the *dollar change* for a financial statement item as follows:

**Example:** What is a more significant change, a 70% increase on a $1,000 expense or a 30% increase on a $400,000 expense? *Answer:* The 30% increase.

$$\text{Dollar change} = \text{Analysis period amount} - \text{Base period amount}$$

*Analysis period* is the point or period of time for the financial statements under analysis, and *base period* is the point or period of time for the financial statements used for comparison purposes. The prior year is commonly used as a base period. We compute the *percent change* by dividing the dollar change by the base period amount and then multiplying this quantity by 100 as follows:

$$\text{Percent change (\%)} = \frac{\text{Analysis period amount} - \text{Base period amount}}{\text{Base period amount}} \times 100$$

We can always compute a dollar change, but we must be aware of a few rules in working with percent changes. To illustrate, look at four separate cases in this chart:

| Case | Analysis Period | Base Period | Change Analysis Dollar | Change Analysis Percent |
|---|---|---|---|---|
| A | $ 1,500 | $(4,500) | $ 6,000 | — |
| B | (1,000) | 2,000 | (3,000) | — |
| C | 8,000 | — | 8,000 | — |
| D | 0 | 10,000 | (10,000) | (100%) |

When a negative amount appears in the base period and a positive amount in the analysis period (or vice versa), we cannot compute a meaningful percent change; see cases A and B. Also, when no value is in the base period, no percent change is computable; see case C. Finally, when an item has a value in the base period and zero in the analysis period, the decrease is 100 percent; see case D.

**Example:** When there is a value in the base period and zero in the analysis period, the decrease is 100%. Why isn't the reverse situation an increase of 100%? *Answer:* A 100% increase of zero is still zero.

It is common when using horizontal analysis to compare amounts to either average or median values from prior periods (average and median values smooth out erratic or unusual fluctuations).[1] We also commonly round percents and ratios to one or two decimal places, but practice on this matter is not uniform. Computations are as detailed as necessary, which is judged by whether rounding potentially affects users' decisions. Computations should not be excessively detailed so that important relations are lost among a mountain of decimal points and digits.

**Comparative Balance Sheets**  Comparative balance sheets consist of balance sheet amounts from two or more balance sheet dates arranged side by side. Its usefulness is often improved by showing each item's dollar change and percent change to highlight large changes.

Analysis of comparative financial statements begins by focusing on items that show large dollar or percent changes. We then try to identify the reasons for these changes and, if possible, determine whether they are favorable or unfavorable. We also follow up on items with small changes when we expected the changes to be large.

**Point:** Spreadsheet programs can help with horizontal, vertical, and ratio analyses, including graphical depictions of financial relations.

[1] *Median* is the middle value in a group of numbers. For instance, if five prior years' incomes are (in 000s) $15, $19, $18, $20, and $22, the median value is $19. When there are two middle numbers, we can take their average. For instance, if four prior years' sales are (in 000s) $84, $91, $96, and $93, the median is $92 (computed as the average of $91 and $93).

**EXHIBIT 17.1**

Comparative Balance Sheets

**RIM**

| RESEARCH IN MOTION<br>Comparative Balance Sheets<br>February 27, 2010 and February 28, 2009 | | | | |
|---|---|---|---|---|
| ($ thousands) | 2010 | 2009 | Dollar<br>Change | Percent<br>Change |
| **Assets** | | | | |
| Cash and cash equivalents ..................... | $ 1,550,861 | $ 835,546 | $ 715,315 | 85.6% |
| Short-term investments ...................... | 360,614 | 682,666 | (322,052) | (47.2) |
| Accounts receivable, net ..................... | 2,593,742 | 2,112,117 | 481,625 | 22.8 |
| Other receivables .......................... | 206,373 | 157,728 | 48,645 | 30.8 |
| Inventories .............................. | 621,611 | 682,400 | (60,789) | (8.9) |
| Other current assets ........................ | 285,539 | 187,257 | 98,282 | 52.5 |
| Deferred income tax asset .................... | 193,916 | 183,872 | 10,044 | 5.5 |
| Total current assets ...................... | 5,812,656 | 4,841,586 | 971,070 | 20.1 |
| Long-term investments ...................... | 958,248 | 720,635 | 237,613 | 33.0 |
| Property, plant and equipment, net .............. | 1,956,581 | 1,334,648 | 621,933 | 46.6 |
| Intangible assets, net ....................... | 1,326,363 | 1,066,527 | 259,836 | 24.4 |
| Goodwill ............................... | 150,561 | 137,572 | 12,989 | 9.4 |
| Deferred income tax asset .................... | 0 | 404 | (404) | (100.0) |
| Total assets ............................. | $10,204,409 | $8,101,372 | $2,103,037 | 26.0 |
| **Liabilities** | | | | |
| Accounts payable .......................... | $ 615,620 | $ 448,339 | $ 167,281 | 37.3% |
| Accrued liabilities .......................... | 1,638,260 | 1,238,602 | 399,658 | 32.3 |
| Income taxes payable ....................... | 95,650 | 361,460 | (265,810) | (73.5) |
| Deferred revenue .......................... | 67,573 | 53,834 | 13,739 | 25.5 |
| Deferred income tax liability .................. | 14,674 | 13,116 | 1,558 | 11.9 |
| Total current liabilities ..................... | 2,431,777 | 2,115,351 | 316,426 | 15.0 |
| Deferred income tax liability .................. | 141,382 | 87,917 | 53,465 | 60.8 |
| Income taxes payable ....................... | 28,587 | 23,976 | 4,611 | 19.2 |
| Total liabilities ........................... | 2,601,746 | 2,227,244 | 374,502 | 16.8 |
| **Shareholders' Equity** | | | | |
| Capital stock ............................. | 2,207,609 | 2,208,235 | (626) | 0.0 |
| Treasury stock ............................ | (94,463) | 0 | (94,463) | — |
| Retained earnings .......................... | 5,274,365 | 3,545,710 | 1,728,655 | 48.8 |
| Additional paid-in capital ..................... | 164,060 | 119,726 | 44,334 | 37.0 |
| Accumulated other comprehensive income ........ | 51,092 | 457 | 50,635 | 11,079 |
| Total stockholders' equity ................... | 7,602,663 | 5,874,128 | 1,728,535 | 29.4 |
| Total liabilities and stockholders' equity ........... | $10,204,409 | $8,101,372 | $2,103,037 | 26.0 |

**Point:** Business consultants use comparative statement analysis to provide management advice.

Exhibit 17.1 shows comparative balance sheets for **Research In Motion** (RIM). A few items stand out. Many asset categories substantially increase, which is probably not surprising because RIM is a growth company. Much of the increase in current assets is from the 85.6% increase in cash and equivalents and the 22.8% increase in accounts receivable; although the 47.2% decline in short-term investments dampened this growth. The long-term assets of property, plant and equipment, intangible assets, and long-term investments also markedly increased. Of course, its sizeable total asset growth of 26.0% must be accompanied by future income to validate RIM's growth strategy.

We likewise see substantial increases on the financing side, the most notable ones (in amount) being accounts payable and accrued liabilities totaling $566,939 thousand. The increase in these items is probably related to the recessionary period covering this report. RIM also reinvested much of its income as reflected in the $1,728,655 thousand increase in retained earnings. Again, we must monitor these increases in investing and financing activities to be sure they are reflected in increased operating performance.

**Comparative Income Statements** Comparative income statements are prepared similarly to comparative balance sheets. Amounts for two or more periods are placed side by side, with additional columns for dollar and percent changes. Exhibit 17.2 shows Research In Motion's comparative income statements.

| RESEARCH IN MOTION<br>Comparative Income Statements<br>For Years Ended February 27, 2010 and February 28, 2009 | | | | |
|---|---|---|---|---|
| ($ thousands, except per share data) | 2010 | 2009 | Dollar Change | Percent Change |
| Revenue | $14,953,224 | $11,065,186 | $3,888,038 | 35.1% |
| Cost of sales | 8,368,958 | 5,967,888 | 2,401,070 | 40.2 |
| Gross profit | 6,584,266 | 5,097,298 | 1,486,968 | 29.2 |
| Research and development | 964,841 | 684,702 | 280,139 | 40.9 |
| Selling, marketing, and administration | 1,907,398 | 1,495,697 | 411,701 | 27.5 |
| Amortization | 310,357 | 194,803 | 115,554 | 59.3 |
| Litigation | 163,800 | — | 163,800 | — |
| Income from operations | 3,237,870 | 2,722,096 | 515,774 | 18.9 |
| Investment income | 28,640 | 78,267 | (49,627) | (63.4) |
| Income before income taxes | 3,266,510 | 2,800,363 | 466,147 | 16.6 |
| Provision for income taxes | 809,366 | 907,747 | (98,381) | (10.8) |
| Net income | $ 2,457,144 | $ 1,892,616 | 564,528 | 29.8 |
| Basic earnings per share | $ 4.35 | $ 3.35 | $ 1.00 | 29.9 |
| Diluted earnings per share | $ 4.31 | $ 3.30 | $ 1.01 | 30.6 |

**EXHIBIT 17.2**

Comparative Income Statements

**RIM**

RIM has substantial revenue growth of 35.1% in 2010. This finding helps support management's growth strategy as reflected in the comparative balance sheets. RIM evidences some ability to control costs of selling, marketing, and administration, which increased 27.5% (versus the 35.1% revenue increase). However, cost of sales increased 40.2% and other expenses also increased at a rate more than that for sales. RIM's net income growth of 29.8% on revenue growth of 35.1% is still good.

**Point:** Percent change can also be computed by dividing the current period by the prior period and subtracting 1.0. For example, the 35.1% revenue increase of Exhibit 17.2 is computed as: ($14,953,224/$11,065,186) − 1.

## Trend Analysis

*Trend analysis,* also called *trend percent analysis* or *index number trend analysis,* is a form of horizontal analysis that can reveal patterns in data across successive periods. It involves computing trend percents for a series of financial numbers and is a variation on the use of percent changes. The difference is that trend analysis does not subtract the base period amount in the numerator. To compute trend percents, we do the following:

1. Select a *base period* and assign each item in the base period a weight of 100%.
2. Express financial numbers as a percent of their base period number.

Specifically, a *trend percent,* also called an *index number,* is computed as follows:

$$\text{Trend percent (\%)} = \frac{\text{Analysis period amount}}{\text{Base period amount}} \times 100$$

To illustrate trend analysis, we use the **Research In Motion** data shown in Exhibit 17.3.

**Point:** *Index* refers to the comparison of the analysis period to the base period. Percents determined for each period are called *index numbers.*

| (in thousands) | 2010 | 2009 | 2008 | 2007 | 2006 |
|---|---|---|---|---|---|
| Revenue | $14,953,224 | $11,065,186 | $6,009,395 | $3,037,103 | $2,065,845 |
| Cost of sales | 8,368,958 | 5,967,888 | 2,928,814 | 1,379,301 | 925,598 |
| Operating expenses | 3,346,396 | 2,375,202 | 1,349,422 | 850,974 | 523,155 |

**EXHIBIT 17.3**

Revenue and Expenses

These data are from RIM's current and prior financial statements. The base period is 2006 and the trend percent is computed in each subsequent year by dividing that year's amount by its 2006 amount. For instance, the revenue trend percent for 2010 is 723.8%, computed as $14,953,224/$2,065,845. The trend percents—using the data from Exhibit 17.3—are shown in Exhibit 17.4.

**EXHIBIT 17.4**

Trend Percents for Revenue and Expenses

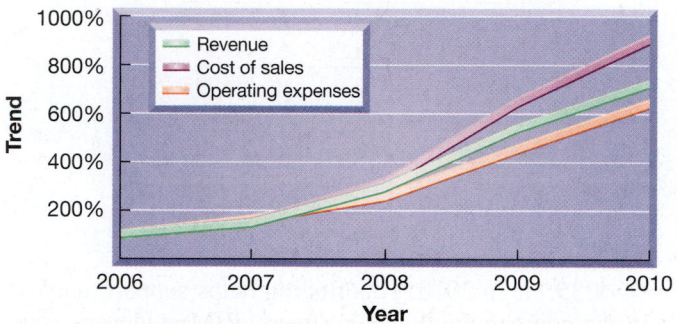

|  | 2010 | 2009 | 2008 | 2007 | 2006 |
|---|---|---|---|---|---|
| Revenue ................. | 723.8% | 535.6% | 290.9% | 147.0% | 100.0% |
| Cost of sales .............. | 904.2 | 644.8 | 316.4 | 149.0 | 100.0 |
| Operating expenses ........ | 639.7 | 454.0 | 257.9 | 162.7 | 100.0 |

**Point:** Trend analysis expresses a percent of base, not a percent of change.

Graphical depictions often aid analysis of trend percents. Exhibit 17.5 shows the trend percents from Exhibit 17.4 in a *line graph,* which can help us identify trends and detect changes in direction or magnitude. It reveals that the trend line for revenue consistently falls short of that for cost of sales. Moreover, the magnitude of that difference has slightly grown. This result does not bode well for RIM because its cost of sales are by far its largest cost, and the company fails to show an ability to control these expenses as it expands. The line graph also reveals a consistent increase in each of these accounts, which is typical of growth companies. The trend line for operating expenses is more encouraging because it falls short of the revenue trend line in 2008, 2009 and 2010. Still, the bad news is that much of the shift in cost of sales occurred in the most recent two years. Management must try to better control those costs in future years.

**EXHIBIT 17.5**

Trend Percent Lines for Revenue and Expenses of Research In Motion

Exhibit 17.6 compares **RIM**'s revenue trend line to that of **Apple** and **Palm** for this same period. RIM's revenues sharply increased over this time period while those of Apple exhibited less growth, and those for Palm were declining. These data indicate that RIM's products and services have met with considerable consumer acceptance.

Trend analysis of financial statement items can include comparisons of relations between items on different financial statements. For instance, Exhibit 17.7 compares RIM's revenue and total assets. The rate of increase in total assets (440.9%) is less than the increase in revenues (723.8%) since 2006. Is this result favorable or not? The answer is that RIM was *more* efficient in using its assets in 2010. Management has generated revenues sufficient to compensate for this asset growth.

**EXHIBIT 17.6**

Trend Percent Lines—Research In Motion, Apple and Palm

**RIM**

Apple

**Palm**

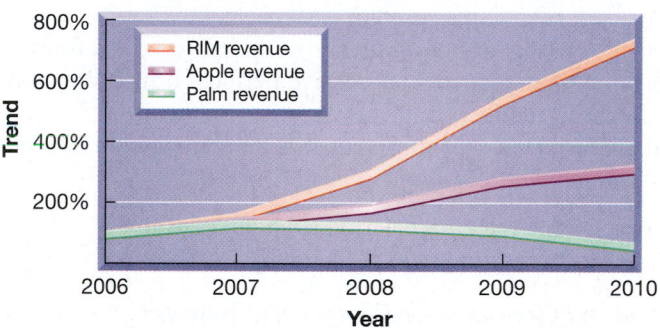

**EXHIBIT 17.7**

Revenue and Asset Data for Research In Motion

| ($ thousands) | 2010 | 2006 | Trend Percent (2010 vs. 2006) |
|---|---|---|---|
| Revenue .......... | $14,953,224 | $2,065,845 | **723.8%** |
| Total assets ........ | 10,204,409 | 2,314,349 | **440.9** |

Overall we must remember that an important role of financial statement analysis is identifying questions and areas of interest, which often direct us to important factors bearing on a company's future. Accordingly, financial statement analysis should be seen as a continuous process of refining our understanding and expectations of company performance and financial condition.

 **Decision Maker**                                     Answer — p. 712

**Auditor** Your tests reveal a 3% increase in sales from $200,000 to $206,000 and a 4% decrease in expenses from $190,000 to $182,400. Both changes are within your "reasonableness" criterion of ±5%, and thus you don't pursue additional tests. The audit partner in charge questions your lack of follow-up and mentions the *joint relation* between sales and expenses. To what is the partner referring? ■

# VERTICAL ANALYSIS

Vertical analysis is a tool to evaluate individual financial statement items or a group of items in terms of a specific base amount. We usually define a key aggregate figure as the base, which for an income statement is usually revenue and for a balance sheet is usually total assets. This section explains vertical analysis and applies it to **Research In Motion**. [The term *vertical analysis* arises from the up-down (or down-up) movement of our eyes as we review common-size financial statements. Vertical analysis is also called *common-size analysis*.]

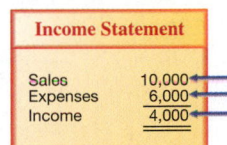

## Common-Size Statements

The comparative statements in Exhibits 17.1 and 17.2 show the change in each item over time, but they do not emphasize the relative importance of each item. We use **common-size financial statements** to reveal changes in the relative importance of each financial statement item. All individual amounts in common-size statements are redefined in terms of common-size percents. A *common-size percent* is measured by dividing each individual financial statement amount under analysis by its base amount:

**P2** Describe and apply methods of vertical analysis.

$$\text{Common-size percent (\%)} = \frac{\text{Analysis amount}}{\text{Base amount}} \times 100$$

**Common-Size Balance Sheets** Common-size statements express each item as a percent of a *base amount,* which for a common-size balance sheet is usually total assets. The base amount is assigned a value of 100%. (This implies that the total amount of liabilities plus equity equals 100% since this amount equals total assets.) We then compute a common-size percent for each asset, liability, and equity item using total assets as the base amount. When we present a company's successive balance sheets in this way, changes in the mixture of assets, liabilities, and equity are apparent.

Exhibit 17.8 shows common-size comparative balance sheets for RIM. Some relations that stand out on both a magnitude and percentage basis include (1) a 4.9% point increase in cash and equivalents, which is likely balanced with a 4.9% point decline in short-term investments, (2) a 2.3% point decline in inventories, (3) a 2.7% point increase in net property, plant and equipment, (4) a 3.6% point decline in taxes payable, and (5) a marked increase in retained earnings. Many of these changes are characteristic of a growth/stable company. The concern, if any, is whether RIM can continue to generate sufficient revenue and income to support its asset buildup within a very competitive industry.

**Point:** The *base* amount in common-size analysis is an *aggregate* amount from that period's financial statement.

**Point:** Common-size statements often are used to compare two or more companies in the same industry.

**Point:** Common-size statements are also useful in comparing firms that report in different currencies.

**Common-Size Income Statements** Analysis also benefits from use of a common-size income statement. Revenue is usually the base amount, which is assigned a value of 100%. Each common-size income statement item appears as a percent of revenue. If we think of the 100%

**EXHIBIT 17.8**

Common-Size Comparative
Balance Sheets

**RIM**

| | | | Common-Size Percents* | |
|---|---|---|---|---|
| (in thousands) | 2010 | 2009 | 2010 | 2009 |
| **Assets** | | | | |
| Cash and cash equivalents | $ 1,550,861 | $ 835,546 | 15.2% | 10.3% |
| Short-term investments | 360,614 | 682,666 | 3.5 | 8.4 |
| Accounts receivable, net | 2,593,742 | 2,112,117 | 25.4 | 26.1 |
| Other receivables | 206,373 | 157,728 | 2.0 | 1.9 |
| Inventories | 621,611 | 682,400 | 6.1 | 8.4 |
| Other current assets | 285,539 | 187,257 | 2.8 | 2.3 |
| Deferred income tax asset | 193,916 | 183,872 | 1.9 | 2.3 |
| Total current assets | 5,812,656 | 4,841,586 | 57.0 | 59.8 |
| Long-term investments | 958,248 | 720,635 | 9.4 | 8.9 |
| Property, plant and equipment, net | 1,956,581 | 1,334,648 | 19.2 | 16.5 |
| Intangible assets, net | 1,326,363 | 1,066,527 | 13.0 | 13.2 |
| Goodwill | 150,561 | 137,572 | 1.5 | 1.7 |
| Deferred income tax asset | 0 | 404 | 0.0 | 0.0 |
| Total assets | $10,204,409 | $8,101,372 | 100.0% | 100.0% |
| **Liabilities** | | | | |
| Accounts payable | $   615,620 | $  448,339 | 6.0% | 5.5% |
| Accrued liabilities | 1,638,260 | 1,238,602 | 16.1 | 15.3 |
| Income taxes payable | 95,650 | 361,460 | 0.9 | 4.5 |
| Deferred revenue | 67,573 | 53,834 | 0.7 | 0.7 |
| Deferred income tax liability | 14,674 | 13,116 | 0.1 | 0.2 |
| Total current liabilities | 2,431,777 | 2,115,351 | 23.8 | 26.1 |
| Deferred income tax liability | 141,382 | 87,917 | 1.4 | 1.1 |
| Income taxes payable | 28,587 | 23,976 | 0.3 | 0.3 |
| Total liabilities | 2,601,746 | 2,227,244 | 25.5 | 27.5 |
| **Shareholders' Equity** | | | | |
| Capital stock | 2,207,609 | 2,208,235 | 21.6 | 27.3 |
| Treasury stock | (94,463) | 0 | (0.9) | 0.0 |
| Retained earnings | 5,274,365 | 3,545,710 | 51.7 | 43.8 |
| Additional paid-in capital | 164,060 | 119,726 | 1.6 | 1.5 |
| Accumulated other comprehensive income | 51,092 | 457 | 0.5 | 0.0 |
| Total stockholders' equity | 7,602,663 | 5,874,128 | 74.5 | 72.5 |
| Total liabilities and stockholders' equity | $10,204,409 | $8,101,372 | 100.0% | 100.0% |

**RESEARCH IN MOTION**
**Common-Size Comparative Balance Sheets**
**February 27, 2010 and February 28, 2009**

\* Percents are rounded to tenths and thus may not exactly sum to totals and subtotals.

revenue amount as representing one sales dollar, the remaining items show how each revenue dollar is distributed among costs, expenses, and income.

Exhibit 17.9 shows common-size comparative income statements for each dollar of RIM's revenue. The past two years' common-size numbers are similar with a few exceptions. The bad news is that RIM has given up 0.7 cent in earnings per revenue dollar—evidenced by the 17.1% to 16.4% decline in earnings as a percentage of revenue. This implies that management is not effectively controlling costs. Much of this is attributed to the rise in cost of sales from 53.9% to 56.0% as a percentage of revenue. This is a concern given the price-competitive smartphone market. Some good news is apparent with the decline in selling, marketing, and administration expenses as a percentage of revenue. Analysis here shows that common-size percents for successive income statements can uncover potentially important changes in a company's expenses. Evidence of no changes, especially when changes are expected, is also informative.

**Global:** International companies sometimes disclose "convenience" financial statements, which are statements translated in other languages and currencies. However, these statements rarely adjust for differences in accounting principles across countries.

| **RESEARCH IN MOTION** <br> Common-Size Comparative Income Statements <br> For Years Ended February 27, 2010 and February 28, 2009 | | | Common-Size Percents* | |
|---|---|---|---|---|
| ($ thousands) | 2010 | 2009 | 2010 | 2009 |
| Revenue | $14,953,224 | $11,065,186 | 100.0% | 100.0% |
| Cost of sales | 8,368,958 | 5,967,888 | 56.0 | 53.9 |
| Gross margin | 6,584,266 | 5,097,298 | 44.0 | 46.1 |
| Research and development | 964,841 | 684,702 | 6.5 | 6.2 |
| Selling, marketing, and administration | 1,907,398 | 1,495,697 | 12.8 | 13.5 |
| Amortization | 310,357 | 194,803 | 2.1 | 1.8 |
| Litigation | 163,800 | — | 1.1 | 0.0 |
| Income from operations | 3,237,870 | 2,722,096 | 21.7 | 24.6 |
| Investment income | 28,640 | 78,267 | 0.2 | 0.7 |
| Income before income taxes | 3,266,510 | 2,800,363 | 21.8 | 25.3 |
| Provision for income taxes | 809,366 | 907,747 | 5.4 | 8.2 |
| Net income | $ 2,457,144 | $ 1,892,616 | 16.4% | 17.1% |

**EXHIBIT 17.9**

Common-Size Comparative Income Statements

*RIM*

\* Percents are rounded to tenths and thus may not exactly sum to totals and subtotals.

## Common-Size Graphics

Two of the most common tools of common-size analysis are trend analysis of common-size statements and graphical analysis. The trend analysis of common-size statements is similar to that of comparative statements discussed under vertical analysis. It is not illustrated here because the only difference is the substitution of common-size percents for trend percents. Instead, this section discusses graphical analysis of common-size statements.

An income statement readily lends itself to common-size graphical analysis. This is so because revenues affect nearly every item in an income statement. Exhibit 17.10 shows **RIM**'s 2010 common-size income statement in graphical form. This pie chart highlights the contribution of each cost component of revenue for net income, excluding investment income.

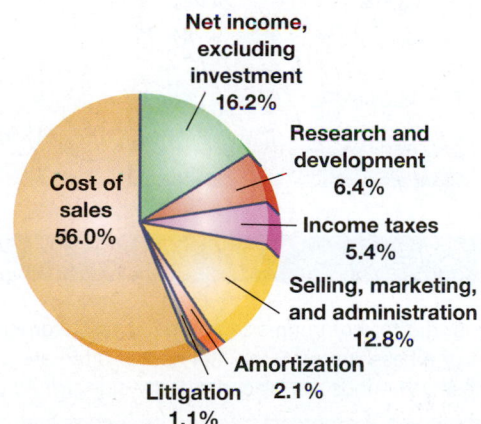

**EXHIBIT 17.10**

Common-Size Graphic of Income Statement

Exhibit 17.11 previews more complex graphical analyses available and the insights they provide. The data for this exhibit are taken from **RIM**'s *Segments* footnote. RIM has at least two reportable segments: (1) United States, and (2) outside the United States (titled Non-U.S.).

**EXHIBIT 17.11**

Revenue and Total Asset Breakdown by Segment

**EXHIBIT 17.12**

Common-Size Graphic of
Asset Components

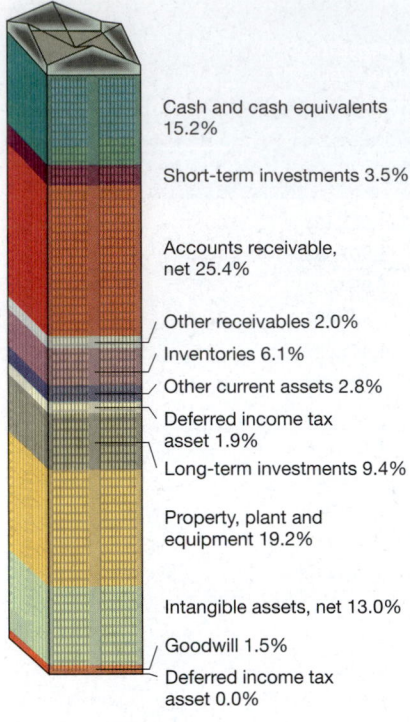

Cash and cash equivalents
15.2%

Short-term investments 3.5%

Accounts receivable,
net 25.4%

Other receivables 2.0%

Inventories 6.1%

Other current assets 2.8%

Deferred income tax
asset 1.9%

Long-term investments 9.4%

Property, plant and
equipment 19.2%

Intangible assets, net 13.0%

Goodwill 1.5%

Deferred income tax
asset 0.0%

The upper set of bars in Exhibit 17.11 shows the percent of revenues from, and the assets invested in, its U.S. segment. Its U.S. segment generates 57.7% of its revenue, while only 39.8% of its assets are in the United States. The lower set of bars shows that 42.3% of its revenue is generated outside the United States, while 60.2% of its assets are outside the United States. This can lead to questions about the revenue generated per assets invested across different countries. This type of information can help users in determining strategic analyses and actions.

Graphical analysis is also useful in identifying (1) sources of financing including the distribution among current liabilities, noncurrent liabilities, and equity capital and (2) focuses of investing activities, including the distribution among current and noncurrent assets. To illustrate, Exhibit 17.12 shows a common-size graphical display of RIM's assets. Common-size balance sheet analysis can be extended to examine the composition of these subgroups. For instance, in assessing liquidity of current assets, knowing what proportion of *current* assets consists of inventories is usually important, and not simply what proportion inventories are of *total* assets.

Common-size financial statements are also useful in comparing different companies. Exhibit 17.13 shows common-size graphics of **RIM**, **Apple** and **Nokia** on financing sources. This graphic highlights the larger percent of equity financing for RIM and Apple than for Nokia. It also highlights the much larger noncurrent (debt) financing of Nokia and Apple versus RIM. Comparison of a company's common-size statements with competitors' or industry common-size statistics alerts us to differences in the structure or distribution of its financial statements but not to their dollar magnitude.

**EXHIBIT 17.13**

Common-Size Graphic of Financing
Sources—Competitor Analysis

*RIM*

Apple

NOKIA

**Quick Check**          Answers — p. 713

5. Which of the following is true for common-size comparative statements? (*a*) Each item is expressed as a percent of a base amount. (*b*) Total assets often are assigned a value of 100%. (*c*) Amounts from successive periods are placed side by side. (*d*) All are true. (*e*) None is true.

6. What is the difference between the percents shown on a comparative income statement and those shown on a common-size comparative income statement?

7. Trend percents are (*a*) shown on comparative income statements and balance sheets, (*b*) shown on common-size comparative statements, or (*c*) also called *index numbers*.

## RATIO ANALYSIS

 **P3** Define and apply ratio analysis.

Ratios are among the more widely used tools of financial analysis because they provide clues to and symptoms of underlying conditions. A ratio can help us uncover conditions and trends difficult to detect by inspecting individual components making up the ratio. Ratios, like other analysis tools, are usually future oriented; that is, they are often adjusted for their probable future trend and magnitude, and their usefulness depends on skillful interpretation.

A ratio expresses a mathematical relation between two quantities. It can be expressed as a percent, rate, or proportion. For instance, a change in an account balance from $100 to $250 can be expressed as (1) 150% increase, (2) 2.5 times, or (3) 2.5 to 1 (or 2.5:1). Computation of a ratio is a simple arithmetic operation, but its interpretation is not. To be meaningful, a ratio must refer to an economically important relation. For example, a direct and crucial relation exists between an item's sales price and its cost. Accordingly, the ratio of cost of goods sold to sales is meaningful. In contrast, no obvious relation exists between freight costs and the balance of long-term investments.

This section describes an important set of financial ratios and its application. The selected ratios are organized into the four building blocks of financial statement analysis: (1) liquidity and efficiency, (2) solvency, (3) profitability, and (4) market prospects. All of these ratios were explained at relevant points in prior chapters. The purpose here is to organize and apply them under a summary framework. We use four common standards, in varying degrees, for comparisons: intracompany, competitor, industry, and guidelines.

**Point:** Some sources for industry norms are *Annual Statement Studies* by Robert Morris Associates, *Industry Norms & Key Business Ratios* by Dun & Bradstreet, *Standard & Poor's Industry Surveys*, and Reuters.com/finance.

## Liquidity and Efficiency

*Liquidity* refers to the availability of resources to meet short-term cash requirements. It is affected by the timing of cash inflows and outflows along with prospects for future performance. Analysis of liquidity is aimed at a company's funding requirements. *Efficiency* refers to how productive a company is in using its assets. Efficiency is usually measured relative to how much revenue is generated from a certain level of assets.

Both liquidity and efficiency are important and complementary. If a company fails to meet its current obligations, its continued existence is doubtful. Viewed in this light, all other measures of analysis are of secondary importance. Although accounting measurements assume the company's continued existence, our analysis must always assess the validity of this assumption using liquidity measures. Moreover, inefficient use of assets can cause liquidity problems. A lack of liquidity often precedes lower profitability and fewer opportunities. It can foretell a loss of owner control. To a company's creditors, lack of liquidity can yield delays in collecting interest and principal payments or the loss of amounts due them. A company's customers and suppliers of goods and services also are affected by short-term liquidity problems. Implications include a company's inability to execute contracts and potential damage to important customer and supplier relationships. This section describes and illustrates key ratios relevant to assessing liquidity and efficiency.

**Working Capital and Current Ratio** The amount of current assets less current liabilities is called **working capital,** or *net working capital*. A company needs adequate working capital to meet current debts, to carry sufficient inventories, and to take advantage of cash discounts. A company that runs low on working capital is less likely to meet current obligations or to continue operating. When evaluating a company's working capital, we must not only look at the dollar amount of current assets less current liabilities, but also at their ratio. The *current ratio* is defined as follows (see Chapter 3 for additional explanation):

$$\text{Current ratio} = \frac{\text{Current assets}}{\text{Current liabilities}}$$

Drawing on information in Exhibit 17.1, **RIM**'s working capital and current ratio for both 2010 and 2009 are shown in Exhibit 17.14. Also, **Apple** (2.74), **Palm** (1.03), and the Industry's current ratio (2.4) are shown in the margin. RIM's 2010 ratio (2.39) is between the competitors' ratios, and it does not appear in danger of defaulting on loan payments. A high current ratio suggests a strong liquidity position and an ability to meet current obligations. A company can, however, have a current ratio that is too high. An excessively high current ratio means that the company has invested too much in current assets compared to its current obligations.

| ($ thousands) | 2010 | 2009 |
|---|---|---|
| Current assets . . . . . . . . . | $ 5,812,656 | $ 4,841,586 |
| Current liabilities . . . . . . . | 2,431,777 | 2,115,351 |
| **Working capital** . . . . . . | **$3,380,879** | **$2,726,235** |
| **Current ratio** | | |
| $5,812,656/$2,431,777 = | **2.39 to 1** | |
| $4,841,586/$2,115,351 = | | **2.29 to 1** |

**EXHIBIT 17.14**

RIM's Working Capital and Current Ratio

**Current ratio**
**Apple = 2.74**
**Palm = 1.03**
**Industry = 2.4**

An excessive investment in current assets is not an efficient use of funds because current assets normally generate a low return on investment (compared with long-term assets).

Many users apply a guideline of 2:1 (or 1.5:1) for the current ratio in helping evaluate a company's debt-paying ability. A company with a 2:1 or higher current ratio is generally thought to be a good credit risk in the short run. Such a guideline or any analysis of the current ratio must recognize at least three additional factors: (1) type of business, (2) composition of current assets, and (3) turnover rate of current asset components.

**Type of business.**    A service company that grants little or no credit and carries few inventories can probably operate on a current ratio of less than 1:1 if its revenues generate enough cash to pay its current liabilities. On the other hand, a company selling high-priced clothing or furniture requires a higher ratio because of difficulties in judging customer demand and cash receipts. For instance, if demand falls, inventory may not generate as much cash as expected. Accordingly, analysis of the current ratio should include a comparison with ratios from successful companies in the same industry and from prior periods. We must also recognize that a company's accounting methods, especially choice of inventory method, affect the current ratio. For instance, when costs are rising, a company using LIFO tends to report a smaller amount of current assets than when using FIFO.

**Composition of current assets.**    The composition of a company's current assets is important to an evaluation of short-term liquidity. For instance, cash, cash equivalents, and short-term investments are more liquid than accounts and notes receivable. Also, short-term receivables normally are more liquid than inventory. Cash, of course, can be used to immediately pay current debts. Items such as accounts receivable and inventory, however, normally must be converted into cash before payment is made. An excessive amount of receivables and inventory weakens a company's ability to pay current liabilities. The acid-test ratio (see below) can help with this assessment.

**Turnover rate of assets.**    Asset turnover measures a company's efficiency in using its assets. One relevant measure of asset efficiency is the revenue generated. A measure of total asset turnover is revenues divided by total assets, but evaluation of turnover for individual assets is also useful. We discuss both receivables turnover and inventory turnover on the next page.

> **◻ Decision Maker**                                          Answer — p. 713
>
> **Banker**    A company requests a one-year, $200,000 loan for expansion. This company's current ratio is 4:1, with current assets of $160,000. Key competitors carry a current ratio of about 1.9:1. Using this information, do you approve the loan application? Does your decision change if the application is for a 10-year loan? ■

**Acid-Test Ratio**    Quick assets are cash, short-term investments, and current receivables. These are the most liquid types of current assets. The *acid-test ratio,* also called *quick ratio,* and introduced in Chapter 5, reflects on a company's short-term liquidity.

$$\text{Acid-test ratio} = \frac{\text{Cash + Short-term investments + Current receivables}}{\text{Current liabilities}}$$

RIM's acid-test ratio is computed in Exhibit 17.15. RIM's 2010 acid-test ratio (1.94) is between that for Apple (2.33) and Palm (0.94), and greater than the 1:1 common guideline for an

**Point:** When a firm uses LIFO in a period of rising costs, the standard for an adequate current ratio usually is lower than if it used FIFO.

**EXHIBIT 17.15**

Acid-Test Ratio

| ($ thousands) | 2010 | 2009 |
|---|---|---|
| Cash and equivalents . . . . . . . . . . | $1,550,861 | $ 835,546 |
| Short-term investments . . . . . . . . | 360,614 | 682,666 |
| Current receivables . . . . . . . . . . . | 2,800,115 | 2,269,845 |
| Total quick assets . . . . . . . . . . . . . | $4,711,590 | $3,788,057 |
| Current liabilities . . . . . . . . . . . . . | $2,431,777 | $2,115,351 |
| **Acid-test ratio** | | |
| $4,711,590/$2,431,777 . . . . . . . | 1.94 to 1 | |
| $3,788,057/$2,115,351 . . . . . . . | | 1.79 to 1 |

**Acid-test ratio**
Apple = 2.33
Palm = 0.94
Industry = 1.5

acceptable acid-test ratio. The ratios for both RIM and Apple exceed the 1.5 industry norm. As with analysis of the current ratio, we need to consider other factors. For instance, the frequency with which a company converts its current assets into cash affects its working capital requirements. This implies that analysis of short-term liquidity should also include an analysis of receivables and inventories, which we consider next.

**Accounts Receivable Turnover**   We can measure how frequently a company converts its receivables into cash by computing the *accounts receivable turnover*. This ratio is defined as follows (see Chapter 9 for additional explanation):

$$\text{Accounts receivable turnover} = \frac{\text{Net sales}}{\text{Average accounts receivable, net}}$$

Short-term receivables from customers are often included in the denominator along with accounts receivable. Also, accounts receivable turnover is more precise if credit sales are used for the numerator, but external users generally use net sales (or net revenues) because information about credit sales is typically not reported. RIM's 2010 accounts receivable turnover is computed as follows ($ millions).

$$\frac{14,953,224}{(\$2,593,742 + \$2,112,117)/2} = 6.4 \text{ times}$$

RIM's value of 6.4 is between that of Apple's 14.8 and Palm's 8.0. Accounts receivable turnover is high when accounts receivable are quickly collected. A high turnover is favorable because it means the company need not commit large amounts of funds to accounts receivable. However, an accounts receivable turnover can be too high; this can occur when credit terms are so restrictive that they negatively affect sales volume.

**Inventory Turnover**   How long a company holds inventory before selling it will affect working capital requirements. One measure of this effect is *inventory turnover,* also called *merchandise turnover* or *merchandise inventory turnover,* which is defined as follows (see Chapter 6 for additional explanation):

$$\text{Inventory turnover} = \frac{\text{Cost of goods sold}}{\text{Average inventory}}$$

Using RIM's cost of goods sold and inventories information, we compute its inventory turnover for 2010 as follows (if the beginning and ending inventories for the year do not represent the usual inventory amount, an average of quarterly or monthly inventories can be used).

$$\frac{\$8,368,958}{(\$621,611 + \$682,400)/2} = 12.84 \text{ times}$$

RIM's inventory turnover of 12.84 is less than Apple's 53.28, but similar to Palm's 13.22, and the industry's 10.1. A company with a high turnover requires a smaller investment in inventory than one producing the same sales with a lower turnover. Inventory turnover can be too high, however, if the inventory a company keeps is so small that it restricts sales volume.

**Days' Sales Uncollected**   Accounts receivable turnover provides insight into how frequently a company collects its accounts. Days' sales uncollected is one measure of this activity, which is defined as follows (Chapter 8 provides additional explanation):

$$\text{Days' sales uncollected} = \frac{\text{Accounts receivable, net}}{\text{Net sales}} \times 365$$

Any short-term notes receivable from customers are normally included in the numerator.

**Global:** Ratio analysis helps overcome currency translation problems, but it does *not* overcome differences in accounting principles.

**Point:** Some users prefer using gross accounts receivable (before subtracting the allowance for doubtful accounts) to avoid the influence of a manager's bad debts estimate.

**Accounts receivable turnover**
Apple = 14.8
Palm = 8.0
Industry = 6.6

**Point:** Ending accounts receivable can be substituted for the average balance in computing accounts receivable turnover if the difference between ending and average receivables is small.

**Inventory turnover**
Apple = 53.28
Palm = 13.22
Industry = 10.1

RIM's 2010 days' sales uncollected follows.

$$\frac{\$2,593,742}{\$14,953,224} \times 365 = 63.31 \text{ days}$$

Both Apple's days' sales uncollected of 28.59 days and Palm's 32.96 days are less than the 63.31 days for RIM. Days' sales uncollected is more meaningful if we know company credit terms. A rough guideline states that days' sales uncollected should not exceed $1\frac{1}{3}$ times the days in its (1) credit period, *if* discounts are not offered or (2) discount period, *if* favorable discounts are offered.

**Days' Sales in Inventory**   *Days' sales in inventory* is a useful measure in evaluating inventory liquidity. Days' sales in inventory is linked to inventory in a way that days' sales uncollected is linked to receivables. We compute days' sales in inventory as follows (Chapter 6 provides additional explanation).

$$\text{Days' sales in inventory} = \frac{\textbf{Ending inventory}}{\textbf{Cost of goods sold}} \times 365$$

RIM's days' sales in inventory for 2010 follows.

$$\frac{\$621,611}{\$8,368,958} \times 365 = 27.1 \text{ days}$$

If the products in RIM's inventory are in demand by customers, this formula estimates that its inventory will be converted into receivables (or cash) in 27.1 days. If all of RIM's sales were credit sales, the conversion of inventory to receivables in 27.1 days *plus* the conversion of receivables to cash in 63.31 days implies that inventory will be converted to cash in about 90.41 days (27.1 + 63.31).

**Total Asset Turnover**   *Total asset turnover* reflects a company's ability to use its assets to generate sales and is an important indication of operating efficiency. The definition of this ratio follows (Chapter 10 offers additional explanation).

$$\text{Total asset turnover} = \frac{\textbf{Net sales}}{\textbf{Average total assets}}$$

RIM's total asset turnover for 2010 follows and is greater than that for both Apple (1.03) and Palm (0.81).

$$\frac{\$14,953,224}{(\$10,204,409 + \$8,101,372)/2} = 1.63 \text{ times}$$

## Quick Check Answers — p. 713

8. Information from Paff Co. at Dec. 31, 2010, follows: cash, $820,000; accounts receivable, $240,000; inventories, $470,000; plant assets, $910,000; accounts payable, $350,000; and income taxes payable, $180,000. Compute its (a) current ratio and (b) acid-test ratio.

9. On Dec. 31, 2011, Paff Company (see question 8) had accounts receivable of $290,000 and inventories of $530,000. During 2011, net sales amounted to $2,500,000 and cost of goods sold was $750,000. Compute (a) accounts receivable turnover, (b) days' sales uncollected, (c) inventory turnover, and (d) days' sales in inventory.

## Solvency

*Solvency* refers to a company's long-run financial viability and its ability to cover long-term obligations. All of a company's business activities—financing, investing, and operating—affect its solvency. Analysis of solvency is long term and uses less precise but more encompassing measures than liquidity. One of the most important components of solvency analysis is the composition of a company's capital structure. *Capital structure* refers to a company's financing sources. It ranges from relatively permanent equity financing to riskier or more temporary short-term financing. Assets represent security for financiers, ranging from loans secured by specific assets to the assets available as general security to unsecured creditors. This section describes the tools of solvency analysis. Our analysis focuses on a company's ability to both meet its obligations and provide security to its creditors *over the long run*. Indicators of this ability include *debt* and *equity* ratios, the relation between *pledged assets and secured liabilities,* and the company's capacity to earn sufficient income to *pay fixed interest charges.*

**Debt and Equity Ratios**  One element of solvency analysis is to assess the portion of a company's assets contributed by its owners and the portion contributed by creditors. This relation is reflected in the debt ratio (also described in Chapter 2). The *debt ratio* expresses total liabilities as a percent of total assets. The **equity ratio** provides complementary information by expressing total equity as a percent of total assets. **RIM**'s debt and equity ratios follow.

**Point:** For analysis purposes, Minority Interest is usually included in equity.

| ($ thousands) | 2010 | Ratios | |
|---|---|---|---|
| Total liabilities | $ 2,601,746 | 25.5% | [Debt ratio] |
| Total equity | 7,602,663 | 74.5 | [Equity ratio] |
| Total liabilities and equity | $10,204,409 | 100.0% | |

**Debt ratio :: Equity ratio**
**Apple = 33.4% :: 66.6%**
**Industry = 40% :: 60%**

RIM's financial statements reveal more equity than debt. A company is considered less risky if its capital structure (equity and long-term debt) contains more equity. One risk factor is the required payment for interest and principal when debt is outstanding. Another factor is the greater the stockholder financing, the more losses a company can absorb through equity before the assets become inadequate to satisfy creditors' claims. From the stockholders' point of view, if a company earns a return on borrowed capital that is higher than the cost of borrowing, the difference represents increased income to stockholders. The inclusion of debt is described as *financial leverage* because debt can have the effect of increasing the return to stockholders. Companies are said to be highly leveraged if a large portion of their assets is financed by debt.

**Point:** Bank examiners from the FDIC and other regulatory agencies use debt and equity ratios to monitor compliance with regulatory capital requirements imposed on banks and S&Ls.

**Debt-to-Equity Ratio**  The ratio of total liabilities to equity is another measure of solvency. We compute the ratio as follows (Chapter 14 offers additional explanation).

$$\text{Debt-to-equity ratio} = \frac{\text{Total liabilities}}{\text{Total equity}}$$

RIM's debt-to-equity ratio for 2010 is

$$\$2,601,746/\$7,602,663 = 0.34$$

**Debt-to-equity**
**Apple = 0.50**
**Industry = 0.7**

RIM's 0.34 debt-to-equity ratio is less than the 0.50 ratio for Apple, and less than the industry ratio of 0.7. Consistent with our inferences from the debt ratio, RIM's capital structure has more equity than debt, which decreases risk. Recall that debt must be repaid with interest, while equity does not. These debt requirements can be burdensome when the industry and/or the economy experience a downturn. A larger debt-to-equity ratio also implies less opportunity to expand through use of debt financing.

**Times Interest Earned**  The amount of income before deductions for interest expense and income taxes is the amount available to pay interest expense. The following *times interest earned* ratio reflects the creditors' risk of loan repayments with interest (see Chapter 11 for additional explanation).

$$\text{Times interest earned} = \frac{\text{Income before interest expense and income taxes}}{\text{Interest expense}}$$

The larger this ratio, the less risky is the company for creditors. One guideline says that creditors are reasonably safe if the company earns its fixed interest expense two or more times each year. RIM's times interest earned ratio follows; its value suggests that its creditors have little risk of nonrepayment.

**Times interest earned**
**Apple = n.a.**

$$\frac{\$2,457,144 + {\sim}\$0 \text{ (see RIM note \#16)} + \$809,366}{{\sim}\$0} = \text{"infinite" (not applicable)}$$

**Decision Insight**

**Bears and Bulls**    A *bear market* is a declining market. The phrase comes from bear-skin jobbers who often sold the skins before the bears were caught. The term *bear* was then used to describe investors who sold shares they did not own in anticipation of a price decline. A *bull market* is a rising market. This phrase comes from the once popular sport of bear and bull baiting. The term *bull* came to mean the opposite of *bear*. ∎

## Profitability

We are especially interested in a company's ability to use its assets efficiently to produce profits (and positive cash flows). *Profitability* refers to a company's ability to generate an adequate return on invested capital. Return is judged by assessing earnings relative to the level and sources of financing. Profitability is also relevant to solvency. This section describes key profitability measures and their importance to financial statement analysis.

**Profit Margin**    A company's operating efficiency and profitability can be expressed by two components. The first is *profit margin,* which reflects a company's ability to earn net income from sales (Chapter 3 offers additional explanation). It is measured by expressing net income as a percent of sales (*sales* and *revenues* are similar terms). **RIM**'s profit margin follows.

**Profit margin**
**Apple = 19.2%**
**Industry = 3%**

$$\text{Profit margin} = \frac{\text{Net income}}{\text{Net sales}} = \frac{\$2,457,144}{\$14,953,224} = 16.4\%$$

To evaluate profit margin, we must consider the industry. For instance, an appliance company might require a profit margin between 10% and 15%; whereas a retail supermarket might require a profit margin of 1% or 2%. Both profit margin and *total asset turnover* make up the two basic components of operating efficiency. These ratios reflect on management because managers are ultimately responsible for operating efficiency. The next section explains how we use both measures to analyze return on total assets.

**Return on Total Assets**    *Return on total assets* is defined as follows.

$$\text{Return on total assets} = \frac{\text{Net income}}{\text{Average total assets}}$$

RIM's 2010 return on total assets is

**Return on total assets**
**Apple = 19.7%**
**Industry = 4%**

$$\frac{\$2,457,144}{(\$10,204,409 + \$8,101,372)/2} = 26.8\%$$

RIM's 26.8% return on total assets is higher than that for many businesses and is higher than Apple's return of 19.7% and the industry's 4% return. We also should evaluate any trend in the rate of return.

The following equation shows the important relation between profit margin, total asset turnover, and return on total assets.

**Point:** Many analysts add back *Interest expense × (1 − Tax rate)* to net income in computing return on total assets.

$$\textbf{Profit margin} \times \textbf{Total asset turnover} = \textbf{Return on total assets}$$

or

$$\frac{\textbf{Net income}}{\textbf{Net sales}} \times \frac{\textbf{Net sales}}{\textbf{Average total assets}} = \frac{\textbf{Net income}}{\textbf{Average total assets}}$$

Both profit margin and total asset turnover contribute to overall operating efficiency, as measured by return on total assets. If we apply this formula to RIM, we get

$$16.4\% \times 1.63 = 26.8\% \text{ (with rounding error)}$$

**Apple: 19.2% × 1.03 = 19.7%**<br>**(with rounding)**

This analysis shows that RIM's superior return on assets versus that of Apple is driven mainly by its higher total asset turnover.

**Return on Common Stockholders' Equity**  Perhaps the most important goal in operating a company is to earn net income for its owner(s). *Return on common stockholders' equity* measures a company's success in reaching this goal and is defined as follows.

$$\textbf{Return on common stockholders' equity} = \frac{\textbf{Net income} - \textbf{Preferred dividends}}{\textbf{Average common stockholders' equity}}$$

RIM's 2010 return on common stockholders' equity is computed as follows:

$$\frac{\$2,457,144 - \$0}{(\$5,874,128 + \$7,602,663)/2} = 36.5\%$$

**Return on common equity**<br>**Apple = 30.5%**<br>**Industry = 6%**

The denominator in this computation is the book value of common equity (minority interest is often included in common equity for this ratio). In the numerator, the dividends on cumulative preferred stock are subtracted whether they are declared or are in arrears. If preferred stock is noncumulative, its dividends are subtracted only if declared.

---

**Decision Insight**

**Wall Street**  *Wall Street* is synonymous with financial markets, but its name comes from the street location of the original New York Stock Exchange. The street's name derives from stockades built by early settlers to protect New York from pirate attacks. ■

## Market Prospects

Market measures are useful for analyzing corporations with publicly traded stock. These market measures use stock price, which reflects the market's (public's) expectations for the company. This includes expectations of both company return and risk—as the market perceives it.

**Price-Earnings Ratio**  Computation of the *price-earnings ratio* follows (Chapter 13 provides additional explanation).

$$\textbf{Price-earnings ratio} = \frac{\textbf{Market price per common share}}{\textbf{Earnings per share}}$$

**Point:** PE ratio can be viewed as an indicator of the market's expected growth and risk for a stock. High expected risk suggests a low PE ratio. High expected growth suggests a high PE ratio.

**PE (year-end)**
**Apple = 13.9**

**Point:** Some investors avoid stocks with high PE ratios under the belief they are "overpriced." Alternatively, some investors *sell these stocks short*—hoping for price declines.

**Dividend yield**
**Apple = 0.0%**
**Palm = 0.0%**

**Point:** Corporate PE ratios and dividend yields are found in daily stock market quotations listed in *The Wall Street Journal, Investor's Business Daily,* or other publications and Web services.

Predicted earnings per share for the next period is often used in the denominator of this computation. Reported earnings per share for the most recent period is also commonly used. In both cases, the ratio is used as an indicator of the future growth and risk of a company's earnings as perceived by the stock's buyers and sellers.

The market price of RIM's common stock at the start of fiscal year 2010 was $50.84. Using RIM's $4.35 basic earnings per share, we compute its price-earnings ratio as follows (some analysts compute this ratio using the median of the low and high stock price).

$$\frac{\$50.84}{\$4.35} = 11.7$$

RIM's price-earnings ratio is less than that for Apple, but is slightly higher than the norm for the recessionary period 2009–2010. (Palm's ratio is negative due to its abnormally low earnings.) RIM's middle-of-the-pack ratio likely reflects investors' expectations of stagnant growth but normal earnings.

**Dividend Yield**    *Dividend yield* is used to compare the dividend-paying performance of different investment alternatives. We compute dividend yield as follows (Chapter 13 offers additional explanation).

$$\text{Dividend yield} = \frac{\text{Annual cash dividends per share}}{\text{Market price per share}}$$

RIM's dividend yield, based on its fiscal year-end market price per share of $50.84 and its policy of $0.00 cash dividends per share, is computed as follows.

$$\frac{\$0.00}{\$50.84} = 0.0\%$$

Some companies do not declare and pay dividends because they wish to reinvest the cash.

## Summary of Ratios

Exhibit 17.16 summarizes the major financial statement analysis ratios illustrated in this chapter and throughout the book. This summary includes each ratio's title, its formula, and the purpose for which it is commonly used.

---

**Decision Insight**

**Ticker Prices**    *Ticker prices* refer to a band of moving data on a monitor carrying up-to-the-minute stock prices. The phrase comes from *ticker tape,* a 1-inch-wide strip of paper spewing stock prices from a printer that ticked as it ran. Most of today's investors have never seen actual ticker tape, but the phrase survives. ■

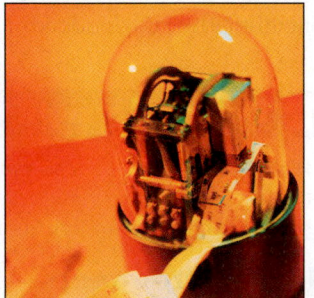

---

**Quick Check**                                                    Answers — p. 713

10. Which ratio best reflects a company's ability to meet immediate interest payments? (*a*) Debt ratio. (*b*) Equity ratio. (*c*) Times interest earned.
11. Which ratio best measures a company's success in earning net income for its owner(s)? (*a*) Profit margin. (*b*) Return on common stockholders' equity. (*c*) Price-earnings ratio. (*d*) Dividend yield.
12. If a company has net sales of $8,500,000, net income of $945,000, and total asset turnover of 1.8 times, what is its return on total assets?

## EXHIBIT 17.16

Financial Statement Analysis Ratios*

| Ratio | Formula | Measure of |
|---|---|---|
| **Liquidity and Efficiency** | | |
| Current ratio | $= \dfrac{\text{Current assets}}{\text{Current liabilities}}$ | Short-term debt-paying ability |
| Acid-test ratio | $= \dfrac{\text{Cash} + \text{Short-term investments} + \text{Current receivables}}{\text{Current liabilities}}$ | Immediate short-term debt-paying ability |
| Accounts receivable turnover | $= \dfrac{\text{Net sales}}{\text{Average accounts receivable, net}}$ | Efficiency of collection |
| Inventory turnover | $= \dfrac{\text{Cost of goods sold}}{\text{Average inventory}}$ | Efficiency of inventory management |
| Days' sales uncollected | $= \dfrac{\text{Accounts receivable, net}}{\text{Net sales}} \times 365$ | Liquidity of receivables |
| Days' sales in inventory | $= \dfrac{\text{Ending inventory}}{\text{Cost of goods sold}} \times 365$ | Liquidity of inventory |
| Total asset turnover | $= \dfrac{\text{Net sales}}{\text{Average total assets}}$ | Efficiency of assets in producing sales |
| **Solvency** | | |
| Debt ratio | $= \dfrac{\text{Total liabilities}}{\text{Total assets}}$ | Creditor financing and leverage |
| Equity ratio | $= \dfrac{\text{Total equity}}{\text{Total assets}}$ | Owner financing |
| Debt-to-equity ratio | $= \dfrac{\text{Total liabilities}}{\text{Total equity}}$ | Debt versus equity financing |
| Times interest earned | $= \dfrac{\text{Income before interest expense and income taxes}}{\text{Interest expense}}$ | Protection in meeting interest payments |
| **Profitability** | | |
| Profit margin ratio | $= \dfrac{\text{Net income}}{\text{Net sales}}$ | Net income in each sales dollar |
| Gross margin ratio | $= \dfrac{\text{Net sales} - \text{Cost of goods sold}}{\text{Net sales}}$ | Gross margin in each sales dollar |
| Return on total assets | $= \dfrac{\text{Net income}}{\text{Average total assets}}$ | Overall profitability of assets |
| Return on common stockholders' equity | $= \dfrac{\text{Net income} - \text{Preferred dividends}}{\text{Average common stockholders' equity}}$ | Profitability of owner investment |
| Book value per common share | $= \dfrac{\text{Shareholders' equity applicable to common shares}}{\text{Number of common shares outstanding}}$ | Liquidation at reported amounts |
| Basic earnings per share | $= \dfrac{\text{Net income} - \text{Preferred dividends}}{\text{Weighted-average common shares outstanding}}$ | Net income per common share |
| **Market Prospects** | | |
| Price-earnings ratio | $= \dfrac{\text{Market price per common share}}{\text{Earnings per share}}$ | Market value relative to earnings |
| Dividend yield | $= \dfrac{\text{Annual cash dividends per share}}{\text{Market price per share}}$ | Cash return per common share |

* Additional ratios also examined in previous chapters included credit risk ratio; plant asset useful life; plant asset age; days' cash expense coverage; cash coverage of growth; cash coverage of debt; free cash flow; cash flow on total assets; and payout ratio.

# GLOBAL VIEW

The analysis and interpretation of financial statements is, of course, impacted by the accounting system in effect. This section discusses similarities and differences for analysis of financial statements when prepared under U.S. GAAP vis-à-vis IFRS.

**Horizontal and Vertical Analyses**   Horizontal and vertical analyses help eliminate many differences between U.S. GAAP and IFRS when analyzing and interpreting financial statements. Financial numbers are converted to percentages that are, in the best case scenario, consistently applied across and within periods. This enables users to effectively compare companies across reporting regimes. However, when fundamental differences in reporting regimes impact financial statements, such as with certain recognition rule differences, the user must exercise caution when drawing conclusions. Some users will reformulate one set of numbers to be more consistent with the other system to enable comparative analysis. This reformulation process is covered in advanced courses. The important point is that horizontal and vertical analyses help strip away differences between the reporting regimes, but several key differences sometimes remain and require adjustment of the numbers. **Nokia** reports the following partial vertical analysis to its shareholders as part of its MD&A report.

**NOKIA**

| As a Percentage of Revenue | 2010 |
| --- | --- |
| Research and development . . . . . . . . . . . . . . . . . . | 6.5% |
| Selling, marketing and administration . . . . . . . . . | 12.8 |
| Amortization . . . . . . . . . . . . . . . . . . . . . . . . . . . . | 2.1 |
| Litigation . . . . . . . . . . . . . . . . . . . . . . . . . . . . . . | 1.1 |
| Total operating expenses . . . . . . . . . . . . . . . . . . | 22.5% |

**Ratio Analysis**   Ratio analysis of financial statement numbers has many of the advantages and disadvantages of horizontal and vertical analyses discussed above. Importantly, ratio analysis is useful for business decisions, with some possible changes in interpretation depending on what is and what is not included in accounting measures across U.S. GAAP and IFRS. Still, we must take care in drawing inferences from a comparison of ratios across reporting regimes because what a number measures can differ across regimes. **Nokia** offers the following example of its own ratio analysis applied to gross margin: "Consolidated gross margin increased by $1.48 billion, or 29.2%, to $6.58 billion, or 44.0% of revenue, in fiscal 2010, compared to $5.10 billion, or 46.1% of revenue, in fiscal 2009. The decrease of 2.1% in consolidated gross margin percentage was primarily due to a decrease in the blended device margins."

## Decision Insight

**Not Created Equal**   Financial regulation has several goals. Two of them are to ensure adequate accounting disclosure and to strengthen corporate governance. For disclosure purposes, companies must now provide details of related-party transactions and material off-balance-sheet agreements. This is motivated by several major frauds. For corporate governance, the CEO and CFO must now certify the fairness of financial statements and the effectiveness of internal controls. Yet, concerns remain. A study reports that 23% of management and administrative employees observed activities that posed a conflict of interest in the past year (KPMG 2009). Another 12% witnessed the falsifying or manipulating of accounting information. The bottom line: All financial statements are not of equal quality. ■

## Decision Analysis                                     Analysis Reporting

**A1**   Summarize and report results of analysis.

Understanding the purpose of financial statement analysis is crucial to the usefulness of any analysis. This understanding leads to efficiency of effort, effectiveness in application, and relevance in focus. The purpose of most financial statement analyses is to reduce uncertainty in business decisions through a rigorous and sound evaluation. A *financial statement analysis report* helps by directly addressing the building blocks of analysis and by identifying weaknesses in inference by requiring explanation: It forces us to organize our reasoning and to verify its flow and logic. A report also serves as a communication link with readers, and the writing process reinforces our judgments and vice versa. Finally, the report helps us (re)evaluate evidence and refine conclusions on key building blocks. A good analysis report usually consists of six sections:

1. **Executive summary**—brief focus on important analysis results and conclusions.

2. **Analysis overview**—background on the company, its industry, and its economic setting.

3. **Evidential matter**—financial statements and information used in the analysis, including ratios, trends, comparisons, statistics, and all analytical measures assembled; often organized under the building blocks of analysis.

4. **Assumptions**—identification of important assumptions regarding a company's industry and economic environment, and other important assumptions for estimates.

5. **Key factors**—list of important favorable and unfavorable factors, both quantitative and qualitative, for company performance; usually organized by areas of analysis.

6. **Inferences**—forecasts, estimates, interpretations, and conclusions drawing on all sections of the report.

We must remember that the user dictates relevance, meaning that the analysis report should include a brief table of contents to help readers focus on those areas most relevant to their decisions. All irrelevant matter must be eliminated. For example, decades-old details of obscure transactions and detailed miscues of the analysis are irrelevant. Ambiguities and qualifications to avoid responsibility or hedging inferences must be eliminated. Finally, writing is important. Mistakes in grammar and errors of fact compromise the report's credibility.

---

### Decision **Insight**

**Short Selling**   *Short selling* refers to selling stock before you buy it. Here's an example: You borrow 100 shares of Nike stock, sell them at $40 each, and receive money from their sale. You then wait. You hope that Nike's stock price falls to, say, $35 each and you can replace the borrowed stock for less than you sold it for, reaping a profit of $5 each less any transaction costs. ∎

---

## DEMONSTRATION PROBLEM

Use the following financial statements of Precision Co. to complete these requirements.

1. Prepare comparative income statements showing the percent increase or decrease for year 2011 in comparison to year 2010.

2. Prepare common-size comparative balance sheets for years 2011 and 2010.

3. Compute the following ratios as of December 31, 2011, or for the year ended December 31, 2011, and identify its building block category for financial statement analysis.

   **a.** Current ratio

   **b.** Acid-test ratio

   **c.** Accounts receivable turnover

   **d.** Days' sales uncollected

   **e.** Inventory turnover

   **f.** Debt ratio

   **g.** Debt-to-equity ratio

   **h.** Times interest earned

   **i.** Profit margin ratio

   **j.** Total asset turnover

   **k.** Return on total assets

   **l.** Return on common stockholders' equity

**PRECISION COMPANY**
**Comparative Income Statements**
**For Years Ended December 31, 2011 and 2010**

| | 2011 | 2010 |
|---|---|---|
| Sales . . . . . . . . . . . . . . . . . . . . . . . . . . . . . | $2,486,000 | $2,075,000 |
| Cost of goods sold . . . . . . . . . . . . . . . . | 1,523,000 | 1,222,000 |
| Gross profit . . . . . . . . . . . . . . . . . . . . . . . | 963,000 | 853,000 |
| Operating expenses | | |
| Advertising expense . . . . . . . . . . . . . . | 145,000 | 100,000 |
| Sales salaries expense . . . . . . . . . . . . . | 240,000 | 280,000 |
| Office salaries expense . . . . . . . . . . . | 165,000 | 200,000 |
| Insurance expense . . . . . . . . . . . . . . . | 100,000 | 45,000 |
| Supplies expense . . . . . . . . . . . . . . . . . | 26,000 | 35,000 |
| Depreciation expense . . . . . . . . . . . . . | 85,000 | 75,000 |
| Miscellaneous expenses . . . . . . . . . . . | 17,000 | 15,000 |
| Total operating expenses . . . . . . . . . | 778,000 | 750,000 |
| Operating income . . . . . . . . . . . . . . . . . | 185,000 | 103,000 |
| Interest expense . . . . . . . . . . . . . . . . . . . | 44,000 | 46,000 |
| Income before taxes . . . . . . . . . . . . . . . | 141,000 | 57,000 |
| Income taxes . . . . . . . . . . . . . . . . . . . . . | 47,000 | 19,000 |
| Net income . . . . . . . . . . . . . . . . . . . . . . | $ 94,000 | $ 38,000 |
| | | |
| Earnings per share . . . . . . . . . . . . . . . . | $ 0.99 | $ 0.40 |

**PRECISION COMPANY**
**Comparative Balance Sheets**
**December 31, 2011 and 2010**

| | 2011 | 2010 |
|---|---|---|
| **Assets** | | |
| Current assets | | |
| Cash . . . . . . . . . . . . . . . . . . . . . . . . | $ 79,000 | $ 42,000 |
| Short-term investments . . . . . . . . . . | 65,000 | 96,000 |
| Accounts receivable, net . . . . . . . . . . | 120,000 | 100,000 |
| Merchandise inventory . . . . . . . . . . . | 250,000 | 265,000 |
| Total current assets . . . . . . . . . . . . . | 514,000 | 503,000 |
| Plant assets | | |
| Store equipment, net . . . . . . . . . . . . | 400,000 | 350,000 |
| Office equipment, net . . . . . . . . . . . . | 45,000 | 50,000 |
| Buildings, net . . . . . . . . . . . . . . . . . | 625,000 | 675,000 |
| Land . . . . . . . . . . . . . . . . . . . . . . . . | 100,000 | 100,000 |
| Total plant assets . . . . . . . . . . . . . . | 1,170,000 | 1,175,000 |
| Total assets . . . . . . . . . . . . . . . . . . | $1,684,000 | $1,678,000 |
| **Liabilities** | | |
| Current liabilities | | |
| Accounts payable . . . . . . . . . . . . . . . | $ 164,000 | $ 190,000 |
| Short-term notes payable . . . . . . . . . | 75,000 | 90,000 |
| Taxes payable . . . . . . . . . . . . . . . . . | 26,000 | 12,000 |
| Total current liabilities . . . . . . . . . . . | 265,000 | 292,000 |
| Long-term liabilities | | |
| Notes payable (secured by mortgage on buildings) . . . . . . . . . | 400,000 | 420,000 |
| Total liabilities . . . . . . . . . . . . . . . . . | 665,000 | 712,000 |
| **Stockholders' Equity** | | |
| Common stock, $5 par value . . . . . . . . | 475,000 | 475,000 |
| Retained earnings . . . . . . . . . . . . . . . . | 544,000 | 491,000 |
| Total stockholders' equity . . . . . . . . . | 1,019,000 | 966,000 |
| Total liabilities and equity . . . . . . . . . | $1,684,000 | $1,678,000 |

## PLANNING THE SOLUTION

- Set up a four-column income statement; enter the 2011 and 2010 amounts in the first two columns and then enter the dollar change in the third column and the percent change from 2010 in the fourth column.
- Set up a four-column balance sheet; enter the 2011 and 2010 year-end amounts in the first two columns and then compute and enter the amount of each item as a percent of total assets.
- Compute the required ratios using the data provided. Use the average of beginning and ending amounts when appropriate (see Exhibit 17.16 for definitions).

## SOLUTION TO DEMONSTRATION PROBLEM

1.

**PRECISION COMPANY**
**Comparative Income Statements**
**For Years Ended December 31, 2011 and 2010**

| | | | Increase (Decrease) in 2011 | |
|---|---|---|---|---|
| | 2011 | 2010 | Amount | Percent |
| Sales . . . . . . . . . . . . . . . . . . . . . . . . | $2,486,000 | $2,075,000 | $411,000 | 19.8% |
| Cost of goods sold . . . . . . . . . . . . . . | 1,523,000 | 1,222,000 | 301,000 | 24.6 |
| Gross profit . . . . . . . . . . . . . . . . . . . | 963,000 | 853,000 | 110,000 | 12.9 |

[continued on next page]

[continued from previous page]

| Operating expenses | | | | |
|---|---|---|---|---|
| Advertising expense . . . . . . . . . . . . | 145,000 | 100,000 | 45,000 | 45.0 |
| Sales salaries expense . . . . . . . . . . . | 240,000 | 280,000 | (40,000) | (14.3) |
| Office salaries expense . . . . . . . . . | 165,000 | 200,000 | (35,000) | (17.5) |
| Insurance expense . . . . . . . . . . . . . . | 100,000 | 45,000 | 55,000 | 122.2 |
| Supplies expense . . . . . . . . . . . . . . . | 26,000 | 35,000 | (9,000) | (25.7) |
| Depreciation expense . . . . . . . . . . . | 85,000 | 75,000 | 10,000 | 13.3 |
| Miscellaneous expenses . . . . . . . . . | 17,000 | 15,000 | 2,000 | 13.3 |
| Total operating expenses . . . . . . . . | 778,000 | 750,000 | 28,000 | 3.7 |
| Operating income . . . . . . . . . . . . . . . . | 185,000 | 103,000 | 82,000 | 79.6 |
| Interest expense . . . . . . . . . . . . . . . | 44,000 | 46,000 | (2,000) | (4.3) |
| Income before taxes . . . . . . . . . . . . . | 141,000 | 57,000 | 84,000 | 147.4 |
| Income taxes . . . . . . . . . . . . . . . . . . | 47,000 | 19,000 | 28,000 | 147.4 |
| Net income . . . . . . . . . . . . . . . . . . | $   94,000 | $   38,000 | $ 56,000 | 147.4 |
| Earnings per share . . . . . . . . . . . . . . | $      0.99 | $      0.40 | $     0.59 | 147.5 |

2.

**PRECISION COMPANY**
**Common-Size Comparative Balance Sheets**
**December 31, 2011 and 2010**

| | December 31 | | Common-Size Percents | |
|---|---|---|---|---|
| | 2011 | 2010 | 2011* | 2010* |
| **Assets** | | | | |
| Current assets | | | | |
| Cash . . . . . . . . . . . . . . . . . . . . . . . | $   79,000 | $   42,000 | 4.7% | 2.5% |
| Short-term investments . . . . . . . . . . . | 65,000 | 96,000 | 3.9 | 5.7 |
| Accounts receivable, net . . . . . . . . . . | 120,000 | 100,000 | 7.1 | 6.0 |
| Merchandise inventory . . . . . . . . . . . . | 250,000 | 265,000 | 14.8 | 15.8 |
| Total current assets . . . . . . . . . . . . . . | 514,000 | 503,000 | 30.5 | 30.0 |
| Plant assets | | | | |
| Store equipment, net . . . . . . . . . . . . | 400,000 | 350,000 | 23.8 | 20.9 |
| Office equipment, net . . . . . . . . . . . . | 45,000 | 50,000 | 2.7 | 3.0 |
| Buildings, net . . . . . . . . . . . . . . . . . . | 625,000 | 675,000 | 37.1 | 40.2 |
| Land . . . . . . . . . . . . . . . . . . . . . . . | 100,000 | 100,000 | 5.9 | 6.0 |
| Total plant assets . . . . . . . . . . . . . . | 1,170,000 | 1,175,000 | 69.5 | 70.0 |
| Total assets . . . . . . . . . . . . . . . . . . . | $1,684,000 | $1,678,000 | 100.0 | 100.0 |
| **Liabilities** | | | | |
| Current liabilities | | | | |
| Accounts payable . . . . . . . . . . . . . . | $ 164,000 | $ 190,000 | 9.7% | 11.3% |
| Short-term notes payable . . . . . . . . . | 75,000 | 90,000 | 4.5 | 5.4 |
| Taxes payable . . . . . . . . . . . . . . . . . | 26,000 | 12,000 | 1.5 | 0.7 |
| Total current liabilities . . . . . . . . . . . . | 265,000 | 292,000 | 15.7 | 17.4 |
| Long-term liabilities | | | | |
| Notes payable (secured by mortgage on buildings) . . . . . . . . . . | 400,000 | 420,000 | 23.8 | 25.0 |
| Total liabilities . . . . . . . . . . . . . . . . . | 665,000 | 712,000 | 39.5 | 42.4 |
| **Stockholders' equity** | | | | |
| Common stock, $5 par value . . . . . . . . | 475,000 | 475,000 | 28.2 | 28.3 |
| Retained earnings . . . . . . . . . . . . . . . | 544,000 | 491,000 | 32.3 | 29.3 |
| Total stockholders' equity . . . . . . . . . | 1,019,000 | 966,000 | 60.5 | 57.6 |
| Total liabilities and equity . . . . . . . . . | $1,684,000 | $1,678,000 | 100.0 | 100.0 |

* Columns do not always exactly add to 100 due to rounding.

**3. Ratios for 2011:**

  **a.**  Current ratio: $514,000/$265,000 = 1.9:1 (liquidity and efficiency)

  **b.**  Acid-test ratio: ($79,000 + $65,000 + $120,000)/$265,000 = 1.0:1 (liquidity and efficiency)

  **c.**  Average receivables: ($120,000 + $100,000)/2 = $110,000
     Accounts receivable turnover: $2,486,000/$110,000 = 22.6 times (liquidity and efficiency)

  **d.**  Days' sales uncollected: ($120,000/$2,486,000) $\times$ 365 = 17.6 days (liquidity and efficiency)

  **e.**  Average inventory: ($250,000 + $265,000)/2 = $257,500
     Inventory turnover: $1,523,000/$257,500 = 5.9 times (liquidity and efficiency)

  **f.**  Debt ratio: $665,000/$1,684,000 = 39.5% (solvency)

  **g.**  Debt-to-equity ratio: $665,000/$1,019,000 = 0.65 (solvency)

  **h.**  Times interest earned: $185,000/$44,000 = 4.2 times (solvency)

  **i.**  Profit margin ratio: $94,000/$2,486,000 = 3.8% (profitability)

  **j.**  Average total assets: ($1,684,000 + $1,678,000)/2 = $1,681,000
     Total asset turnover: $2,486,000/$1,681,000 = 1.48 times (liquidity and efficiency)

  **k.**  Return on total assets: $94,000/$1,681,000 = 5.6% or 3.8% $\times$ 1.48 = 5.6% (profitability)

  **l.**  Average total common equity: ($1,019,000 + $966,000)/2 = $992,500
     Return on common stockholders' equity: $94,000/$992,500 = 9.5% (profitability)

---

**APPENDIX**

# 17A

# Sustainable Income

| **A2** | Explain the form and assess the content of a complete income statement. |
|---|---|

When a company's revenue and expense transactions are from normal, continuing operations, a simple income statement is usually adequate. When a company's activities include income-related events not part of its normal, continuing operations, it must disclose information to help users understand these events and predict future performance. To meet these objectives, companies separate the income statement into continuing operations, discontinued segments, extraordinary items, comprehensive income, and earnings per share. For illustration, Exhibit 17A.1 shows such an income statement for ComUS. These separate distinctions help us measure *sustainable income,* which is the income level most likely to continue into the future. Sustainable income is commonly used in PE ratios and other market-based measures of performance.

**Continuing Operations**   The first major section (①) shows the revenues, expenses, and income from continuing operations. Users especially rely on this information to predict future operations. Many users view this section as the most important. Earlier chapters explained the items comprising income from continuing operations.

**Discontinued Segments**   A **business segment** is a part of a company's operations that serves a particular line of business or class of customers. A segment has assets, liabilities, and financial results of operations that can be distinguished from those of other parts of the company. A company's gain or loss from selling or closing down a segment is separately reported. Section ② of Exhibit 17A.1 reports both (1) income from operating the discontinued segment for the current period prior to its disposal and (2) the loss from disposing of the segment's net assets. The income tax effects of each are reported separately from the income taxes expense in section ①.

**Extraordinary Items**   Section ③ reports **extraordinary gains and losses,** which are those that are *both unusual* and *infrequent.* An **unusual gain or loss** is abnormal or otherwise unrelated to the company's regular activities and environment. An **infrequent gain or loss** is not expected to recur given the company's operating environment. Reporting extraordinary items in a separate category helps users predict future performance, absent the effects of extraordinary items. Items usually considered extraordinary include (1) expropriation (taking away) of property by a foreign government, (2) condemning of property by a domestic government body, (3) prohibition against using an asset by a newly enacted law, and (4) losses and gains from an unusual and infrequent calamity ("act of God"). Items *not* considered extraordinary include (1) write-downs of inventories and write-offs of receivables, (2) gains and losses from disposing of segments, and (3) financial effects of labor strikes.

**EXHIBIT 17A.1**

Income Statement (all-inclusive) for a Corporation

**ComUS**
**Income Statement**
**For Year Ended December 31, 2011**

| | | |
|---|---:|---:|
| Net sales | | $8,478,000 |
| **Operating expenses** | | |
| Cost of goods sold | $5,950,000 | |
| Depreciation expense | 35,000 | |
| Other selling, general, and administrative expenses | 515,000 | |
| Interest expense | 20,000 | |
| ① Total operating expenses | | (6,520,000) |
| **Other gains (losses)** | | |
| Loss on plant relocation | | (45,000) |
| Gain on sale of surplus land | | 72,000 |
| Income from continuing operations before taxes | | 1,985,000 |
| Income taxes expense | | (595,500) |
| Income from continuing operations | | 1,389,500 |
| | | |
| **Discontinued segment** | | |
| ② Income from operating Division A (net of $180,000 taxes) | 420,000 | |
| Loss on disposal of Division A (net of $66,000 tax benefit) | (154,000) | 266,000 |
| Income before extraordinary items | | 1,655,500 |
| | | |
| **Extraordinary items** | | |
| ③ Gain on land expropriated by state (net of $85,200 taxes) | 198,800 | |
| Loss from earthquake damage (net of $270,000 tax benefit) | (630,000) | (431,200) |
| Net income | | $1,224,300 |
| | | |
| **Earnings per common share (200,000 outstanding shares)** | | |
| Income from continuing operations | | $ 6.95 |
| ④ Discontinued operations | | 1.33 |
| Income before extraordinary items | | 8.28 |
| Extraordinary items | | (2.16) |
| Net income (basic earnings per share) | | $ 6.12 |

Gains and losses that are neither unusual nor infrequent are reported as part of continuing operations. Gains and losses that are *either* unusual *or* infrequent, but *not* both, are reported as part of continuing operations *but* after the normal revenues and expenses.

 **Decision Maker**     Answer — p. 713

**Small Business Owner**   You own an orange grove near Jacksonville, Florida. A bad frost destroys about one-half of your oranges. You are currently preparing an income statement for a bank loan. Can you claim the loss of oranges as extraordinary? ■

**Earnings per Share**   The final section ④ of the income statement in Exhibit 17A.1 reports earnings per share for each of the three subcategories of income (continuing operations, discontinued segments, and extraordinary items) when they exist. Earnings per share is discussed in Chapter 13.

**Changes in Accounting Principles**   The *consistency concept* directs a company to apply the same accounting principles across periods. Yet a company can change from one acceptable accounting principle (such as FIFO, LIFO, or weighted-average) to another as long as the change improves the usefulness of information in its financial statements. A footnote would describe the accounting change and why it is an improvement.

Changes in accounting principles require retrospective application to prior periods' financial statements. *Retrospective application* involves applying a different accounting principle to prior periods as if that principle had always been used. Retrospective application enhances the consistency of financial information between periods, which improves the usefulness of information, especially with comparative

**Point:** Changes in principles are sometimes required when new accounting standards are issued.

analyses. (Prior to 2005, the cumulative effect of changes in accounting principles was recognized in net income in the period of the change.) Accounting standards also require that *a change in depreciation, amortization, or depletion method for long-term operating assets is accounted for as a change in accounting estimate*—that is, prospectively over current and future periods. This reflects the notion that an entity should change its depreciation, amortization, or depletion method only with changes in estimated asset benefits, the pattern of benefit usage, or information about those benefits.

## Quick Check                                                              Answers — p. 713

13. Which of the following is an extraordinary item? (*a*) a settlement paid to a customer injured while using the company's product, (*b*) a loss to a plant from damages caused by a meteorite, or (*c*) a loss from selling old equipment.
14. Identify the four major sections of an income statement that are potentially reportable.
15. A company using FIFO for the past 15 years decides to switch to LIFO. The effect of this event on prior years' net income is (*a*) reported as if the new method had always been used; (*b*) ignored because it is a change in an accounting estimate; or (*c*) reported on the current year income statement.

# Summary

**C1** **Explain the purpose and identify the building blocks of analysis.** The purpose of financial statement analysis is to help users make better business decisions. Internal users want information to improve company efficiency and effectiveness in providing products and services. External users want information to make better and more informed decisions in pursuing their goals. The common goals of all users are to evaluate a company's (1) past and current performance, (2) current financial position, and (3) future performance and risk. Financial statement analysis focuses on four "building blocks" of analysis: (1) liquidity and efficiency—ability to meet short-term obligations and efficiently generate revenues; (2) solvency—ability to generate future revenues and meet long-term obligations; (3) profitability—ability to provide financial rewards sufficient to attract and retain financing; and (4) market prospects—ability to generate positive market expectations.

**C2** **Describe standards for comparisons in analysis.** Standards for comparisons include (1) intracompany—prior performance and relations between financial items for the company under analysis; (2) competitor—one or more direct competitors of the company; (3) industry—industry statistics; and (4) guidelines (rules of thumb)—general standards developed from past experiences and personal judgments.

**A1** **Summarize and report results of analysis.** A financial statement analysis report is often organized around the building blocks of analysis. A good report separates interpretations and conclusions of analysis from the information underlying them. An analysis report often consists of six sections: (1) executive summary, (2) analysis overview, (3) evidential matter, (4) assumptions, (5) key factors, and (6) inferences.

**A2ᴬ** **Explain the form and assess the content of a complete income statement.** An income statement has four *potential* sections: (1) continuing operations, (2) discontinued segments, (3) extraordinary items, and (4) earnings per share.

**P1** **Explain and apply methods of horizontal analysis.** Horizontal analysis is a tool to evaluate changes in data across time. Two important tools of horizontal analysis are comparative statements and trend analysis. Comparative statements show amounts for two or more successive periods, often with changes disclosed in both absolute and percent terms. Trend analysis is used to reveal important changes occurring from one period to the next.

**P2** **Describe and apply methods of vertical analysis.** Vertical analysis is a tool to evaluate each financial statement item or group of items in terms of a base amount. Two tools of vertical analysis are common-size statements and graphical analyses. Each item in common-size statements is expressed as a percent of a base amount. For the balance sheet, the base amount is usually total assets, and for the income statement, it is usually sales.

**P3** **Define and apply ratio analysis.** Ratio analysis provides clues to and symptoms of underlying conditions. Ratios, properly interpreted, identify areas requiring further investigation. A ratio expresses a mathematical relation between two quantities such as a percent, rate, or proportion. Ratios can be organized into the building blocks of analysis: (1) liquidity and efficiency, (2) solvency, (3) profitability, and (4) market prospects.

## Guidance Answers to **Decision Maker**

**Auditor**   The *joint relation* referred to is the combined increase in sales and the decrease in expenses yielding more than a 5% increase in income. Both *individual* accounts (sales and expenses) yield percent changes within the ±5% acceptable range. However, a joint

analysis suggests a different picture. For example, consider a joint analysis using the profit margin ratio. The client's profit margin is 11.46% ($206,000 − $182,400/$206,000) for the current year compared with 5.0% ($200,000 − $190,000/$200,000) for the prior year—yielding a 129% increase in profit margin! This is what concerns the partner, and it suggests expanding audit tests to verify or refute the client's figures.

**Banker** Your decision on the loan application is positive for at least two reasons. First, the current ratio suggests a strong ability to meet short-term obligations. Second, current assets of $160,000 and a current ratio of 4:1 imply current liabilities of $40,000 (one-fourth of current assets) and a working capital excess of $120,000. This working capital excess is 60% of the loan amount. However, if the application is for a 10-year loan, our decision is less optimistic. The

current ratio and working capital suggest a good safety margin, but indications of inefficiency in operations exist. In particular, a 4:1 current ratio is more than double its key competitors' ratio. This is characteristic of inefficient asset use.

**Small Business Owner** The frost loss is probably not extraordinary. Jacksonville experiences enough recurring frost damage to make it difficult to argue this event is both unusual and infrequent. Still, you want to highlight the frost loss and hope the bank views this uncommon event separately from continuing operations.

## Guidance Answers to Quick Checks

1. General-purpose financial statements are intended for a variety of users interested in a company's financial condition and performance—users without the power to require specialized financial reports to meet their specific needs.

2. General-purpose financial statements include the income statement, balance sheet, statement of stockholders' (owners') equity, and statement of cash flows plus the notes related to these statements.

3. *a*

4. Data from one or more direct competitors are usually preferred for comparative purposes.

5. *d*

6. Percents on comparative income statements show the increase or decrease in each item from one period to the next. On common-size comparative income statements, each item is shown as a percent of net sales for that period.

7. *c*

8. (*a*) ($820,000 + $240,000 + $470,000)/
   ($350,000 + $180,000) = 2.9 to 1.

   (*b*) ($820,000 + $240,000)/($350,000 + $180,000) = 2:1.

9. (*a*) $2,500,000/[($290,000 + $240,000)/2] = 9.43 times.
   (*b*) ($290,000/$2,500,000) × 365 = 42 days.
   (*c*) $750,000/[($530,000 + $470,000)/2] = 1.5 times.
   (*d*) ($530,000/$750,000) × 365 = 258 days.

10. *c*

11. *b*

12. $\text{Profit margin} \times \dfrac{\text{Total asset}}{\text{turnover}} = \dfrac{\text{Return on}}{\text{total assets}}$

    $\dfrac{\$945,000}{\$8,500,000} \quad \times \quad 1.8 \quad = \quad 20\%$

13. (*b*)

14. The four (potentially reportable) major sections are income from continuing operations, discontinued segments, extraordinary items, and earnings per share.

15. (*a*); known as retrospective application.

## Multiple Choice Quiz          Answers on p. 729          mhhe.com/wildFAP20e

Additional Quiz Questions are available at the book's Website.

1. A company's sales in 2010 were $300,000 and in 2011 were $351,000. Using 2010 as the base year, the sales trend percent for 2011 is:
   **a.** 17%
   **b.** 85%
   **c.** 100%
   **d.** 117%
   **e.** 48%

Use the following information for questions 2 through 5.

### GALLOWAY COMPANY
### Balance Sheet
### December 31, 2011

**Assets**

| | |
|---|---|
| Cash . . . . . . . . . . . . . . . . . . . . . . . . | $ 86,000 |
| Accounts receivable . . . . . . . . . . . . | 76,000 |
| Merchandise inventory . . . . . . . . . . | 122,000 |
| Prepaid insurance . . . . . . . . . . . . . . | 12,000 |
| Long-term investments . . . . . . . . . . | 98,000 |
| Plant assets, net . . . . . . . . . . . . . . . . | 436,000 |
| Total assets . . . . . . . . . . . . . . . . . . | $830,000 |

**Liabilities and Equity**

| | |
|---|---|
| Current liabilities . . . . . . . . . . . . . . . | $124,000 |
| Long-term liabilities . . . . . . . . . . . . . | 90,000 |
| Common stock . . . . . . . . . . . . . . . . | 300,000 |
| Retained earnings . . . . . . . . . . . . . . | 316,000 |
| Total liabilities and equity . . . . . . . . | $830,000 |

**2.** What is Galloway Company's current ratio?
  **a.** 0.69
  **b.** 1.31
  **c.** 3.88
  **d.** 6.69
  **e.** 2.39

**3.** What is Galloway Company's acid-test ratio?
  **a.** 2.39
  **b.** 0.69
  **c.** 1.31
  **d.** 6.69
  **e.** 3.88

**4.** What is Galloway Company's debt ratio?
  **a.** 25.78%
  **b.** 100.00%
  **c.** 74.22%
  **d.** 137.78%
  **e.** 34.74%

**5.** What is Galloway Company's equity ratio?
  **a.** 25.78%
  **b.** 100.00%
  **c.** 34.74%
  **d.** 74.22%
  **e.** 137.78%

---

<sup>A</sup> *Superscript letter A denotes assignments based on Appendix 17A.*

🛈 Icon denotes assignments that involve decision making.

## Discussion Questions

**1.** What is the difference between comparative financial statements and common-size comparative statements?

**2.** Which items are usually assigned a 100% value on (*a*) a common-size balance sheet and (*b*) a common-size income statement?

**3.** Explain the difference between financial reporting and financial statements.

**4.** 🛈 What three factors would influence your evaluation as to whether a company's current ratio is good or bad?

**5.** 🛈 Suggest several reasons why a 2:1 current ratio might not be adequate for a particular company.

**6.** 🛈 Why is working capital given special attention in the process of analyzing balance sheets?

**7.** 🛈 What does the number of days' sales uncollected indicate?

**8.** 🛈 What does a relatively high accounts receivable turnover indicate about a company's short-term liquidity?

**9.** 🛈 Why is a company's capital structure, as measured by debt and equity ratios, important to financial statement analysts?

**10.** 🛈 How does inventory turnover provide information about a company's short-term liquidity?

**11.** 🛈 What ratios would you compute to evaluate management performance?

**12.** 🛈 Why would a company's return on total assets be different from its return on common stockholders' equity?

**13.** Where on the income statement does a company report an unusual gain not expected to occur more often than once every two years or so?

**14.** Use **Research In Motion**'s financial statements in Appendix A to compute its return on total assets for **RIM** fiscal years ended February 27, 2010, and February 28, 2009. Total assets at March 1, 2008, were $5,511,187 (in thousands).

**15.** Refer to **Palm**'s financial statements in Appendix A to compute its equity ratio as of May 31, 2009 and **Palm** May 31, 2008.

**16.** Refer to **Nokia**'s financial statements in Appendix A. Compute its debt ratio as of December 31, **NOKIA** 2009, and December 31, 2008.

**17.** Refer to **Apple**'s financial statements in Appendix A. Compute its profit margin for the fiscal year **Apple** ended September 26, 2009.

**connect**

Which of the following items (1) through (9) are part of financial reporting but are *not* included as part of general-purpose financial statements? (1) stock price information and analysis, (2) statement of cash flows, (3) management discussion and analysis of financial performance, (4) income statement, (5) company news releases, (6) balance sheet, (7) financial statement notes, (8) statement of shareholders' equity, (9) prospectus.

**QUICK STUDY**

**QS 17-1**
Financial reporting  **C1**

What are four possible standards of comparison used to analyze financial statement ratios? Which of these is generally considered to be the most useful? Which one is least likely to provide a good basis for comparison?

**QS 17-2**
Standard of comparison  **C2**

Use the following information for Tipster Corporation to determine the 2010 and 2011 trend percents for net sales using 2010 as the base year.

**QS 17-3**
Trend percents
**P1**

| ($ thousands) | 2011 | 2010 |
|---|---|---|
| Net sales ............... | $201,600 | $114,800 |
| Cost of goods sold ........ | 109,200 | 60,200 |

Refer to the information in QS 17-3. Use that information for Tipster Corporation to determine the 2010 and 2011 common-size percents for cost of goods sold using net sales as the base.

**QS 17-4**
Common-size analysis  **P2**

Compute the annual dollar changes and percent changes for each of the following accounts.

**QS 17-5**
Horizontal analysis
**P1**

| | 2011 | 2010 |
|---|---|---|
| Short-term investments ........ | $217,800 | $165,000 |
| Accounts receivable ........... | 42,120 | 48,000 |
| Notes payable ............... | 57,000 | 0 |

For each ratio listed, identify whether the change in ratio value from 2010 to 2011 is usually regarded as favorable or unfavorable.

**QS 17-6**
Ratio interpretation
**P3**

| Ratio | 2011 | 2010 | Ratio | 2011 | 2010 |
|---|---|---|---|---|---|
| 1. Profit margin | 8% | 6% | 5. Accounts receivable turnover | 5.4 | 6.6 |
| 2. Debt ratio | 45% | 40% | 6. Basic earnings per share | $1.24 | $1.20 |
| 3. Gross margin | 33% | 45% | 7. Inventory turnover | 3.5 | 3.3 |
| 4. Acid-test ratio | 0.99 | 1.10 | 8. Dividend yield | 1% | 0.8% |

The following information is available for Silverado Company and Titan Company, similar firms operating in the same industry. Write a half-page report comparing Silverado and Titan using the available information. Your discussion should include their ability to meet current obligations and to use current assets efficiently.

**QS 17-7**
Analysis of short-term financial condition
**A1**

Microsoft Excel - Book1
File  Edit  View  Insert  Format  Tools  Data  Accounting  Window  Help

| | Silverado | | | Titan | | |
|---|---|---|---|---|---|---|
| | 2012 | 2011 | 2010 | 2012 | 2011 | 2010 |
| Current ratio | 1.6 | 1.7 | 2.0 | 3.1 | 2.6 | 1.8 |
| Acid-test ratio | 0.9 | 1.0 | 1.1 | 2.7 | 2.4 | 1.5 |
| Accounts receivable turnover | 29.5 | 24.2 | 28.2 | 15.4 | 14.2 | 15.0 |
| Merchandise inventory turnover | 23.2 | 20.9 | 16.1 | 13.5 | 12.0 | 11.6 |
| Working capital | $60,000 | $48,000 | $42,000 | $121,000 | $93,000 | $68,000 |

Sheet1 / Sheet2 / Sheet3 /

**Team Project:** Assume that the two companies apply for a one-year loan from the team. Identify additional information the companies must provide before the team can make a loan decision.

**QS 17-8<sup>A</sup>**

Error adjustments

A2

A review of the notes payable files discovers that three years ago the company reported the entire amount of a payment (principal and interest) on an installment note payable as interest expense. This mistake had a material effect on the amount of income in that year. How should the correction be reported in the current year financial statements?

---

**QS 17-9**

International ratio analysis

C2

Answer each of the following related to international accounting and analysis.

a.  Identify an advantage to using horizontal and vertical analyses when examining companies reporting under different currencies.

b.  Identify a limitation to using ratio analysis when examining companies reporting under different accounting systems such as IFRS versus U.S. GAAP.

---

Mc Graw Hill **connect**™

# EXERCISES

**Exercise 17-1**

Building blocks of analysis

C1

Match the ratio to the building block of financial statement analysis to which it best relates.

**A.** Liquidity and efficiency        **C.** Profitability

**B.** Solvency                         **D.** Market prospects

**1.** _____ Book value per common share        **6.** _____ Gross margin ratio

**2.** _____ Days' sales in inventory            **7.** _____ Acid-test ratio

**3.** _____ Accounts receivable turnover        **8.** _____ Equity ratio

**4.** _____ Debt-to-equity                       **9.** _____ Return on total assets

**5.** _____ Times interest earned                **10.** _____ Dividend yield

---

**Exercise 17-2**

Identifying financial ratios

C2

**1.** Which two short-term liquidity ratios measure how frequently a company collects its accounts?

**2.** What measure reflects the difference between current assets and current liabilities?

**3.** Which two ratios are key components in measuring a company's operating efficiency? Which ratio summarizes these two components?

---

**Exercise 17-3**

Computation and analysis of trend percents

P1

Compute trend percents for the following accounts, using 2009 as the base year. State whether the situation as revealed by the trends appears to be favorable or unfavorable for each account.

|  | 2013 | 2012 | 2011 | 2010 | 2009 |
|---|---|---|---|---|---|
| Sales . . . . . . . . . . . . . . . . . . . . . | $283,880 | $271,800 | $253,680 | $235,560 | $151,000 |
| Cost of goods sold . . . . . . . . . | 129,200 | 123,080 | 116,280 | 107,440 | 68,000 |
| Accounts receivable . . . . . . . . | 19,100 | 18,300 | 17,400 | 16,200 | 10,000 |

---

**Exercise 17-4**

Determination of income effects from common-size and trend percents

P1  P2

Common-size and trend percents for Aziz Company's sales, cost of goods sold, and expenses follow. Determine whether net income increased, decreased, or remained unchanged in this three-year period.

|  | Common-Size Percents | | | Trend Percents | | |
|---|---|---|---|---|---|---|
|  | 2012 | 2011 | 2010 | 2012 | 2011 | 2010 |
| Sales . . . . . . . . . . . . . . . . . . | 100.0% | 100.0% | 100.0% | 104.4% | 103.2% | 100.0% |
| Cost of goods sold . . . . . . . . | 62.4 | 60.9 | 58.1 | 102.0 | 108.1 | 100.0 |
| Total expenses . . . . . . . . . . . | 14.3 | 13.8 | 14.1 | 105.9 | 101.0 | 100.0 |

Express the following comparative income statements in common-size percents and assess whether or not this company's situation has improved in the most recent year.

**Exercise 17-5**
Common-size percent computation and interpretation

P2

| GERALDO CORPORATION Comparative Income Statements For Years Ended December 31, 2011 and 2010 | | |
|---|---|---|
| | **2011** | **2010** |
| Sales .................... | $720,000 | $535,000 |
| Cost of goods sold ......... | 475,200 | 280,340 |
| Gross profit .............. | 244,800 | 254,660 |
| Operating expenses ........ | 151,200 | 103,790 |
| Net income .............. | $ 93,600 | $150,870 |

Rolf Company and Kent Company are similar firms that operate in the same industry. Kent began operations in 2011 and Rolf in 2008. In 2013, both companies pay 7% interest on their debt to creditors. The following additional information is available.

**Exercise 17-6**
Analysis of efficiency and financial leverage

A1

| | **Rolf Company** | | | **Kent Company** | | |
|---|---|---|---|---|---|---|
| | **2013** | **2012** | **2011** | **2013** | **2012** | **2011** |
| Total asset turnover .......... | 3.0 | 2.7 | 2.9 | 1.6 | 1.4 | 1.1 |
| Return on total assets ........ | 8.9% | 9.5% | 8.7% | 5.8% | 5.5% | 5.2% |
| Profit margin ratio ........... | 2.3% | 2.4% | 2.2% | 2.7% | 2.9% | 2.8% |
| Sales ..................... | $400,000 | $370,000 | $386,000 | $200,000 | $160,000 | $100,000 |

Write a half-page report comparing Rolf and Kent using the available information. Your analysis should include their ability to use assets efficiently to produce profits. Also comment on their success in employing financial leverage in 2013.

Sanderson Company's year-end balance sheets follow. Express the balance sheets in common-size percents. Round amounts to the nearest one-tenth of a percent. Analyze and comment on the results.

**Exercise 17-7**
Common-size percents

P2

| At December 31 | 2012 | 2011 | 2010 |
|---|---|---|---|
| **Assets** | | | |
| Cash ...................................... | $ 30,800 | $ 35,625 | $ 36,800 |
| Accounts receivable, net ................... | 88,500 | 62,500 | 49,200 |
| Merchandise inventory .................... | 111,500 | 82,500 | 53,000 |
| Prepaid expenses ....................... | 9,700 | 9,375 | 4,000 |
| Plant assets, net ......................... | 277,500 | 255,000 | 229,500 |
| Total assets ............................ | $518,000 | $445,000 | $372,500 |
| **Liabilities and Equity** | | | |
| Accounts payable ....................... | $128,900 | $ 75,250 | $ 49,250 |
| Long-term notes payable secured by mortgages on plant assets .............. | 97,500 | 102,500 | 82,500 |
| Common stock, $10 par value ............. | 162,500 | 162,500 | 162,500 |
| Retained earnings ....................... | 129,100 | 104,750 | 78,250 |
| Total liabilities and equity ................. | $518,000 | $445,000 | $372,500 |

Refer to Sanderson Company's balance sheets in Exercise 17-7. Analyze its year-end short-term liquidity position at the end of 2012, 2011, and 2010 by computing (1) the current ratio and (2) the acid-test ratio. Comment on the ratio results. (Round ratio amounts to two decimals.)

**Exercise 17-8**
Liquidity analysis

P3

**Exercise 17-9**
Liquidity analysis and interpretation

**P3**

Refer to the Sanderson Company information in Exercise 17-7. The company's income statements for the years ended December 31, 2012 and 2011, follow. Assume that all sales are on credit and then compute: (1) days' sales uncollected, (2) accounts receivable turnover, (3) inventory turnover, and (4) days' sales in inventory. Comment on the changes in the ratios from 2011 to 2012. (Round amounts to one decimal.)

| For Year Ended December 31 | 2012 | | 2011 | |
|---|---|---|---|---|
| Sales .......................... | | $672,500 | | $530,000 |
| Cost of goods sold .............. | $410,225 | | $344,500 | |
| Other operating expenses ........ | 208,550 | | 133,980 | |
| Interest expense ................ | 11,100 | | 12,300 | |
| Income taxes ................... | 8,525 | | 7,845 | |
| Total costs and expenses ......... | | 638,400 | | 498,625 |
| Net income .................... | | $ 34,100 | | $ 31,375 |
| Earnings per share .............. | | $    2.10 | | $    1.93 |

**Exercise 17-10**
Risk and capital structure analysis  **P3**

Refer to the Sanderson Company information in Exercises 17-7 and 17-9. Compare the company's long-term risk and capital structure positions at the end of 2012 and 2011 by computing these ratios: (1) debt and equity ratios, (2) debt-to-equity ratio, and (3) times interest earned. Comment on these ratio results.

**Exercise 17-11**
Efficiency and profitability analysis  **P3**

Refer to Sanderson Company's financial information in Exercises 17-7 and 17-9. Evaluate the company's efficiency and profitability by computing the following for 2012 and 2011: (1) profit margin ratio, (2) total asset turnover, and (3) return on total assets. Comment on these ratio results.

**Exercise 17-12**
Profitability analysis

**P3**

Refer to Sanderson Company's financial information in Exercises 17-7 and 17-9. Additional information about the company follows. To help evaluate the company's profitability, compute and interpret the following ratios for 2012 and 2011: (1) return on common stockholders' equity, (2) price-earnings ratio on December 31, and (3) dividend yield.

| | |
|---|---|
| Common stock market price, December 31, 2012 ........ | $15.00 |
| Common stock market price, December 31, 2011 ........ | 14.00 |
| Annual cash dividends per share in 2012 ............... | 0.30 |
| Annual cash dividends per share in 2011 ............... | 0.15 |

**Exercise 17-13ᴬ**
Income statement categories

**A2**

In 2011, Jin Merchandising, Inc., sold its interest in a chain of retail outlets, taking the company completely out of the retailing business. The company still operates its wholesale outlets. A listing of the major sections of an income statement follows:

**A.** Income (loss) from continuing operations

**B.** Income (loss) from operating, or gain (loss) from disposing, a discontinued segment

**C.** Extraordinary gain (loss)

Indicate where each of the following income-related items for this company appears on its 2011 income statement by writing the letter of the appropriate section in the blank beside each item.

| Section | Item | Debit | Credit |
|---|---|---|---|
| _____ | 1. Net sales ................................... | | $3,000,000 |
| _____ | 2. Gain on state's condemnation of company property (net of tax) ............. | | 330,000 |
| _____ | 3. Salaries expense .......................... | $ 640,000 | |
| _____ | 4. Income taxes expense .................... | 117,000 | |
| _____ | 5. Depreciation expense .................... | 432,500 | |
| _____ | 6. Gain on sale of retail business segment (net of tax) ..................... | | 875,000 |
| _____ | 7. Loss from operating retail business segment (net of tax) ..................... | 544,000 | |
| _____ | 8. Cost of goods sold ....................... | 1,580,000 | |

Use the financial data for Jin Merchandising, Inc., in Exercise 17-13 to prepare its income statement for calendar year 2011. (Ignore the earnings per share section.)

**Exercise 17-14^A**
Income statement presentation
A2

**Nintendo Company, Ltd.**, reports the following financial information as of, or for the year ended, March 31, 2008. Nintendo reports its financial statements in both Japanese yen and U.S. dollars as shown (amounts in millions).

**Exercise 17-15**
Ratio analysis under different currencies
P3

| | | |
|---|---|---|
| Current assets | ¥1,646,834 | $16,468.348 |
| Total assets | 1,802,490 | 18,024.903 |
| Current liabilities | 567,222 | 5,672.229 |
| Net sales | 1,672,423 | 16,724.230 |
| Net income | 257,342 | 2,573.426 |

1. Compute Nintendo's current ratio, net profit margin, and sales-to-total-assets using the financial information reported in (a) yen and (b) dollars.
2. What can we conclude from a review of the results for part 1?

**connect**

Selected comparative financial statements of Bennington Company follow.

**PROBLEM SET A**

**Problem 17-1A**
Ratios, common-size statements, and trend percents
P1  P2  P3

**eXcel**
mhhe.com/wildFAP20e

**BENNINGTON COMPANY**
**Comparative Income Statements**
**For Years Ended December 31, 2012, 2011, and 2010**

| | 2012 | 2011 | 2010 |
|---|---|---|---|
| Sales | $444,000 | $340,000 | $236,000 |
| Cost of goods sold | 267,288 | 212,500 | 151,040 |
| Gross profit | 176,712 | 127,500 | 84,960 |
| Selling expenses | 62,694 | 46,920 | 31,152 |
| Administrative expenses | 40,137 | 29,920 | 19,470 |
| Total expenses | 102,831 | 76,840 | 50,622 |
| Income before taxes | 73,881 | 50,660 | 34,338 |
| Income taxes | 13,764 | 10,370 | 6,962 |
| Net income | $ 60,117 | $ 40,290 | $ 27,376 |

**BENNINGTON COMPANY**
**Comparative Balance Sheets**
**December 31, 2012, 2011, and 2010**

| | 2012 | 2011 | 2010 |
|---|---|---|---|
| **Assets** | | | |
| Current assets | $ 48,480 | $ 37,924 | $ 50,648 |
| Long-term investments | 0 | 500 | 3,720 |
| Plant assets, net | 90,000 | 96,000 | 57,000 |
| Total assets | $138,480 | $134,424 | $111,368 |
| **Liabilities and Equity** | | | |
| Current liabilities | $ 20,200 | $ 19,960 | $ 19,480 |
| Common stock | 72,000 | 72,000 | 54,000 |
| Other paid-in capital | 9,000 | 9,000 | 6,000 |
| Retained earnings | 37,280 | 33,464 | 31,888 |
| Total liabilities and equity | $138,480 | $134,424 | $111,368 |

*Required*

1. Compute each year's current ratio. (Round ratio amounts to one decimal.)
2. Express the income statement data in common-size percents. (Round percents to two decimals.)

**Check**   (3) 2012, Total assets trend, 124.34%

**3.** Express the balance sheet data in trend percents with 2010 as the base year. (Round percents to two decimals.)

*Analysis Component*

**4.** Comment on any significant relations revealed by the ratios and percents computed.

**Problem 17-2A**

Calculation and analysis of trend percents

A1   P1

Selected comparative financial statements of Sugo Company follow.

| SUGO COMPANY Comparative Income Statements For Years Ended December 31, 2012–2006 | | | | | | | |
|---|---|---|---|---|---|---|---|
| ($ thousands) | 2012 | 2011 | 2010 | 2009 | 2008 | 2007 | 2006 |
| Sales . . . . . . . . . . . . . . . . . . . . | $1,594 | $1,396 | $1,270 | $1,164 | $1,086 | $1,010 | $828 |
| Cost of goods sold . . . . . . . . | 1,146 | 932 | 802 | 702 | 652 | 610 | 486 |
| Gross profit . . . . . . . . . . . . . . | 448 | 464 | 468 | 462 | 434 | 400 | 342 |
| Operating expenses . . . . . . . . | 340 | 266 | 244 | 180 | 156 | 154 | 128 |
| Net income . . . . . . . . . . . . . . | $ 108 | $ 198 | $ 224 | $ 282 | $ 278 | $ 246 | $214 |

| SUGO COMPANY Comparative Balance Sheets December 31, 2012–2006 | | | | | | | |
|---|---|---|---|---|---|---|---|
| ($ thousands) | 2012 | 2011 | 2010 | 2009 | 2008 | 2007 | 2006 |
| **Assets** | | | | | | | |
| Cash . . . . . . . . . . . . . . . . . . . . . . | $ 68 | $ 88 | $ 92 | $ 94 | $ 98 | $ 96 | $ 99 |
| Accounts receivable, net . . . . . . . . . | 480 | 504 | 456 | 350 | 308 | 292 | 206 |
| Merchandise inventory . . . . . . . . . . | 1,738 | 1,264 | 1,104 | 932 | 836 | 710 | 515 |
| Other current assets . . . . . . . . . . . . | 46 | 42 | 24 | 44 | 38 | 38 | 19 |
| Long-term investments . . . . . . . . . . | 0 | 0 | 0 | 136 | 136 | 136 | 136 |
| Plant assets, net . . . . . . . . . . . . . . . | 2,120 | 2,114 | 1,852 | 1,044 | 1,078 | 960 | 825 |
| Total assets . . . . . . . . . . . . . . . . . . | $4,452 | $4,012 | $3,528 | $2,600 | $2,494 | $2,232 | $1,800 |
| **Liabilities and Equity** | | | | | | | |
| Current liabilities . . . . . . . . . . . . . . | $1,120 | $ 942 | $ 618 | $ 514 | $ 446 | $ 422 | $ 272 |
| Long-term liabilities . . . . . . . . . . . . | 1,194 | 1,040 | 1,012 | 470 | 480 | 520 | 390 |
| Common stock . . . . . . . . . . . . . . . . | 1,000 | 1,000 | 1,000 | 840 | 840 | 640 | 640 |
| Other paid-in capital . . . . . . . . . . . . | 250 | 250 | 250 | 180 | 180 | 160 | 160 |
| Retained earnings . . . . . . . . . . . . . . | 888 | 780 | 648 | 596 | 548 | 490 | 338 |
| Total liabilities and equity . . . . . . . . | $4,452 | $4,012 | $3,528 | $2,600 | $2,494 | $2,232 | $1,800 |

*Required*

**Check**   (1) 2012, Total assets trend, 247.3%

**1.** Compute trend percents for all components of both statements using 2006 as the base year. (Round percents to one decimal.)

*Analysis Component*

**2.** Analyze and comment on the financial statements and trend percents from part 1.

**Problem 17-3A**

Transactions, working capital, and liquidity ratios

P3

mhhe.com/wildFAP20e

Park Corporation began the month of May with $650,000 of current assets, a current ratio of 2.50:1, and an acid-test ratio of 1.10:1. During the month, it completed the following transactions (the company uses a perpetual inventory system).

May   2   Purchased $75,000 of merchandise inventory on credit.
     8   Sold merchandise inventory that cost $58,000 for $103,000 cash.
   10   Collected $19,000 cash on an account receivable.
   15   Paid $21,000 cash to settle an account payable.

17 Wrote off a $3,000 bad debt against the Allowance for Doubtful Accounts account.
22 Declared a $1 per share cash dividend on its 40,000 shares of outstanding common stock.
26 Paid the dividend declared on May 22.
27 Borrowed $75,000 cash by giving the bank a 30-day, 10% note.
28 Borrowed $90,000 cash by signing a long-term secured note.
29 Used the $165,000 cash proceeds from the notes to buy new machinery.

**Check** May 22: Current ratio, 2.12; Acid-test ratio, 1.04

May 29: Current ratio, 1.82; Working capital, $320,000

### Required

Prepare a table showing Park's (1) current ratio, (2) acid-test ratio, and (3) working capital, after each transaction. Round ratios to two decimals.

---

Selected year-end financial statements of McCord Corporation follow. (All sales were on credit; selected balance sheet amounts at December 31, 2010, were inventory, $32,400; total assets, $182,400; common stock, $90,000; and retained earnings, $31,300.)

**Problem 17-4A**
Calculation of financial statement ratios

P3

mhhe.com/wildFAP20e

| McCORD CORPORATION Income Statement For Year Ended December 31, 2011 | |
|---|---:|
| Sales ..................... | $348,600 |
| Cost of goods sold .......... | 229,150 |
| Gross profit ................ | 119,450 |
| Operating expenses ......... | 52,500 |
| Interest expense ........... | 3,100 |
| Income before taxes ........ | 63,850 |
| Income taxes .............. | 15,800 |
| Net income .............. | $ 48,050 |

| McCORD CORPORATION Balance Sheet December 31, 2011 | | | |
|---|---:|---|---:|
| **Assets** | | **Liabilities and Equity** | |
| Cash ........................ | $ 9,000 | Accounts payable .................... | $ 16,500 |
| Short-term investments .......... | 7,400 | Accrued wages payable ................ | 2,200 |
| Accounts receivable, net .......... | 28,200 | Income taxes payable ................ | 2,300 |
| Notes receivable (trade)* ........ | 3,500 | Long-term note payable, secured | |
| Merchandise inventory ........... | 31,150 |   by mortgage on plant assets .......... | 62,400 |
| Prepaid expenses ............... | 1,650 | Common stock .................... | 90,000 |
| Plant assets, net ................ | 152,300 | Retained earnings .................... | 59,800 |
| Total assets .................... | $233,200 | Total liabilities and equity ............. | $233,200 |

* These are short-term notes receivable arising from customer (trade) sales.

### Required

Compute the following: (1) current ratio, (2) acid-test ratio, (3) days' sales uncollected, (4) inventory turnover, (5) days' sales in inventory, (6) debt-to-equity ratio, (7) times interest earned, (8) profit margin ratio, (9) total asset turnover, (10) return on total assets, and (11) return on common stockholders' equity.

**Check** Acid-test ratio, 2.3 to 1; Inventory turnover, 7.2

---

Summary information from the financial statements of two companies competing in the same industry follows.

**Problem 17-5A**
Comparative ratio analysis

A1 P3

|  | Ryan Company | Priest Company |  | Ryan Company | Priest Company |
|---|---|---|---|---|---|
| **Data from the current year-end balance sheets** | | | **Data from the current year's income statement** | | |
| **Assets** | | | Sales . . . . . . . . . . . . . . . . . . . . . . . . . | $660,000 | $780,200 |
| Cash . . . . . . . . . . . . . . . . . . . . . . . . . . . . . | $ 18,500 | $ 33,000 | Cost of goods sold . . . . . . . . . . . . . . . | 485,100 | 532,500 |
| Accounts receivable, net . . . . . . . . . . . . . . . | 36,400 | 56,400 | Interest expense . . . . . . . . . . . . . . . . . | 6,900 | 11,000 |
| Current notes receivable (trade) . . . . . . . . | 8,100 | 6,200 | Income tax expense . . . . . . . . . . . . . . . | 12,800 | 19,300 |
| Merchandise inventory . . . . . . . . . . . . . . . | 83,440 | 131,500 | Net income . . . . . . . . . . . . . . . . . . . . . | 67,770 | 105,000 |
| Prepaid expenses . . . . . . . . . . . . . . . . . . . | 4,000 | 5,950 | Basic earnings per share . . . . . . . . . . . . . | 1.94 | 2.56 |
| Plant assets, net . . . . . . . . . . . . . . . . . . . . | 284,000 | 303,400 | | | |
| Total assets . . . . . . . . . . . . . . . . . . . | $434,440 | $536,450 | | | |
| | | | **Beginning-of-year balance sheet data** | | |
| **Liabilities and Equity** | | | Accounts receivable, net . . . . . . . . . . . . . | $ 28,800 | $ 53,200 |
| Current liabilities . . . . . . . . . . . . . . . . . . . . | $ 60,340 | $ 92,300 | Current notes receivable (trade) . . . . . . . . | 0 | 0 |
| Long-term notes payable . . . . . . . . . . . . . . | 79,800 | 100,000 | Merchandise inventory . . . . . . . . . . . . . . | 54,600 | 106,400 |
| Common stock, $5 par value . . . . . . . . . . . | 175,000 | 205,000 | Total assets . . . . . . . . . . . . . . . . . . . . | 388,000 | 372,500 |
| Retained earnings . . . . . . . . . . . . . . . . . . . | 119,300 | 139,150 | Common stock, $5 par value . . . . . . . . . . . | 175,000 | 205,000 |
| Total liabilities and equity . . . . . . . . . . . . . | $434,440 | $536,450 | Retained earnings . . . . . . . . . . . . . . . . | 94,300 | 90,600 |

**Required**

**Check** (1) Priest: Accounts
receivable turnover, 13.5; Inventory
turnover, 4.5

(2) Ryan: Profit margin,
10.3%; PE, 12.9

1. For both companies compute the (*a*) current ratio, (*b*) acid-test ratio, (*c*) accounts (including notes) receivable turnover, (*d*) inventory turnover, (*e*) days' sales in inventory, and (*f*) days' sales uncollected. Identify the company you consider to be the better short-term credit risk and explain why.

2. For both companies compute the (*a*) profit margin ratio, (*b*) total asset turnover, (*c*) return on total assets, and (*d*) return on common stockholders' equity. Assuming that each company paid cash dividends of $1.50 per share and each company's stock can be purchased at $25 per share, compute their (*e*) price-earnings ratios and (*f*) dividend yields. Identify which company's stock you would recommend as the better investment and explain why.

**Problem 17-6A<sup>A</sup>**
Income statement computations and format

A2

Selected account balances from the adjusted trial balance for Zen Corporation as of its calendar year-end December 31, 2011, follow.

| | Debit | Credit |
|---|---|---|
| a. Income taxes expense . . . . . . . . . . . . . . . . . . . . . . . . . . . . . . . . . . . . . . . . . . . | $ ? | |
| b. Correction of overstatement of prior year's sales (pretax) . . . . . . . . . . . . . . . . . . . . | 17,000 | |
| c. Loss on sale of machinery . . . . . . . . . . . . . . . . . . . . . . . . . . . . . . . . . . . . . . . . | 26,850 | |
| d. Loss from settlement of lawsuit . . . . . . . . . . . . . . . . . . . . . . . . . . . . . . . . . . . . | 24,750 | |
| e. Other operating expenses . . . . . . . . . . . . . . . . . . . . . . . . . . . . . . . . . . . . . . . | 107,400 | |
| f. Accumulated depreciation—Machinery . . . . . . . . . . . . . . . . . . . . . . . . . . . . . . . . | | $ 72,600 |
| g. Gain from settlement of lawsuit . . . . . . . . . . . . . . . . . . . . . . . . . . . . . . . . . . . . | | 45,000 |
| h. Accumulated depreciation—Buildings . . . . . . . . . . . . . . . . . . . . . . . . . . . . . . . . | | 175,500 |
| i. Loss from operating a discontinued segment (pretax) . . . . . . . . . . . . . . . . . . . . . . | 19,250 | |
| j. Gain on insurance recovery of tornado damage (pretax and extraordinary) . . . . . . . . | | 30,120 |
| k. Net sales . . . . . . . . . . . . . . . . . . . . . . . . . . . . . . . . . . . . . . . . . . . . . . . . . . . | | 999,500 |
| l. Depreciation expense—Buildings . . . . . . . . . . . . . . . . . . . . . . . . . . . . . . . . . . . | 53,000 | |
| m. Depreciation expense—Machinery . . . . . . . . . . . . . . . . . . . . . . . . . . . . . . . . . . | 35,000 | |
| n. Gain on sale of discontinued segment's assets (pretax) . . . . . . . . . . . . . . . . . . . . . | | 35,000 |
| o. Accounts payable . . . . . . . . . . . . . . . . . . . . . . . . . . . . . . . . . . . . . . . . . . . . . | | 45,000 |
| p. Interest revenue . . . . . . . . . . . . . . . . . . . . . . . . . . . . . . . . . . . . . . . . . . . . . . | | 15,000 |
| q. Cost of goods sold . . . . . . . . . . . . . . . . . . . . . . . . . . . . . . . . . . . . . . . . . . . . | 483,500 | |

**Required**

Answer each of the following questions by providing supporting computations.

1. Assume that the company's income tax rate is 30% for all items. Identify the tax effects and after-tax amounts of the four items labeled pretax.
2. What is the amount of income from continuing operations before income taxes? What is the amount of the income taxes expense? What is the amount of income from continuing operations?
3. What is the total amount of after-tax income (loss) associated with the discontinued segment?
4. What is the amount of income (loss) before the extraordinary items?
5. What is the amount of net income for the year?

**Check**  (3) $11,025
(4) $241,325
(5) $262,409

---

Selected comparative financial statement information of Sawgrass Corporation follows.

**PROBLEM SET B**

**Problem 17-1B**
Ratios, common-size statements, and trend percents

P1  P2  P3

| SAWGRASS CORPORATION | | | |
|---|---|---|---|
| Comparative Income Statements | | | |
| For Years Ended December 31, 2012, 2011, and 2010 | | | |
|  | 2012 | 2011 | 2010 |
| Sales ......................... | $199,800 | $167,000 | $144,800 |
| Cost of goods sold ............. | 109,890 | 87,175 | 67,200 |
| Gross profit .................... | 89,910 | 79,825 | 77,600 |
| Selling expenses ............... | 23,680 | 20,790 | 19,000 |
| Administrative expenses ......... | 17,760 | 15,610 | 16,700 |
| Total expenses ................ | 41,440 | 36,400 | 35,700 |
| Income before taxes ............ | 48,470 | 43,425 | 41,900 |
| Income taxes .................. | 5,050 | 4,910 | 4,300 |
| Net income ................... | $ 43,420 | $ 38,515 | $ 37,600 |

| SAWGRASS CORPORATION | | | |
|---|---|---|---|
| Comparative Balance Sheets | | | |
| December 31, 2012, 2011, and 2010 | | | |
|  | 2012 | 2011 | 2010 |
| **Assets** | | | |
| Current assets ................... | $ 55,860 | $ 33,660 | $ 37,300 |
| Long-term investments ........... | 0 | 2,700 | 11,600 |
| Plant assets, net ................. | 113,810 | 114,660 | 80,000 |
| Total assets .................... | $169,670 | $151,020 | $128,900 |
| **Liabilities and Equity** | | | |
| Current liabilities ............... | $ 23,370 | $ 20,180 | $ 17,500 |
| Common stock ................. | 47,500 | 47,500 | 38,000 |
| Other paid-in capital ............. | 14,850 | 14,850 | 12,300 |
| Retained earnings ............... | 83,950 | 68,490 | 61,100 |
| Total liabilities and equity ......... | $169,670 | $151,020 | $128,900 |

**Required**

1. Compute each year's current ratio. (Round ratio amounts to one decimal.)
2. Express the income statement data in common-size percents. (Round percents to two decimals.)
3. Express the balance sheet data in trend percents with 2010 as the base year. (Round percents to two decimals.)

**Check**  (3) 2012, Total assets trend, 131.63%

**Analysis Component**

4. Comment on any significant relations revealed by the ratios and percents computed.

**Problem 17-2B**

Calculation and analysis of trend percents

A1  P1

Selected comparative financial statements of Deuce Company follow.

| DEUCE COMPANY | | | | | | | |
|---|---|---|---|---|---|---|---|
| **Comparative Income Statements** | | | | | | | |
| **For Years Ended December 31, 2012–2006** | | | | | | | |
| ($ thousands) | 2012 | 2011 | 2010 | 2009 | 2008 | 2007 | 2006 |
| Sales ..................... | $660 | $710 | $730 | $780 | $840 | $870 | $960 |
| Cost of goods sold ......... | 376 | 390 | 394 | 414 | 440 | 450 | 480 |
| Gross profit .............. | 284 | 320 | 336 | 366 | 400 | 420 | 480 |
| Operating expenses ........ | 184 | 204 | 212 | 226 | 240 | 244 | 250 |
| Net income .............. | $100 | $116 | $124 | $140 | $160 | $176 | $230 |

| DEUCE COMPANY | | | | | | | |
|---|---|---|---|---|---|---|---|
| **Comparative Balance Sheets** | | | | | | | |
| **December 31, 2012–2006** | | | | | | | |
| ($ thousands) | 2012 | 2011 | 2010 | 2009 | 2008 | 2007 | 2006 |
| **Assets** | | | | | | | |
| Cash ...................... | $ 34 | $ 36 | $ 42 | $ 44 | $ 50 | $ 52 | $ 58 |
| Accounts receivable, net ......... | 120 | 126 | 130 | 134 | 140 | 144 | 150 |
| Merchandise inventory .......... | 156 | 162 | 168 | 170 | 176 | 180 | 198 |
| Other current assets ........... | 24 | 24 | 26 | 28 | 28 | 30 | 30 |
| Long-term investments .......... | 26 | 20 | 16 | 100 | 100 | 100 | 100 |
| Plant assets, net ............... | 410 | 414 | 420 | 312 | 320 | 328 | 354 |
| Total assets .................. | $770 | $782 | $802 | $788 | $814 | $834 | $890 |
| **Liabilities and Equity** | | | | | | | |
| Current liabilities .............. | $138 | $146 | $176 | $180 | $200 | $250 | $270 |
| Long-term liabilities ............ | 82 | 110 | 132 | 138 | 184 | 204 | 250 |
| Common stock ................ | 150 | 150 | 150 | 150 | 150 | 150 | 150 |
| Other paid-in capital ............ | 60 | 60 | 60 | 60 | 60 | 60 | 60 |
| Retained earnings ............. | 340 | 316 | 284 | 260 | 220 | 170 | 160 |
| Total liabilities and equity ........ | $770 | $782 | $802 | $788 | $814 | $834 | $890 |

**Required**

**Check**  (1) 2012, Total assets trend, 86.5%

**1.** Compute trend percents for all components of both statements using 2006 as the base year. (Round percents to one decimal.)

*Analysis Component*

**2.** Analyze and comment on the financial statements and trend percents from part 1.

---

**Problem 17-3B**

Transactions, working capital, and liquidity ratios  P3

**Check**  June 1: Current ratio, 3.19; Acid-test ratio, 2.21

Ready Corporation began the month of June with $280,000 of current assets, a current ratio of 2.8:1, and an acid-test ratio of 1.2:1. During the month, it completed the following transactions (the company uses a perpetual inventory system).

| June | 1 | Sold merchandise inventory that cost $62,000 for $101,000 cash. |
|---|---|---|
| | 3 | Collected $78,000 cash on an account receivable. |
| | 5 | Purchased $130,000 of merchandise inventory on credit. |
| | 7 | Borrowed $90,000 cash by giving the bank a 60-day, 10% note. |
| | 10 | Borrowed $180,000 cash by signing a long-term secured note. |
| | 12 | Purchased machinery for $280,000 cash. |
| | 15 | Declared a $1 per share cash dividend on its 60,000 shares of outstanding common stock. |
| | 19 | Wrote off a $7,000 bad debt against the Allowance for Doubtful Accounts account. |
| | 22 | Paid $11,000 cash to settle an account payable. |
| | 30 | Paid the dividend declared on June 15. |

June 30: Working capital, $59,000; Current ratio, 1.19

**Required**

Prepare a table showing the company's (1) current ratio, (2) acid-test ratio, and (3) working capital after each transaction. Round ratios to two decimals.

Selected year-end financial statements of Overland Corporation follow. (All sales were on credit; selected balance sheet amounts at December 31, 2010, were inventory, $16,400; total assets, $95,900; common stock, $41,500; and retained earnings, $19,800.)

**Problem 17-4B**
Calculation of financial statement ratios

P3

### OVERLAND CORPORATION
### Income Statement
### For Year Ended December 31, 2011

| | |
|---|---:|
| Sales . . . . . . . . . . . . . . . . . . . . . . | $215,500 |
| Cost of goods sold . . . . . . . . . | 136,100 |
| Gross profit . . . . . . . . . . . . . . . . | 79,400 |
| Operating expenses . . . . . . . . . | 50,200 |
| Interest expense . . . . . . . . . . . . | 1,200 |
| Income before taxes . . . . . . . . . | 28,000 |
| Income taxes . . . . . . . . . . . . . . . | 2,200 |
| Net income . . . . . . . . . . . . . . . . | $ 25,800 |

### OVERLAND CORPORATION
### Balance Sheet
### December 31, 2011

| Assets | | Liabilities and Equity | |
|---|---:|---|---:|
| Cash . . . . . . . . . . . . . . . . . . . . . . | $ 5,100 | Accounts payable . . . . . . . . . . . . . . . . . . . . . | $ 10,500 |
| Short-term investments . . . . . . . . . . | 5,900 | Accrued wages payable . . . . . . . . . . . . . . . | 2,300 |
| Accounts receivable, net . . . . . . . . . . | 11,100 | Income taxes payable . . . . . . . . . . . . . . . . | 1,600 |
| Notes receivable (trade)* . . . . . . . . | 2,000 | Long-term note payable, secured | |
| Merchandise inventory . . . . . . . . . . . | 12,500 | by mortgage on plant assets . . . . . . . . . | 25,000 |
| Prepaid expenses . . . . . . . . . . . . . . . | 1,000 | Common stock, $5 par value . . . . . . . . . . . | 41,000 |
| Plant assets, net . . . . . . . . . . . . . . . . | 72,900 | Retained earnings . . . . . . . . . . . . . . . . . . . . | 30,100 |
| Total assets . . . . . . . . . . . . . . . . . . . | $110,500 | Total liabilities and equity . . . . . . . . . . . . . | $110,500 |

\* These are short-term notes receivable arising from customer (trade) sales.

### Required

Compute the following: (1) current ratio, (2) acid-test ratio, (3) days' sales uncollected, (4) inventory turnover, (5) days' sales in inventory, (6) debt-to-equity ratio, (7) times interest earned, (8) profit margin ratio, (9) total asset turnover, (10) return on total assets, and (11) return on common stockholders' equity.

**Check** Acid-test ratio, 1.7 to 1; Inventory turnover, 9.4

---

Summary information from the financial statements of two companies competing in the same industry follows.

**Problem 17-5B**
Comparative ratio analysis

A1 P3

| | Loud Company | Clear Company | | Loud Company | Clear Company |
|---|---:|---:|---|---:|---:|
| **Data from the current year-end balance sheets** | | | **Data from the current year's income statement** | | |
| **Assets** | | | Sales . . . . . . . . . . . . . . . . . . . . . . . . . . . . | $395,600 | $669,500 |
| Cash . . . . . . . . . . . . . . . . . . . . . . . . . | $ 22,000 | $ 38,500 | Cost of goods sold . . . . . . . . . . . . . . . . . . . | 292,600 | 482,000 |
| Accounts receivable, net . . . . . . . . . . . . . | 79,100 | 72,500 | Interest expense . . . . . . . . . . . . . . . . . . . . | 7,900 | 12,400 |
| Current notes receivable (trade) . . . . . . . . | 13,600 | 11,000 | Income tax expense . . . . . . . . . . . . . . . . . . | 7,700 | 14,300 |
| Merchandise inventory . . . . . . . . . . . . . . | 88,800 | 84,000 | Net income . . . . . . . . . . . . . . . . . . . . . . . | 35,850 | 63,700 |
| Prepaid expenses . . . . . . . . . . . . . . . . . . | 11,700 | 12,100 | Basic earnings per share . . . . . . . . . . . . . . | 1.33 | 2.23 |
| Plant assets, net . . . . . . . . . . . . . . . . . . . | 178,900 | 254,300 | | | |
| Total assets . . . . . . . . . . . . . . . . . . . . | $394,100 | $472,400 | | | |
| | | | **Beginning-of-year balance sheet data** | | |
| **Liabilities and Equity** | | | Accounts receivable, net . . . . . . . . . . . . . . | $ 74,200 | $ 75,300 |
| Current liabilities . . . . . . . . . . . . . . . . . . | $ 92,500 | $ 99,000 | Current notes receivable (trade) . . . . . . . . | 0 | 0 |
| Long-term notes payable . . . . . . . . . . . . . | 95,000 | 95,300 | Merchandise inventory . . . . . . . . . . . . . . | 107,100 | 82,500 |
| Common stock, $5 par value . . . . . . . . . . | 135,000 | 143,000 | Total assets . . . . . . . . . . . . . . . . . . . . . . | 385,400 | 445,000 |
| Retained earnings . . . . . . . . . . . . . . . . . . | 71,600 | 135,100 | Common stock, $5 par value . . . . . . . . . . . | 135,000 | 143,000 |
| Total liabilities and equity . . . . . . . . . . . . | $394,100 | $472,400 | Retained earnings . . . . . . . . . . . . . . . . . . | 51,100 | 111,700 |

**Required**

**1.** For both companies compute the (*a*) current ratio, (*b*) acid-test ratio, (*c*) accounts (including notes) receivable turnover, (*d*) inventory turnover, (*e*) days' sales in inventory, and (*f*) days' sales uncollected. Identify the company you consider to be the better short-term credit risk and explain why.

**2.** For both companies compute the (*a*) profit margin ratio, (*b*) total asset turnover, (*c*) return on total assets, and (*d*) return on common stockholders' equity. Assuming that each company paid cash dividends of $3.00 per share and each company's stock can be purchased at $25 per share, compute their (*e*) price-earnings ratios and (*f*) dividend yields. Identify which company's stock you would recommend as the better investment and explain why.

**Problem 17-6B**<sup>A</sup>

Income statement computations and format

A2

Selected account balances from the adjusted trial balance for Halogen Corp. as of its calendar year-end December 31, 2011, follow.

| | Debit | Credit |
|---|---|---|
| a. Other operating expenses | $ 338,000 | |
| b. Depreciation expense—Buildings | 110,000 | |
| c. Loss from settlement of lawsuit | 46,000 | |
| d. Income taxes expense | ? | |
| e. Loss on hurricane damage (pretax and extraordinary) | 74,000 | |
| f. Accumulated depreciation—Buildings | | $ 230,000 |
| g. Accumulated depreciation—Equipment | | 410,000 |
| h. Interest revenue | | 30,000 |
| i. Net sales | | 2,650,000 |
| j. Gain from settlement of lawsuit | | 78,000 |
| k. Loss on sale of building | 34,000 | |
| l. Loss from operating a discontinued segment (pretax) | 130,000 | |
| m. Accounts payable | | 142,000 |
| n. Correction of overstatement of prior year's expense (pretax) | | 58,000 |
| o. Cost of goods sold | 1,050,000 | |
| p. Loss on sale of discontinued segment's assets (pretax) | 190,000 | |
| q. Depreciation expense—Equipment | 166,000 | |

**Required**

Answer each of the following questions by providing supporting computations.

**1.** Assume that the company's income tax rate is 25% for all items. Identify the tax effects and after-tax amounts of the four items labeled pretax.

**2.** What is the amount of income from continuing operations before income taxes? What is the amount of income taxes expense? What is the amount of income from continuing operations?

**3.** What is the total amount of after-tax income (loss) associated with the discontinued segment?

**4.** What is the amount of income (loss) before the extraordinary items?

**5.** What is the amount of net income for the year?

## SERIAL PROBLEM
Business Solutions

P3

*(This serial problem began in Chapter 1 and continues through most of the book. If previous chapter segments were not completed, the serial problem can begin at this point. It is helpful, but not necessary, to use the Working Papers that accompany the book.)*

**SP 17** Use the following selected data from Business Solutions' income statement for the three months ended March 31, 2012, and from its March 31, 2012, balance sheet to complete the requirements below: computer services revenue, $25,307; net sales (of goods), $18,693; total sales and revenue, $44,000; cost of goods sold, $14,052; net income, $18,833; quick assets, $90,924; current assets, $95,568; total assets, $120,268; current liabilities, $875; total liabilities, $875; and total equity, $119,393.

**Required**

**1.** Compute the gross margin ratio (both with and without services revenue) and net profit margin ratio.

**2.** Compute the current ratio and acid-test ratio.

**3.** Compute the debt ratio and equity ratio.

**4.** What percent of its assets are current? What percent are long term?

## Beyond the Numbers

**BTN 17-1**  Refer to **Research In Motion** financial statements in Appendix A to answer the following.

1. Using fiscal 2008 as the base year, compute trend percents for fiscal years 2008, 2009, and 2010 for revenues, cost of sales, operating expenses, income taxes, and net income. (Round percents to one decimal.)

2. Compute common-size percents for fiscal years 2009 and 2010 for the following categories of assets: (*a*) total current assets, (*b*) property and equipment, net, and (*c*) intangible assets. (Round to the nearest tenth of a percent.)

3. Comment on any notable changes across the years for the income statement trends computed in part 1 and the balance sheet percents computed in part 2.

### Fast Forward

4. Access Research In Motion's financial statements for fiscal years ending after February 27, 2010, from its Website (**RIM.com**) or the SEC database (**www.SEC.gov**). Update your work for parts 1, 2, and 3 using the new information accessed.

**REPORTING IN ACTION**

A1  P1  P2

*RIM*

---

**BTN 17-2**  Key figures for **Research In Motion** and **Apple** follow.

| ($ millions) | Research In Motion | Apple |
|---|---|---|
| Cash and equivalents ........... | $ 1,551 | $ 5,263 |
| Accounts receivable, net ......... | 2,594 | 3,361 |
| Inventories ................... | 622 | 455 |
| Retained earnings ............. | 5,274 | 23,353 |
| Cost of sales ................. | 8,369 | 25,683 |
| Revenues .................... | 14,953 | 42,905 |
| Total assets ................. | 10,204 | 47,501 |

**COMPARATIVE ANALYSIS**

C2  P2

*RIM*

Apple

### Required

1. Compute common-size percents for each of the companies using the data provided. (Round percents to one decimal.)
2. Which company retains a higher portion of cumulative net income in the company?
3. Which company has a higher gross margin ratio on sales?
4. Which company holds a higher percent of its total assets as inventory?

---

**BTN 17-3**  As Baldwin Company controller, you are responsible for informing the board of directors about its financial activities. At the board meeting, you present the following information.

**ETHICS CHALLENGE**

A1

| | 2011 | 2010 | 2009 |
|---|---|---|---|
| Sales trend percent .................. | 147.0% | 135.0% | 100.0% |
| Selling expenses to sales .............. | 10.1% | 14.0% | 15.6% |
| Sales to plant assets ratio ............. | 3.8 to 1 | 3.6 to 1 | 3.3 to 1 |
| Current ratio ...................... | 2.9 to 1 | 2.7 to 1 | 2.4 to 1 |
| Acid-test ratio ..................... | 1.1 to 1 | 1.4 to 1 | 1.5 to 1 |
| Inventory turnover .................. | 7.8 times | 9.0 times | 10.2 times |
| Accounts receivable turnover ......... | 7.0 times | 7.7 times | 8.5 times |
| Total asset turnover ................ | 2.9 times | 2.9 times | 3.3 times |
| Return on total assets ............... | 10.4% | 11.0% | 13.2% |
| Return on stockholders' equity......... | 10.7% | 11.5% | 14.1% |
| Profit margin ratio .................. | 3.6% | 3.8% | 4.0% |

After the meeting, the company's CEO holds a press conference with analysts in which she mentions the following ratios.

|  | 2011 | 2010 | 2009 |
|---|---|---|---|
| Sales trend percent . . . . . . . . . . . . . . | 147.0% | 135.0% | 100.0% |
| Selling expenses to sales . . . . . . . . . . | 10.1% | 14.0% | 15.6% |
| Sales to plant assets ratio . . . . . . . . . | 3.8 to 1 | 3.6 to 1 | 3.3 to 1 |
| Current ratio . . . . . . . . . . . . . . . . . . | 2.9 to 1 | 2.7 to 1 | 2.4 to 1 |

**Required**

1. Why do you think the CEO decided to report 4 ratios instead of the 11 prepared?
2. Comment on the possible consequences of the CEO's reporting of the ratios selected.

---

**COMMUNICATING IN PRACTICE**
A1  P3

**BTN 17-4**  Each team is to select a different industry, and each team member is to select a different company in that industry and acquire its financial statements. Use those statements to analyze the company, including at least one ratio from each of the four building blocks of analysis. When necessary, use the financial press to determine the market price of its stock. Communicate with teammates via a meeting, e-mail, or telephone to discuss how different companies compare to each other and to industry norms. The team is to prepare a single one-page memorandum reporting on its analysis and the conclusions reached.

---

**TAKING IT TO THE NET**
P3

**BTN 17-5**  Access the February 19, 2010, filing of the December 31, 2009, 10-K report of **The Hershey Company** (ticker HSY) at **www.sec.gov** and complete the following requirements.

**Required**

Compute or identify the following profitability ratios of Hershey for its years ending December 31, 2009, *and* December 31, 2008. Interpret its profitability using the results obtained for these two years.

1. Profit margin ratio.
2. Gross profit ratio.
3. Return on total assets. (Total assets at year-end 2007 were $4,247,113,000.)
4. Return on common stockholders' equity. (Total shareholders' equity at year-end 2007 was $592,922,000.)
5. Basic net income per common share.

---

**TEAMWORK IN ACTION**
P1  P2  P3

**BTN 17-6**  A team approach to learning financial statement analysis is often useful.

**Required**

1. Each team should write a description of horizontal and vertical analysis that all team members agree with and understand. Illustrate each description with an example.
2. *Each* member of the team is to select *one* of the following categories of ratio analysis. Explain what the ratios in that category measure. Choose one ratio from the category selected, present its formula, and explain what it measures.

   **a.** Liquidity and efficiency     **c.** Profitability

   **b.** Solvency                     **d.** Market prospects

3. Each team member is to present his or her notes from part 2 to teammates. Team members are to confirm or correct other teammates' presentation.

**Hint:** Pairing within teams may be necessary for part 2. Use as an in-class activity or as an assignment. Consider presentations to the entire class using team rotation with transparencies.

---

**ENTREPRENEURIAL DECISION**
A1  P1  P2  P3

**BTN 17-7**  Assume that David and Tom Gardner of **The Motley Fool** (**Fool.com**) have impressed you since you first heard of their rather improbable rise to prominence in financial circles. You learn of a staff opening at The Motley Fool and decide to apply for it. Your resume is successfully screened from the thousands received and you advance to the interview process. You learn that the interview consists of analyzing the following financial facts and answering analysis questions. (*Note:* The data are taken from a small merchandiser in outdoor recreational equipment.)

| | 2010 | 2009 | 2008 |
|---|---|---|---|
| Sales trend percents ................... | 137.0% | 125.0% | 100.0% |
| Selling expenses to sales ............... | 9.8% | 13.7% | 15.3% |
| Sales to plant assets ratio .............. | 3.5 to 1 | 3.3 to 1 | 3.0 to 1 |
| Current ratio ....................... | 2.6 to 1 | 2.4 to 1 | 2.1 to 1 |
| Acid-test ratio ...................... | 0.8 to 1 | 1.1 to 1 | 1.2 to 1 |
| Merchandise inventory turnover ........ | 7.5 times | 8.7 times | 9.9 times |
| Accounts receivable turnover .......... | 6.7 times | 7.4 times | 8.2 times |
| Total asset turnover ................. | 2.6 times | 2.6 times | 3.0 times |
| Return on total assets ............... | 8.8% | 9.4% | 11.1% |
| Return on equity .................... | 9.75% | 11.50% | 12.25% |
| Profit margin ratio ................... | 3.3% | 3.5% | 3.7% |

### Required

Use these data to answer each of the following questions with explanations.

**1.** Is it becoming easier for the company to meet its current liabilities on time and to take advantage of any available cash discounts? Explain.

**2.** Is the company collecting its accounts receivable more rapidly? Explain.

**3.** Is the company's investment in accounts receivable decreasing? Explain.

**4.** Is the company's investment in plant assets increasing? Explain.

**5.** Is the owner's investment becoming more profitable? Explain.

**6.** Did the dollar amount of selling expenses decrease during the three-year period? Explain.

**HITTING THE ROAD**
C1 P3

**BTN 17-8** You are to devise an investment strategy to enable you to accumulate $1,000,000 by age 65. Start by making some assumptions about your salary. Next compute the percent of your salary that you will be able to save each year. If you will receive any lump-sum monies, include those amounts in your calculations. Historically, stocks have delivered average annual returns of 10–11%. Given this history, you should probably not assume that you will earn above 10% on the money you invest. It is not necessary to specify exactly what types of assets you will buy for your investments; just assume a rate you expect to earn. Use the future value tables in Appendix B to calculate how your savings will grow. Experiment a bit with your figures to see how much less you have to save if you start at, for example, age 25 versus age 35 or 40. (For this assignment, do not include inflation in your calculations.)

**GLOBAL DECISION**
A1

**NOKIA**
**RIM**
Apple

**BTN 17-9** **Nokia** (www.Nokia.com), which is a leading manufacturer of mobile devices and services, along with **Research In Motion** and **Apple** are competitors in the global marketplace. Key figures for Nokia follow (in Euro millions).

| | |
|---|---|
| Cash and equivalents ........... | 1,142 |
| Accounts receivable, net ......... | 7,981 |
| Inventories ................... | 1,865 |
| Retained earnings ............. | 10,132 |
| Cost of sales ................. | 27,720 |
| Revenues .................... | 40,984 |
| Total assets .................. | 35,738 |

### Required

**1.** Compute common-size percents for Nokia using the data provided. (Round percents to one decimal.)

**2.** Compare the results with Research In Motion and Apple from BTN 17-2.

## ANSWERS TO MULTIPLE CHOICE QUIZ

**1.** d; ($351,000/$300,000) × 100 = 117%

**2.** e; ($86,000 + $76,000 + $122,000 + $12,000)/$124,000 = 2.39

**3.** c; ($86,000 + $76,000)/$124,000 = 1.31

**4.** a; ($124,000 + $90,000)/$830,000 = 25.78%

**5.** d; ($300,000 + $316,000)/$830,000 = 74.22%

# Financial Statement Information

This appendix includes financial information for (1) **Research In Motion**, (2) **Apple**, (3) **Palm**, and (4) **Nokia**. This information is taken from their annual 10-K reports (20-F for Nokia) filed with the SEC. An **annual report** is a summary of a company's financial results for the year along with its current financial condition and future plans. This report is directed to external users of financial information, but it also affects the actions and decisions of internal users.

A company often uses an annual report to showcase itself and its products. Many annual reports include photos, diagrams, and illustrations related to the company. The primary objective of annual reports, however, is the *financial section,* which communicates much information about a company, with most data drawn from the accounting information system. The layout of an annual report's financial section is fairly established and typically includes the following:

- Letter to Shareholders
- Financial History and Highlights
- Management Discussion and Analysis
- Management's Report on Financial Statements and on Internal Controls
- Report of Independent Accountants (Auditor's Report) and on Internal Controls
- Financial Statements
- Notes to Financial Statements
- List of Directors and Officers

This appendix provides the financial statements for Research In Motion (plus selected notes), Apple, Palm, and Nokia. The appendix is organized as follows:

- **Research In Motion** **A-2** through **A-18**
- **Apple** **A-19** through **A-23**
- **Palm** **A-24** through **A-28**
- **Nokia** **A-29** through **A-33**

*RIM*

Apple

**Palm**

**NOKIA**

Many assignments at the end of each chapter refer to information in this appendix. We encourage readers to spend time with these assignments; they are especially useful in showing the relevance and diversity of financial accounting and reporting.

---

*Special note:* The SEC maintains the EDGAR (**E**lectronic **D**ata **G**athering, **A**nalysis, and **R**etrieval) database at **www.SEC.gov**. (Over the next few years, the SEC will be moving to IDEA, short for Interactive Data Electronic Applications, which will eventually replace the EDGAR system.) The **Form 10-K** is the annual report form for most companies. It provides electronically accessible information. The **Form 10-KSB** is the annual report form filed by small businesses. It requires slightly less information than the Form 10-K. One of these forms must be filed within 90 days after the company's fiscal year-end. (Forms 10-K405, 10-KT, 10-KT405, and 10-KSB405 are slight variations of the usual form due to certain regulations or rules.)

RESEARCH IN MOTION

# Research In Motion Financial Report

RESEARCH IN MOTION

Research In Motion Limited
Summary Data—Management's Discussion and Analysis of Financial Condition and Results of Operations

| As at and for the Fiscal Year Ended | February 27, 2010 | February 28, 2009 | March 1, 2008 | March 3, 2007 | March 4, 2006 |
|---|---|---|---|---|---|
| | (in thousands, except for per share amounts) | | | | |
| Revenue | $ 14,953,224 | $ 11,065,186 | $ 6,009,395 | $ 3,037,103 | $ 2,065,845 |
| Cost of sales | 8,368,958 | 5,967,888 | 2,928,814 | 1,379,301 | 925,598 |
| Gross margin | 6,584,266 | 5,097,298 | 3,080,581 | 1,657,802 | 1,140,247 |
| Operating expenses | | | | | |
| Research and development | 964,841 | 684,702 | 359,828 | 236,173 | 158,887 |
| Selling, marketing and administration | 1,907,398 | 1,495,697 | 881,482 | 537,922 | 314,317 |
| Amortization | 310,357 | 194,803 | 108,112 | 76,879 | 49,951 |
| Litigation | 163,800 | — | — | — | 201,791 |
| Total operating expenses | 3,346,396 | 2,375,202 | 1,349,422 | 850,974 | 724,946 |
| Income from operations | 3,237,870 | 2,722,096 | 1,731,159 | 806,828 | 415,301 |
| Investment income | 28,640 | 78,267 | 79,361 | 52,117 | 66,218 |
| Income before income taxes | 3,266,510 | 2,800,363 | 1,810,520 | 858,945 | 481,519 |
| Provision for income taxes | 809,366 | 907,747 | 516,653 | 227,373 | 106,863 |
| Net income | $ 2,457,144 | $ 1,892,616 | $ 1,293,867 | $ 631,572 | $ 374,656 |
| Earnings per share | | | | | |
| Basic | $ 4.35 | $ 3.35 | $ 2.31 | $ 1.14 | $ 0.66 |
| Diluted | $ 4.31 | $ 3.30 | $ 2.26 | $ 1.10 | $ 0.64 |
| Weighted-average number of shares outstanding (000's) | | | | | |
| Basic | 564,492 | 565,059 | 559,778 | 556,059 | 566,742 |
| Diluted | 569,759 | 574,156 | 572,830 | 571,809 | 588,468 |
| Total asset | $ 10,204,409 | $ 8,101,372 | $ 5,511,187 | $ 3,088,949 | $ 2,314,349 |
| Total liabilities | $ 2,601,746 | $ 2,227,244 | $ 1,577,621 | $ 605,449 | $ 318,934 |
| Total long-term liabilities | $ 169,969 | $ 111,893 | $ 103,190 | $ 58,874 | $ 34,709 |
| Shareholders' equity | $ 7,602,663 | $ 5,874,128 | $ 3,933,566 | $ 2,483,500 | $ 1,995,415 |

## REPORT OF
## INDEPENDENT REGISTERED PUBLIC ACCOUNTING FIRM

To the Shareholders of **Research In Motion Limited**

We have audited the accompanying consolidated balance sheets of **Research In Motion Limited** [the "Company"] as at February 27, 2010 and February 28, 2009, and the related consolidated statements of operations, shareholders' equity and cash flows for the years ended February 27, 2010, February 28, 2009 and March 1, 2008. These financial statements are the responsibility of the Company's management. Our responsibility is to express an opinion on these financial statements based on our audits.

We conducted our audits in accordance with Canadian generally accepted auditing standards and the standards of the Public Company Accounting Oversight Board (United States). Those standards require that we plan and perform the audit to obtain reasonable assurance about whether the financial statements are free of material misstatement. An audit includes examining, on a test basis, evidence supporting the amounts and disclosures in the financial statements. An audit also includes assessing the accounting principles used and significant estimates made by management, as well as evaluating the overall financial statement presentation. We believe that our audits provide a reasonable basis for our opinion.

In our opinion, the consolidated financial statements referred to above present fairly, in all material respects, the financial position of the Company as at February 27, 2010 and February 28, 2009, and the results of its operations and its cash flows for the years ended February 27, 2010, February 28, 2009 and March 1, 2008, in conformity with United States generally accepted accounting principles.

We also have audited, in accordance with the standards of the Public Company Accounting Oversight Board (United States), the Company's internal control over financial reporting as of February 27, 2010, based on criteria established in Internal Control-Integrated Framework issued by the Committee of Sponsoring Organizations of the Treadway Commission and our report dated April 1, 2010 expressed an unqualified opinion thereon.

*Ernst & Young LLP*

Kitchener, Canada,
April 1, 2010.

Chartered Accountants
Licensed Public Accountants

**RESEARCH IN MOTION**

### REPORT OF
### INDEPENDENT REGISTERED PUBLIC ACCOUNTING FIRM
### ON INTERNAL CONTROL OVER FINANCIAL REPORTING

To the Shareholders of **Research In Motion Limited**

We have audited **Research In Motion Limited's** [the "Company"] internal control over financial reporting as of February 27, 2010, based on criteria established in Internal Control — Integrated Framework issued by the Committee of Sponsoring Organizations of the Treadway Commission ["the COSO criteria"]. The Company's management is responsible for maintaining effective internal control over financial reporting, and for its assessment of the effectiveness of internal control over financial reporting. Our responsibility is to express an opinion on the Company's internal control over financial reporting based on our audit.

We conducted our audit in accordance with the standards of the Public Company Accounting Oversight Board (United States). Those standards require that we plan and perform the audit to obtain reasonable assurance about whether effective internal control over financial reporting was maintained in all material respects. Our audit included obtaining an understanding of internal control over financial reporting, assessing the risk that a material weakness exists, testing and evaluating the design and operating effectiveness of internal control based on the assessed risk, and performing such other procedures as we considered necessary in the circumstances. We believe that our audit provides a reasonable basis for our opinion.

A company's internal control over financial reporting is a process designed to provide reasonable assurance regarding the reliability of financial reporting and the preparation of financial statements for external purposes in accordance with generally accepted accounting principles. A company's internal control over financial reporting includes those policies and procedures that [1] pertain to the maintenance of records that, in reasonable detail, accurately and fairly reflect the transactions and dispositions of the assets of the company; [2] provide reasonable assurance that transactions are recorded as necessary to permit preparation of financial statements in accordance with generally accepted accounting principles, and that receipts and expenditures of the company are being made only in accordance with authorizations of management and directors of the company; and [3] provide reasonable assurance regarding prevention or timely detection of unauthorized acquisition, use or disposition of the company's assets that could have a material effect on the financial statements.

Because of its inherent limitations, internal control over financial reporting may not prevent or detect misstatements. Also, projections of any evaluation of effectiveness to future periods are subject to the risk that controls may become inadequate because of changes in conditions, or that the degree of compliance with the policies or procedures may deteriorate.

In our opinion, the Company maintained, in all material respects, effective internal control over financial reporting as of February 27, 2010, based on the COSO criteria.

We also have audited, in accordance with the standards of the Public Company Accounting Oversight Board (United States), the consolidated balance sheets of the Company as at February 27, 2010 and February 28, 2009, and the consolidated statements of operations, shareholders' equity and cash flows for the years ended February 27, 2010, February 28, 2009 and March 1, 2008 of the Company and our report dated April 1, 2010 expressed an unqualified opinion thereon.

*Ernst + Young LLP*

Kitchener, Canada,
April 1, 2010.

Chartered Accountants
Licensed Public Accountants

## Research In Motion Limited
## Consolidated Balance Sheets

| ($US, in thousands) | February 27, 2010 | February 28, 2009 |
|---|---|---|
| **Assets** | | |
| **Current** | | |
| Cash and cash equivalents | $ 1,550,861 | $ 835,546 |
| Short-term investments | 360,614 | 682,666 |
| Accounts receivable, net | 2,593,742 | 2,112,117 |
| Other receivables | 206,373 | 157,728 |
| Inventories | 621,611 | 682,400 |
| Other current assets | 285,539 | 187,257 |
| Deferred income tax asset | 193,916 | 183,872 |
| Total current assets | 5,812,656 | 4,841,586 |
| **Long-term investments** | 958,248 | 720,635 |
| **Property, plant and equipment, net** | 1,956,581 | 1,334,648 |
| **Intangible assets, net** | 1,326,363 | 1,066,527 |
| **Goodwill** | 150,561 | 137,572 |
| **Deferred income tax asset** | — | 404 |
| Total assets | $10,204,409 | $8,101,372 |
| **Liabilities** | | |
| **Current** | | |
| Accounts payable | $   615,620 | $  448,339 |
| Accrued liabilities | 1,638,260 | 1,238,602 |
| Income taxes payable | 95,650 | 361,460 |
| Deferred revenue | 67,573 | 53,834 |
| Deferred income tax liability | 14,674 | 13,116 |
| Total current liabilities | 2,431,777 | 2,115,351 |
| **Deferred income tax liability** | 141,382 | 87,917 |
| **Income taxes payable** | 28,587 | 23,976 |
| Total liabilities | 2,601,746 | 2,227,244 |
| **Shareholders' Equity** | | |
| **Capital stock** | | |
| Preferred shares, authorized unlimited number of non-voting, cumulative, redeemable and retractable | — | — |
| Common shares, authorized unlimited number of non-voting, redeemable, retractable Class A common shares and unlimited number of voting common shares. Issued — 557,328,394 voting common shares (February 28, 2009 — 566,218,819) | 2,207,609 | 2,208,235 |
| **Treasury stock** | | |
| February 27, 2010 — 1,458,950 (February 28, 2009 — nil) | (94,463) | — |
| **Retained earnings** | 5,274,365 | 3,545,710 |
| **Additional paid-in capital** | 164,060 | 119,726 |
| **Accumulated other comprehensive income** | 51,092 | 457 |
| Total shareholders equity | 7,602,663 | 5,874,128 |
| Total liabilities and shareholders' equity | $10,204,409 | $8,101,372 |

RESEARCH IN MOTION

**Research In Motion Limited**
**Consolidated Statements of Operations**

($US, in thousands, except per share data)

| For the Year Ended | February 27, 2010 | February 28, 2009 | March 1, 2008 |
|---|---|---|---|
| **Revenue** | | | |
| Devices and other | $12,535,998 | $ 9,410,755 | $4,914,366 |
| Service and software | 2,417,226 | 1,654,431 | 1,095,029 |
| Total revenue | $14,953,224 | 11,065,186 | 6,009,395 |
| **Cost of sales** | | | |
| Devices and other | 7,979,163 | 5,718,041 | 2,758,250 |
| Service and software | 389,795 | 249,847 | 170,564 |
| Total cost of sales | 8,368,958 | 5,967,888 | 2,928,814 |
| **Gross margin** | 6,584,266 | 5,097,298 | 3,080,581 |
| **Operating expenses** | | | |
| Research and development | 964,841 | 684,702 | 359,828 |
| Selling, marketing and administration | 1,907,398 | 1,495,697 | 881,482 |
| Amortization | 310,357 | 194,803 | 108,112 |
| Litigation | 163,800 | — | — |
| Total operating expenses | 3,346,396 | 2,375,202 | 1,349,422 |
| **Income from operations** | 3,237,870 | 2,722,096 | 1,731,159 |
| Investment income | 28,640 | 78,267 | 79,361 |
| **Income before income taxes** | 3,266,510 | 2,800,363 | 1,810,520 |
| **Provision for income taxes** | 809,366 | 907,747 | 516,653 |
| **Net income** | $ 2,457,144 | $ 1,892,616 | $1,293,867 |
| **Earnings per share** | | | |
| Basic | $      4.35 | $      3.35 | $      2.31 |
| Diluted | $      4.31 | $      3.30 | $      2.26 |

## Research In Motion Limited

### Consolidated Statements of Shareholders' Equity

| ($US, in thousands) | Capital Stock | Additional Paid-In Capital | Treasury Stock | Retained Earnings | Accumulated Other Comprehensive Income (Loss) | Total |
|---|---|---|---|---|---|---|
| Balance as at March 3, 2007 | $2,099,696 | $ 36,093 | $ — | $ 359,227 | $(11,516) | $2,483,500 |
| **Comprehensive income (loss):** | | | | | | |
| Net income | — | — | — | 1,293,867 | — | 1,293,867 |
| Net change in unrealized gains on available-for-sale investments | — | — | — | — | 13,467 | 13,467 |
| Net change in fair value of derivatives designated as cash flow hedges during the year | — | — | — | — | 37,564 | 37,564 |
| Amounts reclassified to earnings during the year | — | — | — | — | (9,232) | (9,232) |
| Other paid-in capital | — | 9,626 | — | — | — | 9,626 |
| **Shares issued:** | | | | | | |
| Exercise of stock options | 62,889 | — | — | — | — | 62,889 |
| Transfers to capital stock from stock option exercises | 7,271 | (7,271) | — | — | — | — |
| Stock-based compensation | — | 33,700 | — | — | — | 33,700 |
| Excess tax benefits from stock-based compensation | — | 8,185 | — | — | — | 8,185 |
| Balance as at March 1, 2008 | $2,169,856 | $ 80,333 | $ — | $1,653,094 | $ 30,283 | $3,933,566 |
| **Comprehensive income (loss):** | | | | | | |
| Net income | — | — | — | 1,892,616 | — | 1,892,616 |
| Net change in unrealized gains on available-for-sale investments | — | — | — | — | (7,161) | (7,161) |
| Net change in fair value of derivatives designated as cash flow hedges during the year | — | — | — | — | (6,168) | (6,168) |
| Amounts reclassified to earnings during the year | — | — | — | — | (16,497) | (16,497) |
| **Shares issued:** | | | | | | |
| Exercise of stock options | 27,024 | — | — | — | — | 27,024 |
| Transfers to capital stock from stock option exercises | 11,355 | (11,355) | — | — | — | — |
| Stock-based compensation | — | 38,100 | — | — | — | 38,100 |
| Excess tax benefits from stock-based compensation | — | 12,648 | — | — | — | 12,648 |
| Balance as at February 28, 2009 | $2,208,235 | $119,726 | $ — | $3,545,710 | $   457 | $5,874,128 |
| **Comprehensive income:** | | | | | | |
| Net income | — | — | — | 2,457,144 | — | 2,457,144 |
| Net change in unrealized gains on available-for-sale investments | — | — | — | — | 6,803 | 6,803 |
| Net change in fair value of derivatives designated as cash flow hedges during the year | — | — | — | — | 28,324 | 28,324 |
| Amounts reclassified to earnings during the year | — | — | — | — | 15,508 | 15,508 |
| **Shares issued:** | | | | | | |
| Exercise of stock options | 30,246 | — | — | — | — | 30,246 |
| Transfers to capital stock from stock option exercises | 15,647 | (15,647) | — | — | — | — |
| Stock-based compensation | — | 58,038 | — | — | — | 58,038 |
| Excess tax benefits from stock-based compensation | — | 1,943 | — | — | — | 1,943 |
| Purchase of treasury stock | — | — | (94,463) | — | — | (94,463) |
| Common shares repurchased | (46,519) | | | (728,489) | | (775,008) |
| **Balance as at February 27, 2010** | $2,207,609 | $164,060 | $(94,463) | $5,274,365 | $ 51,092 | $7,602,663 |

**Research In Motion Limited**
**Consolidated Statements of Cash Flows**

| For the Year Ended ($US, in thousands) | February 27, 2010 | February 28, 2009 | March 1, 2008 |
|---|---|---|---|
| **Cash flows from operating activities** | | | |
| Net income | $ 2,457,144 | $ 1,892,616 | $ 1,293,867 |
| Adjustments to reconcile net income to net cash provided by operating activities: | | | |
| Amortization | 615,621 | 327,896 | 177,366 |
| Deferred income taxes | 51,363 | (36,623) | (67,244) |
| Income taxes payable | 4,611 | (6,897) | 4,973 |
| Stock-based compensation | 58,038 | 38,100 | 33,700 |
| Other | 8,806 | 5,867 | 3,303 |
| Net changes in working capital items | (160,709) | (769,114) | 130,794 |
| **Net cash provided by operating activities** | 3,034,874 | 1,451,845 | 1,576,759 |
| **Cash flows from investing activities** | | | |
| Acquisition of long-term investments | (862,977) | (507,082) | (757,656) |
| Proceeds on sale or maturity of long-term investments | 473,476 | 431,713 | 260,393 |
| Acquisition of property, plant and equipment | (1,009,416) | (833,521) | (351,914) |
| Acquisition of intangible assets | (421,400) | (687,913) | (374,128) |
| Business acquisitions, net of cash acquired | (143,375) | (48,425) | (6,200) |
| Acquisition of short-term investments | (476,956) | (917,316) | (1,249,919) |
| Proceeds on sale or maturity of short-term investments | 970,521 | 739,021 | 1,325,487 |
| **Net cash used in investing activities** | (1,470,127) | (1,823,523) | (1,153,937) |
| **Cash flows from financing activities** | | | |
| Issuance of common shares | 30,246 | 27,024 | 62,889 |
| Additional paid-in capital | — | — | 9,626 |
| Excess tax benefits from stock-based compensation | 1,943 | 12,648 | 8,185 |
| Purchase of treasury stock | (94,463) | — | — |
| Common shares repurchased | (775,008) | — | — |
| Repayment of debt | (6,099) | (14,305) | (302) |
| **Net cash provided by (used in) financing activities** | (843,381) | 25,367 | 80,398 |
| **Effect of foreign exchange gain (loss) on cash and cash equivalents** | (6,051) | (2,541) | 4,034 |
| **Net increase (decrease) in cash and cash equivalents for the year** | 715,315 | (348,852) | 507,254 |
| **Cash and cash equivalents, beginning of year** | 835,546 | 1,184,398 | 677,144 |
| **Cash and cash equivalents, end of year** | $ 1,550,861 | $   835,546 | $ 1,184,398 |

**RIM—SELECTED Notes to the Consolidated Financial Statements**

*$US in thousands, except share and per share data, and where otherwise indicated*

## 1.  RESEARCH IN MOTION LIMITED AND SUMMARY OF SIGNIFICANT ACCOUNTING POLICIES

Research In Motion Limited ("RIM" or the "Company") is a leading designer, manufacturer and marketer of innovative wireless solutions for the worldwide mobile communications market. Through the development of integrated hardware, software and services that support multiple wireless network standards, RIM provides platforms and solutions for seamless access to time-sensitive information including email, phone, short messaging service (SMS), Internet and intranet-based applications. RIM technology also enables a broad array of third party developers and manufacturers to enhance their products and services with wireless connectivity to data. RIM's portfolio of award-winning products, services and embedded technologies are used by thousands of organizations and millions of consumers around the world and include the BlackBerry wireless solution, and other software and hardware. The Company's sales and marketing efforts include collaboration with strategic partners and distribution channels, as well as its own supporting sales and marketing teams, to promote the sale of its products and services.

### Basis of presentation and preparation

The consolidated financial statements include the accounts of all subsidiaries of the Company with intercompany transactions and balances eliminated on consolidation. All of the Company's subsidiaries are wholly-owned. These consolidated financial statements have been prepared by management in accordance with United States generally accepted accounting principles ("U.S. GAAP") on a basis consistent for all periods presented except as described in note 2. Certain of the comparative figures have been reclassified to conform to the current year presentation. The Company's fiscal year end date is the 52 or 53 weeks ending on the last Saturday of February, or the first Saturday of March. The fiscal years ended February 27, 2010, February 28, 2009, and March 1, 2008 comprise 52 weeks.

The significant accounting policies used in these U.S. GAAP consolidated financial statements are as follows:

### Use of estimates

The preparation of the consolidated financial statements requires management to make estimates and assumptions with respect to the reported amounts of assets, liabilities, revenues and expenses and the disclosure of contingent assets and liabilities. Significant areas requiring the use of management estimates relate to the determination of reserves for various litigation claims, provisions for excess and obsolete inventories and liabilities for purchase commitments with contract manufacturers and suppliers, fair values of assets acquired and liabilities assumed in business combinations, royalties, amortization expense, implied fair value of goodwill, provision for income taxes, realization of deferred income tax assets and the related components of the valuation allowance, provisions for warranty and the fair values of financial instruments. Actual results could differ from these estimates.

### Foreign currency translation

The U.S. dollar is the functional and reporting currency of the Company. Foreign currency denominated assets and liabilities of the Company and all of its subsidiaries are translated into U.S. dollars. Accordingly, monetary assets and liabilities are translated using the exchange rates in effect at the consolidated balance sheet date and revenues and expenses at the rates of exchange prevailing when the transactions occurred. Remeasurement adjustments are included in income. Non-monetary assets and liabilities are translated at historical exchange rates.

### Cash and cash equivalents

Cash and cash equivalents consist of balances with banks and liquid investments with maturities of three months or less at the date of acquisition.

### Accounts receivable, net

The accounts receivable balance which reflects invoiced and accrued revenue is presented net of an allowance for doubtful accounts. The allowance for doubtful accounts reflects estimates of probable losses in accounts receivables. The Company is dependent on a number of significant customers and on large complex contracts with respect to sales of the majority of its products, software and services. The Company expects the majority of its accounts receivable balances to continue to come from large customers as it sells the majority of its devices and software products and service relay access through network carriers and resellers rather than directly.

The Company evaluates the collectability of its accounts receivables based upon a combination of factors on a periodic basis such as specific credit risk of its customers, historical trends and economic circumstances. The Company, in the normal course of business, monitors the financial condition of its customers and reviews the credit history of each new

*$US in thousands, except share and per share data, and where otherwise indicated*

customer. When the Company becomes aware of a specific customer's inability to meet its financial obligations to the Company (such as in the case of bankruptcy filings or material deterioration in the customer's operating results or financial position, and payment experiences), RIM records a specific bad debt provision to reduce the customer's related accounts receivable to its estimated net realizable value. If circumstances related to specific customers change, the Company's estimates of the recoverability of accounts receivables balances could be further adjusted. The allowance for doubtful accounts as at February 27, 2010 is $2.0 million (February 28, 2009- $2.1 million).

### Investments

The Company's investments, other than cost method investments of $2.5 million and equity method investments of $4.1 million, consist of money market and other debt securities, and are classified as available-for-sale for accounting purposes. The Company does not exercise significant influence with respect to any of these investments.

Investments with maturities one year or less, as well as any investments that management intends to hold for less than one year, are classified as short-term investments. Investments with maturities in excess of one year are classified as long-term investments.

The Company determines the appropriate classification of investments at the time of purchase and subsequently reassesses the classification of such investments at each balance sheet date. Investments classified as available-for-sale are carried at fair value with unrealized gains and losses recorded in accumulated other comprehensive income (loss) until such investments mature or are sold. The Company uses the specific identification method of determining the cost basis in computing realized gains or losses on available-for-sale investments which are recorded in investment income.

The Company assesses individual investments in an unrealized loss position to determine whether the unrealized loss is other-than-temporary. The Company makes this assessment by considering available evidence, including changes in general market conditions, specific industry and individual company data, the length of time and the extent to which the fair value has been less than cost, the financial condition, the near-term prospects of the individual investment and the Company's intent and ability to hold the investments. In the event that a decline in the fair value of an investment occurs and the decline in value is considered to be other-than-temporary, an impairment charge is recorded in investment income equal to the difference between the cost basis and the fair value of the individual investment at the balance sheet date of the reporting period for which the assessment was made. The fair value of the investment then becomes the new cost basis of the investment.

Effective in the second quarter of fiscal 2010, if a debt security's market value is below its amortized cost and the Company either intends to sell the security or it is more likely than not that the Company will be required to sell the security before its anticipated recovery, the Company records an other-than-temporary impairment charge to investment income for the entire amount of the impairment. For other-than-temporary impairments on debt securities that the Company does not intend to sell and it is not more likely than not that the entity will be required to sell the security before its anticipated recovery, the Company would separate the other-than-temporary impairment into the amount representing the credit loss and the amount related to all other factors. The Company would record the other-than-temporary impairment related to the credit loss as a charge to investment income and the remaining other-than-temporary impairment would be recorded as a component of accumulated other comprehensive income.

### Derivative financial instruments

The Company uses derivative financial instruments, including forward contracts and options, to hedge certain foreign currency exposures. The Company does not use derivative financial instruments for speculative purposes.

### Inventories

Raw materials are stated at the lower of cost and replacement cost. Work in process and finished goods inventories are stated at the lower of cost and net realizable value. Cost includes the cost of materials plus direct labour applied to the product and the applicable share of manufacturing overhead. Cost is determined on a first-in-first-out basis.

### Property, plant and equipment, net

Property, plant and equipment is stated at cost less accumulated amortization. No amortization is provided for construction in progress until the assets are ready for use. Amortization is provided using the following rates and methods:

| | |
|---|---|
| Buildings, leaseholds and other . . . . . . . . . . . . . . . . . . . . . . | Straight-line over terms between 5 and 40 years |
| BlackBerry operations and other information technology. . . | Straight-line over terms between 3 and 5 years |
| Manufacturing equipment, R&D equipment and tooling . . . | Straight-line over terms between 2 and 8 years |
| Furniture and fixtures. . . . . . . . . . . . . . . . . . . . . . . . . . . . . | Declining balance at 20% per annum |

*$US in thousands, except share and per share data, and where otherwise indicated*

### Intangible assets, net

Intangible assets are stated at cost less accumulated amortization and are comprised of acquired technology, licenses, and patents. Acquired technology consists of purchased developed technology arising from the Company's business acquisitions. Licenses include licenses or agreements that the Company has negotiated with third parties upon use of third parties' technology. Patents comprise trademarks, internally developed patents, as well as individual patents or portfolios of patents acquired from third parties. Costs capitalized and subsequently amortized include all costs necessary to acquire intellectual property, such as patents and trademarks, as well as legal defense costs arising out of the assertion of any Company-owned patents.

Intangible assets are amortized as follows:

| | |
|---|---|
| Acquired technology . . . . . . . . . . | Straight-line over 2 to 5 years |
| Licenses . . . . . . . . . . . . . . . . . . . . | Straight-line over terms of the license agreements or on a per unit basis based upon the anticipated number of units sold during the terms, subject to a maximum of 5 years |
| Patents . . . . . . . . . . . . . . . . . . . . . | Straight-line over 17 years or over estimated useful life |

### Goodwill

Goodwill represents the excess of the purchase price of business acquisitions over the fair value of identifiable net assets acquired. Goodwill is allocated as at the date of the business combination. Goodwill is not amortized, but is tested for impairment annually, or more frequently if events or changes in circumstances indicate the asset may be impaired.

### Impairment of long-lived assets

The Company reviews long-lived assets such as property, plant and equipment and intangible assets with finite useful lives for impairment whenever events or changes in circumstances indicate that the carrying amount may not be recoverable. If the total of the expected undiscounted future cash flows is less than the carrying amount of the asset, a loss is recognized for the excess of the carrying amount over the fair value of the asset.

### Income taxes

The Company uses the liability method of tax allocation to account for income taxes. Deferred income tax assets and liabilities are recognized based upon temporary differences between the financial reporting and tax bases of assets and liabilities, and measured using enacted tax rates and laws that will be in effect when the differences are expected to reverse. The Company records a valuation allowance to reduce deferred income tax assets to the amount that is more likely than not to be realized. The Company considers both positive evidence and negative evidence, to determine whether, based upon the weight of that evidence, a valuation allowance is required. Judgment is required in considering the relative impact of negative and positive evidence.

### Revenue recognition

The Company recognizes revenue when it is realized or realizable and earned. The Company considers revenue realized or realizable and earned when it has persuasive evidence of an arrangement, the product has been delivered or the services have been provided to the customer, the sales price is fixed or determinable and collectability is reasonably assured. In addition to this general policy, the following paragraphs describe the specific revenue recognition policies for each major category of revenue.

#### Devices

Revenue from the sales of BlackBerry devices is recognized when title is transferred to the customer and all significant contractual obligations that affect the customer's final acceptance have been fulfilled. For hardware products for which software is deemed not to be incidental, the Company recognizes revenue in accordance with industry specific software revenue recognition guidance. The Company records reductions to revenue for estimated commitments related to price protection and for customer incentive programs, including reseller and end-user rebates. The estimated cost of the incentive programs are accrued based on historical experience, as a reduction to revenue in the period the Company has sold the product and committed to a plan. Price protection is accrued as a reduction to revenue based on estimates of future price reductions and certain agreed customer inventories at the date of the price adjustment. In addition, provisions are made at the time of sale for warranties and royalties.

#### Service

Revenue from service is recognized rateably on a monthly basis when the service is provided. In instances where the Company bills the customer prior to performing the service, the prebilling is recorded as deferred revenue.

#### Software

Revenue from licensed software is recognized at the inception of the license term and in accordance with industry

*$US in thousands, except share and per share data, and where otherwise indicated*

specific software revenue recognition guidance. When the fair value of a delivered element has not been established, the Company uses the residual method to recognize revenue if the fair value of undelivered elements is determinable. Revenue from software maintenance, unspecified upgrades and technical support contracts is recognized over the period that such items are delivered or that services are provided.

### Other

Revenue from the sale of accessories is recognized when title is transferred to the customer and all significant contractual obligations that affect the customer's final acceptance have been fulfilled. Technical support ("T-Support") contracts extending beyond the current period are recorded as deferred revenue. Revenue from repair and maintenance programs is recognized when the service is delivered which is when the title is transferred to the customer and all significant contractual obligations that affect the customer's final acceptance have been fulfilled. Revenue for non-recurring engineering contracts is recognized as specific contract milestones are met. The attainment of milestones approximates actual performance.

### Shipping and handling costs

Shipping and handling costs charged to income are included in cost of sales where they can be reasonably attributed to certain revenue; otherwise they are included in selling, marketing and administration.

### Multiple-element arrangements

The Company enters into transactions that represent multiple-element arrangements which may include any combination of hardware and/or service or software and T-Support. These multiple-element arrangements are assessed to determine whether they can be separated into more than one unit of accounting or element for the purpose of revenue recognition. When the appropriate criteria for separating revenue into more than one unit of accounting is met and there is vendor specific objective evidence of fair value for all units of accounting or elements in an arrangement, the arrangement consideration is allocated to the separate units of accounting or elements based on each unit's relative fair value. When the fair value of a delivered element has not been established, the Company uses the residual method to recognize revenue if the fair value of undelivered elements is determinable. This vendor specific objective evidence of fair value is established through prices charged for each revenue element when that element is sold separately. The revenue recognition policies described above are then applied to each unit of accounting.

### Research and development

Research costs are expensed as incurred. Development costs for BlackBerry devices and licensed software to be sold, leased or otherwise marketed are subject to capitalization beginning when a product's technological feasibility has been established and ending when a product is available for general release to customers. The Company's products are generally released soon after technological feasibility has been established and therefore costs incurred subsequent to achievement of technological feasibility are not significant and have been expensed as incurred.

### Comprehensive income (loss)

Comprehensive income (loss) is defined as the change in net assets of a business enterprise during a period from transactions and other events and circumstances from non-owner sources and includes all changes in equity during a period except those resulting from investments by owners and distributions to owners. The Company's reportable items of comprehensive income are cash flow hedges and changes in the fair value of available-for-sale investments. Realized gains or losses on available-for-sale investments are reclassified into investment income using the specific identification basis.

### Earnings per share

Earnings per share is calculated based on the weighted-average number of shares outstanding during the year. The treasury stock method is used for the calculation of the dilutive effect of stock options.

### Stock-based compensation plans

The Company has stock-based compensation plans.

### Warranty

The Company provides for the estimated costs of product warranties at the time revenue is recognized. BlackBerry devices are generally covered by a time-limited warranty for varying periods of time. The Company's warranty obligation is affected by product failure rates, differences in warranty periods, regulatory developments with respect to warranty obligations in the countries in which the Company carries on business, freight expense, and material usage and other related repair costs. The Company's estimates of costs are based upon historical experience and expectations of future return rates and unit warranty repair cost. If the Company experiences increased or decreased warranty activity, or increased or decreased costs associated with servicing those obligations, revisions to the estimated warranty liability would be recognized in the reporting period when such revisions are made.

### Advertising costs

The Company expenses all advertising costs as incurred. These costs are included in selling, marketing and administration.

*$US in thousands, except share and per share data, and where otherwise indicated*

## 4.   CASH, CASH EQUIVALENTS AND INVESTMENTS

The components of cash, cash equivalents and investments were as follows:

| | Cost Basis | Unrealized Gains | Unrealized Losses | Recorded Basis | Cash and Cash Equivalents | Short-term Investments | Long-term Investments |
|---|---|---|---|---|---|---|---|
| **As at February 27, 2010** | | | | | | | |
| Bank balances | $ 535,445 | $ — | $ — | $ 535,445 | $ 535,445 | $ — | $ — |
| Money market fund | 3,278 | — | — | 3,278 | 3,278 | — | — |
| Bankers acceptances and term deposits/certificates | 377,596 | — | — | 377,596 | 377,596 | — | — |
| Commercial paper and corporate notes/bonds | 855,145 | 6,528 | (49) | 861,624 | 472,312 | 187,369 | 201,943 |
| Treasury bills/notes | 203,514 | 129 | (12) | 203,631 | 92,272 | 50,786 | 60,573 |
| Government sponsored enterprise notes | 447,131 | 2,590 | (13) | 449,708 | 69,958 | 111,977 | 267,773 |
| Asset-backed securities | 393,751 | 5,280 | (50) | 398,981 | — | 10,482 | 388,499 |
| Auction-rate securities | 40,527 | — | (7,688) | 32,839 | — | — | 32,839 |
| Other investments | 6,621 | — | — | 6,621 | — | — | 6,621 |
| | $2,863,008 | $14,527 | $ (7,812) | $2,869,723 | $1,550,861 | $360,614 | $958,248 |

Realized gains and losses on available-for-sale securities comprise the following:

| For the year ended | February 27, 2010 | February 28, 2009 | March 1, 2008 |
|---|---|---|---|
| Realized gains | $439 | $ 158 | $ 10 |
| Realized losses | (17) | (1,801) | (410) |
| Net realized gains (losses) | $422 | $(1,643) | $(400) |

The contractual maturities of available-for-sale investments at February 27, 2010 were as follows:

| | Cost Basis | Fair Value |
|---|---|---|
| Due in one year or less | $1,371,047 | $1,372,752 |
| Due in one to five years | 773,471 | 783,451 |
| Due after five years | 173,146 | 168,176 |
| No fixed maturity date | 3,278 | 3,278 |
| | $2,320,942 | $2,327,657 |

## 5.   FAIR VALUE MEASUREMENTS

The Company defines fair value as the price that would be received to sell an asset or paid to transfer a liability in an orderly transaction between market participants at the measurement date. When determining the fair value measurements for assets and liabilities required to be recorded at fair value, the Company considers the principal or most advantageous market in which it would transact and considers assumptions that market participants would use in pricing the asset or liability such as inherent risk, non-performance risk and credit risk. The Company applies the following fair value hierarchy, which prioritizes the inputs used in the valuation methodologies in measuring fair value into three levels:

- Level 1 — Unadjusted quoted prices at the measurement date for identical assets or liabilities in active markets.

- Level 2 — Observable inputs other than quoted prices included in Level 1, such as quoted prices for similar assets and liabilities in active markets; quoted prices for identical or similar assets and liabilities in markets that are not active; or other inputs that are observable or can be corroborated by observable market data.

- Level 3 — Significant unobservable inputs which are supported by little or no market activity.

The fair value hierarchy also requires the Company to maximize the use of observable inputs and minimize the use of unobservable inputs when measuring fair value. The carrying amounts of the Company's cash and cash equivalents, accounts receivable, other receivables, accounts payable and accrued liabilities, approximate fair value due to their short maturities. When determining the fair value of its investments held, the Company primarily relies on an independent third party valuator for the fair valuation of securities.

*$US in thousands, except share and per share data, and where otherwise indicated*

## 6.  INVENTORIES

Inventories were comprised as follows:

|  | February 27, 2010 | February 28, 2009 |
|---|---|---|
| Raw materials | $ 490,063 | $464,497 |
| Work in process | 231,939 | 250,728 |
| Finished goods | 17,068 | 35,264 |
| Provision for excess and obsolete inventories | (117,459) | (68,089) |
|  | $ 621,611 | $682,400 |

## 7.  PROPERTY, PLANT AND EQUIPMENT, NET

Property, plant and equipment were comprised of the following:

| February 27, 2010 | Cost | Accumulated amortization | Net book value |
|---|---|---|---|
| Land | $ 104,254 | $ — | $ 104,254 |
| Buildings, leaseholds and other | 926,747 | 115,216 | 811,531 |
| BlackBerry operations and other information technology | 1,152,637 | 484,180 | 668,457 |
| Manufacturing equipment, research and development equipment, and tooling | 347,692 | 182,228 | 165,464 |
| Furniture and fixtures | 346,641 | 139,766 | 206,875 |
|  | $2,877,971 | $921,390 | $1,956,581 |

As at February 27, 2010, the carrying amount of assets under construction was $254.3 million (February 28, 2009 — $88.9 million). Of this amount, $110.9 million (February 28, 2009 — $50.0 million) was included in buildings, leaseholds and other; $102.5 million (February 28, 2009 - $35.8 million) was included in BlackBerry operations and other information technology; and $40.9 million (February 28, 2009 — $3.2 million) was included in manufacturing equipment, research and development equipment, and tooling. As at February 27, 2010, $31.7 million has been classified as an asset held for sale and accordingly has been reclassified from property, plant and equipment to other current assets. For the year ended February 27, 2010, amortization expense related to property, plant and equipment was $344.5 million (February 28, 2009 — $203.4 million; March 1, 2008 — $133.1 million).

## 8.  INTANGIBLE ASSETS, NET

Intangible assets were comprised of the following:

| February 27, 2010 | Cost | Accumulated amortization | Net book value |
|---|---|---|---|
| Acquired technology | $ 165,791 | $ 70,777 | $ 95,014 |
| Licenses | 711,969 | 196,618 | 515,351 |
| Patents | 889,467 | 173,469 | 715,998 |
|  | $1,767,227 | $440,864 | $1,326,363 |

For the year ended February 27, 2010, amortization expense related to intangible assets was $271.1 million (February 28, 2009 — $124.5 million; March 1, 2008 — $44.3 million). Total additions to intangible assets in fiscal 2010 were $531.0 million (2009 — $721.1 million). Based on the carrying value of the identified intangible assets as at February 27, 2010 and assuming no subsequent impairment of the underlying assets, the annual amortization expense for the next five fiscal years is expected to be as follows: 2011 — $324 million; 2012 — $275 million; 2013 — $227 million; 2014 — $139 million; and 2015 — $61 million. The weighted-average remaining useful life of the acquired technology is 3.4 years (2009 – 3.7 years).

*$US in thousands, except share and per share data, and where otherwise indicated*

## 10.  INCOME TAXES

The difference between the amount of the provision for income taxes and the amount computed by multiplying income before income taxes by the statutory Canadian tax rate is reconciled as follows:

| For the year ended | February 27, 2010 | February 28, 2009 |
|---|---|---|
| Statutory Canadian tax rate | 32.8% | 33.4% |
| Expected income tax provision | $1,072,395 | $935,881 |
| Differences in income taxes resulting from: | | |
| Impact of Canadian U.S. dollar functional currency election | (145,000) | — |
| Investment tax credits | (101,214) | (81,173) |
| Manufacturing and processing activities | (52,053) | (49,808) |
| Foreign exchange | 2,837 | 99,575 |
| Foreign tax rate differences | 5,291 | (16,273) |
| Non-deductible stock compensation | 9,600 | 10,500 |
| Adjustments to deferred tax balances for enacted changes in tax laws and rates | 7,927 | 1,260 |
| Other differences | 9,583 | 7,785 |
| | $  809,366 | $907,747 |

## 11.  CAPITAL STOCK

### (a) Capital stock

The Company is authorized to issue an unlimited number of non-voting, redeemable, retractable Class A common shares, an unlimited number of voting common shares and an unlimited number of non-voting, cumulative, redeemable, retractable preferred shares. At February 27, 2010 and February 28, 2009, there were no Class A common shares or preferred shares outstanding. The Company declared a 3-for-1 stock split of the Company's outstanding common shares on June 28, 2007. The stock split was implemented by way of a stock dividend. Shareholders received an additional two common shares of the Company for each common share held. The stock dividend was paid on August 20, 2007 to common shareholders of record at the close of business on August 17, 2007. All share, earnings per share and stock option data have been adjusted to reflect this stock dividend.

The following details the changes in issued and outstanding common shares for the year ended February 27, 2010:

| | Capital Stock | | Treasury Stock | |
|---|---|---|---|---|
| | Stock Outstanding (000's) | Amount | Stock Outstanding (000's) | Amount |
| Common shares outstanding as at February 28, 2009 | 566,219 | 2,208,235 | — | — |
| Exercise of stock options | 3,408 | 30,246 | — | — |
| Conversion of restricted share units | 2 | — | — | — |
| Transfers to capital stock resulting from stock option exercises | — | 15,647 | — | — |
| Restricted share unit plan purchase of shares | — | — | 1,459 | (94,463) |
| Common shares repurchased | (12,300) | (46,519) | — | — |
| Common shares outstanding as at February 27, 2010 | 557,329 | $2,207,609 | 1,459 | $(94,463) |

On November 4, 2009, the Company's Board of Directors authorized a Common Share Repurchase Program for the repurchase and cancellation, through the facilities of the NASDAQ Stock Market, common shares having an aggregate purchase price of up to $1.2 billion, or approximately 21 million common shares based on trading prices at the time of the authorization. This represents approximately 3.6% of the outstanding common shares of the Company at the time of the authorization. All common shares repurchased by the Company pursuant to the Common Share Repurchase Program have been cancelled. The Common Share Repurchase Program will remain in place for up to 12 months from November 4, 2009 or until the purchases are completed or the program is terminated by the Company.

### (b) Stock-based compensation

#### Stock Option Plan

The Company recorded a charge to income and a credit to paid-in-capital of $37.0 million in fiscal 2010 (fiscal 2009 — $38.1 million; fiscal 2008 — $33.7 million) in relation to stock-based compensation expense.

The Company has not paid a dividend in the previous twelve fiscal years and has no current expectation of paying cash dividends on its common shares.

#### Restricted Share Unit Plan

During fiscal 2010, the trustee purchased 1,458,950 common shares for total consideration of approximately $94.5 million

*$US in thousands, except share and per share data, and where otherwise indicated*

to comply with its obligations to deliver shares upon vesting. These purchased shares are classified as treasury stock for accounting purposes and included in the shareholders' equity section of the Company's consolidated balance sheet. The Company recorded compensation expense with respect to RSUs of $21.0 million in the year ended February 27, 2010 (February 28, 2009 — $196; March 1, 2008 — $33).

*Deferred Share Unit Plan*

The Company issued 14,593 DSUs in the year ended February 27, 2010. There are 34,801 DSUs outstanding as at February 27, 2010 (February 28, 2009 — 20,208). The Company had a liability of $2.5 million in relation to the DSU plan as at February 27, 2010 (February 28, 2009 — $834).

## 12.   COMMITMENTS AND CONTINGENCIES

### (a) Credit Facility

The Company has $150.0 million in unsecured demand credit facilities (the "Facilities") to support and secure operating and financing requirements. As at February 27, 2010, the Company has utilized $6.9 million of the Facilities for outstanding letters of credit, and $143.1 million of the Facilities are unused.

### (b) Lease commitments

The Company is committed to future minimum annual lease payments under operating leases as follows:

| For the years ending | Real Estate | Equipment and other | Total |
|---|---|---|---|
| 2011 | $ 35,088 | $1,917 | $ 37,005 |
| 2012 | 30,611 | 1,202 | 31,813 |
| 2013 | 27,841 | 163 | 28,004 |
| 2014 | 26,178 | — | 26,178 |
| 2015 | 21,755 | — | 21,755 |
| Thereafter | 63,631 | — | 63,631 |
| | $205,104 | $3,282 | $208,386 |

For the year ended February 27, 2010, the Company incurred rental expense of $39.6 million (February 28, 2009 — $22.7 million; March 1, 2008 — $15.5 million).

### (c) Litigation

The Company is involved in litigation in the normal course of its business, both as a defendant and as a plaintiff. The Company may be subject to claims (including claims related to patent infringement, purported class actions and derivative actions) either directly or through indemnities against these claims that it provides to certain of it partners.

## 13.   PRODUCT WARRANTY

The Company estimates its warranty costs at the time of revenue recognition based on historical warranty claims experience and records the expense in cost of sales. The warranty accrual balance is reviewed quarterly to establish that it materially reflects the remaining obligation based on the anticipated future expenditures over the balance of the obligation period. Adjustments are made when the actual warranty claim experience differs from estimates. The change in the Company's warranty expense and actual warranty experience from March 3, 2007 to February 27, 2010 as well as the accrued warranty obligations as at February 27, 2010 are set forth in the following table:

| | |
|---|---|
| Accrued warranty obligations as at March 3, 2007 | $  36,669 |
| Actual warranty experience during fiscal 2008 | (68,166) |
| Fiscal 2008 warranty provision | 116,045 |
| Accrued warranty obligations as at March 1, 2008 | 84,548 |
| Actual warranty experience during fiscal 2009 | (146,434) |
| Fiscal 2009 warranty provision | 258,757 |
| Adjustments for changes in estimate | (12,536) |
| Accrued warranty obligations as at February 28, 2009 | 184,335 |
| Actual warranty experience during fiscal 2010 | (416,393) |
| Fiscal 2010 warranty provision | 462,834 |
| Adjustments for changes in estimate | 21,541 |
| Accrued warranty obligations as at February 27, 2010 | $ 252,317 |

*$US in thousands, except share and per share data, and where otherwise indicated*

## 14.  EARNINGS PER SHARE

The following table sets forth the computation of basic and diluted earnings per share:

| For the year ended | February 27, 2010 | February 28, 2009 | March 1, 2008 |
|---|---|---|---|
| Net income for basic and diluted earnings per share available to common shareholders | $2,457,144 | $1,892,616 | $1,293,867 |
| Weighted-average number of shares outstanding (000's) — basic | 564,492 | 565,059 | 559,778 |
| Effect of dilutive securities (000's) — stock-based compensation | 5,267 | 9,097 | 13,052 |
| Weighted-average number of shares and assumed conversions (000's) — diluted | 569,759 | 574,156 | 572,830 |
| Earnings per share — reported | | | |
| Basic | $ 4.35 | $ 3.35 | $ 2.31 |
| Diluted | $ 4.31 | $ 3.30 | $ 2.26 |

## 15.  COMPREHENSIVE INCOME (LOSS)

The components of comprehensive income (loss) are shown in the following table:

| For the year ended | February 27, 2010 | February 28, 2009 | March 1, 2008 |
|---|---|---|---|
| Net income | $2,457,144 | $1,892,616 | $1,293,867 |
| Net change in unrealized gains (losses) on available-for-sale investments | 6,803 | (7,161) | 13,467 |
| Net change in fair value of derivatives designated as cash flow hedges during the year, net of income taxes of $13,190 (February 28, 2009 - tax recovery of $8,641; March 1, 2008 - income taxes of $19,238) | 28,324 | (6,168) | 37,564 |
| Amounts reclassified to earnings during the year, net of income tax recovery of $6,079 (February 28, 2009 - income taxes of $4,644; March 1, 2008 - income taxes of $5,142) | 15,508 | (16,497) | (9,232) |
| Comprehensive income | $2,507,779 | $1,862,790 | $1,335,666 |

The components of accumulated other comprehensive income (loss) are as follows:

| | February 27, 2010 | February 28, 2009 | March 1, 2008 |
|---|---|---|---|
| Accumulated net unrealized gains (losses) on available- for-sale investments | $ 6,715 | $ (88) | $ 7,073 |
| Accumulated net unrealized gains on derivative instruments designated as cash flow hedges | 44,377 | 545 | 23,210 |
| Total accumulated other comprehensive income | $51,092 | $457 | $30,283 |

## 16.  SUPPLEMENTAL INFORMATION

(a) Cash flows resulting from net changes in working capital items are as follows:

| For the year ended | February 27, 2010 | February 28, 2009 | March 1, 2008 |
|---|---|---|---|
| Accounts receivable | $(480,610) | $(936,514) | $(602,055) |
| Other receivables | (44,719) | (83,039) | (34,515) |
| Inventories | 60,789 | (286,133) | (140,360) |
| Other current assets | (52,737) | (50,280) | (26,161) |
| Accounts payable | 167,281 | 177,263 | 140,806 |
| Accrued liabilities | 442,065 | 506,859 | 383,020 |
| Income taxes payable | (266,517) | (113,868) | 401,270 |
| Deferred revenue | 13,739 | 16,598 | 8,789 |
| | $(160,709) | $(769,114) | $ 130,794 |

(b) Certain statement of cash flow information related to interest and income taxes paid is summarized as follows:

| For the year ended | February 27, 2010 | February 28, 2009 | March 1, 2008 |
|---|---|---|---|
| Interest paid during the year | $ — | $ 502 | $ 518 |
| Income taxes paid during the year | $1,081,720 | $946,237 | $216,095 |

RESEARCH IN MOTION

*$US in thousands, except share and per share data, and where otherwise indicated*

(c) The following items are included in the accrued liabilities balance:

|  | February 27, 2010 | February 28, 2009 |
|---|---|---|
| Marketing costs | $ 91,554 | $ 91,160 |
| Vendor inventory liabilities | 125,761 | 18,000 |
| Warranty | 252,316 | 184,335 |
| Royalties | 383,939 | 279,476 |
| Rebates | 146,304 | 134,788 |
| Other | 638,386 | 530,843 |
|  | $1,638,260 | $1,238,602 |

Other accrued liabilities as noted in the above chart, include, among other things, salaries, payroll withholding taxes and incentive accruals, none of which are greater than 5% of the current liability balance.

(d) Additional information

Advertising expense, which includes media, agency and promotional expenses totalling $790.8 million (February 28, 2009 — $718.9 million; March 1, 2008 — $336.0 million) is included in selling, marketing and administration expense.

Selling, marketing and administration expense for the fiscal year includes $58.4 million with respect to foreign exchange losses (February 28, 2009 – loss of $6.1 million; March 1, 2008 – loss of $5.3 million). For the year ended February 27, 2010, the Company recorded a $54.3 million charge primarily relating to the reversal of foreign exchange gains previously recorded in fiscal 2009 on the revaluation of Canadian dollar denominated tax liability balances.

## 17.  DERIVATIVE FINANCIAL INSTRUMENTS

The Company uses derivative instruments to manage exposures to foreign exchange risk resulting from transactions in currencies other than its functional currency, the U.S. dollar. The Company's risk management objective in holding derivative instruments is to reduce the volatility of current and future income as a result of changes in foreign currency. To limit its exposure to adverse movements in foreign currency exchange rates, the Company enters into foreign currency forward and option contracts.

## 18.  SEGMENT DISCLOSURES

The Company is organized and managed as a single reportable business segment. The Company's operations are substantially all related to the research, design, manufacture and sales of wireless communications products, services and software. Selected financial information is as follows:

Revenue, classified by major geographic segments in which our customers are located, was as follows:

| For the year ended | February 27, 2010 | February 28, 2009 | March 1, 2008 |
|---|---|---|---|
| Revenue |  |  |  |
| Canada | $ 843,762 | $ 887,005 | $ 438,302 |
| United States | 8,619,762 | 6,967,598 | 3,528,858 |
| United Kingdom | 1,447,417 | 711,536 | 461,592 |
| Other | 4,042,283 | 2,499,047 | 1,580,643 |
|  | $14,953,224 | $11,065,186 | $6,009,395 |

| | February 27, 2010 | February 28, 2009 |
|---|---|---|
| Total assets |  |  |
| Canada | $ 4,502,522 | $3,218,640 |
| United States | 4,059,174 | 2,646,783 |
| United Kingdom | 1,195,534 | 1,931,387 |
| Other | 447,179 | 304,562 |
|  | $10,204,409 | $8,101,372 |

# Apple Financial Report

APPLE

**APPLE INC.**
**CONSOLIDATED BALANCE SHEETS**
(in millions, except share amounts)

| | September 26, 2009 | September 27, 2008 |
|---|---|---|
| **ASSETS** | | |
| Current assets | | |
| Cash and cash equivalents | $ 5,263 | $11,875 |
| Short-term marketable securities | 18,201 | 10,236 |
| Accounts receivable, less allowances of $52 and $47, respectively | 3,361 | 2,422 |
| Inventories | 455 | 509 |
| Deferred tax assets | 1,135 | 1,044 |
| Other current assets | 3,140 | 3,920 |
| Total current assets | 31,555 | 30,006 |
| Long-term marketable securities | 10,528 | 2,379 |
| Property, plant and equipment, net | 2,954 | 2,455 |
| Goodwill | 206 | 207 |
| Acquired intangible assets, net | 247 | 285 |
| Other assets | 2,011 | 839 |
| Total assets | $47,501 | $36,171 |
| **LIABILITIES AND SHAREHOLDERS' EQUITY** | | |
| Current liabilities | | |
| Accounts payable | $ 5,601 | $ 5,520 |
| Accrued expenses | 3,852 | 4,224 |
| Deferred revenue | 2,053 | 1,617 |
| Total current liabilities | 11,506 | 11,361 |
| Deferred revenue – non-current | 853 | 768 |
| Other non-current liabilities | 3,502 | 1,745 |
| Total liabilities | 15,861 | 13,874 |
| Shareholders' equity | | |
| Common stock, no par value; 1,800,000,000 shares authorized; 899,805,500 and 888,325,973 shares issued and outstanding, respectively | 8,210 | 7,177 |
| Retained earnings | 23,353 | 15,129 |
| Accumulated other comprehensive income/(loss) | 77 | (9) |
| Total shareholders' equity | 31,640 | 22,297 |
| Total liabilities and shareholders' equity | $47,501 | $36,171 |

## APPLE INC.
## CONSOLIDATED STATEMENTS OF OPERATIONS
(in millions, except share amounts which are reflected in thousands and per share amounts)

| For fiscal year ended | September 26, 2009 | September 27, 2008 | September 29, 2007 |
|---|---|---|---|
| Net sales | $ 42,905 | $ 37,491 | $ 24,578 |
| Cost of sales | 25,683 | 24,294 | 16,426 |
| Gross margin | 17,222 | 13,197 | 8,152 |
| | | | |
| Operating expenses | | | |
| Research and development | 1,333 | 1,109 | 782 |
| Selling, general and administrative | 4,149 | 3,761 | 2,963 |
| Total operating expenses | 5,482 | 4,870 | 3,745 |
| | | | |
| Operating income | 11,740 | 8,327 | 4,407 |
| Other income and expense | 326 | 620 | 599 |
| | | | |
| Income before provision for income taxes | 12,066 | 8,947 | 5,006 |
| Provision for income taxes | 3,831 | 2,828 | 1,511 |
| | | | |
| Net income | $ 8,235 | $ 6,119 | $ 3,495 |
| | | | |
| | | | |
| Earnings per common share: | | | |
| Basic | $ 9.22 | $ 6.94 | $ 4.04 |
| Diluted | $ 9.08 | $ 6.78 | $ 3.93 |
| Shares used in computing earnings per share: | | | |
| Basic | 893,016 | 881,592 | 864,595 |
| Diluted | 907,005 | 902,139 | 889,292 |

**APPLE**

## APPLE INC.
## CONSOLIDATED STATEMENTS OF SHAREHOLDERS' EQUITY
(in millions, except share amounts which are reflected in thousands)

| | Common Stock | | Retained Earnings | Accumulated Other Comprehensive Income | Total Shareholders' Equity |
|---|---|---|---|---|---|
| | Shares | Amount | | | |
| Balances as of September 30, 2006 | 855,263 | $ 4,355 | $ 5,607 | $    22 | $ 9,984 |
| Components of comprehensive income: | | | | | |
| Net income | — | — | 3,495 | — | 3,495 |
| Change in foreign currency translation | — | — | — | 51 | 51 |
| Change in unrealized loss on available-for-sale securities, net of tax | — | — | — | (7) | (7) |
| Change in unrealized gain on derivative instruments, net of tax | — | — | — | (3) | (3) |
| Total comprehensive income | | | | | 3,536 |
| Stock-based compensation | — | 251 | — | — | 251 |
| Common stock issued under stock plans, net of shares withheld for employee taxes | 17,066 | 364 | (2) | — | 362 |
| Tax benefit from employee stock plan awards | — | 398 | — | — | 398 |
| Balances as of September 29, 2007 | 872,329 | 5,368 | 9,100 | 63 | 14,531 |
| Cumulative effect of change in accounting principle | — | 45 | 11 | — | 56 |
| Components of comprehensive income: | | | | | |
| Net income | — | — | 6,119 | — | 6,119 |
| Change in foreign currency translation | — | — | — | (28) | (28) |
| Change in unrealized loss on available-for-sale securities, net of tax | — | — | — | (63) | (63) |
| Change in unrealized gain on derivative instruments, net of tax | — | — | — | 19 | 19 |
| Total comprehensive income | | | | | 6,047 |
| Stock-based compensation | — | 513 | — | — | 513 |
| Common stock issued under stock plans, net of shares withheld for employee taxes | 15,888 | 460 | (101) | — | 359 |
| Issuance of common stock in connection with an asset acquisition | 109 | 21 | — | — | 21 |
| Tax benefit from employee stock plan awards | — | 770 | — | — | 770 |
| Balances as of September 27, 2008 | 888,326 | 7,177 | 15,129 | (9) | 22,297 |
| Components of comprehensive income: | | | | | |
| Net income | — | — | 8,235 | — | 8,235 |
| Change in foreign currency translation | — | — | — | (14) | (14) |
| Change in unrealized loss on available-for-sale securities, net of tax | — | — | — | 118 | 118 |
| Change in unrealized gain on derivative instruments, net of tax | — | — | — | (18) | (18) |
| Total comprehensive income | | | | | 8,321 |
| Stock-based compensation | — | 707 | — | — | 707 |
| Common stock issued under stock plans, net of shares withheld for employee taxes | 11,480 | 404 | (11) | — | 393 |
| Tax benefit from employee stock plan awards, including transfer pricing adjustments | — | (78) | — | — | (78) |
| Balances as of September 26, 2009 | 899,806 | $ 8,210 | $23,353 | $    77 | $31,640 |

## APPLE INC.
## CONSOLIDATED STATEMENTS OF CASH FLOWS
(in millions)

| For fiscal year ended | September 26, 2009 | September 27, 2008 | September 29, 2007 |
|---|---|---|---|
| Cash and cash equivalents, beginning of the year . . . . . . . . . . . . . . . . . | $ 11,875 | $ 9,352 | $ 6,392 |
| **Operating Activities** | | | |
| Net income. . . . . . . . . . . . . . . . . . . . . . . . . . . . . . . . . . . . . . . . . . | 8,235 | 6,119 | 3,495 |
| Adjustments to reconcile net income to cash | | | |
| generated by operating activities | | | |
| Depreciation, amortization and accretion . . . . . . . . . . . . . . . . . | 734 | 496 | 327 |
| Stock-based compensation expense. . . . . . . . . . . . . . . . . . . . . . | 710 | 516 | 242 |
| Deferred income tax expense. . . . . . . . . . . . . . . . . . . . . . . . . . | 1,040 | 398 | 73 |
| Loss on disposition of property, plant and equipment . . . . . . . . | 26 | 22 | 12 |
| Changes in operating assets and liabilities | | | |
| Accounts receivable, net . . . . . . . . . . . . . . . . . . . . . . . . . . . . . | (939) | (785) | (385) |
| Inventories . . . . . . . . . . . . . . . . . . . . . . . . . . . . . . . . . . . . . . . | 54 | (163) | (76) |
| Other current assets . . . . . . . . . . . . . . . . . . . . . . . . . . . . . . . . | 749 | (274) | (1,279) |
| Other assets . . . . . . . . . . . . . . . . . . . . . . . . . . . . . . . . . . . . . . | (902) | 289 | 285 |
| Accounts payable. . . . . . . . . . . . . . . . . . . . . . . . . . . . . . . . . . | 92 | 596 | 1,494 |
| Deferred revenue . . . . . . . . . . . . . . . . . . . . . . . . . . . . . . . . . . | 521 | 718 | 566 |
| Other liabilities. . . . . . . . . . . . . . . . . . . . . . . . . . . . . . . . . . . | (161) | 1,664 | 716 |
| Cash generated by operating activities . . . . . . . . . . . . . . . . | 10,159 | 9,596 | 5,470 |
| **Investing Activities** | | | |
| Purchases of marketable securities . . . . . . . . . . . . . . . . . . . . . . . . | (46,724) | (22,965) | (11,719) |
| Proceeds from maturities of marketable securities . . . . . . . . . . . . . | 19,790 | 11,804 | 6,483 |
| Proceeds from sales of marketable securities . . . . . . . . . . . . . . . . | 10,888 | 4,439 | 2,941 |
| Purchases of other long-term investments . . . . . . . . . . . . . . . . . . | (101) | (38) | (17) |
| Payments made in connection with business acquisitions, | | | |
| net of cash acquired . . . . . . . . . . . . . . . . . . . . . . . . . . . . . . . . | — | (220) | — |
| Payment for acquisition of property, plant and equipment . . . . . . . | (1,144) | (1,091) | (735) |
| Payment for acquisition of intangible assets . . . . . . . . . . . . . . . . | (69) | (108) | (251) |
| Other . . . . . . . . . . . . . . . . . . . . . . . . . . . . . . . . . . . . . . . . . . . | (74) | (10) | 49 |
| Cash used in investing activities . . . . . . . . . . . . . . . . . . . . . | (17,434) | (8,189) | (3,249) |
| **Financing Activities** | | | |
| Proceeds from issuance of common stock. . . . . . . . . . . . . . . . . . . | 475 | 483 | 365 |
| Excess tax benefits from stock-based compensation . . . . . . . . . . . . | 270 | 757 | 377 |
| Cash used to net share settle equity awards. . . . . . . . . . . . . . . . . . | (82) | (124) | (3) |
| Cash generated by financing activities. . . . . . . . . . . . . . . . | 663 | 1,116 | 739 |
| (Decrease)/increase in cash and cash equivalents . . . . . . . . . . . . . . . | (6,612) | 2,523 | 2,960 |
| Cash and cash equivalents, end of the year . . . . . . . . . . . . . . . . . . . | $ 5,263 | $11,875 | $ 9,352 |
| **Supplemental cash flow disclosures:** | | | |
| Cash paid for income taxes, net. . . . . . . . . . . . . . . . . . . . . . . . . . | $ 2,997 | $ 1,267 | $ 863 |

APPLE

# Palm Financial Report

## Palm, Inc.

### Consolidated Balance Sheets
(In thousands, except par value amounts)

| | May 31, 2009 | May 31, 2008 |
|---|---|---|
| **ASSETS** | | |
| Current assets | | |
| Cash and cash equivalents | $ 152,400 | $ 176,918 |
| Short-term investments | 102,733 | 81,830 |
| Accounts receivable, net of allowance for doubtful accounts of $350 and $1,169, respectively | 66,452 | 116,430 |
| Inventories | 19,716 | 67,461 |
| Deferred income taxes | 174 | 82,011 |
| Prepaids and other | 12,104 | 15,436 |
| Total current assets | 353,579 | 540,086 |
| Restricted investments | 9,496 | 8,620 |
| Non-current auction rate securities | 6,105 | 29,944 |
| Deferred costs | 14,896 | — |
| Property and equipment, net | 31,167 | 39,636 |
| Goodwill | 166,320 | 166,332 |
| Intangible assets, net | 48,914 | 61,048 |
| Deferred income taxes | 331 | 318,850 |
| Other assets | 12,428 | 15,746 |
| Total assets | $ 643,236 | $1,180,262 |
| **LIABILITIES AND STOCKHOLDERS' EQUITY (DEFICIT)** | | |
| Current liabilities | | |
| Accounts payable | $ 105,628 | $ 161,642 |
| Income taxes payable | 475 | 1,088 |
| Deferred revenues | 18,429 | 4,080 |
| Accrued restructuring | 6,090 | 8,058 |
| Current portion of long-term debt | 4,000 | 4,000 |
| Other accrued liabilities | 207,820 | 232,478 |
| Total current liabilities | 342,442 | 411,346 |
| Non-current liabilities | | |
| Long-term debt | 390,000 | 394,000 |
| Non-current deferred revenues | 13,077 | — |
| Non-current tax liabilities | 5,783 | 6,127 |
| Other non-current liabilities | — | 2,098 |
| Series B redeemable convertible preferred stock, $0.001 par value, 325 shares authorized and outstanding; aggregate liquidation value: $325,000 | 265,412 | 255,671 |
| Series C redeemable convertible preferred stock, $0.001 par value, 100 shares authorized; outstanding: 51 shares and 0 shares, respectively; aggregate liquidation value: $51,000 and $0, respectively | 40,387 | — |
| Stockholders' equity (deficit) | | |
| Preferred stock, $0.001 par value, 125,000 shares authorized: | | |
| Series A: 2,000 shares authorized, none outstanding | — | — |
| Common stock, $0.001 par value, 2,000,000 shares authorized; outstanding: 139,687 shares and 108,369 shares, respectively | 140 | 108 |
| Additional paid-in capital | 854,649 | 659,141 |
| Accumulated deficit | (1,269,672) | (537,484) |
| Accumulated other comprehensive income (loss) | 1,018 | (10,745) |
| Total stockholders' equity (deficit) | (413,865) | 111,020 |
| Total liabilities and stockholders' equity (deficit) | $ 643,236 | $1,180,262 |

PALM

## Palm, Inc.

### Consolidated Statements of Operations
(In thousands, except per share amounts)

| Years Ended May 31 | 2009 | 2008 | 2007 |
|---|---|---|---|
| Revenues | $ 735,872 | $1,318,691 | $1,560,507 |
| Cost of revenues | 576,113 | 916,810 | 985,369 |
| Gross profit | 159,759 | 401,881 | 575,138 |
| Operating expenses | | | |
| Sales and marketing | 174,052 | 229,702 | 248,685 |
| Research and development | 177,210 | 202,764 | 190,952 |
| General and administrative | 55,923 | 60,778 | 59,762 |
| Amortization of intangible assets | 3,054 | 3,775 | 1,981 |
| Restructuring charges | 16,134 | 30,353 | — |
| Casualty recovery | (268) | — | — |
| Patent acquisition cost (refund) | (1,537) | 5,000 | — |
| Gain on sale of land | — | (4,446) | — |
| In-process research and development | — | — | 3,700 |
| Total operating expenses | 424,568 | 527,926 | 505,080 |
| Operating income (loss) | (264,809) | (126,045) | 70,058 |
| Impairment of non-current auction rate securities | (35,885) | (32,175) | — |
| Interest (expense) | (25,299) | (20,397) | (1,970) |
| Interest income | 5,840 | 21,860 | 25,958 |
| Loss on series C derivative | (2,515) | — | — |
| Other income (expense), net | (5,255) | (1,471) | (1,619) |
| Income (loss) before income taxes | (327,923) | (158,228) | 92,427 |
| Income tax provision (benefit) | 404,265 | (52,809) | 36,044 |
| Net income (loss) | (732,188) | (105,419) | 56,383 |
| Accretion of series B and series C redeemable convertible preferred stock | 21,285 | 5,516 | — |
| Net income (loss) applicable to common shareholders | $(753,473) | $ (110,935) | $  56,383 |
| | | | |
| Net income (loss) per common share: | | | |
| Basic | $   (6.51) | $   (1.05) | $    0.55 |
| Diluted | $   (6.51) | $   (1.05) | $    0.54 |
| Shares used to compute net income (loss) per common share: | | | |
| Basic | 115,725 | 105,891 | 102,757 |
| Diluted | 115,725 | 105,891 | 104,442 |

PALM

## Palm, Inc.
### Consolidated Statements of Stockholders' Equity (Deficit) and Comprehensive Income (Loss)
(In thousands)

| | Common Stock | Additional Paid-In Capital | Unamortized Deferred Stock-Based Compensation | Accumulated Deficit | Accumulated Other Comprehensive Income (Loss) | Total |
|---|---|---|---|---|---|---|
| Balances, May 31, 2006 | $   103 | $1,475,319 | $   (2,752) | $   (488,081) | $   (684) | $   983,905 |
| Components of comprehensive income: | | | | | | |
| Net income | — | — | — | 56,383 | — | 56,383 |
| Net unrealized gains on available-for-sale investments | — | — | — | — | 1,522 | 1,522 |
| Recognized gains included in results of operations | — | — | — | — | (110) | (110) |
| Accumulated translation adjustments | — | — | — | — | 915 | 915 |
| Total comprehensive income | — | — | — | — | — | 58,710 |
| Common stock issued under stock plans, net | 3 | 21,923 | — | — | — | 21,926 |
| Stock-based compensation expense | — | 21,503 | 2,752 | — | — | 24,255 |
| Tax benefit from employee stock options | — | 4,578 | — | — | — | 4,578 |
| Shares repurchased and retired | (2) | (30,961) | | | | (30,963) |
| Balances, May 31, 2007 | 104 | 1,492,362 | — | (431,698) | 1,643 | 1,062,411 |
| Components of comprehensive loss: | | | | | | |
| Net loss | — | — | — | (105,419) | — | (105,419) |
| Net unrealized losses on available-for-sale investments | — | — | — | — | (1,261) | (1,261) |
| Net unrealized losses in value of non-current auction rate securities | — | — | — | — | (44,706) | (44,706) |
| Net recognized losses on non-current auction rate securities included in results of operations | — | — | — | — | 32,175 | 32,175 |
| Net recognized gains on available-for-sale investments included in results of operations | — | — | — | — | (68) | (68) |
| Accumulated translation adjustments | — | — | — | — | 1,472 | 1,472 |
| Total comprehensive loss | — | — | — | — | — | (117,807) |
| Common stock issued under stock plans, net | 4 | 28,433 | — | — | — | 28,437 |
| Stock-based compensation expense | — | 32,181 | — | — | — | 32,181 |
| Tax deficiency from employee stock options | — | (3,663) | — | — | — | (3,663) |
| Cash distribution to stockholders | — | (949,691) | — | — | — | (949,691) |
| Discount recognized on issuance of series B redeemable convertible preferred stock | — | 65,035 | — | — | — | 65,035 |
| Accretion of series B redeemable convertible preferred stock | — | (5,516) | — | — | — | (5,516) |
| Adjustment to accumulated deficit due to adoption of FIN No. 48 (see Note 16) | — | — | — | (367) | — | (367) |
| Balances, May 31, 2008 | 108 | 659,141 | — | (537,484) | (10,745) | 111,020 |
| Components of comprehensive loss: | | | | | | |
| Net loss | — | — | — | (732,188) | — | (732,188) |
| Net unrealized losses on available-for-sale investments | — | — | — | — | (1,649) | (1,649) |
| Net unrealized losses in value of non-current auction rate securities | — | — | — | — | (23,354) | (23,354) |
| Net recognized losses on non-current auction rate securities included in results of operations | — | — | — | — | 35,885 | 35,885 |
| Net recognized losses on available-for-sale investments included in results of operations | — | — | — | — | 3,594 | 3,594 |
| Accumulated translation adjustments | — | — | — | — | (2,713) | (2,713) |
| Total comprehensive loss | — | — | — | — | — | (720,425) |
| Common stock issued under stock plans, net | 5 | 15,531 | — | — | — | 15,536 |
| Stock-based compensation expense | — | 23,853 | — | — | — | 23,853 |
| Tax benefit from employee stock options | — | 1,924 | — | — | — | 1,924 |
| Distribution liability related to canceled shares of restricted stock | — | 34 | — | — | — | 34 |
| Accretion of series B and series C redeemable convertible preferred stock | — | (21,285) | — | — | — | (21,285) |
| Warrants recorded in connection with issuance of series C units | — | 21,966 | — | — | — | 21,966 |
| Conversion of series C units and issuance of additional common stock, net | 27 | 101,544 | — | — | — | 101,571 |
| Discount recognized on issuance of series C redeemable convertible preferred stock | — | 51,941 | — | — | — | 51,941 |
| Balances, May 31, 2009 | $   140 | $   854,649 | $   — | $   (1,269,672) | $   1,018 | $   (413,865) |

PALM

## Palm, Inc.

## Consolidated Statements of Cash Flows

### (In thousands)

| Years Ended May 31 | 2009 | 2008 | 2007 |
|---|---|---|---|
| **Cash flows from operating activities** | | | |
| Net income (loss) | $(732,188) | $(105,419) | $ 56,383 |
| Adjustments to reconcile net income (loss) to net cash flows from operating activities | | | |
| Depreciation | 19,677 | 19,699 | 13,316 |
| Stock-based compensation | 23,853 | 32,181 | 24,255 |
| Amortization of intangible assets | 12,134 | 16,510 | 8,315 |
| Amortization of debt issuance costs | 3,139 | 1,834 | — |
| In-process research and development | — | — | 3,700 |
| Deferred income taxes | 401,670 | (58,227) | 11,313 |
| Realized (gain) loss on short-term investments | 3,594 | (68) | (110) |
| Excess tax benefit related to stock-based compensation | (142) | (40) | (5,241) |
| Realized loss (gain) on disposition of property and equipment and sale of land | 619 | (4,446) | — |
| Impairment of non-current auction rate securities | 35,885 | 32,175 | — |
| Loss on series C derivative | 2,515 | — | — |
| Changes in assets and liabilities | | | |
| Accounts receivable | 48,425 | 89,312 | 2 |
| Inventories | 47,571 | (28,147) | 18,842 |
| Prepaids and other | 4,542 | 736 | 1,790 |
| Accounts payable | (54,883) | (35,840) | 11,654 |
| Income taxes payable | (346) | 3,033 | 16,421 |
| Accrued restructuring | (361) | 6,303 | (1,803) |
| Deferred revenues/costs, net | 12,530 | — | — |
| Other accrued liabilities | (16,746) | 12,866 | 9,354 |
| Net cash provided by (used in) operating activities | (188,512) | (17,538) | 168,191 |
| **Cash flows from investing activities** | | | |
| Purchase of brand name intangible asset | — | (1,500) | (44,000) |
| Purchase of property and equipment | (13,452) | (22,999) | (24,651) |
| Proceeds from sale of land | — | 64,446 | — |
| Cash paid for business acquisitions | — | (495) | (19,000) |
| Purchase of short-term investments | (112,385) | (517,104) | (682,882) |
| Sales/maturities of short-term investments | 88,109 | 777,917 | 671,623 |
| Purchase of restricted investments | (2,000) | (8,951) | — |
| Sale of restricted investments | 1,124 | 331 | — |
| Proceeds related to investments in non-current auction rate securities | 485 | 250 | — |
| Net cash provided by (used in) investing activities | (38,119) | 291,895 | (98,910) |
| **Cash flows from financing activities** | | | |
| Proceeds from issuance of common stock, net | 104,049 | — | — |
| Proceeds from issuance of common stock, employee stock plans | 15,536 | 28,437 | 21,926 |
| Purchase and subsequent retirement of common stock | — | — | (30,963) |
| Excess tax benefit related to stock-based compensation | 142 | 40 | 5,241 |
| Proceeds from issuance of redeemable convertible preferred stock and series C units, net | 99,173 | 315,190 | — |
| Proceeds from issuance of debt, net | — | 381,107 | — |
| Repayment of debt | (14,446) | (3,089) | (50,816) |
| Cash distribution to stockholders | (439) | (948,949) | — |
| Net cash provided by (used in) financing activities | 204,015 | (227,264) | (54,612) |
| Effects of exchange rate changes on cash and cash equivalents | (1,902) | 1,695 | — |
| Change in cash and cash equivalents | (24,518) | 48,788 | 14,669 |
| Cash and cash equivalents, beginning of period | 176,918 | 128,130 | 113,461 |
| Cash and cash equivalents, end of period | $ 152,400 | $ 176,918 | $ 128,130 |
| **Supplemental cash flow information:** | | | |
| Cash paid for income taxes | $ 3,402 | $ 3,391 | $ 8,900 |
| Cash paid for interest | $ 21,828 | $ 18,042 | $ 1,741 |
| **Non-cash investing and financing activities:** | | | |
| Liability for property and equipment acquired | $ — | $ 3,334 | $ 2,309 |

PALM

# Nokia Financial Report

**Nokia Corporation and Subsidiaries**
**Consolidated Statements of Financial Position**

| December 31 | 2009 EURm | 2008 EURm |
|---|---|---|
| **ASSETS** | | |
| **Non-current assets** | | |
| Capitalized development costs | 143 | 244 |
| Goodwill | 5 171 | 6 257 |
| Other intangible assets | 2 762 | 3 913 |
| Property, plant and equipment | 1 867 | 2 090 |
| Investments in associated companies | 69 | 96 |
| Available-for-sale investments | 554 | 512 |
| Deferred tax assets | 1 507 | 1 963 |
| Long-term loans receivable | 46 | 27 |
| Other non-current assets | 6 | 10 |
| | 12 125 | 15 112 |
| **Current assets** | | |
| Inventories | 1 865 | 2 533 |
| Accounts receivable, net of allowances for doubtful accounts (2009: EUR 391 million, 2008: EUR 415 million) | 7 981 | 9 444 |
| Prepaid expenses and accrued income | 4 551 | 4 538 |
| Current portion of long-term loans receivable | 14 | 101 |
| Other financial assets | 329 | 1 034 |
| Investments at fair value through profit and loss, liquid assets | 580 | — |
| Available-for-sale investments, liquid assets | 2 367 | 1 272 |
| Available-for-sale investments, cash equivalents | 4 784 | 3 842 |
| Bank and cash | 1 142 | 1 706 |
| | 23 613 | 24 470 |
| **Total assets** | 35 738 | 39 582 |
| **SHAREHOLDERS' EQUITY AND LIABILITIES** | | |
| **Capital and reserves attributable to equity holders of the parent** | | |
| Share capital | 246 | 246 |
| Share issue premium | 279 | 442 |
| Treasury shares, at cost | (681) | (1 881) |
| Translation differences | (127) | 341 |
| Fair value and other reserves | 69 | 62 |
| Reserve for invested non-restricted equity | 3 170 | 3 306 |
| Retained earnings | 10 132 | 11 692 |
| | 13 088 | 14 208 |
| **Minority interests** | 1 661 | 2 302 |
| **Total equity** | 14 749 | 16 510 |
| **Non-current liabilities** | | |
| Long-term interest-bearing liabilities | 4 432 | 861 |
| Deferred tax liabilities | 1 303 | 1 787 |
| Other long-term liabilities | 66 | 69 |
| | 5 801 | 2 717 |
| **Current liabilities** | | |
| Current portion of long-term loans | 44 | 13 |
| Short-term borrowings | 727 | 3 578 |
| Other financial liabilities | 245 | 924 |
| Accounts payable | 4 950 | 5 225 |
| Accrued expenses | 6 504 | 7 023 |
| Provisions | 2 718 | 3 592 |
| | 15 188 | 20 355 |
| **Total shareholders' equity and liabilities** | 35 738 | 39 582 |

NOKIA

## Nokia Corporation and Subsidiaries
### Consolidated Income Statements

| Financial Year Ended December 31 | 2009 EURm | 2008 EURm | 2007 EURm |
|---|---|---|---|
| Net sales | 40 984 | 50 710 | 51 058 |
| Cost of sales | (27 720) | (33 337) | (33 781) |
| Gross profit | 13 264 | 17 373 | 17 277 |
| Research and development expenses | (5 909) | (5 968) | (5 636) |
| Selling and marketing expenses | (3 933) | (4 380) | (4 379) |
| Administrative and general expenses | (1 145) | (1 284) | (1 165) |
| Impairment of goodwill | (908) | — | — |
| Other income | 338 | 420 | 2 312 |
| Other expenses | (510) | (1 195) | (424) |
| Operating profit | 1 197 | 4 966 | 7 985 |
| Share of results of associated companies | 30 | 6 | 44 |
| Financial income and expenses | (265) | (2) | 239 |
| Profit before tax | 962 | 4 970 | 8 268 |
| Tax | (702) | (1 081) | (1 522) |
| Profit | 260 | 3 889 | 6 746 |
| Profit attributable to equity holders of the parent | 891 | 3 988 | 7 205 |
| Loss attributable to minority interests | (631) | (99) | (459) |
|  | 260 | 3 889 | 6 746 |

| | 2009 EUR | 2008 EUR | 2007 EUR |
|---|---|---|---|
| **Earnings per share** | | | |
| (for profit attributable to the equity holders of the parent) | | | |
| Basic | 0.24 | 1.07 | 1.85 |
| Diluted | 0.24 | 1.05 | 1.83 |

| | 2009 | 2008 | 2007 |
|---|---|---|---|
| **Average number of shares (000's shares)** | | | |
| Basic | 3 705 116 | 3 743 622 | 3 885 408 |
| Diluted | 3 721 072 | 3 780 363 | 3 932 008 |

## Nokia Corporation and Subsidiaries
### Consolidated Statements of Comprehensive Income

| Financial Year Ended December 31 | 2009 EURm | 2008 EURm | 2007 EURm |
|---|---|---|---|
| Profit | 260 | 3 889 | 6 746 |
| Other comprehensive income | | | |
| Translation differences | (563) | 595 | (151) |
| Net investment hedge gains (losses) | 114 | (123) | 51 |
| Cash flow hedges | 25 | (40) | (7) |
| Available-for-sale investments | 48 | (15) | 49 |
| Other increase (decrease), net | (7) | 28 | (46) |
| Income tax related to components of other comprehensive income | (44) | 58 | (12) |
| Other comprehensive income (expense), net of tax | (427) | 503 | (116) |
| Total comprehensive income (expense) | (167) | 4 392 | 6 630 |
| Total comprehensive income (expense) attributable to: | | | |
| Equity holders of the parent | 429 | 4 577 | 7 073 |
| Minority interests | (596) | (185) | (443) |
|  | (167) | 4 392 | 6 630 |

NOKIA

**Nokia Corporation and Subsidiaries**
**Consolidated Statements of Changes in Shareholders' Equity**

| | Number of shares (000's) | Share capital | Share issue premium | Treasury shares | Translation differences | Fair value and other reserves | Reserve for invested non-restrict. equity | Retained earnings | Before minority interests | Minority interests | Total |
|---|---|---|---|---|---|---|---|---|---|---|---|
| Balance at December 31, 2007 | 3 845 950 | 246 | 644 | (3 146) | (163) | 23 | 3 299 | 13 870 | 14 773 | 2 565 | 17 338 |
| Translation differences | | | | | 595 | | | | 595 | | 595 |
| Net investment hedge gains, net of tax | | | | | (91) | | | | (91) | | (91) |
| Cash flow hedges, net of tax | | | | | | 42 | | | 42 | (67) | (25) |
| Available-for-sale investments, net of tax | | | | | | (3) | | | (3) | (2) | (5) |
| Other increase, net | | | | | | | | 46 | 46 | (17) | 29 |
| Profit | | | | | | | | 3 988 | 3 988 | (99) | 3 889 |
| Total comprehensive income | | — | — | | 504 | 39 | — | 4 034 | 4 577 | (185) | 4 392 |
| Stock options exercised | 3 547 | | | | | | 51 | | 51 | | 51 |
| Stock options exercised related to acquisitions | | | 1 | | | | | | 1 | | 1 |
| Share-based compensation | | | 74 | | | | | | 74 | | 74 |
| Excess tax benefit on share-based compensation | | | (117) | | | | | | (117) | (6) | (124) |
| Settlement of performance and restricted shares | 5 622 | | (179) | 154 | | | (44) | | (69) | | (69) |
| Acquisition of treasury shares | (157 390) | | | (3 123) | | | | | (3 123) | | (3 123) |
| Reissuance of treasury shares | 143 | | | 2 | | | | | 2 | | 2 |
| Cancellation of treasury shares | | | 0 | 4 232 | | | | (4 232) | — | | |
| Dividend | | | | | | | | (1 992) | (1 992) | (35) | (2 027) |
| Acquisitions and other change in minority interests | | | | | | | | | | (37) | (37) |
| Vested portion of share-based payment awards related to acquisitions | | | 19 | | | | | | 19 | | 19 |
| Acquisition of Symbian | | | | | | | | 12 | 12 | | 12 |
| Total of other equity movements | | — | (202) | 1 265 | — | — | 7 | (6 212) | (5 142) | (78) | (5 220) |
| Balance at December 31, 2008 | 3 697 872 | 246 | 442 | (1 881) | 341 | 62 | 3 306 | 11 692 | 14 208 | 2 302 | 16 510 |
| Translation differences | | | | | (552) | | | | (552) | (9) | (561) |
| Net investment hedge gains, net of tax | | | | | 84 | | | | 84 | | 84 |
| Cash flow hedges, net of tax | | | | | | (35) | | | (35) | 49 | 14 |
| Available-for-sale investments, net of tax | | | | | | 42 | | | 42 | 2 | 44 |
| Other decrease, net | | | | | | | | (1) | (1) | (7) | (8) |
| Profit | | | | | | | | 891 | 891 | (631) | 260 |
| Total comprehensive income | | — | — | | (468) | 7 | — | 890 | 429 | (596) | (167) |
| Stock options exercised | 7 | | | | | | — | | | | |
| Stock options exercised related to acquisitions | | | (1) | | | | | | (1) | | (1) |
| Share-based compensation | | | 16 | | | | | | 16 | | 16 |
| Excess tax benefit on share-based compensation | | | (12) | | | | | | (12) | (1) | (13) |
| Settlement of performance and restricted shares | 10 352 | | (166) | 230 | | | (136) | | (72) | | (72) |
| Acquisition of treasury shares | | | | | | | | | — | | |
| Reissuance of treasury shares | 31 | | | 1 | | | | | 1 | | 1 |
| Cancellation of treasury shares | | | | 969 | | | | (969) | — | | |
| Dividend | | | | | | | | (1 481) | (1 481) | (44) | (1 525) |
| Total of other equity movements | | — | (163) | 1 200 | — | — | (136) | (2 450) | (1 549) | (45) | (1 594) |
| Balance at December 31, 2009 | 3 708 262 | 246 | 279 | (681) | (127) | 69 | 3 170 | 10 132 | 13 088 | 1 661 | 14 749 |

Dividends declared per share were EUR 0.40 for 2009 (EUR 0.40 for 2008 and EUR 0.53 for 2007), subject to shareholders' approval.

## Nokia Corporation and Subsidiaries
## Consolidated Statements of Cash Flows

| Financial Year Ended December 31 | 2009 EURm | 2008 EURm | 2007 EURm |
|---|---|---|---|
| **Cash flow from operating activities** | | | |
| Profit attributable to equity holders of the parent | **891** | 3 988 | 7 205 |
| Adjustments, total | **3 390** | 3 024 | 1 159 |
| Change in net working capital | **140** | (2 546) | 605 |
| Cash generated from operations | **4 421** | 4 466 | 8 969 |
| Interest received | **125** | 416 | 362 |
| Interest paid | **(256)** | (155) | (59) |
| Other financial income and expenses, net received | **(128)** | 250 | 67 |
| Income taxes paid, net received | **(915)** | (1 780) | (1 457) |
| **Net cash from operating activities** | **3 247** | 3 197 | 7 882 |
| **Cash flow from investing activities** | | | |
| Acquisition of Group companies, net of acquired cash | **(29)** | (5 962) | 253 |
| Purchase of current available-for-sale investments, liquid assets | **(2 800)** | (669) | (4 798) |
| Purchase of investments at fair value through profit and loss, liquid assets | **(695)** | — | — |
| Purchase of non-current available-for-sale investments | **(95)** | (121) | (126) |
| Purchase of shares in associated companies | **(30)** | (24) | (25) |
| Additions to capitalized development costs | **(27)** | (131) | (157) |
| Long-term loans made to customers | **—** | — | (261) |
| Proceeds from repayment and sale of long-term loans receivable | **—** | 129 | 163 |
| Proceeds from (+) / payment of (-) other long-term receivables | **2** | (1) | 5 |
| Proceeds from (+) / payment of (-) short-term loans receivable | **2** | (15) | (119) |
| Capital expenditures | **(531)** | (889) | (715) |
| Proceeds from disposal of shares in associated companies | **40** | 3 | 6 |
| Proceeds from disposal of businesses | **61** | 41 | — |
| Proceeds from maturities and sale of current available-for-sale investments, liquid assets | **1 730** | 4 664 | 4 930 |
| Proceeds from maturities and sale of investments at fair value through profit and loss, liquid assets | **108** | — | — |
| Proceeds from sale of non-current available-for-sale investments | **14** | 10 | 50 |
| Proceeds from sale of fixed assets | **100** | 54 | 72 |
| Dividends received | **2** | 6 | 12 |
| **Net cash used in investing activities** | **(2 148)** | (2 905) | (710) |
| **Cash flow from financing activities** | | | |
| Proceeds from stock option exercises | **—** | 53 | 987 |
| Purchase of treasury shares | **—** | (3 121) | (3 819) |
| Proceeds from long-term borrowings | **3 901** | 714 | 115 |
| Repayment of long-term borrowings | **(209)** | (34) | (16) |
| Proceeds from (+) / repayment of (-) short-term borrowings | **(2 842)** | 2 891 | 661 |
| Dividends paid | **(1 546)** | (2 048) | (1 760) |
| **Net cash used in financing activities** | **(696)** | (1 545) | (3 832) |
| **Foreign exchange adjustment** | **(25)** | (49) | (15) |
| **Net increase (+) / decrease (-) in cash and cash equivalents** | **378** | (1 302) | 3 325 |
| **Cash and cash equivalents at beginning of period** | **5 548** | 6 850 | 3 525 |
| **Cash and cash equivalents at end of period** | **5 926** | 5 548 | 6 850 |
| | | | |
| Cash and cash equivalents comprise of: | | | |
| Bank and cash | **1 142** | 1 706 | 2 125 |
| Current available-for-sale investments, cash equivalents | **4 784** | 3 842 | 4 725 |
| | **5 926** | 5 548 | 6 850 |

NOKIA

## CAP

### CONCEPTUAL

**C1** Describe the earning of interest and the concepts of present and future values. (p. B-1)

### PROCEDURAL

**P1** Apply present value concepts to a single amount by using interest tables. (p. B-3)

**P2** Apply future value concepts to a single amount by using interest tables. (p. B-4)

**P3** Apply present value concepts to an annuity by using interest tables. (p. B-5)

**P4** Apply future value concepts to an annuity by using interest tables. (p. B-6)

The concepts of present and future values are important to modern business, including the preparation and analysis of financial statements. The purpose of this appendix is to explain, illustrate, and compute present and future values. This appendix applies these concepts with reference to both business and everyday activities.

### Time Value of Money

| Present and Future Value Concepts | Value of a Single Amount | Value of an Annuity |
| --- | --- | --- |
| • Time is money<br>• Concept of interest | • Present value of a single amount<br>• Future value of a single amount | • Present value of an annuity<br>• Future value of an annuity |

# PRESENT AND FUTURE VALUE CONCEPTS

The old saying "Time is money" reflects the notion that as time passes, the values of our assets and liabilities change. This change is due to *interest,* which is a borrower's payment to the owner of an asset for its use. The most common example of interest is a savings account asset. As we keep a balance of cash in the account, it earns interest that the financial institution pays us. An example of a liability is a car loan. As we carry the balance of the loan, we accumulate interest costs on it. We must ultimately repay this loan with interest.

**C1** Describe the earning of interest and the concepts of present and future values.

Present and future value computations enable us to measure or estimate the interest component of holding assets or liabilities over time. The present value computation is important when we want to know the value of future-day assets *today.* The future value computation is important when we want to know the value of present-day assets *at a future date.* The first section focuses on the present value of a single amount. The second section focuses on the future value of a single amount. Then both the present and future values of a series of amounts (called an *annuity*) are defined and explained.

### Decision Insight

**Keep That Job** Lottery winners often never work again. Kenny Dukes, a recent Georgia lottery winner, doesn't have that option. He is serving parole for burglary charges, and Georgia requires its parolees to be employed (or in school). For his lottery winnings, Dukes had to choose between $31 million in 30 annual payments or $16 million in one lump sum ($10.6 million after-tax); he chose the latter. ■

# PRESENT VALUE OF A SINGLE AMOUNT

We graphically express the present value, called *p,* of a single future amount, called *f,* that is received or paid at a future date in Exhibit B.1.

**EXHIBIT B.1**

Present Value of a Single Amount Diagram

The formula to compute the present value of a single amount is shown in Exhibit B.2, where $p$ = present value; $f$ = future value; $i$ = rate of interest per period; and $n$ = number of periods. (Interest is also called the *discount,* and an interest rate is also called the *discount rate.*)

**EXHIBIT B.2**

Present Value of a Single Amount Formula

$$p = \frac{f}{(1 + i)^n}$$

To illustrate present value concepts, assume that we need $220 one period from today. We want to know how much we must invest now, for one period, at an interest rate of 10% to provide for this $220. For this illustration, the $p$, or present value, is the unknown amount—the specifics are shown graphically as follows:

Conceptually, we know $p$ must be less than $220. This is obvious from the answer to this question: Would we rather have $220 today or $220 at some future date? If we had $220 today, we could invest it and see it grow to something more than $220 in the future. Therefore, we would prefer the $220 today. This means that if we were promised $220 in the future, we would take less than $220 today. But how much less? To answer that question, we compute an estimate of the present value of the $220 to be received one period from now using the formula in Exhibit B.2 as follows:

$$p = \frac{f}{(1 + i)^n} = \frac{\$220}{(1 + 0.10)^1} = \$200$$

We interpret this result to say that given an interest rate of 10%, we are indifferent between $200 today or $220 at the end of one period.

We can also use this formula to compute the present value for *any number of periods.* To illustrate, consider a payment of $242 at the end of two periods at 10% interest. The present value of this $242 to be received two periods from now is computed as follows:

$$p = \frac{f}{(1 + i)^n} = \frac{\$242}{(1 + 0.10)^2} = \$200$$

Together, these results tell us we are indifferent between $200 today, or $220 one period from today, or $242 two periods from today given a 10% interest rate per period.

The number of periods ($n$) in the present value formula does not have to be expressed in years. Any period of time such as a day, a month, a quarter, or a year can be used. Whatever period is used, the interest rate ($i$) must be compounded for the same period. This means that if a situation expresses $n$ in months and $i$ equals 12% per year, then $i$ is transformed into interest earned per month (or 1%). In this case, interest is said to be *compounded monthly.*

A present value table helps us with present value computations. It gives us present values (factors) for a variety of both interest rates ($i$) and periods ($n$). Each present value in a present value table assumes that the future value ($f$) equals 1. When the future value ($f$) is different from 1, we simply multiply the present value ($p$) from the table by that future value to give us the estimate. The formula used to construct a table of present values for a single future amount of 1 is shown in Exhibit B.3.

**EXHIBIT B.3**

Present Value of 1 Formula

$$p = \frac{1}{(1 + i)^n}$$

This formula is identical to that in Exhibit B.2 except that *f* equals 1. Table B.1 at the end of this appendix is such a present value table. It is often called a **present value of 1 table**. A present value table involves three factors: *p*, *i*, and *n*. Knowing two of these three factors allows us to compute the third. (A fourth is *f*, but as already explained, we need only multiply the 1 used in the formula by *f*.) To illustrate the use of a present value table, consider three cases.

> **P1** Apply present value concepts to a single amount by using interest tables.

**Case I**   (solve for *p* when knowing *i* and *n*). To show how we use a present value table, let's look again at how we estimate the present value of $220 (the *f* value) at the end of one period (*n* = 1) where the interest rate (*i*) is 10%. To solve this case, we go to the present value table (Table B.1) and look in the row for 1 period and in the column for 10% interest. Here we find a present value (*p*) of 0.9091 based on a future value of 1. This means, for instance, that $1 to be received one period from today at 10% interest is worth $0.9091 today. Since the future value in this case is not $1 but $220, we multiply the 0.9091 by $220 to get an answer of $200.

**Case 2**   (solve for *n* when knowing *p* and *i*). To illustrate, assume a $100,000 future value (*f*) that is worth $13,000 today (*p*) using an interest rate of 12% (*i*) but where *n* is unknown. In particular, we want to know how many periods (*n*) there are between the present value and the future value. To put this in context, it would fit a situation in which we want to retire with $100,000 but currently have only $13,000 that is earning a 12% return and we will be unable to save any additional money. How long will it be before we can retire? To answer this, we go to Table B.1 and look in the 12% interest column. Here we find a column of present values (*p*) based on a future value of 1. To use the present value table for this solution, we must divide $13,000 (*p*) by $100,000 (*f*), which equals 0.1300. This is necessary because *a present value table defines f equal to 1, and p as a fraction of 1*. We look for a value nearest to 0.1300 (*p*), which we find in the row for 18 periods (*n*). This means that the present value of $100,000 at the end of 18 periods at 12% interest is $13,000; alternatively stated, we must work 18 more years.

**Case 3**   (solve for *i* when knowing *p* and *n*). In this case, we have, say, a $120,000 future value (*f*) worth $60,000 today (*p*) when there are nine periods (*n*) between the present and future values, but the interest rate is unknown. As an example, suppose we want to retire with $120,000, but we have only $60,000 and we will be unable to save any additional money, yet we hope to retire in nine years. What interest rate must we earn to retire with $120,000 in nine years? To answer this, we go to the present value table (Table B.1) and look in the row for nine periods. To use the present value table, we must divide $60,000 (*p*) by $120,000 (*f*), which equals 0.5000. Recall that this step is necessary because a present value table defines *f* equal to 1 and *p* as a fraction of 1. We look for a value in the row for nine periods that is nearest to 0.5000 (*p*), which we find in the column for 8% interest (*i*). This means that the present value of $120,000 at the end of nine periods at 8% interest is $60,000 or, in our example, we must earn 8% annual interest to retire in nine years.

---

**Quick Check**                                       Answer — p. B-7

> **1.** A company is considering an investment expected to yield $70,000 after six years. If this company demands an 8% return, how much is it willing to pay for this investment?

---

## FUTURE VALUE OF A SINGLE AMOUNT

We must modify the formula for the present value of a single amount to obtain the formula for the future value of a single amount. In particular, we multiply both sides of the equation in Exhibit B.2 by $(1 + i)^n$ to get the result shown in Exhibit B.4.

$$f = p \times (1 + i)^n$$

**EXHIBIT B.4**

Future Value of a Single Amount Formula

The future value ($f$) is defined in terms of $p$, $i$, and $n$. We can use this formula to determine that $200 ($p$) invested for 1 ($n$) period at an interest rate of 10% ($i$) yields a future value of $220 as follows:

$$f = p \times (1 + i)^n$$
$$= \$200 \times (1 + 0.10)^1$$
$$= \$220$$

**P2** Apply future value concepts to a single amount by using interest tables.

This formula can also be used to compute the future value of an amount for *any number of periods* into the future. To illustrate, assume that $200 is invested for three periods at 10%. The future value of this $200 is $266.20, computed as follows:

$$f = p \times (1 + i)^n$$
$$= \$200 \times (1 + 0.10)^3$$
$$= \$266.20$$

A future value table makes it easier for us to compute future values ($f$) for many different combinations of interest rates ($i$) and time periods ($n$). Each future value in a future value table assumes the present value ($p$) is 1. As with a present value table, if the future amount is something other than 1, we simply multiply our answer by that amount. The formula used to construct a table of future values (factors) for a single amount of 1 is in Exhibit B.5.

**EXHIBIT B.5**

Future Value of 1 Formula

$$f = (1 + i)^n$$

Table B.2 at the end of this appendix shows a table of future values for a current amount of 1. This type of table is called a **future value of 1 table**.

There are some important relations between Tables B.1 and B.2. In Table B.2, for the row where $n = 0$, the future value is 1 for each interest rate. This is so because no interest is earned when time does not pass. We also see that Tables B.1 and B.2 report the same information but in a different manner. In particular, one table is simply the *inverse* of the other. To illustrate this inverse relation, let's say we invest $100 for a period of five years at 12% per year. How much do we expect to have after five years? We can answer this question using Table B.2 by finding the future value ($f$) of 1, for five periods from now, compounded at 12%. From that table we find $f = 1.7623$. If we start with $100, the amount it accumulates to after five years is $176.23 ($100 \times 1.7623$). We can alternatively use Table B.1. Here we find that the present value ($p$) of 1, discounted five periods at 12%, is 0.5674. Recall the inverse relation between present value and future value. This means that $p = 1/f$ (or equivalently, $f = 1/p$). We can compute the future value of $100 invested for five periods at 12% as follows: $f = \$100 \times (1/0.5674) = \$176.24$ (which equals the $176.23 just computed, except for a 1 cent rounding difference).

A future value table involves three factors: $f$, $i$, and $n$. Knowing two of these three factors allows us to compute the third. To illustrate, consider these three possible cases.

**Case 1**   (solve for $f$ when knowing $i$ and $n$). Our preceding example fits this case. We found that $100 invested for five periods at 12% interest accumulates to $176.24.

**Case 2**   (solve for $n$ when knowing $f$ and $i$). In this case, we have, say, $2,000 ($p$) and we want to know how many periods ($n$) it will take to accumulate to $3,000 ($f$) at 7% ($i$) interest. To answer this, we go to the future value table (Table B.2) and look in the 7% interest column. Here we find a column of future values ($f$) based on a present value of 1. To use a future value table, we must divide $3,000 ($f$) by $2,000 ($p$), which equals 1.500. This is necessary because *a future value table defines* p *equal to 1, and* f *as a multiple of 1*. We look for a value nearest to 1.50 ($f$), which we find in the row for six periods ($n$). This means that $2,000 invested for six periods at 7% interest accumulates to $3,000.

**Case 3**   (solve for $i$ when knowing $f$ and $n$). In this case, we have, say, $2,001 ($p$), and in nine years ($n$) we want to have $4,000 ($f$). What rate of interest must we earn to accomplish this? To answer that, we go to Table B.2 and search in the row for nine periods. To use a future value table, we must divide $4,000 ($f$) by $2,001 ($p$), which equals 1.9990. Recall that this is necessary because a future value table defines *p* equal to 1 and *f* as a multiple of 1. We look for a value nearest to 1.9990 (*f*), which we find in the column for 8% interest (*i*). This means that $2,001 invested for nine periods at 8% interest accumulates to $4,000.

**2.** Assume that you win a $150,000 cash sweepstakes. You decide to deposit this cash in an account earning 8% annual interest, and you plan to quit your job when the account equals $555,000. How many years will it be before you can quit working?

# PRESENT VALUE OF AN ANNUITY

An *annuity* is a series of equal payments occurring at equal intervals. One example is a series of three annual payments of $100 each. An *ordinary annuity* is defined as equal end-of-period payments at equal intervals. An ordinary annuity of $100 for three periods and its present value (*p*) are illustrated in Exhibit B.6.

**EXHIBIT B.6**

Present Value of an Ordinary Annuity Diagram

One way to compute the present value of an ordinary annuity is to find the present value of each payment using our present value formula from Exhibit B.3. We then add each of the three present values. To illustrate, let's look at three $100 payments at the end of each of the next three periods with an interest rate of 15%. Our present value computations are

**P3** Apply present value concepts to an annuity by using interest tables.

$$p = \frac{\$100}{(1 + 0.15)^1} + \frac{\$100}{(1 + 0.15)^2} + \frac{\$100}{(1 + 0.15)^3} = \$228.32$$

This computation is identical to computing the present value of each payment (from Table B.1) and taking their sum or, alternatively, adding the values from Table B.1 for each of the three payments and multiplying their sum by the $100 annuity payment.

A more direct way is to use a present value of annuity table. Table B.3 at the end of this appendix is one such table. This table is called a **present value of an annuity of 1 table**. If we look at Table B.3 where *n* = 3 and *i* = 15%, we see the present value is 2.2832. This means that the present value of an annuity of 1 for three periods, with a 15% interest rate, equals 2.2832.

A present value of an annuity formula is used to construct Table B.3. It can also be constructed by adding the amounts in a present value of 1 table. To illustrate, we use Tables B.1 and B.3 to confirm this relation for the prior example:

| From Table B.1 | | From Table B.3 | |
|---|---|---|---|
| *i* = 15%, *n* = 1 . . . . . . . . | 0.8696 | | |
| *i* = 15%, *n* = 2 . . . . . . . . | 0.7561 | | |
| *i* = 15%, *n* = 3 . . . . . . . . | 0.6575 | | |
| Total . . . . . . . . . . . . . . | 2.2832 | *i* = 15%, *n* = 3 . . . . . . . . | 2.2832 |

We can also use business calculators or spreadsheet programs to find the present value of an annuity.

**Decision Insight**

**Better Lucky Than Good**   "I don't have good luck—I'm blessed," proclaimed Andrew "Jack" Whittaker, 55, a sewage treatment contractor, after winning the largest ever undivided jackpot in a U.S. lottery. Whittaker had to choose between $315 million in 30 annual installments or $170 million in one lump sum ($112 million after-tax). ■

**Quick Check**                                                          Answer — p. B-7

3.  A company is considering an investment paying $10,000 every six months for three years. The first payment would be received in six months. If this company requires an 8% annual return, what is the maximum amount it is willing to pay for this investment?

# FUTURE VALUE OF AN ANNUITY

The future value of an *ordinary annuity* is the accumulated value of each annuity payment with interest as of the date of the final payment. To illustrate, let's consider the earlier annuity of three annual payments of $100. Exhibit B.7 shows the point in time for the future value ($f$). The first payment is made two periods prior to the point when future value is determined, and the final payment occurs on the future value date.

**EXHIBIT B.7**

Future Value of an Ordinary
Annuity Diagram

One way to compute the future value of an annuity is to use the formula to find the future value of *each* payment and add them. If we assume an interest rate of 15%, our calculation is

$$f = \$100 \times (1 + 0.15)^2 + \$100 \times (1 + 0.15)^1 + \$100 \times (1 + 0.15)^0 = \$347.25$$

This is identical to using Table B.2 and summing the future values of each payment, or adding the future values of the three payments of 1 and multiplying the sum by $100.

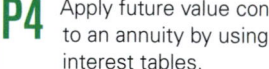 Apply future value concepts to an annuity by using interest tables.

A more direct way is to use a table showing future values of annuities. Such a table is called a **future value of an annuity of 1 table**. Table B.4 at the end of this appendix is one such table. Note that in Table B.4 when $n = 1$, the future values equal 1 ($f = 1$) for all rates of interest. This is so because such an annuity consists of only one payment and the future value is determined on the date of that payment—no time passes between the payment and its future value. The future value of an annuity formula is used to construct Table B.4. We can also construct it by adding the amounts from a future value of 1 table. To illustrate, we use Tables B.2 and B.4 to confirm this relation for the prior example:

| From Table B.2 | | From Table B.4 | |
|---|---|---|---|
| $i = 15\%, n = 0$ ......... | 1.0000 | | |
| $i = 15\%, n = 1$ ......... | 1.1500 | | |
| $i = 15\%, n = 2$ ......... | 1.3225 | | |
| Total ............... | 3.4725 | $i = 15\%, n = 3$ ........ | 3.4725 |

Note that the future value in Table B.2 is 1.0000 when $n = 0$, but the future value in Table B.4 is 1.0000 when $n = 1$. Is this a contradiction? No. When $n = 0$ in Table B.2, the future value is determined on the date when a single payment occurs. This means that no interest is earned because no time has passed, and the future value equals the payment. Table B.4 describes an-nuities with equal payments occurring at the end of each period. When $n = 1$, the annuity has one payment, and its future value equals 1 on the date of its final and only payment. Again, no time passes between the payment and its future value date.

## Quick Check                                    Answer — p. B-7

**4.** A company invests $45,000 per year for five years at 12% annual interest. Compute the value of this annuity investment at the end of five years.

# Summary

**C1** **Describe the earning of interest and the concepts of present and future values.** Interest is payment by a borrower to the owner of an asset for its use. Present and future value computations are a way for us to estimate the interest component of holding assets or liabilities over a period of time.

**P1** **Apply present value concepts to a single amount by using interest tables.** The present value of a single amount received at a future date is the amount that can be invested now at the speci-fied interest rate to yield that future value.

**P2** **Apply future value concepts to a single amount by using interest tables.** The future value of a single amount invested

at a specified rate of interest is the amount that would accumulate by the future date.

**P3** **Apply present value concepts to an annuity by using interest tables.** The present value of an annuity is the amount that can be invested now at the specified interest rate to yield that series of equal periodic payments.

**P4** **Apply future value concepts to an annuity by using interest tables.** The future value of an annuity invested at a specific rate of interest is the amount that would accumulate by the date of the final payment.

## Guidance Answers to Quick Checks

**1.** $70,000 × 0.6302 = $44,114 (use Table B.1, $i = 8\%$, $n = 6$).

**2.** $555,000/$150,000 = 3.7000; Table B.2 shows this value is not achieved until after 17 years at 8% interest.

**3.** $10,000 × 5.2421 = $52,421 (use Table B.3, $i = 4\%$, $n = 6$).

**4.** $45,000 × 6.3528 = $285,876 (use Table B.4, $i = 12\%$, $n = 5$).

## ■ connect

Assume that you must make future value estimates using the *future value of 1 table* (Table B.2). Which interest rate column do you use when working with the following rates?

**1.** 8% compounded quarterly

**2.** 12% compounded annually

**3.** 6% compounded semiannually

**4.** 12% compounded monthly

**QUICK STUDY**

**QS B-1**
Identifying interest rates in tables
**C1**

---

Ken Francis is offered the possibility of investing $2,745 today and in return to receive $10,000 after 15 years. What is the annual rate of interest for this investment? (Use Table B.1.)

**QS B-2**
Interest rate on an investment   **P1**

---

Megan Brink is offered the possibility of investing $6,651 today at 6% interest per year in a desire to accumulate $10,000. How many years must Brink wait to accumulate $10,000? (Use Table B.1.)

**QS B-3**
Number of periods of an investment   **P1**

---

Flaherty is considering an investment that, if paid for immediately, is expected to return $140,000 five years from now. If Flaherty demands a 9% return, how much is she willing to pay for this investment?

**QS B-4**
Present value of an amount   **P1**

---

CII, Inc., invests $630,000 in a project expected to earn a 12% annual rate of return. The earnings will be reinvested in the project each year until the entire investment is liquidated 10 years later. What will the cash proceeds be when the project is liquidated?

**QS B-5**
Future value of an amount   **P2**

| | |
|---|---|
| **QS B-6**<br>Present value<br>of an annuity   P3 | Beene Distributing is considering a project that will return $150,000 annually at the end of each year for six years. If Beene demands an annual return of 7% and pays for the project immediately, how much is it willing to pay for the project? |
| **QS B-7**<br>Future value<br>of an annuity   P4 | Claire Fitch is planning to begin an individual retirement program in which she will invest $1,500 at the end of each year. Fitch plans to retire after making 30 annual investments in the program earning a return of 10%. What is the value of the program on the date of the last payment? |

## EXERCISES

| | |
|---|---|
| **Exercise B-1**<br>Number of periods<br>of an investment   P2 | Bill Thompson expects to invest $10,000 at 12% and, at the end of a certain period, receive $96,463. How many years will it be before Thompson receives the payment? (Use Table B.2.) |
| **Exercise B-2**<br>Interest rate on<br>an investment   P2 | Ed Summers expects to invest $10,000 for 25 years, after which he wants to receive $108,347. What rate of interest must Summers earn? (Use Table B.2.) |
| **Exercise B-3**<br>Interest rate on<br>an investment   P3 | Jones expects an immediate investment of $57,466 to return $10,000 annually for eight years, with the first payment to be received one year from now. What rate of interest must Jones earn? (Use Table B.3.) |
| **Exercise B-4**<br>Number of periods<br>of an investment   P3 | Keith Riggins expects an investment of $82,014 to return $10,000 annually for several years. If Riggins earns a return of 10%, how many annual payments will he receive? (Use Table B.3.) |
| **Exercise B-5**<br>Interest rate on<br>an investment   P4 | Algoe expects to invest $1,000 annually for 40 years to yield an accumulated value of $154,762 on the date of the last investment. For this to occur, what rate of interest must Algoe earn? (Use Table B.4.) |
| **Exercise B-6**<br>Number of periods<br>of an investment   P4 | Kate Beckwith expects to invest $10,000 annually that will earn 8%. How many annual investments must Beckwith make to accumulate $303,243 on the date of the last investment? (Use Table B.4.) |
| **Exercise B-7**<br>Present value<br>of an annuity   P3 | Sam Weber finances a new automobile by paying $6,500 cash and agreeing to make 40 monthly payments of $500 each, the first payment to be made one month after the purchase. The loan bears interest at an annual rate of 12%. What is the cost of the automobile? |
| **Exercise B-8**<br>Present value of bonds<br>P1  P3 | Spiller Corp. plans to issue 10%, 15-year, $500,000 par value bonds payable that pay interest semiannually on June 30 and December 31. The bonds are dated December 31, 2011, and are issued on that date. If the market rate of interest for the bonds is 8% on the date of issue, what will be the total cash proceeds from the bond issue? |
| **Exercise B-9**<br>Present value<br>of an amount   P1 | McAdams Company expects to earn 10% per year on an investment that will pay $606,773 six years from now. Use Table B.1 to compute the present value of this investment. (Round the amount to the nearest dollar.) |
| **Exercise B-10**<br>Present value of<br>an amount and<br>of an annuity   P1  P3 | Compute the amount that can be borrowed under each of the following circumstances:<br>**1.** A promise to repay $90,000 seven years from now at an interest rate of 6%.<br>**2.** An agreement made on February 1, 2011, to make three separate payments of $20,000 on February 1 of 2012, 2013, and 2014. The annual interest rate is 10%. |
| **Exercise B-11**<br>Present value<br>of an amount   P1 | On January 1, 2011, a company agrees to pay $20,000 in three years. If the annual interest rate is 10%, determine how much cash the company can borrow with this agreement. |

Find the amount of money that can be borrowed today with each of the following separate debt agreements *a* through *f.* (Round amounts to the nearest dollar.)

| Case | Single Future Payment | Number of Periods | Interest Rate |
|---|---|---|---|
| a. ........ | $40,000 | 3 | 4% |
| b. ........ | 75,000 | 7 | 8 |
| c. ........ | 52,000 | 9 | 10 |
| d. ........ | 18,000 | 2 | 4 |
| e. ........ | 63,000 | 8 | 6 |
| f. ........ | 89,000 | 5 | 2 |

C&H Ski Club recently borrowed money and agrees to pay it back with a series of six annual payments of $5,000 each. C&H subsequently borrows more money and agrees to pay it back with a series of four annual payments of $7,500 each. The annual interest rate for both loans is 6%.

1. Use Table B.1 to find the present value of these two separate annuities. (Round amounts to the nearest dollar.)

2. Use Table B.3 to find the present value of these two separate annuities. (Round amounts to the nearest dollar.)

Otto Co. borrows money on April 30, 2011, by promising to make four payments of $13,000 each on November 1, 2011; May 1, 2012; November 1, 2012; and May 1, 2013.

1. How much money is Otto able to borrow if the interest rate is 8%, compounded semiannually?

2. How much money is Otto able to borrow if the interest rate is 12%, compounded semiannually?

3. How much money is Otto able to borrow if the interest rate is 16%, compounded semiannually?

Mark Welsch deposits $7,200 in an account that earns interest at an annual rate of 8%, compounded quarterly. The $7,200 plus earned interest must remain in the account 10 years before it can be withdrawn. How much money will be in the account at the end of 10 years?

Kelly Malone plans to have $50 withheld from her monthly paycheck and deposited in a savings account that earns 12% annually, compounded monthly. If Malone continues with her plan for two and one-half years, how much will be accumulated in the account on the date of the last deposit?

Starr Company decides to establish a fund that it will use 10 years from now to replace an aging production facility. The company will make a $100,000 initial contribution to the fund and plans to make quarterly contributions of $50,000 beginning in three months. The fund earns 12%, compounded quarterly. What will be the value of the fund 10 years from now?

Catten, Inc., invests $163,170 today earning 7% per year for nine years. Use Table B.2 to compute the future value of the investment nine years from now. (Round the amount to the nearest dollar.)

For each of the following situations, identify (1) the case as either (*a*) a present or a future value and (*b*) a single amount or an annuity, (2) the table you would use in your computations (but do not solve the problem), and (3) the interest rate and time periods you would use.

a. You need to accumulate $10,000 for a trip you wish to take in four years. You are able to earn 8% compounded semiannually on your savings. You plan to make only one deposit and let the money accumulate for four years. How would you determine the amount of the one-time deposit?

b. Assume the same facts as in part (*a*) except that you will make semiannual deposits to your savings account.

c. You want to retire after working 40 years with savings in excess of $1,000,000. You expect to save $4,000 a year for 40 years and earn an annual rate of interest of 8%. Will you be able to retire with more than $1,000,000 in 40 years? Explain.

d. A sweepstakes agency names you a grand prize winner. You can take $225,000 immediately or elect to receive annual installments of $30,000 for 20 years. You can earn 10% annually on any investments you make. Which prize do you choose to receive?

## TABLE B.1

Present Value of 1

$$p = 1/(1 + i)^n$$

| | Rate | | | | | | | | | | | |
|---|---|---|---|---|---|---|---|---|---|---|---|---|
| Periods | 1% | 2% | 3% | 4% | 5% | 6% | 7% | 8% | 9% | 10% | 12% | 15% |
| 1 | 0.9901 | 0.9804 | 0.9709 | 0.9615 | 0.9524 | 0.9434 | 0.9346 | 0.9259 | 0.9174 | 0.9091 | 0.8929 | 0.8696 |
| 2 | 0.9803 | 0.9612 | 0.9426 | 0.9246 | 0.9070 | 0.8900 | 0.8734 | 0.8573 | 0.8417 | 0.8264 | 0.7972 | 0.7561 |
| 3 | 0.9706 | 0.9423 | 0.9151 | 0.8890 | 0.8638 | 0.8396 | 0.8163 | 0.7938 | 0.7722 | 0.7513 | 0.7118 | 0.6575 |
| 4 | 0.9610 | 0.9238 | 0.8885 | 0.8548 | 0.8227 | 0.7921 | 0.7629 | 0.7350 | 0.7084 | 0.6830 | 0.6355 | 0.5718 |
| 5 | 0.9515 | 0.9057 | 0.8626 | 0.8219 | 0.7835 | 0.7473 | 0.7130 | 0.6806 | 0.6499 | 0.6209 | 0.5674 | 0.4972 |
| 6 | 0.9420 | 0.8880 | 0.8375 | 0.7903 | 0.7462 | 0.7050 | 0.6663 | 0.6302 | 0.5963 | 0.5645 | 0.5066 | 0.4323 |
| 7 | 0.9327 | 0.8706 | 0.8131 | 0.7599 | 0.7107 | 0.6651 | 0.6227 | 0.5835 | 0.5470 | 0.5132 | 0.4523 | 0.3759 |
| 8 | 0.9235 | 0.8535 | 0.7894 | 0.7307 | 0.6768 | 0.6274 | 0.5820 | 0.5403 | 0.5019 | 0.4665 | 0.4039 | 0.3269 |
| 9 | 0.9143 | 0.8368 | 0.7664 | 0.7026 | 0.6446 | 0.5919 | 0.5439 | 0.5002 | 0.4604 | 0.4241 | 0.3606 | 0.2843 |
| 10 | 0.9053 | 0.8203 | 0.7441 | 0.6756 | 0.6139 | 0.5584 | 0.5083 | 0.4632 | 0.4224 | 0.3855 | 0.3220 | 0.2472 |
| 11 | 0.8963 | 0.8043 | 0.7224 | 0.6496 | 0.5847 | 0.5268 | 0.4751 | 0.4289 | 0.3875 | 0.3505 | 0.2875 | 0.2149 |
| 12 | 0.8874 | 0.7885 | 0.7014 | 0.6246 | 0.5568 | 0.4970 | 0.4440 | 0.3971 | 0.3555 | 0.3186 | 0.2567 | 0.1869 |
| 13 | 0.8787 | 0.7730 | 0.6810 | 0.6006 | 0.5303 | 0.4688 | 0.4150 | 0.3677 | 0.3262 | 0.2897 | 0.2292 | 0.1625 |
| 14 | 0.8700 | 0.7579 | 0.6611 | 0.5775 | 0.5051 | 0.4423 | 0.3878 | 0.3405 | 0.2992 | 0.2633 | 0.2046 | 0.1413 |
| 15 | 0.8613 | 0.7430 | 0.6419 | 0.5553 | 0.4810 | 0.4173 | 0.3624 | 0.3152 | 0.2745 | 0.2394 | 0.1827 | 0.1229 |
| 16 | 0.8528 | 0.7284 | 0.6232 | 0.5339 | 0.4581 | 0.3936 | 0.3387 | 0.2919 | 0.2519 | 0.2176 | 0.1631 | 0.1069 |
| 17 | 0.8444 | 0.7142 | 0.6050 | 0.5134 | 0.4363 | 0.3714 | 0.3166 | 0.2703 | 0.2311 | 0.1978 | 0.1456 | 0.0929 |
| 18 | 0.8360 | 0.7002 | 0.5874 | 0.4936 | 0.4155 | 0.3503 | 0.2959 | 0.2502 | 0.2120 | 0.1799 | 0.1300 | 0.0808 |
| 19 | 0.8277 | 0.6864 | 0.5703 | 0.4746 | 0.3957 | 0.3305 | 0.2765 | 0.2317 | 0.1945 | 0.1635 | 0.1161 | 0.0703 |
| 20 | 0.8195 | 0.6730 | 0.5537 | 0.4564 | 0.3769 | 0.3118 | 0.2584 | 0.2145 | 0.1784 | 0.1486 | 0.1037 | 0.0611 |
| 25 | 0.7798 | 0.6095 | 0.4776 | 0.3751 | 0.2953 | 0.2330 | 0.1842 | 0.1460 | 0.1160 | 0.0923 | 0.0588 | 0.0304 |
| 30 | 0.7419 | 0.5521 | 0.4120 | 0.3083 | 0.2314 | 0.1741 | 0.1314 | 0.0994 | 0.0754 | 0.0573 | 0.0334 | 0.0151 |
| 35 | 0.7059 | 0.5000 | 0.3554 | 0.2534 | 0.1813 | 0.1301 | 0.0937 | 0.0676 | 0.0490 | 0.0356 | 0.0189 | 0.0075 |
| 40 | 0.6717 | 0.4529 | 0.3066 | 0.2083 | 0.1420 | 0.0972 | 0.0668 | 0.0460 | 0.0318 | 0.0221 | 0.0107 | 0.0037 |

## TABLE B.2

Future Value of 1

$$f = (1 + i)^n$$

| | Rate | | | | | | | | | | | |
|---|---|---|---|---|---|---|---|---|---|---|---|---|
| Periods | 1% | 2% | 3% | 4% | 5% | 6% | 7% | 8% | 9% | 10% | 12% | 15% |
| 0 | 1.0000 | 1.0000 | 1.0000 | 1.0000 | 1.0000 | 1.0000 | 1.0000 | 1.0000 | 1.0000 | 1.0000 | 1.0000 | 1.0000 |
| 1 | 1.0100 | 1.0200 | 1.0300 | 1.0400 | 1.0500 | 1.0600 | 1.0700 | 1.0800 | 1.0900 | 1.1000 | 1.1200 | 1.1500 |
| 2 | 1.0201 | 1.0404 | 1.0609 | 1.0816 | 1.1025 | 1.1236 | 1.1449 | 1.1664 | 1.1881 | 1.2100 | 1.2544 | 1.3225 |
| 3 | 1.0303 | 1.0612 | 1.0927 | 1.1249 | 1.1576 | 1.1910 | 1.2250 | 1.2597 | 1.2950 | 1.3310 | 1.4049 | 1.5209 |
| 4 | 1.0406 | 1.0824 | 1.1255 | 1.1699 | 1.2155 | 1.2625 | 1.3108 | 1.3605 | 1.4116 | 1.4641 | 1.5735 | 1.7490 |
| 5 | 1.0510 | 1.1041 | 1.1593 | 1.2167 | 1.2763 | 1.3382 | 1.4026 | 1.4693 | 1.5386 | 1.6105 | 1.7623 | 2.0114 |
| 6 | 1.0615 | 1.1262 | 1.1941 | 1.2653 | 1.3401 | 1.4185 | 1.5007 | 1.5869 | 1.6771 | 1.7716 | 1.9738 | 2.3131 |
| 7 | 1.0721 | 1.1487 | 1.2299 | 1.3159 | 1.4071 | 1.5036 | 1.6058 | 1.7138 | 1.8280 | 1.9487 | 2.2107 | 2.6600 |
| 8 | 1.0829 | 1.1717 | 1.2668 | 1.3686 | 1.4775 | 1.5938 | 1.7182 | 1.8509 | 1.9926 | 2.1436 | 2.4760 | 3.0590 |
| 9 | 1.0937 | 1.1951 | 1.3048 | 1.4233 | 1.5513 | 1.6895 | 1.8385 | 1.9990 | 2.1719 | 2.3579 | 2.7731 | 3.5179 |
| 10 | 1.1046 | 1.2190 | 1.3439 | 1.4802 | 1.6289 | 1.7908 | 1.9672 | 2.1589 | 2.3674 | 2.5937 | 3.1058 | 4.0456 |
| 11 | 1.1157 | 1.2434 | 1.3842 | 1.5395 | 1.7103 | 1.8983 | 2.1049 | 2.3316 | 2.5804 | 2.8531 | 3.4785 | 4.6524 |
| 12 | 1.1268 | 1.2682 | 1.4258 | 1.6010 | 1.7959 | 2.0122 | 2.2522 | 2.5182 | 2.8127 | 3.1384 | 3.8960 | 5.3503 |
| 13 | 1.1381 | 1.2936 | 1.4685 | 1.6651 | 1.8856 | 2.1329 | 2.4098 | 2.7196 | 3.0658 | 3.4523 | 4.3635 | 6.1528 |
| 14 | 1.1495 | 1.3195 | 1.5126 | 1.7317 | 1.9799 | 2.2609 | 2.5785 | 2.9372 | 3.3417 | 3.7975 | 4.8871 | 7.0757 |
| 15 | 1.1610 | 1.3459 | 1.5580 | 1.8009 | 2.0789 | 2.3966 | 2.7590 | 3.1722 | 3.6425 | 4.1772 | 5.4736 | 8.1371 |
| 16 | 1.1726 | 1.3728 | 1.6047 | 1.8730 | 2.1829 | 2.5404 | 2.9522 | 3.4259 | 3.9703 | 4.5950 | 6.1304 | 9.3576 |
| 17 | 1.1843 | 1.4002 | 1.6528 | 1.9479 | 2.2920 | 2.6928 | 3.1588 | 3.7000 | 4.3276 | 5.0545 | 6.8660 | 10.7613 |
| 18 | 1.1961 | 1.4282 | 1.7024 | 2.0258 | 2.4066 | 2.8543 | 3.3799 | 3.9960 | 4.7171 | 5.5599 | 7.6900 | 12.3755 |
| 19 | 1.2081 | 1.4568 | 1.7535 | 2.1068 | 2.5270 | 3.0256 | 3.6165 | 4.3157 | 5.1417 | 6.1159 | 8.6128 | 14.2318 |
| 20 | 1.2202 | 1.4859 | 1.8061 | 2.1911 | 2.6533 | 3.2071 | 3.8697 | 4.6610 | 5.6044 | 6.7275 | 9.6463 | 16.3665 |
| 25 | 1.2824 | 1.6406 | 2.0938 | 2.6658 | 3.3864 | 4.2919 | 5.4274 | 6.8485 | 8.6231 | 10.8347 | 17.0001 | 32.9190 |
| 30 | 1.3478 | 1.8114 | 2.4273 | 3.2434 | 4.3219 | 5.7435 | 7.6123 | 10.0627 | 13.2677 | 17.4494 | 29.9599 | 66.2118 |
| 35 | 1.4166 | 1.9999 | 2.8139 | 3.9461 | 5.5160 | 7.6861 | 10.6766 | 14.7853 | 20.4140 | 28.1024 | 52.7996 | 133.1755 |
| 40 | 1.4889 | 2.2080 | 3.2620 | 4.8010 | 7.0400 | 10.2857 | 14.9745 | 21.7245 | 31.4094 | 45.2593 | 93.0510 | 267.8635 |

$$p = \left[1 - \frac{1}{(1+i)^n}\right]/i$$

**TABLE B.3**

Present Value of an Annuity of 1

| Periods | 1% | 2% | 3% | 4% | 5% | 6% | 7% | 8% | 9% | 10% | 12% | 15% |
|---|---|---|---|---|---|---|---|---|---|---|---|---|
| | | | | | | Rate | | | | | | |
| 1 | 0.9901 | 0.9804 | 0.9709 | 0.9615 | 0.9524 | 0.9434 | 0.9346 | 0.9259 | 0.9174 | 0.9091 | 0.8929 | 0.8696 |
| 2 | 1.9704 | 1.9416 | 1.9135 | 1.8861 | 1.8594 | 1.8334 | 1.8080 | 1.7833 | 1.7591 | 1.7355 | 1.6901 | 1.6257 |
| 3 | 2.9410 | 2.8839 | 2.8286 | 2.7751 | 2.7232 | 2.6730 | 2.6243 | 2.5771 | 2.5313 | 2.4869 | 2.4018 | 2.2832 |
| 4 | 3.9020 | 3.8077 | 3.7171 | 3.6299 | 3.5460 | 3.4651 | 3.3872 | 3.3121 | 3.2397 | 3.1699 | 3.0373 | 2.8550 |
| 5 | 4.8534 | 4.7135 | 4.5797 | 4.4518 | 4.3295 | 4.2124 | 4.1002 | 3.9927 | 3.8897 | 3.7908 | 3.6048 | 3.3522 |
| 6 | 5.7955 | 5.6014 | 5.4172 | 5.2421 | 5.0757 | 4.9173 | 4.7665 | 4.6229 | 4.4859 | 4.3553 | 4.1114 | 3.7845 |
| 7 | 6.7282 | 6.4720 | 6.2303 | 6.0021 | 5.7864 | 5.5824 | 5.3893 | 5.2064 | 5.0330 | 4.8684 | 4.5638 | 4.1604 |
| 8 | 7.6517 | 7.3255 | 7.0197 | 6.7327 | 6.4632 | 6.2098 | 5.9713 | 5.7466 | 5.5348 | 5.3349 | 4.9676 | 4.4873 |
| 9 | 8.5660 | 8.1622 | 7.7861 | 7.4353 | 7.1078 | 6.8017 | 6.5152 | 6.2469 | 5.9952 | 5.7590 | 5.3282 | 4.7716 |
| 10 | 9.4713 | 8.9826 | 8.5302 | 8.1109 | 7.7217 | 7.3601 | 7.0236 | 6.7101 | 6.4177 | 6.1446 | 5.6502 | 5.0188 |
| 11 | 10.3676 | 9.7868 | 9.2526 | 8.7605 | 8.3064 | 7.8869 | 7.4987 | 7.1390 | 6.8052 | 6.4951 | 5.9377 | 5.2337 |
| 12 | 11.2551 | 10.5753 | 9.9540 | 9.3851 | 8.8633 | 8.3838 | 7.9427 | 7.5361 | 7.1607 | 6.8137 | 6.1944 | 5.4206 |
| 13 | 12.1337 | 11.3484 | 10.6350 | 9.9856 | 9.3936 | 8.8527 | 8.3577 | 7.9038 | 7.4869 | 7.1034 | 6.4235 | 5.5831 |
| 14 | 13.0037 | 12.1062 | 11.2961 | 10.5631 | 9.8986 | 9.2950 | 8.7455 | 8.2442 | 7.7862 | 7.3667 | 6.6282 | 5.7245 |
| 15 | 13.8651 | 12.8493 | 11.9379 | 11.1184 | 10.3797 | 9.7122 | 9.1079 | 8.5595 | 8.0607 | 7.6061 | 6.8109 | 5.8474 |
| 16 | 14.7179 | 13.5777 | 12.5611 | 11.6523 | 10.8378 | 10.1059 | 9.4466 | 8.8514 | 8.3126 | 7.8237 | 6.9740 | 5.9542 |
| 17 | 15.5623 | 14.2919 | 13.1661 | 12.1657 | 11.2741 | 10.4773 | 9.7632 | 9.1216 | 8.5436 | 8.0216 | 7.1196 | 6.0472 |
| 18 | 16.3983 | 14.9920 | 13.7535 | 12.6593 | 11.6896 | 10.8276 | 10.0591 | 9.3719 | 8.7556 | 8.2014 | 7.2497 | 6.1280 |
| 19 | 17.2260 | 15.6785 | 14.3238 | 13.1339 | 12.0853 | 11.1581 | 10.3356 | 9.6036 | 8.9501 | 8.3649 | 7.3658 | 6.1982 |
| 20 | 18.0456 | 16.3514 | 14.8775 | 13.5903 | 12.4622 | 11.4699 | 10.5940 | 9.8181 | 9.1285 | 8.5136 | 7.4694 | 6.2593 |
| 25 | 22.0232 | 19.5235 | 17.4131 | 15.6221 | 14.0939 | 12.7834 | 11.6536 | 10.6748 | 9.8226 | 9.0770 | 7.8431 | 6.4641 |
| 30 | 25.8077 | 22.3965 | 19.6004 | 17.2920 | 15.3725 | 13.7648 | 12.4090 | 11.2578 | 10.2737 | 9.4269 | 8.0552 | 6.5660 |
| 35 | 29.4086 | 24.9986 | 21.4872 | 18.6646 | 16.3742 | 14.4982 | 12.9477 | 11.6546 | 10.5668 | 9.6442 | 8.1755 | 6.6166 |
| 40 | 32.8347 | 27.3555 | 23.1148 | 19.7928 | 17.1591 | 15.0463 | 13.3317 | 11.9246 | 10.7574 | 9.7791 | 8.2438 | 6.6418 |

$$f = [(1+i)^n - 1]/i$$

**TABLE B.4**

Future Value of an Annuity of 1

| Periods | 1% | 2% | 3% | 4% | 5% | 6% | 7% | 8% | 9% | 10% | 12% | 15% |
|---|---|---|---|---|---|---|---|---|---|---|---|---|
| | | | | | | Rate | | | | | | |
| 1 | 1.0000 | 1.0000 | 1.0000 | 1.0000 | 1.0000 | 1.0000 | 1.0000 | 1.0000 | 1.0000 | 1.0000 | 1.0000 | 1.0000 |
| 2 | 2.0100 | 2.0200 | 2.0300 | 2.0400 | 2.0500 | 2.0600 | 2.0700 | 2.0800 | 2.0900 | 2.1000 | 2.1200 | 2.1500 |
| 3 | 3.0301 | 3.0604 | 3.0909 | 3.1216 | 3.1525 | 3.1836 | 3.2149 | 3.2464 | 3.2781 | 3.3100 | 3.3744 | 3.4725 |
| 4 | 4.0604 | 4.1216 | 4.1836 | 4.2465 | 4.3101 | 4.3746 | 4.4399 | 4.5061 | 4.5731 | 4.6410 | 4.7793 | 4.9934 |
| 5 | 5.1010 | 5.2040 | 5.3091 | 5.4163 | 5.5256 | 5.6371 | 5.7507 | 5.8666 | 5.9847 | 6.1051 | 6.3528 | 6.7424 |
| 6 | 6.1520 | 6.3081 | 6.4684 | 6.6330 | 6.8019 | 6.9753 | 7.1533 | 7.3359 | 7.5233 | 7.7156 | 8.1152 | 8.7537 |
| 7 | 7.2135 | 7.4343 | 7.6625 | 7.8983 | 8.1420 | 8.3938 | 8.6540 | 8.9228 | 9.2004 | 9.4872 | 10.0890 | 11.0668 |
| 8 | 8.2857 | 8.5830 | 8.8923 | 9.2142 | 9.5491 | 9.8975 | 10.2598 | 10.6366 | 11.0285 | 11.4359 | 12.2997 | 13.7268 |
| 9 | 9.3685 | 9.7546 | 10.1591 | 10.5828 | 11.0266 | 11.4913 | 11.9780 | 12.4876 | 13.0210 | 13.5795 | 14.7757 | 16.7858 |
| 10 | 10.4622 | 10.9497 | 11.4639 | 12.0061 | 12.5779 | 13.1808 | 13.8164 | 14.4866 | 15.1929 | 15.9374 | 17.5487 | 20.3037 |
| 11 | 11.5668 | 12.1687 | 12.8078 | 13.4864 | 14.2068 | 14.9716 | 15.7836 | 16.6455 | 17.5603 | 18.5312 | 20.6546 | 24.3493 |
| 12 | 12.6825 | 13.4121 | 14.1920 | 15.0258 | 15.9171 | 16.8699 | 17.8885 | 18.9771 | 20.1407 | 21.3843 | 24.1331 | 29.0017 |
| 13 | 13.8093 | 14.6803 | 15.6178 | 16.6268 | 17.7130 | 18.8821 | 20.1406 | 21.4953 | 22.9534 | 24.5227 | 28.0291 | 34.3519 |
| 14 | 14.9474 | 15.9739 | 17.0863 | 18.2919 | 19.5986 | 21.0151 | 22.5505 | 24.2149 | 26.0192 | 27.9750 | 32.3926 | 40.5047 |
| 15 | 16.0969 | 17.2934 | 18.5989 | 20.0236 | 21.5786 | 23.2760 | 25.1290 | 27.1521 | 29.3609 | 31.7725 | 37.2797 | 47.5804 |
| 16 | 17.2579 | 18.6393 | 20.1569 | 21.8245 | 23.6575 | 25.6725 | 27.8881 | 30.3243 | 33.0034 | 35.9497 | 42.7533 | 55.7175 |
| 17 | 18.4304 | 20.0121 | 21.7616 | 23.6975 | 25.8404 | 28.2129 | 30.8402 | 33.7502 | 36.9737 | 40.5447 | 48.8837 | 65.0751 |
| 18 | 19.6147 | 21.4123 | 23.4144 | 25.6454 | 28.1324 | 30.9057 | 33.9990 | 37.4502 | 41.3013 | 45.5992 | 55.7497 | 75.8364 |
| 19 | 20.8109 | 22.8406 | 25.1169 | 27.6712 | 30.5390 | 33.7600 | 37.3790 | 41.4463 | 46.0185 | 51.1591 | 63.4397 | 88.2118 |
| 20 | 22.0190 | 24.2974 | 26.8704 | 29.7781 | 33.0660 | 36.7856 | 40.9955 | 45.7620 | 51.1601 | 57.2750 | 72.0524 | 102.4436 |
| 25 | 28.2432 | 32.0303 | 36.4593 | 41.6459 | 47.7271 | 54.8645 | 63.2490 | 73.1059 | 84.7009 | 98.3471 | 133.3339 | 212.7930 |
| 30 | 34.7849 | 40.5681 | 47.5754 | 56.0849 | 66.4388 | 79.0582 | 94.4608 | 113.2832 | 136.3075 | 164.4940 | 241.3327 | 434.7451 |
| 35 | 41.6603 | 49.9945 | 60.4621 | 73.6522 | 90.3203 | 111.4348 | 138.2369 | 172.3168 | 215.7108 | 271.0244 | 431.6635 | 881.1702 |
| 40 | 48.8864 | 60.4020 | 75.4013 | 95.0255 | 120.7998 | 154.7620 | 199.6351 | 259.0565 | 337.8824 | 442.5926 | 767.0914 | 1,779.0903 |

# Glossary

**Absorption costing** Costing method that assigns both variable and fixed costs to products. *(p. 915)*

**Accelerated depreciation method** Method that produces larger depreciation charges in the early years of an asset's life and smaller charges in its later years. *(p. 400)*

**Account** Record within an accounting system in which increases and decreases are entered and stored in a specific asset, liability, equity, revenue, or expense. *(p. 51)*

**Account balance** Difference between total debits and total credits (including the beginning balance) for an account. *(p. 55)*

**Account form balance sheet** Balance sheet that lists assets on the left side and liabilities and equity on the right. *(p. 18)*

**Account payable** Liability created by buying goods or services on credit; backed by the buyer's general credit standing. *(p. 50)*

**Accounting** Information and measurement system that identifies, records, and communicates relevant information about a company's business activities. *(p. 4)*

**Accounting cycle** Recurring steps performed each accounting period, starting with analyzing transactions and continuing through the post-closing trial balance (or reversing entries). *(p. 146)*

**Accounting equation** Equality involving a company's assets, liabilities, and equity; Assets = Liabilities + Equity; also called *balance sheet equation*. *(p. 14)*

**Accounting information system** People, records, and methods that collect and process data from transactions and events, organize them in useful forms, and communicate results to decision makers. *(p. 272)*

**Accounting period** Length of time covered by financial statements; also called *reporting period*. *(p. 94)*

**Accounting rate of return** Rate used to evaluate the acceptability of an investment; equals the after-tax periodic income from a project divided by the average investment in the asset; also called *rate of return on average investment*. *(p. 1039)*

**Accounts payable ledger** Subsidiary ledger listing individual creditor (supplier) accounts. *(p. 277)*

**Accounts receivable** Amounts due from customers for credit sales; backed by the customer's general credit standing. *(p. 360)*

**Accounts receivable ledger** Subsidiary ledger listing individual customer accounts. *(p. 277)*

**Accounts receivable turnover** Measure of both the quality and liquidity of accounts receivable; indicates how often receivables are received and collected during the period; computed by dividing net sales by average accounts receivable. *(p. 375)*

**Accrual basis accounting** Accounting system that recognizes revenues when earned and expenses when incurred; the basis for GAAP. *(p. 95)*

**Accrued expenses** Costs incurred in a period that are both unpaid and unrecorded; adjusting entries for recording accrued expenses involve increasing expenses and increasing liabilities. *(p. 101)*

**Accrued revenues** Revenues earned in a period that are both unrecorded and not yet received in cash (or other assets); adjusting entries for recording accrued revenues involve increasing assets and increasing revenues. *(pp. 103 & 960)*

**Accumulated depreciation** Cumulative sum of all depreciation expense recorded for an asset. *(p. 97)*

**Acid-test ratio** Ratio used to assess a company's ability to settle its current debts with its most liquid assets; defined as quick assets (cash, short-term investments, and current receivables) divided by current liabilities. *(p. 196)*

**Activity-based budgeting (ABB)** Budget system based on expected activities. *(p. 960)*

**Activity-based costing (ABC)** Cost allocation method that focuses on activities performed; traces costs to activities and then assigns them to cost objects. *(p. 861)*

**Activity cost driver** Variable that causes an activity's cost to go up or down; a causal factor. *(p. 861)*

**Activity cost pool** Temporary account that accumulates costs a company incurs to support an activity. *(p. 861)*

**Adjusted trial balance** List of accounts and balances prepared after period-end adjustments are recorded and posted. *(p. 106)*

**Adjusting entry** Journal entry at the end of an accounting period to bring an asset or liability account to its proper amount and update the related expense or revenue account. *(p. 96)*

**Aging of accounts receivable** Process of classifying accounts receivable by how long they are past due for purposes of estimating uncollectible accounts. *(p. 368)*

**Allowance for Doubtful Accounts** Contra asset account with a balance approximating uncollectible accounts receivable; also called *Allowance for Uncollectible Accounts*. *(p. 365)*

**Allowance method** Procedure that (a) estimates and matches bad debts expense with its sales for the period and/or (b) reports accounts receivable at estimated realizable value. *(p. 364)*

**Amortization** Process of allocating the cost of an intangible asset to expense over its estimated useful life. *(p. 409)*

**Annual financial statements** Financial statements covering a one-year period; often based on a calendar year, but any consecutive 12-month (or 52-week) period is acceptable. *(p. 94)*

**Annual report** Summary of a company's financial results for the year with its current financial condition and future plans; directed to external users of financial information. *(p. A-1)*

**Annuity** Series of equal payments at equal intervals. *(p. 571)*

**Appropriated retained earnings** Retained earnings separately reported to inform stockholders of funding needs. *(p. 525)*

**Asset book value** (See *book value.*)

**Assets** Resources a business owns or controls that are expected to provide current and future benefits to the business. *(p. 14)*

**Audit** Analysis and report of an organization's accounting system, its records, and its reports using various tests. *(p. 12)*

**Auditors** Individuals hired to review financial reports and information systems. *Internal auditors* of a company are employed to assess and evaluate its system of internal controls, including the resulting reports. *External auditors* are independent of a company and are hired to assess and evaluate the "fairness" of financial statements (or to perform other contracted financial services) *(p. 13).*

**Authorized stock** Total amount of stock that a corporation's charter authorizes it to issue. *(p. 511)*

**Available-for-sale (AFS) securities** Investments in debt and equity securities that are not classified as trading securities or held-to-maturity securities. *(p. 600)*

**Average cost** See *weighted average.*

**Avoidable expense** Expense (or cost) that is relevant for decision making; expense that is not incurred if a department, product, or service is eliminated. *(p. 1053)*

**Bad debts** Accounts of customers who do not pay what they have promised to pay; an expense of selling on credit; also called *uncollectible accounts.* *(p. 363)*

**Balance column account** Account with debit and credit columns for recording entries and another column for showing the balance of the account after each entry. *(p. 58)*

**Balance sheet** Financial statement that lists types and dollar amounts of assets, liabilities, and equity at a specific date. *(p. 19)*

**Balance sheet equation** (See *accounting equation.*)

**Balanced scorecard** A system of performance measurement that collects information on several key performance indicators within each of four perspectives: customer, internal processes, innovation and learning, and financial. *(p. 874)*

**Bank reconciliation** Report that explains the difference between the book (company) balance of cash and the cash balance reported on the bank statement. *(p. 331)*

**Bank statement** Bank report on the depositor's beginning and ending cash balances, and a listing of its changes, for a period. *(p. 330)*

**Basic earnings per share** Net income less any preferred dividends and then divided by weighted-average common shares outstanding. *(p. 527)*

**Batch processing** Accumulating source documents for a period of time and then processing them all at once such as once a day, week, or month. *(p. 286)*

**Bearer bonds** Bonds made payable to whoever holds them (the *bearer*); also called *unregistered bonds.* *(p. 566)*

**Benchmarking** Practice of comparing and analyzing company financial performance or position with other companies or standards. *(p. 1002)*

**Betterments** Expenditures to make a plant asset more efficient or productive; also called *improvements.* *(p. 405)*

**Bond** Written promise to pay the bond's par (or face) value and interest at a stated contract rate; often issued in denominations of $1,000. *(p. 552)*

**Bond certificate** Document containing bond specifics such as issuer's name, bond par value, contract interest rate, and maturity date. *(p. 554)*

**Bond indenture** Contract between the bond issuer and the bondholders; identifies the parties' rights and obligations. *(p. 554)*

**Book value** Asset's acquisition costs less its accumulated depreciation (or depletion, or amortization); also sometimes used synonymously as the *carrying value* of an account. *(p. 100)*

**Book value per common share** Recorded amount of equity applicable to common shares divided by the number of common shares outstanding. *(p. 528)*

**Book value per preferred share** Equity applicable to preferred shares (equals its call price [or par value if it is not callable] plus any cumulative dividends in arrears) divided by the number of preferred shares outstanding. *(p. 528)*

**Bookkeeping** (See *recordkeeping.*)

**Break-even point** Output level at which sales equals fixed plus variable costs; where income equals zero. *(p. 915)*

**Break-even time (BET)** Time-based measurement used to evaluate the acceptability of an investment; equals the time expected to pass before the present value of the net cash flows from an investment equals its initial cost. *(p. 1055)*

**Budget** Formal statement of future plans, usually expressed in monetary terms. *(p. 946)*

**Budget report** Report comparing actual results to planned objectives; sometimes used as a progress report. *(p. 990)*

**Budgetary control** Management use of budgets to monitor and control company operations. *(p. 990)*

**Budgeted balance sheet** Accounting report that presents predicted amounts of the company's assets, liabilities, and equity balances as of the end of the budget period. *(p. 958)*

**Budgeted income statement** Accounting report that presents predicted amounts of the company's revenues and expenses for the budget period. *(p. 958)*

**Budgeting** Process of planning future business actions and expressing them as formal plans. *(p. 946)*

**Business** An organization of one or more individuals selling products and/or services for profit. *(p. 10)*

**Business entity assumption** Principle that requires a business to be accounted for separately from its owner(s) and from any other entity. *(p. 11)*

**Business segment** Part of a company that can be separately identified by the products or services that it provides or by the geographic markets that it serves; also called *segment*. *(p. 710)*

**C corporation** Corporation that does not qualify for nor elect to be treated as a proprietorship or partnership for income tax purposes and therefore is subject to income taxes; also called *C corp*. *(p. 482)*

**Call price** Amount that must be paid to call and retire a callable preferred stock or a callable bond. *(p. 521)*

**Callable bonds** Bonds that give the issuer the option to retire them at a stated amount prior to maturity. *(p. 566)*

**Callable preferred stock** Preferred stock that the issuing corporation, at its option, may retire by paying the call price plus any dividends in arrears. *(p. 521)*

**Canceled checks** Checks that the bank has paid and deducted from the depositor's account. *(p. 331)*

**Capital budgeting** Process of analyzing alternative investments and deciding which assets to acquire or sell. *(p. 1036)*

**Capital expenditures** Additional costs of plant assets that provide material benefits extending beyond the current period; also called *balance sheet expenditures*. *(p. 404)*

**Capital expenditures budget** Plan that lists dollar amounts to be both received from disposal of plant assets and spent to purchase plant assets. *(p. 956)*

**Capital leases** Long-term leases in which the lessor transfers substantially all risk and rewards of ownership to the lessee. *(p. 577)*

**Capital stock** General term referring to a corporation's stock used in obtaining capital (owner financing). *(p. 511)*

**Capitalize** Record the cost as part of a permanent account and allocate it over later periods.

**Carrying (book) value of bonds** Net amount at which bonds are reported on the balance sheet; equals the par value of the bonds less any unamortized discount or plus any unamortized premium; also called *carrying amount or book value*. *(p. 556)*

**Cash** Includes currency, coins, and amounts on deposit in bank checking or savings accounts. *(p. 321)*

**Cash basis accounting** Accounting system that recognizes revenues when cash is received and records expenses when cash is paid. *(p. 95)*

**Cash budget** Plan that shows expected cash inflows and outflows during the budget period, including receipts from loans needed to maintain a minimum cash balance and repayments of such loans. *(p. 956)*

**Cash disbursements journal** Special journal normally used to record all payments of cash; also called *cash payments journal*. *(p. 284)*

**Cash discount** Reduction in the price of merchandise granted by a seller to a buyer when payment is made within the discount period. *(p. 183)*

**Cash equivalents** Short-term, investment assets that are readily convertible to a known cash amount or sufficiently close to their maturity date (usually within 90 days) so that market value is not sensitive to interest rate changes. *(p. 321)*

**Cash flow on total assets** Ratio of operating cash flows to average total assets; not sensitive to income recognition and measurement; partly reflects earnings quality. *(p. 650)*

**Cash Over and Short** Income statement account used to record cash overages and cash shortages arising from errors in cash receipts or payments. *(p. 323)*

**Cash receipts journal** Special journal normally used to record all receipts of cash. *(p. 281)*

**Change in an accounting estimate** Change in an accounting estimate that results from new information, subsequent developments, or improved judgment that impacts current and future periods. *(pp. 403 & 525)*

**Chart of accounts** List of accounts used by a company; includes an identification number for each account. *(p. 54)*

**Check** Document signed by a depositor instructing the bank to pay a specified amount to a designated recipient. *(p. 328)*

**Check register** Another name for a cash disbursements journal when the journal has a column for check numbers. *(pp. 284 & 340)*

**Classified balance sheet** Balance sheet that presents assets and liabilities in relevant subgroups, including current and noncurrent classifications. *(p. 147)*

**Clock card** Source document used to record the number of hours an employee works and to determine the total labor cost for each pay period. *(p. 782)*

**Closing entries** Entries recorded at the end of each accounting period to transfer end-of-period balances in revenue, gain, expense, loss, and withdrawal (dividend for a corporation) accounts to the capital account (to retained earnings for a corporation). *(p. 143)*

**Closing process** Necessary end-of-period steps to prepare the accounts for recording the transactions of the next period. *(p. 142)*

**Columnar journal** Journal with more than one column. *(p. 278)*

**Committee on Sponsoring Organizations (COSO)** Committee devoted to improving the quality of financial reporting through effective internal controls, consisting of five interrelated components, along with other mechanisms (www.COSO.org). *(p. 315)*

**Common stock** Corporation's basic ownership share; also generically called *capital stock*. *(pp. 12 & 510)*

**Common-size financial statement** Statement that expresses each amount as a percent of a base amount. In the balance sheet, total assets is usually the base and is expressed as 100%. In the income statement, net sales is usually the base. *(p. 693)*

**Comparative financial statement** Statement with data for two or more successive periods placed in side-by-side columns, often with changes shown in dollar amounts and percents. *(p. 688)*

**Compatibility principle** Information system principle that prescribes an accounting system to conform with a company's activities, personnel, and structure. *(p. 273)*

**Complex capital structure** Capital structure that includes outstanding rights or options to purchase common stock, or securities that are convertible into common stock. *(p. 527)*

**Components of accounting systems** Five basic components of accounting systems are source documents, input devices, information processors, information storage, and output devices. *(p. 273)*

**Composite unit** Generic unit consisting of a specific number of units of each product; unit comprised in proportion to the expected sales mix of its products. *(p. 922)*

**Compound journal entry** Journal entry that affects at least three accounts. *(p. 61)*

**Comprehensive income** Net change in equity for a period, excluding owner investments and distributions. *(p. 604)*

**Computer hardware** Physical equipment in a computerized accounting information system.

**Computer network** Linkage giving different users and different computers access to common databases and programs. *(p. 286)*

**Computer software** Programs that direct operations of computer hardware.

**Conceptual framework** A written framework to guide the development, preparation, and interpretation of financial accounting information. *(p. 9)*

**Conservatism constraint** Principle that prescribes the less optimistic estimate when two estimates are about equally likely. *(p. 238)*

**Consignee** Receiver of goods owned by another who holds them for purposes of selling them for the owner. *(p. 228)*

**Consignor** Owner of goods who ships them to another party who will sell them for the owner. *(p. 228)*

**Consistency concept** Principle that prescribes use of the same accounting method(s) over time so that financial statements are comparable across periods. *(p. 237)*

**Consolidated financial statements** Financial statements that show all (combined) activities under the parent's control, including those of any subsidiaries. *(p. 603)*

**Contingent liability** Obligation to make a future payment if, and only if, an uncertain future event occurs. *(p. 448)*

**Continuous budgeting** Practice of preparing budgets for a selected number of future periods and revising those budgets as each period is completed. *(p. 949)*

**Continuous improvement** Concept requiring every manager and employee continually to look to improve operations. *(p. 748)*

**Contra account** Account linked with another account and having an opposite normal balance; reported as a subtraction from the other account's balance. *(p. 99)*

**Contract rate** Interest rate specified in a bond indenture (or note); multiplied by the par value to determine the interest paid each period; also called *coupon rate, stated rate,* or *nominal rate. (p. 555)*

**Contributed capital** Total amount of cash and other assets received from stockholders in exchange for stock; also called *paid-in capital. (p. 13)*

**Contributed capital in excess of par value** Difference between the par value of stock and its issue price when issued at a price above par.

**Contribution margin** Sales revenue less total variable costs.

**Contribution margin income statement** Income statement that separates variable and fixed costs; highlights the contribution margin, which is sales less variable expenses.

**Contribution margin per unit** Amount that the sale of one unit contributes toward recovering fixed costs and earning profit; defined as sales price per unit minus variable expense per unit. *(p. 914)*

**Contribution margin ratio** Product's contribution margin divided by its sale price. *(p. 914)*

**Control** Process of monitoring planning decisions and evaluating the organization's activities and employees. *(p. 733)*

**Control principle** Information system principle that prescribes an accounting system to aid managers in controlling and monitoring business activities. *(p. 272)*

**Controllable costs** Costs that a manager has the power to control or at least strongly influence. *(pp. 737 & 875)*

**Controllable variance** Combination of both overhead spending variances (variable and fixed) and the variable overhead efficiency variance. *(p. 1003)*

**Controlling account** General ledger account, the balance of which (after posting) equals the sum of the balances in its related subsidiary ledger. *(p. 277)*

**Conversion costs** Expenditures incurred in converting raw materials to finished goods; includes direct labor costs and overhead costs. *(p. 743)*

**Conversion costs per equivalent unit** The combined costs of direct labor and factory overhead per equivalent unit. *(p. 829)*

**Convertible bonds** Bonds that bondholders can exchange for a set number of the issuer's shares. *(p. 566)*

**Convertible preferred stock** Preferred stock with an option to exchange it for common stock at a specified rate. *(p. 520)*

**Copyright** Right giving the owner the exclusive privilege to publish and sell musical, literary, or artistic work during the creator's life plus 70 years. *(p. 410)*

**Corporation** Business that is a separate legal entity under state or federal laws with owners called *shareholders* or *stockholders. (pp. 12 & 508)*

**Cost** All normal and reasonable expenditures necessary to get an asset in place and ready for its intended use. *(p. 395)*

**Cost accounting system** Accounting system for manufacturing activities based on the perpetual inventory system. *(p. 776)*

**Cost-based transfer pricing** A form of pricing transfers between divisions of the same company based on costs to the transferring division; typically used when the transferring division has excess capacity. *(p. 883)*

**Cost-benefit constraint** Notion that only information with benefits of disclosure greater than the costs of disclosure need be disclosed. *(p. 12)*

**Cost-benefit principle** Information system principle that prescribes the benefits from an activity in an accounting system to outweigh the costs of that activity. *(p. 273)*

**Cost center** Department that incurs costs but generates no revenues; common example is the accounting or legal department. *(p. 865)*

**Cost object** Product, process, department, or customer to which costs are assigned. *(p. 737)*

**Cost of capital** Rate the company must pay to its long-term creditors and shareholders; also called *hurdle rate. (p. 1041)*

**Cost of goods available for sale** Consists of beginning inventory plus net purchases of a period.

**Cost of goods manufactured** Total manufacturing costs (direct materials, direct labor, and factory overhead) for the period plus beginning goods in process less ending goods in process; also called *net cost of goods manufactured* and *cost of goods completed. (p. 827)*

**Cost of goods sold** Cost of inventory sold to customers during a period; also called *cost of sales. (p. 180)*

**Cost principle** Accounting principle that prescribes financial statement information to be based on actual costs incurred in business transactions. *(p. 10)*

**Cost variance** Difference between the actual incurred cost and the standard cost. *(p. 997)*

**Cost-volume-profit (CVP) analysis** Planning method that includes predicting the volume of activity, the costs incurred, sales earned, and profits received. *(p. 908)*

**Cost-volume-profit (CVP) chart** Graphic representation of cost-volume-profit relations. *(p. 916)*

**Coupon bonds** Bonds with interest coupons attached to their certificates; bondholders detach coupons when they mature and present them to a bank or broker for collection. *(p. 566)*

**Credit** Recorded on the right side; an entry that decreases asset and expense accounts, and increases liability, revenue, and most equity accounts; abbreviated Cr. *(p. 55)*

**Credit memorandum** Notification that the sender has credited the recipient's account in the sender's records. *(p. 189)*

**Credit period** Time period that can pass before a customer's payment is due. *(p. 183)*

**Credit terms** Description of the amounts and timing of payments that a buyer (debtor) agrees to make in the future. *(p. 183)*

**Creditors** Individuals or organizations entitled to receive payments. *(p. 52)*

**Cumulative preferred stock** Preferred stock on which undeclared dividends accumulate until paid; common stockholders cannot receive dividends until cumulative dividends are paid. *(p. 519)*

**Current assets** Cash and other assets expected to be sold, collected, or used within one year or the company's operating cycle, whichever is longer. *(p. 148)*

**Current liabilities** Obligations due to be paid or settled within one year or the company's operating cycle, whichever is longer. *(p. 149 & 437)*

**Current portion of long-term debt** Portion of long-term debt due within one year or the operating cycle, whichever is longer; reported under current liabilities. *(p. 445)*

**Current ratio** Ratio used to evaluate a company's ability to pay its short-term obligations, calculated by dividing current assets by current liabilities. *(p. 150)*

**Curvilinear cost** Cost that changes with volume but not at a constant rate. *(p. 910)*

**Customer orientation** Company position that its managers and employees be in tune with the changing wants and needs of consumers. *(p. 747)*

**Cycle efficiency (CE)** A measure of production efficiency, which is defined as value-added (process) time divided by total cycle time. *(p. 750)*

**Cycle time (CT)** A measure of the time to produce a product or service, which is the sum of process time, inspection time, move time, and wait time; also called *throughput time*. *(p. 749)*

**Date of declaration** Date the directors vote to pay a dividend. *(p. 515)*

**Date of payment** Date the corporation makes the dividend payment. *(p. 515)*

**Date of record** Date directors specify for identifying stockholders to receive dividends. *(p. 515)*

**Days' sales in inventory** Estimate of number of days needed to convert inventory into receivables or cash; equals ending inventory divided by cost of goods sold and then multiplied by 365; also called days' *stock on hand. (p. 241)*

**Days' sales uncollected** Measure of the liquidity of receivables computed by dividing the current balance of receivables by the annual credit (or net) sales and then multiplying by 365; also called *days' sales in receivables. (p. 335)*

**Debit** Recorded on the left side; an entry that increases asset and expense accounts, and decreases liability, revenue, and most equity accounts; abbreviated Dr. *(p. 55)*

**Debit memorandum** Notification that the sender has debited the recipient's account in the sender's records. *(p. 184)*

**Debt ratio** Ratio of total liabilities to total assets; used to reflect risk associated with a company's debts. *(p. 69)*

**Debt-to-equity ratio** Defined as total liabilities divided by total equity; shows the proportion of a company financed by non-owners (creditors) in comparison with that financed by owners. *(p. 567)*

**Debtors** Individuals or organizations that owe money. *(p. 51)*

**Declining-balance method** Method that determines depreciation charge for the period by multiplying a depreciation rate (often twice the straight-line rate) by the asset's beginning-period book value. *(p. 400)*

**Deferred income tax liability** Corporation income taxes that are deferred until future years because of temporary differences between GAAP and tax rules. *(p. 460)*

**Degree of operating leverage (DOL)** Ratio of contribution margin divided by pretax income; used to assess the effect on income of changes in sales. *(p. 924)*

**Departmental accounting system** Accounting system that provides information useful in evaluating the profitability or cost effectiveness of a department. *(p. 864)*

**Departmental contribution to overhead** Amount by which a department's revenues exceed its direct expenses. *(p. 871)*

**Depletion** Process of allocating the cost of natural resources to periods when they are consumed and sold. *(p. 408)*

**Deposit ticket** Lists items such as currency, coins, and checks deposited and their corresponding dollar amounts. *(p. 328)*

**Deposits in transit** Deposits recorded by the company but not yet recorded by its bank. *(p. 331)*

**Depreciable cost** Cost of a plant asset less its salvage value.

**Depreciation** Expense created by allocating the cost of plant and equipment to periods in which they are used; represents the expense of using the asset. *(pp. 99 & 397)*

**Diluted earnings per share** Earnings per share calculation that requires dilutive securities be added to the denominator of the basic EPS calculation. *(p. 527)*

**Dilutive securities** Securities having the potential to increase common shares outstanding; examples are options, rights, convertible bonds, and convertible preferred stock. *(p. 527)*

**Direct costs** Costs incurred for the benefit of one specific cost object. *(p. 737)*

**Direct expenses** Expenses traced to a specific department (object) that are incurred for the sole benefit of that department. *(p. 865)*

**Direct labor** Efforts of employees who physically convert materials to finished product. *(p. 742)*

**Direct labor costs** Wages and salaries for direct labor that are separately and readily traced through the production process to finished goods. *(p. 742)*

**Direct material** Raw material that physically becomes part of the product and is clearly identified with specific products or batches of product. *(p. 742)*

**Direct material costs** Expenditures for direct material that are separately and readily traced through the production process to finished goods. *(p. 742)*

**Direct method** Presentation of net cash from operating activities for the statement of cash flows that lists major operating cash receipts less major operating cash payments. *(p. 638)*

**Direct write-off method** Method that records the loss from an uncollectible account receivable at the time it is determined to be uncollectible; no attempt is made to estimate bad debts. *(p. 363)*

**Discount on bonds payable** Difference between a bond's par value and its lower issue price or carrying value; occurs when the contract rate is less than the market rate. *(p. 555)*

**Discount on note payable** Difference between the face value of a note payable and the (lesser) amount borrowed; reflects the added interest to be paid on the note over its life.

**Discount on stock** Difference between the par value of stock and its issue price when issued at a price below par value. *(p. 513)*

**Discount period** Time period in which a cash discount is available and the buyer can make a reduced payment. *(p. 183)*

**Discount rate** Expected rate of return on investments; also called *cost of capital, hurdle rate,* or *required rate of return.* *(p. B-2)*

**Discounts lost** Expenses resulting from not taking advantage of cash discounts on purchases. *(p. 341)*

**Dividend in arrears** Unpaid dividend on cumulative preferred stock; must be paid before any regular dividends on preferred stock and before any dividends on common stock. *(p. 519)*

**Dividends** Corporation's distributions of assets to its owners.

**Dividend yield** Ratio of the annual amount of cash dividends distributed to common shareholders relative to the common stock's market value (price). *(p. 528)*

**Double-declining-balance (DDB) depreciation** Depreciation equals beginning book value multiplied by 2 times the straight-line rate.

**Double taxation** Corporate income is taxed and then its later distribution through dividends is normally taxed again for shareholders.

**Double-entry accounting** Accounting system in which each transaction affects at least two accounts and has at least one debit and one credit. *(p. 55)*

**Earnings** (See *net income.*)

**Earnings per share (EPS)** Amount of income earned by each share of a company's outstanding common stock; also called *net income per share.* *(p. 527)*

**Effective interest method** Allocates interest expense over the bond life to yield a constant rate of interest; interest expense for a period is found by multiplying the balance of the liability at the beginning of the period by the bond market rate at issuance; also called *interest method.* *(p. 572)*

**Efficiency** Company's productivity in using its assets; usually measured relative to how much revenue a certain level of assets generates. *(p. 687)*

**Efficiency variance** Difference between the actual quantity of an input and the standard quantity of that input. *(p. 1010)*

**Electronic funds transfer (EFT)** Use of electronic communication to transfer cash from one party to another. *(p. 329)*

**Employee benefits** Additional compensation paid to or on behalf of employees, such as premiums for medical, dental, life, and disability insurance, and contributions to pension plans. *(p. 445)*

**Employee earnings report** Record of an employee's net pay, gross pay, deductions, and year-to-date payroll information. *(p. 456)*

**Enterprise resource planning (ERP) software** Programs that manage a company's vital operations, which range from order taking to production to accounting. *(p. 287)*

**Entity** Organization that, for accounting purposes, is separate from other organizations and individuals.

**EOM** Abbreviation for *end of month;* used to describe credit terms for credit transactions. *(p. 183)*

**Equity** Owner's claim on the assets of a business; equals the residual interest in an entity's assets after deducting liabilities; also called *net assets.* *(p. 14)*

**Equity method** Accounting method used for long-term investments when the investor has "significant influence" over the investee. *(p. 602)*

**Equity ratio** Portion of total assets provided by equity, computed as total equity divided by total assets. *(p. 701)*

**Equity securities with controlling influence** Long-term investment when the investor is able to exert controlling influence over the investee; investors owning 50% or more of voting stock are presumed to exert controlling influence. *(p. 603)*

**Equity securities with significant influence** Long-term investment when the investor is able to exert significant influence over the investee; investors owning 20 percent or more (but less than 50 percent) of voting stock are presumed to exert significant influence. *(p. 602)*

**Equivalent units of production (EUP)** Number of units that would be completed if all effort during a period had been applied to units that were started and finished. *(p. 821)*

**Estimated liability** Obligation of an uncertain amount that can be reasonably estimated. *(p. 445)*

**Estimated line of cost behavior** Line drawn on a graph to visually fit the relation between cost and sales. *(p. 912)*

**Ethics** Codes of conduct by which actions are judged as right or wrong, fair or unfair, honest or dishonest. *(pp. 8 & 736)*

**Events** Happenings that both affect an organization's financial position and can be reliably measured. *(p. 15)*

**Expanded accounting equation** Assets = Liabilities + Equity; Equity equals [Owner capital − Owner withdrawals + Revenues − Expenses] for a noncorporation; Equity equals [Contributed capital + Retained earnings + Revenues − Expenses] for a corporation where dividends are subtracted from retained earnings. *(p. 14)*

**Expense recognition** (or **matching**) **principle** (See *matching principle.*) *(pp. 11 & 96)*

**Expenses** Outflows or using up of assets as part of operations of a business to generate sales. *(p. 14)*

**External transactions** Exchanges of economic value between one entity and another entity. *(p. 15)*

**External users** Persons using accounting information who are not directly involved in running the organization. *(p. 5)*

**Extraordinary gains or losses** Gains or losses reported separately from continuing operations because they are both unusual and infrequent. *(p. 710)*

**Extraordinary repairs** Major repairs that extend the useful life of a plant asset beyond prior expectations; treated as a capital expenditure. *(p. 405)*

**Factory overhead** Factory activities supporting the production process that are not direct material or direct labor; also called *overhead and manufacturing overhead.* *(p. 742)*

**Factory overhead costs** Expenditures for factory overhead that cannot be separately or readily traced to finished goods; also called *overhead costs.* *(p. 742)*

**Fair value option** Reporting option that permits a company to use fair value in reporting certain assets and liabilities, which is presently based on a 3-level system to determine fair value. *(p. 565)*

**Favorable variance** Difference in actual revenues or expenses from the budgeted amount that contributes to a higher income. *(p. 991)*

**Federal depository bank** Bank authorized to accept deposits of amounts payable to the federal government. *(p. 453)*

**Federal Insurance Contributions Act (FICA) Taxes** Taxes assessed on both employers and employees; for Social Security and Medicare programs. *(p. 442)*

**Federal Unemployment Taxes (FUTA)** Payroll taxes on employers assessed by the federal government to support its unemployment insurance program. *(p. 444)*

**FIFO method** (See *first-in, first-out.*) *(pp. 233 & 833)*

**Financial accounting** Area of accounting aimed mainly at serving external users. *(p. 5)*

**Financial Accounting Standards Board (FASB)** Independent group of full-time members responsible for setting accounting rules. *(p. 9)*

**Financial leverage** Earning a higher return on equity by paying dividends on preferred stock or interest on debt at a rate lower than the return earned with the assets from issuing preferred stock or debt; also called *trading on the equity.* *(p. 521)*

**Financial reporting** Process of communicating information relevant to investors, creditors, and others in making investment, credit, and business decisions. *(p. 687)*

**Financial statement analysis** Application of analytical tools to general-purpose financial statements and related data for making business decisions. *(p. 686)*

**Financial statements** Includes the balance sheet, income statement, statement of owner's (or stockholders') equity, and statement of cash flows.

**Financing activities** Transactions with owners and creditors that include obtaining cash from issuing debt, repaying amounts borrowed, and obtaining cash from or distributing cash to owners. *(p. 634)*

**Finished goods inventory** Account that controls the finished goods files, which acts as a subsidiary ledger (of the Inventory account) in which the costs of finished goods that are ready for sale are recorded. *(pp. 741 & 779)*

**First-in, first-out (FIFO)** Method to assign cost to inventory that assumes items are sold in the order acquired; earliest items purchased are the first sold. *(p. 233)*

**Fiscal year** Consecutive 12-month (or 52-week) period chosen as the organization's annual accounting period. *(p. 95)*

**Fixed budget** Planning budget based on a single predicted amount of volume; unsuitable for evaluations if the actual volume differs from predicted volume. *(p. 991)*

**Fixed budget performance report** Report that compares actual revenues and costs with fixed budgeted amounts and identifies the differences as favorable or unfavorable variances. *(p. 991)*

**Fixed cost** Cost that does not change with changes in the volume of activity. *(p. 736)*

**Flexibility principle** Information system principle that prescribes an accounting system be able to adapt to changes in the company, its operations, and needs of decision makers. *(p. 273)*

**Flexible budget** Budget prepared (using actual volume) once a period is complete that helps managers evaluate past performance; uses fixed and variable costs in determining total costs. *(p. 992)*

**Flexible budget performance report** Report that compares actual revenues and costs with their variable budgeted amounts based on actual sales volume (or other level of activity) and identifies the differences as variances. *(p. 994)*

**FOB** Abbreviation for *free on board;* the point when ownership of goods passes to the buyer; *FOB shipping point* (or *factory*) means the buyer pays shipping costs and accepts ownership of goods when the seller transfers goods to carrier; *FOB destination* means the seller pays shipping costs and buyer accepts ownership of goods at the buyer's place of business. *(p. 185)*

**Foreign exchange rate** Price of one currency stated in terms of another currency. *(p. 610)*

**Form 940** IRS form used to report an employer's federal unemployment taxes (FUTA) on an annual filing basis. *(p. 453)*

**Form 941** IRS form filed to report FICA taxes owed and remitted. *(p. 453)*

**Form 10-K (or 10-KSB)** Annual report form filed with SEC by businesses (small businesses) with publicly traded securities. *(p. A-1)*

**Form W-2** Annual report by an employer to each employee showing the employee's wages subject to FICA and federal income taxes along with amounts withheld. *(p. 455)*

**Form W-4** Withholding allowance certificate, filed with the employer, identifying the number of withholding allowances claimed. *(p. 458)*

**Franchises** Privileges granted by a company or government to sell a product or service under specified conditions. *(p. 410)*

**Full disclosure principle** Principle that prescribes financial statements (including notes) to report all relevant information about an entity's operations and financial condition. *(p. 11)*

**GAAP** (See *generally accepted accounting principles.*)

**General accounting system** Accounting system for manufacturing activities based on the *periodic* inventory system. *(p. 776)*

**General and administrative expenses** Expenses that support the operating activities of a business. *(p. 193)*

**General and administrative expense budget** Plan that shows predicted operating expenses not included in the selling expenses budget. *(p. 955)*

**General journal** All-purpose journal for recording the debits and credits of transactions and events. *(pp. 56 & 276)*

**General ledger** (See *ledger.*) *(p. 51)*

**General partner** Partner who assumes unlimited liability for the debts of the partnership; responsible for partnership management. *(p. 481)*

**General partnership** Partnership in which all partners have mutual agency and unlimited liability for partnership debts. *(p. 481)*

**Generally accepted accounting principles (GAAP)** Rules that specify acceptable accounting practices. *(p. 8)*

**Generally accepted auditing standards (GAAS)** Rules that specify auditing practices.

**General-purpose financial statements** Statements published periodically for use by a variety of interested parties; includes the income statement, balance sheet, statement of owner's equity (or statement of retained earnings for a corporation), statement of cash flows, and notes to these statements. *(p. 687)*

**Going-concern assumption** Principle that prescribes financial statements to reflect the assumption that the business will continue operating. *(p. 11)*

**Goods in process inventory** Account in which costs are accumulated for products that are in the process of being produced but are not yet complete; also called *work in process inventory.* *(pp. 741 & 778)*

**Goodwill** Amount by which a company's (or a segment's) value exceeds the value of its individual assets less its liabilities. *(p. 411)*

**Gross margin** (See *gross profit.*)

**Gross margin ratio** Gross margin (net sales minus cost of goods sold) divided by net sales; also called *gross profit ratio.* *(p. 196)*

**Gross method** Method of recording purchases at the full invoice price without deducting any cash discounts. *(p. 341)*

**Gross pay** Total compensation earned by an employee. *(p. 442)*

**Gross profit** Net sales minus cost of goods sold; also called *gross margin.* *(p. 180)*

**Gross profit method** Procedure to estimate inventory when the past gross profit rate is used to estimate cost of goods sold, which is then subtracted from the cost of goods available for sale. *(p. 252)*

**Held-to-maturity (HTM) securities** Debt securities that a company has the intent and ability to hold until they mature. *(p. 600)*

**High-low method** Procedure that yields an estimated line of cost behavior by graphically connecting costs associated with the highest and lowest sales volume. *(p. 912)*

**Horizontal analysis** Comparison of a company's financial condition and performance across time. *(p. 688)*

**Hurdle rate** Minimum acceptable rate of return (set by management) for an investment. *(pp. 873 & 1045)*

**Impairment** Diminishment of an asset value. *(pp. 404 & 410)*

**Imprest system** Method to account for petty cash; maintains a constant balance in the fund, which equals cash plus petty cash receipts.

**Inadequacy** Condition in which the capacity of plant assets is too small to meet the company's production demands. *(p. 397)*

**Income** (See *net income.*)

**Income statement** Financial statement that subtracts expenses from revenues to yield a net income or loss over a specified period of time; also includes any gains or losses. *(p. 19)*

**Income Summary** Temporary account used only in the closing process to which the balances of revenue and expense accounts (including any gains or losses) are transferred; its balance is transferred to the capital account (or retained earnings for a corporation). *(p. 143)*

**Incremental cost** Additional cost incurred only if a company pursues a specific course of action. *(p. 1048)*

**Indefinite life** Asset life that is not limited by legal, regulatory, contractual, competitive, economic, or other factors. *(p. 409)*

**Indirect costs** Costs incurred for the benefit of more than one cost object. *(p. 737)*

**Indirect expenses** Expenses incurred for the joint benefit of more than one department (or cost object). *(p. 865)*

**Indirect labor** Efforts of production employees who do not work specifically on converting direct materials into finished products and who are not clearly identified with specific units or batches of product. *(p. 742)*

**Indirect labor costs** Labor costs that cannot be physically traced to production of a product or service; included as part of overhead. *(p. 742)*

**Indirect material** Material used to support the production process but not clearly identified with products or batches of product. *(p. 740)*

**Indirect method** Presentation that reports net income and then adjusts it by adding and subtracting items to yield net cash from operating activities on the statement of cash flows. *(p. 638)*

**Information processor** Component of an accounting system that interprets, transforms, and summarizes information for use in analysis and reporting. *(p. 274)*

**Information storage** Component of an accounting system that keeps data in a form accessible to information processors. *(p. 274)*

**Infrequent gain or loss** Gain or loss not expected to recur given the operating environment of the business. *(p. 710)*

**Input device** Means of capturing information from source documents that enables its transfer to information processors. *(p. 274)*

**Installment note** Liability requiring a series of periodic payments to the lender. *(p. 562)*

**Institute of Management Accountants (IMA)** A professional association of management accountants. *(p. 736)*

**Intangible assets** Long-term assets (resources) used to produce or sell products or services; usually lack physical form and have uncertain benefits. *(pp. 149 & 409)*

**Interest** Charge for using money (or other assets) loaned from one entity to another. *(p. 370)*

**Interim financial statements** Financial statements covering periods of less than one year; usually based on one-, three-, or six-month periods. (*pp. 94 & 251*)

**Internal controls** or **Internal control system** All policies and procedures used to protect assets, ensure reliable accounting, promote efficient operations, and urge adherence to company policies. (*pp. 272 & 736*)

**Internal rate of return (IRR)** Rate used to evaluate the acceptability of an investment; equals the rate that yields a net present value of zero for an investment. (*p. 1043*)

**Internal transactions** Activities within an organization that can affect the accounting equation. (*p. 15*)

**Internal users** Persons using accounting information who are directly involved in managing the organization. (*p. 6*)

**International Accounting Standards Board (IASB)** Group that identifies preferred accounting practices and encourages global acceptance; issues International Financial Reporting Standards (IFRS). (*p. 9*)

**International Financial Reporting Standards (IFRS)** International Financial Reporting Standards (IFRS) are required or allowed by over 100 countries; IFRS is set by the International Accounting Standards Board (IASB), which aims to develop a single set of global standards, to promote those standards, and to converge national and international standards globally. (*p. 9*)

**Inventory** Goods a company owns and expects to sell in its normal operations. (*p. 181*)

**Inventory turnover** Number of times a company's average inventory is sold during a period; computed by dividing cost of goods sold by average inventory; also called *merchandise turnover*. (*p. 241*)

**Investing activities** Transactions that involve purchasing and selling of long-term assets, includes making and collecting notes receivable and investments in other than cash equivalents. (*p. 634*)

**Investment center** Center of which a manager is responsible for revenues, costs, and asset investments. (*p. 865*)

**Investment center residual income** The net income an investment center earns above a target return on average invested assets. (*p. 873*)

**Investment center return on total assets** Center net income divided by average total assets for the center. (*p. 873*)

**Investment turnover** The efficiency with which a company generates sales from its available assets; computed as sales divided by average invested assets. (*p. 878*)

**Invoice** Itemized record of goods prepared by the vendor that lists the customer's name, items sold, sales prices, and terms of sale. (*p. 339*)

**Invoice approval** Document containing a checklist of steps necessary for approving the recording and payment of an invoice; also called *check authorization*. (*p. 339*)

**Job** Production of a customized product or service. (*p. 776*)

**Job cost sheet** Separate record maintained for each job. (*p. 778*)

**Job lot** Production of more than one unit of a customized product or service. (*p. 777*)

**Job order cost accounting system** Cost accounting system to determine the cost of producing each job or job lot. (*pp. 778 & 817*)

**Job order production** Production of special-order products; also called *customized production*. (*p. 776*)

**Joint cost** Cost incurred to produce or purchase two or more products at the same time. (*p. 883*)

**Journal** Record in which transactions are entered before they are posted to ledger accounts; also called *book of original entry*. (*p. 56*)

**Journalizing** Process of recording transactions in a journal. (*p. 56*)

**Just-in-time (JIT) manufacturing** Process of acquiring or producing inventory only when needed. (*p. 748*)

**Known liabilities** Obligations of a company with little uncertainty; set by agreements, contracts, or laws; also called *definitely determinable liabilities*. (*p. 438*)

**Land improvements** Assets that increase the benefits of land, have a limited useful life, and are depreciated. (*p. 396*)

**Large stock dividend** Stock dividend that is more than 25% of the previously outstanding shares. (*p. 516*)

**Last-in, first-out (LIFO)** Method to assign cost to inventory that assumes costs for the most recent items purchased are sold first and charged to cost of goods sold. (*p. 233*)

**Lean business model** Practice of eliminating waste while meeting customer needs and yielding positive company returns. (*p. 747*)

**Lease** Contract specifying the rental of property. (*pp. 411 & 576*)

**Leasehold** Rights the lessor grants to the lessee under the terms of a lease. (*p. 411*)

**Leasehold improvements** Alterations or improvements to leased property such as partitions and storefronts. (*p. 411*)

**Least-squares regression** Statistical method for deriving an estimated line of cost behavior that is more precise than the high-low method and the scatter diagram. (*p. 913*)

**Ledger** Record containing all accounts (with amounts) for a business; also called *general ledger*. (*p. 51*)

**Lessee** Party to a lease who secures the right to possess and use the property from another party (the lessor). (*p. 411*)

**Lessor** Party to a lease who grants another party (the lessee) the right to possess and use its property. (*p. 411*)

**Liabilities** Creditors' claims on an organization's assets; involves a probable future payment of assets, products, or services that a company is obligated to make due to past transactions or events. (*p. 14*)

**Licenses** (See *franchises*.) (*p. 410*)

**Limited liability** Owner can lose no more than the amount invested. (*p. 11*)

**Limited liability company** Organization form that combines select features of a corporation and a limited partnership; provides limited liability to its members (owners), is free of business tax, and allows members to actively participate in management. (*p. 482*)

**Limited liability partnership** Partnership in which a partner is not personally liable for malpractice or negligence unless that partner is responsible for providing the service that resulted in the claim. (*p. 481*)

**Limited life** (See *useful life*.)

**Limited partners** Partners who have no personal liability for partnership debts beyond the amounts they invested in the partnership. (*p. 481*)

**Limited partnership** Partnership that has two classes of partners, limited partners and general partners. (*p. 481*)

**Liquid assets** Resources such as cash that are easily converted into other assets or used to pay for goods, services, or liabilities. *(p. 321)*

**Liquidating cash dividend** Distribution of assets that returns part of the original investment to stockholders; deducted from contributed capital accounts. *(p. 516)*

**Liquidation** Process of going out of business; involves selling assets, paying liabilities, and distributing remainder to owners.

**Liquidity** Availability of resources to meet short-term cash requirements. *(pp. 321 & 687)*

**List price** Catalog (full) price of an item before any trade discount is deducted. *(p. 182)*

**Long-term investments** Long-term assets not used in operating activities such as notes receivable and investments in stocks and bonds. *(pp. 149 & 596)*

**Long-term liabilities** Obligations not due to be paid within one year or the operating cycle, whichever is longer. *(pp. 149 & 437)*

**Lower of cost or market (LCM)** Required method to report inventory at market replacement cost when that market cost is lower than recorded cost. *(p. 237)*

**Maker of the note** Entity who signs a note and promises to pay it at maturity. *(p. 370)*

**Management by exception** Management process to focus on significant variances and give less attention to areas where performance is close to the standard. *(p. 995)*

**Managerial accounting** Area of accounting aimed mainly at serving the decision-making needs of internal users; also called *management accounting*. *(pp. 6 & 732)*

**Manufacturer** Company that uses labor and operating assets to convert raw materials to finished goods.

**Manufacturing budget** Plan that shows the predicted costs for direct materials, direct labor, and overhead to be incurred in manufacturing units in the production budget. *(p. 966)*

**Manufacturing statement** Report that summarizes the types and amounts of costs incurred in a company's production process for a period; also called *cost of goods manufacturing statement*. *(p. 745)*

**Margin of safety** Excess of expected sales over the level of break-even sales. *(p. 920)*

**Market-based transfer price** The market price of a good or service being transferred between divisions within a company; typically used when the transferring division does not have excess capacity. *(p. 883)*

**Market prospects** Expectations (both good and bad) about a company's future performance as assessed by users and other interested parties. *(p. 687)*

**Market rate** Interest rate that borrowers are willing to pay and lenders are willing to accept for a specific lending agreement given the borrowers' risk level. *(p. 555)*

**Market value per share** Price at which stock is bought or sold. *(p. 511)*

**Master budget** Comprehensive business plan that includes specific plans for expected sales, product units to be produced, merchandise (or materials) to be purchased, expenses to be incurred, plant assets to be purchased, and amounts of cash to be borrowed or loans to be repaid, as well as a budgeted income statement and balance sheet. *(p. 950)*

**Matching (or expense recognition) principle** Prescribes expenses to be reported in the same period as the revenues that were earned as a result of the expenses. *(pp. 11 & 364)*

**Materiality constraint** Prescribes that accounting for items that significantly impact financial statement and any inferences from them adhere strictly to GAAP. *(pp. 12 & 364)*

**Materials consumption report** Document that summarizes the materials a department uses during a reporting period; replaces materials requisitions. *(p. 818)*

**Materials ledger card** Perpetual record updated each time units are purchased or issued for production use. *(p. 780)*

**Materials requisition** Source document production managers use to request materials for production; used to assign materials costs to specific jobs or overhead. *(p. 781)*

**Maturity date of a note** Date when a note's principal and interest are due. *(p. 370)*

**Measurement principle** Accounting information is based on cost with potential subsequent adjustments to fair value; see also *cost principle*. *(p. 10)*

**Merchandise** (See *merchandise inventory*.) *(p. 180)*

**Merchandise inventory** Goods that a company owns and expects to sell to customers; also called *merchandise* or *inventory*. *(p. 181)*

**Merchandise purchases budget** Plan that shows the units or costs of merchandise to be purchased by a merchandising company during the budget period. *(p. 953)*

**Merchandiser** Entity that earns net income by buying and selling merchandise. *(p. 180)*

**Merit rating** Rating assigned to an employer by a state based on the employer's record of employment. *(p. 444)*

**Minimum legal capital** Amount of assets defined by law that stockholders must (potentially) invest in a corporation; usually defined as par value of the stock; intended to protect creditors. *(p. 511)*

**Mixed cost** Cost that behaves like a combination of fixed and variable costs. *(p. 909)*

**Modified Accelerated Cost Recovery System (MACRS)** Depreciation system required by federal income tax law. *(p. 402)*

**Monetary unit assumption** Principle that assumes transactions and events can be expressed in money units. *(p. 11)*

**Mortgage** Legal loan agreement that protects a lender by giving the lender the right to be paid from the cash proceeds from the sale of a borrower's assets identified in the mortgage. *(p. 564)*

**Multinational** Company that operates in several countries. *(p. 610)*

**Multiple-step income statement** Income statement format that shows subtotals between sales and net income, categorizes expenses, and often reports the details of net sales and expenses. *(p. 192)*

**Mutual agency** Legal relationship among partners whereby each partner is an agent of the partnership and is able to bind the partnership to contracts within the scope of the partnership's business. *(p. 480)*

**Natural business year** Twelve-month period that ends when a company's sales activities are at their lowest point. *(p. 95)*

**Natural resources** Assets physically consumed when used; examples are timber, mineral deposits, and oil and gas fields; also called *wasting assets*. *(p. 408)*

**Negotiated transfer price** A price, determined by negotiation between division managers, to record transfers between divisions; typically lies between the variable cost and the market price of the item transferred. *(p. 883)*

**Net assets** (See *equity*.)

**Net income** Amount earned after subtracting all expenses necessary for and matched with sales for a period; also called *income, profit,* or *earnings*. *(p. 14)*

**Net loss** Excess of expenses over revenues for a period. *(p. 14)*

**Net method** Method of recording purchases at the full invoice price less any cash discounts. *(p. 341)*

**Net pay** Gross pay less all deductions; also called *take-home pay*. *(p. 442)*

**Net present value (NPV)** Dollar estimate of an asset's value that is used to evaluate the acceptability of an investment; computed by discounting future cash flows from the investment at a satisfactory rate and then subtracting the initial cost of the investment. *(p. 1041)*

**Net realizable value** Expected selling price (value) of an item minus the cost of making the sale. *(p. 228)*

**Noncumulative preferred stock** Preferred stock on which the right to receive dividends is lost for any period when dividends are not declared. *(p. 519)*

**Noninterest-bearing note** Note with no stated (contract) rate of interest; interest is implicitly included in the note's face value.

**Nonparticipating preferred stock** Preferred stock on which dividends are limited to a maximum amount each year. *(p. 520)*

**Nonsufficient funds (NSF) check** Maker's bank account has insufficient money to pay the check; also called *hot check*.

**Non-value-added time** The portion of cycle time that is not directed at producing a product or service; equals the sum of inspection time, move time, and wait time. *(p. 750)*

**No-par value stock** Stock class that has not been assigned a par (or stated) value by the corporate charter. *(p. 511)*

**Not controllable costs** Costs that a manager does not have the power to control or strongly influence. *(p. 737)*

**Note** (See *promissory note*.)

**Note payable** Liability expressed by a written promise to pay a definite sum of money on demand or on a specific future date(s).

**Note receivable** Asset consisting of a written promise to receive a definite sum of money on demand or on a specific future date(s).

**Objectivity principle** Principle that prescribes independent, unbiased evidence to support financial statement information. *(p. 9)*

**Obsolescence** Condition in which, because of new inventions and improvements, a plant asset can no longer be used to produce goods or services with a competitive advantage. *(p. 397)*

**Off-balance-sheet financing** Acquisition of assets by agreeing to liabilities not reported on the balance sheet. *(p. 577)*

**Online processing** Approach to inputting data from source documents as soon as the information is available. *(p. 286)*

**Operating activities** Activities that involve the production or purchase of merchandise and the sale of goods or services to customers, including expenditures related to administering the business. *(p. 633)*

**Operating cycle** Normal time between paying cash for merchandise or employee services and receiving cash from customers. *(p. 147)*

**Operating leases** Short-term (or cancelable) leases in which the lessor retains risks and rewards of ownership. *(p. 576)*

**Operating leverage** Extent, or relative size, of fixed costs in the total cost structure. *(p. 924)*

**Opportunity cost** Potential benefit lost by choosing a specific action from two or more alternatives. *(p. 738)*

**Ordinary repairs** Repairs to keep a plant asset in normal, good operating condition; treated as a revenue expenditure and immediately expensed. *(p. 404)*

**Organization expenses (costs)** Costs such as legal fees and promoter fees to bring an entity into existence. *(pp. 509 & 514)*

**Other comprehensive income** Equals net income less comprehensive income; includes unrealized gains and losses on available-for-sale securities, foreign currency adjustments, and pension adjustments. *(p. 604)*

**Out-of-pocket cost** Cost incurred or avoided as a result of management's decisions. *(p. 738)*

**Output devices** Means by which information is taken out of the accounting system and made available for use. *(p. 275)*

**Outsourcing** Manager decision to buy a product or service from another part of a *make-or-buy* decision; also called *make or buy*.

**Outstanding checks** Checks written and recorded by the depositor but not yet paid by the bank at the bank statement date. *(p. 331)*

**Outstanding stock** Corporation's stock held by its shareholders.

**Overapplied overhead** Amount by which the overhead applied to production in a period using the predetermined overhead rate exceeds the actual overhead incurred in a period. *(p. 787)*

**Overhead cost variance** Difference between the total overhead cost applied to products and the total overhead cost actually incurred. *(p. 1002)*

**Owner, Capital** Account showing the owner's claim on company assets; equals owner investments plus net income (or less net losses) minus owner withdrawals since the company's inception; also referred to as *equity*. *(p. 14)*

**Owner investment** Assets put into the business by the owner. *(p. 14)*

**Owner's equity** (See *equity*.)

**Owner, withdrawals** Account used to record asset distributions to the owner. (See also *withdrawals*.) *(p. 14)*

**Paid-in capital** (See *contributed capital*.) *(p. 512)*

**Paid-in capital in excess of par value** Amount received from issuance of stock that is in excess of the stock's par value. *(p. 513)*

**Par value** Value assigned a share of stock by the corporate charter when the stock is authorized. *(p. 511)*

**Par value of a bond** Amount the bond issuer agrees to pay at maturity and the amount on which cash interest payments are based; also called *face amount* or *face value* of a bond. *(p. 552)*

**Par value stock** Class of stock assigned a par value by the corporate charter. *(p. 511)*

**Parent** Company that owns a controlling interest in a corporation (requires more than 50% of voting stock). *(p. 603)*

**Participating preferred stock** Preferred stock that shares with common stockholders any dividends paid in excess of the percent stated on preferred stock. *(p. 520)*

**Partner return on equity** Partner net income divided by average partner equity for the period. *(p. 492)*

**Partnership** Unincorporated association of two or more persons to pursue a business for profit as co-owners. *(pp. 11 & 480)*

**Partnership contract** Agreement among partners that sets terms under which the affairs of the partnership are conducted; also called *articles of partnership*. *(p. 480)*

**Partnership liquidation** Dissolution of a partnership by (1) selling noncash assets and allocating any gain or loss according to partners' income-and-loss ratio, (2) paying liabilities, and (3) distributing any remaining cash according to partners' capital balances. *(p. 489)*

**Patent** Exclusive right granted to its owner to produce and sell an item or to use a process for 20 years. *(p. 410)*

**Payback period (PBP)** Time-based measurement used to evaluate the acceptability of an investment; equals the time expected to pass before an investment's net cash flows equal its initial cost. *(p. 1037)*

**Payee of the note** Entity to whom a note is made payable. *(p. 370)*

**Payroll bank account** Bank account used solely for paying employees; each pay period an amount equal to the total employees' net pay is deposited in it and the payroll checks are drawn on it. *(p. 458)*

**Payroll deductions** Amounts withheld from an employee's gross pay; also called *withholdings*. *(p. 442)*

**Payroll register** Record for a pay period that shows the pay period dates, regular and overtime hours worked, gross pay, net pay, and deductions. *(p. 455)*

**Pension plan** Contractual agreement between an employer and its employees for the employer to provide benefits to employees after they retire; expensed when incurred. *(p. 578)*

**Period costs** Expenditures identified more with a time period than with finished products costs; includes selling and general administrative expenses. *(p. 738)*

**Periodic inventory system** Method that records the cost of inventory purchased but does not continuously track the quantity available or sold to customers; records are updated at the end of each period to reflect the physical count and costs of goods available. *(p. 182)*

**Permanent accounts** Accounts that reflect activities related to one or more future periods; balance sheet accounts whose balances are not closed; also called *real accounts*. *(p. 142)*

**Perpetual inventory system** Method that maintains continuous records of the cost of inventory available and the cost of goods sold. *(p. 182)*

**Petty cash** Small amount of cash in a fund to pay minor expenses; accounted for using an imprest system. *(p. 326)*

**Planning** Process of setting goals and preparing to achieve them. *(p. 732)*

**Plant asset age** Estimate of the age of a company's plant assets, computed by dividing accumulated depreciation by depreciation expense. *(p. 413)*

**Plant assets** Tangible long-lived assets used to produce or sell products and services; also called *property, plant and equipment (PP&E)* or *fixed assets*. *(pp. 99 & 394)*

**Pledged assets to secured liabilities** Ratio of the book value of a company's pledged assets to the book value of its secured liabilities.

**Post-closing trial balance** List of permanent accounts and their balances from the ledger after all closing entries are journalized and posted. *(p. 146)*

**Posting** Process of transferring journal entry information to the ledger; computerized systems automate this process. *(p. 56)*

**Posting reference (PR) column** A column in journals in which individual ledger account numbers are entered when entries are posted to those ledger accounts. *(p. 58)*

**Predetermined overhead rate** Rate established prior to the beginning of a period that relates estimated overhead to another variable, such as estimated direct labor, and is used to assign overhead cost to production. *(p. 784)*

**Preemptive right** Stockholders' right to maintain their proportionate interest in a corporation with any additional shares issued. *(p. 510)*

**Preferred stock** Stock with a priority status over common stockholders in one or more ways, such as paying dividends or distributing assets. *(p. 518)*

**Premium on bonds** Difference between a bond's par value and its higher carrying value; occurs when the contract rate is higher than the market rate; also called *bond premium*. *(p. 558)*

**Premium on stock** (See *contributed capital in excess of par value*.) *(p. 513)*

**Prepaid expenses** Items paid for in advance of receiving their benefits; classified as assets. *(p. 97)*

**Price-earnings (PE) ratio** Ratio of a company's current market value per share to its earnings per share; also called *price-to-earnings*. *(p. 527)*

**Price variance** Difference between actual and budgeted revenue or cost caused by the difference between the actual price per unit and the budgeted price per unit. *(p. 995)*

**Prime costs** Expenditures directly identified with the production of finished goods; include direct materials costs and direct labor costs. *(p. 743)*

**Principal of a note** Amount that the signer of a note agrees to pay back when it matures, not including interest. *(p. 370)*

**Principles of internal control** Principles prescribing management to establish responsibility, maintain records, insure assets, separate record-keeping from custody of assets, divide responsibility for related transactions, apply technological controls, and perform reviews. *(p. 317)*

**Prior period adjustment** Correction of an error in a prior year that is reported in the statement of retained earnings (or statement of stockholders' equity) net of any income tax effects. *(p. 525)*

**Pro forma financial statements** Statements that show the effects of proposed transactions and events as if they had occurred. *(p. 142)*

**Process cost accounting system** System of assigning direct materials, direct labor, and overhead to specific processes; total costs associated with each process are then divided by the number of units passing through that process to determine the cost per equivalent unit. *(p. 817)*

**Process cost summary** Report of costs charged to a department, its equivalent units of production achieved, and the costs assigned to its output. *(p. 826)*

**Process operations** Processing of products in a continuous (sequential) flow of steps; also called *process manufacturing* or *process production*. *(p. 814)*

**Product costs** Costs that are capitalized as inventory because they produce benefits expected to have future value; include direct materials, direct labor, and overhead. *(p. 738)*

**Production budget** Plan that shows the units to be produced each period. *(p. 966)*

**Profit** (See *net income*.)

**Profit center** Business unit that incurs costs and generates revenues. *(p. 865)*

**Profit margin** Ratio of a company's net income to its net sales; the percent of income in each dollar of revenue; also called *net profit margin*. *(pp. 109 & 878)*

**Profitability** Company's ability to generate an adequate return on invested capital. *(p. 687)*

**Profitability index** A measure of the relation between the expected benefits of a project and its investment, computed as the present value of expected future cash flows from the investment divided by the cost of the investment; a higher value indicates a more desirable investment, and a value below 1 indicates an unacceptable project. *(p. 1043)*

**Promissory note** (or **note**) Written promise to pay a specified amount either on demand or at a definite future date; is a *note receivable* for the lender but a *note payable* for the lendee. *(p. 370)*

**Proprietorship** (See *sole proprietorship*.) *(p. 11)*

**Proxy** Legal document giving a stockholder's agent the power to exercise the stockholder's voting rights. *(p. 509)*

**Purchase discount** Term used by a purchaser to describe a cash discount granted to the purchaser for paying within the discount period. *(p. 183)*

**Purchase order** Document used by the purchasing department to place an order with a seller (vendor). *(p. 338)*

**Purchase requisition** Document listing merchandise needed by a department and requesting it be purchased. *(p. 338)*

**Purchases journal** Journal normally used to record all purchases on credit. *(p. 283)*

**Quantity variance** Difference between actual and budgeted revenue or cost caused by the difference between the actual number of units and the budgeted number of units. *(p. 995)*

**Ratio analysis** Determination of key relations between financial statement items as reflected in numerical measures. *(p. 688)*

**Raw materials inventory** Goods a company acquires to use in making products. *(p. 740)*

**Realizable value** Expected proceeds from converting an asset into cash. *(p. 365)*

**Receiving report** Form used to report that ordered goods are received and to describe their quantity and condition. *(p. 339)*

**Recordkeeping** Part of accounting that involves recording transactions and events, either manually or electronically; also called *bookkeeping*. *(p. 4)*

**Registered bonds** Bonds owned by investors whose names and addresses are recorded by the issuer; interest payments are made to the registered owners. *(p. 566)*

**Relevance principle** Information system principle prescribing that its reports be useful, understandable, timely, and pertinent for decision making. *(p. 272)*

**Relevant benefits** Additional or incremental revenue generated by selecting a particular course of action over another. *(p. 1047)*

**Relevant range of operations** Company's normal operating range; excludes extremely high and low volumes not likely to occur. *(p. 917)*

**Report form balance sheet** Balance sheet that lists accounts vertically in the order of assets, liabilities, and equity.

**Responsibility accounting budget** Report of expected costs and expenses under a manager's control. *(p. 876)*

**Responsibility accounting performance report** Responsibility report that compares actual costs and expenses for a department with budgeted amounts. *(p. 876)*

**Responsibility accounting system** System that provides information that management can use to evaluate the performance of a department's manager. *(p. 864)*

**Restricted retained earnings** Retained earnings not available for dividends because of legal or contractual limitations. *(p. 524)*

**Retail inventory method** Method to estimate ending inventory based on the ratio of the amount of goods for sale at cost to the amount of goods for sale at retail. *(p. 251)*

**Retailer** Intermediary that buys products from manufacturers or wholesalers and sells them to consumers. *(p. 180)*

**Retained earnings** Cumulative income less cumulative losses and dividends. *(p. 512)*

**Retained earnings deficit** Debit (abnormal) balance in Retained Earnings; occurs when cumulative losses and dividends exceed cumulative income; also called *accumulated deficit*. *(p. 515)*

**Return** Monies received from an investment; often in percent form. *(p. 26)*

**Return on assets** (See *return on total assets*) *(p. 22)*

**Return on equity** Ratio of net income to average equity for the period.

**Return on total assets** Ratio reflecting operating efficiency; defined as net income divided by average total assets for the period; also called *return on assets* or *return on investment*. *(p. 605)*

**Revenue expenditures** Expenditures reported on the current income statement as an expense because they do not provide benefits in future periods. *(p. 404)*

**Revenue recognition principle** The principle prescribing that revenue is recognized when earned. *(p. 10)*

**Revenues** Gross increase in equity from a company's business activities that earn income; also called *sales*. *(p. 14)*

**Reverse stock split** Occurs when a corporation calls in its stock and replaces each share with less than one new share; increases both market value per share and any par or stated value per share. *(p. 518)*

**Reversing entries** Optional entries recorded at the beginning of a period that prepare the accounts for the usual journal entries as if adjusting entries had not occurred in the prior period. *(p. 154)*

**Risk** Uncertainty about an expected return. *(p. 26)*

**Rolling budget** New set of budgets a firm adds for the next period (with revisions) to replace the ones that have lapsed. *(p. 949)*

**S corporation** Corporation that meets special tax qualifications so as to be treated like a partnership for income tax purposes. *(p. 482)*

**Safety stock** Quantity of inventory or materials over the minimum needed to satisfy budgeted demand. *(p. 953)*

**Sales** (See *revenues.*)

**Sales budget** Plan showing the units of goods to be sold or services to be provided; the starting point in the budgeting process for most departments. *(p. 952)*

**Sales discount** Term used by a seller to describe a cash discount granted to buyers who pay within the discount period. *(p. 183)*

**Sales journal** Journal normally used to record sales of goods on credit. *(p. 278)*

**Sales mix** Ratio of sales volumes for the various products sold by a company. *(p. 921)*

**Salvage value** Estimate of amount to be recovered at the end of an asset's useful life; also called *residual value* or *scrap value.* *(p. 397)*

**Sarbanes-Oxley Act (SOX)** Created the *Public Company Accounting Oversight Board,* regulates analyst conflicts, imposes corporate governance requirements, enhances accounting and control disclosures, impacts insider transactions and executive loans, establishes new types of criminal conduct, and expands penalties for violations of federal securities laws. *(pp. 12 & 316)*

**Scatter diagram** Graph used to display data about past cost behavior and sales as points on a diagram. *(p. 911)*

**Schedule of accounts payable** List of the balances of all accounts in the accounts payable ledger and their totals. *(p. 284)*

**Schedule of accounts receivable** List of the balances of all accounts in the accounts receivable ledger and their totals. *(p. 279)*

**Section 404 (of SOX)** Section 404 of SOX requires that company management document and assess the effectiveness of all internal control processes that can affect financial reporting; company auditors express an opinion on whether management's assessment of the effectiveness of internal controls is fairly stated. *(p. 317)*

**Secured bonds** Bonds that have specific assets of the issuer pledged as collateral. *(p. 566)*

**Securities and Exchange Commission (SEC)** Federal agency Congress has charged to set reporting rules for organizations that sell ownership shares to the public. *(p. 9)*

**Segment return on assets** Segment operating income divided by segment average (identifiable) assets for the period. *(p. 288)*

**Selling expense budget** Plan that lists the types and amounts of selling expenses expected in the budget period. *(p. 954)*

**Selling expenses** Expenses of promoting sales, such as displaying and advertising merchandise, making sales, and delivering goods to customers. *(p. 193)*

**Serial bonds** Bonds consisting of separate amounts that mature at different dates. *(p. 566)*

**Service company** Organization that provides services instead of tangible products.

**Shareholders** Owners of a corporation; also called *stockholders.* *(p. 12)*

**Shares** Equity of a corporation divided into ownership units; also called *stock.* *(p. 12)*

**Short-term investments** Debt and equity securities that management expects to convert to cash within the next 3 to 12 months (or the operating cycle if longer); also called *temporary investments* or *marketable securities.* *(p. 596)*

**Short-term note payable** Current obligation in the form of a written promissory note. *(p. 439)*

**Shrinkage** Inventory losses that occur as a result of theft or deterioration. *(p. 190)*

**Signature card** Includes the signatures of each person authorized to sign checks on the bank account. *(p. 328)*

**Simple capital structure** Capital structure that consists of only common stock and nonconvertible preferred stock; consists of no dilutive securities. *(p. 527)*

**Single-step income statement** Income statement format that includes cost of goods sold as an expense and shows only one subtotal for total expenses. *(p. 193)*

**Sinking fund bonds** Bonds that require the issuer to make deposits to a separate account; bondholders are repaid at maturity from that account. *(p. 566)*

**Small stock dividend** Stock dividend that is 25% or less of a corporation's previously outstanding shares. *(p. 516)*

**Social responsibility** Being accountable for the impact that one's actions might have on society. *(p. 8)*

**Sole proprietorship** Business owned by one person that is not organized as a corporation; also called *proprietorship.* *(p. 11)*

**Solvency** Company's long-run financial viability and its ability to cover long-term obligations. *(p. 687)*

**Source documents** Source of information for accounting entries that can be in either paper or electronic form; also called *business papers.* *(p. 50)*

**Special journal** Any journal used for recording and posting transactions of a similar type. *(p. 276)*

**Specific identification** Method to assign cost to inventory when the purchase cost of each item in inventory is identified and used to compute cost of inventory. *(p. 231)*

**Spending variance** Difference between the actual price of an item and its standard price. *(p. 1010)*

**Spreadsheet** Computer program that organizes data by means of formulas and format; also called *electronic work sheet.*

**Standard costs** Costs that should be incurred under normal conditions to produce a product or component or to perform a service. *(p. 995)*

**State Unemployment Taxes (SUTA)** State payroll taxes on employers to support its unemployment programs. *(p. 444)*

**Stated value stock** No-par stock assigned a stated value per share; this amount is recorded in the stock account when the stock is issued. *(p. 512)*

**Statement of cash flows** A financial statement that lists cash inflows (receipts) and cash outflows (payments) during a period; arranged by operating, investing, and financing. *(pp. 19 & 632)*

**Statement of owner's equity** Report of changes in equity over a period; adjusted for increases (owner investment and net income) and for decreases (withdrawals and net loss). *(p. 19)*

**Statement of partners' equity** Financial statement that shows total capital balances at the beginning of the period, any additional investment by partners, the income or loss of the period, the partners' withdrawals, and the partners' ending capital balances; also called *statement of partners' capital*. *(p. 485)*

**Statement of retained earnings** Report of changes in retained earnings over a period; adjusted for increases (net income), for decreases (dividends and net loss), and for any prior period adjustment.

**Statement of stockholders' equity** Financial statement that lists the beginning and ending balances of each major equity account and describes all changes in those accounts. *(p. 525)*

**Statements of Financial Accounting Standards (SFAS)** FASB publications that establish U.S. GAAP.

**Step-wise cost** Cost that remains fixed over limited ranges of volumes but changes by a lump sum when volume changes occur outside these limited ranges. *(p. 910)*.

**Stock** (See *shares*.) *(p. 12)*

**Stock dividend** Corporation's distribution of its own stock to its stockholders without the receipt of any payment. *(p. 516)*

**Stock options** Rights to purchase common stock at a fixed price over a specified period of time. *(p. 525)*

**Stock split** Occurs when a corporation calls in its stock and replaces each share with more than one new share; decreases both the market value per share and any par or stated value per share. *(p. 518)*

**Stock subscription** Investor's contractual commitment to purchase unissued shares at future dates and prices.

**Stockholders** (See *shareholders*.) *(p. 12)*

**Stockholders' equity** A corporation's equity; also called *shareholders' equity* or *corporate capital*. *(p. 512)*

**Straight-line depreciation** Method that allocates an equal portion of the depreciable cost of plant asset (cost minus salvage) to each accounting period in its useful life. *(pp. 99 & 398)*

**Straight-line bond amortization** Method allocating an equal amount of bond interest expense to each period of the bond life. *(p. 556)*

**Subsidiary** Entity controlled by another entity (parent) in which the parent owns more than 50% of the subsidiary's voting stock. *(p. 603)*

**Subsidiary ledger** List of individual subaccounts and amounts with a common characteristic; linked to a controlling account in the general ledger. *(p. 276)*

**Sunk cost** Cost already incurred and cannot be avoided or changed. *(p. 738)*

**Supplementary records** Information outside the usual accounting records; also called *supplemental records*. *(p. 186)*

**Supply chain** Linkages of services or goods extending from suppliers, to the company itself, and on to customers.

**T-account** Tool used to show the effects of transactions and events on individual accounts. *(p. 55)*

**Target cost** Maximum allowable cost for a product or service; defined as expected selling price less the desired profit. *(p. 777)*

**Temporary accounts** Accounts used to record revenues, expenses, and withdrawals (dividends for a corporation); they are closed at the end of each period; also called *nominal accounts*. *(p. 142)*

**Term bonds** Bonds scheduled for payment (maturity) at a single specified date. *(p. 566)*

**Throughput time** (See *cycle time*.)

**Time period assumption** Assumption that an organization's activities can be divided into specific time periods such as months, quarters, or years. *(pp. 11 & 94)*

**Time ticket** Source document used to report the time an employee spent working on a job or on overhead activities and then to determine the amount of direct labor to charge to the job or the amount of indirect labor to charge to overhead. *(p. 782)*

**Times interest earned** Ratio of income before interest expense (and any income taxes) divided by interest expense; reflects risk of covering interest commitments when income varies. *(p. 450)*

**Total asset turnover** Measure of a company's ability to use its assets to generate sales; computed by dividing net sales by average total assets. *(p. 413)*

**Total quality management (TQM)** Concept calling for all managers and employees at all stages of operations to strive toward higher standards and reduce number of defects. *(p. 748)*

**Trade discount** Reduction from a list or catalog price that can vary for wholesalers, retailers, and consumers. *(p. 182)*

**Trademark** or **trade (brand) name** Symbol, name, phrase, or jingle identified with a company, product, or service. *(p. 411)*

**Trading on the equity** (See *financial leverage*.)

**Trading securities** Investments in debt and equity securities that the company intends to actively trade for profit. *(p. 599)*

**Transfer price** The price used to record transfers of goods or services between divisions in the same company. *(p. 882)*

**Transaction** Exchange of economic consideration affecting an entity's financial position that can be reliably measured.

**Treasury stock** Corporation's own stock that it reacquired and still holds. *(p. 522)*

**Trial balance** List of accounts and their balances at a point in time; total debit balances equal total credit balances. *(p. 65)*

**Unadjusted trial balance** List of accounts and balances prepared before accounting adjustments are recorded and posted. *(p. 106)*

**Unavoidable expense** Expense (or cost) that is not relevant for business decisions; an expense that would continue even if a department, product, or service is eliminated. *(p. 1053)*

**Unclassified balance sheet** Balance sheet that broadly groups assets, liabilities, and equity accounts. *(p. 147)*

**Uncontrollable costs** Costs that a manager does not have the power to determine or strongly influence. *(p. 875)*

**Underapplied overhead** Amount by which overhead incurred in a period exceeds the overhead applied to that period's production using the predetermined overhead rate. *(p. 787)*

**Unearned revenue** Liability created when customers pay in advance for products or services; earned when the products or services are later delivered. *(pp. 52 & 100)*

**Unfavorable variance** Difference in revenues or costs, when the actual amount is compared to the budgeted amount, that contributes to a lower income.

**Unit contribution margin** Amount a product's unit selling price exceeds its total unit variable cost.

**Units-of-production depreciation** Method that charges a varying amount to depreciation expense for each period of an asset's useful life depending on its usage. *(p. 399)*

**Unlimited liability** Legal relationship among general partners that makes each of them responsible for partnership debts if the other partners are unable to pay their shares. *(p. 481)*

**Unrealized gain (loss)** Gain (loss) not yet realized by an actual transaction or event such as a sale. *(p. 599)*

**Unsecured bonds** Bonds backed only by the issuer's credit standing; almost always riskier than secured bonds; also called *debentures*. *(p. 566)*

**Unusual gain or loss** Gain or loss that is abnormal or unrelated to the company's ordinary activities and environment. *(p. 710)*

**Useful life** Length of time an asset will be productively used in the operations of a business; also called *service life* or *limited life*. *(p. 397)*

**Value-added time** The portion of cycle time that is directed at producing a product or service; equals process time. *(p. 750)*

**Value chain** Sequential activities that add value to an entity's products or services; includes design, production, marketing, distribution, and service. *(p. 748)*

**Variable cost** Cost that changes in proportion to changes in the activity output volume. *(p. 736)*

**Variable costing income statement** An income statement which reports variable costs and fixed costs separately; also called a *contribution margin income statement*. *(p. 915)*

**Variance analysis** Process of examining differences between actual and budgeted revenues or costs and describing them in terms of price and quantity differences. *(p. 995)*

**Vendee** Buyer of goods or services. *(p. 339)*

**Vendor** Seller of goods or services. *(p. 338)*

**Vertical analysis** Evaluation of each financial statement item or group of items in terms of a specific base amount. *(p. 688)*

**Volume variance** Difference between two dollar amounts of fixed overhead cost; one amount is the total budgeted overhead cost, and the other is the overhead cost allocated to products using the predetermined fixed overhead rate. *(p. 1003)*

**Voucher** Internal file used to store documents and information to control cash disbursements and to ensure that a transaction is properly authorized and recorded. *(p. 325)*

**Voucher register** Journal (referred to as *book of original entry*) in which all vouchers are recorded after they have been approved. *(p. 340)*

**Voucher system** Procedures and approvals designed to control cash disbursements and acceptance of obligations. *(p. 324)*

**Wage bracket withholding table** Table of the amounts of income tax withheld from employees' wages. *(p. 458)*

**Warranty** Agreement that obligates the seller to correct or replace a product or service when it fails to perform properly within a specified period. *(p. 446)*

**Weighted average** Method to assign inventory cost to sales; the cost of available-for-sale units is divided by the number of units available to determine per unit cost prior to each sale that is then multiplied by the units sold to yield the cost of that sale. *(pp. 234 & 824)*

**Weighted-average contribution margin** Contribution margin for a multiproduct company; computed based on each products' percentage of the company's sales mix. *(p. 922)*

**Weighted-average method** (See *weighted average*.)

**Wholesaler** Intermediary that buys products from manufacturers or other wholesalers and sells them to retailers or other wholesalers. *(p. 180)*

**Withdrawals** Payment of cash or other assets from a proprietorship or partnership to its owner or owners. *(p. 14)*

**Work sheet** Spreadsheet used to draft an unadjusted trial balance, adjusting entries, adjusted trial balance, and financial statements. *(p. 138)*

**Working capital** Current assets minus current liabilities at a point in time. *(p. 697)*

**Working papers** Analyses and other informal reports prepared by accountants and managers when organizing information for formal reports and financial statements. *(p. 138)*

# Credits

Note: Page numbers followed by *n* indicate information found in footnotes; **bold-face** entries indicate defined terms.

# A Rose by Any Other Name

**The same financial statement sometimes receives different titles. Following are some of the more common aliases.***

| | |
|---|---|
| **Balance Sheet** | Statement of Financial Position<br>Statement of Financial Condition |
| **Income Statement** | Statement of Income<br>Operating Statement<br>Statement of Operations<br>Statement of Operating Activity<br>Earnings Statement<br>Statement of Earnings<br>Profit and Loss (P&L) Statement |
| **Statement of Cash Flows** | Statement of Cash Flow<br>Cash Flows Statement<br>Statement of Changes in Cash Position<br>Statement of Changes in Financial Position |
| **Statement of Owner's Equity** | Statement of Changes in Owner's Equity<br>Statement of Changes in Owner's Capital<br><br>Statement of Shareholders' Equity[†]<br>Statement of Changes in Shareholders' Equity[†]<br>Statement of Stockholders' Equity and Comprehensive Income[†]<br>Statement of Changes in Capital Accounts[†] |

*The term **Consolidated** often precedes or follows these statement titles to reflect the combination of different entities, such as a parent company and its subsidiaries.
[†] For corporations only.

*We thank Dr. Louella Moore from Arkansas State University for suggesting this listing.*

# Chart of Accounts

Following is a typical chart of accounts, which is used in several assignments. Every company has its own unique accounts and numbering system.

## Assets

### Current Assets

101 Cash
102 Petty cash
103 Cash equivalents
104 Short-term investments
105 Fair value adjustment, _____ securities (S-T)
106 Accounts receivable
107 Allowance for doubtful accounts
108 Legal fees receivable
109 Interest receivable
110 Rent receivable
111 Notes receivable
119 Merchandise inventory
120 _____ inventory
121 _____ inventory
124 Office supplies
125 Store supplies
126 _____ supplies
128 Prepaid insurance
129 Prepaid interest
131 Prepaid rent
132 Raw materials inventory
133 Goods in process inventory, _____
134 Goods in process inventory, _____
135 Finished goods inventory

### Long-Term Investments

141 Long-term investments
142 Fair value adjustment, _____ securities (L-T)
144 Investment in _____
145 Bond sinking fund

### Plant Assets

151 Automobiles
152 Accumulated depreciation—Automobiles
153 Trucks
154 Accumulated depreciation—Trucks
155 Boats
156 Accumulated depreciation—Boats
157 Professional library
158 Accumulated depreciation—Professional library
159 Law library
160 Accumulated depreciation—Law library
161 Furniture
162 Accumulated depreciation—Furniture
163 Office equipment
164 Accumulated depreciation—Office equipment
165 Store equipment

166 Accumulated depreciation—Store equipment
167 _____ equipment
168 Accumulated depreciation—_____ equipment
169 Machinery
170 Accumulated depreciation—Machinery
173 Building _____
174 Accumulated depreciation—Building _____
175 Building _____
176 Accumulated depreciation—Building _____
179 Land improvements _____
180 Accumulated depreciation—Land improvements _____
181 Land improvements _____
182 Accumulated depreciation—Land improvements _____
183 Land

### Natural Resources

185 Mineral deposit
186 Accumulated depletion—Mineral deposit

### Intangible Assets

191 Patents
192 Leasehold
193 Franchise
194 Copyrights
195 Leasehold improvements
196 Licenses
197 Accumulated amortization—_____

## Liabilities

### Current Liabilities

201 Accounts payable
202 Insurance payable
203 Interest payable
204 Legal fees payable
207 Office salaries payable
208 Rent payable
209 Salaries payable
210 Wages payable
211 Accrued payroll payable
214 Estimated warranty liability
215 Income taxes payable
216 Common dividend payable
217 Preferred dividend payable
218 State unemployment taxes payable
219 Employee federal income taxes payable
221 Employee medical insurance payable

222 Employee retirement program payable
223 Employee union dues payable
224 Federal unemployment taxes payable
225 FICA taxes payable
226 Estimated vacation pay liability

### Unearned Revenues

230 Unearned consulting fees
231 Unearned legal fees
232 Unearned property management fees
233 Unearned _____ fees
234 Unearned _____ fees
235 Unearned janitorial revenue
236 Unearned _____ revenue
238 Unearned rent

### Notes Payable

240 Short-term notes payable
241 Discount on short-term notes payable
245 Notes payable
251 Long-term notes payable
252 Discount on long-term notes payable

### Long-Term Liabilities

253 Long-term lease liability
255 Bonds payable
256 Discount on bonds payable
257 Premium on bonds payable
258 Deferred income tax liability

## Equity

### Owner's Equity

301 _____, Capital
302 _____, Withdrawals
303 _____, Capital
304 _____, Withdrawals
305 _____, Capital
306 _____, Withdrawals

### Paid-In Capital

307 Common stock, $_____ par value
308 Common stock, no-par value
309 Common stock, $_____ stated value
310 Common stock dividend distributable
311 Paid-in capital in excess of par value, Common stock

312 Paid-in capital in excess of stated value, No-par common stock
313 Paid-in capital from retirement of common stock
314 Paid-in capital, Treasury stock
315 Preferred stock
316 Paid-in capital in excess of par value, Preferred stock

### Retained Earnings

318 Retained earnings
319 Cash dividends (or Dividends)
320 Stock dividends

### Other Equity Accounts

321 Treasury stock, Common
322 Unrealized gain—Equity
323 Unrealized loss—Equity

## Revenues

401 _____ fees earned
402 _____ fees earned
403 _____ services revenue
404 _____ services revenue
405 Commissions earned
406 Rent revenue (or Rent earned)
407 Dividends revenue (or Dividend earned)
408 Earnings from investment in _____
409 Interest revenue (or Interest earned)
410 Sinking fund earnings
413 Sales
414 Sales returns and allowances
415 Sales discounts

## Cost of Sales

### Cost of Goods Sold

502 Cost of goods sold
505 Purchases
506 Purchases returns and allowances
507 Purchases discounts
508 Transportation-in

### Manufacturing

520 Raw materials purchases
521 Freight-in on raw materials
530 Factory payroll
531 Direct labor
540 Factory overhead
541 Indirect materials
542 Indirect labor
543 Factory insurance expired
544 Factory supervision
545 Factory supplies used
546 Factory utilities
547 Miscellaneous production costs
548 Property taxes on factory building
549 Property taxes on factory equipment
550 Rent on factory building
551 Repairs, factory equipment
552 Small tools written off
560 Depreciation of factory equipment
561 Depreciation of factory building

### Standard Cost Variance

580 Direct material quantity variance
581 Direct material price variance
582 Direct labor quantity variance
583 Direct labor price variance
584 Factory overhead volume variance
585 Factory overhead controllable variance

## Expenses

### Amortization, Depletion, and Depreciation

601 Amortization expense—_____
602 Amortization expense—_____
603 Depletion expense—_____
604 Depreciation expense—Boats
605 Depreciation expense—Automobiles
606 Depreciation expense—Building _____
607 Depreciation expense—Building _____
608 Depreciation expense—Land improvements _____
609 Depreciation expense—Land improvements _____
610 Depreciation expense—Law library
611 Depreciation expense—Trucks
612 Depreciation expense—_____ equipment
613 Depreciation expense—_____ equipment
614 Depreciation expense—_____
615 Depreciation expense—_____

### Employee-Related Expenses

620 Office salaries expense
621 Sales salaries expense
622 Salaries expense
623 _____ wages expense
624 Employees' benefits expense
625 Payroll taxes expense

### Financial Expenses

630 Cash over and short
631 Discounts lost
632 Factoring fee expense
633 Interest expense

### Insurance Expenses

635 Insurance expense—Delivery equipment
636 Insurance expense—Office equipment
637 Insurance expense—_____

### Rental Expenses

640 Rent expense
641 Rent expense—Office space
642 Rent expense—Selling space
643 Press rental expense
644 Truck rental expense
645 _____ rental expense

### Supplies Expenses

650 Office supplies expense
651 Store supplies expense
652 _____ supplies expense
653 _____ supplies expense

### Miscellaneous Expenses

655 Advertising expense
656 Bad debts expense
657 Blueprinting expense
658 Boat expense
659 Collection expense
661 Concessions expense
662 Credit card expense
663 Delivery expense
664 Dumping expense
667 Equipment expense
668 Food and drinks expense
671 Gas and oil expense
672 General and administrative expense
673 Janitorial expense
674 Legal fees expense
676 Mileage expense
677 Miscellaneous expenses
678 Mower and tools expense
679 Operating expense
680 Organization expense
681 Permits expense
682 Postage expense
683 Property taxes expense
684 Repairs expense—_____
685 Repairs expense—_____
687 Selling expense
688 Telephone expense
689 Travel and entertainment expense
690 Utilities expense
691 Warranty expense
695 Income taxes expense

## Gains and Losses

701 Gain on retirement of bonds
702 Gain on sale of machinery
703 Gain on sale of investments
704 Gain on sale of trucks
705 Gain on _____
706 Foreign exchange gain or loss
801 Loss on disposal of machinery
802 Loss on exchange of equipment
803 Loss on exchange of _____
804 Loss on sale of notes
805 Loss on retirement of bonds
806 Loss on sale of investments
807 Loss on sale of machinery
808 Loss on _____
809 Unrealized gain—Income
810 Unrealized loss—Income
811 Impairment gain
812 Impairment loss

## Clearing Accounts

901 Income summary
902 Manufacturing summary

# SELECTED TRANSACTIONS AND RELATIONS

## ① Merchandising Transactions Summary

| Merchandising Transactions | | Merchandising Entries | Dr. | Cr. |
|---|---|---|---|---|
| **Purchases** | Purchasing merchandise for resale. | • Merchandise Inventory ............... <br> Cash or Accounts Payable ......... | # | # |
| | Paying freight costs on purchases; FOB shipping point. | • Merchandise Inventory ............... <br> Cash ...................... | # | # |
| | Paying within discount period. | • Accounts Payable ..................... <br> Merchandise Inventory ............. <br> Cash ....................... | # | # <br> # |
| | Recording purchase returns or allowances. | • Cash or Accounts Payable ............. <br> Merchandise Inventory ............. | # | # |
| **Sales** | Selling merchandise. | • Cash or Accounts Receivable ......... <br> Sales ...................... <br> • Cost of Goods Sold.................... <br> Merchandise Inventory ............. | # <br><br> # | # <br><br> # |
| | Receiving payment within discount period. | • Cash ............................. <br> Sales Discounts ..................... <br> Accounts Receivable .............. | # <br> # | # |
| | Granting sales returns or allowances. | • Sales Returns and Allowances.......... <br> Cash or Accounts Receivable ....... <br> • Merchandise Inventory ............... <br> Cost of Goods Sold ............... | # <br><br> # | # <br><br> # |
| | Paying freight costs on sales; FOB destination. | • Delivery Expense .................... <br> Cash ............................. | # | # |

| Merchandising Events | | Adjusting and Closing Entries | Dr. | Cr. |
|---|---|---|---|---|
| **Adjusting** | Adjusting due to shrinkage (occurs when recorded amount larger than physical inventory). | Cost of Goods Sold .................... <br> Merchandise Inventory .............. | # | # |
| **Closing** | Closing temporary accounts with credit balances. | Sales ................................ <br> Income Summary ................... | # | # |
| | Closing temporary accounts with debit balances. | Income Summary ...................... <br> Sales Returns and Allowances ........ <br> Sales Discounts .................... <br> Cost of Goods Sold ................ <br> Delivery Expense .................. <br> "Other Expenses" ................. | # | # <br> # <br> # <br> # <br> # |

## ② Merchandising Cash Flows

## ③ Credit Terms and Amounts

*Discount refers to a purchase discount for a buyer and a sales discount for a seller.

## ④ Bad Debts Estimation

**Bad Debts Estimation**

- Income Statement Focus
  - **Percent of Sales** [Emphasis on Matching]
    - Sales × Rate = Bad Debts Expense
- Balance Sheet Focus
  - **Percent of Receivables** [Emphasis on Realizable Value]
    - Accounts Receivable × Rate = Allowance for Doubtful Accounts
  - **Aging of Receivables** [Emphasis on Realizable Value]
    - Accounts Receivable (by Age) × Rates (by Age) = Allowance for Doubtful Accounts

## ⑤ Bond Valuation

| Bond Sets | Market Sets | Bond Price Determined | |
|---|---|---|---|
| Contract rate | Market rate | Contract rate > Market rate | Bond sells at Premium |
| | | Contract rate = Market rate | Bond sells at Par |
| | | Contract rate < Market rate | Bond sells at Discount |

## ⑥ Stock Transactions Summary

| Stock Transactions | | Stock Entries | Dr. | Cr. |
|---|---|---|---|---|
| **Issue Common Stock** | Issue par value common stock at par (par stock recorded at par). | Cash ............................. <br> Common Stock ................ | # | # |
| | Issue par value common stock at premium (par stock recorded at par). | Cash ........................... <br> Common Stock ................... <br> Paid-In Capital in Excess of Par Value, Common Stock ..... | # | # <br> # |
| | Issue no-par value common stock (no-par stock recorded at amount received). | Cash ............................. <br> Common Stock ................. | # | # |
| | Issue stated value common stock at stated value (stated stock recorded at stated value). | Cash ............................. <br> Common stock ................. | # | # |
| | Issue stated value common stock at premium (stated stock recorded at stated value). | Cash ............................. <br> Common Stock ................. <br> Paid-In Capital in Excess of Stated Value, Common Stock .... | # | # <br> # |
| **Issue Preferred Stock** | Issue par value preferred stock at par (par stock recorded at par). | Cash ............................. <br> Preferred Stock ................ | # | # |
| | Issue par value preferred stock at premium (par stock recorded at par). | Cash ............................. <br> Preferred Stock ................ <br> Paid-In Capital in Excess of Par Value, Preferred Stock ..... | # | # <br> # |
| **Reacquire Common Stock** | Reacquire its own common stock (treasury stock recorded at cost). | Treasury Stock, Common ........... <br> Cash ......................... | # | # |
| **Reissue Common Stock** | Reissue its treasury stock at cost (treasury stock removed at cost). | Cash .............................. <br> Treasury Stock, Common ....... | # | # |
| | Reissue its treasury stock above cost (treasury stock removed at cost). | Cash ............................. <br> Treasury Stock, Common ....... <br> Paid-In Capital, Treasury ......... | # | # <br> # |
| | Reissue its treasury stock below cost (treasury stock removed at cost; if paid-in capital is insufficient to cover amount below cost, retained earnings is debited for remainder). | Cash ............................. <br> Paid-In Capital, Treasury ........ <br> Treasury Stock, Common ....... <br> Retained Earnings (if necessary) ... | # <br> # | # <br> # |

## ⑦ Dividend Transactions

| | Type of Dividend | | |
|---|---|---|---|
| **Account Affected** | **Cash Dividend** | **Stock Dividend** | **Stock Split** |
| Cash ............. | Decrease | — | — |
| Common Stock .... | — | Increase | — |
| Retained Earnings .. | Decrease | Decrease | — |

## ⑧ A Rose by Any Other Name

The same financial statement sometimes receives different titles. Following are some of the more common aliases.*

| | |
|---|---|
| **Balance Sheet** | Statement of Financial Position <br> Statement of Financial Condition |
| **Income Statement** | Statement of Income <br> Operating Statement <br> Statement of Operations <br> Statement of Operating Activity <br> Earnings Statement <br> Statement of Earnings <br> Profit and Loss (P&L) Statement |
| **Statement of Cash Flows** | Statement of Cash Flow <br> Cash Flows Statement <br> Statement of Changes in Cash Position <br> Statement of Changes in Financial Position |
| **Statement of Owner's Equity** | Statement of Changes in Owner's Equity <br> Statement of Changes in Owner's Capital <br><br> Statement of Shareholders' Equity† <br> Statement of Changes in Shareholders' Equity† <br> Statement of Stockholders' Equity and Comprehensive Income† <br> Statement of Changes in Capital Accounts† |

*The term **Consolidated** often precedes or follows these statement titles to reflect the combination of different entities, such as a parent company and its subsidiaries.

† Corporation only.

# MANAGERIAL ANALYSES AND REPORTS

## ① Cost Types

| | |
|---|---|
| Variable costs: | Total cost changes in proportion to volume of activity |
| Fixed costs: | Total cost does not change in proportion to volume of activity |
| Mixed costs: | Cost consists of both a variable and a fixed element |

## ② Cost Sources

| | |
|---|---|
| Direct materials: | Raw materials costs directly linked to finished product |
| Direct labor: | Employee costs directly linked to finished product |
| Overhead: | Costs indirectly linked to finished product |

## ③ Costing Systems

| | |
|---|---|
| Job order costing: | Costs assigned to each unique unit or batch of units |
| Process costing: | Costs assigned to similar products that are mass-produced in a continuous manner |

## ④ Costing Ratios

Contribution margin ratio = (Net sales − Variable costs)/Net sales
Predetermined overhead rate = Estimated overhead costs/Estimated activity base
Break-even point in units = Total fixed costs/Contribution margin per unit

## ⑤ Planning and Control Metrics

Cost variance = Actual cost − Standard (budgeted) cost
Sales (revenue) variance = Actual sales − Standard (budgeted) sales

## ⑥ Capital Budgeting

Payback period = Time expected to recover investment cost
Accounting rate of return = Expected annual net income/Average annual investment
Net present value (NPV) = Present value of future cash flows − Investment cost
NPV rule:   1. Compute net present value (NPV in $)
            2. If NPV ≥ 0, then accept project; If NPV < 0, then reject project
Internal rate   1. Compute internal rate of return (IRR in %)
of return rule: 2. If IRR ≥ hurdle rate, accept project; If IRR < hurdle rate, reject project

## ⑦ Costing Terminology

| | |
|---|---|
| Relevant range: | Organization's normal range of operating activity. |
| Direct cost: | Cost incurred for the benefit of one cost object. |
| Indirect cost: | Cost incurred for the benefit of more than one cost object. |
| Product cost: | Cost that is necessary and integral to finished products. |
| Period cost: | Cost identified more with a time period than with finished products. |
| Overhead cost: | Cost not separately or directly traceable to a cost object. |
| Relevant cost: | Cost that is pertinent to a decision. |
| Opportunity cost: | Benefit lost by choosing an action from two or more alternatives. |
| Sunk cost: | Cost already incurred that cannot be avoided or changed. |
| Standard cost: | Cost computed using standard price and standard quantity. |
| Budget: | Formal statement of an organization's future plans. |
| Break-even point: | Sales level at which an organization earns zero profit. |
| Incremental cost: | Cost incurred only if the organization undertakes a certain action. |
| Transfer price: | Price on transactions between divisions within a company. |

## ⑧ Standard Cost Variances

| Total materials variance | = | Materials price variance + Materials quantity variance |
|---|---|---|

| Total labor variance | = | Labor (rate) variance + Labor efficiency (quantity) variance |
|---|---|---|

| Total overhead variance | = | Overhead controllable variance + Fixed overhead volume variance |
|---|---|---|

Overhead controllable variance = Actual total overhead − Applied total overhead from flexible budget

Fixed overhead volume variance = Budgeted fixed overhead − Applied fixed overhead

Variable overhead variance = Variable overhead spending variance + Variable overhead efficiency variance

Fixed overhead variance = Fixed overhead spending variance + Fixed overhead volume variance

} = Total overhead variance

| Materials price variance | = [AQ × AP] − [AQ × SP] |
|---|---|
| Materials quantity variance | = [AQ × SP] − [SQ × SP] |
| Labor (rate) variance | = [AH × AR] − [AH × SR] |
| Labor efficiency (quantity) variance | = [AH × SR] − [SH × SR] |

Variable overhead spending variance = [AH × AVR] − [AH × SVR]
Variable overhead efficiency variance = [AH × SVR] − [SH × SVR]
Fixed overhead spending variance = Actual fixed overhead − Budgeted fixed overhead

where AQ is actual quantity of materials; AP is actual price of materials; AH is actual hours of labor; AR is actual rate of wages; AVR is actual variable rate of overhead; SQ is standard quantity of materials; SP is standard price of materials; SH is standard hours of labor; SR is standard rate of wages; SVR is standard variable rate of overhead.

## ⑨ Sales Variances

| Sales price variance | = [AS × AP] − [AS × BP] |
|---|---|
| Sales volume variance | = [AS × BP] − [BS × BP] |

where AS = actual sales units; AP = actual sales price; BP = budgeted sales price;
BS = budgeted sales units (fixed budget)

---

## Manufacturing Statement
### For _period_ Ended _date_

| | | |
|---|---|---|
| Direct materials | | |
| Raw materials inventory, Beginning | $ | # |
| Raw materials purchases | | # |
| Raw materials available for use | | # |
| Raw materials inventory, Ending | | (#) |
| Direct materials used | | # |
| Direct labor | | # |
| Overhead costs | | |
| Total overhead costs | | # |
| Total manufacturing costs | | # |
| Add goods in process inventory, Beginning | | # |
| Total cost of goods in process | | # |
| Deduct goods in process inventory, Ending | | (#) |
| Cost of goods manufactured | $ | # |

---

## Contribution Margin Income Statement
### For _period_ Ended _date_

| | | |
|---|---|---|
| Net sales (revenues) | $ | # |
| Total variable costs | | # |
| Contribution margin | | # |
| Total fixed costs | | # |
| Net income | $ | # |

---

## Flexible Budget
### For _period_ Ended _date_

| | Flexible Budget | | Flexible Budget for Unit Sales of # |
|---|---|---|---|
| | Variable Amount per Unit | Fixed Cost | |
| Sales (revenues) | $ # | | $ # |
| Variable costs | | | |
| Examples: Direct materials, Direct labor, | | | |
| Other variable costs | # | | # |
| Total variable costs | # | | # |
| Contribution margin | $ # | | # |
| Fixed costs | | | |
| Examples: Depreciation, Manager | | $ # | # |
| salaries, Administrative salaries | | # | # |
| Total fixed costs | | $ # | # |
| Income from operations | | | $ # |

---

## Fixed Budget Performance Report
### For _period_ Ended _date_

| | Fixed Budget | Actual Performance | Variances[†] |
|---|---|---|---|
| Sales: In units | # | # | |
| In dollars | $ # | $ # | $ # F or U |
| Cost of sales | | | |
| Direct costs | # | # | # F or U |
| Indirect costs | # | # | # F or U |
| Selling expenses | | | |
| Examples: Commissions, | # | # | # F or U |
| Shipping expenses | # | # | # F or U |
| General and administrative expenses | | | |
| Examples: Administrative salaries | # | # | # F or U |
| Total expenses | $ # | $ # | $ # F or U |
| Income from operations | $ # | $ # | $ # F or U |

[†] F = Favorable variance; U = Unfavorable variance.

---

## Master Budget Sequence

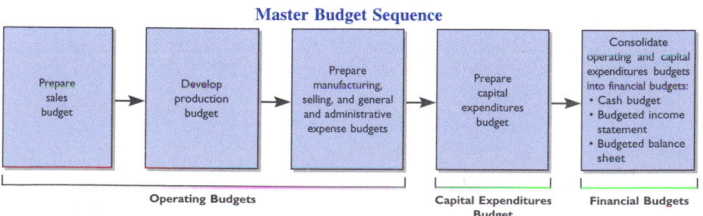

# FUNDAMENTALS

## ① Accounting Equation

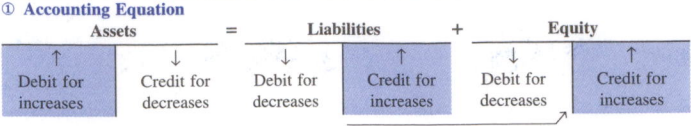

| Assets | = | Liabilities | + | Equity |
|--------|---|-------------|---|--------|
| ↑ Debit for increases | ↓ Credit for decreases | ↓ Debit for decreases | ↑ Credit for increases | ↓ Debit for decreases | ↑ Credit for increases |

|  | Owner's Capital* | − | Owner's Withdrawals* | + | Revenues | − | Expenses |
|--|-----------------|---|---------------------|---|----------|---|----------|
| | ↓ Dr. for decreases | ↑ Cr. for increases | ↑ Dr. for increases | ↓ Cr. for decreases | ↓ Dr. for decreases | ↑ Cr. for increases | ↑ Dr. for increases | ↓ Cr. for decreases |

Indicates normal balance.

*Comparable corporate accounts are Common Stock (Paid-In Capital) and Dividends.

## ② Accounting Cycle

1. Analyze transactions
2. Journalize
3. Post
4. Prepare unadjusted trial balance
5. Adjust
6. Prepare adjusted trial balance
7. Prepare statements
8. Close
9. Prepare post-closing trial balance
10. Reverse (Optional)

Accounting Cycle

## ③ Adjustments and Entries

| Type | Adjusting Entry | |
|------|-----------------|--|
| Prepaid Expenses | Dr. Expense | Cr. Asset* |
| Unearned Revenues | Dr. Liability | Cr. Revenue |
| Accrued Expenses | Dr. Expense | Cr. Liability |
| Accrued Revenues | Dr. Asset | Cr. Revenue |

*For depreciation, credit Accumulated Depreciation (contra asset).

## ④ 4-Step Closing Process

1. Transfer revenue and gain account balances to Income Summary.
2. Transfer expense and loss account balances to Income Summary.
3. Transfer Income Summary balance to Owner's Capital.
4. Transfer Withdrawals balance to Owner's Capital.

## ⑤ Accounting Concepts

| Characteristics | Assumptions | Principles | Constraints |
|-----------------|-------------|------------|-------------|
| Relevance | Business entity | Historical cost | Cost-benefit |
| Reliability | Going concern | Revenue recognition | Materiality |
| Comparability | Monetary unit | Expense recognition | Industry practice |
| Consistency | Periodicity | Full disclosure | Conservatism |

## ⑥ Ownership of Inventory

| | Ownership Transfers When Goods Passed To | Transportation Costs Paid By |
|--|------------------------------------------|------------------------------|
| FOB Shipping Point | Carrier | Buyer |
| FOB Destination | Buyer | Seller |

## ⑦ Inventory Costing Methods

- Specific Identification
- First-In, First-Out (FIFO)
- Weighted-Average
- Last-In, First-Out (LIFO)

## ⑧ Depreciation and Depletion

Straight-Line:
$$\frac{\text{Cost} - \text{Salvage value}}{\text{Useful life in periods}} \times \text{Periods expired}$$

Units-of-Production:
$$\frac{\text{Cost} - \text{Salvage value}}{\text{Useful life in units}} \times \text{Units produced}$$

Declining-Balance: Rate* × Beginning-of-period book value
*Rate is often double the straight-line rate, or $2 \times (1/\text{Useful life})$

Depletion:
$$\frac{\text{Cost} - \text{Salvage value}}{\text{Total capacity in units}} \times \text{Units extracted}$$

## ⑨ Interest Computation

Interest = Principal (face) × Rate × Time

## ⑩ Accounting for Investment Securities

| Classification* | Accounting |
|-----------------|------------|
| **Short-Term Investment in Securities** | |
| Held-to-maturity (debt) securities | **Cost** (without any discount or premium amortization) |
| Trading (debt and equity) securities | **Fair value** (with fair value adjustment to income) |
| Available-for-sale (debt and equity) securities | **Fair value** (with fair value adjustment to equity) |
| **Long-Term Investment in Securities** | |
| Held-to-maturity (debt) securities | **Cost** (with any discount or premium amortization) |
| Available-for-sale (debt and equity) securities | **Fair value** (with fair value adjustment to equity) |
| Equity securities with significant influence | Equity method |
| Equity securities with controlling influence | Equity method (with consolidation) |

*A *fair value option* allows companies to report HTM and AFS securities much like trading securities.

# ANALYSES

## ① Liquidity and Efficiency

Current ratio $= \dfrac{\text{Current assets}}{\text{Current liabilities}}$ — p. 148

Working capital = Current assets − Current liabilities — p. 697

Acid-test ratio $= \dfrac{\text{Cash} + \text{Short-term investments} + \text{Current receivables}}{\text{Current liabilities}}$ — p. 196

Accounts receivable turnover $= \dfrac{\text{Net sales}}{\text{Average accounts receivable, net}}$ — p. 375

Credit risk ratio $= \dfrac{\text{Allowance for doubtful accounts}}{\text{Accounts receivable, net}}$ — p. 375

Inventory turnover $= \dfrac{\text{Cost of goods sold}}{\text{Average inventory}}$ — p. 241

Days' sales uncollected $= \dfrac{\text{Accounts receivable, net}}{\text{Net sales}} \times 365^*$ — p. 335

Days' sales in inventory $= \dfrac{\text{Ending inventory}}{\text{Cost of goods sold}} \times 365^*$ — p. 241

Total asset turnover $= \dfrac{\text{Net sales}}{\text{Average total assets}}$ — p. 413

Plant asset useful life $= \dfrac{\text{Plant asset cost}}{\text{Depreciation expense}}$ — p. 413

Plant asset age $= \dfrac{\text{Accumulated depreciation}}{\text{Depreciation expense}}$ — p. 413

Days' cash expense coverage $= \dfrac{\text{Cash and cash equivalents}}{\text{Average daily cash expenses}}$ — p. 322

*360 days is also commonly used.

## ② Solvency

Debt ratio $= \dfrac{\text{Total liabilities}}{\text{Total assets}}$    Equity ratio $= \dfrac{\text{Total equity}}{\text{Total assets}}$ — pp. 69 & 701

Debt-to-equity $= \dfrac{\text{Total liabilities}}{\text{Total equity}}$ — p. 567

Times interest earned $= \dfrac{\text{Income before interest expense and income taxes}}{\text{Interest expense}}$ — p. 450

Cash coverage of growth $= \dfrac{\text{Cash flow from operations}}{\text{Cash outflow for plant assets}}$ — p. 651

Cash coverage of debt $= \dfrac{\text{Cash flow from operations}}{\text{Total noncurrent liabilities}}$ — p. 646

## ③ Profitability

Profit margin ratio $= \dfrac{\text{Net income}}{\text{Net sales}}$ — p. 109

Gross margin ratio $= \dfrac{\text{Net sales} - \text{Cost of goods sold}}{\text{Net sales}}$ — p. 196

Return on total assets $= \dfrac{\text{Net income}}{\text{Average total assets}}$ — p. 22

$= $ Profit margin ratio × Total asset turnover — p. 703

Return on common stockholders' equity $= \dfrac{\text{Net income} - \text{Preferred dividends}}{\text{Average common stockholders' equity}}$ — p. 703

Book value per common share $= \dfrac{\text{Stockholders' equity applicable to common shares}}{\text{Number of common shares outstanding}}$ — p. 528

Basic earnings per share $= \dfrac{\text{Net income} - \text{Preferred dividends}}{\text{Weighted-average common shares outstanding}}$ — p. 527

Cash flow on total assets $= \dfrac{\text{Cash flow from operations}}{\text{Average total assets}}$ — p. 650

Payout ratio $= \dfrac{\text{Cash dividends declared on common stock}}{\text{Net income}}$ — p. 528

## ④ Market

Price-earnings ratio $= \dfrac{\text{Market value (price) per share}}{\text{Earnings per share}}$ — p. 527

Dividend yield $= \dfrac{\text{Annual cash dividends per share}}{\text{Market price per share}}$ — p. 528

Residual income = Net income − Target net income